SOUTH-WESTERN

Law for Business

14TH EDITION

Norbert J. Mietus

Professor of Law Emeritus
School of Business Administration
California State University, Sacramento

John E. Adamson

Assistant Professor of Business and Law
Finance and General Business Department
Southwest Missouri State University

Edward J. Conry

Associate Professor
College of Business and Administration
University of Colorado at Denver

ISBN: 0-538-63311-5

1 2 3 4 5 6 AGK 99 98 97 96 95 94

Printed in the United States of America

South-Western Publishing Co.

I(T)P
International Thomson Publishing
South-Western Publishing Co. is an ITP Company.
The ITP trademark is used under license.

South-Western's *Law for Business* Integrates the Strongest Content With the Most Complete Teaching Plan on the Market Today

The wraparound **Teacher Edition** for *Law for Business* has been developed to provide instructors of business law with a variety of teaching techniques, activities, and suggestions to support and extend your classroom readings, lectures, and discussions. The margin notes, corresponding to the student text on a page-by-page basis, are offered as suggestions to enhance your classroom instruction. Feel free to select the sequence of chapters that best meets your instructional needs and, within each chapter, to choose those activities that appear most relevant and meaningful to your students' learning experience. It is unnecessary and impractical to try to implement all of the activities given the time constraints of a typical class period. Instead, we recommend that you preview the wide selection of activities prior to starting a chapter and mark those that appeal to you most.

Special-feature interleaf sections precede each unit and chapter of the program. They contain a variety of creative activities, from portfolio assessment opportunities to the study of careers related to business law. In addition, comprehensive chapter organizers help you identify and select from the wealth of teaching materials offered for each lesson. Each chapter of the **Teacher Edition** follows a consistent, multi-part lesson plan: TEACH, APPLY, ASSESS, RETEACH, and ENRICH, ensuring you that key concepts are taught, developed, practiced, assessed and, if desired, retaught or enriched during every class period.

Before beginning a unit of instruction or assigning specific activities, please familiarize yourself with the corresponding sections of the student text. Herein lie the fully developed, authoritative explanations of the law, on which you may rely for definitive legal material and explanations for each concept.

The ©1995 Wraparound **Teacher Edition** of South-Western's *Law for Business* brings to your fingertips a winning combination of superior student text; innovative teaching strategies; and a wealth of outstanding, creative activities to "drive home" key concepts for your students.

***Law for Business* Makes a Case for Integrating the Strongest Content With the Best Teaching Tools and Techniques on the Market!**

Authors and Reviewers

***O**ur Outstanding Authorship Team and Program Reviewers Developed the Topics and Content YOU Asked For!*

Program Authors

Norbert J. Mietus is Professor of Law Emeritus at the School of Business Administration at California State University, Sacramento. A graduate of Marquette (B.S.), Harvard (M.B.A.), and UCLA (J.D.), Mietus is a member of the California Bar. He has taught at Loyola Marymount, the University of California at Berkeley, and California State University at Sacramento, and has written numerous books on the law and business.

John E. Adamson is Assistant Professor of Business and Law in the Department of Finance and General Business at Southwest Missouri State University. Adamson received a B.S. from the U.S. Military Academy at West Point, NY; an M.A. from Georgetown University; and an M.B.A. and J.D. from the University of Virginia at Charlottesville. A decorated, disabled Vietnam veteran and current mayor and school board member of Miller, MO, Adamson is author of numerous business law publications, with a concentration on environmental law.

Edward J. Conry is Associate Professor at the College of Business and Administration at the University of Colorado at Denver. He earned a B.A. from California State University at Fullerton, a J.D. at the University of California at Davis, and an M.B.A. from the University of California at Berkeley. Conry, a former Research Fellow at Yale. University, is author of more than 20 books and 200 professional articles on the law.

Program Reviewers

Sheri Alford
B. F. Terry HS
Lamar C.I.S.D., TX

Jerry Bryant
Merritt Island HS
Merritt Island, FL

Carole Bushert
Bloomington HS So.
Bloomington, IN

Marianne Failla
Dulles HS
Fort Bend I.S.D., TX

Patsy Goss
George Jenkins HS
Lakeland, FL

Patricia Heller
Broomfield HS
Boulder, CO

Jim MacNeal
Waterloo HS
Waterloo, NY

Roy Russell
Arroyo HS
El Monte, CA

Ofelia Salazar
Donna HS
Donna I.S.D., TX

John Scally
G. Ray Bodley HS
Fulton, NY

John Sprenger
La Grande HS
La Grande, OR

Virginia Weber
St. Amant HS
St. Amant, LA

Features of the Student Text

A Wealth of Special-Purpose Features Focus and Enhance Students' Learning in Every Chapter

Learning Objectives for every chapter ensure that your students understand their instructional goals and priorities—before they begin each chapter.

Learning Objectives

When you complete this chapter, you will be able to

1. Describe how disputes can be resolved without courts.
2. Explain how courts operate.
3. Distinguish between trial courts and appellate courts.
4. State the jurisdictions of federal, state, and local courts.
5. Understand how a juvenile court differs from criminal and civil courts.
6. Discuss the various procedures used in juvenile, ...nd civil trials.

Embedded in every chapter are several **Ethics Issues**—ideal vehicles for leading classroom discussions on the ethical issues and concerns related to the points of law under study. In addition, Chapter 2 is devoted to ethics and law—providing students with concrete methods to help them resolve ethical issues related to business law.

2 ETHICS ISSUE Walter owed $17 to Olivia. Walter knew that it would not be worthwhile for Olivia to sue for this small amount of money. Although Olivia might recover the $17 and court costs, she could earn more money by spending the time working. Why should Walter pay the money even though Olivia may not sue? Does Olivia have a duty to sue even though she could make better financial use of her time?

Preventing Legal Difficulties presents a variety of helpful and informative tips and suggestions for avoiding legal problems. Based on the relevant and personally useful information offered in each chapter, you and your students will practice applying elements of business and personal law to your own lives.

Preventing Legal Difficulties

1 As you travel from state to state, the minimum age for full adult responsibility for criminal acts, torts, voting, driving, drinking, and many other forms of conduct varies greatly. Become familiar with the appropriate laws in each jurisdiction you enter.

A boxed **PROBLEM** presents a realistic scenario to highlight and focus the topic question for every section.

PROBLEM

Will is a junior in high school and has lived in the same New Hampshire community all his life. In October, his mother learns that the plant in which she has been a manager for over twenty years is closing. She has accepted a new position at company headquarters 1,200 miles away. Rather than leave his friends, Will tells his mother that he wants to remain where they are and finish high school there. His mother insists she has the right to force him to move. Can she legally do so?

SPECIAL SECTION

CAREERS IN LAW

research, and appears in court or before administrative agencies when required.

Specialized Practice

The complexity of the law requires that some lawyers concentrate on a specific area of law. Specialists work almost exclusively in a particular area, such as domestic relations (family) law, criminal law, labor law, debt collection, or copyright law.

At the end of each unit, a **Special Section** presents an in-depth look at a related topic of interest, such as environmental law, criteria for selecting and dealing with one's own attorney, how to litigate in small claims court, and computer law—information you and your students will apply *personally*, time and time again.

Features of the Teacher Edition Unit Interleaf

Special Activities and Features for Each Unit Help You Identify and Prioritize the Chapters and Content to Maximize Benefits for You and Your Students

Unit Overview sections provide a comprehensive, at-a-glance overview of each unit. Each overview summarizes the content and points of business law covered in subsequent chapters, providing a focus for your classroom instruction. It's the perfect vehicle to help you identify the materials you wish to use to prepare for class!

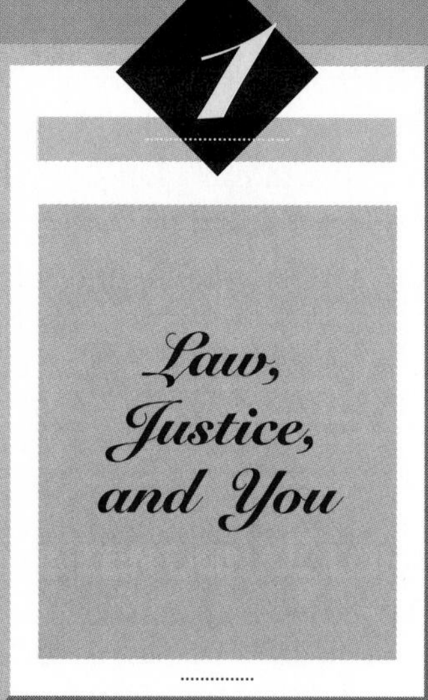

Unit Overview

Unit 1, *Law, Justice, and You*, contains information that creates the foundation of the student text. In this unit, students will learn how our nation's laws were formed, the ethics behind our laws, our kinds of law, how laws are enforced, and the difference between crimes and torts.

The Constitution, the Bill of Rights, and subsequent amendments form the shield of U.S. liberty. In Chapter 1, *The Shield of the Constitution*, students will learn that the U.S. Constitution is the keystone of our nation. They'll discover how the Constitution came into being, how the Bill of Rights enhanced the original Constitution, and the problems that required more amendments be added to the Constitution.

Consequential and deontological forms of ethics are reflected in—and compel us to obey—our laws. In Chapter 2, *Ethics in Our Law*, students will study how we reason about right and wrong. In addition, students will study how ethical goals are reflected in our laws.

Criminal, civil, and business law are just a few kinds of law reflected in constitutions, statutes, and rulings by administrative agencies. In Chapter 3, *Kinds of Law*, students will discover how our laws developed and what types of law we have today. Students will learn which type of law is valid when laws conflict, how criminal and civil laws differ, how procedural and substantive laws differ, and what business law is.

In Chapter 4, *Enforcing the Law*, students will study our court system. They will have the opportunity to learn how a juvenile court differs from others, what the procedures are in criminal and civil actions, how a civil case is tried, and how a judgment is satisfied.

In Chapter 5, *Crimes*, students will understand how crimes are classified, what business-related crimes are, and what rights a person has when arrested. They will be actively involved in defining when one party is responsible for the criminal conduct of another, what the defenses are to criminal charges, and what the punishments are for crimes.

Torts fall under a variety of classifications. In Chapter 6, *Torts*, students will learn what the elements of a tort are, what common intentional torts are, what negligence is, what strict liability is, when a person is responsible for the torts of another, and what a victim of a tort can collect.

At the end of the unit, you'll find a special section, *Pressing Issue: Environmental Law,* which can be used at any time during the study of Unit 1. You may wish to assign its accompanying *Teacher Edition* activity to give students an opportunity to research an environmental issue and present their findings as a unit project to the class.

1A

Annotated Bibliography

- ***Banco Nacional de Cuba v. Sabbatino*, 376 U.S. 398 (1964).**
It is a violation of the international law for a country to fail to pay adequate compensation for the property it seizes from a particular class of aliens, when the purpose of the seizure is to retaliate against the homeland of those aliens and the result of such seizure discriminates against them only. (Chapter 1)

- ***Miranda v. Arizona*, 384 U.S. 436 (1966).**
The privilege against self-incrimination is the essential mainstay of our adversary system and guarantees to the individual the "right to remain silent unless he or she chooses to speak in the unfettered exercise of his own will." Statements of an accused may not be used against the accused unless he or she has been clearly informed that he or she has the right to remain silent, that anything he or she says will be used against him or her in a court, that he or she has the right to consult with a lawyer and have the lawyer present during interrogation, and that, if he or she is indigent, a lawyer will be appointed to represent him or her. (Chapter 5)

The **Annotated Bibliography** provides additional, annotated court cases of importance related to the unit. Full case citations allow you and your students access to each case of interest.

A **Portfolio Assessment** opportunity related to the content of each unit provides you with a cumulative and comprehensive vehicle for assessing student performance. Based on a FOCUS, SELECT, COLLECT, and SAVE format, these activities allow you to collect documentary evidence of students' growth in the areas of literacy development, thinking skills, and extension and application of content knowledge. Writing assignments range from letters and essays on business law topics at the beginning of the year, to more complex formats, such as contracts, speeches, and handbooks. Use our suggestions—or create your own from our formats!

Portfolio Assessment

Have students skim current newspapers or news magazines to find a controversial political case or timely issue that interests them or affects their daily lives. Have students collect five to ten articles about the case to familiarize themselves with the issue. To understand how the law is involved in the issues, ask students to think about questions such as: How is the law being enforced? Is the case criminal or civil? If criminal, what kind of crime was committed? If civil, what type of tort was committed? Is this an ethical issue? Using a computer, if possible, have students exercise their First Amendment rights by writing a letter to their mayor, governor, or senator expressing their point of view on the issue. Encourage students to send their letters. Have students put a copy of their letter in portfolios or law journals labeled *The Law & You.* Tell students that, at the end of each unit, they will complete a writing assignment and add it to their portfolio.

Careers

Police Officer
Our country's laws include not only the rules of conduct for its people but also the means of enforcing those rules. It is the duty of police officers to know the law, to protect the lives and property of citizens, prevent crimes, apprehend law-breakers, maintain order, and testify in court.

Many police departments require at least a high-school education of their officers. A candidate should be at least 21 years old, meet minimum height and weight requirements, pass a physical exam and a civil-service test. Entry-level salaries are between $18,000 and $22,000.

Have each student skim through newspapers looking for articles involving police action. Have them highlight the sections that discuss what law was broken, what procedural and substantive laws were used, and the results. Then, have students create a large chart with the categories: *Civil* and *Criminal*, and secure the clipped articles to it.

Careers features profile a business law career related to the content of each unit. A description of the job responsibilities, educational and training requirements, and starting salaries is followed by a hands-on activity that involves students in finding out more about that occupation. Who knows...you may inspire future police officers, consumer rights activists, and human resource managers!

Features of the Teacher Edition Chapter Interleaf

Chapter Interleaf Sections Facilitate Planning, Conducting, and Assessing Your Lessons

Directed Study Questions parallel the key section topics and provide a focus for your classroom instruction.

Reteach and **Enrich** opportunities are springboards for informal, daily assessment opportunities. Now you can monitor—every class day—how your students are doing and have at your fingertips activities for enriching their class performance.

Chapter Themes preview the content in each chapter

Six **Special Features**—Writing Connections, Ethics Issue, Personal Perspectives, Multicultural Highlights, Thinking Critically Through Visuals, and Preventing Legal Difficulties—extend instruction in each chapter to other content areas and integrate additional topics of relevance and interest into your business law class.

Additional Resources are provided for each chapter. Consisting of print, computer-based, and multimedia references, you and your students can select from a wealth of content-based references to extend and apply the concepts developed in each chapter.

CHAPTER 2 ORGANIZER

Chapter Theme

Consequential and deontological forms of ethics are reflected in—and compel us to obey—our laws.

DIRECTED STUDY QUESTIONS	SPECIAL FEATURES	PROGRAM RESOURCES			
		Reteach	Enrich	S N	A M
What is ethics?		✔	✔		
How do we reason about right and wrong?	Personal Perspectives, p. 29 Ethics Issue, p. 30	✔	✔	✔	
How do our laws reflect consequential ethics?	Thinking Critically Through Visuals, p. 33	✔	✔		
How do our laws reflect deontological ethics?		✔	✔		A
How are other ethical goals reflected in our laws?		✔	✔		
Why are we obligated to obey laws?		✔	✔		
Are we ever justified in violating the law?	Writing Connection, p 38 Multicultural Highlights, p. 39 Thinking Critically Through Visuals, p. 39 Preventing Legal Difficulties, p. 40	✔	✔		V K

Additional Resources

- *An Amazing Grace.* Detroit, MI: MultiMedia Education Inc.
- Aristotle, *The Nicomachean Ethics.* New York: Oxford University Press, 1925.
- Ferrell, O.C. and Gardiner, Gareth. *In Pursuit of Ethics: Tough Choices in the World of Work.* Springfield, IL: Smith Collins, 1991.
- Frankena, William K. *Ethics.* Englewood Cliffs, NJ: Prentice-Hall, 1963.

uthentic Cooperative Learning ctivities support and extend your assroom instruction. ecommendations for assigning les, tasks, and goals are entified for each activity, guiding our students to work together, pplying key concepts to complete e activities.

Assessment is built into your teaching plan. From informal assessment opportunities for each lesson, to student-directed chapter reviews, to more formal print chapter tests and our computerized *MicroExam*, you and your students have the opportunity to monitor progress and target areas of weakness for reteaching and reinforcement.

One- and two-semester Chapter Pacing Guides help you project number of class days for each chapter of instruction.

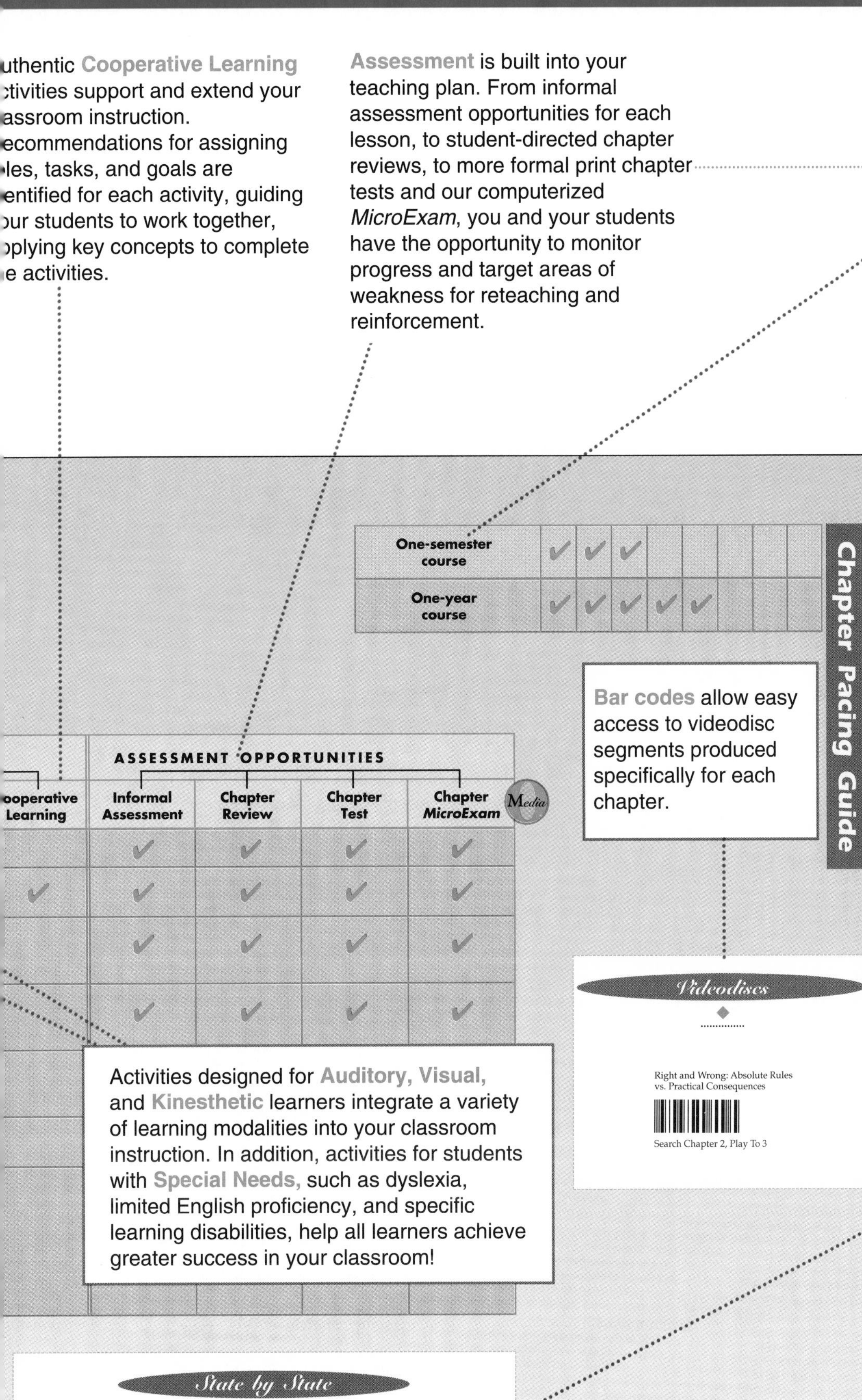

Bar codes allow easy access to videodisc segments produced specifically for each chapter.

Videodiscs

Right and Wrong: Absolute Rules vs. Practical Consequences

Search Chapter 2, Play To 3

Activities designed for Auditory, Visual, and Kinesthetic learners integrate a variety of learning modalities into your classroom instruction. In addition, activities for students with Special Needs, such as dyslexia, limited English proficiency, and specific learning disabilities, help all learners achieve greater success in your classroom!

State by State

Voters of Jefferson County, AL, challenged the Alabama legislature for failing to reflect increases in the county population. The Alabama legislature was reapportioned.

State by State references provide insights into specific state laws related to the content of each chapter. Use this space to record specific curriculum objectives for your state or district!

Features of the Teacher Edition by Chapter

Fully Developed, On-Page Lesson Plans Put a Wealth of Teaching Suggestions and Activities at Your Fingertips

Teacher planning and preparation is simplified by up-front identification of **Teaching Materials:** applicable program resources, outside materials, and formal assessment opportunities for each chapter of instruction.

Media icons integrate technology and multimedia into your classroom—from computers to publisher-supplied transparency masters and outlines, videotapes, and videodisc resources!

Vocabulary terms—and corresponding page references to the student text—are identified for each boldfaced vocabulary word in every chapter.

A **Chapter Self-Test** enables instructors to gauge what content-related information—and how much—each student brings to class prior to beginning a chapter. From the first moments of class, your students are involved, thinking critically about the issues and content of the chapter.

Teaching Materials

Student text, pp. 24–45

Overhead transparency masters

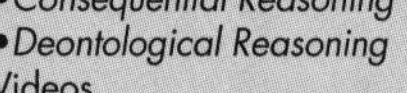

- *Consequential Reasoning*
- *Deontological Reasoning*

Videos

- *Our Legal System* Videotape
- *Law for Business* Videodisc

Workbook, pp. 3–4

Outside Resources

- Copy of minutes from recent town/city council meeting
- Index cards

- *An Amazing Grace*, videotape from Multi-Media Education, Inc.

Assessment

- Chapter Test

- Chapter *MicroExam*

Vocabulary

ethics, p. 26
impartiality, p. 27
consequential reasoning, p. 28
deontology, p. 28
The Good, p. 29
universalizing, p. 31
moral rights, p. 31
natural rights, p. 32
natural law, p. 32
false rights, p. 32
majority rule, p. 33
civil rights, p. 34
unconstitutional, p. 35
integrity, p. 37

Learning Objectives

When you complete this chapter, you will be able to

1. Recognize when ethics should affect a decision.
2. Determine when a person acts without regard to ethics.
3. Describe the basic forms of ethical reasoning.
4. Identify the ethical justification for many laws.
5. Explain why we are obligated to obey the law.
6. Distinguish between a scofflaw and civil disobedience.

24

Chapter Self-Test

Assess students' understanding of ethics, especially as applied to the law, before they begin Chapter 2 by asking them briefly to describe one circumstance in which people might believe it would be proper to break a rule or a law. (Answers may include to save someone from harm or for self-protection.) Before continuing with the chapter, review and discuss students' responses without making judgments.

24

Ethics Issue questions are integrated throughout each chapter, encouraging students to think ethically about the implication and consequences of their legal decisions.

Focus activities get students started with the chapter—even before the class bell rings! By making use of prior knowledge, building interest, and serving as a springboard to new learning, these activities engage your students in the learning process from the moment they enter your classroom.

CHAPTER 2 ETHICS IN OUR LAW

1 ETHICS ISSUE Mario was awarding end-of-year bonuses. As he looked over the list of employees, he rated each one based on how he felt about them. The political views of some of the employees affected his feelings. So did their physical attractiveness. Ultimately, Mario awarded the bonuses in proportion to the employee ratings. Has Mario made ethical decisions?

2 ETHICS ISSUE Sharon is knowledgeable about tax laws and how the Internal Revenue Service (IRS) audits tax returns. She knows a way to cheat on her tax return that would save her almost $2,000. She thinks her chance of being caught is about one in 100. Would it be ethical for Sharon to prepare her tax return in this way? Why, or why not?

3 James owns four dry cleaning

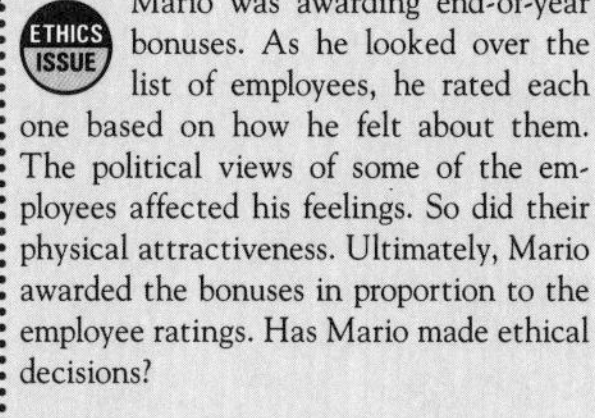

FOCUS

Begin Chapter 2 by having students write a brief response to this question: **Why, do you think, does this chapter on ethics follow the chapter on the U.S. Constitution?** (Answers may include that the law expresses society's basic ethical standards, and so on.)

After discussing the above question, direct students' attention to the statement on p. vii: *In our society the law is the official statement of what is right and wrong ...* Ask: **How do we know what is right and what is wrong?** (Answers may include religious teachings, community standards, family traditions and customs, and so on.)

Focusing on key concepts to be developed and reinforced, You Decide provides suggested answers to the three, open-ended teaser questions at the beginning of each chapter. You and your students will delight in applying your knowledge of business law to answer these dilemmas.

You Decide

1 ETHICS ISSUE Mario has not made ethical decisions. He relied on emotions rather than reason and he has not been impartial.

2 ETHICS ISSUE Sharon's actions are unethical because they injure the law, they injure other taxpayers who must pay more than their fair share, and because Sharon has, as a citizen, promised to obey her country's laws.

3 ETHICS ISSUE Ethically, James should hire the best qualified person. He should obey the law even if it is not enforced. Ethical reasoning demands that James should give the job to a woman, even if there were not a law.

Thinking Critically Through Visuals allows students to build and apply higher-level critical thinking skills to respond to each of the visuals in the text—from photographs and illustrations to figures, charts, and diagrams.

Thinking Critically Through Visuals

Ask students if they have ever seen a statue like the one on p. 25. Then ask the following questions: **Where did you see this kind of statue?** (Answers should indicate near or in a court house.) **Why are balanced scales and a blindfolded woman often used as symbols of courts of law?** (The blindfold over the eyes is the symbol of the impartiality of the law and the scales represent the law's commitment to weighing decisions carefully.)

Every question has a suggested answer to help you guide students to the most complete response.

25

Features of the Teacher Edition Lesson Plans

A Fully Developed, Multi-Step Teaching Plan for Each Instructional Lesson Provides a Blueprint to Teach, Apply, Assess, Reteach, and Enrich Key Business Law Concepts During Every Class Period—As Learning Happens!

Following a multi-step lesson plan, TEACH activities synthesize content and provide you with a variety of teaching suggestions to communicate the main points to your students.

Guided Practice activities allow you to direct and focus students' efforts as they begin to APPLY the concepts developed in the lesson. Pick and choose the activities that best meet your class's individual needs.

Writing Connections activities apply students' process writing skills to link other curricular areas to business law.

Independent Practice opportunities encourage students to apply business law concepts on their own, in a supportive learning environment.

On-page ASSESS activities help you informally monitor and evaluate students' understanding of key concepts and learning objectives on a daily basis—before you proceed with the next section.

Media icons highlight activities that integrate technology and multimedia resources into your business law curriculum.

38 UNIT 1 • LAW, JUSTICE, AND YOU

TEACH

Ask students to jot down one to three situations or instances that they think would justify violating the law. Discuss their responses. Help them identify acts of true civil disobedience.

APPLY

Have students form groups of four or five students and create and dramatize a situation and its ethical outcome. Each group must pick a director, a playwright who will put together the basic outline that the group as a whole will flesh out, and actors. **Guided Practice**

Writing Connections

Reading/Language Arts Edmund Burke, the 18th century English philosopher, wrote, *"The only thing necessary for the triumph of evil is for good men to do nothing."* As an independent writing activity, ask students to create an essay using the computer, if possible, connecting Burke's statement to the concept of civil disobedience. They may agree with or refute Burke's statement.

Independent Practice

death. While these penalties are widely known, there are many less well-known penalties imposed on criminals. For instance, persons convicted of serious crimes may be barred from jobs that require a security clearance. In many companies and governmental agencies, a security clearance is required for every employee. Also, some industries automatically exclude persons with criminal records from employment consideration. Banks, savings and loan associations, credit unions, and finance companies are but a few examples.

Employers often purchase fidelity bonds for persons who handle large sums of money, such as cashiers, managers of movie theaters, or supervisors of restaurants. A **fidelity bond** is an insurance policy that pays the employer money in the case of theft by employees. Generally, those convicted of a serious crime cannot qualify for a fidelity bond.

Also, many professions are closed to those who are convicted of serious crimes. For example, before being licensed, prospective lawyers, public accountants, and medical doctors are subject to a background check, which includes a check for criminal convictions. In the problem, if Clementine is caught and convicted, her biggest penalty could be the one she would "pay" outside the judicial system: the probable loss of many future job opportunities and her lasting embarrassment.

ARE WE EVER JUSTIFIED IN VIOLATING THE LAW?

PROBLEM

In the early 1960s, Martin Luther King, Jr., wanted to lead a march into Birmingham, Alabama, to protest racial segregation in that city. When he applied for a parade permit, his request was denied. Dr. King, knowing that his conduct was illegal, led the nonviolent march anyway. He was at the front of the line and allowed himself to be arrested, although he could have easily escaped. He went to jail. Community leaders were highly critical of Dr. King because he had violated the law. In response and while in jail, he wrote a famous letter attacking segregation laws as inconsistent with consequential and deontological ethical reasoning. Is there an ethical justification for Dr. King's violation of the law?

Some persons care passionately about human rights and justice. Their concern for justice sometimes compels them to violate what they consider a clearly unjust law. They violate the law by engaging in acts of civil disobedience. **Civil disobedience** is an open, peaceful, violation of a law to protest

ASSESS

Learning Objective 6 Ask students to write a response to the question: **Are we ever justified in breaking the law?** (Answers should reflect understanding of the seriousness of obeying the law.) For a wrap-up discussion on this objective, ask volunteers to share their answers to this question.

38

Use **Thinking Critically Through Visuals** to direct critical thinking toward visuals and informational graphics.

its alleged injustice. The goal of those who engage in civil disobedience is not to advance their self-interest but rather to make the legal system more just. Th... e arrested in order to test ...

Dr. ... ermine when a law is just o... res with the moral law or t... t of harmony with the mo... Aquinas, an unjust law is a... ural law. Any law that up... des human personality is ... y inflicts on a minority t... ade legal. On the

RETEACH and **ENRICH** activities use alternate teaching modalities to help students more fully grasp important concepts or extend and enrich understanding beyond the basic course content.

Thinking Critically Through Visuals

Have students review pp. 38–39 about **civil disobedience** and write a caption evaluating what is happening in the photograph. (Answers may include that Dr. King successfully used civil disobedience to fight for equal rights.)

Multicultural Highlights

Martin Luther King, Jr., often said that he based his nonviolent civil disobedience on the example of Mahatma Gandhi, the leader of India's independence movement. A trained attorney, Gandhi spent some time in British prisons for his actions. The Indian struggle was not without violence, but Gandhi felt that only nonviolent disobedience to Britain's restrictive colonial laws would be successful. One of Gandhi's major influences was Henry David Thoreau's essay "On Civil Disobedience." Ask students how King appeared to follow Gandhi's principles.

Multicultural Highlights focus on the contributions of women and various cultural and ethnic groups to our society. Also examined are the effects laws have had on these groups of people.

▼RETEACH Present a situation, such as parking in a handicapped zone without a permit. Ask: **Can this violation be justified?** (No, not ethically under the law) **Can you think of a situation when violation of the law would be justified?** (Answers should reflect understanding of civil disobedience.)

▼ENRICH Have students role-play a judge and a defendant. The situation is one in which a minor law has been violated. The violator must explain why the violation was justified. The judge must explain why it was not. Present the skits to the class.

Special Features in the Teacher Edition

Six High-Interest Features Supplement and Extend Instruction to Other Content Areas and Integrate Topics of Interest into Each Chapter

Ethics Issue activities provide opportunities for students to use their critical thinking skills to analyze ethical issues and offer opinions based on their understanding of right, wrong, and the law.

Preventing Legal Difficulties activities give students a head start in applying useful tips to avoid common legal problems.

Multicultural Highlights lend a real-life perspective and real-world focus to issues and contributions that affect America's women and cultural and ethnic groups as related to business law.

Personal Perspectives link chapter concepts to personal law applications and home-connection activities.

Thinking Critically Through Visuals encourages students to really seek the meaning behind the visuals and informational graphics that support the text activities.

Writing Connections to other disciplines, such as social studies, science, and language arts, allow students to use process writing and critical thinking to respond in a personally meaningful way to business law issues.

ETHICS ISSUE

Ethics Issue

Remind students that the chapter is entitled *Ethics in* ***Our*** *[emphasis added] Law*. Ask: **What, do you think, happens when people from cultures that value different goods must interact with one another or seek common goals?** (Answers may include developing awareness and understanding of

Multicultural Highlights

The law that ended slavery was the Thirteenth Amendment to the Constitution, which took effect on December 18, 1865. Because the Constitution is the supreme law of the land, no state or local area could vote to initiate or maintain slavery from that time forward. Ask: **Why would modern-day seekers of civil rights laws want such laws to be enacted at the federal level?** (Answers may include to ensure country-wide compliance.) **Independent Practice**

Preventing Legal Difficulties

After students have read the section on pp. 40–41, initiate a discussion by asking: **By accepting the benefits of a society, are we obligated to obey its laws?** (Answers should include that

Writing Connections

Reading/ Language Arts
Edmund Burke, the 18th century English philosopher, wrote, *"The only thing necessary for the triumph of evil is for good men to do nothing."* As an independent writing activity, ask students to create an essay using the computer, if possible, connecting Burke's state-

Personal Perspectives

Have students poll family members and/or friends to find out if white-collar crimes should carry greater, lesser, or the same punishment as other types of crime. Have students tabulate and present their findings as a bar chart, using graphics or spreadsheet software, if possible.

Independent Practice

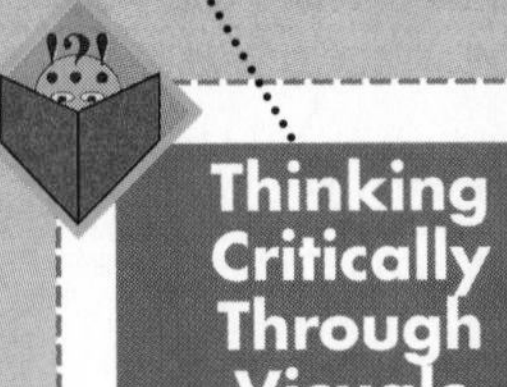

Thinking Critically Through Visuals

Discuss with students where they have seen graffiti art. Then ask: **Do you think that graffiti artists have a right to display their art in public places?** (Answers might include that graffiti is another example of

A Wealth of Instructional Media Components Support and Enhance Learning Every Class Period

Consumable copies of the student ***Workbook*** include chapter outlines and a variety of questioning techniques to reinforce and assess key learning objectives and content taught in each chapter.

Media In ***Mock Trial: A Question of Facts***, students view a realistic videotaped incident, then role-play trial procedures and apply critical thinking skills—firsthand opportunities to practice business law!

Media The ***Law for Business Videodisc*** is comprised of full-motion video that is barcoded and correlated to each chapter of the *Student Text. Mock Trial: A Question of Facts* is also included on the videodisc.

A comprehensive teacher ***Manual*** provides you with teaching essentials in one volume, including activity suggestions, answers to *Tests* and chapter review questions in the *Student Text*, the *Teacher Edition of the Workbook*, chapter outlines, overhead transparency masters, and bibliography references.

Tests and our computerized ***MicroExam*** for each chapter of instruction provide multiple evaluation and assessment opportunities in your choice of formats—both print and on-line for MS-DOS, Macintosh, and Apple.

Media Two videos, ***Our Legal System*** and ***Contracts, Warranties, and Credit,*** correlate real-world examples of business law applications to the *Student Text*.

Ordering Information

Need More Information? To Order or Find Out More About South-Western's Law for Business Components, Call the Following Toll-Free Number or Your Local Sales Representative: 1-800-543-7972.

Component	ISBN
Student Text (LA25NA)	0-538-60956-7
Abridged Student Text (LA26NA)	0-538-60958-3
Wraparound Teacher Edition (LA25NW)	0-538-63311-5
Manual (LA25NX)	0-538-60960-5
Workbook (LA25ND)	0-538-60957-5
Abridged Workbook (LA26ND)	0-538-60959-1
Tests (LA25NG)	0-538-61285-1
Abridged Tests (LA26NG)	0-538-61286-X
Our Legal System videotape (LA10AN1)	0-538-62008-0
Contracts, Warranties, and Credit videotape(LA10AN2)	0-538-62009-9
Law for Business videodisc (LA25NV)	0-538-63397-2
A Question of Facts: Mock Trial videotape (LA25NN1)	0-538-61759-4
MicroExam, Apple (LA25NH73T)	0-538-61289-4
MicroExam II, MS-DOS (LA25NH81T)	0-538-61287-8
MicroExam II, Macintosh (LA25NH71T)	0-538-61796-9
MicroExam, Abridged, Apple (LA26NH73T)	0-538-61290-8
MicroExam II, Abridged, MS-DOS (LA26NH81T)	0-538-61288-6
MicroExam II, Abridged, Macintosh (LA26NH71T)	0-538-61799-3

Law for Business

14TH EDITION

Norbert J. Mietus
Professor of Law Emeritus
School of Business Administration
California State University, Sacramento

John E. Adamson
Assistant Professor of Business and Law
Finance and General Business Department
Southwest Missouri State University

Edward J. Conry
Associate Professor
College of Business and Administration
University of Colorado at Denver

South-Western Publishing Co.

Credits:
Managing Editor: Robert E. Lewis
Developmental Editor: Nancy A. Long
Production Editor: Karen E. Davis
Associate Director/Design: Darren K. Wright
Associate Director/Photo Editing: Devore M. Nixon
Associate Editor/Educational Media: Christine Kunz
Marketing Manager: Donald H. Fox

ISBN: 0-538-60956-7

Library of Congress Catalog Card Number: 91-61755

2 3 4 5 6 D 97 96 95 94 93 92

Printed in the United States of America

Contents

iii

UNIT 4 CONTRACTS: BUYING AND SELLING GOODS 317

UNIT 5 USING CREDIT 383

UNIT 6 WORKING FOR OTHERS 427

UNIT 7 PROPERTY LAWS 525

UNIT 8 CHECKS AND OTHER COMMERCIAL PAPER 595

UNIT 9 PROTECTING AGAINST LOSS 653

UNIT 10 BUSINESS ORGANIZATIONS 729

Preface to Teachers

We are confident that you will find this fourteenth edition of *Law for Business,* with its supplements, to be the most effective instructional package in the field. The pedagogy of the book has been carefully designed to create a comprehensive learning system.

THE LEARNING PACKAGE

This system includes the following features.

Full Color

The textbook is printed in full color for heightened student interest. Photographs and a visually attractive layout increase both student interest and concentration.

Mock Trial

Materials for conducting a mock trial in the classroom are available to use with this learning package. The trial is based on a videotaped incident viewed by witnesses. During the mock trial, issues are raised relating to rules of evidence, biased witnesses, depositions, and physical evidence. Individual students participate as the plaintiff, defendant, witnesses, attorneys, and bailiff. The rest of the class acts as the jury. After rendering its verdict, the class is shown the actual videotaped incident. This exercise teaches both trial procedure and critical thinking. The jurors see how important and difficult it is to make accurate *inferences*—to construct pictures of reality from incomplete information.

Ethics

This edition presents, for the first time, *a complete chapter* on ethics and law. Chapter 2 provides students with concrete methods to use when resolving ethical issues.

Ethics is the study of what is right and wrong conduct. In our society the law is an official statement of what is right and wrong, so a law course is a great place to address ethics. The focus here is on determining what is right and wrong when the law is silent. Every chapter presents ethics questions in the introductory teasers and end-of-chapter activities. These ethics questions are marked by this symbol:

Mock Trial

Search Chapter 51, Play To 52

The teacher's manual also contains additional exercises designed to explore ethical issues. This depth of ethics coverage is greater than in any other high school text.

Critical Thinking

This book involves students in studying rules of law and how those rules apply to different factual situations, particularly in the end-of-chapter cases. When students apply the law to facts, they must make reasonable inferences. This is a central skill in critical thinking. These end-of-chapter activities, the teasers and problems presented in each chapter, the mock trial, factual examples of the application of the law, and many homework assignments will build the students' skills in critical thinking.

Chapter Structure

Each chapter incorporates special features that increase attention and foster retention. Three introductory teasers (short scenarios that pose legal questions) appear at the beginning of every chapter. These instantly capture reader interest, stimulate curiosity, and encourage careful reading. In a variation of the Socratic method of teaching, every section heading is expressed in the form of a question. It is followed by a legal problem phrased in understandable language. These challenge the students to think analytically and to check their mastery of the material in the section before proceeding. Thus students form the "connection of interest with materials" that is so important for durable learning. Key vocabulary words appear in the text in **boldface** and are followed by their definitions. All key terms are included in the Glossary at the end of the book for easy reference.

At the end of each chapter the very popular (for students and their parents) Preventing Legal Difficulties feature remains, along with Reviewing Important Points. The matching exercise Strengthening Your Legal Vocabulary reinforces the definitions of key terms introduced in the chapter. The fascinating hypothetical situations in Applying Law to Everyday Life and the carefully selected actual appellate cases in Solving Case Problems challenge students to apply what they have studied, analyze facts, and think critically. The case problems include shortened versions of old classics that are used in our nation's leading law schools, as well as recently decided cases that demonstrate the continuing evolution of the law.

Manual and Tests

Other new features for this edition include individual chapter tests (both printed and computerized) and two transparency masters for each chapter. The manual's Teaching Tools and Tips offers numerous suggestions for enriching your presentations by the use of nontraditional learning experiences. Detailed answers to Teasers and the end-of-chapter exercises, ethics questions, and legal cases are provided. Think Tank questions that are designed to stimulate class discussion are also provided. A bibliography provides additional references.

Student Workbook

The workbook is geared toward presenting questions and exercises that facilitate retention. Summary and review exercises are included in the workbook at appropriate intervals. New to this edition, a complete outline of each chapter provides room for the student to take notes.

Varied Pedagogy

This law package incorporates carefully balanced pedagogical approaches. *Interest-heightening* features include four-color print and realistic problems, examples, teasers, and cases. These are keyed to high school students whenever possible. *Review and repetition* is an integral part of the book's structure. The end-of-chapter materials, tests, and workbook exercises review and reinforce in ways which address the same concepts from a different perspective. *Visual and auditory* learning opportunities are provided with overhead transparency masters, the mock trial, and the nontraditional teaching suggestions in Teaching Tools and Tips. *Important points* are emphasized with headings, photographs, figures, and factual illustrations.

The total effect is a powerful learning system to support your classroom presentations. With this package, your students will have a sense of accomplishment as they progress through the course.

CONTENT COVERAGE

Experienced teachers know that our laws are made by fifty different states, the federal courts, and administrative agencies. Every law is subject to judicial interpretation and human beings engage in an infinite variety of activities under the law. Therefore, it is impossible to cover every possibility with precision. Exceptions, distinctions, and variations exist in even the simplest rules. Where *important* differences exist, an attempt has been made to present the generally prevailing view, as well as major exceptions. But a textbook of this nature is intended neither to be definitive nor to take the place of professional legal counsel for the resolution of specific legal problems.

Students who conscientiously read this book and successfully do the assigned work will better understand the legal world in which they live. They will expand their vocabularies and sharpen their abilities to think critically, analytically, and systematically. They will be better equipped to recognize legal problems and to utilize professional counsel.

To those many dedicated teachers who have worked with our book in the past and to those teachers and other friends who have been so generous with suggestions for its continued improvement, we express our sincere gratitude.

Norbert J. Mietus • John E. Adamson • Edward J. Conry

Introduction to Students

You will soon find that business law is one of your most interesting subjects. The problems you will study reflect true situations where business law has a major impact on the lives of young persons, such as you and your friends, as well as on adults and business firms. The learning materials will help you to achieve an understanding of legal principles which will be useful throughout your life. Below is a plan for effectively studying the text material.

HOW TO STUDY BUSINESS LAW

1. Each chapter is introduced by three questions that you should be able to answer from what you already know or what you think is fair or reasonable. In your mind, answer each question before you read the chapter. Refer back to these three questions after you have completed your study of the chapter and see if your answers have changed.
2. After you have answered the three introductory questions, scan the topic headings to get a general idea of what is included in the chapter.
3. After you have scanned the chapter, read it slowly and carefully. Make notes of the important points. (In the student workbook, there is an outline of every chapter with room to take notes.) Topic headings are stated in the form of a question and problems are presented in each chapter section. Try to answer each question and understand the solution to each problem before you study the next topic. If in doubt, read the topic again and, if necessary, ask someone to help you with it. If you do not know the meaning of a legal word, look it up in the glossary.
4. As you read, try to apply the rules to yourself or to your family and friends. Think about situations within your own experience to which the rules apply.
5. After you have carefully studied the chapter, read the section entitled Reviewing Important Points to refresh your memory and complete the activity entitled Strengthening Your Legal Vocabulary.
6. Examples of legal problems from real life are included in the section entitled Applying Law to Everyday Life and actual case problems can be solved in the section entitled Solving Case Problems. These appear at the end of each chapter. Each case or problem relates to the law discussed in that chapter. You can sharpen your wits by being the judge and solving them. Make a note of the page on which you think the answer to each is found.

xi

HOW YOU CAN SOLVE LEGAL PROBLEMS

Following each chapter, you will find a number of real-life problems under the heading Applying Law to Everyday Life. You will also find actual cases that have been decided by courts, headed Solving Case Problems. The method of solving is the same for both problems and cases.

To answer the question raised in a problem or case, first read it carefully. Be sure you understand the question. Then analyze the situation, determine the rule of law involved, and reach a decision. You will find it helpful to answer these five questions:

1. What are the facts?
2. What is the disputed point?
3. What rule of law is involved?
4. How does this rule apply to the facts?
5. What is the answer or decision?

A NOTE ON CASE CITATIONS

Law cases are referenced in a way that makes them easy for lawyers to find. There are four parts to a citation. For example, *28 A2d 309* identifies (1) a *series* of law books, (2) one *volume* in that series, and (3) the *page number* where the case begins in that volume.

In the example, *A2d* identifies the series of books that report the decisions of certain courts. The A stands for *Atlantic Reporter,* a series that reports the cases of appellate courts in the North Atlantic Region of the country. The *2d* indicates that the case appears in the second series of the *Atlantic Reporter.* The 28 in this example citation refers to Volume 28 in the series. The case begins on page 309.

LEGAL ADVICE

1. Choose a family lawyer.
2. Consult your lawyer if you have any doubts about your rights or duties when your property, life, or liberty is endangered or if significant changes occur in your circumstances.
3. Familiarize yourself with local, state, and federal laws to help avoid violations. Ignorance of the law is normally no excuse.
4. Remember that a minor is generally liable for crimes and torts and may also be bound by contracts.

5 If you are involved in a legal dispute, try to learn the other person's version and honestly seek a friendly solution out of court. In every court action at least one person loses—and often both find the costs burdensome.

6 If someone injures you or your property, do not rush to sign a statement releasing the person from liability in exchange for some payment of money. The damages may be greater than they appear at first. Consult your attorney immediately.

7 Although oral agreements can be legally binding, it is prudent to write out all contracts which involve significant time, money, or detail and to have both parties sign and receive copies.

Law, Justice, and You

Unit Overview

Unit 1, *Law, Justice, and You*, contains information that creates the foundation of the student text. In this unit, students will learn how our nation's laws were formed, the ethics behind our laws, our kinds of law, how laws are enforced, and the difference between crimes and torts.

The Constitution, the Bill of Rights, and subsequent amendments form the shield of U.S. liberty. In Chapter 1, *The Shield of the Constitution*, students will learn that the U.S. Constitution is the keystone of our nation. They'll discover how the Constitution came into being, how the Bill of Rights enhanced the original Constitution, and the problems that required more amendments be added to the Constitution.

Consequential and deontological forms of ethics are reflected in—and compel us to obey—our laws. In Chapter 2, *Ethics in Our Law*, students will study how we reason about right and wrong. In addition, students will study how ethical goals are reflected in our laws.

Criminal, civil, and business law are just a few kinds of law reflected in constitutions, statutes, and rulings by administrative agencies. In Chapter 3, *Kinds of Law*, students will discover how our laws developed and what types of law we have today. Students will learn which type of law is valid when laws conflict, how criminal and civil laws differ, how procedural and substantive laws differ, and what business law is.

In Chapter 4, *Enforcing the Law*, students will study our court system. They will have the opportunity to learn how a juvenile court differs from others, what the procedures are in criminal and civil actions, how a civil case is tried, and how a judgment is satisfied.

In Chapter 5, *Crimes*, students will understand how crimes are classified, what business-related crimes are, and what rights a person has when arrested. They will be actively involved in defining when one party is responsible for the criminal conduct of another, what the defenses are to criminal charges, and what the punishments are for crimes.

Torts fall under a variety of classifications. In Chapter 6, *Torts*, students will learn what the elements of a tort are, what common intentional torts are, what negligence is, what strict liability is, when a person is responsible for the torts of another, and what a victim of a tort can collect.

At the end of the unit, you'll find a special section, *Pressing Issue: Environmental Law,* which can be used at any time during the study of Unit 1. You may wish to assign its accompanying *Teacher Edition* activity to give students an opportunity to research an environmental issue and present their findings as a unit project to the class.

Portfolio Assessment

Have students skim current newspapers or news magazines to find a controversial political case or timely issue that interests them or affects their daily lives. Have students collect five to ten articles about the case to familiarize themselves with the issue. To understand how the law is involved in the issues, ask students to think about questions such as: How is the law being enforced? Is the case criminal or civil? If criminal, what kind of crime was committed? If civil, what type of tort was committed? Is this an ethical issue? Using a computer, if possible, have students exercise their First Amendment rights by writing a letter to their mayor, governor, or senator expressing their point of view on the issue. Encourage students to send their letters. Have students put a copy of their letter in portfolios or law journals labeled *The Law & You.* Tell students that, at the end of each unit, they will complete a writing assignment and add it to their portfolio.

Careers

Police Officer

Our country's laws include not only the rules of conduct for its people but also the means of enforcing those rules. It is the duty of police officers to know the law, to protect the lives and property of citizens, prevent crimes, apprehend law-breakers, maintain order, and testify in court.

Many police departments require at least a high-school education of their officers. A candidate should be at least 21 years old, meet minimum height and weight requirements, pass a physical exam and a civil-service test. Entry-level salaries are between $18,000 and $22,000.

Have each student skim through newspapers looking for articles involving police action. Have them highlight the sections that discuss what law was broken, what procedural and substantive laws were used, and the results. Then, have students create a large chart with the categories: *Civil* and *Criminal*, and secure the clipped articles to it.

Annotated Bibliography

- ***Banco Nacional de Cuba v. Sabbatino*, 376 U.S. 398 (1964).**
  It is a violation of the international law for a country to fail to pay adequate compensation for the property it seizes from a particular class of aliens, when the purpose of the seizure is to retaliate against the homeland of those aliens and the result of such seizure discriminates against them only. (Chapter 1)

- ***Miranda v. Arizona,* 384 U.S. 436 (1966).**
  The privilege against self-incrimination is the essential mainstay of our adversary system and guarantees to the individual the "right to remain silent unless he or she chooses to speak in the unfettered exercise of his own will." Statements of an accused may not be used against the accused unless he or she has been clearly informed that he or she has the right to remain silent, that anything he or she says will be used against him or her in a court, that he or she has the right to consult with a lawyer and have the lawyer present during interrogation, and that, if he or she is indigent, a lawyer will be appointed to represent him or her. (Chapter 5)

Law, Justice, and You

- The Shield of the Constitution
- Ethics in Our Law
- Kinds of Law
- Enforcing the Law
- Crimes
- Torts

UNIT 1
LAW, JUSTICE, AND YOU

CHAPTER 1 ORGANIZER

Chapter Theme

The Constitution, the Bill of Rights, and subsequent amendments form the shield of U.S. liberty.

DIRECTED STUDY QUESTIONS	SPECIAL FEATURES	PROGRAM RESOURCES				
		Reteach	Enrich	SN	AM	
What makes our nation great?	Writing Connections, p. 5	✓	✓			
How did the Constitution come into being?	Thinking Critically Through Visuals, p. 8	✓	✓			
Did the Constitution give total governing power to the federal government?		✓	✓			
How did the Bill of Rights enhance the original Constitution?	Ethics Issue, p. 11 Thinking Critically Through Visuals, p. 14 Personal Perspectives, p. 14	✓	✓	✓	A V	
What problems required more amendments to the Constitution?	Multicultural Highlights, p. 15 Preventing Legal Difficulties, p. 17	✓	✓		K	

Additional Resources

- ABC News Interactive™. *Martin Luther King Jr., HyperCard* stack and videodisc. ABC News.
- Alderman, Ellen and Kennedy, Caroline. *In Our Defense: the Bill of Rights in Action*. NY: Morrow, 1991.
- *Born Yesterday*. Videotape, Warner Bros,: 1993
- Bowen, Catherine Drinker. *Miracle at Philadelphia: The Story of the Constitutional Convention*, May to September, 1787. Boston: Little, Brown, 1966.
- Peters, William. *A More Perfect Union.* New York: Crown Publishers, 1987.
- Rhodehamel, John H. *Letters of Liberty: A Documentary History of the United States Constitution*. Los Angeles, CA: Constitutional Rights Foundation, 1988.

Chapter Pacing Guide

One-semester course	✔	✔	✔					
One-year course	✔	✔	✔	✔	✔			

	ASSESSMENT OPPORTUNITIES			
Cooperative Learning	**Informal Assessment**	**Chapter Review**	**Chapter Test**	**Chapter *MicroExam*** (Media)
	✔	✔	✔	✔
✔	✔	✔	✔	✔
	✔	✔	✔	✔
	✔	✔	✔	✔
	✔	✔	✔	✔

Videodiscs

Three Key Features of the U.S. Legal System

Search Chapter 1, Play To 2

State by State

Amendment XXVII, proposed in 1789, was added to the Constitution in 1992 when Michigan became the 38th state to ratify it. Now there can be no mid-term pay cuts or raises for Congress.

Teaching Materials

Student text, pp. 2–23

Overhead transparency masters
• *The Three Branches of Our Government in a Unique System of Checks and Balances*
• *The Legal Shield of Our Freedom*

Videos
• *Our Legal System* Videotape
• *Law for Business* Videodisc

Workbook, pp. 1–2

Outside Resources
• Poster board
• Blank overhead transparencies
• Flip chart
• Voter registration materials
• Copies of state constitution
• Newspaper articles dealing with application of federal or state law

• Camcorder
• VCR
• *Born Yesterday,* videotape from Warner Bros.
• ABC News InterActive™: *Martin Luther King Jr., HyperCard* stack and videodisc from ABC News

Assessment
• Chapter Test

• Chapter *MicroExam*

Vocabulary

U.S. Constitution, p. 5
Bill of Rights, p. 5
Declaration of Independence, p. 5
War of Independence, p. 5
Articles of Confederation, p. 6
system of checks and balances, p. 6
Senate, p. 7
House of Representatives, p. 7
Democratic and Republican political parties, p. 7
political party, p. 7
amendment, p. 8
pure democracy, p. 8
republic, p. 8
sovereignty, p. 9
state constitution, p. 10
legal rights, p. 13
legal duties, p. 13
due process of law, p. 13
civil rights, p. 13

Learning Objectives

When you complete this chapter, you will be able to

1. Explain how the U.S. Constitution has contributed to the development of one of the greatest countries in the history of the world.
2. Explain the relationship between the Declaration of Independence and the Constitution.
3. Identify how the Constitution has been a shield against possible violations of basic human rights.
4. Identify the three major parts of the Constitution.
5. Explain how power to govern and make laws is divided between the federal and state governments.
6. Identify the principal human rights protected by the Bill of Rights and by subsequent amendments.
7. Explain how additional amendments improved the Constitution.

2

Chapter Self-Test

Assess students' understanding of the Constitution and the Bill of Rights before they begin Chapter 1 by posing the following questions to the class. As you read aloud each question, have students jot down *True* or *False* on a sheet of paper. **(1) The Bill of Rights is the name given to the first 15 amendments.** (False); **(2) The Fifteenth Amendment was a deliberate exclusion of "gender" in the denial of voting rights to women of all races.** (True); and **(3) The legislative branch of the U.S. government consists of the Senate and the House of Representatives.** (True) Before continuing with the chapter, review and discuss students' responses. At this time, you may wish to assign the *Law for Business Pretest,* found on the first two pages of the Tests booklet.

THE SHIELD OF THE CONSTITUTION

1 Each of our fifty states is equal in its sovereign (supreme) governing status within its own borders. However, some states, such as Alaska and Wyoming, are greatly outnumbered in eligible voters by a few very populous states, such as California and New York. How does the U.S. Constitution protect the rights of all states in terms of congressional power?

2 ETHICS ISSUE Nanette and Philo were seriously discussing legal rights and duties. "We are lucky because we have a Bill of Rights that guarantees at least all human rights for our citizens!" said Nanette. "No, no, Nanette," Philo protested, "that's not true!" Who is correct? Does the Bill of Rights, along with other amendments, uphold high standards of ethical conduct?

3 At the time of the American Revolution, no American was serving in the British Parliament, yet taxes had been imposed on the colonists. As a result, one rallying cry for revolution was "Taxation without representation is tyranny!" Recently, Jake recalled this historical fact when he received his paycheck. "Look at that," he grumbled. "Deductions for federal income taxes, state income taxes, and social security taxes. And I pay sales taxes and property taxes. What we need is another revolution!" What might you say to calm Jake down?

3

FOCUS

Pair students as they enter the classroom and ask each pair to think of as many amendments to the U.S. Constitution as they can. Have them jot down any information about the amendment, along with its corresponding number, if they know it.

When class begins, poll students to determine with which amendments they are most familiar. Lead a brief discussion on why the amendments were written and whom they benefited.

You Decide

1 Each state, regardless of population, has two senators in the Senate; membership in the House is determined by state population. Therefore, the large number of less populous states have proportionately greater power in the Senate; the more populous states have greater power in the House.

2 ETHICS ISSUE Philo; Some rights are in the original Constitution, others in the Bill of Rights, and still others are identified and applied through detailed laws enacted by Congress or added to state constitutions.

3 Jake is represented at the federal, state, and local levels by the representatives his fellow voters and he elect (if he is of legal voting age and exercises this right). If Jake is unhappy, there are several accepted ways to express his disapproval, including the right to write or phone his protests to his representatives, to attend rallies, or to give speeches. Before he proceeds, however, it would be prudent for Jake to gather the facts and to determine how his tax revenue is actually used.

Thinking Critically Through Visuals

The individuals in this photograph appear to be attending a convention of one of the U.S political parties. Which party— the Democratic party or the Republican party—do you think, is holding the convention? What clues in the photograph let you know? (The Republican party. Its symbol is an elephant. An elephant logo is pictured in the foreground above the names of the states of Louisiana and Kansas.)

▼ TEACH

Tell students that our nation is great for a variety of reasons, including our various heritages, cultures, religions, and vast natural resources as well as our freedom to compete, progress, and be educated. Explain, however, that the keystone of the United States of America is the U.S. Constitution including the Bill of Rights—its first 10 amendments.

▼ APPLY

The technical and archaic language of the Constitution may pose some difficulties for students reading the document independently. Preview with students this document, which is found in Appendix A, pp. 785–804. Explain, or even omit, some of the more technical procedural passages so that students get a feel for the intent, but are not bogged down by the language. **Guided Practice**

[I]ts soul, its climate, its equality, liberty, laws, people, and manners. My God! how little do my countrymen know what precious blessings they are in possession of, and which no other people on earth enjoy![1]

—Thomas Jefferson
Author of the Declaration of Independence

▼ WHAT MAKES OUR NATION GREAT?

PROBLEM

Students in a high school class had just seen and heard the President of the United States' televised State of the Union message. The President spoke to the Senate and the House of Representatives meeting in a joint session of Congress, along with the nine Justices of the Supreme Court. Also attending were ambassadors from the world's leading countries.

The class period was almost over when the instructor flicked off the television. Then she said, "Thanks to television, we have just witnessed history in the making and law in action. Attending this meeting were key personnel from the three branches of our government: the legislative, the executive, and the judicial. The President spoke as the head of what most people—correctly, I think—regard as the greatest country in the history of the world. So, your special assignment for our next class is to answer this question: If indeed we are 'the greatest,' what one factor or reason best explains this greatness?"

At the next class meeting, students presented the following reasons:

- "Our melting pot of people. In this class we have thirty students. I'll bet our ancestors came from at least fifteen different countries. They brought with them a great variety of useful knowledge, talent, and skills."
- "Our nation's unique combination of cultures—races, religions, customs—all blended into one dynamic AMERICAN culture. There has been friction, but it has encouraged competition and progress."
- "Our natural resources: millions of acres of rich, productive land, both clear and forested; mountains containing needed minerals; an abundance of coal, natural gas, and petroleum; and many freshwater lakes and rivers."

[1]Excerpt from a letter to James Monroe, fifth President of the United States, dated June 17, 1785.

▼ ASSESS

Learning Objective 1 Have students respond orally to the following question: **How did our Constitution contribute to making our country one of the greatest in the history of the world?** (Answers may include that our Constitution is able to change with the times; it provides us with justice, liberty, and defense as well as many other rights.) For students having difficulty verbalizing their understanding, assign the reteaching activity on p. 5. For students who have mastered the concept, an enrichment activity is offered.

- "Saltwater, too, off our coasts. The oceans have provided insulation that's kept the two world wars off our soil."
- "Thanks to free public education, individuals are not frozen into place on the economic or social ladders. Ability coupled with hard work does pay off."

Other reasons were added. Finally the instructor said, "Those are very good answers. But no one has mentioned what is perhaps the paramount reason for our greatness and good fortune. It is the keystone, the reason that makes the others possible, usable, or meaningful. That reason is the **U.S. Constitution** including amendments starting with the **Bill of Rights**—the popular name given to the first ten amendments. The Constitution, as amended and as interpreted by the U.S. Supreme Court, is the supreme law of our country. It has been a veritable shield for our liberty."

In this chapter, we study that shield by examining the three major segments of that document, together with important amendments. A copy of the U.S. Constitution is provided in Appendix A.

HOW DID THE CONSTITUTION COME INTO BEING?

PROBLEM

June and Max happened to be born during the same week some eighteen years ago. Both will soon legally become adults. "That means we can vote," said June. "I plan to register as a Democrat, since we live in a democracy. How will you register?" Max replied, "Nonsense, we don't live in a democracy. We live in a republic. We should both register as Republicans." Who is correct about our system of government?

1. The Birth of a Nation Under Law

The **Declaration of Independence** was formally adopted on July 4, 1776, by delegates from the thirteen original American colonies meeting in Philadelphia. The Declaration charged the King of Great Britain with "a History of repeated Injuries and Usurpations, all having in direct Object the Establishment of an absolute Tyranny. . . ." It proclaimed the existence of "certain unalienable Rights" and declared that "to secure these Rights, Governments are instituted among Men, deriving their just Powers from the Consent of the Governed, that whenever any Form of Government becomes destructive of these Ends, it is the Right of the People to alter or to abolish it, and to institute new Government. . . ."

At the time the Declaration was adopted, the American **War of Independence** had already begun (in April 1775), when British troops marched

Writing Connections

Language Arts/ Social Studies
Have students skim the U.S. Constitution found in Appendix A of the student text. Using a computer, if possible, have students write a personal response to the following statement: **The U.S. Constitution is an obsolete relic of the past.** After volunteers have read their essays aloud, discuss students' reactions. Display the essays on a bulletin board entitled *Our Constitution: Passé or for Today?*
Media **Independent Practice**

TEACH

Be sure students understand the 11 vocabulary terms from pp. 5–9. Discuss the steps of how today's Constitution came into being. Display the overhead transparency, *The Three Branches of Our Government in a Unique System of Checks and Balances,* as a visual aid to help explain the division and balance of power. Stress to students the importance of voting—and voting intelligently—if democracy is to survive and thrive in the United States.

RETEACH Have students create a poster to illustrate what makes our nation great. Encourage students to add to the poster their own reasons for our country's greatness.

ENRICH Media Display the overhead transparency, *The Legal Shield of Our Freedom.* Ask students to brainstorm what the three symbols (shield, olive branch, and dove) represent. Then, have students skim the amendments in Appendix A for key words or phrases that make these symbols meaningful.

APPLY

On the chalkboard, draw a cause-and-effect chart. Accurately list each vocabulary word in this section in one of the two columns. Then have students give you its correct counterpart. Continue with this pattern until each of the vocabulary words and its cause or effect has been added to the chart. **Guided Practice**

Have students create a timeline to illustrate how the Constitution came into being. On an overhead transparency or on the chalkboard, write the following information: **(1776) Declaration of Independence formally adopted; (1789) Congress declared Constitution effective; (1787) U.S. Constitution drafted; (1775) War of Independence begins; (1788) U.S. Constitution ratified by nine states; (1781) Articles of Confederation formed.** Encourage students to be creative by using computer graphics, three-dimensional techniques, and so on.

Independent Practice

some seventeen miles from Boston through Lexington and on to Concord. Their mission was to destroy rebel military stores at Concord. The resulting war lasted more than eight long years before the last British forces left New York. However, a battle of words continued among the thirteen sovereign states. They had united loosely in 1781 under a charter called the **Articles of Confederation.** Many felt a need for a stronger central government with uniform laws on immigration, money standards, postal service, taxes on imports, and—notably in a war-torn world—an adequate national army and navy.

As a result, the U.S. Constitution was finally drafted by a special convention of delegates from the original thirteen states meeting in Philadelphia during the hot summer of 1787. By June 1788, their work had been ratified by delegates to special conventions in nine of the states. Accordingly, our existence as a truly united country began on March 4, 1789, when Congress declared the Constitution effective and binding on the nine states that had ratified it. More than a year later, Rhode Island became the last of the original thirteen states to ratify.

2. The Original Constitution and the Bill of Rights

The seven articles of the initial document provided an eminently workable framework for a federal government "of the people, by the people, and for the people."[2] However, although the Constitution defined and established our new government, critics in some states feared future violation of fundamental rights by the strong central power. Therefore, the Bill of Rights was enacted as a shield against the possible violation of specified human rights by the federal government.

3. Additional Amendments

Subsequent amendments made important improvements in the Constitution. Especially noteworthy are the Thirteenth, Fourteenth, and Fifteenth Amendments, enacted shortly after the Civil War. All three were designed to end slavery and to provide a shield against the violation of human rights by state governments.

4. Division and Balance of Powers

Warren E. Burger, former Chief Justice of the U.S. Supreme Court, has pointed out that at the time the Constitution was drafted and adopted, "there was no country in the world that governed with separated and divided powers providing checks and balances on the exercise of authority by those who governed." Thus, the fifty-five delegates who drafted the U.S. Constitution displayed rare genius and foresight in devising a unique **system**

[2]From President Abraham Lincoln's Gettysburg Address, November 19, 1863.

ASSESS

Learning Objective 2 Read aloud the following statements and have students answer *True* or *False*. If a statement is false, have students change one word to make it true. **(1) The Declaration of Independence was adopted on July 4, 1776, by delegates from 10 original colonies.** (False/13); **(2) The Senate and House of Representatives are parts of the executive branch.** (False/legislative); and **(3) We live in a republic, not a pure democracy.** (True)

of checks and balances, which endures even now. In this system, specific authority is given to each of the three basic branches of government: the legislative, the executive, and the judicial.

The legislative branch is the Congress. Convention delegates from states with small populations were understandably concerned that they would lose some measure of the sovereignty and independence of action each had been enjoying under the Articles of Confederation. On the other hand, the few states with large populations feared they would be dominated by the many more less populous states if each state were to be given an equal number of votes regardless of the number of its citizens. The solution? The national legislature would consist of two bodies: (1) a **Senate**, with two members from every state regardless of population, and (2) a **House of Representatives,** with seats allocated to the states in proportion to their population.[3] In effect, the Senate may block any action of the House, and vice versa. All bills for taxing or appropriating funds must originate in the House, but a majority vote of both chambers is required for passage of any bill.

A further check is available to the House of Representatives. The House has the power to initiate the impeachment of any civil officer of the United States, including the President and the Vice President, for treason, bribery, or other high crimes and misdemeanors. However, the Senate has the sole power to try all impeachments, and conviction requires a two-thirds vote of the members present. Finally, the people who vote may "throw the rascals out" in elections to the House (for a two-year term), the Senate (for a six-year term), and the executive office (for a four-year term).

The executive branch is headed by the President and Vice President, who are elected by popular vote of all the people. This is accomplished through a process whereby citizens vote for the actual electors who are pledged to support candidates selected by political parties.[4] Although the **Democratic and Republican political parties** select candidates for President and Vice President, parties are not even mentioned in the Constitution. Nevertheless, over the years, many political parties have sought general public support. A **political party** is a group of citizens who are loosely affiliated in a private organization to select and promote for election to public office candidates who agree with them on important governmental policies and legislation.

The third branch of government is the judiciary, headed by the Supreme Court of the United States. Ultimately, it is the Supreme Court that decides whether a statute passed by the legislative branch—the Congress—and signed by the President as head of the executive branch is in fact

[3]There are fifty Senators and 435 members of the House of Representatives.

[4]The process is prescribed in Article II, Section 1, of the U.S. Constitution, as amended by the Twelfth, Twentieth, Twenty-second, and Twenty-fifth Amendments.

Have students draw a graphic organizer to outline and summarize the three branches of government. Give students the following instructions to draw a fishbone map: In a rectangle at the far left of the paper, write **Checks and Balances.** Draw a horizontal line from the right of the rectangle across the paper and add one diagonal branch (like a fishbone) for each of the three branches of government. Add horizontal writing lines connected to the diagonal lines to add supporting details regarding checks and balances.

Students may be amazed that each of the three branches of government is subject to limiting guidance and control by the other two, yet there has never been a deadlock or breakdown in the activity of any of the three. Have students brainstorm a plausible response to this phenomenon.

RETEACH Have students create a poster, bulletin board, poem, or rap to describe the functions of the three branches of government. Have students share their selection with the class.

ENRICH On poster board, have students create a flowchart to illustrate how the U.S. Constitution came into being. Display the flowcharts on the walls of your classroom as you complete this chapter.

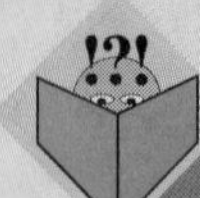

Thinking Critically Through Visuals

The woman in the photograph is voting at a local polling place. Is she exercising a right or a duty? (Answers may include either or both responses because voting may be considered both a right and a duty.)

Hold a class election for a Business Law Class President. Divide the class into groups of three or four students. Except for one group, assign the following roles in each group: publicity manager to create ad campaign, candidate to give a speech and participate in a debate, speech writer to write persuasive speeches for the candidate, and campaign manager (optional) to keep everyone on task. Each student in the remaining group will have two roles: voter to choose the best candidate plus one of the following: engineer/architect to design and "construct" the polling place; newspaper journalist to write news articles on the candidates; camera person to videotape the debates and speeches; television reporter to interview candidates; or election coordinator to schedule debates, speeches, interviews, and so on. Play the videotape to other business law classes.

Cooperative Learning

unconstitutional and therefore void. The Supreme Court can also be called on to decide if a particular action or decision of the President exceeds the powers granted to the executive branch under the Constitution and, if so, is therefore void.

Finally, a major check is provided by the power of **amendment**, meaning change or alteration. The Constitution may be amended in either of two ways. The first way has been used for all amendments adopted to date: the amendment is proposed by a two-thirds majority vote in both the Senate and the House. The second way requires the legislatures of two-thirds of all the states to call a convention of all the states and the convention may propose one or more amendments. Thereafter, under either method of proposal, the amendment becomes a valid part of the U.S. Constitution only if it is ratified by the legislatures of three-fourths of the states, or if it is ratified by conventions in three-fourths of the states.[5]

In a **pure democracy,** every adult citizen may vote on all issues. This is practically impossible in our nation of more than 250 million persons. Instead, we have a **republic** (as stated in the Pledge of Allegiance to the flag of the United States), or representative democracy, in which voters democratically select persons to represent them in the legislative, executive, and judicial branches of government. Thus, the sovereign power ultimately resides in the people. Practically, this means that the highest final authority to decide what the law shall be rests with those citizens who exercise their

[5]The particular mode for ratification is specified by Congress. In practice, Congress has permitted the states to follow their own state constitutional requirements for ratification. Some have ratifying conventions; others permit ratification by the state legislatures. Congress stipulates the time limit for ratification of proposed amendments. The time limit has usually been seven years from the date of submission to the state legislatures. In the case of the Equal Rights Amendment (ERA), Congress extended the time to ten years. However, only thirty-five states had ratified it by the second deadline, and approval of thirty-eight was necessary to make it law. The ERA provided: "Equality of rights under the law shall not be denied or abridged by the United States or by any State on account of sex."

▼ ASSESS

Learning Objective 3 As you read aloud the following statements, have students state whether they are *True* or *False:* **(1)** ***Amendment*** **means a change or alteration.** (True); **(2) A representative democracy is one in which voters democratically select persons to represent them.** (True); and **(3) An amendment can become a valid part of the Constitution if it is ratified by the legislatures of only one-half of the states.** (False) right and duty to vote. This is often only a minority of the total number who are eligible.

In the problem, neither June nor Max had a correct impression of our form of government or what the political parties represent. Think about the significance of what Chief Justice Burger also said: "The work of 55 men at Philadelphia in 1787 marked the beginning of the end of the concept of the divine right of kings. In place of the absolutism of monarchy, the freedom flowing from this document created a land of opportunities. Ever since then, discouraged and oppressed people from every part of the world have made a beaten path to our shores. This is the meaning of our Constitution."

Using a computer, if possible, have students write an essay on why they think only a minority of the total number of U.S. citizens who are eligible to vote actually do so. Ask students to offer suggestions on how to encourage adult citizens

to participate in this democratic right and duty.

▼ DID THE CONSTITUTION GIVE TOTAL GOVERNING POWER TO THE FEDERAL GOVERNMENT?

PROBLEM

It was July 4th. Several thousand people had assembled in the park for the annual celebration, complete with speeches and a band concert. The state's senior federal senator opened the ceremonies. "On this day, on all days," he said, "I am proud and pleased to be a citizen of the United States of America. I feel no less proud and fortunate to be a citizen of this great sovereign state that is ours. But I tell you: before I am a citizen of either the state or the country, I am a human being. And so too are you who hear my voice. By divine providence we share with mankind the gifts of reason and freedom of will that dignify and unite us. Our humanity precedes our citizenship. Government exists only by the will and consent of the people. It is the people who control the government. Any control by the government of the people is by virtue of permission granted and maintained." Does the governmental structure created by the U.S. Constitution conform to the senator's outspoken analysis?

▼ TEACH

Read aloud the Ninth and Tenth Amendments and Article VI, found in quotations on pp. 9–10. Ask students to interpret the meanings. Clarify any misconceptions. Explain that, although the U.S. Constitution is the supreme law of the land, state constitutions are also supreme within their limited spheres of authority. Point out that the U.S. Constitution gives the federal government *enumerated powers,* or those powers specifically delegated to it; all other powers remain with the states and the people.

1. Sovereignty of the States

The Constitution and the Bill of Rights were drafted by representatives of the people elected by voters in the thirteen original states. There is a priority in time, in scope, and in the nature of the basic rights of human beings when they act as individuals or in concert with each other. The Ninth Amendment recognizes this priority when it states, "The enumeration in the Constitution, of certain rights, shall not be construed to deny or disparage others retained by the people."

The Tenth Amendment acknowledges the continued sovereignty of all of the states to govern their own citizens within their own borders. **Sovereignty** is freedom from external control. The Tenth Amendment declares:

▼RETEACH Discuss the advantages and disadvantages of a pure democracy and a republic as well as the differences between the two. Then, in small groups, have students make graphic organizers comparing the two types of democracies.

▼ENRICH Have students find out how to register to vote, or provide voter registration materials. Using a computer, if possible, have students create a brochure showing how to become a registered voter. Encourage them to use the power of the vote to vote in student government elections.

▼ APPLY

On the chalkboard, create a two-column chart with the headings: **State Laws** and **Federal Laws.** As a class, list in the appropriate columns instances or areas in which each state rules supreme and those in which the federal government rules supreme. Have students brainstorm examples of business and contractual law, criminal and tort law, real property and probate law, and domestic relations law. **Guided Practice**

Obtain and distribute copies of your state constitution to groups of four or five. (If state history is taught at your school, that textbook usually contains the state constitution.) Then, have students compare it to the U.S. Constitution. Discuss the differences and similarities. **Independent Practice**

▼ TEACH

Explain to students that the original Constitution failed to include important human rights included in the Declaration of Independence, which were later added by the *Bill of Rights*—the first 10 amendments. Explain the difference between *legal rights* and *legal duties*. Explain that *due process of law* and *civil rights* are both important concepts found in the Bill of Rights.

"The powers not delegated to the United States by the Constitution, nor prohibited by it to the States, are reserved to the States respectively, or to the people." Here it is evident that the Constitution is a shield against unlimited power of the federal government.

Nevertheless, in Article VI, the U.S. Constitution is recognized as "the supreme law of the land," and it prevails over any possible contrary state constitution or law. At the same time, every **state constitution** and the respective statutes are supreme on matters that have not been delegated to the federal government. Powers retained by the states include control over most business law and contract law, most criminal and tort law, real property and probate law, and domestic relations law.

2. Powers of the Federal Government

The federal government has the duty to protect every state against invasion, and it may raise and support armies, a navy, and an air force for national defense. The federal government has exclusive power to regulate interstate (i.e., between states) and foreign commerce, but each state retains authority to regulate intrastate commerce (i.e., within its own borders). The federal government alone may establish post offices, coin money, and tax imports and exports, but both federal and state legislatures may impose other taxes (on sales and on incomes).

Congress has the power to make detailed laws it considers appropriate for executing its enumerated powers. The people, through their votes, ultimately control the entire governmental structure. Each adult retains power over choice of a place to live and to work, a career, friends, travel, holiday activities, and many other ingredients that determine one's personal life-style.

It is evident that in the problem, the senator's comments accurately reflect the reality of the relationship between citizens and our government today. However, even after the Bill of Rights was added to the Constitution, certain serious deficiencies existed in the Constitution and in the resulting life of our nation.

▼ HOW DID THE BILL OF RIGHTS ENHANCE THE ORIGINAL CONSTITUTION?

PROBLEM

The Constitution was drafted in 1787. It was ratified by the ninth state, New Hampshire, in 1788, and immediately thereafter became effective for all nine states that had ratified it. But the four other states took longer; the vote of approval finally became unanimous in 1790 when Rhode Island became the thirteenth state to ratify. What caused the delay?

▼ ASSESS

Learning Objective 5 Have students work together to create a graphic organizer on the chalkboard, a flip chart, or an overhead transparency that graphically illustrates how the power to govern and make laws is divided between the federal and state governments.

Critics complained that the Constitution failed to mention the human rights proclaimed by these memorable words in the Declaration of Independence: "We hold these Truths to be self-evident, that all Men are created equal, that they are endowed by their Creator with certain unalienable Rights, that among these are Life, Liberty, and the Pursuit of Happiness." How was this fundamental deficiency in the Constitution corrected? The shortcoming of the Constitution referred to in the problem was corrected by adoption of the first ten amendments, the Bill of Rights. As noted earlier, they are a shield against possible abusive conduct by the federal government.

AMENDMENT I.

Congress shall make no law respecting an establishment of religion, or prohibiting the free exercise thereof; or abridging the freedom of speech, or of the press, or the right of the people peaceably to assemble, and to petition the Government for a redress of grievances.

AMENDMENT II.

A well regulated Militia, being necessary to the security of a free State, the right of the people to keep and bear Arms, shall not be infringed.

AMENDMENT III.

No Soldier shall, in time of peace be quartered in any house, without the consent of the Owner, nor in time of war, but in a manner to be prescribed by law.

AMENDMENT IV.

The right of the people to be secure in their persons, houses, papers, and effects, against unreasonable searches and seizures, shall not be violated, and no Warrants shall issue, but upon probable cause, supported by Oath or affirmation, and particularly describing the place to be searched, and the persons or things to be seized.

AMENDMENT V.

No person shall be held to answer for a capital, or otherwise infamous crime, unless on a presentment or indictment of a Grand Jury, except in cases arising in the land or naval forces, or in the Militia, when in actual service in time of War or public danger; nor shall any person be subject for the same offence to be twice put in jeopardy of life or limb, nor shall be compelled in any criminal case to be a witness against himself, nor be deprived of life, liberty, or property, without due process of law; nor shall private property be taken for public use without just compensation.

APPLY

Students are probably familiar with the phrase, *"I take the Fifth."* Have students read the Fifth Amendment and take turns interpreting and applying it to various scenarios that students create. **Guided Practice**

ETHICS ISSUE

Ethics Issue

The National Rifle Association (NRA) heavily lobbies Congress on issues dealing with individuals' rights to keep and bear arms—in effect, to buy, own, and use guns. Divide the class into two groups to debate the firearms issue. Have one group support and defend the NRA's position on gun control, and have the opponents counter the claims. Have both sides refer to the Second Amendment as a starting point for developing their position statements.

RETEACH Clip newspaper articles that deal with the application of federal or state law, masking out references to which has jurisdiction. Have students identify which courts would hear the cases.

ENRICH Have students play a *Jeopardy*-style game in which there are only two answers: *What is the federal government?* and *What are the state governments?* Divide the class into four teams: one to research and write the statements, two to play the game, and a fourth to serve as announcer and control the game board.

At this point, you may wish to show the videotape, *Born Yesterday*, a 1993 film starring John Goodman and Melanie Griffith. Griffith learns about the Constitution and the Bill of Rights firsthand and shares her knowledge at a dinner attended by Washington's most powerful politicians. Have students use her unique way of remembering each amendment.

On an overhead transparency or on a flip chart, create a two-column chart with the headings: **Amendment** and **Interpretation.** Ask student volunteers to read aloud the first 10 amendments found on pp. 11–12. Then, work with students to write a brief interpretation for each one. Have students copy the chart in their notebooks.

Save this chart for use in the first activity on p. 13.

To assist limited English proficient students or those who are having reading comprehension difficulties with the Bill of Rights, have the class devise symbols for each amendment. For example, lips, a cross, a newspaper, a cluster of stick figures, and a petition could symbolize the First Amendment. After symbols for all 10 amendments have been agreed upon, have students use them to create a large poster. Keep the poster on a classroom wall so students can

refer to it while studying this chapter.

AMENDMENT VI.

In all criminal prosecutions, the accused shall enjoy the right to a speedy and public trial, by an impartial jury of the State and district wherein the crime shall have been committed; which district shall have been previously ascertained by law, and to be informed of the nature and cause of the accusation; to be confronted with the witnesses against him; to have compulsory process for obtaining witnesses in his favor, and to have the assistance of counsel for his defence.

AMENDMENT VII.

In Suits at common law, where the value in controversy shall exceed twenty dollars, the right of trial by jury shall be preserved, and no fact tried by a jury shall be otherwise re-examined in any Court of the United States, than according to the rules of the common law.

AMENDMENT VIII.

Excessive bail shall not be required, nor excessive fines imposed, nor cruel and unusual punishments inflicted.

AMENDMENT IX.

The enumeration in the Constitution of certain rights shall not be construed to deny or disparage others retained by the people.

AMENDMENT X.

The powers not delegated to the United States by the Constitution, nor prohibited by it to the States, are reserved to the States respectively, or to the people.

1. Due Process of Law

The Fifth Amendment is especially important. It states: "No person shall be . . . deprived of life, liberty, or property, without due process of law. . . ." Note that the Constitution, unlike the Declaration of Independence, does not mention happiness. However, respect by others for one's life, liberty, and property surely helps one to be secure and content, if not consciously happy. It was the insightful former U.S. Supreme Court Justice Louis D. Brandeis who opined, "Those who won our independence . . . believed liberty to be the secret of happiness and courage to be the secret of liberty."[6] Brandeis also penned the related comment that the makers of the Constitution "conferred, as against the Government, the right to be let alone—the most comprehensive of rights and the right most valued by civilized men."[7]

[6]*Whitney v. California*, 274 U.S. 357.
[7]*Olmstead v. United States*, 277 U.S. 438.

ASSESS

Learning Objective 6 In writing, using a computer, if possible, have students identify the principal human rights protected by each of the 10 amendments contained in the Bill of Rights and explain how each amendment improved the Constitution.

Legal rights are the benefits to which a person is justly entitled by law. **Legal duties** are obligations or conduct toward other persons that is enforceable by law. Everyone should understand that the legal right of one person generally imposes a legal duty on others. Frequently, legal rights and duties are also moral rights and duties—but not necessarily so. My right to life, for example, imposes a duty on you not to injure or to kill me. But no right is absolute. Thus, if I attack you without justification and threaten your life, you may reasonably defend yourself—even if it appears necessary to take my life. However, a person who unjustly kills another may be prosecuted for murder. Then the arrest, trial, and punishment of the alleged wrongdoer must be in accordance with due process of law. **Due process of law** requires fundamental fairness in compliance with reasonable and just laws. If convicted, the criminal may be deprived of property by fine, of liberty by imprisonment, and even of life by lawful execution.

Due process of law is a concept embodied throughout the Constitution. It is assured in the amendments by recognizing

1. "[T]he right of the people peaceably to assemble..." (First Amendment).
2. "The right of the people to be secure in their persons, houses, papers, and effects, against unreasonable searches and seizures..." (Fourth Amendment).
3. "No person...shall be compelled in any criminal case to be a witness against himself..." (Fifth Amendment).
4. "In all criminal prosecutions, the accused shall enjoy the right to a speedy and public trial, by an impartial jury of the State and district wherein the crime shall have been committed...and to be informed of the nature and cause of the accusation; to be confronted with the witnesses against him; to have compulsory process for obtaining witnesses in his favor, and to have the assistance of counsel for his defence" (Sixth Amendment).
5. In civil suits "where the value in controversy shall exceed twenty dollars...," either plaintiff or defendant may require trial by jury (Seventh Amendment).
6. "Excessive bail shall not be required nor excessive fines imposed, nor cruel and unusual punishments inflicted" (Eighth Amendment).

2. Civil Matters

Since most persons do not engage in criminal conduct, the Constitution's shield for civil rights is generally much more important to them. **Civil rights**

Refer to the amendment chart that the class completed on p. 12. On the overhead transparency or flip chart, add third and fourth columns and the following headings: **Due Process** and **Civil Rights**. Have students determine in which category each amendment belongs. Place a check mark in the appropriate column. Have students add this information to the charts in their notebooks. Save this chart for use on p. 16.

At this time, you may wish to use the *HyperCard* stack and videodisc by ABC News InterActive™: *Martin Luther King Jr.*, to acquaint students with this prominent civil rights leader and his accomplishments and goals, and the application of the First Amendment guaranteeing civil rights.

▼RETEACH Have students role-play scenarios in which they demonstrate a person's legal rights, corresponding legal duties, and due process of law. Have students identify where in the scenarios these concepts are demonstrated.

▼ENRICH Media: Have students prioritize the first 10 amendments in descending order—from most important (1) to least important (10). Using a computer, if possible, have students write an essay discussing why they made the selections they did.

Thinking Critically Through Visuals

The family members in the photograph are sharing a meal as part of a religious celebration. Which amendment gives them the right to practice their religion freely? (First)

Divide the class into two groups. Have students debate the issue of the right to privacy by individuals vs. the freedom of speech and press exercised in newspapers, TV, and radio.

Personal Perspectives

Encourage students to use the five steps of the writing process (prewrite, write, revise, edit, and publish) to write using a computer, if possible, about their personal experiences exercising one of the following freedoms: religion, speech, the press, peaceful assembly, and petition of the government. Then, have students rank each right on a scale from one to five, with one being the most important. Share students' rankings and discuss.

Independent Practice

are personal natural rights guaranteed by the Constitution. Preeminent is the shield of the First Amendment, which declares: "Congress shall make no law . . . abridging the freedom of speech, or of the press; or the right of the people peaceably to assemble . . . ." Former U.S. Supreme Court Chief Justice Charles E. Hughes once wrote, "The greater the importance of safeguarding the community from incitements to the overthrow of our institutions by force and violence, the more imperative is the need to preserve inviolate the constitutional rights of free speech, free press, and free assembly in order to maintain the opportunity for free political discussion to the end that government may be responsive to the will of the people and that changes, if desired, may be obtained by peaceful means. Therein lies the security of the Republic, the very foundation of Constitutional government."[8] Former Supreme Court Justice Benjamin N. Cardozo once wrote that the freedom of thought and speech "is the matrix, the indispensable condition, of nearly every other form of freedom."[9]

The First Amendment also states: "Congress shall make no law respecting an establishment of religion, or prohibiting the free exercise thereof . . . ." Mankind's universal religious impulse has led to the construction of some of the most beautiful and enduring temples throughout the world. Religion has inspired men, women, and children to their most noble and compassionate

[8] *DeJonge v. Oregon,* 299 U.S. 353.

[9] *Palko v. Connecticut,* 302 U.S. 319.

ASSESS

Learning Objective 6 On a sheet of paper, have students identify a list of five personal, natural rights guaranteed by the Constitution under the First Amendment. (Religion, speech, press, assembly, and petition)

conduct toward their fellow beings. Paradoxically, misguided religious zeal has caused great violence and destruction over the centuries in wars ostensibly designed to win converts or to eliminate heathens. Here again, the founders of our republic recognized this deep-seated religious impulse but wisely imposed a role of neutrality for the government; a wall of separation between church and state. The government tolerates all and supports none in any strictly religious efforts. The Constitution is the shield of protection for both believers and agnostics.

WHAT PROBLEMS REQUIRED MORE AMENDMENTS TO THE CONSTITUTION?

PROBLEM

Ida presented a controversial talk before her high school class. "You speak of the shield of the Constitution. Maybe that's true today, but it was not so in days gone by. Originally, more than half of the adults over twenty-one—the women of our country—could not vote. The situation was much worse for women and men who happened to be black. They were slaves, and the Constitution validated that terrible practice." Several students protested. "That can't be true!" one said. Was Ida telling the truth?

Among the nations of the world there is no monopoly on virtue or on vice. Man's inhumanity to man is evident in the enslavement and maltreatment of human beings of all colors and of all races in ancient, medieval, and modern times. As recently as World War II, some eleven million innocent men, women, and children were slaughtered by Nazis. Included were some six million persons who were murdered simply because they were Jewish. Today in India, despite formal legal bans on the custom, millions of people are still classified as untouchables. They are relegated to menial work and are the victims of other discrimination.

1. Slavery Is Abolished

In our country, despite the solemn affirmation in the Declaration of Independence that "all Men are created equal . . . ," the evil practice of slavery for black men, women, and children was tolerated by the Constitution. It continued until the issue was resolved through the bloodshed of our Civil War, which preserved the Union and abolished slavery.

In the problem, Ida told the truth. Under pressure by delegates from states where many slaves did menial labor, the Constitution provided that

TEACH

Explain to students that one of the greatest benefits of our Constitution is that it allows us to change it, by way of amendment, which makes the Constitution a living document that can change with the times.

Multicultural Highlights

In September, 1992, Carrie Meek, 66, (D-FL), became Florida's first African American woman elected to Congress. One of 24 women of the 110 members of the freshman class of the House of Representatives, Meek also carried the distinction of being a senior citizen. A former college gym teacher and school administrator, this sharecropper's daughter was assigned to sit on the powerful House Appropriations Committee. She vowed to push job training and economic aid for her Miami district, which recently had been ravaged by hurricanes and civil unrest.

RETEACH Have students create a graphic organizer to illustrate the five freedoms of the First Amendment—religion, speech, press, assembly, and petition.

ENRICH Have students respond in writing to the following statement about the First Amendment: **The Constitution is the shield of protection for both believers and agnostics.**

APPLY

Explain why more amendments were added to the Constitution by creating on the chalkboard a two-column chart with the headings **Amendment** and **Reason(s) for Passage**. List the amendment number in the first column and the reason or reasons for passage in the second column. **Guided Practice**

In small groups, have students create a poster to illustrate the following six amendments: Thirteenth, Fourteenth, Fifteenth, Nineteenth, Twenty-fourth, and Twenty-sixth. Have groups exchange posters and write headline-news copy to accompany the poster illustrations. Display students' work on a bulletin board called *Extending the Constitution to All.*

Independent Practice

Have students add their interpretations of the six amendments that they have just learned about in this section to their amendment charts in their notebooks and to the class chart, which they started in the activities on pp. 12 and 13.

Congress could not prohibit, prior to 1808, "[t]he Migration or Importation of such Persons. . . ." Slaves were further dehumanized by a provision in Article I that counted only three-fifths of each slave as a person when determining a state's population for the purpose of apportioning representatives to Congress. Finally, under Article IV, a slave who escaped to another state had to be returned to "the Party to whom such Service or Labour may be due."

These provisions were negated by the Thirteenth Amendment, which states, in part: "Neither slavery nor involuntary servitude, except as a punishment for a crime whereof the party shall have been duly convicted, shall exist within the United States, or any place subject to their jurisdiction."

2. The Right to Vote

The Fifteenth Amendment provided the newly freed slaves the legal right to vote. It decreed: "The right of citizens of the United States to vote shall not be denied or abridged by the United States or by any State on account of race, color or previous condition of servitude."

The exclusion of "gender" in the Fifteenth Amendment was a deliberate denial of voting rights to women of all races. This injustice was removed fifty years later when the Nineteenth Amendment provided: "The right of citizens of the United States to vote shall not be denied or abridged by the United States or by any State on account of sex."

Although the Thirteenth Amendment abolished slavery, racial discrimination continued in both the North and the South. For example, some southern states enacted the poll tax. It was a fixed amount per head or person, payment of which was required before the person could vote. Money needed by very poor black people for bread and shoes could not be spent to pay a tax in order to vote. Ultimately—more than 100 years after the Civil War began with the attack on Fort Sumter—the Twenty-fourth Amendment provided that the right to vote in federal elections "shall not be denied or abridged . . . by reason of failure to pay any poll tax or other tax."

The Supreme Court subsequently applied the same rule to all state elections, declaring such taxes unconstitutional under the Fourteenth Amendment.[10] In their ongoing struggle for genuine equality in civil rights, blacks have also advanced the cause of women and other victims of discrimination. The Civil Rights Act of 1964, for example, is comprehensive in its coverage (see Chapter 21).

An interesting result of the student protests against U.S. involvement in the Vietnam War was the hasty enactment of an amendment that gave all citizens who are age eighteen or older the right to vote. The Twenty-sixth

[10] *Harper v. Virginia Board of Elections,* 383 U.S. 663.

ASSESS

Learning Objective 7 In small groups, have students create a cause-and-effect chart to show why the Thirteenth, Fourteenth, Fifteenth, Nineteenth, Twenty-fourth, and Twenty-sixth amendments were added to the Constitution.

Amendment was approved overwhelmingly by the Senate and House in March 1971, and was ratified by thirty-eight states within three months.

3. Protection of Rights Extended to Limit Power of States

The Fourteenth Amendment opens with these sweeping provisions: "All persons born or naturalized in the United States and subject to the jurisdiction thereof, are citizens of the United States and of the State wherein they reside. No State shall make or enforce any law which shall abridge the privileges or immunities of citizens of the United States; nor shall any State deprive any person of life, liberty, or property, without due process of law; nor deny to any person within its jurisdiction the equal protection of the laws."

The Fourteenth Amendment was a gigantic step forward because, by its terms, all *state* governments are barred from depriving any person of life, liberty, or property without due process of law. Recall that the Fifth Amendment had previously applied only to the powers of the federal government. The Fourteenth Amendment subjects the states to the same restraints.

Due process, as outlined in the Fifth Amendment, is not the only constitutional protection that state governments are now required to respect. Other relevant amendments in the Bill of Rights have also been applied to the states. As a result, today the shield of the Constitution is effective against abuse of power by *both* the federal and state governments. And at both levels, statutes have been enacted to provide comparable protection against abuse of power by private individuals and corporations. Prime examples are civil rights statutes discussed in Chapter 21.

Preventing Legal Difficulties

1. Carefully read and reread the Constitution as it has been amended to become a properly informed citizen and voter of the United States of America, and of the state and local community in which you reside.
2. Pay special attention to the Bill of Rights and the Fourteenth Amendment to better appreciate their value in assuring our liberty and to be alert to possible threats that could erode vital freedoms for you and others.
3. As a minimum, when eligible, participate in government as a conscientious voter. If you are able and willing, participate in the work of the political party of your choice. If you are one of the dedicated few, become a candidate for public office. Those elected as representatives or executives should be truly dedicated to public service in the tradition of such immortal patriots as Washington, Lincoln, and the Roosevelts.

Preventing Legal Difficulties

To prepare students to be informed and intelligent citizens and voters, have them work in small groups to create a public service announcement (PSA) for the radio, TV, or newspaper about voting rights and duties. Have students use the hints in this special section as a guide.

▼ CLOSE

As a whole-class activity, have students create a class constitution. Have the class decide on classroom rules, students' and instructor's legal duties, and students' and instructor's legal and civil rights. Have students follow the format of their state constitution or the U.S. Constitution. Encourage students to use a computer, if possible, to create their class constitution in final form. After its completion, have students review their constitution

and allow them to add amendments to it.

Assign the following end-of-chapter materials:
Student text review activities, pp. 18–23
Workbook, pp. 1–2
Chapter Test

Chapter *MicroExam*

▼RETEACH

In writing, using a computer, if possible, have students describe how our country would be different if the Thirteenth, Fourteenth, Fifteenth, Nineteenth, Twenty-fourth, and Twenty-sixth amendments had *not* been added to the Constitution.

▼ENRICH

Have students discuss in writing, using a computer, if possible, how the Vietnam War was the catalyst for the Twenty-sixth Amendment.

Strengthening Your Legal Vocabulary

1. Senate
2. U.S. Constitution
3. Bill of Rights
4. republic
5. amendments
6. due process of law
7. sovereignty
8. system of checks and balances
9. pure democracy
10. civil rights

Applying Law to Everyday Life

1. If the very next phrase is added, the statement becomes more credible and clear. It then reads "... all Men are created equal ... endowed by their Creator with certain unalienable Rights, that among these are Life, Liberty, and the Pursuit of Happiness ...." The U.S. Constitution later declared that "No person shall be ... deprived of life, liberty, or property, without due process of law ...." Regrettably and, indeed hypocritically, the Constitution tolerated slavery for many years. This gross aberration was later corrected by the Thirteenth, Fourteenth, Fifteenth, and Twenty-fourth Amendments.

REVIEWING IMPORTANT POINTS

1. The U.S. Constitution, as amended, is the shield of U.S. liberty.
2. A vigorous and useful balance of power exists among the three basic branches of government: legislative, executive, and judicial.
3. The Bill of Rights is the popular name of the first ten amendments to the U.S. Constitution.
4. Under the First Amendment, Congress is barred from making any law to establish a public religion or to prohibit the free exercise of any private religion.
5. The First Amendment also protects free speech, free press, and freedom to assemble peaceably and the right to petition the government for redress if one is wronged.
6. The Fifth Amendment provides that no person shall be deprived of life, liberty, or property without due process of law.
7. Due process of law is assured by the First, Fourth, Fifth, Sixth, Seventh, and Eighth Amendments.
8. Slavery was finally banned by the Thirteenth Amendment, which was reinforced by the Fourteenth, Fifteenth, and Twenty-fourth Amendments.
9. The Fourteenth Amendment applied to the states the rule that no person shall be deprived of life, liberty, or property without due process of law.
10. In 1920, the fundamental right of women citizens to vote was recognized by ratification of the Nineteenth Amendment. In 1971, the voting age for all citizens was lowered to eighteen by the Twenty-sixth Amendment.

STRENGTHENING YOUR LEGAL VOCABULARY

Match each term with the statement that best defines that term. Some terms may not be used.

amendments
Articles of Confederation
Bill of Rights
civil rights
Declaration of Independence
Democratic party
due process of law

House of Representatives
legal duties
legal rights
political party
pure democracy
republic
Republican party

2. ETHICS ISSUE Mrs. Miller is probably correct. But the First Amendment to the U.S. Constitution is the same throughout the country. By means of clever, albeit somewhat belabored logic, the shield of the Constitution is the same across the United States, but its operation depends on the community involved. In the case of *Miller v. California* (413 U.S. 15, 1973), the U.S. Supreme Court ruled that obscenity is not protected by the First Amendment to the Constitution.

Senate	system of checks and balances
sovereignty	U.S. Constitution
state constitution	War of Independence

1. Upper chamber of Congress in which every state has two members.
2. The supreme law of the land.
3. First ten amendments to the U.S. Constitution.
4. Country or state in which ultimate power resides in the people who elect representatives to enact and enforce the laws that govern all.
5. Additions to and/or changes in the Constitution.
6. Rules that require fundamental fairness in the conduct of governmental officers when depriving any person of life, liberty, or property.
7. Freedom from external control.
8. System that distributes specific authority among the legislative, executive, and judicial branches of government in order to separate and divide power.
9. Government in which every qualified voter votes on every issue.
10. Personal natural rights guaranteed by the U.S. Constitution.

APPLYING LAW TO EVERYDAY LIFE

1. Paula Bell maintains that when the authors of the Declaration of Independence wrote "that all Men are created equal...," they were either (a) lying, (b) exaggerating, or (c) simply wishing it could be so. How do you read their words?
2. ETHICS ISSUE After driving from their home in a small city in the Northeast, teenagers Don and Donna Miller were sightseeing in New York City's Times Square with their parents. Within minutes, all four were shocked by the profusion of shows and other advertised attractions that blatantly portrayed sexual practices. "Holy smokes! What's going on here?!" their father asked. "You mean, 'What's coming off!'" Don quipped. Donna frowned and punched him in his ribs. Their mother said, "They'd never get away with this stuff back home in Centerville.... Come on, let's get out of here!" Is their mother's statement correct? If so, does it mean the First Amendment to the U.S. Constitution is not the same in all states?
3. After a worried rap session on the money problem of schools in their area, a group of high school students decided to act. They agreed to

3 Although the goal of universal education through the college level may be commendable, there are serious flaws in the plan.
a) Even if all of the congressional representatives from the students' state support the idea, two senators out of 100 and 10 representatives out of 435 are not likely to succeed in convincing the required two-thirds majority of each respective chamber to endorse the proposal.
b) Letters to senators and representatives are more likely to be effective if personalized rather than in a standardized form.
c) Congress cannot amend the Constitution; it can only submit proposed amendments to the states.
d) Although the federal government has assisted education in many ways, the states and local governments retain control over public education and finance it in accord with the availability of local resources.
e) Many persons are convinced that, in most states, adequate funds are already being appropriated for schooling.
f) The federal government is already burdened by a national debt that exceeds three trillion (3,000,000,000,000) dollars.
g) Not all persons desire, need, or qualify for education from kindergarten through college.

contact the other five secondary schools in their city to obtain cooperation in a letter-writing campaign. Every student would be committed to sign and mail one copy of a standard form letter to each of their senators and to at least two of their ten representatives in Congress. The letters would urge their congressional representatives to get the full Congress to enact an amendment to the Constitution. That amendment would recognize the human right of every person to formal education from kindergarten through the senior year at college, to be financed from the general funds of the federal government. Is there any flaw in the students' plan?

4 Glen Turner is twenty-eight years old. He lives with his wife and young son in a small one-company town in the Appalachian Mountains. Glen and his family are very poor. He is a coal miner but has no job because the mine where he worked shut down when the last veins of coal were cleaned out. Glen's wife also lost her job in the company office. Glen mournfully says, "Our threesome sort of enjoys life and liberty. But as to property, we haven't got any to speak of. The government's not going to deprive us of something we haven't got. So when you say owning property's a right under the Constitution, maybe that's true. But it's nothing for us. Nothing." Is Glen wrong? What could you say to him?

5 It started as a fraternity stunt at a local college. But the stunt gained momentum over the next few days as other students took it seriously. The key idea was to tie up the evening rush-hour traffic at the busiest intersection in the city's business district as a protest against U.S. involvement in the Middle East. "We'll stage a surprise rally," Ollie Blarnie proposed, "then march back to the campus."

About 600 students gathered as planned. They took over the intersection and all traffic stopped. Within minutes, the police moved in and forced the crowd to disperse. Several individuals who dropped their signs and "went limp" on the pavement were arrested. Did the police action violate the protesters' First Amendment Constitutional right "peaceably to assemble?"

6 ETHICS ISSUE The Equal Rights Amendment (ERA) was formally proposed in 1972. It provided: "Equality of rights under the law shall not be denied or abridged by the United States or by any state on account of sex." For more than ten years, proponents and opponents conducted vigorous campaigns in all states. When the time limit for approval elapsed in 1982, only thirty-five of the required state legislatures had voted in favor. Women in a sorority at a nearby college now wonder if another campaign should be launched to pass the ERA. How would you advise them? With or without an equal rights amendment, is it ethical to draft only men in time of war?

4 Yes, fortunately Glen is wrong. When one has life and liberty, coupled with youth and a willingness and ability to work, there is a strong possibility, indeed a probability, of acquiring property. Moreover, Glen and his wife are free to move where there are likely to be new opportunities. They may have to learn new skills, either on the job or in school.

5 No; The right of peaceable assembly is subject to reasonable regulations enacted to maintain orderly flow of traffic and to preserve the peace. Communities generally require that sponsors of planned outdoor assemblies or rallies in public places obtain licenses in advance. No license had been obtained by the group or by its leaders.

6 ETHICS ISSUE **a)** Another effort to pass an ERA amendment could be made, but only if the necessary initial support could be obtained.
b) If women are equal in ability to do work traditionally done by men—as they indeed appear to be—it would be unfair, hence unethical, to draft only men.

7 It is highly doubtful that the nation would approve a new prohibition law. Alternative approaches might include: (1) public education encouraging moderation or abstinence; (2) more stringent enforcement of existing laws against driving while drunk; and (3) encouraging campaigns by liquor manufacturers and others to convince all persons to follow this advice: "If you drink, don't drive."

8 No; The Declaration of Independence lists serious abuses by the British under King George III of citizens in the American Colonies. As stated in the Declaration of Independence, "... when a long train of Abuses and Usurpations, pursuing invariably the same Object, evinces a Design to reduce them under absolute Despotism, it is their Right, it is their Duty, to throw off such Government, and to provide new Guards for their future Security." This the colonists did in the War of Independence.

7 In 1919 the Eighteenth Amendment outlawed "the manufacture, sale, or transportation of intoxicating liquors...." On the supply side, this law led to widespread bootlegging or illegal traffic in liquor by criminals. On the demand side, the controversial law led to tacit approval of the illicit trade by many otherwise law-abiding citizens who continued to buy and consume the illegal liquor. In 1933, after fourteen years of mixed enforcement, the Eighteenth Amendment was repealed by the Twenty-first Amendment, but individual states were permitted to continue to enforce Prohibition within their borders. By 1966, all individual states had abandoned Prohibition. Medical and legal experts say abuse in the use of alcoholic beverages is the most serious drug problem in overall harmful effect on our society. Should Prohibition be reinstated? If not, what should be done?

8 The Declaration of Independence led to the violent overthrow of British rule over the thirteen original American colonies. In 1940, the U.S. Congress enacted the Smith Act, which forbade persons to advocate, teach, or advise the violent overthrow of the government. When this legal history was recently mentioned in a high school class, student Tom Pane said, "That's hypocrisy. It condemns the very behavior that gave us liberty!" Do you agree?

9 Headlines in the morning paper told of how a local judge had ordered the release of a person accused of dealing in cocaine. A large quantity of the drug had been found in his garage, but the police had no search warrant when they seized it and arrested the accused. The evidence was therefore illegal and inadmissible in court. Accordingly, the judge ordered the police to release the defendant. Madeline Quinn was boiling mad. "There we go again," she said. "Our crazy due process laws protect the criminal, not the innocent victims!" Is Madeline right?

10 ETHICS ISSUE

a. What was the dual purpose of the Civil War in the opinion of people living at that time in the northern states of our country?

b. In your opinion, has our history since the Civil War demonstrated the wisdom and ethical propriety of the northern cause?

▼ SOLVING CASE PROBLEMS

1 In 1951, during the Korean War, a dispute arose between our nation's leading steel mills and their employees, represented by the United Steelworkers of America, C.I.O. It concerned the terms of a new collective bargaining agreement. Prolonged negotiations failed to resolve the dispute. Governmental mediation efforts and recommendations were also

10 ETHICS ISSUE **a)** The dual purpose was: (1) to restore and maintain the Union of all of the states under one federal government; legislative leaders from the South had argued that among the sovereign rights retained by every state under the Constitution was the right to secede; and (2) to abolish slavery; some may say that slavery had already been abolished in most of the civilized world by legislation and that, therefore, its termination by peaceful means was inevitable in our country.
b) Student answers will vary.

Solving Case Problems

1 Yes, the President acted beyond his powers. Justice Hugo Black noted that "the Founders of this Nation entrusted the lawmaking power to the Congress alone in both good and bad times. It would do us good to recall the historical events, the fear of power and the hopes for freedom that lay behind their choice."

9 No; A fundamental tenet of our law is that a person is presumed to be innocent of crime until proven to be guilty beyond a reasonable doubt. The law of the Fourth Amendment against unreasonable searches and seizures is designed to protect the population against this type of abusive conduct by police.

2 Yes; The judgment was reversed and the case remanded (sent back) with orders to issue the writ (injunction) ending the practice. The U.S. Supreme Court declared that permitting release time for religious instruction during regular public school hours "... is beyond all question a utilization of the tax-established and tax-supported public school system to aid religious groups to spread their faith. And it falls squarely under the ban of the First Amendment (made applicable to the states by the Fourteenth Amendment)."

3 No, the judgment was affirmed. The motel was engaged in interstate commerce and therefore is subject to federal regulation.

4 The U.S. Supreme Court ruled in favor of Gideon and remanded (sent back) the case for a new trial. The right of an indigent defendant in a criminal trial to have assistance of counsel is a fundamental right essential to a fair trial. Conviction without the assistance of counsel violated the Fourteenth Amendment of the U.S. Constitution. Assistance of counsel "... is one of the safeguards of the Sixth Amendment deemed necessary to assure fundamental human rights of life and liberty."

fruitless. When the union gave notice of a nationwide strike to begin in five days, President Harry Truman issued an executive order directing the Secretary of Commerce to seize and operate most of the steel mills. The President believed a work stoppage would jeopardize our national defense. The steel companies complied with the executive order, but they claimed (a) that the seizure was unlawful because it violated the U.S. Constitution and (b) that Congress alone has power to make laws. Therefore, they requested and obtained a preliminary court injunction to end the seizure. However, the injunction was stayed (stopped or held in abeyance) while the U.S. Supreme Court reviewed the matter. Did the President act beyond his powers under the Constitution? (*Youngstown Sheet & Tube Company v. Sawyer*, 343 U.S. 579)

2 A board of education in Champaign County, Illinois, granted permission to religious teachers to give religious instruction in public school buildings in grades four to nine. The instruction would last thirty minutes for lower grades, forty-five minutes for higher grades, once each week. Subject to approval of and supervision by the superintendent of schools, the teachers were employed by a private religious group and included representatives of the Catholic, Jewish, and Protestant faiths. Only pupils whose parents requested religious instruction were required to attend the religious classes; other pupils continued with their regular public school duties.

McCollum, a resident with a pupil who was enrolled in one of the public schools, sued for a writ (i.e., court order) to end the religious instruction as a violation of the First Amendment to the Constitution. The writ was denied, and the Illinois Supreme Court upheld the denial. The parent appealed to the U.S. Supreme Court. Should the writ have been granted to end the practice as a violation of the First Amendment? (*McCollum v. Board of Education*, 333 U.S. 203)

3 In 1964, the owner of a motel in Atlanta restricted its clientele to white persons, three-fourths of whom were interstate travelers. Officers of the U.S. government charged that this policy violated the Civil Rights Act of 1964, which forbids such discrimination against blacks. The trial court ordered the motel to stop refusing blacks as guests because of their race or color. The motel owner appealed to the U.S. Supreme Court, claiming the Civil Rights Act was unconstitutional. Was it? (*Heart of Atlanta Motel, Inc. v. United States*, 379 U.S. 241)

4 Gideon was charged in a Florida court with a noncapital felony, which is a serious crime but not one punishable by death. Gideon appeared in court without legal counsel and requested the court to appoint a lawyer to defend him, since he had no funds to hire one. His request was

denied because Florida state law permitted such appointment for indigent defendants only in capital felony cases. Gideon then conducted his own defense.

Gideon was convicted and sentenced to prison. He then applied to the Florida Supreme Court for a writ of habeas corpus, which sought an order to bring him before the Supreme Court for a hearing of his claim that he was unlawfully imprisoned. He claimed his conviction had violated his rights under the federal Constitution. The state supreme court denied all relief. Thereafter, Gideon wrote a letter to the U.S. Supreme Court from his prison cell, asking it to review his case. The Supreme Court responded favorably to his petition. It appointed legal counsel, who submitted briefs and oral arguments. How should the U.S. Supreme Court have ruled on the Florida case? (*Gideon v. Wainwright*, 372 U.S. 335)

5 Cleveland police had received information that a person wanted for questioning about a recent bombing was hiding in a particular two-family dwelling. Also, there was said to be a large quantity of illegal lottery materials hidden in the home. Upon arrival, three officers knocked on the door and demanded entrance. Mapp, who lived on the top floor with her daughter, telephoned her attorney and then refused to admit the officers without a search warrant.

Three hours later, reinforced by additional officers, the police returned. When Mapp did not answer immediately, they tried to kick in the door, then broke its glass pane, reached in, unlocked it, and entered. Meanwhile Mapp's attorney had arrived, but the officers would not let him see his client or enter the house. Mapp demanded to see a search warrant and when an officer held up a paper claiming it to be a warrant, Mapp grabbed the paper and placed it in her bosom. A struggle ensued during which the officer recovered the paper, and Mapp was handcuffed for resisting the officer. The entire house was searched, but all that was found were certain allegedly "lewd and lascivious books and pictures." Mapp was convicted of knowingly having them in her possession. At the trial, no search warrant was produced nor was the failure to produce one explained. Mapp appealed to the U.S. Supreme Court for a reversal of her conviction because it was based on a search that was illegal under the U.S. Constitution. (a) Was the evidence for conviction obtained in violation of the U.S. Constitution? (b) If so, was it admissible in the trial against the defendant Mapp? (*Mapp v. Ohio*, 367 U.S. 643)

5 **a)** Yes, the evidence had been obtained in violation of the Fourth Amendment prohibition of unreasonable searches and seizures. **b)** The illegally seized evidence was not admissible. The U.S. Supreme Court had previously held "... that all evidence obtained by an unconstitutional search and seizure was inadmissible in a federal court regardless of its source." Judgment against defendant Mapp was reversed.

Chapter Theme

Consequential and deontological forms of ethics are reflected in—and compel us to obey—our laws.

DIRECTED STUDY QUESTIONS	SPECIAL FEATURES	PROGRAM RESOURCES				
		Reteach	Enrich	SN	AM	
What is ethics?		✔	✔			
How do we reason about right and wrong?	Personal Perspectives, p. 29 Ethics Issue, p. 30	✔	✔	✔		
How do our laws reflect consequential ethics?	Thinking Critically Through Visuals, p. 33	✔	✔			
How do our laws reflect deontological ethics?		✔	✔		A	
How are other ethical goals reflected in our laws?		✔	✔			
Why are we obligated to obey laws?		✔	✔			
Are we ever justified in violating the law?	Writing Connections, p. 38 Thinking Critically Through Visuals, p. 39 Multicultural Highlights, p. 39 Preventing Legal Difficulties, p. 40	✔	✔		V K	

Additional Resources

- *An Amazing Grace.* Detroit, MI: MultiMedia Education Inc.
- Aristotle, *The Nicomachean Ethics.* New York: Oxford University Press, 1925.
- Ferrell, O.C. and Gardiner, Gareth. *In Pursuit of Ethics: Tough Choices in the World of Work.* Springfield, IL: Smith Collins, 1991.
- Frankena, William K. *Ethics.* Englewood Cliffs, NJ: Prentice-Hall, 1963.
- Madsen, Peter, ed. and Shafritz, Jay M., ed. *Essentials of Business Ethics.* NY: New American Library, 1990.
- Rachels, James. *The Elements of Moral Philosophy.* New York: McGraw-Hill, 1986.

One-semester course	✔	✔	✔					
One-year course	✔	✔	✔	✔	✔			

		ASSESSMENT OPPORTUNITIES			
	Cooperative Learning	Informal Assessment	Chapter Review	Chapter Test	Chapter *MicroExam* (Media)
		✔	✔	✔	✔
	✔	✔	✔	✔	✔
		✔	✔	✔	✔
		✔	✔	✔	✔
		✔	✔	✔	✔
		✔	✔	✔	✔
		✔	✔	✔	✔

Videodiscs

Right and Wrong: Absolute Rules vs. Practical Consequences

Search Chapter 2, Play To 3

State by State

Jefferson County, AL, challenged the Alabama legislature for failing to reflect increases in the county population. The Alabama legislature was reapportioned.

Teaching Materials

Student text, pp. 24–45

Overhead transparency masters
- *Consequential Reasoning*
- *Deontological Reasoning*

Videos
- *Our Legal System* Videotape
- *Law for Business* Videodisc

Workbook, pp. 3–4

Outside Resources
- Copy of minutes from recent town/city council meeting
- Index cards

- *An Amazing Grace*, videotape from Multi-Media Education, Inc.

Assessment
- Chapter Test

- Chapter *MicroExam*

Vocabulary

ethics, p. 26
impartiality, p. 27
consequential reasoning, p. 28
deontology, p. 28
The Good, p. 29
universalizing, p. 31
moral rights, p. 31
natural rights, p. 32
natural law, p. 32
false rights, p. 32
majority rule, p. 33
civil rights, p. 34
unconstitutional, p. 35
integrity, p. 37
fidelity bond, p. 38
civil disobedience, p. 38
scofflaws, p. 40

Learning Objectives

When you complete this chapter, you will be able to

1. Recognize when ethics should affect a decision.
2. Determine when a person acts without regard to ethics.
3. Describe the basic forms of ethical reasoning.
4. Identify the ethical justification for many laws.
5. Explain why we are obligated to obey the law.
6. Distinguish between a scofflaw and civil disobedience.

24

Chapter Self-Test

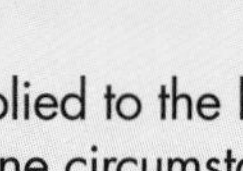

Assess students' understanding of ethics, especially as applied to the law, before they begin Chapter 2 by asking them briefly to describe one circumstance in which people might believe it would be proper to break a rule or a law. (Answers may include to save someone from harm or for self-protection.) Before continuing with the chapter, review and discuss students' responses without making judgments.

CHAPTER 2

ETHICS IN OUR LAW

❶ ETHICS ISSUE Mario was awarding end-of-year bonuses. As he looked over the list of employees, he rated each one based on how he felt about them. The political views of some of the employees affected his feelings. So did their physical attractiveness. Ultimately, Mario awarded the bonuses in proportion to the employee ratings. Has Mario made ethical decisions?

❷ ETHICS ISSUE Sharon is knowledgeable about tax laws and how the Internal Revenue Service (IRS) audits tax returns. She knows a way to cheat on her tax return that would save her almost $2,000. She thinks her chance of being caught is about one in 100. Would it be ethical for Sharon to prepare her tax return in this way? Why, or why not?

❸ ETHICS ISSUE James owns four dry cleaning stores and employs twenty-two people. He needs a bookkeeper and advertises for one in the local newspaper. Twelve persons respond, and Joni is clearly the best qualified. However, James prefers to hire a man. The law requires James to hire Joni, but he is confident that he will not be caught if he hires a less qualified male instead. Whom should he hire? Why?

25

▼ FOCUS

Begin Chapter 2 by having students write a brief response to this question: **Why, do you think, does this chapter on ethics follow the chapter on the U.S. Constitution?** (Answers may include that the law expresses society's basic ethical standards, and so on.)

After discussing the above question, direct students' attention to the statement on p. vii: *In our society the law is the official statement of what is right and wrong ...* Ask: **How do we know what is right and what is wrong?** (Answers may include religious teachings, community standards, family traditions and customs, and so on.)

You Decide

❶ ETHICS ISSUE Mario has not made ethical decisions. He relied on emotions rather than reason and he has not been impartial.

❷ ETHICS ISSUE Sharon's actions are unethical because they injure the law, they injure other taxpayers who must pay more than their fair share, and because Sharon has, as a citizen, promised to obey her country's laws.

❸ ETHICS ISSUE Ethically, James should hire the best qualified person. He should obey the law even if it is not enforced. Ethical reasoning demands that James should give the job to a woman, even if there were not a law.

Thinking Critically Through Visuals

Ask students if they have ever seen a statue like the one on p. 25. Then ask the following questions: **Where did you see this kind of statue?** (Answers should indicate near or in a court house.) **Why are balanced scales and a blindfolded woman often used as symbols of courts of law?** (The blindfold over the eyes is the symbol of the impartiality of the law and the scales represent the law's commitment to weighing decisions carefully.)

TEACH

Many students may have difficulty accepting the definition of **ethics** given in the text because emotions may be their only guide to right and wrong. Use the example of Sharon on p. 25 to help students make the distinction between emotional feeling and thoughtful (logical) reason.

APPLY

Hold a class discussion about instances when students responded with emotions rather than in a style of ethical reasoning. Ask students to recall the results of their emotional decision and what, if anything, they would change about their actions. **Guided Practice**

**Note: Margin illustrations can be enlarged on a photocopier as necessary.*

WHAT IS ETHICS?

PROBLEM

While working in the school office, Jane discovered a copy of the exam to be given in one of her classes. She thought she could take it home with little chance of being caught. In thinking about whether to take the test home, she weighed how helpful an A on the test would be and how important grades are to her. In the end, she stole the test. Later she told a friend, "It just felt so good to know that I wouldn't need to spend all that time studying to get an A, that I didn't have any real choice." Has Jane made an ethical decision?

Ethics is determining what is right or wrong action in a reasoned, impartial manner. Consider the three important elements in this definition: (1) a decision about right and wrong action; (2) a reasoned decision; and (3) a decision that is impartial. The following sections discuss each of these important elements.

1. Decisions About Right or Wrong Action

Many of our decisions have little effect on other persons or ourselves. For example, your decision to buy blue jeans with wide, instead of narrow, pant legs has no ethical component. On the other hand, your decision to discontinue medical support for an unconscious, terminally ill relative is an intensely ethical decision. To involve ethics, a decision must affect you or others in some significant way.

2. Reasoned Decisions

Often we act in response to our emotions. For example, after watching a film, we recommend it to friends with such words as, "It really made me feel good." Or when someone asks us why we bought a particular brand of bread, we respond, "I don't really know, I just felt like it." What we are saying is that our emotions have guided these decisions. Our *feelings* have directed our actions. But to make ethical decisions, we must base our decisions on reason, not on emotion.

This does not mean that emotional decisions are usually wrong, only that emotions cannot be the foundation for serious ethical consideration. For many people, emotions vary from one time to another. Further, emotions vary greatly from one person to another. So when emotions guide decisions, they often define right or wrong differently for different persons or differ-

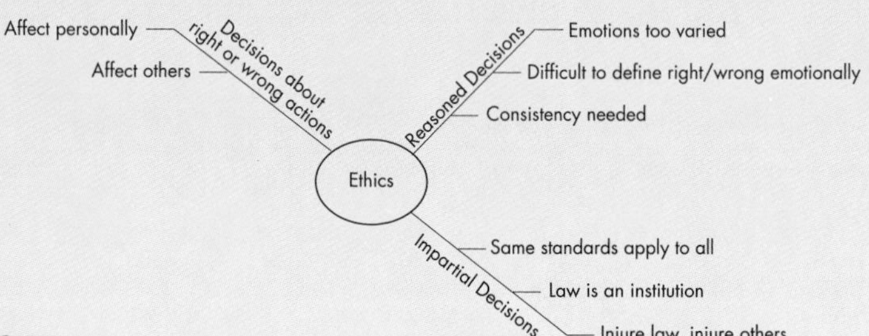

ASSESS

Learning Objective 1 Copy the base of this spider map on the chalkboard and write **Ethics** in the center circle. Have students complete the map to depict the elements in the definition of **ethics**. Each element is written on one of the spokes. Students may add more lines with supporting details if they wish.

ently for the same person at different times. This makes emotions inconsistent guides to serious decisions that affect people.

Almost all philosophers agree that *reasoning* differs from emotion in important ways. One way is that reasoning is more consistent from person to person and over time. Suppose I say, “If I am in Denver, then I must be in Colorado; however, I am not in Denver so I must not be in Colorado.” You would recognize that my reasoning is faulty. You might say, “But you could be in Aspen, Colorado!” and reason would compel me to agree. So reasoning provides a way to be consistent. It lets us consistently determine what is right and wrong. If reason and emotion conflict, reason should prevail.

Often people reason about right and wrong by referring to a written authority that provides consistency. The law is such an authority. So are the Torah, the Bible, the Koran, and the Bhagavad Gita. For example, a person might reason, “I believe that God is the source of the Bible and the Bible tells me not to lie; therefore, it would be ethically wrong for me to lie.” Other persons might reason that they have promised to obey the laws of their country; therefore, it would be unethical to violate such laws.

3. Impartial Decisions

Impartiality is the idea that the same ethical standards are applied to everyone. If it is wrong for you to engage in a certain action, then in the same circumstance it is also wrong for me. This means that by definition ethics does not value one person or group of persons more than any other. Men are not more valuable than women. Caucasians are not entitled to greater consideration than persons of another race. Each person is an individual and is to be accorded equal consideration and human respect.

Impartiality requires that in making ethical decisions, we balance our self-interest with the interests of others. To do this, we must develop skill in recognizing the interests of others. Sometimes this is difficult. Self-interest can cloud perceptions and our ability to reason impartially. For example, some people might think, “I know my religion requires me to tell the truth. But in this situation it would cost me more than $100 if I admitted that I ran into Mrs. Anderson’s fence. I can’t afford that, but she can! So it must be okay to deny my beliefs here.” On the other hand, the same people might condemn someone else who engaged in such conduct. If they were in Mrs. Anderson’s shoes, they would be outraged to discover that the guilty person remained silent. One who behaves in this manner is not being impartial.

Impartiality is particularly important when the other persons are represented by *institutions* instead of real people, such as Mrs. Anderson. When we think about Mrs. Anderson, our emotions help us understand that she is a person who is entitled to the same treatment as you and I. But when people’s interests are represented by organizations, self-interest can make

During the year, ask students to keep a law journal in which they summarize current newspaper or magazine articles pertaining to topics mentioned in their text or discussed in class. Have them exchange journals with classmates and add their comments to the journal they are reading. Journals can be used for informal assessment, and can be completed using a computer, if possible.

Media **Independent Practice**

▼RETEACH Pair a student who has difficulty understanding the concept of ethics with another who has mastered the concept. Have the pair create an example to illustrate each of the elements of the spider map made in the ASSESS activity.

▼ENRICH Ask students to dramatize the statement *When we injure the law, ... we injure many other people.* Then ask: **Which of the three elements of ethics are applied?** (All three)

TEACH

As students read the introduction to *How Do We Reason About Right and Wrong?* on pp. 28–29, write the following statements on the chalkboard:

The end justifies the means.

The means are not justified by the end.

Explain, if necessary, that the end is the result of an action. The means is the action itself. Ask students to identify the type of ethical reasoning expressed in each statement.

APPLY

Have students follow the steps in consequential reasoning to respond to the PROBLEM on p. 28 and analyze the solutions given on pp. 29–30. **Guided Practice**

Display the overhead transparency, *Consequential Reasoning*. Using a computer, if possible, ask students to use the steps shown to write their own solutions to the problem developed on p. 28. Have students exchange papers and critique their partners' work.

Independent Practice

people conclude that their actions really do not injure other people. "It was only the school's property," or "It doesn't matter, it was just the insurance company that was cheated." In truth, behind all organizations there are many persons, such as taxpayers, employees, and customers. They are injured when the organization is injured. Property taxes may go up or insurance rates may be raised. So when dealing with institutions, being impartial means seeing how others are affected by our actions.

The law is an institution. It represents all the people in our country. When we injure the law, perhaps by violating it, or by laughing at it, or by encouraging others to violate it, we injure many other people.

HOW DO WE REASON ABOUT RIGHT AND WRONG?

PROBLEM

Tab built a tool shed in the yard between his house and his neighbors' property line. Later, when he decided to build a fence on the border, he discovered that the shed was too close to the property line. He would not be able to drive his car between the fence and the shed. So, he built the fence one foot onto the neighbors' property. Tab lived alone and three people lived on the neighboring property. How can we evaluate the ethical character of Tab's action?

Ethical reasoning about right and wrong takes two basic forms. One form is **consequential reasoning.** In this style of ethical reasoning, particular acts have no moral character. Rightness or wrongness is based only on *consequences* or the results of the action. In consequential reasoning, an act that produces good consequences is good. An act that produces bad consequences is bad.

The other form of moral reasoning is **deontology**. This style of moral reasoning asserts that acts are inherently right or wrong (e.g., that lying is always wrong). In deontology, good consequences cannot justify wrong or bad acts. For example, in deontology, you cannot justify lying by showing that it produces good consequences.

For almost all ethical decisions, these two forms of moral reasoning reach the same conclusion. Therefore, consequentialists and deontologists usually agree that one should not lie. The consequentialists justify this position by recognizing that lying usually produces bad consequences. Deontologists say that lying is inherently wrong.

These two forms of ethical reasoning occasionally conflict. When they do, we face the most difficult moral decisions. Because these decisions are

ASSESS

Learning Objectives 2 & 3 Prepare to display the overhead transparency, *Consequential Reasoning*. Present it with everything but the title covered by a sheet of paper. Lower the cover step-by-step and have students explain or describe each step using terms such as *forecasting, standards, counting people*, and ***The Good***.

so difficult, they receive great publicity. Unfortunately, this causes many people to wrongly conclude that ethics is not a reliable guide. These people notice only the well-publicized issues where even experts on ethics debate at length about what is truly right. Critics fail to realize that in almost all cases, different forms of ethical or moral reasoning reach the same conclusion.

1. Consequential Reasoning

Consequential reasoning first describes alternative ways to alter the current situation. Then, it attempts to forecast the future consequences arising from each alternative. Finally, it evaluates all those future consequences to select the alternative that generates the greatest good. These steps in consequential reasoning are described in the following paragraphs.

Describe alternative actions. First, one must describe alternative actions that would improve things. For example, in the problem two of the many alternatives Tab might have considered are (1) building the fence on the neighbors' property without telling them or (2) offering to buy a one-foot strip of the neighbors' property. In order to decide what is the best thing to do, consequentialists must describe the alternatives so they can be evaluated.

Forecast consequences. Second, one must describe the consequences flowing from each alternative. This requires skill in forecasting the future. It requires an ability to see things such as, "If I build the fence one foot inside my neighbors' property, they probably won't notice." Or "If they do discover that the fence was built on their property, they will probably make me pay for the one-foot strip of property instead of making me tear it down."

Evaluate consequences. Third, the consequences for each alternative must be evaluated. There are two elements to the evaluation process: (1) selecting the *standard* for judging consequences as right or wrong and (2) *counting the persons* affected.

Philosophers usually call the standard for judging right or wrong **The Good.** The Good is the primary goal toward which human life ought to be directed. Many philosophers assert a single Good while others claim that there are multiple goods. Alternative goods include such basic goals as:

- beauty
- justice
- knowledge
- liberty
- love
- pleasure
- power
- salvation
- truth

Personal Perspectives

High school graduation is an important event full of traditions which, in the past, often included prayers by local clergy. In 1992, the Supreme Court declared that nonsectarian prayer at public high school graduations violated the First Amendment, which guaranteed the separation of church and state. In June, 1993 the Supreme Court declared that the opinion of the majority of students—whether in favor of or opposed to prayer—would determine whether school functions would include prayer. The preference of school officials was not to determine the outcome of this issue. Ask students to comment on the ethical reasoning displayed by those in favor of, and opposed to, school prayer.

▼RETEACH In pairs, have students select a school rule or a class procedure and explain its ethical reasoning. Have each pair share its rule with the entire group and give the reasoning behind it.

▼ENRICH Bring to class, or have students bring, articles on contemporary issues to be analyzed using the forms of ethical reasoning. You may wish to distribute photocopies of the overhead transparency master, *Consequential Reasoning*, for students to follow as they explain their analyses.

Discuss possible difficulties in arriving at ethical decisions using consequential reasoning. Have students consider such questions as: **How do we recognize the fundamental character of a true good? Can we be sure that all alternatives have been considered? Are most ethical decisions direct and clear cut?** Help students recognize that there are no simple answers to these questions.

Ethics Issue

Remind students that the chapter is entitled *Ethics in* ***Our*** *[emphasis added] Law*. Ask: **What, do you think, happens when people from cultures that value different goods must interact with one another or seek common goals?** (Answers may include developing awareness and understanding of differences, agreeing to third-party arbitration, or creating organizations such as the United Nations. Students may also mention negative examples.)

The feature that determines whether a particular goal is a true good is its fundamental character. A good is something that motivates most of a person's actions or important decisions. So it would be incorrect to call "the desire to be nicely dressed" a good. It is simply not basic. In the problem, Tab must choose a good to evaluate the alternative actions. Let's assume Tab chooses *pleasure (from use of the land)*.

Most consequentialists judge by the standard of "the greatest good for the greatest number" of people. Thus, for each alternative we must determine how many people will be positively and negatively affected. In the problem, if Tab builds the fence on the neighbors' land without their consent, his pleasure—one person's—is increased. But the pleasure of his three neighbors is decreased. Tab receives the benefit while his three neighbors bear the cost. So this alternative is ethically wrong.

To evaluate the consequences of buying the strip of land, we compare both *the costs and the benefits* for each person. For Tab, essentially the cost is the price paid for the land and the benefit is the ability to use the strip of land for his fence. For his neighbors, the cost is the loss of the land and the benefit is the money they receive for it. For the parties to agree voluntarily, Tab must prefer the land to the money and the neighbors must prefer the money to the land. If the sale can be voluntarily completed, four parties are positively benefited. This makes this alternative ethically good.

It is a mistake in reasoning to *not count* all the persons affected by a decision. Similarly, it is an error in reasoning to ignore important *ways* in which persons are affected. These two problems arise when the effects are indirect. Thus, it is easy for employees in a large firm to ignore the effects of their actions on the owners. Problems can also arise when the effects are associated with mere risks or only probabilities.

Gerry was late for a job interview. The rural road she was driving down was not heavily traveled. The posted speed limit was fifty-five miles per hour. She reasoned that by speeding she could benefit both herself and the interviewer. Gerry would make a better impression by arriving on time and the interviewer would not waste her time waiting for Gerry to arrive. So she sped up to seventy miles per hour.

Gerry made an error in her ethical reasoning. She ignored some of the ways her actions affected other people. By speeding, she imposed a substantially greater risk of an accident and injury on the other drivers on the road. Since she did not see this effect, she also failed to count some of the people affected by her decision. Also, she ignored the way her actions undermine respect for law. When these effects and people are counted, the action seems ethically wrong.

ASSESS

Learning Objective 3 Read question 5 of APPLYING LAW TO EVERYDAY LIFE on p. 43 aloud to students. Ask: **What errors in consequential reasoning, do you think, did Rosanna make?** (Answers may include that she was both selfish and emotional.) Require each student to make a brief response (orally or in writing) to your question.

2. Deontological Reasoning

In this form of ethical reasoning, the acts themselves are judged as right or wrong. The standard for judging usually comes from one of two sources—a recognized authority or human reasoning.

Decisions based on authority. An authority, such as the law or scripture, can mandate (i.e., command or order) that stealing is wrong. When there is an accepted authority speaking directly to an issue, such as stealing, it is relatively easy to decide what is right and wrong. The act of building a fence on a neighbor's property without permission would be condemned by all religious authorities and all legal systems as a form of stealing. The act is inherently wrong. In deontology, the act is wrong even if it benefits more people than it injures. Unfortunately, recognized authorities do not always take positions about specific behavior, or if they do, the positions are unclear.

Decisions based on reasoning. In addition to an authority, human reasoning can also show that some things are inherently wrong. Many people agree that the capacity to reason is the central and distinguishing characteristic of human beings. The most human thing a person can do is to reason about right and wrong. Therefore, things inconsistent with reason are ethically wrong.

A test has been devised to determine whether an action is inconsistent with reason. This is the test of universalizing. **Universalizing** is a mental test that magnifies the illogical character of acts to make this lack of logic easier to see. The test involves making the action universal; that is, picturing in your mind everyone doing it. Then you ask, "Is this universalized world irrational, illogical, or self-defeating?" If it is any of the three, the action is inconsistent with reason and ethically wrong.

We can universalize lying by imagining a world where everyone lies. Such a world would be illogical because there would be no point in lying, since no one would believe anyone. Similarly, if we imagine a world where everyone takes her or his neighbor's land, there would be no point in taking the land because another neighbor would promptly take it from you. These pictures help us see that the actions of lying and stealing are inconsistent with human reason. Accordingly, in deontological reasoning, they are inherently wrong.

Both religions and reasoning conclude that all human beings have enormous dignity and intrinsic worth. Religions usually assert that humans are "made in the image of God" or "of Allah" and therefore must be treated with profound respect. Reason says that humans are unique because of their potential for reasoning about right and wrong. Both of these lines of argument lead to the conclusion that humans have moral rights. **Moral rights** are legitimate claims on other persons, which flow from each person's status

It is probable that the word **deontology** is new to most of your students, especially those that have limited English proficiency. It might help to say it several times and to write the pronunciation on the chalkboard: dee-on-tol'-o-jee.

Divide the class into four groups for a portion of this class period. For each of the two situations that follow, ask one group to decide if the action is ethical using consequential reasoning and the other group to decide if the action is ethical using deontological reasoning. Have each group identify a moderator and recorder. Remaining students in each group are members of the decision-making team. Each group should present its decision, and the rationale for its decision, to the entire class.

1. You lie about your whereabouts to your parents.

2. You drive 80 mph in a 55 mph zone to impress your friends.

Cooperative Learning

RETEACH For students who have not grasped consequential reasoning, use the overhead transparency master *Consequential Reasoning* to help them work their way through question 5 of APPLYING LAW TO EVERYDAY LIFE.

ENRICH Have students who have grasped consequential reasoning meet in small groups to create three ethical issues. Have them explain to the class the steps taken to reach an ethical conclusion for each issue.

▼ TEACH

After reading the PROBLEM on p. 32, ask students if they agree that the noise law is an ethical law. Have students explain their answers. Remind them that sound ethical reasoning is rational, not emotional.

▼ APPLY

Ask students how this law passed by the city council could be enforced. (Answers may include that police officers could issue a summons to those they find breaking the law.) Ask: **Is a law passed to satisfy a majority—though difficult to enforce—an ethical law?** (Answers may include that such laws might not be ethical because they failed to forecast or evaluate the consequences.) **Guided Practice**

Contact, or have small groups of students contact, your local town or city hall for a copy of the minutes from the most recent town/city council meeting. After making individual student copies of the minutes, ask students to find any mention of new legislation discussed, voted on, or passed. Then, as a group, have students evaluate the legislation by the ethical standards they have been studying. **Independent Practice**

as a human being. Deontologists acknowledge that humans have moral rights that others must not violate. For deontologists, human rights cannot be violated even if doing so generates the greatest good for the greatest number. **Natural rights** is a name most often used to describe moral rights that are protected by law. Sometimes **natural law** is also used as a synonym for moral rights.

The school board's greatest problem in preparing an annual budget was allocating funds for a program for severely handicapped students. Some board members argued that since these children would never be able to contribute to society through work, could never carry their own weight, the budget for their education should be minimized. This would allow the board to significantly increase the quality of education for the vast majority of students.

Other board members conceded that these handicapped students would always be a financial drain on society. But they said, because these children are human beings, they have the right to develop their minds. Therefore, the program should be well funded even if doing so injures the majority of students. The first group of board members used consequential reasoning. The second group used deontological reasoning based on human rights.

Sometimes people assert false rights. **False rights** are claims based on the desires of a particular individual instead of the basic needs of humanity. Thus, intoxicated persons sometimes claim that they have the right to be drunk in public. A worker may claim that she has the right to work at her own pace. But these claims are justified only by the desires of the individual. They are not claims arising out of the status of these persons as human beings.

▼ HOW DO OUR LAWS REFLECT CONSEQUENTIAL ETHICS?

PROBLEM

In a coastal city of California, residents often could not sleep because people were driving late at night with their car windows down and their stereos playing full blast. On holidays, people put large home stereos in the back of their pickup trucks and played them as loud as possible. In response, the city council enacted a law making it illegal to generate noise in public above a certain decibel (level of loudness). Is there an ethical justification for this law?

▼ ASSESS

Learning Objectives 3 & 4 After reading on p. 32 about the school board and its budget problems, have students analyze the steps in ethical reasoning each group might have used to reach its decisions.

In our country, the people—directly or indirectly—determine the laws that bind them. They do this by electing representatives to lawmaking bodies, such as city councils, state legislatures, or the Congress of the United States. In these elections and in the legislative bodies, **majority rule** prevails. The elected representatives must vote for laws acceptable to the majority of people they represent if they expect to be reelected.

Because this system is grounded on majority rule, it displays many of the features of consequential ethics. In this system, laws are not inherently right or wrong. Rather laws are judged to be good when the consequence is that they affect the majority of the people positively. The laws are judged to be wrong when the consequence is to affect the majority negatively.

The Constitution of the United States seeks to ensure that our federal lawmaking system reflects the desires of our citizens. It does this by creating a national legislature composed of two bodies—the House of Representatives and the Senate. Together, these bodies are called Congress. The Constitution provides for the election of the members of Congress by the citizenry. States have similar legislative structures. This legislative structure promotes ethical consequentialism.

In the problem, the members of the city council tried to determine what the majority of citizens wanted. Some wanted the pleasure of playing their music loudly in public. But many more wanted the pleasure of a quiet community. So the law was passed in response to the majority will. It is ethically justified by consequential ethics. It produces the greatest good for the greatest number. Clearly, this law restricts the conduct of those who want

Thinking Critically Through Visuals

Discuss with students where they have seen graffiti art. Then ask: **Do you think that graffiti artists have a right to display their art in public places?** (Answers might include that graffiti is another example of anti-social "noise" and should not be allowed, or that this type of art is an expression of free speech that should be encouraged.)

RETEACH Help students who are having difficulty grasping the role of ethics and the forms of ethical reasoning by having them complete with you the first two sections of the chapter outline found on p. 139 in the Workbook.

ENRICH Pair students who have an understanding of the forms of ethical reasoning. One student should prepare a situation in which ethical reasoning can be used. The partner should orally explain how ethical reasoning can be used in the situation.

TEACH

Review with students the Constitutional amendments that specifically protect certain basic civil rights (First, Fourth, Fifth, Sixth, Eighth, Fourteenth, and Fifteenth amendments). Prepare an overhead transparency with those amendments and have students determine, orally or in writing, which civil rights are being protected. (First—freedom of speech, Fourth—unreasonable search, Fifth—testifying against oneself, Sixth—right to a speedy trial and to legal counsel, Eighth—excessive bail, Fourteenth—equal protection of the laws, Fifteenth—right to vote)

APPLY

Have students compare the statement of fundamental rights in the Declaration of Independence with the amendments listed on pp. 34–35. Discuss how the amendments appear to be a natural progression from the Declaration. Remind students that many leaders of the Revolution did not want to ratify the Constitution until the first 10 amendments had been added. **Guided Practice**

to play loud music. But does it violate their moral rights? No. Freedom to play very loud music in public is not essential for the maintenance of human dignity; therefore, it is not a right.

HOW DO OUR LAWS REFLECT DEONTOLOGICAL ETHICS?

PROBLEM

Almost everyone in a small community belonged to the same church. When members of a different denomination were considering buying land to erect a church, the city conducted a referendum (a direct vote by all the citizens on a proposed law). The referendum was on a zoning law that made it illegal to use any land in the city for any purpose other than residential housing. The law was enacted by majority vote. The effect of the law was to prohibit the construction of the proposed church in that city. Is such a law ethically justified? Is such a law legal?

While most laws reflect the desires of the people governed, the laws desired by the majority sometimes conflict with moral rights or natural rights. Stated another way, the majority may benefit from unjust laws. For example, the wealth of the majority of persons in this country might increase if we were to enslave some minority percentage of the population—say fifteen percent. They could be forced to work for free. Then the benefits of their free labor could be distributed to the majority. Historically, many countries adopted such laws. While these laws might benefit the majority, they would violate the natural rights of the minority. The majority would be treating the minority in a manner inconsistent with their status as human beings.

Under the U.S. Constitution, the courts would declare such laws invalid because they deny "equal protection of the law" to the minority. Other concepts of natural rights are used to protect political minorities from exploitation by those who make up the political majority. For example, the Fifth Amendment to the U.S. Constitution declares: "No person shall be . . . deprived of life, liberty, or property, without due process of law."

The United States of America is a country that recognizes and supports human rights. Other countries vary dramatically in the extent to which they do so. **Civil rights** (or civil liberties) generally are personal, human rights recognized and guaranteed by our Constitution. Among the civil rights so recognized are the following:

1. "Congress shall make no law respecting an establishment of religion . . . or abridging the freedom of speech, or of the press . . . " (First Amendment).

ASSESS

Learning Objective 4 Ask students to write a response to the following question: **How do the amendments make the Constitution a more ethical document?** (Answers may include that they protect civil rights or that they can protect the minority from the power of the majority.)

2 "The right of the people to be secure in their persons, houses, papers, and effects, against unreasonable searches and seizures, shall not be violated, and no Warrants shall issue, but upon probable cause . . . " (Fourth Amendment).

3 "No person . . . shall be compelled in any criminal case to be a witness against himself . . . " (Fifth Amendment).

4 "In all criminal prosecutions, the accused shall enjoy the right to a speedy and public trial, by an impartial jury . . . and to have the Assistance of Counsel . . . " (Sixth Amendment).

5 "Excessive bail shall not be required, nor excessive fines imposed, nor cruel and unusual punishments inflicted" (Eighth Amendment).

6 "No state shall . . . deny to any person . . . the equal protection of the laws" (Fourteenth Amendment).

7 "The right of citizens of the United States to vote shall not be denied or abridged . . . on account of race [or] color . . . " (Fifteenth Amendment).

Natural rights are usually protected by the courts. When the people or legislatures pass laws that undermine human rights, they are usually declared **unconstitutional**. This means that a court finds that the law conflicts with a constitutional provision, such as those listed above. Thus, in the problem, the zoning law adopted by majority vote is invalid. It is unconstitutional because it undermines freedom of religion.

Because courts perform the important duty of protecting natural rights, we sometimes try to insulate judges from the will of the majority. Many judges are *appointed*, rather than *elected*. Federal judges are appointed for life, so they are free from the influence of the populace and elected officials. This permits judges to protect human rights without risking their jobs.

Our legal system is one that *primarily* advances the will of the majority. It does this through the legislative process. But in this country we recognize that there are limits to majority rule. When the will of the majority conflicts with basic human rights, our legal system, particularly the judiciary, protects the individuals' rights. Our Declaration of Independence recognized these fundamental rights when it stated: "We hold these truths to be self-evident, that all men are created equal, that they are endowed by their Creator with certain unalienable Rights, that among these are Life, Liberty, and the pursuit of Happiness."

Make students aware that the U.S. Constitution is open to judicial interpretation. Divide the class into two groups. Have one group research the interpretation of the Constitution proposed by Alexander Hamilton. The other group should research Thomas Jefferson's opinions on the same subject. Have each group present its findings to the class. (Answers should include that Hamilton favored a loose, liberal interpretation and Jefferson a strict, literal interpretation.)

Independent Practice

Arrange a student debate on the pros and cons of the following statement: **The rights of the individual would be better protected if federal judges served a limited specified term, rather than serving a term for life.**

RETEACH Have students identify an important civil right, write it on a sheet of paper, and exchange the paper with another student completing this activity. Using the partial list of amendments on pp. 34–35, or the full list on pp. 795–804, have students note on paper the number of the amendment that protects the right and explain why or how it does.

ENRICH Have groups of three or four students make a bulletin board display featuring important Supreme Court decisions that have protected civil rights or liberties.

TEACH

Distribute index cards. Have each student write one current school rule on the card. Collect the cards and discard duplicates or frivolous responses. Use the remaining cards as the basis for a discussion on how rules help ensure order and greater efficiency in learning.

APPLY

Have students work in groups of three or four to create five class rules. Each group should choose a moderator to chair the discussion, a notetaker to record the proceedings, and a reporter to present the group's rules and rationale to the rest of the class. As a whole-class activity, combine and amend the responses into one set of rules. **Guided Practice**

Ask individual students to respond in writing to the following questions, using a computer, if possible: **What would happen if there were no school rules?** (Answers should show awareness of the chaos that could result if there were no rules.) **Why do you have to obey school rules?** (Answers should show an awareness that being part of a group requires adherence to all the group's rules.)

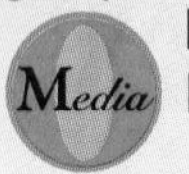
Independent Practice

HOW ARE OTHER ETHICAL GOALS REFLECTED IN OUR LAWS?

PROBLEM

Smyth was stopped for suspicion of drunk driving. The breathalyzer tests showed a blood alcohol level of 0.099 percent. State law defined drunkenness at .100 percent, so Smyth was not charged. Brown was stopped ten minutes later at the same location. Her test showed a .101 percent blood level and she was arrested, tried, and found guilty. Her driver's license was revoked for one year. Is there any ethical justification for treating Smyth and Brown so differently?

Often, matters simply need a consistent rule to assure order and predictability. The rule need not be based on majority rule or on natural rights. Sometimes this means that the rule or law is arbitrary. For example, teachers are required to award grades on exams and for courses. Assume that the cutoff point between an *A* and a *B* is a 90-percent average. A student who has an 89-percent average and therefore receives a *B* may argue that this grade is unfair because it is arbitrary. After all, the student who receives an *A* for a 90-percent average has not done substantially better work. Yet the letter grades indicate a substantial difference. If the grade for the student with an 89-percent average is changed to an *A*, then the argument for the student with the 88-percent average must be addressed and resolved the same way. In the end, everyone would receive the same grade.

A clear rule is needed, and it is perhaps more important that the rule exist than it is that the rule be completely fair. To be just, such rules of law must be communicated in advance and they must be applied consistently. In the problem, the law is clear and has been communicated to all drivers; so it is just to treat Smyth and Brown differently.

WHY ARE WE OBLIGATED TO OBEY LAWS?

PROBLEM

During Christmas vacation, Clementine worked part-time as a salesclerk in the jewelry department of a large department store. It was a busy time of the year and there were many opportunities for her to put a watch in her purse without being detected. There was one watch that she wanted very much but could not afford. She was convinced that the store management had not treated her fairly. Should she take the watch if she thinks there is no chance of being caught?

ASSESS

Learning Objectives 4 & 5 Have students review the PROBLEM presented on the bottom of p. 36 and review the reasons why Clementine should obey the law. Ask: **Is fear of getting caught the most important reason for obeying a law?** (Encourage free expression of opinion. Let any judgmental comments come from peers rather than from you.)

We are obligated to obey the law because ethical reasoning demands it, because we have agreed to obey it, and because by obeying it we avoid punishment.

1. Ethics Demands That We Obey

Both consequential ethics and deontological ethics conclude that we are obligated to obey the law. Consequentialists state that when the law is violated, many more people are injured than are benefited. Deontologists say that we have agreed to obey the law and that if we violate it, we are breaking our promise. If we universalize promise breaking—imagining that everyone always breaks promises—there would be no point to promising. So promise breaking is illogical and inherently wrong. It is deontologically wrong.

Persons who embrace formal religious principles (e.g., Buddhists, Christians, Hindus, Jews, and Muslims) are required to live in a manner that helps others. Hence, many religious persons feel particularly obligated to obey the law in order to help others.

2. We Consent to Be Governed by Laws

Socrates was a philosopher who lived in Athens, Greece, from 470–399 B.C. He believed that he had consented, had promised, to be governed by the laws of Athens. He expressed this promise by living in Athens and accepting the benefits of that society. Socrates believed that he should leave Athens, or not accept the benefits that it conferred on citizens, if he was not willing to obey all of its laws. Through this type of reasoning, Socrates concluded that it would be ethically wrong for him to violate the law of Athens. Socrates was charged with a crime and unjustly sentenced to death. When given the opportunity to escape, he declined, saying that to do so would be inconsistent with his moral beliefs. As a result, he was executed.

Socrates is widely regarded as a person of great integrity. **Integrity** is the capacity to do what is right even in the face of temptation or pressure to do otherwise. By giving up his life for his ethical beliefs, Socrates displayed the highest degree of integrity.

In the problem, Clementine is required to obey the law because she has accepted the benefits of the society that made the law. Free schooling is one benefit this society has provided Clementine. Other benefits include police protection, safe roads, welfare systems, social security, and protection from foreign enemies in times of war. By accepting the benefits, Clementine has demonstrated her consent to be governed by our laws.

3. We Want to Avoid Punishment

Some persons comply with the law primarily to avoid punishment. A person convicted of a crime may be fined, jailed, or, in some instances, put to

▼ TEACH

On the chalkboard, write the three reasons (numbered 1, 2, and 3) given on p. 37 for obeying the law. Then ask: **Is personal integrity important in a well-ordered, civilized society?** (Yes) **Is fear of punishment an important deterrent to breaking the law?** (Probably, for many people)

▼ APPLY

Write the following statements on the chalkboard. Ask students to respond in writing to one of the statements using arguments based on ethical reasoning.

1. If everyone obeyed the 10 commandments, we wouldn't need any other laws.
2. Socrates was a fool not to escape.
3. If you're not caught, you have not broken the law.

Divide the class into three groups, based on the statement students selected, and hold a discussion based on their responses. **Guided Practice**

In the opinion of many people, integrity is largely lacking in contemporary society. Share this comment with students and ask them to individually respond to the statement. **Independent Practice**

▼RETEACH Ask students who are having difficulty with understanding the importance of obeying laws to create a poster visually summarizing one of the three reasons listed on pp. 37–38.

▼ENRICH Have students needing a challenge role-play the situation and characters in question 9 of APPLYING LAW TO EVERYDAY LIFE on pp. 43–44. Ask students participating in this activity to respond orally to the final questions.

TEACH

Ask students to jot down one to three situations or instances that they think would justify violating the law. Discuss their responses. Help them identify acts of true civil disobedience.

APPLY

Have students form groups of four or five students and create and dramatize a situation and its ethical outcome. Each group must pick a director, a playwright who will put together the basic outline that the group as a whole will flesh out, and actors. **Guided Practice**

Writing Connections

Reading/ Language Arts
Edmund Burke, the 18th century English philosopher, wrote, *"The only thing necessary for the triumph of evil is for good men to do nothing."* As an independent writing activity, ask students to create an essay using the computer, if possible, connecting Burke's statement to the concept of civil disobedience. They may agree with or refute Burke's statement.

Independent Practice

death. While these penalties are widely known, there are many less well-known penalties imposed on criminals. For instance, persons convicted of serious crimes may be barred from jobs that require a security clearance. In many companies and governmental agencies, a security clearance is required for every employee. Also, some industries automatically exclude persons with criminal records from employment consideration. Banks, savings and loan associations, credit unions, and finance companies are but a few examples.

Employers often purchase fidelity bonds for persons who handle large sums of money, such as cashiers, managers of movie theaters, or supervisors of restaurants. A **fidelity bond** is an insurance policy that pays the employer money in the case of theft by employees. Generally, those convicted of a serious crime cannot qualify for a fidelity bond.

Also, many professions are closed to those who are convicted of serious crimes. For example, before being licensed, prospective lawyers, public accountants, and medical doctors are subject to a background check, which includes a check for criminal convictions. In the problem, if Clementine is caught and convicted, her biggest penalty could be the one she would "pay" outside the judicial system: the probable loss of many future job opportunities and her lasting embarrassment.

ARE WE EVER JUSTIFIED IN VIOLATING THE LAW?

PROBLEM

In the early 1960s, Martin Luther King, Jr., wanted to lead a march into Birmingham, Alabama, to protest racial segregation in that city. When he applied for a parade permit, his request was denied. Dr. King, knowing that his conduct was illegal, led the nonviolent march anyway. He was at the front of the line and allowed himself to be arrested, although he could have easily escaped. He went to jail. Community leaders were highly critical of Dr. King because he had violated the law. In response and while in jail, he wrote a famous letter attacking segregation laws as inconsistent with consequential and deontological ethical reasoning. Is there an ethical justification for Dr. King's violation of the law?

Some persons care passionately about human rights and justice. Their concern for justice sometimes compels them to violate what they consider a clearly unjust law. They violate the law by engaging in acts of civil disobedience. **Civil disobedience** is an open, peaceful, violation of a law to protest

ASSESS

Learning Objective 6 Ask students to write a response to the question: **Are we ever justified in breaking the law?** (Answers should reflect understanding of the seriousness of obeying the law.) For a wrap-up discussion on this objective, ask volunteers to share their answers to this question.

its alleged injustice. The goal of those who engage in civil disobedience is not to advance their self-interest but rather to make the legal system more just. The participants may be willing, or even eager, to be arrested in order to test the validity of the law in court.

Dr. Martin Luther King, Jr., wrote, "How does one determine when a law is just or unjust? A just law is a man-made code that squares with the moral law or the law of God. An unjust law is a code that is out of harmony with the moral law. To put it in the terms of Saint Thomas Aquinas, an unjust law is a human law that is not rooted in eternal and natural law. Any law that uplifts human personality is just. Any law that degrades human personality is unjust.... An unjust law is a code that a majority inflicts on a minority that is not binding on itself. This is difference made legal. On the other hand, a just law is a code that a majority compels a minority to follow that it is willing to follow itself. This is sameness made legal."

Thinking Critically Through Visuals

Have students review pp. 38–39 about **civil disobedience** and write a caption evaluating what is happening in the photograph. (Answers may include that Dr. King successfully used civil disobedience to fight for equal rights.)

Multicultural Highlights

Martin Luther King, Jr., often said that he based his nonviolent civil disobedience on the example of Mahatma Gandhi, the leader of India's independence movement. A trained attorney, Gandhi spent some time in British prisons for his actions. The Indian struggle was not without violence, but Gandhi felt that only nonviolent disobedience to Britain's restrictive colonial laws would be successful. One of Gandhi's major influences was Henry David Thoreau's essay "On Civil Disobedience." Ask students how King appeared to follow Gandhi's principles.

▼RETEACH Present a situation, such as parking in a handicapped zone without a permit. Ask: **Can this violation be justified?** (No, not ethically under the law) **Can you think of a situation when violation of the law would be justified?** (Answers should reflect understanding of civil disobedience.)

▼ENRICH Have students role-play a judge and a defendant. The situation is one in which a minor law has been violated. The violator must explain why the violation was justified. The judge must explain why it was not. Present the skits to the class.

You may wish to show a filmstrip or video that presents the highlights of Martin Luther King, Jr.'s, struggle in the civil rights movement. *An Amazing Grace*, available as a videotape from Multi-Media Education, Inc. (19363 Livenois, Detroit, MI 48221), details King's involvement from the Montgomery, AL bus boycott in 1955 to the march from Selma.

Preventing Legal Difficulties

After students have read the section on pp. 40–41, initiate a discussion by asking: **By accepting the benefits of a society, are we obligated to obey its laws?** (Answers should include that by accepting the benefits of society we imply that we will obey its laws.)

Like others, Dr. King believed that civil disobedience is justified only in extremely limited circumstances. He and others conclude that civil disobedience is ethical only when:

1. a written law is in conflict with ethical reasoning,
2. there are no effective political methods available to change the law,
3. the civil disobedience is nonviolent,
4. it does not advance one's immediate self-interest, and
5. the civil disobedience is public and one willingly accepts the punishment for violating the law.

In the problem, Martin Luther King, Jr., engaged in civil disobedience. As a result of efforts like his, many human rights were extended for the first time to several minority groups in this country.

In contrast with Dr. King, some persons are mere **scofflaws**. These are persons who do not respect the law. They simply assess the risk of being caught against the benefits they obtain by breaking the law. They think they are smart because they frequently violate valid laws without being caught. A scofflaw is never ethically justified in violating the law.

Preventing Legal Difficulties

As a citizen...

You have certain human rights protected by our Constitution, including:

1. The right to equal protection of laws and equal justice in the courts.
2. The right to be free from arbitrary search or arrest.
3. The right to equal educational and economic opportunities.
4. The right to choose public officers in free elections.
5. The right to own, use, and dispose of property.
6. The right of free speech, press, and assembly.
7. The right to freedom of religion.
8. The right to have legal counsel of your choice and a prompt trial if accused of a crime.

With your rights as a citizen go individual responsibilities. Every American shares them. Only by fulfilling our duties are we able to maintain our rights. Your duties as a citizen include the following:

1. The duty to obey the law.
2. The duty to respect the rights of others.
3. The duty to inform yourself on political issues.
4. The duty to vote in elections.
5. The duty to serve on juries if called.
6. The duty to serve and defend your country.
7. The duty to assist agencies of law enforcement.

—Adapted from *Law Day USA*
American Bar Association

▼ REVIEWING IMPORTANT POINTS

1. Ethics applies when decisions affect people.
2. Ethical decisions must be grounded on reason and impartiality.
3. There are two basic forms of ethics: consequential and deontological.
4. Consequential ethics evaluates only the results or effects of acts.
5. It is an error in consequential reasoning not to count all persons affected or to ignore some of the ways persons are affected.
6. Deontological ethics evaluates the acts themselves.
7. It is an error in deontological reasoning to assert false rights.
8. The legislative process is sometimes very consequential in operation.
9. The judicial process is sometimes very deontological in operation.
10. The law tries to advance the goals of:
    a. reflecting the will of those governed
    b. preserving natural rights
    c. maintaining order
11. Both consequential and deontological ethics compel us to obey the law.
12. We are obligated to obey the law because, by accepting society's benefits, we have consented to be bound by its laws.
13. We are obligated to obey the law if we believe in helping others. Civil disobedience is only justified in rare and extraordinary circumstances.
14. We should obey the law if we desire to avoid punishment.
15. Integrity is the capacity to do what is right even in the face of temptation or pressure to do what is wrong.
16. Civil disobedience is the open, peaceful violation of a law to protest its alleged injustice or unfairness.

▼ CLOSE

Use this closed-book activity to review the vocabulary terms for the chapter. Divide the class into three groups and split the vocabulary words (listed on p. 24 of the Teacher Edition) among them. Each group should draw on a sheet of paper a definition for the assigned terms. Collect the drawings and have the

class as a whole decide if they are appropriate.

Assign the following end-of-chapter materials:
Student text review activities, pp. 41–45
Workbook, pp. 3–4
Chapter Test

Chapter *MicroExam*

STRENGTHENING YOUR LEGAL VOCABULARY

Match each term with the statement that best defines that term. Some terms may not be used.

civil disobedience
civil rights
consequential reasoning
deontology
ethics
false rights
fidelity bond
integrity
impartiality
majority rule
moral rights
natural law
natural rights
scofflaw
the Good
unconstitutional
universalizing

1. Ethical conduct in violation of the law.
2. Claims based on the desires of a particular individual instead of the basic needs of humanity.
3. Ethics that evaluates the results of an action.
4. Making decisions that treat everyone the same.
5. A mental test to identify illogical actions.
6. Laws that reflect ethical principles.
7. Ethical decisions that evaluate only the act and not its consequences.
8. The capacity to do what is right even under pressure.
9. A person who does not respect the law.
10. Determining what is right or wrong action in a reasoned, impartial manner.

APPLYING LAW TO EVERYDAY LIFE

1. ETHICS ISSUE Jan was trying to decide who to vote for in an upcoming election. After reviewing the candidates, she said, "I've decided to vote for Gary because I just *feel* better about him." Is Jan's decision based on ethics? If not, why?

2. ETHICS ISSUE Jared was trying to decide who to hire. He had narrowed it down to two male finalists. One seemed better qualified to do the work. But the other candidate, like Jared, had played high school football. Because of this shared experience, Jared chose the other athlete. Is the decision by Jared based on ethics? If not, why?

Strengthening Your Legal Vocabulary

1. civil disobedience
2. false rights
3. consequential reasoning
4. impartiality
5. universalizing
6. natural law
7. deontological reasoning
8. integrity
9. scofflaw
10. ethics

Applying Law to Everyday Life

1. ETHICS ISSUE Jan's decision is based on emotion, not reason. So, it is not an ethical decision.
2. ETHICS ISSUE Jared's decision is not based on ethics because he is not being impartial. He uses a factor in his decision making that is not related to the applicants' abilities to perform the job.
3. ETHICS ISSUE Susan is using consequential reasoning. She forecasts that there is a chance she might get caught if she speeds. Then she evaluates this consequence. In her reasoning, Susan sees the consequences as negative. Therefore, she decides speeding is wrong.

4. 

Carol is using deontological reasoning in making this decision. She judges cheating to be a form of lying and, therefore, inherently wrong.

5. 

Rosanna has made several errors if she thinks she is making an ethical decision. She only counts herself in making the decision. This is a blatant mistake in consequential reasoning. Further, she bases her decision on emotion instead of reason.

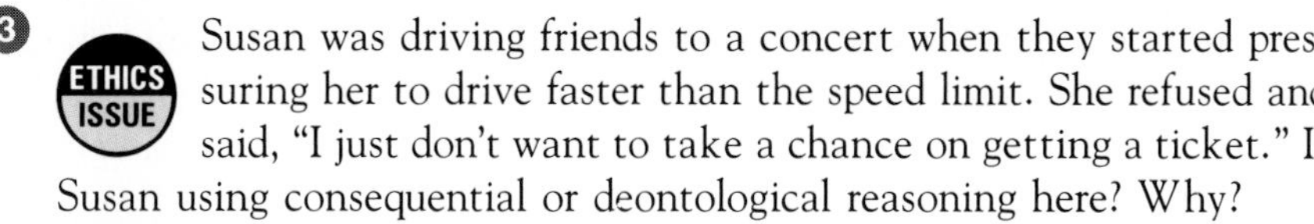

3 ETHICS ISSUE Susan was driving friends to a concert when they started pressuring her to drive faster than the speed limit. She refused and said, "I just don't want to take a chance on getting a ticket." Is Susan using consequential or deontological reasoning here? Why?

4 ETHICS ISSUE Carol found a copy of the answer key for an exam she was scheduled to take the next day in a trash basket she was emptying after school. Instead of using it, she returned it to the teacher, explaining how she found it. When the teacher asked why she did not use it to cheat, Carol said, "I just think it is wrong to cheat. When I take tests I am telling the teacher how much I really know. If I cheated it would be a form of lying. I believe lying is wrong. I won't lie even if it might help me." Is Carol using consequential or deontological reasoning here? Why?

5 ETHICS ISSUE Rosanna was trying to decide whether to share part of her lunch with Sheila and Fran, who had forgotten theirs. She decided not to, saying, "I just don't like Sheila, so I won't share with anyone." Has Rosanna made any errors in consequential reasoning? If so, which errors?

6 ETHICS ISSUE A new principal established the rule that no one could eat in the hallways between classes. Students protested, saying that the rule violated their rights. Is eating in the hallway a right or simply a desire?

7 ETHICS ISSUE An ordinance of Walker County provided that all automobiles must pass a smog emissions test once a year. Ross was ticketed because his car had not been inspected and approved at an emissions testing center. Ross claimed to be a skilled mechanic who kept his car well tuned and "cleaner" than the law required. According to Ross, the law violated his natural rights. Explain why you agree or disagree with Ross.

8 ETHICS ISSUE Crawford was caught shoplifting by a store detective. The police were called, and he was arrested. When his parents came to bail him out of jail, they asked him why he did it. Crawford responded that he had applied for a summer job at the store, but he was not hired. He thought he was treated unfairly, and this justified the shoplifting. What do you think of Crawford's justification?

9 ETHICS ISSUE Staub, Conly, and Winfield were employees of the Prime Time Restaurant. They were aware that the owner never checked the totals on the sales checks against the cash in the register. Therefore, it would be very easy to steal from the cash register. However, they did not steal. When asked why, they gave the following reasons. Staub said he did not take the money because he was afraid of

6 ETHICS ISSUE Eating in the hallway is not a right. It is not something which is basic to human dignity. So, students would not be justified in saying that the rule does anything more than make them uncomfortable.

7 ETHICS ISSUE Ross does not have a natural right to ignore the law. He does not have this right even when, while ignoring the law, he causes no injury. The law regarding the smog emissions test must be followed by everyone or there will be little order.

8 ETHICS ISSUE Crawford is not engaging in an ethical decision-making process. Instead, he is thinking only about himself and his feelings. If he were to evaluate the consequences for himself and the store, he would conclude that shoplifting is wrong.

9 ETHICS ISSUE There is no right answer to this question. It just asks students to choose the reason for not stealing with which they identify most closely. All are valid reasons; many thinking persons are influenced by all three reasons.

10  If the Seymours did not send Anna to school they probably would not be scofflaws. They would not receive a benefit from violating the law. On the other hand, for their actions to qualify as civil disobedience, the Seymours must declare their objection to the law and try to get it changed through the legal system. If they are unsuccessful, they could make public their plans and accept the punishment for violating this law. Then their actions might qualify as civil disobedience.

being caught. Conly said she did not take the money because she felt obligated to obey the law. Winfield said he did not take the money because of his religious beliefs. To which person do you best relate? Why?

10 ETHICS ISSUE The Seymours wanted their fifteen-year-old daughter, Anna, to help out in the family business, a convenience grocery store which was open twenty-four hours every day. The Seymours thought Anna could learn the business best this way. Since they would be paying Anna, they would not be benefiting financially. They insisted that state school attendance rules interfered both with parental rights to educate their children and with the children's right to get ahead faster. If the Seymours did not send Anna to school, would they be engaging in civil disobedience or acting as scofflaws? What action could the Seymours ethically take in response to the situation?

SOLVING CASE PROBLEMS

1. Poppy Construction Company was engaged in the business of developing, building, and selling a tract of houses in San Francisco. Mr. and Mrs. Burks, who were black, offered to purchase one of the houses. Poppy had a policy and practice of refusing to sell housing in the tract to blacks on the same conditions that the company applied to others. When their offer was rejected, Mr. and Mrs. Burks sued on the ground of racial discrimination. Racial discrimination was contrary to the law of California as well as to the U.S. Constitution. Poppy was required to accept the Burkses' offer to purchase the house. Is this law best justified by consequential or deontological reasoning? (*Burks v. Poppy Construction Company,* 307 P.2d 313, Cal.)

2. The city of Chicago sued to stop the operation of the Commonwealth Edison Company's coal-burning, electricity-generating plant in nearby Hammond, Indiana. Chicago claimed that the plant emitted too much smoke, sulfur dioxide, and other harmful substances. The city also claimed that the plant was a common-law public nuisance because it caused "an unreasonable interference with a right common to the general public" to clean, unpolluted air. Edison argued that it had spent much money to reduce harmful emissions and that the emissions were now well below the levels prescribed by federal clean air regulations and by the city of Hammond. Edison also pointed out that "unpleasant odors, smoke, and film" already characterized the area in which the plant was located. The trial court refused to issue an injunction. Therefore, the city of Chicago appealed to a higher court, which affirmed (upheld) the trial court. How can this legal action be ethically justified? (*City of Chicago v. Commonwealth Edison Company,* 321 N.E.2d 412, Ill.)

Solving Case Problems

1. The law in *Burks v. Poppy Construction Company* is probably best justified by deontology. Human beings have certain natural rights. One of the most basic is the right to be evaluated on the basis of one's ability, or merit, rather than on the basis of arbitrary factors over which one has no control. Judging the Burks on the basis of their gender, race, religion, or other factors not related to housing would violate this basic right and therefore be ethically wrong. It is also possible to justify the law using consequentialism. Racial discrimination has produced terrible consequences for societies.

2. The law in *City of Chicago v. Commonwealth Edison Co.* can be ethically justified by consequentialism. The residents of Chicago are injured by being required to breathe slightly polluted air. But the residents of the city of Hammond are benefited by being able to work. Further, everyone is benefited by the electricity produced by the Edison plant. Deontologists would argue that the benefits of the employment and electricity cannot be used to justify the pollution. They would say that basic human rights cannot be traded for good consequences.

3 Briney owned an old farmhouse in Iowa, which had been unoccupied for years. Although he had posted "No Trespassing" signs outside, there were intruders. So, Briney set a loaded shotgun inside the building and rigged it to fire when the bedroom door was opened. Soon after, Katko and a companion burglar broke into the house to steal old bottles they considered antiques. As Katko started to open the bedroom door, the shotgun blasted him, blowing off much of one leg. Katko sued Briney for damages and won. Is there a form of ethical reasoning that justifies this legal result? (*Katko v. Briney,* 183 N.W.2d 657, Iowa)

4 Reader's Digest Association, Inc., promoted magazine subscriptions in 1970 by sending materials that included "simulated checks" to potential subscribers. The government concluded that use of the simulated checks was, for some consumers, unfair and deceptive and thus illegal. Therefore, the government ordered the Digest to stop using "simulated checks or any confusingly simulated item of value." The Digest agreed to be bound to this governmental order. Later, the Digest mailed promotional material that used misleading "travel checks." After the government notified the Digest that these travel checks were illegal, the Digest mailed millions of additional checks to consumers. Was the conduct of the Digest that of a scofflaw or was the Digest engaged in civil disobedience? Explain. (*United States v. Reader's Digest Association, Inc.,* 662 F.2d 955)

5 Ford Motor Company designed and manufactured a car named Pinto. It weighed less than 2,000 pounds and cost less than $2,000. The fuel tank was located between the rear bumper and the rear axle. In crash tests, Ford learned that rear-end collisions could cause the fuel tank to rupture, spilling gas. The spillage could be prevented by spending between $4 and $8 to cover the fuel tank with a protective device. Total cost for the devices on all the vehicles manufactured would amount to $20.9 million. Ford declined to spend the money. In 1982, Richard Grimshaw, age thirteen, was riding in a new Pinto when it was struck in the rear by a car traveling between twenty-eight and thirty-seven miles per hour. The impact ruptured the fuel tank, causing gasoline to spill into the passenger compartment. When Richard emerged from the car, his clothing was almost completely burned off. He had to undergo numerous and extensive surgical procedures and skin grafts. The driver of the car suffered severe burns and died a few days after the accident. Discuss Ford Motor Company's decision not to cover the fuel tanks with the protective devices in terms of consequential and deontological ethics. (*Grimshaw v. Ford Motor Company,* 174 Cal. Reptr. 348, Cal.)

3 The law in *Katko v. Briney* can be justified by deontological reasoning. Even burglars are human beings and have rights. The most basic right is to life. Since this is the most basic right it cannot be violated, particularly to protect mere property.

Consequential reasoning probably reaches the opposite conclusion. If burglars could be killed with impunity, there would be fewer burglars, and fewer burglaries.

4 In *United States v. Reader's Digest Association, Inc.,* the Association was acting as a scofflaw. It was not engaged in civil disobedience for the following reasons: 1) Its actions were designed to benefit itself; the goal of the Association was profit. 2) The Association didn't first try to change the law. 3) The Association did not willingly accept the punishment for violating the law.

5 The facts in *Grimshaw v. Ford Motor Co.* suggest that Ford was engaged only in self-interested thinking. The decision not to protect the fuel tank saved Ford about $21 million, so it was in Ford's financial self-interest to let consumers bear the risk. It is easy to see that this decision could be justified by looking at the large number of people who benefited by the decision and the few who were injured. Accordingly, the decision can be justified by consequential ethics. This decision cannot be justified by deontological ethics. Ford 's decision caused some people to suffer physical injury. That is inherently wrong. The injuries cannot be justified by Ford's increased profits. Reason also condemns Ford's conduct. As humans, the victims have rights. One right is the right not to be intentionally or negligently injured by others. Ford violated this right and therefore its conduct was unethical.

CHAPTER 3 ORGANIZER

Chapter Theme

Criminal, civil, and business law are just a few kinds of law reflected in constitutions, statutes, and rulings by administrative agencies.

DIRECTED STUDY QUESTIONS	SPECIAL FEATURES	PROGRAM RESOURCES: Reteach	Enrich	SN	AM	
How did our law develop?		✔	✔			
What types of law do we have today?	Thinking Critically Through Visuals, pp. 50, 51, 52 Personal Perspectives, p. 54	✔	✔	✔	V A	
Which type of law is valid when laws conflict?	Multicultural Highlights, p.55	✔	✔		K	
How do criminal and civil laws differ?	Writing Connections, p. 56	✔	✔			
How do procedural and substantive laws differ?	Thinking Critically Through Visuals, p. 58	✔	✔			
What is Business Law?	Ethics Issue, p. 58 Preventing Legal Difficulties, p. 59	✔	✔			

Additional Resources

- *Black's Law Dictionary*, 6th ed. St. Paul, MN: West Publishing Co., 1990.
- Frascona, Conry, et al. *Business Law.* Boston: Allyn & Bacon, 1991.
- *June 15, 1215*. Newscast from the Past. AIT The Learning Source.
- Schwartz, Bernard, ed. *Statutory History of the United States: Civil Rights.* NY: Chelsea House Publishers, 1970.
- Smith, Len Young and Roberson, G. Gale. *Business Law: Uniform Commercial Code,* 4th ed. St. Paul, MN: West Publishing Co., 1977.

One-semester course	✔	✔	✔					
One-year course	✔	✔	✔	✔				

Chapter Pacing Guide

	ASSESSMENT OPPORTUNITIES			
Cooperative Learning	**Informal Assessment**	**Chapter Review**	**Chapter Test**	**Chapter *MicroExam***
	✔	✔	✔	✔
✔		✔	✔	✔
	✔	✔	✔	✔
	✔	✔	✔	✔
	✔	✔	✔	✔
	✔	✔	✔	✔

Videodiscs

Distribution of Legal Power between States and Federal Government

Search Chapter 3, Play To 4

Four Types of Law: Constitutional, Statutory, Administration Regulations, and Case Law

Search Chapter 4, Play To 5

State by State

Louisiana, a state with ties to civil law systems such as that of France, has adopted only a part of the Uniform Commercial Code (UCC).

Teaching Materials

Student text, pp. 46–63

Overhead transparency masters
- *Evolution of Our Legal System*
- *Hierarchy, Levels, and Sources of Law*

Videos
- *Our Legal System* Videotape
- *Law for Business* Videodisc

Workbook, pp. 5–6

Outside Resources
- Game pieces
- VCR
- AIT's *June 15, 1215*, video
- Tape recorder
- Various newspapers and news magazines (include business sections)
- Poster boards and index cards
- Copies of school constitution

Assessment
- Chapter Test
- Chapter *MicroExam*

Vocabulary

common law, p. 48
Magna Carta, p. 48
Roman civil law, p. 48
money damages, p. 48
specific performance, p. 49
injunction, p. 49
equity, p. 49
constitutional law, p. 51
interstate commerce, p. 52
intrastate commerce, p. 52
statutes, p. 53
ordinance, p. 53
administrative agencies, p. 53
administrative laws, p. 53
rules and regulations, p. 53
case law, p. 53
appellate review, p. 53
stare decisis, p. 54
supremacy, p. 55
unconstitutional, p. 55
constitutional, p. 55
civil law, p. 56
liable, p. 56
criminal law, p. 56
procedural law, p. 57
substantive law, p. 57
business law, p. 59
torts, p. 59
Uniform Commercial Code (UCC), p. 59

Learning Objectives

When you complete this chapter, you will be able to

1. Describe the difference between law courts and equity courts.
2. Explain how constitutional, statutory, case, and administrative laws are created.
3. Explain how we resolve conflicts among constitutional, statutory, case, and administrative laws.
4. Describe the difference between civil and criminal law.
5. Describe the difference between substantive and procedural laws.
6. Understand when business law regulates a situation.

Chapter Self-Test

Orally assess students' understanding of the historical roots of the U.S. legal system before they begin Chapter 3 by asking the following: **(1) The foundation of present-day U.S. law is based on which country's system of law—France, England, or Spain?** (England); and **(2) Is U.S. law based mainly on the common-law principles of the Magna Carta or Roman civil law?** (The Magna Carta)

Before continuing with the chapter, review and discuss students' rationale for choosing their responses.

CHAPTER

3

KINDS OF LAW

1 Sperry rented an apartment from Yu. When Sperry fell behind in her monthly rental payments, Yu threatened to call the police and have Sperry arrested. Can Sperry be arrested for failing to pay her rent?

2 While driving toward an intersection, Landrum sees the green traffic light change to yellow. Attempting to "beat the signal," he accelerates, racing well above the posted speed limit. But the light turns red seconds before he reaches it. Brakes screech, then Landrum smashes into the side of a sedan moving across the intersection. Landrum is knocked unconscious and partially paralyzed. The other driver is killed, and two passengers are seriously injured. What kinds of law have been violated?

3 
For twenty minutes, Agusto drove around downtown looking for a parking space. Finally, he gave up and parked near a fire hydrant. The curb beside his car was painted red. From past experience, he knew the fine for blocking a fire hydrant was only $10. Agusto was more than willing to pay $10 to end his frustrating search. Was Agusto's conduct ethical?

FOCUS

Divide the classroom into four or five workstations. When students come into the classroom, direct them to choose a seat in one of the stations. Give each group a set of game pieces such as dice, spinners, and poster board. Allow 10 minutes for groups to devise a board game of their choosing.

Have each group explain its game to the class. Ask students: **What are the two main things that you need to decide when devising a new game?** (The goal of the game; the rules) Ask: **Why is it important to have rules?** (Answers may include that it isn't fair if everyone plays by different rules; no one will know how to proceed.) Draw analogies between the need for game rules and the need for rules and laws for civilized society.

You Decide

1 No, this is a civil matter, a private conflict between Yu and Sperry. The police will not involve themselves in a purely civil matter.

2 Both criminal and civil laws—criminal: speeding, "running a red light," causing death of one passenger and injuring two others; civil: (torts) causing death of the other driver and injuring two passengers, and destroying the other car.

3 
No, the conduct was not ethical. Personal frustration is not justification for violating the law.

Thinking Critically Through Visuals

Tell students to note the body language of the people in the photograph. Ask: **What feelings might each person be expressing?** (Answers may include the following: judge—desire to be fair but determined to enforce the law; parents—desire to be protective and supportive, worried; boy—answers should reflect independent thinking.)

TEACH

Explain to students that English common law is judge-made law, or case law. Point out that English common law, along with the principles of the Magna Carta, are the foundation of our legal system.

To provide students with a feeling for the time period in which the Magna Carta was conceived and signed, show program 2, *June 15, 1215*, from the video series Newscast from the Past, distributed by AIT The Learning Source. After showing the video, have student volunteers share what they think would be the most difficult daily law-related stress to deal with during this early historic time.

Explain the difference between common-law courts and equity courts. Point out that common-law courts limited themselves to granting only the remedy of money damages, and equity courts—sometimes called courts of equity or chancery courts—could grant a decree of **specific performance** (an order to do something) or an **injunction** (an order not to do something.)

HOW DID OUR LAW DEVELOP?

PROBLEM

The labor strike was in its fifth bitter week. The strikers were as tense and angry as the workers who had remained on the job. For several days, about a thousand picketers gathered at the company's main gate, chanting slogans and jeering those who entered the plant. Then a company truck was set on fire and destroyed. Management went to court seeking protection. What could a court do?

1. English Common Law: Our Legal Heritage

The United States uses a legal system called the **common law.** This system developed in England and was later adopted by our nation. Before there was a written law in England, barons acted as the judges within their territories. Disputes were settled on the basis of local customs and the barons' judgments. Therefore, the laws of England tended to differ by region or by territory. In some places, such practices as trial by ordeal (e.g., determining innocence by the ability to walk barefoot across hot coals) were used. Eventually the king established a system of courts that enforced a uniform or "common" law throughout England. To promote uniformity, rules of law stated by judges in one territory became precedents (i.e., examples) for settling future, similar cases in all territories. This resulted in what has come to be known as the common law or judge-made law or case law.

In 1215, the barons forced King John to accept the **Magna Carta** (Latin for "great charter"). It provided protection against unreasonable acts by kings. When the thirteen American colonies broke away from Great Britain, the colonists adopted the common law and important principles from the Magna Carta. These principles became the foundation of our legal system. The principles are the basis for our federal laws and for the laws of all the states except Louisiana, where French influence and Roman civil law prevail.

Today, the world's two great systems of law are the English common law and the **Roman civil law.** Countries with civil law systems adopted written, well-organized, comprehensive sets of statutes called codes. This contrasts with common-law countries, where judges make a series of decisions, one at a time, gradually expanding the law. Also, English common law was unique in providing for trial by a jury of one's peers (i.e., one's equals).

2. Equity: Alternative to the Common Law

The common-law courts carefully followed prior cases in deciding similar new cases. But in doing so these courts became quite rigid. They limited themselves to granting only the remedy of **money damages.** Money dam-

ASSESS

Learning Objective 1 Have students respond orally to the following: Which type of court, common-law or equity, would grant each of the following: money damages (Common–law), **specific performance** (Equity), and **injunction** (Equity)?

ages basically consists of a court-ordered payment by the defendant to the plaintiff. This rigidity meant that common-law courts were sometimes unable to correct certain obvious wrongs. For example, if Smyth promised to sell land to Jones, and then Smyth refused to complete the deal, the common-law courts would not force Smyth to deliver the deed to the land.

Because there were many instances where the common-law courts would not aid those with valid claims, the king began providing help. Thus, Jones could appeal his case to the king, who would refer the matter to his chancellor. The chancellor was usually a high clergyman respected for fairness or equity. The chancellor would conduct a hearing under rules somewhat different from those of a common-law trial. These chancery courts could grant more remedies. Jones could now win a decree of specific performance from the king compelling Smyth to deliver the deed to the land. A decree of **specific performance** is an order from the king to *do* something. In another type of case a chancellor might issue an **injunction** (a command to *not do* something). The chancellors heard these cases without a jury. These hearings developed into a separate system of courts, called **equity** or courts of equity or chancery courts.

In the United States today, law courts and equity courts are generally merged. Most American courts can provide the help common-law courts gave, such as money damages. Thus, in the problem at the beginning of this section, the judge might grant the company money damages for the loss of the truck. The same court could also provide the help that equity courts granted, such as an injunction limiting the number of picketers at the plant's entrance to perhaps ten. Strikers who violated the injunction would then risk a jail sentence for contempt of court if they failed to obey the injunction. As in England, there is no right to a trial by jury in suits for specific performance or injunctions because these suits have their roots in the English equity courts.

WHAT TYPES OF LAW DO WE HAVE TODAY?

PROBLEM

Congress requires cigarette makers to print these words on every cigarette package: "Warning: the Surgeon General has determined that cigarette smoking is dangerous to your health." What type of law requires this?

There are three levels of legal systems in the United States: federal, state, and local (city or county). Among the levels, there is a hierarchy of authority. Thus, federal law generally prevails over state and local law. State law prevails over local law.

APPLY

Create situations that illustrate examples of money damages, specific performance, and injunction. For example, for specific performance, you might say, "Person A agrees to sell Person B an antique bicycle for a specific price and later wants to back out of the deal. The judge orders Person A to go through with the sale." Read each aloud and ask students to identify which of the three judgments the situation illustrates. Discuss answers. **Guided Practice**

Bring to class newspapers and news magazines. Have students work in pairs using these resources to identify examples of cases that involve money damages, specific performance, or injunction. Have students label clippings and display them on a bulletin board called *Court-ordered Remedies.* **Independent Practice**

TEACH

To reinforce the concept that laws are created by three levels of government—federal, state, and local—take time whenever a law comes up as part of a class discussion to ask students at which level of government the law was created. Then, ask what was the probable source of the law. (Judge, city council, congress, and so on)

RETEACH

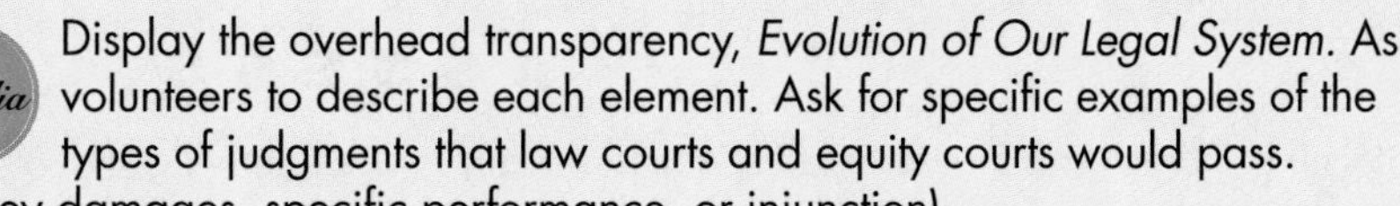

Media: Display the overhead transparency, *Evolution of Our Legal System.* Ask volunteers to describe each element. Ask for specific examples of the types of judgments that law courts and equity courts would pass. (Money damages, specific performance, or injunction)

ENRICH

Direct students to work in pairs to list examples of school rules or regulations related to money damages, specific performance, or injunction. (Answers may include library fines, required attendance, no smoking, and so on.)

On the chalkboard, list in one vertical column the three levels of law—federal, state, and local. Beside each level, list the four types of law—constitutions, statutes, administrative regulations, and case law. Point out that some form of all four kinds of law are found at each of the three levels. For example, at the constitutional level there is the U.S. Constitution, state constitutions, and city constitutions or charters.

Tell students that each of the four types of law has a specific source, specific powers, and is associated with specific terms and procedures. Have them note these during their reading and class discussions and write them in their notebooks.

Thinking Critically Through Visuals

In this photograph, a lawyer is meeting with her client and her assistant. Where is this meeting probably taking place? (The lawyer's office) **Why, do you think, do lawyers keep so many books in their offices?** (Answers may include that practicing law requires frequent referral to past cases and current statutes.)

The types of laws at each level consist of the following:

1. *Constitutions:* These documents define the fundamental laws of our country and each state. There are also charters or constitutions for cities or counties.
2. *Statutes:* These are the laws enacted by our elected representatives at the federal and state levels. At the local level, they are called ordinances.
3. *Administrative regulations:* These are laws created by administrative agencies at the federal, state, and local levels.
4. *Case law:* This is the law stated by judges in court opinions.

These four types of laws—constitutional, statutory, administrative, and case—are created by federal, state, and local governments. Figure 3-1 shows this relationship and presents an example for each level. The following paragraphs describe in detail the ways these laws are created.

1. Constitutional Law

Law is created when people adopt constitutions or amend existing constitutions. You are governed by both the Constitution of the United States and the constitution of the state in which you live. The Supreme Court of the United States is the final interpreter of the federal Constitution and each state supreme court is the final authority on the meaning of its state

▼ ASSESS

Learning Objective 2 Have students respond orally to the following: **(1) What type of law defines the fundamental laws of our country and each state?** (Constitutional law); and **(2) Define the source of constitutional law by naming three ways it is made.** (When constitutions are adopted; when constitutions are amended; and when courts interpret constitutions)

	Constitutions	Statutes	Administrative Regulations	Case Law
Federal Level	U.S. Constitution	U.S. Code	Regulations of the Internal Revenue Service (IRS)	*Brown v. Board of Education* decided by the U.S. Supreme Court
State Level	Florida's State Constitution	Colorado Revised Statutes	Regulations of the Department of Agriculture in Texas	Decisions of the New Mexico Supreme Court
Local Level	Detroit City Charter	New York City Zoning Ordinances	Rules of the Department of Parks and Recreation in Hamilton County	Small Claims Court of Jefferson County

Figure 3-1
Examples of constitutions, statutes, administrative regulations, and case law at each level of government.

constitution. When constitutions are adopted or amended, or when courts interpret constitutions, **constitutional law** is made.

The federal and state constitutions are concerned primarily with defining and allocating certain powers in our society. Our constitutions allocate powers:

1. between the people and their governments,
2. between state governments and the federal government, and
3. among the branches of the governments.

The federal Constitution is the main instrument for allocating powers between persons and their governments. It does this with its first ten amendments, called the Bill of Rights. As described in Chapter 1, the Bill of Rights protects people from actions of their governments. Among these rights are the following:

1. freedom of religion;
2. freedom of speech, press, and peaceable assembly;
3. security in person and property against unreasonable searches and seizures;
4. right to remain silent if accused of a crime and to enjoy a speedy and public trial by an impartial jury;

▼ APPLY

Write the terms **adopted, amended,** and **interpreted** on the chalkboard. Tell students that these are key terms in describing the possible sources of constitutional law. Read aloud the following examples and have students identify which of the terms best applies:
1. The people voted to make some changes to the constitution under which they lived. (Amended)
2. The people of a new nation all agreed to live by the presented constitution. (Adopted)
3. The supreme court conferred and decided exactly what the words in a specific part of the constitution meant. (Interpretation) **Guided Practice**

Thinking Critically Through Visuals

This chart summarizes the three levels of law. What example of a federal statute is given? (U.S. code) **What example of case law is provided for the state level?** (Decisions of the New Mexico Supreme Court) **At what level of law is the Detroit City Charter?** (Local level)

Have students make a poster summarizing the sources, powers, and terms associated with constitutional law.

Ask small groups to brainstorm examples of the three sources of law at the federal level related to the U.S. Constitution. (Answers may include adoption—ratification in 1788; adaptation—Bill of Rights; and interpretation—U.S. Supreme Court declared poll taxes unconstitutional.)

To help students with reading comprehension difficulties or limited English proficiency, write the two prefixes **inter-** (between) and **intra-** (within) on the chalkboard. Discuss the meaning of the terms **interstate commerce** and **intrastate commerce**. Ask for other examples of terms that incorporate these prefixes. (Answers may include international, interracial, intramural, intrapersonal, and so on.) Relate the original terms to

the powers of state and federal constitutions.

Thinking Critically Through Visuals

Police officers often check documentation for vehicles carrying interstate or intrastate commerce. What might the officer be checking? (Answers may include what is being carried on the truck, where it is going, if the driver has a valid license, and so on.)

5. protection from cruel or unusual punishment if convicted of a crime;
6. right to fair compensation for private property taken by the government for a public purpose; and
7. protection from the taking of life, liberty, or property without due process of law.

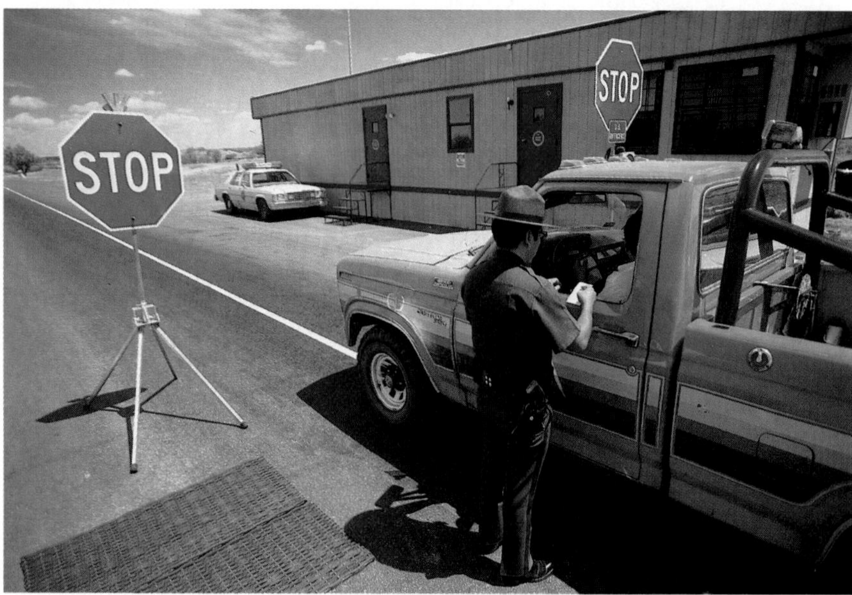

The federal Constitution also allocates powers among the federal and state governments. For example, many governmental powers over business are divided between state governments and the federal government on the basis of commerce. In general, the Constitution gives the federal government the power to regulate foreign and interstate commerce. **Interstate commerce** occurs between two or more states. Regulation of **intrastate commerce,** which occurs within one state, is left to the states.

State and federal constitutions also allocate governmental powers among the three branches of government: the executive, the legislative, and the judicial. Constitutions do this to create a system of checks and balances among the branches so that no branch of government becomes too powerful.

> Suppose Congress held hearings and determined that a certain person was a drug dealer. If Congress then passed a statute sentencing that person to prison, the courts would declare that statute unconstitutional and therefore invalid. The Constitution gives the courts, not Congress, the authority to conduct trials.

ASSESS

Learning Objective 2 On an overhead transparency, write terms A–D in one column and phrases 1–4 in a second column: **(A) constitutional law; (B) statutory law; (C) administrative law; and (D) case law; (1) Enacted by Congress; (2) Enacted by agencies; (3) Enacted by the people;** and **(4) Enacted by judges.** On a separate sheet of paper, ask students to match terms with phrases by pairing appropriate letters with numbers. (1B, 2C, 3A, 4D)

2. Statutory Law

The federal Constitution created the Congress of the United States. State constitutions created the state legislatures. These state and federal legislatures are composed of elected representatives of the people. Acting for their citizens, these legislatures enact laws called **statutes.**

All states have delegated some of their legislative authority to local governments. Thus, towns, cities, and counties can legislate on matters over which the state has given them authority. These laws then are effective only within the boundary of the county or city. Such legislation is created by a town or city council or by a county board or commission. Legislation of this type is usually called an **ordinance** rather than a statute.

3. Administrative Law

Federal, state, and local legislatures all create administrative agencies. **Administrative agencies** are governmental bodies formed to carry out particular laws. The federal Social Security Administration, your state's division of motor vehicles, and your county's zoning commission are examples of administrative agencies. Although they are created by legislatures, administrative agencies are usually operated by the executive branch of the government. Thus, the President, governor, or mayor will supervise the agency's activities. For example, the U.S. Congress created the Internal Revenue Service (an agency) and directed that the President appoint and supervise the staff of the agency.

Legislatures sometimes give administrative agencies legislative powers and limited judicial powers. Legislative power means the agency is authorized to create **administrative laws,** which are also called **rules and regulations.** For example, the Social Security Administration might establish rules for determining *when* a student is a dependent of a widow or widower and qualified to receive social security payments. The rules and regulations established by an administrative agency generally have the force of law.

If an agency has judicial power, it can hold hearings, make determinations of fact, and apply the law to particular cases. So, the Social Security Administration might hold a hearing that decides whether a *particular* student is, in fact, dependent on her mother and therefore entitled to social security payments.

4. Case Law

Case law is created by the judicial branches of our governments. Federal courts establish federal case law and, similarly, each state creates case law through its state courts. **Case law** is usually made after a trial has ended and one of the parties has appealed to a higher court. This may result in a review of parts of the trial in a process called **appellate review.** When the

Have students work in groups of three or four to brainstorm and compile a list of laws, rules, and regulations and their probable sources. (Answers may include statutes and case law.) Then, allow a representative of each group to tape record its list. Play back the tapes and have students judge the accuracy of each other's work. **Independent Practice**

Divide the class into groups of three or four. Assign or have students choose the following roles: a fact checker to check facts, an artist to draw the illustrations, a copywriter to write the copy, and a facilitator to keep everyone on task (optional). Have groups create a chart, graphic organizer, or poster that compares case law and statutory law. You also may wish to have students consider and compare the probable effect of social, economic, and political forces on the making of specific laws in each category. Allow each group to make a five- to 10-minute presentation to the class. **Cooperative Learning**

Ask students which type of law would most likely apply to each of the following: **(1) A person's rights as a citizen** (Constitutional), **(2) A car parked in a restricted zone** (Statutory), **(3) A restaurant owner's handling of food** (Administrative), and **(4) A conflict between a landlord and a tenant** (Case).

Have students assume the role of a specific type of law maker and orally give a brief description of the final form of the law maker's work. (Answers may include senator who would make state statutes such as tax laws.)

Personal Perspectives

Ask a student volunteer to read the case example found on p. 54 about the borrowed car. After you are sure students understand the case, direct students to discuss it with adult family members at home. Have them discuss whether or not a family member's view of a circumstance (there was no theft) should override the judge's view (there was theft). In class, have volunteers share their discussions. Ask students how many families were surprised to learn that the law might override their personal agreements on what is or is not happening within their own family.

▼ TEACH

Discuss how rules and regulations at school reflect a hierarchy of power. Teachers make rules for their class that do not conflict with school rules; schools make rules that do not conflict with district rules, and so on. Explain that hierarchy also exists in law. Sometimes the laws of different levels of government conflict, as do the types of laws created by the same level. In these situations, supremacy rules determine which is valid.

appellate court publishes its opinion on a case, that opinion may state new rules, thereby creating new case law.

> Carol borrowed her stepfather's car without his express permission. The police stopped her, discovered the car was not registered in her name, then phoned her stepfather. When he said he did not know where his car was, Carol was arrested. At her trial, Carol and her stepfather testified that she had his permission to use the car without asking each time. The trial judge nevertheless found Carol guilty of auto theft, which, the judge stated, occurs when one person takes the car of another without express permission. Carol appealed to the state supreme court. That appellate court issued an opinion stating that implied permission is enough and therefore Carol was innocent. This rule then becomes case law.

The effectiveness of case law arises out of the doctrine of **stare decisis.** This is Latin for "to adhere to decided cases." This doctrine requires that once case law is stated, it must be followed by lower courts in other similar cases. Thus, in the illustration about auto theft, all the trial courts in that state would be required to follow as case law the rule that one is not guilty of auto theft if she or he has implied permission to use the car.

The doctrine of stare decisis generally does not bind supreme courts; they can modify or overturn their own case law. In the illustration, the same supreme court could rule in a later but similar case that implied permission is not enough. Supreme courts are not bound by their own prior decisions. Generally, however, most case law doctrines are carefully established and seldom revoked.

▼ WHICH TYPE OF LAW IS VALID WHEN LAWS CONFLICT?

PROBLEM

> When adopted, the U.S. Constitution provided that there could be no income tax. So when the Congress levied a two percent income tax in 1894, the U.S. Supreme Court declared it unconstitutional. Many people wanted the federal government to raise money by taxing incomes because then the burden imposed would be according to one's ability to pay. Was there anything the people could do to change the effect of the Supreme Court's decision?

▼ ASSESS

Learning Objective 3 Have students orally identify which of the laws will prevail in each of the following situations: **(1) A statute conflicts with a state constitution.** (State constitution), **(2) A state constitution conflicts with the federal Constitution.** (Federal Constitution), and **(3) A local ordinance conflicts with a state statute.** (State statute)

Sometimes the laws of the differing levels of government conflict. For example, a city ordinance may conflict with a state statute on speed limits. Sometimes different types of laws created by the same level of government conflict. A federal administrative regulation may conflict with a federal court decision. In these situations, the legal rules for determining **supremacy** establish which law is valid.

1. Constitutions and Validity

Constitutions are the highest sources of law, and the federal Constitution is "the supreme law of the land." This means that any federal, state, or local law—including a part of a state constitution—is void to the extent that it conflicts with the federal Constitution. Thus, for example, no New York statute, no federal administrative regulation, and no city court decision is valid if it conflicts with the federal Constitution.

Similarly, within each state, the state constitution is supreme to all other state laws. When a law is invalid because it conflicts with a constitution, it is **unconstitutional**. The appropriate supreme court determines when a law is unconstitutional.

2. Statutes and Validity

To be valid, the statute or ordinance must be **constitutional**. In addition, ordinances must not exceed the powers delegated to local governments by the states. The courts will determine the constitutionality of statutes and ordinances and whether local ordinances exceed the scope of powers delegated by the state.

> The city of Sparrow enacted a law that made it illegal to sell gasoline for more than $1 per gallon and another law that made the death penalty mandatory for persons who commit murder within the city limits. Both ordinances were challenged in court. The first was declared invalid because it conflicted with the federal Constitution, which gives the power to regulate interstate commerce to the federal government. The second was invalidated because it was outside the scope of the city's powers. Only the state had the power to set penalties for murder.

3. Administrative Regulations and Validity

Like statutes and ordinances, administrative regulations can be reviewed by courts to determine whether they are constitutional. In addition, the courts may invalidate a rule or regulation if it is outside the scope of powers delegated by the legislature.

▼ APPLY

Provide students with copies of your school constitution or student conduct policy. In small groups, ask students to examine the document and circle any conflicts with higher governing bodies. Then, have them amend any sections they would like to change. As a class, discuss the conflicts that students discovered and the amendments they wrote.

Guided Practice

Multicultural Highlights

The law that ended slavery was the Thirteenth Amendment to the Constitution, which took effect on December 18, 1865. Because the Constitution is the supreme law of the land, no state or local area could vote to initiate or maintain slavery from that time forward. Ask: **Why would modern-day seekers of civil rights laws want such laws to be enacted at the federal level?** (Answers may include to ensure country-wide compliance.) **Independent Practice**

Cover the boxed labels on the overhead transparency, *Hierarchy, Levels, and Sources of Law.* Display the transparency and uncover each label as students offer answers.

Ask students to turn to the Constitution of the United States in Appendix A of their texts. Have them find which article and amendment define the relation between federal and state laws (Article VI and Amendment XIV).

▼ TEACH

Compare civil and criminal laws. Violations of an individual's private rights are governed by civil law, and civil courts mainly grant money damages. Offenses against society usually are governed by criminal law, and criminal courts impose fines, imprisonment and, in some states, execution. Give examples of civil and criminal laws.

▼ APPLY

Examine newspapers for one example in which civil law governs and one in which criminal law does. Read pertinent facts to the class. Have students categorize the facts as raising a civil or a criminal issue, then explain their reasons. **Guided Practice**

Social Studies
Direct students to write, on computers, if possible, scenarios that describe each of the following: a violation of only civil law, a violation of only criminal law, and a violation of both civil and criminal law. Then, have small groups meet to share their work.

Independent Practice

4. Case Law and Validity

In addition to determining constitutionality, courts often interpret the meaning of *legislative* language. Thus, a court may be required to determine whether the word "people" in a statute is intended to include business organizations. But courts are not the final authority on the effect of statutes. Legislative bodies have the power to nullify a court's interpretation of its statute or ordinance by abolishing or rewriting it. Similarly, administrative agencies can revise their regulations when they are challenged.

Even when interpreting constitutions, the courts are not the ultimate authority. The people, through votes for their elected representatives, have the power to amend constitutions if they disagree with the way courts have interpreted them. In the problem, the Sixteenth Amendment to the U.S. Constitution was adopted in 1913 to give Congress the power to lay and collect an income tax. In effect, this nullified the decision of the U.S. Supreme Court.

▼ HOW DO CRIMINAL AND CIVIL LAWS DIFFER?

PROBLEM

Worthington was driving down the road well within the speed limit. At a stop sign he slowed to about fifteen miles per hour, but did not stop. As a result, he smashed into the side of Bates's Mercedes, causing $12,000 in damages. Has Worthington violated either the civil or criminal law?

When the private legal rights of an individual are violated, the matter is governed by civil law. **Civil law** refers to wrongs against individual persons. It applies whenever one person has a right to sue another person. An example of such a situation is when a tenant fails to pay the rent. The police will not take any action in civil conflicts. If a defendant loses a civil case, we say that she or he is **liable**. This means that she or he must pay money to the plaintiff. This is the main help that courts grant in civil matters. Civil law in this sense differs from the comprehensive system of Roman civil law mentioned earlier in this chapter.

A crime is an offense against society. When the rights of the public—society as a whole—are violated, the offense is governed by **criminal law.** The government, acting in the name of all the people, investigates the alleged wrongdoer and, if found guilty, prosecutes him or her. Conviction of a crime can result in a fine, imprisonment, and in some states execution.

Usually, when a crime occurs, private rights of the victim are violated also. The violation may be both a crime and a civil offense. Thus, the civil

▼ ASSESS

Learning Objectives 4 & 5 Ask students to write the term—*criminal law, civil law, procedural law,* or *substantive law*—that would play a major role in each of the following: **(1) A is accusing B of breach of contract.** (Substantive); **(2) C is accused of computer theft.** (Criminal); **(3) D wants his tenants out because they haven't paid the rent.** (Civil); and **(4) E and F are protesting the circumstances under which they were arrested.** (Procedural) law may also apply. The victim of the crime may sue the wrongdoer. Often, though, that does not happen because it is difficult to collect damages from criminals.

In the problem, Worthington committed both a crime and a civil offense. Driving through the stop sign was a crime. Worthington could be arrested, convicted in a criminal trial, and fined. In addition, Worthington committed a civil offense when he carelessly smashed into the side of Bates's Mercedes. Bates could probably win a separate civil trial and recover the $12,000 from Worthington.

HOW DO PROCEDURAL AND SUBSTANTIVE LAWS DIFFER?

PROBLEM

Robertson, a builder, contracted with McGee to construct a building to be occupied by one of McGee's Hamburger Havens. A short time later, the state revealed plans to build a super highway nearby. The proposed highway would isolate the site and make access to it difficult. Therefore, McGee canceled the construction contract. Robertson had already bought some materials for the job, but they were usable elsewhere. Although McGee indicated that she would consider Robertson for a future job, she refused to pay him for anything for this one. So he lost the hoped-for profit. What can he do to collect the anticipated profit?

Procedural law deals with methods of *enforcing* legal rights and duties. Laws that specify how and when police can make arrests and what methods can be used in a trial are procedural laws. Procedural laws determine whether the equitable remedies of injunction or specific performance are available. The doctrine of stare decisis is a procedural law. Rules for determining the supremacy of conflicting laws are procedural laws. In contrast, **substantive law** defines rights and duties; it is concerned with all the rules of conduct except those involved in enforcement. Substantive laws *define* offenses, such as murder, theft, vehicular homicide, breach of contract, and negligence.

There are two types of procedural law—civil procedure and criminal procedure. Criminal procedure defines the process for enforcing the law when someone is charged with a crime. Since a crime is an offense against society, representatives of society—such as city police, the state highway patrol, or Federal Bureau of Investigation (FBI) agents—investigate alleged criminal conduct. They try to arrest those who commit criminal acts. Other

TEACH

Compare procedural law and substantive law. Point out that civil law and criminal law include both substantive and procedural laws.

APPLY

Write on the chalkboard the following list of phrases, omitting the answers in parentheses: procedural law (p.l.) or substantive law (s.l.).
- **Defines offenses** (s.l.)
- **Determines whether the equitable remedies of injunction or specific performance are available** (p.l.)
- **The doctrine of stare decisis is an example** (p.l.)
- **Defines rights and duties** (s.l.)
- **Determines the supremacy of conflicting laws** (p.l.)

Then, have students write the term in their notebooks next to each phrase most associated with that term. **Guided Practice**

Have students take turns describing a situation that is governed by either procedural or substantive law. Have the class label the presented situation. Then, have the presenter explain why he or she agrees or disagrees with the label. **Independent Practice**

RETEACH Have students work in pairs and copy the following terms from pp. 56–58 on a sheet of paper: **civil law, criminal law, civil substantive law, civil procedural law, criminal substantive law,** and **criminal procedural law**. Have them write a definition and an example for each term.

ENRICH Have students write statements that describe an offense. Under each statement have them tell why each is part of civil or criminal law and whether substantive or procedural law would probably be involved and why.

Thinking Critically Through Visuals

This chart shows the classifications of the law. Why isn't the *Criminal* heading of *Procedural* subdivided into *Law* and *Equity?* (Law courts grant money damages and equity courts grant decrees of specific performance and injunctions. Rulings of this type are not part of criminal law.)

▼ TEACH

Business law is mainly concerned with contracts and torts. Ask the class to define **tort**. Introduce the Uniform Commercial Code.

▼ APPLY

Ethics Issue

Sometimes a tort involves an injured party who accuses a manufacturer of knowingly selling a dangerous product. Discuss situations in which a manufacturer should be liable for an injury caused by its product. **Guided Practice**

representatives of society—city prosecutors, state attorneys general, and U.S. attorneys—may try to convict the alleged criminal during a criminal trial. The law of criminal procedure controls each of these activities.

Civil procedure is used when a civil law has been violated. Because civil law is concerned only with private offenses, when a civil law is violated the injured party (not a public official) must protect his or her rights. Police and public prosecutors generally do not involve themselves in the dispute. Figure 3-2 depicts the relationships among these categories of law.

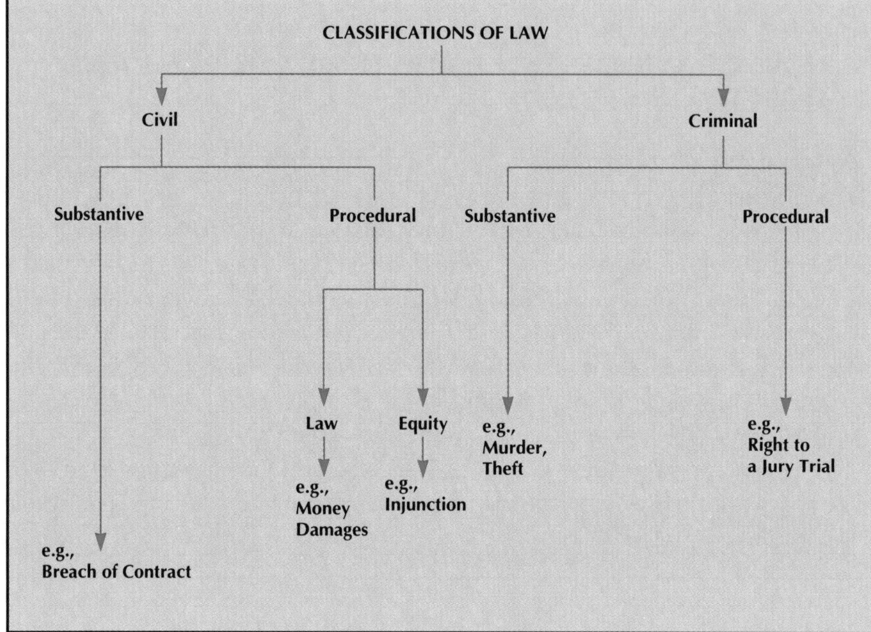

Figure 3-2
Relationships among criminal, civil, procedural, and substantive law, with examples of each.

In the earlier problem, Robertson's claim against McGee is a civil matter for breach of contract. Therefore, police and prosecutors will not become involved. If Robertson initiates a lawsuit to recover lost profits, the rules of civil procedure will govern the trial.

▼ WHAT IS BUSINESS LAW?

PROBLEM

Royal, a teacher, agreed to buy a new subcompact automobile from Morgan Motors on a time payment plan. Royal signed a lengthy printed form with specific terms of the transaction typed in. However, he was uncertain about the full meaning of the contents of the document. How would a knowledge of business law have helped?

▼ ASSESS

Learning Objective 6 Ask students to indicate (by voting thumbs up for *regulated* or thumbs down for *not regulated*) whether or not each of the following situations is governed by business law: **(1) There is a contract dispute between a manufacturer and a distributor.** (Regulated); **(2) A person steals candy bars from a store.** (Not regulated); and **(3) A store is accused of selling used merchandise as "new."** (Regulated)

Business law (also known as commercial law) covers rules that apply to business situations and transactions. A look at the table of contents of this book will show that the scope of business law is very broad.

While some students may think that business law concerns only people planning to go into business, this is not so. Most business transactions involve both a merchant and a consumer. As you study business law, you will gain legal knowledge which will make you a more competent consumer.

Business law is largely concerned with civil law, especially contracts. Torts is another category of business law. **Torts** are private wrongs (i.e., civil offenses) against people or organizations. Torts are distinct from breaches of contracts. For example, a tort may occur when a manufacturer makes a defective product that injures a user. Criminal law sometimes governs business-related activities, too. For example, criminal law would punish a firm that conspires with competitors to fix prices or an employee who steals company tools.

Although generally the laws of our fifty states are similar, there are state-to-state differences. With the growth of interstate commerce and large business firms, greater uniformity of laws governing business and commercial transactions became necessary. In response, all states adopted all or at least parts of the Uniform Commercial Code. The **Uniform Commercial Code (UCC)** is a large set of business statutes which simplified, clarified, and modernized many laws relating to commercial transactions.

Preventing Legal Difficulties

As a citizen...

1. When moving to a new location, find out which county or city makes laws that may affect you.
2. Before beginning a new business, consult an attorney to learn about city, county, state, and federal laws and how they may affect you.
3. Study business law diligently so you can become an informed consumer who is knowledgeable about legal matters.

▼ REVIEWING IMPORTANT POINTS

1. The two great systems of law in the world are the English common law and the Roman civil law. The federal government and all states except Louisiana follow the common law.
2. The common law operates through the doctrine of stare decisis.

Display pages from the business section of a newspaper. In pairs, have students choose an article and circle sections that describe various situations in which business law might apply. Also, have students label examples of *torts* and *breaches of contract.* Ask the class to accept or challenge the labeling. **Independent Practice**

Preventing Legal Difficulties

Discuss each of the three suggestions for preventing legal difficulties. Ask students to suggest the possible consequences of not following each of these suggestions.

▼ CLOSE

Ask small groups to present skits of situations that could prompt legal action. Have the class name the kind of law—civil, criminal, constitutional, statutory, administrative, case, procedural, substantive, or business—that has jurisdiction over the situation.

Assign the following end-of-chapter materials:
Student text review activities, pp. 59–63
Workbook, pp. 5–6
Chapter Test

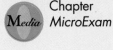

Chapter *MicroExam*

▼RETEACH

On a computer, if possible, have students write 10 terms that come to mind when they think of *business law*. Then, have students use these terms to describe an imaginary business scenario.

▼ENRICH

Have students write, on a computer, if possible, then read aloud summaries of personal business situations in which a knowledge of business law at the time would have altered their actions. Have them explain what they would now do differently and why.

Strengthening Your Legal Vocabulary

1. unconstitutional
2. stare decisis
3. statute
4. interstate commerce
5. ordinance
6. common law
7. business law
8. Uniform Commercial Code (UCC)
9. injunction
10. case law

Applying Law to Everyday Life

1. Juan can sue and recover his father's ring with a suit for specific performance. A suit for specific performance would be allowed in this case because the ring is unique and has primarily sentimental value. (p. 49)
2. The federal level of government created the law that makes this religious activity illegal in a public school. The Bill of Rights, a part of our Constitution, requires this ruling. (p. 51)
3. No; The conduct by the city of Oakland violates the prohibition in the Bill of Rights against "deprivation of … property without due process." With due process and the payment of reasonable compensation, the city would be able to condemn Slovin's property for a public use such as a wider road. (pp. 51–52)
4. No, in interstate commerce the federal law is supreme. The state law is invalid. (p. 52)
5. The legal speed limit is 55 miles per hour. All of a county's legal powers are derived from the state government. State laws are superior to those of their counties or cities. Therefore, the Sonoma County speed limit must yield to the state speed limit. (p. 49)

3. When no adequate remedy was available through the common law, a person could often obtain relief through a supplementary system of justice known as equity.
4. Law is found in constitutions, statutes, cases decided by appellate courts, and regulations and rulings of administrative agencies.
5. Constitutions are the supreme source of law.
6. Civil law governs relations between individuals. Criminal law governs violations of duties owed to society as a whole.
7. Business law is concerned with the rules that apply to business situations and transactions. The UCC is an important part of business law.

STRENGTHENING YOUR LEGAL VOCABULARY

Match each term with the statement that best defines that term. Some terms may not be used.

administrative agencies	liable
administrative laws	Magna Carta
appellate review	money damages
business law	ordinance
case law	procedural law
civil law	Roman civil law
common law	rules and regulations
constitutional	specific performance
constitutional law	stare decisis
criminal law	statute
equity	substantive law
injunction	supremacy
interstate commerce	Uniform Commercial Code (UCC)
intrastate commerce	unconstitutional

1. Term classifying statutes as invalid because they conflict with the federal Constitution or a state constitution.
2. Principle under which new cases are treated in ways consistent with prior case law.
3. A law of Congress or state legislature.
4. Commerce between two or more states.
5. A law of a local governmental body.
6. Case decisions and opinions reflecting customs and practices of the people.

7 Rules of law that apply to business situations and transactions.

8 Name of a code of laws that simplifies, clarifies, and modernizes the laws affecting commercial transactions.

9 A command from a court to not do something.

10 Laws made by court opinions.

APPLYING LAW TO EVERYDAY LIFE

1 Jose promised his brother Juan that he would sell to him the wedding ring of their deceased father for $250. Juan agreed and paid the money. Later Jose refused to deliver the ring. What order from a court would help Juan get the *ring* as opposed to the money?

2 Suppose the principal of your public school required all students to recite a prayer at the beginning of each school day. What level of government (federal, state, or local) is most likely to rule against such action? What type of law (constitutional, statutory, administrative, or case) requires such a ruling?

3 The city of Oakland needed land to widen an important road. Without prior notice, a public hearing, or payment of compensation, it seized a four-foot-wide strip of Slovin's land for the road. Do governments have the power to take private property in this manner?

4 A statute of a certain state limited the number of box cars on all freight trains within its borders to seventy-five. The federal government had no such limitation. Northern Atlantic Railways was running a 100-car train from Chicago to Los Angeles. Did Northern Atlantic have to stop the train at the border of the state that had imposed the limitations and divide the train into two sections?

5 Sonoma County passed a law making it legal to drive sixty-five miles per hour on freeways inside the county. A state law limited all vehicles anywhere in the state to fifty-five miles per hour. What is the legal speed limit on freeways inside Sonoma County?

6 A defect in the fuel line caused a fire which destroyed Jiminez's automobile when it was beyond the one-year warranty period. Although Jiminez was not the original owner of the car, she sued and obtained a judgment against the manufacturer. The case was appealed and affirmed. May owners of the same model of car in the same state rely on the rule of strict liability declared by the trial court in this case and collect damages if they have similar trouble?

8 The following are possible answers and references to appropriate chapters for further investigation.
(a) for an architect
•torts (Chapter 6)
•contracts (Unit 3)
•real property (Chapter 28)
•employment and agency (Unit 6)
•insurance (Unit 9)
•law of business organization (Unit 10)
(b) for a farmer
•real property (Chapter 28)
•contracts (Unit 3)
•sales (Unit 4)
•employment and agency (Unit 6)
•insurance (Unit 9)
(c) for a motel owner
•contracts (Unit 3)
•bailments (Chapter 27)
•employment and agency (Unit 6)
•real property (Chapter 28)
•checks and credit instruments (Unit 8)
•insurance (Unit 9)
(d) for a taxicab driver
•contracts (Unit 3)
•crimes and torts (Chapters 5 and 6)
•bailments (Chapter 27)
•insurance (Unit 9)
(e) for consumers
•all of the above

6 Yes, a significant and important rule of common law is the doctrine of stare decisis (by precedent), which means like cases in the future are to be decided in like manner. (p. 54)

7 ETHICS ISSUE **(a)** Both; Criminal law has been violated because such littering on a public road violates a public duty (p. 56); civil law has been violated because the resulting destruction of the bike tires and personal injury of a bicyclist violate a private duty to respect others' property and other persons (pp. 56–57). **(b)** Their conduct was unethical. It violated the bicyclists' natural rights.

9 ETHICS ISSUE Socrates said we should think of the law as our moral teacher. And, since laws are usually carefully thought out, they often provide good standards for moral conduct.

10  Majority rule is not always morally right. That is one reason we have the Bill of Rights. It protects individuals who may be in minority positions from the possibility of "tyranny of the majority."

Solving Case Problems

1 Yes, our legal roots in courts of equity determines whether, in civil cases, a jury trial is available. In the Memorex case, the court decided that on retrial there should not be a jury. (p. 49)

2 Yes, in instances of conflict between the state and federal constitutions, the provisions of the federal Constitution govern. (p. 55)

7 ETHICS ISSUE A group of people cruising in a car intentionally threw empty pop bottles in front of a group of bicyclists who were moving fast down a hill behind the car. The glass shattered, and almost every bike tire was cut beyond repair. One rider was badly injured after skidding and falling. Were the car occupants guilty of violating the civil law, the criminal law, or both? Was their conduct ethical?

8 What business law topics in the Table of Contents of this book would the following people find helpful?

a. Architect
b. Farmer
c. Motel owner
d. Taxicab driver
e. Consumer

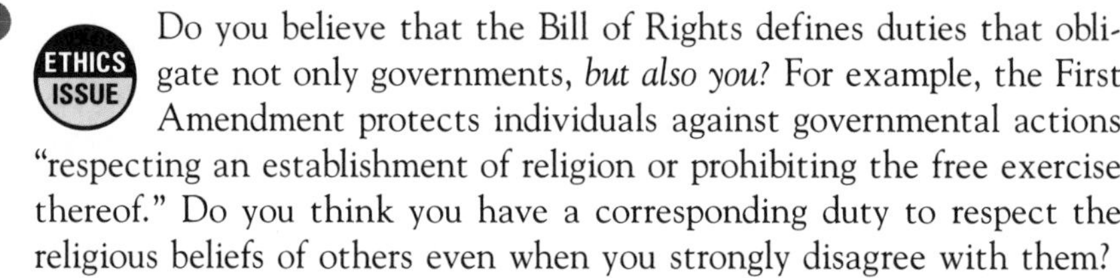

9 ETHICS ISSUE Do you believe that the Bill of Rights defines duties that obligate not only governments, *but also you?* For example, the First Amendment protects individuals against governmental actions "respecting an establishment of religion or prohibiting the free exercise thereof." Do you think you have a corresponding duty to respect the religious beliefs of others even when you strongly disagree with them?

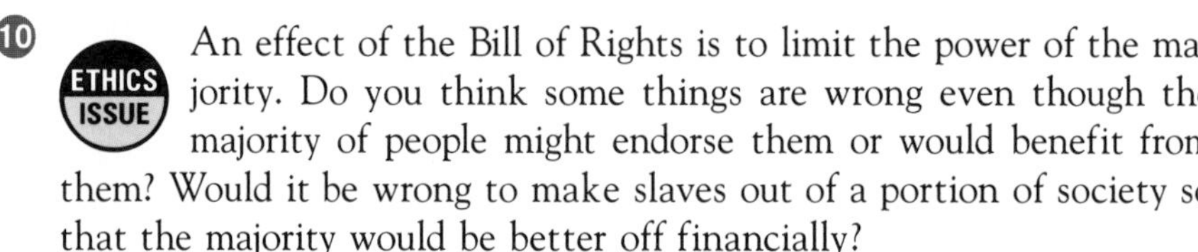

10 ETHICS ISSUE An effect of the Bill of Rights is to limit the power of the majority. Do you think some things are wrong even though the majority of people might endorse them or would benefit from them? Would it be wrong to make slaves out of a portion of society so that the majority would be better off financially?

▼ SOLVING CASE PROBLEMS

1 Memorex Corporation sued IBM for monopolization. The trial lasted five months, during which eighty-seven witnesses were called. There were 19,000 written pages of testimony and 2,300 exhibits. At the trial's conclusion, the jury deadlocked (i.e., they could not reach a decision). Is there anything in the legal history of this country that would permit the retrial to be heard without a jury? (*Memorex Corporation v. IBM Corporation*, 408 F. Supp. 423)

2 Andrews was stopped by a police officer on the street in an area where a murder had been committed a few hours earlier. The officer had no search warrant but arrested Andrews for carrying a concealed weapon—a .38 caliber Cobra revolver. The officer relied on a clause in the Michigan Constitution concerning the use of search warrants. The clause exempted from the requirement of a search warrant in "any

criminal proceeding, any...firearm...seized by a peace officer outside the...[yard] of any dwelling house in this state." However, the U.S. Supreme Court had earlier held that the Fourth Amendment to the U.S. Constitution, which prohibits unreasonable searches and seizures, applied to the states through the Fourteenth Amendment. Also, a U.S. court of appeals had previously held in another case that the clause in the Michigan Constitution relied on by the officer was in conflict with the U.S. Constitution. Must the Michigan courts recognize the superior authority of the U.S. Supreme Court and the U.S. Constitution? (*People v. Andrews,* 21 Mich. App. 731, 176 N.W.2d 460)

3 Alaska enacted a statute known as "Alaska Hire." It required employers in the state to hire qualified Alaskan residents in preference to nonresidents. Hicklin, a nonresident, sued Orbeck, the state official charged with enforcing the statute. After the Supreme Court of Alaska found the statute constitutional, Hicklin appealed to the U.S. Supreme Court, which found the statute to be in conflict with the U.S. Constitution. Which supreme court is the final authority in this case? (*Hicklin v. Orbeck,* 437 U.S. 518)

4 The statute enacted by the U.S. Congress that created the Selective Service authorized it to register and classify draft-age men. It also authorized the Service to reclassify persons who fail to appear before the Service or who fail to provide it with certain information. Peter Wolff was registered with the Selective Service. During the Vietnam War, he received a deferment for being a student at the University of Michigan. When Wolff participated in a demonstration protesting U.S. involvement in the war, the Service eliminated his deferment. Is it legal for the Selective Service to do this? (*Wolff v. Selective Service,* 372 F.2d 817)

5 In 1896, the U.S. Supreme Court held in *Plessy v. Ferguson,* 163 U.S. 537, that equality of treatment of different races in our country is provided when public and semipublic facilities, even though separate, are substantially equal in quality. For years, railroad cars, buses, restaurants, schools, and other facilities in many states had separate and supposedly equal facilities for blacks. In 1954, fifty-eight years later, black plaintiffs in Delaware, Kansas, South Carolina, and Virginia sought admission for their children to public schools on a nonsegregated basis. Does the doctrine of stare decisis bar the U.S. Supreme Court from changing the law declared in *Plessy v. Ferguson?* (*Brown v. Board of Education,* 347 U.S. 483)

3 The supremacy clause of the U.S. Constitution makes federal law, in general, superior to state law. Therefore the opinion of the U.S. Supreme Court is superior to that of the Supreme Court of Alaska. (p. 55) (Note: The "Alaska Hire" statute was invalidated because it violated the "privileges and immunities" clause of the U.S. Constitution. This clause requires states to grant to citizens of other states the same privileges and immunities that are granted to their own citizens.)

4 The Selective Service, an administrative agency of the federal government, acted outside the scope of the powers granted to it by Congress. Therefore, its reclassification of Peter Wolff is invalid. (p. 55) Congress authorized the agency to reclassify people who failed to register or who failed to provide information. Congress did not authorize the Selective Service to reclassify people who engaged in a political demonstration. Even if Congress had so authorized the agency, it is likely that such congressional action would violate the First Amendment rights of freedom of speech and assembly. (p. 55)

5 No, established rules of law must change with changing conditions and more enlightened views of problems. The doctrine of stare decisis does not bind supreme courts. (p. 54)

Chapter Theme

The federal government, each state, and some cities and counties have separate court systems where cases are tried and judgments are satisfied.

DIRECTED STUDY QUESTIONS	SPECIAL FEATURES	PROGRAM RESOURCES: Reteach	Enrich	SN	AM	
How can disputes be resolved privately?	Thinking Critically Through Visuals, p. 66	✔	✔			
What is a court?		✔	✔	✔		
What is our system of courts?	Personal Perspectives, p. 69 Thinking Critically Through Visuals, pp. 69, 70 Ethics Issue, p. 70	✔	✔		K	
How does a juvenile court differ from others?		✔	✔			
What is the procedure in a criminal action?	Thinking Critically Through Visuals, p. 72	✔	✔			
What is the procedure in a civil action?	Thinking Critically Through Visuals, p. 73	✔	✔		A	
How is a civil case tried?	Multicultural Highlights, p. 75 Writing Connections, p. 76	✔	✔		V	
How is a judgment satisfied?	Thinking Critically Through Visuals, p. 77 Preventing Legal Difficulties, p. 77	✔	✔			

Additional Resources

- Eldefonso, Edward. *Law Enforcement and the Youthful Offender: Delinquency and Juvenile Justice*. NY: John Wiley & Sons, 1983.
- Hall, Kermit L., ed. *The Oxford Companion to the Supreme Court of the United States*. NY: Oxford University Press, 1992.
- *United States Government Manual*. Washington, DC: U.S. Government Printing Office.
- *You & the Law*. Pleasantville, NY: The Readers' Digest Association, 1984.

One-semester course	✔	✔	✔					
One-year course	✔	✔	✔	✔				

Chapter Pacing Guide

	ASSESSMENT OPPORTUNITIES			
Cooperative Learning	**Informal Assessment**	**Chapter Review**	**Chapter Test**	**Chapter *MicroExam*** (Media)
	✔	✔	✔	✔
	✔	✔	✔	✔
	✔	✔	✔	✔
	✔	✔	✔	✔
	✔	✔	✔	✔
✔	✔	✔	✔	✔
	✔	✔	✔	✔
	✔	✔	✔	✔

Videodiscs

Criminal Law and Civil Law

Search Chapter 5, Play To 6

State by State

In Mississippi, justice courts are used instead of small claims courts. Their civil jurisdiction is limited to $1,000.

Teaching Materials

Student text, pp. 64–83

Overhead transparency masters
• *Complaint and Answer, United States District Court, Southern District of Indiana, Indianapolis Division* (2)

Videos
• *Our Legal System* Videotape
• *Mock Trial: A Question of Facts* Videotape
• *Law for Business* Videodisc

Workbook, pp. 7–8

Outside Resources

• Camcorder
• Articles on trial and appellate court cases, state and federal courts, and judgments awarded in civil cases
• Phone numbers of local court houses

Assessment

• Chapter Test

• Chapter *MicroExam*

Vocabulary

litigate, p. 66
mediator, p. 66
arbitrator, p. 67
court, p. 67
trial court, p. 67
appellate court, p. 68
transcript, p. 68
jurisdiction, p. 68
small claims court, p. 70
juveniles, p. 71
juvenile delinquent, p. 71
criminal action, p. 72
proof beyond a reasonable doubt, p. 72
plaintiff, p. 73
defendant, p. 73
complaint, p. 73
summons, p. 74
discovery procedures, p. 74
answer, p. 74
deposition, p. 74
jury, p. 75
opening statements, p. 75
evidence, p. 75
testimony, p. 75
witness, p. 75
expert witness, p. 75
subpoena, p. 75
contempt of court, p. 75
closing statements, p. 76
instructions to the jury, p. 76
preponderance of the evidence, p. 76
verdict, p. 76
judgment, p. 76
writ of execution, p. 77

Learning Objectives

When you complete this chapter, you will be able to

1. Describe how disputes can be resolved without courts.
2. Explain how courts operate.
3. Distinguish between trial courts and appellate courts.
4. State the jurisdictions of federal, state, and local courts.
5. Understand how a juvenile court differs from criminal and civil courts.
6. Discuss the various procedures used in juvenile, criminal, and civil trials.
7. Describe how judgments are rendered by courts.

64

Chapter Self-Test

Assess students' understanding of our court system before they begin Chapter 4 by posing the following situations to the class. After reading each situation, ask students to determine if a juvenile court, an intermediate court of appeals, or a small claims court would be involved. Only one of the three courts is applicable for each situation and each type of court is used only once. **(1) A 14-year-old steals a pair of pants.** (Juvenile court); **(2) A person is dissatisfied with a trial court decision.** (Intermediate court of appeals); and **(3) A person sues a dry cleaner for ruining a $75.00 shirt.** (Small claims court)

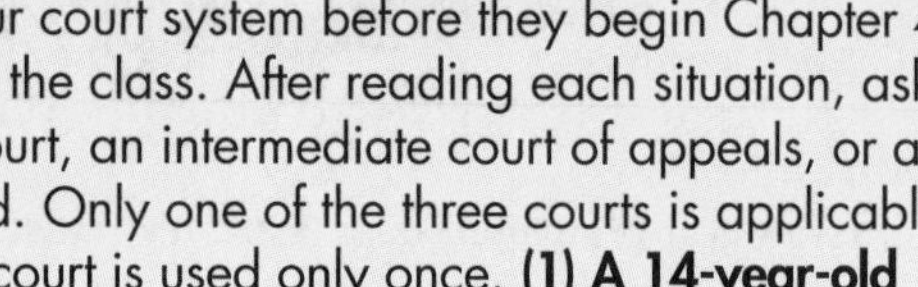

CHAPTER

4 ENFORCING THE LAW

1 Woody sold Ed a used car for $1,500. Two days after the sale, the engine failed and needed to be rebuilt. Ed thought Woody had misrepresented the car's mechanical condition and should pay for the necessary repairs. After arguing about the situation, they decided to let a third party, Dennis, decide how to resolve their dispute. Dennis decided that they should split the cost of a new engine. Ed did not like the decision. Is he nevertheless bound by Dennis's decision?

2 ETHICS ISSUE Walter owed $17 to Olivia. Walter knew that it would not be worthwhile for Olivia to sue for this small amount of money. Although Olivia might recover the $17 and court costs, she could earn more money by spending the time working. Why should Walter pay the money even though Olivia may not sue? Does Olivia have a duty to sue even though she could make better financial use of her time?

3 Whipple sued her employer for discrimination. She claimed her employer paid higher wages to male employees who did identical work. The judge ruled that Whipple was entitled to receive $15,000 in damages from her employer. Six months after the trial Whipple still had not been paid the $15,000. What can she do to get the money?

65

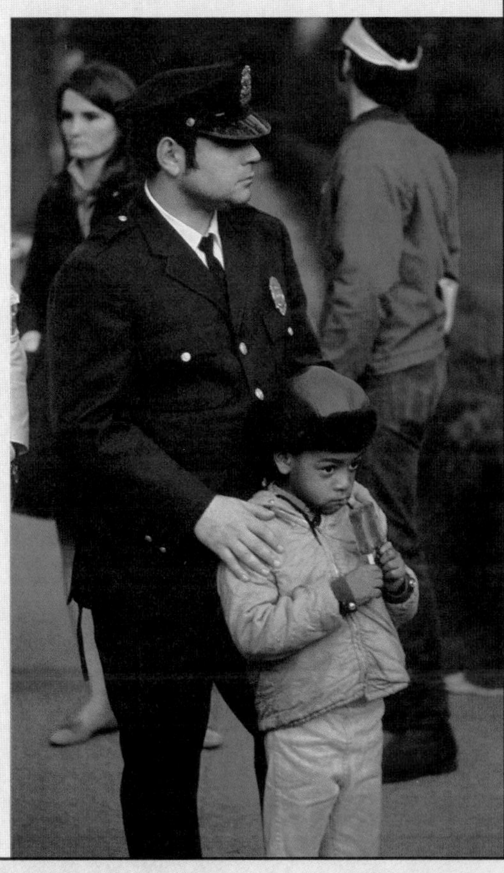

FOCUS

To get students started, write the following question on the chalkboard: **Under what circumstances might you use our court system?** (Answers may include to provide testimony in a trial, to sue someone for damages, or to defend yourself in either case.)

Record students' responses to the question above on the chalkboard or on chart paper. You may wish to ask the same question at the end of the chapter and compare how students responses have changed.

You Decide

1 Woody and Ed intended that Dennis's decision should be binding upon them. Therefore, Dennis would be an arbitrator rather than a mediator. Accordingly, the parties would be bound by this arbitrator's decision. Courts will generally enforce the arbitrator's decision.

2 ETHICS ISSUE Walter should pay the money even though Olivia may not sue for it because he has a moral duty to do so. That duty was created by Walter's promise to repay the money. Olivia may have a duty to sue even if that isn't the best use of her time.

3 The court can help Whipple collect the judgment. She could obtain a writ of execution. Then assets may be seized and sold to pay Whipple.

Thinking Critically Through Visuals

Direct students to the photograph on this page and ask: **What, do you think, should children be taught about the role of police officers?** (Answers may include that the police provide a variety of services to the community, the most important of which is safety.)

▼ TEACH

Help students to understand that litigation is costly and should be avoided, when possible. Many disputes can be settled by mediation or arbitration. Be sure students understand these terms.

▼ APPLY

Have students brainstorm ways to resolve disputes other than by taking their disputes to court. (Answers may include coming to a mutually–agreed upon decision or using an arbitrator.) **Guided Practice**

HOW CAN DISPUTES BE RESOLVED PRIVATELY?

PROBLEM

7-Eleven sold franchises for stores bearing its name. The franchise agreement specified that disputes between 7-Eleven and those who bought a franchise should be settled by arbitration rather than by a trial in court. Can 7-Eleven compel its franchisees to use arbitration instead of litigation?

Many persons decide too quickly to **litigate** their disputes; that is, to take their disputes to court. When someone injures another person or fails to keep a binding agreement, it usually makes sense to first try to settle by direct negotiation. The injured person should try to discuss the problem calmly with the wrongdoer. Together, they can often reach a mutually acceptable solution.

In some cases, the parties may invite an independent third party to act as **mediator**. The mediator tries to develop a solution acceptable to both sides of the dispute. The actions of a mediator are merely advisory. They do not bind the parties.

Thinking Critically Through Visuals

Have students recall the definition of **mediator** on p. 66, then ask: **Who, do you think, is the mediator in the photograph? Why?** (Answers may include that any of the three people could be the mediator; the dress and position of the individuals have no bearing on who mediates.)

▼ ASSESS

Learning Objective 3 Bring to class current newspaper articles dealing with trial and appellate court cases (three of each kind should be sufficient). Have students work in pairs, reading the articles and identifying in which court each case was tried. Then, as a class, discuss how students determined which court was involved.

In other cases, the parties may retain an **arbitrator**. Arbitrators usually hold an informal hearing to determine what happened. The arbitrator's decision, unlike that of a mediator, is binding on both parties. The decision can be enforced by court order if necessary. Sometimes a provision for arbitration is included in the original agreement between the parties. In the problem, 7-Eleven could require buyers of its franchises to use arbitration. By using negotiation, mediation, or arbitration, the disputing parties may avoid the costs, delays, and difficulties of a trial in court.

WHAT IS A COURT?

PROBLEM

Doyle made an illegal U-turn. A police officer saw it and gave him a citation (i.e., an order to appear in court). Doyle claimed that the sign forbidding a U-turn at that intersection was obstructed by a tree branch. The officer replied, "Sorry, you can tell it to the judge in court." Why is a court necessary in this situation?

A **court** is a tribunal established to administer justice under the law. Courts decide civil disputes and criminal cases. A court may award damages in civil cases, impose punishment in criminal cases, or grant other appropriate relief. In the problem, a court was necessary to decide whether Doyle was telling the truth and whether the blocked sign would be a valid defense. Courts attempt to use impartial and thorough procedures to make decisions. For example, witnesses can be compelled to give testimony and an accused party is allowed equal opportunity to argue her or his side of the case. There are two different levels of courts: trial courts and appellate courts.

1. Trial Courts

A **trial court** is the first court to hear a dispute. Witnesses testify and other information is presented to prove the alleged facts. A trial court consists not only of a judge but also of lawyers, who are officers of the court, and others who are necessary for the court's operation. The words *court* and *judge* are often used to mean the same thing. While presiding, the judge may be referred to as "The Court" or "Your Honor."

Working in small groups, take one class period and have students role-play the scenario that follows. You and a friend form a lawn care business. Your friend habitually shows up 10 minutes late for one-hour jobs. You do not want to pay your friend a full half of the proceeds. After students have role-played, ask: **How can this dispute be resolved?** (Answers may include that the two parties will agree on an amount on their own, or that the friend will go to court to be paid his or her "full share.") **Independent Practice**

TEACH

Before students read *What Is a Court?* on pp. 67–68, discuss students' views of the functions of courts. Base the discussion on any prior knowledge students may have about courts from actual experiences, television shows, or reading materials. Review students' responses after they have read the section.

APPLY

After reading pp. 67–68, assist students in creating a list of differences between a trial court and an appellate court. (Unlike trial courts, appellate courts only review decisions made in trial courts, do not hear witnesses, do not accept new evidence, and normally are not concerned with determining questions of fact.) **Guided Practice**

RETEACH To help differentiate between a trial court and an appellate court, have students make a comparison table. Under the heads **Trial** and **Appellate** have students list the kinds of cases that each court would hear.

ENRICH Individually or in small groups, have students research how one goes about having a case reviewed by a small claims court. Then, have students create a flowchart showing the steps of the process. Display students' work in the classroom.

Ask students with limited-English proficiency who are having trouble dealing with the terminology in this chapter to first deal with the root word of the difficult term. For example, to understand what an **appellate court** is have them look up the definition of *appeal* in a dictionary.

Independent Practice

▼ TEACH

Some students may not understand why different types of courts and more than one level of appellate court are necessary. As you teach this lesson, you may wish to review with students figures 4-1 and 4-2, which show the framework of the federal and state court systems.

▼ APPLY

Refer to figures 4-1 and 4-2—diagrams of the federal court system and a typical state court system. Assist students in creating a flowchart showing the course of action one would take if a case was lost in small claims court.

Guided Practice

2. Appellate Courts

An **appellate court** reviews decisions of trial courts when a party claims an error was made during the trial. Appellate courts do not hear witnesses. Generally, they do not accept new evidence and normally are not concerned with questions of fact. Instead, appellate review is normally limited to correcting errors of law. These courts examine the **transcript** (i.e., the word-for-word written record of what was said at the trial). They also read appellate briefs, which are written arguments on the issues of law submitted by the opposing attorneys. Then the appellate courts listen to oral arguments of the attorneys and may question them about the case. Finally, the appellate courts decide whether the decision of the trial court should be affirmed (upheld), reversed (overturned), amended (changed), or remanded (sent back to the trial court for corrective action, possibly including a new trial).

3. Jurisdiction

Courts vary in **jurisdiction**. Jurisdiction is the authority to decide types of cases. For example, a juvenile court does not have the jurisdiction to hear cases involving adults. Small claims courts are limited to civil matters involving small amounts, such as $3,000. Supreme courts are typically limited to appellate jurisdiction.

▼ WHAT IS OUR SYSTEM OF COURTS?

PROBLEM

During a trip to Europe, Wendy purchased several clocks. When she returned with the clocks, she claimed that they were more than 100 years old. If true, this would exempt them from import duties (i.e., taxes). The collector of customs disagreed. He demanded payment of the assessed tax. Did Wendy have any recourse from the collector's ruling?

As described in Chapter 3, in this country courts exist on the federal, state, and local levels.

1. Federal Courts

The Constitution of the United States provides: "The judicial power of the United States, shall be vested in one Supreme Court, and in such inferior courts as the Congress may from time to time ordain and establish." The Supreme Court's decisions about federal constitutional law are final. This Court is composed of nine judges appointed for life by the President.

▼ ASSESS

Learning Objective 4 Bring, or have students bring to class, newspaper or magazine articles on a variety of court cases involving either state or federal courts. Then have students categorize the cases by the court involved. Create a classroom bulletin board display identifying in which court each case was tried.

From time to time, Congress has created other federal courts below the Supreme Court. The present federal court system includes thirteen intermediate U.S. courts of appeals. Most are located in circuits; that is, designated areas in different parts of the country. They receive most of the appeals from the federal trial courts. Most federal trials occur in U.S. district courts. There are district courts in all states, as well as in the District of Columbia and in U.S. overseas territories. In general, federal courts hear cases that involve rights created by the Constitution or by other federal laws. Figure 4-1 is a diagram of the federal court system.

In the problem, Wendy could appeal the ruling of the collector of customs to the Customs Court. If dissatisfied with the decision of the Customs Court, she could appeal to the Court of Appeals for the Federal Circuit, and ultimately to the U.S. Supreme Court.

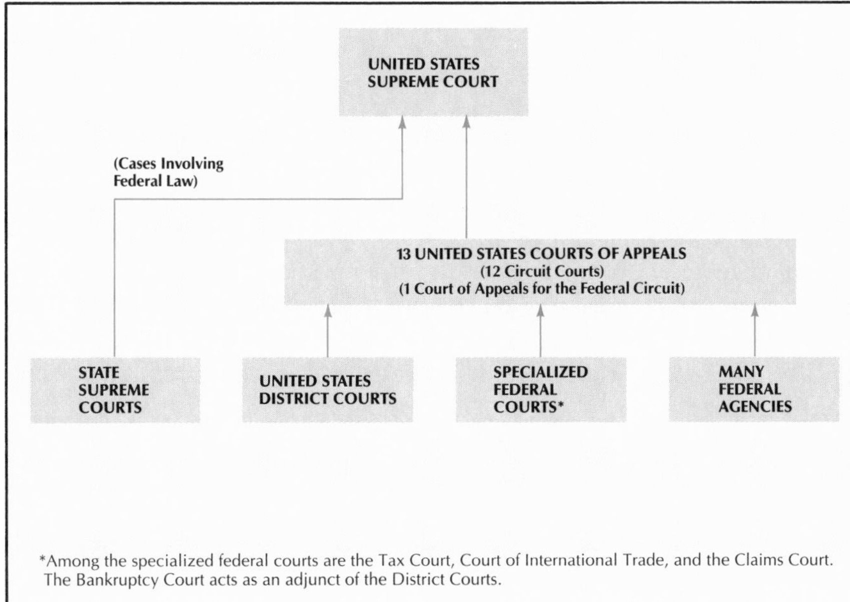

Figure 4-1
A simplified diagram of the federal court system.

2. State and Local Courts

The systems of courts in the different states are organized in ways similar to the federal courts. Each state ordinarily has (1) a supreme court; (2) trial courts—they are variously named county, circuit, superior, or district courts and have general jurisdiction over most important cases; and (3) courts of limited jurisdiction—such as juvenile courts. Most of the populous states also have intermediate courts of appeals, which ease the work load of the state supreme court.

Thinking Critically Through Visuals

Ask students to use Figure 4-1 on this page to answer the following questions:
1. Which is the highest court of our country? (U.S. Supreme Court)
2. What kinds of cases from the state supreme courts will the U.S. Supreme Court hear? (Answers may include cases involving the U.S. Constitution and other federal laws.)

Personal Perspectives

Individually, ask each student to interview a family member or a friend to find out about any court experiences they may have had, such as in small claims court or traffic court. Students should identify the court involved, the problem, the process followed in deciding the case, and the outcome. Have students share the information with the class, perhaps in the form of a flowchart. Keep the identity of the person they interviewed confidential. **Independent Practice**

RETEACH Have students who need help understanding jurisdiction orally list the types of cases that would come under the federal and state court systems. Have them create, then review, a table showing the types of cases tried in each court system.

ENRICH Select a recent court case in your state and bring information about that case to class. Have students, working in small groups of three or four, prepare a chart showing the progress of the case up to the final appellate court.

Thinking Critically Through Visuals

Ask students to find the names of the courts of limited jurisdiction on Figure 4-2. (Family, juvenile, municipal, probate, and criminal court)

Ethics Issue

In 1991, Clarence Thomas was nominated for the Supreme Court. During his confirmation hearings, he was accused of having sexually harassed a woman he had once supervised. Thomas denied the charges and, after a lengthy hearing, was confirmed. Have each student develop guidelines for evaluating a Supreme Court candidate's ethics.

TEACH

Discuss with students how serving time in a prison or jail for adults might affect a convicted minor. (Answers may include that a minor could be physically, and/or psychologically abused in an adult jail.)

Figure 4-2
A typical state court system.

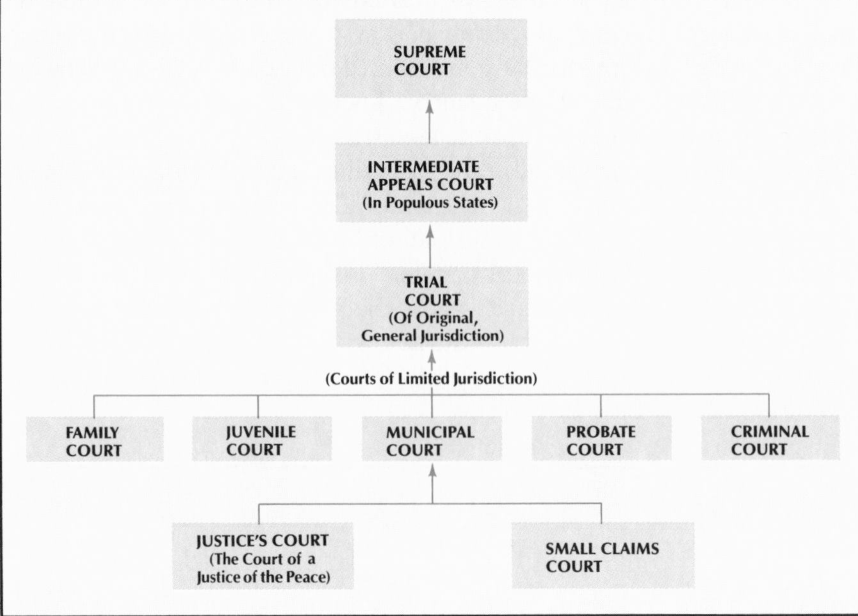

Many cities or counties have small claims courts. In a **small claims court,** a civil action for a small amount, typically up to $3,000, can be filed. Each party may represent himself or herself. In some states attorneys are not permitted unless they are acting on their own behalf or for an employer, such as a corporation. The proceedings of such courts are conducted informally, quickly, and economically. Figure 4-2 presents a typical structure for a state court system.

Arnold owed Bruce $150 for a bicycle Bruce had sold and delivered. Since the county where they live has a small claims court, Bruce filed a suit against Arnold in that court. Bruce received a judgment for $150 plus $11.50 in court costs.

HOW DOES A JUVENILE COURT DIFFER FROM OTHERS?

PROBLEM

Reid, age fifteen, was detained by the police for shoplifting and was referred to the juvenile court. Would Reid be treated differently there than in a criminal court for adults?

ASSESS

Learning Objectives 2 & 6 Independently, have students create a chart like the following, showing the two phases in a juvenile court hearing. Their charts should include the steps involved in each phase.

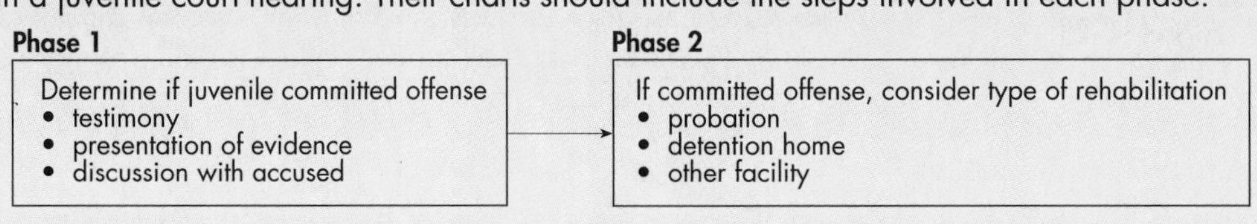

Phase 1
Determine if juvenile committed offense
• testimony
• presentation of evidence
• discussion with accused
Phase 2
If committed offense, consider type of rehabilitation
• probation
• detention home
• other facility

All states have special courts with exclusive jurisdiction over juveniles charged with criminal acts. **Juveniles** are persons under the age of majority. They are also called minors. In most states, the age of majority is eighteen years old. All states provide that for certain crimes, notably murder, the juvenile court may transfer a minor to a regular criminal court to be tried as an adult. Depending on the state, the minimum age for such a transfer may be as low as thirteen or as high as sixteen. The transfer can be made if it has been determined that the minor had the maturity and moral perception (1) to distinguish between right and wrong and (2) to understand the legal consequences of her or his acts.

Minors who commit criminal acts are treated not as criminals but as juvenile delinquents. The legal definition of **juvenile delinquent** varies among the states. However, in general the term means a child under a specified age who commits a criminal act or is incorrigible (i.e., is ungovernable or uncontrollable).

Generally, juvenile courts protect minors from the results of their own immaturity. The court may serve as the guardian of children who are abandoned, orphaned, or incapable of self-support. The juvenile court seeks to provide guidance and rehabilitation rather than to fix criminal responsibility and impose punishment. Accordingly, in the problem, Reid would not be treated as an adult. Instead he would be entitled to a juvenile court hearing where his age and level of maturity would be taken into consideration.

The first purpose of the juvenile court hearing is to determine whether the juvenile committed the offense. This part of the hearing includes testimony of witnesses, presentation of evidence, and discussion with the accused minor. If the juvenile is found to have committed the offense, then the court moves to the second purpose of the hearing and considers ways to rehabilitate the juvenile. Professional specialists, such as psychologists, social workers, and physicians, may be consulted. The juvenile may be placed on probation or committed to a detention home or other facility such as a psychiatric hospital. Often the child is placed in the home of a relative or in a foster family home. When a minor is involved in a civil matter, the case is heard by a regular civil court.

▼ WHAT IS THE PROCEDURE IN A CRIMINAL ACTION?

PROBLEM

Teresa was suspected of deliberately failing to file and pay her income tax—a criminal offense. What steps must be taken to determine whether Teresa committed a crime?

▼ APPLY

As a class, discuss why a juvenile court system is necessary. Focus on the juvenile court's role in offering guidance and rehabilitation. **Guided Practice**

Have individual students contact their local court house to find out their state's legal definition of **juvenile delinquent**. (You may wish to ask students to use a computer, if possible, to type a summary of their findings.)

Independent Practice

In groups of three or four, have students brainstorm criminal conduct for which a minor would be tried in the juvenile court system or as an adult. (Responses may include: juvenile court— stealing from a store, or adult court— committing murder.)

▼ TEACH

Students are probably familiar with the phrase, **proof beyond a reasonable doubt** (vast majority of evidence supports a guilty verdict). Before reading *What Is the Procedure in a Criminal Action?* on pp. 71–72, discuss students' ideas on what the phrase means.

▼RETEACH Have students reread the fourth paragraph on p. 71 and look for the purpose of a juvenile court hearing. Create an overhead transparency of the chart used in the ASSESS on p. 70. Review each phase of the chart with the students as they reread the text.

▼ENRICH Have students contact your county court to get information on the rights of an accused minor in your state. Students should create a poster from the information they receive.

Thinking Critically Through Visuals

This photograph shows a chalk outline of an accident victim. Why, do you think, is an outline made of the victim's body? (Answers may include so they can remove the body and still have a visual of the body's position.)

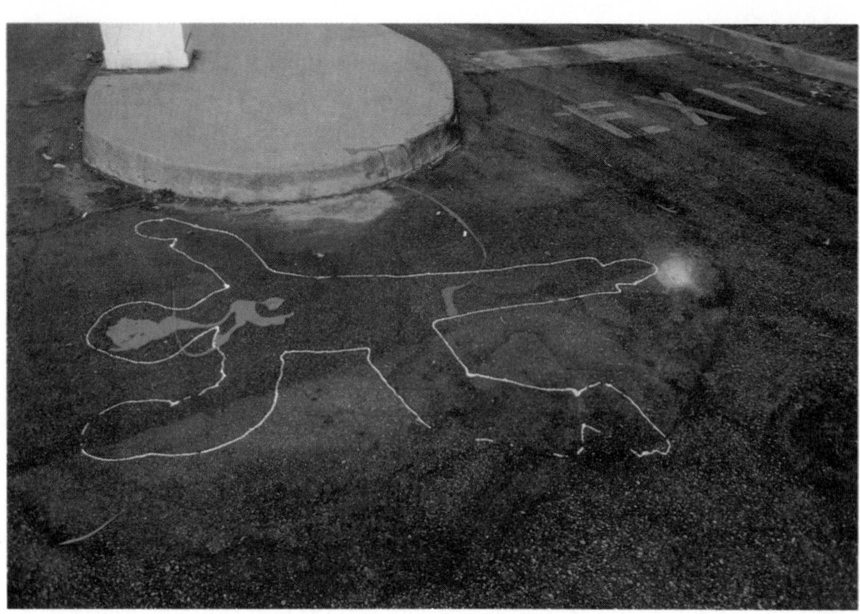

A **criminal action** is a lawsuit brought by the state (also known as *the people*) against a person accused of a crime. In criminal cases, the defendant is presumed innocent. Therefore, the state has the burden of proving the defendant's guilt. Thus, in the problem, if Teresa does not admit that she deliberately failed to file and pay her income tax, the government must submit evidence proving the charges during a trial.

To convict a person of a crime, the evidence must establish guilt with **proof beyond a reasonable doubt.** This means the vast majority of the evidence (perhaps ninety percent) supports the guilty verdict. Defendants have a constitutional right to a trial by jury. There will be a jury if either the state prosecutor or the defendant requests one. In jury trials, the defendant is usually found guilty only if all the jurors vote to convict. Defendants need not testify against themselves, and they are entitled to be represented by lawyers. The procedural law of each state specifies the process to be followed in state criminal trials.

WHAT IS THE PROCEDURE IN A CIVIL ACTION?

PROBLEM

Loo owed Kim $15,000, which she did not pay when it came due. How could Kim compel Loo to pay?

APPLY

Pose the following question: **Why, do you think, is "the state" referred to as "the people"?** (Answers should include an understanding that the officials of the state represent the people of the state.) **Guided Practice**

Referring to the PROBLEM on p. 71, have students create a body of evidence that would be **proof beyond a reasonable doubt** against Teresa. **Independent Practice**

TEACH

Emphasize the difference between a civil action (a lawsuit brought by an injured, private individual against another private individual) and a **criminal action** (a lawsuit brought by the state against a person accused of a crime).

ASSESS

Media

Learning Objectives 2 & 6 Divide the class into three or four groups for a portion of a class period. Assign each group a civil action to role-play. Within each group have students choose one of the following roles: plaintiff (writes complaint), defendant (writes answer), two attorneys (question witnesses and write out-of-court settlement), one to three witnesses (give depositions), and recorder (takes notes on procedure). You may wish to videotape each group's proceedings. **Cooperative Learning**

A person injured by the wrongful conduct of another may be able to obtain relief by having a lawyer bring a civil action against the wrongdoer. In the problem, Kim could bring a civil suit against Loo.

A civil action involves two parties. The party who brings a civil action to enforce a private right is the **plaintiff**. The party against whom the civil action is brought is the **defendant**.

Taylor and Shannon negligently ran their motorboat near a beach area and injured Peter, who was swimming. Peter, the plaintiff, sued to collect for doctor and hospital bills and for pain and suffering. Taylor and Shannon were the defendants.

In state courts, a civil action begins with the filing of the plaintiff's complaint with the clerk of the court (see Figure 4-3). The **complaint** states the plaintiff's claims, which allegedly justify the relief demanded. It is

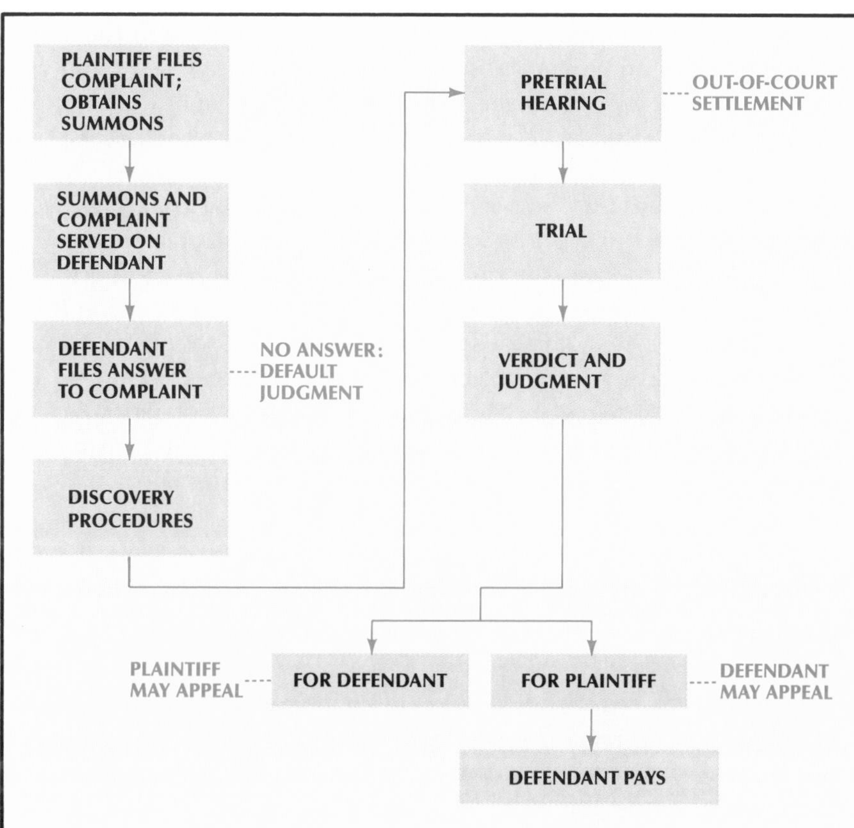

Figure 4-3
Civil action procedure.

▼ APPLY

Display the two overhead transparencies *Complaint and Answer, United States District Court, Southern District of Indiana, Indianapolis Division.* As a class, review each part of the complaint and its corresponding answer.

Guided Practice

Working in pairs, have students write a complaint and an answer. Complaints should focus on the plaintiff's claims, such as loss of property or the defendant's negligence. Have students use a computer, if possible, for this activity.

Independent Practice

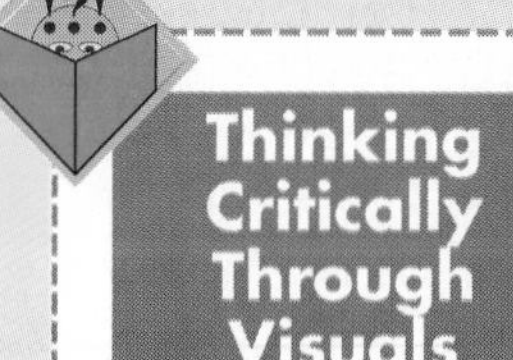

Not every civil action goes all the way through this procedure. Ask: **What happens if the defendant does not answer the complaint?** (Plaintiff may win by default) Then ask: **What advantages are there for the plaintiff if the case is settled out of court?** (Reduces cost of litigation; Plaintiff's settlement cannot be appealed.)

▼RETEACH Pair a student having trouble understanding the procedure in a civil action with a peer-tutor who demonstrates understanding. Have them review the procedure. Using Figure 4-3 on p. 73 as a guide, have students create a chart of the procedure that includes an explanation for each step.

▼ENRICH Individually, have students rethink Figure 4-3 on p. 73 and create a diagram to show changes they would make to refine, contract, or expand the procedure for civil actions.

Divide the class into groups of three. Take one class period and have groups role-play a deposition. One student in each group will act as the court reporter, one will be the person giving the deposition, and one will be the questioning attorney. Tape record the depositions and play them back for the court reporters. Discuss how much easier it is to transcribe the deposition from the tape recording rather than to rely only on the reporters' notes.

▼ TEACH

As students read *How Is a Civil Case Tried?* on pp. 74–76, emphasize the importance of the jury and evidence in a civil trial. Point out the difference between the verdict and the judgment. To illustrate the point, bring to class some newspaper articles that give verdicts and judgments made in local courts.

▼ APPLY

Ask students to brainstorm characteristics of jurors which would undermine their impartiality in the case of *Claxon v. Da Lucia*. Then ask them to list qualifications they think are important for a juror in this case. **Guided Practice**

written by the plaintiff's lawyer and tells the plaintiff's version of what happened. Next, the defendant is served with a copy of the complaint and with a summons. The **summons** is a court order that directs the defendant to answer the complaint. An **answer** is the defendant's statement in reply to the complaint. If the defendant does not answer the complaint within the time allowed (generally twenty days), the plaintiff may automatically win the lawsuit by default. In a timely answer, the defendant may do any one of the following:

1. Deny the truth of the facts alleged in the complaint. This raises an issue of fact that can be resolved during the trial.
2. Declare that even if the facts alleged in the complaint are true, they do not violate the law. This is an issue of law, which is decided by the judge in the course of the trial.
3. Admit the facts alleged but introduce other facts that excuse the defendant from liability.

In the problem, Kim, the plaintiff, must file a complaint with the appropriate court and obtain a summons from the court directing Loo to answer. Kim would have a process server deliver the summons and a copy of the complaint to the defendant. Loo would then have to answer the complaint or he would lose by default.

Both parties may use discovery procedures before the trial. **Discovery procedures** are used to obtain information and clarify the facts. Discovery also helps identify the issues in dispute that require decision at the trial. A commonly used discovery procedure is the deposition. In a **deposition**, parties or witnesses are questioned under oath by the opposing attorney. A court reporter makes a written record of this testimony. Depositions and other discovery procedures, such as physical examinations of persons claiming they were injured, greatly assist attorneys for both sides in preparing for the trial. Discovery also often leads to out-of-court settlements.

▼ HOW IS A CIVIL CASE TRIED?

PROBLEM

Claxon's car collided with Da Lucia's in an intersection that had four-way stop signs. Claxon's car was badly damaged by Da Lucia's car, so she sued for damages. Claxon claimed Da Lucia was going at least twenty miles per hour and had not stopped for the sign but had merely

▼ ASSESS

Learning Objectives 2 & 6 Have students choose a topic for a civil lawsuit. Working in small groups, have students develop a body of evidence for the case and create at least three key witnesses. Another group of students can serve as a jury, listening to the evidence presented and listening to the testimony of the witnesses. After the jury delivers its verdict, you may wish to poll other class members for their opinions on the case.

slowed down. Da Lucia claimed he had stopped and had not reached five miles per hour. He said he entered the intersection first and Claxon tried to swing around his front end but had failed. Two witnesses saw the accident and could testify. How can the court determine what really happened?

Judges and juries play different roles in trials. Judges always decide any issues of law. A **jury** is a body of impartial citizens (usually twelve) who listen to the witnesses, review physical evidence, and decide the issues of fact. In civil cases, there is not always a right to a trial by jury. Even when there is a right to a civil trial by jury, both the plaintiff and the defendant may decide to forgo this right. When there is no jury, the judge decides the issues of both law and fact. In the problem, if the parties agreed to waive a jury trial, the judge would listen to the witnesses, including Claxon and Da Lucia, and then decide the issues of fact and the issues of law.

After the jury for a specific case has been selected, the attorneys make opening statements. These **opening statements** briefly outline what the plaintiff or the defendant will try to prove. The evidence is then presented to the jury, first by the plaintiff and then by the defendant. **Evidence** includes anything that the judge allows to be presented to the jury that helps to prove or disprove the alleged facts. Evidence may consist of written documents, records, charts, weapons, photographs, and other objects. Testimony of witnesses is the most common form of evidence. **Testimony** consists of statements made by witnesses under oath. A **witness** is someone who has personal knowledge of the facts. Sometimes an **expert witness** (i.e., a witness who possesses superior knowledge about important facts) will give an opinion. For example, an engineer may be an expert witness testifying that the skid marks left by braking tires indicate a car was going seventy miles per hour before the collision.

A **subpoena** is a written order by the judge commanding a witness to appear in court to give testimony. Willful, unexcused failure to appear is **contempt of court.** The judge can punish persons guilty of contempt of court by jailing them without a trial.

While waiting for a bus, Charles observed a collision. If there is a suit because of this accident, Charles could be subpoenaed as a witness by either side. Charles would be required to tell, under oath, the truth as to what he observed. If he failed to respond to the subpoena, he could be held in contempt of court, arrested, and jailed.

Multicultural Highlights

Are people being kept off juries because of their race? For many years, lawyers were able to exclude potential jurors (up to a limit) without giving a reason. This changed in 1986 when the Supreme Court ruled that, in criminal cases, jurors could not be excluded from a jury solely because of race. In 1991, this ruling was expanded to include civil cases. Have students hypothesize why this ruling is important. (Answers should include that this ruling lessens the possibility of racial discrimination in jury selection and in the subsequent verdict.)

Without advance notice, arrange to have a colleague come into your classroom, pick something up from a specified spot, and then leave the room. Then have each student write a description of the person and the event. Point out how witnesses, seeing the same incident, can describe the event differently. **Independent Practice**

▼RETEACH In small groups, have students create a poster illustrating each of the vocabulary terms used in the section *How Is a Civil Case Tried?* You may wish to award a prize for the most complete or most creative poster.

▼ENRICH Take the ASSESS on p. 74 one step further by having students decide if a monetary judgment would be appropriate and, if so, how much it should be. Have students give reasons to support their analyses.

Writing Connections

Social Studies
Have students react in writing to the following statement, using the computer, if possible: **As Americans, we are guaranteed the right to a trial by jury, with certain exceptions.** Have students give reasons for their answers. (Answers should include mention of the U.S. Constitution, specifically the Sixth and Seventh amendments.) Have several volunteers

read their answers aloud.

Arrange with a judge to have students visit a civil court in session. Try to obtain copies of the complaint and answers beforehand. If it is to be a long trial, try to attend at a special time, such as

during opening or closing statements.

▼ TEACH

Have volunteers share with the class any experiences they may have had with someone failing to pay what was owed to them. Discuss the action they took. Then discuss the PROBLEM on p. 76 and the recourse Stevens would have to take.

Following the presentation of the evidence, the attorney for each side gives a closing statement. During **closing statements,** each attorney summarizes the case, trying to persuade the judge (and the jury if there is one) to favor his or her side. After consultation with the attorneys, the judge then gives instructions to the jury. These **instructions to the jury** tell the jury what rules of law apply to the case. They also tell the jury what issues of fact they must decide. For example, in a civil case involving an auto accident, the judge might instruct the jury that exceeding the speed limit in bad weather is negligence (a rule of law). The judge may also tell the jury to decide if the weather was bad at the time of the accident (a question of fact) and whether the defendant was exceeding the speed limit at the time of the accident (a question of fact). The jury then retires to the jury room for secret deliberation. In deciding, each juror must determine whether a **preponderance of the evidence** supports the plaintiff's case. This means at least a majority (fifty-one percent) of the evidence. In a civil action, a majority vote of the jurors is usually required to find for the plaintiff. The **verdict** is the jury's decision.

After the verdict of a jury has been returned, the judge, in accordance with the verdict, renders a judgment. The **judgment** is the final result of the trial. It will normally be for a sum of money if the plaintiff wins. If the defendant wins, the judgment will merely be "judgment for the defendant."

If either party believes the judge made a mistake, an appeal may be made to a higher court. Examples of judicial error include incorrect instructions to the jury, admission of evidence that should have been rejected, or exclusion of evidence that should have been admitted. When there has been an error, the appellate court may modify or reverse the judgment of the lower court. Or it may order a new trial. If there is no error in the record, the reviewing court will affirm the judgment of the lower court. Figure 4-4 presents the steps in a jury trial.

▼ HOW IS A JUDGMENT SATISFIED?

PROBLEM

Stevens brought a civil suit against Alvarez for breach of contract in building a warehouse. Stevens won a judgment for $35,000. Alvarez objected to the decision. However, she did not appeal because her lawyer told her that there was no basis for appeal. Nevertheless, Alvarez stubbornly refused to pay Stevens. What steps could Stevens take to collect the judgment?

Ordinarily, when a civil judgment for the plaintiff becomes final, the defendant will pay the judgment. If the defendant does not pay, the plaintiff may

▼ ASSESS

Learning Objective 7 Have students create a chart showing the steps one can take after a judgment is rendered, including the causes for each step (such as appeal— incorrect jury instructions).

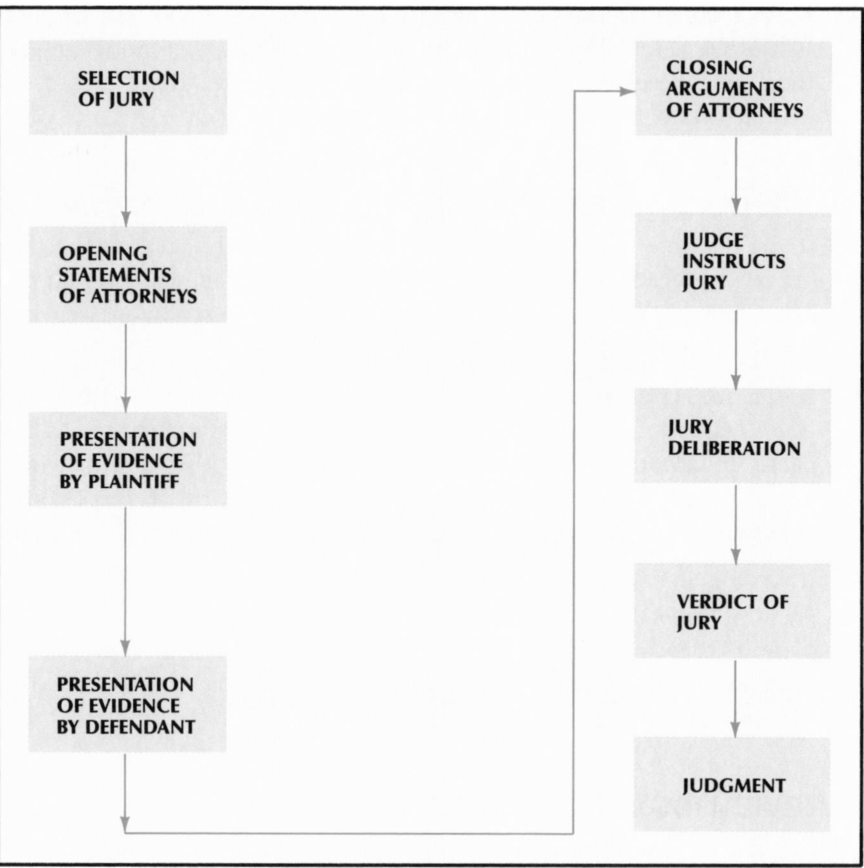

Figure 4-4
*Jury **trial** procedure.*

obtain a **writ of execution.** Execution is the process by which a judgment for money is enforced. The court directs the sheriff, or other officer, to seize and sell property (e.g., a savings account or car) of the defendant. The proceeds, after deducting the costs of seizure and sale, are used to pay the judgment. In the problem, Stevens could get a writ of execution, since Alvarez refused to pay voluntarily.

Preventing Legal Difficulties

If you are a party to a court action . . .

1. Hire a lawyer who is competent and experienced for the kind of case in which you are involved. It helps if you already have a family lawyer whom you can call in a legal emergency.

APPLY

Thinking Critically Through Visuals

The role of the jury is very important in a trial. Ask: **How many of the steps in Figure 4-4 specifically mention the jury?** (Four) Then ask students how many of the steps, do they think, involve the jury. (All of them)

Have two groups debate if the actions of Alvarez (in the PROBLEM on p. 76) are morally correct. **Guided Practice**

Independently, have students brainstorm reasons why someone might not pay a judgment. (Child-custody cases, inability to pay, and so on) Ask: **Do any of these reasons excuse the defendant from his or her obligation to pay?** (Legally, no, but students should be able to defend their responses.) **Independent Practice**

Preventing Legal Difficulties

To help students know what to do if involved in a court action, hold a class discussion on each of the points on pp. 77–78.

Bring to class some recent national and local newspapers. To help students better understand what a judgment is, have them find articles that identify the judgments awarded in civil cases. Ask students to write a summary of one judgment, using a computer, if available.

Using the same newspapers, students should select an article and explain in writing why the judgment should be accepted or appealed. (Students may wish to use a computer to write their rationale.)

▼ CLOSE

As a class, close the chapter by having students discuss the similarities and differences between the procedures for a criminal action and those for a civil action. Then, in writing, have students answer this question: **Why is our right to bring a case to court so important?** (Answers may include the importance of being able to bring our differences before an independent third party.) Close the chapter by reviewing key points for students.

Assign the following end-of-chapter materials:
Student text review activities, pp. 78–83
Workbook, pp. 7–8
Chapter Test

Chapter *MicroExam*

2 Keep accurate records of all events related to any important dispute. While the details are still fresh in your memory, put them in writing. If there are witnesses, ask them to do the same. Give these records to your attorney.

3 Try to become familiar with the terminology and legal procedure of the case.

4 If you disagree with your lawyer about a legal matter, realize that the lawyer is probably right. If you are in serious doubt, you can consult another lawyer. You can change lawyers, but you must pay for services previously received.

5 If you are a plaintiff, do not delay in consulting a lawyer. This is because evidence may be lost. Also, you may forfeit your right to sue because of a statute of limitations (see pages 306–307). If you win a judgment, press promptly for payment, through a writ of execution if necessary.

6 If you are a prospective defendant, promptly consult a lawyer when you get into legal difficulty. If served with process (i.e., summons and a copy of the complaint), immediately give the papers to your lawyer. Your lawyer can then file a timely answer so that you will not lose your case by default.

▼ REVIEWING IMPORTANT POINTS

1 Law includes not only the rules of conduct but also the means for enforcing those rules. Any set of rules would be useless without machinery for enforcement.

2 Civil law is enforced through the courts at the request of the injured party. Criminal law is enforced through the courts by the prosecuting attorney.

3 The federal government and each state, and some cities or counties, have separate court systems.

4 In every state, there are juvenile courts with special jurisdiction over persons under the age of majority. These courts emphasize rehabilitation.

5 Juvenile courts treat minors as delinquents if they commit offenses that would be crimes for adults.

6 In a criminal action, the state must prove "beyond a reasonable doubt" that the defendant is guilty.

7 A civil action begins when the plaintiff files a complaint. The defendant must answer the complaint or lose the case by default.

8 Evidence usually consists of testimony, but it may include documents, objects, pictures, etc.

9 Persons who have knowledge of the facts in a case may be ordered by subpoena to appear in court as witnesses and to give testimony.

10 Most litigation ends with a judgment by the trial court. However, any judgment can be appealed to a higher court.

11 Judgment in a criminal action consists of a finding of not guilty or sentencing by the judge. Judgment in a civil action normally consists of a finding for the defendant or a judgment for money.

▼ STRENGTHENING YOUR LEGAL VOCABULARY

Match each term with the statement that best defines that term. Some terms may not be used.

answer	juvenile delinquent
appellate court	juveniles
arbitrator	litigate
closing statement	mediator
complaint	opening statement
contempt of court	plaintiff
court	preponderance of the evidence
criminal action	proof beyond a reasonable doubt
defendant	small claims court
deposition	subpoena
discovery procedures	summons
evidence	testimony
expert witness	transcript
instructions to the jury	trial court
judgment	verdict
jurisdiction	witness
jury	writ of execution

1 A summary of what the plaintiff or defendant will be trying to prove during the trial.

2 Decision of a jury.

Strengthening Your Legal Vocabulary

1 opening statement
2 verdict
3 juvenile delinquent
4 instructions to the jury
5 subpoena
6 testimony
7 plaintiff
8 arbitrator
9 writ of execution
10 jury

Applying Law to Everyday Life

1. Direct negotiation, mediation, or arbitration (pp. 66–67)
2. ETHICS ISSUE Yes, if by suing them you reduce the chance that they will cheat others in a similar way.
3. ETHICS ISSUE Yes, the moral duty to tell the truth is greater than the duty to help friends.
4. No, only trial courts hear, testimony. (p. 68)
5. Both; Able could be arrested for assault and battery. Beta could try to collect for the injuries suffered. (pp. 72–74)

3. A person under a certain age who commits a criminal act.
4. A statement by the judge telling the jury what rules of law apply to the case.
5. A written order commanding a person to appear in court as a witness and to give testimony.
6. Oral statements given as evidence by witnesses under oath.
7. Party who brings a civil action against another.
8. One, other than a judge or jury, who can make a decision that is binding on the parties to a dispute.
9. Process by which a judgment for money is enforced.
10. Person who testifies about the facts being litigated.

APPLYING LAW TO EVERYDAY LIFE

1. Gomez wanted to sue Shapiro for breach of contract but could not afford the expenses and time delays associated with litigation. What alternatives are available to resolve this matter?
2. ETHICS ISSUE When someone has injured you, do you have a duty to sue them for the injury even when the costs of the trial may be more than you can recover?
3. ETHICS ISSUE If you were a witness to an incident involving a friend, would you be obligated to tell the complete truth even if it might cause your friend to lose the case? Would you have the moral strength to do that?
4. June lost her case in the trial court. She thought that the plaintiff, Sid, had lied during the trial. On appeal, she requested that she be allowed to appear and explain why she thought Sid had lied. Will her request be granted?
5. Able and Beta were neighbors who did not like each other. One day as Beta was driving to work on his motorcycle, Able tried to run him down in his pickup truck. After three tries, Able was successful and caused serious personal injury and property damage. Is this a civil or criminal matter—or both?

6 Glen was an alcoholic and a penniless ne'er-do-well. One night while drunk, he stole Buchanan's pickup truck and crashed into Goldman's Pharmacy. When the police arrived, Glen resisted arrest. Which of Glen's acts are civil offenses and which are criminal offenses? Is anyone likely to collect damages?

7 The Spirit Club of Central High contracted with Martínez and her rock band to play at the homecoming dance. The price agreed upon was $750. One week before the event, Martínez notified the club president that the band members were ill and could not play. In reality, they appeared at another event. The club hastily hired a replacement band that charged $1,000. Is the club justified in suing Martínez? If so, in what court would the club probably sue and for how much? What would happen if the club did file suit and Martínez ignored the summons and the complaint filed by the club?

8 Wilson, age twelve, was habitually running away from home and was repeatedly truant from school. His parents and teachers thought he was incorrigible. Can he be placed under the jurisdiction of a juvenile court?

9 Mike ran into the rear of Sharon's new car, causing $32,000 in personal injury and property damage. Sharon won a civil judgment for the amount of the damages, but weeks have passed and Mike still has not paid. What can Sharon do?

▼ SOLVING CASE PROBLEMS

1 Taylor and Fitz Coal Company had a dispute over the amount of money due under a mineral lease. They submitted the dispute to arbitration according to the provisions of the lease. The arbitrators awarded the lessor, Taylor, $37,214.67. Taylor did not like the amount awarded and filed suit in court. Will the court conduct a trial to determine whether the amount is fair? (*Taylor v. Fitz Coal Company*, 618 S.W.2d 432, Ky.)

2 New Jersey enacted an environmental protection statute making it illegal to bring solid waste from another state to be buried in New Jersey's landfill sites. Philadelphia became a plaintiff in a New Jersey trial court by filing a complaint claiming that the statute violated New Jersey's constitution. The state of New Jersey was the defendant and filed an answer. Philadelphia won a judgment at the trial. New Jersey then appealed to the New Jersey Supreme Court, which reversed the trial court

6 Criminal offenses—auto theft, driving under the influence of alcohol, reckless driving, and trespass; he can be prosecuted by the state for his crimes. (p. 72) It is unlikely anyone would be able to collect anything from Glen. (pp. 73–74)

7 The club could sue Martínez for breach of contract; the club would probably sue in small claims court and collect $250 (p. 70); the club would win a default judgment. (p. 74)

8 Yes, Wilson's conduct makes him a juvenile delinquent. (p. 71)

9 Sharon can obtain a writ of execution and take Mike's property and sell it to satisfy the judgment. (p. 77)

▼ Solving Case Problems ▼

1 No; The decisions of arbitrators are binding on the parties. (p. 67)

2 The New Jersey statute created a burden on interstate commerce. It gave preferential treatment to residents of New Jersey over residents of other states. So, the New Jersey statute was declared unconstitutional by the United States Supreme Court. (pp. 68–69)

3 No; Although a juvenile court has considerable latitude in deciding whether it should keep jurisdiction over a child, the court must satisfy the basic requirements of due process and fairness and must comply with statutory requirements of a full investigation. (p. 71)

4 Yes, Dorsey is entitled to the court order directing Pearl to provide information related to the matter being litigated. (p. 74)

5 Douglas is correct. This is an issue of fact. Therefore it will be decided by a jury rather than by the judge. (pp. 75–77)

and held that the statute *is* consistent with the New Jersey Constitution. Philadelphia then appealed to the U.S. Supreme Court, arguing that the statute violated the U.S. Constitution because it restricts interstate commerce. Can you see the relationships among trial and appellate courts in this situation? Do you think the New Jersey statute restricts interstate commerce so that it is unconstitutional? (*City of Philadelphia v. New Jersey,* 437 U.S. 617)

3 Kent, a sixteen-year-old boy, was taken into custody by the police of Washington, D.C. He was held and questioned about breaking into an apartment, raping the occupant, and stealing a wallet. He admitted the offenses and volunteered information on several similar offenses. At the time, Kent was on probation for housebreaking and attempted purse snatching. Under the Juvenile Court Act, the case of any child sixteen years of age or older who is charged with an offense that in the case of an adult would be a felony may, after an investigation by the juvenile court judge, be transferred by the juvenile court to the district court. The juvenile court waived its jurisdiction in Kent's case, and he was tried and found guilty by a jury in the district court. Kent, admitting through his attorney that the juvenile court had the right to waive its jurisdiction, claimed nevertheless that the juvenile court had acted in an arbitrary manner by transferring him to the jurisdiction of the district court. Was the court within its rights in waiving jurisdiction? (*Kent v. United States,* 383 U.S. 541)

4 Bruce Mincey was killed by the explosion of a steel drum that he was cutting with a power saw. His wife, Pearl, filed suit against his employer, Dorsey Trailers. She alleged Dorsey was responsible for the death. Dorsey initiated discovery procedures, but Pearl did not respond to them. Dorsey asked for a court order instructing Pearl to respond. Will the court grant such an order? (*Mincey v. Dorsey Trailers, Inc.,* 367 So. 2d 98, Ala.)

5 A government-owned P-51 fighter plane landed at a Los Angeles airport and, on instructions from the tower, waited on a runway for a tow truck. Shortly thereafter, a plane owned by Douglas Aircraft Company began approaching the airfield to land. The Douglas aircraft struck the P-51, which was parked on the runway. The United States brought suit against Douglas, claiming that the Douglas pilot was negligent. During the trial, evidence was introduced indicating that the Douglas pilot was careless in not seeing the parked P-51, but that the airport was covered with a haze and the P-51 was painted in camouflage colors. Also, the

Douglas pilot had "zigzagged" his plane while taxiing in order to improve his forward vision. The trial was conducted before a jury. The government claimed that the issue of whether the Douglas pilot was negligent was an issue of law for the judge to decide. Douglas claimed that it was an issue of fact for the jury to decide. Which one is correct? (*United States v. Douglas Aircraft Company,* 169 F.2d 755, 9th Cir.)

CHAPTER 5 ORGANIZER

Chapter Theme

Crimes, usually classified as felonies or misdemeanors, are punishable by fine, imprisonment, or both, after the accused has been afforded his or her constitutional rights.

DIRECTED STUDY QUESTIONS	SPECIAL FEATURES	PROGRAM RESOURCES				
		Reteach	Enrich	SN	AM	
What are crimes?	Thinking Critically Through Visuals, p. 87	✔	✔		V	
How are crimes classified?		✔	✔			
What are business-related crimes?	Ethics Issue, p. 90 Personal Perspectives, p. 91 Multicultural Highlights, p. 92 Thinking Critically Through Visuals, p. 93	✔	✔		A K	
What rights does a person have when arrested?		✔	✔	✔		
When is one party responsible for the criminal conduct of another?		✔	✔			
What are defenses to criminal charges?	Writing Connections, p. 96	✔	✔			
What are the punishments for crimes?	Preventing Legal Difficulties, p. 97	✔	✔			

Additional Resources

- *Black's Law Dictionary*, 6th ed. St. Paul, MN: West Publishing Co., 1990.
- *Elements of Conspiracy Investigation.* Washington, D.C.: Dept. of Treasury, Bureau of Alcohol, Tobacco & Firearms, 1988.
- Mungo, Paul and Clough, Bryan. *Approaching Zero: The Extraordinary Underworld of Hackers, Phreakers, Virus Writers, and Keyboard Criminals.* NY: Random House, 1992.

Chapter Pacing Guide

One-semester course	✓	✓	✓					
One-year course	✓	✓	✓	✓				

	ASSESSMENT OPPORTUNITIES			
Cooperative Learning	Informal Assessment	Chapter Review	Chapter Test	Chapter *MicroExam* (Media)
	✓	✓	✓	✓
	✓	✓	✓	✓
✓	✓	✓	✓	✓
	✓	✓	✓	✓
	✓	✓	✓	✓
	✓	✓	✓	✓
	✓	✓	✓	✓

Videodiscs

Defenses in Criminal Law

Search Chapter 6, Play To 7

State by State

In Arkansas, burglary is "entering or remaining unlawfully in an occupiable structure of another person with the purpose of committing therein any offense punishable by imprisonment."

Teaching Materials

Student text, pp. 84–101

Overhead transparency masters
- *Criminal Intent and Age*
- *Important Due Process Rights*

Videos
- *Contracts, Warranties, and Credit* Videotape
- *Law for Business* Videodisc

Workbook, pp. 9–10

Outside Resources
- Magazine or newspaper articles about corporations being convicted of a criminal act
- Newspaper articles on white-collar crime
- 3 × 5 index cards
- Community newspaper articles on violations of local ordinances
- Telephone book
- Miranda rights

Assessment
- Chapter Test

- Chapter *MicroExam*

Vocabulary

crime, p. 86
criminal act, p. 86
criminal battery, p. 86
criminal intent, p. 87
vicarious criminal liability, p. 87
embezzlement, p. 89
felony, p. 89
perjury, p. 89
misdemeanor, p. 89
infractions, p. 89
white-collar crimes, p. 90
antitrust laws, p. 90
larceny, p. 90
robbery, p. 90
burglary, p. 90
receiving stolen property, p. 91
false pretenses, p. 91
forgery, p. 91
bribery, p. 91
extortion, p. 91
conspiracy, p. 92
arson, p. 92
defense, p. 95
procedural defenses, p. 95
substantive defenses, p. 95
self-defense, p. 96
criminal insanity, p. 96
immunity, p. 96
contempt of court, p. 96
punishment, p. 96
plea bargaining, pp. 96–970

Learning Objectives

When you complete this chapter, you will be able to

1. Define the elements present in all crimes.
2. Distinguish between a felony and a misdemeanor.
3. Describe crimes that commonly occur in the business environment.
4. Explain the rights of a person who has been arrested.
5. Understand when one party is responsible for the criminal acts of another.
6. Discuss defenses to criminal charges.
7. Describe the punishments for crimes.

84

Chapter Self-Test

Assess students' understanding of crimes before they begin Chapter 5 by asking them to define the following terms based on their current knowledge of each word: **(1) criminal intent** (The defendant intended to commit the act and intended to do evil); **(2) felony** (A serious crime punishable by confinement for more than one year or by execution); **(3) misdemeanor** (A less serious crime punishable by confinement in jail for less than one year, a fine, or both); **(4) burglary** (Entering a building without permission to commit a crime); and **(5) robbery** (Taking property from another's person or immediate presence, against the victim's will). Using the glossary or a dictionary, ask students to review their responses with a partner before continuing with the chapter.

CHAPTER 5

CRIMES

1. A woman was shopping in the local grocery store with her four-year-old daughter. The mother's purse was in the shopping cart. When the mother was not looking, the tot put $2 worth of candy in her purse. The mother did not see the candy in her purse, and when they left the store she was arrested for shoplifting. Has either the mother or the daughter committed a crime?

2. Two students, ages thirteen and fourteen, broke into their school building one weekend and vandalized it. They smashed equipment, sprayed paint on walls, broke furniture, and started fires in trash cans. The damage totalled $12,700. Are the students criminally responsible?

3. ETHICS ISSUE Suppose you could commit a crime and be absolutely sure you would not be caught. Would you do it? What if it caused physical injury to another human being? What if it caused only financial injury to another human being? What if the loss was insured so the victim was not injured? Should it make a difference if the victim was a stranger to you?

FOCUS

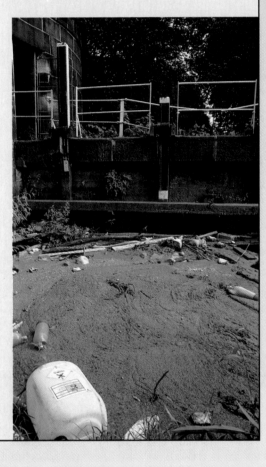

Write the following question on the chalkboard prior to the beginning of class: **What is a good definition of "crime"?** (An offense against society, such as robbery, trespassing, or murder)

Begin class by reviewing students' ideas of what **crime** means. If necessary, have them skim the section, *Offenses Against Society*, p. 86, to get started. On chart paper, create a class list of the types of crimes students suggest. As crimes are mentioned in the text, check them off or add them to the list as necessary.

You Decide

1. No; The mother did not engage in shoplifting because she did not perform a criminal act and she lacked criminal intent. Her daughter is too young to form criminal intent.
2. Yes, clearly both committed acts which are criminal; the issue is whether or not they possessed criminal intent. In this case, the conduct—particularly smashing the equipment and setting the fires—indicates criminal intent.
3. ETHICS ISSUE None of the questions present moral justifications for violating the law. Instead, they present reasons which might tempt someone to violate the law.

Thinking Critically Through Visuals

This is a photograph of an area that has been destroyed by illegal dumping. What picture caption might you write to describe what you see? (Answers may include, "The beauty of this area was destroyed by illegal dumping of waste materials" and so on.)

TEACH

Review the concept of *civil law* (concerned with private wrongs against individuals) presented in Chapter 4. Then help students to understand how criminal law and civil law differ by summarizing points 1–3 on pp. 86–89.

Explain to students that corporate employees—as well as the corporation itself—can both be judged to have had criminal intent to commit a crime. To clarify how a business as well as a person can possess intent, provide examples of recent scandals involving products or consumer goods. Have students mentally walk through the processes.

APPLY

After reading the PROBLEM on p. 86, ask the class to apply the three elements of a crime to determine if a crime was committed. (Yes; She had a duty not to embezzle, she violated that duty, and possessed criminal intent.)
Guided Practice

Assign individual students to investigate organizations in their community or state that aid victims of crimes. Starting with the telephone book as a resource, have them create a master list of the available agencies, including phone numbers and addresses.
Independent Practice

WHAT ARE CRIMES?

PROBLEM

Davis, the chief accountant of the Del Norte Credit Union, cleverly juggled the company records over a period of years. During that time, she took at least $35,000 belonging to the credit union. When the theft was discovered by outside auditors, Davis repaid the money with interest. Has she committed a crime despite the repayment?

1. Offenses Against Society

The most fundamental characteristic of a **crime** is that it is an offense against society. Consequently, when a crime occurs, society, acting through such employees as police and prosecutors, attempts to identify, arrest, prosecute, and punish the criminal. These efforts are designed to protect society rather than to aid the victim of the crime. For almost all crimes, the victim can sue identified criminals for civil damages. However, victims seldom do so because few criminals have the money to pay judgments. Crimes contrast with *civil offenses,* which are offenses against just the victim, not society.

2. Elements of Every Crime

Before anyone can be convicted of a crime, three elements usually must be proved at the trial. They are the following:

1. a duty to do (or not to do) a certain thing,
2. an act or omission in violation of that duty, and
3. criminal intent.

Duty. The duty is usually described by *state* statutes that prohibit certain conduct. Less frequently, federal statutes or city ordinances identify criminal behavior. To establish the duty in a trial, the prosecutor would simply cite a statute to the judge.

Violation of the duty. The breach of duty is the **criminal act;** the specific conduct that violates the statute. For example, all states have statutes that make battery a crime. These statutes often define **criminal battery** as "the intentional causing of bodily harm to another person." A breach of this duty could be proved in a trial by the testimony of a witness who saw the defendant punch the victim.

ASSESS

Learning Objective 1 Individually, have students identify and explain in writing, using a computer, if possible, the three elements that must be present to convict someone of a crime. (See p. 86.)

Criminal intent. The third element, criminal intent, must be proved in most cases. **Criminal intent** generally means that the defendant (1) intended to commit the act and (2) intended to do evil. If in a basketball game you deliberately punch an opposing player, you display criminal intent. You have committed a crime. On the other hand, if you lost your balance and while flailing your arms, you hit the nose of a bystander, there would be no criminal intent. You did not intend the act nor did you intend to do evil. So there is no crime.

Criminal intent creates two issues for corporations. First, can a corporation, an organization, form criminal intent the way humans can? The answer is yes. If the corporation's employees have criminal intent, their employer may be judged to have criminal intent. If the employees were doing their assigned duties and the criminal act benefits the organization, most courts will find criminal intent in the organization. The second issue relates to corporate officers. When a corporate employee commits a crime, can officers be held criminally responsible? The answer is often yes. In many situations, the officer will be held criminally liable under the doctrine of **vicarious criminal liability.** Vicarious means "substituted." Thus, the criminal intent of the employee is used as a substitute for the requirement of criminal intent for an officer. Suppose the president of a company knows generally about very dangerous working conditions, but does nothing to protect workers from the risks. If a worker is killed because a supervisor failed to take safety precautions, the president may be charged with the crime of homicide.

Thinking Critically Through Visuals

The use of handcuffs is a common procedure when arresting someone. Why do you think handcuffs are used? Do you think they are necessary? (Students should note that a police officer never knows whether a suspect will become violent and, if so, when. The use of handcuffs protects the officer from possible attack and keeps the accused from getting into more trouble.)

RETEACH Have students fold a piece of paper in half horizontally. On the top half, students should illustrate a criminal act that shows criminal intent. On the bottom half, students should draw an act that was not intended to do evil.

ENRICH Bring to class, or have students bring, magazine or newspaper articles about a corporation convicted of a criminal act. Independently or in small groups, students should make a running list of examples of criminal intent and the type of crime mentioned in each article.

Display the overhead transparency, *Criminal Intent and Age*. Referring to this transparency, have students orally explain the difference between common law and contemporary law as they pertain to age and its effect on criminal intent.

To be found not guilty of a crime by reason of insanity, it must be proved that the defendant did not know the difference between right and wrong and, therefore, did not have criminal intent (the intention to commit the act and do evil). This is often very hard to prove. Have students debate the following question: **Should the insanity defense be allowed in a murder case?** (Answers should reflect independent thinking but be supported by students.)

Criminal intent is also related to age. Under early common law, children less than age seven were considered below the age of reason. Therefore, they were not capable of having the criminal intent necessary for crimes. Those over age fourteen were presumed to know the difference between right and wrong and so were accountable as adults for their acts. For children ages seven through fourteen, such knowledge had to be proved. Today, statutes in most states fix the age of criminal liability at eighteen, but the figure ranges from sixteen to nineteen. As you will learn in Chapter 7, statutes often provide that minors as young as thirteen may be tried and punished as adults if they are accused of serious crimes, such as murder. Generally, however, what is a crime for adults is juvenile delinquency for minors.

To have criminal intent, one must have sufficient mental capacity to know the difference between right and wrong. Accordingly, insane persons are not held responsible for their criminal acts. Normally, neither voluntary intoxication nor use of drugs affects one's criminal intent.

A few crimes do not require the element of criminal intent. For the less serious crimes where being sentenced to jail is very unlikely, criminal intent is not required. Traffic offenses are an example. A speeding driver who did not intend to speed or intend evil has still committed a traffic offense. Another exception applies to actions involving extreme carelessness. Suppose you drove eighty miles per hour through a residential neighborhood while drunk and killed a pedestrian. While you may not have intended to speed or intended evil, your conduct is so careless that some courts treat it as the same thing as criminal intent. You could be convicted of the crime of vehicular homicide.

3. Overview of Criminal Conduct

Criminal conduct may be classified in various ways. One type of classification follows:

1. crimes against a person (assault and battery, kidnapping, rape, murder);
2. crimes against property (theft, robbery, embezzlement, receiving stolen property);
3. crimes against the government and the administration of justice (treason, tax evasion, bribery, counterfeiting, perjury);
4. crimes against public peace and order (rioting, carrying concealed weapons, drunk and disorderly conduct, illegal speeding);
5. crimes against realty (burglary, arson, criminal trespass);
6. crimes against consumers (fraudulent sale of worthless securities, violation of pure food and drug laws); or

ASSESS

Learning Objective 2 Have students write two scenarios, using a computer, if possible. The first should illustrate a felony and the second should illustrate a misdemeanor. Students' scenarios should clearly show that they understand the difference between the two types of crimes. Have students share their scenarios, then compile the hard copy in a booklet called *Crime and Punishment.*

7 crimes against decency (bigamy, obscenity, prostitution, contributing to the deliquency of a minor).

In the problem, Davis owed a duty, defined by state statute, to not take the credit union's money. Violation of this duty, the criminal conduct, is **embezzlement**. This act could be proved with the testimony of the auditors. Davis's criminal intent can be established by her conduct; the acts were intentional and she intended to do the evil. So Davis did commit a crime. Her return of the money does not alter this fact.

HOW ARE CRIMES CLASSIFIED?

PROBLEM

Murdock was a witness at a civil trial for damages. As all witnesses do before testifying, he took an oath "to tell the truth, the whole truth, and nothing but the truth." Nevertheless, while being questioned by one of the attorneys, Murdock deliberately lied, hoping to help the defendant. If this could be proved, could he be punished for a crime?

Crimes are classified as (1) felonies or (2) misdemeanors.

1. Felonies

A **felony** is a very serious crime punishable either by confinement for more than one year in a state prison or by execution. Murder, kidnapping, arson, rape, robbery, burglary, embezzlement, forgery, theft of large sums, and perjury are examples of felonies. A person who lies under oath, as Murdock did in the problem, commits **perjury**. He may be imprisoned for two or three years.

2. Misdemeanors

A **misdemeanor** is a less serious crime. It is usually punishable (1) by confinement in a county or city jail for less than one year, (2) by fine, or (3) by both confinement and fine. Such crimes as disorderly conduct and speeding are usually misdemeanors. Some states classify lesser misdemeanors as **infractions**. Persons convicted of infractions can only be fined. They cannot be jailed. Since there is no risk of being jailed, the defendant charged with an infraction is not entitled to a jury trial. Parking violations, failing to clear snow from sidewalks, and littering are examples of infractions.

TEACH

Explain to students how crimes are classified as either a **felony** or a **misdemeanor**. Give examples of each so students understand how the two classifications of crimes differ. (Felonies are very serious crimes; misdemeanors are less serious crimes.)

APPLY

Draw the following graphic organizer without the entries on the chalkboard and have students copy it in their notebooks. As a group, assist students in filling in this organizer by having them list five felony crimes and five misdemeanors. **Guided Practice**

Felony	Misdemeanor
Murder Robbery Kidnapping Arson Rape Burglary Embezzlement Forgery Theft of Large Sums Perjury	Disorderly Conduct Speeding Shoplifting Vandalism Jaywalking

Have students exchange their lists with those of their classmates. Students should compare the similarities and differences between the two lists. Have students check to make sure the crimes they list under each category fit the definitions on p. 89. **Independent Practice**

RETEACH

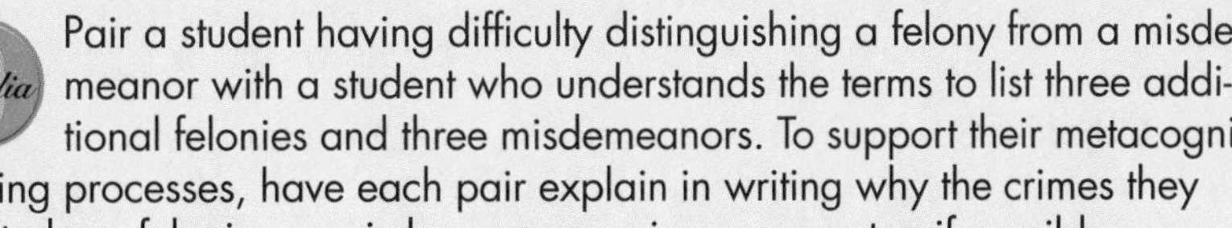

Pair a student having difficulty distinguishing a felony from a misdemeanor with a student who understands the terms to list three additional felonies and three misdemeanors. To support their metacognitive thinking processes, have each pair explain in writing why the crimes they selected are felonies or misdemeanors, using a computer, if possible.

ENRICH

Have students find out which misdemeanors, if any, are classified as infractions in their state. Have each person report his or her findings to the class.

TEACH

Draw the following (base only) chart on the chalkboard for students to copy in their notebooks. As you introduce and explain each of the ten business-related crimes mentioned on pp. 90–93, add the name to the chart.

Business-Related Crimes	
Larceny	Felony or Misdemeanor
False Pretenses	Misdemeanor
Bribery	Felony
Conspiracy	Felony or Misdemeanor
Buy/Sell Narcotics	Felony
Receive Stolen Property	Felony or Misdemeanor
Forgery	Felony
Extortion	Felony or Misdemeanor
Arson	Felony
Computer Crime	Felony or Misdemeanor

APPLY

ETHICS ISSUE

Ethics Issue

Discuss whether or not white-collar crime, such as using inside information for financial gain, is just as unlawful as any other crime, and if the courts are too lenient with white-collar criminals. (Judge students' responses on the thought processes they follow.) **Guided Practice**

WHAT ARE BUSINESS-RELATED CRIMES?

PROBLEM

Officers of six competing cosmetics manufacturers met at a trade convention. All of the officers agreed to use the same wholesale prices. They also agreed to follow the lead of the biggest company in making future price changes. Each officer agreed to promote sales by advertising only within an assigned geographical region. Were the officers and their companies guilty of any crime?

A business, like any person, is subject to general criminal law. So business persons and firms can commit crimes. Because such criminals are generally well-educated, respected members of the community, the offenses are called **white-collar crimes.** Common examples of white-collar crimes are evading income taxes, defrauding consumers, cheating with false weighing machines, conspiring to fix prices, making false fire insurance and auto insurance claims, engaging in false advertising, committing bribery, engaging in political corruption, and embezzling. Normally, physical violence is not involved. Therefore, courts tend to be more lenient with the criminals, punishing them with fines or short prison sentences.

In the problem, the six manufacturers and their involved officers were guilty of violating criminal portions of the antitrust laws. **Antitrust laws** state that competing companies may not cooperate in fixing prices or in dividing sales regions. Antitrust laws require that business firms compete with one another. Some of the more common business-related crimes are discussed below.

1. Larceny

Larceny (commonly known as theft) is the wrongful taking of money or personal property belonging to someone else, with intent to deprive the owner of possession. **Robbery** is a variation of larceny. It is the taking of property from *another's person or immediate presence,* against the victim's will, by force or by causing fear. **Burglary** is another variation of larceny. It is *entering a building* without permission when intending to commit a crime. Other types of larceny include shoplifting, pickpocketing, and purse snatching.

Larceny may be either a felony or a misdemeanor. The classification is determined by the value of the property stolen and other circumstances. However, robbery and burglary are always felonies. If the thief sells the stolen goods, he or she is guilty of a separate crime, selling stolen property.

ASSESS

Learning Objective 3 Have students refer to the fishbone map they completed in the TEACH activity, above. Based on their understanding of the section, have students add horizontal lines to each crime then label whether each crime is a felony, a misdemeanor, or perhaps both.

2. Receiving Stolen Property

Knowingly **receiving stolen property** consists of either receiving or buying property known to be stolen, with intent to deprive the rightful owner of the property. One who receives stolen property is known as a fence.

3. False Pretenses

One who obtains money or other property by lying about a past or existing fact is guilty of **false pretenses.** This crime differs from larceny because the victim parts with the property voluntarily. False pretenses is a type of fraud (see page 111).

Al went to a credit union and filled out a credit application. Although he was unemployed, on the application he wrote that he was earning a salary of $1,200 per month. By error, the credit union did not verify his employment. Al was thereby allowed to borrow $6,000, which he was unable to repay. Al was guilty of obtaining the money under false pretenses.

4. Forgery

Forgery is falsely making or materially altering a writing to defraud another. The most common forgeries are found on checks when one signs another's name without permission to do so. Forgery also includes altering a check, such as changing "$7" to "$70" and "Seven" to "Seventy." Forgery is usually a felony. Of course, if others authorize you to sign their names, there is no forgery.

5. Bribery

Bribery is unlawfully offering or giving to a governmental official anything of value to influence performance of an official duty. Soliciting or accepting the bribe is also criminal. In many states, bribing private parties is also a form of bribery called commercial bribery. Thus, paying a private company's purchasing agent to obtain a sale may be bribery. It is usually bribery when a professional gambler pays an athlete to lose a game intentionally. The federal Foreign Corrupt Practices Act of 1977 condemns bribery in foreign countries by U.S. companies.

6. Extortion

Extortion (commonly known as blackmail) is obtaining money or other property from a person by wrongful use of force, fear, or the power of office.

Divide students into groups of six or seven to role-play then discuss the PROBLEM posed on p. 90. One person should represent each cosmetic manufacturer and a seventh person, if possible, can serve as facilitator/recorder. Discuss each group's deliberations with the class as a whole. **Cooperative Learning**

Some students may have difficulty taking useful notes in class. Suggest that they take notes and tape record a class discussion on business-related crimes. Then have them listen to the tape, take new notes, and compare them to their original set. Have students determine which captured the most important points.

Personal Perspectives

Have students poll family members and/or friends to find out if white-collar crimes should carry greater, lesser, or the same punishment as other types of crime. Have students tabulate and present their findings as a bar chart, using graphics or spreadsheet software, if possible. **Independent Practice**

RETEACH Bring in newspaper articles that deal with the types of white-collar crimes listed on pp. 90–91. Working with a peer-tutor, have students prepare a written summary of one of the articles, using a computer to write their summaries, if possible.

ENRICH Have students work in pairs to create a poster that graphically illustrates the difference between robbery and burglary, both of which are types of larceny.

Assign groups of two or three students one or more of the white-collar crimes discussed in this section. Have each group write and perform a skit showing the crime taking place—without mentioning the type of crime. If possible, videotape each skit. As a class, view the skits (or videotapes) and identify the types of crime portrayed.

Multicultural Highlights

In 1993, Janet Reno, daughter of a Danish immigrant, became the first female U.S. Attorney General. Reno's office advises the President on legal issues, enforces federal laws, and prosecutes criminal cases that involve the U.S. government. Prior to her appointment, Reno was state attorney for Dade County, FL, the first woman to hold that post. Reno made great strides in improving relations between the police and Miami's African American and Hispanic communities. Ask students to brainstorm a list of qualifications a U.S. Attorney General should possess.

The extortionist (blackmailer) may threaten to inflict bodily injury. Sometimes the extortionist threatens to expose a secret crime or embarrassing fact if payment is not made.

> The head of a labor union threatened to call a costly strike among employees of a company unless she was paid $10,000 by the employer. This was extortion.

7. Conspiracy

Conspiracy is an agreement between two or more persons to commit a crime. Usually the agreement is secret. The conspiracy is a crime separate from the crime the parties planned to commit. Depending on the circumstances, the crime may be either a felony or a misdemeanor. Business executives of competing corporations sometimes conspire to fix prices or to divide markets.

> Thompson and two others were convicted of conspiring to smuggle heroin into the United States and planning to distribute the drug. Thompson appealed the conviction. She claimed that no heroin was introduced as evidence to prove that the conspiracy was carried out; therefore, the accused persons could not be guilty. The court held that the crime of conspiracy is not dependent on the *success* of the planned scheme.

8. Arson

Arson is the willful and illegal burning of a building. Arson occurs when someone intentionally starts a fire and burns a structure without the owner's consent. In some states, arson also occurs if you burn your own building to defraud an insurer.

9. Selling and Buying Narcotics

Selling, offering to sell, or possessing illegal narcotics is a crime. So is transporting or giving illegal narcotics. Violations of narcotics laws are usually felonies. Adults who supply others with narcotic drugs are usually dealt with harshly. Some states make prison sentences mandatory for those convicted of distributing narcotics. Also, in some states, increased punishment is required by statute if one has a prior narcotics conviction. Life imprisonment is prescribed in some cases. In some foreign countries, the penalty is execution.

▼ ASSESS

Learning Objective 3 Have students write a one-sentence definition for each of the white-collar crimes mentioned in this section: larceny, receiving stolen property, false pretenses, forgery, bribery, extortion, conspiracy, arson, selling/buying narcotics, and computer crime.

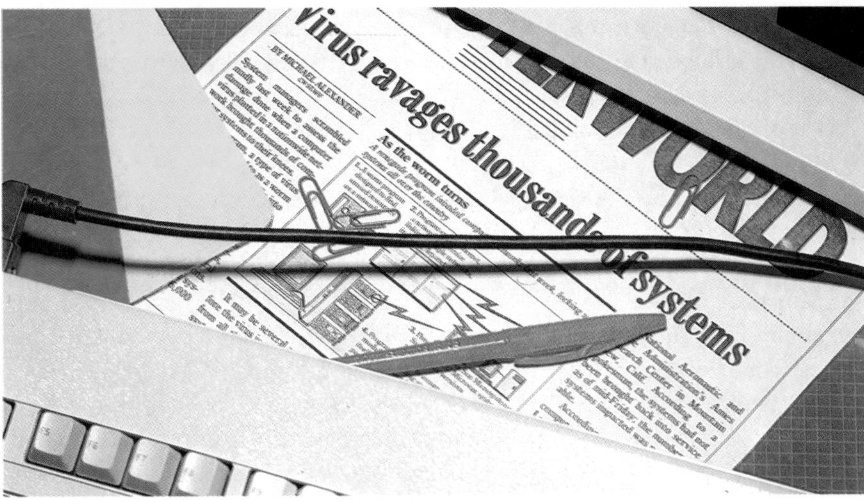

10. Computer Crime

The computer revolution has created a range of problems for the criminal law. For example, larceny is "the wrongful taking of the personal property of others." This traditional definition of the crime made it difficult to prosecute those who steal computer data for two reasons. First, many courts concluded that there was not a "taking" if an intruder merely *copied* the information in the computer. Second, even if an intruder copied and erased computer information, some courts concluded that there was no taking of "personal property" but only the loss of electrical impulses which no one really owns. In response, many states have created new criminal laws. For example, Arizona enacted a statute that states that "accessing, altering, damaging, or destroying without authorization any computer... [is criminal conduct]...." Notice that under such statutes merely "accessing" another's computer without authorization is a crime.

▼ WHAT RIGHTS DOES A PERSON HAVE WHEN ARRESTED?

PROBLEM

A state law makes "hit-and-run" driving a crime. The law requires any driver of a motor vehicle involved in an accident to stay at the scene, give their name and address, and show their driver's licenses. Barlow, who was arrested for violating this law, claimed that the law was unconstitutional. He said that the law violated the right against self-incrimination, as provided in the Fifth Amendment to the U.S. Constitution. Is he correct?

▼RETEACH Using a peer-tutoring approach, have a student who understands the terms listed under ASSESS on p. 92 write each term on individual 3 × 5 index cards and the definition for each term on others. The student needing assistance should use his or her textbook or class notes to match the term with its correct definition.

▼ENRICH In small groups, using a computer, if possible, have students create a collaborative story that uses all of the terms in the ASSESS activity.

Thinking Critically Through Visuals

Computer viruses have caused chaos in businesses around the country. Discuss the following: **If you were a lawmaker, how would you help guard against computer crimes?** (Answers may include prosecuting those who illegally copy software or willfully pass along a computer virus.) **Guided Practice**

Have students find an article about computer crime and summarize it for the class. Then, determine the extent of the crime and its implications. **Independent Practice**

▼ TEACH

Review *due process of law* on pp. 12–13 of Chapter 1. Apply this to a discussion of a person's rights when arrested. Contact your local police station for a copy of the adult and juvenile versions of the Miranda rights.

▼ APPLY

Display the overhead transparency, *Important Due Process Rights*. Have students restate each right in their own words. **Guided Practice**

Using the overhead transparency, *Important Due Process Rights* as a reference, have students make a chart illustrating the rights of the accused. **Independent Practice**

When a person is arrested, he or she is entitled to understand his or her rights under the law. If the suspect does not speak English, this means translating the information into a language the suspect does understand. Obtain a copy of translations of the Miranda rights from your local police department for each of your students

whose native language is not English.

One of the major objectives of the Constitution of the United States is to protect individuals from certain actions of the federal government. These constitutional limitations now also apply to state and local governments. The authors of the Constitution believed it was better for our society to give individuals too much liberty than to allow the government too much power. Thus, in this country, persons suspected or accused of criminal conduct have rights that are not available to people in many other countries.

The constitutional right to due process (discussed in Chapter 1) requires fundamental fairness in governmental actions. It requires fair procedures during an investigation and in court. For example, criminal defendants may not be compelled to testify against themselves. And they have the right to cross-examine witnesses. Perhaps the most important right is the right of the accused criminal to be represented by a lawyer. For a person who cannot afford to hire a lawyer, a public defender or a private lawyer is provided by the state.

The rights of accused persons are subject to reasonable limitations. In the problem, Barlow's right against self-incrimination was not violated by the law that requires one to remain at the scene of the accident and identify oneself. It is true that such actions would indicate involvement and could lead to criminal prosecution if a crime has been committed. However, the right against self-incrimination applies only to statements that would implicate the person in a crime. Merely identifying oneself as a party to an accident does not in itself indicate guilt.

▼ TEACH

Before reading *When Is One Party Responsible for the Criminal Conduct of Another?* on pp. 94–95, ask the class to respond to the PROBLEM on p. 94. Then discuss students' opinions after they have completed the section.

▼ WHEN IS ONE PARTY RESPONSIBLE FOR THE CRIMINAL CONDUCT OF ANOTHER?

PROBLEM

Musk, a career criminal, planned a bank robbery. He sent Spiro and Adams to do the "job." He also had Greene steal a car and serve as chauffeur and lookout. Spiro killed a bank guard during the getaway. Who is guilty of what crime(s)?

A person who aids another in the commission of a crime is also guilty of criminal wrongdoing. For example, one who acts as a lookout to warn a burglar of the approach of the police is an accomplice in the burglary. Similarly, one who plans the crime, or otherwise intentionally helps, is guilty of the same crime. In most jurisdictions, if someone is killed during a felony, all accomplices are guilty of the homicide. Thus, in the problem, all four persons were guilty of car theft and armed bank robbery. All four might also be guilty of murder.

▼ APPLY

Pose the following situation to the class: **Joe agrees to let Mary copy from his test paper. They are caught in the act and both fail the test. Why does Joe also fail?** (Answers may include that Joe allowed Mary to cheat.) Discuss how the scenario relates to criminal actions. **Guided Practice**

▼ ASSESS

Learning Objective 6 Independently, have students write an explanation of the difference between a procedural defense and a substantive defense. (A procedural defense is based on problems with the way the evidence is obtained or the way an accused person is arrested, questioned, tried, or punished. Substantive defenses disprove, justify, or excuse the alleged crime.) Have students give examples of each defense.

As discussed on page 87, corporations can be criminally liable for the conduct of their employees. Also, officers of corporations may be criminally liable for their actions as managers.

WHAT ARE DEFENSES TO CRIMINAL CHARGES?

PROBLEM

Will and Zack, who were arrested for possession of cocaine, signed confessions at the police station. At their trial, they claimed that their right to due process had been violated. They said they had not been advised of their right to remain silent and to have a lawyer present when questioned. If true, are those good defenses?

Of course, the state must prove that the defendant is guilty beyond a reasonable doubt. But even when it appears the state has done this, the defendant may escape criminal liability by subsequently establishing a defense. A **defense** often proves the innocence of the defendant. The defendant must produce the evidence to support any defense. There are two types of defenses: (1) procedural defenses and (2) substantive defenses.

1. Procedural Defenses

Procedural defenses are based on problems with the way evidence is obtained or the way the accused person is arrested, questioned, tried, or punished. For example, a defendant who had confessed to a crime might assert the defense that he signed the confession only because he was threatened by the police. This would be a procedural defense.

Ignorance of the law is not a defense. The legal system assumes that everyone knows the law. Thus if you park in a no-parking area because you did not see the sign, you have no defense.

In the problem, Will and Zack should have been advised of their rights at the time of the arrest. If they were not so advised, their procedural rights under the U.S. Constitution were violated. Such a violation would be a valid defense.

2. Substantive Defenses

Substantive defenses disprove, justify, or excuse the alleged crime. Most substantive defenses discredit the facts that the state sought to establish. For example, an eyewitness may have placed the defendant at the scene of the crime. The defendant may establish a substantive defense by showing that she was in the hospital at the time of the alleged crime. Self-defense, criminal insanity, and immunity are other examples of substantive defenses.

Individually, have students create a flowchart showing the events as presented in the PROBLEM on p. 94 through the arrest of the criminals and the charges made in court. **Independent Practice**

TEACH

Discuss with students the fact that even an individual who confesses to a crime is entitled to have the best possible defense in court. Ask: **Why, do you think, is this important?** (Answers may include that a lawyer will help to protect the accused against procedural and/or substantive violations of the law.)

APPLY

Discuss the PROBLEM on p. 95 and ask students whether or not they think it is fair for people who have confessed to a crime to get away with that crime because they were not advised of their rights. **Guided Practice**

In writing, using a computer, if possible, have students create two situations: one in which a procedural defense is used and one in which a substantive defense is used. Have students create a list of their classmates' examples and record them in their notebooks.

Independent Practice

RETEACH As a group, have students create a bulletin board display that visually explains procedural and substantive defenses. Encourage them to use drawings, cartoons, photographs, and newspaper articles to help with their explanations.

ENRICH Working in groups of two or three, have students role-play a scenario in which they use either a procedural defense or a substantive defense. After presenting their skits, poll the audience to determine which defense was used.

Writing Connections

Language Arts
Ask students, imagining that they are lawyers, to prepare a closing argument explaining why their client was unjustly accused of a certain crime. Have them cite a specific procedural or substantive defense. Have students prepare their arguments in writing, using a computer, if possible, prior to

presenting them orally to the class.

TEACH

Discuss with the class the term **punishment** and its rationale (to discipline the wrongdoer). Ask if students know the meaning of the phrase *"an eye for an eye."* (A punishment for a crime that is equivalent to the crime committed) Then, ask them if they know where this phrase originates. (The Koran and the Old Testament of the Bible)

Self-defense is the use of the force that appears to be reasonably necessary to the victim to prevent death, serious bodily harm, kidnapping, or rape. This defense also extends to members of one's family and household and to others whom one has a legal duty to protect. One may not use deadly force if nondeadly force appears reasonably sufficient. Moreover, only nondeadly force may be used to protect or recover property. Thus, one may not set deadly traps or "spring guns" to protect unoccupied buildings. In addition, a civilian may not shoot a thief who is escaping with stolen property.

Criminal insanity generally exists when the accused does not know the difference between right and wrong. If that is true, there is no criminal intent and therefore no crime. At a trial, the defendant must prove the criminal insanity.

Immunity is freedom from prosecution even when one has committed the crime charged. Sometimes one criminal may be granted immunity in exchange for an agreement to testify about the criminal conduct of several other criminals. In other instances, there is no agreement. Instead, the government grants immunity to a reluctant witness to remove the privilege against self-incrimination. If the witness refuses to testify after the grant of immunity, he or she would be in **contempt of court.** Contempt of court is action that hinders the administration of justice. It is a crime punishable by imprisonment.

WHAT ARE THE PUNISHMENTS FOR CRIMES?

PROBLEM

To conserve water, a city ordinance prohibited the wasteful practice of allowing it to run into the streets and sewers. Gill turned the water sprinklers on in his garden and forgot to turn them off. The water ran into the street all night, making a considerable stream. Gill was cited for violating the ordinance. What is an appropriate penalty for an offense of this nature?

"Let the punishment fit the crime" is more easily said than done. **Punishment** is any penalty provided by law and imposed by a court. The purpose is not to remedy the wrong but rather to discipline the wrongdoer. If reasonably swift and certain, punishment should deter others from similar behavior in the future. In the problem, Gill was guilty of an infraction, which did not require criminal intent. Nevertheless, his conduct was illegal and so he would probably be fined. Criminal statutes ordinarily set maximum limits for punishment, but allow a judge discretion within those limits.

Often an accused person will agree to plead guilty to a less serious crime in exchange for having a more serious charge dropped. This is called **plea**

ASSESS

Learning Objective 7 Present students with a list of offenses against their community or their school, such as stealing a pocketbook, robbing a church poor box, shoplifting, or cheating on a test. Then have students, working in groups of two or three, identify and justify a fitting punishment. As a class, review each group's punishments and discuss whether or not they match the crime.

bargaining. The accused voluntarily gives up the right to a public trial to avoid the risk of a greater penalty if convicted.

> Piper was cited for drunk driving, which carried a penalty of automatic suspension of her driver's license for one year. Mitsu, the prosecuting attorney, knew the state's evidence was weak. Therefore, she offered to drop the charge if the defendant would plead guilty to the lesser charge of reckless driving and a fine of $2,000. The judge agreed. Piper pleaded guilty to reckless driving and paid the fine.

Preventing Legal Difficulties

As a business person...

1. Study business law carefully, particularly when an activity is identified as criminal in nature.
2. Never intentionally do something illegal.
3. Never misrepresent a fact to obtain the goods or services of others.
4. Never threaten others with an illegal act to compel them to do something.
5. If arrested, immediately contact a lawyer.

REVIEWING IMPORTANT POINTS

1. A crime is an offense against society. In order to convict, the prosecution must establish a duty, an act or omission in violation of the duty, and, in most cases, criminal intent.
2. Crimes are generally divided into (a) felonies and (b) misdemeanors. Some states also recognize infractions.
3. Some crimes in which a business may be the victim are robbery, burglary, shoplifting, employee theft, passing bad checks, vandalism, receiving stolen property, and embezzlement.
4. Some crimes in which a business person or firm may be the perpetrator are income tax evasion, consumer fraud, price fixing, antitrust violations, false insurance claims, false advertising, embezzlement, and bribery.
5. Generally, any adult capable of knowing the difference between right and wrong is responsible for his or her crimes.

APPLY

Review the PROBLEM on p. 96 and discuss what kind of penalty students believe should be imposed on Gill if he is convicted. (Answers may include fines, community service, and so on.) **Guided Practice**

Have students create a three-panel cartoon illustrating how crime does not pay. In a humorous but convincing manner, have them show a crime in the first panel, the result of that action in the second panel, and the consequences of the act in the third panel. **Independent Practice**

Preventing Legal Difficulties

Review the five suggestions for preventing legal difficulties, as listed on p. 97. Discuss why this list is good advice for everyone—not just businesspeople—to follow. (Answers may include that these are practical, simple, and honest practices to follow in both our personal and professional lives.)

RETEACH Have students look through the community newspapers you or they brought to class previously. This time, scan for articles on violations of local, city, or town ordinances. Have students list the types of ordinances most often violated and, if possible, the penalties imposed.

ENRICH Divide students into two groups to research and debate the pros and cons of capital punishment (the death penalty). Students should express their views clearly and cite reasons for their views.

▼ CLOSE

As a class, close the chapter by having a spelldown, using the new vocabulary terms listed in the chapter. Divide the class into two teams. Teams accumulate points for correct responses that can be used toward a predetermined award. Orally, give one word to the first student on the first team. The student should respond by correctly spelling the word, giving a definition, and using the word in a sentence. If he or she misses, the opposing team has a chance to respond correctly. Continue until all words have been reviewed.

Assign the following end-of-chapter materials:
Student text review activities, pp. 97–101
Workbook, pp. 9–10
Chapter Test

Chapter *MicroExam*

Strengthening Your Legal Vocabulary

1. larceny
2. crime
3. antitrust laws
4. white-collar crimes
5. perjury
6. bribery
7. forgery
8. felony
9. conspiracy
10. immunity

6. Anyone accused of committing a crime has certain constitutional rights, including freedom from arrest without probable cause; the right to be represented by a lawyer; the right to cross-examine witnesses; the right to not testify against oneself; and the right to a speedy, public, fair trial.
7. Common substantive defenses are self-defense, criminal insanity, and immunity.
8. Crimes are punishable by fine, imprisonment, or both. Some states execute certain criminals.

▼ STRENGTHENING YOUR LEGAL VOCABULARY

Match each term with the statement that best defines that term. Some terms may not be used.

antitrust laws
arson
bribery
burglary
conspiracy
contempt of court
crime
criminal act
criminal battery
criminal insanity
criminal intent
defense
embezzlement
extortion
false pretenses
felony
forgery
immunity
infraction
larceny
misdemeanor
perjury
plea bargaining
procedural defenses
punishment
receiving stolen property
robbery
self-defense
substantive defenses
vicarious criminal liability
white-collar crimes

1. Wrongful taking of another's personal property.
2. Breach of duty to society for which punishment may be imposed.
3. Laws designed to foster business competition.
4. Nonviolent crimes committed by business persons.
5. Lying while testifying under oath.
6. Crime of giving or receiving money to illegally influence a governmental action.
7. Making or materially altering a writing, with intent to defraud.
8. Serious crime punishable by imprisonment in a state prison for more than one year or by execution.

9 Agreement, usually secret, between two or more people to do an unlawful act.

10 Freedom from prosecution.

APPLYING LAW TO EVERYDAY LIFE

1 Mary received a citation for failing to remove the snow from the sidewalk in front of her dress shop. The fine was $60. Mary thought the citation was unfair because she did not have enough time to shovel the snow. She received the citation five hours after the snowstorm ended. In court she protested and asked for a jury trial. When she was told that the matter would be heard only by a judge, she said her constitutional right to a trial by jury in criminal matters was being violated. Is she right?

2 ETHICS ISSUE Al started a trash collection business. After two successful years, he purchased a personal computer to handle his accounting. Later he used the computer to prepare and mail letters soliciting new customers. By mistake he merged the mailing lists of existing customers and prospective customers. As a result, 195 prospective customers received bills for trash collection services that were never provided. Twenty-seven of these people paid these bills. Did Al commit a crime when he sent out the bills? Would Al be acting unethically if he kept the money? Why or why not?

3 Phillips developed a scheme to generate funds by sending bogus bills for relatively small amounts for "District Sanitation Services" to residents of certain affluent neighborhoods. Enough people paid these bills to make the practice quite profitable. Has Phillips committed a crime? If so, what crime? How does the law distinguish between Al in Question 2 and Phillips?

4 A corporation was cited and charged with illegal pollution for dumping chemical wastes into a river. The dumping happened when an employee had mistakenly opened the wrong valve. The company pleaded not guilty because the dumping was not intentional. Moreover, neither the company nor the employee knew of the ban on dumping this particular chemical. Is either argument a good defense?

5 Baxter became intoxicated while celebrating on New Year's Eve. He drove his car the wrong way on a one-way street, struck another car head-on, and killed the other driver. Was Baxter's intoxication a good defense against a criminal charge?

6 There was nothing Love wanted more than a stereo sound system. When Harper, an older student, offered to sell him a practically new deluxe system for just $100, Love agreed to buy. But then Love said,

Applying Law to Everyday Life

1 No, Mary is not entitled to a jury trial because her offense is an infraction and there is not a risk of jail. (p. 89)

2  No, Al has not committed a crime. While the act violates the criminal law, Al lacks criminal intent. He merely made a mistake in programming his computer. Therefore, he could not be convicted of a crime. Due to a mistake, Al obtained money which he did not earn. Therefore, he can and should return the money to the rightful owners. (p. 87)

3 Yes, Phillips has committed the crime of false pretenses. Phillips's act is exactly the same as the act of Al in the previous question; however, Phillips engaged in the act with the intent to cheat people out of money. Al did not. (p. 87)

4 Neither the company nor the employee can assert as a valid defense the fact that it did not know that this particular act was criminal. Ignorance of the law is no excuse. (p. 87) However, the employee and business may escape criminal responsibility on the grounds that there was no criminal intent. The dumping of the chemical into the river was accidental. (pp. 87–88) In many instances, criminal intent is not necessary to convict a business of crime.

5 No, intoxication is ordinarily not a good defense against a criminal charge, especially when the intoxication was voluntary. (p. 88)

6 Yes, Love has committed the crime of receiving stolen goods. He should have known from the price of the stereo and the statements of Harper that the goods were stolen. (p. 91)

7 False pretenses; Buttler obtained possession of property by making a false representation and without intending to pay for the property. The jury could infer from the act of moving the plywood and hiding it that Buttler had criminal intent. (p. 91) He also committed larceny.

"Hey, how come so cheap?" Harper replied, "Had some happy hunting, and now I've got surplus stock." Later that day, the deal was completed. Has any crime been committed?

7 Buttler, a contractor, ordered $24,600 worth of plywood from K.C. Lumber Company without intending to pay for it. Buttler told the company it was to be used in building houses in a subdivision. When Buttler failed to pay for the plywood, the lumber company investigated. Its investigation revealed that after the plywood was delivered to the building site, Buttler had it transported across the state line, hidden, and resold for cash. A criminal complaint was then filed against Buttler. With what crimes could she be charged?

8 ETHICS ISSUE Sharon spent the weekend with her friend Amelia. Amelia proposed a plan for shoplifting compact disks (CDs) from a local music store. Sharon was to go to the store clerk, say she felt very ill, then pretend to faint. This distraction would allow Amelia—at the other end of the store—to place CDs in her shopping bag without risk of being seen. At first Sharon said she could not do something like that because it is against the law. Amelia argued that Sharon would not be breaking the law, only Amelia would. Is Amelia right? If a person can think of a way to profit by violating the law without risk, what reasons are there for not breaking the law?

9 Sal was trying to win a major contract for his small printing company from a large aerospace company. He had taken the purchasing agent to lunch, taken her sailing, and entertained her in his home. But from the purchasing agent's comments, Sal sensed that a competitor would get the work. So Sal sent the purchasing agent three $500 savings bonds issued in the name of her daughter as a birthday gift. Has Sal committed a crime? If so, what crime?

10 Bif was in Gail's office waiting to go to lunch with her. Gail owned a business in competition with Bif's business. When Gail excused herself to go to the restroom, Bif looked at her computer screen and saw part of a customer list. Bif had a blank 3-1/2-inch diskette which he inserted into an empty drive on the computer. He quickly typed instructions into the computer telling it to copy the file onto his diskette. Then he put his diskette in his pocket. The entire action took only twenty seconds. Bif finished long before Gail returned. Has Bif committed a crime? If so, what crime?

SOLVING CASE PROBLEMS

1 The Royal Scotsman Inn built a motel that did not comply with the building code. Therefore, Scotsman was refused an occupancy permit.

8 ETHICS ISSUE No, Amelia is wrong. Sharon would also be engaged in criminal conduct. Sharon would be an accomplice. (p. 94) Committing a crime and profiting from it is wrong because it violates the duty that we owe to our country to comply with its laws. When we commit a crime, we also injure other human beings. This violates the most fundamental moral laws.

9 Yes, Sal has committed the crime of commercial bribery. (p. 91)

10 Yes, Bif committed the crime of illegal access to a computer. (p. 93)

The chair of the county council approached a representative of the motel and offered to have "everything taken care of" in exchange for the payment of $12,000. Scotsman was faced with the possibility of a large loss of revenue. Therefore, Scotsman agreed to pay the money. The Federal Bureau of Investigation arrested the council chairperson after tape recording the discussion and seeing the exchange of the money. What crime did the council chairperson commit? (*United States v. Price,* 507 F.2d 1349)

2. Basic Construction Company was engaged in the road-paving business. Two of its lower level managers rigged bids by giving competitors the prices that Basic would bid for work. That is a criminal violation of the Sherman Antitrust Act. Will Basic be criminally liable for the conduct of its managers? (*United States v. Basic Construction Company,* 711 F.2d 570)

3. Caesar's Palace is a gambling resort in Las Vegas. Boueri was a vice president there. His job was to act as the host for special, rich guests. As part of his job he would often arrange free airfare to Las Vegas as well as free food and free shows. Evidence was presented in a criminal trial which showed that Boueri also obtained free airline tickets for people who never received them. What crime has Boueri committed? (*State of Nevada v. Boueri,* 672 P.2d 33)

4. Pack was the president of Acme Markets, Inc., a large national retail food chain. Both Pack and Acme were charged with violating criminal provisions of the federal Food, Drug, and Cosmetics Act. They were charged with allowing interstate shipments of food contaminated by rodents in an Acme warehouse. Pack defended himself by stating that although he was aware of the problem, he had delegated responsibility for the sanitary conditions of food storage to responsible subordinates. Can Pack be criminally liable in these circumstances? (*United States v. Pack,* 95 S. Ct. 1903)

5. Feinberg owned a cigar store in a very poor neighborhood of Philadelphia. He sold cans of Sterno, which contains about four percent alcohol, to people in the neighborhood who mixed it with water and drank it to become intoxicated. After conducting this business for some time, Feinberg purchased a quantity of "Institutional Sterno." It contained 54 percent alcohol. While the cans were marked "Danger," "Poison," and displayed a picture of a skull and crossbones, Feinberg did not warn his customers of the difference between the old Sterno and the Institutional Sterno. As a result, thirty-three persons died from alcohol poisoning. Did Feinberg commit a crime? (*Commonwealth v. Feinberg,* 234 A.2d 913, Pa.)

Solving Case Problems

1. Extortion; The motel was pressured into paying the money by fear of large monetary loss. (pp. 91–92)
2. Yes, Basic is criminally liable because the managers' actions advanced the interests of the corporation. (pp. 87, 90)
3. Bovueri has committed the crimes of larceny, false pretenses, and, probably, embezzlement. (pp. 90, 91)
4. Yes, Pack was liable. Delegation of responsibility is not a defense. Since Pack was aware of the problem, he is subject to criminal sanction. (pp. 87, 94–95)
5. Although Feinberg did not intend to take the lives of his customers, he acted with such gross negligence that he committed manslaughter. For this form of criminal homicide, it is enough that the defendant acted with gross disregard for the lives of others. It is an exception to the general rule that there must be criminal intent. (p. 88) In a sense, the law concludes that there are situations where we can act with such disregard for others that our carelessness becomes the legal equivalent of criminal intent.

CHAPTER 6 ORGANIZER

Chapter Theme

Torts fall under a variety of classifications and individuals may be held responsible for their own torts and, sometimes, the torts of others.

DIRECTED STUDY QUESTIONS	SPECIAL FEATURES	PROGRAM RESOURCES				
		Reteach	Enrich	SN	AM	
How do crimes and torts differ?	Thinking Critically Through Visuals, p. 103	✔	✔		V	
What are the elements of a tort?	Writing Connections, p. 105	✔	✔		K	
What are some common intentional torts?	Multicultural Highlights, p. 108 Thinking Critically Through Visuals, p. 109 Ethics Issue, pp. 109, 110	✔	✔	✔		
What is negligence?	Thinking Critically Through Visuals, p. 113	✔	✔			
What is strict liability?		✔	✔			
When is a person responsible for the torts of another?	Personal Perspectives, p. 116	✔	✔		A	
What can the victim of a tort collect?	Preventing Legal Difficulties, p. 117	✔	✔			

Additional Resources

- *Black's Law Dictionary*, 6th ed. St. Paul, MN: West Publishing Co., 1990.
- Forer, Lois G. *A Chilling Effect: The Mounting Threat of Libel and Invasion of Privacy Actions to the First Amendment.* NY: Norton, 1987.
- Lewis, Anthony. *Make No Law: The Sullivan Case and the First Amendment.* NY: Random House, 1991.
- Robinson, Joan, LL.B. *An American Legal Almanac.* Dobbs Ferry, NY: Oceana Publications, Inc., 1978.

One-semester course	✔	✔	✔					
One-year course	✔	✔	✔	✔	✔			

		ASSESSMENT OPPORTUNITIES			
	Cooperative Learning	**Informal Assessment**	**Chapter Review**	**Chapter Test**	**Chapter *MicroExam*** (Media)
		✔	✔	✔	✔
		✔	✔	✔	✔
	✔	✔	✔	✔	✔
		✔	✔	✔	✔
		✔	✔	✔	✔
		✔	✔	✔	✔
		✔	✔	✔	✔

Videodiscs

Torts: Civil Wrongs Committed by an Individual

Search Chapter 7, Play To 8

State by State

Kentucky is a state that uses comparative negligence.

Teaching Materials

Student text, pp. 102–124

Overhead transparency masters
- *Types of Torts*
- *Elements of Negligence*

Videos
- *Our Legal System* Videotape
- *Law for Business* Videodisc

Workbook, pp. 11–14

Outside Resources
- Chart paper
- Art supplies
- Newspaper tabloids
- Newspaper articles on tort cases
- Outside speakers: law enforcement officer and school counselor, vice principal, or other school administrator
- Class trip to civil court

- Camcorder
- VCR and videotapes of television shows

Assessment
- Chapter Test

- Chapter *MicroExam*

Vocabulary

tort, p. 104
proximate cause, p. 106
intentional torts, p. 106
assault, p. 107
battery, p. 107
false imprisonment, p. 107
defamation, p. 108
slander, p. 108
libel, p. 108
invasion of privacy, p. 110
trespass, p. 110
conversion, p. 111
interference with contractual relations, p. 111
fraud, p. 111
negligence, p. 112
reasonable-man standard, p. 112
contributory negligence, p. 114
comparative negligence, p. 114
assumption of the risk, p. 114
strict liability, p. 115
vicarious liability, p. 116
damages, p. 116
punitive damages, p. 117

Learning Objectives

When you complete this chapter, you will be able to

1. Explain the difference between crimes and torts.
2. Describe the elements of a tort.
3. Discuss the most common intentional torts.
4. Understand when one person is responsible for the torts of another.
5. Determine what the victim of a tort can recover.

102

Chapter Self-Test

Assess students' understanding of torts before they begin Chapter 6 by recording on the chalkboard students' oral responses to this question: **What kind of offense, do you think, is a tort?** Give them this hint: **A tort is a different kind of offense than a crime.** Before continuing with the chapter, review and discuss students' responses.

CHAPTER 6

TORTS

1 A motorcyclist deliberately rides at high speed toward a group of young people standing on a sidewalk. Frightened, the youngsters scatter, but a girl is struck and injured. What legal wrong has the motorcyclist committed?

2 Your best friend is very interested in computers. He learns the password required to gain access to your school's computer. Out of curiosity, he attempts to look at the grades of his friends. In doing this, he accidentally erases the computer records for seventy-four students. When the school discovers the problem, it spends $6,800 in overtime pay to reconstruct the records. Is your friend liable for the $6,800 even though he did not intend to erase the records?

3 

Your neighbor is using a multipurpose woodcutting machine in her basement hobby shop. Suddenly, a metal clamp from the machine breaks and strikes her left eye, badly injuring it. The defective machine is beyond the manufacturer's one-year warranty period. Can your neighbor win a suit against the manufacturer for her injury? If the manufacturer is not legally liable, do you think it would be morally obligated to pay for your neighbor's medical expenses?

FOCUS

Have this question written on the chalkboard when students arrive in class: **What examples of torts, or private or civil wrongs, can you name?** (Answers may include assault, battery, and other examples identified in the chapter.)

Introduce the discussion on torts by drawing the following chart on chart paper:

TORTS		
Known	Want to Know	Learned

Survey students on what they know about torts and those things that they want to know. Record this information in the first two columns of the chart. Keep this chart posted, and add to the columns as students progress through the chapter. Have students copy the information in their notebooks.

You Decide

1 By intentionally driving at the group, the motorcyclist committed the tort of assault. When the girl was struck, the tort of battery occurred. While the motorcyclist may not have intended to cause the injury, he or she did intend the act and is therefore liable.

2 Yes, your friend is liable for the $6,800. He committed the tort of negligence, so intent to injure is not required. He probably has also committed a computer crime.

3 

If the woodcutting machine was defectively manufactured or designed, the manufacturer is strictly liable for the injury. Your neighbor can recover even though the warranty period has expired. Even if the manufacturer were not legally liable, it would still be morally obligated to pay your neighbor's medical expenses.

Thinking Critically Through Visuals

Imagine that the photograph is a visual image of the start of what a witness observed. Putting all the clues together, what else, do you think, did the witness report? (Answers may include that the person in the doorway disregarded the *Wet Floor* sign, slipped on the wet floor and fell.)

HOW DO CRIMES AND TORTS DIFFER?

PROBLEM

After an exhausting day of skiing, Josephina was driving home near sunset. She dozed off momentarily and crossed the highway dividing lane. She then crashed head-on into John's panel truck. Both drivers were seriously injured, and their vehicles were "totaled." Although Josephina was asleep at the time, has she violated any rights of the other driver?

In Chapter 5, you learned that a crime is an offense against society. It is a public wrong. A **tort**, in contrast, is a private or civil wrong; it is an offense only against an individual. If someone commits a tort, the person injured can sue and obtain a judgment for money damages. The money is intended to compensate for the injury.

One act can be both a tort and a crime. In the problem, Josephina committed an offense against society—the crime of "reckless driving." Police will investigate the crime, then give her a ticket or possibly arrest her. A county or district attorney will prosecute her in a criminal trial. If convicted, she may be fined or jailed. But Josephina also committed a tort by injuring John and his property. John may bring a civil suit against Josephina. If John wins, he can obtain a judgment against her as compensation for his injuries. Thus, Josephina's one act caused her to be criminally liable (for a fine and/or a jail sentence) and civilly liable (for monetary damages).

WHAT ARE THE ELEMENTS OF A TORT?

PROBLEM

On a windy autumn day, Mason was burning dry leaves in his backyard. When he went inside to answer a telephone call, flames from the fire leaped to the next-door neighbor's fence and then to a tool shed where a small can of gasoline exploded. Soon the neighbor's house was ablaze, and it burned to the ground. Was a tort committed by Mason?

Like criminal law, tort law is a broad legal category. Just as there are many specific crimes, such as murder and larceny, there are many specific

TEACH

After distinguishing between a tort and a crime, you may wish to anticipate and eliminate students' confusion by emphasizing up front that while a tort is not the same as a crime, one act may be both a tort and crime.

APPLY

Ask a student volunteer to read aloud the PROBLEM on the top of p. 104. Begin a class discussion by asking students to answer the question at the end of the PROBLEM. Ask them to defend their answers. (Yes, Josephina committed a tort against John.) **Guided Practice**

Ask students to restate in writing, in their own words, using a computer, if possible, how Josephina's one act caused her to be both criminally and civilly liable.

Independent Practice

TEACH

Ask students if they know what elements need to be present for an action to be considered a tort. Remind students that the four elements of a tort are: duty, breach, injury, and causation. Make sure students understand that all these elements must be proved to establish liability.

ASSESS

Learning Objective 1 Check students' understanding of the difference between torts and crimes by asking them to write the following statements as you read them aloud. Then have students mark *T* next to the ones that apply to torts, and *C* next to the ones that apply to crimes. **(1) It is an offense against society.** (C); **(2) It is a private or civil wrong.** (T); **(3) It is punishable by monetary damages.** (T); and **(4) It is punishable by a fine and/or a jail sentence.** (C) torts. There are, however, certain elements that are common to most torts. In a trial, these elements must be proved to establish liability (i.e., legal responsibility) for any specific tort. The elements of a tort are the following:

1. duty: a legal obligation owed another to do (or not to do) something,
2. breach: a violation of the duty,
3. injury: a harm that is recognized by the law, and
4. causation: proof that the breach caused the injury.

Thus, in the problem, Mason committed a tort because: (1) he owed a duty to the neighbors not to injure their property; (2) he breached the duty when he left the fire unattended so it spread to the neighbor's property; (3) the injury occurred when the neighbor's house was burned; and (4) leaving the fire unattended was a cause of the burning. Therefore, the neighbor can obtain a judgment against Mason for the value of the fence, the tool shed, and the house.

1. The Duty

By law, everyone has certain rights. Since everyone has the duty to respect the rights of others, everyone therefore has certain related duties. The following are the principal duties created by tort law:

1. the duty not to injure another: this includes bodily injury, injury to someone's reputation, or invasion of someone's privacy;
2. the duty not to interfere with the property rights of others, for example, by trespassing on their land; and
3. the duty not to interfere with the economic rights of others, such as the right to contract.

Whether or not a duty exists in a certain situation is a question of law for the judge to decide. A judge will make this decision by consulting state case law and state statutory law. Only occasionally is federal law the basis for a tort suit.

2. Violation of the Duty

A breach, or violation of the duty, must be proved before the injured party can collect damages. Whether there has been a breach of a tort duty is almost always a question of fact for a jury to decide.

▼APPLY

Write on the chalkboard the four common elements of a tort as they appear in the student text on p. 105. Then write their corresponding definitions in a different order. Have students copy the terms and write the correct definition next to the corresponding term. **Guided Practice**

Have students work in groups of three or four to create one- or three-dimensional art, such as pictures, clay scenes, or montages, that depict one or more of the three principal duties required by tort law. Have students label their artwork with the appropriate duty or duties.

Independent Practice

Language Arts/ Music

Have students work in groups of three or four to compose a riddle, poem, rap, or song that helps them remember the four elements of a tort. Then, ask student volunteers to perform their projects for the class. If possible, videotape the performances to use as a

review at the end of this chapter.

▼RETEACH Pair students to create a graphic organizer to compare the characteristics of torts and crimes.

▼ENRICH Divide students into groups of two or three. Assign each group to write a scenario for one of the following: a tort, only; a crime, only; and both a tort and a crime. Ask one volunteer from each group to read aloud and lead a discussion on his or her scenario.

In groups of three or four, have students brainstorm a scenario in which a tort is committed. Then have them write it in their notebooks. Have one member of each group read aloud his or her group's scenario to the class. Have students in other groups point out the four elements that characterize each scenario as a tort.

Many torts acknowledge a breach only when the defendant possesses a particular mental state at the time of the breach. Some torts require that the breach be intentional. In other torts, intent is not required; it is enough if the breach occurred because someone was careless or negligent. In still other torts, even carelessness is not required. Liability is imposed simply because a duty was violated and this caused injury. Torts are often classified on the basis of these varying mental requirements. One group of torts is called intentional torts. Another tort is called negligence. The last group, where neither intent nor carelessness is required, is called strict liability.

3. Injury

Generally, injury resulting from the breach of duty must be proved. Thus, if you act very recklessly, but no one is injured, there is usually no tort.

4. Causation

Causation is simply the idea that breach of the duty caused the injury. There are degrees of causation. For example, one can argue that the first people on earth are the ultimate causes of every injury that occurs in the world today. When the amount of causation is great enough for it to be recognized by the law, it is called **proximate cause.** Generally, proximate cause exists when it is reasonably foreseeable that a particular breach of duty will result in a particular injury.

TEACH

Direct students' attention to the section title *What Are Some Common Intentional Torts?* Ask: **What does intentional mean?** (Answers may include that a person intends, or means, to do something or does it willfully, deliberately, or knowingly.)

Make certain that students understand that there are two types of intent: intent to do the act, and intent to injure the victim. Review with students the five common intentional torts against persons (assault, battery, false imprisonment, defamation, and invasion of privacy). Ask students if they can name the four common intentional torts against property. Remind them that they are trespass, conversion, interference with contractual relations, and fraud.

WHAT ARE SOME COMMON INTENTIONAL TORTS?

PROBLEM

During deer-hunting season, Hart drove miles into the country in search of game. He parked his pickup truck alongside a dirt road, climbed a fence, and hiked into the woods. Hart thought the land was part of a national forest. However, it actually belonged to Quincy, who had posted "No Trespassing" signs. Confronted by Quincy, Hart apologized for his mistake and left. Was Hart guilty of a tort?

Intentional torts are those where the defendant intended either the injury or the act. These torts contrast with negligence and strict liability,

ASSESS

Learning Objective 2 Have students work in pairs. After students list from memory the four elements of a tort and their definitions, they should review the information on pp. 104–106, correcting their own work. Have students exchange papers and discuss any questions or problems with their partners.

where intent to engage in the act or to produce the injury is not required. Specific intentional torts against persons are presented below. They are followed by intentional torts against property.

1. Assault

The tort of **assault** occurs when one person intentionally *threatens to injure another.* The threat can be made with words or gestures. The threat must be believable, so there must be an apparent ability to carry it out. The threatened injury can be physical (e.g., a stab) or it can be offensive sexual touching (threatening to kiss someone).

Spencer, elderly and totally blind, thought Wills had swindled him. Spencer told Wills that he was going to "beat your face to a pulp." Because it was obvious that Spencer could not carry out his threat, there was no assault.

2. Battery

A person has the right to be free from harmful or offensive touching. An intentional breach of the duty is a **battery**. Shooting, pushing in anger, spitting on, or throwing a pie in the face are all batteries. An assault frequently precedes a battery. Thus, angrily raising a clenched fist and then striking someone in the face involves first an assault (the raised fist) and then a battery (the blow to the face). When the victim is hit without warning from behind, there is a battery without assault.

Even though there is harmful or offensive touching, there may be no battery. If the contact is not intentional, there is no battery. Also, the contact may be justified. For example, when you act in self-defense, you have not committed a battery. Further, there may be consent to the contact. Thus, in a boxing contest, there is no battery because the boxers consent to the offensive touching.

3. False Imprisonment

False imprisonment is depriving a person of freedom of movement without consent and without privilege.

▼ APPLY

Direct students' attention to the first two boldfaced terms—**assault** and **battery**—on p. 107. Ask student volunteers to explain, perhaps visually, how each term fits the general definition of tort. **Guided Practice**

Copy the following graphic organizer (without the answers) on the chalkboard. Have students complete it by writing words that describe the terms **assault** and **battery**. **Independent Practice**

Assault	Battery
Threats Gestures Intent to harm	Pushing Harmful touching Offensive touching

Present the following situations to the class and ask students if the cases would be considered assault, battery, or assault and battery: **The quarterback gets his leg broken in the Super Bowl right after a tackle.** (Neither; football players consent to offensive touching.) **You are walking in a deserted shopping center parking lot when a man approaches you from behind and hits you over the head with a baseball bat.** (Only battery; no threat or warning was given.) Have student volunteers role-play other torts for the class.

▼RETEACH Direct students' attention to the four terms at the top of p. 105. As you call out a term in random order, have students say the corresponding definition.

▼ENRICH Challenge students to think of a creative mnemonic device to remember the four elements of a tort, such as *Dogs Bark In Cars* (Duty, Breach, Injury, and Causation).

Multicultural Highlights

During the Civil Rights Movement of the 1960s, Dr. Martin Luther King, Jr., called for his followers, including fellow African Americans, to practice nonviolence and non-hatred in the face of assault, battery, and false imprisonment. King's dream was to peacefully end discrimination so that all Americans could enjoy the freedoms promised by the U.S. Constitution. Ask: **What examples can you give that King's dreams have or have not become realities in today's society?** (Answers may include the Los Angeles riots and a reduction in state-sanctioned segregation.)

Ask students: **What do assault and battery and false imprisonment have in common?** (All are threats to personal safety.) Have students brainstorm ways a person could be falsely imprisoned. (Kidnapped, held hostage, abducted) Discuss with students how they can lessen their chances of being a victim of such personal torts.

> While Augusto was driving Sharon on a date to the theater, she became angry and told him to stop the car and let her out. Augusto refused and increased his speed to make it impossible for Sharon to get out. He kept her in the car this way for one-half hour. Augusto has falsely imprisoned Sharon.

Persons are deprived of freedom of movement when they are handcuffed; locked in a room, car, or jail; told in a threatening way to stay in one place; or otherwise deprived of their liberty. Consent occurs, for example, when a suspected shoplifter voluntarily stays in the store in an attempt to establish innocence. When a burglary suspect sits voluntarily in a police car to describe his actions over the last hour, the suspect consents to being detained. If either suspect is prevented from leaving when they want to, their consent evaporates.

Privilege justifies the imprisonment of a person. When the police have probable cause to arrest people, they are privileged to imprison them. But if the police mistake the identity of one person for another, they may commit false imprisonment in the course of the arrest. Merchants in many states have a privilege to detain a person if they have a reasonable basis for believing the person was shoplifting. If they detain persons against their will without a reasonable basis, they falsely imprison them.

> Edna was dressed in jeans, old tennis shoes, and a torn, faded shirt when she went shopping in an expensive high-fashion department store. A security officer became suspicious of her because of her mode of dress. As Edna was leaving, she was stopped and asked to empty her pockets. Outraged, she said, "Leave me alone." When she tried to leave, the security officer produced handcuffs and said, "If you don't cooperate, I'll cuff you until the police get here." The security officer did not have a reasonable basis for detaining Edna. Therefore, she was falsely imprisoned.

4. Defamation

Statements about people can injure them. If a false statement injures one's reputation, it may constitute the tort of **defamation**. If the defamation is spoken, it is **slander**. If the defamation is written or printed, it is **libel**. To be legally defamatory, the statement must (1) be false (truth is a

ASSESS

Media After covering up all the terms except *Intentional Torts* and *Torts Against Property,* display the overhead transparency *Types of Torts.* Have students copy the graphic organizer as it appears on the screen. Then, have students fill in the four torts against persons that they have learned about so far. After students have completed their organizers, call on volunteers to write the correct terms on the transparency. Instruct students to hold onto their graphic organizers for future completion.

complete defense), (2) be communicated to a third person (one's reputation is not harmed if no other person hears or reads the lie), and (3) bring the victim into disrepute, contempt, or ridicule by others.

> A news commentator reported on a radio program that an officer of a local corporation had a conflict of interest. The commentator said that a small company secretly owned by the officer was selling goods to the corporation at a high profit to the officer. This was true. Therefore, the news commentator was not guilty of defamation. Truth is a complete defense to a charge of defamation.

An exception to the definition of defamation exists for statements about public officials or prominent personalities. There is no liability in such cases unless the statement was made with actual malice; that is, the statement was known to be false when made. This exception is intended to encourage free discussion of issues of public concern. For the same reason, legislators' statements, even those made with malice, are immune from liability if made during legislative meetings. Judges, lawyers, jurors, witnesses, and other parties in judicial proceedings are also immune from liability for statements made during the actual trial or hearing.

Thinking Critically Through Visuals

Former President George Bush set as one of the goals of his Presidency the improvement of education. What mistake does the cartoon show President Bush making? (Spelling mistakes) **Is the cartoon ethical if it misrepresents the President's spelling ability?** (No)

ETHICS ISSUE

Ethics Issue

You may wish to bring to class videotapes of skits from current popular television shows that are spoofs of celebrities. In selecting and playing the videotapes, the class discussion should focus on the ethical issues involved in these portrayals,

even when there is no defamation.

Assign to each of four groups responsibility for summarizing and reporting orally and visually, by using the chalkboard, flip chart, or overhead projector, a different one of these four intentional torts: **assault, battery, false imprisonment,** and **defamation.**

Have students create and videotape a skit that incorporates the four common intentional torts. Remind students that they should be sensitive to the feelings of group members and the people they portray.

Ethics Issue

Check with your school administrators or school-board policy on bringing tabloids to class. If permissible, then hand out a few articles from this type of newspaper for students to quickly peruse. Ask students to imagine what it would be like if they found similar invasive stories written about them in their school newspaper. Ask students if buying the "scandal sheets," while not making the buyer legally responsible for invasion of privacy, does make the buyer morally responsible by keeping the papers in business. Ask and discuss: **Should people boycott such newspapers?**

To help limited English proficiency students and students with a minimal command of English, ask student volunteers to pantomime the nine intentional torts, one at a time. After the class has determined which tort is being acted out, have a student write on the

chalkboard the term that describes the tort.

5. Invasion of Privacy

People are entitled to keep personal matters private. This is the right to privacy. Congress has stated that "the right of privacy is a personal and fundamental right protected by the Constitution of the United States." Invasion of this right is the tort of **invasion of privacy.** This tort is defined as the unwelcome and unlawful intrusion into one's private life so as to cause outrage, mental suffering, or humiliation.

This right includes freedom from unnecessary publicity regarding personal matters. Notice that, unlike defamation, publication of a true statement may be an invasion of privacy. The right protects us from being spied upon when we do not expect that. Thus two-way mirrors in the women's restroom of a gas station would constitute an invasion of privacy. On the other hand, a two-way mirror in the dressing room of a department store would not be an invasion of privacy if signs informed customers of that fact. The right to privacy also includes freedom from commercial exploitation of one's name, picture, or endorsement without permission. The right to privacy bans illegal eavesdropping by any listening device, interference with telephone calls, and unauthorized opening of letters and telegrams.

However, the right of privacy is not unlimited. For example, the police are permitted to tap telephone lines secretly if they have a warrant to do so. Also, public figures, such as politicians, actors, and people in the news, give up some of their right to privacy when they step into the public domain.

6. Trespass

The tort of **trespass** is entry onto the realty of another without the owner's consent. However, trespass may consist of other forms of interference with the possession of property. Dumping rubbish on the land of another or breaking the windows of a neighbor's house are also trespasses.

Of course, intent is required to commit the tort of trespass. However, the only requirement is that the intruder intended to be on the particular property. If a person was thrown onto another's land, there would be no intent and no trespass. If a person thought she was walking on her own property, but was mistaken, there would be a trespass because she intended to be on that particular property. Thus, in the problem, Hart was guilty of trespass, even though he thought he was in a national forest.

7. Conversion

People who own personal property, such as diamond rings, have the right to control their possession and their use. This right is violated if the property is stolen, destroyed, or used in a manner inconsistent with the owner's

▼ ASSESS

Learning Objective 3 Display the overhead transparency *Types of Torts.* Have students take out their copies of the graphic organizer and review the information completed so far. Then, direct them to complete the information on *Intentional Torts.* After completing *Torts Against Persons* and *Torts Against Property* on their organizers, ask volunteers to write the correct terms on the transparency. Tell students to keep their graphic organizers for future additions.

rights. If that happens, a **conversion** occurs. A thief is always a converter. Conversion occurs even when the converter does not know that there is a conversion. So, the innocent buyer of stolen goods is a converter. Intent to do just the act is enough. The party injured by the conversion can recover damages. Or the converter can, in effect, be compelled to purchase the converted goods from their owner.

Sanchez went on a three-week vacation. He left the key to his house with his neighbor, Buckley. Without permission, Buckley used the key to get into Sanchez's garage to borrow Sanchez's new chain saw. Buckley used the chain saw for two weeks to cut up nine cords of firewood. When Sanchez returned home and discovered what had happened, he sued Buckley. Sanchez could recover the rental value of the chain saw. Or he could let Buckley keep the chain saw and sue for the price of a new one.

8. Interference With Contractual Relations

Every individual has the legal right to enter into contracts. Parties to a contract may be able to breach the contract if they pay for the injury suffered by the other party; that is, if they pay contract damages. But if a third party entices or encourages the breach, that third party may be liable in tort to the nonbreaching party. This is called the tort of **interference with contractual relations.**

A brilliant scientist had a long-term employment contract to do genetic research at a famous university. A competing research laboratory persuaded the scientist to breach the agreement and come to work for it. As a result, the university could sue the scientist for breach of contract. In addition, the university could sue the laboratory for the tort of interference with contractual relations.

9. Fraud

Fraud occurs when there is an intentional misrepresentation of an existing important fact (i.e., a lie). The misrepresentation must be relied on and cause financial injury.

▼ APPLY

Divide the class into two groups and hold a 15-minute debate on the following topic: *Should a public figure have the right to privacy?* Have students choose one of these roles: facilitator (one), recorders (two), debaters (two), timekeeper (one), impartial scorers/panel of judges (five), researchers (all others). If students are unfamiliar with debate procedure, you may wish to provide direction and guidance. **Cooperative Learning**

Provide information for students or have them do research about local ordinances dealing with the crime of fraud. You may wish to invite a local law enforcement officer or criminal lawyer to class to discuss the tort and crime of fraud.

▼RETEACH Divide the class into two teams. On the chalkboard, write two headings: **Common Intentional Torts Against Persons** and **Common Intentional Torts Against Property**. Have each team send representatives to the chalkboard, one at a time, to write a common intentional tort under the correct heading.

Using computers if possible, have students create a flier or brochure titled *Know Your Rights* describing what intentional torts are and how they violate a person's rights.

▼ TEACH

Make certain that students understand the meaning of **negligence** and can differentiate between negligence and intent. Point out to students that the difference between a negligent tort and an intentional tort has to do with motivation. The person who commits a negligent tort does not deliberately set out to cause personal or property injury, but causes injury through carelessness. The person who commits an intentional tort, on the other hand, commits a deliberate injury.

▼ APPLY

Direct students' attention to the PROBLEM on p. 112. Have students discuss whether Britt committed a negligent or intentional tort. Make certain that students refer to all the relevant pieces of information, and note the role alcohol played in the scenario. **Guided Practice**

Smith is trying to sell her home. While showing the property to Hernandez, Smith said, "This roof is in very good repair and has never leaked." Hernandez buys the house and later learns that the roof leaks and is in need of repairs costing $8,500. Hernandez also learns that Smith was given an estimate for similar repairs before the sale occurred. Smith committed fraud and is liable to Hernandez.

▼ WHAT IS NEGLIGENCE?

PROBLEM

Britt was driving home late one rainy night after drinking alcohol all evening. She raced down residential streets at speeds up to fifty miles per hour with only one working headlight. Meanwhile, Yee was slowly backing her station wagon out of her driveway, but she failed to look both ways when she should have. Britt rammed into the right rear end of Yee's car. Yee's station wagon was badly damaged, and she was injured. Can Yee collect from Britt?

Negligence is the most common tort. Intent is not required for this tort, only carelessness. Like the other torts, negligence involves the elements of a duty, breach of the duty, causation, and injury.

1. The Duty in Negligence

The general duty imposed by negligence law is the **reasonable-man standard.** This duty requires that we act with the care, prudence, and good judgment of a reasonable person so as not to cause injury to others.

For certain individuals, a different degree of care is applied. For example, children under age seven are presumed incapable of negligence. Older children are only required to act with the care that a reasonable child of like age, intelligence, and experience would act. If, however, a child undertakes an adult activity, such as driving a boat or a car, the child is held to the adult standard.

Professionals and skilled tradespersons are held to a higher degree of care in their work. These persons are required to work with the degree of care and skill that is normally possessed by members of the profession or trade. Thus, an attorney must act with the care and skill normally possessed by

▼ ASSESS

Media

After covering over the terms *duty, breach of duty, injury, and causation,* distribute to students copies of the overhead transparency master *Elements of Negligence.* Have students recall and write above the definitions (in the space where the terms originally appeared on the overhead transparency) the four elements of negligence defined in their texts on pp. 112–113. Remind students that these four elements of negligence are the same four elements of any tort.

other attorneys in his or her community. Similarly, a plumber must perform work with the care and skill normally exercised by other plumbers in the community.

2. The Breach of Duty in Negligence

The reasonable-man standard defines the duty. A defendant's conduct, such as that of Britt in the problem, is compared with the reasonable-man standard to determine whether a violation of the duty has occurred. We could conclude that a reasonable person would drive a car only at a safe speed, only when sober, and at night only when the car's lights work. Since Britt engaged in speeding, driving while intoxicated, and driving at night without proper lights, she clearly violated the reasonable-man standard.

3. Causation and Injury in Negligence

As with other torts, the violation of the duty must be the cause of the injury. In the problem, Britt's speeding was a breach of the duty and it is reasonably foreseeable that speeding will cause injury. In fact, speeding was the cause of the property damage to the station wagon and the personal injury to Yee.

Thinking Critically Through Visuals

The woman in the photograph is using a soldering iron. What might she do with this tool that might be considered negligent? (Answers may include act recklessly, carelessly, without good judgment, and so on.)

Direct students' attention to the chapter-opening visual on p. 103. Ask: **Now that you have studied duty, breach of duty, causation, and injury in negligence, was there negligence involved if the person standing in the doorway slipped and fell on the floor?** (Answers may include a reference to whether the person who mopped the floor and the person who put the sign on the floor acted with care and good judgment so as not to hurt themselves or others.) Tell students to withhold final judgment until they discuss the next section, *Defenses to Negligence.*

▼RETEACH Media Distribute to students copies of the *Elements of Negligence* overhead transparency master, on which you have covered the descriptions of the four elements of negligence. Working in pairs, have students use their textbooks to write notes about the elements in the boxes.

▼ENRICH Have students create a graphic organizer on which they compare intentional and negligent torts.

With students' help, outline on the chalkboard the three defenses to negligence. Ask: **Which of these defenses pertains to the incident pictured on p. 103?** (Assumption of the risk)

In view of what students now know about defenses to negligence in general, and assumption of the risk, in particular, ask students to rethink their positions concerning the negligence involved in the incident pictured on p. 103. Have students use a computer, if possible, to compose a few paragraphs on their decisions.

Independent Practice

▼ TEACH

Make sure that students understand **strict liability**, liability that exists even though the defendant was not negligent. Emphasize that the plaintiff is not required to prove either intent or negligence in strict liability cases.

4. Defenses to Negligence

In many states, a plaintiff cannot recover for loss caused by another's negligence if the plaintiff was **contributorily negligent.** This occurs when the plaintiff's own negligence was a partial cause of the injury. For example, in the problem, Yee backed up without looking behind her. That and Britt's speeding were causes of the accident. So Yee was contributorily negligent. If she lived in a state that recognizes contributory negligence, she could not recover from Britt. Under this legal rule, it does not matter that one party, like Britt, was very negligent and primarily responsible for causing the collision while the other, like Yee, was only slightly negligent.

Most states have substituted **comparative negligence** for contributory negligence. Comparative negligence applies when a plaintiff in a negligence action is partially at fault. Then the plaintiff is awarded damages, but they are reduced in proportion to the plaintiff's negligence.

Curtis tripped over an electric cord lying across a walkway in Emerson's Electric Shop and suffered a broken hip. The cord was visible, and Curtis would have noticed it if she had not been wearing dark sunglasses indoors. In a legal action, the jury found her damages to be $50,000. But the jury concluded that she contributed sixty percent of the total negligence. Therefore, the judge deducted $30,000 and awarded Curtis judgment for $20,000.

Assumption of the risk is another defense to negligence. If plaintiffs are aware of a danger, but decide to subject themselves to the risk, that is a defense. Suppose you walk into a fast food restaurant and see a sign stating "Danger! This floor is slippery due to mopping." Then, as you walk through the wet area, you slip, fall, and break your arm. The danger was created by the restaurant but you assumed the risk after being informed of the danger. You could not recover in negligence because of the defense of assumption of the risk.

▼ WHAT IS STRICT LIABILITY?

PROBLEM

Mrs. Lamb went to a grocery store and placed a carton of a carbonated soft drink in her shopping cart. One of the bottles exploded and the broken glass cut her leg. Can she collect in tort from the grocery store or the bottler?

▼ ASSESS

Display the overhead transparency *Types of Torts* that has been partially filled in by students in previous assessment activities. Have students name the other two types of torts (negligence and strict liability) and write those terms on the transparency.

Sometimes the law holds one liable in tort on the basis of absolute or **strict liability.** This is liability that exists even though the defendant was not negligent. In essence, strict liability makes the defendant liable if he or she engaged in a particular activity that resulted in injury. In strict liability, proof of both the activity and the injury substitutes for proof of a violation of a duty.

Engaging in abnormally dangerous activities, such as target practice, blasting, crop burning, or storing flammable liquids in large quantities, gives rise to strict liability. If you engage in activities of this type and someone is injured as a result, you will be liable.

Ownership of dangerous animals also subjects one to strict liability. Domesticated animals are not considered dangerous unless the owner knows that a particular animal is dangerous. Dogs, cats, cows, and horses are domesticated animals. Bears, tigers, snakes, elephants, and monkeys are wild or dangerous animals. If the dangerous animal causes injury, the owner is strictly liable.

A third strict-liability activity is the sale of goods that are unreasonably dangerous. If the goods are defective, the defect makes them dangerous, and this causes an injury, any merchant who sold those goods is strictly liable, as is the manufacturer.

Under strict liability, the manufacturer and any seller in the chain of distribution are liable to any buyer of the defective product who is injured by it. The effect of strict liability is that the manufacturer held liable will increase the price and thus spread the cost to all consumers of the product. Without strict liability, the victim might receive no compensation because negligence may be difficult to prove. In the problem, Mrs. Lamb could collect from either the store or the bottler under strict liability. The bottle was defective, and this defect made the product unreasonably dangerous.

WHEN IS A PERSON RESPONSIBLE FOR THE TORTS OF ANOTHER?

PROBLEM

Hunt was taking riding lessons from Saddleback Stables. Patterson, the Saddleback instructor, was a skilled rider although only seventeen years old. Nevertheless, Patterson negligently lost control of the horse that Hunt was riding. As a result, Hunt was thrown to the ground and injured. Who was liable for Hunt's injuries?

In general, all persons, including minors, are responsible for their conduct and are therefore liable for their torts. Thus, even children or insane persons

APPLY

Direct students' attention to the sentence on p. 115 that contains the vocabulary term **strict liability.** Ask: **What is a synonym for this term?** (Absolute liability) **Guided Practice**

Divide the class into four groups. Assign each group to role-play a tort that would fall under strict liability. Ask the class to identify the evidence needed to prove the tort in court. **Independent Practice**

TEACH

Remind students that their discussion of responsibility for torts has focused on the individual committing the tort. Ask: **Can you think of a situation in which one person is responsible for the torts committed by others?** (Answers may include examples of corporations being responsible for injury caused by their employees.)

Write the term **vicarious liability** on the chalkboard. Ask students to make educated guesses on the term's definition based on the sentence: *The servant lived vicariously through the prince's adventure stories.*

RETEACH Assign to each of five groups the responsibility for summarizing and reporting orally and visually one of the five common intentional torts discussed on pp. 110–111. Have a sixth group review the four intentional torts discussed on pp. 106–109: **assault, battery, false imprisonment,** and **defamation**.

ENRICH Bring in newspapers for students to find articles on torts. Have students clip articles, categorize them according to type of tort, and create a bulletin board titled "Here a Tort, There a Tort."

▼ APPLY

Invite a school administrator or law-enforcement representative to discuss school-related torts for which parents would be responsible. Have students prepare questions to ask the speaker.

Guided Practice

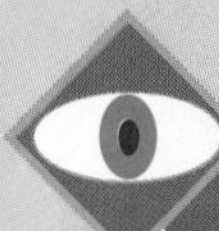

Personal Perspectives

Have students use the information they learned from the speaker to initiate a discussion with their parents or guardians on **vicarious liability.** Ask students to write in their journals the results of their at-home conversations. **Independent Practice**

▼ TEACH

Review with students what the victim of a tort can collect. (Damages and/or punitive damages)

may be held liable for injuring others. So in the problem, Patterson would be liable to Hunt even though he was only seventeen years old.

When one person is liable for the torts of another, the liability is called **vicarious liability.** With some exceptions, parents are not liable for the torts of their children. In some states, by statute, parents are liable up to a specified amount of money for property damage by their minor children. This is usually designed to cover vandalism and malicious destruction of school property. Most states also provide that parents are liable, up to the limits of financial responsibility laws, for damages negligently caused by their children while operating motor vehicles. Parents may also be liable if they give their children "dangerous instrumentalities," such as guns, without proper instructions. Similarly, parents may be liable for their children's continuing dangerous habits, such as throwing rocks at trains and vehicles, if they fail to stop the behavior.

The most common example of vicarious liability is the liability of an employer for the acts of employees committed within the scope of the employment. In the problem, Saddleback Stables was liable for the negligence of its employee Patterson. In such situations, the injured party may sue both the employer and the employee.

▼ WHAT CAN THE VICTIM OF A TORT COLLECT?

PROBLEM

Horsley, the owner of a dry cleaning store, lived next door to Early, who was the editor of a small newspaper in their town. The two quarreled frequently and became enemies. As a consequence, when Early published a story on the drug problem in the town, he identified Horsley as "a drug dealer." This statement was untrue. What can Horsley collect from Early?

Damages are awarded to the injured party to compensate for loss caused by tort. The purpose of the award is to place the injured party in the same financial position as if the tort had not occurred. In many cases, the loss may be difficult to measure. An example is where negligence causes bodily injury with ongoing pain and suffering or even death. However, the dollar value of the injury or loss must be set. This value is usually decided by a jury.

In the problem, if Horsley could prove that Early's defamation injured her business, she could probably get damages as compensation. If Horsley could

▼ ASSESS

Learning Objectives 4 & 5 As you read the following statements, have students copy and then answer these true or false questions on a sheet of paper: **(1) The victim of a tort is barred from collecting monetary compensation for an injury.** (False); and **(2) Parents are the only individuals held responsible for the torts of others.** (False) prove that Early acted with malice (deliberate intention to cause injury), the jury might award her additional **punitive damages.** These damages would be awarded as punishment for Early's malicious defamation and as an example to deter others. Malice or gross negligence must usually be proved to collect punitive damages.

Preventing Legal Difficulties

In the world of torts, remember...

1. Avoid legal liability for torts by consistently respecting other persons and their property.
2. Ignorance of the law is no excuse for any violation of the law.
3. If you commit a tort or are the victim of a tort that may lead to a lawsuit, promptly consult a lawyer. Critical evidence may be lost if you delay.
4. In some states, your own negligence—however slight—may bar any recovery under the doctrine of contributory negligence. However, in many states, the doctrine of comparative negligence may permit recovery. Check with your lawyer.
5. If you injure a third party while on the job, both you and your employer may be liable. The employer, or an insurer, would probably pay, but the incident could cost you your job.
6. Minors are generally liable for their torts.
7. The automobile is the principal source of tort liability for most persons, young and old. Drive carefully.
8. If you are injured by a tort, do not be rushed by insurance adjusters or others into signing a statement releasing the other party from liability. Let your lawyer decide if the settlement offer is fair.

▼ REVIEWING IMPORTANT POINTS

1. A tort is an unlawful act that causes private injury to the person or property of another.
2. Most crimes are also torts, but not all torts are crimes.
3. Torts may be broadly classified as intentional torts, negligence, or strict liability.

▼ APPLY

Read aloud the PROBLEM on p. 116. Ask: **Who is the victim of the tort?** (Horsley) **Why?** (Because Early identified him unjustly as "a drug dealer") **Guided Practice**

Ask student volunteers to research and assess no-fault car insurance to determine what the victim of a tort can collect. Have students write a report, on the computer if possible, about the rights of a car accident victim.

Independent Practice

Preventing Legal Difficulties

Working in pairs, have students select, discuss, and record in their notebooks one of the points to remember about torts. Ask for volunteers to present advice for preventing three specific torts.

Divide the class into groups of four. Have half create PROBLEM activities dealing with **vicarious liability** and the other half with **damages**. Have volunteers act out scenarios and lead discussions on the solutions.

Have students refer to the PROBLEM activities on pp. 104, 106, 112, and 114–116. Have students write an essay called "Commit a Tort, See You in Court" describing damages they would reward to the plaintiffs and why.

▼ CLOSE

On clean copies of the overhead transparency master, *Types of Torts* (with all the type except the title covered), have students work in groups of three to complete the organizer without the use of notes or books. Display and review

the overhead transparency with the answers.

You may wish to show the videotape on the tort

presentations that students made earlier.

Assign the following end-of-chapter materials:
Student text review activities, pp. 117–122
Workbook, pp. 11–12
Chapter Test

Chapter *MicroExam*

▼ Strengthening Your Legal Vocabulary ▼

1. assumption of the risk
2. false imprisonment
3. defamation
4. negligence
5. trespass
6. contributory negligence
7. proximate cause
8. damages
9. battery
10. vicarious liability

4. The most common tort is negligence, which is the failure to act with reasonable care, thus causing a foreseeable injury to another.

5. In a tort caused by negligence, the negligent act (or failure to act) must be the proximate cause of the injury. That is, the injury must follow as a natural and reasonably foreseeable effect of the act (or failure to act).

6. Generally every individual is personally responsible for damage resulting from any torts committed by that individual. Employers are also liable for the torts of their employees if the torts are committed within the scope of the employees' employment.

7. In some states, if the injured person was also negligent and the negligence contributed to the injury, the injured person may be barred from recovering damages. In many states today, however, some recovery may be obtained under the doctrine of comparative negligence.

8. A person injured by a tort is entitled to damages—monetary compensation for the loss or injury suffered. The amount of damages is determined by the jury.

▼ STRENGTHENING YOUR LEGAL VOCABULARY

Match each term with the statement that best defines that term. Some terms may not be used.

assault
assumption of the risk
battery
comparative negligence
contributory negligence
conversion
damages
defamation
false imprisonment
fraud
intentional torts
interference with contractual relations
invasion of privacy
libel
negligence
proximate cause
punitive damages
reasonable-man standard
slander
strict liability
tort
trespass
vicarious liability

1. A defense to negligence based on the plaintiff knowingly subjecting himself or herself to the dangers created by the defendant.

2. Depriving a person of freedom of movement without their consent and without privilege.

3 Injury of a person's reputation by false oral or written statements.

4 Failure to use reasonable care.

5 Temporary or partial interference with the right to possession and use of one's property.

6 Plaintiff's failure to exercise reasonable care to avoid injury, which bars recovery of any damages.

7 Natural and foreseeable cause of injury.

8 Compensation for injury.

9 Harmful or offensive personal touching without consent or legal justification.

10 Responsibility of one person for the torts of another.

APPLYING LAW TO EVERYDAY LIFE

1 ETHICS ISSUE Suppose your home had been burgled and you lost about $2,000 worth of personal property. Many months later, a criminal was arrested and confessed to the burglary of your home. But by then, your property had been disposed of long ago. He was tried, convicted, and sentenced to four years in prison. Do you think you should sue the criminal in tort to win a judgment for the $2,000 you lost? Can you state reasons, other than to benefit yourself, why you might be obligated to do this?

2 ETHICS ISSUE Suppose you were involved in an accident where you scratched the fender of a parked car and no one saw what you had done. The law requires that you leave a note on the damaged car identifying yourself. If you were certain you could just drive away without anyone knowing what had happened, would you do it? What reasons can you state for the action you would take?

3 Philip drove a tractor-trailer rig onto a ferry boat and left the rig in gear because of a problem with his brakes. Posted regulations prohibited the starting of engines before docking. But when the ferry was about fifty feet from the dock, Philip started his engine. That caused the tractor-trailer to jump forward and strike Herrick's car, which in turn hit Patton's car. Patton's car, at the head of the line, crashed through the ferry's barricades and plunged into the water. The car could not be recovered. What was the tort duty in this case? Where was the breach of

Applying Law to Everyday Life

1 
This is an ethics question. By making the burglar repay you for the conversion of your lost property, you make criminal activity less profitable and less attractive.

2 
This is an ethics question with many possible answers. One mature answer is that we owe an obligation to those we injure to compensate them for the injury. In addition, we are morally obligated to obey the law because we consent to society's laws when we accept the benefits of society. Free public education is just one example of the benefits of society.

3 Philip owed two duties here. One was to obey the posted regulations. A second was to act reasonably in operating the truck on the ferry. Both duties were breached by starting a truck (without properly functioning brakes) when the ferry wasn't docked. The injuries were the damages to Herrick's car, Patton's car, and the ferry's barricades. Philip's act of starting the truck without brakes was the proximate cause of the damages to Patton's car. (pp. 104–106)

the duty? What were the injuries? What was the proximate cause of the injury to Patton's car?

4 Betty was at a baseball game seated one row behind a famous movie star. When she stood up to cheer, she was bumped by the person beside her. She lost her balance and fell into the lap of the movie star. He sued her for the tort of assault. Who prevails?

5 McDonald and Beck were sitting in a bar watching a professional football game. When they discovered they were rooting for opposing teams, Beck hit McDonald in the face, breaking McDonald's glasses and nose. McDonald called the police, who arrested Beck. Does McDonald have any legal claims against Beck?

6 Every morning on the way to work, Sharon rode an elevator up fourteen floors. Sometimes, when it was crowded, the elevator operator would intentionally touch her in an offensive way. What can Sharon do besides making a scene in the elevator?

7 Jackson was a lawyer, respected by his peers. He successfully represented several persons who were charged with income tax evasion. All three defendants were reputed to be leaders of an organized crime syndicate. The local newspaper then printed an editorial calling for the tightening of tax laws "to protect society against mobsters and shyster lawyers—we think of Jackson—who would sell their souls to the devil for thirty pieces of silver." Was this a tort?

8 Ham was a guest in Lane's home. While leaving the house, Ham was injured when she slipped on some ice that had formed on the steps leading from the door. Lane had cautioned Ham about the possibility of the steps being slippery, and Ham admitted seeing the ice. In a legal action claiming negligence, would Lane be liable?

9 Yardly and Whiple, ages twelve and thirteen, intentionally threw stones which smashed fifty-seven windows in an old warehouse. The warehouse had been standing vacant for nine months. Yardly and Whiple were caught and disciplined by the juvenile court. Then the owner of the warehouse sued them and their parents for damages. The girls said they were "just having fun and not hurting anyone because the place was empty." Who, if anyone, is liable and why?

▼ SOLVING CASE PROBLEMS

1 Town Finance Corporation (TFC) foreclosed on a mortgage following a dispute with Hughes as to whether a loan had been repaid. TFC had a

4 Betty prevails. She did not intend to put the movie star in fear of offensive or harmful touching. She did not cause the touching, and she did not intend the act of touching. (p. 107)

5 Yes, McDonald could sue for the tort of assault and the tort of battery. In addition, he could sue to recover the cost of new glasses. McDonald would probably win damages for all three. Thus, Beck's action could lead to a fine, imprisonment, and civil damages. (pp. 107, 116–117)

6 Sharon can sue the elevator operator for the torts of assault and battery. This type of touching is clearly a tort. Since Sharon probably is not as interested in money as she is in avoiding future incidents, she might also ask for an injunction to prevent future assaults. (p. 107)

7 Yes; It was the form of defamation called libel. (p. 108) A person accused of crime is presumed to be innocent until proven guilty in court beyond a reasonable doubt. Even confessed criminals are entitled to legal counsel. A lawyer who takes the case has a duty to defend the client as well as possible. The jury (or judge if there is no jury), not the lawyer, decides whether the defendant is guilty.

8 No, Ham could not recover because of assumption of the risk. After receiving a warning and seeing the ice, Ham should have exercised more care in walking on the ice. (p. 114)

locksmith remove the locks of Hughes's dwelling. TFC personnel then entered the house, seized household goods, and left the inside of the house in disarray. No one was home when this was done. Hughes filed suit over the debt. The court held that the finance company had been paid and thus had no further right of action against Hughes. Hughes thereupon filed this action, which claimed malicious and willful trespass and asked both actual (compensatory) and punitive damages. Was Hughes entitled to judgment? (*Town Finance Corporation v. Hughes*, 214 S.E.2d 387)

2 Lewis, an undercover police officer carrying a concealed pistol, went shopping in a Dayton Hudson department store. There, a security officer became suspicious that he was a shoplifter. Lewis took some clothing into a fitting room, where there were signs stating, "This area is under surveillance by Hudson's personnel." In fact, the security guard observed Lewis from a grille in the ceiling. After he saw Lewis place the gun on a chair, he called the police. Eventually, Lewis was identified as an undercover officer. But he sued Dayton Hudson claiming that the spying in the fitting room was an invasion of his privacy. Will he recover? (*Lewis v. Dayton Hudson Corporation*, 128 Mich. App. 165)

3 A train stopped at the defendant's railroad platform. As it started up again, a man carrying a small package jumped aboard. He appeared unsteady and about to fall. Therefore a guard on the train, holding the door open, reached out to help him. Another guard, standing on the platform, pushed the man from behind. The man made it onto the train, but he dropped the package, which was about fifteen inches long. The package was wrapped in newspaper and contained fireworks that exploded when the package hit the rails. The shock of the explosion caused some scales at the other end of the platform, many feet away, to fall down. As they fell, they struck the plaintiff, injuring her. She sued the railroad, claiming the guards were negligent. Is the railroad liable? (*Palsgraf v. Long Island Railroad Company*, 162 N.E. 99, N.Y.)

4 An operator of an earth-moving vehicle was severely injured when his left pants leg caught between the rotating drums of the clutch, pulling his leg through the drums. The operator and his wife sued the manufacturer, claiming there was a defect in the design of the vehicle. They also claimed that the manufacturer knew of this defect. The evidence showed that a perforated guard was installed on the right side but not on the left. The evidence also showed that if there had been a guard on the left side, the accident would not have occurred. Should the operator be awarded damages? (*Carpenter v. Koehring Company*, 391 F. Supp. 206)

9 Yardly and Whiple are liable for the tort of trespass. Throwing rocks which hit windows is trespassing. It does not matter whether the building is occupied or not. Their parents may also be liable for the damages if the girls have a habit of throwing rocks at buildings or if their state has a statute making parents liable for the torts of their children. (pp. 110, 116)

Solving Case Problems

1 Yes, Hughes was entitled to the judgment. The jury awarded both compensatory and punitive damages for the illegal entry and seizure of goods because the trespass was malicious, willful, and without cause. (pp. 110, 116–117)

2 Lewis did not recover. The signs in the fitting room deprived him of the expectation that he was in an area of privacy. The judge stated that without the signs, or if there had been observation by a member of the opposite sex, there might have been an invasion of privacy. (pp. 110, 114)

3 No; For negligence, the defendant must reasonably perceive a risk to the plaintiff. The injury must be reasonably foreseeable. Here, the guards could not possibly have anticipated the chain of events that followed their successful effort to protect the boarding passenger. There was no proximate causation. (p. 106)

4 Yes; The evidence showed that the manufacturer knew that all sides should be covered and was negligent in not installing guards on both sides even though it was feasible to do so. Failure to install the guard was the proximate cause of the injury. (pp. 106, 115)

⑤ No; Dogs are domestic animals. Owners are not liable for injuries caused by their dogs unless the owners know that their dogs are dangerous. Since Whitehead did not know that the animal was dangerous, he is not liable for the injuries to David. (p. 115)

5 David Allen, age two, was attacked and severely bitten in the face and ear by a dog owned by Joseph Whitehead. Whitehead admitted that the dog barked frequently, was large, looked mean, and chased cars. On the other hand, no one had ever complained about the dog, it had never bitten anyone before, and it frequently played with other children. Is Whitehead liable for the injuries to David? (*Allen v. Whitehead*, 423 So. 2d 835, Ala.)

SPECIAL SECTION

PRESSING ISSUE: ENVIRONMENTAL LAW

The problems are on a scale that tends to dwarf us and leaves us feeling powerless. Huge, growing holes in the ozone layer allowing cancer-fostering ultraviolet rays to penetrate our skin. Cancer- and birth-defect-causing residues from herbicide and pesticide use lacing the waters of even the purest looking mountain streams. "Progress," slashing thousands of acres per day from the oxygen-producing forests of the planet we inhabit. Countless tons of pollutants given off daily into the very air we breathe from the factories and modes of transportation that sustain our modern life-style....

Solutions to these potential catastrophes can come only from changes in that life-style; changes that can be fostered now by education and law. Where foresight fails, changes will come at some point in the future out of the desperate anger and frenzy of survival instincts. In the United States, the legal framework for a balanced and orderly response to the environmental problems at hand was laid out over two decades ago. Since that time, the proper utilization of that framework has been stymied by questionable economic conditions and a consequential reluctance to sacrifice our present affluence for the well-being of future generations.

Regardless, the linchpin for any coordinated national response to our environmental problems is the Environmental Protection Agency (EPA). The EPA was founded in 1970 in an executive branch reorganization intended to place federal environmental regulatory authority into one agency. The EPA is expected to coordinate actions against toxic wastes, air and water pollution, radiation hazards, noise pollution, and many other concerns. To give assistance to the EPA in its mission, Congress passed the National Environmental Policy Act (NEPA). This act set up the Council on Environmental Quality (CEQ). The CEQ advises the President on environmental matters and issues regulations on how the federal agencies are to

Special Section: Pressing Issue: Environmental Law

After students have read the Special Section *Pressing Issue: Environmental Law*, have them brainstorm possible topics for discussion gleaned from pp. 123–124. In addition, you may wish to ask students to use library reference materials to come up with more possibilities. You may wish to suggest that students restrict their topics to the United States (perhaps focusing on their city, state, or region) or to think globally; to think about current history, or to look back at past events (litigation involving the Nevada Test Site used in atomic tests in the United States in 1953–1961, for instance).

After students have listed on the chalkboard or flip chart all their possibilities, ask for a volunteer to type (or neatly write) all the topics on a sheet of paper. Distribute copies to students, asking them to number, from one to three, their three favorite topics. Use their preferences to determine which three topics the class will research.

Divide the class into three groups, assigning students to each group, as much as possible, according to their favorite topics. Once students have been assigned to a group, have students within each group assign roles such as researchers, recorder, and presenter. Encourage students to make their presentations as creatively as possible, using media (music, computers, and videos).

Cooperative Learning

integrate the achievement of environmental goals with the pursuit of technical and economic development.

To assist in this integration, the NEPA created the environmental impact statement. An environmental impact statement (EIS) is required for any legislation or major federal action that would significantly affect the quality of the environment. Each EIS must contain a description of the intended project, its purpose, and need. The EIS then must describe the environment of the affected area and discuss in detail the environmental consequences of and the alternatives to the project. The U.S. Supreme Court has determined that the environmental aspects of the project do not have to be given overriding concern by the agency and the filing of the EIS is to be considered merely procedural. However, the information contained in the EIS greatly assists groups wary of the environmental consequences of the action.

The Noise Control Act of 1972 and the Clean Air and Clean Water Acts and Amendments of 1977 furthered the regulatory powers of the EPA in these important areas. Solid waste problems were addressed in the Resource Conservation and Recovery Act (RCRA) of 1976. The RCRA requires the EPA to identify the hazardous wastes that most threaten the human environment and then to require permits for hazardous waste treatment and storage facilities. The information and sensitivity thus developed led to the passage of the Comprehensive Environmental Response, Compensation, and Liability Act (CERCLA) of 1980. CERCLA created the Hazardous Substance Response Trust Fund (Superfund). Financial resources to clean up hazardous waste sites, if those responsible for their creation will not voluntarily clean them up or cannot be found, are available from this Superfund. Reimbursement for the cleanup costs is then sought in court from the polluters.

These acts and policies at the federal level are mirrored and augmented by agencies and laws at the state level throughout our country. Nonetheless, they represent only a partial, unilateral, response to a worldwide environmental crisis that is growing in intensity, severity, and perhaps, irreversibility, every day.

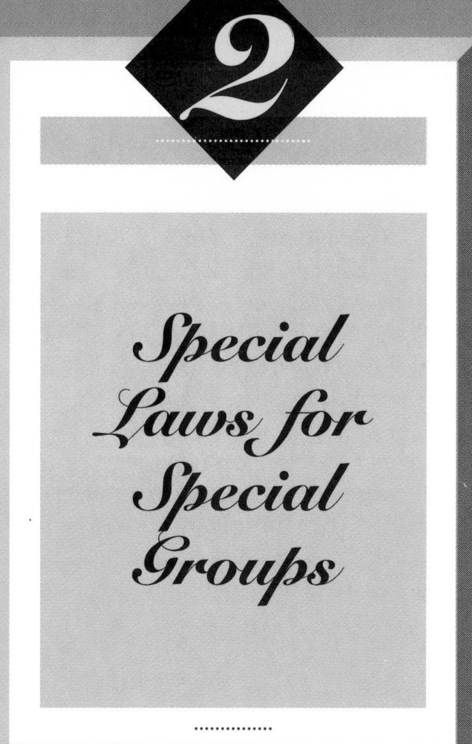

Unit Overview

In Unit 2, *Special Laws for Special Groups*, students will read about the different laws for minors, families, and consumers. In this unit, students will learn about juvenile delinquency, marriage, wills, and consumer protection agencies. They will become immediately involved in the applicability and relevancy of the chapter topics, as students are most likely members of several of the special groups studied.

Minors and their parents are required to obey the law, and have certain rights and duties. In Chapter 7, *Laws for Minors*, students will understand the legal rights and duties of minors. In addition, students will also learn about the rights and duties of parents and students, and what a minor's rights and duties are as drivers of motor vehicles.

Our laws determine the legal status of our personal relationships before, during, and after marriage, and even impact our loved ones after our death. In Chapter 8, *Laws for Families*, students will study how the law affects premarital relationships, legal aspects of the marital contract, what the rights and duties of wives and husbands are, and how a marriage is legally ended. Other coverage includes what the legal consequences of a person's death are, and how a decedent's estate is managed.

Laws protect consumers against unscrupulous merchants, defective merchandise, and unfair trade practices. In Chapter 9, *Laws for Consumers*, students will discover why the law protects consumers and how the law protects against substandard consumer goods. Topics include what trade practices are prohibited by consumer law and which agreements in restraint in trade are valid. In addition, the chapter surveys the scope of various consumer laws. It closes with a survey of the activities of state and local governments in promoting compliance with consumer protection statutes.

At the end of the unit, you'll find a special section, *Careers in Law*, which can be used at any time during the study of Unit 2. You may wish to assign its accompanying *Teacher Edition* activity to give students an opportunity to hold a law career fair.

Portfolio Assessment

Ask students to think about how the law exists and is reflected in every aspect and stage of their lives—even at their age. Using a computer, if possible, ask students to write an essay on how special laws for special groups affects them, as well as other minors, students, drivers, consumers, marriage partners, and parents. Have them include how the law still affects us, and our loved ones, even after we die. Then, have students describe how the law has already affected their lives or predict how it may do so in the future. Have students proofread and edit their first drafts to check their spelling, punctuation, grammar, and for clarity. Then, have students make the needed changes and put the final draft of the essay in their portfolios or law journals.

Careers

Truant Officer

Our society prides itself in providing a free, K–12 education to its youth. Truant officers are called upon to enforce state education compulsory attendance laws. The duties of a truant officer are to record student absences, investigate reasons for the absences, meet with parents or guardians, analyze and evaluate individual situations, confer with other school specialists, and take legal action when necessary.

Truant officers often have a college degree in education; advanced courses in psychology, sociology, and law are also beneficial. Salary ranges vary according to education and experience.

Begin a discussion on the importance of obtaining an education and the need for compulsory attendance laws. As a follow-up, invite a truant officer from your school district to speak to your class about the responsibilities of the job and the adverse consequences of habitually missing school.

Annotated Bibliography

- ***Brown v. Board of Education*, 347 U.S. 483 (1954).** The Court overruled the "separate but equal" doctrine of *Plessy v. Ferguson*, holding that segregation of children in the public schools solely on the basis of race, even though the physical facilities and other "tangible" factors may be equal, deprives the children of the minority group equal educational opportunities. (Chapter 7)
- ***Plessy v. Ferguson*, 163 U.S. 537 (1896).** The Supreme Court sustained a Louisiana law of 1890 that required "equal but separate accommodations" for "white" and "colored" railroad passengers. (Chapter 7)

Special Laws for Special Groups

- Laws for Minors
- Laws for Families
- Laws for Consumers

SPECIAL LAWS FOR SPECIAL GROUPS

CHAPTER 7 ORGANIZER

Chapter Theme

Minors and their parents are required to obey the law, and have certain rights and duties.

DIRECTED STUDY QUESTIONS	SPECIAL FEATURES	PROGRAM RESOURCES				
		Reteach	Enrich	SN	AM	
What are the legal rights and duties of minors?	Thinking Critically Through Visuals, p. 129 Personal Perspectives, p. 130	✔	✔	✔	A	
What are the rights and duties of parents?	Writing Connections, p.132	✔	✔		K V	
What are the rights and duties of students?	Multicultural Highlights, p. 133 Thinking Critically Through Visuals, p. 134 Ethics Issue, p. 134	✔	✔			
What are a minor's rights and duties as a driver?	Preventing Legal Difficulties, p. 136	✔	✔			

Additional Resources

- Englebardt, Leland S. *You Have a Right: A Guide for Minors.* NY: Lothrop, Lee & Shepard Co., 1979.
- Fox, Ken. *Everything You Need to Know About Your Legal Rights.* NY: Rosen Publishing Group, 1992.
- Jackson, Michael. *"Heal the World"* from *Dangerous*. Sony/Epic Records, 1991.
- *You & the Law*. Pleasantville, NY: The Readers' Digest Association, 1984.

Chapter Pacing Guide

One-semester course	✓	✓						
One-year course	✓	✓	✓					

		ASSESSMENT OPPORTUNITIES			
	Cooperative Learning	Informal Assessment	Chapter Review	Chapter Test	Chapter *MicroExam* 
	✓	✓	✓	✓	✓
		✓	✓	✓	✓
		✓	✓	✓	✓
		✓	✓	✓	✓

Videodiscs

Juvenile Court

Search Chapter 8, Play To 9

Civil Disobedience

Search Chapter 9, Play To 10

State by State

In the northeastern states, typically you must be 18 years old to contract, write a will, and marry without parental consent. At 16, you can usually drive and marry with parental consent.

Teaching Materials

Student text, pp. 126–141

Overhead transparency masters
- *The Law and the Minor*
- *How the State Laws Vary for Minors*

Videos
- *Our Legal System* Videotape
- *Law for Business* Videodisc

Workbook, pp. 15–16, p. 151

Outside Resources
- Juvenile court officer to speak to the class
- State driver's manual
- Index cards
- Highlighter marking pens
- Assorted cookbooks

- Recording of *Heal the World* by Michael Jackson
- VCR
- Camcorder
- Cassette recorder or CD player

Assessment
- Chapter Test

- Chapter *MicroExam*

Vocabulary

minors, p. 128
majority, p. 128
juvenile delinquent, p.128
guardian, p. 130
guardian ad litem, p. 130
annulment, p. 130
adoption, p. 132
emancipation, p. 133
truants, p. 133
financial responsibility, p. 135
reckless driving, p. 136

Learning Objectives

When you complete this chapter, you will be able to

1. Understand the reasons for the special status and protection afforded minors in our society.
2. State the legal rights and duties of minors and their parents.
3. Explain the rights and duties of minors as students and drivers.

126

Chapter Self-Test

Assess students' understanding of their rights under the law before they begin Chapter 7 by asking them orally to answer the following questions: **(1) Are parents responsible for their child's school attendance?** (Yes); **(2) Are parents obligated to allow their child to apply for a driver's license?** (No); and **(3) Are the earnings of a child the property of the child?** (No).

CHAPTER 7 LAWS FOR MINORS

❶ Your friend, Eric, rides his motorcycle back and forth to school. Yesterday, an elderly woman in a large four-door sedan negligently pulled out of her driveway into his path. Eric's motorcycle slammed into the side of her car, and he suffered severe head and back injuries. Must Eric, a minor, have adult assistance to bring suit against the driver?

❷ ETHICS ISSUE When you were ten years old, your parents bought your first computer. After helping you learn the basics of programming, they sent you to several summer computer camps to further develop your skills. You recently finished writing a computer game program called Destiny, and a major software dealer agreed to produce and distribute it. Your first royalty check, for $17,254, just arrived. You are still a minor. Ethically, should your parents control how the money is spent? Does the money legally belong to your parents?

❸ Carried away with school spirit, you spray paint derogatory slogans about a rival school's team across the new artificial grass of its football field. A security guard catches you in the act. The cost of the repairs runs well over $10,000. A friend tells you not to worry; you are not liable "because you're a minor." Is your friend correct?

127

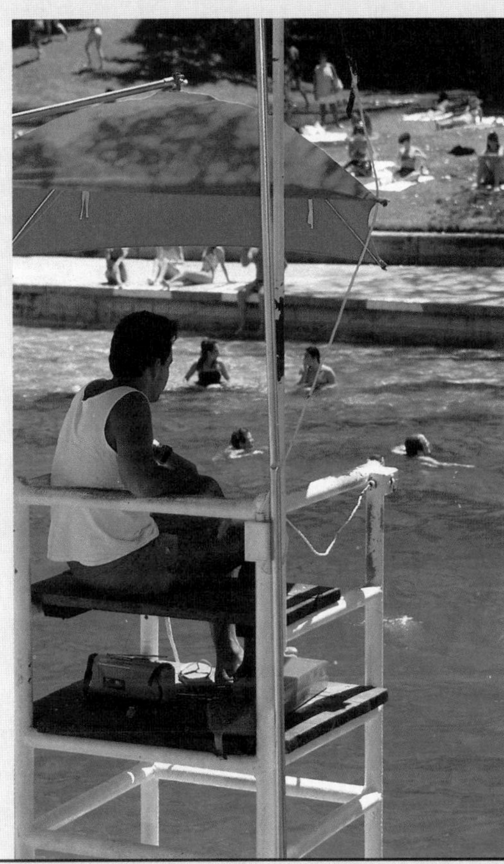

FOCUS

Ask the class to make a list of the legal rights it thinks are withheld from minors. (Answers may include voting, purchasing and consuming alcohol, and so on.)

Record students' responses on a transparency or on a large sheet of chart paper. Students will review and revise their list in the CLOSE activity at the end of the chapter.

You Decide

❶ Yes, a minor must have an adult bring suit on his or her behalf.

❷ ETHICS ISSUE Legally, the money earned by the minor child belongs to the parents. Consequential reasoning also supports this law because parents may be more able to invest the funds wisely.

❸ No, minors are generally held responsible for their torts.

Thinking Critically Through Visuals

Tell students: **Society often assumes responsibility for the safety of its citizens, especially its youth. How does this photograph reflect that concept?** (Answers may include that the lifeguard, representing our society, protects swimmers [citizens] by seeing that pool rules and laws are obeyed.)

TEACH

Display and review the overhead transparency, *The Law and the Minor.* Society withholds full adult rights and duties from minors as a form of protection, not punishment. Discuss the advantages and disadvantages to minors of society's attempt to protect them until they reach adulthood.

APPLY

Have students respond to the PROBLEM on p. 128. Ask: **What advantages do you think Celeste felt she had lost?** (Answers may include not being bound legally to contract promises, or having her basic needs taken care of by others.) **Guided Practice**

Invite a juvenile court officer to speak to your class. Have the officer stress the rehabilitative philosophy behind the juvenile court system.

Have each student write a response to the following statement, using a computer, if possible: **Children who commit adult crimes, such as felonies, should be tried and sentenced as adults.** (Whether students agree or disagree is less important than the thinking skills they apply to support their responses.)

Independent Practice

WHAT ARE THE LEGAL RIGHTS AND DUTIES OF MINORS?

PROBLEM

One evening at a dance you run into Celeste, a woman you have not seen since she was a senior at your high school four years ago. When you tell her you will be glad to turn eighteen next year, she surprises you by saying that she feels like she lost a lot of advantages by reaching the age of adulthood. Did she?

Our legal system will generally withhold full adult rights and duties from individuals until they reach a certain age. In such areas as being held responsible for criminal acts, being bound to contracts, voting, getting married, drinking alcoholic beverages, or even bringing lawsuits, society tries to protect young adults from the full consequences of their acts. Individuals who are under the age at which they acquire full adult rights and duties are **minors**.

Depending on the jurisdiction involved, statutes may set different minimum ages for the time of full accountability that is called adulthood. For example, in most states the age for voting differs from the age for liability for crimes or torts. In a few states, minors become legal adults upon marriage. In most states, minors who are veterans or in the armed forces are given adult rights, such as the power to buy and sell real estate. In some states, California for instance, a minor who is an actor or an actress may be given certain adult rights by court order.

The effects of adulthood vary according to the area of law as well. Under contract law, minors can avoid (i.e., block the enforcement of) contracts that they have willfully entered. However, once individuals reach adulthood, which is termed the age of **majority**, they generally are bound by law to the contracts they enter.

In criminal law, a minor who is arrested is typically kept apart from adult inmates. Also, in most cases, if a minor commits what would be a punishable crime for adults, society handles that underage person as a **juvenile delinquent** through the juvenile court system. Runaways (i.e., minors who leave home without parental consent), once they are found by the police, can also be placed under the control of a juvenile court. In such juvenile delinquency proceedings the emphasis is on helping, guiding, and reforming rather than on punishing the offenders.

In the problem, then, Celeste's feelings are understandable. On attaining the age of majority, Celeste gained more individual freedom but lost the protection the law affords minors. At times, however, society strips away such protection even before an individual reaches legal adulthood. For example,

ASSESS

Learning Objective 1 Have students orally explain why minors who are arrested for a punishable crime are often treated differently than adults by police and representatives of the law. (It is an attempt to keep a minor apart from adult inmates; juvenile delinquency proceedings emphasize helping, guiding, and reforming, rather than punishing, offenders.)

most states permit transfer of a minor from a juvenile court to an adult criminal court when the offense is a particularly serious one, such as murder. In some states, the transfer takes place if the minor is a repeat offender or if the offense would be a felony if committed by an adult. Depending on the state, the minor could be as young as thirteen, but sixteen is the usual age for eligibility for transfer.

A group of five high school students, all ages sixteen and seventeen, were arrested for rioting, seriously injuring a teacher, and destroying thousands of dollars of school property. The state law provided that minors age sixteen and older charged with felonies could be tried as adults in criminal court rather than as juveniles in juvenile court. Upon recommendation by the prosecutor and review and approval by the court, the students were tried, convicted, and punished as adults.

If minors commit torts and thereby injure another person or property, they are usually liable for the loss. This could happen, for example, while a minor is driving an automobile. Although a claim for damages against a minor with no assets might not be immediately collectible, the judgment would remain in effect for many years as a claim against his or her future earnings. As discussed later in this chapter, at times even the minor's parents may also be held liable for the minor's wrongdoing.

Thinking Critically Through Visuals

Society sometimes uses special markings or designations to alert the public when someone is learning something new. Have you ever seen a car marked like the one in this photograph? After an affirmative response, ask: **Why is it important to mark these cars clearly?** (To let other drivers know that the person driving the car is an inexperienced driver and may behave accordingly)

Assist visually impaired students with the THINKING CRITICALLY THROUGH VISUALS activity by seating them next to a sighted student. Have the peer quietly explain the details of the visual.

Divide the class into groups of three or four students. Each group will be responsible for creating a poster on the rights and duties of minors. Each group should choose a facilitator, a writer, and an artist. A fourth person, if necessary, can serve as a proofreader. **Cooperative Learning**

RETEACH Photocopy text pp. 128–132 for students who do not understand Learning Objective 1. Model how to search for and highlight key information. Guide students in completing the first section of p. 151 of the Workbook.

ENRICH Have students debate the following issue: **The Juvenile Justice system was created to protect juveniles from adult criminals. Has society gone too far by allowing some juveniles to go virtually unpunished for their criminal actions? Does this contribute to an increase in juvenile crime?**

Display the overhead transparency, *How the State Laws Vary for Minors.* Students may have difficulty understanding the rationale behind using age as an arbitrary standard for recognizing adulthood, especially since the standards vary from state to state. Add to the transparency your state's minimum age for each activity and have students copy this in their notebooks.

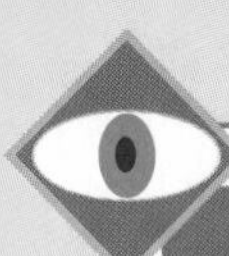

Personal Perspectives

Courts appoint guardians for minors who have no living parents. Ask students to brainstorm a list of qualifications they would expect a legal guardian to have. Then, have them review their list with their own guardian (most likely a parent) and bring their lists to class. Encourage students to discuss the differences between their responses and those of their guardians.

For many purposes, an adult must represent or act for a minor. Courts regularly appoint guardians for minors who have no living parents. The **guardian** acts in place of the parents or may perform some special service, such as suing on behalf of the minor.

The parents of Flood, age fifteen, were killed in a two-car accident. A court appointed her grandparents as her guardians. Thus it became their duty to take care of her, to act in the capacity of parents, and to be responsible for her estate. This guardianship will last until Flood reaches adulthood. The court also named her adult uncle, White, **guardian ad litem**—Latin words meaning "for the suit." This gave the uncle the power to sue, on behalf of Flood, the driver of the other car who had allegedly been negligent in causing the accident.

With parental consent, a minor between ages sixteen and eighteen is generally permitted to marry. Some states require authorization of a court as well as the consent of the parents.

McCarver and Gibson, both minors, eloped to a distant city and were married without their parents' consent. Either spouse, as well as the parents of either, could probably obtain a court-ordered **annulment** (i.e., judicial declaration that a marriage never existed) of the matrimonial union if the application came before the couple became adults.

Although they are often given special treatment under our laws, it is important to remember that minors, like other citizens, retain their constitutional rights. When arrested, for example, minors have the same rights as adults. They are presumed to be innocent unless proved guilty beyond a reasonable doubt. They, and their parents, are entitled to adequate notice of charges, so that they can prepare a defense. They also have the right to be represented by qualified lawyers, who will be provided without charge if the minors (or their parents) cannot afford to hire one. Minors also have a right to confront adverse witnesses in court. In addition, minors cannot be compelled to testify in their own defense because such testimony could lead to self-incrimination.

Minors have other rights upon attaining ages specified by statute. For example, usually at age sixteen, minors may be employed full-time, although there may be restrictions as to hours and kinds of work. Minors under age sixteen may be employed part-time when the work does not interfere with required attendance at school. However, a work permit is often required.

ASSESS

Learning Objective 1 Have students give three examples to support the following statement from the text: **The intent of the laws ... is to create for minors the best legal environment for their growth.** (Answers may include that special courts deal with their problems; there are restrictions on the kinds of labor minors may perform; and society tries to protect minors from the consequences of their actions, such as marriage, drinking, and criminal acts.)

Minors also have the right to obtain a motor vehicle operator's license upon meeting statutory age and other requirements.

The intent of the laws mentioned in this section is to create for minors the best legal environment for their growth. The laws allow for mistakes, some punishment, and, in the long run, forgiveness for errors. While the laws might appear to be too restrictive at times, their intent is to steer minors through the very difficult transition from youth to adulthood. Society wants each person to reach adulthood free from legal burdens he or she might have unwisely incurred while young and relatively naive.

WHAT ARE THE RIGHTS AND DUTIES OF PARENTS?

PROBLEM

Will is a junior in high school and has lived in the same New Hampshire community all his life. In October, his mother learns that the plant in which she has been a manager for over twenty years is closing. She has accepted a new position at company headquarters 1,200 miles away. Rather than leave his friends, Will tells his mother that he wants to remain where they are and finish high school there. His mother insists she has the right to force him to move. Can she legally do so?

Society gives parents legal control over their children provided they do not abuse it. By statute, all states routinely allow qualified parents to have custody and responsibility for their natural and adopted children. This means that parents have authority to restrain their children, to administer reasonable punishment if necessary, and to compel obedience to reasonable directions. These rights continue until the children reach their majority or until the parents give up or are denied their rights by court order. Parents also have the right to determine the residence of their children. Thus, in the problem, Will's mother can compel him to move.

In addition, the services of minors belong to their parents. Children who live at home owe assistance to their parents as requested and without payment. By agreement, children may be paid by their parents for the work they perform, but this is usually done voluntarily. Minor children working for their parents are not covered by most child labor laws. Further, the income a child earns outside the home legally belongs to the parents. The laws of most states require an employer to pay a minor's wages to the parents, if they so request.

This right to the services of their children makes it possible for parents to claim damages when they are wrongfully deprived of the child's services due to a third party's tort.

RETEACH To summarize the law's responsibility to its youth, have students create a poster titled *How the Law Protects Minors.* Students, working in small groups, should include the following topics: contracts, guardians, employment, and constitutional rights.

ENRICH Ask students who have a grasp of the concept of law for minors to develop a daily bulletin board for this chapter, displaying legal issues of special interest to young people. Use recent newspapers and teen magazines as resources.

TEACH

To introduce the section, *What Are the Rights and Duties of Parents?* on pp. 131–133, discuss with students the story of Jackie Coogan, a famous child star who made millions of dollars in the 1920s. When he was 21, he sued to get control of his trust fund, but no trace of it was found. After a long court battle, he and his mother split $250,000—all that was left of the $4 million he said he had earned. Give examples of other parental rights and duties, such as the right to discipline a child and the duty to educate and take care of that child.

APPLY

Assist students in creating a three-column chart listing the rights of parents in one column, parents' obligations to the child in a second column, and, in a third column, the possible legal punishment for not fulfilling their obligations. **Guided Practice**

Have students independently make up a "recipe" for an effective parent or guardian. Bring to class cookbooks (for format) and index cards (for the recipes). Have students list the ingredients and proportions (such as one cup of love and a tablespoon of discipline) and write the recipe directions. Collate individual recipes into a class recipe book.

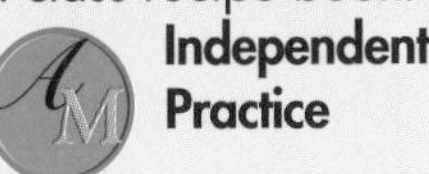

Independent Practice

Writing Connections

Language Arts
Sometimes children are brought under the control of a juvenile court because the authorities believe the children need help that their parents or legal guardians cannot, or will not, provide. In some states, in legal terms, the child becomes a *MINS*—a Minor In Need of Supervision. Have students write a story, poem, rap, song, or essay about the feelings of a MINS, using a computer, if possible. If students write a song, encourage them to tape it and play it for the class.

Have pairs of students act out for the class a situation showing neglect by parents of their legal obligations to their children, such as not providing sufficient food or proper supervision. After watching each skit, have the class discuss possible negative results of the situation and how they might have been avoided. Videotape the skits, if possible.

Bertram, age seventeen, had been helping to do preliminary interviews in his family's income tax preparation service for two years. One rainy day Brock, who had negligently run a red light, rammed his small pickup into Bertram's van. Bertram fractured his collarbone and right arm in the collision and could not help at tax time. His parents were forced to hire another worker to take his place. Bertram's parents are legally entitled to collect from Brock the cost of such replacement services.

In return for all the above-mentioned rights, parents owe certain legal obligations to their children. Included are the duties to protect and take care of them; to provide food, clothing, and shelter according to the parents' financial means; and to see that the children are educated. Finally, we all hope that parents and children will give affection and moral support to one another, although these expectations are not legally enforceable by any means.

Willful failure by parents to care for their children, as through neglect, desertion, or child abuse, subjects the parents to legal punishment. Parents who do not require their children to attend school during the years prescribed by statute are subject to fine or imprisonment. In addition, society expects parents to properly supervise their minor children. If damage to others results from the lack of this supervision, parents may be subject to a limited dollar amount of liability. If parents entrust their minor children with a dangerous instrument, such as a gun, without proper instructions as to its use, the parents may be subject to liability for the harm to others that results.

Normally, the mother and father share the rights and duties in the care and custody of their children. However, these responsibilities may be given up or lost in several ways. For example, if either parent dies, the survivor receives all the parental rights and duties previously shared with the deceased. Also, children who are abused or unreasonably treated by their parents may be taken away by juvenile court order and placed in foster homes or in other protective custody. If the parents divorce or legally separate, the custody of each child is awarded to the parent best qualified to fulfill the child's day-to-day needs. The other parent, however, retains the right to visit the child.

In turn, the legal process of **adoption** allows the parents to relinquish all rights and free themselves of all duties by giving their children to other adults. Such an act is fairly common when the mother is very young and unmarried. Even if the mother is a minor, her consent must be given or the adoption process cannot occur.

▼ ASSESS

Learning Objective 2 Have students read about Bertram, at the top of p. 132. Ask students to respond in writing to the following question: **On what grounds are Bertram's parents entitled to collect payment from Brock?** (Wrongfully deprived of their child's services due to a third-party tort)

Finally, parents may voluntarily surrender responsibility for the care, custody, and control of a minor child as well as claims for the child's earnings by **emancipation**. A minor naturally becomes emancipated upon reaching the age of majority. But a minor may also be emancipated before that time if the minor is legally married or, with parental consent, is self-supporting. Some states recognize partial emancipation, which may consist of allowing minors to retain their earnings and to spend them as they please. This is because "at some point," as stated in a recent court decision, "minors must have some right to their own views and needs for their independent and painful transition from minority to adulthood."

WHAT ARE THE RIGHTS AND DUTIES OF STUDENTS?

PROBLEM

Ted and Eileen Shannon, ages thirteen and fifteen, worked in their parents' video production business. Although frequently absent from the classroom as a consequence, the children loved the work and enjoyed their parents' blessing in doing it. Are Ted and Eileen truants?

Our society endeavors to provide a free education for its young citizens. This, in turn, places a duty on parents to see that their children receive that education. The instruction may take place in a public school system, through qualified private schools, by parents, or by tutors, but it must be given.

Minors who do not attend school when lawfully required to do so are **truants**, and their parents are held responsible. Accordingly, in the problem, the Shannon children are truants. Their parents can be fined or jailed for failing to see that their children attend school. If truancy is habitual, the parents can be charged with child neglect. The child can then be declared delinquent and placed under the jurisdiction of the juvenile court.

Other than the basic claim to a free education, minors also possess the right to participate in normal school activities. As students, they must be allowed access to an environment in which study and learning are facilitated. Also, school personnel must provide reasonable supervision to assure the physical safety of students. Such personnel may be liable if a student is injured.

In addition to the rights that minors have as students, they also have duties to fulfill to avoid disruptions of the common educational environment that benefits all. These duties center on the rules that need to be followed for the orderly and efficient functioning of the school. School authorities are authorized by statute to make such rules. However, the rules must not

TEACH

Free public education (K–12) is accessible to practically everyone in the United States, but certain responsibilities accompany this right. Ask your school principal to speak to students about rights and responsibilities at school.

Multicultural Highlights

Brown v. Board of Education of Topeka (1954) was a landmark Supreme Court decision. It ended legal tolerance of "separate but equal" segregation permitted by *Plessy v. Ferguson* (1896).

APPLY

Have students list their rights at school. Then, have them identify their duties at school. (The right to participate in normal school activities, the duty of obeying classroom rules, and so on) **Guided Practice**

Ask: **If you were your school principal, what changes would you make to the school rules?** (Answers should reflect an understanding of the importance of the school functioning in an orderly and efficient manner.) **Independent Practice**

RETEACH Have students make up five true or false statements (with answers) on the rights and duties of parents. After exchanging papers, have students explain whether each statement is true or false, and why. Review conflicting responses.

ENRICH  Play for the class Michael Jackson's *Heal the World*, sung at halftime during SuperBowl XXVII. Have students interpret the lyrics, then relate them to the rights and duties of society and parents towards children.

Thinking Critically Through Visuals

Newspapers are an excellent outlet for expressing opinions. Ask: **When can our rights to free speech and free press conflict with school regulations?** (When the activity disrupts school functions or jeopardizes the safety of others)

Ethics Issue

A school board pulled *Down These Mean Streets* from the school library because they found the details of life in Spanish Harlem objectionable. A group brought suit against the board and lost. The Supreme Court refused to review the case, but Justice Douglas stated, "*... Are we sending children to school to be educated by the norms of the School Board or are we educating our youth to ... explore all forms of thought, and to find solutions to our world's problems?*" Have students respond to his query.

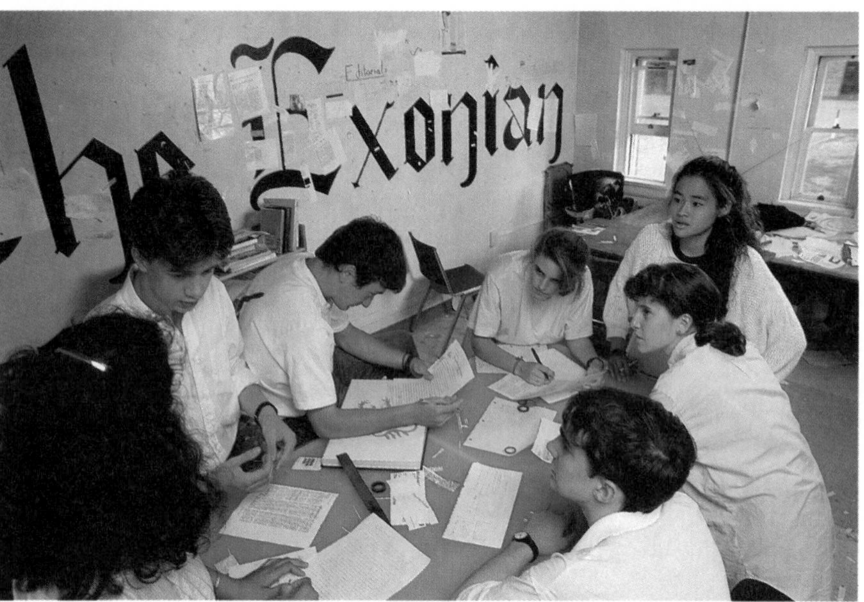

be arbitrary and capricious. For example, according to the U.S. Constitution and the U.S. Supreme Court, students are entitled to free speech, such as wearing a black armband in support of a cause, unless it is evident such an activity will cause "a material and substantial disruption" of the work of the school. Likewise, rules prohibiting extreme styles of dress or personal grooming must be shown to be supported by more than an administrator's dislike of the styles involved.

Within the above boundaries, the power to make the rules and decisions determining school regulations, curriculum matters, and the control of school property belongs to the school administration. Often, however, as a real-life learning experience, schools delegate to student governmental bodies some of these responsibilities. From their experiences in such groups, students learn the wisdom of and the need for compromise in resolving conflicting points of view.

However, even where school administrators delegate to students the power to make rules and provide punishment for disobedience, the ultimate responsibility for the just and reasonable conduct of the day-to-day business of the school rests with the administration. Due process in the form of a notice and a hearing is required before drastic disciplinary action, such as suspension or expulsion, can take place. Where necessary though, a troublemaking student may be temporarily barred from classes and sent home with little delay or formality. Such action legitimately occurs when the student's continued presence poses a danger to persons or to property or when it threat-

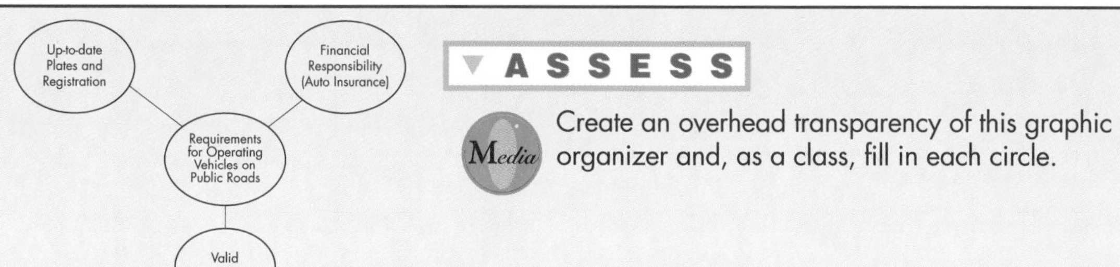

▼ ASSESS

Media Create an overhead transparency of this graphic organizer and, as a class, fill in each circle.

ens to disrupt the academic process and thereby the future chances of the students at the school.

WHAT ARE A MINOR'S RIGHTS AND DUTIES AS A DRIVER?

PROBLEM

Your father restored a large classic English luxury car. You recently obtained your driver's license and have decided to open a summer business driving people to special occasions in the vehicle. On one such trip, you are involved in a minor accident. Even though the wreck was not your fault, the police officer cites you for driving without a proper license. Why?

In owning a motor vehicle, a minor is generally treated as an adult. Regardless of age, a person may hold simple title to an automobile, truck, motorcycle, motorbike, snowmobile, or any other type of transport that various states classify as a motor vehicle. A document of title showing ownership is generally all that is necessary.

But if the minor wishes to operate the vehicle on the public roads, other items are required. First, an up-to-date license plate showing proof of registration of the vehicle with the government must be acquired and displayed. Second, the driver must demonstrate proof of the ability to pay at least a specified minimum amount of damages if at fault in an auto accident. This is termed **financial responsibility** and is often shown by acquiring an insurance policy with the amount of coverage required by state law. Third, and most important, a valid driver's license must be obtained. In the problem, although you had a valid ordinary license, state laws require special licenses for those who operate trucks, buses, limousines, or other vehicles as chauffeurs. Stricter standards, including advanced age criteria, are often demanded of such drivers.

In contrast, most states issue learner's permits to younger inexperienced drivers to help them acquire the skills necessary to assume the responsibility of driving a motor vehicle. A fully licensed driver must be present when such permit recipients are driving.

Even the best prepared driver makes mistakes, however. Insurance company statistics indicate that younger drivers in particular have a high accident rate. As a consequence, their premiums are significantly greater than those of most other age groups.

At times, drivers willfully or carelessly violate the safety standards expected of all those who use our public roads. When they do so, they become

TEACH

Summarize for students the three requirements necessary to operate a vehicle on public roads. (Up-to-date license plates and registration; financial responsibility, such as auto insurance; and a valid driver's license)

APPLY

Ask volunteers to discuss examples of reckless driving that they either witnessed or committed. Guide students to see the risks reckless driving creates for others by making a class list of the negative outcomes of this behavior. **Guided Practice**

If possible, obtain copies of your state's motor vehicle laws, often found in your state's driver's manual. (A driver education teacher may be a good resource.) Allow students time to study the laws. Then have each student write, using a computer, if possible, one multiple choice question (and answer) for a driver's license exam. Have students compile the test questions into one test, take the test individually, then check their responses against the answer key.

Independent Practice

RETEACH

Ask students to respond in writing to the following statement, using a computer, if possible: **Driving an automobile is a privilege, not a right.** (Answers may include that people agree to perform certain responsible acts in exchange for the privilege of driving.)

Have students work as a group to create a serious, yet effective, skit on the hazards of reckless driving. Videotape the skit, perhaps to be used by the driver's education instructor in future classes.

In some states, minors who can prove hardship can receive their driver's licenses early, sometimes before age 15. Hold a discussion on the rationale and benefits of such an exception to the law. (Answers may include that minors who are farm workers, or those who can prove hardship, such as needing to drive to work to help support their family, may do so.)

Preventing Legal Difficulties

Display the overhead transparency, *How the State Laws Vary for Minors* as you reemphasize the first point on p. 136 of the text. Then, to help students practice what to do in a vehicular emergency, assign pairs of students to role-play points 2, 3, and 4. Have students copy the key information onto an index card and keep it in the car in case of an emergency.

potentially liable both civilly and criminally for their actions. In particular, anyone who fails to exercise reasonable care, unreasonably interferes with the use of a public road by others, or deliberately disregards their own safety or that of others may be prosecuted for **reckless driving.** Generally, being convicted of reckless driving three times in twelve to eighteen months results in the loss of a driver's license. Other circumstances that cause the state to take away the driving privilege include the following:

1. driving a car while under the influence of alcohol or other drugs,
2. killing someone while driving negligently,
3. committing a felony while using a car, and
4. repeatedly violating traffic ordinances or regulations.

Responsibie driving habits are required of everyone. Proper care and understanding by any competent individual can ensure that the privilege of operating a motor vehicle on our highways is never lost.

Preventing Legal Difficulties

1. As you travel from state to state, the minimum age for full adult responsibility for criminal acts, torts, voting, driving, drinking, and many other forms of conduct varies greatly. Become familiar with the appropriate laws in each jurisdiction you enter.

If you become involved in an automobile accident...

2. Do not leave the scene unless it is absolutely necessary to seek medical treatment. Contact the police and have a report made of the incident.
3. Exchange identifications and insurance company information with any other involved drivers. Obtain the names and addresses of all witnesses. In addition, write down the license number and description of each car involved and its part in the accident.
4. Do not say anything or sign any statement regarding responsibility for the accident until you have discussed the matter with your attorney. Do not admit fault to the other driver, any witness, an insurance adjuster, or even the police, since you may not know or understand all the facts.

▼ REVIEWING IMPORTANT POINTS

1. A minor is a person from whom certain legal rights and duties are withheld due to being under a legally specified age.

2. Minors and adults alike are required to obey the law and generally are held responsible for their failure to do so.
3. Upon arrest and thereafter, minors, although often subject to the control of a juvenile court system, have constitutional rights similar to those of adults.
4. Parents have the right to the custody and control of their minor children and are entitled to their services and earnings until the children become emancipated.
5. Students may not be denied their constitutional rights, but school authorities have the power to make reasonable rules to ensure the proper maintenance of the educational environment.
6. In owning and driving a car, a minor is subject to the same duty of obeying traffic regulations as an adult. Like an adult, a minor's driver's license may be suspended or revoked if he or she repeatedly violates such regulations.

▼ STRENGTHENING YOUR LEGAL VOCABULARY

Match each term with the statement that best defines that term. Some terms may not be used.

adoption
annulment
emancipation
financial responsibility
guardian
guardian ad litem
juvenile delinquent
majority
minor
reckless driving
truants

1. Minors who fail to attend school when legally required to do so.
2. Person who has not yet reached majority.
3. Adult appointed to sue or defend on behalf of a minor.
4. Age at which one is legally bound by one's contracts.
5. Voluntary surrender by the parents of the rights to care, custody, control, and earnings of a minor child.
6. Adult appointed by a court to have custody of and care for a child during his or her minority.
7. Deliberately driving a vehicle without reasonable care, thus disregarding one's own safety and that of others.
8. Legally taking another's child as one's own.

▼ CLOSE

Display the list of rights withheld from minors that students created in the FOCUS activity at the beginning of this chapter. Have them amend and modify their class list based on the information they discussed in the chapter.

Assign the following end-of-chapter materials:
Student text review activities, pp. 137–141
Workbook, pp. 15–16
Chapter Test

Chapter *MicroExam*

▼ Strengthening Your Legal Vocabulary ▼

1. truants
2. minor
3. guardian ad litem
4. majority
5. emancipation
6. guardian
7. reckless driving
8. adoption
9. annulment
10. financial responsibility

Applying Law to Everyday Life

1. As a minor, she will generally not be charged with or prosecuted for crimes. But she can be found guilty of juvenile delinquency in a juvenile or children's court and committed to a correctional facility. (p. 128)
2. Yes; Unless a minor is emancipated, a minor's earnings belong to the parents. (p.131)
3. No; Although the parents are responsible for their daughter's room and board, they have provided for it in their contract with the school. (p. 132)
4. Yes; A student who is suspended or expelled is entitled to due process, including a conference informing the student of the nature of the offense and an opportunity to give that student's side of the story. (p. 134)
5. No; The ban was an arbitrary exercise of authority and violated the students' right to freedom of the press. (p. 134)
6. Reasonable regulations to prevent interference with a school's operations are not contrary to the U.S. Constitution. When there is a history of disruptions and a breakdown of discipline, as here, reasonable rules to restore and maintain order are proper. (p. 133)

9. Court declaration that a valid marriage never existed.
10. Ability to pay damages.

APPLYING LAW TO EVERYDAY LIFE

1. Shultz, a computer genius and longtime computer hacker, is seventeen years old. Late one evening, she breaks into the school office and steals the access passwords for the school's computer. The next day, she uses her personal computer and modem to erase the past ten years' worth of student grades and other records of the school. It will cost over $300,000 to restore the files. Through telephone company records, Shultz is identified. Can she be prosecuted as an adult?
2. Nguyen, age sixteen, has worked as a clerk in a legal clinic for several months. She earns $70 a week and saves it for her college education. Her father, who needs money to pay an overdue debt, claims that all of her wages legally belong to her parents. Is he correct?
3. The Cuellars strongly disapproved of the life-style of their sixteen-year-old daughter. Therefore, they sent her to a boarding school in another state. Once there she began to do well in her classes, but, unable to stand the food served at the school, she built up sizable credit accounts at nearby restaurants. Because she is unable to pay the debts, the restaurants demand that her parents pay them. Must they do so?
4. Nickie, a high school senior, was suspended from school and not allowed to graduate with her class because she intentionally disabled a teacher's car. Nickie insisted that she was innocent but was never given an opportunity by the school principal to tell her version of what happened. Were her constitutional rights violated?
5. Warwick was editor of the school newspaper. In order to write an editorial on crime on the school grounds, she requested that the administration provide her with the relevant statistics it had. When it refused, she sued for the information on behalf of the paper and won. The administration promptly suspended publication of the paper. Was the suspension a valid exercise of the school officials' authority?
6. Simmons and some other students came to school wearing buttons proclaiming their position on abortion. They did this in defiance of a school regulation prohibiting the wearing of insignia of a controversial nature. The regulation was adopted after similar conduct had resulted in many previous school disturbances. A proper hearing was held, and the students were suspended. They claimed they had been denied their right to freedom of speech. Do you agree?

7 Spezio, age seventeen, had an unblemished safety record for the year he had been a licensed driver. To reward him, his parents bought him a new sports car. Late one evening, on a nearly deserted interstate highway, Spezio pushed his new car to its limit and was caught speeding at over 115 miles per hour. What should he be charged with?

8 Simone and Chuck, both age sixteen, slipped away one day and were married. Their parents did not find out until one year later. Can the parents still get a court order to annul the marriage?

9 ETHICS ISSUE Your friend, Bill, is a star end on the football team but has been struggling to maintain the C-minus average required for eligibility to play. One day he mentions to you that his coach has provided him with answers to the upcoming history exam. He asks if you want the answers. Should you use them? Should you report the coach's conduct to the proper authorities?

10 ETHICS ISSUE Jill's parents' car was damaged by a hit-and-run driver while Jill was using the car. Her mother and father want her to tell their insurance agent that the car's cracked front windshield was part of the resulting damage. Jill knows the windshield was cracked long before the incident. What should she do?

SOLVING CASE PROBLEMS

1 Ohio statutes provide for free education for all children from ages six to twenty-one. The statutes also empower the principal of a public school to suspend for up to ten days or to expel a pupil who misbehaves. In either case, the student's parents must be notified within twenty-four hours, and the reason for the action must be stated. The suspended or expelled pupil, or the parents, may appeal the decision to the board of education. Nine suspended students of high schools in Columbus sued to have the statute declared unconstitutional. They claimed that the statute permitted public school administrators to deprive, without a hearing, the students of their rights to an education, a violation of due process. The nine students' alleged offenses varied from physical attack on a police officer to being bystanders, according to their claims, at disturbances. None of the students was told the reasons for suspension. A three-judge district court held that the students had been denied due process. The court held that in connection with a suspension of up to ten days, students must be given oral or written notice of the charges against them. If the students deny the charges, they must be given a hearing of the evidence and an opportunity to present statements in their defense. The decision of the district court was appealed. Should

7 Spezio should be charged with reckless driving. Regardless of the number of cars on a public highway, his speed showed a deliberate disregard for the safety of others and, of course, himself. (p. 136)

8 Yes; Since Simone and Chuck are still minors, their parents could legally annul the marriage. (p. 130)

9 ETHICS ISSUE Fairness would require you to turn down the offer and report the coach. From a utilitarian standpoint, it would depend on how much good would be done for the greatest number through each alternative.

10 ETHICS ISSUE The admonition against bearing false witness would preclude making such a statement. Deontologically, lying is wrong and unethical.

Solving Case Problems

1 Yes, education is a property right conferred by the state, and it cannot be withdrawn except by due process of law. This due process can be minimal, however, and for short-term suspensions does not require a formal proceeding. (p. 134)

2 Yes; The court stated that neither the Bill of Rights nor the Fourth Amendment is for adults alone. Due process, in the case of juveniles, requires that the parents be notified when the juvenile is taken into custody, and that they be given sufficient advance notice of the court hearing. Before and during the hearing, the juvenile is entitled to counsel. (p. 130)

3 No; Once brought under the jurisdiction of the juvenile system, the defendant could be tried as an adult only by qualifying him under already established juvenile court standards. (pp. 128–129)

4 The court held that the juveniles had a right to privacy as afforded other citizens under the Constitution. This right extended to whether or not they had obtained contraceptives and superseded the right of parents to care and custody. (p. 130)

the Supreme Court uphold the decision of the lower court? (*Goss v. Lopez,* 419 U.S. 565)

2 On the complaint of Cook, Gault, age fifteen, was taken to the Children's Detention Home. Cook claimed that Gault had telephoned her and made obscene remarks—a violation of Arizona law. Gault's parents were not notified of his arrest but learned of it through a friend. At the time, Gault was on probation as a result of being in the company of another boy who, four months earlier, had stolen a wallet from a woman. A hearing date was set, but Gault's parents were not notified of the hearing until two or three days before it took place. At the informal hearing, no attorney was present to represent Gault. Nor was Cook, the complaining witness, present. Gault was found to be delinquent even though he did not admit to the charges, and he was committed to the State Industrial School "for the period of his minority" unless discharged sooner. The judge found Gault delinquent because he was "habitually involved in immoral matters." Under Arizona law, there is no appeal from the decisions of a juvenile court. Gault claimed that he had been denied due process of law. He claimed that he was entitled to the same constitutional rights as adults even though hearings for juvenile offenders are more informal than are criminal trials. Is he right? (*Application of Gault,* 187 S. Ct. 1428)

3 When he was twenty years old, Carlton Smith was proceeded against in juvenile court for the murder of three of his relatives. He confessed that he committed these acts when he was fifteen. After the initiation of the juvenile court proceedings, enough time lapsed for Smith to become twenty-one. The government then dismissed the juvenile charges and indicted Smith as an adult for the alleged murders. Should the government be allowed to try him as an adult? (*United States v. Smith,* 851 F.2d 706)

4 The administrators of the state-supported Tri-County Family Planning Center in Lansing, Michigan, were sued by a group of parents. The parents alleged that their constitutional rights were violated by the center's admitted practice of distributing contraceptive devices and medication to unemancipated minors without notifying the minors' parents. The parents requested that the court order the center to stop the practice. In the fiscal year prior to the filing of the action, the center had in fact distributed contraceptive devices to 623 females who were seventeen years old, 466 who were sixteen, 210 who were fifteen, and 74 who were fourteen. All of the recipients had been counseled, and it was found that 89 percent still lived with their parents, with 88 percent having had intercourse at least once before visiting the center. In deciding the suit, the trial court had to consider that the U.S.

Supreme Court had declared unconstitutional a law that forbade the teaching of foreign languages to pupils who had not passed the eighth grade and a law that required all children between ages eight and sixteen to attend the public schools. These laws were held unconstitutional because they violated the right of the parents to the care and custody of their children under the Fourteenth Amendment. How should this court decide? (*Doe v. Irwin*, 615 F.2d 1162)

5 In 1966, Catherine and William Franz were married. Before they were divorced in 1976, the couple had three children. Catherine retained custody of the children, and William was awarded visitation rights, which he exercised regularly. Prior to the divorce, Catherine developed a "personal relationship" with Charles Allen. Allen later confessed to authorities that he was a "contract killer" and involved with organized crime leaders. In return for the relocation and protection of himself, Catherine, and the three children under the Federal Witness Protection Program, Allen testified in an important criminal trial. Therefore, in early 1978, federal marshals moved Allen, Catherine, and the three children to a new, undisclosed location and provided them with new identities. This was allegedly accomplished without the participation or consent of William or the children. Thereafter, William brought suit against the United States, the Attorney General of the United States, and the Department of Justice to be allowed to exercise his court-granted right to visit his children. He also sued for money damages. The District Court dismissed the case. Franz has appealed. How should the appellate court rule? (*Franz v. United States*, 707 F.2d 582)

5 This is an excellent discussion case due to the lack of easy answers. The appellate court reversed and remanded the case to the district court. The court stated that Mr. Franz did have a cause of action, and that he could sue the government for a violation of Fifth and Fourteenth amendment rights to maintain a relationship with his children. (p. 131) These rights would be violated if he was not afforded procedural protections, such as a hearing. Particular emphasis would need to be placed on whether or not there existed a legitimate state interest to justify infringement of the parental rights, and whether there was equally effective alternative solutions, less restrictive of the father's and children's rights. Note that in a supplemental decision, the court held that the U.S. Attorney General, in accordance with the witness relocation program, could act at odds with visitation rights created by state law.

CHAPTER 8 ORGANIZER

Chapter Theme

Our laws determine the legal status of our personal relationships before, during, and after marriage, and even impact our loved ones after our death.

DIRECTED STUDY QUESTIONS	SPECIAL FEATURES	PROGRAM RESOURCES				
		Reteach	Enrich	SN	AM	
How does the law affect premarital relationships?	Personal Perspectives, p. 144	✔	✔		V K	
How do you get married?	Multicultural Highlights, p. 145 Thinking Critically Through Visuals, p. 146	✔	✔			
What are the rights and duties of wives and husbands?	Writing Connections, p. 147	✔	✔		A	
How is a marriage legally ended?		✔	✔	✔		
What are the legal consequences of a person's death?	Thinking Critically Through Visuals, pp. 149, 151 Ethics Issue, p. 151	✔	✔			
How is a decedent's estate managed?	Preventing Legal Difficulties, p. 153	✔	✔			

Additional Resources

- Clifford, Denis. *Simple Will Book: How to Prepare a Legally Valid Will.* Berkeley, CA: Nolo Press, 1989.
- Leonard, Robin D. and Elias, Stephen. *Family Law Dictionary.* Berkeley, CA: Nolo Press, 1990.
- Robinson, Joan, LL.B. *An American Legal Almanac.* Dobbs Ferry, NY: Oceana Publications, Inc., 1978.
- *You & the Law.* Pleasantville, NY: The Readers' Digest Association, 1984.

One-semester course	✔	✔						
One-year course	✔	✔	✔					

Chapter Pacing Guide

	ASSESSMENT OPPORTUNITIES			
Cooperative Learning	**Informal Assessment**	**Chapter Review**	**Chapter Test**	**Chapter *MicroExam*** 
	✔	✔	✔	✔
	✔	✔	✔	✔
	✔	✔	✔	✔
✔	✔	✔	✔	✔
	✔	✔	✔	✔
	✔	✔	✔	✔

Videodiscs

Marriage

Search Chapter 10, Play To 11

Death and Probate

Search Chapter 11, Play To 12

State by State

In Mississippi, a "Universal Life" minister, ordained by mail, can legitimize vows. However, in New York a marriage solemnized by a Universal Life minister was declared void.

Teaching Materials

Student text, pp. 142–157

Overhead transparency masters
- *How the Marital Relationship Is Terminated*
- *Distribution of a Decedent's Estate*

Videos
- *Our Legal System* Videotape
- *Law for Business* Videodisc

Workbook, pp. 17–18

Outside Resources

- Tape recorder
- Camcorder

Assessment
- Chapter Test

- Chapter *MicroExam*

Vocabulary

annulled, p. 144
common-law marriages, p. 145
marital consortium, p. 146
prenuptial contract, p. 147
voidable marriage, p. 147
void marriage, p. 148
bigamist, p. 148
divorce, p. 148
no-fault divorce, p. 148
separation, p. 148
alimony, p. 148
intestate, p. 149
administrator, p. 149
administratrix, p. 149
estate, p. 149
testate, p. 150
will, p. 150
testator, p. 150
testatrix, p. 150
testamentary intent, p. 150
testamentary capacity, p. 150
holographic will, p. 151
nuncupative will, p. 151
codicil, p. 152
executor, p. 153
executrix, p. 153

Learning Objectives

When you complete this chapter, you will be able to

1. Understand how the law affects premarital and marital relationships.
2. Define the rights and duties of wives and husbands.
3. Describe how a marriage is legally ended.
4. Explain the legal consequences of a person's death.
5. Know the legal definition of a will and why a person makes one.
6. Describe how a decedent's estate is managed.

Chapter Self-Test

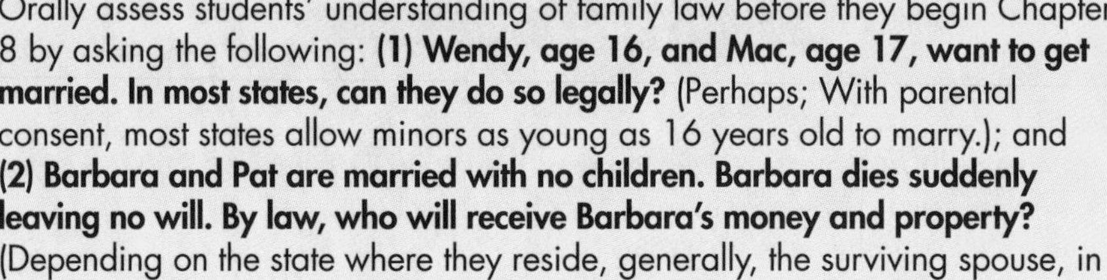

Orally assess students' understanding of family law before they begin Chapter 8 by asking the following: **(1) Wendy, age 16, and Mac, age 17, want to get married. In most states, can they do so legally?** (Perhaps; With parental consent, most states allow minors as young as 16 years old to marry.); and **(2) Barbara and Pat are married with no children. Barbara dies suddenly leaving no will. By law, who will receive Barbara's money and property?** (Depending on the state where they reside, generally, the surviving spouse, in this case Pat, receives one-third to one-half. The remaining share goes to the decedent's parents or siblings.)

CHAPTER 8

LAWS FOR FAMILIES

1 ETHICS ISSUE Your friend, Ramón, falls in love with Susan. She feels the same way about him. They discuss marriage during Christmas vacation. On that holiday she gives him an expensive watch, and he presents her with a pearl necklace. On New Year's Eve, they decide to be married, and Ramón gives Susan a $5,000 engagement ring. A few months later, after a long argument, Susan calls off the engagement. Ramón asks Susan to return the necklace and the ring. Ethically, should Susan return them? Will the law compel her to do so?

2 Harold and Denise are legally separated. Denise takes care of the couple's three young children and does not work outside of the home. One fall, she buys school clothing for the three children on credit. If Denise cannot pay the bill, is Harold legally responsible for paying it?

3 Nick became angry with his wife and wrote a will that left her nothing. Does he have the legal power to disinherit her?

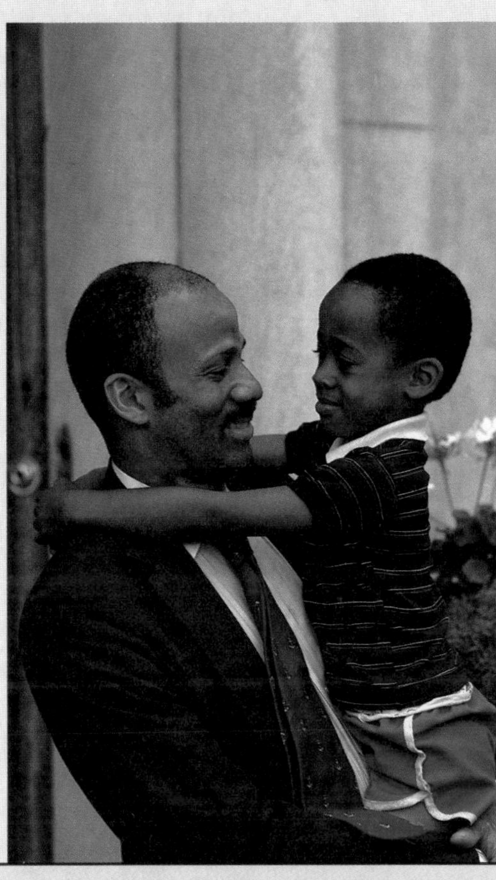

▼ FOCUS

On a sheet of paper, have each student list three things they now own or plan to acquire in the near future. Tell them to choose things that are very important to them.

Have students discuss how they might feel if their former spouse laid claim to these possessions after their marriage had ended in divorce. Ask students how they think they could prevent such claims. (Answers may include signing a prenuptial agreement.)

You Decide

1 ETHICS ISSUE In most states the legal and ethical requirements closely parallel one another. If gifts are given in anticipation of marriage, then they should be returned.

2 The wage earner, in this case the father, remains legally responsible for such debts regardless of the separation.

3 No; Generally, spouses may not disinherit one another—a surviving spouse can elect to receive, under the will or what statutes and case law in the state allow, one third of the estate.

Thinking Critically Through Visuals

In the photograph, it appears that this father and son have a loving relationship. What evidence supports that statement? (Answers may include the father and son are smiling at one another, dad is holding his son, and the boy appears clean, healthy, happy, and well-nourished.) **Is parents' support of children a legal or an ethical responsibility?** (Both)

TEACH

Make sure students understand that when a marriage proposal has been accepted, a premarital contract is formed. Explain to students that if both parties agree to end the contract, then the law considers the agreement **annulled**, or void and to have never existed.

APPLY

Choose students to role-play the following scenario: **Two months ago, Michael proposed to Maria and gave her an engagement ring. She accepted his proposal. Recently, Maria met Phil and called off the wedding.** Have the class debate the rights of Michael and Maria.

Guided Practice

Personal Perspectives

Ask students to discuss with adult family members the role and rights of parents in their children's dating choices and conduct. Have them consider the legal, ethical, and cultural aspects of these issues. Have students create a chart comparing their views with those of their family members. **Independent Practice**

HOW DOES THE LAW AFFECT PREMARITAL RELATIONSHIPS?

PROBLEM

Jim and Mary are both sixteen years old. While dating they have intimate relations, and Mary becomes pregnant. Will the law compel them to marry?

In times past, parents selected mates for their children based on such criteria as social standing, wealth, and religion. The feelings of the husband- and wife-to-be were seldom considered. When a child married at an early age, the parents' blessing, in the form of legal permission for the minor to enter matrimony, was necessary. Marriage was intended to last for the lifetime of the husband and wife. Divorce was socially stigmatizing and, in many countries, illegal.

Times have changed. The primary responsibility for selecting a mate now rests with those whom it will affect the most. No law specifies a minimum age for dating or restricts the choice of marital partners (except in certain cases involving close relatives). If parents tell their minor child not to date or not to see a specific person, they can enforce that order only with the "reasonable force" that they may use to see that their other directions are carried out. If that fails, parents have no legal means to achieve their ends short of having their child labeled incorrigible in a juvenile delinquency proceeding. Parental use of excessive force may result in charges of child abuse.

Laws against premarital sexual intercourse have generally been eliminated over the past fifteen years. However, if pregnancy results and the male responsible is identified, he will be required to pay the female's medical bills and to contribute to the child's support until the child reaches adulthood. This is true even if the father is a minor. Beyond that requirement, no law exists to force the parents of an illegitimate child to marry. In the problem, Mary and Jim may remain single.

However, if one party in a heterosexual relationship proposes marriage and the other accepts, a binding contract results. If both later mutually agree to end their engagement, the contract is **annulled**, which means that the law considers their agreement void and never to have existed. If only one party wants out of the contract and refuses to perform, a breach-of-promise suit may be brought by the other party. Such suits at one time were notorious because juries set abnormally high figures to compensate the jilted party (usually the woman) for the actual damages, humiliation, and hurt feelings that accompanied the breakup. Today, some states allow such suits only where the woman is pregnant and her ex-fiancé is the father.

ASSESS

Learning Objective 1 Have students respond orally to the following: **One month before the ceremony, Tim cancels the wedding, leaving Ann devastated. Is their premarital contract considered annulled?** (No, there was not mutual consent to break the contract.) **Sue and Lou lived together for eight years pretending to be husband and wife. Then, Lou packed and left. Can Sue marry someone else?** (Yes, as long as the state in which they live does not recognize their union as a marriage.)

Other states have placed a cap on the amount of damages that can be awarded. Many states have banned breach-of-promise suits altogether.

If third parties interfere with the engagement, a few states allow damage suits against the intruders. Such suits, however, cannot be brought against the parents who try to prevent their son or daughter from marrying.

When a relationship breaks down, gifts given by one party to the other often create legal problems. If the gift, such as an engagement ring, is given in expectation of marriage, the courts will generally order it to be returned. However, a few jurisdictions allow the woman to retain the ring if it is the man who broke off the engagement. Gifts other than those given in expectation of marriage can be kept by the recipient.

HOW DO YOU GET MARRIED?

PROBLEM

Zed, a friend of yours, lived with Tamra for more than two years. Although they never applied for a marriage license, they told everyone that they were married. Recently, they split up, and now Tamra is about to marry another man. However, Zed claims that she cannot enter another marriage because she is his common-law wife. Is he correct?

Most couples begin the process of becoming wife and husband by appearing before the city or town clerk and applying for a marriage license. In the vast majority of states, if they are over eighteen years of age, they do not need their parents' consent. With parental consent, most states allow minors as young as sixteen years old to marry.

Many states require a blood test to show that the applicants are free from various communicable diseases before the license is issued. A mandatory waiting period of three days from application to issuance is common. Once the license has been issued, any authorized religious or civil official can perform the ceremony. Court clerks, mayors, judges, rabbis, ministers, priests, and even ship captains at sea may then legally tie the knot.

Due to the absence of suitable authority on the frontier, many pioneers could not follow legal methods for becoming husband and wife. As a consequence, the law recognized **common-law marriages** when a single woman and a single man lived together, shared common property, and held themselves out as husband and wife over a prolonged period of time (usually ten years or longer). Today, approximately one-fourth of our states still allow such marriages, although all states must recognize such a union if it is legal in the state in which it occurred. In the problem, Tamra and Zed, even if they lived in a state that allowed common-law marriages, did not remain

TEACH

Marriage is a binding contract. A license, blood test, and parental consent (in some situations) are needed. Explain, however, that some states recognize common-law marriages.

APPLY

Draw a Venn diagram on the chalkboard. Label one circle *Common-law* and the other *Traditional*. Fill in the diagram as students discuss the two types of marriage. **Guided Practice**

Multicultural Highlights

Read aloud the following from *Youth in China* by Beverley Hooper. "'I've heard that quite a few women become single mothers in the West, ... But in China it's against both traditional morality and socialist ethics ... The woman would be ... a social outcast ... Without formal marriage registration, a woman is not entitled to paid maternity leave or subsidized hospital costs and child care.'" Have students compare our societal values and laws with those in China. **Independent Practice**

RETEACH Have students create a flowchart showing the steps from a premarital relationship through a traditional marriage. (Engagement—Parental consent—License—Blood test, if required—Authorized official)

ENRICH

Ask students to think about the legal, economic, and moral aspects of living together versus being married. Have students choose a point of view and defend it in writing, using the computer, if possible, in a one-page essay.

Thinking Critically Through Visuals

The couple in the photograph has just become husband and wife. What leads you to believe that this is a traditional marriage? Explain. (Answers may include that the people are dressed for a traditional wedding ceremony, and so on.)

▼ TEACH

Point out that the law recognizes procreation, raising children, and filling sexual, economic, and companionship needs as the purpose of marriage. Both spouses are to meet these obligations, known as the **marital consortium**. Each spouse also is responsible for debts that were jointly incurred. Ask students if they know what a **prenuptial contract** is.

▼ APPLY

Have each student create a two-column chart headed **My Duties** and **Spouse's Duties**. Have them list their personal expectations for marriage. Discuss whether the law backs up their expectations.

Guided Practice

together long enough to be considered married under common law. Therefore, Tamra is free to marry.

▼ WHAT ARE THE RIGHTS AND DUTIES OF WIVES AND HUSBANDS?

PROBLEM

Your friend Bill's mother died three years ago. Now his father plans to remarry, and Bill is concerned that his father's fiancée will have a claim against the family home and other property. Is there anything Bill can do to prevent such a claim?

Traditionally, the law sees husband and wife as parties to a marriage contract for life and for the benefit of each other. Procreation, raising children, and filling sexual, economic, and companionship needs all provide the practical and legally recognized purposes for marriage.

The law sees these purposes as mutual obligations of the wife and husband and labels them the **marital consortium.** In most states, if either spouse suffers an injury that prevents fulfillment of these marital duties, the other can sue the party who caused the harm for damages for loss of consortium.

▼ ASSESS

Learning Objective 2 Ask students: **(1) Angie works outside the home and her husband, Joey, takes care of their children. Joey breaks his eyeglasses and expects Angie to pay for a new pair. Is she legally obligated to do so?** (Yes, she is responsible for meeting the family's needs.); and **(2) Mary and Jim—married and both gainfully employed—signed a contract to buy a car. They agreed to use part of both salaries to make the payments. After three months, Mary quit her job. Is Jim legally obligated to pay the whole car payment?** (Yes, they jointly incurred the expense.)

Property acquired during the marriage may be kept in the name of the husband, the wife, or both. Either marital partner can buy and sell property of all types in her or his own name and have sole control of the respective earnings and credit. Such was not always the case, especially for the woman in the relationship. The rights of each spouse in the property of the other upon divorce or death are discussed later in this chapter.

At times, spouses bring property into marriage that they want to retain in their own names without the other spouse having claim over it, especially in the event of death or divorce. This can be legally accomplished with a **prenuptial contract.** The marital partners-to-be, by entering into such a contract, typically give up any future claim they might have to part or all of the other's property. Such a contract is especially useful when one or both are entering into their second marriage and want to reserve their property from the first marriage for the children of that bond. In the problem, Bill could recommend that his father enter a prenuptial agreement with his fiancée by which she would give up any property claims she might acquire by the marriage.

As discussed in Chapter 7, the most important duty of both spouses is to provide for the support, nurture, welfare, and education of their children. Other obligations jointly entered into, such as contracts, notes, and income tax returns, are also the mutual responsibility of the marital partners. Finally, the actions of one spouse may incur liability for the other, such as when the wife or husband is left in charge of the household while the other works. This often happens when there are young children in the family. In such a circumstance, the wage-earning spouse is legally responsible for the debts incurred by the other in purchasing food, clothing, medical care, furniture, and any other items necessary to such an undertaking.

HOW IS A MARRIAGE LEGALLY ENDED?

PROBLEM

After they were married a short time, Samuel told Susan that he did not want to have children. Despite several months of discussion, he remained firm. Can Susan end their marriage due to his firm decision?

A marriage may end several ways. The death of either spouse, annulment, divorce, or a variety of illegalities may bring it about. The legal consequences of the spouse's death are discussed later in this chapter.

Annulment ends many marriages. Such problems as refusal to have children or fraudulent grounds for the marriage contract may produce a **void-**

Writing Connections

Social Science
Pair male and female students to create a model prenuptial agreement, using the computer, if possible. Assume the students marry and have one child. Then, in small groups, have students discuss the possible difficulties the couples may have in anticipating and meeting future needs of the family.

Independent Practice

TEACH

Tell students that a marriage can end by death, annulment, divorce, or illegality. Explain the difference between a **voidable marriage** and a **void marriage**.

APPLY

Help students with reading comprehension difficulties to understand the terms void marriage and voidable marriage by reading aloud the definition of *void*. Then have students read the definition for the suffix *-able*.

Guided Practice

RETEACH Have students draw up a contract, on the computer, if possible, listing spousal obligations. Remind students to write clearly, concisely, and specifically. (Answers may include providing for children, meeting joint obligations, paying all debts to meet household needs.)

ENRICH Ask students to collect and compile the lists created in the APPLY activity on p. 146. Have students create two posters showing the top 10 duties of wives and husbands. Have students discuss the stereotypes of each role.

Write the following divorce rate statistics on the chalkboard. 1950 (2.6%); 1960 (2.2%); 1970 (3.5%); 1980 (5.2%); 1990 (4.7%). Have students use these figures to design a line graph. Some students may want to use a computer graphics or spreadsheet program to create their graphs.

Independent Practice

Have students role-play divorce proceedings in class. It is important to emphasize to students the necessity of being sincere, sensitive, and realistic during this role-play activity. The issues examined here are extremely important, but also extremely personal. Choose a judge and a court recorder. Divide the remainder of the class into groups of four or five students. Assign the following roles in each group: facilitator, to keep everyone on task and make sure requirements are met; one male and one female litigant; and two attorneys. After each 10-minute role-play presentation, let the class debate how the issues of alimony, child custody and support, visitation, and property division should be settled.

Cooperative Learning

able marriage. Fraudulent grounds for marriage include either spouse lying to the other as to wealth, condition of pregnancy, freedom from disease, willingness to have a child, past marriage, or age. Such a marriage may be terminated within a reasonable time by an annulment proceeding, but stays valid until then. In the problem, Susan could avoid her marriage by annulment on the grounds that Samuel refused to have children.

A **void marriage,** on the other hand, creates no rights or duties for either party and is considered invalid from the beginning. Such a marriage typically occurs whenever laws are violated by the matrimonial union; for example, when one partner is already married when the second marriage occurs. A person who knowingly marries a second spouse while still married to the first is a **bigamist**. Bigamy is a crime.

The method usually used to end a marriage is **divorce**. This is a court action that terminates the marriage and divides the property and remaining responsibilities between the parties. Divorce has been made even more available with **no-fault divorce.** In such a proceeding, the requesting spouse does not have to list a grievance, such as adultery, desertion, or cruelty, against the other. Instead the court recognizes the right of either the wife or the husband to terminate a failed marriage unilaterally or by mutual agreement.

The usual first step toward divorce is **separation**. In such an event the spouses maintain separate living quarters, but their marital rights and obligations remain intact. To alter these rights and obligations, the parties or their lawyers must negotiate a legal separation agreement. This separation agreement contains terms covering such items as child custody and support, **alimony** (i.e., support paid by the wage earner of the family to the other spouse), and property division. If the parties fail to reconcile their differences during the period of separation and instead go through with a divorce proceeding, the separation agreement often becomes the basis for the final divorce decree.

WHAT ARE THE LEGAL CONSEQUENCES OF A PERSON'S DEATH?

PROBLEM

Dennis, a bachelor living in Maine, often thought he should make a will but repeatedly put off doing so. In the meantime he amassed considerable property. One day, without warning, Dennis died of a heart attack. How will his estate be handled?

When a person dies, the law looks for instructions to resolve some basic legal issues that necessarily arise. These issues include how the debts of the

ASSESS

Learning Objective 3 Ask students to describe, in writing, the ways a marriage can end. (Annulment: judicial declaration that a marriage never existed; void marriage: judicial declaration that the marriage was invalid from the beginning; or divorce: a court action that terminates the marriage and divides the property and remaining responsibilities between parties; and death of a spouse.) Discuss students' responses.

decedent—the deceased person—are to be paid and what is to be done with the remaining property. The necessary instructions are found either in the wishes of the decedent as expressed in a valid will, in statutes, or in both.

1. Death Without a Will

Those who die without a valid will are said to have died **intestate**. When a person dies intestate, as in the problem, a special court (generally called a probate court or surrogate's court) has the power to settle the affairs of the decedent. This court appoints a personal representative known as an **administrator** (if male) or **administratrix** (if female) to take charge of the intestate's property. This representative uses the property of the deceased, called the **estate**, to pay all debts, including the costs of administering the estate. The remainder of the property will then be distributed in accordance with the state's intestacy statute. Dying without a professionally drafted will can cause the beneficiaries to pay considerable administrative expenses and needlessly large estate taxes.

Generally, intestacy statutes call for a surviving spouse to receive one-third to one-half of the estate with the remainder divided equally among the children. If there are no surviving children or grandchildren, then that share goes to the decedent's parents or, if they are dead as well, to the decedent's sisters and brothers and their children.

▼ TEACH

Explain to students that when a person dies it is important that he or she has previously prepared a will. A **will** is a legal expression, usually in writing, directing how the decedent wishes his or her property to be distributed after death. If there is no will, then the person is said to have died **intestate**. All of the decedent's property, called the **estate**, is controlled and distributed by a court-appointed person known as an **administrator** or **administratrix**. Tell students that the suffix *-tor* designates male, *-trix* female.

▼ APPLY

Thinking Critically Through Visuals

The decedent in the photograph is being laid to rest. What does the visual evidence tell you about the decedent's life? (The men in uniform and the clergyman indicate that religion and the military were probably important aspects of the decedent's life.) **Does death end the decedent's power concerning how his or her property is to be distributed?** (No, not if there is a will.)

▼RETEACH

Display the overhead transparency, *How the Marital Relationship Is Terminated.* Have students offer definitions and examples of the terms.

▼ENRICH

Have students examine the graphs they created in the APPLY on p. 148. In an essay, using the computer, if possible, have students speculate about why the divorce rates have risen over the last four decades. (Answers may include that fewer women are as financially dependent on men and divorce is more socially accepted.)

Copy the base and labels for the following graphic organizer onto a transparency. Ask students to add details from pp. 148–152 on the horizontal lines. You may wish to have students copy the completed graphic organizer in their notebooks.

Guided Practice

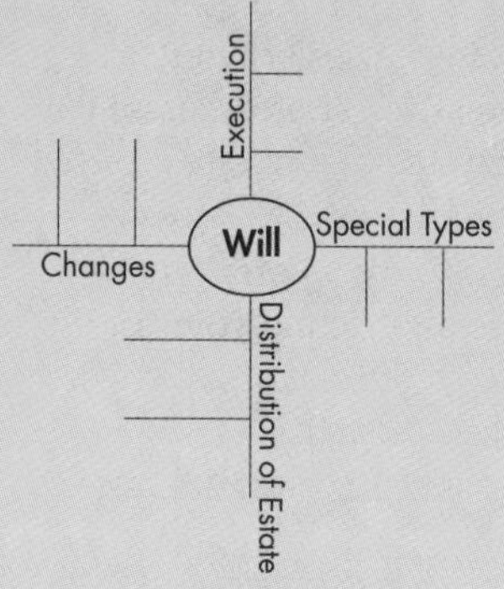

Have students write a model will, using a computer, if possible. Because of the sensitivity of this activity, you may wish to have students assume the identity of a historical or fictional character. The purpose of the activity is to meet basic will requirements and to compose with clarity. Even a humorous will can be evaluated for these principles.

Independent Practice

2. A Will Allows the Maker to Direct the Distribution of the Estate

It is usually much to the advantage of all concerned if the decedent died **testate** (i.e., leaving a valid will). A **will** is a legal expression, usually in writing, by which a person directs how her or his property is to be distributed after death (see Figure 8-1). The maker of the will is called the **testator** (if male) or the **testatrix** (if female). In contrast to the intestacy statutes (which distribute a decedent's estate without regard for need), a will allows a person to direct his or her estate's resources to where they can do the most good.

3. A Will Goes Into Effect Upon Death

A will takes effect only upon the death of the maker. Therefore, it can be changed or canceled at any time during the maker's life. However, this ability to change the document as often as desired, coupled with the fact that the contents of a will are proved only after the death of the maker, opens the way to potentially false claims under forged documents.

4. Execution of a Valid Will

To counteract the possibility of forgery, the law has strict requirements regarding the preparation and execution of valid wills. The most basic requirements (holding true in almost every state) are the following:

1. The testatrix or testator must have **testamentary intent.** A person must not be pressured into signing the document against his or her desires by the undue influence of others. Likewise, the signer must not be misled into thinking that the document is something other than a will.

2. The testator or testatrix, at the time the will is executed, must have **testamentary capacity** to make the will. The maker must know, in a general way at least, the kind and extent of the property involved, the persons who stand to benefit, and that he or she is making arrangements to dispose of his or her property after death. Lapses into senility by the maker often bring the will of an elderly person into question due to the possible lack of capacity. In most states a person under age eighteen does not have testamentary capacity by law.

3. The will must be in writing and, in most states, signed at the end of the document to prevent unauthorized additions. The signing must be witnessed by at least two adults. These witnesses should not be individuals who will inherit under the will and must be advised that they are watching the testator's or testatrix's will being signed.

ASSESS

Learning Objectives 4 & 5 Have students write answers to complete the following statements as you read them aloud: **1. Those who have died intestate have died _____.** (Without a will); **2. The property of the deceased is called his or her _____.** (Estate); **3. The purpose of a will is to allow the maker to _______.** (Direct the distribution of his or her estate); and **4. Compare the following roles: administrator and administratrix.** (Both are personal representatives appointed by the court to take charge of the intestate's property and to pay all debts; *administrator* is male and *administratrix* is female.)

WILL
OF
REBECCA BIRK FAULSTICH

I, Rebecca Birk Faulstich, of 1875 El Rey Way, San Francisco, California, declare that this is my will. I revoke all wills and codicils that I have previously made.

FIRST: I am married to Kevin Alan Faulstich and we have one child, Jeffrey Michael, born March 12, 19--.

SECOND: After payment of all my debts, I give my estate as follows:

(A) To my twin sister, Rachel Ann Wilson, I give my personal clothing, jewelry, and sporting equipment, if she should survive me.

(B) To my beloved husband, Kevin, I give all the residue if he should survive me for thirty (30) days.

(C) To our son, Jeffrey Michael, I give all the residue if my husband should not survive me for thirty days and if my son should survive me for thirty days.

(D) To the Regents of the University of California (to provide student scholarships and awards without reference to financial need, in order to encourage excellence of effort and achievement), I give all the residue if neither my husband nor my son should survive me for thirty days.

THIRD: I nominate my husband as the executor of this will. If for any reason he should fail to qualify or cease to act as such, I nominate my sister, Rachel, as executrix. If for any reason she should fail to qualify or cease to act as such, I nominate the Central City Bank, a California corporation, to act as executor. I direct that neither my husband nor my sister be required to post bond as executor or executrix.

IN WITNESS WHEREOF, I have hereunto set my hand this 18th day of January, 19--, in San Francisco, California.

Rebecca Birk Faulstich
Rebecca Birk Faulstich

The foregoing instrument was subscribed on the date which it bears by the testatrix, Rebecca Birk Faulstich, and at the time of subscribing was declared by her to be her last will. The subscription and declaration were made in our presence, we being present at the same time; and we, at her request and in her presence and in the presence of each other, have affixed our signatures hereto as witnesses:

Diana P. Davis residing at 432 Third Street San Francisco Calif.
Adam T. Price residing at 436 Third Street San Francisco, Calif.

Figure 8-1
The properly executed formal will of Rebecca Birk Faulstich directs how her property is to be distributed after death.

5. Special Types of Wills

There are exceptions to the rules for the execution of a valid will. For example, many states recognize a holographic will as valid even without witnesses. A **holographic will** is one that was written entirely by the decedent's own hand and signed by him or her. A **nuncupative** (oral) **will** is

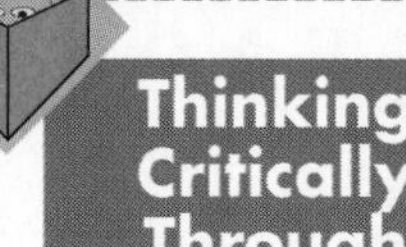

Thinking Critically Through Visuals

This will allows the testatrix to distribute her estate according to her wishes. Who is Rebecca's first choice to be the executor of her will? (Her husband) **If Rebecca and her husband die simultaneously, what happens to her estate?** (Her son inherits everything except her personal clothing, jewelry, and sporting equipment.)

ETHICS ISSUE

Ethics Issue

Have students examine the will on p. 151. Ask them to debate the following: **1. Was it ethical for Rebecca to leave some things to her sister?** (Answers may include yes, because the sister was a beloved family member, too.) **2. If Rebecca had two sisters, would she be ethically obligated to divide her belongings between the two sisters?** (Answers may include no, because relationships between family members are unique.)

▼RETEACH Using the model wills from the APPLY on p. 150, ask students to write an explanation and/or definition next to each section of the will.

▼ENRICH Have students consider the consequences of using computer software and electronic data storage for preparing a will. Ask them to brainstorm and debate the issues that might arise from wills that are composed on the computer. (Answers may include that the decedent's computer file could be tampered with, witnesses and lawyers are excluded from the process, and so on.)

▼ TEACH

The probate court handles estates whether or not there is a will. Tell students that when a person dies with a valid will, the probate court gives the responsibility of the estate to an **executor** (male) or **executrix** (female). This person's duties are to preserve the estate's assets, to inventory the estate, pay all debts, and distribute property according to the will. Point out to students that the probate court oversees the executor or executrix as he or she carries out his or her duties.

▼ APPLY

Display the overhead transparency, *Distribution of a Decedent's Estate.* Ask student volunteers to offer definitions or examples of the following terms: **estate, will, intestacy, testator, testatrix, executrix, executor, administrator,** and **administratrix**.

Guided Practice

Ask students to make a comparison table to compare the terms **executor, executrix, administrator,** and **administratrix**. (All are appointed by the court and are charged with similar duties. The executor or executrix is appointed when there is a will. The administrator or administratrix is appointed when there is no will.)
Independent Practice

recognized in some states if proclaimed during the maker's last illness or by service personnel on active duty. However, the will must be witnessed and is often limited to controlling the distribution of personal property.

Lee was fatally injured in an automobile accident late one evening. As she lay dying, she told three witnesses that she was making a will and that she wanted her valuable collection of paintings to go to her good friend Anne. In a state that allowed nuncupative wills, if the witnesses' testimonies were properly and promptly reduced to writing, Lee's dying wish as to the disposition of her property would be carried out.

6. Keeping the Will Current

Regardless of its form, it is important that the maker of a will keep it current. Marriage, divorce, the birth of children, and other significant changes in a person's life should be reflected in the document by periodic amendments. Where a valid holographic will is utilized, changes require appropriate additions or deletions (before witnesses if necessary) in the handwriting of the maker. In states requiring a formal will, changes must be made using a **codicil**, which is a formal, written, and witnessed amendment.

7. Revoking a Will

A will may be completely revoked, rather than amended, in several ways. Doing something to the will that clearly indicates an intent to revoke it, such as destroying it or defacing it, will accomplish this end. Also, according to some state statutes, the marriage of the maker or the birth or adoption of a child by that individual works an automatic termination. Divorce, on the other hand, does not produce such an automatic revocation. However, a divorce settlement does revoke the parts of a will with which the settlement conflicts once the divorce occurs. Finally, a will may be revoked by a written revocation in a later will. Such a document must either explicitly state, "I hereby revoke all prior wills," or contain provisions that conflict with the prior will so that it impliedly revokes the preceding document.

▼ HOW IS A DECEDENT'S ESTATE MANAGED?

PROBLEM

Benson owed Cane $1,750. Cane did not learn of Benson's death until eight months after it occurred. By that time, the period for presenting claims against the estate had elapsed. Can Cane still legally collect the $1,750 from the estate?

▼ ASSESS

Learning Objective 6 Ask students to indicate whether the following statements are true, by raising a hand with fingers spread for true ,or false by raising a tight fist. **An executor or executrix acts out of respect for the deceased and his or her actions carry no liability.** (False) **A probate court will handle the decedent's estate whether or not he or she died with a valid will.** (True)

Whether a person dies with or without a valid will, a probate court will supervise the handling of the decedent's estate. If there is a will, the court will place the estate in the hands of a qualified personal representative of the deceased called an **executor** (male) or **executrix** (female). Often the executrix or executor is named in the will itself, as shown in Figure 8-1. As with the administrator or administratrix discussed earlier in this chapter, this personal representative's duties extend to (1) assembling and preserving the assets of the estate (which include collecting debts owed to it), (2) inventorying the estate, (3) paying the debts owed by it, and (4) distributing the remaining property according to the will or statute.

The executrix or executor will be liable for failure to reasonably carry out her or his duties. Depending on the size and types of property in the estate, the task can be quite complex. For instance, the personal representative must properly give public notice that all creditors of the estate have a set time, typically six months, to file a claim or go unpaid. He or she must then determine which claims are valid and pay them where possible. In the problem, because Cane did not file within the proper period, the $1,750 will not be paid by the estate.

In addition, even if there is a will, there may be statutory provisions allowing certain relatives to override the will's terms and receive more of the estate than the will provided. For example, in some states the surviving spouse may elect to receive one-third to one-half of the decedent's property instead of the share provided under the will.

Because of the number of technicalities and potential problems, the settling of a decedent's estate with or without a will is an undertaking best carried out with the professional help of a lawyer.

Preventing Legal Difficulties

1. Realize that hasty, ill-considered decisions in selecting a marital partner may become life-long mistakes. Make your decisions with the long-term good of both you and your partner in mind.
2. Consider marriage a serious contract between the husband and wife that requires each to fulfill their duties with mutual concern and respect for each other.
3. Use prenuptial agreements, where appropriate, to avoid subsequent conflicts over property ownership and division.
4. In the event of divorce, seek legal counsel and carefully consider and fulfill the obligations, such as child support and alimony, being assumed.
5. For the good of those you leave behind upon death, consult an attorney and make a will. Remember to update it as your circumstances change.

Preventing Legal Difficulties

Discuss each of the five suggestions for preventing legal difficulties. Ask students to suggest scenarios that reflect the possible consequences of not following each of these suggestions.

▼ CLOSE

Divide the class into six groups and assign one of the six sections in the chapter to each group. Have each student think of one *Jeopardy*-style question for that section. When finished, have each student read aloud his or her question while others write down their answers. When finished, have each student provide the answer to his or her question.

Assign the following end-of-chapter materials:
Student text review activities, pp. 154–157
Workbook, pp. 17–18
Chapter Test

Chapter *MicroExam*

▼RETEACH

Using the *Glossary of Legal Terms* on pp. 809–836, have students create a crossword puzzle for the following terms: **executor, executrix, will, administrator, administratrix,** and **estate.**

▼ENRICH

Have students exchange their model wills from the APPLY on p. 150. Have each student imagine that he or she is the executor or executrix of his or her partner's will. Ask students to describe in writing, using the computer, if possible, how they would carry out those duties.

Strengthening Your Legal Vocabulary

1. holographic will
2. divorce
3. bigamist
4. administratrix
5. alimony
6. marital consortium
7. testator
8. codicil
9. nuncupative will
10. no-fault divorce

REVIEWING IMPORTANT POINTS

1. In most jurisdictions, a gift given by one party in a relationship to the other in anticipation of marriage has to be returned to the giver if the parties do not marry.
2. Parental consent to marry is generally required for individuals between ages sixteen and eighteen.
3. Suits involving loss of consortium may succeed against individuals who cause harm that prevents a spouse from fulfilling marital duties.
4. In a prenuptial contract, marital partners-to-be may renounce any claim to the property of their intended they might acquire through marriage.
5. Even though a married couple may separate or divorce, such obligations as alimony and child support, where appropriate, remain legally enforceable.
6. The basic requirements for a valid, formal will are testamentary intent and capacity, a general knowledge of what is being done, and a signed writing with witnesses.
7. A will can be revoked or changed at any time prior to the testator's (testatrix's) death.
8. Creditors' rights against the estate and the rights of a surviving spouse to a share of the estate may not be defeated by a will that attempts to give the property to others.

STRENGTHENING YOUR LEGAL VOCABULARY

Match each term with the statement that best defines that term. Some terms may not be used.

administrator
administratrix
alimony
annulled
bigamist
codicil
common-law
divorce
estate
executor
executrix
holographic
intestate
marital consortium
no-fault divorce
nuncupative
prenuptial contract
separation
testamentary capacity
testamentary intent
testate
testator
testatrix
void
voidable
will

1. A handwritten will.
2. Method usually used to end a marriage.
3. Person who knowingly marries a second spouse while still married to the first.
4. Woman appointed by the court to manage the estate of a person who died without a valid will.
5. Support paid by the wage earner of the family to the other spouse during separation or after divorce.
6. Mutual obligations of the husband and wife to each other under the marriage contract.
7. Male maker of a will.
8. Formal, written, and witnessed amendment to a will.
9. An oral will.
10. Divorce proceeding in which the requesting spouse does not have to list a grievance against the other.

APPLYING LAW TO EVERYDAY LIFE

1. ETHICS ISSUE Becky and Tom are engaged. Tom has told her he does not want children. Becky knows that she cannot conceive because of an illness she had a few years ago. Should she tell Tom that she cannot have children?
2. ETHICS ISSUE Maria is an only child. Her mother died when she was eight years old. Now, seven years later, her father is engaged to remarry, and Maria objects. She is afraid that her father's new wife will come between her and her father and that the new wife will end up with the family home after her father dies. Ethically, should Maria try to persuade her father not to marry? Is there a legal device that would help resolve part of her worries?
3. Marcel is twenty-two years old and Heather is sixteen. After Heather's parents refused to consent to her marriage, Heather and Marcel eloped. Can Heather's parents have the marriage annulled even though Marcel is an adult?
4. The night after Zeke and Shanda were married, Shanda admitted that she was pregnant by another man. Can Zeke end their marriage? How?

Applying Law to Everyday Life

1. ETHICS ISSUE Ethically, the concealment of such a fundamental problem is improper but legally would not provide grounds for an annulment unless she lied to him about it. (pp. 147–148)
2. ETHICS ISSUE From the standpoint of the egoist (emphasis on self-interest), the answer would be yes. Even a utilitarian (emphasis on seeking the greatest good for the greatest number) would urge that she make her viewpoint known to the father, as his actions might result in severe future problems for all concerned. Legally, a properly negotiated prenuptial agreement (p. 147) might prevent conflict.
3. Yes. Either of her parents could bring suit to annul the marriage. (pp. 145, 148)
4. Yes; by seeking an annulment due to her pregnancy. (pp. 147–148)

5 Yes, and the support of the two children, if they ended up in Ben's custody. (p. 148)
6 No; The father lacked testamentary capacity due to his weak, drugged condition. Testamentary intent was also absent. The father's property would be distributed according to the intestacy statute of the state. (p. 150)
7 No; Without proper execution before witnesses the will is invalid. (p. 150)
8 Generally, this would be a valid holographic will, and Toa's property would be distributed accordingly. Due to the fluctuations in state law pertaining to holographic wills, however, it is wise to consult with an attorney to formulate and properly execute a valid, enforceable will. (p. 151)
9 Hilda's last will, dated the first day of June, is the will which governs the distribution of her estate. The second will, due to its conflicts with the first, implies that it revoked the earlier will even if this was not expressly stated. (p. 152)
10 Yes; State statutory provisions allow certain relatives to override the will's terms and receive more of the estate. (p. 153)

5 Ben Thomas was a writer. He was married to Agnes, a stockbroker. Ben stayed home to write and to take care of their two children. But since Ben's writings had not sold, Agnes provided the sole financial support to the family. If Ben and Agnes ever divorce, would Agnes have to pay for Ben's support?

6 The Corleys had placed their father in a nursing home because he required round-the-clock medical attention. When he was near death, the family decided to have him make a will. While he was weak and so heavily sedated that he was unaware of what was happening, one of his daughters placed a pen in his hand and told him to sign the document. He did so. Is this document a valid will? Why or why not?

7 Sid went to his attorney's office and described in detail how he wanted his estate distributed upon his death. The lawyer made extensive notes and prepared a twelve-page will. He called Sid and read it to him over the phone. Sid made a few minor changes. The lawyer then prepared a final copy. On his way to the lawyer's office to sign the document, Sid died of a heart attack. Was the final copy a valid will? Why or why not?

8 Toa was ill. She did not think she could afford an attorney, so she sat down and wrote on notebook paper what she wanted done with all of her property upon her death. She signed and dated at the end of the document in front of four neighbors, who also signed as witnesses. Will Toa's estate be distributed according to her wishes or in some other manner?

9 Hilda executed a will on the first day of January. On the first day of June in the same year she executed a second will, which contained many provisions in conflict with the first will. She died on the first day of December. Which will governs the distribution of her estate?

10 Eric executed a valid will dividing his property among his wife and three children. The will was not altered for twenty-two years. Then Eric separated from his wife but did not divorce her. He wrote a second will, which left all of his property to their children. After Eric's death, his wife sued to receive a fair share of his estate. Will she succeed?

SOLVING CASE PROBLEMS

1 More than four years after they were married, George Woy sought an annulment of his marriage to Linda Woy on the basis of fraud. In his petition he alleged that at the time of the marriage ceremony he was unaware that she had a dependence on illegal drugs, and that, had

she not concealed the fact from him, he would have refused to marry her. Should the court grant an annulment on this basis? (*Woy v. Woy,* 737 S.W.2d 769)

2 When they remarried each other, Robert Root owed Nila Root several thousand dollars of unpaid child support from their first marriage. A month and a half after their second marriage ceremony, Nila filed to dissolve their second marriage and demanded payment of the back child support. Should the court allow her to collect the money, since she is still married to Robert? (*In re Marriage of Root,* 774 S.W.2d 521)

3 James and Anna Nesbit were contemplating divorce. They entered into a property settlement agreement, but James died before the divorce became final. His will provided a greater amount of property for Anna than did the settlement agreement. Which document should be enforced? (*Crist v. Nesbit,* 352 S.W.2d 53)

4 Ralph Mangan was wounded by a gunshot in 1971. He was hospitalized and later moved to a nursing home. There, he executed a will dated February 23, 1972. After his release from the nursing home, he was cared for by his brother for a short time. Because of Ralph's advanced age and medical problems, he was again hospitalized. In May 1972, he returned to the nursing home and in June was adjudicated incompetent. He died in August 1972. His will was filed for probate and was contested on the grounds that Ralph was disoriented because of his advanced age, heart disease, and the gunshot wound. The will left property to someone described as a nephew when there was no such nephew. Witnesses testified that during Ralph's first stay in the nursing home he was self-reliant and was able to handle his own business affairs. Ralph's attorney testified that Ralph appeared to be of sound mind at the time he executed the will. Ralph had discussed the details of the will with the attorney and had mentioned a number of nephews, cousins, and other distant relatives. Ralph's physicians testified that Ralph had periods of disorientation and periods of lucidity. Is Ralph's will valid? (*Edward L. Mangan v. Joseph J. Mangan, Jr.,* 554 S.W.2d 418)

Solving Case Problems

1 No; There was no evidence she had lied to him about the matter—she had only concealed it from him. Therefore, she had not defrauded him. (p. 148)

2 Yes; A woman's property rights are not canceled just because she marries. (p. 147)

3 The will; The property settlement agreement would take effect only upon the divorce. (p. 152)

4 Yes; Ralph's will is valid. The law requires only that the testator have testamentary capacity at the time the will is executed, not later at the time of death. The fact that one of the persons named in the will was described as a nephew, when he in fact was not, is a mistake easily made by a person with a number of nephews, cousins, and other distant relatives. (p. 150)

CHAPTER 9 ORGANIZER

Chapter Theme

Laws protect consumers against unscrupulous merchants, defective merchandise, and unfair trade practices.

DIRECTED STUDY QUESTIONS	SPECIAL FEATURES	PROGRAM RESOURCES				
		Reteach	Enrich	SN	AM	
Why does the law protect consumers?	Multicultural Highlights, pp. 160, 162 Thinking Critically Through Visuals, pp. 161, 162 Writing Connections, p. 162	✔	✔			
How does the law protect against substandard consumer goods?	Thinking Critically Through Visuals, p. 164 Personal Perspectives, p. 165	✔	✔		V K	
What trade practices are prohibited by consumer law?	Ethics Issue, p. 167	✔	✔	✔	A	
Are any agreements in restraint of trade valid?		✔	✔			
How do state and local governments promote compliance with consumer protection statutes?	Thinking Critically Through Visuals, p. 173 Preventing Legal Difficulties, p. 174	✔	✔			

Additional Resources

- *America at Risk: A History of Consumer Protest*, videotape. Chicago, IL: Public Media Inc.
- *Little Injustices*, videotape. Alexandria, VA: PBS Video.
- Oliver, Daniel. "How Regulation Affects the Consumer." *Consumers' Research Magazine*, July 1993, pp. 14–18.
- *The Smart Consumer's Directory*, 1993 ed. Nashville, TN: Thomas Nelson Publishers, 1992.

One-semester course	✔	✔	✔					
One-year course	✔	✔	✔	✔	✔			

	ASSESSMENT OPPORTUNITIES			
Cooperative Learning	Informal Assessment	Chapter Review	Chapter Test	Chapter *MicroExam*
	✔	✔	✔	✔
✔	✔	✔	✔	✔
	✔	✔	✔	✔
	✔	✔	✔	✔
	✔	✔	✔	✔

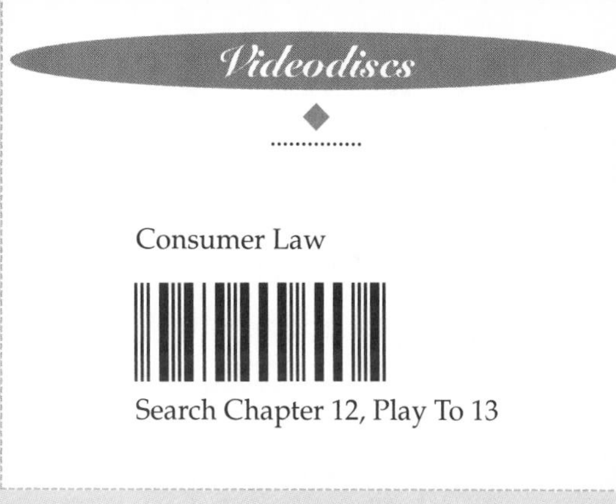

Videodiscs
Consumer Law
Search Chapter 12, Play To 13

State by State

In New Jersey, a person who took money from others to buy tickets in the lotteries of other states committed an illegal act.

Teaching Materials

Student text, pp. 158–182

Overhead transparency masters
- *Consumer Contact Points*
- *The Protective Shield of Consumer Laws*

Videos
- *Our Legal System* Videotape
- *Law for Business* Videodisc

Workbook, pp. 19–24

Outside Resources
- Blank overhead transparencies
- Magazines and newspapers
- Package labels from food, over-the-counter drugs, and cosmetics
- Props, such as a potato chip bag, motor oil, and hair spray
- Outside speaker: representative from Better Business Bureau, chamber of commerce, or state attorney general's office
- Government directories and telephone books
- Copies of public building codes

- *America at Risk: A History of Consumer Protest,* videotape from Public Media Inc.
- *Little Injustices,* videotape from PBS Video
- Tape recorder
- Camcorder
- VCR

Assessment
- Chapter Test

- Chapter *MicroExam*

Vocabulary

consumer, p. 160
caveat emptor, p. 160
class actions, p. 161
cease-and-desist order, p. 161
consent order, p. 162
restitution, p. 162
adulterated, p. 164
unfair trade practice, p. 165
false and misleading advertising, p. 167
bait and switch, p. 167
corrective advertising, p. 167
lottery, p. 167
confidence game, p. 168
loss leaders, p. 169

Learning Objectives

When you complete this chapter, you will be able to

1. Understand why the law focuses on the protection of consumers.
2. Describe how the law protects against substandard consumer goods.
3. Know the trade practices that are prohibited by consumer law.
4. Appreciate the contribution of local and state governments to consumer protection.

158

Chapter Self-Test

Assess students' understanding of consumer law before they begin Chapter 9 by asking them to identify the following federal agencies and to describe briefly their function: FDA, EPA, and FTC. (The Food and Drug Administration ensures purity of food, drugs, and cosmetics; the Environmental Protection Agency controls air and water pollution; and the Federal Trade Commission restrains unfair trade practices and monopolies.) Before continuing with the chapter, review and discuss students' responses.

CHAPTER

9

LAWS FOR CONSUMERS

1 ETHICS ISSUE A nearby resort offers a prize of either $5,000 in cash or a home spa if you will attend a sales presentation. You attend and are persuaded to buy a resort property. After you sign the contract, the salesperson informs you that you have won a home spa. She retrieves a large box and fits it into your car trunk. When you inspect your prize, you discover that it is simply an inflatable pool. You also realize what a hardship it will be to make the payments on the property. Legally you have five days to back out of the contract. Ethically, should you do so?

2 A newspaper ad promises to sell a computer, at $750 below its regular price, to the first ten customers who enter the store on Saturday. You are second in line when the store opens, but the store is sold out of the advertised computer. Can you legally force the store to sell you the advertised computer at the promised price?

3 You receive a "chain letter" in the mail that promises you will make thousands of dollars if you send $10 to the name at the top of an enclosed list. You are then to put your name and address at the bottom of the list, delete the name you sent money to, and send the new list and a copy of the letter to ten of your friends. If you comply, will you be violating the law?

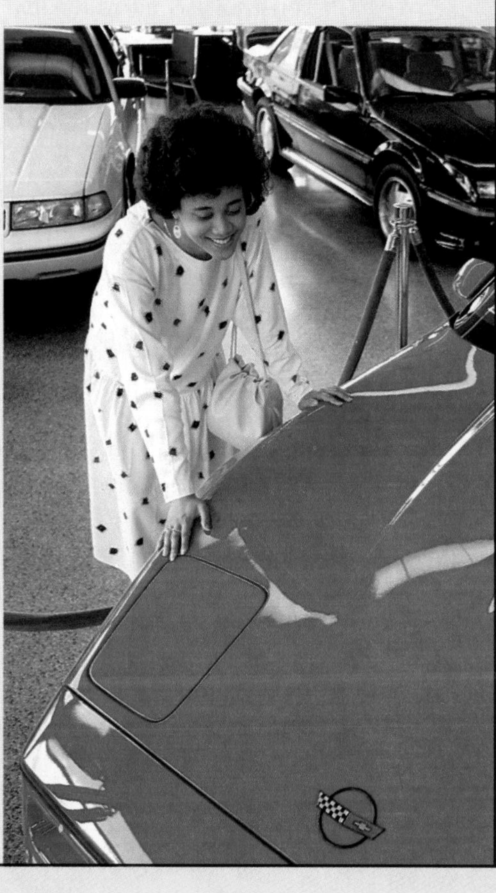

FOCUS

Pair students as they enter the classroom. Have the pairs brainstorm and list on a sheet of paper all federal agencies that they can name that provide consumer protection.

Have one student from each pair read aloud their list. Instruct all students to cross out any duplicate agency that they also have listed. Continue until all pairs have had a turn to read their lists. Reward pairs that listed agencies that were not identified by others.

You Decide

1 ETHICS ISSUE Yes; The five-day grace period was the result of a study of contract situations by the state legislature. It was decided that such legislation provided the greatest good for the greatest number. From that standpoint, avoiding the contract would be ethical. The salesperson certainly must have known about the period for possible withdrawal, and that the "home spa" certainly was not what one would have expected.

2 Yes; Understocking advertised items in order to sell similar goods to responding customers at higher prices is a punishable offense. In order to avoid bait-and-switch charges, most stores will offer rainchecks.

3 Yes; A chain letter is considered a pyramid sales scheme, and is a felony in most states.

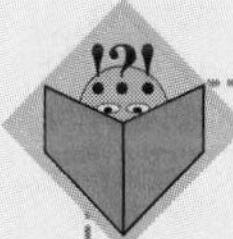

Thinking Critically Through Visuals

The woman in the photograph is shopping for a new car. What laws, do you think, protect the car-buying consumer? (Answers may include "lemon laws", and so on.)

▼ **TEACH**

Tell students that buyers have long lived by the Latin words *caveat emptor* meaning "let the buyer beware." The complexity of today's products and the inaccessibility of manufacturers now require consumers not only to be wary, but also to be aware of the various laws designed to inform and protect them. On the chalkboard, differentiate between the four ways that laws and agencies protect against sellers' abuse (pp. 160–162): **class action**, **cease-and-desist order**, **consent order**, and **restitution**.

Multicultural Highlights

Women often pay more than men do for many goods and services. Women buy nearly 50 percent of the new cars sold each year. Yet, according to *Why Women Pay More*, published by the Center for Responsive Law, a Ralph Nader organization, when compared with a male car buyer, an Anglo woman will pay about $150 more and an African American woman will pay nearly $800 more for the same model.

WHY DOES THE LAW PROTECT CONSUMERS?

PROBLEM

Simmons wanted his car painted. He saw a newspaper advertisement for "car painting, $99.99 complete." He went to the place of business, contracted for the service, and selected a dark blue metallic finish. However, when the paint job was completed and Simmons examined the car, the color was obviously light blue. Simmons complained, but the manager claimed the color was close enough to the color Simmons had selected and refused to make any correction. What should Simmons do?

A **consumer** is an individual who acquires goods that are primarily intended for personal, family, or household use. Until recent decades, the relationship between sellers and consumers was governed primarily by the legal maxim **caveat emptor**—Latin words meaning "let the buyer beware." It was once thought that consumers, so forewarned, would be adequately protected by their own ability to judge a product's safety and utility. In addition, the forces of supply and demand in a competitive marketplace were supposed to keep product makers and sellers committed to producing and marketing the best product for the money so as to maintain their reputation with individual customers.

Unfortunately, these measures proved to be inadequate. In our modern, affluent, technology-oriented society, the complexity and sheer abundance of products leave the consumer unable to properly judge quality or comparative advantage. Products are often so complex that most people cannot determine if they are substandard and could not repair them if they were to break down.

In addition, the products are often offered by huge corporations that are capable of manipulating the marketplace rather than being controlled by it. As a consequence, they are not always responsive to consumer complaints. The sales volume of giant corporations is not as dependent on their reputations with consumers as it once was. Many sellers rely heavily on intensive advertising campaigns costing millions of dollars. Such advertising can be more effective in creating consumer attitudes toward the product than actual first-hand experience or word-of-mouth recommendations. *Caveat emptor* is thereby sometimes subverted by well-chosen television camera angles and seemingly sincere celebrities describing products in glowing terms.

In response, local, state, and federal governments have passed legislation to help restore a balance of power between sellers and buyers in the market-

▼ **ASSESS**

Learning Objective 1 Have students respond in writing to the question: **Why has it become necessary to establish agencies and pass laws to protect consumers?** (Answers may include that today's products are too complex, the marketplace may be manipulated, intensive advertising may be false or misleading, and so on. Historically, laws were created to protect consumers against monopolies, unsanitary production practices, and so on.)

Federal Statute	Basic Objective
Consumer Credit Protection Act	Full disclosure of cost of credit and loans.
Consumer Product Safety Act	Safety of consumer products.
Equal Credit Opportunity Act	Equal access to credit regardless of sex or marital status.
Fair Credit Billing Act	Accuracy and fairness in billing credit accounts.
Fair Credit Reporting Act	Accuracy and fairness in credit agency records.
Fair Debt Collection Practices Act	Elimination of unfair harassment of debtors.
Fair Packaging and Labeling Act	Accuracy and fairness in labels and containers.
Federal Trade Commission Act (as amended)	Protection against unfair methods of competition.
Magnuson-Moss Warranty Act	Clarity of rights under full and limited warranties in sales.
Motor Vehicle Information and Cost Saving Act	Disclosure of factory-recommended prices of various components of new cars.
National Traffic and Motor Vehicle Safety Act	Higher safety standards for automobiles and tires.
Wholesome Meat Act	Upgrading of state inspection standards to federal level.

Figure 9-1
Important federal consumer legislation is designed to ensure a balance of power between sellers and buyers.

place. Some relevant federal statutes are listed in Figure 9-1. In addition, numerous administrative agencies, such as the federal Office of Consumer Affairs, assist and protect consumers. Some of the more important of these agencies are listed in Figure 9-2.

These laws and agencies augment the protection against such abuses that continues to be provided by traditional contract, tort, and criminal laws. For example, anyone who has been deceived while contracting may still sue the wrongdoer for fraud rather than waiting for a governmental agency to act. However, an individual court action to correct a consumer's problem is generally costly and time-consuming. When the product in question costs very little or the potential damage claims are very low, court action is often not worth the required effort and expense. To help overcome this problem, **class actions** have been authorized by court rules. A class action allows one or several persons to sue not only on behalf of themselves, but also on behalf of many others similarly wronged.

When the government acts on behalf of the injured consumer through the proceedings of an administrative agency, it may investigate and issue a **cease-and-desist order** to a company. This is an order requiring the company to stop the specified conduct. If the defendant violates the order,

APPLY

On the chalkboard, write the phrase, *Let the buyer beware.* Ask: **Why isn't this, alone, a good rule for the buyer of a car or a stereo system to follow?** (Answers may include that the average consumer doesn't know enough about the complexities of such products to evaluate them.)

Guided Practice

At this time, you may wish to show the videotape, *America at Risk: A History of Consumer Protest* (color, 60 min.), from Public Media Inc., 5547

N. Ravenswood, Chicago, IL 60640.

Thinking Critically Through Visuals

This chart shows several federal statutes that protect consumers. What statute protects consumers from being denied a credit card because they are divorced? (Equal Credit Opportunity Act) **What statute protects consumers from purchasing inferior car tires?** (Answers may include the National Traffic and Motor Vehicle Safety Act and the Consumer Product Safety Act.)

RETEACH Have students create a cause-and-effect chart to describe how laws have changed to protect consumers. Have students verbally explain their charts to other group members.

ENRICH Have students create a *Mad Magazine*-style, humorous poster illustrating the concept of *caveat emptor*. Display the posters in the hallways or public areas of your school.

Thinking Critically Through Visuals

Which of the agencies listed in this chart would you notify to report that industrial waste had leaked into a reservoir? (Environmental Protection Agency)

Writing Connections

Language Arts
Have students write sample letters of complaint, using the following guidelines:
- Include your name, address, and telephone number.
- Name the product and date and location of purchase.
- State reason for complaint and action you want taken. **Independent Practice**

Multicultural Highlights

Little Injustices is a video that compares Mexican and American systems of settling disputes and complaints. Obtain it from PBS Video, 1320 Braddock Place, Alexandria, VA 22314.

Figure 9-2
Federal agencies provide consumer protection.

Agency	***Area of Consumer Protection***
Consumer Product Safety Commission	Assurance of safety of consumer products.
Department of Agriculture	Assurance of wholesomeness of meat and poultry.
Department of Housing and Urban Development	Establishment of minimum building standards for mobile homes.
Department of Justice—Antitrust Division	Prevention of monopolies.
Department of Labor	Assurance of payment of private pensions.
Environmental Protection Agency	Control over pollution of air and water.
Federal Deposit Insurance Corporation	Control over insurance of bank deposits.
Federal Reserve Board	Control over money supply and inflation.
Federal Savings and Loan Insurance Corporation	Control over insurance of savings accounts.
Federal Trade Commission	Restraint of unfair trade practices and monopolies.
Food and Drug Administration	Assurance of purity of foods, drugs, and cosmetics.
National Highway Traffic Safety Administration	Assurance of safety of motor vehicles and tires.
Securities and Exchange Commission	Regulation of stock and bond sales.
U. S. Postal Service	Control over mail fraud.

heavy civil penalties may be imposed. Often a defendant will sign a consent order rather than resist the charge in a long legal battle. A **consent order** is a voluntary, court-enforceable agreement to stop an illegal or questionable practice. An agency may also order **restitution**—the return to customers of money wrongfully obtained—or some of the other remedies discussed later in this chapter.

In settling a dispute with a business, a consumer may seek help or advice from the state attorney general's office (many maintain toll-free consumer hot lines), the local Better Business Bureau, and, if appropriate, even the customer service department of the corporation involved. In the problem, Simmons might take any of these actions, and as a last resort, he might take his problem to small claims court (see page 426).

Overall, consumer laws provide protection in several basic ways: (1) they help protect against the production and sale of substandard or dangerous consumer goods, (2) they prohibit improper trade practices, (3) they require licenses and inspections to help ensure compliance with the law, and (4) they provide remedies for persons injured. The remainder of this chapter examines these basic protections in detail.

▼ ASSESS

Learning Objective 1 As a group, have students create a graphic organizer showing the actions or orders that can be taken to protect consumers. Then have them copy it in their notebooks. (Answers may include class action, cease-and-desist order, consent order, and restitution.)

HOW DOES THE LAW PROTECT AGAINST SUBSTANDARD CONSUMER GOODS?

PROBLEM

The Annihilator Pest Company developed and sold thousands of robot cockroach traps called the Terminator. The device was mobile and had special sensors and a microprocessor memory. The human user of the trap simply placed it on the floor of the room and the device would pursue, kill, and consume any roaches on the surface it occupied. Unfortunately, recent consumer reports have shown that the integrated circuit chip that controls the trap is too sensitive to vibration and causes the Terminator to go out of control and attack mice, house pets, and even furry house slippers. What is Annihilator required to do?

Although the ultimate responsibility for protection against substandard goods rests with the consumer, the law helps in the following ways.

1. Making and Enforcing Safety Standards

Each year millions of people are injured and thousands are killed by products in use around the home. As a response, in 1972 the Consumer Product Safety Act was made law. The Act created the Consumer Product Safety Commission (CPSC) and gave it authority to issue and enforce safety standards for most consumer products. However, drugs, food, cosmetics, motor vehicles, airplanes, boats, firearms, auto safety seats, and warranties are not under the CPSC's supervision because other agencies are responsible for their regulation.

The CPSC requires any manufacturer, distributor, or retailer that discovers that its product fails to comply with safety regulations to report that fact to the commission. The CPSC also receives reports on product-caused injuries from a computer system tied into the nation's hospitals. If the CPSC determines that a product is substantially hazardous, the manufacturer, distributors, and retailers of the product must notify purchasers of the hazard and then either recall and repair the product, replace it, or refund the purchase price. Often the mere threat of CPSC action causes responsible parties to recall their product "voluntarily." Therefore, in the problem, Annihilator must notify those concerned and implement an appropriate remedy. Failure to comply could lead to fine and imprisonment. If necessary, the CPSC has the power to seize the hazardous product and ban it from the marketplace.

TEACH

On an overhead transparency, draw the following chart to help explain to students how federal agencies protect consumers against substandard goods.

Federal Agency	Duty
Consumer Product Safety Commission (CPSC)	Makes and enforces safety standards
Food and Drug Adminstration (FDA)	Regulates the development, production, and sale of drugs, food, and cosmetics
National Bureau of Standards	Standardizes weights and measures

APPLY

Before showing the overhead transparency, *Consumer Contact Points*, cover the second column that lists the contact agency. In random order, write the names of these agencies on the chalkboard. Have students determine which agency they would contact for each problem listed in the first column. **Guided Practice**

RETEACH On the graphic organizer from the previous ASSESS activity, have students add horizontal lines to each identified action. Then have them add their own examples.

ENRICH Have students use Figures 9-1 and 9-2 to create a poster-size chart showing the relationship between specific federal statutes and agencies that provide consumer protection. For example, the Department of Agriculture and the Wholesome Meat Act protect consumers in the area of meat and poultry.

Consumers who think the CPSC is not taking action where needed may sue in federal district court to have a protective rule established. If victorious, consumers may be awarded an amount to cover reasonable attorney's fees, as well as their court costs.

The CPSC maintains an extensive toll-free telephone service. By requesting CPSC's current number from toll-free information (1-800-555-1212), the consumer can call the CPSC and, among other things, report claims concerning unsafe products, find out about product recalls occurring in the last few months, and get information about unsafe children's products.

2. Regulating the Development, Production, and Sale of Drugs, Food, and Cosmetics

The federal Food and Drug Administration (FDA) requires that the production facilities for cosmetics, food, and drugs be clean and that the products be prepared from ingredients fit for human use or consumption. A product that does not meet the minimum standards for purity and quality set by the FDA is considered **adulterated** and may be confiscated by the government. The U.S. Department of Agriculture also inspects canners, packers, and processors of poultry and meat entering interstate commerce to help ensure that the products are free of disease and were processed under sanitary conditions.

"OUCH!...THE FDA SURE ISN'T PULLING ANY PUNCHES THESE DAYS!!"

Distribute package labels from food, over-the-counter drugs, and cosmetics to small groups. Using these labels, have each group create a collage. Have each group select a facilitator to keep everyone on task; a creative director to arrange and display labels; an editorial director to write a one-paragraph synopsis explaining the artwork; an FDA representative to determine if products meet standards and to label accordingly; and a presenter to give a report. **Cooperative Learning**

Thinking Critically Through Visuals

This cartoon exaggerates the labeling and warnings required by the FDA to be displayed on food products. What message, do you think, is the artist trying to convey? (Answers may include criticism of the FDA's strict labeling regulations and the need for more accurate labeling.)

Invite students to draw their own cartoons pertaining to one of the subheads in this section.

Independent Practice

ASSESS

Learning Objective 2 Independently, have students review this section (pp. 163–165), then create a chart that consists of the following: the three key ways the law helps protect against substandard consumer goods, applicable federal agencies involved, objectives of each, and examples of how these laws protect consumers.

In addition, the FDA requires that labels on regulated products give the name and address of the manufacturer, packager, or distributor, and reveal the quantity, such as the weight or the fluid ounces. Although not required for most foods, the FDA also encourages nutritional labeling. Such labels typically include the caloric, protein, carbohydrate, and fat content of the product as well as the percentage of the recommended daily allowances of protein and nineteen minerals and vitamins provided by a serving.

Drugs are regulated by the FDA to ensure their safety for users and to be certain of their effectiveness for the purpose sold. Without FDA approval, new drugs cannot be marketed in this country. In addition, the FDA determines which drugs are prescription and which may be sold "over-the-counter." The FDA has been criticized for its extremely cautious approach to granting new drug approval because its procedures have led some Americans to go beyond our national borders for certain drugs alleged to be life-saving and pain-easing.

3. Standardizing Weights and Measures

The U.S. Constitution gave Congress the power to fix standards of weights and measures. To do so, Congress created the National Bureau of Standards. This governmental body provides standardized sets of actual weights and measures to the state and local governments. With proper inspection, testing, and enforcement at these levels, the measurement of a gallon of gasoline, pound of bananas, or foot of rope is uniform throughout the country.

Most states inspect and test weighing and measuring devices at least once a year. Seals certify the accuracy of such devices as gasoline pumps, supermarket scales, and taxicab meters. Violations of the weights and measures laws are punishable by fine, imprisonment, or both. In addition, the goods involved may be confiscated.

WHAT TRADE PRACTICES ARE PROHIBITED BY CONSUMER LAW?

Generally, an **unfair trade practice** is any method of business that is dishonest or fraudulent or that illegally limits free competition. To protect consumers, the federal and state governments have enacted numerous laws prohibiting such practices. Chief among these are federal antitrust laws and the Federal Trade Commission Act. They are designed to prevent unfair trade practices in interstate commerce (i.e., business conducted between persons in two or more states). States have similar laws for intrastate com-

Personal Perspectives

Tell students that both Thomas Jefferson and John Quincy Adams suggested that the United States accept metric measurement as the national standard. Ask: **What is metric measurement? In what ways would conversion to metric measurement affect your life?** (Discuss students' responses, which should reflect independent thinking.)

TEACH

Tell students that an **unfair trade practice** is a method of business that is dishonest, fraudulent, or that illegally limits free competition. On the chalkboard or an overhead transparency, copy the following graphic organizer to explain the

different types of unfair trade practices.

Seven Unfair Trade Practices
• Unfair Pricing Methods • Mislabeling Goods • Selling Used Articles as New • Illegal Lotteries or Confidence Games • False or Misleading Advertising • Price Controlling or Fixing • Other

RETEACH

Using a computer, if possible, ask students to write brief descriptions of how the Consumer Product Safety Commission, the Food and Drug Administration, and the National Bureau of Standards affect their lives as consumers. Have volunteers share their reports with the class.

ENRICH

Using a computer, if possible, have students write a one-page essay on whether or not they think the FDA is too cautious in granting new drug approval, especially in light of the AIDS and cancer crises.

▼ APPLY

Add branching lines to the graphic organizer from the TEACH activity in this section. Using text on pp. 166–171 as a reference, have students add details for each of the seven unfair trade practices.

Guided Practice

Tell students to imagine that they live in a country where there is no economic competition, and that the government controls and sets fixed prices. Have students orally describe how this would affect their lives as consumers, and how it might affect product quality.

Using a computer, if possible, have students create false and/or misleading advertisements for items visible in the classroom. Encourage students to use electronic clip art or a draw, paint, or desktop publishing program to enhance their ads. Then, ask students to exchange their ads and

identify the deception in each other's work.

merce (i.e., business conducted wholly within one state). Unfair trade practices take many forms. The more serious types are discussed in the following sections.

1. Making Agreements to Control or Fix Prices

PROBLEM

After lengthy study by a committee and a vote of approval by members of the medical association, the doctors in your community published a list of recommended fees for most of the services they provide. A practitioner charging less than the recommended amount would be considered unethical and subject to censure and possible loss of license. Is this an unfair trade practice?

The part of the free market system that serves the consumer best is competition. Competition is the force that drives efficient businesses to create new and better products and services. Competition also drives the inefficient firms out of business. Some individuals and companies enter into agreements to control or fix prices and thereby try to ensure their survival by eliminating competition. Such agreements, like the scheme mentioned in the problem, are illegal and unenforceable. Violators are subject to criminal penalties.

2. Using False or Misleading Advertising

PROBLEM

A leading national retailer advertised that one of its lawn mowers would be on sale at a very low price beginning on Saturday. Ted Sargent walked into his local store less than fifteen minutes after the store opened that day, went directly to the lawn mower section, and offered to buy one. The store clerk told him that the store's stock of two had already been sold, but there was a better model available for $120 more. Ted spent several minutes looking at the other model. As he was doing so, several other would-be buyers showed up for the advertised lawn mower. Curious, Ted found out from a friend of his who was an employee of the retailer that it purposely drastically understocked the sale items so that salespersons could talk would-be buyers into purchasing more expensive models once they were in the store. Is such a practice illegal?

▼ ASSESS

Learning Objective 3 Have students work in small groups to role-play and present to the class one of the three unfair trade practices discussed on pp. 166–167. Have the audience identify which practice is portrayed and what penalties or corrective practices may be warranted.

False and misleading advertising is advertising that intentionally deceives, makes untrue claims of quality or effectiveness, or fails to reveal critically important facts. Claiming that a mouthwash prevents and cures colds and sore throats when it does not is one example of such advertising. In the problem, the store was guilty of a false and misleading advertising scheme called bait and switch. A store practices **bait and switch** when it uses an understocked, low-priced "come-on" to lure prospective buyers into the store. Once there, the would-be buyers find that the advertised item has been sold out and then are deftly redirected to a better, but more expensive (and profitable) product. The advertisement, however, is not considered deceptive if it states how many of the advertised item are available or otherwise states that the supply of the item is limited. To their credit, many stores that want to maintain customer goodwill give rain checks when even reasonably stocked items are exhausted. Rain checks permit customers to purchase the items later at the advertised price.

The Federal Trade Commission (FTC) has the main responsibility for preventing false and misleading advertising. If necessary, the FTC may order an advertisement terminated. Where the advertiser has created a false impression that will persist even without the advertisement being run any more, the FTC may order corrective advertising. **Corrective advertising** requires the advertiser to admit the wrongdoing and state the truth in a prescribed number of future advertisements.

3. Conducting Illegal Lotteries or Confidence Games

PROBLEM

A national magazine planned to increase the number of its subscribers by giving away prizes of up to $1 million in a drawing. People contacted in a huge mail campaign could enter the drawing by return mail whether or not they actually subscribed to the magazine. However, instructions on how to enter would be placed in the text of the promotional material so a person contacted would have to read about the magazine in order to find out how to enter the drawing. A senior officer of the magazine canceled the plans because she thought it was an illegal lottery. Was she correct?

To be a **lottery**, a gambling scheme or game must have three elements: (1) a required payment of money or something else of value to participate, (2) the winner or winners to be determined by chance rather than by skill, and (3) a prize to be won.

Have students, playing the role of advertisers, admit the deception in the advertisements that they created in the previous APPLY activity. Using a computer, if possible, have students admit to their wrongdoing in a written form and reissue the ads for their products more truthfully.

ETHICS ISSUE

Ethics Issue

Tell students that lotteries and other forms of gambling, long considered illegal, are now being run by a number of our state governments to enhance revenues for specific causes, such as education. Ask: **Ethically, is something good or bad depending only on who profits from it?** Encourage students who take opposite points of view to debate the issue.

RETEACH In pairs, ask students to role-play situations that describe each of the following illegal trade practices: *price fixing, false and misleading advertising,* and *bait and switch.* Have observers guess the practice.

ENRICH Supply students with magazines, newspapers, and newspaper circulars. Have students find advertisements they think could be false or misleading, cut them out, and post them on a bulletin board. Have students circle the ambiguous or deceptive information in each ad.

To alert students to the ease with which they may be deliberately deceived, divide students into pairs to simulate a confidence game. (You may wish to clear this activity with your school administrators or local school board before conducting it.) Have one student role-play the victim and the other the swindler. Have student pairs decide on the method (phone, letter, or in person) and devise a scenario to perform for the class. After each scenario, have the class discuss what the victim did, or could have done, to avoid being victimized. On the chalkboard, make a list of the class's advice.

In order to help ESL students understand important vocabulary related to unfair trade practices, write the following on the chalkboard: **chain letter, swindler, confidence game, loss leaders, mislabeling,** and **lottery**. Have student volunteers explain what the terms mean, give examples, and use the terms in sentences. Then, have ESL students restate, in their own words, what they think the terms mean.

Holding or participating in such a gambling scheme is illegal and violators are subject to fine and imprisonment. However, many states have exempted by statute certain religious and benevolent groups from the lottery prohibition. These groups are allowed to run bingo and other games to produce revenue for their activities. Also, several states are holding their own lotteries to generate revenue for state projects, most notably the funding of educational programs.

The use of lotteries by businesses to promote sales remains an unfair method of competition. In the problem, the promotion was legal because no payment was required to participate. Even so, the FTC would monitor such a game to ensure that all promised prizes are awarded.

Another prohibited scheme often disguised as a legitimate business undertaking is the **confidence game.** Such a game typically involves a fraudulent device whereby the victim is persuaded to trust the swindler with the victim's money or other valuables in hopes of a quick gain. One good example of the confidence game is the chain letter, whereby the sender swindles the recipient by convincing him or her to send money to the person whose name appears at the top of an enclosed list. After sending the money, the recipient is supposed to place his or her name at the bottom of the list and mail copies of the letter and the list to friends. The swindler's name and aliases comprise the first two or more names on the initial list. Initiating or participating in such a scheme is a felony under the law in most states.

4. Using Unfair Pricing Methods

PROBLEM

The Travel Shop, Ltd., priced its luggage at what it claimed to be retail prices and then gave prospective buyers membership in a special club. Members were able to purchase the luggage at "wholesale prices" of one-third off the marked amount. In truth, the marked price less the discount equaled the retail price in other stores and approximately twice the wholesale price. Is this an unfair pricing scheme?

Some of the more common unfair pricing methods include intentionally misrepresenting that goods are being sold at a considerable discount and stating that the price charged for the goods is a wholesale price. Both of these unfair pricing schemes are illustrated in the problem and both are illegal.

Representing goods or services as being free when purchased with another good that is sold at an inflated price to cover the cost of the first is

ASSESS

Learning Objective 3 Explain *pantomime* to students. (Acting that consists primarily of gesture without benefit of spoken dialogue) Have students select one of the three prohibited trade practices discussed on pp. 168–169 and pantomime an example, using props, body language, and visual cues, as necessary. Have the audience identify the practice portrayed, then discuss personal experiences, if any, with each.

also an unfair pricing method. Reputable merchants often give away truly free samples to introduce new products and may have legitimate "two-for-one" and "one-cent" sales as long as the cost of the main item is not artificially raised for the sale.

Some states have unfair sales acts. These acts prevent retailers from selling goods at prices less than their cost plus some minimum markup if the seller's intent is to harm competition. These acts are used to prevent the seller from using well-known brands as loss leaders. **Loss leaders** are used to attract customers into the store to shop. These customers then pay regular or inflated prices for other goods in the store. It has been shown, however, that at times such unfair sales acts inhibit competition. This has resulted in the acts being declared invalid.

Divide the class into four or five groups. Distribute to each group a prop, such as a potato chip bag, motor oil, or hair spray, with the labels covered or removed. Have students create "mislabels" for their item and attach each to the appropriate product. Then, have groups exchange their products and identify the incorrect information on the label.

5. Mislabeling Goods

PROBLEM

Acme Tire Company bought used tires, retreaded them, and sold them as new Acme Supertreads. Was this illegal mislabeling?

Mislabeling a good to make it more marketable is an unfair method of competition that occurs frequently and is prohibited by law. The mislabeling in the problem is a good example. Even the shape or size of a container must not mislead the consumer into thinking the package has more contents than it does. However, some empty space in a package may be necessary to prevent breakage of its contents or may legitimately result from the settling of the contents after filling.

The law also requires that certain products carry warning labels. Poisons and insecticides must have appropriate "Danger" labels. Cigarette packaging and advertisements must carry warnings indicating the danger smoking poses to the health of the user and to others.

6. Selling Used Articles as New

PROBLEM

A large automobile manufacturer allowed its executives to drive the current model year's cars for several months, then rolled back the odometers and sold them as new. Is such an activity illegal?

RETEACH Have students discuss how the practice of comparison shopping can protect consumers from unfair pricing methods, mislabeled goods, and the selling of used articles as new. Have students brainstorm effective ways to shop wisely.

Have pairs of students write a public service announcement warning consumers about unfair trade practices. Have students tape record or videotape their announcements and share them with the class.

Divide the class into seven groups. Have each create a skit showing an unfair trade practice. Assign each group one of the seven trade practices prohibited by law, presented on pp. 166–171. Allow the groups 20 minutes to prepare, then present, their skits. Have the class determine what unfair trade practice is being portrayed. You may wish to videotape the presentations.

Independent Practice

Have students choose a brand name or trademark that already exists, then create a new one so similar that it could confuse or deceive the public. Then, display on a wall a combination of different, original brand names or trademarks and the students' bogus creations. Have the class examine the display and jot down on a sheet of paper the difference between the originals and students' versions.

Many illegal misrepresentations involve selling used, secondhand, or rebuilt articles as if they were new or in a better condition than they are. The most common instance occurs when no indication is given that the goods are secondhand. For example, in used cars, odometers, which show total miles the car has traveled, are turned back, and the cars are then sold for a much higher price. This activity, as depicted in the problem, is illegal.

7. Engaging in Other Unfair Trade Practices

PROBLEM

Superior Cars, Inc., had been selling different models of its luxury limousine called the Excelsior to the very wealthy for more than fifty years. When it discovered that another company was making and selling Excelsior-brand dog food, Superior sued and asked the court to prohibit such use of the Excelsior trademark. Superior claimed that such use was unfair competition, since it misused the good name of Excelsior and thereby undermined the car's reputation as a luxury item. Is Superior correct?

There are many other forms of unfair trade practices and unfair competition. One is the use of a brand name or trademark so similar to a competitor's that it confuses or deceives the public. In the problem, however, the court would hold against Superior because the products involved—cars and dog food—were not in the same area of commerce. If they were competitors in the automobile marketplace, the ruling would go the other way.

Sending unordered merchandise and demanding payment for it or its return is also an unfair trade practice. According to federal law, when someone deliberately sends unordered merchandise through the mail, the recipient is under no obligation to return it or to pay for it. This is true even if the merchandise cannot be returned.

Another unfair practice is commercial bribery, which occurs in several different situations. When a supplier pays a corporation's purchasing agent money "under the counter" in exchange for an order from the supplier, it is commercial bribery. When a manufacturer pays a retail salesperson "push money" for extra effort in promoting the manufacturer's product, commercial bribery is involved. When a spy is employed in "industrial espionage" to find out a competitor's secrets, it is also commercial bribery. In all these instances and others, such bribery is prohibited by law.

▼ ASSESS

Learning Objective 4 Have students complete the fourth section, *Are Any Agreements in Restraint of Trade Valid?*, of the chapter outline on p. 155 of the Workbook. Ask student volunteers to collect, then correct and return other class members' outlines.

In addition, the FTC has adopted many guidelines and regulations that are intended to correct abusive trade practices by requiring businesses to act in certain ways. These include the following:

1. Would-be creditors must explain to their intended borrowers the methods of figuring finance charges (see page 392).

2. Under certain circumstances, sellers, manufacturers, or both must provide written warranties to their customers (see Chapter 18).

3. Businesses selling door-to-door must give purchasers three days to cancel their contracts.

ARE ANY AGREEMENTS IN RESTRAINT OF TRADE VALID?

PROBLEM

Morris employed Weber as an apprentice horseshoer. As part of the bargain, Weber agreed that if he left Morris's shop after completing his apprenticeship, he would not open his own shop to compete with Morris within the county for one year. If Weber failed to keep his promise, could Morris get a court order to end the competition?

Not all agreements that restrain trade are illegal. That is because some trade practices of this nature are believed to be socially and economically desirable if they are reasonable. For example, a person who obtains a patent from the federal government has an exclusive right to make and sell the product for seventeen years. This encourages invention. Similar protection is given to writers, composers, and artists through copyrights.

The government also authorizes certain monopolies by granting exclusive permits for such purposes as transportation, communication, and energy distribution. It would be economically inefficient to have two or more gas or electric companies serve the same block or town. Instead, an exclusive franchise is given to one company, and the government regulates its rates and services.

In the problem, the restraint agreed to by Weber was valid. That is because it was reasonable in terms of area and time and was necessary to protect Morris's business.

TEACH

Explain to students that not all agreements that restrain trade are illegal. Copyrights, patents, and certain monopolies are valid restraints if they are reasonable and are believed to be socially and economically desirable.

APPLY

Tell the class that, at one time, the American Telephone and Telegraph Company (AT&T) had a communications monopoly in the United States. In 1984, in response to a court order, AT&T divested itself of the Bell System—its local telephone companies. Ask: **How, do you think, did this change the communications industry?** (Answers may include the creation of competing phone companies that give consumers a choice of services, increased cost to consumers, and so on.) **Guided Practice**

Divide the class into two debate squads. Have students debate whether or not they think the federal government has the right to authorize certain monopolies and to grant trade restraints to protect those who own patents and copyrights. **Independent Practice**

RETEACH In small groups, ask students to create a graphic organizer to illustrate which agreements in restraint of trade are valid.

ENRICH

In a one-page essay, using a computer, if possible, have students discuss the issue of competition versus government-approved restraint of trade.

TEACH

Tell students that there are laws at the state and local levels that protect consumers. On the chalkboard or an overhead transparency, copy, then discuss, the following graphic organizer:

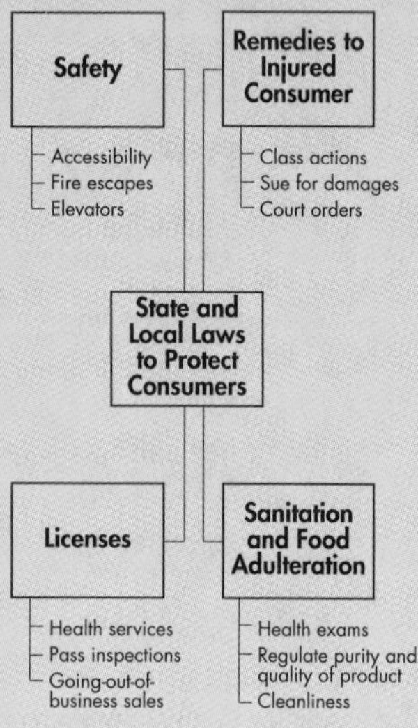

APPLY

Invite a speaker from the Better Business Bureau, chamber of commerce, or state attorney general's office to talk with the class about the organization's purpose, functions, and benefits to consumers. As a whole-class activity, have students prepare questions in advance to ask the speaker. **Guided Practice**

Have students keep a written record for one week of all the people and businesses with which they come in contact, who or which must be licensed. Generate a class list and discuss the extent of this type of consumer protection afforded by licensing laws. **Independent Practice**

HOW DO STATE AND LOCAL GOVERNMENTS PROMOTE COMPLIANCE WITH CONSUMER PROTECTION STATUTES?

PROBLEM

As Wilson and Pequot were driving past the Downtown Electronics Warehouse, Pequot commented that the Warehouse was having another going-out-of-business sale. "They had a sale like this last year and I bought a tape player. I thought I was getting a great deal because they were trying to get rid of all their merchandise. It turned out they stayed in business, and the price I paid was above the regular price for the same tape player at other stores." Are such sales by the Downtown Electronics Warehouse legal?

A variety of state and local laws protect consumers. The extent of that protection is discussed in the following sections.

1. Licensing Laws

Consumer protection often begins with the licensing of suppliers of consumer goods and services. This is particularly true for those who provide health services, such as physicians, dentists, nurses, psychologists, laboratory technicians, and pharmacists. Outside the health professions, teachers, lawyers, morticians, accountants, contractors, plumbers, electricians, realtors, insurance agents, and beauticians, among others, are licensed in most jurisdictions.

Certain businesses and institutions also must pass inspection before they receive their operating licenses. Examples include hospitals, rest homes, private schools, check-cashing services, and insurance companies. Failure to maintain minimum standards may cause suspension or even the permanent cancellation of the license.

Businesses offering repairs on cars, electronic equipment, watches, and the like are often required to give written estimates and detailed bills for all work performed. Similarly, states regulate special sales by retail businesses, such as bankruptcy sales and going-out-of-business sales. Often a special license is required and the businesses must shut down after the sale or be guilty of fraud, as would likely be the case in the problem.

ASSESS

Learning Objective 4 Ask students to list five examples in which state and local governments protect the consumer. (Answers may include licensing suppliers of goods and services, inspection to see that standards are maintained, regulation of repair services, class action suits, inspection of food handlers, and safety regulations for public gathering places.)

2. Laws That Increase the Remedies Available to Injured Consumers

Instead of compelling consumers to rely on various officials to take appropriate legal steps to prevent or remedy harm, many states have given consumers rights against those who take unfair advantage or cause injury. Using these rights in situations where an agency has not acted, the victim may sue for damages and get a court order preventing future violation of the statute the agency was supposed to enforce. These remedies are especially useful when consumers join together in a class action.

3. Sanitation and Food Adulteration Laws

States and localities usually provide for the inspection of businesses where food is handled. Meat markets, bakeries, restaurants, hotels, and other businesses are rated on their cleanliness and are required to display their ratings. Food handlers may be subject to periodic health examinations.

Laws also regulate the purity and quality of such products as milk, meat, fruit, and vegetables that are sold in such businesses.

If possible, have students use a hypermedia program to create a stack/folder of consumer protection agencies that exist on all governmental levels. Refer to Figure 9-2 or p. 162 for a listing of federal agencies.) The first card/page should have a button for each area of consumer protection. The second card/page should contain the names of individual agencies. Subsequent cards provide the addresses, phone numbers, and so on. Have students add and link cards as they wish. Provide government directories and telephone books that list addresses and telephone numbers for federal, state, and local agencies.

Thinking Critically Through Visuals

During the 1980s, federal regulations of financial institutions were eased, but many made poor investments. What evidence in this photograph would lead you to believe that some people no longer believe that their money is protected? (Hundreds of financial institutions have collapsed; today, even the rumor of a bank's weakness has people running to withdraw their savings.)

▼RETEACH

Have students role-play a consumer watchdog and write an article, using a computer, if possible, identifying a (fictitious) violation of consumer laws or rights. Display articles on a bulletin board entitled *Eye on Business.*

▼ENRICH

Supply students with copies of building codes for local public buildings (available from your local government building inspector). Have students identify the safety laws for public buildings, then summarize them on a class chart.

Preventing Legal Difficulties

Encourage students to tell of experiences they have had that pertain to the first five items. Duplicate the overhead transparency master, *Consumer Contact Points*, and distribute copies. If they completed the hypermedia activity on p. 173, allow students to use their hypermedia stack/folder to add the addresses, and keep them for future reference.

▼ CLOSE

As a whole-class activity, have students, in turn, orally summarize how various consumer agencies and laws protect the rights of consumers. On the chalkboard, copy the four bulleted points on the overhead transparency master, *The Protective Shield of Consumer Laws.* Have students complete as much as they can of the sections. Then, show the overhead transparency to compare with the class's version.

Assign the following end-of-chapter materials:
Student text review activities, pp. 174–180
Workbook, pp. 19–24
Chapter Test

Chapter *MicroExam*

4. Safety Laws

To offer additional protection, especially in emergencies, laws govern the type of construction, location, accessibility, occupancy rate, and type of use of buildings where the public gathers. Detailed regulations apply to fire escapes, elevators, parking, sprinkler systems, exit location and marking, and even sanitary facilities.

All of these safety laws, like the other laws mentioned in this chapter, are designed to protect consumers and to assist them in deciding which products and services best meet their needs.

Preventing Legal Difficulties

To avoid being victimized...

1. Practice comparison shopping for value and price and never purchase on impulse, in haste, or in frustration. Remember that self-protection through prior knowledge about the needed product or service is the consumer's best protection.
2. Be cautious of "bargains." Usually they are authentic, but occasionally they are a part of a bait-and-switch scheme or they are loss leaders surrounded by overpriced goods.
3. Do not gamble. Remember that even in free and honest gambling contests, the vast majority of participants receive nothing.
4. Never sign an agreement or other document that you have not read or do not understand.
5. Read labels, warranties, ingredients lists, and other product information carefully.
6. When you have a valid complaint about a fraudulent or unfair business practice, take action, both for yourself and for others who may be similarly victimized in the future. Complain to the business involved, the Better Business Bureau, the local prosecutor, the state attorney general, the FTC, the CPSC, and any other governmental body with jurisdiction. If all else fails, carefully consider taking direct legal action.

▼ REVIEWING IMPORTANT POINTS

1. Buyers have long been urged to beware by the Latin phrase *caveat emptor.* The complexity of today's products and the inaccessibility of their

makers now require consumers not only to beware but to be aware of the various federal, state, and local laws designed to inform and protect them.

2 Unfair trade practices include fixing prices, using false advertising and illegal lotteries to promote products, improperly labeling goods, and selling used articles as new.

3 Many businesses are licensed. Reports of improper goods or services can be made to their licensing authorities at the state and local levels.

4 The CPSC, the FDA, other federal agencies, and state and local governments all work together to ensure safe products, services, stores, sanitary facilities, and access for consumers.

5 The National Bureau of Standards and assisting state agencies set and enforce regulations to ensure uniformity of weights and measures throughout the country.

STRENGTHENING YOUR LEGAL VOCABULARY

Match each term with the statement that best defines that term. Some terms may not be used.

adulterated	consumer
bait and switch	corrective advertising
caveat emptor	false and misleading advertising
cease-and-desist order	loss leaders
class action	lottery
confidence game	restitution
consent order	unfair trade practice

1 A game involving a prize, the requirement that something of value be paid in order to play, and the use of chance to determine the winner.

2 "Let the buyer beware."

3 Repayment of money obtained by illegal means.

4 Goods, usually well-known brands, sold below cost to attract buyers into a store.

5 A product whose purity and quality are below minimum standards, generally because of the addition of another substance.

6 Legal suit brought by one or several persons on behalf of themselves and other similarly affected persons.

Strengthening Your Legal Vocabulary

1 lottery
2 caveat emptor
3 restitution
4 loss leaders
5 adulterated
6 class action
7 consent order
8 false and misleading advertising
9 bait and switch
10 unfair trade practice

7 A court order, agreed to by a governmental body and a defendant, whereby the defendant voluntarily agrees to stop an illegal or questionable practice. Such an agreement typically avoids a long and expensive court battle.

8 Advertising that makes untrue or deceptive claims of quality or effectiveness about the item being offered for sale.

9 Advertising low-priced, understocked goods in an attempt to lure customers into a store and then persuade them to buy costlier goods.

10 Dishonest or illegal method of competition in business.

▼ APPLYING LAW TO EVERYDAY LIFE

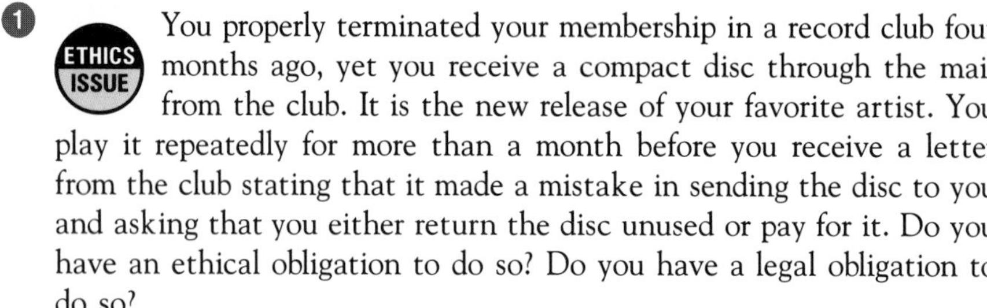
1 ETHICS ISSUE You properly terminated your membership in a record club four months ago, yet you receive a compact disc through the mail from the club. It is the new release of your favorite artist. You play it repeatedly for more than a month before you receive a letter from the club stating that it made a mistake in sending the disc to you and asking that you either return the disc unused or pay for it. Do you have an ethical obligation to do so? Do you have a legal obligation to do so?

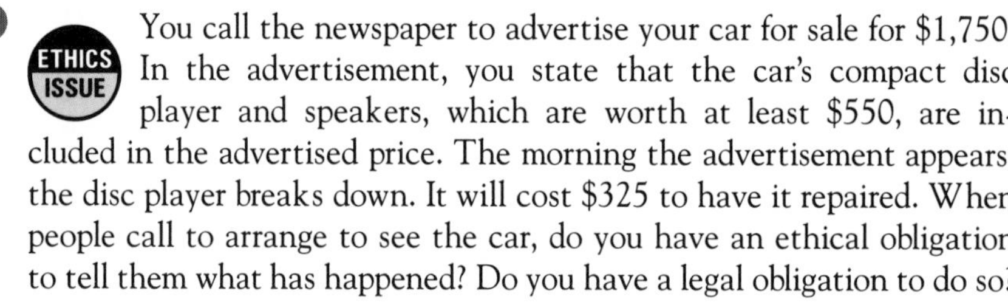
2 ETHICS ISSUE You call the newspaper to advertise your car for sale for $1,750. In the advertisement, you state that the car's compact disc player and speakers, which are worth at least $550, are included in the advertised price. The morning the advertisement appears, the disc player breaks down. It will cost $325 to have it repaired. When people call to arrange to see the car, do you have an ethical obligation to tell them what has happened? Do you have a legal obligation to do so?

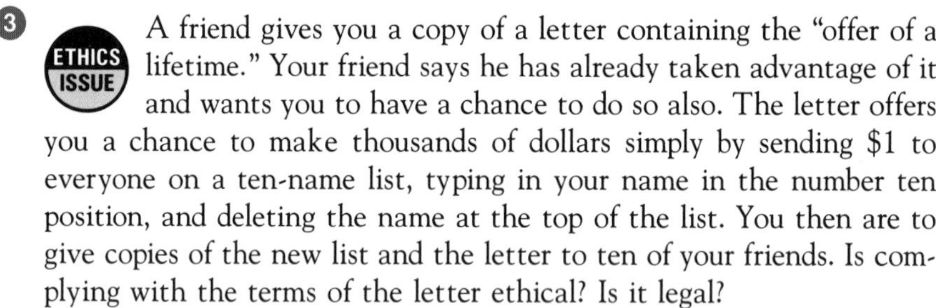
3 ETHICS ISSUE A friend gives you a copy of a letter containing the "offer of a lifetime." Your friend says he has already taken advantage of it and wants you to have a chance to do so also. The letter offers you a chance to make thousands of dollars simply by sending $1 to everyone on a ten-name list, typing in your name in the number ten position, and deleting the name at the top of the list. You then are to give copies of the new list and the letter to ten of your friends. Is complying with the terms of the letter ethical? Is it legal?

4 A computer store chain buys "factory rebuilt" computers and sells them to customers without disclosing their origin or used condition. Is this practice illegal?

▼ Applying Law to Everyday Life ▼

1 ETHICS ISSUE From the perspective of the utilitarian ethic (the greatest good for the greatest number) and according to applicable law, you do not. Our government has determined that sending unordered merchandise and then demanding its return or payment is an unfair trade practice. (p. 170) Honest and efficient dealing is encouraged by these positions, and that benefits all concerned. However, noting that the record club still owns the disc, and that you have the responsibility of being a good steward of those things placed in your control, might cause you to reach a different conclusion.

2 ETHICS ISSUE Concealing the fact cannot be ethically justified, even if saying nothing makes it far more likely the car will sell. The money thus acquired can be utilized to satisfy the seller's desires.

Legally, there was no intent to deceive when the ad was placed, so it could not be considered false and misleading. (p. 167) Beyond that, there is no legal requirement to voluntarily disclose the condition of the player.

3 
The behavior would be illegal and a felony in most states. (p. 168)

5 The Baby-Bright Crib was banned as a hazardous product by the CPSC because of its sharp hardware, lead-containing enamel, and improperly spaced slats. The Sabatinas bought one of the cribs and then learned of the ban. What should they do now?

6 A coffee manufacturer incorrectly stated the volume of coffee in one of its packages. Thousands of these packages are on the market. If necessary, can the packages be confiscated by the government to remedy the situation?

7 Packages of crackers were prominently labeled "Diet Thin Matzo Crackers." Other wording on the label indicated the vitamin content of a cracker. The FDA held that the package was misbranded. The FDA said that the label implied that Diet Thins were lower in caloric content than other matzos and, thus, were useful in weight-control diets. In fact, the crackers had the same caloric content as did plain matzos made by the same company. The FDA filed suit in a federal district court to confiscate 423 cases of Diet Thin Matzos. Should the court uphold the FDA?

8 In a national television advertising campaign, FunTime fruit drink was said to contain "natural food energy." The FTC discovered that the "natural food" providing the energy was sugar and held that the advertisement therefore created a false impression. What remedy would you recommend that the FTC use to correct the situation?

9 The manufacturer of Sweet-Tooth candy bars printed a number on the inside of each wrapper. Buyers who sent in twenty-five clipped-off numbers received a free ball-point pen. Those who returned a number ending in two 2s received a full carton of candy bars. Is this promotional scheme a lottery?

10 Late one evening, the Arnos signed a contract to buy magazine subscriptions. The contract was for one-year subscriptions to ten different magazines to be purchased "at the bargain price of only $4.95 a week." The Arnos signed the contract after an hour of persistent persuasion by a door-to-door salesperson. The next morning, the Arnos did some quick calculating and were appalled to discover that they had agreed to spend $257.40—a sum they could not afford—for magazines. Moreover, they had been buying only one of the magazines at their supermarket. Can the Arnos cancel the contract without being liable for damages?

5 Return the crib to the seller for a refund of the purchase price. If problems arise, complain to the Consumer Product Safety Commission and the Better Business Bureau. (pp. 162, 163)

6 Yes, the government could confiscate the packages. (p. 165)

7 Yes; The claims were false. (p. 167)

8 The FTC should order corrective advertising to supplant the false impression. (p. 167)

9 Giving the pen is merely promotional, and as legal as giving a discount or refund. However, giving a prize (the carton of candy bars) to the person who must pay money for the chance to win it is an illegal lottery. (p. 168)

10 Yes; The law permits a three-day period during which time a person may cancel or avoid such a home solicitation sale. (p. 171)

4 Selling used or rebuilt merchandise as new is an unfair trade practice. (p. 170)

Solving Case Problems

1. Yes; The advertising was deceptive because the claims were not supported by substantial evidence or scientific test data. Ten tests do not constitute scientific test data. (p. 167)
2. Yes; This was a classic case of bait-and-switch advertising, which is illegal. (p. 167) The defendants were convicted of misdemeanors.

SOLVING CASE PROBLEMS

1. The FTC ordered Firestone Tire and Rubber Company to cease and desist from certain advertising. Firestone appealed to the Federal Court of Appeals to have the order set aside. Firestone had advertised "The Safe Tire, Firestone." It also advertised that its Wide Oval Tire "Stops 25% Quicker." The FTC claimed that the "Safe Tire" advertisement implied that the tires would be safe under all conditions without regard to conditions of use. The FTC said the "advertisement gives no indication that there is any limit to the safety of this tire or what such limits might be." Firestone emphasized that a large majority of persons interviewed concerning the "Safe Tire" advertisement thought it meant something less than a guarantee of absolute safety. The FTC also claimed that the "Stops 25% Quicker" advertisement was unfair and deceptive to consumers because it was "without substantial scientific test data to support it." Firestone, thus, submitted evidence of ten tests. The tests showed an average stopping distance on a wet smooth concrete surface to be 29.8 percent less for the Wide Oval tire than that for a Firestone Super Sports tire of standard tread width. Should the court uphold the FTC? (*Firestone Tire and Rubber Company v. FTC*, 481 F.2d 246)

2. Through radio and television, the defendant stores advertised a "top quality . . . Queen Anne Console Magic Stitcher" sewing machine, along with a sewing chair, for the "close-out price of just $29.50." Under the sales plan, a "lead person" would accept the customer's order, taking a deposit as small as 25 cents. After that, a demonstrator would visit the customer and "kill the sale" by having the machine jam in use. The demonstrator would tell the customer that the customer's television set would be damaged if it was left on during the demonstration and that the machine would have to be oiled every few minutes. The demonstrator would also say that a five-pound can of grease would be needed to pack the bearings and that the customer could lose an eye if the machine jammed. Then the demonstrator would attempt to "step-up" the sale and persuade the customer to buy a higher priced machine. In about nineteen months, only twenty-six of the advertised machines were sold, although 10,951 customers entered into conditional sales contracts for such machines. The twenty-six advertised machines were sold at a time when the defendants had received complaints from the television station and the Better Business Bureau. The defendants were

prosecuted for conspiring to sell merchandise by means of deceptive and misleading advertising. The prosecutor gave evidence that the defendants never intended to sell the advertised machines, which actually cost them $45 each. Are the defendants guilty as charged? (*People v. Glubo, Exelbert, Epstein, and Atlantic Sewing Stores, Inc.*, 158 N.E.2d 699)

3 When registration of a "MONOPOLY" trademark for use on men's, women's, and children's wearing apparel was sought by a New York-based corporation, Tuxedo Monopoly, Inc., the makers of the "MONOPOLY" board game, General Mills Fun Group, opposed the application. The Patent and Trademark Office Trademark Trial and Appeal Board sustained the opposition and would not allow the registration. On appeal to the U.S. Court of Customs and Patent Appeals, Tuxedo's attorneys argued that monopoly was a common term and that, regardless, there was very little likelihood of confusion between a trademark used on a game and one used on clothing. They also pointed out that the court had previously allowed the registration of the famous "DIXIE" cup mark by a company using it as its mark on waxed paper. If the court finds a likelihood of confusion exists, it should affirm the Board's decision. How did the court rule? (*Tuxedo Monopoly, Inc. v. General Mills Fun Group, Inc.*, 648 F.2d 1335)

4 When Brenda Lee Suits bought a used car from the Little Motor Company, the company provided her with a mileage disclosure form. The form stated that the mileage reading on the vehicle she was buying was unknown because the actual mileage varied from the odometer reading for reasons "other than odometer calibration error." The odometer of the ten-year-old car showed seventy-three miles at the time of purchase by Suits. In fact, when Donald Little, Little Motor's owner, had purchased the car ten days earlier from Leiphart Chevrolet, he had received a mileage disclosure form warranting the mileage at 100,073. However, as was common practice, Little had asked Leiphart Chevrolet to mail the form to him so that he could sell the car prior to receiving the mailed form and thus be able to indicate that the vehicle's true mileage was unknown. The success of Brenda Suits' lawsuit for damages under the Motor Vehicle Information and Cost Saving Act hinges on whether or not an intent to defraud can be inferred from Little's actions. Little has stated that his reason for failing to disclose the 100,073 mileage was that the buyer of a ten-year-old car with an odometer reading seventy-three miles knows it has turned over. Will Suits recover? (*Suits v. Little Motor Company*, 642 F.2d 883)

3 The court affirmed the holding of the Board as the use of the "MONOPOLY" mark implied the endorsement of the mark holder. The court noted that General Mills Fun Group had acted against such unauthorized use before, and had turned down requests for licenses to utilize its mark on T-shirts and other novelty clothing. (p. 170)

4 Yes; The court pointed out that the odometer could have turned over twice, and the mileage the consumer would normally assume to be correct would, therefore, be grossly inaccurate and detrimental to Suits. (p. 170)

5 Yes; Without the ease of availability of the free entry forms, the necessary result was to require a payment for a chance to win the prize—in short, an illegal lottery. (p. 168)

5 A Chicago newspaper contained a game called Pick and Play. Under the rules of the game, a contestant picked the winners of selected upcoming college and professional football games. The teams were handicapped with various "point spreads" and cash prizes of up to $1,000 were awarded depending on the number of winners selected. The newspaper cost $2, but the contest instructions provided that free entry forms were available at the newspaper's office or in the Chicago public libraries. When a police officer visited the newspaper's office during regular business hours, he found no sign identifying the office, no newspaper employees present, and no certain way to obtain a free entry form. In addition, none of the branches of the Chicago public libraries subscribed to the paper. Should the court consider this an illegal lottery? (*Dreem Arts, Inc. v. City of Chicago*, 637 F. Supp. 53)

SPECIAL SECTION

CAREERS IN LAW

One can pursue a variety of careers in the field of law. Generally, these can be divided into careers involving the direct practice of law and careers involving the support of that practice.

POSITIONS IN THE DIRECT PRACTICE OF LAW

Opportunities in the direct practice of law include independent general practice, specialized practice, practice as legal counsel for a corporation, and practice for the government or quasi-public sector.

General Practice

For many persons, the first mental image of an attorney is in a court scene, usually in a dramatic criminal trial. In fact, many lawyers seldom, if ever, appear in court. The general practitioner works to keep clients out of the courtroom by providing accurate and timely advice. A general practitioner counsels clients, prepares legal documents, does research, and appears in court or before administrative agencies when required.

Specialized Practice

The complexity of the law requires that some lawyers concentrate on a specific area of law. Specialists work almost exclusively in a particular area, such as domestic relations (family) law, criminal law, labor law, debt collection, or copyright law.

Corporate Counsel

Large corporations or other organizations typically have their own "in-house" attorneys, who are salaried employees. Such counsel handle the day-to-day legal problems of the corporation, labor union, university, or other organization and provide legal advice to its executives. A career as a corporate counsel is usually more stable than that of the general practitioner, but the income may be more limited.

Special Section: Careers in Law

Why not have your students hold a law career fair? The fair will provide students with the opportunity to learn about the various careers in law and law-related fields.

The first step in preparing for a career fair is to help students decide on a time and place to hold the event, and to create a guest list. Ask a student volunteer to check with your building administrator for appropriate locations on your school campus and necessary approvals to hold the fair. The school cafeteria, gymnasium, foyer, or another area where large numbers of people can safely and comfortably view students' work might be possible locations. Have the class decide on the following: Will the fair be held during the day, after school hours, or both? What guests of honor, such as your mayor, superintendent of schools, distinguished local judge, or prominent attorneys, will be invited?

Divide the class into five committees and assign each committee one of the following law careers: general practice lawyers; specialized practice lawyers; corporate counsel lawyers; governmental or quasi-public sector lawyers; and other law-related positions, such as court reporters, legal secretaries, and so on. Have committees plan booths to display interesting articles, books, college and law school information, videos, posters, and so on.

Encourage students to invite guest speakers, such as law school students and recent graduates, to their law career fair.

Have students invite other classmates, teachers, faculty members, parents, community members, and even the local media to participate in this special career fair.

Governmental or Quasi-Public Sector Lawyers

Most legislative and executive levels of government and most administrative agencies employ full-time services of prosecutors, legal aid attorneys, judges, and public defenders. In the quasi-public sector, attorneys represent special-interest groups in such areas as the environment, business, civil rights, and consumer rights.

LAW-RELATED POSITIONS

Many careers that support the practice of law are available to persons who need not be trained as attorneys. Court reporter, legal secretary, paralegal, and court administrator are positions involved in law.

Regardless of what specific career path a person follows, law—dynamic and demanding—is a fascinating, absorbing, and rewarding field.

3

Contracts: Making Binding Agreements

Unit Overview

In Unit 3, *Contracts: Making Binding Agreements*, students will read about how contracts—the keystone in the structure of business law—are formed and ended. In this unit, students will learn about different types of contracts, interest rates, and damages.

Offer and acceptance of a contract, the essential elements of a contract, must meet certain standards and conditions in order to be legally valid. In Chapter 10, *Offer and Acceptance*, students will study what a contract is, who enters into contracts, and what the requirements of an offer are. They will also learn how an offer is ended, how an offer can be kept open, what is required for acceptance, and what the effect of acceptance is.

Lawful consideration is necessary to make a promise binding. In Chapter 11, *Mutual Consideration*, students will discover what consideration is, why it is required, and what the exceptions to the requirement of mutual consideration are.

When certain conditions are not met, or when it violates the law, a contract may be considered void or voidable. In Chapter 12, *Void and Voidable Agreements*, students will learn what makes an agreement void or voidable. Other topics of interest include when a minor can or cannot disaffirm a voidable contract, and whether misstating one's age binds a minor.

Contracts must be expressed in a certain form—sometimes verbal and other times written—to be valid and enforceable. In Chapter 13, *Proper Form*, students will study any special form for contracts, learn what the statue of frauds is, and how written contracts are interpreted.

Contractual duties and obligations can be discharged in a variety of different ways. In Chapter 14, *Ending Contractual Obligations*, students will read whether or not contractual rights can be assigned, if contractual duties can be delegated, and what the rights of an assignee are.

Generally, persons who are parties to a contract have certain rights or duties under the contract. In Chapter 15, *Remedies for Breach of Contract*, students will understand who has the rights under a contract, and what remedies are available to a party injured by a breach of contract.

At the end of the unit, you'll find a special section, *International Business Law*, which can be used at any time during the study of Unit 3. You may wish to assign its accompanying *Teacher Edition* activity to give students an opportunity to brainstorm recommendations for improving a particular issue of international business law and write an editorial expressing their views.

Portfolio Assessment

To reflect their understanding of the law as related to making binding contractual agreements, have students create a scenario based on the need for a binding written agreement. (Topics may include buying and selling goods for $500 or more, buying and selling real property, participating in an activity that cannot be performed within one year after being made, paying a debt for a legal obligation of another person, and so on.) Using a computer, if possible, have students draw up a fictitious but valid contract using proper form to show an offer, an acceptance, and mutual consideration. Have students include the final contract in their portfolios or law journals.

Careers

Arbitrator

When a binding agreement is broken, negotiation is often the most advantageous way to resolve the issue. In these cases, an arbitrator, or an unbiased third party, is called upon to settle the dispute between the parties. Arbitrators must attend and participate in the hearings, determine the sufficiency of the evidence, and make a binding decision.

The education and experience for an arbitrator varies, although a degree in dispute resolution provides good background. A master's degree in labor relations or business administration is desirable as is a law degree. To qualify as an arbitrator, one must be well known, well respected, and considered an expert in his or her field. Salary ranges vary according to education and experience.

Divide the class into groups of three or four. Assign each group an issue to dispute. Have one student in each group role play an arbitrator and the other students role play the disputing parties. Encourage the parties to come to an amicable resolution of the problem.

Annotated Bibliography

- ***Kiefer v. Fred Howe Motors*, 39 Wis.2d 20, 158 N.W.2d 288 (1968).**
  A contract entered into by a minor, other than for necessaries, is either void or voidable at the other's option; the other party may, however, have a tort remedy for a minor's misrepresentation of his or her age. (Chapter 12)

- ***Fuentes v. Shevin*, 407 U.S. 67 (1972).**
  A state's replevin provisions are invalid and unconstitutional if they deprive the owner of the property of due process of law by denying him or her the right to a hearing before the property is taken. (Chapter 13)

- ***McCallister v. Patton*, 215 S.W.2d 701 (Ark. 1948).**
  Specific performance is an adequate remedy for a breach of a contract relating to personal property only when the property has a peculiar, unique, or sentimental value to the buyer which is not measurable in money damages. (Chapter 15)

Contracts: Making Binding Agreements

- Offer and Acceptance
- Mutual Consideration
- Void and Voidable Agreements
- Proper Form
- Ending Contractual Obligations
- Remedies for Breach of Contract

CONTRACTS: MAKING BINDING AGREEMENTS

CHAPTER 10 ORGANIZER

Chapter Theme

Offer and acceptance of a contract, the promises we live by in a civilized society, must meet certain standards and conditions in order to be legal.

DIRECTED STUDY QUESTIONS	SPECIAL FEATURES	PROGRAM RESOURCES				
		Reteach	Enrich	SN	AM	
What is a contract?		✔	✔		A	
Who may enter into contracts?	Multicultural Highlights, p. 188 Thinking Critically Through Visuals, p. 188 Ethics Issue, p. 189 Personal Perspectives, p. 189	✔	✔			
What are the requirements of an offer?	Ethics Issue, p. 191	✔	✔	✔		
How is an offer ended?	Thinking Critically Through Visuals, p. 193	✔	✔		V	
How can an offer be kept open?		✔	✔			
What is required for acceptance?	Writing Connections, p. 199	✔	✔		K	
What is the effect of acceptance?	Preventing Legal Difficulties, p. 201	✔	✔			

Additional Resources

- Calamari, John D., and Perillo, Joseph M. *Calamari and Perillo's Hornbook on Contracts*, 3rd ed. St. Paul, MN: West Publishing Co., 1987.
- Corbin. *Corbin on Contracts*. St. Paul, MN: West Publishing Co., 1970.
- Neubert, Christopher. *How to Handle Your Own Contracts.* NY: Sterling Publishing Co., 1991.
- Privette, Mari W. *Sign Here?: Everything You Need to Know About Contracts.* Garden City, NY: Doubleday, 1985.
- *Restatement of the Law, Contracts*, 2nd ed. St. Paul, MN: American Law Institute Publishers, 1981.

One-semester course	✔	✔	✔					
One-year course	✔	✔	✔	✔	✔			

	ASSESSMENT OPPORTUNITIES			
Cooperative Learning	Informal Assessment	Chapter Review	Chapter Test	Chapter *MicroExam* (Media)
	✔	✔	✔	✔
	✔	✔	✔	✔
✔	✔	✔	✔	✔
	✔	✔	✔	✔
	✔	✔	✔	✔
	✔	✔	✔	✔
	✔	✔	✔	✔

Videodiscs

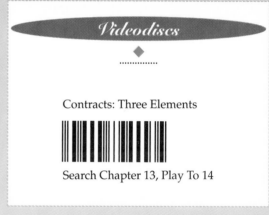

Contracts: Three Elements

Search Chapter 13, Play To 14

State by State

In Alabama, an offer is definite if the court can fix an exact meaning upon its terms.

Teaching Materials

Student text, pp. 184–207

Overhead transparency masters
- *How Can an Offer Be Kept Open? (Part One)*
- *How Can an Offer Be Kept Open? (Part Two)*

Videos
- *Contracts, Warranties, and Credit* Videotape
- *Law for Business* Videodisc

Workbook, pp. 25–26

Outside Resources
- Index cards
- Sample advertisements, letters, and handbills
- Sample contract
- Poster boards

- VCR
- Video recordings of television commercials
- Camcorder
- Tape recorder

Assessment
- Chapter Test

- Chapter *MicroExam*

Vocabulary

contract, p. 186
offeror, p. 186
offerees, p. 186
capacity, p. 187
legally competent, p. 187
offer, p. 190
counteroffer, p. 195
revocation, p. 195
option, p. 196
firm offer, p. 196
acceptance, p. 197
unilateral contract, p. 199
bilateral contract, p. 199
valid contract, p. 200
void agreement, p. 201
voidable contract, p. 201
unenforceable contract, p. 201

Learning Objectives

When you complete this chapter, you will be able to

1. Explain the nature and importance of contracts.
2. Tell who may make contracts.
3. List the requirements of an offer.
4. Outline ways an offer is ended, and how it can be kept open.
5. List the requirements of an acceptance and explain how they result in a valid contract.

184

Chapter Self-Test

Assess students' understanding of contracts before they begin Chapter 10 by having them respond orally to the following: **(1) Is every written agreement an enforceable contract?** (No, minors, intoxicated persons, and insane persons lack the capacity to contract.); and **(2) Is the right to make and enforce contracts open to all citizens?** (No, a person must have the legal capacity to contract.) Review and discuss students' responses before continuing with the chapter.

CHAPTER

10

OFFER AND ACCEPTANCE

1 After lunch, Rick and Mary stretched out in the sun on the school lawn. "It's an adult world," Rick said. "Contracts—stuff like that—have nothing to do with high school students like us." Mary answered, "You're right and you're wrong. The world is run by adults, but we make lots of contracts. Even babies are affected by contracts." Whose opinion is correct?

2 The owner of a small, color television offers to sell it to a neighbor for $75. As the neighbor rubs his jaw, thinking, a bystander says, "That's a bargain. I'll take it!" Is there a contract between the bystander and the owner?

3 ETHICS ISSUE The law protects minors, intoxicated persons, and insane persons by generally permitting them to back out of unfavorable contracts. E. Z. Marque is an adult, perfectly sober, and of normal intelligence. Yet he makes a foolish and extravagant purchase of a product he really does not need. May the seller legally hold him to the contract? Is it ethical for the seller to do so?

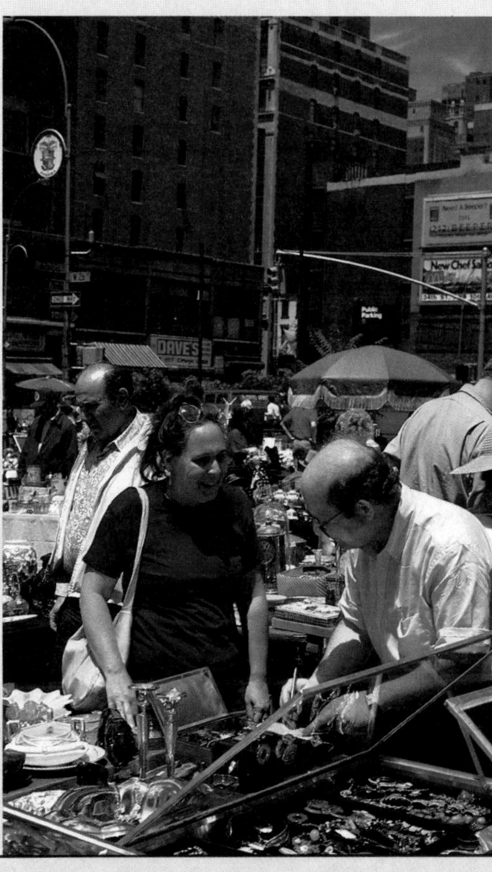

▼ FOCUS

As students enter the classroom, pair them and have each pair write on the chalkboard the name of a good and a service that are related to each other, such as paint and house painting. Ask: **What types of agreements are necessary to provide those goods and services?** (Answers may include agreements on quality, delivery time, price, and warranties.) Have students, in pairs, choose a product or service from the list on the chalkboard and orally trace its path, noting a need for agreements along the way. For example, the path for the good paint and the service house painting could go like this: "Painter and house owner agree on time, quality of paint, and price. Painter and paint supplier agree on delivery of paint and price." Relate the agreements to a need for contracts.

You Decide

1 Mary's opinion is correct. Minors may and do make contracts, some of which are binding.

2 No; The offer can be accepted only by the offeree to whom it was made, or by his or her authorized agent.

3 ETHICS ISSUE Yes, the seller may hold him to the contract. Yes, there is nothing unethical in holding the buyer responsible.

Thinking Critically Through Visuals

Contracts require an agreement between the buyer and the seller. In this photograph, is the man displaying his wares obligated to sell the things on display if he hasn't placed a price on them? (No, no contract has been made.)

TEACH

On the chalkboard or on an overhead transparency, write the following important points about contracts, noted on p. 186. Discuss each statement before writing the next.
1. A contract is an agreement that is enforceable by law.
2. To have an agreement there must be an offer and an acceptance on mutually satisfactory terms.
3. The person who makes the offer is the offeror and the person to whom the offer is made is the offeree.
4. It is the indication of intent to contract, rather than particular language, that is most important in a contract.

APPLY

Have the class brainstorm acts that do and do not result in contracts. Write the two lists on the chalkboard and discuss responses. **Guided Practice**

To reinforce that it is the manifestation of intent rather than particular language that is important, divide the class into small groups. Ask each to compose and tape record three different ways to word the same enforceable oral contract. Play the tapes to the class and have students identify the offeror and offeree. **Independent Practice**

WHAT IS A CONTRACT?

PROBLEM

Lorenzo and Bixby were chatting during the break between classes at Bay View High School. "Remember 'Great Moments in Sports,' the videocassette that I showed you last week?" asked Bixby. "You thought it was super and said you wished it was yours. I'll let you have it for fifteen bucks. Want it?" "Sure! Wow!" Lorenzo answered. "Bring it to school tomorrow, okay?" Did the two friends make a contract?

Have you ever wondered how it is possible that most persons eat a variety of foods, many of which are produced in distant places? That most homes have radios and television sets which bring news, entertainment, and advertisements throughout the day and night? That streets are paved, crowded with vehicles, lined with buildings? That people are dressed in a great variety of garments, most of which are made by others? That there is fresh running water in kitchens and bathrooms, and an underground water supply and waste disposal system?

These and other marvels of modern civilization are the result of the output of work by countless millions of persons throughout the world. Over the years, people have produced and distributed these goods and services through ongoing, intricate, yet fundamentally simple exchanges. The legal links among and between the individuals who, and companies that, produce and consume these many goods and services are contracts.

A **contract** is an agreement that is enforceable by law. It normally results from an exchange of promises to do something or to give something of value. For example, a married couple may want their home painted with a particular color, quality, and brand of outdoor paint. A painter measures the exterior of their house and promises to do the specified job within a designated time for $2,000. A contract arises when the couple agrees to pay the requested price. The painter as **offeror** made a definite proposal. The couple as **offerees** (i.e., persons to whom the offer is made) accepted it exactly as presented. The parties might have negotiated over the details. The couple might have declined the painter's proposal. Or they may have demanded a lower price and an earlier date of completion. The painter, in turn, could accept or reject their proposal. Without both offer and acceptance on mutually satisfactory terms, there is no agreement. No particular language need be used. The intent of the parties is what is important. In the problem, Lorenzo and Bixby made a contract even though delivery of the services and payment for them are to be made later.

ASSESS

Learning Objective 1 Ask students to respond in writing to the following questions: **(1) What distinguishes a contractual agreement from other agreements?** (A contract is enforceable by law, in contrast to a social agreement.); **(2) What two actions are necessary for a legal contract?** (An offer and an acceptance); and **(3) Do contracts require particular language?** (No).

Working at home over several months, Komuro had assembled a stereo sound system with professional-quality recording capabilities. After following the progress of Komuro's work and admiring it, Komuro's friend Feldman wrote a letter to Komuro asking him how much he would want for his new stereo system. Komuro replied by mail: "Including parts and my labor at only $10 an hour, I'd say I have at least $4,500 invested in it. Is it worth that much to you?" Feldman immediately wrote his reply: "It sure is! I accept your offer. I'll bring cash or a certified check for $4,500 if you tell me when to come for the whole system." Here, no contract was formed. Komuro had merely stated an estimate of his cost, which included his labor at $10 an hour but no profit. Since he made *no clear offer to sell,* Feldman could not accept. However, under these circumstances, Feldman's words could be interpreted as *an offer to buy* the complete system for $4,500. Komuro, now acting as the offeree, could accept Feldman's offer and thus make a contract.

▼ WHO MAY ENTER INTO CONTRACTS?

PROBLEM

Purcell developed a taste for fast cars and alcoholic beverages. Over the years, drinking to excess became an uncontrollable habit for him. Eventually, a guardian was appointed to take care of Purcell and his estate and a proper legal notice of this fact was published in the local newspaper. Subsequently, Purcell signed an agreement to buy a new car. Is this agreement valid and binding?

For agreements to be valid contracts, enforceable in court, the persons who make them must have the capacity to contract. **Capacity** means the ability to understand one's actions and the effects of those actions. Persons with the capacity to contract are **legally competent.** Adults are presumed to be legally competent. Minors, intoxicated persons, and insane persons lack capacity, at least to some degree.

For their own protection, such persons are restricted in their freedom to contract. As a form of punishment some states also limit the right of those convicted of major crimes to contract. In most states, aliens from countries at war with the United States lack capacity to contract. This restriction is a means of supporting the nation's war effort.

▼ TEACH

On the chalkboard, list the three types of people who may not legally enter a contract without any restrictions. (Minors, intoxicated persons, and insane or seriously mentally deranged persons) Discuss in detail the laws governing minors and contracts and the responsibility of parents and guardians when a minor makes a contract.

Poll the class to determine how many students have ever sought to disaffirm a contract. The results should demonstrate that minors seldom exercise this right or even feel the need to do so. Nevertheless, you might point out that if the right of disaffirmance did not exist, there probably would be many cases of exploitation of minors in contracts with adults.

▼RETEACH

Discuss why each of the following is or is not an enforceable contract. **(1) Nick and Kim promise to meet for lunch.** (Not enforceable, social agreement); **(2) Tim offers to buy Blake's car.** (Not enforceable, no acceptance); and **(3) José says to Wanda, "Five dollars and my hat is yours." Wanda says, "Sold!"** (Enforceable, includes both offer and acceptance)

▼ENRICH

Have students draw a flowchart of the production of a product. Then have them identify each step in which contracts might be used.

Multicultural Highlights

Prior to 1866, African Americans were prohibited from making and enforcing contracts. This restriction ended with The Civil Rights Act of 1866. That law reads in part, "...and such citizens, of every race and color, without regard to any previous condition of slavery or involuntary servitude shall have the same right, in every State and Territory in the United States, to make and enforce contracts...." The Supreme Court has held that this prohibits private schools from denying admission to minorities.

▼ APPLY

Thinking Critically Through Visuals

Why might the salespeople in this store be apprehensive about selling directly to the girl in the photograph rather than to the adult? (Usually, contracts with minors are not enforceable.)

Young people have limited experience and are more vulnerable to exploitation than are adults. Therefore, although minors are free to make contracts, the law generally gives them the legal right to *disaffirm* (i.e., set aside, void, or nullify) most of their contractual agreements. For example, in most states, minors can demand a full refund if they return their unwanted purchases. Even when the goods involved have been consumed or destroyed, most states permit minors to disaffirm and get their money back.

Realistically, minors seldom disaffirm their contracts. Most are not even aware of this legal right. Agreements they enter and purchases they make are usually fair. They want to enjoy their purchases by using or consuming the products. Moreover, they typically desire the self-confidence and respect of others that come from responsible business conduct. Also, minors may sense that although disaffirmance may be legally permitted, it is not necessarily right and may be difficult to accomplish.

If the minor lied about his or her age when making a contract, many states require the minor to pay for the use of or damage to returned property. Some states flatly deny the right to disaffirm in such situations and require full payment.

If a contract is made between a minor and an adult, only the minor may disaffirm; the adult is bound. A minor who wants to disaffirm a contract must do so while still a minor or within a reasonable time after becoming an adult. Otherwise the agreement is binding.

Businesses that make important contracts with minors often insist that an adult also sign and agree to be bound. The adult may then be held liable

▼ ASSESS

Learning Objective 2 Read the following sentences aloud and have students jot down whether or not each person in these statements is legally bound by the contract entered, then tell why: **(1) A professional decorator has signed a contract to wallpaper a house for a fixed price.** (Bound); **(2) An adult was intoxicated when he signed a contract to buy a car.** (Not bound); and **(3) An adult made a contract with a minor.** (Adult is bound, minor is not).

for damages if the minor disaffirms or fails to pay. Thus, parents are frequently asked to join in signing their children's important contracts. Otherwise parents are not liable for the contracts of their children unless, as explained later in Chapter 12, the contracts are for the purchase of certain important goods and services.

Bailey tried to buy a motor scooter, but the dealer refused to sell it to him because he was a minor. After Bailey persuaded his father to sign as a co-buyer on the contract, the dealer gladly made the sale because the dealer could then hold Bailey's father liable if Bailey failed to pay as promised.

As noted earlier, two other important types of legally incompetent persons are (1) those who are intoxicated by alcohol or other drugs and (2) those who are insane or seriously mentally deranged. In both categories, if guardians (or, in some states, conservators for adults) have been appointed, then only contracts made by the guardians are binding. Contracts made by wards are void. In the problem, Purcell's purchase was void. This is because the contract was made by Purcell, not by his guardian, and it was not for a necessary good or service.

Guardians seldom are appointed for persons who drink too much; they are not always appointed for persons who are insane. When such persons without guardians make contracts, their agreements can be set aside by them if, at the time of contracting, the incompetent could not understand the nature and legal effect of the contract. If the contracts are disaffirmed, anything received by either party to the contract must be returned.

Persons who are being "wined and dined" may sign agreements they would not have signed if they had been sober. Nevertheless, they are bound if they understood the nature and general effects of their agreements.

WHAT ARE THE REQUIREMENTS OF AN OFFER?

PROBLEM

Anchors Aweigh, a boat retailer, advertised a one-day sale of cabin cruisers for the "bargain price" of $12,500 each. The dealer had five cruisers in stock, but they were sold within one hour. During the rest of the day, seven other would-be buyers came in to purchase a bargain cruiser. Is Anchors Aweigh bound by contract to the would-be buyers?

On index cards, write scenarios that outline enforceable and unenforceable contracts involving minors. Divide the class into pairs. Have each choose a card and improvise a skit based on that situation. Discuss why the contract depicted is or is not enforceable. **Guided Practice**

ETHICS ISSUE

Ethics Issue

Set up panels to debate these issues:
1. When a minor signs a contract with an adult, is it fair that the adult is bound and the minor is not?
2. When a person signs a contract as a minor and then comes of age, is it fair that the contract becomes enforceable?
Independent Practice

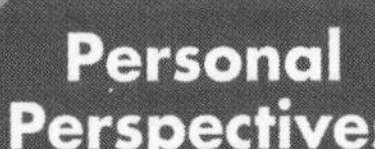

Personal Perspectives

Have students discuss this with adult family members: **Considering the laws regarding minors and contracts, what behaviors characterize responsible business conduct on the part of minors?** Ask students to share points raised in their family discussions.

RETEACH

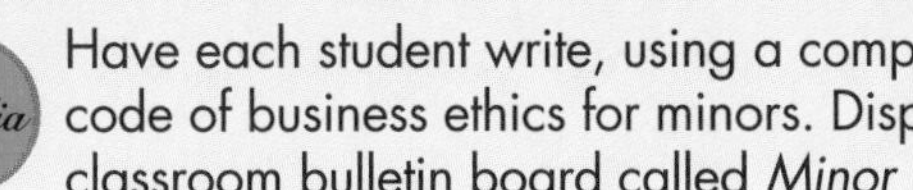

Media: Tell students to skim the section, *Who May Enter Into Contracts?* Display a blank transparency on an overhead projector and have students take turns helping to compose, on the transparency, an outline of the section. Have all students copy the outline in their notebooks.

ENRICH

Media: Have each student write, using a computer, if possible, a personal code of business ethics for minors. Display students' work on a classroom bulletin board called *Minor League Ethics.*

▼ TEACH

Write the three requirements of a valid offer on the chalkboard. Discuss and note exceptions to each requirement. Provide examples to help students understand that social obligations do not create legal obligations. Use the overhead projector to show samples of advertisements, letters, and handbills to teach students the difference between an offer and an invitation to make an offer.

▼ APPLY

Make an overhead transparency of a short, sample contract. Have student volunteers identify the elements that meet the requirements of a valid offer on the transparency and circle them.

Guided Practice

Have groups of two or three students write a scenario to demonstrate a valid offer. Have students act out their scenarios, deliberately leaving out one of the three essential elements for it to be a valid offer. Have the rest of the class determine which element is missing. **Independent Practice**

An **offer** is a proposal by an offeror to do or not to do some specified thing in the future, provided the offeree complies with stated conditions. If the offeree accepts the proposal, a contract arises. Generally, for a valid offer:

1. the offeror must intend to create a legal obligation,
2. the terms must be definite and complete, and
3. the offer must be communicated to the offeree.

1. The Offeror Must Intend to Create a Legal Obligation

The offeror must intend, or must appear to a reasonable person to intend, to create a legal obligation if the proposal is accepted. People often make agreements that no one considers legally enforceable. For example, if two friends agree to go to the movies, no contract is intended or formed. If either breaks the date, the other may be offended but cannot sue. There is no *legal remedy* (i.e., legal means to enforce a right) because social invitations do not create legal obligations.

Certain words that may seem to create offers do not. Before making important contracts, parties often discuss possible terms. The bargaining may become lively as proposals, rejections, and counter-proposals fly back and forth. Sometimes one party states tentative terms, inviting others to make offers. Advertisements in newspapers and magazines, on radio or television, or in catalogs or direct mailings are generally invitations to others to make offers. They are not offers themselves. A person who advertises something for sale cannot be expected to sell to the many thousands who theoretically might reply to the advertisement. Perhaps the seller has only a limited number of items or wants to check the credit of all who want to buy on credit.

In the problem, in answering the advertisement and in *tendering* (i.e., presenting for acceptance) the purchase price of the cabin cruiser, the buyers and would-be buyers were the offerors. Thus, Anchors Aweigh was bound by contract only to the five buyers whose offers it accepted. To promote good customer relations, however, business firms attempt to deliver merchandise as advertised to all who seek to buy. They may give *rain checks,* which permit customers to buy at the sale price in the future when more goods become available. Recall, also, that statutes forbid false and misleading advertising (see page 167).

Sometimes an advertisement is worded so that readers reasonably believe *it is an offer* rather than the customary invitation *to make an offer* (e.g., an advertisement that clearly promises to pay a reward for the return of a lost pet). Or direct-mail advertisements sent to one or to a select few prospects may in fact be legal offers. Another example is someone trying to sell an expensive yacht by mailing a promotional letter to ten prospects. The letter

▼ ASSESS

Learning Objective 3 Read the following aloud and have students indicate orally if the requirements of an offer have been met: **(1) An injured person requests and receives treatment from a doctor without asking the fee.** (Yes); **(2) A newspaper ad urges readers to buy potatoes at $1.00 per pound.** (No); and **(3) A computer programmer offers to create a specific program for a specific fee.** (Yes).

describes the yacht and offers it for a stated price to the first person whose acceptance is received on or before a stated date. This letter is an offer.

If a statement sounds like an offer but is made in obvious jest or in frenzied terror, the words cannot be transformed into a contract by acceptance. A reasonable listener would realize that no offer was intended.

At Cape Cod in Massachusetts, a toddler is playing in the water along the shore. Suddenly he is swept into the sea by an undertow. His terrified mother screams, "Oh my God! Help! Someone please save Timmy! I'll give anything if you'll save him!" You plunge in and rescue Timmy. Later you ask his mother for $10,000. You have no legal basis for collecting.

2. The Terms of the Offer Must Be Definite and Complete

PROBLEM

The Delgados agreed to buy, and Oaknoll, Inc., agreed to sell, one lot from among the 200 in a large suburban subdivision. Using their credit card, the Delgados paid $1,000 as a down payment and were given a receipt. The lots shown on the preliminary subdivision plan were of various sizes, shapes, and prices, but no particular lot was specified in the agreement. Had the parties made a valid, binding contract?

If a vague or incomplete offer is accepted, courts will not enforce the apparent agreement against either party. The terms must be sufficiently definite and complete to allow a court (1) to determine what was intended by the parties and (2) to state their resulting legal rights and duties. Thus, there is no contract in the problem. Neither party is bound because essential terms (notably identity of the specific lot, the price, and full terms for payment and delivery of title) have not been agreed upon.

There are, however, important exceptions to the requirement of definiteness. For example, medical, dental, and legal fees and other professional charges are often set only after the requested service is completed. Similarly, many ordinary workers are employed on an at-will basis, from payday to payday. The actual length of such employment remains uncertain. Generally, in such cases, on any payday, the employee may quit or be fired without further legal obligation for either party. In contracts between merchants, when either the price or the credit and delivery terms are not specified, current market prices and trade customs may be used to provide such details.

To assist ESL and other students who may have difficulty understanding suffixes and prefixes, write the terms **offer, offeror,** and **offeree** on the chalkboard. Have students look up in a dictionary the suffixes *-ee* (recipient of action) and *-or* (doer of action). Write these definitions next to the suffixes. Then, have students act out an offer and acceptance. Ask students what the offer was and who were the offeree and offeror.

ETHICS ISSUE

Ethics Issue

Read to students the following scenario: **Shelley planned an extravagant party. The food was expensive, so she wanted to order only enough for the people attending. So, she requested R.S.V.P.s in writing. Although they *had* written R.S.V.P., several people didn't show. Shelley said their R.S.V.P. was written acceptance of her offer and that they had broken a contract.** Ask: **Were the people legally or ethically obligated to attend the party?** (Ethically, yes; but, social agreements are not legally binding.)

Have students summarize in writing, using a computer, if possible, the three requirements of a valid offer.

▼ENRICH

Videotape one or more television commercials. Show the clips in class and ask students to identify the words that make the commercials appear to be offers or invitations to deal.

Divide the class into groups of five or six to compose and write original contracts. Assign the following roles in each group: facilitator to keep everyone on task; one or two attorneys to check requirements; offeror to state offer; offeree to state acceptance; and recorder to input the document on a computer, if possible. Allow 20 to 30 minutes for students to complete their contracts. Display contracts on a classroom bulletin board.

Cooperative Learning

3. The Offer Must Be Communicated to the Offeree

PROBLEM

Skatter was talking and laughing with four other students at the entrance to their high school. When a bell called them to class, she absentmindedly left her handbag behind. It contained a pocket calculator, her driver's license, and other items of value only to her. After class she posted an advertisement on a student bulletin board, offering $25 to whoever returned her bag. Major, another student, had not seen the advertisement but he found the bag and returned it to Skatter. Is Major legally entitled to the reward?

A person who is not the intended offeree or authorized representative cannot accept the offer. Nor can a person accept an offer without knowing it has been made. That is because any action taken would not have been a response to the offer. Thus, an offer of a reward that is made to certain persons or even to the general public cannot be accepted by someone who has never seen or heard of the offer. In such cases, the offeror may get what was sought, but most courts require that anyone who claims the reward must have known of the offer and acted in response to it when performing the requested act. Therefore, in the problem, Major was not entitled to the reward. However, he was legally and ethically bound to return the bag, if possible, after taking possession of it. Skatter may have been ethically bound to pay a reasonable reward. Indeed, statutes in some states require payment of a reward even if not offered by the owner. Moreover, if the owner fails to claim the property that is properly advertised for a legally specified time, the finder gets legal title to the goods.

▼ TEACH

On an overhead transparency, list or draw cartoon ideas of the six ways an offer can be ended (pp. 192–196). Display the transparency and, as you discuss each point, indicate which party's action (offeree or offeror) ends the contract.

▼ HOW IS AN OFFER ENDED?

Once made, an offer does not last forever. Possible reasons for its termination are explained in the following sections.

1. An Offer Ends at the Time Stated in the Offer

PROBLEM

On October 10, the Macro-Mercantile Bank sent a letter to Boggs, who had applied for a loan. In the letter, Macro-Mercantile offered

▼ ASSESS

Learning Objective 4 Orally assess students' understanding of the role of passing time in terminating contracts by writing the following on the chalkboard: **(1) Contract to deliver bricks**; **(2) Contract to deliver fresh cream puffs**; and **(3) Contract to deliver seedlings for spring planting.** Have students sequence the three contracts in the order in which they would terminate because a reasonable time has elapsed. (2,3,1) Ask students to explain their answers.

to lend $50,000 on specified terms and stated that the acceptance had to be received no later than October 18. Boggs mailed an acceptance on October 17, but the letter was delayed and did not arrive until October 20. Was there a contract?

In making an offer, the offeror may state how and when the offer must be accepted. In the problem, Macro-Mercantile did not receive Bogg's reply by the time specified. Therefore there was no contract.

2. An Offer Not Stating How Long It Will Remain Open Terminates After a Reasonable Length of Time

PROBLEM

Farman, a produce broker in New Jersey, telephoned Dandelo in Florida one morning and offered to sell him a truckload of blueberries. Farman then phoned her next-door neighbor, Sheldon, and made an offer to sell him a used truck and trailer. Both Dandelo and Sheldon told Farman they would "think about it" and "get back later." How long would Farman's offers remain open?

▼ APPLY

Ask students to review the PROBLEM on the bottom of pp. 192–193 and note the action that ended the offer. Have them suggest modifications in the PROBLEM that would have prevented the termination of the offer. **Guided Practice**

Thinking Critically Through Visuals

Business transactions require an offer and an acceptance. Suppose the seller in this photo had advertised his produce in the newspaper for a certain price. Is he—or is the woman doing the buying—the offeror? (He is.)

▼RETEACH Have students call out various goods and services and estimate what might be a "reasonable length of time" after which an offer would be considered legally terminated. Discuss rationale for determining termination time.

▼ENRICH In small groups, ask students to tell of personal, social, and business experiences in which vague time agreements led to misunderstandings or problems. Ask students to relate this potential problem to offers that do not state specific times.

Review the PROBLEM activities on pp. 194–195 with students. Then, have students write, using the computer, if possible, suggestions on how they could change each PROBLEM to make the offers valid.

Divide the class into six groups. Assign each group one of the six ways an offer can end and have students create a poster to depict it. Have each group present its poster to the class. Have the class decide what the poster shows. Display students' posters around the classroom.

What is a reasonable length of time depends on all the surrounding circumstances. In the problem, if the offer to sell the blueberries was not accepted within an hour, and possibly within minutes, it probably would terminate automatically. That is because blueberries are perishable produce, which must be marketed quickly. The seller may be in touch with many prospective buyers throughout the United States and Canada.

In contrast, an offer to sell expensive durable equipment, such as the truck and trailer, would not terminate until a longer time had elapsed. At least several days would probably be reasonable. If the parties had bargained about the sale over a period of months, a week or longer might be appropriate. To avoid misunderstandings, it is prudent to specify the available time at the outset.

3. An Offer Ends If It Is Rejected by the Offeree

PROBLEM

Kempsky offered to sell Del Rey a bicycle for $75, but Del Rey replied, "No, too much." The next day, Del Rey called Kempsky and said, "I've changed my mind. I'll take your bike for $75." Was a contract formed?

When an offeree clearly rejects the offer, the offer is terminated. This occurs even if a time limit set by the offeror has not expired. In the problem, if Del Rey had said, "That is too much. Would you take less?" he would still be negotiating on the original terms. But he flatly said "No." This refusal was a *rejection*, which ended the offer.

4. An Offer Ends If the Offeree Makes a Counteroffer

PROBLEM

Dee Haviland submitted a written offer to Ping-lin Pai, a wealthy Hong Kong real estate investor. The property for sale was a twenty-unit luxury apartment building, priced at $5.5 million, with credit terms available. Pai was represented by the San Francisco real estate agency Kuo & Chou. On Pai's behalf, the agency replied by certified mail offering to pay $4.4 million in cash. Haviland rejected this counteroffer. Pai's agents then wrote: "Our client is shocked by your price but must move assets out of Hong Kong before the British turn the colony over to China. Therefore, he accepts your offer and will pay $5.5 million cash at close of escrow." Was a contract formed?

▼ ASSESS

Learning Objective 4 Have students orally indicate legal terms for what ended each of these offers: **(1) Raff offered his baseball card for $35. Garbo said, "Too much, I'll pay $20."** (Counteroffer); **(2) Wake offered to shovel Soo's walk for $10. Before Soo could reply, Wake said, "Make that $15."** (Modified by the offeror); and **(3) Jones offered her racquet for $70. Wonka said, "No," but later called to accept.** (Rejected by offeree).

Generally an offeree who accepts an offer must accept it exactly as made. If the offeree changes the offeror's terms in any important way, the result is a **counteroffer**. In making a counteroffer, as in the problem, the offeree says in legal effect, "I refuse your offer; here is my proposal." The counteroffer terminates the original offer. Then the counteroffer becomes a new offer. The original offer can no longer be accepted by the offeree, unless it is renewed by the original offeror. In the problem, Haviland did not renew the original offer, so no contract was made.

5. An Offer Usually Ends If It Is Revoked or Modified by the Offeror Before the Offeree Has Accepted

PROBLEM

Perez offered to build twenty concrete mini-storage warehouses on Ander's land, at a fixed price of $11,500 each. Two weeks later, and before Ander had accepted the offer, the price of concrete mix and steel bars had gone up by 10 percent. Perez telephoned Ander and said she would have to boost the price of each unit by $1,000. Can Perez change her offer without liability?

Ordinarily, an offer can be revoked or modified by the offeror at any time before it has been accepted. This is true even if the offeror said the offer would remain open for a definite longer time. Thus, in the problem, Perez could modify her offer to Ander. The right to withdraw an offer before it is accepted is known as the right of **revocation**. A revocation or a modification is not effective until notice of it is communicated to the offeree or received at the offeree's mailing address. Until then, the offeree may accept the offer as originally made.

6. An Offer Is Terminated by Death or Insanity of Either the Offeror or Offeree

PROBLEM

In a telegram to "Lonely Lon" Lando, a famous country-western singing star, New York theatrical producer Hoffman offered him the lead in a new stage show. When Hoffman received no reply, and could not reach Lando by telephone, he left New York for Nashville, Tennessee, in his private jet. He hoped to persuade Lando in person. Unfortunately, all aboard the plane died when it crashed during a severe thunderstorm in the Appalachian Mountains. Did Hoffman's death end the offer?

On the chalkboard, write the following ways an offer can be ended:

1. By time deadline
2. By passage of a reasonable length of time
3. By rejection by offeree
4. By counteroffer by offeree
5. By revocation by offeror
6. By death or by insanity.

Have students count off by number from one to six. Tell students to compose, on a computer, if possible, a scenario of an ended offer that corresponds with "their" numbered statement on the chalkboard. Display students' writing on a bulletin board.

Independent Practice

On the chalkboard, draw the base of the following chart with the heading shown. Then, have students complete the chart.

How and When an Offer Ends
• Death or Insanity • At time stated in offer • After reasonable length of time • If rejected by offeree • If offeree makes counteroffer • If revoked or modified before acceptance of offeree

▼RETEACH Have students work in pairs to make an outline of six ways an offer can be ended. If they need to, have students refer back to pp. 192–195 for information.

▼ENRICH Have students share personal recollections of social and business offers that were ended. Discuss specific reasons why the offer ended and relate them to business offers.

TEACH

Introduce option contracts and firm offers as mechanisms for keeping an offer open. Explain the details of each and point out that, generally, neither death nor insanity of either party terminates an option contract or a firm offer. Have students tell how this differs from a regular offer. (Terminates with death or mental disability)

APPLY

Display parts one and two of the overhead transparency, *How Can an Offer Be Kept Open?* Have students take turns explaining the important points shown in each example. Then, ask students to compare the two. Be sure that the difference between the option contract and firm offer are emphasized. (In the option contract example, the potential buyer gives money.)

Guided Practice

Have students write two paragraphs, using a computer, if possible, describing an offer to sell a used car. Tell them to make the first paragraph a firm offer and the second an option contract.

Independent Practice

Contracts are agreements voluntarily entered into by the parties and subject to their control. Death or insanity obviously eliminates such control. Therefore the law acts for these parties when they can no longer act and terminates their *offers*. In the problem, Hoffman's death terminated his offer to Lando.

HOW CAN AN OFFER BE KEPT OPEN?

PROBLEM

The Downings had placed their idle factory building on the market for $950,000. Robinson, a developer, was interested in buying it, but she needed time to persuade a group of investors to join her in a syndicate to purchase the building. Robinson offered $10,000 to the Downings to keep the offer open to her alone for sixty days. The Downings accepted the money. Are they now legally bound to keep the offer open to Robinson even if someone else offers a much higher price?

Generally, an offeror is not obliged to keep an offer open for a specified time even if the offeror has promised to do so. Why? Because the offeree has given nothing in exchange for the promise. However, if the offeree gives the offeror something of value in return for a promise to keep the offer open, this underlying agreement itself is a binding contract. It is called an **option**. The offer may not be withdrawn during the period of the option. In the problem, Robinson held an option to buy the factory building. Thus, the Downings could not legally withdraw the offer. If they sold to a third party (who was unaware of the option) during the sixty-day period, they would be liable to Robinson for damages. The original offeror keeps the payment received for the option even if the offeree decides not to exercise the right to buy. Usually, if the original offer is accepted within the span of time allowed, money paid for the option is applied to the purchase price. However, this must be agreed to in advance.

In some states, statutes provide that a firm offer cannot be revoked within the stated period. A **firm offer** is a *binding offer* stating in writing how long it is to stay open. The Uniform Commercial Code (UCC) applies this rule to merchants selling or buying goods who agree in a signed writing to keep an offer open for a definite time (not more than three months) even when nothing is paid by the offeree. Generally, neither death nor insanity of either party terminates an option contract or a *firm* offer. This is true when the personal representative of the deceased or the guardian of the insane person can perform the contract if necessary.

ASSESS

Learning Objective 4 Read each of the following statements aloud and have students orally label each *a regular offer, an option contract,* or *a firm offer:* **(1) This signed promise gives you seven days to decide.** (Firm offer); **(2) I will supply all materials and labor for $500.** (Regular offer); and **(3) I'll take $2,000, which I'll apply to the price of the car if you decide to buy it.** (Option contract)

On April 10, Grundig, a merchant dealing in corn products, offered to sell a year's supply of corn oil to Navarro at a certain fixed price. The written and signed offer stated: "Price quoted is firm for one week from this date." Two days later, and before Navarro had accepted, the market price of corn went up sharply because of a published prediction of a very poor corn crop. Grundig immediately phoned Navarro and said, "Our deal is off. I cannot afford to sell at the price I quoted. I'd lose big bucks on every shipment." Navarro nevertheless accepts. Grundig is bound. She may not legally revoke her offer because she is a merchant and the offer was made in writing and signed, effective until April 17.

WHAT IS REQUIRED FOR ACCEPTANCE?

Acceptance occurs when a party *to whom an offer has been made* agrees to the proposal or does what is proposed. To create an enforceable agreement, acceptance must be

1. made only by the person or persons to whom the offer was made,
2. unconditional and match the offer, and
3. communicated to the offeror.

1. Acceptance Must Be by the Person(s) to Whom the Offer Was Made

PROBLEM

Darrow offered to trade his single-lens reflex camera to Monette in exchange for her camcorder with power zoom lens. Schorling, who had a camcorder of the same make and model, overheard the offer and said she would make the swap. Did a contract result from Schorling's acceptance?

An offer made to one person cannot be accepted by another. Accordingly, no contract resulted in the problem. Only Monette, not Schorling, could have accepted Darrow's offer.

Sometimes, however, an offer is made to a particular group or to the public and not to an individual. For example, a reward offer may be made to the general public. Any member of the general public who knows of the offer may accept it by doing whatever the offer requires.

TEACH

On the chalkboard, list the following requirements for acceptance to create an enforceable agreement:
1. Acceptance must be made only by the person or persons to whom the offer was made.
2. Acceptance must be unconditional and match the offer.
3. Acceptance must be communicated to the offeror.

Write the prefixes *uni-* and *bi-* on the chalkboard along with their definitions. Ask students to suggest words that incorporate these prefixes and discuss the commonalities to help students understand the difference between unilateral and bilateral contracts. (Answers may include unisex, unicycle, biannual, biaxial, bicycle, binary, and so on.) Ask students why it is important to know exactly when the acceptance of a contract occurs. Have students skim p. 200 to find when acceptance is effective in each of the following forms: oral (The instant words are spoken), mail (When properly posted), telegram (When handed or told to the clerk at the telegraph office), and fax (Instantaneous when transmission lines are both open and working).

RETEACH Have students role-play the making of regular offers, option contracts, and firm offers. Discuss the words and actions that characterize each type of offer. Have students identify offerors and offerees.

ENRICH Media: Have students imagine that they have been asked to write statutes for the Uniform Commercial Code (UCC) on how to keep an offer valid. Using a computer, if possible, have students work in pairs to write a one-page document to be included in the UCC.

APPLY

Have students suggest various versions of the offer and acceptance of a social date in order to illustrate the three points required of an acceptance to create an enforceable agreement. Have students voice both acceptable and unacceptable versions for each point. **Guided Practice**

Have student volunteers act out the negotiation of a contract. Instruct them to include counteroffers, significant changes that would cancel the acceptance, and suggestions or requests related to routine details of carrying out the contract that would not end the original offer. Have the class identify each.

RING LOST at Zuma Beach in front of beach house. Lady's yellow-gold band with 12 small diamonds. Inside inscribed: "Like diamonds. Forever. Yours, J. R. J." $1,000 reward. Call 555-8142.

Dowell saw this newspaper advertisement and rushed to the beach with a home-made sand sifter. About ten others were also searching, using various devices. After four hours, Dowell shouted, "Eureka! I've found it!" She promptly returned the ring to its owner. She alone was legally entitled to the reward.

2. Acceptance Must Be Unconditional and Must Match the Offer

PROBLEM

Schneider offered to sell his motor home to Nunzio for $28,000, but specified that the entire amount was to be paid within thirty days. Nunzio accepted the offer but changed the terms to $8,000 down and the balance in twenty equal monthly payments with interest at 10 percent a year on the unpaid balance. Was there an acceptance?

The offeror may specify precisely when and how the acceptance is to be made. To complete the agreement, the offeree must then comply with such terms. Any change by the offeree in important terms of the offer, as in the problem, ends the original offer and results in a counteroffer. This is so even if the change is advantageous to the original offeror. Suggestions or requests as to routine details of carrying out the contract, or other unimportant matters, do not end the original offer.

On Thursday, the manager of Volume Value Vacuum, Inc., offered to sell a vacuum cleaner to Susan at the bargain price of $129, on a cash-and-carry basis. Susan accepted, but then she added, "I'll have to pay you with a traveler's check. And my husband won't be able to pick up the vacuum until Saturday when he's off from work." A contract resulted because Susan's changes were unimportant.

ASSESS

Learning Objective 5 Tell students to summarize in writing the following: **(1) The three requirements that an acceptance must meet to create an enforceable agreement.** (Made only by the person or persons to whom the offer was made, must be unconditional and match the offer, and must be communicated to the offeror) and **(2) The difference between promises made in a unilateral contract with those in a bilateral contract.** (Unilateral: one party promises; bilateral: both parties make promises).

3. Acceptance Must Be Communicated to the Offeror

PROBLEM

Kulich, an art dealer, wrote Chiang, "I understand you are interested in selling your four-panel Chinese lacquer screen. I sold it to you in 1980 for $500 and said it would go up in value. Now I offer to buy it back for $3,000. Unless I hear from you to the contrary, I'll send my truck to pick it up next Monday morning. The driver will bring my certified check for the full amount." Chiang did not reply. Is she bound by a contract?

An acceptance must be more than a mental decision. It must be communicated to the offeror. Moreover, one is not obliged to reply to offers made by others. The offeror generally may not word the offer so that silence would appear to be acceptance. Thus, in the problem, Chiang would not be bound to sell the screen in accordance with Kulich's offer.

Sometimes, in a continuing relationship, the parties may agree that silence is to be regarded as acceptance. For example, in a monthly book or compact disc sales club, it may be agreed that failure to say "no" to a proposed shipment is to be regarded as "yes." Or a food market may have a standing order to have a wholesaler ship a certain amount of fresh produce every day unless the retailer breaks the silence with some notice. Only in situations such as these, where the parties have agreed in advance, can silence be acceptance.

In certain transactions, only one of the parties makes a promise. Such a transaction is called a **unilateral contract.** The offeror in a unilateral contract *promises something in return for the performance of a specified act by the offeree.* For example, the offeror may publicly promise to pay a $100 reward to anyone who returns a lost dog. Many persons learn of the offer; all may join the search. But no one promises to look, and no one is required to look. Only one person may find and return the dog, thus performing the act required to earn the reward. When the act requires substantial time and resources, sometimes the offer cannot be revoked until an offeree who has begun performance has had a reasonable amount of time to complete it.

In most cases, the agreement is a **bilateral contract** where both parties make promises. For example, a seller promises to deliver a load of topsoil in exchange for a homeowner's promise to pay $65. Or a dog owner promises to pay someone $10 an hour to look for a lost dog. The fee is due for the time spent looking for the dog even if it is not found. Bilateral contracts require that the offeree make and communicate the requested acceptance promise to the offeror. Until this is done, there is no contract.

Writing Connections

Language Arts
Divide the class into pairs. Assign one person in each pair to be the offeror and the other to be the offeree. Have each pair write, using a computer, if possible, a series of letters that record a valid offer and acceptance. To extend this activity, ask each pair to incorporate one or more of the following: counter-offer, option, firm offer, unilateral contract, and bilateral contract. Have each pair make a cover for their series of letters and bind them in chronological order. Display on a table and encourage students to read each other's work.

Independent Practice

▼RETEACH Review, one at a time, the three PROBLEM activities on pp. 197-199. For each, discuss the requirement for acceptance that was not met and have students suggest alternate scenarios that would have created an enforceable agreement.

▼ENRICH Ask students to brainstorm examples of unilateral contracts and bilateral contracts in everyday life. (Answers may include unilateral: newspaper ads promising rewards for returning lost articles; bilateral: promise to pay money if daily newspaper is delivered.)

TEACH

On the chalkboard, write the terms **valid contract, voidable contract, void agreement**, and **unenforceable contract**. Discuss the meaning of each and draw comparisons with the explanation of the terms *void marriage* and *voidable marriage* in Chapter 8, *Laws for Families.*

APPLY

Make up, or have students make up, situations that are examples of **void agreements, voidable contracts,** and **unenforceable contracts.** For example, for **voidable contracts,** you might describe to students the following: **The Williams Company misrepresented its finances to Ms. Smith, a potential investor.** Orally share these scenarios and ask students to identify which of the terms is depicted. **Guided Practice**

Have students draw cartoon panels to illustrate events that would result in at least two of the following: a valid contract, a void agreement, a voidable contract, or an unenforceable contract. Display their work on a bulletin board. **Independent Practice**

An acceptance may be communicated orally, in person, or by telephone. Or it may be communicated in writing and sent by mail, telegraph, or facsimile (fax) machine. The offeror may specify which method the offeree is to use. If not stated, and if business custom does not govern, most courts say the acceptance may be made by the same means used for the offer, or by faster means. The UCC provides that an acceptance of an offer to buy or sell *goods* (i.e., tangible personal property) may be made "in any manner and by any medium reasonable in the circumstances" unless otherwise clearly "indicated by the language or circumstances." Some experts anticipate that this commonsense rule may some day also be applied to contracts not covered by the UCC, notably for the sale of real property (i.e., land and interests in land).

It sometimes becomes important to determine exactly when acceptance is made and the contract arises. Oral acceptances are effective at the moment the words are spoken to the offeror. Acceptances sent by mail generally take effect when properly posted (i.e., placed under the control of the U.S. Postal Service, with correct address and sufficient postage). A telegram takes effect as an acceptance when it is handed to the clerk at the telegraph office or telephoned to the telegraph office. A fax transmission is instantaneous when the transmission lines are open and both sending and receiving equipment work properly. Therefore the effect is similar to instantaneous oral communication, but in a more durable form.

The offeror may specify that an acceptance will not be binding until it is actually received. This avoids the confusion that arises when an acceptance is mailed yet never reaches the offeror because it is lost in the mail. Legally, such acceptance would otherwise be effective. Mailing could however be proved by testimony of the offeree and by other evidence.

WHAT IS THE EFFECT OF ACCEPTANCE?

PROBLEM

Whitaker offered to buy the Melody Music Shop for $52,000. She gave Melody a check for $2,000 as a down payment, with the balance to be paid in ten monthly installments of $5,000 each starting July 1. The agreement provided that if the offer was not accepted by June 1, the check "shall be returned." Melody cashed the check before June 1, but did not notify Whitaker. What effect did cashing the check have on the offer?

A valid acceptance of a valid offer results in a valid contract. A **valid contract** is one that is legally effective and enforceable in court. Thus, in

ASSESS

Learning Objective 5 Have students jot down *True* or *False* to indicate the accuracy of the following: **(1) A valid contract is enforceable in court.** (True); **(2) An unenforceable contract could have once been a valid contract** (True); **(3) An invalid agreement is another name for a voidable contract.** (False); and **(4) A void agreement can be enforced.** (False).

the problem, cashing the check indicated assent, so there was a valid acceptance when the check was cashed.

A **void** (also called *invalid*) **agreement** cannot be enforced in court by either party. It has no legal force or effect.

Under certain circumstances, only one of the parties has the power to compel legal enforcement. If that party chooses otherwise, or decides to withdraw from the transaction, then the contract will not be enforced. Such an agreement is a **voidable contract.** For example, when one party persuades the other to contract by means of fraud, the sales contract is voidable by the buyer who has been misled.

The difference between a void agreement and a voidable contract is important. A voidable contract can be enforced or avoided by one of the parties. A void agreement, on the other hand, cannot be enforced by either party. A valid contract sometimes becomes an **unenforceable contract** because the time limit for filing suit to enforce it has passed. Sometimes the defendant has gone bankrupt and a judgment usually cannot be obtained in such case.

Preventing Legal Difficulties

When you enter into a contract...

1. Assume the worst possible developments in the performance of a prospective important contract. If feasible, forestall problems in advance by changing terms or by including suitable language in the contract that is clear and fair to both parties.
2. For important contracts, put offers and acceptances in writing. If either an offer or an acceptance is made orally, promptly confirm it in writing.
3. Obtain and keep a copy of every important document you sign.
4. Express your intentions in offers and acceptances with clear, complete, and understandable language. Vague and incomplete terms cause confusion and may lead to disagreements and costly litigation.
5. Remember that the offeror may specify how and when the offer must be accepted; otherwise the offeree may use the same means used by the offeror, or faster means. The UCC logically permits acceptance in such case by any means "reasonable in the circumstances."
6. When appropriate, buy an option, if one is available, to keep the offer open for as long as you need.
7. For an offeror to withdraw or revoke an offer, the offeree must receive the notice. For speed, use the telephone, telegraph, or fax machine to withdraw or revoke an offer. Likewise, promptly give notice of your

Preventing Legal Difficulties

Have students rewrite condensed versions of the eight suggestions for preventing legal difficulties. Instruct them to reduce the list, as much as possible, to a list of actions to take. Discuss and make a composite list on the chalkboard.

▼ CLOSE

Divide the class into groups of three or four. Have each group create a *Contract Caper* radio script—a complex contract that is valid in all aspects except one. Each script can contain only one error that would make the contract transaction incomplete or invalid. Have groups tape record or videotape their *Contract Caper* scripts. Play back the tapes and have the class try to identify the error, as well as verify that no other errors were made  that would render the transaction invalid.

Assign the following end-of-chapter materials:
Student text review activities, pp. 202–207
Workbook, pp. 25–26
Chapter Test
 Chapter *MicroExam*

▼RETEACH

Have students take turns giving oral definitions for the terms **valid contract, void agreement, voidable contract**, and **unenforceable contract.**

▼ENRICH

As a group, ask students to brainstorm which term—**void agreement, voidable contract,** or **unenforceable contract**—best applies to a contract between a minor and an adult. Then, independently, have students explain why in writing, using a computer, if possible. (Voidable contract; Only the minor can choose to withdraw.)

Strengthening Your Legal Vocabulary

1. offeror
2. void agreement
3. offeree
4. voidable contract
5. counteroffer
6. option
7. acceptance
8. capacity
9. valid contract
10. offer

Applying Law to Everyday Life

1. Yes, minors generally can disaffirm contracts. It makes no difference if both parties are minors; in such a case, either party can disaffirm. (p. 188)
2. Black is legally bound. Black was not so drunk that he could not understand the nature and the consequences of the contract. He may not disaffirm. (p. 189)
3. ETHICS ISSUE No, this was a social engagement, not a contract. (p. 190) Tony was not legally liable. There is a tort of inducing someone to breach a contract with a third party, but here there was no contract. Lorene's conduct was rude and displayed a lack of sensitivity for Bill's feelings and finances. It is doubtful that she was "terribly sorry," and to claim that she "just couldn't say no" to Tony was immature. Altogether her conduct was dishonest and unethical. If Tony was aware of Lorene's prior promise to attend the concert with Bill, his conduct was also unethical.
4. Yes, an offer can be withdrawn before it is accepted unless there is an underlying option contract that keeps the offer open. (p. 196)
5. Yes, a contract arises when an offer is accepted. Acceptance by mail is effective when the letter is properly posted with correct address and sufficient postage. Here, Bryant acted within the permitted time. Alber should have telephoned or wired his revocation, which is effective only when received. The

intentions to accept by telephone. Confirm your acceptance by telegram, fax, or mail.

8. To facilitate proof of your acceptance by mail, use certified mail with return receipt requested. Also, keep a copy of your acceptance letter and other documents, including the offer.

REVIEWING IMPORTANT POINTS

1. Contracts are the promises we live by in civilized society. Our interdependent world economy is built on a foundation of contracts—past, present, and future.
2. There can be no contract without a mutual agreement.
3. A contract is a legally enforceable agreement between two or more parties. It results from a valid offer and acceptance.
4. Generally all persons who can understand the nature of a contract and its consequences have the capacity to contract. Such persons are said to be legally competent.
5. Minors, insane persons, and seriously intoxicated persons lack full capacity to contract. Convicts and aliens who are citizens of a country at war with the United States are subject to similar limitations.
6. An offer must be (*a*) made with the offeror's apparent intention to be bound by it, (*b*) definite, and (*c*) communicated to the offeree.
7. If not accepted, an offer is ended (*a*) at the time stated in the offer, (*b*) at the end of a reasonable time if no time is stated, (*c*) by rejection, (*d*) by counteroffer, (*e*) by the offeror's revocation or modification, or (*f*) by death or insanity of either of the parties.
8. Generally the offeree must accept the offer unconditionally and in the exact form and manner indicated by the offeror.
9. An acceptance must be communicated to the offeror. If it is sent by mail (or by wire) it is effective at the time it is properly sent unless the offeror specified that it had to be received to be effective.
10. Agreements that are enforceable by the courts are valid contracts. Those that are not enforceable by either party are void agreements. Contracts enforceable by only one party are also voidable by such party. Unenforceable contracts are those that are valid but cannot be enforced in court.
11. Freedom of contract is basic to life in a democracy. Our economy is built on contracts.

STRENGTHENING YOUR LEGAL VOCABULARY

Match each term with the statement that best defines that term. Some terms may not be used.

acceptance	offeror
bilateral contract	option
capacity	revocation
contract	unenforceable contract
counteroffer	unilateral contract
firm offer	valid contract
legally competent	void agreement
offer	voidable contract
offeree	

1. Party who makes an offer.
2. Agreement that is not enforceable by either party.
3. Party to whom an offer is made.
4. Contract that may be avoided by only one of the parties.
5. Response by offeree, with new terms, which ends the original offer.
6. Contract to keep an offer open a specified length of time.
7. Affirmative response necessary to transform an offer into a contract.
8. Ability to understand the nature and effects of one's actions.
9. Agreement that is legally effective and enforceable in court.
10. Proposal that expresses willingness of the offeror to enter into a legally binding agreement.

APPLYING LAW TO EVERYDAY LIFE

1. Jim and Gary, both minors, were members of an American Legion-sponsored baseball team. When Jim was shifted to the outfield, he bought Gary's fielder's mitt for $25. Later, when Jim was moved back to first base, he told Gary that he wanted his money back and offered to return the glove. Can Jim disaffirm the contract this way?
2. For months Bovard had tried to persuade Black to purchase a computerized system for all accounting records of Black's plastic manufacturing company in New Hampshire. Finally, he persuaded Black to visit New York in order to inspect a similar installation already in use. That night Bovard took Black and his wife to dinner at an exclusive restaurant and

revocation was received on June 6, but the offer had been accepted on June 5. (pp. 199–200) If Bryant had used an incorrect address or amount of postage, there would be no contract because of improper posting of the letter of acceptance. (pp. 199–200)

6. Yes, an acceptance of an offer may be made in the same manner as the offer unless the offeree stipulates otherwise. By sending the offer via fax, the offeror authorizes the telephone company to serve as agent and to receive an acceptance on behalf of the offeror. A fax takes effect as an acceptance when it is sent to the offeree's fax machine. (p. 200)

7. Yes, this was a binding unilateral contract. The offer required the performing of an act, and the offerees did what was requested. (pp. 199, 200)

8. Yes, Barbara's option is still valid. Generally neither physical death of either party nor insanity terminates an option contract. A representative of the estate of the deceased or the guardian of the insane person can perform the sales contract. No unique personal service is required. The option would also be valid if Barbara had died within the 10-day period. The personal representative of her estate could exercise the option, but is not likely to do so under the circumstances. If the goods were truly unique, or if the purchase was a very good bargain, the personal representative might exercise the option and thereby increase the value of Barbara's estate. (p. 196)

9. 

The sequence of events in this little drama unfolded as follows:

MONDAY

ACTION: ABNER offers to sell Track to BOB for $300 cash, "offer open until we go hunting on Saturday."

LEGAL EFFECT: 1. BOB, as offeree, may accept the offer before he and ABNER go hunting on Saturday.
2. ABNER is free to sell to anyone before BOB accepts.

then to a Broadway play. After the play they went to a night club and had several drinks. Before the party ended, Black had signed the contract saying, "Let me sign that contract and let's get on with the fun." Is he legally bound or may he disaffirm?

3 ETHICS ISSUE Bill spent most of his month's allowance for expensive tickets to a rock concert after Lorene said she would go with him. On the morning of the event, Lorene phoned and said she was terribly sorry, but Tony, the high school's star fullback, had also asked her to go and she "just couldn't say no." Did she breach a contract? Could Tony be held legally liable if he knew Lorene had already promised to go with Bill? Was Lorene's conduct ethical? Was Tony's conduct ethical?

4 When Wood was at Prescott's garage sale, he noticed a large, metal tool chest in the corner, complete with about 400 standard and metric tools. Wood offered to buy it for $1,250 and said, "You can take a week to think about it before you decide whether to accept." Four days later, and before Prescott had responded, Wood told Prescott that he had found another set for less money and withdrew his offer. Can he legally do this?

5 On Monday, June 1, Alber sent Bryant an offer by mail to sell his graphite and fiberglass tennis racket for $50. He said, "Take a few days to think about it." The letter arrived on Wednesday, June 3. On Thursday, June 4, Alber wrote again saying, "My offer is canceled." Bryant received this letter on Saturday, June 6. Bryant had properly posted his letter of acceptance on Friday, June 5. Alber received Bryant's letter of acceptance on Monday, June 8. Is there a contract? What if Bryant had used the wrong address or insufficient postage on his letter of June 5?

6 Mid-East Traders, Inc., sent a fax to Starr offering her a job as a translator in Istanbul for three years. The salary of $4,000 a month was specified and other details were given. A reply was requested. Starr immediately sent her acceptance using Mid-East Traders' fax number. Was this a valid acceptance?

7 Colton, an elderly widower, wrote his daughter Janine, saying that if she and her husband would leave their home in Missouri and come to Massachusetts to care for him, they would have the use of his house for the rest of his life. Also, he said that he would will the house to them. Therefore Janine and her husband moved to Massachusetts and began taking care of her father. Was this a binding contract?

8 Sam advertised his ski boat for sale, priced at $4,500 complete with outboard engine and trailer. Barbara paid Sam $100 for a ten-day op-

3. Since BOB paid nothing for an option to buy, ABNER may revoke his offer anytime before BOB accepts.

TUESDAY
ACTION: 1. CARL offers ABNER $400 for Track, to be paid in eight equal installments.
2. ABNER says, "Sorry, my price is $300 cash."
LEGAL EFFECT: 1. Valid offer to buy
2. ABNER rejects CARL's offer, which ends it. Under the circumstances, his statement, "Sorry, my price is $300 cash," would probably be construed as an offer to sell to CARL for $300 cash.

WEDNESDAY
ACTION: 1. DAN learns that ABNER has offered to sell Track, and so he says, "I'll pay $300 cash when you deliver the dog at the end of this year's duck-hunting season."
2. ABNER says, "Okay—you now own Track."
3. ABNER phones BOB and tells him of the sale.
LEGAL EFFECT: 1. Valid offer to buy
2. ABNER accepts Dan's offer. Delivery and payment of $300 cash to take place at the end of this year's duck-hunting season.
3. A courtesy call, which was not essential; ABNER's offer to BOB was not exclusive, nor did BOB have an option to buy. The offer ended when Track was sold to DAN.

THURSDAY
ACTION: 1. CARL phones and says, "I accept your offer. I'll pay $300 cash."
LEGAL EFFECT: 1. A futile effort by CARL because even if ABNER offered to sell Track to CARL, he retained the right to sell it to anyone else before CARL accepted his offer. This ABNER did, on new terms, which he was free to accept.

Abner has not breached a contract with Bob or Carl because he had not made a contract with either of them, hence there was no contract that could be breached.

Yes, Abner has been open and honest in his dealings. He did change his mind and the terms of his original offer when he accepted Dan's offer. But this was his right as the owner of Track, since he had not tied his hands in any previous option contract. Both Bob and Carl knew, should have known, or could have tion, the money to be applied to the purchase price if she exercised her right to buy. Two days later, Sam was killed in a motorcycle accident. Is Barbara's option still valid? If Barbara had died within the ten-day period, would the option still be valid?

9 ETHICS ISSUE On Monday, Abner offers to sell his trained golden retriever, Track, to Bob for $300 cash. "My offer is open until we go hunting next Saturday." On Tuesday, Carl offers Abner $400 for Track, in eight equal monthly payments of $50. Abner says "Sorry, my price is $300 cash." On Wednesday, Dan learns that Abner has offered to sell Track. Dan tells Abner, "I'll pay $300 cash when you deliver the dog at the end of this year's duck hunting season. But you can keep Track until then." Abner says, "Sounds like a good deal. Okay, you now own Track." He phones Bob and tells him of the sale. On Thursday, Carl phones Abner and says, "I accept your offer. I'll pay $300 cash. When can I pick up Track?" Abner replies, "Sorry, but Track's been sold." Has Abner breached a contract with Bob or Carl? Has he been ethical in his conduct?

10 After Greg LeMond won his third Tour de France bicycle race, the G. E. E. Whiz Discount Sports Shop published this advertisement in the local newspaper: "Congratulations to the winners of the Tour de France! Now you too can be a champ! Get your 12-speed Blue Lightning bicycle for only $595, marked down from $795, the manufacturer's suggested retail price. What a bargain! Come and get it! and Go-Go-Go!" Baxter visited the discount store after work the following day and said, "I'll take one of the Blue Lightning bikes." The clerk replied, "Sorry, we had only ten bikes in stock and they've all been sold." Was the advertisement an offer? Is there a contract between Baxter and the G. E. E. Whiz Discount Sports Shop?

SOLVING CASE PROBLEMS

1 On December 23, the First National Bank had its sales agent Wyman mail a written offer to Zeller to sell a parcel of real property for $240,000. On January 10, Zeller had his purchasing agent mail a written offer to buy the property for $230,000. The same counteroffer was made in a telephone conversation on that day to Wyman, but Wyman told Zeller's agent that the offer to sell the land was no longer in effect. When Zeller's agent reported this news to Zeller, he promptly told his agent to wire an acceptance of the original offer at $240,000. Zeller's agent did as ordered and the telegram of acceptance arrived before the letter containing Zeller's counteroffer. The bank refused to sell,

determined, the applicable contract law. Bob is the only party who might have felt badly treated, because Abner had told him the offer was good until Saturday. Abner was not legally or morally obligated to inform Bob of the prior sale, any more than Bob was legally or morally bound to respond or to purchase Track before that deadline. But, Abner courteously did inform Bob of the sale. There was no similar relationship with Carl because Abner had never mentioned the Saturday deadline to Carl, and Carl had no right to assume it also applied to him.

10 No, most advertisements, such as this one, are not offers but rather invitations to the public to come in and "deal," by making offers to buy. If G.E.E. Whiz had only one or two Blue Lightning bicycles in stock, and if it had no plans, or ability, to get more of them from the wholesaler or manufacturer, and if it could conservatively assume that the advertisement would attract many prospective buyers to whom other bicycles could be sold, the firm might be faulted for unethical and illegal (false and misleading) advertising (a tactic called "bait and switch" advertising, p. 167).

Since the ad was not an offer, Baxter could not respond with an acceptance, and therefore there was no contract. (p. 190)

Solving Case Problems

1 The trial court ruled for the defendant, First National Bank; the appellate court affirmed this judgment. "It is elementary that for a contract to exist," the appellate court stated, "there must be an offer and acceptance. Moreover, to create a binding contract, an acceptance must comply strictly with the terms of the offer. An acceptance requesting modification or containing terms that vary from those offered constitutes a

rejection of the original offer, and becomes a counterproposal, which must be accepted by the original offeror before a valid contract is formed." On January 10, Zeller's agent had told the bank through its agent, Wyman, of the counteroffer. "This operated as a rejection and terminated plaintiff's power to accept ...." the bank's offer. Note that the original offer did not require acceptance to be in writing. Therefore. the oral communication of Zeller's counteroffer was an effective rejection. (p. 195)

2 Judgment for CBC; acceptance must be made in the manner specified by the offeror. (p. 198) Where the terms of an option contract clearly state that the intent to exercise the option must be in writing and that a deposit of money must be made, the optionee must comply with these terms.

3 Judgment for Marchiondo; the case was sent back to the trial court for further proceedings. Since the trial court found that Marchiondo had begun performance of the unilateral contract by spending time and money to get the prospect's acceptance, then a contract with a condition results. (p. 199) The condition is full performance by the offeree (Marchiondo) and this is a question of fact to be determined by the trial court. Scheck must give the offeree a reasonable opportunity to perform within the time allowed. The appellate court noted that some states—not New Mexico—additionally require that the agency contract of the broker be exclusive. (Under New Mexico law, this particular contract was actually exclusive, giving Marchiondo alone the right to obtain the prospect's acceptance, or to receive his commission, even if Scheck or anyone else sold the property within the six-day period.)

reminding Zeller that the offer to sell had been revoked and that its agent Wyman had so informed Zeller's agent in the telephone conversation on January 10. Nevertheless, Zeller sued the bank for specific performance and for damages. Who should win? (*Zeller v. First National Bank*, 79 Ill. App. 3d 170, 398 N.E.2d 148)

2. Epton orally bargained for an option to buy a 54-percent share of the ownership of the Chicago White Sox baseball club for $4.8 million from the defendant, CBC Corporation. The option, which was to have been reduced to writing, was to last one week in exchange for the payment of $1,000 by Epton. To exercise the option within the week, Epton was supposed to give CBC a certified or cashier's check for $99,000 as a down payment. Epton was also to notify the corporation in writing that he was exercising his option. Twice during the week, Epton orally assured CBC of his intent to exercise the option and he also offered to pay the $99,000 as soon as the option was signed by CBC. After the week had passed, CBC refused to sell, and Epton sued. He claimed that his oral notice of intent to exercise the option was sufficient. He said that failure of CBC to sign a written option agreement excused both the requirement of a written exercise of the option by him and the necessity of the $99,000 deposit. Who should win? (*Epton v. CBC Corporation*, 48 Ill. App. 2d 274, 197 N.E.2d 727)

3. Scheck wanted to sell a parcel of his real property. He agreed to pay a commission to Marchiondo, a real estate broker, if Marchiondo obtained acceptance from a prospective buyer within six days of Scheck's written sales offer. However, Scheck revoked his offer on the morning of the sixth day. Later that day, Marchiondo obtained the prospect's acceptance, but Scheck refused to pay the commission. Marchiondo sued, claiming breach of contract. The trial court dismissed the complaint. The court stated that a unilateral contract had been formed and that Scheck could revoke his offer at any time before performance of the requested act. Marchiondo appealed. You decide. (*Marchiondo v. Scheck*, 78 N.M. 440, 432 P.2d 405)

4. In newspaper advertisements for two successive Saturdays, the defendant, Great Minneapolis Surplus Store, Inc., offered a fur stole for sale. The advertisements said, "1 Black Lapin Stole, Beautiful, Worth $139.50...$1.00 FIRST COME FIRST SERVED." Leftkowitz was first in line on both Saturdays. The first time, the defendant said "a house rule" limited the offer to women exclusively. The second time the defendant refused to sell, saying Leftkowitz knew the house rule. Leftkowitz sued for damages. You decide. (*Leftkowitz v. Great Minneapolis Surplus Store, Inc.*, 251 Minn. 188, 86 N.W.2d 689)

5 Lee Calan Imports, Inc., advertised a 1964 Volvo station wagon for sale in a Chicago newspaper. Because of an error by the newspaper, the price was listed at $1,095 instead of $1,795. The advertisement made no mention of such material matters as equipment to be furnished or warranties to be offered. Plaintiff O'Brien came in and said he wished to buy the station wagon. One of the defendant's salesmen at first agreed but, upon discovering the erroneous price, refused to sell. Was there a binding contract? (*O'Keefe—Administrator of Estate of O'Brien v. Lee Calan Imports, Inc.*, 128 Ill. App. 2d 410, 262 N.E.2d 758)

5 No, a newspaper advertisement that contains an erroneous purchase price, through no fault of the defendant advertiser, and that contains no other terms is not an offer. The advertisement cannot be accepted to form a contract. It is only an invitation to make an offer. (p. 190) When the salesperson at first agreed to make the sale, he was mistaken as to the true price. The plaintiff buyer was also mistaken as to the true price. As will be discussed in Chapter 12, when there is such a mutual mistake about the material fact (in this case, the price of the car), either party can disaffirm the contract if one has arisen. Here, no contract arose because the plaintiff could not accept as an offer the erroneous advertisement. Moreover, note that there was no crime of false advertising because the price was innocently misstated.

4 Judgment for plaintiff Leftkowitz for $138.50 (the fur was valued at $139.50, and $1 was deducted from the purchase price); athough most advertisements are invitations to make offers, a court may find that a given advertisement is a clear, definite offer that leaves nothing open for negotiation. Therefore, as here, the advertisement is an offer, the acceptance of which completes the contract. The "house rule" did not appear in the advertisement and may not be added after acceptance of the offer by Leftkowitz. (pp. 200–201)

CHAPTER 11 ORGANIZER

Chapter Theme

Lawful consideration is necessary to make a promise binding.

DIRECTED STUDY QUESTIONS	SPECIAL FEATURES	PROGRAM RESOURCES				
		Reteach	Enrich	SN	AM	
What is consideration?	Thinking Critically Through Visuals, p. 210	✔	✔			
Why is consideration required?		✔	✔	✔	K	
What is sufficient consideration?		✔	✔			
Is an existing obligation consideration?	Personal Perspectives, p. 214 Writing Connections, p. 215	✔	✔			
Is past performance consideration?		✔	✔			
What are exceptions to the requirement of mutual consideration?	Ethics Issue, p. 217 Thinking Critically Through Visuals, pp. 217, 218 Multicultural Highlights, p. 219 Preventing Legal Difficulties, p. 220	✔	✔		V A	

Additional Resources

- Calamari, John D., and Perillo, Joseph M. *Calamari and Perillo's Hornbook on Contracts*, 3rd ed. St. Paul, MN: West Publishing Co., 1987.
- Corbin. *Corbin on Contracts*. St. Paul, MN: West Publishing Co., 1970.
- Howell, John Cotton. *The Complete Guide to Business Contracts.* Englewood Cliffs, NJ: Prentice Hall, 1980.
- *Restatement of the Law, Contracts*, 2nd ed. St. Paul, MN: American Law Institute Publishers, 1981.
- Smith, Len Young and Roberson, G. Gale. *Business Law: Uniform Commercial Code,* 4th ed. St. Paul, MN: West Publishing Co., 1977.

One-semester course	✔	✔						
One-year course	✔	✔	✔					

Chapter Pacing Guide

	ASSESSMENT OPPORTUNITIES			
Cooperative Learning	**Informal Assessment**	**Chapter Review**	**Chapter Test**	**Chapter *MicroExam***
	✔	✔	✔	✔
	✔	✔	✔	✔
✔	✔	✔	✔	✔
	✔	✔	✔	✔
	✔	✔	✔	✔
	✔	✔	✔	✔

Media

Videodiscs

Exception to Mutual Consideration

Search Chapter 14, Play To 15

State by State

A court in Massachusetts held that a bank employee's oral promise to a customer that the bank would lend more money to pay the interest on a loan was void. The customer's hope was neither legal detriment nor reliance, required as consideration.

Teaching Materials

Student text, pp. 208–225

Overhead transparency masters
- *Consideration*
- *Composition of Creditors*

Videos
- *Contracts, Warranties, and Credit* Videotape
- *Law for Business* Videodisc

Workbook, pp. 27–32

Outside Resources
- Copies of various contracts
- Wax, wood, rubber, ink, paint, or other materials to carve and print seals
- Pledge cards from various organizations
- Index cards

Assessment
- Chapter Test
- Chapter *MicroExam*

Vocabulary

promisor, p. 210
promisee, p. 210
consideration, p. 210
forbearance, p. 210
gift, p. 211
seal, p. 212
nominal consideration, p. 213
compromise of a disputed claim, p. 215
composition of creditors, p. 215
past consideration, p. 216
promissory estoppel, p. 218

Learning Objectives

When you complete this chapter, you will be able to

1. Understand the nature of consideration in contracts.
2. Know why consideration is essential.
3. Recognize unacceptable types of consideration.
4. Recognize exceptions to the requirement of

consideration.

208

Chapter Self-Test

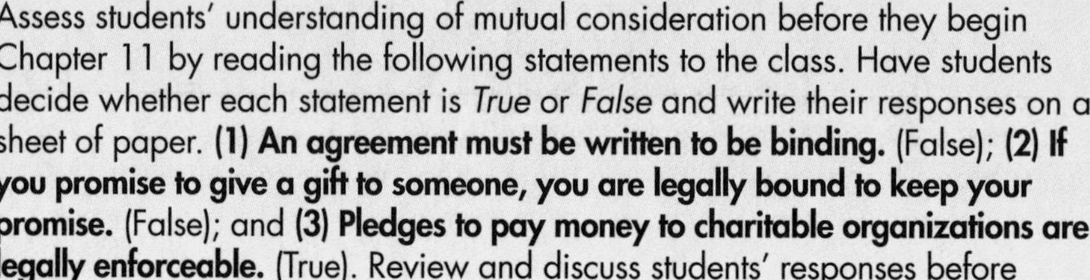

Assess students' understanding of mutual consideration before they begin Chapter 11 by reading the following statements to the class. Have students decide whether each statement is *True* or *False* and write their responses on a sheet of paper. **(1) An agreement must be written to be binding.** (False); **(2) If you promise to give a gift to someone, you are legally bound to keep your promise.** (False); and **(3) Pledges to pay money to charitable organizations are legally enforceable.** (True). Review and discuss students' responses before starting the chapter.

CHAPTER 11

MUTUAL CONSIDERATION

1 After graduation from high school in June, you and three classmates plan to "see America first." The plan is to visit the capital cities of our forty-eight contiguous states, taking numerous pictures along the way. The Sure-Shot Camera Shop offers to give you free a dozen rolls of 36-exposure color film for the trip if you agree to let it develop and print all the rolls you use, for a stated price per roll. You agree. Are both you and the Sure-Shot Camera Shop legally bound?

2 A four-piece high school rock band practices for at least one hour most days of the week. Its studio is the garage of the drummer's home. Several neighbors offered to pay the rent of a local mini-warehouse as a practice room for a year if the group agreed to stop practicing at the drummer's home. The players agreed. Is there a binding contract?

3 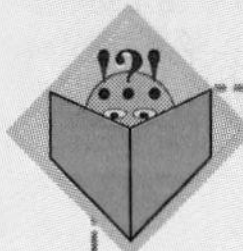
A motorist and her two young children are stranded in the parking lot of a shopping mall because her car battery is dead. You connect the batteries of the two vehicles with your jumper cable. With your engine running, she turns her ignition key and her engine starts smoothly. Grateful, she asks for your address and promises to send you $25. Is she legally bound to keep her promise? Is she ethically bound to do so?

209

▼ FOCUS

Write the following on the chalkboard before class begins and have students list their answers on a sheet of paper: **Identify five things you have made agreements to buy, sell, or do.** (Answers may include agreements to perform work, do household chores, babysit, complete homework, buy things, and so on.)

Begin class by discussing students' lists of agreements. Determine if students know what is legally needed to make a promise or agreement binding. Ask: **Are the agreements you listed binding by law?** Analyze several student agreements to determine if the parties involved both gave and received consideration.

You Decide

1 Yes; Although you get the film "free," you have promised to give the camera shop the developing and printing job. The shop will do the work and you will pay them, so mutual consideration exists and you are both legally bound.

2 Yes; If the rock group accepts the offer, the consideration would be a forbearance—giving up the legal right to practice at home.

3 ETHICS ISSUE No, she is not legally bound. An act that was performed in the past cannot serve as consideration for a promise in the present. However, from an ethical standpoint, she should keep her promise.

Thinking Critically Through Visuals

Ask students to explain what is happening in this photograph. (The woman has just entered into a verbal agreement to have her lawn cut by the man.) Ask: **Is this handshake agreement binding?** (Yes, we must assume that this is a binding agreement because both parties have given and received consideration. The woman is giving money to the man in exchange for his prior promise to cut her lawn, and the man has cut the lawn in exchange for her prior promise to pay the money.)

TEACH

Read the PROBLEM on p. 210. Point out that both parties give consideration. After explaining the six kinds of consideration, found on p. 211, ask students to identify the type of consideration in the example. (The promises exchanged) Then ask: **What are some other examples of consideration?** (Answers may include paying to purchase an item in a store, cash, an agreement to provide a service, and so on.)

APPLY

Copy the overhead transparency master *Consideration* and distribute it to students. Have students work in pairs to identify the consideration in the example. (Money and property)

Guided Practice

Thinking Critically Through Visuals

The female customer in the photograph is making a purchase at a movie theater. What consideration is given and received? (Goods for money; The customer gives money and receives popcorn; the salesperson gives popcorn and receives money.)

WHAT IS CONSIDERATION?

PROBLEM

Your neighbors are going skiing in the Canadian Rockies near Calgary, Alberta. Their vacation will last ten days and so they ask you to watch their house, pick up their mail, and clear the sidewalk of any snow while they are gone. They promise to pay you $50 and you agree. Is this a contract? What consideration is given and received?

In a typical agreement, one party, in effect, says to another, "If you do this for me, I shall do that for you." The promise or action that one person (the **promisor**) gives in exchange for the promise or action of another person (the **promisee**) is **consideration**. In the problem, there was a contract. The promises exchanged, one for the other, were the consideration.

In performing those promises, your neighbors will pay money; you will watch the house, pick up mail, and possibly clear snow. They get your services; you get their $50. Both parties give consideration; both parties receive consideration. There has been a bargained-for exchange.

Consideration may consist of some right or benefit to one party (the promisor), or some duty or detriment (i.e., cost) to the other party (the promisee). Thus, consideration may consist of **forbearance**—that is, refraining from doing what one has a right to do. Frequently, in simple "fender

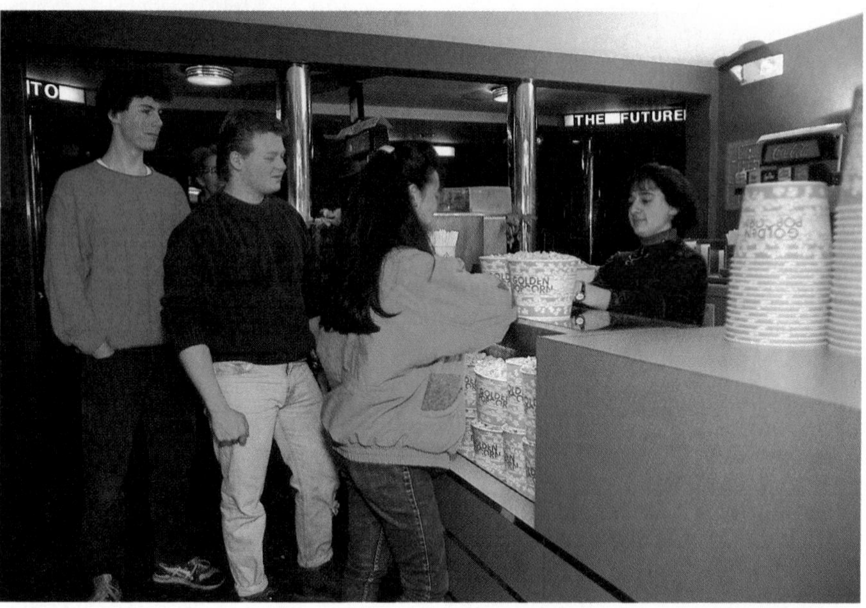

ASSESS

Learning Objective 1 Have students orally identify the six kinds of consideration that make a promise enforceable and give examples of each one. (Consideration—A return promise, an act other than a promise, forbearance, change in legal relation, money, or other property; Examples—A promise to exterminate insects, caring for a child, giving up your right to sue, a marriage, ten dollars, a car, and so on.)

bender" accidents, the guilty party promises to pay an agreed-upon sum to the innocent party in exchange for the latter's promise not to sue. The victim's forbearance is consideration for payment by the wrongdoer or the wrongdoer's automobile insurance company.

The consideration required to make a promise enforceable may consist of (1) a return promise, (2) an act other than a promise, (3) forbearance, (4) a change in a legal relation of the parties (e.g., when A and B mutually agree to marry), (5) money, or (6) other property.

WHY IS CONSIDERATION REQUIRED?

PROBLEM

For a college graduation present, a wealthy aunt promised to give Maureen two round-trip tickets for a cruise for her and any friend of her choice. The promised trip was to be along the "Mexican Riviera" from Long Beach, California, to Acapulco, in the state of Guerrero. At the graduation exercises, however, her aunt gave her a kiss instead and said, "The stock market is down. Sorry, darling!" Although not likely to do so, could Maureen successfully sue her aunt for breach of contract?

In relations with each other, people generally expect to get something of value when they give something of value, unless a gift is intended. Thus consideration is required for a valid, enforceable contract. It must be *mutual* (also called *reciprocal*). This means that each party must give consideration, and each must receive consideration. The presence or absence of consideration is one test of whether a contract has been made. If either of the parties does not give consideration, the other has no duty to perform as promised. In the problem, Maureen promised nothing of value in exchange for her aunt's promise of the tickets. (A "thank you" and continued love and affection do not suffice as consideration in most states. That is because such things lack determinable market value.) Therefore Maureen and her aunt did not make a contract. Instead, the aunt merely promised to make a gift.

A **gift** is the voluntary transfer of ownership of property without receiving consideration in return. Generally, a promise to make a gift is not enforceable, but property actually transferred by gift cannot be recovered by the donor. One who receives property by gift gets the title to the goods. While Maureen's aunt could not be forced to keep her promise or to pay damages, if she had delivered the cruise tickets she could not compel Maureen to return them.

Bring several different types of contracts to class. Have students work in groups of three or four to make a chart identifying the consideration given and received in each contract. **Independent Practice**

TEACH

After summarizing this section, ask: **How would a court use consideration to determine whether or not a contract exists?** (By asking if each party involved has given and received consideration; this reciprocal consideration is essential for every valid contract.)

APPLY

Discuss with students why a promise of a gift probably is not legally enforceable. (Mutual consideration is not present.) Ask: **Is a person bound morally to keep his or her promise of a gift?** (Students may base their responses to this ethical question on deontological reasoning, as discussed in Chapter 2.) **Guided Practice**

Have students with limited English proficiency, who are having trouble with the terminology in this section, copy the PROBLEM on p. 210 onto a sheet of paper. Then, have them highlight and label the parts of the PROBLEM that show the

promisor, the **promisee,** and the **consideration.**

RETEACH Divide students who are having difficulty understanding the concept of **consideration** into six groups. Have each group create a poster illustrating one of the six types of consideration. Have each group share its poster with the others.

Using a computer, if possible, have students write two examples of verbal agreements noting what consideration is given and received.

After discussing seals and the fact that, in some states, consideration is presumed to exist under seal, have students design their own seals. They could carve seals into wax, wood, rubber, or some other material that, when dipped in ink or paint, will imprint the seals on paper. They could also create seals by using computers with graphic capabilities. Then, create a bulletin board display of the seals. **Independent Practice**

In some states, consideration is presumed to exist in contracts under seal. A **seal** may be

1. an impression on the document, or
2. a paper or wax affixed to the document (perhaps inscribed with a design), or
3. the word "Seal" or the letters "L.S." (an abbreviation for the Latin words meaning "place of the seal") on the document.

Seals were used more frequently many years ago when few people could read or write. Persons who wished to be legally bound by some agreement would affix their seals to the writing. The seal was often an elaborate wax impression. Sometimes a colorful ribbon was attached. Such formalities indicated that the parties intended to be bound. Therefore the old common-law courts did not demand proof that both parties had given and received consideration. In most states today, however, the seal is not a substitute for consideration. In these states, while seals are sometimes used, they neither add nor detract from the validity of the contract.

In several states, consideration is presumed when a merchant makes the promise in writing and signs the document. As noted on page 199, this is called a firm offer.

▼ TEACH

Students may have trouble understanding why consideration does not have to be sufficient. To explain this concept, relate the fact that consideration given and received by the promisor and promisee must have legal value but need not be equal in value. As a result, courts generally do not inquire into the sufficiency or the fairness of consideration (in effect, *caveat emptor*).

▼ WHAT IS SUFFICIENT CONSIDERATION?

PROBLEM

While cleaning out his garage, Shreve found an old glass lampshade. He showed it to Laval, who thought it was an authentic Tiffany antique. Laval offered to buy it for $150, and Shreve accepted. When Shreve later learned that it was worth at least $450, he tried to cancel the contract and reclaim the lampshade. "Your miserable $150 was not a fair price!" he said. "That shade is worth at least three times as much as you paid me!" If Shreve sues, will he win?

The values that persons place on the same property may vary widely. For example, one fashion-conscious person might gladly pay $10,000 for an original and exclusive *haute couture* (i.e., high-fashion) gown by a famous designer. Other persons would not be interested in owning such a gown even if they could afford the price. Also, for good reasons, a person may place a higher value on a product at one time than at another. For example, when

▼ APPLY

Discuss with students times when the consideration they received was not of equal value to the service, money, or product they provided. You may wish to give a small prize to the student who received the least "considerate" consideration. **Guided Practice**

▼ ASSESS

Learning Objective 2 Have students respond in writing to the following questions: **(1) Why is consideration important?** (It must be present to make a contract binding.); and **(2) Is the actual dollar value of consideration important? Explain.** (No; As long as both parties have agreed to the consideration and there is no evidence of fraud or duress, its actual value is not important.)

you have been baking for hours on the sunny side of a stadium, you willingly pay three times the grocery-store price for an ice-cold soft drink.

Generally, what the parties give and get as consideration need not be of equal value. The actual value of consideration is unimportant as long as the contracting parties have voluntarily agreed. Thus, in the problem, Shreve is bound by the contract because he voluntarily agreed to the price of $150. It was a freely bargained-for exchange.

What is acceptable consideration to the parties, and therefore sufficient, depends on many variables. These variables include market supply and demand, personal needs and desires, and an individual's ability to evaluate. Generally, courts will not question the sufficiency or fairness of consideration. Courts will question the consideration if there is evidence of fraud or duress, or if the consideration received by one of the parties is so grossly inadequate as to shock the conscience of the court.

In certain written contracts, such as publicly recorded deeds, consideration from one party may be identified as "one dollar ($1) and other good and valuable consideration." In such situations, the actual consideration may be substantially more. However, the parties either cannot state the amount precisely or do not want to publicize it. This token amount is known as **nominal consideration.** Courts enforce contracts supported by nominal consideration if circumstances indicate that, in fact, consideration was given.

IS AN EXISTING OBLIGATION CONSIDERATION?

PROBLEM

Vork was employed under a three-year contract to manage a motel for Lemsky at $25,000 a year, in addition to receiving a free apartment. After six months, Flemming offered Vork $30,000 a year to manage a larger motel. Upon learning of the offer, Lemsky said to Vork, "You're competent. You're honest. I need you. I'll meet any offer you get from anyone else." Vork remains on the job. Must Lemsky pay her the higher salary?

A person sometimes promises to do something that he or she is already bound to do by law or by prior contract. Such a promise, or act, cannot serve as consideration in exchange for a new promise by any other person. This rule applies in the problem. Vork was still bound to work for Lemsky for an additional thirty months under the original contract. Therefore Lemsky's promise to pay more money is unenforceable. To hold him to the new promise, Vork would have to provide new, additional consideration. Otherwise Vork is obligated to carry out the contract as originally agreed upon.

In writing, have individual students identify the three variables used to determine sufficient consideration. Then, ask volunteers to share their responses. (Market supply and demand, personal needs and desires, and an individual's ability to evaluate, and so on) **Independent Practice**

Working in groups of three or four, take part of one class period to have students write and perform short skits to demonstrate various types of consideration, including nominal consideration. Each group should have a director, a scriptwriter, a timekeeper, and a props manager. You may wish to videotape the skits.

Cooperative Learning

TEACH

Discuss with students options for collecting partially paid or unpaid bills. (Answers may include collecting only what the person can afford to pay, setting up a payment schedule, or suing the person in small claims court.) Be sure students understand the difference between a *creditor* and a *debtor.*

RETEACH Have students identify the variable that primarily influences the dollar amount of the following considerations: **A baseball pitcher makes $5 million a year.** (Market supply and demand) and **A minister performs a marriage ceremony for a modest fee.** (Personal dedication to service, rather than profit)

ENRICH

Using a computer, if possible, have students write a creative short story to illustrate the concept of **nominal consideration**. Remind students to first choose the variable that will influence the amount of consideration.

Working in pairs, have students create a scenario in which the parties involved do not agree on the amount of a debt. Then have students decide on a compromise to their disputed claim. Have volunteer pairs present their problems to the class. However, before each pair shares its solution, have members of the audience tell what they think a fair compromise to the dispute would be. **Guided Practice**

Personal Perspectives

Sometimes people feel that they have not received the goods or services that were promised to them. Have students survey family members and/or friends who have been in such situations. Students should ask what was done to remedy the situation, record their findings, and bring the information to class. Then, as a class, discuss each situation and the legal problem to be learned from it, and determine other courses of action that might have been used, such as a compromise of the disputed claim or going to small claims court.

The same rule holds true when a person demands further compensation for carrying out a contract already made.

> Overman contracted with a corporation to build a float for a nationally televised New Year's Day parade. Two weeks before the parade, because the cost of materials had gone up, Overman refused to complete the float unless the corporation promised to pay an extra $15,000. The corporation made the promise in writing. However, Overman could not compel payment of the additional money by suing, simply because there was no consideration. Overman was already obligated to complete the float under the original contract.

This rule is also applied when a *creditor* (i.e., a person to whom a debt is owed) agrees to accept less than the total amount due in full settlement from a *debtor* (i.e., a person who owes money to a creditor). For example, assume that Shawver borrows $1,000 from Reno. The loan is to be paid in one year with interest at 10 percent per year, or a total amount of $1,100. On the due date, Shawver sends Reno a check for only $1,000, saying "Sorry; I'm strapped for cash. You will have to accept this in full payment." Reno *indorsed* (i.e., signed) and cashed the check. Under the rule of most courts, Reno may later sue and recover the unpaid balance of $100. She received no consideration for the suggested agreement to reduce the amount due. Courts in all states permit a debtor to settle a claim by paying less than the full amount due before the due date. But there must be mutual agreement between the creditor and debtor to do so. Valid consideration exists because the creditor is satisfied by getting the money sooner. Similarly, if something extra is given by the debtor, the new consideration supports a voluntary release by the creditor.

> Bennett owed Huff $500 but said he could pay only $300. Huff agreed to accept the lower sum together with a silver ball-point pen in payment of the entire debt. The pen, although not worth $200, was sufficient new consideration for Huff's release from the remaining debt.

In some cases, there is a genuine dispute between the parties as to how much is owed. In such case, partial payment offered in full settlement by the debtor and accepted by a creditor settles the claim. Thus, a debtor may in good faith claim that a certain debt is $50. The creditor in good faith contends that it is $100. If the parties agree, respectively, to pay and to accept $75, their agreement is binding. Consideration is found in their mutual for-

ASSESS

Have groups of three or four students create comic strip stories that illustrate a payment problem and how its settlement involved either a compromise of a disputed claim or a composition of creditors.

bearance from taking the matter to court. This is known as **compromise of a disputed claim.** Also, the disputed claim would be settled if the debtor paid by check and made a clear notation that read: "In full settlement of all claims outstanding." The notation should preferably be on the back of the check where the creditor indorses it. The disputed claim is settled even if the creditor disagrees with the notation and crosses it out before cashing the check.

> Gilbert repaired Sullivan's leaky roof and submitted a bill for $500. Sullivan claimed that the bill should be for only $300 because water still seeped through and further repairs might cost as much as $200 more. Sullivan, therefore, sent a check for $300 with a notation on the back that it was "in full settlement of all accounts due." Gilbert crossed out the words, cashed the check, and filed suit in small claims court for $200. The judge denied the claim. Crossing out the terms did not invalidate them. If Gilbert disagreed, he should not have cashed the check.

In contrast, some states say that with such an indorsement the debt is discharged even when the claim is not in dispute. The Uniform Commercial Code (UCC) adopts this rule. However, under the UCC, if the amount of the debt is not disputed, the creditor may cash the check and still sue for the balance if the creditor adds appropriate words, such as "under protest" and/or "without prejudice" before indorsing. As an alternative, the creditor could send the check back and sue for the full amount.

Occasionally, a group of creditors will cooperatively agree to accept less than what they are entitled to, in full satisfaction of their claims against a debtor. In return, the debtor agrees not to go bankrupt. This is called a **composition of creditors.** Consideration for the promise of each creditor to release the debtor from full payment is found in the reciprocal promises of the other creditors to refrain from suing for the entire amounts due them. If the creditors did not agree to this arrangement, the debtor could go bankrupt, and the creditors might receive much less (see Chapter 19).

> Eubank was in financial trouble. She owed Murray $15,000; Irwin, $10,000; Bunker, $3,000; and Grummand, $2,000. To enable Eubank to stay in business, all the creditors except Grummand agreed to accept 50 percent of their claims in full settlement. The first three agreed to let Eubank pay Grummand 100 percent of his claim. Their agreement was a composition of creditors, and none of the cooperating creditors could legally demand the remaining 50 percent.

Writing Connections

Economics
Using a computer, if possible, have students write a position paper in response to the following statement: **Accepting partial payment of a debt as payment in full may be better than going to court to get the full amount due.** (Answers may include that it is better to accept partial payment and be assured of receiving some money immediately, or that it is better to spend the time and money to go to court in order to try to get the full amount.)

Independent Practice

Display the overhead transparency, *Composition of Creditors.* Have students read the case study on the bottom of p. 215 and, using the transparency chart, identify the role each person in the case study played. (Eubank was a debtor; Murray, Irwin, Bunker, and Grummand were creditors.)

RETEACH Have students work with a peer-tutor to summarize in writing one of the case studies on pp. 214–215. The summary should include whether the problem was solved using a compromise of a disputed claim, a composition of creditors, or neither method.

ENRICH Have students who need a challenge contact a local attorney or court system to find out the legal avenues available to a person with a disputed claim. Then have students create a bulletin board illustrating their findings.

▼ TEACH

Clarify the difference between the terms **consideration** and **past consideration** by giving students an example in which an act has already been performed, such as driving someone home from the airport a week ago (past consideration). Then change the example slightly (offering to drive someone home from the airport in two weeks in exchange for a stated charge), so that it becomes consideration. Provide similar examples as necessary.

▼ APPLY

Ask students to give some examples of past consideration related to school or home, and record their responses on the chalkboard. (Answers may include asking to use the family car for chores performed months earlier, and so on.) **Guided Practice**

Have students work in pairs to explain, in writing, why the example mentioned above is of past consideration, rather than of consideration. Have them use a computer if possible.

Independent Practice

▼ TEACH

Discuss the following: **Should a promise of a gift or pledge to a charitable organization be binding?** (Allow for differences of opinion, but refer students to information on p. 217.)

▼ IS PAST PERFORMANCE CONSIDERATION?

PROBLEM

While the Griffins were out of the country on a business trip, a fire broke out in their unoccupied home. Hiller, a neighbor who had a key to the house, called the fire department. She then risked her life to save three valuable paintings from the living room before the building was destroyed. When the Griffins returned, they thanked Hiller profusely and promised to pay her with a valuable Japanese tea service, which was being shipped. When the tea set arrived, they changed their minds and gave Hiller nothing. Will Hiller win if she sues to get either the tea set or damages for breach of contract?

Recall that consideration is what one person asks of another in return for a promise. The bargaining takes place now, in the present, for immediate or future performance by both parties. Therefore, an act that has already been performed cannot serve as consideration for a promise made now. Such act is called **past consideration.** It is not acceptable as consideration. Thus, in the problem, Hiller was being a good neighbor when she voluntarily saved the paintings. However, her deed could not serve as consideration for any subsequent promise made by the Griffins. When they returned, their promise of the tea service was unenforceable because Hiller's good deed was past consideration. Of course, the Griffins might properly feel ethically obliged to keep their promise.

▼ WHAT ARE EXCEPTIONS TO THE REQUIREMENT OF MUTUAL CONSIDERATION?

PROBLEM

The Branyan family pledged $25,000 to the building fund of the community hospital. Relying on this and other pledges, the board of directors of the hospital entered into a contract for construction of a new section. Can the Branyans be held to their pledge?

Following are important exceptions to the general rule that mutual consideration is necessary for a valid contract or binding promise.

▼ ASSESS

Learning Objective 3 Have students write their own definition for, and provide an example of, **past consideration**.

1. Promises of Financial Support to Charitable Organizations

Individuals and business firms often contribute to charitable organizations, such as churches, schools, and hospitals not operated for profit. The contributions may be outright gifts or promises (i.e., pledges) to pay in the future. Because the party who makes the pledge receives nothing of monetary value in return, one might assume that the pledge is unenforceable. In fact, however, courts generally enforce such promises provided the charity states a specific use for money sought, and then actually acts in reliance on promises made by pledgors. For example, a hospital may have contracted for new facilities, as in the problem. It would be unjust to deprive the hospital of promised support it reasonably relied on.

Some courts hold that the promise of each donor (i.e., contributor) was given in exchange for the promises of all others. Or they point to the donor's personal pride and enjoyment of public esteem. In reality, these courts enforce promises of donations to charities as a matter of public policy. However, this rule may discourage some contributors from pledging substantial payments to be made in the future because they fear they might be unable to pay. Accordingly, many charities simply waive their legal rights to enforce the pledges, as indicated in Figure 11-1.

▼ APPLY

Ethics Issue

Charitable and nonprofit organizations must pay for expenses such as rent, utilities, salaries, and advertising. Donations go, in part, toward these expenses. Some organizations are very conservative. Others have been criticized for extravagance. Ask: **Is it ethical for these organizations to spend their funds on promotion, generous salaries, and expenses?** (Answers may include yes, since the organizations must attract and keep employees; or no, since their goal should be to spend as much money as possible on their causes.)

Thinking Critically Through Visuals

Ask: **Is mutual consideration taking place in this photograph? Explain.** (Yes; Both parties are giving and receiving consideration.)

▼RETEACH Pair students having difficulty understanding **past consideration** with students who have exhibited mastery of the concept. Partners should share the definitions and examples they created for ASSESS on p. 216. Have students amend their definitions and examples to reflect their new understanding of the concept.

▼ENRICH Have students reread the first PROBLEM on p. 216. Then, hold a debate on the moral aspects of the Griffins' decision. Have class members not involved in the debate determine which side presented the best support for its position.

Thinking Critically Through Visuals

Have students read the pledge card on p. 218. Ask: **Does the town have the right to enforce this pledge? Why or why not?** (No, because of the waiver that appears above the donor's signature)

Obtain several pledge cards from various organizations or institutions such as a hospital, a church, United Way, or the YMCA/YWCA. Divide the class into small groups and give each group a pledge card. Help each group identify what considerations, if any, are stated on its pledge card. Then, compare the policies of the organizations.
Guided Practice

Figure 11-1
This pledge card contains a clause that waives the legal rights of Old Town Rehabilitation Foundation to enforce the voluntary pledges of contributors.

OLD TOWN REHABILITATION FOUNDATION

To help restore historic, publicly owned buildings in the Old Town section of Pioneerville, and in consideration of the gifts of others, I (we) subscribe to the OLD TOWN REHABILITATION FUND

the sum of** Five thousand **Dollars ($**5,000**)

TOTAL SUBSCRIPTION	$5,000
AMOUNT PAID	$1,000
BALANCE	$4,000

***Balance to be paid:** $1,000 annually, beginning August 1, 19--*

It is understood and agreed that if the donor's economic circumstances change, making payment impracticable in his/her sole judgment, this pledge will not be enforced. All contributions are tax deductible.*

Ellen Yates — *(Donor's Signature)* 5/1/-- *(Date)*

OLD TOWN REHABILITATION FOUNDATION

BY: James P. Roston — *(Authorized Solicitor)* 5/1/-- *(Date)*

*Note that not all pledge forms contain this waiver clause.

2. Promissory Estoppel

Even though consideration is not present, a promise may be enforced under the doctrine of **promissory estoppel** when the following conditions are met:

a. the promisor should reasonably foresee that the promisee will rely on the promise,

▼ ASSESS

Learning Objective 4 In random order, read students the summaries of the four exceptions to the general rule that mutual consideration is necessary for a binding agreement. Have students orally identify each exception as you read it. (Promises of financial support to charitable organizations, promissory estoppel, commercial paper, and state statutory exceptions)

b. the promisee does, in fact, act in reliance on the promise,
c. the promisee would suffer a substantial economic loss if the promise is not enforced, and
d. injustice can be avoided only by enforcement of the promise.

Silvertone, a wealthy financier, strongly believes that world travel is essential for a balanced education. Accordingly, he told his twin niece and nephew that if they would "cap" their college degrees with a trip around the world, he would pay all their expenses upon their return, up to $9,500 for each. Using savings and some borrowed money, the twins took off on a ninety-day journey. Total reasonable expenses for each exceeded $9,500 by the time they returned home. Silvertone is legally bound to reimburse each with $9,500. Although he received no consideration for his promise, he is *estopped* (i.e., barred) from denying his liability.

3. Commercial Paper

The government tries to encourage ready acceptance of commercial paper, such as bank checks. Accordingly, suppose a person signs and issues (i.e., gives) a check to a swindler who never delivers goods as promised. The swindler promptly negotiates (i.e., transfers) the check to an innocent third party, who gives full value in exchange. Although the writer of the check received no consideration for the check when it was issued, she or he must honor (i.e., pay) it when it is presented by the innocent third party. Commercial paper is discussed more fully in Unit 8.

4. State Statutory Exceptions

A few states exclude certain contracts from the requirement of consideration. An example is when a party, in a signed writing, states the intention to be legally bound. Also, under the UCC, no consideration need be given for a new promise by a debtor to pay a debt when collection is barred by the statute of limitations (discussed on page 306). Likewise under the UCC, a good-faith agreement that modifies an existing contract for the sale of goods needs no new consideration. For example, *after* a sale has been made, a seller could agree to give the buyers a valid warranty without further charge. Also (as discussed on page 199), a merchant who makes a *firm* offer in writing to buy or sell goods is bound for up to three months even when no payment or other consideration has been given by the other party for such offer.

Multicultural Highlights

Marian Wright Edelman was the first African American woman to be admitted to the Mississippi bar and the first African American, and second woman, to chair the Board of Trustees of Spelman College. An accomplished lawyer and writer, she is perhaps best known as the founder and president of the Children's Defense Fund (CDF). More than half of CDF's funds come from foundation grants and pledges. Dubbed "the children's crusader," Edelman hopes CDF will help children before they get sick, drop out of school, become teenage parents, or get into trouble with the law. Have students work in small groups to research the founders and goals of other humanitarian nonprofit organizations such as Amnesty International, Greenpeace, the American Heart Association, and so on. **Independent Practice**

▼RETEACH Give each student a sheet of paper. Tell students to scan the information on pp. 217–219 and list the four exceptions to the requirement of mutual consideration. Then have students exchange papers and correct their work.

▼ENRICH Have students make pledge cards for fund-raising events sponsored by school groups such as the band, drama group, or business club. The cards should include the name of the organization, what the funds will be used for, the amount of the pledge, how the pledge will be paid, and a waiver clause.

Preventing Legal Difficulties

Divide the class into six groups and assign to each group one of the six items on p. 220. After students have discussed the information, ask a volunteer from each group to explain his or her item to the class.

▼ CLOSE

Give each student three index cards. Have students write three scenarios that illustrate either *mutual consideration*, ***past consideration, nominal consideration, a gift,*** or *an exception to the requirement of mutual consideration.* Make sure students include the appropriate term on each card. Collect all the cards and divide the class into two teams. Read each scenario aloud and award one point for each correct answer. The team with the highest score after

all the cards have been read wins.

Assign the following end-of-chapter materials:
Student text review activities, pp. 220–225
Workbook, pp. 27–32
Chapter Test

Chapter *MicroExam*

Preventing Legal Difficulties

To prevent misunderstandings about contracts, remember that . . .

1. Generally both parties must give and receive consideration if their agreement is to be enforceable as a contract.
2. Adequacy or equality of consideration is generally unnecessary. It is sufficient when something of value is given and received.
3. Accepting money or other value in exchange for giving up a legal right, such as the right to sue for damages after an accident, constitutes consideration and is binding. Consult a lawyer before making such an agreement in any major dispute.
4. A pledge to a charitable institution is generally binding and should not be made unless you intend to fulfill it.
5. Promises to make gifts cannot be enforced by the intended donee (i.e., receiver). An exception is made under the unusual conditions of promissory estoppel.
6. You should use care and good judgment in making contracts. Courts generally will not rescue you from "bad bargains" or unfavorable deals voluntarily made.

▼ REVIEWING IMPORTANT POINTS

1. Lawful consideration is necessary to make a promise binding. Such consideration may consist of a return promise, an act, a forbearance, a change in a legal relation of the parties, money, or property.
2. Each party to the contract gives consideration; each party receives consideration. Such exchange is a test of the existence of a contract. It is the reason for the performance of the contract.
3. The adequacy, equality, or fairness of the consideration given and received is immaterial as long as the consideration has value and is voluntarily agreed to by both parties.
4. Performing or promising to perform an existing obligation is not consideration.
5. Past performance is not consideration for a promise given now or in the future.

6. Pledges to pay money to charitable organizations are usually enforceable even though no consideration was given to the pledgors for their promises.
7. Agreements modifying contracts for the sale of goods need no consideration to be binding.
8. Under special circumstances, promises of gifts are enforceable under the doctrine of promissory estoppel.

STRENGTHENING YOUR LEGAL VOCABULARY

Match each term with the statement that best defines that term. Some terms may not be used.

composition of creditors
compromise of a disputed claim
consideration
forbearance
gift
nominal consideration
past consideration
promisee
promisor
promissory estoppel
seal

1. An agreement by all creditors to accept something less than the total amount of their claims in full satisfaction of a debtor's obligations.
2. Token consideration, which bears no relation to the real value of the contract.
3. The promise or action of one person in exchange for the promise or the action of another person.
4. Refraining from doing what one has a right to do.
5. Voluntary transfer of ownership of property without consideration.
6. Mutual promises of a debtor and creditor not to go to court to settle a disagreement regarding the amount of a debt.
7. Act that has already been performed and thus cannot be consideration for a promise in the present.
8. When a promise is enforced to avoid injustice, even though no consideration is given for it.
9. Person who makes a promise.
10. Person to whom a promise is made.

Strengthening Your Legal Vocabulary

1. composition of creditors
2. nominal consideration
3. consideration
4. forbearance
5. gift
6. compromise of a disputed claim
7. past consideration
8. promissory estoppel
9. promisor
10. promisee

▼ APPLYING LAW TO EVERYDAY LIFE

1. Glenn contracted to add a room to Reid's home for $10,000. When Glenn was partway through, he realized that the job was more time-consuming than anticipated. Therefore he refused to continue until Reid promised to pay an additional $2,000. Is Glenn legally entitled to the extra $2,000?

2. Shea owed Barlow $1,200 that was due and payable. Shea had been furloughed (i.e., laid off temporarily) at work, so he asked Barlow to extend the due date for six months. Barlow agreed, but a month later sued Shea to collect the debt. Will she win?

3. Lemke's son bought a videocassette recorder from Dyer on an installment plan. When her son was unable to keep up the payments, Dyer came to repossess the recorder. Lemke promised in writing to make the payments if Dyer would allow her son to keep the recorder. If Dyer agreed, could Lemke hold him to his promise?

4. Kamiar owed Rubio $5,000, which was due in one year. There was no dispute as to the amount. However, Rubio needed money immediately, so Kamiar offered to pay $4,000 early in full settlement of the debt. If Kamiar pays the $4,000 now, may Rubio sue and collect the remaining $1,000 later?

5. Mackey, who had no children, told Lark that if she would attend his alma mater—Ahoya College—and graduate, he would pay all expenses she incurred. Relying on loans and some of her own funds, she financed her way through college and earned the degree. Now Mackey says Lark suffered no detriment and he got no benefit. Since there was no consideration, he need not pay as promised. Do you agree?

6. When they were both freshmen in college, Steiner borrowed $200 from Faber so he could attend the big game in Chicago. Steiner never repaid the debt, and after five years it was barred by the statute of limitations. Then Steiner sent Faber a Christmas card on which he added this note: "I haven't forgotten those four 50's I borrowed from you for the big game. Now that I am working, I'll pay you. In addition, I'll take you to this year's big game at my expense." Are Steiner's promises enforceable?

7. Kari promised to deed ten acres of land to the Ezlers. In reliance on the promise, they took possession of the land, cleared it, installed an irrigation system over a one-acre section, and planted fifty young fruit trees. Then Kari, seeing the improved property, changed her mind. May the Ezlers compel the transfer even though they gave Kari no consideration?

Applying Law to Everyday Life

1. Probably not; mere difficulty in performing an act that one is already legally bound to do is not consideration to support a promise to pay more. Under some circumstances, a contractor might be able to collect an additional amount for work if he or she runs into problems that are unknown and unforeseen by both parties and would cause a serious hardship. Such was not the case in this problem. (p. 214)
2. Yes; Shea gave no consideration for Barlow's promise to extend the date of payment. (p. 211)
3. Yes; The mother's promise to make the remaining payments was consideration to support Dyer's promise (forbearance) not to repossess the recorder. (pp. 210–211)
4. No; Consideration for the $1,000 waived by Rubio is found in the early payment by Kamiar, one year before the money was due. (p. 214)
5. No; Mackey persuaded Lark to attend his alma mater and thereby gained a legal benefit by getting her to do what he wanted. Therefore, Mackey must pay. Note that some courts would also hold him liable under promissory estoppel. It would be a gross injustice if Lark were compelled to pay for four years of college after assuming in good faith that Mackey would do so. (pp. 213, 218–219)
6. Steiner's promise in writing to pay the debt barred by the statute of limitations revives the debt. (p. 219) It is again enforceable without new consideration. However, his promise to see the big game is an unenforceable promise of a gift. (p. 211)

8 ETHICS ISSUE Mary received a diamond brooch from the estate of her maternal grandmother. It was appraised at $7,500. Because it did not fit in with her sports-oriented life-style, Mary sold the brooch to a jeweler who told her, "The setting is old-fashioned, but the diamond is forever the same. I'll give you $3,500 cash." Later Mary wondered whether she received legally sufficient consideration. Did she? Did the jeweler act ethically?

9 ETHICS ISSUE When Bob began college, his godmother promised to give him $1,000 at the end of each of the following four years if he remained in school and refrained from smoking tobacco. She also promised a bonus of $1,000 if and when he received his bachelor of science degree. Are the godmother's promises legally enforceable? What are the ethical implications of her promises?

10 George negligently misjudged the distance between the side of his car and Brian who was on his bicycle. George sideswiped Brian, who was knocked to the ground and injured. An adjuster for George's insurance company persuaded Brian to accept and cash a check for $1,250 in exchange for full release of George and his insurer from further liability. The payment covered Brian's out-of-pocket losses, including the cost of repairing his bike. Later a friend told him he probably could have sued and obtained damages for pain and suffering as well. May Brian legally reopen the matter and successfully sue for more money?

▼ SOLVING CASE PROBLEMS

1 Marine Contractors Company, Inc., did various marine repair work within a 100-mile radius of Boston. The company maintained a trust fund for the benefit of retired employees. The trust agreement provided that employees who resigned could withdraw their share of the fund after waiting five years. Hurley, general manager of the company, had accumulated $12,000 in the trust fund. When Hurley resigned, the president of Marine offered to pay his $12,000 immediately if he would agree not to compete with Marine directly or indirectly within 100 miles of Boston for five years. The parties made a written contract which set forth a "consideration of One Dollar and other good and valuable consideration." It also stated that the parties have "set their hands and seals" to this contract. Within four months after leaving Marine's employ, Hurley began doing repair work similar to that of Marine. Soon after, he organized his own company, hiring two supervisors of Marine. Marine sued to stop Hurley from breaking his contract. Hurley

8 ETHICS ISSUE Yes, Mary received sufficient consideration. Consideration generally need not be fair, reasonable, or adequate. (p. 213) Yes, the jeweler probably acted ethically. The jeweler offered and paid a wholesale-level price which is what he would routinely pay for additions to his inventory.

9 ETHICS ISSUE Yes, the promises are legally enforceable. All four elements of promissory estoppel are present. (p. 218) She is acting ethically, because considerable scientific evidence indicates that smoking is seriously harmful to the health of the user and may injure persons who inhale smoke produced by others. Although the avoidance of smoking, if generalized, would harm the tobacco industry, they have no moral basis for complaining because tobacco is so dangerous.

10 No; His forbearance (from suing) was given in exchange for the payment. The sum paid need not be adequate. There was no evidence of fraud or coercion. (p. 213)

7 Yes; All four elements necessary for promissory estoppel are present. (pp. 218–219)

defended with a plea of no consideration. Do you agree with Hurley? (*Marine Contractors Company, Inc. v. Hurley,* 310 N.E.2d 915)

2. Under a written contract with the Robert Chuckrow Construction Company, Gough agreed to do the carpentry work on a commercial building. Gough was to supply all necessary labor, materials, and other requirements to complete the work "in accordance with the drawings and specifications." After Gough's employees had erected thirty-eight trusses, thirty-two trusses fell off the building. Gough did not claim that the plans or specifications were defective or that Chuckrow was to blame for the collapse. Gough was told by a Chuckrow representative to remove the fallen trusses and to rebuild and reerect them. Gough was also told to submit an additional bill for this work. He completed the job and submitted the additional bill. However, Chuckrow paid only the amount promised under the original written contract. Therefore Gough sued Chuckrow for the extra costs of reconstruction. Is he entitled to the added money? (*Robert Chuckrow Construction Company v. Gough,* 159 S.E.2d 469, Ga.)

3. Hoffman and his wife owned a bakery in Wautoma, Wisconsin. Lukowitz, an agent for Red Owl Stores, Inc., represented to and agreed with Hoffman that Red Owl would erect a grocery store building for them in Chilton and stock it with merchandise. In return, the Hoffmans were to invest $18,000 and Hoffman was to operate the store as a Red Owl franchise. In reliance on Red Owl's assurances and advice, the Hoffmans sold their bakery, paid $1,000 down on a lot in Chilton, and rented a residence there. In negotiations over some seventeen months, Red Owl boosted the required investment to $24,100; then to $26,000; and finally to $34,000, which was to include $13,000 from Hoffman's father-in-law. Red Owl insisted the $13,000 must either be a gift or a loan, which would be inferior in claim to all general creditors. Hoffman balked and sued for damages. Should the Hoffmans win? If so, on what grounds? (*Hoffman v. Red Owl Stores,* 133 N.W.2d 267, 26 Wis. 2d 683)

4. Petty, a general contractor, made a series of purchases from Field Lumber Company. Field's records showed a total price of $1,752.21. Petty admitted he owed $1,091.96, but denied liability for the difference of $660.25. He claimed the difference was a result of an unauthorized $292.60 purchase by an employee, plus related finance charges. Petty sent a check for $500 along with a letter stating that the check must be accepted in full settlement of the total claim or returned. Field phoned to say the lumber company required full payment, but nevertheless Field cashed the check and sued for the full balance it claimed was due. You decide. (*Field Lumber Company v. Petty,* 512 P.2d 764, Wash.)

Solving Case Problems

1. No; Forbearance was consideration for the promise. There was a forbearance of the right to withhold payment of the defendant's vested interest in the trust fund for five years in exchange for his promise not to compete. Further, in some states, making a promise under seal means consideration is presumed. (pp. 210–212)
2. No; Although a written contract may be modified by an oral agreement, in this case Gough merely did what he had originally promised to do—namely, erect the trusses and do related carpentry work. There was no consideration received by Chuckrow for its implied promise to pay the added costs, because Gough was already legally bound to complete the job properly. (p. 214)
3. Yes, the Hoffmans should win. This is a classic case of promissory estoppel. (pp. 218–219) Lukowitz, on behalf of Red Owl, made a number of promises and assurances to the Hoffmans which they relied on reasonably and acted on to their substantial detriment. Important details of the franchise contract (such as specifications of the grocery store building and the terms of the lease) had not been agreed upon, so the promises of Red Owl did not amount to an offer that would have resulted in a contract if the Hoffmans had accepted.

5 Burt made two pledges of $50,000 each to the Mt. Sinai Hospital of Greater Miami "in consideration of and to induce the subscriptions of others." Nothing was said as to how the funds were to be used. Mt. Sinai Hospital did not use his pledge to induce others to subscribe. Nor did the hospital undertake any work in reliance on Burt's pledge. By the time Burt died in the following year, he had paid $20,000 on his pledge. The executors of his estate now refuse to pay the balance. Must they do so? (*Mount Sinai Hospital of Greater Miami, Inc. v. Jordan*, 290 So. 2d 484, Fla.)

4 Judgment for Field Lumber Company; The court held that the $500 was no more than a payment on account of the $1,091.96, which both parties agreed was owed by Petty. Thus, the $500 payment was not made in compromise of a disputed claim. Moreover, Petty gave no new consideration for the release or discharge of the $591.96 ($1,091.96 less the $500 paid) he indisputably owes Field. (p. 215)

5 No; "A gratuitous promise of a future gift, lacking consideration, is a nudum pactum" (Latin: a naked pact or bare agreement without consideration supporting it). To be enforceable after donor Burt's death: (1) The pledge to the charitable hospital would have to state "the specific purpose for which the funds are to be used." (2) The donee hospital would have to show it actually relied on the pledge to further or advance the purpose specified in the pledge. Neither condition was met. Therefore, the pledge need not be fulfilled by payment. (p. 217)

Chapter Theme

When certain conditions are not met, or when it violates the law, a contract may be considered void or voidable.

DIRECTED STUDY QUESTIONS	SPECIAL FEATURES	PROGRAM RESOURCES				
		Reteach	Enrich	SN	AM	
What makes an agreement void or voidable?		✓	✓			
What types of agreements are illegal?	Ethics Issue, p. 229 Writing Connections, p. 230 Multicultural Highlights, p. 231	✓	✓		V	
When may courts help parties to illegal agreements?		✓	✓			
What is fraud?	Thinking Critically Through Visuals, p. 236	✓	✓	✓	A	
What are the rights of the defrauded party?		✓	✓			
What is duress? Undue influence?		✓	✓			
What is the effect of mistake?		✓	✓			
What mistakes make agreements void or voidable?		✓	✓			

Additional Resources

- *Atocha: Quest for Treasure*, videotape. Washington, DC: National Geographic Society, Educational Division.
- Chapman, Michael. "Telemarketing Fraud: A Network of Lies." *Consumers' Research Magazine*, April 1993, pp. 10–14.
- Ortiz, Darwin. *Gambling Scams: How They Work, How to Detect Them, How to Protect Yourself.* NY: Dodd, Mead, 1984.

Chapter Pacing Guide

One-semester course	✔	✔	✔					
One-year course	✔	✔	✔	✔	✔			

	ASSESSMENT OPPORTUNITIES			
Cooperative Learning	**Informal Assessment**	**Chapter Review**	**Chapter Test**	**Chapter *MicroExam*** 
	✔	✔	✔	✔
	✔	✔	✔	✔
	✔	✔	✔	✔
✔	✔	✔	✔	✔
	✔	✔	✔	✔
	✔	✔	✔	✔
	✔	✔	✔	✔
	✔	✔	✔	✔

Videodiscs

Voidable Contracts

Search Chapter 15, Play To 16

Fraud: Five Points

Search Chapter 16, Play To 17

State by State

A job seeker in New York lied in writing his name and qualifications on the application form. The resulting employment contract was void because it was procured by committing a crime.

CHAPTER 12 ORGANIZER (continued)

DIRECTED STUDY QUESTIONS	SPECIAL FEATURES	PROGRAM RESOURCES				
		Reteach	Enrich	SN	AM	
When can a minor disaffirm a voidable contract?	Ethics Issue, p. 241 Thinking Critically Through Visuals, p. 241 Personal Perspectives, p. 242	✔	✔			
What contract of minors cannot be disaffirmed?		✔	✔			
Can minors disaffirm contracts for necessaries?		✔	✔			
Does misstating one's age bind a minor?	Preventing Legal Difficulties, p. 245	✔	✔		K	

	ASSESSMENT OPPORTUNITIES			
Cooperative Learning	Informal Assessment	Chapter Review	Chapter Test	Chapter *MicroExam* Media
	✔	✔	✔	✔
	✔	✔	✔	✔
	✔	✔	✔	✔
	✔	✔	✔	✔

Teaching Materials

Student text, pp. 226–251

Overhead transparency masters
- *Requirements for the Tort of Fraud*
- *Five-Star Ways to Defend Yourself Against Fraud and Folly in Buying*

Videos
- *Contracts, Warranties, and Credit* Videotape
- *Law for Business* Videodisc

Workbook, pp. 33–34

Outside Resources
- Play money
- Newspapers and news or business magazines
- Classified advertisements
- Sample contracts
- Poster board
- Guest speakers: local merchants or representatives of local merchants' association
- Copy of the *Uniform Commercial Code*
- Art supplies

- Tape recorder
- VCR
- Camcorder
- *Atocha: Quest for Treasure*, videotape from the National Geographic Society

Assessment
- Chapter Test

- Chapter *MicroExam*

Vocabulary

genuine assent, p. 228
disaffirmance, p. 228
compounding a crime, p. 229
maximum rate of interest, p. 230
usury, p. 230
legal rate of interest, p. 231
small loan rate of interest, p. 231
wager, p. 231
fraud, p. 233
personal opinions, p. 234
material fact, p. 234
duress, p. 238
undue influence, p. 238
unilateral mistake, p. 238
mutual mistake, p. 239
ratification, p. 240
necessaries, p. 243

Learning Objectives

When you complete this chapter, you will be able to

1. Explain what makes an agreement void or voidable.
2. List and describe types of illegal agreements.
3. Identify exceptions where courts help parties to illegal agreements.
4. Define fraud by tracing its essential elements.
5. Distinguish between duress and undue influence.
6. Demonstrate the effect of mistakes.
7. Analyze the effect of minority on the voidability of contracts, including those made for necessaries.
8. Understand the effect of misstating one's age as a minor.

226

Chapter Self-Test

Assess students' understanding of void and voidable agreements before they begin Chapter 12 by asking students to share their experiences and knowledge about disaffirming a contract. Review and discuss students' responses before continuing with the chapter.

CHAPTER

12

VOID AND VOIDABLE AGREEMENTS

1 Planning to marry, two minors pool their savings to make a down payment on a used recreational vehicle (RV) to use as their first home. Under parental pressure, they agree not to marry until both finish high school and get steady jobs. Can they return the RV and get their money back?

2 An adult friend of yours buys a single-lens reflex camera outfit for $519.97, including a carrying case and a special lens. In her excitement, she fails to note that the case and special lens are advertised as "optional equipment." The two items cost an additional $122.94, which is listed on the contract she signs. When the bill for $642.91 plus sales tax arrives, your friend objects. Is she bound by the contract?

3 
A friend offers you $100 if you will "get rid of" a neighbor's barking dog. "You'll be the hero of this whole block," your friend says. "Just take it far out of town and give it to some farmer." If you do as asked, will you have a legal right to collect the money? Will you have acted ethically?

FOCUS

Before class begins, write the following question on the chalkboard or a transparency: **What, do you think, is the difference between a void and a voidable agreement?** As students arrive in class, direct them to answer the question on a sheet of paper. (Answers may include that a *void agreement* means that there is no contract that a court will recognize, whereas a *voidable*

agreement means that the agreement could be voided by one party.)

Introduce the chapter by having students skim the section titles. Ask students to orally suggest words or phrases that they think will be important to learn in this chapter.

You Decide

1 Yes, the RV is not a necessary. Therefore the minors may disaffirm their contract by returning the property and get their money back. In some states, a minor is liable for housing for his or her family. In this case, the minors had not yet married.

2 Probably; In the absence of fraud or trickery, failure to read what one signs is carelessness and is no defense against enforcement. One has a duty to read what one signs.

3 
No; The dog is private property and belongs to its owners. This would be an agreement to commit both a tort and a crime; hence, it is an illegal agreement. You will not have acted ethically. The crime of larceny is clearly unethical regardless of your misguided motivation.

Thinking Critically Through Visuals

The person in this photograph is a used-car salesperson. Why, do you think, would used-car sales be connected with a chapter on void and voidable agreements? (Answers may include that buyers sometimes want to return used cars with which they are dissatisfied; that is, they want to cancel or disaffirm the contracts and get their money back.)

TEACH

Call students' attention to the three italicized terms on p. 228: *valid, voidable,* and *void.* Remind students that they learned about void and voidable marriages in Chapter 8. Review with students the meanings of these words before you introduce the new terms: **genuine assent** and **disaffirmance**.

APPLY

Have students look up in the glossary the following terms: *valid contract, voidable contract,* and *void agreement.* Ask student volunteers to read aloud their definitions and others to use these terms in sentences. **Guided Practice**

Working in pairs, have students write, using a computer, if possible, two scenarios: the first showing understanding of **genuine assent** and the second illustrating **disaffirmance.**

Independent Practice

TEACH

Have students survey the numbered headings on pp. 229–231 as you list the eight types of illegal agreements on an overhead transparency. Stress that these are illegal agreements and therefore void and unenforceable.

Discuss the boldfaced vocabulary terms.

WHAT MAKES AN AGREEMENT VOID OR VOIDABLE?

PROBLEM

Ricardo, a minor, worked in a fast-food outlet until he had saved enough money to buy a racing bicycle. Then he paid $650 cash for a ten-speed imported Italian model at the WHEEL Shop. When he brought home the bicycle, his father pointed out to him that there were no opportunities in their town to race bicycles. His older sister added, "That's true. And if you take it to school or to the mall, some thief is likely to rip it off!" Convinced, Ricardo reluctantly returned his prized possession to the WHEEL Shop and asked for a refund of the purchase price. Does he legally have a right to a full refund?

A *valid* (i.e., legally effective) offer and acceptance generally result in an enforceable contract. However, sometimes the agreement may be void or voidable because it violates the law as stated in constitutions, statutes, or court opinions. Sometimes one of the parties lacked capacity to contract or failed to give consideration. The contract also may be void or voidable because one of the parties failed to genuinely assent to the agreement. **Genuine assent** exists when consent is not clouded by fraud, duress, undue influence, or mistake.

Generally, if there is no genuine assent, the victim may cancel or disaffirm the contract. As noted in Chapter 10, if the agreement is *void,* there simply is no contract and neither party is bound. Normally, any consideration received must be returned, as in Ricardo's case in the problem. If the agreement is *voidable,* generally only the party who has been victimized in some way may cancel or disaffirm the contract and demand return of any consideration given. **Disaffirmance** is a refusal to carry out or to comply with the terms of a voidable contract, without any liability to pay damages. However, if not disaffirmed, both parties are legally bound to perform.

WHAT TYPES OF AGREEMENTS ARE ILLEGAL?

PROBLEM

E. L. Razer agreed with several published articles that criticized laws prohibiting the production, possession, and use of marijuana. The authors of the articles claimed such legislation was unrealistic and often violated. Razer agreed so heartily that he bought several dozen marijuana plants from a friend "with connections." Then he rented a patch of isolated land and persuaded the owner to accept a share of the anticipated crop as rent. After harvesting the first crop, Razer sold his share to his friend with connections. Were any of his agreements legal? Were any ethical?

ASSESS

Learning Objective 1 Using a computer, if possible, have students use all the italicized and boldfaced terms on p. 228 to write the solution to the first PROBLEM found at the top of the page.

Agreements that are illegal and therefore void and unenforceable include the following:

1. Agreements to Commit Crimes or Torts

Any agreement to commit a crime or a tort is illegal. It would be absurd for the law to prohibit crimes and torts yet enforce agreements to commit such acts.

In the problem, all of Razer's agreements were criminal and therefore void. As such, they were unethical, and the harmful effect on the health of ultimate users of the drug aggravated the offense. Citizens may not violate laws with which they disagree without risking punishment. Unfortunately, such criminal activity often is completed without detection, and the wrongdoers retain their tainted profits. Moreover, they typically evade related income taxes, and this places a greater burden on law-abiding citizens.

2. Agreements That Obstruct Legal Procedures

Agreements that delay or prevent the achievement of justice are void. Examples include promises to (1) pay witnesses in a trial to testify falsely, (2) bribe jurors, and (3) refrain from informing on or prosecuting one for an alleged crime in exchange for money or other valuable consideration (called **compounding a crime**). This sometimes happens when the criminal makes restitution by returning stolen property to the victim. A court may legitimately order a convicted criminal to make restitution as part of the punishment.

3. Agreements That Injure Public Service

A prime example of an agreement that injures public service is a legislator's agreement to vote in a particular way on a bill in exchange for a bribe (i.e., an illicit payment). A contract to use corrupt means in lobbying governmental officials is also illegal. However, many honest persons and organizations legitimately act on their own or through hired specialists to influence legislation that concerns their special interests. They present useful information and arguments, both for and against particular laws, to legislators and governmental officials.

Kabazian was a nationally known expert on nuclear power plants that produce electricity. She was offered $5,000 to present her analysis of certain data to a joint Senate-House committee that was considering a major energy appropriation bill. If Kabazian accepted the offer, the contract would be enforceable.

▼APPLY

On the chalkboard or on a transparency, work with students to construct a graphic organizer that best shows the three examples of agreements that obstruct legal procedure.

Guided Practice

Ask a student volunteer to read aloud the PROBLEM on the bottom of p. 228, then ask: **Was Razer's agreement illegal because it was criminal, it obstructed legal procedures, or it injured public service?** (Criminal) Using a computer, if possible, have students rewrite the PROBLEM so that some part or parts create a legal agreement. Discuss students' revisions.

Ethics Issue

To breach a contract is not a tort or a crime. But, to agree to perform an act contrary to good morals and/or public policy is unethical and may even be a crime. Using the computer, if possible, have students write a one-page essay explaining the rationale for this difference.

Independent Practice

▼RETEACH Have student groups list in writing at least three answers to the section-title question: *What Makes an Agreement Void or Voidable?* (Agreement violates law, one party lacks capacity to contract, one party failed to give consideration, one party failed to genuinely assent to agreement, and so on)

▼ENRICH As a group, have students create a survey to informally poll three to five minors about their experiences with **disaffirmance.** Students will have an opportunity to share results at the end of this chapter.

Call on student volunteers to list on the chalkboard occupations and businesses that require competency licenses. (Answers may include doctors, teachers, lawyers, plumbers, and electricians.) Ask students to discuss the reasons for their answers.

Writing Connections

Social Studies
Once you are certain that students understand the term *restraint of trade*, have students write a short essay, using a computer, if possible, in which they defend or refute the wisdom of laws that render illegal agreements in restraint of trade. You may wish to help set the stage for this writing activity by asking students if they ever shop for a bargain before buying clothing, CDs, and so on. Ask students to imagine what the effect on their search for special values would be if all the businesses got together and set the same price for any given item.

4. Agreements Made Without a Required Competency License

To protect the public from incompetent service, all states require that persons in specified occupations and businesses have a license or permit. Included are physicians, teachers, lawyers, plumbers, electricians, pharmacists, real estate brokers, insurance agents, and building contractors. Persons who lack the required competency licenses may not enforce the contracts they make in doing the regulated work. However, when the purpose of the license is to raise revenue rather than to protect the public, contracts made by the unlicensed person are valid. Generally, the only penalty for failure to get such a license is a higher fee when the license is later obtained.

5. Agreements That Restrain Trade Unreasonably

Agreements between competing business firms to restrict competition by limiting production, fixing prices, or assigning exclusive marketing areas are illegal under both state and federal laws. Our economic system is based on the concept of free and open competition, which benefits consumers by rewarding efficient producers. It seeks to ensure all business firms of an equal opportunity to trade. This tends to protect consumers in their search for quality goods at fair prices. Hence, both state and federal laws seek to prevent monopolies and combinations that either restrict competition unreasonably or that deprive a person of the means of earning a livelihood. There is no legal limit on growth from open and fair competition.

All ten pharmacy owners in the city of Weston met to discuss common problems. During the discussion, they agreed that all the stores would match the prices charged for certain items by a multiservice discount outlet that had recently opened in Weston. They also agreed that they would charge no less than specified minimum prices for some fifty other high-volume items. Because these agreements restrained free trade and controlled prices, they were illegal and void.

6. Agreements to Pay Usurious Interest

Almost all states provide that, with certain exceptions, lenders of money may not charge more than a specified **maximum rate of interest.** This rate varies among the states; 8 percent to 16 percent a year are common maximums. Lending money at a rate higher than the state's maximum rate is **usury**. Generally, the penalty for usury is that the lender cannot collect some or all of the interest. However, the borrower must usually pay the principal.

ASSESS

Learning Objective 2 Using a computer, if possible, have students list and explain the eight types of agreements that are illegal. (See pp. 229–231.)

Sometimes a person borrows money for which interest is charged but no exact rate is stated. The rate to be paid is the **legal rate of interest,** which is specified by state statute. In more than one-half of the states, including the most populous ones, this rate is 7 percent or less per year. In most of the other states, the legal rate ranges between 8 and 12 percent.

Many states permit licensed loan companies and pawnbrokers to charge a **small loan rate of interest.** This rate is typically 36 percent a year, usually on loans of up to $300 or $500. The overhead cost per dollar loaned is high, and presumably the risk of loss from defaults is also high on such loans. This concession by the states is made to protect people against criminal loan sharks, who illegally charge extremely high rates (often 100 percent annually, and sometimes more).

7. Agreements That Involve Illegal Gambling, Wagers, or Lotteries

Every state either forbids or regulates gambling. Gambling involves an agreement with three elements: payment to participate; a chance to win, based on luck rather than on skill; and a prize for one or more winners. A **wager**, one of the most common forms of gambling, is a bet on the uncertain outcome of an event, such as a football game.

Most states have legalized some form of gambling under regulated conditions. Pari-mutuel betting (i.e., a form of betting on races in which those who bet on the winner share the total amount bet) at race tracks is sometimes permitted. State-run lotteries are becoming more common as a means of raising money. Although large prizes are offered to encourage ticket sales, little publicity is given to the fact that the chance to "win big" may be one in millions. Lotteries are not intrinsically immoral, but they are ethically suspect because they are, in effect, a tax on many poor participants who could better use their game money for more important purchases. Bingo, likewise, is permitted in some states, usually on a modest scale, for financing charitable, religious, or educational projects.

Unless specifically permitted by law, the winners in illegal gambling agreements cannot enforce payment of their winnings through court action. Nevertheless, illegal gambling evidently thrives even when state-sponsored, legal alternatives are available. A possible reason for this phenomenon is that the illegal winnings are not always properly reported as taxable income.

8. Agreements That Affect Marriage Negatively

The family is the basic unit of society; therefore public policy encourages marriage and family life. It would be an illegal contract if A agreed to pay B a sum of money in exchange for B's promise never to marry. Similarly, it would be illegal for C to agree to pay D money in exchange for D's promise to divorce D's spouse.

Multicultural Highlights

Steering is the practice by real estate agents of directing prospective homebuyers into or out of a particular neighborhood or area because of their race, color, religion, gender, national origin, handicap, or familial status. This practice was outlawed by the Federal Fair Housing Act of 1968. Ask: **Why, do you think, does the law forbid "steering"?** (Answers may include that it violates a person's right to choose where to live and reinforces segregation.)

Divide the class into four groups. Assign each group one of the following rates of interest—maximum rate of interest, legal rate of interest, small loan rate of interest, and the illegal form of usury. Give each group some play money to allow students to visually grasp the difference between rates. Divide a sheet of poster board into four panels. Have each group create a visual to  illustrate its form of interest in one of the panels.

RETEACH

Display the transparency you created for the TEACH activity on p. 228. Revealing only one illegal agreement at a time, have students review orally what they have learned about it.

ENRICH

Have students clip, label, and display newspaper or magazine articles relating to illegal agreements. Invite students to brainstorm a creative name for the bulletin-board display.

TEACH

Emphasize that courts ordinarily do not help either party seeking to enforce an illegal agreement. However, there are exceptions to this rule, such as when a contract contains a combination of legal and illegal provisions. Identify and explain instances when courts do provide assistance to parties seeking to enforce illegal agreements. (See p. 232 for examples.)

APPLY

Work with students to create a two-column chart. In the first column, have students list examples of situations in which a court will help enforce an illegal agreement, and in the second column, when a court will not. **Guided Practice**

Individually, have students jot down a scenario that contains a combination of legal and illegal provisions and share it aloud with the class. Have volunteers orally identify the legal and illegal aspects of the scenario. **Independent Practice**

WHEN MAY COURTS HELP PARTIES TO ILLEGAL AGREEMENTS?

PROBLEM

A young married couple, the Pathsies, wanted to provide for the college education of their infant daughter. They received this offer in the mail from the True Bonanza Mining Corporation of America, which seemed perfect for their need: "Join us now for only 10 cents a share of stock. Become part owner of a gold and silver mine with already proven mineral deposits. In ten years, you will be rich enough to retire!" The Pathsies used all their savings to buy 10,000 shares of Bonanza stock. Months later they learned that Bonanza had violated the law. Its "mineral deposits" were commercially worthless aluminum oxides. The sales agreement was illegal. Can the Pathsies demand the return of their $1,000?

Generally, courts will not help either party seeking to enforce an illegal agreement. However, there are exceptions to this rule. A contract might contain a combination of legal and illegal provisions. If the illegal part does not taint the entire agreement, courts may enforce the legal part. For example, a retailer contracts to sell a complete camping and hunting outfit, including a gun that is subject to special regulation. The seller fails to comply with a law that requires a thirty-day waiting period and a police clearance of the gun sale, but there is no problem with the other items of the contract. Consequently, a court would probably enforce the *legal* provisions of the contract. The retailer who violated the law would be subject to the sanctions specified in the statute, possibly a fine or loss of license to sell guns if she or he is a repeat offender.

Sometimes the parties to an illegal agreement are not equally blameworthy. For example, one party might persuade an innocent and gullible person to enter an illegal agreement by lying or by applying improper psychological pressure. Sometimes the law that was violated was designed to protect one of the parties. A common example is the *blue-sky law,* which prohibits white-collar criminal promoters from selling worthless stocks and bonds. Such securities have no more value than a section of the blue sky. The victim may disaffirm the contract and sue to recover money paid. Thus, court relief would be available to the Pathsies in the problem. Unfortunately, the criminals in such scams are often judgment proof, or they may have disappeared when pursued.

ASSESS

Learning Objective 3 Have students work together to create a graphic organizer showing the generalizations and exceptions of court involvement with parties involved in illegal agreements.

WHAT IS FRAUD?

PROBLEM

When Graffter sold a used car to Camacho, he told her that the car had been driven only 50,000 miles, had never been in an accident, and had the original paint. He said that the car had new steel-belted radial tires and that the engine had been overhauled. In fact, Graffter had stolen the car, set back the odometer from 90,000 miles, and repainted the exterior in the original color. The tires were a retreaded glass-belted type; the engine had merely been tuned and steam cleaned. Moreover, Graffter had stood between Camacho and the right rear end of the car, so that she would not see a crudely repaired fender, which had been damaged in an accident. After Camacho learns the truth and if she can find Graffter, can she avoid the contract?

The basis of **fraud** is false representation or concealment of a material fact. However, not every misrepresentation or concealment amounts to fraud. All of the following elements must be present for fraud to exist.

1. The False Representation or Concealment of a Past or Present Fact Must Be Deliberate

Fraud results from deliberate lies. It also results from deliberate concealment of unfavorable facts that otherwise could be noticed by a reasonable person. Generally, neither seller nor buyer is obliged to reveal all good or bad facts about the subject matter of the contract. It would be practically impossible for courts to define all that must be known by the seller and disclosed to the buyer in every case. Moreover, buyers should investigate and ask questions before they invest. The seller who responds has a duty to speak honestly. But the seller may decline to answer or may truthfully disclaim necessary knowledge. A prudent buyer who is alerted to a possible serious problem should get the facts by other means or simply walk away from a possible deal.

Normally, silence is not blameworthy. But fraud may result when the party has a duty to speak yet does not. For example, basic honesty requires a seller to tell about a concealed defect not readily discoverable by a reasonably alert buyer.

In addition, the seller must not volunteer false information or act to prevent the other party from learning important facts. In the problem, Graffter was a criminal who acted fraudulently. He lied about the car and actively concealed the damaged rear fender. Accordingly, if Camacho could find

TEACH

When defining the boldfaced term **fraud**, make certain that students understand that, while fraud always involves false representation or concealment of a material fact, not every instance of misrepresentation or concealment of a material fact constitutes fraud.

Before displaying the overhead transparency, *Requirements for the Tort of Fraud*, cover it with a sheet of paper. Uncovering one requirement at a time, discuss the answers to each of the corresponding PROBLEM activities found on pp. 233–236. Call students' attention to the fact that the transparency divides the fifth requirement

in the text into two parts—action and injury.

APPLY

Have the class brainstorm a list of reasons why a person generally is not legally required to tell all he or she knows about a product or service being bought or sold. If students have difficulty generating ideas, ask them to imagine that they are buying a car from an auto mechanic or a computer from a computer whiz. Ask if they would want to hear everything that the salesperson knows about the product. **Guided Practice**

RETEACH Have students outline the section, *When May Courts Help Parties to Enforce Illegal Agreements?* by skimming the text, highlighting the key points, and summarizing them in a standard outline format.

ENRICH

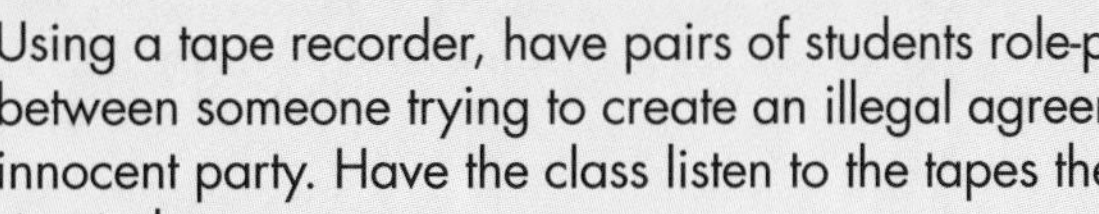

Using a tape recorder, have pairs of students role-play scenarios between someone trying to create an illegal agreement and an innocent party. Have the class listen to the tapes then act as the court to determine judgment.

Explain to students that fraud requires the deliberate misrepresentation or concealment of a present, material fact or past fact. Normally, this does not include personal opinions of value. To help auditory learners differentiate between fact and opinion, read examples of facts and opinions from ads in newspapers or magazines. Ask for volunteers to identify each example as either fact or opinion. Have students explain their reasons for identifying each statement as fact or opinion for the benefit of those students who may be unfamiliar with idioms and other figures of speech used in advertising language.

Graffter, she could disaffirm the contract and sue for damages for the tort of fraud. Graffter should be prosecuted as a criminal, and the stolen car should be returned to its true owner.

If a seller innocently misrepresents a material fact, the buyer may avoid the contract or collect compensatory damages for the injury suffered. However, because no tort has been committed, the buyer is not entitled to punitive damages. On the other hand, one may not claim fraud when the means were readily available for determining the truth, as by simply reading a document before signing it.

The deliberate false representation or concealment must be of a present or past fact. Normally, this does not include personal opinions of value or predictions of what will happen in the future. For example, suppose a salesperson tells you that a certain computer "is the best on the market, a super value that will pay for itself!" You, as a reasonable person, have no legal right to rely on these exaggerated remarks. Such superlatives are usually **personal opinions** reflecting that individual's self-serving and often inflated notion of value. They are not statements of fact. As opinions, if later proved to be false, they normally do not constitute fraud. However, a person may claim to be an expert in, for example, the appraisal (i.e., estimating the value) of ancient African art. An uninformed buyer may hold such expert liable for damages if a requested opinion proves to be erroneous and the buyer thereby suffers a loss.

Two college students, Art and Bond, were negotiating the sale of a set of Chemistry I class notes. Art had purchased the notes from Samantha, who was now a graduate student in chemical engineering. "Listen," Art said, "I paid $100 for these notes. It was a bargain, but I'm asking only $75, and I'll throw in my own notes free. This Samantha is another Isaac Asimov; she really makes sense. Read her notes and the textbook becomes a piece of cake. I got an A for the course. Believe me, you will too!" Bond bought the notes but flunked Chemistry I. Art is not guilty of fraud because he told the truth about the price ($100), the author (Samantha, a graduate student in chemical engineering), and his own A grade. His overzealous endorsement of Samantha and the comparison to Asimov, as well as the other claims and predictions of an A grade for Bond, were personal opinions of a nonexpert and therefore not fraudulent.

2. The Misrepresented or Concealed Fact Must Be Material

To be fraudulent, the statement must be about a past or present **material fact.** A fact is material if it significantly influences the victim's decision.

▼ ASSESS

Learning Objective 4 Have students write five *True* or *False* statements (with answers) concerning the act of fraud. Collect the papers, select the five best statements, and write them on the chalkboard. Have students answer them on a sheet of paper before reviewing the responses as a class.

The person who was defrauded would not have entered into the contract if he or she had known the truth. For example, the seller of a baseball card showing Jose Canseco tells the buyer that the star's signature on the card is his authentic autograph, when in fact it is a forgery.

3. The Person Making the False Representation Must Know It Is False or Make It Recklessly Without Regard to Its Possible Falsity

PROBLEM

Dimmer was a new sales agent for Proto Metal Supply Company. Mitsui was the purchasing agent for Space-Age Specialties Corporation. Eager to make a sale, Dimmer told Mitsui that certain steel sheets and rods had a high chromium content and would not rust. Actually, she did not know the chemical content but said what Mitsui wanted to hear. Mitsui believed her and ordered a carload shipment. When the facts were discovered after many Space-Age customers had complained, Space-Age sued Proto Metal and Dimmer for fraud. Should Space-Age win the suit?

Fraud clearly exists when a person deliberately lies or conceals a material fact. Fraud also exists if a person makes a statement of fact rashly, without determining its truth or falsity.

In the problem, Dimmer, acting as an agent for Proto Metal, made the statements about the steel products with reckless disregard to the truth. Hence, Space-Age was justified in claiming fraud and should win the suit against Proto Metal and Dimmer.

4. The Misrepresentation Must Be Made With the Intention of Influencing the Other Person to Act Upon It

PROBLEM

Braak was deep in debt and needed more credit to keep his business going. He gave Central Credit Controls (CCC) false information that showed his financial condition to be good. Sanchez subsequently obtained a credit report on Braak from CCC. Relying on the report, Sanchez sold a costly in-house telephone answering system to Braak on credit. Within a month, Braak became *insolvent* (i.e., unable to pay debts) and failed to make a payment. Sanchez then learned the truth about Braak's financial condition. Claiming fraud, Sanchez sued to repossess the equipment. Should she succeed?

Divide the class into groups of three or four. Assign the following roles: a director who will serve as facilitator, a person who commits fraud, a person on whom the fraud is committed, and a reporter, if necessary. Have students create a PROBLEM that focuses on the first, second, and third elements of fraud discussed on pp. 234–235. Then have each group role-play the PROBLEM. Have students in the other groups determine which of the three elements of fraud are portrayed. Allow 10 minutes to create the skits and 20 to 30 minutes for the role play. **Cooperative Learning**

▼RETEACH Have individual students re-skim the section, then create their own graphic organizer showing the five elements of fraud. Share organizers with other members of the group and compare responses.

▼ENRICH Have students skim classified advertisements to find five examples of fact versus personal opinion. Have students take turns reading the ads aloud, while the remainder of the group determines which part of the ad is fact and which part is personal opinion.

Divide the class into two groups. Have each group create two scenarios: one that describes a misrepresentation (or a concealment that deceives) and another that shows a misrepresentation (or a concealment that doesn't). Call on student volunteers from each group to role-play the scenarios. **Independent Practice**

Thinking Critically Through Visuals

The crowd of people in the photograph is waiting in line for refunds or new tickets after all airline flights were canceled due to inclement weather. Is it fraudulent for an airline to cancel flights for such a reason? (No, there is no misrepresentation or concealment; The cancellations were caused by an "act of God.")

For a statement to be fraudulent, the person making the statement must intend that it be relied on and acted on. Generally, the false statement is made directly to the intended victim. However, this is not essential. One party (Braak) may tell a second party (CCC) something with the intent that the message be repeated to a third party (Sanchez and other suppliers), whose conduct is to be thereby influenced. Such was the case with Braak in the problem, so Sanchez should succeed in repossessing the telephone equipment.

5. The Misrepresentation or Concealment Must Induce Action and Cause Injury to the Other Party

PROBLEM

In bargaining to sell his sailboat, Martz deliberately tried to deceive Andza by saying it was one of a limited edition of deluxe Mariners. Andza knew it was the cheaper Islander model, but he bought it anyway. Later, when Andza became dissatisfied with the boat, he claimed fraud and sought to disaffirm the contract. Can he do so?

A misrepresentation or concealment is not fraudulent unless it deceives. There is no fraud if the intended victim is not misled. Likewise, there is no fraud if the wrongful concealment or misrepresentation did not affect the buyer's decision to enter into a contract. In the problem, Martz's misrepresentation did not influence Andza's decision to buy. Therefore Andza may not disaffirm the contract. Moreover, if a defrauded party suffers no injury,

ASSESS

Learning Objective 4 Divide the class into five groups. Quietly assign each group one of the five elements of fraud on pp. 233–237. Have each group, using a computer, if possible, write a mock newspaper article (complete with a headline) reflecting the type of fraud. Circulate the newspaper articles and have the remaining groups guess which element of fraud is depicted. Reward the most creative group.

there is no need to sue for damages. An example is the receipt of goods that are worth more than the price paid for them.

To recover damages, there must be proof of injury. Recall, however, that since fraud is an intentional tort, the court may award substantial punitive or exemplary damages even though the actual damages were very limited.

WHAT ARE THE RIGHTS OF THE DEFRAUDED PARTY?

PROBLEM

Cheatta fraudulently induced Kreduloss to buy a painting falsely described as an authentic Van Gogh. Kreduloss discovered the fraud before payment or delivery, and notified Cheatta that she was canceling the contract. Was she within her rights?

Contracts entered into as a result of fraud are voidable by the injured party. Thus, the victim, such as Kreduloss in the problem, may *repudiate* (i.e., disaffirm) the agreement. Normally upon disaffirmance, anything that had been received must be returned. A deceived party who has performed part of the contract may recover what has been paid or given. A defrauded party who has done nothing, like Kreduloss, may cancel the contract and be released with no obligation to pay. If sued on the contract, the defrauded party can plead fraud as a defense. In either case, the victim may sue in tort and collect damages caused by the fraud.

A defrauded person may choose not to disaffirm but instead to ratify the agreement. Either party may then enforce it. However, a defrauded party who decides to ratify an agreement may seek *reimbursement* (i.e., financial compensation) for any loss suffered.

WHAT IS DURESS? UNDUE INFLUENCE?

PROBLEM

Cameron owned a promising racehorse that Link had offered to buy for undisclosed parties. When Cameron refused to sell, Link lowered his voice and slowly said, "Listen, the people I represent don't take 'no' for an answer. If you don't sell, they'll hurt you; they'll hurt your family. Like a good friend, I'm telling you to sell. You're getting a fair price." Cameron, who had secretly recorded the conversation, sold. Then he called the police. Can he now disaffirm the contract and get his horse back?

TEACH

Display the overhead transparency, *Five-Star Ways to Defend Yourself Against Fraud and Folly in Buying,* and discuss with students how to protect themselves. (Answers may include getting and checking references, checking with the local Better Business Bureau, and so on.) Explain that an injured party may *repudiate* (or disaffirm) the agreement or ratify it.

APPLY

Have students create and videotape infomercials dramatizing the five-star ways to defend oneself against fraud and folly. Have students vote on the best infomercial.

Guided Practice

As students view the infomercials, have them note how the "actors" defend themselves against fraud.

Independent Practice

TEACH

Review with students the definition of *fraud,* then introduce the terms **duress** and **undue influence**. Call students' attention to the meanings of the italicized words *coercion* and *illegal imprisonment* on the top of p. 238. Discuss how each applies to duress.

RETEACH Pair a student who understands the five elements of fraud with one who is having difficulty. Have the student who understands help the other list the elements, then create five scenarios, one for each of the elements.

ENRICH Have students brainstorm different types of fraud and suggest defenses against them. Then, in small groups, have students create a public-service radio announcement (PSA) to illustrate solutions on how to avoid being a victim of a fraud. Record and play the PSAs for the class.

APPLY

Work with the class to outline on the chalkboard or an overhead transparency the information in the text on duress and undue influence.

Guided Practice

Have students make a two-column chart listing the characteristics and examples of duress and of undue influence. **Independent Practice**

TEACH

On the chalkboard, write **unilateral mistake**. Ask students if they recall (from Chapter 10) what the term means (*uni-* one; *-lateral* related to one side). Explain that a unilateral mistake occurs when one of the parties to a contract holds an erroneous idea about the facts of the contract.

APPLY

Write on the chalkboard: **Ignorance of the law is no excuse.** Ask: **How, do you think, does this statement relate to a person's failure to read a contract and the voidability of that contract?** Emphasize that failure to read a contract does not, in most cases, relieve the signer from liability. Lead students to conclude that, in making contracts, persons ordinarily are bound by a contract they sign, even if they were careless or negligent in reading it, or failed to read it. **Guided Practice**

An agreement is made under **duress** if one person compels another to enter into it through *coercion* (i.e., threat of force or an act of violence) or by *illegal imprisonment* (i.e., unlawful arrest or detention). The victim has been denied the exercise of free will and can disaffirm the resulting contract.

The threatened or actual violence may be to the life, liberty, or property of (1) the victim, (2) the victim's immediate family, or (3) the victim's near relatives. In the problem, Cameron acted under duress in making the contract and therefore could avoid it.

A person usually is not guilty of duress when the act or threat is to do something the person has a legal right to do. Thus, to persuade another to contract under threat of a justifiable civil lawsuit is permissible. To threaten to have another arrested if the contract is not signed would be duress and possibly criminal coercion.

Undue influence occurs when one person insidiously, or by wrongful persuasion and control over the free will of another, gets the other to make a contract that is unfavorable.

It is more likely to be present when a relationship of trust, confidence, or authority exists between two parties. Thus, it is presumed to exist in unfavorable contracts between attorney and client, wife and husband, parent and child, guardian and ward, physician and patient. When a contract is made as a result of undue influence, the contract is voidable by the victim.

A charge of undue influence can be overcome by proving that the contract is fair and benefits both parties. To forestall a claim of undue influence, the stronger party should act with scrupulous honesty, fully disclose all important facts, and insist that the other party talk to independent counsel before contracting.

WHAT IS THE EFFECT OF MISTAKE?

PROBLEM

Baglio wanted the gutters of his new house to be free of rust. The specifications in the contract he signed called for "rust-resistant steel gutters galvanized with zinc." After the house was built, he learned that the gutters would eventually rust and require replacement. Aluminum or copper gutters would not rust but would be costlier. Baglio now sues the contractor claiming a breach of contract. Will he win?

When there is a **unilateral mistake,** one of the parties has an erroneous idea about the facts of a contract. Generally, this does not affect the validity of the contract. Thus, in the problem Baglio alone was mistaken and will lose the lawsuit.

ASSESS

Learning Objectives 5 & 6 Using their textbooks as a reference, have students write, using a computer, if possible, their solutions to the PROBLEM activities on pp. 237–238. Make sure students substantiate their solutions.

Failure to read a contract before signing, or a hurried or careless reading of it, may result in obligations that a person had no intention of assuming. In making contracts, persons are ordinarily bound by what they outwardly do and say, regardless of what they may inwardly think, understand, or intend. However, if the mistake is a major one and is recognized by the other party to the contract, a court may declare the contract void.

Galaxie Genetic Products, Inc., asked for bids (i.e., offers to build) on construction of its new office building. Eight bids were received. Seven of them were within $100,000 under or over the architect's estimate of $3 million. However, the bid from New Horizon Builders was $500,000 below the architect's estimate. New Horizon's chief estimator had made a gross error which had reduced its bid far below those of all other competitors. Galaxie recognized this and may not seize upon New Horizon's unilateral mistake to demand performance for the erroneous bargain price.

Frequently a party to a contract has erroneous expectations of high profits. For example, suppose a person buys some corporate stock, confidently expecting the price to go up. If the price goes down, the buyer alone suffers the loss. Or again, suppose a building contractor bids to do a job for $10,000. Actual costs run up to $12,000. The mistaken contractor alone suffers the loss. These are examples of unilateral mistakes.

WHAT MISTAKES MAKE AGREEMENTS VOID OR VOIDABLE?

PROBLEM

In a large metropolis in the Midwest, there were two streets named "Highland." Fisher owned the lot at 231 Highland Avenue. Neece, who lived in New York City, wanted to buy the lot at 231 Highland Boulevard. He wrote to Fisher, offering "to buy your lot on Highland" on specified terms. Fisher promptly mailed her acceptance of the offer. Was there a contract?

When there is a **mutual mistake** (also called a *bilateral mistake*) of material fact, both parties are wrong about some important facts. Either party may disaffirm. Thus, in the problem, the parties' mutual mistake as to the *identity* of the subject matter made the contract void. Neece, in his offer, was referring to the lot on Highland Boulevard; Fisher, in her acceptance, was referring to the lot on Highland Avenue.

Distribute sample contracts, such as insurance policies, car rental agreements, or credit card applications to small groups. Remind students of the importance of carefully reading contracts to avoid making unilateral mistakes. Have students review the contracts and make a list of questions that they would ask before signing the contract. **Independent Practice**

TEACH

Make certain that students understand that if both parties make a mistake—hence, a mutual mistake as to the identity of or the existence of the subject matter in a contract—then either party may disaffirm.

APPLY

On the chalkboard, an overhead transparency, or chart paper, display the base and the type in only the first circle of the following graphic organizer. Have students complete the graphic organizer, adding other categories for comparison, if they wish.

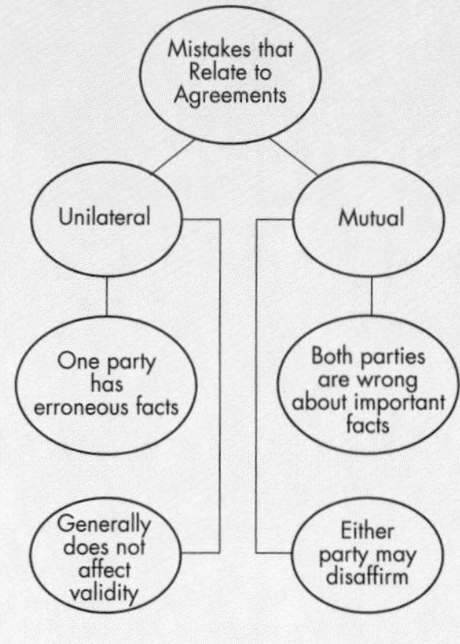

RETEACH

Have students write a short essay, using a computer, if possible, describing a situation in which a person under duress or undue influence could make a unilateral mistake related to a contract.

ENRICH

Have students create contracts in which they contract with you for a project of their choice in exchange for a grade. Then, have them exchange contracts, question any ambiguities, and sign only when they are satisfied. When students complete the terms, they receive the agreed-upon grade.

Help students create a two-column chart on the chalkboard. In one column, have them list examples of a mutual mistake as to the *identity* of the contract's subject matter (such as the unclear description of real property in the PROBLEM on p. 239). In the other column, have students list examples as to the *existence* of the contract's subject matter (such as the scenario in the boxed activity on p. 240). **Guided Practice**

Divide the class into four groups. Assign two groups responsibility for creating a PROBLEM dealing with the identity of the subject matter, and the other two groups responsibility for creating a PROBLEM dealing with the existence of the subject matter. Call on a member from each group to present, solve, and analyze for the class the PROBLEM that the group created. **Independent Practice**

TEACH

Make certain that students understand the terms *minor* and *reaching [the age of] majority* as they relate to themselves and to the disaffirmation and ratification of contracts.

Mutual mistake as to the *existence* of the subject matter has the same effect, as shown in the follow example.

Falkhausen, who lived in Indianapolis, owned a Formula One racing car which he kept in Miami. On March 18, he sold the car to Firenzi. Unknown to either party, the car had been destroyed in an accident on March 17. Because of the mutual mistake as to the existence of the car, there was no contract.

Some states hold that when the mutual mistake was one of fact concerning applicable law, the contract is valid. This would be true, for example, if both parties to a real estate sale mistakenly believed that local zoning laws permitted construction of duplexes on a large lot that was being transferred. All persons are presumed to know the law. The buyer, at least, should have checked the statutes before signing.

WHEN CAN A MINOR DISAFFIRM A VOIDABLE CONTRACT?

PROBLEM

While still a minor, Beach bought a stereo sound system on credit from McReam's Electronic Cloud for $500. The annual percentage rate credit charge was 18 percent. Beach paid $100 down and promised to pay $50 a month on the unpaid balance until the debt was paid. After making four payments, two of which were made after he reached the age of majority, Beach decided to disaffirm the contract and return the equipment. Can he legally do this?

Generally, a minor can disaffirm a voidable contract any time while still a minor or within a reasonable time after reaching majority. As an exception, a minor who has transferred real property usually cannot disaffirm the contract until reaching majority. Likewise, a minor cannot disaffirm a contract made with court approval, nor a contract to enter the armed services, nor—in some states—insurance contracts.

If a minor decides to disaffirm a contract, the entire agreement must be disaffirmed. It does not matter whether the contract has been fully performed.

After reaching majority, a person may ratify a voidable contract made while a minor. **Ratification** is the approval of a voidable contract in its entirety. One may not disaffirm one part and ratify another, unless the other party agrees. Once properly made, ratification may not be withdrawn.

ASSESS

Learning Objective 7 In writing, have students list from memory five facts they have learned about a minor disaffirming a voidable contract. (Anytime while a minor or within a reasonable time after reaching majority, ratifying a voidable contract when reaching majority, enforcing a contract against an adult, not disaffirming contracts made with court approval or those made to enter the armed services, and so on)

Ratification may consist of any of the following:

1. an express new promise to perform as agreed,
2. silence, or the failure to disaffirm, for an unreasonably long time after attaining majority, or
3. any act (such as continued use of the property) that clearly indicates the person's intention to be bound.

In the problem, Beach had ratified the contract by making payments after reaching majority.

As already noted, a minor's contracts are generally voidable by the minor, yet the minor can enforce them against adults. On the other hand, generally adults can neither enforce nor avoid all or any part of a contract with a minor.

> Kent, a minor, sold her used science encyclopedia set to Blum, age twenty-two. Blum paid $125, which was about one-half the original price. Three months later, a new, expanded edition of the same encyclopedia set appeared on the market. Blum told Kent that he was returning the books and wanted the money back. He claimed the set was obsolete, and moreover, Kent—being a minor—could not make a binding contract. Blum was wrong. Kent could indeed sell her books, and she alone could disaffirm the contract.

Thinking Critically Through Visuals

The woman and the man (center) shown in the photograph are discussing with an enlistment officer the possibility of joining the Navy. Is it necessary, do you think, for this enlistment officer to know if the enlistees are minors before they sign a contract to enter the military? (No; While ordinarily a minor can disaffirm a contract, there are exceptions, such as entering the military. Of course, a minimum age is still specified.)

▼ APPLY

Ethics Issue

Remind students that contracts entered into with a minor are usually voidable only by the minor, yet the minor can enforce them against adults. Ask: **In your opinion, is this ethical?** (Answers may include reference to the motivation of the minors and adults in making and breaking the contracts.) **Guided Practice**

▼RETEACH Have students work together to create an acronym to illustrate under what circumstances a minor can disaffirm a voidable contract. Have them memorize it for later use.

▼ENRICH Media: Point out that existentialists, such as Camus (*The Stranger*), believe that not doing something is actually doing something. Challenge students to create, using a computer, if possible, an example illustrating how doing nothing about a contract actually can be doing something.

Ask student volunteers to orally state how a minor who has entered into a voidable contract can ratify the contract upon reaching majority.
Independent Practice

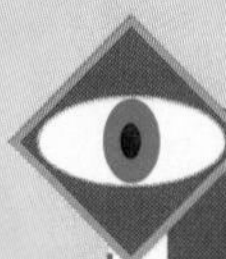

Personal Perspectives

Invite local merchants or representatives of your local merchants' association to share with students their experiences in dealing with minors. Ask them to address the class about the special policies they follow in contracts with minors who make substantial purchases. In preparation for the guest speakers, have students prepare related questions.

▼ TEACH

As a cautionary piece of advice for minor students who have entered—or will enter—into contracts, remind them of the types of contracts that minors cannot disaffirm.

In all states, when a minor disaffirms, anything of value that the minor received and still has must be returned. The minor is then entitled to get back everything that was given to the other party. *In some states,* however, a minor must return everything received in a condition as good as it was when it was received. If this cannot be done, the minor must pay the difference in value, or deduct the difference from the amount to be refunded. *In most states,* a minor can legally refuse to pay for goods received or can get back all money paid. This is true even if the minor returns used or damaged goods. It is also true even if the minor returns nothing because the goods have been lost, consumed, destroyed, or sold to an innocent third party.

Lamon, a minor, bought a diamond engagement ring and a necklace for his fiancée, Morgan. He paid for the items in weekly installments of $10. On the day of Lamon's majority, Lamon and Morgan quarreled. Morgan returned the ring to Lamon but refused to part with the necklace. She was legally entitled to keep the necklace because it was an ordinary gift not connected with the proposed marriage. The next day, Lamon returned the ring to the jeweler and demanded a refund of the money he had paid for both pieces of jewelry. Lamon was entitled to the money he had paid on the ring. In most states, he was even entitled to what he had paid on the necklace. That is because he returned everything that was still in his possession. In a few states, he could be held liable for the price of the necklace.

▼ WHAT CONTRACTS OF MINORS CANNOT BE DISAFFIRMED?

PROBLEM

Upon graduation from high school, Vukovich, age seventeen, became a sales representative of the Muller Broom Company. She was required to buy a $375 kit containing samples of household brushes, brooms, and other supplies for house-to-house selling. The venture was a disappointing failure. Discouraged after a month, Vukovich asked Muller to take back the samples and to return her $375 payment. Must Muller do so?

Some contracts of minors cannot be disaffirmed. Generally, minors cannot void any contracts approved for them by a court. For example, minors who are employed as actors or actresses or as professionals in sports usually

▼ ASSESS

Learning Objective 7 Have students respond by a show of hands if they agree with the following statements: **(1) The laws governing the disaffirmance of contracts by minors are the same in all states.** (Disagree); **(2) There are no contracts that a minor cannot disaffirm.** (Disagree); and **(3) Necessaries are goods and services that are reasonably required to maintain one's lifestyle.** (Agree) have their contracts approved by a court. Once approved, these contracts may not be disaffirmed.

A minor who owns real property may not sell it or borrow money against it without a court's approval. The minor would be bound by the court-approved contract.

In most states, minors who engage in a business or trade cannot disaffirm agreements involving their business. Accordingly, in the problem, Vukovich would not be able to avoid her contract if she lived in a state with such a law.

More than one-half of the states provide that minors who are over a certain age may not disaffirm certain contracts of life insurance. Minors are generally permitted to make deposits in banks and in savings and loan associations. Most states also permit minors to make withdrawals as if they were adults, without any right to disaffirm these transactions. Contracts to enlist in the armed services and contracts for educational loans cannot be disaffirmed.

CAN MINORS DISAFFIRM CONTRACTS FOR NECESSARIES?

PROBLEM

Against their parents' wishes, Garcia and Soto—both minors—left home. Together, they signed a twelve-month lease to rent a nearby furnished apartment from Krohn for $350 a month. Krohn thought that both teenagers looked like young adult college students, so he never asked their ages. After three months, the teenagers ran out of money and returned to their homes. Krohn could not find new tenants. Could he hold the minors or their parents liable for the rent?

Although the law permits minors to disaffirm most of their contracts, it does not allow them to avoid responsibility when they buy truly needed goods or services. Without this rule business firms might understandably refuse to supply goods and services that are necessary for life. Therefore one who supplies to a minor necessaries can collect from the minor or from parents of the minor. **Necessaries** are goods and services that are reasonably required to maintain one's life-style. The law says the parents—who are responsible for the care of their children—have, in effect, authorized the children to make such purchases if not otherwise provided or made available. However, the goods or services must in fact be necessary in the eyes of the law and the supplier is entitled only to their reasonable value, which might not be the contract price.

APPLY

Have students take turns orally brainstorming a list of examples of contracts that minors cannot disaffirm. (Answers may include contracts approved by a court, enlisting in the armed services, educational loans, and so on.) **Guided Practice**

Have students explain in writing why they think that certain contracts that minors enter into cannot be disaffirmed. **Independent Practice**

TEACH

Discuss with students the meaning of the term *necessaries* before discussing the four requirements that must be met before a minor or parent can be held responsible for payment.

In small groups, have students write and record a song, a rap, or poem called, "Warning! You're Not Too Young," warning other minors about contracts that cannot be disaffirmed because of their age. Play the recordings for the class.

Have students skim the chapter on Contractual Capacity of the UCC to find information on ratification, disaffirmance, and necessaries of minors. Ask them to report on any new information they think students, as minors, should know.

▼ APPLY

On the chalkboard or an overhead transparency, create with students a two-column chart that shows items that courts have ruled to be necessaries and non-necessaries for minors. (food, clothing, shelter, education, medical care, and tools used to earn a living; cosmetics, jewelry, liquor, tobacco and other drugs, televisions and audio equipment, pleasure trips, and expensive food for parties)

Guided Practice

Divide the class into four groups. Assign each group the responsibility for summarizing on the chalkboard, without use of the textbook, one of the four requirements for necessaries before a minor or parent can be held responsible for payment. **Independent Practice**

In the case of a minor, these necessaries must be suitable to the minor's economic and social status. They must not already be possessed by the minor or be in the process of being supplied by parents or guardians. Courts have found such things as food, clothing, shelter, education, medical care, and tools used to earn a living to be necessaries. In contrast, cosmetics, jewelry, liquor, tobacco and other drugs, televisions and audio equipment, pleasure trips, and expensive food for parties are not necessaries. Some courts hold that an automobile is a necessary when the automobile is essential for the minor to earn a living.

An article must meet all of the following four requirements for necessaries before a minor or parent can be held responsible for payment.

1. The Item Must Be Reasonably Required

Shelter is a basic human requirement. Because it fulfills this need for shelter, housing is clearly a necessary. In the problem, Krohn's claim would meet this first requirement.

2. The Item Must Be Actually Furnished

The minor who agrees to buy is not bound to pay unless the necessary is actually supplied. In the problem, the apartment was occupied for only three months. There is no liability for the remaining nine.

3. The Item Must Be Reasonably Suitable to the Age and Social and Economic Status of the Minor

What is considered a necessary for one person is not always a necessary for another. The apartment rented by Garcia and Soto would have to be in keeping with their families' life-styles to be a necessary. Here, the court could require further evidence as to the families' life-styles and the type of apartment in question.

4. The Item Must Not Be Otherwise Furnished

If the parents of both Garcia and Soto provided adequate shelter, the apartment would not be a necessary. Therefore, neither the minors nor their parents would be legally obliged to pay future rent. In addition, the minors have a valid claim against Krohn for a refund of the $1,050 already paid.

▼ ASSESS

Learning Objectives 7 & 8 In writing, have students, from memory, list the four requirements for necessaries before a minor or parent can be held responsible for payment, then have them respond to the question: **Does misstating one's age bind a minor?** (Answers may include that minors are liable for torts or criminal action, but usually not for contracts.)

DOES MISSTATING ONE'S AGE BIND A MINOR?

PROBLEM

Rombie, a mature-looking minor, *lied* about his age when he bought an extensive wardrobe of summer clothing from the Beau Brummel Shop. As identification, Rombie showed the driver's license he had taken from his adult brother. Rombie had also used the brother's name on the installment contract. By October, Rombie had paid $325 on the $785 contract. But he was bored with the wardrobe, and so he returned it to the store and demanded the return of all payments. Must the store comply?

In most states, minors who lie about their age may nevertheless disaffirm their contracts. However, *also in most states,* a minor who gives a false age may be held liable for the tort of false representation. Minors are liable for their torts and delinquent or criminal conduct, although they are usually not liable for their contracts. Thus, the other party to the contract may collect from a minor any damages suffered because of the minor's fraud even though the minor cannot be held to the contractual agreement. In the problem, Rombie is within his rights as a minor in disaffirming the *contract.* But his act was also a tort of fraud. Therefore *in most states,* the Beau Brummel Shop could probably hold back from the refund an amount of money sufficient to cover the decrease in value of the wardrobe as returned. Or the store could hold back the full amount if nothing was returned. Moreover, because of his tort, Rombie could be held liable in damages for deceiving the seller, and these damages could exceed the price of the goods he lied to get.

On the other hand, some states will not permit adults to collect damages from minors even if they have misrepresented their age. In protecting the minor, one court said it will not close the front door of contract liability, only to open the rear door of tort liability.

Preventing Legal Difficulties

In making contracts . . .

1. Deal only with persons who are reputable and properly licensed when contracting for professional or skilled services.
2. Most states permit a wide range of interest rates, so shop for loans as carefully as you shop for goods and services.

TEACH

In anwering the section-title question, *Does Misstating One's Age Bind a Minor?*, emphasize the following: misstating one's age is deceit; deceit is a tort of false representation; and minors, as well as adults, are generally liable for their torts.

APPLY

Review the PROBLEM on p. 245. Hold a class discussion on why Rombie is guilty of a tort when his contract was disaffirmed. **Guided Practice**

Have students list the possible outcomes for a minor if he or she misstates his or her age. (Answers may include disaffirming a contract, being held liable for tort of false representation, being held liable for damages, and so on.) **Independent Practice**

Preventing Legal Difficulties

Divide the class into eight groups of two or more students. Assign to each group responsibility for creating a cartoon poster, a three-dimensional piece of art, or a videotape that brings to life one of the eight points listed on pp. 245–246.

RETEACH Write and present to students a PROBLEM that requires them to apply the four-requirement test based on the elements listed on p. 244. Guide students to identify and apply each requirement to this situation.

ENRICH Invite students to orally share their personal experiences with disaffirmance. Then, have volunteers analyze and report to the class their findings from the informal polling of minors they began earlier in the ENRICH activity on p. 229.

▼ CLOSE

Make and display an overhead transparency of the Chapter Outline for Chapter 12, found on pp. 159–162 of the Workbook. As a whole-class activity, work with students to complete the outline satisfactorily.

Assign the following end-of-chapter materials:
Student text review activities, pp. 246–251
Workbook, pp. 33–34
Chapter Test

Chapter MicroExam

3. Wagering is illegal in most states. Even where legal, most persons who wager lose in the long run. Therefore do not bet unless you can afford to lose.
4. Always carefully investigate before entering into an important transaction. When appropriate, consult trustworthy, independent experts. The other party in a transaction is seldom primarily concerned with your best interest, and is generally not obligated to volunteer information or to disclose all the facts she or he knows.
5. Do not rush into a decision. Take time to review and understand the advantages and disadvantages of the proposed contract. Legitimate proposals will usually survive a delay.
6. Learn to distinguish between fact and opinion. Do not rely on the other party's opinion unless that party is a trustworthy expert.
7. If you suspect or know of fraud, do not enter into the contract.
8. If you believe you have been defrauded, act promptly to disaffirm the contract and possibly take other steps (such as consulting a lawyer) to protect your rights. "Sitting on your rights" may cause you to lose them.

▼ REVIEWING IMPORTANT POINTS

1. To be valid, a contract must not violate the law (constitutional, statutory, or case), nor be contrary to public policy in its formation, purpose, or performance.
2. Illegal agreements are usually void and therefore not enforceable by either party. Exceptions are sometimes made to this rule when:
   a. the contract is divisible into legal and illegal parts;
   b. the parties are not equally guilty; or
   c. the violated law was meant to protect one of the parties.
3. Among agreements that violate law or public policy and are therefore void and unenforceable are those that
   a. require committing a crime or tort;
   b. obstruct legal procedures;
   c. injure public service;
   d. are made by persons without a required competency license;
   e. involve payment of usurious interest;
   f. involve illegal gambling, wagers, or lotteries, and
   g. threaten the freedom or security of marriage.
4. An offer and its acceptance must be made with genuine assent.

5 A minor may usually disaffirm a voidable contract anytime before becoming of age or within a reasonable time thereafter. In doing so, the minor must return anything that has been received if the minor still possesses it.

6 After reaching majority, a person may ratify a contract made during minority. This can be done either by an express promise or by an act such as payment. In most states, silence or the failure to disaffirm within a reasonable time is considered ratification.

7 Fraud exists when deliberate false representation or concealment of a material fact is intended to and does influence the action of another, causing injury. Contracts induced by fraud are voidable by the victim.

8 Duress consists of either coercion or illegal imprisonment that induces the victim to make an unwanted contract. Such contracts are voidable by the victim.

9 Undue influence exists when one person, because of trust, confidence, or authority, uses an overpowering influence over another, depriving the victim of freedom of will in making a contract. The contract is voidable by the victim.

10 Generally a unilateral mistake of fact does not affect the validity of a contract.

11 Generally a mutual (i.e., bilateral) mistake of material fact (as to identity or existence of the subject matter) makes the agreement void. In some states, if the mistake concerns the applicable law, the contract may be valid.

STRENGTHENING YOUR LEGAL VOCABULARY

Match each term with the statement that best defines that term. Some terms may not be used.

compounding a crime	necessaries
disaffirmance	personal opinion
duress	ratification
fraud	small loan rate of interest
genuine assent	undue influence
legal rate of interest	unilateral mistake
material fact	usury
maximum rate of interest	wager
mutual mistake	

1 A bet on any event that depends on chance or uncertainty.

Strengthening Your Legal Vocabulary

1 wager
2 mutual (bilateral) mistake
3 necessaries
4 genuine assent
5 compounding a crime
6 legal rate of interest
7 usury
8 fraud
9 ratification
10 undue influence

Applying Law to Everyday Life

1 No, the money cannot be recovered because agreements that tend to injure the public service are void and cannot be enforced. (p. 229)

2 

No, the agreement was void. Any agreement to commit a crime or tort, as here, is illegal and unenforceable. (p. 229) Moreover, both Dixon and "Sparky" may be prosecuted for the crime of arson. No, criminal conduct is generally unethical because it deprives innocent victims of life, liberty, property, happiness, and so on. No, Dixon could not collect. No insurance benefits would be paid. (Note: Even if insurance benefits were honestly collectible, the two companies providing coverage would share the loss.)

3 ETHICS ISSUE No, she lacked the required competency license to practice medicine. Under the circumstances, her conduct was unethical. No, she evidently misrepresented her qualifications and, in the opinion of experts on the state examining board, she was not professionally prepared to practice medicine. (p. 230) She had perpetrated a fraud to induce the city council to make the employment contract. Therefore the employment contract was illegal, void, and unenforceable. No, the prior agreement was null and void, and could not be revived. She is free to submit a new application and could be legitimately hired. (p. 230)

4 Yes, the loan required payments of $325 for 12 months, a total of $3,900. Thus the interest was $1,400 ($3,900 – $2,500) for a loan of $2,500. The interest rate would be 56 percent a year if the Franklins were permitted to delay repayment until the end of the year ($1,400 divided by $2,500). In fact, they had the effective use of only $1,250 for the year because they had to pay 1/12 of the $3,900 every month. Consequently, the effective annual rate of interest was 112 percent. Slye was guilty of the crime of usury. (pp. 230–231)

2 Mistake about an important fact believed by both parties to a contract.

3 Goods and services reasonably needed to maintain one's life-style.

4 Consent or agreement not clouded by fraud, duress, undue influence, or mistake.

5 Accepting something of value for a promise not to prosecute a suspected criminal.

6 Rate specified by statute when interest is called for but no percentage is stated in the contract.

7 Charging interest on a loan beyond the legally permitted maximum rate.

8 Deliberate false representation or concealment of a material fact, which is meant to and which does induce another to make an unfavorable contract.

9 Approval of a voidable contract.

10 Overpowering of another's free will by taking unfair advantage to induce the person to make an unfavorable contract.

▼ APPLYING LAW TO EVERYDAY LIFE

1 Crump was the owner of a restaurant. She applied to the state liquor control board for a $500 license to sell alcohol. When the application was denied, Lynch, a customer, told Crump that he knew someone on the board and could get her a license for $7,500. Crump paid Lynch the money but never received the license. Can she recover the money?

2 ETHICS ISSUE Dixon, a wholesaler, was on the brink of bankruptcy. He bought fire insurance policies for more than twice the value of the building and contents from two companies. Then he arranged to pay a character known only as "Sparky" $10,000 to "torch" his business building. The property was leveled to the ground. Was the agreement with Sparky valid? Was it ethical? Could Dixon legally collect on his insurance policies?

3 ETHICS ISSUE A remote community and the surrounding countryside had no doctor. The city council advertised for help, offering free office space, a six-bed infirmary, and a three-year contract. Glorgan applied and was accepted. Three months later, the council learned that although Glorgan had a medical degree, she had failed to pass the state examination required to practice medicine. No patients complained, but the council summarily discharged her. Glorgan sued for breach of con-

5 Yes, as long as Agnes is a minor, she has the right to disaffirm the contract by returning the shoes. No, an adult would be bound on the contract. (p. 228)

6 ETHICS ISSUE Yes, Shawn must return the money to Blick. (pp. 240–242) In most states, Shawn, a minor, could not be liable to another minor for the money if Shawn no longer had it. Either party could have disaffirmed the contract. (pp. 240–242) No, Blick acted illegally and unethically in making a copy of the copyrighted recording. It was a form of larceny even though it probably will never be detected by the victim—the owner of the copyright.

tract. Was Glorgan's conduct ethical? Should she win the lawsuit? If she retakes the state examination and passes, must the city council rehire her if a vacancy exists at the infirmary?

4 The Franklins, Ali and Lomalinda, had no medical insurance and urgently needed money for emergency surgery for their infant child. They could not qualify for a bank loan and they did not belong to a credit union. An acquaintance referred them to someone named "Slye who'll lend you money on sight. No collateral; no credit report. Just show him you've got a steady job." The Franklins borrowed $2,500 from Slye and agreed to pay $325 on the first of each month "in twelve easy installments." Later a lawyer told them that the loan contract was illegal. Was it?

5 Agnes, age sixteen, bought a pair of tinted shoes to match her prom gown and wore them to the prom. She returned the shoes to the store after she realized they would be of no further use to her. She demanded a refund. Must the store give her the money? Would your answer be the same if her mother had made the purchase?

6 ETHICS ISSUE Blick, a minor, bought a copyrighted compact disc recording of a current hit from Shawn, another minor. After making a copy of the disc, Blick tried to return the original CD to Shawn and demanded a full refund. If Shawn still has the money, must the full price be returned? If Shawn does not have the money, what will happen? Did Blick act legally and ethically in making a copy?

7 In western states, water rights are often critical to the use and value of rural land. They determine how much water a landowner may take from surface and underground sources. In negotiations for the purchase of a ranch, Adler, the seller, discussed water rights with Folt, the buyer. Adler never mentioned an on-going dispute she had over such rights with a neighboring rancher. After the purchase, Folt realized that he had "bought a lawsuit" when his neighbor sued him over the water rights. In turn, he therefore sued Adler for rescission of their contract. You decide.

8 During negotiations for the sale of a salt well, Hutton said the well was free of gypsum and that the brine was 90 percent in strength. In fact, the well did contain gypsum and was deficient in strength. Curry, the purchaser, refused to pay, claiming the contract was void because of fraud. Was it?

9 Ashbery, a salesperson, told Gelman that a new computer and its accounting software should do the work of at least five employees, and maybe more. Relying on this statement, Gelman bought the products.

8 Yes, misrepresentation of a material fact constitutes fraud. (pp. 234–235) Had Curry known that the well contained gypsum and was deficient in saline strength, she would not have purchased it. Even if Hutton honestly believed he was telling the truth but was misinformed, Curry could avoid the contract. However, when the misrepresentation is innocent, there is no tort of fraud and no liability for such wrongful conduct. (p. 235)

9 No, statements of opinion or belief which prove to be wrong normally did not constitute fraud. (p. 234) They are sometimes referred to as "trade talk," "puffing," or "sales talk" and should not be believed by reasonable persons.

10 No, it was not duress. Chang had a legal right to sue. (p. 238) Yes, it would have been duress and also criminal coercion. As a good citizen, one may and usually should report criminal acts. However, one may not threaten to do so to induce another to contract. (p. 238)

7 Judgment for Folt; Although, normally, sellers need not say anything about their products, if they speak they must not mislead—as here—by revealing favorable facts only. (pp. 233–237) Indeed, because the problem of water rights was a serious one and the potential lawsuit was not readily discoverable by an alert buyer, Adler had an affirmative duty to disclose it.

Solving Case Problems

1 ETHICS ISSUE Yes, Marin could be held liable. A state statute and court decisions generally make invalid clauses which

exempt one from responsibility for certain willful or negligent acts that affect the public interest. (p. 229) The clause here was invalid as contrary to public policy because:
•"It concerns a business of a type generally thought suitable for public regulation .... Public policy compels landlords to bear the primary responsibility for maintaining safe, clean and habitable housing ...."
•The defendant performs "a service of great importance to the public." Shelter is a basic necessity of life.
•The defendant "holds himself out as willing to perform this service for any member of the public ...."
•The defendant "possesses a decisive advantage of bargaining strength." Because of the severe shortage of low-cost housing, tenants have little bargaining power with landlords.
•The contract "makes no provision whereby a purchaser may pay additional fees and obtain protection against negligence."

When Gelman found that he could eliminate only three employees but needed a new specialist, he claimed fraud. Was fraud committed?

10 Moser had no automobile liability insurance, although it was required by state law. She negligently collided with Chang's car. Chang threatened to sue if Moser failed to pay $1,000 for pain and suffering and $2,000 for car repairs. Moser gave Chang a check for $3,000. Then she stopped payment on it, claiming duress. Was it duress? What would your answer be if Chang threatened to file a criminal complaint unless paid?

SOLVING CASE PROBLEMS

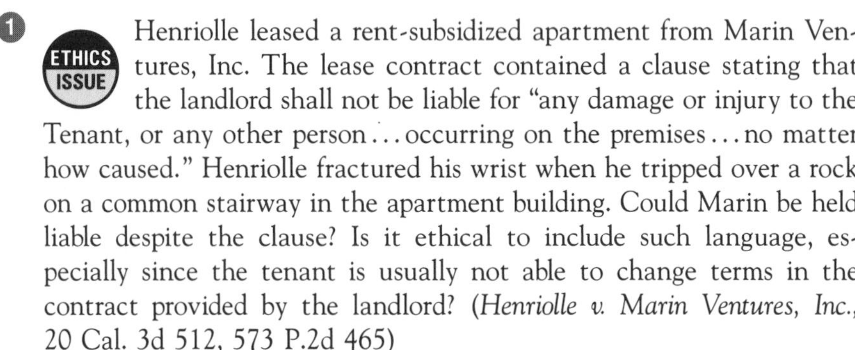

1 ETHICS ISSUE Henriolle leased a rent-subsidized apartment from Marin Ventures, Inc. The lease contract contained a clause stating that the landlord shall not be liable for "any damage or injury to the Tenant, or any other person . . . occurring on the premises . . . no matter how caused." Henriolle fractured his wrist when he tripped over a rock on a common stairway in the apartment building. Could Marin be held liable despite the clause? Is it ethical to include such language, especially since the tenant is usually not able to change terms in the contract provided by the landlord? (*Henriolle v. Marin Ventures, Inc.*, 20 Cal. 3d 512, 573 P.2d 465)

2 Vaughn Turner gave his consent for his son Clifford, age seventeen, to marry Marcella E. Gilbert. After the wedding, Vaughn filed suit to have his consent canceled and the marriage annulled. Vaughn claimed that he was induced by fraud to give his parental consent to the marriage. Clifford and Marcella had represented to him that they had already been married in Tijuana, Mexico. They had also represented that Marcella was pregnant and that Clifford was the father of the expected baby. Because of these representations, Vaughn had given his consent. (Parental consent was required by law because the son was under eighteen.) However, the representation that Clifford was the father was false. Marcella had been about seven months' pregnant when Clifford met her. Indeed, the child's birth certificate listed the name of the mother as Marcella T. Belden and the father as James Taylor Belden. Could the consent be canceled and the marriage annulled? (*Turner v. Turner*, 167 Cal. App. 2d 636, 334 P.2d 1011)

3 Richard purchased a lot and model home from the defendant, a developer of residential real estate. The sales agreement provided that the sale was subject to zoning ordinances. At the time of the sale, the defendant delivered a plot plan to Richard. The plot plan showed a twenty-

•As a result of the contract, the tenant is placed under the control of the landlord subject to the risk of the latter's carelessness. No, it is unethical to include such language in the lease contract. Such clauses are deliberately designed to nullify legislation properly enacted to protect tenants. Often prospective tenants do not understand how the clause, if honored, could deprive them of legitimate rights. Even if they do comprehend the possible consequences, they might not object because of a fear that unscrupulous landlords would refuse to rent the needed housing.

foot side yard, which complied with minimum requirements of the zoning regulations. After taking possession of the house, however, Richard discovered that the building was, in fact, only eighteen feet from the property line. Richard claimed that he relied on the representations of the developer, who should have known that the property did not meet the zoning requirements. Richard sought damages for the misrepresentation. Should he recover? (*Richard v. Waldman and Sons, Inc.*, 155 Conn. 343, 232 A.2d 307)

4 Defendant Darigold Farms was one of several dairies that submitted bids to supply 1.5 million half-pints of milk to the plaintiff, Clover Park School District. Its low bid was $.07013 per half-pint; the next lowest bid was $.072. A usually reliable Darigold secretary had seen penciled figures on a bid form and had erroneously typed them in the bid. The figures were actually the previous year's low price. Because the manager was away at the time, the bid was submitted without review. When the bids were opened on May 25, Darigold's manager immediately recognized the error and on the same day notified Clover Park, asking that the bid be rejected. Nevertheless, it was accepted by the school board on June 11. Darigold's lawyer told Clover Park that Darigold could not supply the milk at the bid price, but that Foremost Dairies would. Then Foremost backed out and Darigold persuaded Sanitary Cloverleaf Dairy to take over. It supplied milk until October, when it became insolvent and went out of business. Clover Park then sued Darigold for breach of contract. You decide. (*Clover Park School District v. Consolidated Dairy Products Company-Darigold Farms*, 550 P.2d 47, Wash.)

5 In 1971, using modern technology, Treasure Salvors, Inc., located a Spanish ship on the ocean bottom in 55 feet of water about 46 miles off the Florida coast. The ship, the *Nuestra Señora de Atocha*, sank in a hurricane while heading from Havana to Spain in 1622. It was carrying "a treasure worthy of Midas: 160 gold bullion pieces, 900 silver ingots, over 250,000 silver coins, 600 copper planks, 350 chests of indigo and 25 tons of tobacco." On the mistaken assumption that the seabed where the *Atocha* lay was state land, Treasure Salvors made a series of contracts with Florida whereby the state was to receive 25 percent of all items recovered. After the U.S. Supreme Court, in another case, had decided that the continental shelf where the ship rested was federal land, Treasure Salvors sued to rescind its contract with Florida and to recover all items as the exclusive owner of the *Atocha*. You decide. (*Florida v. Treasure Salvors, Inc.*, 621 F.2d 1340)

(p. 234) The purchaser who relied on representations by a real estate developer has a right to receive what has been paid for or to receive damages.

4 Judgment for Clover Park School District; Darigold could have rescinded the contract, even though it had made a unilateral mistake. It should have stuck to its resolve not to perform while Clover Park still had the possibility of selecting another bid. Instead, Darigold said it could not perform yet found another dairy. Such conduct was inconsistent with rescission. (p. 238)

5 Judgment for Treasure Salvors; the contracts were based on a mutual mistake: the false assumption that Florida owned the land where the *Atocha* was found. (p. 239) Moreover, there was a failure of consideration; for example, Florida gave no consideration for the 25 percent of the treasure recovered. This is also called a nudum pactum, a naked agreement. (Note: The *Atocha* story appears in the June, 1976, issue of National Geographic. The one-hour videotape *Atocha: Quest for Treasurer* is available from the National Geographic Society, Educational Division, 17th and M Streets, NW, Washington, DC 20036. Media ($26.95 plus mailing costs.)

2 Yes, this was a clear case of fraud. The representations were material, and if the father had known the facts he would not have given his permission for the marriage. The consent must be voluntary and not based on deception. (pp. 234–235) The court said, "To permit a parent to be defrauded into giving his consent would be to deprive him of the control of the marital status of his child which the law has specifically given him."

3 Yes, even an innocent misrepresentation of fact gives the injured party a right to sue for contractual damages if the other party has a means of knowing, ought to know, or has a duty to know the truth.

CHAPTER 13 ORGANIZER

Chapter Theme

Contracts must be expressed in a certain form, sometimes verbal and other times written, to be valid and enforceable.

DIRECTED STUDY QUESTIONS	SPECIAL FEATURES	PROGRAM RESOURCES				
		Reteach	Enrich	SN	AM	
Must contracts be in any special form?		✔	✔			
How are contracts classified?	Thinking Critically Through Visuals, pp. 256, 257, 258	✔	✔	✔	V	
What is the statute of frauds?		✔	✔			
What contracts are subject to the statute of frauds?	Ethics Issue, p. 262 Personal Perspectives, p. 263	✔	✔		A K	
What type of writing is required?		✔	✔			
What is the parol evidence rule?		✔	✔			
How are written contracts interpreted?	Multicultural Highlights, p. 268 Preventing Legal Difficulties, p. 269	✔	✔			

Additional Resources

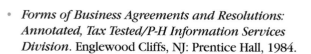

- *Forms of Business Agreements and Resolutions: Annotated, Tax Tested/P-H Information Services Division*. Englewood Cliffs, NJ: Prentice Hall, 1984.
- Sitarz, Daniel, LL.B. *The Complete Book of Small Business Legal Forms.* Carbonsdale, IL: Nova Publishing Co., 1991.

One-semester course	✔	✔	✔					
One-year course	✔	✔	✔	✔	✔			

		ASSESSMENT OPPORTUNITIES			
	Cooperative Learning	Informal Assessment	Chapter Review	Chapter Test	Chapter *MicroExam* (Media)
		✔	✔	✔	✔
		✔	✔	✔	✔
		✔	✔	✔	✔
	✔	✔	✔	✔	✔
		✔	✔	✔	✔
		✔	✔	✔	✔
		✔	✔	✔	✔

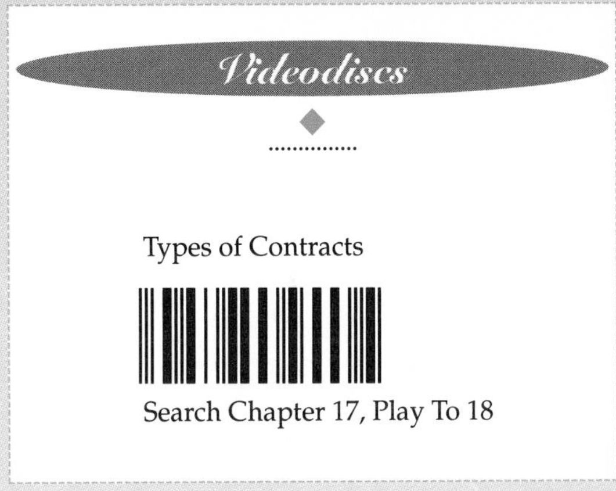

Videodiscs
Types of Contracts
Search Chapter 17, Play To 18

State by State

Credit cards are issued under contracts of adhesion. About 1.1 million cardholders in California recently received refunds because of illegal computation fees by the issuing banks.

Teaching Materials

Student text, pp. 252–275

Overhead transparency masters
• *Forms of Contracts*
• *When There Are Conflicting Inconsistencies in the Wording of Written Contracts, Which Version Prevails?*

Videos
• *Contracts, Warranties, and Credit* Videotape
• *Mock Trial: A Question of Facts* Videotape
• *Law for Business* Videodisc

Workbook, pp. 35–40

Outside Resources

• Sample copies of pre-printed contract forms
• Index cards

• Tape recorder
• Camcorder
• VCR

Assessment

• Chapter Test
• Chapter *MicroExam*

Vocabulary

express contract, p. 255
implied contract, p. 255
quasi contract, p. 256
formal contract, p. 256
notary public, p. 257
simple contract, p. 257
executed contract, p. 258
executory contract, p. 258
statute of frauds, p. 260
parol evidence rule, p. 266
contracts of adhesion, p. 267

Learning Objectives

When you complete this chapter, you will be able to

1. Appreciate the importance of proper form for certain contracts.
2. Classify contracts by their form, how they are made, and the extent of their performance.
3. Identify types of contracts that must be in writing and signed by the defendant to be enforceable.
4. Define and apply the parol evidence rule.
5. Know how courts interpret written contracts.

252

Chapter Self-Test

Assess students' understanding of binding contracts before they begin Chapter 13 by having them respond orally to the following questions: **(1) Must a contract be written and signed by both parties to be legally binding?** (No, there are many circumstances when this is not necessary.); and **(2) Can an enforceable agreement exist without either a spoken or written promise by both parties?** (Yes, in an implied contract) Review and discuss students' responses before continuing with the chapter.

CHAPTER 13

PROPER FORM

1 While dining in a restaurant, a young woman laughed loudly, but humor suddenly turned to horror as she gasped for breath. A piece of food had lodged in her windpipe, and moments later she was unconscious. A licensed surgeon who was present quickly made a lifesaving incision in her windpipe. Although no contractual promise was made, is the surgeon legally entitled to a reasonable fee?

2 A salesperson tries to persuade you, a minor, to buy an electronic musical instrument. The price is $499, plus carrying charges of $72. The salesperson says, "You'll soon be the life of the party. If not, just return it and get your money back." You sign a detailed installment payment contract, which says nothing about a return privilege. Can you hold the salesperson to her promise to accept a return?

3 

During the final week of the star fullback's junior year at Jefferson High, an officer from the Granite Company offered him a full-time job. "After you get that diploma," the officer said, "show up ready for work." "I'll be there," the athlete responded. Was this a legally binding contract? Ethically, should both parties be bound?

▼ FOCUS

Before class begins, list the following forms of contracts on the chalkboard: **written agreement signed by both parties; oral agreement;** and **agreement indicated only by conduct, with no exchange of words**. As students enter the classroom, have them write their initials beside the phrase or phrases that describe a contract form that they think is legally enforceable.

When all have indicated their opinion, explain that all three can be enforceable, but written contracts have the advantage of being most easily proved. Ask students to speculate reasons for this advantage. (Answers may include to prevent confusion, to be used in court, for easy reference, and so on.)

You Decide

1 Yes, the surgeon can recover under a quasi contract to prevent unjust enrichment, even though there was no agreement because the patient was unconscious.

2 Probably not; There is no evidence that the salesperson had authority to promise a return privilege and no such promise appears in the integrated written contract. However, as a minor you have every legal right to disaffirm, return the instrument, and get your money back.

3 ETHICS ISSUE No, because the contract could not be performed within one year under the statute of frauds. Ethically, one may argue that the adult employer should be bound. Because society has given special protection to minors, ethicists would argue that it is quite ethical for the minor to take full advantage of the rules governing minors' contracts.

Thinking Critically Through Visuals

All people have the right and responsibility to ask questions to help them fully understand the details of a contract before they sign it. In this photograph, what evidence is there that the blond-haired woman is helping the other people understand the contract? (Answers may include that she is pointing out and explaining particular points to the others.)

TEACH

Tell students that most contracts are oral and that, unless a particular form is required by statute, such as in the sale of land or buildings, most written and oral forms are enforceable.

Show part II of the overhead transparency, *Forms of Contracts.* Point out that even when a written contract is not required by law, it is good business practice to put it in writing when the agreement involves the three points listed on the transparency.

Have students tell why.

APPLY

Instruct students to close their texts and listen as you read aloud the agreement shown on p. 257. Then, quiz them orally on the details of the agreement. Ask students to make inferences concerning the reliability of oral contracts. **Guided Practice**

Have students brainstorm independently the advantages and disadvantages of both oral and written contracts. Then, have them compile their suggestions into a written class list for future reference. **Independent Practice**

MUST CONTRACTS BE IN ANY SPECIAL FORM?

PROBLEM

While they were playing golf, Hakata orally agreed to buy a triplex apartment building from Simon. In a later telephone conversation, Hakata persuaded Corbin to promise to lend her the $100,000 needed for a down payment on the purchase price. In exchange, Corbin was to be given a promissory note (i.e., a written promise to pay the loan) and a mortgage (i.e., a claim to the building if the note was not paid on time). Hakata and Simon then signed the sales contract. Early the next day, Hakata was stunned when Corbin said he had looked at the apartment and decided not to make the loan. Is Hakata's contract with Corbin enforceable?

Unless a particular form is required by statute, contracts may be oral or written. They may even be implied from conduct. Most contracts are oral. Many are made by telephone; others in face-to-face conversation. For example, in the sale of goods, payment by buyer and delivery by seller often occur when the agreement is made. A person may take a job, rent an apartment, and enter many other business agreements without the formality of a written contract. Sometimes conduct alone is sufficient. For example, a person may hail a bus, board it, deposit the proper coins, and later get off. No words are spoken or written by either passenger or driver, yet there is a valid contract.

There are, however, certain important contracts that will not be enforced in court unless some properly signed writing proves their existence. For example, contracts to transfer an interest in real property (notably land and buildings permanently attached to the land) must be in writing and signed by the party against whom enforcement is sought. (See Chapter 28 for a more complete discussion of real property.) Thus, in the problem, the original oral agreement between Hakata and Simon would not be enforceable. Neither would the oral agreement between Hakata and Corbin be enforceable. Both pertain to an interest in real property: the first, an agreement to buy an apartment building, the second, an agreement to loan money secured by a mortgage on the real property. However, the final signed sales contract between Hakata and Simon is enforceable.

Even when a written contract is not required by law, it is often wise to put the agreement in writing and have a signed copy for each party. This is particularly true if the agreement is complex and contains many details that could lead to later misunderstandings. It also is important when large sums of money or long periods of time are involved. Parties are likely to express

ASSESS

Learning Objective 1 Read aloud the following phrases while students jot down whether or not the contract, according to good business practice, should be in writing and why: **(1) Sale of plants for $5.98** (No, small sum of money, simple agreement); **(2) Agreement to clear land over a three-year period** (Yes, long period of time); and **(3) Agreement to perform services of certain quality, by certain times, and by certain processes** (Yes, complex agreement) their intentions more precisely when they write them down. The possibility of later confusion or disagreement is greatly reduced. Neither party can effectively deny having agreed to particular terms. Also, the added formality encourages the parties to anticipate and provide for problems that could arise later. It is usually easier to settle such matters before either party signs and while both parties are inclined to compromise in order to conclude the agreement. Later, each party tends to demand strict performance of the terms. Finally, their written agreement can be easily referred to and more readily proved in court if necessary. Whenever appropriate, prudent persons seek the aid of a lawyer in the preparation or review of important contracts.

HOW ARE CONTRACTS CLASSIFIED?

PROBLEM

Laredo walked up to a telephone booth in Central Park, dropped a quarter into a receptacle in the phone, and dialed a number. No words were spoken until a party answered the call at the other end of the line. Laredo then chatted briefly, hung up the receiver, and walked away. What kind of contract had Laredo made with the telephone company?

Recall from Chapter 10 that contracts can be classified as either unilateral or bilateral, according to whether one or both parties make a promise. Contracts also can be classified according to enforceability as valid, voidable, unenforceable, or void. Several other ways to classify contracts are presented in the following sections.

1. Method of Creation

The way a contract comes into being gives some idea of its nature. Thus, there are express contracts, implied contracts, and quasi contracts.

Express Contracts. In an **express contract,** the agreement is stated in words—written or spoken. For example, upon graduation from high school, Mary Kelly agrees in a written contract to work as a carpenter's apprentice for three years.

Implied Contracts. In an **implied contract,** the agreement is not stated in words. Instead, the parties express their intent by conduct that is appropriate under the circumstances. For example, Pierre buys a carton of fruit juice in the high school cafeteria by inserting coins into a vending machine.

TEACH

On the chalkboard or on a transparency, draw the following chart to help explain the classifications of contracts. Be sure to define the terms and

explain the concepts listed on the chart.

Parties Bound	Bilateral; unilateral
Enforceability	Valid; void; voidable; unenforceable
Method of Creation	Express; implied; quasi
Formality	Formal; simple
Extent of Performance	Executory; executed

RETEACH Divide the class into pairs. In each pair, have one student orally describe an agreement that must be in writing and properly signed to be enforceable. Have the partner give an opposite example involving the same topic. As a group, discuss why each example does or does not require a written contract.

ENRICH In small groups, have students discuss incidents where conflicting recollections of oral instructions or agreements led to problems. Then have students analyze how these difficulties could have been avoided.

Quasi Contracts. In a **quasi contract,** the parties are bound as though a valid contract exists even though there is none. No true contract exists because some essential element of a contract is missing. Nevertheless, the law imposes a contractual obligation. This is done to prevent unjust enrichment of one of the parties who would otherwise benefit without paying for it. For example, a minor lacks capacity and therefore may usually disaffirm contracts made. In fairness to the other party, however, the minor is held liable for the fair value of any necessaries purchased, as noted in Chapter 12. Otherwise the minor would be unjustly enriched at the expense of the seller. Similarly, a doctor may voluntarily give first aid to a skier who is knocked unconscious in an accident. There is no agreement. Yet the doctor may later collect a reasonable fee for such professional service. Someone who is not a doctor could give similar first aid yet not be entitled to payment because the service was not done by a licensed specialist with the expectation of payment.

2. Formality

A few contracts must meet strict requirements as to formality. They are called formal contracts. Most contracts do not need to meet such requirements. They are called simple contracts.

Formal Contracts. A **formal contract** is a written contract that must be in some special form to be enforceable. Examples are commercial paper

▼ APPLY

Thinking Critically Through Visuals

Contracts take many forms. Into what kind of contract is this man about to enter? Who is it with? (An implied contract with the phone company) **What has he done to indicate his part of the agreement?** (Put a coin in the slot, or provided his credit card number)

On an overhead transparency, list the following statements without the answers in parentheses. Have students identify each as an express contract, implied contract, or quasi contract, then discuss their responses.

1. Zack, an adult, buys a ticket and takes a seat in a roller coaster car. (Implied)
2. Juanita, a physician, renders emergency medical service at the scene of an accident to an unconscious victim. (Quasi)
3. Margo, an adult, signs an installment purchase agreement to buy a used car because she had no other means of transportation to get to work. (Express)

Guided Practice

▼ ASSESS

Learning Objective 2 Have students indicate orally whether or not each of the following describes an express (E), implied (I), quasi (Q), formal (F), or simple contract (S). **(1) A written contract that must be in some special form** (F); **(2) The agreement is stated in words.** (E); **(3) A contract that is not formal** (S); **(4) Parties are bound as though a valid contract exists even though there is none.** (Q); and **(5) The agreement is expressed by conduct rather than words.** (I) and contracts under seal. Commercial paper, such as an ordinary check, must meet certain requirements to be valid. A contract under seal is one with a seal attached or with a similar impression made on the paper. Seals served to validate agreements years ago, when few people could read or write. Today, in most states, the legal effect of the seal on contracts has been limited or ended. Seals are still used by notaries public. A **notary public** is a public officer who formally certifies that the signatures on deeds and other documents are authentic.

Simple Contracts. A contract that is not formal is a **simple contract.** This is true whether the contract is oral, written, or based on conduct. Figure 13-1 is an example of a simple, written contract.

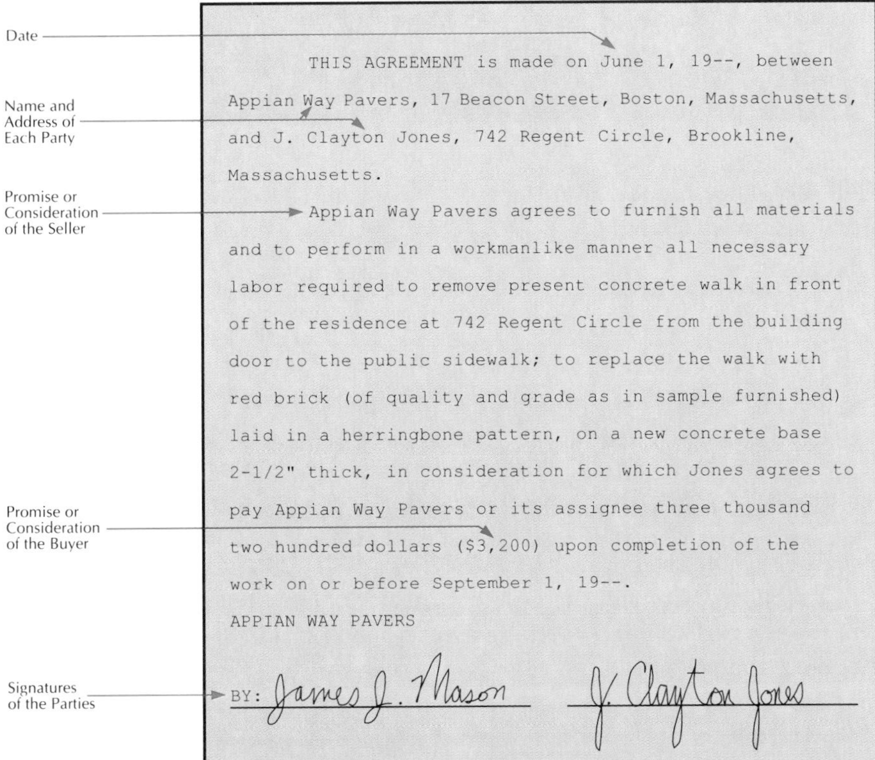

THIS AGREEMENT is made on June 1, 19--, between Appian Way Pavers, 17 Beacon Street, Boston, Massachusetts, and J. Clayton Jones, 742 Regent Circle, Brookline, Massachusetts.

Appian Way Pavers agrees to furnish all materials and to perform in a workmanlike manner all necessary labor required to remove present concrete walk in front of the residence at 742 Regent Circle from the building door to the public sidewalk; to replace the walk with red brick (of quality and grade as in sample furnished) laid in a herringbone pattern, on a new concrete base 2-1/2" thick, in consideration for which Jones agrees to pay Appian Way Pavers or its assignee three thousand two hundred dollars ($3,200) upon completion of the work on or before September 1, 19--.

APPIAN WAY PAVERS

BY: James J. Mason　　J. Clayton Jones

Figure 13-1
A simple, written contract does not have to meet strict requirements as to form.

3. Extent of Performance

Contracts can be classified as either executed or executory, according to whether or not they have been completed. Many contracts are performed almost immediately; others require days, months, or years to complete. Many

Divide the class into groups of three or four. Have each group list the pros and cons of having an express, implied, formal, or simple contract for a given situation. Have each group read aloud its list to the class. Make a class list of the pros and cons on the chalkboard or on chart paper. **Independent Practice**

Thinking Critically Through Visuals

Simple contracts do not have to meet strict requirements of form but do give important information. Who is this contract between? (Appian Way Pavers and J. Clayton Jones) **Who has the authority to sign for Appian Way?** (Mason)

RETEACH Write the five classifications of contracts (pp. 255–259) on the chalkboard. Have students create mnemonic devices for remembering the definitions of each.

ENRICH Have students suggest examples of personal communications that are examples of express, implied, formal, and simple contracts. (Answers may include oral promises [Express, simple]; using an automated teller machine, or ATM [Implied, simple]; waving [implied, simple]; and so on.)

Thinking Critically Through Visuals

Contracts can be classified as either executed or executory. What evidence in this photograph tells you that a contract is being executed? (Both parties have done all they promised to do: the woman gave money and the pizza company delivered pizza.) **When did this contract probably become executory?** (When the woman called to place her order and the order was accepted)

For students who are having reading comprehension difficulties, write contract descriptions on a set of index cards. On each card, list the following: the number of people entering into the contract; how the contract came into being, whether it is written or oral, printed or handwritten; and whether it is completed or in progress. Have students take turns sorting the cards by various classifications. (Unilateral or bilateral, express or implied, written or oral, formal or informal, and executory or executed) Point out that a single contract can have several classifications.

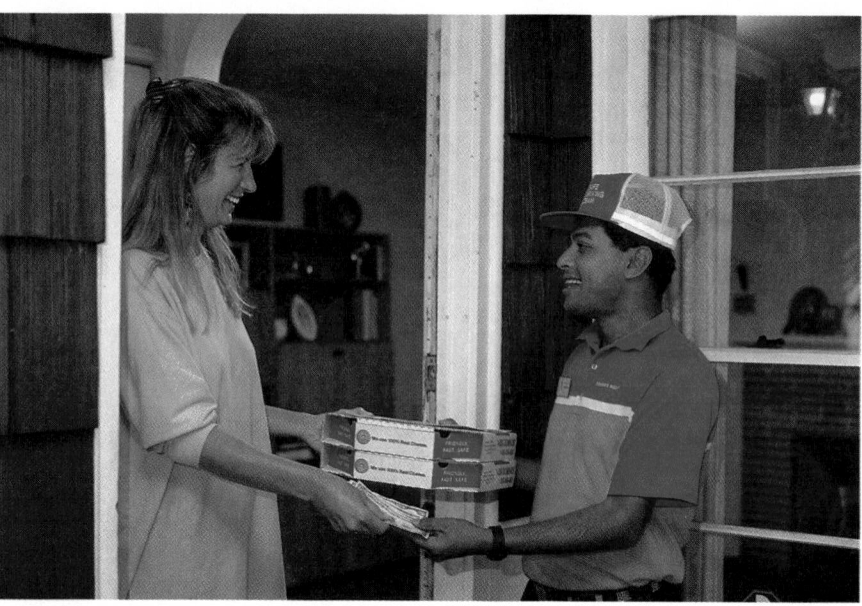

life insurance contracts are not completed until the insured dies, perhaps many decades later.

Executed Contracts. An **executed contract** is one that has been fully performed. Both parties have done all they promised to do.

> You order a five-dish, carryout Chinese dinner at Yutan's Imperial Garden Cafe. When the meal is ready, you give the cashier the purchase price and receive five cartons of food in an insulated bag. This is an executed contract because it has been fully performed by both parties.

Executory Contracts. An **executory contract** is one that has not been fully performed. Something agreed upon remains to be done by one or both of the parties.

> Peg and Paul Powell ordered a "Tasty Treat of the Month" from a mail-order company in New Hampshire. They paid $120 by check, which the seller, Toothsome Treats, Inc., cashed. Just before Christmas, a pound of deluxe assorted truffles was delivered. During each of the following eleven months a different "Treat" will be delivered. The contract will be executory until all promised treats are delivered. Then it will be an executed contract.

Learning Objective 2 Have students write, using a computer, if possible, a definition and an example for an executed contract and an executory contract.

In the problem, the contract Laredo had with the telephone company was bilateral and valid. It was executory when the coins were deposited. It became executed when Laredo finished the conversation and hung up the receiver. As to formality, it was simple; as to method of creation, it was implied from conduct.

WHAT IS THE STATUTE OF FRAUDS?

PROBLEM

When the general manager of Special-Teas Sales Company hired Bellini as advertising manager for a five-year period, the two parties discussed the terms of employment and then they shook hands. As Bellini later recalled, her beginning salary was to be $3,000 a month but would go up annually if, and as, sales rose. At the end of the first year, she expected a pay increase of at least $500 a month, but there was no increase at all. She threatened to quit. The manager admitted that sales were up; however, he claimed that expenses had also risen and therefore profits were down. He threatened to sue Bellini for breach of contract if she left. How could their misunderstanding have been avoided?

An important purpose of business law is to assist persons in their business dealings and to protect them from avoidable injury. One way is to inform the public that certain types of agreements must be in written form and signed to be enforceable in court. A writing is generally more reliable than oral testimony as proof of an executory agreement. The writing is not affected by the absence, illness, or death of parties or of witnesses. A writing helps to dissuade dishonest persons from later deliberately lying about relevant facts. For honest persons, it refreshes the memory and thereby prevents them from later innocently misrepresenting the facts.

A writing takes extra time to prepare and is more likely to reflect greater care in its preparation. It can serve as the medium to provide for alternatives to litigation if a dispute arises. For example, it can require mediation and arbitration. It might also specify that the loser in the event of a trial must pay not only the court costs, but also reasonable attorney's fees for both parties. Thus, the dispute between Bellini and the Special-Teas Sales Company probably would never have occurred if their agreement had been in writing with all important terms and contingencies clearly spelled out.

Many years ago, avoidable injustices resulted from innocent failures of memory. They also resulted from intentional lies in testimony given in court during cases involving important oral contracts. Sometimes plaintiffs and defendants would lie under oath—although perjury is a crime, it was

TEACH

Ask the class why writing is usually a more reliable means of communication than speaking. (Writing is not affected by the absence, illness, or death of the parties and is not subject to memory failure, which leads to innocent misrepresentation of the facts.) Write the term **statute of frauds** on the chalkboard. Explain that its use can be traced back to the English Statute of Frauds and Perjuries adopted in 1677. Explain that the name *statute of frauds* now designates statutes enacted by all states that require specified types of contracts to be in writing. Explain that an oral contract may be used even when statutes call for a written one. However, if the non-signer refuses to perform, the contract might not be enforceable by legal means.

RETEACH Have students enter into oral agreements with one another that will result in immediate action such as one student asking, "Would you like to buy this CD for five dollars?" and another answering "Yes, I'll pay you tomorrow." Have other students identify when the contract becomes executory, then executed.

Using a computer, if possible, have students write three social promises and three personal goals they have made or would like to make, then classify each using the terms **executory** and **executed**.

▼ APPLY

Have students share examples of situations when it would have been to their advantage to have had a written contract. Ask students to decide if an oral contract would have been enforceable. Discuss answers. **Guided Practice**

Have students write slogans or raps, using a computer, if possible, to remind them that contracts subject to the statute of frauds are not illegal if they are oral; they simply may not be enforceable in court. Ask student volunteers to tape record and share their work with the class. Display students' work. **Independent Practice**

▼ TEACH

Display part I of the overhead transparency, *Forms of Contracts*. Tell students that, to be enforceable under the statute of frauds, these five types of executory contracts must be in writing and signed by the party against whom the contract is to be enforced. Discuss each type. Point out that, as an alternative, the contract may be provable by some other writing, such as a letter signed by the party who is being sued.

difficult to prove. To help prevent such injustices, and for certain procedural reasons, England adopted a remedial statute in 1677. The statute required that certain agreements be in writing and be signed by the party against whom the contract was to be enforced in court: the defendant in the action. Because the statute was designed to prevent frauds and perjuries, it was called the Statute of Frauds and Perjuries. The name **statute of frauds** is now commonly used to designate statutes enacted by all states that require certain contracts to be evidenced by a signed writing in order to be enforceable in court.

The Rosenbergs made an offer in writing to sell their house to Chabra. Chabra orally agreed to buy, but since he had not yet signed any purchase agreement he is not legally bound. However, the Rosenbergs would be bound if Chabra accepted their offer in writing within a reasonable time. Meanwhile the Rosenbergs are free to revoke their offer.

The statute of frauds does not prevent the voluntary performance of oral agreements that should have been in writing. It has no effect on oral agreements that have been fully performed. After all, contracts subject to the statute are not illegal if they are oral; they are simply not enforceable in court.

▼ WHAT CONTRACTS ARE SUBJECT TO THE STATUTE OF FRAUDS?

PROBLEM

Cervante and Brecht were good friends. When they graduated from high school, both were eighteen. They planned to marry, but first they wanted to become financially secure. So they shook hands and agreed to become partners in operating a small, iced-tea and lemonade stand at the county fair. "This is just the beginning," Brecht said. "Till death do us part!" both said. Are they legally bound to remain partners in business until one dies?

To be enforceable under the statute of frauds, five important types of executory contracts must be in writing and signed by the party against whom the contract is to be enforced. As an alternative, the contract may be provable by some other writing, such as a letter signed by the party who is being sued. The plaintiff seeking to enforce the contract can readily sign if his or her signature is missing. Since either party might later want to sue for breach, both parties should sign when the contract is made.

▼ ASSESS

Learning Objective 3 As you read aloud the following statements, have students write them in their notebooks and fill in the missing words: **(1) Writing is generally more __ than oral testimony as proof of an executory agreement.** (Reliable); **(2) The statute of frauds requires certain contracts to be __ to be enforceable in court.** (Written and signed by the party to be charged); and **(3) Contracts subject to the statute of frauds are not illegal if they are oral, they simply may not be __.** (Enforceable).

Contracts subject to the statute of frauds include those to:

1. buy and sell goods for a price of $500 or more;[1]
2. buy and sell real property or any interest in real property;
3. do something that cannot be performed within a year;
4. pay the debt or answer for a legal obligation of another person; and
5. give something of value in return for a promise of marriage.

For the sale or purchase of goods for a price of $500 or more, a simple memorandum suffices provided it states the quantity of goods and is properly signed. Other terms, such as price and time and place of delivery, can be added later if necessary. For most other types of contracts, the memorandum must also name the parties, the subject matter, the price or consideration, and other essential terms.

1. Contract for the Sale of Goods for $500 or More

PROBLEM

Khan bought a new car and wanted to sell her old car. She advertised in the local paper and Khazari agreed to buy the car for $1,885. He promised to pay and to take delivery when he received his paycheck in two weeks. Must this contract be in writing to be enforceable?

Goods are tangible personal property. Limited exceptions to this requirement under the statute of frauds are discussed in Chapter 16. In the problem, if Khan refused to sell as promised, Khazari could enforce their agreement only if Khan had signed their agreement. Reciprocally, if Khazari refused to buy as promised, Khan could collect damages only if Khazari had signed.

2. Contract to Sell or Sale of Any Interest in Real Property

PROBLEM

The Schmidts orally agreed to sell their mountain cabin, and the Cardonas orally agreed to buy it. The price agreed upon was $8,950. Before the oral contract was executed, the Schmidts got a better offer in writing from Murata. Could the Cardonas still hold the Schmidts to their original oral promise to sell for the agreed-upon price?

[1]All states except Louisiana have adopted the $500 figure specified by the Uniform Commercial Code. Also, in Louisiana, there is no requirement for a writing.

▼ APPLY

Divide the class into five groups. Assign each group one of the five types of contracts subject to the statute of frauds. Have each group compose and videotape an example of a contract situation that depicts their contract assignment. Play the tapes and assign students to affirm or challenge the accuracy and completeness of the examples. **Guided Practice**

Have students write a one-page essay, on a computer, if possible, to answer the following question: **Is the statute of frauds essential, or could it be abolished without calamitous results?**

▼RETEACH Ask students to skim the section, *What Is the Statute of Frauds?*, and note the arguments given for putting a contract in writing. Have students take turns listing each argument on the chalkboard. Ask them to circle the reasons that prompted the first statute of frauds. (Innocent failures of memory and lying under oath)

▼ENRICH Ask students to discuss reasons why people might purposefully avoid using a written agreement. (Answers may include that they are not fully committed, plan to deceive, unsure of their own ability to interpret language, and so on.)

Ethics Issue

Brenda came from a very small isolated town that had trouble attracting a doctor. She made an oral agreement that if the chamber of commerce would loan her money for her last year of medical school, she would practice in the town for at least two years. The members of the chamber of commerce agreed to pay all of her medical school bills. After Brenda graduated, she decided to join the practice of a doctor in a large city, where she quickly earned enough money to reimburse the chamber of commerce. Ask: **Could the chamber of commerce enforce the agreement? Was Brenda acting ethically?** (No, under statutes of frauds, this oral contract is not enforceable because it could not be performed within one year. Brenda still has a moral obligation to keep her word to practice in the small town.)

Real property includes land and buildings permanently attached to land; personal property includes all other property. Thus there should be written evidence of contracts to transfer title to real property. Likewise, transfers of lesser interests—such as a lease or the right to pump oil or to cut timber—must be in a properly signed writing to be enforceable. In most states, oil leases for one year or less are enforceable. Some states provide that an agreement employing an agent to buy or sell land must also be in a properly signed writing (see Chapter 25).

In the problem, neither the Cardonas nor Murata can hold the Schmidts to their oral promise to sell. However, since Murata made his offer (to buy) in writing, the Schmidts could hold him to this promise. As an exception to the general rule, a court will enforce the oral contract if the buyer has also done all of the following:

a. made partial or full payment,
b. occupied or possessed the land, and
c. made substantial improvements to the land.

3. Contract That Cannot Be Performed Within One Year After Being Made

PROBLEM

Late in March, Bulger, the human resources manager of Data Dot Data, Inc., orally promised to employ Gramling in the company's information processing department. The job was to be for one year at $2,000 a month plus a customary package of fringe benefits. Gramling was to report for work one month after receiving her high school diploma in June. Gramling, a minor, discussed the offer with her parents. The next day she telephoned Bulger and accepted it. When Gramling reported for work as promised, Bulger said, "Sorry; business is too slow. We've changed our minds." Was this agreement an enforceable contract by either Gramling or Data Dot Data, Inc.?

A contract that cannot be performed within one year from the time it is made will not be enforced by courts unless there is a signed writing to prove the agreement. The year is figured from the time the contract is made, not from the time performance is to begin. Accordingly, the oral agreement in the problem was not enforceable against Data Dot Data or its agent Bulger. Nor could the corporation enforce it against Gramling. The fact that she was a minor did not affect the outcome of this case. However, had there been a written contract, signed by both parties, only Gramling could have

ASSESS

Learning Objective 3 In writing, have students list the five types of contracts subject to the statute of frauds. (Those contracts used to: buy and sell goods for a price of $500 or more, buy and sell real property or any interest in real property, do something that cannot be performed within a year, pay a debt or answer for the legal obligation of another person, and give something of value in return for a promise of marriage.)

avoided it without liability. She alone could have claimed incapacity as a minor.

This time provision does not apply to agreements that can be executed within one year. This is true even if such agreements are not actually carried out within that time. The test is not whether the agreement is actually performed within one year, but whether there is a possibility of performance within one year. To illustrate, two persons shake hands and orally agree to be business partners. But they do not say for how long. Because either partner may legally quit within one year, their agreement need not be in writing. On the other hand, their partnership could last indefinitely.

Thus, in the problem on page 260, the partnership agreement between Cervante and Brecht did not have to be in writing. That is because the agreement was for an indefinite time that could be less than one year. Although they said, "Till death do us part," either might die within one year. Because the agreement was for an indefinite time, either partner could withdraw at any time, "at will," without liability to the other for breach of contract. In starting a partnership, it is always prudent to prepare the agreement carefully, spelling out all important terms in the writing. That is because of the complexity of the partnership, the money invested, the possible liabilities incurred, and the long time potentially involved. (Partnerships are discussed more fully in Chapter 37.)

4. Contract to Pay a Debt or to Answer for the Legal Obligation of Another Person

PROBLEM

With so many people living beyond the age sixty-five, Puccini predicted a revival of sweet music by "big bands" as well as "one-man bands" featuring piano accordion music. Mike's Music Box shop had the accordion Puccini needed but it cost $1,495, and he had neither the necessary cash or credit. His friend, Muniz, told the music shop owner, "Sell Puccini the accordion on a fifteen-month installment contract. If he fails to make any payment, I will pay the balance due." After three months, Puccini defaults. Is Muniz liable for the balance due?

One provision of the statute of frauds requires a writing for a promise to answer for the debt or default of another person (see Unit 5). In the problem, the oral promise Muniz made is not enforceable. Had he made the promise in writing and signed it, he would have been bound to pay. Likewise, if he had orally said, "Sell the accordion to Puccini, but bill me. I will

▼RETEACH Describe various business situations, such as selling a car and so on, and ask students to tell if they are subject to the statute of frauds.

▼ENRICH In small groups, have students brainstorm five to ten examples of informal situations that involve a person assuming the legal or financial obligations of another. Share examples.

Distribute to small groups copies of standardized written contracts, letters, or order blanks which you have filled in and signed with fictitious names. (They can be purchased from stationery stores or office supply stores.) Have students analyze these forms to determine whether the transaction is within the statute of frauds, whether the writing satisfies the statute, and whether both parties can enforce the agreement. **Independent Practice**

Personal Perspectives

Have each student create a contract, using a computer, if possible, entering a family member into a contractual arrangement with him or her. Have each student take home the contract and ask adult family members to read it and determine if they would sign such a document. Tell students that they may orally persuade family members to sign it. Poll students on how many of their family members signed their contracts. Discuss whether making oral promises is convincing when trying to get someone to sign a contract.

Media

Divide the class into groups of four or five students. Assign the following roles to each group: plaintiff, defendant, two attorneys, and facilitator, if necessary. Have each group prepare and present skits that depict a contract that is either based on performance, where time is an issue; holds someone liable for another's debt; or promises value in return for a promise to marry. Have the other groups determine enforceability based on text information. **Cooperative Learning**

▼ TEACH

Tell students that, in most states, a signed memorandum satisfies the writing requirement of the statute of frauds for most transactions but is enforceable only against those who have signed it. The memo may be printed, typed, or written by hand and the signature may be written, stamped, engraved, or printed. However, an adequate memo contains the following four items: date and place of contract, names of parties, all material terms of agreement, and the signature of the party against whom the contract is to be enforced.

pay you," it would have been a direct, primary promise to the seller, and as such, enforceable in court.

Sometimes a third party is liable under an oral promise to pay another's debt, but only if the payment serves the promisor's own financial interest. Thus, suppose a buyer of a house under construction is anxious to see it completed. He orally promises to pay a lumberyard for needed supplies after the building contractor fails to pay, and the driver of the delivery truck refuses to unload a shipment. Now, the homeowner is legally bound to pay the lumberyard. Incidentally, if the homeowner breaks this promise, the lumberyard company could file a lien against the house, as discussed later (page 387).

5. Contract for Which the Consideration Is Marriage

PROBLEM

A Hollywood actress, Flora Flambé, promised to marry the wealthy tycoon Mackay Munimint, but only if he would agree to transfer $10 million in U.S. government bonds to her name as her own separate property. Flora's lawyer prepared the necessary document, which Mackay signed. The couple married, but Mackay failed to transfer title to the bonds. Is his promise now enforceable?

A signed writing is required for agreements in which marriage is the consideration for a promise to pay money or to give other valuable consideration to the offeree or to some third party if the offeree marries as requested. It is sometimes made by a parent of the woman or man contemplating marriage. It does not refer to mutual promises of persons to marry. In the problem, Mackay's written promise was enforceable.

In some states, if one party breaches an oral or written contract to marry, the victim of the breach may successfully sue for damages. The trend is to ban such "heart balm" suits. Generally, however, if the man breaches his promise to marry, the woman may keep the engagement ring. If the woman breaches, the ring must be returned. Ordinary gifts from one another need not be returned.

▼ WHAT TYPE OF WRITING IS REQUIRED?

PROBLEM

In June, Bachman orally agreed to sell to Caruso Commodities Company the entire next harvest of wheat from his 640-acre farm. He

▼ ASSESS

Learning Objective 3 Have students respond orally to the following: **(1) Can an informal memo signed by only one party satisfy the requirement of the statute of frauds for evidence?** (Yes, if it is the party against whom the contract is to be enforced); **(2) Does such a memorandum bind both parties?** (No, only the one who signed); and **(3) Name the four items that an adequate memorandum includes.** (See TEACH, above.)

agreed to sell the wheat at the current market price. Later, he changed his mind and wrote to Caruso, "Complications force me to alter plans for the sale of my wheat crop. I will not be able to let you have my harvest at the June price as we discussed. It's a good year. Therefore I trust you'll get all the wheat you can handle from other sources." Bachman then signed his name to the writing. Was this writing sufficient to allow Caruso to enforce the oral contract against Bachman?

In most states, a signed memorandum satisfies the writing requirement of the statute of frauds for evidence of an agreement. Usually, any words that clearly state the important terms of the agreement suffice. However, the memorandum is enforceable only against those who have signed it. Thus, in the problem, the letter Bachman wrote would actually prove the existence of the agreement to sell his wheat to Caruso. Bachman is bound.

The memorandum need not be in any special form. Moreover, a series of writings—such as an exchange of letters, telegrams, or facsimile messages—is sufficient if all essential terms are included. Essential terms would depend on the particular circumstances; in a sale of land, for example, they normally would include the location, legal description, price, and terms of payment. The memorandum may be printed, typed, or written with pen or pencil. The signature may be written, stamped, engraved, or printed. It may consist of any mark that is intended as a signature. An adequate memorandum includes the following items:

1. Date and place of the contract.
2. Names of the parties.
3. All material terms of the agreement. These usually include the subject matter, price, and any special conditions, such as time or method of delivery or terms of payment. (However, in the case of a sale of goods, the Uniform Commercial Code [UCC] provides that the memorandum need only state the quantity of described goods that are involved and indicate that there has been a related sale.)
4. The signature of the party against whom the contract is to be enforced. This signature may be by an agent authorized to sign.

These items do not need to be in a particular order. If custom or business usage is well established, some items may be excluded. For example, such items as terms of payment and delivery, even price, are often omitted from orders for goods. The UCC permits this because such items are governed by trade usage or custom.

▼ APPLY

On the chalkboard, have students write a memorandum that includes the four items that make it enforceable. To the left of the memo, label the date and place, names of parties, material terms of the agreement, and signatures. To the right, list the format options for the memo and the signatures. (Printed, typed, and so on) Determine which parties are bound by the agreement. **Guided Practice**

Writing Connections

Social Studies
Tell students to use a historical incident as the basis of a fictitious memorandum, such as an agreement between the Pony Express and a rider. Have students write the memorandum, using a computer, if possible. Remind students to include the four items that make a memorandum enforceable. Display students' memos on a bulletin board called *Back to the Future: Rewriting History through Memos.*

Independent Practice

▼RETEACH

Using a blank transparency and an overhead projector, have students work together to create a graphic organizer to show the four parts of an adequate memorandum.

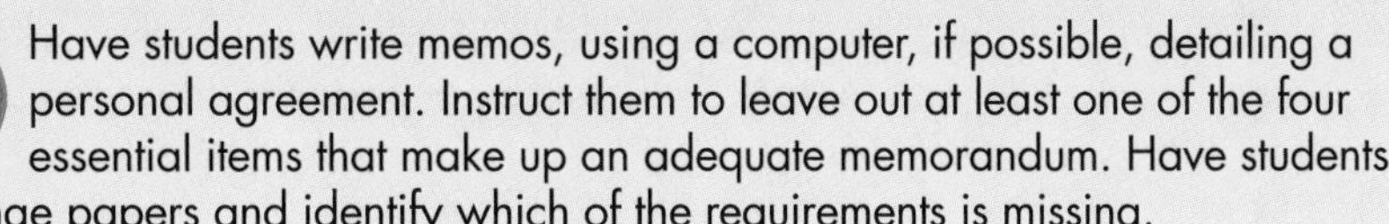

▼ENRICH

Have students write memos, using a computer, if possible, detailing a personal agreement. Instruct them to leave out at least one of the four essential items that make up an adequate memorandum. Have students exchange papers and identify which of the requirements is missing.

TEACH

Tell students that *parol* means "word of mouth" or "oral". Write **parol evidence rule** on the chalkboard. Ask: **What does the name of this rule imply?** (Answers may include that the rule regulates the use of oral evidence.) Explain the details of the parol evidence rule. Point out that a trial judge will sometimes permit parol evidence to be introduced to prove mistake, fraud, illegality, custom and trade usage, clerical errors, and the meaning of terms. Explain *parol*, used here, and *parole*, as used in criminal law.

APPLY

Have students brainstorm reasons why inconsistencies between oral and written agreements might arise in a sales situation. (Answers may include that sales contracts are usually pre-printed forms and, as a result, salespeople often do not add their verbal promises to them.) **Guided Practice**

Have students pretend to be Highman in the PROBLEM on p. 266, and, using a computer, if possible, write a letter of advice to a friend based on personal experience with Advanced Electronics. Tell them to include the term **parol evidence rule** in their letters.

Independent Practice

WHAT IS THE PAROL EVIDENCE RULE?

PROBLEM

Highman bought a new personal computer from Advance Electronics. She signed the store's usual contract, which stated the terms completely. Later, Highman alleged that as part of the bargain, the salesperson orally promised that if the factory list price was reduced within two months, he would refund the same amount to Highman. The factory list price was reduced, but Advanced Electronics refused to pass the savings on to Highman. What were Highman's rights?

The parol evidence rule applies whenever parties put their agreement in writing, whether or not a writing is required under the statute of frauds. With certain exceptions, under the **parol evidence rule** the writing itself is the only evidence allowed in court to prove the terms of a written contract if the writing appears to be the complete agreement between the parties.

This important rule bars the introduction of prior or contemporaneous (i.e., made at the same time) oral or written agreements alleged to be part of a disputed written contract. Unless these agreements were actually referred to or included in that written contract, the court presumes that when the parties put their agreement into written form it was integrated; that is, complete and final. Thus, the writing presumably included all desired terms and excluded all other agreements or comments made while negotiating up to that time. Accordingly, in case of dispute in court, the written contract is the only acceptable evidence of the intent of the parties. In the problem, therefore, Highman loses. She probably could not prove that the salesperson's oral promise was ever made. Moreover, preliminary discussions are often vague and unsettled. Both parties should carefully include in their integrated contract all terms that they deem essential. "When you write, write it right!"

In the interests of justice, however, the trial judge will sometimes permit parol evidence to be introduced to prove certain matters. These include mistake, fraud, illegality, custom and trade usage, clerical errors, and the meaning of terms. Also, when a contract is obviously ambiguous, parol evidence may be used to clarify terms to determine the true intent of the parties. Such evidence explains the meaning of the writing. Sometimes it may prove that the contract is voidable because a party is a minor, or that there never was a valid, enforceable contract.

ASSESS

Learning Objective 4 Have students jot down whether or not the following statements are *True* or *False*: **(1) Under the parol evidence rule, agreements in written form, even when not required to be written under the statute of frauds, are usually considered to be complete.** (True); and **(2) There are no exceptions to the parol evidence rule.** (False; judges sometimes permit parol evidence to be introduced to prove certain matters, such as mistake or fraud.)

HOW ARE WRITTEN CONTRACTS INTERPRETED?

PROBLEM

Milo contracted with Corrigan for the installation of a complete burglar alarm system for $2,900. The printed contract provided that Milo was to pay $900 down and the balance at $100 a month for twenty months. Failure to pay any installment when due would accelerate the debt and make the entire balance due. The payments were to be made on the first day of each month. Milo explained that he did not receive his paycheck until the tenth. Therefore, he said, he would prefer to make the payments on that date. Corrigan agreed and in the margin wrote in "tenth," and initialed it on Milo's copy only. During the first month, Corrigan demanded the full balance when Milo failed to make the payment on the first day. Is Corrigan entitled to the full balance immediately?

Even when parties put their agreement into a signed contract, the written words may be unclear or require interpretation. This sometimes happens when standardized contract forms purchased in stationery stores are used. Filling in blanks on the forms, or modifying terms, may cause contradictions among terms. Also, one party may use a word that seems perfectly clear yet has a totally different meaning for the other party.

In millions of transactions, consumers buy, borrow, and lease goods and services. Usually the consumers are asked to accept and sign **contracts of adhesion.** These are contracts—such as purchases on credit and life insurance policies—that are prepared by the stronger parties (usually the sellers) with the help of skilled lawyers who naturally favor the interests of their clients. Generally, the terms of such contracts cannot be changed; the weaker parties (usually the consumers) must "take it or leave it." Understandably, in later disputes over the meaning of the language in such contracts, courts favor the party who did not prepare the document. Another helpful development is the requirement by statute in some states that the language of consumer contracts be clear, simple, and understandable to the average person.

When required to settle disputes over the correct interpretation of written contracts, courts generally seek to determine and to enforce the intent of the parties by applying the following rules of interpretation.

APPLY

Explain **contracts of adhesion** and point out that they always favor the person providing them, usually the seller. Tell students that when disputes over the correct interpretation of such written contracts arise, there are rules to guide judicial interpretation. Discuss how to review the contract as a whole. Then, show the transparency, *When There Are Conflicting Inconsistencies in the Wording of Written Contracts, Which Version Prevails?*, and discuss why one form prevails over another. Give examples of trade customs or practices and discuss their relation to contracts.

APPLY

Divide the class into an even number of groups of three or four students each. Pair groups. Assign each pair of groups a business situation, such as agreeing to buy a used car on an installment plan. Assign Group A of the pair to represent the buyer and Group B of the pair to represent the seller. On a transparency, have each group write a contract of adhesion that favors itself. Have the paired groups show, read, and compare their contracts.

Guided Practice

RETEACH Pair students to create a contract based, in part, on parol evidence. Have each pair perform their skit. Other students will judge whether the parol evidence should be permitted or not.

ENRICH Ask students to brainstorm wise consumer rules for entering into contracts, especially those implied by the parol evidence rule. Have students collaborate to create a poster illustrating these rules.

On the chalkboard, write the following pairs of terms, and have students respond orally to indicate the form that would prevail. (Answers are underlined.) **figures/words printing/typewriting printing/handwriting typewriting/handwriting Independent Practice**

Multicultural Highlights

In 1967, Margarita Fuentes, a Cuban American living in Miami, bought a gas stove with a service contract on the installment plan from Firestone Corp. She made payments for more than a year—until the stove stopped working. When no one from Firestone Corp. would fix it, Fuentes stopped paying. Firestone, acting within the law, repossessed the stove without warning. Fuentes and her attorney felt this process infringed upon her constitutional right to due process and pursued the matter to the Supreme Court. Her case, *Fuentes v. Shevin,* was won in 1972, and is considered a landmark constitutional victory for ordinary citizens. Discuss how due process relates to contracts.

1. The Writing Is Evaluated as a Single, Whole Document

Each clause is interpreted in the light of all other provisions of the contract. Words are interpreted as they are ordinarily used unless circumstances indicate a different meaning. Legal and other technical terms or abbreviations are given their technical meaning unless the contract as a whole shows that a different meaning is intended.

2. On Printed Forms, Added Typewritten Provisions Prevail Over Contradictory Printed Provisions, and Added Handwritten Ones Prevail Over Both Printed and Typewritten Ones

An individual's typewriting *supersedes* (i.e., replaces) printing because it presumably represents that person's most recent intentions. Similarly, handwriting prevails over both printing and typewriting. Thus, in the problem, Milo's payments were not due until the tenth of the month. The handwritten change to that effect made by Corrigan on Milo's copy of the contract superseded the printed version. Milo did not have to add his initials simply because he was the party who benefited by the change. He could add his initials or signature if requested. Because either party might raise the point, it is a good preventive law practice for both parties to initial all changes and to do this on all copies of the contract.

3. If Words and Figures Are Inconsistent, the Words Prevail

One is less likely to make a mistake in writing a number in words than writing it in figures. Thus, words prevail over figures.

4. Where a Trade Custom or Practice Applies, Both Parties Are Presumed to Know It, and the Contract Is Interpreted in Light of That Trade Custom or Practice

Contracts often include implied terms because of some applicable custom or as a matter of reasonableness and propriety. Thus, a clause requiring "payment in cash" usually may be satisfied by check. Promised services must be performed with reasonable care and skill even when this is not stated. When no time for performance is mentioned, a reasonable time is allowed. Parties are always expected to act legally and fairly.

▼ ASSESS

Learning Objective 5 On the chalkboard, write the following sets of terms (not in the order given, which is correct): **(1) Handwritten additions, typewritten additions, printed provisions;** and **(2) Words, figures.** Have students write them in hierarchical order according to the way courts will interpret them.

By telephone, Swann ordered delivery of the *Daily Tribune* newspaper. He correctly assumed that he would be billed by mail at the end of the month. As was customary, the bill was then payable ten days after receipt.

Preventing Legal Difficulties

When you enter a contract . . .

1. If the contract is complex or involves much time or money, put it in writing even when not required to do so by the statute of frauds. Try to anticipate and provide for all important contingencies and possible problems. When appropriate, obtain the assistance of a qualified lawyer for drafting the contract.
2. If a prepared contract is presented to you for signature, read it carefully and with understanding, especially if it is a contract of adhesion. If the contract is important to you in terms of money, or if it is complex in details, have your lawyer review it before you sign.
3. Insist that any terms of the contract that you do not understand be defined and explained. Make necessary changes, or reject the entire contract.
4. Make sure that all changes are written into the contract on all copies as well as on the original, and that all changes are initialed by both parties.
5. Be sure all desired terms are expressed in the writing or incorporated (meaning included) by specific reference to any other relevant document(s).
6. When any payments have been made in cash, be sure to get a receipt if payment is not acknowledged in the contract. (If payments are made by check, indicate the purpose on the face of the check. The canceled check may serve as your receipt.)

▼ REVIEWING IMPORTANT POINTS

1. Unless so required by law, contracts need not be in writing to be enforceable.

Preventing Legal Difficulties

Discuss each of the six suggestions for preventing legal difficulties. Ask students to suggest scenarios that reflect the possible consequences of not following each of these suggestions.

▼ CLOSE

Have students use index cards to create game cards that contain the following three items, each one written on the faces of 18 cards, for a total of 54 cards: *handwriting, typewriting,* and *printing.* Then pair students, rotating pairs so all students can participate, to play a form of the card game *War* in which both students use their deck of cards and place one card down at the same time. The person who placed the highest card down (from highest to lowest—handwriting, typewriting, and printing) wins the round and the two cards. The student with the most cards at the end of the game wins.

Assign the following end-of-chapter materials:
Student text review activities, pp. 269–275
Workbook, pp. 35–40
Chapter Test

Chapter *MicroExam*

▼RETEACH Tape paper strips over all the boxes in column one on the overhead transparency master, *When There Are Conflicting Inconsistencies in the Wording of Written Contracts, Which Version Prevails?,* then make copies for students. Distribute copies and have students fill in the empty boxes.

▼ENRICH Make copies of the Chapter Outline for Chapter 13, found on pp. 163–165 of the Workbook. As a group activity, have students complete the outline and make copies for all students to keep.

Strengthening Your Legal Vocabulary

1. parol evidence rule
2. express contract
3. formal contract
4. executed contract
5. simple contract
6. implied contract
7. quasi contract
8. statute of frauds
9. executory contract
10. contract of adhesion

2. An express contract is stated in words, written or spoken. An implied contract is shown by conduct of the parties and by surrounding circumstances.
3. A formal contract must be in some special, written form. All contracts that are not formal contracts are simple contracts.
4. An executory contract has not been fully performed. An executed contract has been completed by both parties.
5. A quasi contract exists when some element of a valid contract is missing, yet is enforced as if it were a contract. This is done to prevent unjust enrichment of one party.
6. To be enforceable, the following contracts must be in writing (or evidenced by some other written proof) and signed by the party against whom enforcement is sought:
   - **a.** contracts to buy and sell goods for a price of $500 or more,
   - **b.** contracts to buy and sell real property or any interest in real property,
   - **c.** contracts that cannot be performed within one year after being made,
   - **d.** contracts to pay a debt or answer for a legal obligation of another person, and
   - **e.** contracts having marriage as the consideration.
7. A memorandum of an agreement need not be in any special form. However, it must contain all the material facts and must be signed by the party against whom the contract is to be enforced.
8. The terms of a written contract may not be changed by parol evidence unless the original writing is clearly ambiguous. Parol evidence may also be used to show that a written agreement is not binding because of mistake, fraud, illegality, or because a party was a minor.

STRENGTHENING YOUR LEGAL VOCABULARY

Match each term with the statement that best defines that term. Some terms may not be used.

contract of adhesion
executed contract
executory contract
express contract
formal contract
implied contract
notary public
parol evidence rule
quasi contract
simple contract
statute of frauds

1. Rule under which a written contract cannot be changed by prior oral or written agreements.
2. Contract in which the agreement of the parties is spoken or written.
3. Written contract that must be in a special form to be enforceable.
4. Contract that has been fully performed.
5. Any contract that is not a formal contract.
6. Contract in which intent of the parties is shown by conduct or circumstances.
7. Obligation that is enforced as if it were a contract in order to prevent unjust enrichment of one party.
8. Law stating that certain agreements are not enforceable unless they are in writing and are signed by the party against whom the contract is to be enforced.
9. Contract that has not been fully performed.
10. Contract in which the more powerful party dictates all the important terms.

APPLYING LAW TO EVERYDAY LIFE

1. Vancura and Trickett are competent adults. Under a written contract, Vancura bought Trickett's motor scooter for $800. Vancura gave Trickett a check for $300 as a down payment and took delivery of the scooter. On the way home, Vancura bought some gas at a self-service station. She then got a granola bar from a vending machine. How would these four contracts be classified as to method of creation, formality, and extent of performance?

2. ETHICS ISSUE Bruno bought Hummel's condominium under a written contract. The title was to be transferred in thirty days. Bruno then orally agreed to buy specified items of Hummel's furniture for the lump sum of $2,800. When she took possession of the condominium, however, she decided not to buy any of the furniture. Is Bruno legally permitted to change her mind this way without any legal liability to Hummel? Is such conduct ethical?

3. Central-Cal Lands Corporation orally agreed to sell a 640-acre producing ranch to Ceres, Inc., for $1,280,000. Ceres paid $25,000 and immediately took possession. Can Central-Cal legally withdraw from the

Applying Law to Everyday Life

1. The purchase of the motor scooter was an express (written), simple, executory contract even though the down payment was made by check. The fact that $500 was yet to be paid made the purchase contract executory. The check was an express (written), formal, executory contract ordering Vancura's bank to pay Trickett and to deduct the $300 from Vancura's account. The purchase of the gas was an express (oral) and implied (the self-service conduct), simple, executed contract. Buying the granola bar was a simple, implied, executed contract. Incidentally, all four contracts were bilateral and valid. (pp. 255–259)

2. ETHICS ISSUE Yes, the sale of the furniture was required to be in writing under the statute of frauds because it exceeded $500 in value. (p. 261) No, such conduct is probably not ethical. Because specified conduct is legal does not necessarily mean it is ethical and right. Interestingly, the reverse is also true. Because specified conduct is illegal does not necessarily mean it is unethical and wrong.

3. Yes, the oral contract for sale of land, even if followed by partial

payment and possession, is not enforceable. (p. 262) Yes, when, in addition to partial payment and possession, the buyer makes substantial improvements, the oral contract for land is enforceable. (p. 262)

4 No, the promise of the sons to pay the father's hospital bill was an original, direct, and primary promise; hence it was not required to be in writing. (pp. 263–264)

5 ETHICS ISSUE No, under the statute of frauds, a promise made in consideration of marriage must be in writing and signed by the promisor to be enforceable. (p. 264)

No, he should not break his promise. See answer 2 above. Under these circumstances both Cornelius and Barbara would be acting dishonestly and deceptively. Neither has acted ethically. In a sense, both are responsible for the resulting mess.

6 No, under the parol evidence rule, prior or contemporaneous oral agreements or promises may not be admitted as evidence to contradict an unambiguous, apparently complete, written contract. The writing presumably reflects the final intentions of the parties. (p. 266)

agreement? If Ceres spends $75,000 to level part of the land for improved irrigation purposes, can it now enforce the oral contract?

4 Kelley was admitted to University Hospital as an emergency heart transplant patient. The next day, the hospital's business manager discussed the cost of the surgery with Kelley's two sons. Both sons told the manager, "Do whatever is necessary to save his life, and we will pay you." When the hospital presented the staggering bill to the junior Kelleys, they said the contract was oral and, therefore, they were not liable. A promise to pay the debt of another (their father) had to be in writing. Is that true?

5 ETHICS ISSUE Cornelius, an elderly bachelor, was at the town cafe. In front of several witnesses who will vouch for the story, Cornelius made the following statement to Barbara, a young waitress: "I can't give you a castle in Spain. But, by gosh, if you marry me, I will deed to you a half interest in Meadowland Acres, the best farm in the county. And I'll transfer title to 75 cows, 200 hogs, and 5,000 chickens." Barbara said, "I will, I will," and they were married. Is Cornelius legally bound to keep his promise? If not, would it be ethical for him to break his promise? Would your answer be the same if Barbara had confided to a friend, "I'll marry the old geezer and then divorce him as soon as I can!" and she does just that?

6 In a detailed, written purchase contract, Trans-Continental Supply Corporation, a food distributor, agreed to buy a large quantity of beet sugar from Col-Rocky Mountaineers. Some sugar was delivered, but then Col-Rocky stopped all shipments. It claimed that Trans-Continental had breached an oral promise to make advance cash payments. Trans-Continental denied making the promise, and sued Col-Rocky for breach of contract. At the trial, Col-Rocky sought to introduce evidence of the alleged oral promise. Can it do so?

7 Silvio Development Company bought an insurance policy to cover the risk of damage to its corporate helicopter. For coverage, the standard printed insurance policy required that every pilot of the plane be licensed by the Federal Aviation Agency (FAA) and have a minimum of 500 logged (i.e., recorded by the pilot) *flying* hours. A typewritten addition specified that every pilot had to have a minimum of 200 logged *helicopter flying* hours. When the plane crashed, the pilot had logged only seventy-five helicopter flying hours. However, she was FAA licensed and had logged over 2,000 flying hours in conventional planes. Must the insurance company pay?

7 No, in the interpretation of contracts where the printed form and typewritten provisions conflict, the typewritten provisions prevail. (p. 268)

8 ETHICS ISSUE Arnold's parents adamantly refused to buy, or to let him buy, a car or truck when he turned sixteen. Arnold's second passion was music and he desperately wanted a six-unit audiophile system of computer direct-line components, complete with a digitally operated preamplifier and dual high-resolution 200-watt per channel power amplifier. The price was $1,895, payable over twenty-four months at $79 a month. When the owner of the Hear Here Now: Loud-n-Clear shop phoned, Arnold's father orally agreed to pay if Arnold failed to make any of the payments. Six months later, Arnold lost his part-time job and defaulted on the payment due. Must his father pay? What is an alternative legal solution to Arnold's problem, as a minor? Would it be an ethical solution?

9 When Torres leased an apartment from Leon, they used a printed form provided by Leon, the landlord. One sentence stated: "No advance deposits shall be required other than for one month's rent." However, Leon had typed in: "Tenant shall pay a $400 refundable cleaning and repair deposit upon taking possession. No charge shall be made for ordinary wear and tear." Torres drew a line through the $400 and wrote in $200. Both parties signed and each received a copy of the lease. Which provision governs the refundable deposit, the printed ($0), the typewritten ($400), or the handwritten ($200)?

10 ETHICS ISSUE Under a written contract, Cabrera bought a used sedan from Sharpe's Previously Owned Cars, Inc. The salesperson had knowingly falsely assured her that the car was in "tip-top condition...with just 45,000 miles driven by only one previous owner." Later, in checking official registration records, Cabrera discovered that the sedan had three previous owners and that the odometer had been set back from 70,000 miles. In court, Sharpe's attorney claims that the parol evidence rule bars introduction of the salesperson's false oral statements because there was an integrated written contract. Is the parol evidence admissable? Was the salesperson's conduct unethical? Was it criminal?

SOLVING CASE PROBLEMS

1 Between 1964 and 1973, Kiyosi served as a teaching associate and lecturer at Indiana University, Bloomington. Meanwhile, he continued to study and write to qualify for a Ph.D. degree. He relied on an oral promise by the defendant university that upon obtaining the degree, he would be appointed to a permanent position with perpetual renewals,

9 The handwritten $200 provision; The handwritten version is the most recent in time, and presumably it expresses the current intentions of the parties. (p. 268)

10 ETHICS ISSUE Yes, parol evidence may be introduced to prove fraud in an integrated written contract. (p. 266) The salesperson's conduct (and probably that of her employer) was unethical and criminal.

Solving Case Problems

1 Judgment for Kiyosi; The statute of frauds does not apply to contracts that are capable of being performed within one year. Kiyosi could die at any time and thus the contract for "lifetime employment" could be performed within one year. Death is possible at any time and is therefore the contingency which could render the agreement fully performed within one year. (pp. 262–263)

8 ETHICS ISSUE No, Arnold's father is not legally obligated to pay as he orally promised. However, most persons would probably say that he is ethically bound to pay. (pp. 263–264) As a minor, Arnold could return the equipment and get either a full or partial refund of the money paid to date, depending on the state. The solution would probably not be ethical in the eyes of most minors and adults. The contract was freely entered into by Arnold, with implied parental approval. There was no exploitation or over-reaching by the "Hear Here Now" shop.

starting at the rank of assistant professor. It was customary for the university to make such appointments for terms of three years. When Kiyosi received his Ph.D. in 1973, he was appointed assistant professor, but was told that he would not be reappointed for the following year of 1974–75. He then sued for damages for breach of contract. The university officials claimed that his action was barred by the statute of frauds because a lifetime contract cannot be performed within one year. You decide. (*Kiyosi v. Trustees of Indiana University,* 166 Ind. App. 34, 333 N.E.2d 886)

2 Hanan had been employed as a management consultant by Corning Glass Works for almost two years. On March 14, 1966, after two months of negotiations, Corning entered into an oral agreement to employ Hanan for a third year. The third year was to begin on May 1, 1966, at an annual salary of $25,000. Because this agreement could not be performed within one year, it was void and unenforceable under the statute of frauds. However, Hanan argued that he had already been employed for two years and had then continued on the job for twelve days into the third year. He admitted that there was only an oral contract for the third year. But he claimed that there was a contract implied in fact from the conduct of the parties, and that therefore the statute of frauds did not apply. You decide. (*Hanan v. Corning Glass Works,* 314 N.Y.S.2d 804, 35 A.D.2d 697)

3 Unit, Inc., was the general contractor for a real estate development owned by Sciota Park, Ltd. Unit subcontracted to plaintiff Wilson Floors Company the job of furnishing and installing flooring materials. When Unit fell behind in making promised payments for completed work, Wilson stopped work. The Pittsburgh National Bank had already loaned $7 million to Sciota for the project, which was now two-thirds completed. The bank representatives orally assured Wilson that if it returned to work, it would be paid. Wilson did so and finished the job. When Wilson was not paid, it sued Unit, Sciota Park, and the Pittsburgh Bank for the $15,443.06, plus interest. Wilson received judgment. When Sciota and Unit failed to pay, Wilson sought recovery from the bank. But the bank claimed it was not liable because a promise to pay another's debt had to be in writing. You decide. (*Wilson Floors Co. v. Sciota Park, Ltd.,* 54 Ohio St. 2d 451, 377 N.E.2d 514)

4 For safekeeping, Kula deposited $18,300 with the cashier of a hotel casino and was given a receipt for the money. Kula and a friend, Goldfinger, gambled in the hotel's casino. (Casino gambling is legal in Nevada.) Kula made withdrawals and deposits from time to time with

2 Judgment for Corning; Hanan himself testified that there was an oral contract for the third year. This contradicted any reliance on a contract implied from conduct. The statute of frauds applied, since the contract entered into on March 14 (for one year beginning May 1) obviously could not be completed within one year. The contract would have had to be in writing and signed by Corning to be enforceable. (pp. 262–263)

3 Judgment for plaintiff Wilson; In deciding whether an oral promise to pay the debt of another is enforceable, the court may apply either one of two tests: (1) Did the promisor become primarily liable on the debt? (Here, the bank did not; Both Sciota and Unit were primarily liable.) (2) If the promisor did not become primarily liable, was the oral promise made to serve the promisor's own business or pecuniary interest? (Here, the bank clearly induced Wilson to finish the job in order to serve its own interest as the holder of the mortgage on the construction loan. It must therefore pay Wilson and seek recovery from Sciota and/or Unit. To hold otherwise would be to use the statute of frauds to inflict a wrong rather than to prevent one.) (pp. 263–264)

4 Yes, even if the plaintiff had promised to guarantee the gambling debts of his friend to the amount of $18,000, he was not bound because of a statute which states that "every special promise to answer for the debt, default or miscarriage of another" is void unless evidenced by some note or memorandum in writing. (pp. 263–264) (Note: Although not legally bound to do so, the plaintiff did honor his oral guarantee to pay $1,000 of Goldfinger's debt.)

the casino cashier and at the time had a balance of $18,000. One evening Goldfinger lost $500 in gambling and was unable to pay it. He asked the shift boss, Ponto, to telephone Kula for a guarantee of the loss. Ponto did so and received Kula's authorization to give Goldfinger credit up to $1,000 but no more. Ponto confirmed this but stated that Kula had also said Goldfinger could gamble the entire deposit of $18,000. Goldfinger was permitted to gamble until he lost $18,000. The casino tried to collect the amount from Kula on his alleged oral promise to cover Goldfinger's debt to $18,000. The casino did this by refusing to return to Kula the amount he had on deposit. Kula was willing to honor his oral guarantee of Goldfinger's debt up to $1,000 but no more. Kula sued the hotel for return of his deposit. Should he get it? (*Kula v. Karat, Inc.*, 531 P.2d 1353)

5 Nicolella, a building contractor, was asked by Palmer to submit a bid for the construction of an addition to a food market. After reviewing the plans and specifications for the addition, Nicolella bid $57,027 for the job. Two revisions of the written plans were subsequently made by Palmer. Thereafter, the parties entered into a written contract. At the time of its execution, Nicolella orally asked Palmer if changes in the plans would materially affect the bid and Palmer said no. Palmer added that if there were any substantial changes, the price paid would be adjusted. After the start of construction, Nicolella discovered that 1,340 square feet had been added to the building. Palmer orally urged Nicolella to continue and said that any additional amount claimed would be paid. Upon completion of the job, Nicolella asked for an additional $10,653, based on the original price per square foot. Palmer refused to pay, so Nicolella sued, alleging that Palmer's statements had been made fraudulently. Could the terms of the original written agreement be varied by any prior or contemporaneous promises made by Palmer? Was Palmer bound by his later oral promise to pay any additional amount claimed by Nicolella? (*Nicolella v. Palmer*, 432 Pa. 502, 248 A.2d 20)

5 No, judgment for Palmer; There was an integrated, apparently complete, written contract between the parties. Under the parol evidence rule, it may not be changed by prior or contemporaneous oral agreements as attempted by Nicolella here. An exception is made in the case of fraud, but it is not enough for the plaintiff to say that the oral statement about square footage was false or even that it was made fraudulently. To overcome the parol evidence rule, Nicolella would have to prove that the false statement was fraudulently omitted from the integrated written contract (or omitted by accident or mistake). That was not done. (p. 266)

No, Palmer's oral promise to pay more for completion of the building was likewise unenforceable. Palmer received no consideration for this new promise because Nicolella was already bound by contract to complete the building. (See Chapter 11.)

CHAPTER 14 ORGANIZER

Chapter Theme

Contractual duties and obligations can be ended in a variety of ways.

DIRECTED STUDY QUESTIONS	SPECIAL FEATURES	PROGRAM RESOURCES				
		Reteach	Enrich	SN	AM	
Can contractual rights be assigned?		✔	✔		A	
Can contractual duties be delegated?	Personal Perspectives, p. 280	✔	✔		V	
What are the rights of an assignee?	Thinking Critically Through Visuals, p. 282	✔	✔			
How are contracts usually discharged?	Writing Connections, p. 283	✔	✔			
In what other ways can contracts be discharged?	Multicultural Highlights, p. 286 Thinking Critically Through Visuals, p. 287 Ethics Issue, p. 288	✔	✔		K	
What is the effect of tender of performance?	Preventing Legal Difficulties, p. 289	✔	✔	✔		

Additional Resources

- Calamari, John D., and Perillo, Joseph M. *Calamari and Perillo's Hornbook on Contracts*, 3rd ed. St. Paul, MN: West Publishing Co., 1987.
- Corbin. *Corbin on Contracts*. St. Paul, MN: West Publishing Co., 1970.
- Privette, Mari W. *Sign Here?: Everything You Need to Know About Contracts.* Garden City, NY: Doubleday, 1985.
- *Restatement of the Law, Contracts*, 2nd ed. St. Paul, MN: American Law Institute Publishers, 1981.
- Trachtman, Michael G. *What Every Executive Better Know About the Law.* NY: Simon & Schuster, 1987.

One-semester course	✔	✔	✔					
One-year course	✔	✔	✔	✔				

Chapter Pacing Guide

	ASSESSMENT OPPORTUNITIES			
Cooperative Learning	Informal Assessment	Chapter Review	Chapter Test	Chapter *MicroExam* (Media)
	✔	✔	✔	✔
	✔	✔	✔	✔
	✔	✔	✔	✔
	✔	✔	✔	✔
✔	✔	✔	✔	✔
	✔	✔	✔	✔

Videodiscs

Discharge of Contract

Search Chapter 18, Play To 19

State by State

A court in New York held that a corporation that installed the piping in a nuclear power plant did not breach its contract when its price went from $39 million to $300 million.

Teaching Materials

Student text, pp. 276–295

Overhead transparency masters
- *Assignment of Rights and Delegation of Duties*
- *How Are Contracts Ended?*

Videos
- *Contracts, Warranties, and Credit* Videotape
- *Law for Business* Videodisc

Workbook, pp. 41–42

Outside Resources
- Index cards
- Examples of contracts or legal agreements
- Highlighter marking pens
- Newspaper or magazine articles on contract disputes and/or discharging contracts
- Guest speaker: lawyer, paralegal, or law-school student
- Coat hangers, string, and colored construction paper
- 2′ × 2′ sheets of cardboard
- Post-it™ Brand notes

- Camcorder
- VCR

Assessment
- Chapter Test

- Chapter *MicroExam*

Vocabulary

assignment, p. 278
assignor, p. 278
assignee, p. 278
performance, p. 278
delegation of duties, p. 279
novation, p. 280
obligor, p. 281
discharge of contract, p. 282
substantial performance, p. 282
diminished value rule, p. 282
breach of contract, p. 283
anticipatory breach, p. 283
substitution, p.285
accord, p. 285
satisfaction, p. 285
accord and satisfaction, p. 285
alteration, p. 288
tender, p. 288
legal tender, p. 289

Learning Objectives

When you complete this chapter, you will be able to

1. Explain the difference between assigning contractual rights and delegating related duties.
2. Identify the rights of assignees.
3. Describe customary and unusual ways that contracts are discharged.
4. Discuss tender of performance.

276

Chapter Self-Test

Assess students' understanding of contractual obligations before they begin Chapter 14 by having them brainstorm a class list on a flip chart of terms they associate with contracts. Review and discuss students' responses. In a second column, have students brainstorm how contracts might be terminated. After students complete the chapter, return to the flip chart and revise any misconceptions they had.

CHAPTER 14

ENDING CONTRACTUAL OBLIGATIONS

1 Your parents contract to have a new house built. Shortly after, your father's employer promotes him. The new position requires a move to corporate headquarters in Atlanta, Georgia, which is 2,000 miles away. Must he accept the promotion? If he does, can your parents transfer their rights and duties under the building contract to someone else without becoming liable for breach of contract?

2 ETHICS ISSUE Your school orders fifty new uniforms for its marching band. The contract states that "time is of the essence," and if the goods are not received in time for the first public performance by the band on September 1, the old uniforms will be used for another year. The manufacturer does not deliver the uniforms until September 3. Can the school cancel the contract? Would it be ethical for the supplier to delay the delivery until October 10 because of a rush order from another school which provided a higher profit?

3 A friend of yours is under contract to play professional basketball. His knee is injured during the second game of the season, and he will be unable to play for the remainder of the current season. Does he remain on the team payroll?

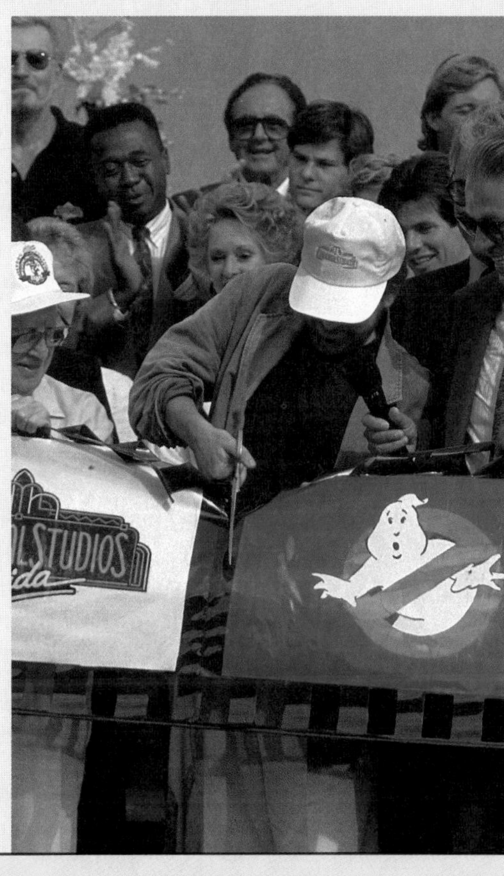

▼ FOCUS

Before class begins, write the following question on the chalkboard for students to answer individually on a sheet of paper: **What kinds of contracts have you entered into?** (Answers may include school contracts to do assignments, sales contracts, employment contracts, and so on.)

Have students share what acts or terms might legally end such contracts. (Paying the outstanding balance, fulfilling the duties of the contract, and so on)

◆ You Decide ◆

1 No, he need not accept unless his employment contract so specifies. Yes; Your parents may assign their rights and duties to another person or arrange a novation.

2 ETHICS ISSUE Probably not; When no significant loss is caused by the delay, time is not critical and the contract cannot be canceled for that reason. No; It would be both unethical and illegal. The time delay of more than a month would properly trigger the essence clause because presumably it would cause a significant loss.

3 Probably, if he is expected to return, but his compensation and status would depend on the terms of his contract.

Thinking Critically Through Visuals

This photograph was taken at the opening of Universal Studios in Florida. If you wanted to use the *Ghostbusters* logo why, do you think, would you have to contact Universal Studios? (Answers may include that Universal Studios owns the logo and all contractual rights to its licensing and usage.)

▼ TEACH

Ensure that students understand that, unless prohibited by statute or contract, a person can often transfer his or her contractual rights to another so long as performance is not materially changed. Provide examples of cases when such assignment would be upheld by a court (such as a bank transferring a mortgage or payment to a car dealer who sells your contract) and when it would not (such as a publisher contracting with a writer to deliver specific services personally).

▼ APPLY

Divide the class into two groups. Ask the first group to brainstorm a written list of five more examples of assignment and the second group to list five examples of contracts that cannot be assigned. Verify students' work before bringing the two groups back together as a class. (Keep the lists for use in the next section.) **Guided Practice**

Ask 10 volunteers (one by one) to read aloud their example. For each, have a trio of students role-play the two parties in the original contract (one of whom is the assignor) and have the third person play the assignee. After role-playing is completed, discuss why each contract could or could not be assigned.

Independent Practice

▼ CAN CONTRACTUAL RIGHTS BE ASSIGNED?

PROBLEM

Whippet bought a high-powered sports coupe from the Oriental Motordome for $32,000. After a down payment of $2,000, the balance, plus a finance charge, was to be paid in installments over the following forty-eight months. Oriental Motordome needed cash to restore its inventory of new cars. Therefore, it immediately sold Whippet's contract to the Jee-Em-See Finance Company and told Whippet to make all installment payments to Jee-Em-See. Is such a transfer of contract rights legal?

Persons frequently have contractual rights that they transfer to others. Such transfer is called an **assignment**. The party who makes the assignment is the **assignor**. The party to whom the assignment is made is the **assignee**.

Generally, unless prohibited by statute or by the contract creating the right, a party may assign any rights to another, provided performance will not be materially changed. **Performance** is the fulfillment of contractual promises as agreed. Frequently, assignments of future wages are prohibited or limited by statute. A right to collect a debt is assignable because performance remains the same after assignment. In the problem, when Whippet was notified of the assignment, he became obligated to pay Jee-Em-See instead of Oriental Motordome. Retailers and restaurants assign to issuers of credit cards the right to collect the amounts due from customers who have used the cards. In exchange, the credit card companies immediately pay the retailers and restaurants the face amount of the credit slips, less an agreed percentage.

Contract rights may not be assigned if performance would be materially (i.e., importantly) changed thereby or become substantially more difficult. For example, *A* has a claim against *B* for $1,000. *A* may not assign that claim in 2,000 parts to the 2,000 students at Central High. Rights that may not be transferred include the following:

1. claims to damages for personal injuries,
2. claims against the United States, and
3. rights to personal services, especially those of a skilled nature, or when personal trust and confidence are involved.

Ford, a dentist, owed Bentin $5,000 for office furniture. Bentin agreed to accept $1,000 in cash and $4,000 in orthodontic services for his

▼ ASSESS

Learning Objective 1 To help students understand the difference between assigning contractual rights and delegating related duties (the law does not usually allow assigning duties), copy the following comparison chart (with side and top headings only) on the chalkboard or an overhead transparency. Have students complete the chart, revising their responses as necessary.

	Assignment of Rights	Delegation of Duties
What Is Transferred	Contractual rights	Routine contractual duties
Exceptions	Provided performance will not be materially changed	Where personal skills or special qualities are required
Responsibilities	Not released from contractual duties	Still liable for proper performance

children as payment for the debt. Soon after, Bentin needed the money, so he assigned his right to receive the dental services to Lakely. Unless Ford consented, this assignment would not be valid because it included rights to personal services of a skilled, professional nature.

Assignment of contractual rights is usually made voluntarily by the assignor. It may also occur automatically by operation of law, as when one of the contracting parties dies. Then the *decedent's* (i.e., deceased person's) rights are assigned to the decedent's personal representative (executor, executrix, administrator, or administratrix of the estate). Assignment also occurs by operation of law when a trustee in bankruptcy receives title to a debtor's assets.

Ordinarily, an assignment may be oral or written, but statutes sometimes require that certain assignments be in writing.

CAN CONTRACTUAL DUTIES BE DELEGATED?

PROBLEM

Ramirez hired Norton to come to her home and care for her two young children while she was at work. Could Norton legally delegate the child-care duties to a well-qualified third party?

Routine contractual duties may be transferred to another party. This is known as **delegation of duties.** However, a person cannot delegate to another any duty where performance requires unique personal skill or special qualifications. Thus, in the problem, Norton cannot delegate the duty of caring for the children because it involves special qualifications of trust and skill.

A person who delegates contract duties remains legally obligated and responsible for proper performance even though someone else may actually do the required work. Thus, a general contractor who agrees to build a house is responsible for providing the finished structure as promised. However, general contractors typically delegate most of the work to independent subcontractors. Subcontractors are specialists who lay foundations and do masonry, carpentry, plumbing, electrical, painting, and other work. The general contractor makes individual contracts with them and pays them as agreed. The subcontractors are responsible to the general contractor for proper performance. But the general contractor remains responsible to the buyer for the finished job. The general contractor, in a separate contract, may also assign to a bank the right to collect all or a percentage of the

TEACH

Point out the difference between assignment (transfer of contractual rights) and delegation (someone other than the original contractor complies with the duties or provides the required services, but the original contractor is still responsible for satisfactory performance to the holder of the contractual rights). Make and distribute two lists of services: one of duties which are often transferred (such as duties of electrical subcontractors) and another of duties which are seldom transferred (such as child-care services). One by one, explain why each of your examples is in its respective list.

APPLY

Display the overhead transparency master, *Assignment of Rights and Delegation of Duties.* As the class views the visual, ask a volunteer to read aloud the last paragraph on p. 279. Verbally, walk through the contract between the home builder and the home buyer. Select individual students to explain the basic contract, the potential assignment of rights, and possible delegation of duties. **Guided Practice**

RETEACH Have students identify the three contractual rights that may not be transferred because performance would be importantly changed. (Claims to damages for personal injuries, claims against the U.S., and rights to personal services)

ENRICH Have individual students make up three examples of each right identified in the RETEACH activity and write each on an index card. Shuffle the cards. Pair each student with a partner who has completed the RETEACH activity and have the partner correctly categorize the example.

Make photocopies of a variety of contracts, such as a credit-card application, car-rental agreement, or health-spa contract, or have students bring in samples. (You may wish to reuse examples of contracts from earlier chapters.) In small groups, have students peruse the documents for language relating to assignment of the contract or delegation of duties and use highlighter marking pens to identify such clauses. In the absence of this language, have students determine whether the duties could be assigned or the rights transferred. **Independent Practice**

Personal Perspectives

Have students ask family members for examples of contracts or agreements into which they may have entered, if they are willing to share this information. Have students find out if any duties of the contract were delegated or transferred. Have students anonymously report their findings to the class by summarizing their examples on a *Home Contracts* tally sheet posted at your classroom door. Tabulate which duties and rights were most frequently delegated or assigned, then have students hypothesize why.

purchase price from the buyer. This is often done even before ground is broken so that the general contractor can buy materials and pay for labor.

Torelli operated a high-quality graphic design and printing shop. Geramov contracted to have Torelli design and print 25,000 brochures in full color promoting a variety of international tours by plane, ship, and chartered bus. Under their contract, Torelli also agreed to address and mail envelopes containing the brochures to a select list of prospects provided by Geramov. Torelli's employees did all the work involved except the addressing, stuffing of the envelopes, and mailing. These tasks were delegated to Moreno Mailers, Inc., a specialist in that field. This was a valid delegation because only the design and production required Torelli's special skills. Moreno was accountable to Torelli for proper mailing; Torelli remained liable to Geramov for proper completion of the entire job.

Sometimes a contracting party will both assign rights and delegate duties.

The Pyramid Builders, a ready-mix concrete company, received more orders than it could fill on schedule. Therefore it arranged to have a competitor, Gibraltar Rock and Stone, Inc., supply certain customers. Pyramid would bill the customers and turn over the proceeds to Gibraltar, after deducting a commission for Pyramid's assistance. If the concrete delivered was faulty, Pyramid remained liable to the customer for damages. In turn, Gibraltar would be liable to Pyramid if Gibraltar were at fault.

A party entitled to receive performance under a contract may release the other party from the duty of performance and accept a substitute party. This is neither assignment nor delegation of duties. It is a **novation**; in effect, a new contract is formed by agreement of the three parties who are involved.

Revell had contracted to install a skylight in the roof of Sinclair's workshop. Because of pressures to complete other jobs before the rainy season began, Revell asked Sinclair if she would accept a qualified substitute carpenter named Lowry. Lowry was willing to do the job for the same price. All three parties were agreeable. By novation, Lowry took Revell's place in the original contract, thus releasing him from all duties to perform and depriving him of all rights to be paid.

▼ ASSESS

Learning Objective 2 Have students create a flowchart to explain their answer to the following question: **What happens to the rights and duties of the obligor, the assignor, and the assignee when an assignment is made?** (Answers may include that the assignor must notify the obligor, preferably in writing; the assignee has the same obligations and rights as the assignor; and the obligor is liable to the assignee for performance.)

WHAT ARE THE RIGHTS OF AN ASSIGNEE?

PROBLEM

Ginsburg, a distinguished concert violinist, purchased "a genuine Stradivarius violin" from Krone for $150,000. Ginsburg paid $50,000 down and agreed to pay the balance in twenty-four equal monthly installments along with an annual carrying charge of 18 percent. Krone knew the violin was not a Stradivarius. Therefore, he immediately assigned his right to collect the balance of $100,000 to the Continental Finance Company. In return, Continental gave Krone $90,000 in cash. Krone then disappeared. Shortly after, Ginsburg discovered the fraud. Can she now refuse to pay Continental if it tries to collect?

Courts sometimes say that the assignee "stands in the shoes of the assignor." This means that the assignee receives exactly the same contractual rights and duties as the assignor had—no more and no less.

To protect newly acquired rights, the assignee should promptly notify the obligor—orally or in writing—of the assignment, preferably before the assignment is made. The **obligor** is the *debtor*—the one who owes the money or other obligation. Until notified, the obligor has no reason to assume that the contractual obligations have been changed and may continue to pay the original creditor. After notification, however, the obligor is liable to the assignee for performance.

In making an assignment, the assignor does not promise to make good if the obligor fails to perform, unless this is specifically required by the assignment. However, the assignor does guarantee that he or she has a right to assign and that the assigned right is legally enforceable. Thereafter, the assignor may not legally or ethically collect the assigned claim unless the money is accepted for prompt payment to the assignee.

In the problem, Ginsburg can claim fraud. Because Continental now stands in the place of Krone, Ginsburg can refuse to pay Continental. This is true even though Continental is an innocent third party. Also, if Krone is located, Ginsburg can sue him for damages caused by the fraud and Continental can sue him for the $90,000. Krone may also be criminally liable.

HOW ARE CONTRACTS USUALLY DISCHARGED?

PROBLEM

Wesley loaned Hudson $900 to be repaid within three months. When the debt was due, Hudson did not have the money. But she offered to

TEACH

Discuss students' ideas of what it means to "stand in someone else's shoes" and relate this to the relationship between an assignee and an assignor. Point out that it is the duty of the assignor to notify the obligor, or debtor, of the change caused by the assignment.

APPLY

Be sure students understand the terms **assignee**, **assignor**, and **obligor** by having them identify the roles of Ginsburg (obligor), Krone (assignor), and Continental (assignee) in the PROBLEM at the top of p. 281. Ask: **What is another name for obligor?** (Debtor) **Guided Practice**

Have students research your state statute(s) as to what happens when a person knowingly and fraudulently assigns a right to an assignee then disappears. Ask students to identify whether or not this is a criminal act in your state (most likely, yes), whether it is a misdemeanor or a felony, and the mandated punishment. **Independent Practice**

TEACH

The overwhelming majority of all contracts are discharged by full performance or by substantial performance. Point out that if most people did not keep their promises, our court system would collapse under the weight of contractual litigation.

RETEACH Assign students to work in small groups to review the first two boxed examples on p. 280. For each, have them identify the **obligor**, the **assignor**, and the **assignee**.

ENRICH Divide the class in two. Have the first group draw a cartoon illustrating a contract in which the assignee *"stands in the shoes"* of the assignor. Have the second group use the same characters, but illustrate a novation. Bring both groups together to compare and contrast their illustrations.

give Wesley an aquamarine ring that had a retail value of about $1,000, and a wholesale value of perhaps $500. Must Wesley accept the ring instead of payment, thus discharging Hudson from her contractual obligation?

When a contract is made, the parties take on certain duties or obligations. **Discharge of contract** is a termination of obligations that occurs when the parties perform as promised. It may also take place when a party is released from contractual responsibilities by action of the other party or by law. Generally, contracts are discharged by full performance; most parties perform as promised. Partial performance does not suffice. Frequently, however, complex contracts are discharged by **substantial performance.** This occurs when there is only a minor modification or failure to fulfill all terms of the contract. The performance is incomplete but substantial. An appropriate allowance is made in the price to cover the deviation. Moreover, the buyer is entitled to the difference in the value of the product (such as a house) as it stands substantially completed, and its value if built in strict compliance with the contract plans and specifications. This is known as the **diminished value rule.** If the deviation is deliberate, the victim may treat it as a breach.

Kitchen Construction Company, Inc., remodeled the kitchen in the Hamill's mid-Victorian house. The new built-in cabinets were made of top-grade plywood instead of solid wood as specified in the contract. (The mistake was caused by an error in the contractor's purchasing

▼ **APPLY**

Have students create a two-column chart. In the first column, have them identify the ways a contract can be discharged, as discussed on pp. 282–284. (Discharge of contract, substantial performance, breach, anticipatory breach) In the second column, have students briefly describe each. **Guided Practice**

Have students add a third column to their charts. Individually, have them give examples of each kind of contract that was discharged. Share responses as a group. **Independent Practice**

Thinking Critically Through Visuals

The pickup in this photograph was ordered in the U.S. from an overseas manufacturer. What legal recourse does the truck-buyer have if the pickup does not arrive exactly as—or when—ordered? (Answers may include discharging the contract by substantial performance or canceling the order due to breach of contract.)

▼ **ASSESS**

Learning Objective 3 Have each student write his or her own learning contract for this course (including all that must be done to receive the desired grade and thus discharge the contract). Then have students identify what actions would constitute a breach of contract. Review the contract with the individual student who wrote it and, if amenable to you, agree to the terms and sign the contract.

department.) The substituted materials were actually more durable. The Hamills were not aware of the difference until a friend whose hobby was woodworking pointed it out. However, the contract had been substantially performed. Therefore, the Hamills were responsible for the full price less a deduction for the lower cost of the plywood.

Failure to perform in accordance with the contractual terms is a **breach of contract;** this gives the other party the right to cancel. Sometimes a party who *defaults* (i.e., fails to perform) notifies the other party to a contract before the time of performance has arrived that he or she will not perform. This is called an **anticipatory breach.** The victim may wait until the promised time of performance, or the victim may treat the default as a breach of contract and immediately sue for damages.

On January 5, Graham Roofers contracted to remove the old shingles and to install a new fireproof roof on the home of the Sterlings. The job was to be completed "by March 30, at the latest," to be ready for anticipated heavy spring rains. Late in February, Graham notified the Sterlings that because of a rush of orders, his crews were "swamped" and could not get to the job until late April or early May. This was an anticipatory breach. The Sterlings have the choice of waiting for performance or immediately proceeding as though Graham had breached the contract.

When one party breaches a contract, the other party may regard her or his obligation as discharged or terminated. In sales contracts under the Uniform Commercial Code (UCC) this is termed a cancellation, which is discussed more fully in Chapter 15.

A contract calling for payment of money requires payment of the exact amount on the specified date. The creditor to whom the money is owed need not accept a substitute. Therefore, in the problem, Wesley need not accept the ring, but if she does, Hudson's obligation to pay the $900 is discharged.

Usually bank checks are given in payment of sizeable debts that are payable in money. Receipt of the check suspends the debt while the check is processed in the banking system. The debt is discharged when the check is honored (i.e., paid) by the bank on which it was drawn.

When a contract states that performance must be completed on or before a specified date, and that "time is of the essence," failure to perform by that date is generally regarded as a breach of contract. However, if no loss is caused by a delay, time is not critical. In such cases, the "essence" clause may be ignored by the courts. When no precise date is specified, performance within a reasonable time suffices. What is "reasonable" depends on all

Writing Connections

Language Arts
Have students brainstorm, write (using a computer, if possible), and exchange with a classmate a business letter about a company that has not fulfilled a contract with them. (Examples might include a yearbook or class-ring order, a purchase of defective goods, and so on.) Using appropriate style for writing a business letter, students should state the terms of the contract, the obligation that was not fulfilled, and what course of action they took or would like to take to end the contractual obligation. Post students' letters on a bulletin board and allow students time to read their classmates' work. Discuss selected letters, the options chosen to end the contracts, and other alternatives students may suggest.

RETEACH Following text pp. 281–284 as a guide, have students work in pairs to outline the key clauses for a contract for a (fictitious) service to be performed by a set date, including a "time is of the essence" clause.

ENRICH Using the RETEACH contracts as a springboard, have students identify in writing, using a computer, if possible, any number of the contracts that might be discharged. Ask students to give an example of how each contract could also be breached.

▼ TEACH

Display the overhead transparency, *How Are Contracts Ended?*, to underscore that contracts can be discharged in ways other than by complete or substantial performance. Give students examples of contracts discharged by agreement, impossibility of performance, or operation of law, using the important points under each numbered section on pp. 284–288 as a guide for a subsequent discussion.

Discuss the concept of *impossibility of performance*. Circumstances may make it extremely difficult, unusual, or impossible for one or both parties to fulfill the terms of the contract; it is immaterial that the terms are too costly or time-consuming.

▼ APPLY

Obtain, or have students obtain, newspaper or magazine articles dealing with contract disputes or methods of discharging contracts. After reading each article, have students suggest clever headlines that include the method of discharge for each contract. Post the article under the headline, created graphically with a graphics computer program, if possible, on a bulletin board for this chapter.

Guided Practice

relevant circumstances. In case of litigated dispute, it becomes a question of fact for the jury to decide.

▼ IN WHAT OTHER WAYS CAN CONTRACTS BE DISCHARGED?

PROBLEM

Diaz was the owner of a landscape service. He contracted to maintain the yard of Reingold while she sailed around the world in a forty-five-foot yacht. Reingold planned to write and take photographs for a national magazine and had no fixed itinerary or schedule for the journey. When would the contract with Diaz terminate?

In addition to discharge by complete or substantial performance, a contract may be discharged by:

1. agreement,
2. impossibility of performance, or
3. operation of law.

1. By Agreement

When the parties prepare their contract, they may agree that it will terminate:

- **a.** on a specified date or upon the expiration of a specified period of time (e.g., a fresh food supply contract on the last day of school);
- **b.** upon the happening of a specified event (in the problem, the contract to maintain the yard would terminate when Reingold returned from her voyage around the world);
- **c.** upon the failure of a certain event to happen (e.g., a construction loan contract upon failure to get a required building permit); or
- **d.** at the free will of either party upon giving notice (e.g., when one partner decides to retire from business and gives the required notice as specified in the partnership agreement with her associates).

The parties who have made a contract may later mutually agree to change either the terms of the contract or the nature of their relationship. They may do so without any liability for breach.

By rescission the parties may agree to unmake or to undo their entire contract from its very beginning. Each party returns any consideration already received, and both are placed in their original positions in so far as possible. (See the fuller discussion of rescission in Chapter 15.) Or they may decide

▼ ASSESS

Learning Objective 3 Have students create a spider map identifying five ways a contract may be discharged. (Complete or substantial performance, agreement, impossibility of performance, and operation of law) Then, have them add an example of each in additional spokes on the map.

that the present contract is not what they want, and so they replace it with a new one. This discharges their original contract by **substitution**. The parties may also agree to change the obligation required by the original contract. An agreement to make such a change is an **accord**. Performance of the new obligation is called a **satisfaction**. A compromise of a disputed claim or a composition of creditors (see pages 214–215) is an accord. Carrying out the new agreement is the satisfaction. Thus, the previous obligation is discharged by an **accord and satisfaction.** Also, as you may recall, a contract can be terminated, and a new one formed, through novation (see page 280).

Vanvoor borrowed $650 from Banta. Vanvoor could not repay the loan on schedule. The parties then agreed that Vanvoor would work off the debt by doing thirty hours of painting, electrical, and plumbing work in Banta's home during the next three months. The agreement to change the required performance was an accord. Vanvoor's completion of the agreed-upon work was the satisfaction. Together, this accord and satisfaction discharged Vanvoor's original obligation to pay $650.

2. By Impossibility of Performance

As a general rule, a contract is not discharged when some unforeseen event makes performance more costly or difficult for one of the parties. For example, increased prices of needed supplies, a strike of needed workers, difficulty in obtaining materials or equipment, or a natural disaster (such as a flood or earthquake) may delay performance. Generally, these events do not discharge the contractual obligations; they should be anticipated as possibilities and be provided for in the contract when it is made. Otherwise, a party who fails to perform because of such events could be held liable for breach of contract.

Sundstrum was a wholesaler. He contracted to supply various airplane parts to Arcadia Airport at a price of $17,686. However, Sundstrum later defaulted. He claimed that it was impossible to deliver at the contract price because manufacturers had increased their prices to him by more than $8,600. The court held him to the contract. The fact that the contract was no longer economically profitable did not mean that it was legally and physically impossible to perform.

However, the parties may, and commonly do, include "escape hatch" language in their contracts. Such language permits modification, or even termination, of performance without liability for damages in the event of

Divide the class into three groups and assign to each group one of the three additional ways in which a contract can be discharged. Have students write and perform a skit about a contract that is discharged by the means assigned to them. Share the skits and have class members share which words or actions indicated the manner of discharge. **Independent Practice**

You may wish to invite a lawyer, paralegal, or law-school student to class to explain the many ways a contract can be discharged. Have class members prepare questions in advance.

Divide the class into groups of four, five, or six students to plan, then visually present, a contract to be discharged. In each group, allow students to select their role: parties to the contract (two) and lawyer (one or two per party). Invite another class to act as the jury, (or have the students who are not currently role-playing do so), by listening to the proceedings, reading applicable law, and determining whether or not the contracts may be discharged as requested. **Cooperative Learning**

▼RETEACH Ask students to reread the five boxed examples on pp. 285–287. Have students give reasons to explain why each contract was discharged as indicated.

▼ENRICH Media Working in pairs, have students brainstorm and write, using a computer, if possible, three examples of contracts discharged by impossibility because of destruction of subject matter, by the performance being declared illegal, or by death or disability of the party providing personal services under the terms of the contract.

Multicultural Highlights

To most people, legal terminology may seem like a foreign language. For others, it really is a foreign language! A person should never sign a contract—or any other document—if he or she does not understand what it states. However, not all people entering into contractual agreements in the United States understand English well enough to be able to interpret the documents they sign. Have students brainstorm and share with the class five suggestions to help limited- or non-English speakers when they find themselves faced with a proposed contract. (Answers may include having an attorney or legal-aid provider read and explain all clauses and provisions of a contract, and so on.) You may wish to have a native speaker of another language translate the class's suggestions into his or her own language for future reference.

inability to perform on schedule because of specified conditions, such as foul weather and labor strikes.

Also, under unusual circumstances recognized by the UCC, a contract for the sale of goods may be discharged by conditions that make performance impracticable. Increased cost alone is not enough. But a possibility not thought of by the parties, such as a surprise war or an unexpected *embargo* (i.e., legal stoppage of commerce) may suffice. Even a shutdown of major supply sources could discharge the contract if it prevented the seller from getting supplies or if it caused an extreme increase in cost beyond what could reasonably be anticipated.

Other situations in which a contract is discharged by impossibility include the following.

Destruction of the Subject Matter. Sometimes performance depends on the continued existence of some specific thing. Destruction of that thing terminates the contract if the destruction was not the fault of the party who is sued for nonperformance.

Blitz was a famous jockey. He contracted to ride the thoroughbred White Flash in the Kentucky Derby. A week before the race, the horse stumbled during a workout, broke a leg, and had to be destroyed. Blitz's employment contract was discharged. He was free to contract to ride another horse in the Derby.

The result of destruction of the subject matter is different if the seller has other sources of supply and the parties did not specify one and only one source as acceptable. For example, suppose that because of a fire, a wholesale lumber broker loses one supply source. If the broker has access to other sources of lumber, and if her contract does not limit her to one particular source, she is legally bound to deliver, at no higher price, lumber previously ordered by a buyer. This is true even if the broker's resulting cost is much higher than she had anticipated.

Performance Declared Illegal. A contract that is legal when made is discharged if and when it later becomes illegal. Illegality might be caused by a new statute, by a court ruling, or by an administrative decision.

Tippner contracted with Barnell to build a warehouse on land owned by Barnell. Before construction began, the city council passed a zoning ordinance restricting the site to residential dwellings. The construction contract was thereby discharged.

ASSESS

Media **Learning Objective 3** Have students create a mobile of the additional ways in which contracts are discharged by impossibility of performance. (Destruction of the subject matter, performance declared illegal, and death or disability) Using a coat hanger, string, and construction paper, have students create one tier for each of the three ways, label it, and provide visual and textual examples. Display the mobiles in your class for the rest of the chapter.

Death or Disability. If the contract requires personal services, death or disability of the party who was to provide such services terminates the agreement. This rule does not apply when others are available to perform, as in partnerships or corporations that continue to do business. Likewise, it does not apply where the contract simply calls for payment of money, delivery of goods, or transfer of title to land by the decedent. In each such case, the decedent's personal representative can and is required to perform.

The *Daily Tribune* contracted for the consulting services of Chi Liang, a computer expert, at a rate of $400 a day. Liang agreed to supervise the installation of a system of computers with integrated software programs. The *Tribune*'s newsroom, pressroom, circulation and advertising departments, and business office were all included. After Liang had completed his work linking the newsroom and pressroom, he suffered a stroke and was unable to continue. Liang's contractual obligation was discharged by impossibility.

3. By Operation of Law

A contract may be discharged or the right to enforce it may be barred by operation of law. This happens when the promisor's debts are discharged in bankruptcy. It also happens when the time allowed for enforcement of the contract has elapsed because of the statute of limitations.

Thinking Critically Through Visuals

This football player was injured during a game and he will be unable to play for several more games. Has he, do you think, breached his contract? (The death or disability clause probably does not apply, as the football player will be able to play again; In the meantime, other players could play his position.)

Divide the class into several smaller groups. Ask each group to create their own board game (such as *Chutes and Ladders*) based on the participants working through a series of contracts that are discharged in one of the manners identified in this chapter. Students may wish to use 2′ x 2′ cardboard to make their gameboard, Post-it™ Brand notes or index cards for game questions, and other classroom items as game pieces. Allow time for students to play each game, then select their favorite.

RETEACH Have students review, outline, and give examples of the ways that a contract can be discharged by impossibility of performance. (See pp. 285–287.)

ENRICH Have students work in pairs to take turns writing, then videotaping, news broadcasts for the evening news. Tell students that their topic is a high-interest (but fictitious) human-interest story on a contract discharged by impossibility of performance. Play the tapes for the class.

Ethics Issue

Unfortunately, some people do not go through appropriate channels to alter a signed contract. This can result in innocent parties believing they have to fulfill the conditions of a changed (and possibly now non-binding) agreement or incur unanticipated legal fees to either defend themselves or have a contract legally discharged. A person who illegally alters a contract can be taken to court and may have to pay damages to the other party or honor the original contract. Have students discuss ways they can protect themselves in future contract situations (such as making sure they understand what they sign, initial changes, and so on). Have students summarize their class discussion on a poster called, *Protect Yourself!*

Alteration of a written agreement also usually discharges the agreement by operation of law. **Alteration** is a material change in the terms of a written contract without consent of the other party. To discharge the contract, the alteration must be:

a. material, thus changing the obligation in an important way;
b. made intentionally, and not by accident or mistake;
c. made by a party to the agreement, or by an authorized agent; and
d. made without consent of the other party.

Carey's Complete Cleaners contracted to clean all rooms and public spaces of Dahl's office building. A contractual clause in small print allowed a 10 percent discount if the charges were paid in advance in one lump sum instead of in twelve monthly installments. After the contract had been signed by both parties, and before giving Dahl her copy, Carey secretly crossed out the clause referring to the discount. This material alteration discharged Dahl from any obligation under the contract. Dahl could thereupon insist on inclusion of the clause or seek damages through court action.

WHAT IS THE EFFECT OF TENDER OF PERFORMANCE?

PROBLEM

Zamorsky, a professional artist, agreed to paint Quincy's portrait for $5,000. Five sittings of two hours each were scheduled at times selected by Quincy, but he failed to appear for any of them. To accommodate her client, Zamorsky then offered to come to Quincy's home or office for rescheduled sittings at his convenience. Quincy rejected this proposal. Is Zamorsky's legal obligation discharged? Is Quincy liable for damages?

An offer to perform an obligation is a **tender**. If the obligation requires the doing of an act, a tender that is made in good faith but is rejected will discharge the obligation of the one offering to perform. In the problem, Quincy refused Zamorsky's offer to perform as agreed. Thus, Zamorsky's obligation was discharged, and Quincy is liable for damages.

If the obligation requires the payment of money, rejection of an offer to pay the money does not discharge the debt nor does it prevent the creditor

TEACH

Point out the difference between an obligation that requires the doing of an act (tender of performance) and an obligation that requires the payment of money (tender of payment).

ASSESS

Learning Objective 4 Have students explain *tender of performance* and what a *tender of payment* does to an obligation. (An offer to perform an obligation; it does not discharge an obligation to pay money, but IT does relieve the debtor of possible court costs and future interest charges that might otherwise become due.)

from collecting later. It merely relieves the debtor of court costs or future interest charges that might otherwise become due. To be valid, the tender of money must consist of the exact amount due in legal tender. **Legal tender** is currency or coins—including Federal Reserve notes—of the United States of America. Checks are not legal tender, but as noted earlier, they are frequently given and accepted, conditional on payment by the bank on which they are drawn.

Preventing Legal Difficulties

To protect yourself...

1. As a prospective assignee, determine whether the assignor is subject to any defense that may affect your claim. Do this by promptly checking with the obligor (i.e., debtor). Remember that you, as the assignee, acquire only such rights as the assignor possessed.
2. Do not forget that the assignor does not agree to pay the debt if the debtor fails to do so. If you wish the assignor to remain liable, include a provision to that effect in the written assignment agreement.
3. Be sure to notify the obligor (i.e., debtor) of the assignment as soon as practicable.
4. Be aware that "time is of the essence" in many contracts. If a contract calls for performance by a certain time, failure to perform may be a breach of contract. When appropriate, include this requirement in your contract, and clearly state that failure to perform at the time agreed upon may be treated as a breach.
5. Remember that hardship and higher costs do not make performance impossible. Hardship could be caused by bad weather, fires, strikes, inability to obtain materials, or similar difficulties. To be protected against damages for failure to fulfill a contract because of such events, include a clause in the contract to that effect.

▼ REVIEWING IMPORTANT POINTS

1. A party may generally assign rights under a contract as long as the performance will not thereby be materially changed. One is not released from contractual duties by making an assignment.

▼ APPLY

Have students read the PROBLEM on p. 288 and identify the tender of performance offered. (The act of painting the portrait) **Guided Practice**

Using a computer, if possible, have individual students explain why personal checks are not legal tender. (Answers may include that a check is not backed by the U.S. government; it can be canceled or not be backed by sufficient funds.)

Independent Practice

Preventing Legal Difficulties

To help prevent legal difficulties when entering into a contract, have students read the five items on p. 289. Have students brainstorm examples that may apply to them, then discuss possible remedies. Have students record their responses in their notebooks or law journals.

Have students who experience difficulty understanding the concept of **tender** carefully reread the paragraphs on pp. 288–289 and outline the two scenarios given: an obligation to perform without payment of money (such as a service) and an obligation requiring the payment of money.

In pairs, have students choose, then write, two scenarios: the first, a situation in which a person's legal obligation requires the payment of money and the second requiring an obligation to perform an act or service.

▼ CLOSE

Much of the conceptual understanding of this chapter revolves around comprehension of the new vocabulary identified on p. 276 of the Teacher Edition. Assist your weak readers, speakers of non-standard English, and dyslexic students to better understand the terms by having them make their own crossword puzzles, using the *Glossary of Legal Terms* as the basis for their definitions. After completing their crossword (with an answer key), have the creator exchange his or her paper with a

partner and complete a puzzle.

Assign the following end-of-chapter materials:
Student text review activities, pp. 289–295
Workbook, pp. 41–42
Chapter Test
Chapter *MicroExam*

2 Some contractual duties may be delegated but duties may not be delegated when they involve personal judgment or skill, as with artists and professional experts. When duties are delegated, the original party remains liable for proper performance.

3 An assignee acquires only such rights as the assignor has under the contract. The assignee takes the rights subject to any existing defenses, such as prior payment or other performance.

4 Until notification of assignment is received, the obligor is justified in believing that performance may still be properly made to the original contracting party.

5 Contracts are usually discharged by performance or by substantial performance.

6 A breach of contract generally permits the other party to regard his or her obligation to perform as discharged. The same is true in anticipatory breach of contract. In either case, the victim may seek damages in court.

7 Discharge by agreement of the parties may be accomplished by doing any of the following:

a. including provisions for termination in the contract,
b. rescinding the existing contract,
c. substituting a new contract,
d. replacing a party through novation, or
e. making an accord and satisfaction.

8 Difficulty of performance of unforeseen high costs generally do not relieve a promisor of the obligation to perform. However, contractual duties may be discharged because of actual impossibility when:

a. the subject matter is destroyed,
b. a change in the law makes performance illegal, or
c. either party dies or becomes disabled, if the contract required the personal services of the individual.

9 The obligation of one party is discharged when a written contract is materially and intentionally altered by the other party without the consent of the former.

10 An obligation calling for an act is discharged by a tender of performance that corresponds exactly to the agreement. A tender of payment does not discharge an obligation to pay money. It does relieve the debtor of possible court costs and future interest charges that might otherwise become due and payable.

STRENGTHENING YOUR LEGAL VOCABULARY

Match each term with the statement that best defines that term. Some terms may not be used.

accord	discharge of contract
accord and satisfaction	legal tender
alteration	novation
anticipatory breach	obligor
assignee	performance
assignment	satisfaction
assignor	substantial performance
breach of contract	substitution
delegation of duties	tender
diminished value rule	

1. Agreement to change a contractual obligation, and the performance of the new obligation.
2. Transaction by which a party transfers contractual rights to another.
3. Notification, before the scheduled time of performance, of refusal to perform contractual terms as agreed upon.
4. Termination of contractual obligations.
5. Currency or coins of the United States.
6. Material change in the terms of a contract, made intentionally by one party without consent of the other.
7. Fulfillment or accomplishment of the contract as promised.
8. One who transfers contractual rights.
9. Turning over to another party one's routine duties under a contract.
10. One to whom contractual rights are transferred.

APPLYING LAW TO EVERYDAY LIFE

1. ETHICS ISSUE Zack bought an automobile insurance policy. The policy contained a clause prohibiting assignment of the policy without written consent of the insurer. Later, when his car was stolen, Zack notified the insurer. After six months, during which the car had not been recovered, Zack assigned to Pragg his claim for payment under the policy. The insurance company refused to pay because it had not given its written consent to the assignment. Must the insurance company pay? Was the insurance company ethical in refusing payment of Zack's claim?

Strengthening Your Legal Vocabulary

1. accord and satisfaction
2. assignment
3. anticipatory breach
4. discharge of contract
5. legal tender
6. alteration
7. performance
8. assignor
9. delegation of duties
10. assignee

Applying Law to Everyday Life

1. Yes; The prohibition against assignment became meaningless after the car was stolen and not recovered during a reasonably long time. Until then, the insurance company could be legitimately concerned about the record and reputation of the insured (Zack) and could reject a substitute. The obligation of the insurance company to pay for the loss arose at the time the theft occurred and was reported. At that time, Zack had not made an assignment. (p. 278) No, it was unethical. Pragg, by virtue of the assignment, was legally and ethically entitled to the payment.

2 No; Because of the anti-assignment clause, the transaction would require the consent of Holee Donuts. Some courts would hold that the assignment could be made without the specified consent, but then the assignor would be liable in damages for any loss proved. (p. 278)

3 No; The employment contract was personal in nature, involving skill and experience and cannot be assigned without the consent of the other contracting party. (p. 278)

4 Yes; Olefson assigned his rights and delegated his duties to Ogden. But Olefson remained responsible for proper performance to Bradmaker after Ogden defaulted. (p. 281)

5 No; Duties under a contract may not be delegated when they involve personal skill. (p. 279) If all parties agreed, a novation or substitution could be negotiated. (p. 280)

6 Probably, yes; Failure by one party to perform the obligations of a contract (breach of contract) gives the other party the right to cancel it. (p. 283) Ohler should not have accepted orders beyond its capacity to deliver. No; The outbreak of war and the resulting government rationing orders would make performance of the contract illegal. (pp. 285–286)

2 Cullen purchased a Holee Donuts franchise. The contract contained a clause that forbade transfer of the business without consent of the franchisor. After six years of successful operation, Cullen wanted to sell the business to his manager. Was he legally permitted to do this?

3 Mercado contracted with Hidden Valley School District to provide a bus and to serve as the driver for a five-year period. After two years, Mercado died and his adult son became owner of the bus. He proposed to become the driver and complete the remaining three years of the contract. Must Hidden Valley accept his services?

4 Bradmaker operated a profitable lunch bar in a downtown business district. He sold the business to Olefson for $60,000. Olefson was to pay 25 percent down and the balance in equal monthly installments over a five-year period, with interest at 10 percent a year on the unpaid balance. Olefson later assigned the contract to Ogden with Bradmaker's knowledge and consent. By then only $30,000 of the debt remained to be paid. Within six months, however, Ogden closed the lunch bar. He also stopped making payments. Bradmaker sued Olefson for the unpaid balance. Is Olefson liable?

5 Ferrazzi, a distinguished Italian sculptor, contracted to create a large bronze abstract design for the lobby of the Martindale Mart. He was to receive $75,000 upon its completion and installation. Shortly thereafter, Ferrazzi was injured in an accident. Unable to fulfill his agreement, he asked his friend Drinano to do the work for him. Drinano was an equally competent sculptor. Must Martindale Mart accept Drinano's services?

6 Ohler Oil Company contracted to sell and to deliver 500 barrels of fuel oil on the first of each month for one year to the Monson Mushroom Factory (an indoor farm). Ohler delivered the oil for the first two months, but none during the third month. Ohler said there was unprecedented demand and it was allocating available supplies to all customers. Monson notified Ohler that it was canceling the contract because of Ohler's breach. Was Monson justified in its action? What would your answer be if a war had broken out in the Middle East and Ohler was simply complying with governmental orders to ration the limited supplies?

7 ETHICS ISSUE The Laroffs had looked for a long time to find the right color paint for the exterior of their recently remodeled home. Finally, they contracted with Redi & Able Painters to do the job. Paint brand, color, and quality were specified in the contract. It was also specified that two coats would be applied by brush, not sprayed or

7 ETHICS ISSUE Redi & Able Painters had breached the contract. The fact that the wrong color was used was a major deviation of the contract terms; therefore, there was no substantial performance. (pp. 282, 283) No, it would not be ethical or legal. It would be highly presumptuous for them to make the changes "because we are experts." Failure to inform the Laroffs would also be unethical and illegal, and tainted by deceit or fraud.

rolled on. One week later, when the Laroffs came home from a vacation, they were dismayed to find their dream house painted in the wrong color. Also, they learned that the paint had been sprayed on and that only one coat had been applied. It was not the brand of paint that the Laroffs had specified. But it was a more expensive brand, and the maker guaranteed that "one coat covers any surface." Had Redi & Able Painters breached, or had they substantially performed the contract? Would it be ethical for Redi & Able to make the changes "because we are experts and are better qualified than you to decide such questions"? What would your answer be if they used the correct color but deliberately failed to inform the Laroffs about the other changes?

8 Davie Dare and his Daredevils, a rock group, attracted record crowds in concert appearances. The quintet signed a contract with Grandiose Studio to appear in three motion pictures for specified salaries plus a percentage of the box-office receipts. Their first movie was a "bomb" and lost money. Davie and his associates blamed the script, the director, the producer, and the advertising and promotional efforts for the film's failure. They found another studio that was willing to star them in the remaining two films. Grandiose is anxious to get out of the project completely. What might be a suitable solution?

9 In January, Doolan Construction Company promised to remodel Kemper's kitchen during July when Kemper would be visiting relatives in Canada. Their written contract called for work to start on July 1, and to be completed before August 2. In April, Doolan phoned and said he could not start the job before July 20, if then. What can Kemper do?

10 Tina, aged seven, was playing accountant at her father's desk in his absence. When she found a stack of interesting papers, she "corrected" all of them, adding zeros to numbers ("500" thus became "5000") and drawing lines through words. The "interesting papers" were promissory notes, owned by her father, representing claims against debtors totaling about $17,000. Have these contractual claims been discharged by the alterations?

▼ SOLVING CASE PROBLEMS

1 Eugene Plante was a general contractor who built a house for Frank and Carol Jacobs for a contract price of $26,765. The buyers paid $20,000 but refused to pay the balance, claiming that the contract had not been substantially performed. Plante sued, and the court ruled in his favor but first deducted the cost of repairing plaster cracks in the ceilings and

8 Grandiose could transfer its rights and duties under the contract to ZYX Productions. It would remain contingently liable to the Dare group, however. Therefore it should enter into a novation, with ZYX Productions replacing Grandiose in the contract with the Daredevils Group. (p. 280)

9 Doolan has committed an anticipatory breach of the contract. Kemper may immediately seek out another contractor who will do the remodeling during July, and then sue Doolan for damages as measured by any extra price Kemper has to pay. Kemper could also permit Doolan to perform late, and then sue for any damages that could be proved. (p. 283)

10 No; The changes were not made by a party to the contracts or by an authorized agent. They were made innocently by a young child with no intent to destroy their legal effect, albeit with misguided intent to improve them. (pp. 278, 284–285)

Solving Case Problems

1 Judgment for plaintiff Plante; There was no evidence that the Jacobses requested or demanded moving the wall while the house was under construction, nor was there any evidence that Plante deliberately deviated from the expressed wishes of the defendants. There were no blueprints and the stock plan provided did not show details of construction. To move the wall now would cause unreasonable and an unjustified economic waste. Under the diminished value rule, the trial court properly found that the defendants had suffered no legal damage since experts agreed that the misplacement of the wall had no effect on the market price of the property. (p. 282)

❷ Judgment for the Walkers, the defendants; As assignee of the contract, Associates got nothing more than the assignor Partin had to give. All of the Walkers' defenses against the assignor, Partin, are also good against the assignee, Associates. Here, the defense was that the condition which had to be met before payment was required—the increase in milk production—was not met. (p. 278)

❸ Judgment reversed; Swanola was awarded $250 plus interest (and 20 percent of the principal and interest as attorney fees provided for in the contract). After Tanner committed the anticipatory breach, Swanola had the option of either canceling the contract and keeping the deposit or enforcing payment of the full consideration—which is what it did. (p. 283) After Tanner's anticipatory breach, Swanola had no duty to complete and deliver the ball gown or otherwise tender performance "because the law does not require a vain and useless act."

❹ No; Difficulty of performance and unprofitability do not make a contract impossible to perform and discharge the obligation. (pp. 285–286)

a number of other defects. The buyers were dissatisfied with the judgment and appealed, notably because the trial court had allowed nothing for the misplacement of a wall between the kitchen and the living room. This enlarged the kitchen and narrowed the living room by one foot. Real estate experts testified during the trial that this did not affect the market price of the house, yet to move the wall would cost about $4,000. How should the appellate court decide? (*Plante v. Jacobs*, 103 N.W.2d 296, Wis.)

❷ Partin sold a mechanical water softener to the defendants, Earl Walker and his wife Billie, for their dairy farm. Although a written installment contract was signed by the Walkers, Partin orally agreed that if milk production did not increase enough to pay for the machine, Partin would remove it without charge. Partin also orally agreed not to assign the contract. In fact, he did assign the contract to the plaintiff, Associates Loan Company. The Walkers made no payments, but Partin and a successor did. Ultimately, the softener was removed because milk production did not go up as promised. Associates sued the Walkers to collect the balance due. Who should win? (*Associates Loan Company v. Walker*, 416 P.2d 529, N.M.)

❸ In August, Tanner contracted to pay $300 to the Swanola Club to have his minor daughter participate as one of eight maids in the following year's carnival ball. Tanner paid $50 down, but one month later, he notified Swanola that his daughter would not participate because it might interfere with her college studies. He failed to pay the balance of $250 due before December 15. The contract gave Swanola "the option either to cancel the agreement and retain the cash portion paid as damages, or, in the alternative, to enforce payment of the entire consideration." Tanner claimed that Swanola was not entitled to the full contract price because it had never tendered performance by delivering the ball gown and other items as agreed. (Tanner's daughter had been measured for her gown by the Swanola dressmaker. Also, the daughter had found time to participate as a maid in a ball sponsored by another organization that same carnival season.) Only seven maids appeared in the Swanola ball. Six months after the ball, Swanola sued for the $250 balance. The trial court allowed Swanola to retain only the $50 deposit. Swanola appealed. You decide. (*Swanola Club v. Tanner*, 209 So. 2d 173, La.)

❹ The defendant, Sunset Packing Company, contracted to buy Schafer's strawberry crop. It also contracted to furnish 150–200 laborers to harvest the crop beginning June 1. A recruiting fee of $15 per laborer was to be paid by Schafer, who gave Sunset a check for $2,000 as advance payment. Sunset recruited the laborers in Texas, but they went to Idaho to work in the sugar beet harvest. Two days before June 1, Sunset notified Schafer that it would be impossible to supply the laborers as agreed upon. Sunset said, however, that it would make available 100 laborers from its own labor force if Schafer would pay Sunset an extra $20 per ton of harvested strawberries. Schafer then recruited his own labor force, but at a greater cost. Later he sued Sunset for $17,880 in lost profits. Sunset claimed that it was discharged from its contractual obligation because of impossibility of performance. Do you agree with Sunset? (*Schafer v. Sunset Packing Company of Oregon*, 474 P.2d 529, Or.)

5 The *Washington Trader* was a giant oil tanker owned by the plaintiff, American Trading and Production Corporation. In March 1967, the defendant, Shell International Marine, Ltd., contracted for the ship to carry a load of oil from Texas to India. The total fee agreed upon was $417,327.36. No reference was made in the contract for the route to be taken; this was to be a decision of the shipping company. The route around Africa's Cape of Good Hope was an acceptable route; however, the price was based on passage through the Suez Canal (the invoice contained a Suez Canal toll charge). The *Washington Trader* headed for the Mediterranean Sea and the Suez. When the ship reached Gibraltar, it was warned of possible violence in the Middle East. Nevertheless, it continued. Upon reaching the Suez Canal, the ship found the canal closed by the Arab-Israeli War. The ship turned back and took the long route around Africa, at an added cost of $131,978.44. It arrived in Bombay some thirty days later than originally expected. American Trading then billed Shell for the full amount; when Shell refused to pay, it sued. American claimed that the war made it impossible to perform as originally agreed. Shell, it said, should pay the extra cost because otherwise Shell would be unjustly enriched. You decide. (*American Trading and Production Corporation v. Shell International Marine, Ltd.*, 453 F.2d 939, 2d Cir.)

5 Judgment for Shell; The contract called for transit to India at a fixed price and made no reference to any particular fixed route. Reference to Suez Canal tolls merely indicated that this would be the probable route because it was the shortest. American Traders was not excused from performance because of strict impossibility. Moreover, the theory of commercial impracticability does not apply. (pp. 285–286) The blockage of the Canal added less than one-third to the original cost. This is not a sufficiently extreme and unreasonable added expense such as would constitute commercial impracticability. (Note: It is noteworthy that the ship's captain had been alerted to the worsening Suez conflict situation when his ship was at the other end of the Mediterranean Sea, at Gibraltar, yet did not change course as he should have.)

CHAPTER 15 ORGANIZER

Chapter Theme

Generally, persons who are parties to a contract have certain rights or duties under the contract; including the right to breach. The injured party has various rights and remedies under the law.

DIRECTED STUDY QUESTIONS	SPECIAL FEATURES	PROGRAM RESOURCES				
		Reteach	Enrich	SN	AM	
Who has rights under a contract?	Thinking Critically Through Visuals, p. 298	✔	✔		V	
What remedies does the injured party have?	Thinking Critically Through Visuals, p. 301 Writing Connections, p. 303	✔	✔	✔	A	
How are damages measured?	Multicultural Highlights, p. 304 Ethics Issue, p. 305	✔	✔			
Can the injured party ever be denied a remedy?	Personal Perspectives, p. 307 Preventing Legal Difficulties, p. 308	✔	✔		K	

Additional Resources

- Calamari, John D., and Perillo, Joseph M. *Calamari and Perillo's Hornbook on Contracts*, 3rd ed. St. Paul, MN: West Publishing Co., 1987.
- Caplan, Suzanne. *Saving Your Business: How to Survive Chapter 11 Bankruptcy and Successfully Reorganize Your Company.* Englewood Cliffs, NJ: Prentice Hall, 1992.
- Corbin. *Corbin on Contracts*. St. Paul, MN: West Publishing Co., 1970.
- *Restatement of the Law, Contracts*, 2nd ed. St. Paul, MN: American Law Institute Publishers, 1981.
- Summers, Mark Steven. *Bankruptcy Explained: A Guide for Businesses.* NY: John Wiley & Sons, 1989.

One-semester course	✔	✔	✔					
One-year course	✔	✔	✔	✔	✔			

	ASSESSMENT OPPORTUNITIES			
Cooperative Learning	**Informal Assessment**	**Chapter Review**	**Chapter Test**	**Chapter *MicroExam*** Media
	✔	✔	✔	✔
✔	✔	✔	✔	✔
	✔	✔	✔	✔
	✔	✔	✔	✔

Videodiscs

Breach of Contract

Search Chapter 19, Play To 20

State by State

In Washington, when contracts call for simultaneous or concurrent performance, the party who fails to pay is barred from suing the other party who fails to render promised services, and vice versa.

Teaching Materials

Student text, pp. 296–316

Overhead transparency masters
- *What Are the Basic Remedies for Breach of Contract?*
- *How May an Injured Party Lose the Remedy for a Breach of Contract?*

Videos
- *Contracts, Warranties, and Credit* Videotape
- *Mock Trial: A Question of Facts* Videotape
- *Law for Business* Videodisc

Workbook, pp. 43–48

Outside Resources
- Blank overhead transparencies
- Poster paper
- Newspaper and magazine articles

- Tape recorder
- Camcorder

Assessment
- Chapter Test

- Chapter *MicroExam*

Vocabulary

incidental beneficiary, p. 298
third-party beneficiary, p. 299
remedy, p. 299
waiver, p. 300
rescission, p. 301
cancellation, p. 301
special or consequential damages, p. 302
mitigate, p. 302
compensatory damages, p. 304
nominal damages, p. 304
liquidated damages, p. 305
outlawed debt, p. 306
bankruptcy, p. 308

Learning Objectives

When you complete this chapter, you will be able to

1. Identify two types of beneficiaries, who are not parties to the contracts.
2. Describe the basic remedies available for victims of breaches.
3. Define four types of damages awarded by courts.
4. Discuss how injured parties can be denied remedy through a delay in suing or through bankruptcy of debtors.

296

Chapter Self-Test

Assess students' understanding of the remedies for breach of contract before they begin Chapter 15 by directing their attention to the Learning Objectives listed on p. 296. Divide the class into four groups, assigning to each group responsibility for carrying out a different learning objective—without making use of material in the chapter. Review and discuss students' responses before continuing with the chapter.

CHAPTER 15

REMEDIES FOR BREACH OF CONTRACT

❶ While under contract with the county, Pyramid Paving improperly applies asphalt to the public gravel road in front of your family's home. Soon after application, large cracks appear and your father sues Pyramid for damages, "asserting his rights as a taxpayer and co-owner of the road." Will he win?

❷ ETHICS ISSUE A college football coach has directed his team to division championships five times. With two years remaining in his current three-year employment contract, he notifies the college president that he is resigning in order to coach a professional team at a higher salary. Is the coach legally free to change employers? Is he acting ethically? Is the professional team legally free to hire him? What can the college legally do?

❸ ETHICS ISSUE You were hired to work as an aide at a youth camp in Alaska for three months, beginning on June 10. Because of an increase in camp fees and air fares, enrollment drops sharply. After the first two-week session, the director no longer needs your help, and so she fires you. Is the director acting legally? Is she acting ethically? Do you have any legal remedy?

Thinking Critically Through Visuals

The building in this photograph, although not yet fully constructed, looks abandoned. What evidence supports this inference? (Answers may include the broken glass, growing grass, and so on.) **Based on the situation you have described, who, do you think, is the injured party?** (Answers may include the construction company, if the buyer breached the contract; or the buyer, if the construction company breached the contract.)

FOCUS

Before class begins, write on the chalkboard the chapter title, *Remedies for Breach of Contract.* Have students use the letters in the title to write as many legal terms as they can. (Answers may include contract, minor, mediator, and crime.)

Direct students to watch the second half of the *Contracts, Warranties, and Credit* videotape. Write the definitions of **breach** and **remedy** on the chalkboard, and ask students to find the definitions in the videotape. Review answers with students, then ask them to discuss information that they learned about remedies for breach of contract. Have a volunteer record the responses on an

overhead transparency or on poster paper to use in the CLOSE activity.

You Decide

❶ No; As a taxpayer he is only an incidental beneficiary of contracts made by government agencies, and he has no "standing to sue."

❷  No; The coach has breached his employment contract. No; He does not have the ethical right to do so. No; It is a tort to intentionally interfere with an existing contractual relationship, as in this case. The college could seek a negative injunction barring the coach from leaving and bringing legal suit.

❸  Although she does not have the legal right to fire you, her action is ethical since your services no longer are required, but you do have legal remedy.

▼ TEACH

Make certain that students understand that all of us are, to some extent, incidental beneficiaries of contracts made by others. A third-party beneficiary under a contract has rights, but not reciprocal duties.

▼ APPLY

Tell students to imagine that a new brand of sneakers called "RunAbouts" are to hit the stores soon. Ask students to name the persons contractually involved in creating and distributing the sneakers. (Answers may include rubber manufacturer, leather manufacturer, and retail stores.) Ask: **Who will be the incidental beneficiaries?** (Athletes, children, and so on) **Guided Practice**

▼ WHO HAS RIGHTS UNDER A CONTRACT?

PROBLEM

Shortly after Royter was born, his elderly uncle bought an endowment life insurance policy naming Royter as the beneficiary. The policy was to mature when Royter reached age eighteen or when the uncle died, whichever came earlier. The proceeds were intended for Royter's college education. Although the insurance company and the uncle were parties to the endowment contract, does Royter have any legal rights under it that he could enforce in court?

When valid contracts are performed, the immediate parties enjoy their legal rights to receive the benefits promised. As explained in Chapter 11, each party gives and each receives valuable consideration. In addition, many persons who are not the contracting parties benefit indirectly from countless contracts executed by others over the years. Our nation's farms and factories; wholesale warehouses and retail stores; and the extensive distribution system utilizing trucks, trains, ships, and planes are the result of a maze of interrelated contracts. Everyone who uses these facilities or enjoys their products and services is an incidental beneficiary of the many related contracts required to do the work involved. An **incidental beneficiary** is a person who benefits from a contract yet is not a party to the contract and may not sue to enforce it.

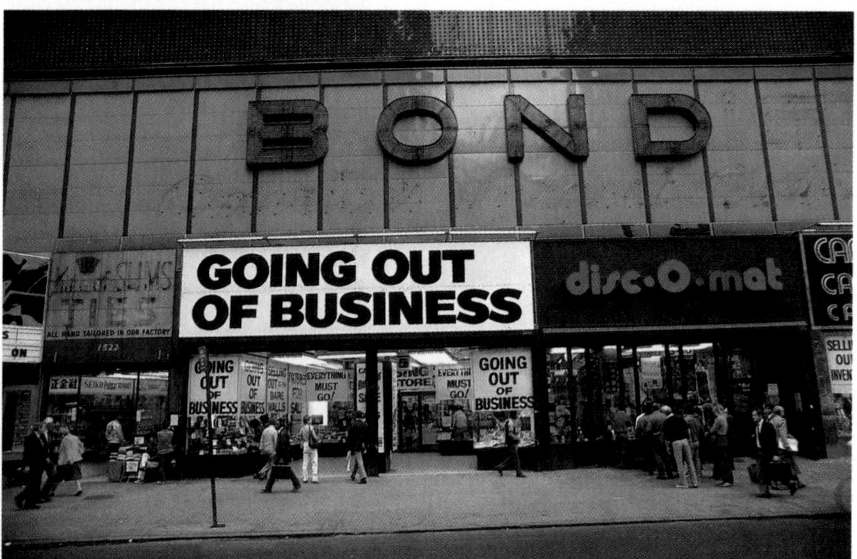

Thinking Critically Through Visuals

A store in this photograph is going out of business. What incidental beneficiaries may be affected by the store's closing? (Answers may include the shoppers, the distributors of the goods sold in the store, truckers who delivered the goods to the store, and others who had shopped at the store.)

▼ ASSESS

Learning Objective 1 Write the following on the chalkboard, and have students complete the sentences on a sheet of paper: **(1) People who benefit from a contract but are not parties to the contract and may not sue to enforce it are ______.** (Incidental beneficiaries); and **(2) Third-parties for whose express benefit the contract is made by others are ______.** (Third-party beneficiaries).

In general, only parties who have entered into a contract have enforceable rights under it. This is true even though other persons gain advantages from the contracts. There are two important exceptions to this rule:

1. most enforceable rights arising under a contract can be transferred to a third person by assignment and can then be enforced by the assignee, as discussed in Chapter 14; and
2. when a contract is made with the primary intention of benefiting a third person, that person is entitled to enforce the agreement.

Accordingly, contracts made specifically for the benefit of a third party can usually be enforced by that person. The **third-party beneficiary,** then, is the one for whose express benefit the contract is made. Life insurance contracts are the most common form of third-party beneficiary agreements. Parents, for example, in contracts with insurance companies, often name their children as beneficiaries. In the problem, because Royter was a third-party beneficiary, he could compel the insurance company to pay him when the policy *matured* and the face value became due.

WHAT REMEDIES DOES THE INJURED PARTY HAVE?

PROBLEM

A large new shopping mall scheduled its grand opening for November 30 to take advantage of the pre-Christmas buying rush. Eve Everling planned to open her Top-T-Bottom sportswear shop in one of the thirty small retail store spaces in the mall. In a construction contract, Designs, Inc., assured her that all cabinets and other interior work would be completed by November 10. On October 15, the manager of Designs, Inc., told Everling that her crews were working double shifts on the two "anchor" department stores in the mall. "Sorry, but we really can't get you in before December 15, if then." Everling immediately hired another firm to do the job. It finished on November 12, but charged 25 percent more. Does Everling have any enforceable claim against Designs, Inc.?

When one party to a contract refuses to perform or fails to perform properly, the other party suffers a legal injury. The injured party is entitled to be "made whole" and to get "the benefit of the bargain." Accordingly, such victim of a breach may seek any one of several remedies. A **remedy** is the means to enforce a right or to compensate for an injury. Remedies vary with

Challenge students to use the terms **incidental beneficiary** and **third-party beneficiary** to state the rule about enforceable contracts. **Independent Practice**

TEACH

Ask students to call out synonyms for the term **remedy**. (Answers may include cure, treatment, or correction.) Discuss the four remedies for breach of contract found on pp. 300–304. Covering the cartoons, display the overhead transparency, *What Are the Basic Remedies for Breach of Contract?*, to explain the four ways to respond to a broken contract. Use the space under each remedy to write definitions and key phrases.

Emphasize that the purpose of damages for breach of contract is to "make whole" the injured party, not to punish the person who breached the contract.

APPLY

Discuss the option of a waiver, found on the top of p. 300, then explain the reasons why someone would give up a contractual right. **Guided Practice**

RETEACH Guide students to create a graphic organizer describing each of the following terms: **incidental beneficiary** and **third-party beneficiary.** Then pair students to compare their graphic organizers and discuss the differences between the two terms.

ENRICH Have students create a rebus or puzzle using new or unfamiliar terms from this section.

Working in groups of four or five, have students brainstorm additional reasons why a person might waive a legal right. On the chalkboard or on an overhead transparency, call on a volunteer from each group to list the group's ideas. Discuss the merits of each reason.

Independent Practice

For the benefit of students with specific learning disabilities who have difficulty using context clues to define words, use peer mentoring to decode the vocabulary word **rescission**. Have students use the context clues provided on pp. 300–301 to define the term. Then, have students use context clues, their vocabulary knowledge, or a dictionary, if necessary, to find the verb form of the word **rescission** (rescind). Help them to connect the meaning of the verb *rescind* with the meaning of the noun **rescission**.

the type of contract and differ in results or benefits provided. In the problem, Designs, Inc., failed to perform its obligation under the contract. Everling had a choice of remedies, as discussed below.

Sometimes a party intentionally and voluntarily gives up a contractual right. This is called a **waiver**. Why should one waive a legal right? The injury is minor and so potential monetary damages are low and not worth fighting for; the costs of suing, including loss of goodwill, may exceed the value of any likely remedy obtained; the outcome of the lawsuit may be "iffy" and problematical; the defendant may be judgment-proof; the victim may actually be glad to be free of any obligations under the contract.

When Lister bought her new automobile, she received a customary limited warranty from the manufacturer. It provided protection against defects in materials or workmanship of most components of the car for one year or 12,000 miles, whichever came first. One door did not fit properly and a whistling of wind could be heard when Lister drove faster than fifty miles per hour. Also, in heavy rains, water leaked into the trunk. Because Lister drove only in town, at low speeds, in good weather, she never bothered to complain about the defects. By her failure to act within one year, she waived her right to claim a breach of warranty.

Remedies for breach of contract include the following:

1. rescission of the contract, either voluntarily or by court order;
2. cancellation of the contract (in cases of sales of goods);
3. recovery of money damages; and
4. court order for specific performance or for an injunction.

1. The Injured Party Has the Right of Rescission

PROBLEM

The Cuddle-Me doll was so popular that the manufacturer could not fill all orders for it. Dealers therefore put their customers on waiting lists. In October, one retailer required a $15 deposit with every order and promised to deliver "no later than December 1." In fact, the supply remained inadequate until the new year. Hundreds of depositors did not get dolls for Christmas. Were they entitled to refunds or must they accept late delivery?

ASSESS

Learning Objective 2 Using a computer, if possible, have students compare the definitions of **rescission** and **cancellation** by creating an anecdotal example of each. (See pp. 300–301.)

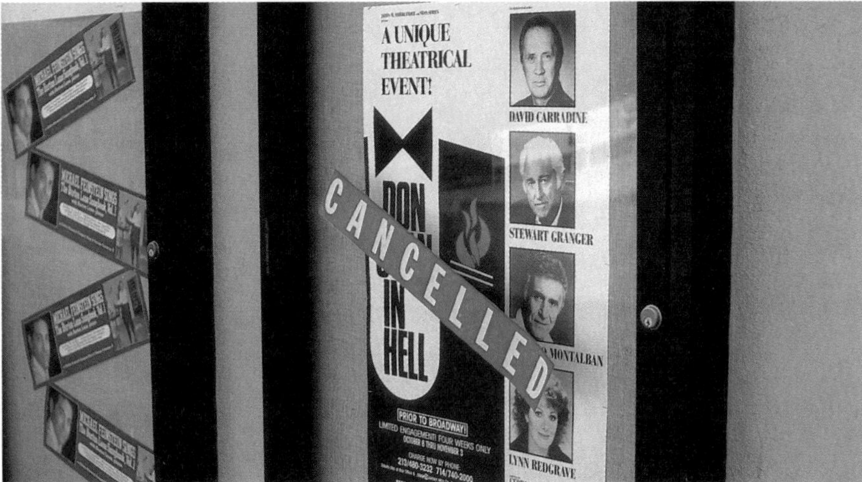

If one party breaches the contract by failure to perform, the other party may usually consider any reciprocal obligation as discharged. Thus, in the problem, customers who received no dolls before Christmas had a right to be restored to their original position—as if there had been no contract—by getting full refunds.

This remedy is the right of **rescission**. Each party returns any consideration received and gives credit for what cannot be returned. The entire contract must be rescinded, not just a part of it. Rescission may be voluntary under an agreement of the parties or it may be done by court order at the request of the injured party. Neither party gets damages.

2. The Injured Party May Have the Right of Cancellation

Cancellation is a variation of rescission. It is authorized by the Uniform Commercial Code (UCC) for breach of contract for the sale of goods. The injured party—either buyer or seller—may cancel the contract, return consideration received, and still retain other remedies.

> Ta-pei Yang ordered 900 solid brass bowls for indoor plants from the East-Meet-West Company, which imports such goods from Singapore. Yang had included the bowls as a special in his holiday gift catalog and expected to generate a net profit of at least $9,000 from their sale. When the shipment arrived and was opened, Yang scratched the bottom of one bowl and determined that it was steel with a surface plating of brass. Yang complained to the supplier, who pleaded ignorance and apologized, but offered no substitute. Yang returned the shipment and canceled his order. He may sue for damages for breach of contract and possibly for the tort of fraud.

Thinking Critically Through Visuals

This photograph shows an advertisement for a theatrical event superimposed with a cancellation notice. Do the ticket holders for the cancelled event have a remedy for breach of contract? (Answers may include yes, because cancellation is a variation of rescission, and, as such, the injured party is entitled to a remedy.)

Divide the class into three groups. Assign to members in each group responsibility for one of these roles: director, recorder, script writer(s), and actor(s). Using a computer, if possible, have students compose scenarios in which someone uses a **waiver**, **rescission**, or **cancellation**. After each group presentation, have the other groups determine which remedy is being portrayed and critique whether the injured party showed good judgment in exercising the right being portrayed.

Cooperative Learning

RETEACH Have students create a chart showing the differences between **rescission** and **cancellation**, terms presented on pp. 301–302.

ENRICH

Working in pairs, have students interview each other on their experiences with breaking a contract, especially the remedies of **cancellation** and **rescission**. Use a tape recorder to record interviews.

Call on student volunteers to explain the meanings of the terms **special** or **consequential damages** and **mitigate**.

Review with students the PROBLEM presented at the top of p. 302. Guide students to apply the terms **special** or **consequential damages** and **mitigate** to the analysis of the solution to the PROBLEM.

Have students rewrite, using a computer, if possible, the PROBLEM at the top of p. 302 so that

the injured party does not have the right to damages.

Have students create a cartoon to visually describe what it means to put the injured party "in the same position he or she would have been in if the contract had been performed" when a breach of contract occurs. (See p. 302.) Students may wish to use one of the PROBLEMS as the basis of their cartoon.

3. The Injured Party Has the Right to Damages

PROBLEM

Rivera had the concession rights to sell food, drinks, and souvenirs at a big football bowl post-season game. Some 60,000 reserved seat tickets had been sold for the event. As part of her preparations, Rivera contracted with Ace High Novelty Company for 10,000 pennants, noisemakers, and other items imprinted with the emblems and using the colors of the two competing teams. Although Rivera had emphasized the absolute necessity of delivery at least eight hours before game time, the goods arrived two days after the game had been played. What rights does Rivera have against Ace High Novelty Company?

When a breach of contract occurs, the injured party is entitled to be put in the same position he or she would have been in if the contract had been performed. After a breach, the parties frequently negotiate an amicable settlement, often with the help of their lawyers. If they do not reach a settlement, the injured party may sue to recover money damages for loss caused by improper or partial performance or by the total failure to perform as promised. In the problem, Rivera could sue Ace High for any injury suffered. This may include the loss of profits reasonably anticipated from the sale of the customized souvenirs which did not arrive in time. Such damages are **special or consequential damages,** which must be reasonably foreseeable by the defaulting seller. Ace High knew or should have known that the goods ordered would be useless to Rivera after the game, yet they could not have been obtained in time from any other source. Thus, Rivera lost all profits anticipated from the sales that could not be made.

Generally, however, the victim of a breach of contract is required to **mitigate** the damages. This means that losses must be reduced, if feasible, by any reasonable and available means under the given circumstances. Accordingly, when a seller fails to deliver, the buyer is legally required to purchase appropriate substitute goods or services from any alternative source. In the problem, Rivera could not obtain suitable substitute souvenirs in time for the game.

In a valid written contract, Allente Associates, an advertising agency, employed DeChant to be its European representative based in Paris, France, for a three-year period. His salary was set at $4,000 a month, plus a housing allowance, travel expenses, and other fringe benefits. After two years, Allente fired DeChant because it had decided to use

▼ ASSESS

Learning Objective 2 Project the overhead transparency, *What Are the Basic Remedies for Breach of Contract?*, covering the numbered terms on the left. Ask students to use the information in the cartoon bubbles to identify the examples of the right to damages and the right to specific performance.

local native talent to perform his customary duties. DeChant was upset by the news but decided to "make lemonade out of the lemons" as he put it. He immediately drove to a resort in Monaco, on the Mediterranean, for twelve months of the three R's; rest, recreation, and recuperation. DeChant's failure to mitigate damages by seeking comparable employment eliminates any damages he might otherwise have recovered from Allente, beyond nominal damages for its breach of his employment contract.

4. The Injured Party May Compel Specific Performance or Get an Injunction

PROBLEM

Kelly contracted to buy 160 acres of land from the McCalls. She planned to develop an amusement park on the land. When the McCalls learned of her plan, they refused to transfer title to the property. Did Kelly have any recourse?

As noted in Chapter 4, sometimes money damages are not an adequate remedy for breach of contract. Therefore a court of equity may give the injured party the special relief of specific performance. In a decree for specific performance, the court orders the defendant to do exactly what she or he had agreed or promised to do in the contract.

Generally, money damages suffice as a remedy for breach of contract in cases involving the sale of personal property. The victim may use the money to buy similar property from someone else. If the property is unique, however, so that it cannot be obtained elsewhere, specific performance may be awarded. An example is a rare work of art. This remedy is also generally available when the contract is for the sale of real property because every parcel of land is distinctively different from all others, if only as to location. Accordingly, in the problem, Kelly could sue the McCalls in a court of equity. The court would order them to transfer title to the property with a properly signed deed delivered to Kelly.

Specific performance is ordinarily denied by the court when:

a. money damages would be an adequate remedy;
b. the court is not able to supervise performance;
c. the contract is immoral, fraudulent, or illegal;
d. specific performance will work undue hardship on the other party to the contract; or
e. the contract involves personal service or employment.

Have students review the definitions of *specific performance* and *injunction* provided in Chapter 3 on p. 49 and in the *Glossary of Legal Terms.*

While the remainder of the class listens, have a volunteer read aloud the first paragraph in section four, *The Injured Party May Compel Specific Performance or Get an Injunction.* On a sheet of paper, have students write what they think *specific performance* means. Discuss students' definitions.

Working in pairs, have students recall from memory and list on paper the five examples of when specific performance ordinarily is denied by the court. Ask for volunteers to list the examples on the chalkboard.

Writing Connections

Language Arts
Using a computer, if possible, have students state, in essay form, their position on the ethics of breaking an employment contract.

Have students create a graphic organizer showing the four remedies listed on pp. 300–304 for breach of contract.

Mimicking the overhead transparency, *What Are the Basic Remedies for Breach of Contract?*, have students make an overhead transparency creating new cartoons for the four remedies.

▼ TEACH

Make certain that students can identify different measures of damages by calling attention to the definitions of these terms: **compensatory, nominal, liquidated,** and **punitive damages.**

▼ APPLY

Multicultural Highlights

In 1990, Public Law 101-503, the Seneca Nation Settlement Act, provided $35 million to the Seneca Nation of Indians of southwestern New York as compensation for federal failures to carry out trust responsibilities and properly protect the Senecas' interests under leasing arrangements made in the late 1800s. These leases were to land on the Seneca reservation from which the Seneca collected either no rent or insignificant amounts. The federal government had abdicated its trust responsibility to the Seneca Nation, so it paid compensatory damages. Discuss whether students think the amount awarded was equal to the extent of the injury.

In employment contracts, the court of equity will not compel a person to work against his or her free will. Such an order would smack of slavery. However, the court may grant an injunction prohibiting the defaulting party—such as an athletic coach or a key laboratory scientist—from working for anyone else during the period of employment agreed to under the contract. The person who breached the contract would still be liable for any money damages suffered by the employer. Thus, the defaulter may decide to perform as agreed, rather than be without work and still be liable for damages.

In some cases when money damages are not an adequate remedy for breach, and an order for specific performance is not appropriate, the court of equity may simply order rescission. Each party returns any consideration received.

▼ HOW ARE DAMAGES MEASURED?

PROBLEM

In a valid contract, Hall agreed in writing to sell his used ski outfit (skis, boots, jacket, and pants) to Cornall for $600. Then Hall changed his mind. He said, "Sue me if you must, but I'm not selling." Cornall, seeking to mitigate damages, immediately searched for comparable equipment. He found a better outfit at a college campus "ski swap," and it cost only $450. Can he still collect damages from Hall?

In awarding damages for breach of contract, the court tries to place the injured party in approximately the position that party would have been in had the breach not occurred. The amount awarded as **compensatory damages** is usually determined by the extent of the injury. One party is not permitted to increase the damages by continuing to perform the contract after notice of the other's breach or intention to cancel. As noted earlier, the injured party is also required to mitigate damages if reasonably possible. Sometimes, however, goods in the process of being made may be completed by the injured party. Such seeming addition to the loss actually reduces the final claim for damages because it makes the goods more salable. This would be true, for example, when a custom set of wooden furniture had been built but the finish of stain and multiple coats of lacquer had not yet been applied.

Failure to perform a duty under a contract is a legal wrong. Therefore courts will award **nominal damages** even when there is no actual injury.

▼ ASSESS

Media

Learning Objective 3 Divide the class into four groups, assigning each group the responsibility for writing, using a computer, if possible, a PROBLEM that illustrates one of the four damages—compensatory, nominal, liquidated, or punitive (exemplary), pp. 300–304. After each group has shared its PROBLEM, have students vote on the best PROBLEM for each damage. Make copies of the best PROBLEM activities for students to keep in their notebooks.

This could happen when, after a breach, the plaintiff finds a satisfactory product at a lower price. Such would be the case with Cornall in the problem. Nominal damages are granted in recognition of the rights that have been violated. Such damages may consist of a few cents or a dollar. The plaintiff is usually pleased to have proved a point or to have established a legal precedent. A litigious or vindictive plaintiff who expects to win no more than nominal damages may sue simply to embarrass the defendant or to force the defendant to hire a lawyer and incur court costs. Such action is legal but generally unethical.

When entering into a contract, the parties may specify the amount of money that is to be paid in the event of a breach. This sum is known as **liquidated damages.** This arrangement is common when actual damages would be difficult to measure and prove. It is enforceable if the amount is reasonable. If damages are not reasonable, the court will deem them to be a penalty and will not enforce the agreement. It will then award reasonable damages but only if proved. Penalties, you will recall, are generally imposed for crimes and intentional torts; they are not imposed for breaches of contract unless the agreement is tainted by some serious intentional wrong. Otherwise people would hesitate to enter contracts, which are necessary for commerce and a prosperous society.

The Bethlehem Steel Company contracted with the city of Chicago to supply and erect the steelwork for a certain section of a superhighway. The price agreed upon was $1,734,200. The contract also provided that the steel company would pay as liquidated damages $1,000 for each day the work was extended and uncompleted beyond a specified date. The work was completed fifty-two days after the date agreed upon. The court held that it would be difficult to determine the actual amount of damages. It also held that the amount of damages provided for in the contract was reasonable, and therefore was not a penalty. The company was liable for $52,000.

Under certain circumstances, such as when an intentional tort is involved in a breach of contract, the courts will award exemplary or punitive damages. Such damages are added to the actual damages. Their purpose is to punish and to make an example of the defendant. This could happen, for example, when a crooked seller cheats a buyer by falsely saying a necklace is made of solid, eighteen-carat gold when in fact it is gold-plated copper or highly polished brass.

On an overhead transparency, draw a spider map with four spokes and **Damages** in the center. Have students complete the organizer on a sheet of paper as you complete it.

Guided Practice

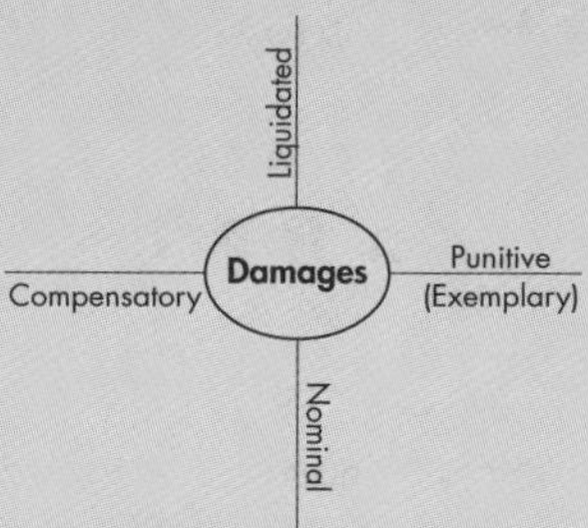

Challenge students to devise and share creative memory aids for recalling the four measures of damages. **Independent Practice**

Ethics Issue

Sometimes a litigious or vindictive plaintiff who sues for nominal damages may do so simply to embarrass the defendant or to force the defendant to hire a lawyer and incur court costs. Such action is legal, but generally unethical. In small groups, have students create and role-play situations in which someone sues for nominal damages for the above reasons. Poll students on whether they think that this type of suit is ethical.

RETEACH Pair students who understand the four types of damages with those who are having difficulty. Have each pair add examples to the spider map they created as **Guided Practice** in the APPLY section on p. 305.

ENRICH Using a computer, if possible, have students write an essay to answer the following question: **Should the party who breaches a contract be required to pay punitive (exemplary) damages as well as compensatory damages?**

TEACH

Display the overhead transparency, *How May an Injured Party Lose the Remedy for a Breach of Contract?*, to introduce the two ways that remedies for breach of contract may be denied or barred.

APPLY

Review the PROBLEM on p. 306. Lead students in a discussion so they understand how the statute of limitations applies to the PROBLEM. **Guided Practice**

Divide the class into three groups. Assign each group one of the following categories: social, psychological, and legal. Have students brainstorm reasons for their category for outlawing obligations, especially debts, after they become "stale" under statutes of limitations. Have students construct on the chalkboard or on an overhead transparency a class graphic organizer that shows their reasons for all three categories. Discuss the reasons as students list them.

Independent Practice

CAN THE INJURED PARTY EVER BE DENIED A REMEDY?

PROBLEM

Raley sold a used videocassette recorder to his friend and neighbor, Parr, for $495 on credit. Over a six-year period, Parr always had some excuse for not paying when Raley tried to collect. Exasperated, Raley finally filed suit in small claims court. Will the court consider the claim even though it is six years old?

Under certain circumstances, a remedy for breach of contract will be denied or barred. For example, a debtor who is too poor to pay a debt may avoid the obligation by having it discharged in bankruptcy. Also, a creditor who is tardy in suing may lose otherwise available legal rights. It would be unfair to permit a person to wait an unreasonable length of time before bringing suit. Circumstances change, witnesses move, memories fade, and records may be lost or destroyed. Then, too, there is a greater tendency toward fraud and perjury in proving stale claims, and many courts are already overcrowded with current cases. The courts do not want to be bothered with stale disputes which often can no longer be decided fairly.

1. The Remedy May Be Barred by a Statute of Limitations

A creditor may lose a legal right of action against a debtor by waiting too long before filing suit. Statutes in all states deny creditors a right of action for damages for breach of contract after the lapse of a specified time. These statutes of limitation prevent harassment of debtors by means of lawsuits and other efforts to collect stale claims. When an injured party fails to sue within the time permitted by law, the claim becomes an **outlawed debt** and the creditor may not sue. The time period varies among the states. Within a given state, the time may vary according to the nature of the contract. Depending on the state, a statute may bar action after two, three, four, five, or six years from the time the debt was due and payable. About one-half the states allow more time to sue on written contracts than on oral ones. In the problem, Raley has probably waited too long to file his suit. The statute of limitations would bar Raley from suing Parr.

The UCC provides that an action for breach of a contract of sale of goods must be *commenced* (i.e., begun) within four years after the cause of action arises. In their original agreement, the parties may shorten the pe-

ASSESS

Media **Learning Objective 4** On the chalkboard or on an overhead transparency, write this paraphrase of a common expression: **Those who hesitate are lost.** Using a computer, if possible, have students write a short paragraph in which they discuss statutes of limitations, incorporating the given expression as the title or main idea.

riod to not less than one year, but may not lengthen it. The statute begins to run from the moment there is a right to sue for a breach or a default.

In the case of minors and others who lack capacity to contract, allowance is made for their period of incapacity. Thus, a minor is given a reasonable time after reaching majority to start the action.

Statutes of limitations ordinarily do not discharge debts. Instead, they merely bar the remedies of the injured parties. The bar may be waived and the right of action may be revived if the debtor makes a new promise. Since the new promise is a waiver, it need not be supported by consideration. However, in some states, it must be in writing. The new promise may be express or implied, as in the case of a partial payment or a payment of interest. The period specified in the statute, during which an action must be commenced, begins to run anew from the date of the new promise.

Fredman borrowed $500 from McNulty for one year at 7 percent interest. Each year for ten years, Fredman sent the interest but no payment on the principal. Finally, McNulty decided she must take steps to collect the debt. So she filed suit. Fredman pleaded that the statute of limitations outlawed the debt. This was not a good defense. His annual payments of interest acknowledged the existence of the debt and kept it alive.

2. The Remedy May Be Barred by Discharge of the Debtor in Bankruptcy

PROBLEM

Greene had overextended himself financially by buying too many items on installment plans. Then he lost his job. His wife required major surgery and was hospitalized for almost two months. Soon after, Greene was found guilty of negligence in an automobile accident and was held liable for $155,000 more than his insurance policy coverage. Greene can see no way of paying his creditors, yet bill collectors are at his door almost daily. Is there anything he can legally do to get rid of his debts?

Years ago, a person who could not or did not pay debts as they came due could be jailed. Such punishment is costly for society, impractical, and unreasonable. A debtor cannot earn money to pay a debt while in prison. Moreover, the debtor's dependents may be forced to rely on public relief for

Personal Perspectives

On the chalkboard or on an overhead transparency, write: **There is a risk of loss in sleeping on one's rights.** Ask: **Does this statement relate to the statute of limitations or to bankruptcy? Why?** (Statute of limitations; taking no action may cause a creditor to lose the right to remedy) Ask students to discuss the statute of limitations at home with their families. Family members may share experiences with waiting too long to seek a remedy for breach of contract. Following the completion of the at-home assignment, have students share examples with the class.

Challenge students to recall from U.S. history the connection between the founding of the United States and this sentence: **Years ago, a person who could not, or did not, pay debts could be jailed.** (Many debtors were forced to colonize the Americas.) Discuss the reality that—with the exception of those sent to the Americas—many debtors never did get out of jail. Have students decide whether such punishment for debts was productive or counterproductive.

▼RETEACH Working in pairs, have students list five things they have learned about statutes of limitations.

▼ENRICH In small groups, have students investigate the specific statutes of limitations on oral and written contracts in their state. Then have each group create a poster illustrating the most interesting or important point.

Working in groups of four or five, have students create sets of scenarios involving petitions of bankruptcy, which demonstrate conditions eligible and ineligible for bankruptcy. Have them dramatize their scenarios for the class.

Preventing Legal Difficulties

To help students better understand how to prevent legal difficulties when seeking a remedy for breach of contract, have them clip (or you may wish to clip and bring to class) and label examples of newspaper or magazine real-life stories that illustrate one of the measures of damages or one of the reasons for losing the right to remedy. Have students report on their findings before displaying the articles creatively on a bulletin board.

support. Under the U.S. Constitution, Congress has established uniform laws on bankruptcies which permit the discharge of (i.e., excuse of) debts. Under these laws, debtors can get a fresh start, and creditors share fairly in whatever assets are available. **Bankruptcy** is a legal proceeding whereby a debtor's assets are distributed among his or her creditors to discharge the debts.

In the problem, Greene should file a proper voluntary petition with the bankruptcy court. If the petition is approved, he possibly would be permanently excused from paying all of his debts. Note that if Greene had willfully and maliciously caused the automobile accident, or if the accident resulted because he was intoxicated, the judgment debt of $155,000 would not be discharged. Bankruptcy is discussed more fully in Chapter 19.

Preventing Legal Difficulties

When seeking a remedy for breach of contract . . .

1. Negotiate, and if feasible, mediate or voluntarily arbitrate, before you litigate. A lawsuit should be the final resort because it is costly in time, money, and goodwill.
2. As a creditor seeking payment of an overdue debt, try to get at least a partial payment. In most states, such payment extends the time for filing suit before the claim is barred by the statute of limitations.
3. Do not delay too long. If the debtor is uncooperative or defiant, sue. To rest on legal rights is to risk losing them.
4. If you wish to rescind or to cancel your obligation, you must show that the other party breached the agreement in a material way. If you have paid anything, you may be able to recover what has been paid. If you have performed any service, you are entitled to be compensated.
5. Always keep accurate records and be prepared to show that you actually suffered a monetary loss if you seek more than nominal damages. You must also show that you made a reasonable effort to mitigate the damages.
6. If you seek specific performance, you must show that money damages will not adequately compensate you for your loss. You must also show that you are able, willing, and ready to fulfill your obligation.

▼ REVIEWING IMPORTANT POINTS

1. As a general rule, one who is not a party to a contract has no rights or duties under the contract. However, a third-party beneficiary may en-

▼ ASSESS

Learning Objective 4 Distribute to students copies of the overhead transparency master, *How May an Injured Party Lose the Remedy for a Breach of Contract?* Have students write a speech-bubble message that includes the terms **bankruptcy** and *discharge (or excuse) of debts* for the figure shown in connection with bankruptcy.

force a contract made for such party's benefit. An assignee may also acquire rights or assume duties under another party's contract.

2 In case of a breach of contract, the injured party has various remedies. An injured party may (*a*) rescind or cancel the contract, (*b*) recover the amount of loss through damages, and (*c*) in certain cases, require specific performance or obtain an injunction.

3 After default, the injured party usually may recover the amount already spent in carrying out the obligations incurred as part of the contract. But the injured party should not increase the damages. Instead, the damages should be mitigated—that is, reduced if reasonably possible.

4 Generally, a party to a contract has the option of breaching it. The courts will not punish such action by awarding punitive or exemplary damages unless an intentional tort or crime is involved. Rather, the court will award compensatory damages, possibly including special consequential damages. Sometimes the court will award either liquidated or nominal damages.

5 When the legal remedy of damages is not adequate, the court may grant the equitable remedy of specific performance, or of rescission, or it may grant an injunction prohibiting specified acts.

6 At the time of entering into a contract, the parties may agree to pay a specified, reasonable amount of damages if actual damages would be difficult to prove in case of default. Such damages are known as liquidated damages. The amount must not be so excessive that it would constitute a penalty.

7 A remedy for breach of contract may be barred (*a*) by the lapse of the time prescribed by a statute of limitations or (*b*) by the debtor's discharge in bankruptcy.

▼ STRENGTHENING YOUR LEGAL VOCABULARY

Match each term with the statement that best defines that term. Some terms may not be used.

bankruptcy
cancellation
compensatory damages
incidental beneficiary
liquidated damages
mitigate
nominal damages
outlawed debt
remedy
rescission
special or consequential damages
third-party beneficiary
waiver

▼ CLOSE

Project on the overhead transparency or the poster paper the responses students created in the FOCUS activity. As a whole-class activity, have students orally review and evaluate the list, modifying, correcting, or adding to their list.

Assign the following end-of-chapter materials:
Student text review activities, pp. 308–314
Workbook, pp. 43–48
Chapter Test

Chapter *MicroExam*

Strengthening Your Legal Vocabulary

1 incidental beneficiary
2 liquidated damages
3 bankruptcy
4 remedy
5 rescission
6 mitigate
7 third-party beneficiary
8 cancellation
9 nominal damages
10 compensatory damages

▼RETEACH

Have students write, using a computer, if possible, an essay applying the definition of **bankruptcy** on p. 308 to the analysis and solution of the PROBLEM presented on p. 307.

▼ENRICH

Have students look ahead to Chapter 19 to discover the reasons for bankruptcy laws and ways in which an obligation may be revived. Have students write their discoveries in their notebooks.

Applying Law to Everyday Life

1. Yes; They were third-party beneficiaries in the contract between Gallo and Blake, and as such they may sue Blake. (p. 299) Note that Gallo also remains responsible for the debts because there was no novation. (Chapter 14) The fact that Blake thinks she was charged too much for the store is of no concern to the book publishers.
2. No; By continuing to use the equipment and not claiming damages, the city waived its rights to any recourse for the breach of contract. (p. 300)
3. Elsen is entitled to damages because Hoglund did breach the sales contract. However, Elsen suffered no out-of-pocket loss because of the breach and in fact profited from it by getting a better vehicle for less money. Therefore Elsen is entitled to no more than nominal damages of perhaps a few cents or one dollar. (p. 305) Moreover, Elsen has to pay her own attorney's fee. She may gain some satisfaction from the fact that Hoglund has probably hired an attorney and, therefore, would be required to pay for the defense attorney's fees, as well as court costs.

1. One who benefits from a contract but is not a party to it and cannot enforce it.
2. Damages that are agreed upon before a possible breach of contract.
3. Legal proceedings discharging debts and distributing assets.
4. Means used to enforce a right or to compensate for an injury.
5. Ending a contract by placing parties in the same position as if there had been no contract; neither party gets damages.
6. To reduce damages if reasonably possible.
7. One who is not a party to a contract but benefits from it and can enforce it.
8. Ending a contract for the sale of goods because of a breach, and returning consideration and retaining other remedies.
9. Token amount awarded when rights have been violated, but there is no actual injury.
10. Amount of money awarded to compensate for a plaintiff's loss.

APPLYING LAW TO EVERYDAY LIFE

1. When Gallo sold his bookstore to Blake, there were balances due to twelve different publishing companies for books sold on account to Gallo. In their contract for sale of the store, Blake agreed to pay these accounts payable, and Gallo reduced his selling price by an equivalent sum. Now Blake refuses to pay the publishers, claiming Gallo overcharged her for the store. Do the publishers have a cause of action against Blake?
2. Fulton sold traffic signal equipment to the city of Philadelphia. The city installed the equipment, put it to use, and found that it did not work satisfactorily. The city claimed the equipment did not meet specifications, so notified Fulton, and refused to pay the purchase price. Nevertheless, the city continued to use the equipment. The city did not claim damages. Was the notice of failure to meet specifications a good defense against a suit for purchase price?
3. Hoglund reneged on his promise to sell his 1992 Camaro to Elsen. Elsen immediately went to nearby Los Angeles and found a 1992 model with lower mileage, in better condition, and priced $600 below Hoglund's. Nevertheless, Elsen was incensed by Hoglund's conduct and was determined to sue him "for all he's got." What damages, if any, is Elsen entitled to?

4. No; She should have mitigated her damages by immediately buying the stock through a broker on the open market. (p. 302) She could then have held Van Den liable for the broker's commission (a small percentage of the selling price). Having procrastinated, she is entitled to no more than the broker's commission calculated as a percentage of the $7 price.
5. Probably not; Damages of $1,500 a day for delay in completion appear unreasonably high and would be regarded as a penalty. (p. 305) If there is any delay in completion, the school district may still sue for damages but would have to prove the amount of damages suffered.

4 Van Den agreed in writing to sell directly to Wall 5,000 shares of stock in a major corporation listed on the New York Stock Exchange. By not going through stockbrokers they would save the usual sales and purchase commissions. The market price of the stock was $7 per share. For reasons he refused to disclose, Van Den told Wall, "Our deal is off. Sue me if you must." Wall could have purchased the shares through a stockbroker, paid the commission, and sued Van Den for reimbursement of the commission. Instead, she hesitated for three weeks, wondering whether she really wanted to buy the stock. By the time she bought, the price had more than doubled to $15 a share. Now she sues Van Den for the extra cost of $8 a share plus the commission she had to pay as a percentage of the total price. Is she entitled to judgment?

5 Madison Unified High School District had plans to build a new high school. Madison awarded the contract for construction to Empire Builders, Inc., which bid $2.6 million. The contract contained a liquidated damage clause that provided for payment of $1,500 a day for every day that completion was delayed beyond the expected twenty-four-month construction period. Could the liquidated damage clause be enforced?

6 ETHICS ISSUE Good contracted to build a house for Stern according to Stern's plans. After the house was completed, there were several defects that Good refused to fix. Stern then contracted with Madden to do the necessary corrective work for $8,000 and then sued Good for $8,000 in compensatory damages. Stern also demanded $10,000 in punitive damages "to punish Good and set an example for others." Is Stern entitled to compensatory damages? Is Stern legally or ethically entitled to punitive damages?

7 ETHICS ISSUE Ender was found guilty of manslaughter for causing the death of another driver in an automobile accident. Ender had been drinking and had been "showing off" his car to the passengers. At the trial, all of the passengers testified that they had tried to get him to stop, but he would not do so. In a separate civil action, judgment was rendered against Ender for a total of $650,000 for willful and malicious battery. Although he had no liability insurance, Ender just laughed. He said that when he got out of jail, he would "go through bankruptcy and shake the debt off." Would Ender's conduct be legal? Would Ender's conduct be ethical?

8 ETHICS ISSUE When Smythe bought a mattress and boxspring at Big Bazaar, a recently hired and soon-to-be-fired clerk mishandled the records of the sale. As a result, the store never charged the price of $475 to Smythe's account. For four years (the statutory period

7 ETHICS ISSUE No; Although judgments for negligent torts are dischargeable in bankruptcy, this is not true for intentional (willful and malicious) torts, as in the case of Ender. He may never be able to pay in full, but, unless he does, the creditors can seize all of his available earnings and assets up to the amount of the judgment. (p. 308) No; Ender's conduct would not be ethical. This would be an abuse of the bankruptcy procedure.

8 ETHICS ISSUE No; The applicable statute of limitations prevents Big Bazaar from suing Smythe for the price of the mattress and boxspring. Big Bazaar probably had a cause of action against its incompetent clerk, but such suits are seldom filed. The clerk may well be judgment-proof. (p. 306) Yes; Ethically, Smythe took unfair advantage of the error made by Big Bazaar's clerk. Although the statute of limitations reflects a good public policy of clearing the slate of stale legal actions, persons who thus are relieved of the legal obligation of paying legitimate debts still have a moral or ethical duty to pay them.

6 ETHICS ISSUE Yes; Stern is entitled to compensatory damages of $8,000, the amount of the loss suffered. The purpose of damages is to place the injured party in the same position as if there had been no breach of contract. (p. 299) No; Punitive damages generally are not awarded for breach of contract alone; there must be an intentional tort (such as fraud) also committed by the defendant. (p. 305) Good had only breached the contract.

of limitation for such accounts), Smythe received no bill and made no payment. Then she boasted to friends about how "sweet it is to snooze at the expense of Big Bazaar." Is Smythe still legally obligated to pay for the goods? Is she ethically obligated to pay?

9 ETHICS ISSUE Sara and John Renfrew were the parents of five-year old twins, Tom and Molly. To provide for the support of their children in case of need, the Renfrews bought term life insurance policies on their own lives. Term life insurance policies are similar to automobile and homeowner insurance policies. All are pure insurance with no savings element. This contrasts with the much more expensive ordinary or straight life insurance policies, which include a savings element. The policies expired after twenty years. By then the Renfrews assumed that Molly and Tom would be self-supporting. Could Tom and Molly collect the value of the insurance policies if their parents died within twenty years? Was it ethical for the Renfrews to buy insurance policies that became worthless after their children reach age twenty-five?

10 ETHICS ISSUE Gordon, a wholesaler of women's clothing, contracted to buy 6,000 woolen wrap-around robes from Shine. Shine, who used nonunion labor in her factory in New York City, had purchased the required bolts of cloth in several colors and her employees had almost completed cutting the cloth into proper pieces. Gordon then surprised and shocked Shine with a letter in which he said, "Let's cancel the deal. I got an offer I couldn't refuse from an outfit in Shanghai. Their price is about half of yours. What could I do? But you'll get my next order, I guarantee you that!" Does Shine have a cause of action (i.e., right to sue) against Gordon? How should Shine mitigate the damages? Did Gordon behave in an ethical manner?

▼ SOLVING CASE PROBLEMS

1 The plaintiffs filed a class action suit against the state of Colorado, certain officials, and the contractors on a tunnel construction project. The purpose of the suit was to seek recovery of funds alleged to have been expended unlawfully in the construction. The plaintiffs claimed that as citizens and taxpayers, they were beneficiaries of the contract for the tunnel construction. Therefore, they claimed, they were entitled to sue on the contract that was made on their behalf even though the contract was made with the state of Colorado and did not mention any individuals by name as beneficiaries. May these plaintiffs properly sue? (*Gallagher v. Continental Insurance Company*, 502 F.2d 827, 10th Cir.)

9 ETHICS ISSUE Yes; Tom and Molly are third-party beneficiaries of the life insurance policies (contracts) made by their parents. As such, they could legally collect the value of the respective policy when a parent dies before the passage of 20 years. (p. 299)

Yes; The Renfrews have no legal obligation, and usually no ethical obligation, to support their children after the children become self-supporting adults. To buy the policies for any period of time provided their children with an added measure of financial protection beyond the call of duty and in excess of what some parents provide. Note that in buying term insurance (which is pure insurance without any savings component) the parents provided the twins with a measure of security. They obtained the maximum possible amount of insurance for the specified term of years at the particular cost in premiums. It is wrong to say the policies were worthless after 20 years since they were intended to last only 20 years.

10 ETHICS ISSUE Yes; Gordon had breached the contract and Shine may sue for damages. (p. 302) Mitigation normally and generally requires the injured party to stop performing the contract or incurring additional expenses. But sometimes that is counterproductive. Here, to discard the bolts of cloth already cut into pieces usable for robes would be wasteful. Shine should complete the robes. As such they could be sold and the proceeds should reduce or even eliminate the loss from Gordon's breached contract. (p. 303)

No; Most ethicists would question the propriety of breaching the original contract and giving the job to a foreign garment manufacturer. This is especially true if the foreign producer operates a sweatshop in which workers are often exploited. They work for very long hours at very low wages, often under unsafe and unsanitary conditions.

2 Seismic & Digital Concepts, Inc., was a manufacturer of computer hardware. Digital Resources Corporation produced computer software. Digital Resources sold software to Seismic and sued when Seismic refused to pay for the software. Seismic countersued for damages because of late delivery of the goods—they were delivered ten to twenty-five days after the date specified in the contract. There was no indication in the contract that "time was of the essence." Moreover, Seismic had accepted and used the software, and for about five months had even asked Digital Resources to do additional work. Is Digital entitled to judgment? (*Seismic & Digital Concepts, Inc. v. Digital Resources Corporation,* 590 S.W.2d 718, Tex.)

3 Union Oil Company was the owner of a truck stop. Union sued the general contractor and subcontractors who had constructed the large service station to recover the cost of repairing the cracked parking area pavement. Union claimed the defendant had not followed specifications for the base material used for fill. When the contractor, Kennon Construction, refused to make the needed repairs, Union had the work done by others at a cost of $58,659 and then sought to recover this sum. The contractor's superintendent admitted under oath that he had not followed the specifications, but he said that Union had approved the substitute material. Union denied this, and the notes of Union's representative supported Union's testimony. The defendant's witnesses could not remember times or dates or present any records on the matter. Should Union win? (*Union Oil Company of California v. Kennon Construction,* 502 F.2d 792, 6th Cir.)

4 Under a written contract, plaintiff Shirley MacLaine Parker agreed to play the female singing-dancing lead in defendant 20th Century-Fox Film Corporation's planned production of a musical entitled "Bloomer Girl," to be filmed in Los Angeles. Fox Films was to pay MacLaine a minimum of $53,571.42 a week for fourteen weeks, starting May 23. Before then, Fox decided not to produce the picture. In a letter dated April 4, Fox offered to employ MacLaine in a dramatic, western-type movie to be produced in Australia instead. She was given one week in which to accept. She did not, and the offer lapsed. She then sued for the agreed-upon $750,000 guaranteed compensation. Fox defended by saying MacLaine had unreasonably refused to mitigate damages by rejecting the substitute role. You decide. (*Parker v. 20th Century-Fox Film Corporation,* 474 P.2d 689, Cal.)

5 Knutton operated a music company. Cofield was the owner of a restaurant. Knutton and Cofield contracted for the installation of a jukebox

Solving Case Problems

1 No; To be permitted to sue on a contract as a third-party beneficiary, the third party must prove that the contract clearly shows that a direct benefit was intended. If any rights existed under this contract for the plaintiffs, the rights came to the plaintiffs as incidental beneficiaries. The contract was with the state of Colorado, not with the people of the state as individuals. (p. 298)

2 Yes; The contract did not specify that "time was of the essence." Even if the initial delay in deliveries was a breach, Seismic waived its right to strict compliance by accepting the goods and continuing to deal with Digital Resources for five months without objection. (p. 300)

3 Yes; For breach of contract, one of the remedies is to sue for damages. The court held that the failure of the contractor and subcontractor to follow the specifications set forth in the contract was the cause of the damage. (p. 302)

4 Summary judgment for MacLaine for $750,000, plus interest and court costs; a wrongfully discharged employee normally is entitled to the agreed-upon compensation less the amount the employee

has earned or might have earned with reasonable effort from other employment. However, the substitute employment must be comparable, and not inferior. Here, the defendant's offer of substitute employment could not be applied in mitigation because working in the Australian production would be both different and inferior. (p. 302)

5 No; The formula under which the liquidated damages were to be calculated was reasonable. If no such formula had been included in the contract, it would have been difficult to determine the amount of damages for the breach. Where the loss for breach is difficult to determine, the courts favor the use of agreements for liquidated damages where they are reasonable. (p. 305)

in the restaurant, agreeing to share the receipts obtained. The contract provided that if Cofield discontinued use of the jukebox before the end of the agreed-upon period, he would pay Knutton a sum of money for the unexpired time. The sum would be based on the average of the amount paid to Knutton per day while the machine had been used. Before the contracted time expired, Cofield disconnected the jukebox and installed one from another supplier. Knutton sued for damages for breach of contract. Cofield claimed the damages sought were a penalty for the breach and not liquidated damages, as claimed by Knutton. Was Cofield correct? (*Knutton v. Cofield*, 160 S.E.2d 29, N.C.)

SPECIAL SECTION

INTERNATIONAL BUSINESS LAW

International business law is at once the most complex and least settled area of the law. It lacks the centralized, precedent-setting, decision-making authority of a supreme court. Yet international business law deals with disputes centering on sophisticated exchanges of technology and other products. Typically, extremely high monetary amounts are at stake and resolutions must be in accordance with agreements negotiated by individuals with vastly different political, cultural, social, and language backgrounds.

In some areas, international treaties—such as those providing for transnational protection of patents, copyrights, and trademarks—have produced a relatively clear framework for the law (in the signatory countries only, however). In other areas, unilateral national actions have created special situations. The antitrust laws of the United States and other nations (e.g., the European Economic Community), the U.S. Foreign Corrupt Practices Act of 1977, tariffs, licensing laws of all kinds, laws relating to the trading status of a nation, laws and regulations relating to the financing of transactions, and many others all impinge on the basic contractual negotiations involved in an international business transaction.

In addition to considering the special situations posed by the types of governmental action illustrated above, an adept international legal adviser will include terms in a contract to cover the following issues.

Choice of Forum

It is wise to predetermine the court system that will have jurisdiction over any dispute that arises under the contract. Realize that the courts of the nation of either litigant might be biased in favor of its citizen or entity. On the other hand, a neutral nation's court system might not have jurisdiction over enough property of the party determined to be at fault to allow for execution of a judgment.

Choice of Laws

The choice of the laws to be used to decide the issue is as important as the choice

Special Section: International Business Law

After students have read the special section, have them work in groups of four or five to identify the problems, difficulties, and challenges associated with international business law. Have each group report on its findings, writing its major points of discussion on the chalkboard or on an overhead transparency. After all groups have presented, ask for one or more volunteers to summarize the class's conclusions. Then, invite students as a group to brainstorm recommendations for improving international business law. Have students research to discover the names and addresses of newspapers, magazines, and journals that deal with international business law. Challenge students to use a computer, if possible, to prepare a letter to the editor of one or more of these publications, expressing their view of the problems and possible solutions in Media regard to international business law.

of the forum for the dispute's resolution. This is because laws vary so widely from nation to nation.

Excused Lack of Performance

Certain situations in which a lack of performance of the contract will be excused and not foster liability on the part of the person unable to perform should be specified. These situations include war, subsequent governmental action precluding the transaction (e.g., failure to issue a license to transfer technology), embargo, fire, flood, destruction of the specific subject matter, and others.

"Official" Contract Version(s)

The contract should stipulate which draft is to be legally effective and the language in which it is to be stated. It is also a good idea to define the terms used in the transaction in the chosen language and version.

Regardless of all the legal precautions a party can take, trust, experience, and reputation remain as the most important elements in international dealings. Avoiding disputes by careful negotiation and verification is far more important and advisable than having to resolve disputes later.

316

Contracts: Buying and Selling Goods

Unit Overview

In Unit 4, *Contracts: Buying and Selling Goods*, students will read about the sales contract, the transfer of ownership and risk of loss, and defective products. In this unit, students will learn about the different types of sales, goods, warranties, and product liabilities.

Contracts for the sale of goods, to sell goods, and to transfer of ownership of other kinds of property are regulated by a variety of laws. In Chapter 16, *The Sales Contract*, students will understand what a sale is. Readers are alerted to the applicability and significance of the statute of frauds, and to important exceptions to this statute that they are likely to encounter in future years.

Certain conditions must be met before the owner of goods can transfer ownership. In Chapter 17, *Transfer of Ownership and Risk of Loss*, students will study who may transfer the ownership of goods. They will learn what is required for transfer of ownership, when ownership and risk of loss transfer, when insurable property interests transfer, when the transfer of ownership and risk of loss occur in specific transactions, and what procedure must be followed in a bulk of transfer of goods.

Express and implied warranties are designed to substantiate product quality or performance; persons injured by defective products may bring suit against manufacturers or merchants in the chain of distribution of the product. In Chapter 18, *Defective Products*, students will discover what express and implied warranties are. They will discuss if sellers' claims are always warranties; what is meant by "caveat emptor," "caveat venditor," and "good faith;" what warranties are implied by law in all sales; what express warranties can be made by all sellers; what additional warranties are implied by law for merchants only; when and how warranties may be excluded; and what product liability is.

At the end of the unit, you'll find a special section, *Choosing an Attorney*, which can be used at any time during the study of Unit 4. You may wish to assign its accompanying *Teacher Edition* activity to give students an opportunity to create a consumer handbook on how to choose an attorney.

Portfolio Assessment

Using a computer, if possible, have students create a consumer pamphlet, *Don't Get Sold Out: Consumer Tips on Buying and Selling Goods*. Tell students to include business law-related topics such as when and why to get a sales contract, when the statute of frauds apply to sales, what to do if you have a defective product, how to transfer ownership, what the differences between warranties are, and what product liability is. Have students provide personal (or fictitious) examples of what can happen if a consumer is uninformed about sales contracts and the buying of goods. Have students add their pamphlets to their portfolios or law journals.

Careers

Consumer Rights Activist

The complexity of products requires consumers not only to beware, but to be aware of the laws designed to protect them. Consumer rights activists protect consumers by ensuring product safety and the appropriateness of goods and services for fair prices. They test potentially hazardous goods, lobby legislation, and publish consumer information.

Consumer rights activists usually have experience in research, public information, or community education, and have college degrees in law, public policy, or political science. Staff members of consumer advocacy groups usually earn an annual salary of between $16,000 and $28,000.

Have students create a newsletter or brochure of consumer tips on service contracts, warranties, and other consumer issues. Encourage students to use sources such as *The Smart Consumer's Directory*, and to contact their Better Business Bureau and local consumer protection agencies for information.

Annotated Bibliography

- ***Courtin v. Sharp*, 365 U.S. 814 (1960).**
  The Court held that the loss of a colt, which accidentally died after the completed sale but while still in the seller's possession, must be borne by the buyer. (Chapter 17)

- ***Duncun v. Cessna Aircraft Co.*, 665 S.W.2d 414 (Tex. 1984).**
  In a plane crash case, the Texas Supreme Court analyzed comparative apportionment in product liability cases. The Court stated that an ideal tort system should impose responsibility on the parties according to their abilities to prevent the harm. Equitable and rational risk distribution depends on the existence of some system for comparing causation. Pure comparative apportionment allows a claimant to recover the percentage of damages caused by the defendants, regardless of the extent of his own causation. In the modified system, a claimant's recovery is entirely barred if his or her share of causation is found to be greater than the total causation attributed to the defendants. (Chapter 18)

Contracts: Buying and Selling Goods

- The Sales Contract
- Transfer of Ownership and Risk of Loss
- Defective Products

UNIT 4 CONTRACTS: BUYING AND SELLING GOODS

CHAPTER 16 ORGANIZER

Chapter Theme

Contracts for the sale of goods, to sell goods, and to transfer of ownership of other kinds of property are generated by a variety of laws.

DIRECTED STUDY QUESTIONS	SPECIAL FEATURES	PROGRAM RESOURCES				
		Reteach	Enrich	SN	AM	
What is a sale?	Thinking Critically Through Visuals, p. 321	✔	✔	✔		
What if the sales contract is unconscionable?		✔	✔		A	
What are the results of ownership?		✔	✔			
How do sales compare with similar transfers of ownership and possession?	Personal Perspectives, p. 324 Thinking Critically Through Visuals, p. 326	✔	✔		V	
Must delivery and payment be made at the same time?		✔	✔			
How does the statute of frauds apply to sales?	Ethics Issue, p. 328	✔	✔			
When is a signed writing not required under the statute?	Writing Connections, p. 330 Thinking Critically Through Visuals, p. 331 Multicultural Highlights, p. 331 Preventing Legal Difficulties, p. 332	✔	✔		K	

Additional Resources

- Elias, Stephen and Stewart, Marcia, LL.B. *Simple Contracts for Personal Use.* Berkeley, CA: Nolo Press, 1991.
- Sack, Steven Mitchell and Steinberg, Howard Jay. *The Salesperson's Legal Guide.* Englewood Cliffs, NJ: Prentice Hall, 1981.

One-semester course	✔	✔	✔					
One-year course	✔	✔	✔	✔	✔			

		ASSESSMENT OPPORTUNITIES			
	Cooperative Learning	**Informal Assessment**	**Chapter Review**	**Chapter Test**	**Chapter *MicroExam***
		✔	✔	✔	✔
		✔	✔	✔	✔
		✔	✔	✔	✔
		✔	✔	✔	✔
		✔	✔	✔	✔
		✔	✔	✔	✔
		✔	✔	✔	✔

Videodiscs
Purchase Contracts
Search Chapter 20, Play To 21

State by State

A Colorado court has held that in suing a buyer for breach of contract to buy natural gas, the seller could testify as to whether the parties intended to include a claimed price increase.

Teaching Materials

Student text, pp. 318–337

Overhead transparency masters
- *Comparing Sales with Similar Transactions*
- *When Is a Signed Writing Not Required for Sales of Goods Priced at $500 or More?*

Videos
- *Contracts, Warranties, and Credit* Videotape
- *Law for Business* Videodisc

Workbook, pp. 49–50

Outside Resources
- Flip chart
- Blank overhead transparency
- Index cards
- Photocopies of a bill of sale
- Posterboard
- Markers

- Camcorder
- VCR
- Tape recorder

Assessment
- Chapter Test

- Chapter *MicroExam*

Vocabulary

sale, p. 320
price, p. 320
barter, p. 320
goods, p. 320
payment, p. 321
receipt of goods, p. 321
acceptance of goods, p. 321
contract to sell, p. 322
vendor, p. 322
vendee, p. 322
unconscionable, p. 322
contracts of adhesion, p. 322
merchant, p. 324
casual seller, p. 325
bill of sale, p. 327

Learning Objectives

When you complete this chapter, you will be able to

1. Define the sale of goods under the Uniform Commercial Code.
2. Identify unconscionable contracts and contracts of adhesion.
3. Recognize the benefits and burdens of ownership of property.
4. Compare the various methods of acquiring property.
5. Appreciate the unique role of merchants and why and how they are treated specially by the law.
6. Distinguish between payment, delivery, and transfer of title of goods.
7. Discuss how the statute of frauds applies to the sale of goods.

318

Chapter Self-Test

Assess students' understanding of sales contracts before they begin Chapter 16 by asking the following *True* or *False* questions. Students should write their answers on a sheet of notepaper. Review and discuss students' responses before continuing with the chapter. **(1) All sales contracts must be written.** (False); and **(2) All transfers of ownership and possession are sales.** (False)

CHAPTER

16

THE SALES CONTRACT

1 ETHICS ISSUE Months before the event, J. J. Smythe buys two tickets to a concert for $70. Two weeks before the concert, J. J. learns that important business will keep her out of town during the event. She calls a friend and agrees to trade the tickets for three videotapes of the singing group to be featured at the concert. J. J. later breaches this promise when a stranger, who is unaware of the previous deal, gives her $175 for the tickets. Was the original agreement a valid sale governed by the Uniform Commercial Code (UCC)? Did J. J. act ethically? What legal and equitable remedies are available to J. J.'s friend?

2 A young couple selects matching wedding bands from a catalog in a jewelry store. In a writing signed by them and the store manager, the couple agrees to pay $1,400 upon delivery. Has a sale been made?

3 A bride-to-be wants her wedding gown to be custom-made from a unique new fabric. A bridal shop quotes a price of $1,750. When she orally agrees, the shop special-orders the fabric and cuts it to fit. Then the wedding is canceled. The bride-to-be seeks to avoid the contract because it was not in writing. May she do so?

319

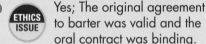

▼ FOCUS

Have students spend a few minutes before class jotting down what they already know about contracts. Discuss their responses. You may wish to use the information you gather to tailor the way you present the chapter to the class.

Have students, working in small groups, write brief scenarios based on the photograph on p. 319 of what they think will happen when the homeowners contract to buy carpeting. (Answers may include that the salesperson will complete a preprinted sales contract, sign it, have the homeowners sign it, collect a deposit, and so on.) Collect the scenarios, or have students keep them in a safe place, since they will be used in the CLOSE activity at the end of this chapter.

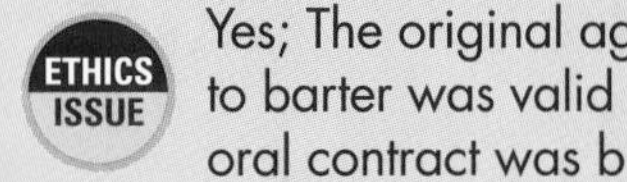

You Decide

1 ETHICS ISSUE Yes; The original agreement to barter was valid and the oral contract was binding. J.J. did not act ethically, since one should not break promises without a proper reason. The friend could go to small claims court to collect monetary damages.

2 No; It was a contract to sell, rather than a sale. However, they are legally bound to pay upon delivery.

3 No; She is liable. Even though oral agreements are enforceable only on goods up to $500 in value, the gown would not be salable to others in the ordinary course of the seller's business.

Thinking Critically Through Visuals

Draw students' attention to the photograph of the homeowners looking at a salesperson's carpet samples. Ask: **What, do you think, must happen for the sale to take place?** (Accept all reasonable answers, but explain to students that goods must be exchanged for a price in order for a sale to take place. The homeowners and the salesperson may sign a sales contract; however, until they exchange payment for goods, a sale will not take place.)

▼ TEACH

Write *Uniform Commercial Code (UCC)* on the chalkboard and ask a volunteer to define the term. (Statutes that simplified, clarified, and modernized many laws relating to commercial transactions) Ask: **Why does the UCC apply to this chapter?** (A sale is a commercial transaction.) Focus on the concept that the UCC deals with sales of goods and with contracts to sell goods in the future. Give examples of goods (such as tangible personal property) and contracts to sell goods (such as sales agreements, purchase orders, and so on).

▼ APPLY

To ensure that students who are dyslexic or who experience difficulty spelling focus on the new vocabulary, create a word search puzzle using the terms on pp. 320–322. The definitions of the terms should be the clues. Distribute copies and allow 10 minutes for work on the puzzle.

Guided Practice

Have small groups brainstorm sales scenarios in which the UCC would apply. Have students identify each of the following: the goods, the contract to sell goods in the future (if applicable), the payment, the receipt of goods, the acceptance of goods, the vendor, and the vendee.
Independent Practice

▼ WHAT IS A SALE?

PROBLEM

At the Dan-Dee Discount Department Store, the Medinas—husband and wife—signed a contract to buy a clothes washer and dryer set. The Dan-Dee salesperson showed them display samples and explained that although their set was not in stock, "We will deliver and install it within two weeks, certain." While shopping at the store, the Medinas had left their car in the store's automobile service department to have the engine's idling speed adjusted and to have squeaks in the door eliminated. The charge for labor was $45; there was no charge for parts or supplies. The service attendant recommended replacement of the car's tires and the Medinas agreed. The cost of the tires was $300, plus $25 for balancing and installation. The Medinas also bought a new battery for $59, and it was installed free of charge. Were all of these agreements sales?

A **sale** is a contract in which *ownership* of (also known as *title* to) goods transfers immediately from the seller to the buyer for a price. **Price** is the consideration for a sale or contract to sell goods. It may be expressed in money, in services, or in other goods. When parties exchange goods for goods, the sale is a **barter**.

The UCC deals with sales of goods and with contracts to sell goods in the future. **Goods** are tangible (i.e., touchable), movable, personal property: such things as airplanes, books, clothing, and dogs. By UCC definition, goods do not include the following:

1. money (except rare currency or rare coins, which are collectible items with value that may exceed their face amounts);
2. intangible (i.e., not touchable) personal property, such as legal rights to performance under a contract, transferred by assignment rather than by sale;
3. patents and copyrights, which are exclusive rights given by the federal government to inventors and writers (see page 531);
4. land and other forms of real property, which are transferred by conveyance and are subject to special rules (as discussed more fully in Chapter 28).

Under the UCC, a sales contract may be made in any manner sufficient to show agreement. The resulting contract suffices if the parties by their actions recognize the existence of a contract. This is true even though a court

▼ ASSESS

Learning Objective 1 Ask students to summarize briefly in writing the functions of **payment, receipt of goods,** and **acceptance of goods** in a sales contract. (Payment—buyer gives seller the agreed price, receipt of goods—buyer takes physical possession of goods, and acceptance of goods—shows by word or conduct that the goods are satisfactory) might not be able to determine precisely when the contract was made, and even though one or more terms are left open in accordance with customs of the trade.

Payment occurs when the buyer delivers the agreed price and the seller accepts it. **Receipt of goods** means that the buyer takes physical possession or control of the goods. Receipt usually involves actual delivery. However, delivery may be constructive. This happens when there is no actual transfer of possession of the goods, but the recipient has the power to control them, as intended by the parties involved. Examples would be when the buyer gets the keys to a car or receives a warehouse receipt for stored goods.

Acceptance of goods means that the buyer has agreed, by words or by conduct, that the goods received are satisfactory. Acceptance is shown when the goods are used, resold, or otherwise treated as if they were owned by the buyer. Acceptance may also be indicated when a buyer fails to reject the goods within a reasonable time, if the buyer has had adequate opportunity to inspect them.

In general, the law of contracts has been simplified and made less strict in its application to sales of goods. For example, the price for goods usually is fixed in the contract. However, the parties may indicate that the price is to be set in a certain way at a later date. This method is especially used in long-term contracts when considerable instability of prices is expected. Ordinarily, when nothing is said about the price, a contract results if all other essentials are present, and provided the parties do not express a contrary intent. In such a case, the buyer is required to pay the price that is reasonable at the time of delivery.

In many situations, the contract is primarily for personal services. Such contracts are not sales because any goods supplied are merely incidental. In

Thinking Critically Through Visuals

Imagine that McKinnon ordered this cake by phone on Monday, paid for it and picked it up on Tuesday morning, and served it at a party on Tuesday night. Describe the specific steps of the sales contract. (The contract to sell was made Monday; payment, receipt, and acceptance of goods took place Tuesday morning; revocation of the acceptance Tuesday night.)

Using a computer, if possible, have half the class write a scenario showing the difference between a sale and personal service contract. (In a sale, goods are exchanged for payment. In a personal service contract, payment is exchanged for a service; any goods received are incidental.) Have the other half show the difference between receipt of goods and acceptance. (Receipt of goods occurs when the buyer takes physical possession of the goods. Acceptance occurs when the buyer indicates by words or actions that the goods are satisfactory.) The two groups should exchange papers and verify the other group's information.

▼RETEACH To help students understand what a sale is, review each event in the PROBLEM on p. 320. For each event ask: **Was there an exchange of goods for a price?** (Washer/dryer—no, engine/door—no, tires—yes, battery—yes)

▼ENRICH Using a computer, if possible, have students explain if, by UCC definition, sales have taken place. For example **If the Squirrels' owner sells the contract of his star pitcher to the Bullets' owner, would the UCC acknowledge the sale?** (No, contract is for an intangible item)

TEACH

On a transparency, list the guidelines a court would apply to a contract to determine if it, or a clause in it, is **unconscionable**. (*Grossly unfair, oppressive, offends an honest person's sense of justice,* and *unethical*) Then, explain how a court could respond to an unconscionable contract,

following the points on pp. 322–323.

APPLY

Distribute one index card to each student. On it, have students write one example of a contract, or a clause in a contract, that would be considered **unconscionable**. Collect the cards, shuffle them, and redistribute them. Have students write, on the back of the card, why they think this example can accurately be called **unconscionable**. Have volunteers read aloud the examples. **Guided Practice**

Read aloud problem 5 on p. 335. Have students indicate, by a show of hands, if the clerk's actions are or are not unconscionable. Ask volunteers to explain their judgment. (Some students may believe that the sale was unconscionable since it "offends an honest person's conscience," whereas others may say that it is not, since it is not "grossly unfair" or "oppressive.")

Independent Practice

the problem, the work on the car engine and the doors was a contract for services: any goods supplied, such as lubricants, were incidental. Even if a specific charge was made for them, the contract would remain one for the services that were the dominant part of that agreement. On the other hand, the transfer to the Medinas of title to the tires was a sale of goods, even though a small charge was made for related labor. The battery was also acquired in a sale of goods, with no charge for labor. The Medinas' agreement to buy the washer and dryer at a later date was not a sale. Instead, it was a **contract to sell**—a contract in which ownership of goods is to transfer in a sale in the future. Both present sales of goods and contracts to sell goods are governed by the law of sales found in the UCC. In both types of transactions, the seller is known as a **vendor**. The buyer is known as the **vendee** (also called the *purchaser*). The transaction involving a vendor and a vendee is called a "sale" by the seller and is called a "purchase" by the buyer.

WHAT IF THE SALES CONTRACT IS UNCONSCIONABLE?

PROBLEM

Frostifresh Corporation sold a refrigerator to Nguyen, a recent immigrant, who spoke, read, and wrote Vietnamese and French, but not English. The refrigerator was sold on an installment payment contract. The negotiations and sale of the refrigerator were made in French. However, the written contract was entirely in English, although the seller knew that Nguyen could not read English. The refrigerator, which cost Frostifresh $348, was sold on the installment plan for $1,146, plus a credit charge of $246. Was this agreement unconscionable?

The UCC provides that a court may find that a contract or a clause of a contract is **unconscionable**—that is, grossly unfair and oppressive. An unconscionable contract or clause offends an honest person's conscience and sense of justice, as in the problem. The terms need not be criminal nor violate a statute, but they are unethical. **Contracts of adhesion** are more likely to be unconscionable. This is so because in such contracts one of the parties dictates all the important terms. The weaker party must generally accept the terms as offered or not contract at all.

If a court decides that a clause of a contract is unconscionable, it may do any of the following:

a. refuse to enforce the contract,
b. enforce the contract without the unconscionable clause, or
c. limit the clause's application so that the contract is no longer unfair.

ASSESS

Learning Objective 3 Have students complete charts such as the one shown here to list the rights/benefits and the duties/burdens of ownership.

OWNERSHIP	
Rights/Benefits	**Duties/Burdens**
• To use, abuse, enjoy • Increase in value	• Taxes • Legal limitations of use • Tortability • Maintenance • Responsibility • Deterioration, obsolescence • Depreciation in value

The law is not designed to relieve a person of a bad bargain. One may still be legally bound by the purchase of overpriced, poor quality, or unneeded goods.

WHAT ARE RESULTS OF OWNERSHIP?

PROBLEM

Leister won $2 million in a state lottery. When he received the first of twenty promised annual payments of $100,000, he went on a spending spree. He bought a new car which he carelessly wrecked, clothes which he never even wore, and a mink coat for a casual friend he met in a bar. He staged a wild New Year's Eve party for fifty new friends, during which the revelers smashed their crystal champagne glasses in a fireplace. Through court action, relatives now seek to stop Leister from using his money and goods so wastefully. Will they succeed?

It is important to know the difference between a sale and a contract to sell because both benefits and burdens generally go with ownership. Therefore it is necessary to know when ownership transfers from one party to another. When one person *sells* (i.e., transfers to another party the ownership of goods), he or she says, in effect, "I hereby transfer to you the legal right to use, control, and dispose of these goods."

Ownership carries valuable rights. Any rise in value (as in prices of securities, output of land, or increase in animal weight or number) belongs to the owner. Moreover, goods generally may be enjoyed and used as the owner pleases. They may be squandered or even destroyed, as in the problem. Leister's relatives will fail unless they can prove he has become mentally incompetent, which is unlikely.

Ownership also involves duties and burdens. The owner may be taxed in proportion to what is owned. The freedom to use one's property may be limited by governmental regulations for the common good, as by speeding and zoning laws. Property should be protected and maintained. If it is cared for improperly or used in a manner that interferes with the rights of others, the owner may be liable for resulting torts (see Chapter 6). In recent years, penalties have also been imposed for violations of environmental protection laws (see page 123). In some cases, the owner's responsibility may extend to cover the use of the goods by other persons. For example, the owner of an automobile may be held responsible for injuries caused by another person operating the car with the owner's permission.

The owner suffers loss when goods deteriorate because of the passage of time and the action of natural forces—sun, wind, rain, snow, oxygen, and

TEACH

Point out to students that the "plusses and minuses" associated with owning a good do not necessarily apply to a contract to buy or sell that good before possession takes place. Discuss the meanings of the terms *benefits, rights, burdens,* and *duties* as they relate to ownership. (Benefit—an advantage, something that promotes well-being; burden—often a heavy responsibility; duty—an obligation; right—in accordance with law, a satisfactory state or condition)

APPLY

Give specific examples of an item owned, such as a home, a bicycle, a swimming pool, a car, and so on, and write them in a vertical column on the chalkboard. In two more columns, have students brainstorm the benefits and burdens associated with ownership of each item. **Guided Practice**

Have students copy the chart in their notebooks. Independently, have them add five more items, including the benefits and burdens, to their lists. Ask volunteers to share new examples with their classmates. **Independent Practice**

RETEACH Have students imagine that they receive a $30,000 sports car as a gift from an anonymous donor. The catch? The student legally cannot drive it until he or she is of legal age. Have students create a comparison chart like the one in the ASSESS activity on p. 322 to identify their rights/benefits and duties/burdens of ownership as related to this gift.

ENRICH Have students create a bulletin board entitled *Know Your Rights* to show the difference between the terms **sale** and **contract to sell.**

other elements in the air. When goods are destroyed or damaged without the legal fault of any person, the owner loses unless covered by insurance. For example, if a storm destroys your camping tent, you suffer the loss unless it was properly insured. The result is the same when your possessions are lost, stolen, or destroyed by fire. In effect, your goods are also under a never-ending assault by the economic forces of obsolescence, (i.e., becoming out-of-date) and depreciation (i.e., declining in value because of wear and tear, and for other reasons).

In spite of all this, ownership does not always determine who shall take losses for goods. As discussed in Chapter 17, the UCC sometimes places the risk of loss on someone other than the owner.

HOW DO SALES COMPARE WITH SIMILAR TRANSFERS OF OWNERSHIP AND POSSESSION?

PROBLEM

Both Brian and Claire became electronic data processing specialists during their service in the U.S. Army. When they retired from the Army, they decided to open a retail electronics specialty store. Using savings, borrowed funds, and (a) money donated by their parents, they (b) purchased a parcel of land that had a suitable building. They (c) rented the empty lot next to the building to use as parking space, under a five-year contract. They (d) bought a supply of personal computers and related equipment and (e) agreed to purchase an equal quantity of a new PC model scheduled for production within six months. They (f) traded their two sports cars for a company truck, and (g) raised additional money by transferring, to a buyer, a note receivable (commercial paper) for $27,000 that Brian had received in partial payment when he sold his house trailer. To get more cash for working capital, (h) Brian and Claire transferred to a bank all rights to collect on a group of accounts receivable they had obtained from sales made on credit. They (i) obtained all their store display cases by renting them from the manufacturer. In every instance noted, Brian and Claire obtained possession of property needed for their business. What types of transactions did they utilize?

In most cases, the UCC treats all buyers and sellers alike. In some cases, it treats merchants differently from casual sellers. A **merchant** is a seller who deals regularly in a particular kind of goods or otherwise claims to have special knowledge or skill in a certain type of sales transaction. In the problem, Brian and Claire became merchants after retirement from the

TEACH

Display the overhead transparency, *Comparing Sales with Similar Transactions.* Discuss the different types of transactions and their similarities. Ask: **In which types of transactions have you participated?** (Answers

may include barter, gift, sale, and so on.)

Discuss any terms with which students may be unfamiliar, such as *bailment* (transfer of possession of personal property without transfer of ownership).

APPLY

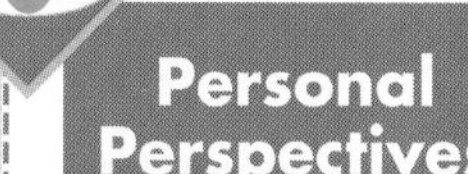

Personal Perspectives

Ask students to share experiences they have had with sales contracts. Ask the following: **Have you ever engaged in barter? Have you had a newspaper route? Have you sold anything to raise money for a school function?** Have students identify their experiences with different sales contracts, then graph the results, using a computer, if possible. Refer to the

types of transactions on p. 325.

ASSESS

Learning Objective 5 Have students summarize in writing, using a computer, if possible, the ways in which a merchant is different from a casual seller. (Casual seller—sells occasionally; Merchant—deals regularly in a particular type of goods, held to higher standards, needs licensing, subject to special taxes, under government regulations)

Army. A **casual seller** is one who sells only occasionally or otherwise does not meet the definition of merchant. For example, you would be a casual seller if you sold your private automobile. A used-car dealer selling the same car would be a merchant. In general, the UCC holds merchants to a higher standard of conduct than it does casual sellers. Merchants may be required to have licenses to sell. They are also usually subjected to special taxation and closer regulation by the government.

In the problem, most of the business transactions Brian and Claire engage in as merchants will be sales, or the reciprocal of sales, namely purchases. This will be true when they acquire inventory and other equipment from suppliers, and when they sell their stock in trade to customers. However, as noted in the problem, they could acquire property in a variety of other transactions. The transactions lettered in the problem are identified as follows and explained more fully in Table 16-1: (a)-gift; (b)-conveyance; (c)-lease; (d)-sale; (e)-contract to sell; (f)-barter; (g)-negotiation; (h)-assignment; and (i)-bailment. Conveyances of real property are discussed in Chapter 28, leases in Chapter 29, negotiation of commercial paper in Chapter 31, and bailments in Chapter 27. For now, you need to know only that these other legal methods of transferring possession and ownership of property do exist.

As already noted, sales contracts may be made through a traditional exchange of offer and acceptance. But the UCC recognizes alternative methods. It adds another way of accepting an offer to buy. Instead of telephoning, sending a facsimile (fax), or mailing an acceptance, the seller may simply ship the goods and thereafter notify the buyer of this action.

> The Tastie Treat Shop mailed an order for 500 one-pound boxes of fruit and nut center candies to the Chocolate Castle Company. Chocolate Castle could have accepted the order by mail, telephone, wire, or fax machine. Instead, it immediately shipped the candy, thus creating a contract. The usual price was simply added to the next invoice mailed to the Tastie Treat Shop.

Under the UCC, an offeror may state that the offer to buy or to sell goods must be accepted exactly as made or not at all. Otherwise the offeree may accept and still change some terms of the contract or add new ones. Recall that in most contract negotiations such changes would end the original offer and would be considered a counteroffer. Under the law of sales of goods, the new term is treated as a proposal for addition to the contract.

This provision of the UCC helps to avoid what courts have called the "battle of the forms." This battle occurs when a merchant buyer makes an offer with a preprinted *purchase order form.* It contains detailed terms, often including many that clearly favor the buyer. In response, a merchant

Refer students to the PROBLEM on p. 324 and the corresponding transactions, found on p. 325. Draw the following graphic organizer on an overhead transparency, on the chalkboard, or on a flip chart (without the responses in the boxes). Have students complete the diagram showing how Brian and Claire went about setting up shop.

Guided Practice

B & C Electronic Specialties

Gift	Sale	Lease
money from parents	computers and equipment	next-door parking lot
Barter	**Conveyance**	**Bailment**
2 cars = 1 truck	purchased land with building	rented display cases
Negotiation	**Contract to sell**	**Assignment**
commercial paper = $27,000	buy more computers in future	rights to collect on accounts goes to bank

Ask: **If you were looking for a computer, what difference in buyers' protection exists, do you think, between buying from a merchant (such as in a computer store) or from a casual seller? Explain your reasons.** (Accept all reasonable responses, but lead students to see that a merchant is held to stricter rules than is a casual seller, and therefore buyers have more protection.)

ENRICH

Have students role-play a negotiation for a final contract between a buyer of a stereo and its casual seller.

Thinking Critically Through Visuals

Ask the following questions based on the information in Table 16-1: **In which transactions is ownership not transferred to the second party?** (Lease, contract to sell, and bailment). **If your grandmother gave you a valuable watch—for which she received nothing in return—what kind of transaction would it be?** (Most likely a gift)

Have students respond *True* or *False* to each of the following. **(1) You own the necklace your mother gave you on your birthday.** (True); **(2) Your father owns the car he is leasing.** (False); **(3) You and your friend executed a contract when you exchanged your hockey stick for his basketball.** (True); and **(4) A bill of sale is legal evidence that a transaction has taken place.** (True)

Independent Practice

Ask students to suggest situations in which the terms of a contract between a merchant buyer and a merchant seller may change. (If the offeree suggests a lower price than that set by the offeror, if the delivery schedule changes, and so on)

Table 16-1
This table summarizes and compares important effects of nine common transactions involving property, both personal and real. Note how the legal effects reflect the intent of the parties.

Transaction	What Type of Property Is Involved?	Is a Contract Involved?	Is Ownership Transferred?	Is Possession Transferred?	What is the Evidence of a Transaction?
(a) Gift	Personal or Real Property	No	Yes	Usually yes	Usually none; Deed for Real Property
(b) Conveyance	Real Property	Usually*	Yes	Usually yes	Contract; Deed
(c) Lease	Real Property	Usually*	No	Yes	Lease (a Contract)
(d) Sale	(Usually) Goods (Tangible Personal Property)	Yes	Yes	Usually yes	Contract; Bill of Sale
(e) Contract to Sell	Goods	Yes	No	Usually yes, but not immediately	Contract
(f) Barter	Goods	Yes	Yes	Usually yes	Contract
(g) Negotiation	Negotiable Instruments	Usually*	Yes	Yes	Commercial Paper (Contracts)
(h) Assignment	Contract Rights	Usually*	Yes	Yes, when contract is performed	Contract
(i) Bailment	Personal Property	Usually*	No	Yes	Contract (in Commercial Bailment)

*May be gratuitous.

seller accepts by using a *sales order form* with differing terms, which favor the seller.

When both parties are merchants, a new term inserted by the offeree automatically becomes part of the contract if the offeror fails to object within a reasonable time. However, the new term must not materially alter the offer, and the original offer must not expressly bar such changes. If the new term is a *material* (i.e., important) alteration, it is included in the contract only if the offeror expressly agrees to be bound by it.

A pottery manufacturer offered to sell red clay flowerpots in three different sizes to a garden supply store. The store accepted the offer but

ASSESS

Have students respond in writing to this statement, using computers, if possible: **Name the nine common transactions involving personal or real property and give an example of each.** (Use Table 16-1 to check answers.)

specified that the pots had to be packaged in sets of three (with one of each size) rather than in bulk as described in the offer. This was a material change in the terms of the contract. The pottery maker did not object or revoke the original offer. Instead it packaged and shipped the goods as requested. Therefore a contract resulted, with no other change in terms.

▼ MUST DELIVERY AND PAYMENT BE MADE AT THE SAME TIME?

PROBLEM

The Baumgartens bought Hannukah gifts for their three young children during the Sunrise Center's October layaway sale. Delivery was scheduled for early December, and payment was due before January 15 of the following year. When did the Baumgartens become owners of the gifts they had purchased?

In the basic sales transaction, payment, *delivery* (i.e., transfer of possession), and transfer of title take place simultaneously at the seller's place of business. Even if payment or delivery, or both, take place later, title still passes when the buyer selects (i.e., identifies to the contract) and agrees to buy the goods in the seller's store. At the appropriate time fixed in the sales contract, normally the buyer has a duty to pay, and the seller has a duty to transfer possession. Generally neither is obligated to perform until the other does. Thus, unless it is otherwise agreed (as when the sale is on credit), or if it is the custom of the trade, the seller may retain the goods until the buyer makes payment in full. Similarly, the buyer may refuse to pay the price until the seller delivers all the goods. The buyer is entitled to a receipt when payment is made.

A **bill of sale** is a receipt that serves as written evidence of the transfer of ownership of (title to) goods. Such a document is sometimes required by statute, as in the case of automobile sales. If a bill of sale is signed by the seller, buyer, or both, it can satisfy the requirements of the statute of frauds for a signed writing. However, neither a sales contract nor a bill of sale necessarily identifies the parties nor explains the terms of the transaction.

A bill of sale makes resale of the property easier because it provides the owner with written evidence of ownership. When goods are lost, stolen, or destroyed, as in a fire, the document can be used to help prove value for insurance purposes. If the owner borrows money and uses the goods as security, the bill of sale helps to assure the creditor that the debtor owns the

▼ TEACH

Discuss the following:
1. In a basic sales transaction, payment, delivery, and transfer of title take place simultaneously at the seller's place of business.
2. A bill of sale is not necessarily proof of ownership, but is evidence of transfer of ownership, because other people may have claims against the goods.

Make an overhead transparency of a bill of sale. Emphasize its value. (Provides written evidence of ownership; if signed, is proof of authorized agreement; helps creditors determine owner of goods)

▼ APPLY

In certain industries, it is customary for buyers to receive goods before paying, such as meals in a restaurant. Ask students to list similar examples on the chalkboard. (Hotel stays, rental cars, and so on) **Guided Practice**

Have students, with prior adult consent and possible supervision, videotape a variety of sales transactions taking place in their community (with permission from the sales establishments). Play the tapes in class and have viewers identify when the payment, delivery, and transfer of title take place in each transaction. **Independent Practice**

▼RETEACH Using a computer, if possible, have pairs of students create a bill of sale, taking care to include all the important characteristics. (Transaction, date, payment, delivery, terms, signatures, "PAID" stamp, and so on) Review bills of sale with students to ensure clear understanding of these elements.

▼ENRICH Have students explain orally why buyers of expensive items should request a bill of sale marked "PAID" when the sale has been completed. (As evidence of a transfer of title, as documentation of payment, and so on)

TEACH

Review the characteristics of the statute of frauds (pp. 259–260). Then, summarize the criteria required for a sales contract to be governed by the statute of frauds. (Written documentation signed by the party being sued that a contract to sell, or a sale, has been made; Between merchants, the signature of the party being sued alone may suffice.)

APPLY

In small groups, guide students to create scenarios about the statute of frauds to share with the class. Ask students why the statute of frauds would or would not apply in each scenario. **Guided Practice**

Ethics Issue

Have students respond to the following statement, using a computer, if possible: **In spite of the fact that ethically we are required to keep the written and oral promises we make, all states have a statute of frauds. Why?** (Answers may include that the statute serves as a preventative law.)

Independent Practice

goods that are being pledged. The bill of sale is not absolute proof of ownership because other persons may have acquired claims against the goods since the bill of sale was issued. Also, dishonest persons may forge such documents to help dispose of stolen property.

To encourage business, most sellers extend credit to qualified buyers, including other business firms. Some retailers do most of their business selling to customers who use credit cards or charge accounts, or who pay in installments (see Unit 5). Thus, the buyer may get both title and possession before payment. In the problem, assuming the goods were set aside for the Baumgartens at the time of the sale, they received title in October, possession in December, and paid for the goods in January.

HOW DOES THE STATUTE OF FRAUDS APPLY TO SALES?

PROBLEM

Chilton orally agreed to buy an imported camera from the Open Shutter Shop for $748.98. The camera she wanted was not in stock, but a shipment was expected any day. Therefore the salesclerk prepared a memorandum of the sale, signed it, and gave Chilton a copy. A week later the clerk phoned and said, "Your camera is ready." Chilton replied that she did not want it because she had learned that the identical model could be purchased for much less by mail from a New York City discount store. Is Chilton liable to Open Shutter for breach of contract?

Sales or contracts to sell, like other contracts, are generally valid and enforceable in court whether they are oral, written, or implied from the conduct of the parties. However, as you may recall, under the statute of frauds sales of goods for $500 or more must be evidenced by a writing to be enforceable in court.

In good business practice, both parties sign if a written sales contract is used and each gets a copy. This provides both parties with a useful legal record, and it reinforces mutual good faith. Normally both parties expect to perform, but either party could breach the contract. If that happens, the injured party can sue for damages, and the written contract helps to prove both the existence and the terms of the agreement.

In the problem, the price of the goods was more than $500. Therefore the sale was governed by the statute of frauds. Open Shutter is bound because its clerk signed the contract. Chilton is not bound because she did not sign, but she could enforce the agreement against Open Shutter if she so desired.

ASSESS

Learning Objective 7 With books closed, have students outline how the statute of frauds applies to sales or contracts to sell. (Barring exceptions discussed on pp. 329–332, it applies to goods over $500; evidenced in writing; signed by party being sued; and indicates that a contract to sell, or a sale, has been made.)

Not all the terms of a sales contract have to be in writing to satisfy the statute of frauds. Essentially, all that is required is a writing, signed by the party being sued, which satisfies the court that a contract to sell, or a sale, has been made. The number or quantity of goods involved in the transaction must be contained in the writing, and the contract is not enforceable beyond the stated quantity. However, the time and manner of performance; credit and warranty terms; packaging, labeling, and shipping instructions; and even the price need not be included for the writing to satisfy the statute. If necessary, this information can be provided later in oral testimony in court.

A unique variation of the statute of frauds applies only to contracts between merchants. You will recall that generally the law requires a signature of the person being sued. Between merchants, however, the signature of the party who is suing may suffice to prove an otherwise unenforceable sales contract. If a merchant sends a written confirmation of an oral contract to another merchant within a reasonable time after this oral agreement was made, the confirmation binds both parties. However, if the second merchant sends a written objection to the confirmation within ten days, the confirmation is not binding.

WHEN IS A SIGNED WRITING NOT REQUIRED UNDER THE STATUTE?

PROBLEM

La Fargo telephoned an order to Hoban's Brick and Tile Works for ceramic tiles imported from Mexico and priced at $663. In accordance with the oral contract order, the proper tiles were delivered. Later that day, La Fargo notified Hoban's that she refused to accept the goods. Hoban's insisted that the oral contract was binding and sued for damages. Who should win?

Under certain circumstances, oral contracts for the sale of goods priced at $500 or more may be valid and enforceable. These exceptions to the requirements of the statute of frauds include the following:

1. When the Goods Have Been Received and Accepted by the Buyer

Receiving the goods does not in itself make an oral contract binding under the statute of frauds. Both receipt and acceptance are necessary. A buyer may receive goods without accepting them.

TEACH

Under four specific circumstances, oral contracts for the sale of goods of $500 or more may be valid and enforceable. These are (numbered subheads 1–4 on pp. 329–332): when the buyer receives and accepts goods, when payment has been given and accepted, when specially made goods cannot be sold to others, and when the existence of an oral contract is admitted in court by the defendant. Summarize these points on the chalkboard.

APPLY

Make and distribute copies of the overhead transparency master, *When Is a Signed Writing Not Required for Sales of Goods Priced at $500 or More?* Tell students to use it as an outline for taking notes on pp. 329–332. Then display the transparency and fill in information as students dictate. Encourage students to amend their notes as needed. Compare this information to your chalkboard summary.
Guided Practice

Divide the class into groups of two or three students and assign each group to role-play one of the case studies on pp. 330–332. Discuss the specifics of each situation that make the sales contract enforceable.

Independent Practice

RETEACH Ask students to respond in writing to the question: **What help is a written contract if a person wants to sue?** (Answers may include that it is evidence that an agreement was made between the parties and it is a statement of terms.)

ENRICH Ask: **How does the statute of frauds differ when it is applied to transactions between merchants?** (In a suit between merchants, written confirmation by the suing party of an oral agreement is binding on both parties unless the other party responds with a written objection within 10 days.)

Writing Connections

Sociology
Divide the class into groups of three or four students and have each group contact merchants in your community by telephone, in person, or in writing, to find out about their sales policies. Have students prepare a written set of interview questions ahead of time. Sample questions might include: Do you and your customers sign all sales contracts? May we have a copy? What are your policies for special orders? Have you ever been to court for breach of a sales contract? and so on. Have each group present its findings to the class in a written report, using a computer, if possible.

Have students design banners and signs on the theme, *It's Best to Get It in Writing*, using posterboard and markers or a graphics program on your computer.

Under the UCC a buyer can accept goods in three ways:

1. after a reasonable opportunity to inspect the goods, the buyer signifies to the seller that the goods conform to the contract, or will be retained in spite of their nonconformity; or
2. the buyer acts inconsistently with the seller's ownership (e.g., uses, consumes, or resells the goods); or
3. the buyer fails to make an effective rejection after having a reasonable opportunity to inspect the goods.

In the problem, La Fargo effectively rejected the goods even though they conformed to the contract. She could legally do this because the statute of frauds required that the contract (for goods priced at $663) be in writing and signed by her as buyer. Alternatively, to make the oral contract binding, La Fargo had to receive and accept the goods. Here, she received the goods but did not accept them. Therefore Hoban's loses the suit. Hoban's could have prevented this costly problem by requiring La Fargo's signature on a suitable writing before shipping the tiles.

Note that if the buyer has received and accepted only some of the goods, the oral contract is enforceable only for those goods received and accepted.

Ramirez visited Petrosiki's Paint Pot and orally ordered forty gallons of shingle stain. The stain was priced at $13 a gallon. It was to be charged to her account and delivered the following Monday. Nothing was signed. Ramirez took one five-gallon can home with her. However, her husband was displeased with the color, and she disliked the way it went on. Therefore she refused to accept the balance of the order. Ramirez was within her rights in doing so. She was bound by the contract only for the five gallons that she had received and accepted.

2. When the Buyer Has Paid for the Goods and the Seller Has Accepted Payment

When payment in full has been accepted by the seller, the oral contract is enforceable in full. When *partial* payment has been accepted by the seller, the oral contract is enforceable only for the goods paid for if the goods can be divided and the price can be apportioned fairly. If the goods are indivisible and there can be no dispute as to quantity, the contract is enforceable in full.

At an auction, Zutto bought a handmade, oak rolltop desk from Winslow for $1,250. Zutto paid $250 and left to get a truck and the

ASSESS

Learning Objective 7 Have students review, under the statute of frauds, the exceptions on pp. 329–332 to the rules for oral contracts for the sale of goods and write five true or false questions (and answers). Have students exchange papers with their classmates and answer each other's questions.

balance still due. When Zutto returned, Winslow told her the desk had been sold to another person for $1,500. He explained that the contract with her was oral and therefore not enforceable. Winslow was wrong; Zutto's partial payment for the indivisible goods (the oak desk) made the oral contract enforceable. If the goods had been divisible (e.g., fifty reams of paper), the contract would be enforceable only for the quantity paid for. Winslow is liable to Zutto for damages measured by the extra amount she must now pay someone else for an equivalent desk.

3. When the Goods to Be Specially Made for the Buyer Are Not Suitable for Sale to Others in the Ordinary Course of the Seller's Business

A seller can enforce an oral contract for nonsalable goods in either of the following two situations:

a. if the seller has made a substantial beginning in manufacturing the goods, or
b. if the seller has made contracts to obtain the goods from third parties.

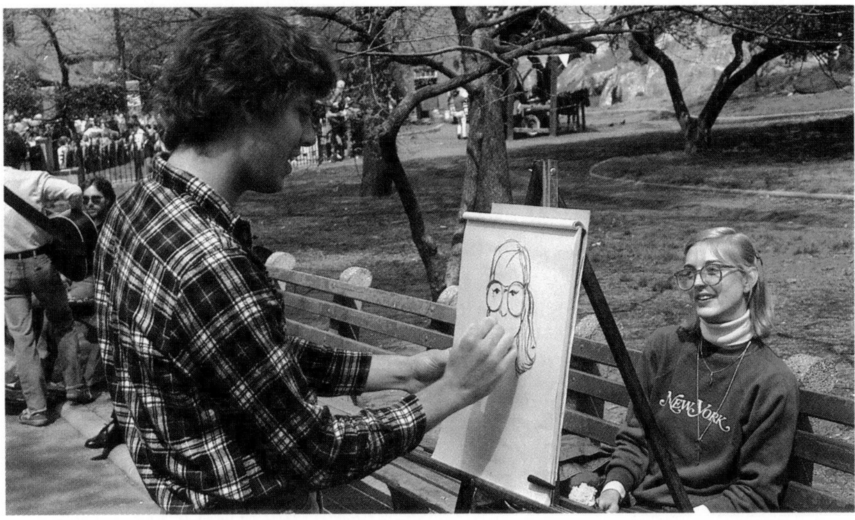

In an oral contract, Lugo ordered a $750 customized silver-plated trophy from Mendoza's Trophy Shop. The trophy was to be awarded to the winner of the Tri-Town Drag Racing Competition. Mendoza had already completed a three-dimensional racing car and mounted it on a black marble base. Then Lugo canceled the order saying the races had

Thinking Critically Through Visuals

What evidence supports the inference that an oral contract exists between this artist and the subject in the photograph? (Subject is posing and so on) **When will the sale be enforceable?** (When the artist has made a substantial beginning on the portrait)

Multicultural Highlights

Ralph Nader, a Lebanese American, is a symbol of unflagging commitment to consumer rights. Nader was directly responsible for the formation of the Consumer Products Safety Commission, which works to recall defective products and to enact and apply consumer protection laws. In writing, have students brainstorm how consumer protection organizations protect buyers against product defects and consumer fraud. Companies may respond to collective complaints more than to individual complaints and so on.)

▼RETEACH Have students outline in detail the section, *When Is a Signed Writing Not Required Under the Statute?* (pp. 329–332). Then, ask them to provide at least one example for each of the four exceptions to the general rule.

▼ENRICH Ask students' opinion: **Mrs. Renza went to La Mode to get a dress made for her son's wedding. The material had to be ordered from Hong Kong. The couple eloped a week before the wedding. Is Mrs. Renza obligated to pay for the $600 dress? Why?** (Yes; The dress was a special order.)

Have students reread the boxed example of Richardson and Olmstead, on p. 332, and ask: **Although written documentation was not required in this case because of the defendant's testimony in court, how, do you think, might Richardson's claim of an agreement for 100 sides of beef have been substantiated in his testimony?** (Answers may include by determining fair-market value of 100 or 300 sides of beef, totaling the contract amount, and so on.)

Preventing Legal Difficulties

In small groups, have students make posters using a rebus (picture symbols) or an acronym to remind them of each of the eight precautions to take in sales-contract situations.

also been canceled. "We expected to sell 5,000 tickets," he said, "but we've unloaded only 500." Lugo is liable to Mendoza for breach of contract because the trophy was not suitable for sale to others in the ordinary course of her business, and she had made a substantial beginning in producing it.

4. When the Party Against Whom Enforcement Is Sought Admits During Legal Proceedings That the Oral Contract Was Made

A party against whom enforcement of an oral contract is sought may admit in legal pleadings or testimony that a contract was made. In this case, a signed writing is not necessary for the enforcement of the part of the contract that was admitted.

Richardson was sued by the seller, Olmstead, for breach of an oral contract to buy 300 sides of prime Kansas beef. Because the order exceeded $500, the contract should have been evidenced by some signed writing to be enforceable. In his testimony during the trial, Richardson admitted that there had been an oral agreement, but he said that it was for only 100 sides. Richardson is bound to perform or pay damages for breach of contract for the reduced quantity because of his admission of the existence of the oral contract.

Preventing Legal Difficulties

In sales, be informed and aware that...

1. During your lifetime, you will probably enter into more sales contracts than any other type of contract (usually as buyer, but often as seller). It helps to know the law of sales.
2. Your best protection against shoddy merchandise is knowledge of goods and their value, followed by careful comparison shopping.
3. Your best protection against sales fraud is the integrity of the seller (as reflected in the seller's established reputation) coupled with your caution.
4. When you make a major purchase, make sure your insurance is adequate. It should provide for coverage against possible loss of valuable purchased property. If appropriate (as in automobile purchases), it should also provide protection against possible liability for injury to others.

5 It is a good idea to put a sales agreement in writing even if it is for goods worth less than $500. Although this is not required by the statute of frauds, doing so can avoid misunderstandings and prevent costly litigation. If the goods are worth $500 or more, insist on compliance with the statute of frauds.

6 The other party should sign the contract or memorandum and give you a copy. The other party may properly require that you sign too.

7 You are bound by an oral contract for goods priced at $500 or more to the extent that you have received them and accepted delivery. You may be bound in full or in part if you have made some payment. You usually are bound when you order custom-made goods.

8 For expensive "big ticket" items, you should get a bill of sale marked "paid" when you pay the full price.

REVIEWING IMPORTANT POINTS

1 Both sales of goods and contracts to sell goods are governed by a combination of basic contract law and special UCC provisions on sales. Transfers of ownership of other types of property, such as intangible personal property and real estate, are governed by different laws.

2 Both benefits and burdens go with ownership of goods.

3 Merchants generally are held to a higher standard of conduct by the UCC than are casual sellers.

4 Neither payment nor delivery is essential for transfer of title.

5 Unless otherwise provided by statute, sales or contracts to sell may be oral, written, or implied from the conduct of the parties.

6 To be enforceable, a sale or contract to sell goods for $500 or more must be evidenced by a writing. The writing must specify at least a quantity of goods involved and must be signed by the party who is sued or by that party's agent. The writing is not essential when:
a. the buyer has received and accepted the goods;
b. the buyer has paid for the goods in full and the seller has accepted payment;
c. the goods are custom-made for the buyer, are not suitable for sale to others in the ordinary course of business, and the seller has begun manufacturing or has contracted to obtain them; or
d. the party seeking to avoid the contract admits during the legal proceedings that the oral agreement was made.

7 Price may consist of anything—such as money, services, or goods—as agreed upon by the parties as consideration.

CLOSE

Have students use the scenarios they wrote in the second FOCUS activity on p. 319. Have them review the scenarios to judge how accurately they described the creation of a contract between the buyers and the seller. Break into the same groups as in the FOCUS activity and allow each group to revise its scenarios before sharing them with the rest of the class. Have students summarize what they have learned from the chapter about sales contracts.

Divide the class into small groups. Tell students that each group is responsible for writing, producing, and delivering one episode of a new TV show, "News in One Minute." Today's topic is "sales contract court cases." Have students select from the following roles: on-air anchor (one or two), producer/director (one), and camera person (one). All members should participate in writing a one-minute script for the broadcast. Have each group videotape or audiotape its script if possible and play the tape for the class.

Cooperative Learning

Assign the following end-of-chapter materials:
Student text review activities, pp. 333–337
Workbook, pp. 49–50
Chapter Test

Chapter *MicroExam*

8. Payment occurs when the buyer delivers the price and the seller accepts it.
9. Receipt of goods occurs when the buyer takes physical possession or control of the goods.
10. Acceptance of the goods occurs when the buyer indicates that the goods received are satisfactory.
11. A bill of sale may provide useful evidence of the transfer of title to goods.

STRENGTHENING YOUR LEGAL VOCABULARY

Match each term with the statement that best defines that term. Some terms may not be used.

acceptance of goods
barter
bill of sale
casual seller
contracts of adhesion
contract to sell
goods
merchant
payment
price
receipt of goods
sale
unconscionable
vendee
vendor

1. Contract in which ownership of goods passes immediately from the seller to the buyer for a price.
2. Consideration in money, goods, or services that is given in return for the transfer of title to goods.
3. Buyer or purchaser.
4. Contract to transfer ownership of goods at a later date.
5. Seller who deals regularly in a particular kind of goods or otherwise claims to have special knowledge or skill in a certain type of transaction.
6. Exchange of goods for goods.
7. Tangible personal property that is movable.
8. Receipt serving as written evidence of the transfer of ownership of goods.
9. Buyer's taking of physical possession or control of goods.
10. Buyer's indication that the goods received are satisfactory.

Strengthening Your Legal Vocabulary

1. sale
2. price
3. vendee
4. contract to sell
5. merchant
6. barter
7. goods
8. bill of sale
9. receipt of goods
10. acceptance of goods

Applying Law to Everyday Life

1. Yes; When the parties fail to state a price in an otherwise complete contract, the price is the reasonable price at the time and place of delivery. (p. 321) With a commodity such as electrolytic copper bars, for which a daily market exists, the figure selected would be the market price on the day and at the time of delivery.
2. No; The doctor was primarily engaged in providing professional services. The goods supplied were merely incidental. (pp. 321–322) The parties who were potentially liable for breach of warranty (as well as for the tort of strict liability) were maker A, wholesaler B, and retailer C. (Chapter 18)
3. No; There was no contract. Brackston had negligently caused the loss and is liable in damages to the Nook and Cranny Shoppe. The sales price would probably be a fair measure of such damages, but there should be no sales tax because there was no sale. (pp. 320–321)

APPLYING LAW TO EVERYDAY LIFE

1 The Caribbean Mill sold a quantity of standard electrolytic copper bars to Pollard. The contract was complete in all respects except that it failed to state the price. Was the contract a valid one, thus enforceable in court?

2 At Ellen Johnson's request, her doctor prescribed and injected her with a drug. The drug had been tested and approved for sale by the federal Food and Drug Administration. It had been manufactured by maker A, sold to wholesaler B, then sold to retail pharmacy C, which sold it to the doctor. The doctor charged Ellen Johnson $15 for the drug and $50 for his services. Twenty years later, Ellen Johnson's daughter developed a cancer traceable to the drug that her mother had taken. Was the doctor a seller and therefore liable for breach of warranty?

3 As Brackston was examining a large Swedish glass vase in the Nook and Cranny Shoppe, the vase slipped from her hands. It smashed into countless pieces when it hit the floor. After the proprietress had swept up the mess, she pointed to a sign on the wall that said, "Handle with Care! If You Break It, You Buy It." She then rang up a sales charge of $300 plus $18 sales tax. Was Brackston the vendee in a sales contract?

4 Every two weeks, Ericson held a garage sale to resell items she had purchased at other such sales. When the city and state governments tried to tax her sales, Ericson claimed that she was merely a casual seller. Therefore, she claimed, she did not have to pay a sales tax. Was she correct?

5 ETHICS ISSUE When Soule bought a sweater for his wife, the clerk deliberately lied to him. She said that the garment was a pure silk and mohair, hand-knitted import from Italy. In fact, it was a machine-made, domestic, polyester-and-wool mix. Did the clerk violate the statute of frauds by her conduct? Did the clerk act ethically?

6 Grant had long admired Kahn's collection of records featuring the big bands of the 1930s. One day Kahn orally agreed to sell the collection to Grant for $275. When Grant appeared with the money, however, Kahn said she had changed her mind and refused to deliver. Moreover, she insisted she was acting within her legal rights. Kahn said she had learned that her collection was worth at least $1,000. Therefore, she said, a signed writing was required to make the contract enforceable. Has Kahn stated the law correctly?

7 Harrison orally agreed to buy two electric guitars and a matched set of drums from Rudolph. The price was $1,250, payable with $800 in cash and a bass saxophone. Harrison paid the price in full. However, Rudolph refused to deliver the guitars and drums, and he sent the

6 No; The amount agreed upon at the time of contracting was under $500 and did not need to be in writing to be enforceable. (p. 328)

7 No; Payment in full, which Rudolph accepted, makes the writing unnecessary under the statute of frauds. (p. 330)

8 Benefits of ownership include the pride in owning expensive and beautiful jewelry and in having others notice, admire, and be impressed by it. The jewelry may also increase in value. It is usually durable, does not deteriorate from action of the elements, and can be easily stored and moved. Burdens of ownership include the comparatively high retail price that must be paid for items which generally produce no economic product or profit, its low resale value, annual premiums for theft and accidental loss insurance, and home alarm systems. (pp. 323–324)

4 No; She has, by the regularity of her conduct and the nature of her business, transformed herself into a merchant, and must pay the sales tax. (pp. 324–325)

5 ETHICS ISSUE No; Although the clerk committed the tort of fraud (Chapter 6) and may also have been guilty of a crime (Chapter 5), the statute of frauds does not apply. (p. 328) The clerk's misrepresentation was clearly unethical.

9 ETHICS ISSUE No; Since the price was more than $500, the contract had to be in writing and signed by Starke to be binding on him. (pp. 328–329)

No; Starke took advantage of Berm's ignorance of the statute of frauds by giving the impression that both of them were bound while he continued to deal with Tremmel, an innocent third party.

10 ETHICS ISSUE In contracts of adhesion prepared by the seller, the buyer generally must agree to the stated terms or not get the goods. However, an eager seller will often be willing to reduce the price rather than lose the sale. Moreover, the buyer has the option of shopping further and buying from another source. (p. 322)

Yes, it is quite ethical for a seller to use contracts of adhesion provided the terms are fair to both parties.

Solving Case Problems

1 Yes; presence of the soft drinks on the shelf in the defendant's self-service store constitutes an offer for sale and delivery at a stated price. (pp. 320, 327) A customer who takes possession with intent to pay at the cashier's counter has accepted the offer and has title. Implied warranties arise under the UCC.

saxophone back and mailed a certified check for $800 to Harrison. He explained that he had decided to start another rock group. Rudolph claimed that their oral agreement was not enforceable. Is he right?

8 Danny Destello received several million dollars as the star and as co-owner of a motion picture that was a box-office sales success. Danny proceeded to spend $2 million on jewelry for friends and for himself. His older brother told him, "I admire your success, and I guess I should envy you and your friends. But I don't. Even assuming the friendships are genuine, believe me pal, burdens of such ownership will exceed the benefits." What are some of the possible burdens and benefits of such legal ownership?

9 ETHICS ISSUE On Monday, Starke dickered with Berm for more than an hour over the sale of a personal computer that had cost Starke $4,750 two years before. Starke alone was aware of the statute of frauds, and he knew Berm was not. Nevertheless when Berm said, "I'll give you $2,200 cash. That's my final offer," Starke replied, "Okay, I accept. You've just bought yourself a bargain." The exchange of the computer for the cash was to be made on Saturday. On Friday, Starke telephoned Berm and said, "Sorry, I've just delivered my PC to Tremmel for $2,500." Has Starke breached a binding contract to sell to Berm? Has Starke behaved ethically in his dealing with Berm?

10 ETHICS ISSUE After their business law class, Alexa and Ronald were discussing contracts of adhesion. Ronald insisted that when a "big ticket item," such as a television, is sold on credit terms, the seller prepares the contract. "You agree to it as written or you're out of luck. No sale." Alexa argued, "That's the truth, but not the whole truth." Can you explain what Alexa meant by her comment? Is it ethical for a seller to use contracts of adhesion?

▼ SOLVING CASE PROBLEMS

1 Gillispie, a minor, was injured when two bottles of a soft drink exploded. The accident occurred as Gillispie was carrying the bottles to the checkout counter in the defendant's self-service store. Had a sale taken place even though Gillispie had not yet paid for the goods? If so, the store could be liable for the injury. You decide. (*Gillispie v. Great Atlantic and Pacific Tea Company*, 187 S.E.2d 441, N.C.)

2 Shriber, an officer of Nelly Don, Inc., orally agreed with a representative of the defendant DHJ Industries, Inc., to buy 75,000 yards of colorfast fabric from DHJ. A few days later, Shriber confirmed this agreement by telephone, and then sent a Nelly Don purchase order form. The form included these words, "This purchase order shall be-

come a binding contract when acknowledged by Seller, or upon whole or partial shipment by Seller." In response, Shriber received a DHJ sales order form. At the bottom, just above the lines for signatures, this statement appeared, "THIS CONTRACT IS SUBJECT TO ALL THE TERMS AND CONDITIONS PRINTED ON THE REVERSE SIDE." On the reverse side was a clause requiring settlement of any controversy by arbitration. Shriber signed. Later, a dispute arose as to whether the fabric delivered was colorfast and machine washable. The plaintiff buyers claimed fraud and sued. The defendant sellers said the dispute had to be settled by arbitration and not in court. Was the arbitration clause binding? (*N & D Fashions, Inc. and Nelly Don, Inc. v. DHJ Industries, Inc.*, 548 F.2d 722)

3 Cargill, Inc., the plaintiff, is a large grain company. Warren, an agent of Cargill, managed its grain elevator in Hingham, Montana. On August 24, Warren orally contracted to buy from Wilson, the defendant farmer, 28,000 bushels of wheat at $1.48 per bushel and 6,000 bushels of higher protein wheat at $1.63 per bushel. Warren prepared two standard grain purchase written contracts. He signed them for Cargill, as its agent, and he also signed Wilson's name. A few days later, he delivered copies to Wilson, who made no objection. On August 30, Wilson received a $10,000 loan from Cargill. The check was attached to a detachable part of the standard grain contract, and it incorporated the two contracts by specific references to their numbers. Wilson indorsed and cashed the check. The loan was interest-free because it was an advance payment for the wheat. During September and October, Wilson delivered 11,000 bushels of ordinary wheat at the agreed-upon price of $1.48, and 6,000 bushels at the then-current, higher market price. Then Wilson refused to deliver any more wheat. Cargill sued for damages. Wilson claimed he was not bound because of the statute of frauds. Who should win? (*Cargill, Inc. v. Wilson*, 532 P.2d 988, Mont.)

4 Smigel orally offered to sell to Lockwood a used Rolls Royce for $11,400. Lockwood orally accepted the offer, paid $100 down, and agreed to pay the balance on delivery. However, Smigel failed to deliver the car and notified Lockwood that he had sold it to someone else. Lockwood sued to enforce the oral contract. You decide. (*Lockwood v. Smigel*, 18 Cal. App. 3d 800, 96 Cal. Rptr.289)

5 Jordan Paper Products, Inc., sued to recover $22,089.48 owed to it under an oral contract by Burger Man, Inc., an Indiana fast-food chain. The contract was for various paper products that Jordan had prepared at Burger Man's order, to specially identify the fast-food chain to its customers. Burger Man maintained that the oral contract was unenforceable because of the statute of frauds. You decide. (*Burger Man, Inc. v. Jordan Paper Products, Inc.*, 352 N.E.2d 821, Ind.)

2 Yes, it was binding. Under the UCC, in dealings between merchants, as here, when an acceptance contains terms which are "additional to or different from" the offer, the additional terms become a part of the agreement provided (a) the original offer did not expressly preclude such additions, (b) the additions do not materially alter the agreement, and (c) no reasonable notice is given of objections to the addition. (pp. 325–326)

3 Cargill should win. Written contracts—signed by the plaintiff's agent Warren—were delivered to Wilson, a merchant farmer, who accepted the contracts without objection. He also accepted and endorsed the check for $10,000. Wilson did not object within ten days, nor even within four months. Under these circumstances, it is not essential that Wilson sign to be bound. (pp. 328–329)

4 Judgment for Lockwood; under the UCC partial payment validates an oral contract if the unit sold is indivisible, as here. (p. 330)

5 Judgment for Jordan Paper Products. Due to the chain's identification being printed on the goods, they were unique and not suitable for resale. As a result, the oral contract is enforceable. (p. 331)

CHAPTER 17 ORGANIZER

Chapter Theme

Certain conditions must be met before the owner of goods can transfer ownership.

DIRECTED STUDY QUESTIONS	SPECIAL FEATURES	PROGRAM RESOURCES				
		Reteach	Enrich			
Who may transfer the ownership of goods?	Multicultural Highlights, p. 340 Thinking Critically Through Visuals, p. 341	✔	✔			
What is required for transfer of ownership?		✔	✔			
When does ownership transfer?		✔	✔			
When does risk of loss transfer?	Thinking Critically Through Visuals, p. 347	✔	✔		V K	
When do insurable property interests transfer?		✔	✔		A	
When do the transfer of ownership and risk of loss occur in specific transactions?	Ethics Issue, p. 350 Personal Perspectives, p. 351	✔	✔	✔		
What procedure must be followed in a bulk transfer of goods?	Writing Connections, p. 353 Preventing Legal Difficulties, p. 354	✔	✔			

Additional Resources

- *American Wholesalers and Distributors Directory*. Detroit, IL: Gale Research, 1992.
- Smith, Len Young and Roberson, G. Gale. *Business Law: Uniform Commercial Code,* 4th ed. St. Paul, MN: West Publishing Co., 1977.
- White, James J., and Summers, Robert S. *White and Summer's Hornbook on the Uniform Commercial Code*, 3d ed. St. Paul, MN: West Publishing Co., 1988.

One-semester course	✔	✔	✔					
One-year course	✔	✔	✔	✔	✔			

		ASSESSMENT OPPORTUNITIES			
	Cooperative Learning	Informal Assessment	Chapter Review	Chapter Test	Chapter *MicroExam* 
		✔	✔	✔	✔
		✔	✔	✔	✔
	✔	✔	✔	✔	✔
		✔	✔	✔	✔
		✔	✔	✔	✔
		✔	✔	✔	✔
		✔	✔	✔	✔

Videodiscs

Selling a Car

Search Chapter 21, Play To 22

Risk of Loss

Search Chapter 22, Play To 23

State by State

For *insurance* purposes, when a car dealer in Montana delivers a vehicle to the buyer, legal title passes, even though the dealer still has to transfer the certificate of title.

Teaching Materials

Student text, pp. 338–359

Overhead transparency masters

• *Who May Transfer Ownership (Clear Title) of Goods?*

• *What Tests Decide if Goods Are Subject to Transfer of Ownership by Sale?*

Videos

• *Law for Business* Videodisc

Workbook, pp. 51–52

Outside Resources

- Poster board
- Newspapers—business and classified sales sections
- Butcher paper
- Markers
- Blank overhead transparencies
- Magazines—business and news
- Scissors and tape
- Play money
- Chart paper

- Tape recorder
- Camcorder
- VCR

Assessment

- Chapter Test

- Chapter *MicroExam*

Vocabulary

good-faith purchaser, p.341
existing goods, p. 342
identified goods, p. 342
future goods, p. 343
fungible goods, p. 343
tender of delivery, p. 344
FOB, p. 347
bailee, p. 348
credit sale, p. 350
COD, p. 351
sale or return, p. 351
sale on approval, p. 352
sale of an undivided interest, p. 352
auction, p. 353
bulk transfer, p. 353

Learning Objectives

When you complete this chapter, you will be able to

1. Discuss who may transfer ownership of goods.
2. Understand what is required for transfer of ownership of goods.
3. Describe various types of goods.
4. Recognize when ownership and risk of loss transfer.
5. Differentiate between routine sales and important special types of sales.
6. Understand the unique problems in a bulk transfer of goods.

338

Chapter Self-Test

Assess students' understanding of ownership and risk of loss before they begin Chapter 17 by asking them to respond orally to the following questions: **(1) When transferring ownership of goods, is there a difference between transferring possession of the goods and transferring title to the goods?** (Yes, a person who buys stolen goods from a thief receives possession, but not title.); and **(2) When a buyer purchases goods on credit, does the buyer or seller carry the risk of loss when the payment is made in full?** (Buyer, ownership and risk usually pass at time of sale transaction, regardless of agreed-upon terms of payment) Review and discuss students' responses before continuing with the chapter.

CHAPTER 17

TRANSFER OF OWNERSHIP AND RISK OF LOSS

1 ETHICS ISSUE During a weekend of skiing at a resort in Vermont, you enjoy hours of skiing with Jack, a newly found friend. In good faith, you buy his cross-country skis for what seems to be a low but fair price. You never meet again. Later you meet Jill, who proves the skis were stolen from her by pointing out that her driver's license number is inscribed on the skis. Legally, who is entitled to the skis? Ethically, who is entitled to the skis?

2 Paying the price in advance, you order a professional-type hair dryer from a mail-order house. If the shipment is lost en route, who bears the loss?

3 You agreed to a ten-day free home trial of a new camcorder. During the trial period, a thief broke into your home. The camcorder, a television, and your stereo system were stolen and never recovered. Must you pay for the camcorder?

▼ FOCUS

As students enter the classroom, have them write on the chalkboard the name of something they own and beside it tell how they could prove ownership.

Discuss the difference between true ownership and possession in relationship to the legal transfer of ownership.

You Decide

1 ETHICS ISSUE Legally and ethically, Jill, the true owner, is entitled to the skis. A thief does not get good title to goods he or she steals, and therefore cannot transfer good title. You are, of course, legally and ethically entitled to recover damages from the loss suffered—but from Jack, the thief, not from Jill, the innocent victim.

2 The mail-order firm bears the loss. In a sale by a merchant to a consumer, the risk of loss normally passes only upon receipt of the goods by the buyer.

3 No; In a sale on approval, ownership and risk of loss do not pass to the buyer until the decision has been made to buy the goods. The buyer would, of course, be liable for loss or damage to the goods if caused by the buyer's negligence. That is not the case here, however.

Thinking Critically Through Visuals

In this photograph, customs officials are examining the contents of goods in transit during transfer of ownership of the goods. What might they discover that would make it important to know if the buyer has full knowledge of the laws governing the transfer of ownership? (If the goods were seized because of some illegality, it is important to know who is at risk of loss.)

TEACH

Write: **Generally one cannot transfer a better title than one possesses.** This sums up legal transfer of ownership, but there are specific exceptions. Discuss the four exceptions on pp. 341–342 using the transparency, *Who May Transfer Ownership (Clear Title) of Goods?*

APPLY

Multicultural Highlights

When the Yurok Indian tribe learned the U.S. Forest Service was building a logging road through federal land, the Yurok, whose religious practices require vast areas of natural setting, went to court to block the construction. The Yurok feared that the road would change the area and interfere with their religion, thus violating the First Amendment. They lost a Supreme Court battle by one vote. Not willing to give up, they challenged the construction on environmental grounds and won. Ask: **Do you consider the Yurok successful? Why?**

WHO MAY TRANSFER THE OWNERSHIP OF GOODS?

PROBLEM

Brad stole a cassette player from Fuller's car. He then sold it to Standon, who knew it was stolen. Did either Brad or Standon receive good title to the cassette player? Would it make any difference if Standon did not know or suspect that the cassette player was stolen?

Generally, only the true owner of goods may legally transfer ownership of those goods. Also, as a general rule, the buyer of goods receives only the property rights that the seller has in the goods and nothing more. Therefore, the person who buys stolen goods from a thief receives possession, but not title, because the thief did not have good title to give. This is true whether the buyer is innocent or, as in the problem, knows that the goods have been stolen and is therefore also guilty of the crime of receiving stolen property (see page 91). Unfortunately, stolen goods are seldom recovered. And if they are recovered, they have often been damaged or stripped of parts, as is often the case with automobiles. Even when recovered in good condition by the police, stolen goods often cannot be clearly identified as property of the victim and therefore are not returned.[1] The police are compelled to sell such goods at public auction.

As with most general rules, there are exceptions to these rules about transfer of ownership. Such exceptions include the following.

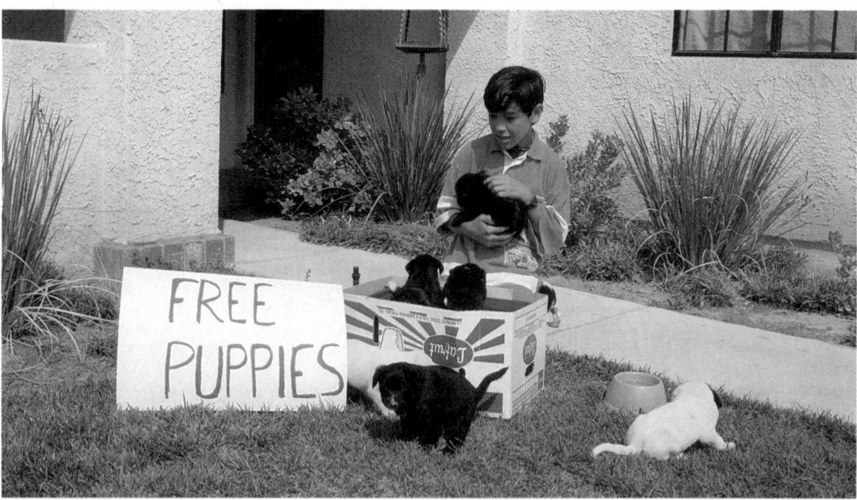

[1]Police authorities advise owners to use an electric engraving tool to inscribe their valuable possessions with the state and number of their automobile driver's license. This enables the police to locate the owners of recovered stolen goods.

ASSESS

Learning Objective 1 Have students write *Yes* or *No* to indicate if each of the following situations denotes a legal transfer of ownership: **(1) A fraudulent buyer sells to a third party good-faith purchaser.** (Yes); **(2) A true owner sells to another party.** (Yes); **(3) A thief sells to a person who knows the goods are stolen.** (No); **(4) A holder of a negotiable document sells the document?** (Yes); and **(5) A sales clerk sells to a customer?** (Yes)

1. Persons Authorized to Do So May Transfer Another's Title

Persons may validly sell what they do not own if the owner has authorized them to do so. Salesclerks in retail stores are so authorized. Auctioneers and sheriffs are also authorized when they sell, under court order, stolen or repossessed goods, or foreclosed property.

2. Fraudulent Buyers May Transfer Better Title Than They Have

If an owner of goods is induced by fraud to sell the goods, the buyer obtains a voidable title (see Chapter 12). Upon discovering the fraud, the victimized seller may cancel the contract and recover the goods unless an innocent third party has already given value and acquired rights in them. Such a third party is known as a **good-faith purchaser.** Thus, a fraudulent buyer with voidable title may transfer valid title to a good-faith purchaser. To act in good faith, the purchaser must not have reason to suspect the person who has the voidable title. The defrauded seller must seek damages from the original fraudulent buyer.

> Downy lied about his income and assets when he bought a dinette from Furniture World on credit. After making the first of twelve payments, Downy defaulted. Furniture World then checked Downy's credit record and discovered the fraud. But Downy had already sold the dinette to Tilly, who honestly thought that Downy was the owner. As a good-faith purchaser, Tilly received good title to the dinette. Furniture World must suffer the loss unless it can locate Downy and recover from him.

3. Holders of Negotiable Documents of Title May Transfer Better Title Than They Have

In business, certain documents are often used as a substitute for possession of goods. Examples are warehouse receipts issued by public warehouses, and bills of lading and airbills issued by common carriers. These documents may be nonnegotiable or negotiable. If the documents are negotiable, the goods are to be delivered to the bearer, who is the person in possession of the document, or to the order of a named party. Such persons, also known as holders, are deemed to have title to the goods. They may transfer ownership of the goods by transferring the documents alone. A holder who is named in the negotiable document must sign as well as deliver the document to transfer it to a third party. Negotiable documents, or instruments, as they are called, are discussed more fully in Unit 8.

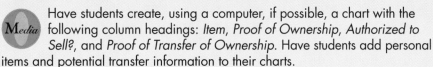

Thinking Critically Through Visuals

The boy in the photograph is offering puppies for free. If a person took a puppy home, would this legally transfer real ownership? (Yes, if the boy had clear title to the puppies.)

On a piece of poster board, print **Clear Title**. On several strips of poster board, write descriptions of possible buyers and sellers. Have students act out various transactions described on pp. 340–341. Use a book as the goods, and the *Clear Title* poster as the title. Assign roles by having students choose strips with buyer and seller descriptions. Make sure students accurately portray transfer of goods and transfer of title. **Guided Practice**

Have students create a flowchart illustrating how a fraudulent buyer with voidable title may transfer valid title to a good-faith purchaser. Check students' flowcharts against the following example. **Independent Practice**

Display the transparency, *Who May Transfer Ownership (Clear Title) of Goods?* Discuss if each person's right to transfer ownership is legal—always, sometimes, or never.

Have students create, using a computer, if possible, a chart with the following column headings: *Item, Proof of Ownership, Authorized to Sell?*, and *Proof of Transfer of Ownership*. Have students add personal items and potential transfer information to their charts.

▼ TEACH

Display the transparency, *What Tests Decide if Goods Are Subject to Transfer of Ownership by Sale?* Discuss the terms **existing goods** and **identified goods**. Circle the word *and* on the transparency and call attention to the fact that both characteristics are required to transfer ownership by sale. Discuss examples of **future goods** (Custom ordered furniture) and **fungible goods** (Boxes of paper cups). Compare contracts to sell with the sale of existing goods.

▼ APPLY

Have pairs of students role-play an attempt to transfer ownership in the following situations: the goods are physically in existence and identified to the contract, the goods are in existence but not identified to the contract, and the goods are not yet in existence. Point out the difficulties that arise and relate to the requirements for transfer of ownership. **Guided Practice**

4. Merchants Who Keep Possession of Goods They Have Sold May Transfer Better Title Than They Have

Occasionally a buyer will allow the merchant seller to temporarily retain possession of the goods after the sale. If, during this period, the merchant resells and delivers these goods to a good-faith purchaser, the latter receives good title. But the merchant must replace the resold goods or be liable in damages for the tort of conversion.

When their new home was almost finished, the Howlands bought a set of new living room furniture from Eaton's Fine Furniture Shop. Eaton was to retain possession of the furniture under a layaway plan until the house was completed. Eaton assumed that she would have no trouble replacing the furniture before this completion date. Therefore she sold the Howlands' furniture to Hopkins, a good-faith purchaser who took immediate delivery. Hopkins thus obtained a valid title. If Eaton is unable to replace the set when the Howlands demand delivery, she will be liable to them for damages for the tort of conversion.

▼ WHAT IS REQUIRED FOR TRANSFER OF OWNERSHIP?

PROBLEM

O'Dell was preparing for a gala New Year's Eve charity ball. He could not decide which of three tuxedos to buy from Signet Styles. At O'Dell's request, the manager set all three aside until the next day so O'Dell's friend could come in to help him decide. That night a fire destroyed the store and its contents. Must O'Dell pay for the tuxedos that were set aside?

For transfer of ownership of goods in a sale, the goods must be both existing and identified. **Existing goods** (1) are physically in existence even though they may not be in a fully assembled and immediately deliverable condition and (2) are owned by the seller. **Identified goods** have been specifically designated as the subject matter of a particular sales contract. The identification of such goods may be done by the buyer, the seller, both, or a mutually agreed-upon third party. Typically, when identified, the goods are marked, separated, or in some way made distinct from similar goods that the seller might have on hand.

In the problem, there was no intent to buy all three tuxedos, and no selection had been made of the one to be bought. Therefore, even though the

▼ ASSESS

Learning Objectives 2 & 3 Ask students to respond orally to the following questions: **(1) Can a seller transfer ownership of goods that are not fully assembled?** (Yes); **(2) Does a contract to sell future goods transfer ownership? Explain.** (No; It is a contract to sell.); and **(3) Is there ever an exception to the process of specific designation to meet the requirement of identified goods? Explain.** (Yes; fungible goods)

goods were existing, they had not been identified. Thus, there never was a contract to buy any one tuxedo. Consequently, ownership and risk of loss for all three items remained in the seller.

Unless goods are both existing and identified, they are **future goods.** Any contract for the sale of future goods is a contract to sell. Neither ownership nor risk of loss passes at the time of the agreement.

An important exception to the process of identification is made for **fungible goods.** These are goods of a *homogeneous* (i.e., essentially identical) nature in which, by nature or trade usage, each unit is regarded as equal to every other unit. Examples are a quantity of corn or oil of a given variety and grade, or thousands of cases of identical canned fruit in a warehouse. In many states, ownership and risk of loss in fungible goods pass without selection or identification of specific goods. The buyer therefore becomes the owner at the time of the agreement.

Bob Kluber produced 12,000 bushels of corn on his farm in Iowa and delivered it to the Golden Grain Granary for storage. It was mingled with even larger shipments from other farmers in the area. Kluber planned to withdraw most of the grain during the months ahead to feed his pigs and hogs. However, he sold 2,000 bushels to a neighbor and another 2,000 bushels to the Golden Granary. Since all of the corn was of the same variety and fungible, no effort was made to identify or to segregate specific additions to and withdrawals from the homogeneous mass.

WHEN DOES OWNERSHIP TRANSFER?

PROBLEM

Chien Huang ordered electronic equipment worth $3,000,275 from Inter-Continental Traders, a Seattle exporter. The equipment was to be shipped to a company in the People's Republic of China. The sales agreement, signed by both parties, stated that title and risk of loss would pass "when all necessary governmental permits are obtained." The Chinese government granted an import permit and necessary clearance to allow the exchange of Chinese currency into dollars to pay for the order. However, the U.S. State Department refused to grant an export permit because of the classified nature of some of the equipment. Did a sale take place?

Divide the class into groups of three or four students. Assign each group a sales situation, such as sale of a custom ordered table, sale of five horses from a herd of 20, or sale of 30 cartons of packages of potato chips. Ask each group to write, using a computer, if possible, a sales memorandum. (See p. 265.) confirming the sale. Have students provide evidence of existing, future, identified, or fungible goods as appropriate in their memos. Display students' memos on a bulletin board.

Independent Practice

TEACH

On the chalkboard, draw a balanced seesaw with a box on either end. In one box write **Rights and Benefits**, in the other box write **Duties and Burdens**. Under the drawing write **Ownership**. Explain that when ownership of goods is transferred, the owner also gains certain rights, benefits, duties, and burdens. Tell students that knowing when title transfers is especially important when goods are lost or damaged. The specifics on when ownership transfers are sometimes part of a sales agreement. When time of transfer is not spelled out, courts refer to the UCC for a solution. Discuss the four common situations of transfer found on pp. 344–345.

RETEACH

On an overhead transparency, write **existing goods**, **identified goods**, **future goods**, and **fungible goods**. Ask volunteers to add the definition and to tell whether it is required for transfer of ownership.

ENRICH

Have students brainstorm examples for the terms **existing goods, identified goods, future goods,** and **fungible goods.** Then have students individually make a three-column chart in which they list the four terms in the first column, their definitions in the second, and examples in the third.

APPLY

Have the class as a group examine the cases described on pp. 344–345 and brainstorm potential problems involving risk of loss that could happen and that would cause concern over the exact moment of transfer of ownership. Relate the discussion to the need for rules governing these situations. **Guided Practice**

Have a panel of students debate orally, or on paper in essay form, using a computer, if possible, the question of whether or not the best practice is to try to state exactly when ownership is transferred during a sale and list all possible circumstances, or to rely on trade custom and the UCC.

Independent Practice

Recall that ownership of goods brings with it a bundle of rights and benefits, offset by a related bundle of duties and burdens. Understandably it is important to know when ownership transfers from one party to another, accompanied by rights and duties.

Once goods are existing and identified, disputes may arise over who has title to the goods at particular times. Sometimes creditors of the seller, or creditors of the buyer, may claim possession in order to collect moneys due. Other disputes may concern who bears the risk of loss if the goods are damaged, stolen, or destroyed before the transaction is completed. A risk-bearer may want or need the protection of casualty insurance. Generally, the person who has title to the goods will bear the loss, but this is not always the case.

In deciding when title transfers from seller to buyer, courts first examine the sales agreement to see if the parties have clearly specified when they intended title to pass. If they have expressed such intent, courts will generally uphold their agreement. In the problem, no sale took place. The agreement said that title and risk of loss would pass "when all necessary permits" were obtained. Therefore Inter-Continental Traders would retain its goods because this condition had not been met.

If the parties do not specify when title is to pass, courts first determine if there is any applicable custom or usage in the particular trade that can settle the question. If there is no agreement on the matter and no available trade custom or usage, courts refer to the Uniform Commercial Code (UCC) for a solution.

Common situations involving transfer of title are discussed below. Note that neither the method of payment nor the time of payment governs the outcome.

1. If the Seller Is to Deliver the Goods to Their Destination

If the contract requires the seller to deliver the goods to their destination, title passes when the goods are tendered at that specified destination. **Tender of delivery** means that the seller (1) places (or authorizes a carrier to place) the proper goods at the buyer's disposal and (2) notifies the buyer so that delivery can be received. The manner, time, and place for tender are determined by the agreement and the UCC. When the seller is required to do additional work, title does not pass until such work is completed.

> Ozark Electric ordered a new electric generator for its power plant. Because of the generator's complexity, the seller was required to deliver it to Ozark's plant site and then install and test run it. Title to the generator passed to Ozark Electric when the delivery, installation, and test run were properly completed.

ASSESS

Learning Objective 4 Read aloud the following situations and have students jot down when title would pass: **(1) If the seller is to deliver the goods to a specified destination; (2) If the seller is to ship, but not deliver, the goods to a specified destination; (3) If the seller is to deliver a document of title; and (4) If the buyer is to take possession of the goods at the place of sale.** (For answers, see pp. 344–345.)

2. If the Seller Is to Ship, But Not Deliver, the Goods to Their Destination

If the contract requires or authorizes the seller to ship the goods but does not obligate the seller to deliver them to the destination, title passes to the buyer at the time and place of shipment, when possession is transferred to the carrier.

The San Pedro Unified School District ordered from the Papyrus Products Company of Quebec, Canada, 5,000 reams of paper suitable for high-speed photocopying. The buyers specified shipment via the Dolphin Lines Steamship Company with transit through the Panama Canal. Title passed when the seller delivered the paper to the carrier.

3. If the Seller Is to Deliver a Document of Title

When it is customary, or when the parties have agreed that the seller is to deliver a document of title (e.g., a negotiable warehouse receipt), title passes when and where the document is delivered.

Degory bought 6,000 tons of rice from the Diamond Delta Rice Growers' Cooperative. The rice was stored in a public grain elevator. Title passed when an authorized agent of Diamond Delta delivered the negotiable warehouse receipt for the goods to Degory. Degory planned to withdraw the goods at a later date. (Warehouse receipts are discussed more fully in Chapter 27.)

4. If the Buyer Is to Take Possession of the Goods at the Place of Sale

If the seller is to tender the goods at the place of sale, title passes at the time and the place where the sales contract is made.

Audugood contracted to buy a variety of 500 live tropical fish for her Pet Palace from a wholesaler. Because the fish required delicate handling, Audugood insisted on first inspecting and selecting the specific fish at the wholesaler's place of business. The sales contract was made and title passed after this was done, whereupon the wholesaler tendered delivery and Audugood took possession of the fish.

Divide the class into an even number of groups of four or five. Tell students they have two tasks:
1. To choose one of the numbered points on pp. 344–345 and to use it as a basis to write a case description of a dispute of ownership sparked by loss or damage to the goods in question.
2. To read and judge ownership and risk in a case description written by another group.

Pair groups for exchange of cases, and assign the following roles in each group: lawyer who checks accuracy of judgment against text; recorder who writes case; presenter who reads case and judgment to class; editor who checks case for completeness and clarity; and, facilitator, if necessary, who keeps everyone on task. Have the judging groups read the cases and judgments. Have the presenting group explain its reasoning. **Cooperative Learning**

RETEACH

On overhead transparencies, draw a diagram, such as a flowchart, to illustrate each of the four transfer-of-title situations described on pp. 344–345. Have volunteers circle the point of title transfer.

Have students imagine that they ordered a good. Have them describe, using a computer, if possible, what they ordered, who and where they ordered it from, where and how it will be delivered, and when ownership and risk of loss is transferred.

TEACH

On the chalkboard, draw the following sequence of events chain. Use the diagram as a guide to discuss the following four possible alternatives as to when the transfer of risk of loss from buyer to seller occurs: (1) if the seller ships the goods by carrier, (2) if the goods are held by a bailee, (3) if either party breaches after the goods are identified, and (4) if the goods are neither to be shipped by carrier nor to be held by a bailee. When discussing situations involving a bailee, list the three events—(a), (b), and (c) on p. 348—that transfer risk of loss. Point out that the risk of loss does not necessarily pass from seller to buyer when title is transferred.

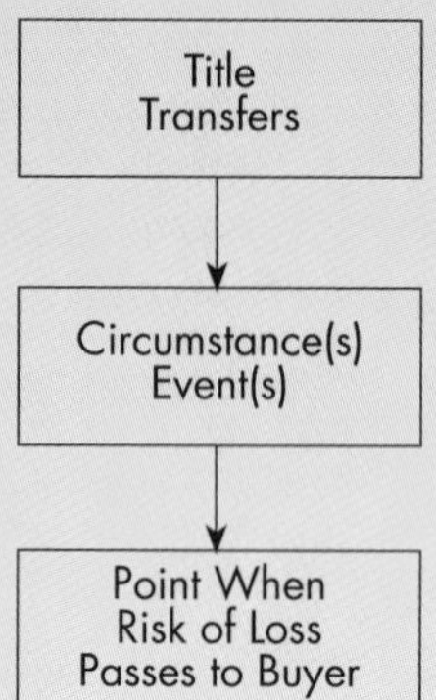

WHEN DOES RISK OF LOSS TRANSFER?

PROBLEM

Alda had stored 200,000 pounds of Idaho potatoes in Berle's B-r-r Cold Storage house. On December 17, Alda sold 25,000 pounds to Clark. On December 20, Alda notified Berle, who issued a negotiable warehouse receipt to Clark for 25,000 pounds. On February 15, Clark paid the storage charges and ordered shipment of the potatoes to New Orleans. On February 16, Berle shipped the goods. When did the risk of loss transfer to the buyer, Clark?

The transfer of the risk of loss from seller to buyer does not always occur when title transfers. Possible alternatives as to when the transfer of risk of loss takes place are discussed below.

1. If the Seller Ships the Goods by Carrier

If the seller is required to deliver the goods to a particular destination but is allowed to use a carrier, such as a railroad, to make the delivery, the risk of loss passes to the buyer at the destination, upon tender of delivery. This is true even if goods that are shipped by carrier are still in possession of the carrier.

Oregon Indian Industries Corporation sold a carload of cedar shingles to Orange County Developers, Inc., a construction company. Oregon Industries was to deliver the goods but could use a carrier to do so. When the railroad (the authorized carrier) delivered the car on a siding at the buyer's warehouse, unloading was delayed. The reason for the delay was that Orange County Developers hoped to save handling costs by transferring the shingles directly to delivery trucks for a subdivision project underway. A week passed before the railroad car was opened. If the contents had been stolen, damaged, or destroyed during those days, Orange County Developers, as the buyer, would have taken the loss. Risk of loss had passed upon the initial tender of delivery by the carrier.

Suppose the seller is not required to deliver the goods to the buyer at a particular destination. If the seller then uses a carrier to transport the goods, the risk of loss passes to the buyer when the goods are delivered to the carrier.

ASSESS

Learning Objective 4 Ask students to respond orally to the following: **Roll On, a Boston skateboard dealer ordered two shipments of skateboard wheels to be carried by Warp Time Express—one from Chicago marked FOB Boston and one from Houston marked FOB, Roll On warehouse, Boston. Where will each be delivered and when will risk of loss transfer?** (Warp Time freight station in Boston; Roll On warehouse in Boston)

Cook's Christmas Tree Corner ordered fifty cases of fragile ornaments from a wholesaler. The contract did not require delivery to Cook's or to any other designated destination. The wholesaler routinely shipped the ornaments using an independent trucker selected by Cook's. The shipment was lost when the trailer that contained the ornaments was stolen at an overnight truck stop. Unless covered by insurance, Cook's must bear the loss because it owned the goods.

Commercial buyers often use the shipment term **FOB**, which means "free on board." Assume (a) that the seller is in Atlanta and the buyer is in New York City. In such case, "FOB Atlanta" means the seller agrees to deliver the goods no further than the carrier's freight station in Atlanta. Title and risk of loss transfer to the buyer at that point. On the other hand, if (b) the terms are "FOB, buyer's warehouse, New York City," the seller must deliver the goods to the buyer's warehouse in New York City. The title and the risk of loss remain with the seller until delivery takes place. In the absence of contrary arrangements, the buyer pays the transportation charges in (a) above, the seller pays the charges in (b).

In shipments from foreign countries, it is not uncommon for the seller to quote a *CIF (cost, insurance, freight)* price. This means that the seller contracts for adequate insurance and for proper shipment to the named destination and then adds these items to the price or cost of the goods. The risk of

▼ APPLY

Thinking Critically Through Visuals

Fireboats in this photograph are working to extinguish a serious fire aboard a cargo ship. To what kinds of damage is the cargo subject? (Fire and water damage; total loss if the ship sinks) **If the seller was not required to deliver the goods to the buyer at a particular destination and chose to use the cargo ship as a common carrier, explain who is at risk of loss.** (The buyer to whom the risk of loss passed when the goods were delivered to the ship)

Pair students and give each pair two blank overhead transparencies and a marking pen. Assign two of the four alternatives for transfer of risk of loss (pp. 346–349) to each pair. Have each pair draw detailed flowcharts to illustrate their two alternatives. Have each pair show and explain their charts. Have students vote on the most cogent charts for each situation.

Guided Practice

▼RETEACH Have students outline the information on pp. 346–349 on the alternatives to when the transfer of risk of loss takes place.

▼ENRICH Have students brainstorm a list of various circumstances and objectives that would motivate a buyer to accept FOB to a destination other than his or her own place of business. (Answers may include that the buyer needs time to prepare space for the items, the destination is used as an intermediate point or as a warehouse, and so on.)

Divide the class into groups of three or four. Provide each group with copies of old business and news magazines, scissors, tape, markers, and blank posterboard. Have students use clipped photos and illustrations and markers to create a graphic-panel storyboard involving damage of goods and transfer of the risk of loss. Tell students that their objective is to incorporate as much as possible of their knowledge of the rules that govern risk of loss transfer.

Independent Practice

loss passes to the buyer when the seller delivers the goods to the carrier, such as a seagoing ship. However, the insurance provides protection against loss from any identified risks.

2. If the Goods Are Held by a Bailee

Sometimes goods are held for a seller by a bailee. A **bailee** has temporary possession of another person's goods, holding them in trust for a specified purpose. A public warehouse is an example of a bailee. The goods may be sold by the owner, yet the contract may call for delivery to the buyer without the goods being moved. The risk of loss transfers to the buyer under such circumstances in any of the following situations:

a. when the buyer receives a negotiable document of title covering the goods (e.g., a negotiable warehouse receipt);
b. when the bailee acknowledges the buyer's right to possession of the goods; or
c. after the buyer receives a nonnegotiable document of title (e.g., a nonnegotiable warehouse receipt) or other written direction to a bailee to deliver the goods. (The buyer must have had a reasonable time to present the document to the bailee, who must have honored it.)

In the problem on page 346, the risk of loss passed from Alda to Clark on December 20, when Berle issued the negotiable warehouse receipt. (Bailments are discussed more fully in Chapter 27.)

3. If Either Party Breaches After the Goods Are Identified

The seller sometimes breaches by providing goods so faulty that the buyer rightly rejects them. The risk of loss then remains with the seller until the defects are corrected.

Galaxy Glamor Furniture Company shipped a truckload of chairs and sofas to Brenda's Bargain Basement. Without unloading the tractor-trailer, inspection disclosed that Galaxy had mistakenly shipped sofas and chairs upholstered in costly Italian leather. Brenda had ordered the durable but much cheaper vinyl upholstery models. Brenda promptly notified Galaxy of the error and asked for instructions on their disposal. After a week, the unloaded trailer was still parked in back of Brenda's warehouse. Then a fire of undisclosed origin destroyed the trailer (along with some other vehicles). Galaxy suffers the loss unless properly insured.

▼ ASSESS

Learning Objective 4 Have students jot down the party who is at risk of loss in each of the following situations: **(1) Seller provides faulty goods and buyer rejects them.** (Seller); **(2) The instant buyer receives a negotiable document of title from a bailee.** (Buyer); and **(3) After the buyer receives a nonnegotiable document of title, a bailee is ordered to release the goods.** (Buyer)

4. If the Goods Are Neither to Be Shipped by Carrier Nor to Be Held by a Bailee

In any case not covered previously, the risk of loss falls on the buyer upon receipt of the goods if the seller is a merchant. If the seller is not a merchant, the risk of loss transfers to the buyer as soon as the seller makes a tender of delivery.

Abigail bought a camper trailer at a garage sale. The seller said that Abigail could take the trailer home at any time. Abigail went home to get a pickup with a trailer hitch. Upon returning, Abigail was told that during her absence, an unidentified person had backed into the trailer and had done extensive damage to it. If the person cannot be found, Abigail will have to bear the loss. That is because the seller was not a merchant and the seller had made an effective tender before Abigail left to get the pickup.

WHEN DO INSURABLE PROPERTY INTERESTS TRANSFER?

PROBLEM

Frosty-Frolic Company was a fresh-food packer and processor. In a sales contract with Goodman, Frosty-Frolic agreed to pack a quantity of head lettuce grown near Salinas, California, and to place the "Soaring Eagle" brand label on the cartons. The lettuce was routinely dehydrated, cooled, packaged, placed in the special cartons, and stacked on pallets in Frosty-Frolic sheds for daily shipment as ordered by Goodman. At what point did Goodman obtain the right to insure the goods against possible loss?

The buyer obtains a special property interest in goods at the time of their identification to the contract. This special interest gives the buyer the right to buy insurance on the goods. The physical act of identifying goods usually takes the form of setting aside, marking, tagging, labeling, boxing, branding, shipping, or in some other way indicating that the specific goods are to be delivered or sent to the buyer in fulfillment of the contract. Thus, in the problem, Goodman obtained an insurable interest when the lettuce was identified as hers, probably when it was placed in "Soaring Eagle" cartons. If the goods already exist and have been identified to the contract, the property interest of the buyer arises when the contract is made.

TEACH

Tell students that to insure goods, a person must have a special property interest in those goods at the time of their identification in the contract. Explain that special interest occurs by the physical act of identifying the goods. Discuss when insurable property interests transfer, how goods are identified, and what rights come to the buyer with insurable interests.

APPLY

On the chalkboard, write the following headings: **When Buyer Obtains a Special Property Interest in Goods, Ways Goods are Identified,** and **Buyer's Rights in Addition to the Insurable Interest**. Have students skim pp. 349–350 and list details under each column. (See pp. 349–350 for answers.) **Guided Practice**

Divide the class into groups of four or five students. Ask each group to prepare and tape record or videotape a mock newscast with related commentary about an insurable property interests transfer event. Play the tapes and have the class comment on the broadcasts' adherence to rules and laws concerning special property interests. **Independent Practice**

RETEACH Draw diagrams that depict transfer of risk of loss when involving a bailee, when either party breaches after goods are identified, and when goods are neither shipped by carrier nor held by bailee. Have students mark when risk of loss transfers and explain answers.

ENRICH Have students brainstorm analogies that characterize transfer of risk of loss. For example, the childhood game of *Hot Potato*, the saying *"left holding the bag,"* and so on. Ask: **When, do you think, does the greatest risk of loss occur?**

▼ TEACH

On the chalkboard, write the seven transactions: **cash-and-carry sales, sales on credit, COD sales, sale or return, sale on approval, sale of an undivided interest**, and **auctions**. Tell students that these transactions merit special attention because of the frequency with which they occur or because of the uniqueness of the rules that apply to them. Discuss transfer of ownership in each.

▼ APPLY

Ethics Issue

Read aloud the following: **Pretend you are the assistant manager of a pasta stand. Customers order, pay for their food, and receive a receipt at window one. At another window, a clerk puts the orders on trays and sets them on the counter for pick-up. Customers carry their trays to their seats. During the noon rush, a customer picked up her slippery tray, lost her grip and dumped her entire order on the floor.** Ask: **When was the risk of loss transferred?** (When the clerk put the tray on the counter) **Guided Practice**

In addition to the insurable interest, the buyer has the following rights:

1. to inspect the identified goods at a reasonable hour,
2. to compel delivery if the seller wrongfully withholds delivery, and
3. to collect damages from third persons who take or injure the goods.

WHEN DO THE TRANSFER OF OWNERSHIP AND RISK OF LOSS OCCUR IN SPECIFIC TRANSACTIONS?

PROBLEM

Cutting Edge, Inc., a manufacturer, sold 250 gasoline-powered chain saws to Valu-Line, a large retailer. The full price was due in six months, and Cutting Edge agreed to accept the return of any saws not sold by then. Two months later, after only twenty-five saws had been sold, Valu-Line filed a bankruptcy petition. Cutting Edge demands return of the unsold saws. Valu-Line's other creditors claim that title to the saws had passed to the retailer. Therefore, under the bankruptcy law, all creditors should share in the claim to the saws. Who is right?

The following transactions merit special attention because of the frequency with which they occur or because of the uniqueness of the rules that apply to them.

1. Cash-and-Carry Sales

When the buyer in a sales contract is a consumer who pays cash and takes immediate delivery, title passes to the buyer at the time of the transaction. This is the most common type of transaction when the goods are groceries or other low-priced items. Risk of loss passes upon the buyer's receipt of the goods from a merchant and on tender of goods by a casual seller.

The seller may insist on payment in legal tender. Checks are commonly used but are not legal tender. Acceptance of a check by the seller is not considered payment until the check is paid at the bank. But use of a check by the consumer in a cash-and-carry sale does not affect the timing of the transfer of title or risk of loss.

2. Sales on Credit

The fact that a sale is made on credit does not affect the passing of title or risk of loss. A **credit sale** is simply a sale that, by agreement of the parties, calls for payment for the goods at a later date. Ownership and risk of loss may pass even though the time of payment or delivery is delayed.

▼ ASSESS

Learning Objective 5 Have students respond orally to identify the moment that transfer of ownership and risk of loss occur in each of the following: **(1) Cash-and-carry sales between merchant and buyer** (On buyer's receipt of goods); **(2) Cash-and-carry sales between casual seller and buyer** (On tender of goods); **(3) Sales on credit** (Same as cash-and-carry); and **(4) COD sales** (On payment to carrier)

3. COD Sales

Goods are often shipped **COD**, which means collect on delivery. The carrier collects the price and transportation charges upon delivery and transmits this amount to the seller. If the buyer does not pay, the goods are not delivered. Thus, in effect, the seller retains control over the possession of the goods until the price is paid. In a COD arrangement, the buyer loses the right otherwise available to inspect the goods before payment. Nevertheless, ownership and risk of loss transfer just as though there were no such provision.

For years Global Reach, Inc., had sold postage stamps to collectors by direct mail. Losses from bad checks and uncollectible accounts continued to grow and were reducing the company's profits. Therefore, the owners adopted a new policy: all sales would be COD. This eliminated bad debt losses but sharply reduced the number of sales.

4. Sale or Return

When goods are delivered to a merchant buyer in a **sale or return,** the ownership and risk of loss pass to the buyer upon delivery. Such a transaction is a true sale. But if the buyer—who has a right to return the goods to the seller—returns the goods within the fixed or a reasonable amount of time, ownership and risk of loss pass back to the seller. This is true whether the sale is made for cash or on credit. The returned goods must be in substantially their original condition. Normally goods held on sale or return are subject to the claims of the buyer's creditors, which can seize the goods under court order. Thus, in the problem, all of Valu-Line's creditors share in the claim to the saws. Cutting Edge was but one of many claimants.

On November 27, Distributors, Inc., sold 100 pairs of ladies' hose, each in Christmas packaging, to Andy's Supermarket. Under the terms of the contract, Distributors, Inc., would buy back all the hose that the supermarket had not sold by January 1. This agreement would be classified as a sale or return.

The sale or return provision should not be confused with the return privilege granted to customers of some retail stores. These stores allow customers to return most purchases that have not been used, even if they are not defective. This return privilege is not required by law, but stores offer it to promote goodwill and increase sales in the long run.

Personal Perspectives

Ask students to share with family members what they have learned about transfer of ownership and risk of loss regarding cash-and-carry sales, COD sales, and sales on credit. Tell students to ask adult family members to offer additional knowledge about these topics and to tell about personal experiences they have had with these types of transactions. Tell students to then ask their family to consider all that has been discussed and to work together to come up with a recommended list of items or circumstances for each transaction type. In class, compile a composite list. **Independent Practice**

RETEACH In small groups, have students incorporate tangible props, including play money, to represent goods and means of payment as they role-play cash-and-carry, credit, COD, and sale or return sales transactions. Have them identify when transfer of ownership and risk of loss occur and explain why.

ENRICH Have students brainstorm and list on the chalkboard various signs and notices restricting acceptable means of payment in local businesses and institutions. Have them speculate and list possible pros and cons of each policy.

For students with specific learning disabilities, write the terms ***sale or return,*** *sale with privilege to return,* and ***sale on approval*** on an overhead transparency. Have students brainstorm to compose sentences that explain the words. Have a volunteer write the explanation on the transparency. For example, for **sale or return**, students could write "Sale or return is between a merchant buyer and a merchant seller. When the buyer receives the goods, the sale is complete, but the buyer has the right to set the sale aside by returning all or a portion of the goods." Photocopy the transparency and distribute a copy to each student.

5. Sale on Approval

Sometimes goods are delivered to the buyer in a **sale on approval,** "on trial," or "on satisfaction." In such a case, prospective ownership and risk of loss do not pass until the prospective buyer approves the goods. This may be done by words, payment, any conduct indicating approval, or retention of the goods beyond a specified or reasonable time. While in possession of the goods, the prospective buyer is liable for any damage to them caused by his or her negligence. Normally, the prospective buyer may reject for any cause, whether or not it is reasonable.

Gardner filled in and mailed a magazine coupon for a series of best-selling books. Both the advertisement and the descriptive folder said the subscriber would have "ten days free trial." When the first book was delivered, Gardner carelessly placed it on the metal cover over a steam radiator in her old Victorian house. She forgot about the book until she returned two weeks later from a winter skiing vacation. By then the heat from the radiator had permanently warped the binding of the book. The loss was Gardner's. Risk of loss had passed to her at the end of ten days. Even if the damage had taken place during the trial period, she would still be responsible because the damage resulted from her negligence.

6. Sale of an Undivided Interest

A person who sells a fractional interest in a single good or in a number of goods that are to remain together makes a **sale of an undivided interest.** Ownership and risk of loss pass to each buyer at the time of the sale of each undivided interest.

Clarke bought a one-half interest in a traveling carnival. On the day after the purchase, the truck and trailer carrying the big tent to the next city were totally destroyed in a crash and fire. Clarke claimed that he should not have to bear any part of the loss because the owners had not yet determined which part of the carnival belonged to whom. However, the contract showed an intent to continue the carnival's operation under joint ownership. There was no intent to divide the various properties into separately owned parts. Therefore Clarke was wrong. From the time of the purchase, he was part owner of all the carnival properties. As such, he had to suffer one-half of the loss.

ASSESS

Learning Objective 6 Read aloud the following questions and have students write answers: **(1) What might be included in a bulk transfer?** (Materials, supplies, merchandise, or equipment); **(2) What are the responsibilities of the seller in a bulk transfer?** (Provide a list of creditors); and **(3) What is the responsibility of the buyer in a bulk transfer?** (Notify the seller's creditors of the forthcoming transfer and to pay their claims or make other credit arrangements with them)

7. Auctions

An **auction** is a public sale to the highest bidder. When an auctioneer decides that no one will bid any higher for the goods on sale, the bidding is closed, usually by the pounding of the auctioneer's gavel. In doing so, the auctioneer accepts the bid on behalf of the owner of the goods, and ownership passes to the buyer at that time. Risk of loss passes whenever the auctioneer acknowledges the buyer's right to possess the goods, typically upon tender of the goods in exchange for payment.

Auction sales are "with reserve" unless specifically announced in advance to be "without reserve." "With reserve" means that if nothing to the contrary is stated in the conditions of the sale, an auctioneer may withdraw the goods anytime before announcing completion of the sale. If "without reserve," the goods must be sold to the person who makes the highest bid even if it is the first and only one, and is ridiculously low.

WHAT PROCEDURE MUST BE FOLLOWED IN A BULK TRANSFER OF GOODS?

PROBLEM

Tinker rented a small retail store building in a resort town in Massachusetts. She planned to stock it with toys and souvenirs and was pleased when Turner, a local merchant, offered to sell her his entire inventory of such goods at his wholesale cost. Turner gave Tinker a list of creditors of his business. What should Tinker do with this list?

A **bulk transfer** is the transfer, generally by sale, of all or a major part of the goods of a business in one unit at one time. Such goods would include materials, supplies, merchandise, and equipment if sold with the inventory.

The law protects creditors of the occasional dishonest merchant who would otherwise sell out secretly, keep the proceeds, and disappear. The UCC requires notice to the seller's creditors before the bulk transfer is made. The seller is required to list all creditors. The buyer is required to notify those creditors of the forthcoming transfer of ownership and to pay their claims or to make other arrangements with them. In the problem, Tinker would be required to take this action. If the buyer does not do this, creditors of the seller may make claims against the inventory and equipment after the buyer takes possession.

An innocent third party who in good faith buys some or all of the goods from a bulk transferee gets good title. But if such third party pays no value or knows that the buyer failed to comply with requirements of the bulk transfer law, the creditors can retake the goods.

TEACH

On the chalkboard, write the definition of **bulk transfer**. (The transfer, generally by sale, of all or a major part of the goods of a business in one unit at one time) Have students brainstorm what those goods might include. (Supplies, merchandise, and so on) List the responsibilities of the buyer and the seller.

APPLY

Have the whole class collaborate on the construction of an outline that summarizes the major points in the section *What Procedure Must Be Followed in a Bulk Transfer of Goods?* Decide on the three main points first and write them in outline form on the chalkboard. Next, add details. **Guided Practice**

Writing Connections

Language Arts
Have students review the PROBLEM on p. 353 and assume the role of Tinker to write, using a computer, if possible, a generic letter to Turner's creditors. Have students exchange papers and check each other's rationale and format.

Independent Practice

RETEACH

Media: Write the term **bulk transfer** on a transparency. Under it, list these phrases: **What it is; What it includes; Responsibilities of the seller; Responsibilities of the buyer**; and **What happens if seller and buyer do not comply**. Have students list details.

ENRICH

Have students brainstorm a list of results of not complying with the requirements in a bulk sale. Discuss the legal and ethical ramifications. (For example, creditors could make claims against the goods after the buyer takes possession.)

Preventing Legal Difficulties

Lead students in a discussion of the seven suggestions for preventing legal difficulties. Ask students to propose ways to remember each item and, when appropriate, to advocate ways to carry out the suggestion. For example, for suggestion six, students could recommend ways to check the buyer's credit. (Consult credit bureaus for credit rating.)

▼ CLOSE

Divide the class into small groups. Have groups brainstorm three to six tips involving transfer of ownership and risk of loss that would be immediately relevant to people their age. Have one person from each group write their tips on the chalkboard. Then have students vote on the most important ones and create a class list on chart paper. Have students illustrate each item on the list. Have students copy the final list in their notebooks.

Assign the following end-of-chapter materials:
Student text review activities, pp. 354–359
Workbook, pp. 51–52
Chapter Test

Chapter *MicroExam*

Preventing Legal Difficulties

When dealing with personal property...

1. Remember that ownership of goods will not necessarily prevent transfer of title to them contrary to your wishes when:
   a. you have authorized others to sell the goods for you. They may violate your instructions.
   b. you have been defrauded in a sales transaction and have given a voidable title to the wrongdoer. Before you cancel the contract and try to get your goods back, the wrongdoer can transfer good title to a good-faith buyer.
   c. someone has wrongfully obtained possession of a negotiable warehouse receipt, a negotiable bill of lading, or a negotiable airbill for your goods. The wrongdoer can give good title by negotiating, that is, transferring, the paper.
   d. you have allowed the person who sold to you to keep possession of your goods. The person who sold them to you might sell them again.

   Be alert to such possibilities.
2. It is generally wise to act promptly in identifying goods to the sales contract and in completing performance. Delay may lead to complications.
3. Ideally, in important written sales contracts specify precisely when title to goods and risk of loss of goods is to transfer.
4. As a buyer or a seller, carry adequate insurance when appropriate to cover any insurable interest you may have in goods that are the subject matter of the sales contract.
5. Assure yourself of the integrity and financial responsibility of buyers before selling goods to them on credit, on sale or return, or on approval.
6. When the buyer's credit is questionable, sell for cash or on a COD basis.
7. If you buy an entire business inventory or a major part of one, be sure to comply with UCC rules governing bulk transfers.

▼ REVIEWING IMPORTANT POINTS

1. Generally the owner of goods is the only one who can legally transfer title to them. Exceptions are made for a party who:
   a. is authorized by the owner to sell the goods,
   b. has obtained good title to the goods by fraud, and sells them to a good faith purchaser,
   c. is the holder of a negotiable document of title, or

d. is a merchant seller who has retained possession of previously sold goods.

2 Before ownership in goods can pass, goods must be both existing and identified.

3 In determining when title and risk of loss pass in a sales transaction, the terms of the sales contract are given top priority. If those terms do not provide an answer, then trade customs and usage may provide the determining customary rule. If not, UCC rules are used to make the determination.

4 A special, insurable property interest is transferred to the buyer at the time of identification of the goods to the contract.

5 In cash-and-carry sales, title passes at the time of the transaction. If a check is used, the payment is conditional until the check is paid by the bank on which it is drawn.

6 COD terms by a seller do not affect the time of transfer of ownership or of risk of loss. But the terms do reserve control of the goods to the seller until payment is received.

7 At an auction, title passes when the auctioneer signifies acceptance of the bidder's offer. Unless otherwise announced, the auctioneer may refuse all bids and withdraw the goods.

8 Notice of a bulk transfer of the inventory and equipment of a business must be given to creditors of the seller before the sale takes place.

9 An innocent third party who in good faith buys some or all of the goods from a bulk transferee gets good title.

▼ STRENGTHENING YOUR LEGAL VOCABULARY

Match each term with the statement that best defines that term. Some terms may not be used.

auction
bailee
bulk transfer
COD
credit sale
existing goods
FOB
fungible goods
future goods
good-faith purchaser
identified goods
sale of an undivided interest
sale on approval
sale or return
tender of delivery

1 Goods of a homogeneous nature in which each unit, by nature or by trade usage, is treated as equal to every other unit in the mass.

Strengthening Your Legal Vocabulary

1 fungible goods
2 COD
3 bulk transfer
4 sale or return
5 auction
6 identified goods
7 future goods
8 credit sale
9 tender of delivery
10 sale of an undivided interest

Applying Law to Everyday Life

1 No; Carr did not have title and therefore could not give title. (p. 340) Properly, the saw should be returned to the neighbor and the sales price to Sutro. Practically, the parties, not aware of the facts or the law, will probably go their separate ways without changing anything.

2 Salmon; Smith's is a merchant seller. Because the Bible has been left in Smith's possession by the buyer in each of the first two instances, Smith's may transfer good title to the Bible to a good-faith purchaser who takes delivery of it, as Salmon did. Note that Smith's is liable in damages to both Aubley and James for breach of contract and for tort. Smith's may also be criminally liable. (p. 342)

2. Shipment term that forces the buyer to pay before being allowed to take delivery of the goods.
3. Transfer of all or a major part of the goods of a business.
4. Completed sale in which the buyer has a right to return goods within a reasonable or fixed amount of time.
5. Sale to the highest bidder.
6. Goods that are selected and designated for a particular contract.
7. Goods that are not identified or are not in existence.
8. Sale in which payment for the goods takes place, by agreement, at a future time.
9. Placing of the proper goods at the buyer's disposal with notification that delivery can be taken.
10. Sale of a fractional interest in a single good or in a number of goods that are to remain together.

▼ APPLYING LAW TO EVERYDAY LIFE

1. After Carr refurbished her home, she held a yard sale of furniture and equipment she no longer needed. Included was a large crosscut saw, which she sold to Sutro, not knowing that her husband had borrowed the tool from a neighbor. Did Sutro become the owner?
2. Smith's Bookstore handled rare books. Needing money desperately, Smith's sold an old edition of the Bible to Aubley, a collector. Smith's received $20,000 as a deposit of one-half the purchase price. The remainder was to be paid upon delivery of the book. Smith's then sold the same book to another collector, James, on the same terms. Finally, Smith's sold and delivered the book to Salmon for the full $40,000. All three buyers acted in good faith and without notice of the other transactions. Who gets title to the book?
3. Some years ago, OPEC (the Organization of Petroleum Exporting Countries) boosted oil prices. Since then, fuel conservation has become increasingly important. Accordingly, the Enterprise Tower Corporation contracted for installation of a computerized system of temperature control for its thirty story office building. The seller, Minnesota Systematics, was required to deliver, install, and successfully test run all equipment involved in the new system. When did Enterprise Tower become the owner of the goods?
4. Donatti, of San Francisco, ordered 400 pounds of fresh blueberries from Margeson, a produce broker in New Zealand. The terms called for ship-

3. Enterprise Tower became the owner only after delivery, installation, and a successful test run of the entire complex system. (p. 344)
4. Initially, Margeson suffers the loss since the berries had not yet arrived at Donatti's cold-storage plant. (p. 346) However, she can probably prove that the airline was at fault and therefore that it was liable. If Margeson had purchased insurance, the insurance company would normally pay and then seek to be indemnified by the airline, by right of what is called subrogation. (Chapter 34)
5. Burby; If Burby is a merchant, risk of loss would pass to the buyer, Buckminster, on receipt of the wood. If Burby is an ordinary, nonprofessional seller, risk of loss would pass to the buyer on tender of delivery. Here, neither receipt nor tender took place. (p. 349)
6. Promptly return the unsold fireworks and get a refund of $2,713.50. In a sale-or-return contract, ownership and risk of loss pass to the buyer upon delivery, but the buyer has a right to return the goods within an agreed or reasonable amount of time. (p. 351)
7. ETHICS ISSUE In a bulk transfer such as this, creditors who have not been given the notice required by statute are not bound by the sale. They may treat it as void and proceed to seize the inventory in order to collect what is due them. (p. 353) No; Ashford lied and deliberately defrauded Bogler. Such conduct is criminal, and clearly unethical.
8. ETHICS ISSUE Yes; The buyers of the furniture and other equipment from the Shwindlers did get good title. Corcoran had been induced by fraud to sell these possessions and they had voidable title. Corcoran could have canceled the contract and recovered his goods, but innocent third-party buyers had already given value and acquired good title to them. Corcoran's only recourse is to pursue

ment by airfreight, FOB Donatti's cold-storage plant, in Los Angeles. The blueberries were properly packed and shipped by airline common carrier, but they were mishandled upon arrival at the Los Angeles International Airport. Delivery was delayed, and when the fruit was finally delivered it was not edible. Who must suffer the loss?

5 Burby was a dealer in fuel and related supplies. Burby sold a quantity of oak firewood to Buckminster. Nothing was said about delivery to a carrier or transfer to a bailee. After the goods were set aside and were ready for delivery, they were stolen by burglars. Who suffers the loss?

6 To finance a trip for the high school band, the director bought "safe and sane fireworks" priced at $4,000 wholesale. The director paid cash in a sale-or-return contract. Band members took turns as salesclerks in the Fourth of July booth provided by the distributor. Several items did not sell at all. The wholesale price of those fireworks sold by midnight on July 4 was only $1,286.50. What should the director do?

7 ETHICS ISSUE After ten years as a retail stationery and gift dealer, Ashford decided to sell out and move to Europe. Shortly before the lease on his store expired, he sold his entire inventory, all cabinets and shelving, accounting equipment, and accounts receivable to Bogler for $48,950. Bogler planned to open a store in a new location under her own name. Ashford owed $13,950 to fourteen trade creditors. He assured Bogler that he would pay them off out of the sales price so that "she would not be pestered and could start out with a clean slate." The creditors were not notified of the bulk transfer. What can they do when they learn that Ashford has disappeared somewhere in Europe with the sales proceeds? Did Ashford act ethically?

8 ETHICS ISSUE Corcoran was suddenly transferred from Portland, Oregon, to company headquarters in Schenectady, New York. Before moving, he hastily rented his house to Mr. and Mrs. A. Shwindler, who had shown him convincing credentials of their credit worthiness. The Shwindlers also bought all the household furniture and equipment for $10,000. They paid 5 percent ($500) down, with the balance to be paid in nineteen equal installments of $500 each. The Shwindlers were prompt in paying the rent and the $500 installment for two months. Then they disappeared. Evidently their credit records were forgeries, and before vanishing they had sold almost all the furniture and kitchen equipment to good-faith purchasers. Did the good-faith purchasers get good title? Did the Shwindlers act ethically?

9 Late one evening, Annette and Barbie were discussing plans each had for an independent mail-order business "some day." They agreed that they would not want to face the headaches and risks of selling goods on

the Shwindlers, sue them for civil damages, and possibly file criminal complaints against them. But this may prove to be impossible. (p. 341) No; The Shwindlers were guilty of crimes, torts, and grossly unethical behavior.

9 No; By offering to sell only for cash or certified check, Annette automatically limits the potential volume of sales. Despite the added cost of credit to consumers, most do buy on credit. Thus Annette may even be unable to cover her overhead expenses (e.g., rent, utilities, insurance) and she could suffer losses that force her out of business or even into bankruptcy. Note also that experts advise against sending cash by mail unless the letter is registered, which is relatively expensive. Otherwise the cash could be lost or stolen en route. Barbie, by selling only on COD terms, would discourage potential sales, with similar results to those experienced by Annette. Then, too, persons who do buy on COD terms sometimes refuse to accept the goods, which are then returned to the seller at the seller's expense. Both Annette and Barbie should consider selling to customers who use valid credit cards and thus have usually established their credit worthiness. (p. 350)

10 Rock is quite wrong. One may indeed have legal possession of property, but that is not the whole story. Enforceable rights and duties of ownership often remain with someone else, as determined by the UCC and by other rules of law. Examples abound:
• When the legal owner rents or leases property to a user or tenant; when one buys a motor vehicle on the installment plan; The seller or finance company retains the legal title until paid in full, and may summarily repossess if there is a default in payments.
• When one buys a residence and pays for it over a period that

credit. Annette said she would "avoid all losses by selling only for cash or certified check." Barbie said she would "avoid all losses by selling only on a COD basis." Will these strategies avoid all losses?

10 Guy D. Rock was big, tough, and outspoken in class. "Why are we dancing around with all this confusing talk about 'title' and 'ownership' and 'transfer' and 'rights and duties' and 'risk of loss'? All you gotta know out there in the cold cruel world is that possession is nine-tenths of the law. And the tenth doesn't count when the chips are down!" Is Rock right?

SOLVING CASE PROBLEMS

1 In 1945, during World War II, Lieber was in the U.S. Army and was one of the first soldiers to occupy Munich, Germany. Lieber entered Adolf Hitler's apartment with some companions and removed some of "der Führer's" clothing, decorations, and jewelry. In 1968, Lieber was living in Louisiana when his chauffeur stole the collection and sold it to a dealer. The dealer then sold the collection to Mohawk, in New York. Mohawk bought the collection in good faith. Through collectors' circles, Lieber learned that Mohawk had his collection. He demanded its return. You decide. (*Lieber v. Mohawk Arms, Inc.*, 314 N.Y.S.2d 510, N.Y.)

2 Lane was in the business of selling boats in North Carolina. In February, he sold a new boat, a 120-HP motor, and a trailer to a man who represented himself to be "John Willis." Willis gave Lane a check for $6,285 and left with the goods. The check proved to be worthless. Less than six months later, Honeycutt bought the three items in South Carolina from a man whom he had known for several years as "John R. Garrett." In fact, this was Willis, using an alias. Later, while searching for Willis under the alias of "John Patterson," the Federal Bureau of Investigation contacted Honeycutt. Honeycutt said that (a) he had paid a full price of only $2,500; (b) Garrett had nothing to show he was the owner; (c) he did not know from whom Garrett got the boat; (d) Garrett said he was selling the boat for someone else; (e) Garrett signed what he called a "title" (the document was nothing more than a "Certificate of Number" issued by the state Wildlife Resources Commission, not the "certificate of title" required by statutes); (f) Garrett forged the signature of the purported owner, John F. Patterson, on the so-called title. Plaintiff Lane now claims that defendant Honeycutt was not a good-faith purchaser and therefore should return the boat to him, with damages for a wrongful detention. You decide. (*Lane v. Honeycutt*, 188 S.E.2d 604, N.C.)

often lasts up to thirty years; Again, in case of default, the property can be legally seized and sold to pay the balance due.

It is true that criminals in our society do not concern themselves with laws governing the legal transfer of title. Criminals get possession of property by illegal means under a code that says might is right and possession is nine-tenths of the law. Of course, only a small segment of society thinks that way. And many from that group are eventually arrested and deprived of both their ill-gotten gains and their liberty.

Solving Case Problems

1 Judgment for the plaintiff, Lieber; his chauffeur, the thief, could not give good title. (p. 340) Even though Lieber's title was open to possible challenge by the occupational military authority in Germany and/or by the German Bavarian government, neither challenged. New York law (Civil Practice Law and Rules, Sec. 7101) provides for the recovery of goods by one who has superior right to possession, and Lieber's right was superior to that of Mohawk. Moreover, Lieber benefits from a Louisiana law (Civil Code 3509) which provides that when "the possessor of any movable whatever has possessed it for ten years without interruption, he shall acquire ownership of it without being obliged to produce a title or to prove that he did not act in bad faith." This is not the law in other states.

2 Judgment for the plaintiff, Lane; Although the plaintiff was defrauded in the original sale in February, John Willis had obtained a voidable title. As such, Willis could have transferred good title to a good-faith purchaser. (p. 341) Here, however, the evidence, including the ridiculously low price, and knowledge of the forgery proved that Honeycutt was not a good-faith purchaser.

3. Consolidated Chemical Industries purchased three heat exchangers at a cost of $12,500 from Falls Industries, in Cleveland. The contract specified that after identification, the machines were to be crated securely. They were then to be delivered, without breakage, to the destination, the Consolidated plant in East Baton Rouge. Because the machines were not crated securely, the exchangers were badly damaged in transit. Consolidated refused to accept them, and Falls sued. Falls claimed that risk of loss had passed when the goods were delivered to the carrier. Do you agree? (*Falls Industries, Inc. v. Consolidated Chemical Industries, Inc.*, 258 F.2d 277)

4. The plaintiff, a Los Angeles manufacturer of men's clothing, sold a variety of clothing to the defendant, a retailer in Westport, Connecticut. The plaintiff prepared four invoices covering the clothing and stamped them "FOB Los Angeles," and added the words "GOODS SHIPPED AT PURCHASER'S RISK." The plaintiff delivered the goods to the Denver-Chicago Trucking Company. When the truck arrived in Connecticut with the goods, the defendant's wife was in charge of the store. She ordered the driver to unload the cartons and place them inside the store. The driver refused and left with the goods. The defendant complained to the plaintiff, who filed a claim against the trucking company. No reimbursement was obtained by the plaintiff, and the defendant never received the goods. Now the plaintiff seller sues the defendant buyer for the purchase price. You decide. (*Ninth Street East, Ltd. v. Harrison*, 259 A.2d 772, Conn.)

5. In June, plaintiff Multiplastics, Inc., contracted with defendant Arch Industries, Inc., to make and to ship 40,000 pounds of plastic pellets, which were to be delivered at the rate of 1,000 pounds a day after Arch gave "release instructions." Multiplastics produced the pellets within two weeks. Arch refused to give the release orders, citing labor difficulties and its vacation schedule. On August 18, Multiplastics wrote, "We have warehoused these products for more than forty days... however we cannot warehouse...indefinitely, and request that you send us shipping instructions." Multiplastics followed this with numerous telephone calls seeking payment and delivery instructions. In response, on August 20, Arch agreed to issue the release orders but never did. On September 22, the Multiplastics factory, including the 40,000 pounds of this order, was destroyed by fire. The pellets were not covered by Multiplastics' fire insurance policy. Therefore Multiplastics sued Arch for breach of contract and also claimed that the risk of loss had passed to the buyer. You decide. (*Multiplastics, Inc. v. Arch Industries, Inc.*, 348 A.2d 618, Conn.)

3. No; When identified existing goods (p. 342) are to be delivered at destination without breakage, the risk of loss from breakage is on the seller until the goods are tendered at the point of delivery. (p. 346)

4. Judgment for the plaintiff seller; The goods were shipped FOB Los Angeles, and so when the goods were duly delivered to the carrier, the risk of loss passed to the defendant buyer. The dispute as to unloading was a problem to be resolved between the buyer and the carrier, which was the buyer's agent. The fact that the plaintiff voluntarily tried to recover from the carrier does not make any difference in the result. (p. 346) (Note: The defendant should pay the plaintiff and file a claim against the common carrier.)

5. Judgment for the plaintiff, Multiplastics; The seller had made a proper tender of delivery under the contract that required the buyer to accept delivery at the indicated rate (1,000 pounds a day). The contract was breached on August 20. The time that elapsed until September 22, the date of the fire, was a commercially reasonable period within which to place the risk of loss on the buyer. After a buyer has breached, the seller must eventually resume full responsibility for goods in his or her possession and obtain appropriate insurance coverage. But the law allows a commercially reasonable time during which this must be done. Meanwhile, the risk of loss remains on the defaulting buyer. (p. 348) Note also that the decision did not depend on whether title had passed to the buyer. This reflects the UCC's philosophy of holding the parties responsible on the basis of "provable circumstances" and "operative facts," rather than on some arbitrarily or mechanically applied standard as to passage of title (as was done before adoption of the UCC).

CHAPTER 18 ORGANIZER

Chapter Theme

Express and implied warranties are designed to substantiate product quality or performance; persons injured by defective products may bring suit against manufacturers or merchants in the chain of distribution of the product.

DIRECTED STUDY QUESTIONS	SPECIAL FEATURES	PROGRAM RESOURCES				
		Reteach	Enrich	SN	AM	
What are express and implied warranties?	Thinking Critically Through Visuals, p. 363	✓	✓		V	
Are sellers' claims always warranties?		✓	✓			
What is meant by "caveat emptor," "caveat venditor,"and "good faith"?	Writing Connections, p. 366	✓	✓	✓		
What warranties are implied by law in all sales?	Ethics Issue, p. 367; Thinking Critically Through Visuals, p. 368	✓	✓			
What express warranties can be made by all sellers?	Personal Perspectives, pp. 368–369	✓	✓			
What additional warranties are implied by law for merchants only?		✓	✓		A	
When and how may warranties be excluded?		✓	✓			
What is product liability?	Thinking Critically Through Visuals, p. 373 Multicultural Highlights, p. 374 Preventing Legal Difficulties, p. 374	✓	✓		K	

Additional Resources

- Ciullo, Peter A. *Low Impact Service: A Guide to Automotive Service & Warranty Complaints, How to Avoid Them, How to Resolve Them.* Naugatuck, CT: Maradin Press, 1992.
- Guaspari, John. *The Customer Connection: Quality for the Rest of Us.* NY: AMACOM, 1988.
- White, James J., and Summers, Robert S. *White and Summer's Hornbook on the Uniform Commercial Code*, 3d ed. St. Paul, MN: West Publishing Co., 1988.

One-semester course	✔	✔	✔					
One-year course	✔	✔	✔	✔	✔			

Chapter Pacing Guide

	ASSESSMENT OPPORTUNITIES			
Cooperative Learning	**Informal Assessment**	**Chapter Review**	**Chapter Test**	**Chapter *MicroExam*** (Media)
	✔	✔	✔	✔
✔	✔	✔	✔	✔
	✔	✔	✔	✔
	✔	✔	✔	✔
	✔	✔	✔	✔
	✔	✔	✔	✔
	✔	✔	✔	✔
	✔	✔	✔	✔

State by State

A trial judge in Mississippi said it was proper to impose absolute liability on cigarette manufacturers for injuries from use of their products.

Videodiscs

Warranties

Search Chapter 23, Play To 24

Teaching Materials

Student text, pp. 360–382

Overhead transparency masters
- *What Is the Implied Warranty of Merchantability?*
- *What Warranties Are Made:*

Videos
- *Contracts, Warranties, and Credit* Videotape
- *Mock Trial:A Question of Facts* Videotape
- *Law for Business* Videodisc

Workbook, pp. 53–58

Outside Resources
- Newspaper and magazine advertisements
- Classified ads for flea markets, garage sales, and other casual sales
- Blank overhead transparencies
- Index cards
- Copies of *Safety Alerts* and *Consumer Reports* magazines
- Poster paper & markers

- Camcorder
- VCR

Assessment
- Chapter Test

- Chapter *MicroExam*

Vocabulary

warranty, p. 362
express warranty, p. 362
full warranty, p. 364
limited warranty, p. 364
implied warranty, p. 364
puffing, p. 364
caveat venditor, p. 366
good faith, p. 366
encumbrances, p. 367
warranty of merchantability, p. 370
disclaimer, p. 372
privity of contract, p. 373
product liability, p. 374

Learning Objectives

When you complete this chapter, you will be able to

1. Distinguish between implied and express warranties and understand the protection they provide.
2. Appreciate the importance of careful, informed buying, even when warranties are available. "Caveat emptor!"
3. Recognize the preeminent importance of the warranty of merchantability, but realize that it is often limited or excluded by sellers.
4. Differentiate between a full warranty and a limited warranty.
5. Know that application of strict liability law can protect consumers injured by defective products, regardless of the presence or absence of warranties or sellers' negligence.

360

Chapter Self-Test

Assess students' understanding of warranties before they begin Chapter 18 by asking them to explain briefly in writing what a **warranty** is and how it protects the buyer against defective products he or she has purchased. (Answers may include that a warranty is a written or oral statement of truth about the qualities and/or performance of a product. A warranty protects the buyer against false sales claims and product defects, depending on the terms of the individual warranty.)

CHAPTER

18

DEFECTIVE PRODUCTS

❶ Shortly after buying a new jacket, you become displeased with its color, fit, style, and price. As you think back, you also decide that the merchant was rude, delivery was slow, and credit terms were harsh. Can you, as a consequence, return the goods and claim a breach of warranty?

❷ ETHICS ISSUE You enter a hardware store and tell the salesperson, "I need some stuff that will remove varnish from an old oak desk I'm refinishing." Although the salesperson had never used the product or seen it demonstrated, he urges you to buy a product called Strippo-Speedo. "It works like a charm," he says. When you apply the product, it gums up the varnish but does not remove it, and it scars the wood. Is the seller liable? Was it ethical for the salesperson to give the advice he did?

❸ Your parents buy a new sofa for the living room. Less than nine weeks after the purchase, they discover that the upholstery is starting to wear thin. In some places, the stitching is unraveling. Do your parents have any legal recourse?

FOCUS

As they enter the classroom, tell students to jot down on a flip chart or an overhead transparency some experiences they or their family and friends have had with defective products and/or warranties. If students have not had any such experiences, ask them to write about what they think should be done if they purchase a product that is defective. Save the list for use in the ENRICH activity on p. 365.

After reviewing the experiences listed above, begin a brief class discussion about defective products and warranties, asking student volunteers to share their experiences.

You Decide

❶ No, warranty protection does not apply to this situation. It is a matter of personal judgment.

❷ ETHICS ISSUE No, the salesperson did not act ethically. The claims went beyond puffing. The buyer clearly stated what the product was expected to accomplish. The salesperson implied that the product in question would do the job. The seller is obligated to support the implication.

❸ Yes; Goods are expected to last for a reasonable time before showing wear and tear.

Thinking Critically Through Visuals

Unpacking a newly purchased item and finding it defective can be very discouraging. What options are available to the buyer of this product? (The mixer is probably covered by a manufacturer's warranty; it may be honored by the store where the mixer was purchased.)

TEACH

Explain to students that a **warranty** is a statement about the product's qualities or performance that the seller assures the buyer is true. Explain the difference between the four types of warranties: **express, full, limited,** and **implied**. Make students aware that sellers are not required to give warranties. However, under the Magnuson-Moss Warranty Act, the Federal Trade Commission has established certain minimum standards that must be met by sellers who give written warranties on products sold to consumers that cost more than $15 and that normally are used for personal, family, or household purposes.

APPLY

On a blank overhead transparency or on the chalkboard, have students list and explain the nine points of information found on pp. 363–364 that are required to be in a single-document warranty.

Guided Practice

WHAT ARE EXPRESS AND IMPLIED WARRANTIES?

PROBLEM

Bligh, a sales agent employed by Total Environments, persuaded the Fletchers to install a central air-conditioning system. Bligh assured them that "this unit will keep all rooms at 68 degrees even on the hottest summer days and the coldest winter mornings." The unit failed to perform as promised. Do the Fletchers have any rights against Total Environments?

To induce prospects to buy, sellers often promise more than their products can provide or do. An example is Bligh's statement in the problem. When such a precise factual claim is part of the bargain, the seller legally promises the buyer that the product will perform as stated. The price paid is consideration for the product and any included warranty. In sales, a **warranty** is a statement about the product's qualities or performance that the seller assures the buyer is true.

Warranties may be either express or implied. Because they involve sales of goods, they are governed by the Uniform Commercial Code (UCC). An assurance of quality or promise of performance explicitly made by the seller is an **express warranty.** An example is: "Use our brand of oil and you won't need to change your engine oil for 10,000 miles." In the problem, Bligh made an express warranty. As Bligh's employer, Total Environments is liable because the warranty was breached. A breach of warranty is a breach of contract. There is no intent to deceive, so it is not the tort of fraud for which punitive damages might be claimed and collected.

An express warranty may be oral or written. (See the example in Figure 18-1.) It may even be implied by conduct. If the contract is written, the warranty must be included in the writing, or it probably will be excluded from the agreement by the parol evidence rule. However, if the warranty is given after the sale, it may be oral even though the sales contract was written. A warranty or any other term may be added to a sales contract later by mutual agreement, and no new consideration is required.

Under the Magnuson-Moss Warranty Act, the Federal Trade Commission has established certain minimum standards that must be met by sellers who give written warranties on products sold to consumers that cost more than $15 and that normally are used for personal, family, or household purposes. Sellers are not required to give warranties, but if they do they must make available to consumers prior to the sale a single document, in simple and readily understandable language, with the following information:

ASSESS

Learning Objectives 1 & 4 Have students write the difference between an **express warranty** and an **implied warranty** and the difference to the buyer between a **full warranty** and a **limited warranty.** (The full express warranty makes specific promises of quality and guarantees replacement or repair without cost within a reasonable time; the limited warranty offers less protection. An implied warranty is imposed on sellers and provides buyers assurance of minimum standards of contractual performance.)

Motorparts PART NO. **CX-83** ADJ. PERIOD **60 MO.**

PLANT CODE GRN 0846

BATTERY LIMITED WARRANTY

This Motorparts Battery is warranted by Steeley Motor Co. to the original retail purchaser for the time shown above when it is used in a private passenger car or light truck. If the battery fails to hold a charge due to a defect in material or workmanship it should be returned to a Motorparts retailer or wholesaler. THIS CARD AND YOUR DATED PURCHASE INVOICE ARE REQUIRED FOR WARRANTY REPLACEMENT.

Name *Al T. Kelley* Date Purchased *3-6-92*
(Date Installed for Service Fleet)

Address *1020 Elm* City *Akron* State *OH*

SERIAL NUMBER A 464476

If a failure occurs, the owner will pay a percentage of the replacement cost based on the Motorparts user exchange price (fleet price for fleet users) at the time of the adjustment. Shown below are the adjustment tables for privately owned passenger cars and light trucks and fleet, farm, marine and other commercial vehicles.

Adjustment Table

Mo.'s After Purch.	0-3	4-5	6-10	11-15	16-20	21-25	26-30	31-35	36-40	41-45	46-50	51-55	56-60
Owner's Percentage Replacement Cost													
Car/Lt. Truck	0%	8%	17%	25%	33%	42%	50%	59%	67%	75%	84%	92%	97%
Fleet/Commercial*	0%	16%	35%	50%	67%	84%	100%	*Farm, Marine & Other Commercial					

IMPORTANT: Further Warranty information is on the reverse side of this card.

NOTE: Detach and KEEP with your purchase invoice.

The Motorparts Limited Battery Warranty does not cover:

1. Failure as a result of use in applications other than those recommended in Motorparts catalogs
2. Damage to case, cover or terminals caused by abuse, negligence, freezing or improper installation
3. Cost of recharging or use of a rental battery
4. Labor to remove and replace battery in the vehicle
5. To the extent allowed by law, loss of time, inconvenience, loss of use of the vehicle or other consequential damages

THERE IS NO OTHER EXPRESS WARRANTY ON MOTORPARTS BATTERIES. ANY IMPLIED WARRANTY OF MERCHANTABILITY OR FITNESS IS LIMITED TO THE DURATION OF THE WRITTEN WARRANTY. SOME STATES DO NOT ALLOW THE EXCLUSION OR LIMITATION OF CONSEQUENTIAL OR INCIDENTAL DAMAGES OR HOW LONG AN IMPLIED WARRANTY LASTS, SO THE ABOVE LIMITATIONS AND EXCLUSIONS MAY NOT APPLY TO YOU.

THIS WARRANTY GIVES YOU SPECIFIC RIGHTS, AND YOU MAY HAVE OTHER RIGHTS WHICH VARY FROM STATE TO STATE.

Inquiries concerning this warranty should be directed to:

Warranty Administration, Steeley Parts and Service Division
7800 River Road Pittsburgh, Pennsylvania 15227

Figure 18-1

This is an example of an express warranty. Note that the seller does not unconditionally agree to repair or replace the battery if it proves to be defective. Instead the buyer-owner is required to pay an increasing percentage of the replacement cost, which grows to 100 percent at the end of sixty months. Also note that this warranty expressly excludes the important warranty of merchantability, which could have extended the warranty protection well beyond sixty months. Therefore this is a limited warranty.

1. to whom the warranty is extended (e.g., if it is limited to the original buyer),
2. a description of the product and any excluded parts,
3. what the *warrantor* (i.e., one who makes a warranty) will and will not do in the event of a breach of warranty,
4. when the warranty begins (if different from purchase date) and when it ends,

Thinking Critically Through Visuals

Figure 18-1 is an example of an express limited warranty. When does this warranty expire? (Five years from date of purchase) **If Al Kelley sells his vehicle before the warranty expires, can this warranty be transferred to the new owner?** (No, the warranty is good only to the original retail purchaser.)

Photocopy the warranty in Figure 18-1 and distribute copies to students. Have them highlight the information on the warranty that matches the nine items listed on pp. 363–364, which are some of the provisions of the Magnuson-Moss Warranty Act. Remind students that not all the numbered items may apply to this warranty. Make and display an overhead transparency of the warranty on an overhead projector and, with students' direction, identify the nine items. Tell students to make any corrections on their paper copies.

Independent Practice

RETEACH Have students imagine a defective product. Then help students write their own warranty for this product. Encourage students to refer to the warranty and minimum standards on pp. 363–364.

ENRICH Have students explain in writing why it is to the consumer's benefit that warranties are governed by federal legislation. (Answers may include that consumers should have some basic protection against defective goods, which then can be enhanced by state laws.)

▼ TEACH

Explain to students that **puffing** is exaggerated sales talk. Make students aware that buyers should not accept personal opinions as warranties or facts. However, if a buyer asks the seller's opinion as an expert, the seller's word as to the quality of the article becomes part of the basis of the bargain and may be taken as a warranty.

▼ APPLY

Role-play or describe a salesperson who uses puffing to sell a student an item visible in the classroom. Repeat this activity using different scenarios, different student buyers, and varying your sales pitch. Have the class differentiate between facts or product warranties and personal opinions. **Guided Practice**

Distribute newspapers and magazines to students and ask them to find advertisements that are good examples of **puffing.** Have them circle these sections in the ads. Then, have students work together to create a bulletin board display called *All Puffed Up.* **Independent Practice**

5. the step-by-step procedure to follow to obtain performance of warranty obligations,
6. the availability of any informal methods of settling disputes,
7. any limitation on how long implied warranties last,
8. any exclusion or limitation on incidental or consequential damages, and
9. the words "This warranty gives you specific legal rights, and you may also have other rights which vary from state to state."

An express warranty that obligates the seller to repair or to replace a defective product without cost to the buyer and within a reasonable time is a **full warranty.** Any warranty that provides less protection than a full warranty is a **limited warranty,** and the seller must identify it as such (see Figure 18-1).

Sellers are free to decide whether to give any express warranties. However, the law compels all sellers to honor certain implicit, unstated warranties, in order to ensure minimal standards of contractual performance. This rule applies whether or not explicit warranties are given by the seller. Such an implicit warranty obligation imposed on all sellers is an **implied warranty.**

▼ ARE SELLERS' CLAIMS ALWAYS WARRANTIES?

PROBLEM

Kanssar was trying to persuade Ana to buy a new car. "Just stand back and admire it," he said. "There's nothing finer on the road. It's sleek as a leopard. Fast as a jaguar. Tough as a tiger. Test drive it and you'll think you're floating on a cloud—at eighty miles per hour. And look at our terms. You can't find a better deal in town!" Not one of these exaggerated claims was literally true. But Ana, who knew little about cars, was persuaded and made the purchase. Does she have any resulting legal rights against Kanssar?

Sellers often enthusiastically overstate the merits of the goods they are trying to sell. The making of such statements as "superb quality," "you can't buy a better book," or "most beautiful" is **puffing**—exaggerated sales talk. Such words are not warranties or statements of fact. They are merely personal opinions. Buyers should not—and generally do not—accept such opinions at face value. In the problem, Kanssar was puffing. Thus Ana has no resulting legal rights.

▼ ASSESS

Learning Objective 2 Have students make a two-column chart. In the first column, have them write *caveat emptor*, **caveat venditor,** and **good faith.** In the second column, have students explain how the law applies to the buyer in each case. (Caveat emptor does not protect the buyer from poor judgment; caveat venditor protects the buyer and the seller by implying important warranties; good faith is defined by the UCC as "honesty in fact.")

Sometimes, however, the buyer has good reason to believe that the seller is an expert. If a buyer asks for the seller's opinion as an expert, the seller's word as to the quality of the article becomes part of the basis of the bargain and may be taken as a warranty. This is particularly true with merchants. For example, a statement by a jeweler that a diamond is flawless may thus be a warranty and may be relied on as such.

WHAT IS MEANT BY "CAVEAT EMPTOR," "CAVEAT VENDITOR," AND "GOOD FAITH"?

PROBLEM

The Stephensons bought a personal computer from Outer Space Outfitters. Within two weeks, the Stephensons learned that although their PC was a standard brand sold nationally, it was not highly regarded by experts in the field. It was comparatively slow, had limited capacity, and could not utilize many of the best software programs. Moreover, it was overpriced. In fact, some stores were selling the same model at 30 percent below the list price paid by the Stephensons. Security analysts predicted that the manufacturer would soon file a bankruptcy petition. Can the Stephensons legally demand and get their money back from Outer Space Outfitters?

Under the old common law, a person who inspects goods or who fails to use the opportunity to inspect them, yet purchases, cannot later complain of defects that would be detectable by ordinary inspection. As you know from Chapter 9, *caveat emptor* is Latin for "let the buyer beware." This warning applies to all buyers. The buyer may get the "worst of the bargain" because of a failure to define needs, to study values, and to compare available brands (and unbranded items) and prices before buying. Persons who fail to observe shortcomings in the quality and value of goods they buy must usually live with their mistakes. Fortunately, many large stores voluntarily accept returns of merchandise. They then permit exchanges, give credit toward future purchases, or reverse credit account charges. Some even give cash refunds. In the problem, the Stephensons cannot recover their purchase price. They could have avoided this outcome by learning more about personal computers before buying one. The law does not protect buyers against bad judgment of value. Nor does it prevent poor choice of color, style, or fit. It cannot direct buyers at various price levels to the most appropriate cars or cakes or computers.

Divide the class into groups of three or four students. Assign the following roles: facilitator (optional), express warranty writer, puffed advertisement writer, and presenter. Assign each group a product and have them write both a piece of puffery and an express warranty for it. Then, have the presenter show and explain the group's work. **Cooperative Learning**

TEACH

Write the terms **caveat emptor** and **caveat venditor** on the chalkboard. Tell students that caveat emptor puts the responsibility in a sale on the buyer and caveat venditor makes the merchant responsible for the quality or performance of the goods. Explain that the UCC enforces **good faith,** or honesty in the conduct or transaction.

APPLY

Read aloud the following scenario: **Smith purchased a diamond ring from a jeweler after being told that it was nearly flawless. When he had the ring appraised, he was told it was worth much less than he paid. Is this a case of caveat emptor or caveat venditor?** (Caveat venditor; the jeweler gave an oral express warranty for the quality of the diamond.) **Guided Practice**

RETEACH Have each student choose one of the following terms: *caveat emptor,* **caveat venditor**, or **good faith** and create a cartoon strip that expresses its meaning in a sales situation. Display students' work and have them explain it.

ENRICH Have students return to the FOCUS activity list created at the beginning of the chapter. For each defective product, have students discuss which of the warnings applies: *caveat emptor* or **caveat venditor.** Have students explain the basis for their responses.

Writing Connections

Economics
Have students prepare a simple questionnaire, then survey local merchants on what warranties (other than manufacturer's warranties), if any, they offer on their products. **Independent Practice**

For limited English proficient students who are having difficulties learning the term **caveat venditor,** provide the following chart:

Language	Term	Meaning
English	Vend	to sell
Italian	Vendere	to sell
Spanish	Vender	to sell

Ask students to use the root word *vend* to list other English words dealing with sales, such as vendee, vendor, vending machine, and so on.

▼ TEACH

Some warranties are implied by law in all sales (pp. 366–368): warranty of title, warranty against encumbrances, and warranty of fitness for a particular purpose. However, these warranties can be excluded from the sales contract only if both parties agree to it.

To a considerable extent, the effect of caveat emptor has been reduced in modern times by **caveat venditor,** which is Latin for "let the seller beware." Under this doctrine, important warranties are implied by law to benefit buyers if the seller is a merchant. Numerous other statutes have also been enacted to protect consumers. Also, courts have helped buyers by expanding consumer rights under the doctrine of strict product liability.

The UCC formally decrees that "[e]very contract or duty within this Act imposes an obligation of good faith in its performance or enforcement." This affirms the necessity of ethical standards of behavior in business. The UCC further explains that **good faith** "means honesty in fact in the conduct or transaction concerned."

▼ WHAT WARRANTIES ARE IMPLIED BY LAW IN ALL SALES?

PROBLEM

While adding a large new family room to their home, the Tanakas asked the Alpha Electric Service Company what size circuit breaker they would need to carry the increased electrical current load. After reviewing the list of equipment planned for the entertainment center of the room, the Alpha expert recommended a fifteen-ampere breaker. Following installation, however, the breaker consistently cut off the power whenever two or more of the listed equipment were operating at the same time. The breaker was mechanically perfect, but it was not adequate for the current load. Do the Tanakas have any legal rights against Alpha?

The three warranties discussed in the following sections are made to all purchasers by all sellers, including casual sellers as well as professional merchants. These warranties are implied by law and need not be mentioned in the contract. Only if the parties specifically agree is any one or more of these warranties excluded.

1. Warranty of Title

In the very act of selling, the seller implicitly warrants that he or she has title to the goods and the right to transfer them. This warranty is implied by law but is excluded when it is obvious that the seller does not have title. An example is when a sheriff, by court order, sells a debtor's goods to satisfy a judgment.

▼ ASSESS

Learning Objective 1 Distribute one index card to each student. Ask students to write five *True* or *False* statements on the front with answers on the back, dealing with the three warranties (pp. 366–368) that are implied by law in all sales. After exchanging cards, have students answer each statement. After verifying the correct response, pair students to discuss the reasons for their responses.

Donnell found a gold ring on a busy downtown street. The ring had no identifying marks. He gave it to the local police, but they returned it after their customary search procedure had failed to locate the owner. Donnell then sold the ring to Leesen. They agreed that since Donnell had found the ring, there would be no warranty of title. If the true owner appeared and could prove ownership, the ring would have to be returned, and Leesen agreed that such loss would be his.

2. Warranty Against Encumbrances

Also implicit in the act of selling is the seller's warranty that the goods shall be delivered free of all **encumbrances** (i.e., claims of third parties, for example for an unpaid balance) of which the buyer is not aware at the time of contracting. This warranty does not ensure that the goods are free of encumbrances at the time of the sale, but rather that they will be free at the time of delivery. This distinction enables the seller to comply with the warranty by paying off any third-party claimants before transferring ownership.

Kossel sold a portable copying machine to Nansen and promised delivery in two weeks. Kossel did not mention that he owed $850 to the bank, with the machine as security. Kossel can avoid breaching the implied warranty against encumbrances by paying off the loan before delivering the machine.

3. Warranty of Fitness for a Particular Purpose

A buyer who needs goods for a specific purpose often tells the seller about that purpose. Then (a) the buyer relies on the seller's skill and judgment for a selection of appropriate goods and (b) the seller has ample reason to know of that reliance. In such circumstances, the seller impliedly warrants that the goods delivered to the buyer are reasonably fit for the stated purpose. If they prove to be unfit, the buyer has a right of action for breach of warranty. Therefore, in the problem, the Tanakas have a right of action for breach of an implied warranty of fitness for a particular purpose.

This warranty does not arise when the buyer

a. personally selects the goods, or
b. orders the goods according to the buyer's own specifications, or
c. does not rely on the skill and judgment of the seller, because of independent testing or for other reasons.

▼APPLY

Copy the base and the title of the following graphic organizer on the chalkboard. Ask students to help you complete the organizer. **Guided Practice**

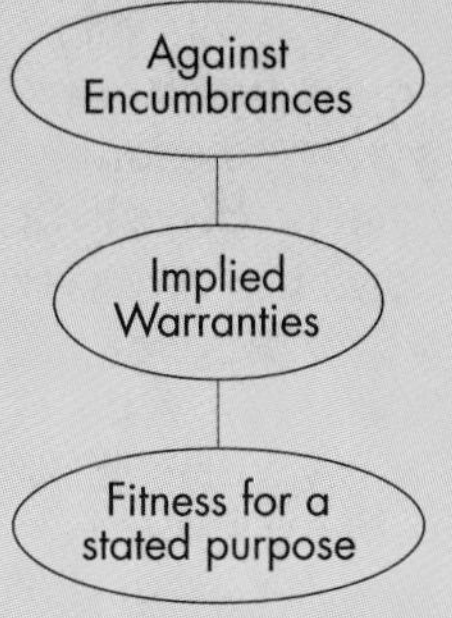

ETHICS ISSUE

Ethics Issue

Using a computer, if possible, have students respond in writing to the following situation: **Babs, who has little sewing experience, buys a complicated dress pattern and an expensive silk fabric at La Mode Fabric Shoppe. Babs botches the job and returns to La Mode to complain. Is the shop legally or ethically required to compensate Babs for her loss?** (No, the shop is not legally responsible. Answers will vary as to ethical responsibility.)

Independent Practice

▼RETEACH Arrange students who need reteaching into three smaller groups. Assign to each group one of the warranties discussed on pp. 366–368. Have each group summarize a consumer's rights, then give examples.

▼ENRICH Have students debate the statement: *It is in a consumer's best interest that all express warranties be implied.* (Arguments could be made that the average consumer is not aware of the warranties implied by law, and is unaware of his or her rights, and, therefore, all warranties should be express.)

Thinking Critically Through Visuals

If the buyer of this new cassette player has only an implied warranty, will he or she, do you think, have a problem getting a replacement product? (Probably not; A cassette player is designed to play tapes, and the law compels all sellers to honor the unstated warranty of merchantability to ensure minimal standards of contractual performance.)

▼ TEACH

Sellers may be bound by two express warranties: the warranty of conformity to seller's statement or promise and the warranty of conformity to description, sample, or model.

▼ APPLY

Personal Perspectives

Ask students to recount any experiences they may have had ordering a product from a catalog or TV ad, or after only seeing a sample of it. Use

(continued)

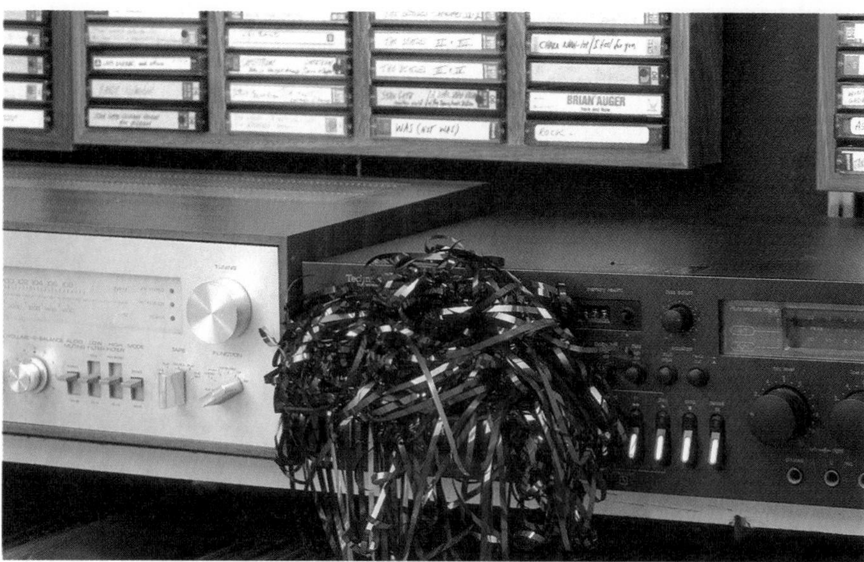

The warranty could arise even when the buyer asks for goods by patent or brand name. However, this variation applies only if the seller knows the purpose for which the goods are required and if the buyer relies on the seller's selection. For example, the buyer might ask for a "BUZZER" brand name chain saw to fell a stand of thirty trees with trunks two feet in diameter. When the seller selects the proper model, the buyer is relying on the seller's judgment, expertise, and implied warranty of fitness for a stated purpose. Contrast this with the case of a buyer who insists on getting goods of a particular brand and specifies the model, size, or number, obviously not relying on the seller's knowledge. Consequently, no warranty of fitness for a particular purpose arises.

▼ WHAT EXPRESS WARRANTIES CAN BE MADE BY ALL SELLERS?

PROBLEM

The Metropolitan Unified School District bought a large quantity of chalk from the Cliffs-of-Dover Corporation. The purchase was based on the sales agent's statement that the chalk was nonirritating, nontoxic, and would not scratch. In fact, however, the chalk often made a loud scratching sound when used. It also produced a fine dust, which caused many users to sneeze and develop skin rashes. Can Metropolitan claim a breach of warranty and obtain a refund?

▼ ASSESS

Learning Objective 1 Have students write brief summaries of why the express warranties described on p. 369 can be made by *all* sellers. (Responses may include that any seller who makes a specific, explicit statement or promise or provides a description, sample, or model should be held to it.)

1. Warranty of Conformity to Seller's Statement or Promise

In addition to warranties implied by law, every seller is bound by any express statement of fact or promise that is part of the bargain. It is desirable to have such statements in writing. Thus, in the problem, Metropolitan is legally entitled to recover money paid for the chalk.

2. Warranty of Conformity to Description, Sample, or Model

When a description of the goods or a sample or model is made part of the contractual agreement, there is an express warranty that all the goods shall conform to the description, sample, or model—whichever is used. This is true even if the words "warrant" or "guarantee" do not appear in the contract. It is also true even if the seller had no intention to give such a warranty.

The Space Rockets, a professional football club, contracted for new uniforms from Arkwright Mills. At the time of the order, sample uniforms in particular colors and fabrics were referred to and included as part of the agreement. Arkwright is legally obligated to provide goods that match the samples.

▼ WHAT ADDITIONAL WARRANTIES ARE IMPLIED BY LAW FOR MERCHANTS ONLY?

PROBLEM

Marquez built and sold to Frobisher, a candy manufacturer, a machine for wrapping individual pieces of candy in foil. The machine was built according to Frobisher's directions and specifications. Unknown to either party, Rodmann, a European candy manufacturer, held a Swiss patent on such a machine. She had also registered it with the U.S. Patent Office to protect the U.S. monopoly rights. Rodmann sued Marquez for an injunction against further production and for damages. Rodmann won the suit. Must Frobisher indemnify Marquez, thus making good his loss?

Merchants are typically held to higher standards in their dealings with consumers than are casual sellers. This is certainly true in the area of warranties. In addition to the warranties previously discussed, which are made by all sellers, the following warranties are, by law, also made by merchants.

these questions to start a class discussion: **Have you purchased a class ring? A band uniform or team jacket? Were you satisfied with the product? Did it fit the description and live up to the seller's promise?** Discuss whether a written warranty accompanied each product. **Guided Practice**

Have students work in small groups to create a Venn diagram to illustrate the similarities and differences between two types of express warranties that can be made by all sellers. Ask for volunteers to draw their organizers on the chalkboard. **Independent Practice**

▼ TEACH

Tell students that the Uniform Commercial Code holds merchants to stricter accountability in the area of warranties than it does casual sellers. Explain that *warranty against infringement* means that the goods in which the merchant deals shall be delivered to a buyer free of any third party claims for patent, copyright, or any other unauthorized use. **Warranty of merchantability** requires that the goods be fit for the ordinary purposes for which such goods are used.

▼RETEACH Divide the class in two and provide poster paper and markers to each group. Assign one of the two warranties on p. 369 to each group. Have students create posters informing other buyers of the sellers' warranties.

▼ENRICH Provide students with copies of classified ads for garage sales, flea markets, and other casual sales. Ask them to identify in writing the protection afforded by implied warranties and to suggest express warranties made by all sellers that would be advisable for the buyers to seek.

▼ APPLY

Before displaying the overhead transparency, *What Is the Implied Warranty of Merchantability?*, cover a key word or two in each statement with masking tape or strips of paper. Have students fill in the blanks. Ask students to define such terms as *pass in the trade* (acceptable to buyers), *fungible* (goods that are interchangeable), and *affirmations of fact* (truthful statements).

Guided Practice

Pair students and assign each pair a product or good that might be sold by both a casual seller and a merchant. Have them decide who is going to play the role of each. Have the "merchant" and the "casual seller" each write a warranty against infringement or of merchantability, using a computer, if possible, for the product he or she is selling. Have each pair read their warranties to the class. Discuss similarities, differences, or discrepancies between the two warranties.

Independent Practice

1. Warranty Against Infringement

A merchant impliedly warrants that the goods in which she or he normally deals shall be delivered to a buyer free of any third party's claims for patent, copyright, or trademark *infringement* (i.e., unauthorized use). This warranty may be excluded by agreement between the parties.

If the buyer furnishes specifications to the seller that lead to a claim of infringement against the seller, the buyer is obligated to indemnify the seller for any loss suffered because of the infringement. Accordingly, in the problem, Frobisher must indemnify Marquez and also pay damages to Rodmann.

2. Warranty of Merchantability

Every merchant who customarily deals in goods of a particular kind makes an implied **warranty of merchantability** to all buyers of the goods. Basically, a warranty of merchantability requires that the goods be fit for the ordinary purposes for which such goods are used. Thus, a radio must bring in broadcasts, soap must clean, and an umbrella must provide protection from rain. All goods sold must pass without objection in the trade under the sales contract description; buyers must not balk at accepting them. If the goods are fungible, like grain, they must be at least of fair, average quality within the description. Within variations permitted by the contract, goods must be of even kind, quality, and quantity. If required by the contract, they must be adequately contained, packaged, and labeled. Finally, they must conform to any promises or affirmations of fact made on the label or on the container.

> Huang owned a gift shop. She bought a shipment of ceramic flower vases from Kwo, a Singapore exporter. After she had sold many of the vases, customers started coming back with the complaint that the vases leaked water. Kwo has breached the warranty of merchantability. He must take back all unsold and returned vases, refunding payment in full. Huang has likewise breached the warranty of merchantability to customers. Therefore, she must make refunds or other adjustments acceptable to the customers.

This important implied warranty of merchantability greatly increases the merchant's duties of care and performance beyond those of the casual seller. It extends, for example, to food sold, which must be wholesome and fit for human consumption. It includes foods and drinks that are sold and served to be consumed elsewhere or on the premises, as in restaurants and in fast-food shops. Drugs for human use must also be safe and wholesome. Buyers

▼ ASSESS

Learning Objective 3 Ask students to respond independently and in writing to the following question: **Can merchants who sell pirated goods (such as unauthorized copies of designer clothes) be held to the implied warranty against infringement and the warranty of merchantability? Explain.** (Yes; Responses should reflect the understanding that the sale of pirated goods is both illegal and unethical.) Correct and return papers.

of perishable foods and drugs must also handle them properly. For example, it is generally known that fresh dairy products should be kept refrigerated, and that food containing mayonnaise, when exposed to prolonged heat or sunshine, may become poisonous.

Merchantability requires that any warranty protection that is customary in the trade be extended to all buyers. For example, the seller of a pedigreed animal, such as a dog or horse, is expected to provide documentation of the lineage of the animal because such proof is customary in the trade.

The warranty of merchantability may be expressly excluded by agreement of the parties. Also, when a buyer has examined the goods, sample, or model before contracting, there is no implied warranty of merchantability as to those defects that a reasonable examination would have revealed. This also applies if the buyer refused to examine the goods, sample, or model before contracting.

Heathe bought a bolt of cloth that was marked down in price because of a flaw in the weave. The flaw was obvious under casual inspection. Heathe cannot later return the goods, claiming a breach of warranty of merchantability.

WHEN AND HOW MAY WARRANTIES BE EXCLUDED?

PROBLEM

At a sale in a discount store, Doty bought twenty pounds of shelled walnuts. They were packed in one-pound sealed plastic bags and were sold at a bargain price "as is." When Doty opened one package, he discovered that the walnuts were edible but were stale and unpalatable. Doty claims a breach of warranty of merchantability. Is he entitled to a refund?

A seller may offer to sell goods without any warranties. This is most likely to occur if the goods are known to have defects or if they are a new design or model. To sell goods without a warranty, the seller must do the following:

1. refrain from making any express warranties, and
2. use appropriate language that will exclude implied warranties.

For example, to exclude or modify the broad warranty of merchantability or any part of it, the seller must mention "merchantability" in a disclaimer.

Divide the class into two groups. The students in one group should prepare to verbalize the effects on consumers if the warranty against infringement did not exist in sales transactions. (Answers may include that consumers might benefit from lower prices; they could also suffer from unknowingly buying inferior goods carrying well-known labels.) The students in the other group are to describe the consumer's situation if the warranty of merchantability did not apply. (Answers may include that consumers could not depend on the fitness of goods, conformity of packaging and labeling, substitution of like goods, and so on.)

TEACH

Tell students that in order to sell goods without a warranty, the seller must refrain from making any express warranties *and* use appropriate language that will exclude implied warranties. Write **Only $1.98—AS IS** on the chalkboard. Tell students that a **disclaimer** is a notice of exclusion. Explain how the statement on the chalkboard is an example of a disclaimer.

RETEACH

On the chalkboard, a flip chart, or an overhead transparency, write the headings *Warranty Against Infringement* and *Warranty of Merchantability*. Have students brainstorm as many examples of each as possible. Review and correct misconceptions as necessary.

ENRICH

Make and distribute copies of the overhead transparency master, *What Is the Implied Warranty of Merchantability?* Ask students to describe a situation for each item on the list and share their scenarios with the class.

▼ APPLY

Draw a three-column chart on the chalkboard. Label the first column **Goods** and list items such as clothing, tools, toys, flowers and plants, cars, radios, and so on. Label the second column **Casual Seller** and the third column **Merchant**. Have students orally describe which warranties may be excluded and, in each case, under what circumstances. Complete the chart with their responses. **Guided Practice**

Have students copy the chart into their notebooks and, working individually, note the items for which merchants and manufacturers likely would be liable should the goods prove defective. (Items that could be proved defective in manufacture could fall under the law of product liability.) **Independent Practice**

A **disclaimer** is a notice of exclusion. To exclude or modify any implied warranty of fitness, the exclusion must be in writing and must be conspicuous (i.e., easily seen or noticed). A statement such as this would suffice for both merchantability and fitness: "There are no warranties of merchantability or fitness that extend beyond the description on the label." (See also the example in Figure 18-1.)

Unless circumstances indicate otherwise, all implied warranties are excluded by such expressions as "with all faults," "as is," or other similar words. Thus, in the problem, Doty is not entitled to a refund because the walnuts were bought "as is."

When express warranties of quality are given, they exclude all inconsistent implied warranties except the one for fitness for a particular purpose. No warranty arises, however, as to fitness for use when a casual seller disposes of used goods. An example is when someone holds a garage sale to dispose of assorted secondhand possessions. On the other hand, if the seller is a merchant, such a warranty would be implied according to the conditions discussed earlier. Note, however, that no disclaimers allow the manufacturer or merchant seller of the goods to avoid liability for injuries caused by defects in those goods.

An automobile manufacturer gave a new-car warranty that limited recovery to replacement of defective parts and necessary labor "for one year or 12,000 miles, whichever occurs first." The manufacturer stated that the warranty was "in lieu of all other warranties, obligations, and liabilities, including the warranty of merchantability." Mackenzie bought one of the cars and operated and maintained it in accordance with the owner's manual. Nevertheless, when Mackenzie was driving at a normal highway speed fourteen months later, the steering wheel suddenly failed to work properly. As a result, the car left the road and overturned. Despite the disclaimer of liability, the manufacturer may be liable in tort on the theory of strict liability.

▼ WHAT IS PRODUCT LIABILITY?

PROBLEM

Tacky removed a safety guard from his electrically powered radial saw. This was contrary to a warning prominently printed on the guard. Because of a manufacturing defect, a saw blade broke. Since the safety guard was not in place, the blade hit and seriously injured Tacky. Can Tacky recover for the injury caused by the defective product?

▼ ASSESS

Learning Objective 5 Have students review how the law of strict liability protects consumers. Then, ask students to write two, three-choice multiple choice questions (with answers) and turn them in to you. Select the top 20 questions, and prepare them as a class quiz on product liability. You may wish to assign extra credit to those students whose questions (including duplicates) you incorporated into the quiz.

The rules for determining who is legally liable for injuries caused by a defective product have been expanded in recent years to protect injured plaintiffs. For example, at common law, warranty liability depended on the contract between the buyer and seller, who were said to be in privity of contract. **Privity of contract** means the relationship or connection that exists only between or among the contracting parties as a result of their legally binding agreement. Only the immediate contracting buyer was permitted to sue and this could be done only against the immediate contracting seller. Thus, an injured consumer could sue the retailer, but not the wholesaler or the manufacturer, which might be primarily responsible for the defect and better able to pay.

Now, however, the UCC broadens the common-law rule so that all injured persons who are in the buyer's family or household, including guests, may sue. Moreover, courts in most states now permit the injured party, even a nonuser, to sue retailers, intermediate sellers, and manufacturers.

Today, a manufacturer or producer that makes inaccurate or misleading statements in advertising or labels is liable for resulting injuries to

▼ TEACH

Any person injured by a defective product may bring suit against anyone in the chain of distribution of that product. There is no liability if the injury was suffered while the product was being used for a purpose for which it was not intended or if the injured person is guilty of improper conduct that caused the accident. Discuss the terms **privity of contract** and **product liability.**

▼ APPLY

Thinking Critically Through Visuals

Neither manufacturer nor seller is responsible for burnt toast. Who is liable if defective wiring in the toaster causes a fire? (The seller, if he or she is a merchant, and the manufacturer might both be liable.) **Guided Practice**

Distribute to students publications such as *Safety Alerts* (published by the Consumer Product Safety Commission) or *Consumer Reports*. In small groups, have students skim this material and make a list of products that have been recalled or cited as unsafe or defective. Discuss product liability. **Independent Practice**

▼RETEACH As a group, have students answer the question, *What Is Product Liability?*, by reviewing pp. 372–375, then creating a section outline to highlight the key points. As you lead a discussion of these points, based on the outline, have students copy the information in their notebooks.

▼ENRICH Using a computer, if possible, have students write a one-page essay on the need for product liability as a form of consumer protection.

Ethics Issue

Divide the class into two groups and ask them to debate this question: **Should state laws regarding strict liability limit the amount of punitive damages that can be placed on a manufacturer found guilty?** (Answers should reflect an understanding of ethical, legal, and monetary ramifications.)

Multicultural Highlights

Sarah Breedlove Walker, better known as Madame C.J. Walker, born in Louisiana in the 1860s, was one of the first American women to become a self-made millionaire. She did this by filling a need among African American women for cosmetic products upon whose purity and safety they could depend. Ask: **Why are manufacturers and sellers of cosmetics and drugs particularly sensitive to laws of strict liability?** (Responses should indicate an awareness that the liability is imposed without reliance on warranties.)

consumers. If the goods are defective and therefore dangerous, the maker is similarly liable for resulting harm. In either case, not only the manufacturer or producer but also intermediate sellers and the immediate supplier may be liable. **Product liability** may be based on a breach of warranty. It may also be based on the torts of fraud or negligence, or, increasingly, on the tort of strict liability.

While there are many alternative legal theories, it may still be difficult for the injured consumer to recover. A person injured by a defective product might find that there is no warranty, that the warranty is not applicable, or that the warranty has expired. The injured person, even if defrauded, might also discover that the seller's misbehavior is difficult to prove. Fraud requires proof of intent, an elusive element. Finally, negligence, even if present, is difficult to prove because the defective product may have been made many months or years before in some distant factory by workers who cannot be identified or located.

Today, a person injured by a defective product is most likely to recover damages by relying on strict liability. The trend in many states is to hold the manufacturer, wholesaler, and retailer strictly liable if someone is injured because of a defective condition in the product that caused it to be unreasonably dangerous to the user or consumer. The liability is imposed without reliance on warranties and regardless of the presence or absence of fraudulent intent or negligence. At the time of the writing of this edition, efforts are being made in Congress and in some state legislatures to limit the scope of strict liability and to require the proof of fault. Some proposals would place ceilings on the amount of punitive damages that could be awarded.[1]

There is no liability if the injury was suffered while the product was being used for a purpose for which it was not intended (e.g., using gasoline to clean clothes or using a screwdriver as a chisel) or which could not reasonably be foreseen (e.g., trying to climb a mountain using ropes made for tying packages). Likewise, liability may be barred if the product has been altered by the user (e.g., lengthening a ladder by nailing extensions to its legs). Liability may also be barred if the injured person is personally found guilty of improper conduct that causes the accident. (Examples of this include driving on a defective tire after discovering the defect, failing to service or to maintain an engine, or taking an overdose of medication.) There is generally no liability if one is hurt when improperly using a product that may be dangerous when misused (e.g., sharp knives and cutting tools, firearms, and various chemicals).

[1]In March 1991, the U.S. Supreme Court upheld the constitutionality of punitive damages in an Alabama case in which the jury awarded a verdict against an insurance company for $840,000, or more than 200 times the $4,000 in out-of-pocket expenses of the plaintiff. (*Pacific Mutual v. Haslip*, No. 89–1729)

▼ ASSESS

Learning Objective 5 Have the class discuss who can sue—and be sued—for damages related to defective products. Make sure that the discussion incorporates the key elements of product liability, found on pp. 373–375.

In the problem, Tacky's removal of the fully adequate safety guard bars his recovery. Legally, the injury was the result of Tacky's foolish action, not the defect in the saw blade.

Preventing Legal Difficulties

When purchasing goods . . .

1. Be aware that not every assurance of quality or performance made by a seller is a warranty. Often such statements are deemed by the law to be "puffing" and cannot be the basis for breach of warranty action.
2. Know the implied warranties and watch for sellers' statements of limitation and exclusion of such warranties.
3. When appropriate, tell the seller how you intend to use the goods. If the seller has superior knowledge and advice upon which you can reasonably rely, you will be protected by an implied warranty of fitness of the goods for your particular purpose.
4. Generally request that express warranties be in writing. This helps to avoid later disputes as to their meaning or existence. If the seller unreasonably refuses to warrant the goods, go elsewhere, or realize that any disappointing product quality and performance will be your burden.
5. Use special care in buying goods "as is." Inspect the goods to be sure that you are willing to take them without the benefit of warranties.

▼ REVIEWING IMPORTANT POINTS

1. Warranties may be express or implied. Express warranties are oral or written promises by the seller of product quality or performance. Implied warranties are imposed by law and are effective even when not mentioned by the seller.
2. The following warranties are made by both casual sellers and merchants:
   a. that the seller has title to the goods and the right to transfer them (implied),
   b. that the goods shall be delivered free of all encumbrances unknown to the buyer (implied),
   c. that the goods are fit for the purpose of the buyer when the seller knows of the buyer's intended use and the buyer relies on the skill and judgment of the seller for selection (implied),

Preventing Legal Difficulties

Have students work in small groups to role-play the advice given in the five items in this section. If possible, videotape the performances for use in a consumer education or life skills class.

▼ CLOSE

Distribute copies of the overhead transparency master, *What Warranties Are Made:*, and review each kind of warranty by having students note those which all consumers should get in writing. (Conformity to seller's statement and conformity to description, sample, or model) Ask students to consider the following question: **Should *all* manufacturers of consumer goods provide *all* consumers with express, full warranties on *all* products sold?**

Assign the following end-of-chapter materials:
Student text review activities, pp. 375–381
Workbook, pp. 53–58
Chapter Test

Chapter *MicroExam*

▼RETEACH Have students brainstorm a definition of **product liability.** Then, have them brainstorm five situations in which a manufacturer, retailer, or wholesaler is liable for a defective product, and five instances in which improper use by the consumer releases the manufacturer from liability.

▼ENRICH Under close supervision, have students role-play using defective products or using products improperly. Have the class determine if there is liability on the part of the manufacturer, wholesaler, or retailer for the product.

Strengthening Your Legal Vocabulary

1. warranty
2. puffing
3. express warranty
4. implied warranty
5. warranty of merchantability
6. privity of contract
7. encumbrances
8. product liability
9. caveat venditor
10. disclaimer

Applying Law to Everyday Life

1 

Yes; A warranty made after the sale does not require new consideration. It becomes part of the original contract. This is a special rule true of any modification of a

d. that the goods will conform to the seller's statements or promises (express), and
e. that goods sold by description, sample, or model will conform to such description, sample, or model (express).

3. The following warranties are made only by merchants:
   a. that the goods are free of any patent, copyright, or trademark infringement claims by third parties (implied), and
   b. that the goods are merchantable; that is, of fair, average, salable quality and fit for the ordinary purpose for which they normally are used (implied).
4. The buyer from a casual seller should examine the goods for defects before making the purchase. That is because the buyer has no legal right (in the absence of fraud by the casual seller) to complain of defects that might have been detected by ordinary inspection. It is prudent to also inspect goods sold by merchants. However, merchant sellers normally are bound by the important implied warranty of merchantability unless explicitly disclaimed.
5. Generally, any person injured by a defective product may bring suit against any manufacturer or merchant in the chain of distribution of that product. Depending on the circumstances, the suit may be based on warranty, fraud, negligence, or strict liability.

STRENGTHENING YOUR LEGAL VOCABULARY

Match each term with the statement that best defines that term. Some terms may not be used.

caveat venditor
disclaimer
encumbrances
express warranty
full warranty
good faith
implied warranty
limited warranty
privity of contract
product liability
puffing
warranty
warranty of merchantability

1. Promise that a statement of product qualities is true.
2. Exaggerated sales talk.
3. Warranty that is explicitly made.
4. Warranty imposed by law.

5 Warranty that goods are fit for the ordinary purposes for which such goods are used.

6 Relationship that exists only between contracting parties as a result of their agreement.

7 Creditors' claims.

8 Liability of manufacturer or producer, wholesaler, or retailer when a defective product causes injury to a consumer or to the consumer's property.

9 "Let the seller beware."

10 Notice of exclusion of a warranty.

APPLYING LAW TO EVERYDAY LIFE

1 ETHICS ISSUE When the Grandiose Motor Car Company introduced its new model, sales lagged. After three months, only 7,500 cars had been sold. To stimulate sales, Grandiose added four years to its standard one-year warranty. It also extended the warranty on the cars already sold. Is Grandiose legally bound to the early buyers for the extra four years even though no new consideration was paid? Is it ethical to sell new cars with only a "one-year-12,000-mile-whichever-comes-first" warranty against defects in materials and workmanship, and to add a disclaimer of this implied warranty of merchantability beyond one year?

2 ETHICS ISSUE It had been an exhausting year of hard work for Dryden. The Paradiso Resort advertisement in a national magazine promised, "The perfect holiday. Escape from it all on the beaches of Kauai—your paradise on earth! Surf and relax in the sun. Dine and dance like royalty. Return refreshed, revitalized, renewed!" Dryden used all his savings for a month-long stay. Now that the vacation is over, Dryden is physically exhausted, and still mentally frustrated with his work. Is the Paradiso Resort liable for breach of an express warranty? Is such puffing in advertising ethical?

3 While in Florida, Van Loon decided to go fishing for tarpon. Visiting Stanton's Sports Shop, Van Loon explained the specific need to the salesperson. Van Loon then bought the rod, reel, and line that the salesperson recommended. During the first trip out, Van Loon had repeated strikes, but the line was too light for the weight of the fish. As a result, the line broke every time even though it was being handled properly. What legal rights, if any, does Van Loon have against Stanton's?

sales agreement and is contrary to the rule for new promises in all other types of contracts, where new consideration is required. (p. 362)

Yes, it is ethical. Generally both minor and major defects in materials and workmanship become evident well within one year or 12,000 miles of operation.

2 ETHICS ISSUE No; The advertisement was a typical example of puffing. A reasonable person should recognize the superlative claims as exaggerated promotional talk reflecting biased personal opinion. (p. 364)

Yes, it is ethical. The puffing here is so obviously exaggeration for effect that no reasonable person is likely to be deceived by it.

3 Stanton's has breached the implied warranty of fitness for a particular purpose as to the line. (pp. 367–368) Van Loon had told Stanton's salesclerk the purpose at hand and had relied on the salesclerk's presumed expert judgment in buying the particular goods. Now proper line must be provided (possibly at a higher price, which Van Loon must pay) or a refund must be made.

4 There was no breach of warranty because the weed killer was advertised as effective only against crabgrass and the other varieties of broad-leaved weeds. (pp. 370–371)
No; A merchant seller is not obligated to volunteer advice.

5 No; Only merchants make the implied warranty of merchantability, and Canby is not a merchant. (pp. 370–371) Note that in most sales of used merchandise, the product is sold "as is," and the buyer may not and does not expect the performance of new goods.

6 Yes; She may sue the operator of the glider port as well as the manufacturer of the glider on the theory of strict liability. (p. 374) There is no warranty in effect; no fraud is involved; and negligence is doubtful and difficult to prove, even if it were present during manufacture of the product.(page 378)

7 No; Mortar is a product that must be used with special care. The damage which arises from its use is caused by the nature of the product and not from a defect in the product. The seller, moreover, had advised against direct contact with the skin and had made no warranty against injuries from misuse or against allergic reactions to the sensitive user. Nor was there negligence, fraud, or any basis for strict liability on the part of the dealer or manufacturer. (p. 374)

8 Gaston was correct. It is true that there is a big difference in the price of the two models, and yet no difference in the basic warranty against defects in materials and workmanship. However, the higher price for the second model can be justified by such features as the use of better materials throughout the vehicle.

4 The Motleys entered Penn's Nursery and asked for a fifty-pound sack of ZAP, a brand-name weed killer, to use to eliminate narrow-leaved devil grass from their lawn. ZAP was advertised as "effective, when properly used, against crabgrass and other broad-leaved weeds and grasses." The Motleys applied the chemical according to directions, but the devil grass survived. Therefore they sued the manufacturer, claiming a breach of warranty. They also sued Penn's for failure to give them proper advice as to what kind of weed killer they should buy. Will the Motleys win their suit against the manufacturer? Will they win their suit against Penn's?

5 Using a newspaper want advertisement, Canby sold his slightly used stereo equipment to Pegler. A week later, Pegler tried to return the merchandise to Canby. Pegler claimed that there was a breach of the warranty of merchantability because the compact disc programmer did not work properly. Is Canby liable?

6 Gallo, an experienced glider pilot, rented a glider at a commercial glider port. While in flight during ideal weather, she lost control because of a defect in the cables for the tail assembly. As a result, the glider crashed while landing, and Gallo was permanently disabled. The glider, which was several years old, had been properly maintained. There was no warranty in effect on the glider. Does Gallo have any legal recourse?

7 When Winslow decided to install a brick walk in front of his home, he bought three sacks of standard Pyramid-brand mortar mix from the U-Can-Do store. Instructions on the bags warned against direct contact with skin. Although Winslow had sensitive skin, he repeatedly touched the wet mix with his bare hands because he was not skilled in using a trowel. This burned his hands and he developed an allergic rash. Is either U-Can-Do or Pyramid liable to him under any theory of product liability?

8 Alfonse and Gaston are at an automobile show. "Look at these prices!" Alfonse says, "Two new cars. Both four-door sedans. Both will get you from here to there, and back again. But this one costs $9,000 and that one costs $90,000. The warranty is the same for both. I say that second price is outrageously high, that it is unethical, and that it should be illegal!" Gaston answers, "Ah, *mon ami*, your facts are right but your conclusion is wrong." With whom do you agree, and why?

9 The students in Ms. Romboldt's law class were writing a script for a skit intended to dramatize points of law about product liability. One idea was to have someone play the role of Barbara Walters interviewing Ralph

Nader, the consumer activist. Student Jack Parish suggested this question: "As a consumer of goods, what *warranty* would you choose to have if you could have only *one*?" How would you answer?

10 ETHICS ISSUE When your friend returned from a trip to mainland China he brought back copies of three recent best-selling American novels. "I paid five bucks for each," he boasted. "They still sell for $29.50 each in the U.S.A." What is the explanation of this bargain? Was the purchase ethical?

SOLVING CASE PROBLEMS

1. Every week for a year and a half, Newmark was given a shampoo and set by employees of Gimbel's. Then a new product ("Candle Wave," made by the Helene Curtis company) was applied to Newmark's hair. As a result, Newmark suffered contact dermatitis of the scalp, with substantial loss of hair. Newmark sued Gimbel's for breach of the implied warranty of fitness for a particular purpose. Gimbel's argued that it was providing a service and not selling goods in this transaction. Therefore it could not be held liable for breach of warranty with reference to the product of Helene Curtis. It could only be held liable, it claimed, if its own employees were proved negligent. Could a jury find Gimbel's liable if the wave solution was defective and caused the injury? (*Newmark v. Gimbel's Inc.*, 258 A.2d 679, N.J.)

2. While trying on a pair of slacks in a Mode O'Day Frock Shop, Flippo was bitten by a poisonous brown recluse spider concealed in the slacks. Flippo was hospitalized for thirty days because of the bite. Was Mode O'Day liable for a breach of the implied warranty of merchantability? (*Flippo v. Mode O'Day Frock Shops of Hollywood*, 248 Ark. 1, 449 S.W.2d 692)

3. Mahaney purchased a used car from Perry Auto Exchange. Mahaney was told that the car was in "perfect, A-1, and first-class condition." A written statement given to Mahaney at the time of the sale described the car as being in "good operating condition." Mahaney had no opportunity to investigate the truth of these statements. Later, it was determined that the car had a bearing knock and a growl in the differential and had no brakes at the time of the sale. Mahaney sued for rescission. Were Perry's statements merely puffing or were they warranties upon which the rescission could be based? (*Mahaney v. Perry Auto Exchange*, 85 N.E.2d 558, Ohio)

9 Any answer could be correct; however, Ralph Nader would probably select the warranty of merchantability. It is the most comprehensive of all and provides assurance that the goods will be reasonably fit for the ordinary purposes for which they are normally used, and that they will serve those purposes for a reasonable length of time. (pp. 370–371)

10 ETHICS ISSUE The explanation of the bargain is that China, and a number of other countries in the world, do not honor the copyright, trademark, and patent laws of the United States, or the rights of persons created under those laws. (page 379) Thus the publisher in China is able to duplicate the text of the best sellers very cheaply by simply not compensating the American owners. Other products are also copied illegally. It is illegal to bring such products into the United States or to sell them here. Both buyers and sellers in such transactions may be guilty of crimes and torts. Their conduct is clearly unethical if done with knowledge of its wrongful nature.

Solving Case Problems

1 Yes; Framers of the Uniform Commercial Code did not intend to limit implied warranties to transactions that technically meet the definition of a sale of goods. One who, in the regular course of business, sells or applies a product in a hybrid or combination sales-service transaction (as did the employee of Gimbel's here) may be liable for breach of the implied warranty of fitness of the product for the normal or ordinary use intended. (pp. 369–370) The merchant may also be liable in strict liability in tort. (p. 374) The retailer may in turn sue the manufacturer, who should bear the primary responsibility for putting the defective product on the market.

❷ No; The slacks were not defective and did not cause the injury. (pp. 369–370) The injury was caused by the spider, which was not part of the goods (as would be, for example, weevils in flour). Moreover, it was not shown that the retailer or manufacturer had any control over the spider or caused it to be in the slacks or was negligent in not keeping it out of the slacks.

❸ In this case, the statements were treated as warranties because of their factual nature, to the lack of an opportunity for Mahaney to investigate the truth of the statements, and, consequently, to the relative position of expertise that the dealer occupied. (pp. 364–365)

❹ **(a)** Yes; After January 1, 1966, when the federal Cigarette Labeling and Advertising Act became effective, consumers were properly warned of the hazards of smoking and so there could be no action against cigarette manufacturers for a failure to warn, or for breach of express warranty, or for intentional tort. (p. 374)
(b) No; There was not sufficient evidence for the trial court to find that the inherently dangerous characteristics of cigarettes were known to the ordinary

❹ Rose Cipollone was born in 1925 and began smoking Chesterfield cigarettes as a teenager in 1942. She smoked between one and two packs daily (reduced in number only during a pregnancy) until she died of lung cancer in 1984. Before she died, she sued the defendants (the Liggett Group, Inc.; Philip Morris, Inc.; and Lorillard, Inc., manufacturers of cigarettes) for damages. After she died, her husband continued the action. A four-month-long trial resulted in a jury verdict of $400,000 for the plaintiff because of the breach of an express warranty of product safety in her smoking before 1966. The court of appeals had previously ruled that the federal Cigarette Labeling and Advertising Act of 1966 preempted (i.e., effectively barred) claims arising from smoking after January 1, 1966.[2] This reflects the fact that the act required cigarette makers to print warnings on packages and in advertisements of the hazards to health from smoking. Since then, smokers knowingly assume the risks. However, initially the required warning merely stated: "Caution: Cigarette Smoking *May* Be Hazardous to Your Health." Later variations stated: "Warning: The Surgeon General Has Determined That Cigarette Smoking *Is* Dangerous to Your Health." Finally, in 1984, the required warning stated: "SURGEON GENERAL'S WARNING: Smoking *Causes Lung Cancer*" (emphases added to all). Both the plaintiff and the defendants appealed, raising the following questions, among others:

a. Was it proper for the trial court to rule that *after January 1, 1966*, the defendants could not be liable for failure to warn users, or for a breach of an express warranty of safety?

b. Was it proper for the trial court to rule that "the inherently dangerous characteristics of cigarettes were known to the ordinary consumer or user *prior to 1966*?"

c. Was it proper for the trial court to rule that the defendant Liggett is not liable for failure to warn of the hazards of smoking *before the act of 1966?*

You decide. (*Cipollone v. Liggett Group, Inc.*, 893 F.2d 541)

❺ On January 1, plaintiff Werner bought the *White Eagle*, a wooden sloop, from defendant Montana, and the parties signed a bill of sale. The previous October they had signed an intent to purchase and sell. During their negotiations, the seller had assured the buyer orally that the hull would "make up" from swelling when placed in the water and would be watertight. At the end of June, Werner put the boat in the water. He

[2]Rose Cipollone did not smoke cigarettes made by Lorillard and Philip Morris until after 1965. This absolved them from liability on the breach of express warranty and failure-to-warn claims of the plaintiff, but they remain potentially liable on the risk-utility claim. The risk-utility claim alleged that the risk of cigarettes outweighs their social value.

allowed more than six weeks—a sufficient time—for the planking to swell to form a watertight hull. But the hull still leaked. The boat could not be sailed. Werner then checked the hull and for the first time discovered extensive dry rot which required substantial repairs. In a letter in September, he demanded that Montana take the boat back and refund the purchase price of $13,250. The defendant refused, and so Werner sued for rescission. Montana argued that the oral assurances he had given of watertightness could not be admitted at the trial because of the parol evidence rule. Who should win? (*Werner v. Montana*, 378 A.2d 1130, N.H.)

consumer or user before 1966 when the warnings began to appear in ads and on cigarette packages. This is an issue of fact for the jury to decide. **(c)** No; A reasonable jury could conclude that Liggett had falsely represented in advertisements that its cigarettes would not endanger the consumer's health. The express warranty claim could not be upheld after January 1, 1966, when the warning ads began to appear. (p. 369) The Court of Appeals ordered a new trial but both parties appealed to the U.S. Supreme Court. The plaintiff dropped the case and, thus, the Supreme Court did not have to render any decision. The issue of liability is still unresolved.

5 Judgment for plaintiff Werner; The oral assurances of the defendant seller that the sloop would become watertight when placed in the water was an express warranty. (pp. 362, 369) Since the documents used (the intent to purchase and sell and the bill of sale) did not constitute a complete and exclusive statement of their agreement, the seller's oral assurances were admissible under the parol evidence rule.

Special Section: Choosing an Attorney

In small groups, have students create a handbook to help consumers choose an attorney. Have students research local lawyers, using the *Martindale-Hubbell* and other resources, write biographies on them, and categorize them according to their specialties. Have students reread the information on p. 382, then create a one-page checklist of questions and important points to consider when choosing an attorney. Have students write the handbook, create a table of contents, supply an index, and design a cover using a computer, if possible. Encourage students to use electronic clip art, or a draw or paint program, to design and create illustrations for the handbook. Display students' work in the library. With prior approval from your administration, you may wish to include notice of this consumer booklet in your next parent letter or in your community newspaper's school-information section.

SPECIAL SECTION

CHOOSING AN ATTORNEY

All too often, individuals find themselves immediately in need of legal services, and they are forced to choose an attorney without the benefit of adequate time to evaluate the alternatives. This may result in an unsatisfactory selection. The prudent person deliberately establishes an ongoing working relationship with a qualified attorney early in adult life and maintains the relationship through the years by practicing preventive law. Preventive law involves consulting your lawyer often in order to anticipate, identify, and confront legal issues before they become legal problems.

Your attorney should be someone with whom you can talk comfortably and in whom you have confidence. Although the working relationship is typically person to person, resources of firms with many members can be important. The size of the firm often affects the size of its library and computer research capability. It also determines the pool of specialized experience available to your lawyer. Inquiries among relatives, friends, perhaps your banker, accountant, and insurance agent can provide information about the reputation of the lawyers you are considering.

The work load of a lawyer is significant because an attorney who is successful but is too busy to give your situation the attention it needs will not be a good choice for you. You may want to visit the offices of more than one attorney to observe how business is handled and to discuss fees before you decide.

Your situation may at times require an attorney who is a specialist in a particular area. Criminal law, environmental law, and antitrust law are all specialized areas.

Attorneys often identify their field(s) of specialization in the Yellow Pages. Also, the multi-volume Martindale-Hubbell directory of attorneys, published annually and available in public libraries, lists most practicing attorneys and law firms in the United States. Local bar associations often can provide lists of attorneys in specialized areas of practice.

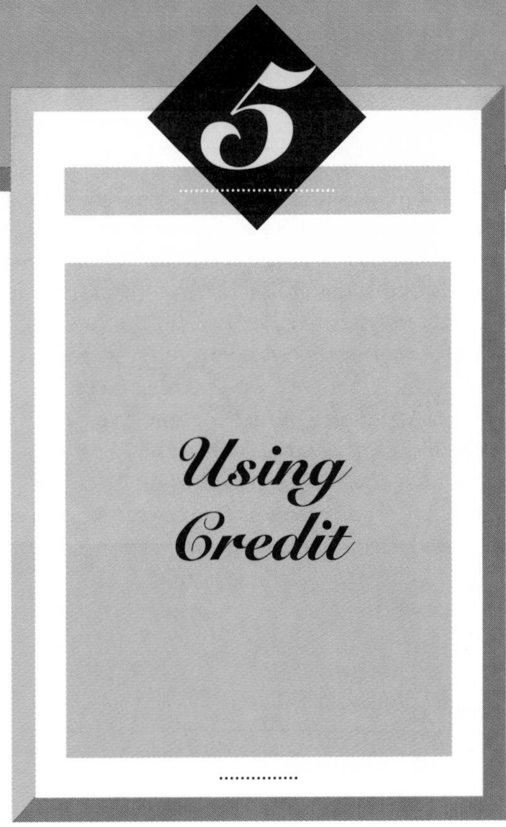

Unit Overview

In Unit 5, *Using Credit*, students will read about debts, bankruptcy, collateral, and repossessions. They will learn about finance charges, credit ratings, federal credit laws, credit cards, and tangible and intangible property. Students will learn the advantages and disadvantages of acquiring money, goods, or services on credit in exchange for the debtor's promise to pay on a later date the amount due plus interest.

The transactions between debtors and creditors—the debts and credit—are governed by a number of laws. In Chapter 19, *Debts and Bankruptcy*, students will study who the debtors and creditors are, which laws at the federal level protect creditors, and which protect debtors, and what special laws apply to credit cards and their use. Students learn that judicious use of credit is of paramount importance.

Specific laws govern secured transactions, security interests, and the termination of secured transactions. In Chapter 20, *Collateral and Repossessions*, students will discover what a secured transaction is, how security interests are created, how a creditor perfects a security interest, and how secured transactions are terminated. They also will learn how requiring collateral before credit is extended impacts both parties to the transaction.

At the end of this unit, you'll find a special section, *How and When to Be Your Own Attorney*, which can be used at any time during the study of Unit 5.

You may wish to assign its accompanying *Teacher Edition* activity to give students an opportunity to create a chart summarizing options to the litigation process.

Portfolio Assessment

Using a computer, if possible, have students write a fictitious story called *From Riches to Rags*. Have students use the knowledge and information gained in their study of this unit, *Using Credit*, to describe how using credit unwisely can lead to substantial debt, bankruptcy, and/or repossession. Tell students to draw from personal experiences about using credit, if possible, to write their stories. Be sure to have students discuss how laws, such as the Fair Credit Reporting Act and Fair Debt Collection Practices Act, protect debtors and creditors. Encourage students to end their stories with a moral. Have students add the story to their portfolios or law journals.

Careers

Bankruptcy Attorney

Bankruptcy laws allow debtors who have become overburdened with debts to be released from most financial obligations. Bankruptcy attorneys specialize in counseling clients on their legal rights and obligations, and suggest actions to be taken.

To practice law in any state, a candidate must be licensed, which requires passing a bar exam. To qualify for the exam, an applicant must have a four-year college degree followed by three years of law school. To become a bankruptcy lawyer, a law school student must take advanced courses in debtor and creditor rights and secured transactions. Proficiency in writing, reading, and analysis are essential skills as is knowledge of bank, federal, and business laws. Depending on the firm and its location, salary ranges vary between $30,000 and $60,000.

Divide students into pairs. Have one student role-play a debtor who creates a bankruptcy scenario. Have the other student role play the bankruptcy attorney who counsels the debtor.

Annotated Bibliography

- ***In Re: Terry*, 603 F.2d 634 (8th Cir. 1980).**
  A debtor who has no excess income out of which to make payments under a Chapter 13 Plan is not eligible for Chapter 13 relief. (Chapter 19)

- ***In Re: Yale Express System, Inc.*, 384 F.2d 990 (2d Cir. 1967).**
  The fundamental purpose of reorganization proceedings is to enable the debtor to continue operations as well as to protect the rights of the creditors. (Chapter 19)

- ***Danns v. Household Finance Corp.*, 558 F.2d 114 (2d Cir. 1977).**
  A discharge in bankruptcy shall release a bankrupt from all of his or her provable debts except such liabilities for obtaining money or property by false pretenses or false representations, or for obtaining money or property on credit or obtaining an extension or renewal of credit in reliance upon a materially false statement in writing respecting his or her financial condition made with intent to deceive. (Chapter 19)

Using Credit

- **Debts and Bankruptcy**
- **Collateral and Repossessions**

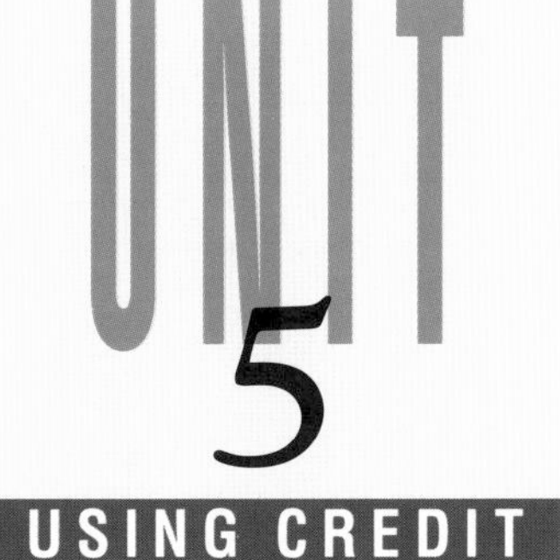

UNIT 5
USING CREDIT

CHAPTER 19 ORGANIZER

Chapter Theme

The transactions between debtors and creditors, debts and credit, are governed by a number of laws.

DIRECTED STUDY QUESTIONS	SPECIAL FEATURES	PROGRAM RESOURCES				
		Reteach	Enrich	SN	AM	
Who are debtors and creditors?		✔	✔			
What laws protect creditors?	Multicultural Highlights, p. 387 Thinking Critically Through Visuals, p. 389	✔	✔		V	
What laws protect debtors?	Ethics Issue, p. 393 Writing Connections, p. 395 Personal Perspectives, p. 396 Thinking Critically Through Visuals, p. 397	✔	✔		K A	
What special laws apply to credit cards and their use?	Thinking Critically Through Visuals, p. 399 Personal Perspectives, p. 400 Preventing Legal Difficulties, p. 401	✔	✔	✔		

Additional Resources

- Aaron, Richard. *Bankruptcy Law Fundamentals*. New York: Clark-Boardman Publishing Co., 1989.
- Epstein, David G. *Debtor-Creditor Law*, 3rd ed. St. Paul, MN: West Publishing Co., 1986.
- Nickel, Gudrun, M. *Debtor's' Rights: A Legal Self Help Guide.* Clearwater, FL: Sphinx International, 1992.
- Topolnicki, Denise, M. and MacDonald, Elizabeth, M. "The Bankruptcy Bonanza!" *Money*, August 1993, pp. 82–94.

Chapter Pacing Guide

One-semester course	✔	✔	✔					
One-year course	✔	✔	✔	✔	✔			

	ASSESSMENT OPPORTUNITIES			
Cooperative Learning	Informal Assessment	Chapter Review	Chapter Test	Chapter *MicroExam* (Media)
	✔	✔	✔	✔
	✔	✔	✔	✔
✔	✔	✔	✔	✔
	✔	✔	✔	✔

Videodiscs
Debt and Credit Cards
Search Chapter 24, Play To 25

State by State

Fraudulently transferring assets before going bankrupt is hard to prove. Judges in California and Illinois have ruled that actual intent may be inferred from actions and proved by circumstantial evidence.

Teaching Materials

Student text, pp. 384–407

Overhead transparency masters
- *What Laws Protect Creditors?*
- *What Laws Protect Debtors?*

Videos
- *Contracts, Warranties, and Credit*
- *Law for Business* Videodisc

Workbook, pp. 59–60

Outside Resources
- Newspaper articles on legislation protecting creditors and bankruptcy
- Federal Truth in Lending disclosure statement
- Poster paper and index cards
- Credit card application forms showing interest rates and finance charges
- Outside speakers: Bankruptcy attorney, banker, or mortgage loan officer
- Comics from a daily newspaper

- Camcorder
- Tape recorder
- VCR

Assessment
- Chapter Test
- Chapter *MicroExam*

Vocabulary

debtor, p. 386
debt, p. 386
creditor, p. 386
security interest, p. 387
secured debt, p. 387
lien, p. 387
pledge, p. 387
pledgor, p. 388
pledgee, p. 388
pawn, p. 388
pawnbroker, p. 388
pawn ticket, p. 388
mechanic's lien, p. 389
artisan's lien, p. 389
suretyship, p. 389
principal debtor, p. 389
surety, p. 390
guaranty, p. 390
guarantor, p. 390
unsecured debt, p. 390
garnishment, p. 391
consumer loan, p. 392
finance charge, p. 392
unconscionable contract, p. 393
credit rating, p. 395
discharge, p. 396
voluntary bankruptcy, p. 397
involuntary bankruptcy, p. 397
credit cards, p. 399

Learning Objectives

When you complete this chapter, you will be able to

1. Define debtors and creditors and understand how debts benefit both.
2. Discuss laws that protect creditors.
3. Discuss laws that protect debtors.
4. Appreciate how bankruptcy law protects both creditors and debtors.
5. Understand why credit cards have become a major substitute for money.

384

Chapter Self-Test

Assess students' understanding of debts and bankruptcy before they begin Chapter 19 by writing the following pairs of words or phrases on the chalkboard. Tell students to take out notepaper and, for each pair, write *Yes* if the terms are synonyms or *No* if the terms have different meanings. Before continuing with the chapter, review and discuss students' responses.

1. debt: lien (No)
2. guarantor: creditor (No)
3. pledgor: debtor (Yes)
4. unconscionable contract: unethical agreement (Yes)
5. garnishment: unsecured debt (No)

CHAPTER

19

DEBTS AND BANKRUPTCY

1 You are thinking of buying an automobile and plan to borrow money to help you pay cash for the purchase. Is there a limit on how much interest a lender can charge you? Suppose you decide to rely on dealer financing, paying the dealer or finance company a series of monthly installments. Is there any limit on the annual percentage rate (APR) of the financing charge the seller may add to the price of the car?

2 ETHICS ISSUE An acquaintance brags that she will finance her college education with government-insured student loans and then go bankrupt after graduation to avoid paying them. Is this possible? Is this ethical?

3 All five of your credit cards are stolen from your motel room while you are skiing. Fortunately you discover the loss within a few hours and immediately notify the credit card companies by telephone. On the following day, you also notify them by mail. However, within a week, the thief uses your credit cards to charge $1,875 in purchases. Eventually, each credit card company bills you for $50 of the purchases made with its card. By what authority did they do this? Must you pay these bills?

FOCUS

Before class begins, write the following question on the chalkboard and have students jot down their responses on notepaper: **Why do people use credit cards?** (Answers may include lack of cash, to keep receipts for business expenses, to buy things they don't have the cash for, and so on.)

Begin class by recording students' responses on the chalkboard, eliminating duplicate answers. Lead a discussion on students' ideas regarding when a credit card should, or should not, be used.

You Decide

1 Yes; Usury laws generally limit the rate of interest lenders may charge. Specially regulated small loan companies, pawnbrokers, and often banks may charge more. Limits may be imposed by state law on how much a seller or finance company may charge.

2 ETHICS ISSUE No; Educational loans for college are generally not dischargeable under the bankruptcy provisions. Deliberate plans to evade payment are clearly unethical. Such actions, if they succeed, would unfairly shift the burden of payment to taxpayers.

3 Under federal law, consumers are liable for unauthorized use of their credit cards, but only up to $50 if certain conditions are met. No; you would not be liable for the bills because the unauthorized purchases were made after you notified the companies that the cards were stolen.

Thinking Critically Through Visuals

These people are attending a farm auction. Why, do you think, do people hold auctions? (Answers may include the need to raise money to pay debts. Point out that creditors may seize a person's belongings and sell them to satisfy a debt.)

▼ TEACH

To introduce the terms **debtor** and **creditor**, ask students to brainstorm instances in which obtaining a loan is usually necessary. Orally, have students identify the debtor and creditor in each situation. (Answers may include buying a car to get to work—bank is creditor, car owner is debtor; medical emergencies—hospital is creditor, patient is debtor; and so on.)

▼ APPLY

Point out that prudent borrowing has several benefits. Have students make a chart on the chalkboard showing some of the advantages. (Answers may include that the debtor gets needed goods or services, the creditor is paid for his or her financial support, the economy is stimulated, more jobs for producers and more goods for consumers are created, and so on.) **Guided Practice**

Have students, working in pairs, orally summarize situations in which they may need to apply for credit. Have students identify the reason for and amount of the debt, the debtor, and the creditor in each case.

Independent Practice

▼ WHO ARE DEBTORS AND CREDITORS?

PROBLEM

Chang, a college student majoring in physics, won a $2,500 prize in a science project competition. She deposited the money in her checking account at the Ranchers and Merchants State Bank. In the resulting relationship with the bank, is the bank a debtor or a creditor of Chang?

A **debtor** is a person or a business that owes money, goods, or services to another. Whatever is owed is generally called the **debt**. The **creditor** is the one to whom the debt is owed.

At first, the debtor-creditor relationship may seem to be heavily weighted in favor of the creditor. In fact, the creditor generally faces a higher risk of loss. However, as in all contracts, both parties benefit. The debtor gets needed or wanted goods or services that might not otherwise be obtainable; the creditor puts available capital to work and is paid for this accommodation. Each needs the other; if either fails to perform their contract as promised, both are likely to suffer some loss. Understandably, default is more likely to be by the debtor who fails to pay when due. But usually creditors can and do screen would-be debtors for creditworthiness, and thus limit defaults to a tolerable level.

A legally enforceable debt normally arises out of a contract where something of value has been exchanged for a promise to provide money, goods, or services. In the problem, Chang transferred her money to the bank in exchange for the bank's promise either to keep it safe and to return it upon demand by Chang or to pay it to someone else as she may order in writing. Therefore, the bank is the debtor and Chang is the creditor in their relationship.

During the Middle Ages, charging any interest on loans was illegal. Today it is legal and very common. Prudent borrowing of money is recognized as beneficial to all parties involved. Extension of credit, whereby a buyer gets goods today and pays later, also facilitates economic growth. This economic growth provides more jobs for producers and more goods for consumers. Accordingly, the debtor-creditor relationship is encouraged and protected by law. This protection makes creditors more secure when lending money or selling on credit. At the same time, the law protects debtors by forbidding unfair credit and collection practices.

▼ ASSESS

Learning Objective 1 Have students work in pairs to write expanded definitions, in their own words, for the terms **debtor** and **creditor** and explain how both parties benefit from their relationship. (A debtor is a person or business that owes money, goods, or services to another; a creditor is one to whom the debt is owed. A debtor gets needed or wanted goods or services; a creditor is paid for use of his or her capital.)

WHAT LAWS PROTECT CREDITORS?

PROBLEM

Spano borrowed $7,500 from Wagner. Spano promised to repay the money in twelve months with interest at 9 percent per year. Spano gave Wagner shares of American Telephone Company common stock, which had a market value of $8,000, to hold as security for the payment. The stock was to be returned when the debt was paid. What was Wagner's legal status?

The primary concern of a typical creditor is that the loan be promptly paid when due. If it is not paid, and especially if costly efforts to collect it prove fruitless, the creditor usually suffers a financial loss. When feasible, such bad debt losses are shifted to other borrowers through higher fees and charges. Thus, it is in the interest of all society that fair and honest loans be collectible with minimum difficulty and expense. Legislation to protect creditors includes the following.

1. Laws Allowing Secured Debts

Probably most helpful for creditors are laws that permit them to acquire a legal interest in (i.e., a right in or a claim to) specific property of the debtor. This is a **security interest**, which is enforceable in court if the debtor defaults (i.e., fails to pay in accordance with the loan agreement or credit extension). The related debt is called a **secured debt.**

A creditor who holds a security interest, as Wagner did in the problem, is a secured creditor. A creditor with a security interest in specific property has a **lien** against that property. A lien gives the creditor the right, in case of default on a payment that is due, to sell the property and to use the proceeds from the sale to pay the debt. Usually, the debtor keeps possession of the liened property as long as the debt is not in default. Mortgages on homes are common examples of this type of secured debt. However, a default occurs if a scheduled payment is missed. The creditor may then exercise her or his right to obtain a court order for sale of the property, as discussed in Chapter 28. If the secured property is personal and movable, such as a car or television, the creditor may peacefully repossess (i.e., seize control or possession of it).

Some secured debt arrangements permit the *creditor* to have possession of the property until the debt is paid. In the **pledge**, for example, personal

▼RETEACH Pair students who understand the creditor-debtor relationship with students who need help with the concept. Using poster board, have each pair create a strip-picture story that illustrates the relationship between a debtor and a creditor.

Media: Using a computer, if possible, have students describe how the creditor-debtor relationship stimulates economic growth or undermines the economy if not managed wisely. (Creation of new businesses and jobs; increased personal debt can reduce further spending, and so on)

▼ TEACH

To help the visual learners, draw a chart on poster paper and fill in the four types of laws that protect creditors. As you discuss each law, fill in details. Have students copy and study the completed chart. They will be asked to fill in

blank versions in the ASSESS activity on p. 388.

Laws that Protect Creditors	
Laws Allowing Secured Debts	liens pledges pawns
Laws Involving Third Parties	suretyship guaranty
Laws Concerning Unsecured Debts	based on oral or written promise costly to collect
Laws Allowing Garnishment of Wages	court hearing 25% of take-home pay

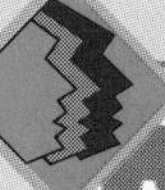

Multicultural Highlights

Many people who live in low-income communities have difficulty obtaining credit. Some of these people are able to go to banks, such as Chicago's South Shore Bank, for loans or credit. Formed in 1973 by Milton Davis, an African American, South Shore was organized to provide loans to people in lower- and moderate-income areas. South Shore has been successful, while also promoting community development.

▼ APPLY

In order to help students learn the many vocabulary terms in this section, play a game of *Twenty Questions* with the class. Select a vocabulary word, such as **pawnbroker** and, as students refer to their books, encourage them to ask you *Yes* or *No* questions to guess the chosen term. Possible questions are: Are you a person? (Yes); Are you a debtor? (No); and Do you work in a bank? (No); Continue answering questions until students guess the term (they win a point) or you answer 20 questions (you win a point). Then, select another term and repeat the process. You may wish to give students a reward if they score more points than you do. **Guided Practice**

Have students research pawnbroker laws in their state. Then, using a graphics or desktop publishing program, have students write ads for a (fictitious) pawn shop. Ads should include such things as items to be pawned, interest rates, and repayment plans. Show students' work in a classroom display.

property is given to a creditor as security for the payment of a debt or for the performance of an obligation. The property may be either goods or documents representing property rights (e.g., corporate stock). The **pledgor** (debtor) voluntarily gives up possession of the property. The **pledgee** (creditor) gets possession. Normally, the debt is paid when due or the legal obligation is performed. Thereupon, the property is returned to the pledgor (debtor).

While the pledge lasts, the pledgee (creditor) must treat the property with reasonable care. The property may, however, be repledged to a third party on terms that do not prevent the pledgor (debtor) from getting the property back when the debt is paid. If the pledgor (debtor) defaults, the pledgee (creditor) may sell the property after giving proper notice to the defaulter. Under the Uniform Commercial Code (UCC), this sale may be either an advertised public sale or a private sale. In either case, the pledgee (creditor) must act in good faith and in a commercially reasonable manner. Then, after deduction of interest due and the expenses of the sale, if the price received is more than the total debt, the excess must be paid to the pledgor (debtor). If the price received is less than the total debt, the pledgor (debtor) remains liable for the unpaid balance.

A **pawn** is a pledge of tangible personal property, usually of small size and comparatively high value. This type of pledge includes such durable and readily resalable items as jewelry, cameras, and musical instruments. It excludes intangible property rights (see page 418), stocks and bonds (which are discussed in Chapter 38), as well as other valuable documents. A **pawnbroker** lends money at interest and takes possession of tangible personal property from the borrower as security for repayment. The borrower who pawns goods gets a receipt known as a **pawn ticket.** When the debt together with interest due is paid, the pawn ticket is exchanged for the goods.

Because thieves sometimes use pawnbroking to convert stolen goods into cash, the business is regulated by special statutes. These laws require that the pawnbroker be licensed, post a bond, and keep accurate records open to police inspection. If stolen goods are found in the pawnshop, they may be seized without compensation to the pawnbroker. Also, maximum limits are imposed on the rate of interest pawnbrokers may charge.

Goods that are pawned must be held by the pawnbroker for a time prescribed by law (four months is typical) before they can be sold. In most states, the rights of the parties to the proceeds of the sale are the same as for ordinary pledges. In some states, the pawnbroker automatically gets title to pawned and unclaimed goods at the end of a specified time.

Although most liens are created with the consent of the debtor-owner, statutes in many states create liens in favor of the creditor without such

▼ ASSESS

Learning Objective 2 Display the chart from the TEACH activity on p. 387. In writing, have students name the four types of laws that protect creditors and explain how each law accomplishes this goal.

consent. These involuntary liens include the mechanic's lien and the artisan's lien. The **mechanic's lien** allows a person who has not been paid for labor or materials furnished to build a home, building, or other real property improvement to file a legal claim or charge against the property. If the debt is not paid, the realty may be sold and the holder of the mechanic's lien gets the amount owed from the proceeds. Thus, such lienholder is entitled to the amount owed from the sale proceeds, even before other claimants such as a bank with a mortgage on the property, gets any money.

The **artisan's lien** allows persons who have not been paid for services, such as repairing a car or providing a hotel room, to retain possession of the car or the luggage that has been brought onto the premises until they are paid. If payment is not made, these retained goods may be sold to pay the debts that are due.

2. Laws Involving Third Parties

In addition to liens, other means of protection are available to creditors. For example, a creditor who wishes assurance beyond the debtor's promise to pay may demand that a creditworthy third party assume the liability. This is **suretyship**, a contractual relation in which a third party agrees to be primarily liable for the debt or obligation if payment or performance becomes overdue. Three parties are involved. The **principal debtor** owes the debt or obligation. The creditor is the one to whom the obligation is owed.

Thinking Critically Through Visuals

Pawnshops are found across the country. Why, do you think, would someone pawn personal property, such as a family heirloom? (Answers may include that many people have tried traditional methods for raising money, and use pawnshops because they are in need of quick cash, but plan to repossess their items in the near future.)

Divide the class into groups of three or four students. Have each group write, then perform, a scenario involving either a mechanic's lien, an artisan's lien, a suretyship, a pledge, a pawn, a guaranty, or a garnishment of wages. (You may wish to videotape students' performances.) Each scenario should be prefaced by a description of the situation, the people involved, and the laws that protect the creditor. Invite groups to present their scenarios to the class. Then, hold a class

discussion on issues that are raised.

RETEACH Working in small groups, have one student be the pawnbroker and the others be borrowers. Have students role-play pawning various (fictitious) items, bargaining over price, interest, and the time limit to buy back the items.

ENRICH Have students work in small groups to create interview questions for pawnbrokers regarding their interest rates and other policies. Have each group telephone or, with adult supervision, visit a pawnbroker and present its findings to the class. Compare interest rates with rates from banks and credit cards.

Divide the class into four groups and assign each group one of the four subsections on pp. 387–391 that describe laws that protect creditors. Have each group write a paragraph, using a computer, if possible, explaining how debts are secured to ensure payment and what collection methods are appropriate in the case of default. Make four copies of each assignment (one for you and one for each of the other three groups) and have all groups read them. Ask a volunteer spokesperson from each group to answer any questions that may arise.

Independent Practice

Have students orally explain the difference between a **suretyship** and a **guaranty**. (Both protect creditors and both involve third parties but, in a suretyship, the third party (the surety) is liable in case of default. In a guaranty, the third party (the guarantor) is liable only after the creditor sues the defaulting debtor.)

The **surety** is the third party who promises to be liable in case of default by the principal debtor. The surety may be bound by an oral contract, since a suretyship is a primary obligation, as you may recall from your study of the statute of frauds in Chapter 13. Nevertheless, such agreements are usually put in writing.

Suretyship contracts are discharged in much the same way as other contracts. If the debtor pays, the surety is discharged. The surety is also discharged if the creditor releases the debtor or alters the obligation, as by extending the time of performance, without the surety's consent. But a surety who is required to pay the creditor has a legal right to collect from the principal debtor.

> Alvarez was the surety on a debt Benitez owed to Cintron. When Benitez failed to pay on the due date, Cintron graciously told Benitez that she could pay the debt with her next month's paycheck. Cintron thus extended the time for payment without notifying and getting Alvarez's consent. As a result, Alvarez was released from her obligation as surety. If Benitez later defaults and goes bankrupt, for example, Cintron cannot demand payment of the debt by Alvarez.

If there are cosureties, any cosurety who pays the full debt may get a judgment against the other cosureties for their proportionate share of the debt. This is called the *right of contribution.*

Like suretyship, the **guaranty** relationship protects the creditor. In it, the third party, the **guarantor**, agrees to pay if the principal debtor fails to do so. But unlike a surety, the guarantor is only secondarily liable. In effect, the guarantor merely promises that the debtor will pay when the debt comes due. However, this means that the creditor must first sue the defaulting debtor and get a judgment that proves to be uncollectible. In contrast, in a suretyship, such a suit is not necessary because the surety in effect insures that the debt will be paid when due, without further proof of his or her primary liability which is equal to that of the debtor. The contract creating the guaranty relationship must be in writing and signed by the guarantor to be enforceable under the statute of frauds (see page 263).

3. Laws Concerning Unsecured Debts

When the debt is small or the credit standing of the borrower is very good, the creditor may be willing to take an **unsecured debt.** This is a debt based only on the oral or written promise of the debtor.

Upon default, an unsecured creditor is in a much weaker position than a secured creditor because, in order to collect, the unsecured creditor must

▼ ASSESS

Learning Objective 2 Independently and in writing, using a computer, if possible, have students identify which of the four types of laws that protect creditors they think is the most important. Have students explain why they chose a particular law. Have students who selected different responses debate their choices.

sue the debtor for breach of contract. Then, upon obtaining judgment, the creditor must take legally prescribed steps to collect. This is costly and time-consuming. Moreover, some debtors may prove to be dishonest and may move without leaving a forwarding address. Or they may have no assets that the creditor can take. In other instances, debtors may even avoid some of their obligations by going into bankruptcy. It is certainly better for the creditor to have a security interest in some asset of the debtor. For example, in the problem at the beginning of this section, the common stock could be converted into cash by the secured creditor (Wagner) if the debtor (Spano) defaults.

4. Laws Allowing Garnishment of Wages

One other method for creditor protection is the **garnishment** of wages. Once a creditor's claim is shown to be legally valid and fair in a court hearing, the creditor may receive a portion of the debtor's wages directly from the debtor's employer. The amount that can be garnished by all creditors, however, is generally limited by the Consumer Credit Protection Act to 25 percent of the debtor's take-home pay.

▼ WHAT LAWS PROTECT DEBTORS?

PROBLEM

The Santaros decided to rent an unfurnished apartment. Reliable Finance Company was among the sources they used for funds to buy the furniture they needed. Reliable gave them a copy of the loan contract showing only the amount to be paid per installment and the number of payments. Could they demand further information?

There are six important types of laws designed to protect debtors. They do this by: (1) setting maximum interest rates, (2) requiring clear and complete advance disclosure of loan terms, (3) changing the terms of unconscionable contracts, (4) correcting specific abuses of the credit system, (5) requiring the creditor to record a public notice when certain debts have been paid, and (6) canceling most debts and giving the debtor's financial life a fresh start.

1. Laws Setting Maximum Interest Rates

Usury laws that set maximum interest rates are discussed in Chapter 12. Usually such laws apply only to loans of money. They do not govern carrying charges imposed on credit purchases of goods and services "on time." A

Discuss with the class the fourth method of creditor protection—the garnishment of wages. Point out that, generally, the total amount of wages that can be garnished by all creditors combined is limited to a maximum of 25 percent of the debtor's take-home (net) pay.

▼ TEACH

Make individual student copies of the overhead transparency master and display the overhead transparency, *What Laws Protect Debtors?*, to aid students in identifying the six types of laws that protect debtors. Help students identify and fill in appropriate details relating to each type of law as you discuss each one, using the information on pp. 391–398 as a resource.

Have the class, using a blank transparency, complete a fishbone map to summarize the six types of laws designed to protect creditors. (Students may refer to transparency masters completed in the previous TEACH activity.)

Gather articles about legislation aimed at protecting creditors. Have volunteers summarize them orally. (*Business Week*, *Money*, *Consumer's Digest*, and *Congressional Quarterly* are possible sources.)

APPLY

Invite a banker or mortgage company representative to speak to the class about the amount of interest paid on home mortgages. Using an example, have the guest speaker walk the class through the calculations used to determine the amount of interest paid over the life of the loan. **Guided Practice**

Obtain from a bank, realtor, or mortgage company a copy of a federal Truth in Lending disclosure statement. Review the statement with students explaining the annual percentage rate, or APR (cost of credit as a yearly rate), finance charge (dollar amount the credit will cost minus loan amount), amount financed (amount of loan minus any prepaid charges such as points), and total of payments (amount paid after all payments are made—loan amount plus interest).

few states do regulate such charges as interest. They do this on the theory that the store—in effect—borrows money and relends it to the customer-debtor to finance the purchase on credit.

2. Laws Requiring Clear and Complete Disclosure of Terms in Loans and Credit Sales

A **consumer loan** arises when a person borrows money primarily for personal, family, household, or agricultural purposes. It is often called a personal loan to distinguish it from a business or commercial loan.

By requiring complete and clear disclosure of loan terms, the federal Truth in Lending Act (which is part of the Consumer Credit Protection Act) best exemplifies laws designed to protect consumers when they become debtors. In particular, it requires creditors to furnish debtors with certain information. This law does not limit the percentage amounts that may be charged. However, creditors must make a full disclosure of interest and finance charges whenever the consumer loan is repayable in four or more installments or carries a finance charge. The **finance charge** is the total added cost when one pays in installments for goods or services. The creditor must also declare the true equivalent annual interest rate or annual percentage rate (APR). Thus, 1½ percent a month must be stated as 18 percent a year. Under the law, a credit sales contract must also state such details as the cash price of the item; the down payment or trade-in allowance, if any; an itemized list of finance charges; and the total amount to be financed. In the problem, Reliable Finance is obligated to tell the Santaros the total cost of their loan expressed in dollars and cents and to show the actual APR.

The Truth in Lending Act does not apply to first mortgage loans on homes. Fortunately, interest rates on home loans are usually comparatively low. No doubt this is true because the security behind such loans—namely the houses—tends to be high and can be protected by insurance (as discussed in Chapter 34).

Any creditor who willfully and knowingly violates the Truth in Lending Act may be fined, imprisoned, or both. The violator must also pay the debtor twice the finance charge (but no less than $100 nor more than $1,000) plus court costs and attorney's fees.

An increasing number of consumers lease automobiles and other equipment instead of buying the items. A big advantage of leasing for some persons is that it requires no down payment. However, in the end, the total price paid in leasing is usually higher than a cash or credit purchase would be. This is especially true for persons who maintain their automobiles properly and keep them for perhaps five or more years.

ASSESS

Media **Learning Objective 3** Using a computer, if possible, have students explain why each of the types of laws from pp. 392–393 is important. (Answers may include that disclosure is important because it requires creditors to furnish debtors with relevant information, laws against unconscionable contracts can prohibit the stronger party from taking undue advantage, and other laws have been enacted to prohibit or correct specific abuses or problems in the current credit system.)

The federal Consumer Leasing Act extends the protection of the Consumer Credit Protection Act to consumer lessees. Before the contract is signed, the lessor must comply with full disclosure requirements.

3. Laws Changing Unconscionable Contracts

The UCC provides that a court may find that a contract or a clause of a contract is unconscionable—that is, grossly unfair and oppressive. An **unconscionable contract** or clause offends an honest person's conscience and sense of justice. The terms need not be criminal nor violate a statute, but simply unethical. Contracts of adhesion are more likely to be unconscionable. This is so because in such contracts one of the parties dictates all the important terms and the weaker party either must take it as offered or not contract. An example is a contract for emergency repairs in which an unscrupulous mechanic may take unfair advantage and grossly overcharge a motorist who is unfamiliar with automobiles and their maintenance and repair. However, if the contract is challenged in court, a judge who decides that a clause of the contract is unconscionable may:

a. refuse to enforce the contract,
b. enforce the contract without the unconscionable clause, or
c. limit the clause's application so that the contract is no longer unfair.

The law is not designed to relieve a person of a bad bargain. One may still be legally bound by the purchase of overpriced, poor quality, or unneeded goods.

4. Laws Prohibiting Specific Abuses in the Credit System

Laws have been enacted to correct such specific problems as the relative inability of women to get credit, unfair debt-collection practices, and inaccurate credit reports.

The Federal Equal Credit Opportunity Act. This act makes it unlawful for any creditor to discriminate against an applicant because of sex or marital status. In the past, women had difficulty in obtaining credit. This was true even for gainfully employed women. It was especially true for married women who worked as homemakers. The act was created to make such discrimination illegal. Major provisions of the act are the following:

1. A creditor may not refuse, on the basis of sex or marital status, to grant a separate account to a creditworthy applicant.
2. A creditor may not ask the applicant's marital status if the applicant applies for an unsecured separate account.

Using blank overhead transparencies and working in pairs, have students write a contract between two parties, one of whom is stronger and one who is weaker, which includes certain unconscionable clauses. Have each pair display its finished contract to the class. Have class members decide how the contract could successfully be challenged in court.

ETHICS ISSUE

Ethics Issue

The federal Equal Credit Opportunity Act has made it illegal for a creditor to discriminate because of gender or marital status. Discuss the problems individuals face if they are denied credit. Discuss students' opinions of why discrimination took place in the past and continues even today. Ask students to find out what people can do to protect themselves against this type of discrimination. (Answers may include obtaining credit in the individual's name alone, maintaining a spotless credit history, establishing sole bank accounts to prove credit worthiness, and so on.)

▼RETEACH Have students create posters for each of the three types of laws explained on pp. 392–393. Have students summarize the laws, explain the potential abuses (the reasons for the law), and penalties for violating the laws.

▼ENRICH Media Using a computer, if possible, have students write a consumer rights bulletin warning against abuses of the three types of laws summarized on pp. 392–393. (Obtain examples from the state attorney general's office or Better Business Bureau.) Tape record these PSAs to share with the class.

Divide the class into groups of three or four. Assign each group one of the four federal laws prohibiting specific abuses in the credit system, outlined on pp. 393–395. Using one class period, have each group work together to prepare a campaign to inform the general public about each law. Once they decide on their strategy, such as creating television or radio ads or using billboards, bumper stickers, and flyers, they should identify what role each person in the group will play. One person can prepare the text for the ads, another can prepare and place the visuals for the ads and a fourth, if necessary, can serve as project director to coordinate the marketing campaign strategy. You may wish to have students import or create computer graphics, if possible to illustrate their ads. Display students' work around the classroom or, if possible, around the school.

Cooperative Learning

3. A creditor may not prohibit a married female applicant from opening or maintaining an account in her maiden name.
4. A creditor shall not request information about birth control practices or childbearing intentions or capability.
5. Married persons who have joint accounts have the right to have credit information reported in both their names in order to provide a credit history for both. In the past, upon divorce or upon death of the husband, the wife would often be denied credit because the joint account had been listed in the husband's name only.

The Federal Fair Debt Collection Practices Act. This act makes abusive and deceptive debt-collection practices illegal. The act applies to professional bill collectors or agencies that regularly try to collect consumer debts for clients. Prohibited practices include the following:

1. Harassment of debtors (as with a series of letters that contain menacing or threatening language, or with repeated telephone calls, especially at night);
2. abusive and profane language;
3. threats of violence;
4. contact with third parties (e.g., relatives, neighbors, friends, and employers); and
5. communication with the debtor at work.

The act is aimed at aggressively insensitive and irresponsible professional collection agencies. It does not apply to individual creditors who personally try to collect money due them. Nor does it apply to "in-house" debt collection efforts of the creditor, or of employees or lawyers of the creditor. However, a seriously abused debtor may sometimes succeed in a civil action against any debt collector for damages. The legal basis could be the tort of defamation, assault, invasion of privacy, or intentional infliction of mental suffering.

The Federal Fair Credit Billing Act. This act provides the following protections to credit card holders:

1. Creditors must mail bills at least fourteen days before the due date, must acknowledge billing inquiries within thirty days, and must settle any complaints within ninety days.
2. Creditors may not send repeated, insistent letters demanding payment until disputes over the billing are settled.

ASSESS

Learning Objective 3 Have students use the information on pp. 393–395 to create a spider or fishbone map identifying the four federal laws that prohibit specific abuses in the credit system (The Equal Credit Opportunity Act, the Fair Debt Collection Practices Act, the Fair Credit Billing Act, and the Fair Credit Reporting Act). Have them fill in details relating to each law on horizontal lines radiating from the appropriate arm and color code the laws, if desired.

3 Credit card holders may withhold payment for items that prove defective without being held liable for the entire amount owed. This applies only in case of purchases of more than $50 made in the buyer's state or within 100 miles of the buyer's home.

The Fair Credit Billing Act also permits merchants to offer discounts to customers who pay cash instead of using credit cards. Thus, gasoline service stations often charge a few cents less per gallon to customers who pay cash. This is fair because extending credit is costly for sellers even though it may increase sales volume.

The Federal Fair Credit Reporting Act. This act regulates credit rating service companies that review personal financial records of credit applicants. Aided by computers, these companies or agencies maintain voluminous files covering pertinent information about millions of individuals and business firms that buy goods and services on credit. Retailers, wholesalers, and manufacturers routinely supply such credit rating agencies with data about their experience with customers. In turn, credit rating agencies relay relevant information to cooperating member firms that request it when someone asks them for a credit purchase.

The Retailers Credit Association, composed of retail merchants who sell on credit, is an example of a credit rating agency. It determines the prospective buyer's credit rating. A **credit rating** reflects the evaluation of one's ability to pay debts. Under the law, if credit is denied because of information in a credit report, the company denying credit must tell the applicant. The applicant may then demand that the reporting agency disclose the general nature of the contents of its file (except medical information) and the names of parties who were given this information. However, names of those who provided the information need not be disclosed. If there is any demonstrated error in the report, the credit reporting agency must correct it. Upon request, it must notify the inquirers who had been misinformed. The agency must make the disclosures and reports without charge if the applicant acted within thirty days of getting notice of a denial of credit. Similar rules apply when an individual is denied an insurance policy or employment contract because of an unfavorable credit report.

5. Laws Requiring Notice of Debt Payment to Be Recorded

As a practical matter, debtors should always request receipts, especially when paying in cash. In some states, a debtor is not required to pay a debt unless such a receipt is given. A check that has been paid and properly canceled is returned to the drawer (writer) of the check by the bank on which

Divide the class into four groups and assign each to role-play a violation of one of the four federal credit laws prohibiting specific abuses in the credit system (outlined on pp. 393–395). Discuss each group's scenario and what the person being discriminated against could have done to stop the violation under the Equal Credit Opportunity Act. Videotape each group's scenario. **Independent Practice**

Writing Connections

Consumer Law
Show students the back of a credit card statement; specifically, the section(s) dealing with withholding payment for items that prove defective. Ask students to write letters, using a computer, if possible, to fictitious credit card companies explaining that they are withholding payment for an item because it is defective. They should identify themselves and the product, and tell when and where it was purchased, what is wrong, and what they did to try to resolve the problem.

RETEACH Working with a peer-tutor, have students write two examples of each law identified in the ASSESS activity (while keeping the law itself anonymous). Have pairs exchange examples to correctly identify the law from each example.

ENRICH Have students fold a sheet of drawing paper in half horizontally. On the top half, have them draw a picture illustrating one of the four laws that prohibit specific abuses in the credit system, outlined on pp. 393–395. On the bottom half, have them illustrate a potential abuse of each law.

Personal Perspectives

Several companies provide your credit history to institutions (such as department stores, banks, or auto dealerships) that request this information. Two that provide this information are TRW (214–235–1200) and Equifax (800–685–1111). Have students discuss with an adult family member the importance of maintaining an accurate credit history.

Give each student four index cards. Have students write four questions that illustrate each of the four forms of discharge of debt for debtors (chapters 7, 11, 12, and 13). Have students identify the appropriate form of relief, by number, on the top of each card. Collect all the cards and divide the class into two teams. Read aloud each question and award one point for each correct response.

As a class, discuss why many people still file for bankruptcy even though a bankruptcy filing remains on your credit report for 10 years. (Answers may include that the stigma once attached to bankruptcy no longer exists, some people have no alternative, and so on.)

it was drawn. Such canceled check serves as a receipt. It is often helpful for this purpose to indicate on the face of the check the purpose for the payment. Even without such notation, it can serve as evidence of payment. When a secured debt (as discussed in Chapter 20) is paid in full, the law generally permits the debtor to require the creditor to record that fact in the public records.

6. Laws Allowing Debtors to Cancel Most Debts and Start Over

Bankruptcy laws have been enacted to help debtors who have become overburdened with debts. These laws allow an individual or business to be released from the obligation to pay most debts when they are overwhelming and might never be paid in any event. At the same time, they provide some protection for creditors by ensuring a fair and orderly distribution of the debtor's available assets among all of the creditors. This release of the debtor from debt is called a **discharge**. Discharges through bankruptcy are available to a particular debtor only once every six years. A record that debts were discharged in bankruptcy generally stays on the debtor's record for ten years. This reduces the debtor's ability to get credit during that period.

Under the U.S. Constitution, Congress has exclusive power to establish uniform laws on bankruptcies. The federal Bankruptcy Code provides the following forms of possible relief for debtors.

Chapter 7 Liquidation, or "Straight Bankruptcy." This relief involves the sale for cash of the nonexempt property of the debtor and the distribution of the proceeds to creditors. Nonexempt property includes such assets as bank accounts, stocks, and bonds (see page 398 for further details). Liquidation results in the discharge of most of the debtor's financial obligations.

Chapter 11 Reorganization of Debtor Business Firms. This relief is designed to keep the corporation, partnership, or sole proprietorship (as described fully in Chapters 37 and 38) in active business with no liquidation. Under Chapter 11, claims of both secured and unsecured creditors, as well as the interests of the owners of the business, may be "impaired," meaning reduced. The plan must be in the best interests of the creditors, and each class of creditors that is adversely affected must accept it. A class of creditors accepts the plan when a majority that represents two-thirds of the amount of that group's total claim votes to approve the plan. Even when only one class (e.g., the bondholders) accepts the plan the Bankruptcy Court may approve it under a so-called cramdown provision. This requires that the creditors or the owners who object are either unaffected by the plan, or are paid in full before any junior (or lower) class of claimant is paid.

ASSESS

Learning Objective 4 In writing, have students identify how bankruptcy laws protect both creditors and debtors. (Answers may include that individuals and businesses are released from most debts, creditors are ensured a fair and orderly distribution of the debtor's available assets, and so on.)

Chapter 13 Proceeding. This relief is available only to individuals and sole proprietors of business firms. This plan also avoids liquidation of assets. The debtor must have regular income, unsecured debts of less than $100,000, and/or secured debts of less than $350,000. The debtor must submit a plan for payment of debts within three years with a possible extension to five years. During this time, the creditors may not file suit for payment of any debts. Both secured and unsecured debts (other than a claim, such as a promissory note and mortgage, secured by the debtor's principal residence) may be reduced in amount or extended in time for payment. The plan must be "in the best interests of the creditors," who might otherwise receive even less in a Chapter 7 liquidation. A major advantage of the Chapter 13 proceeding is that upon completion of payments called for under the plan, the court grants a discharge for almost all debts. The only exceptions are for certain long-term debts, such as payments for a house and payments of alimony and child support.

Chapter 12 Proceeding. This relief was added to the Bankruptcy Code in 1986 for family farm owners. This plan is similar in operation to the Chapter 13 proceeding for other debtors.

Liquidation may be voluntary or involuntary. With a few exceptions, any person, business, or other association may request **voluntary bankruptcy.** Any person or business, except farmers and charitable institutions, owing $5,000 or more and unable to pay debts when they come due may be forced into **involuntary bankruptcy.**

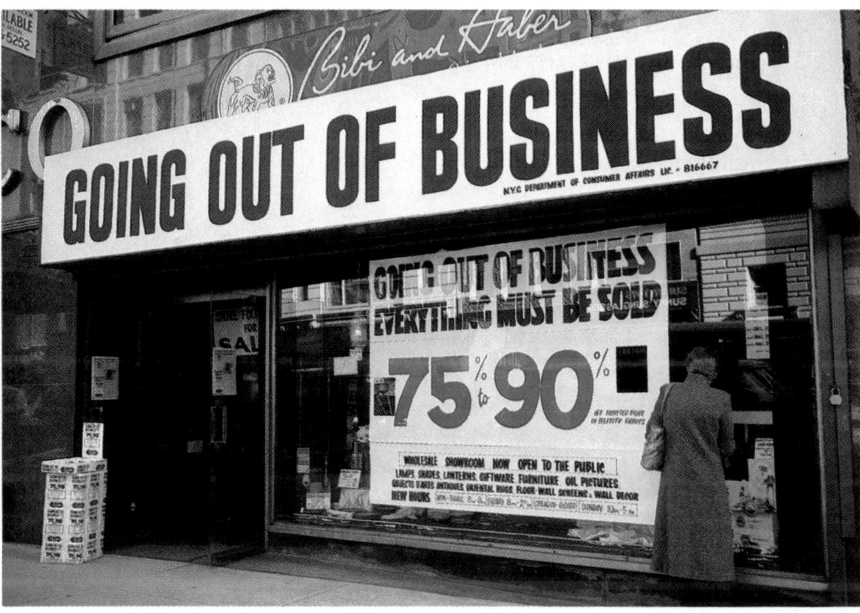

Have students obtain business bankruptcy ads from local newspapers. Have students discuss why some of these businesses remain open even after filing for bankruptcy. (Answers may include that certain types of relief, such as chapters 11 and 13, allow businesses to stay open while they reorganize, so long as two-thirds of the creditors agree to the plan.)

Working in small groups, have students plan, write, and tape record a public service announcement (PSA) on bankruptcy. Their PSA may focus on information such as who may file, how to file, or how to avoid bankruptcy. Each PSA should last about one minute and should open with a catchy phrase or jingle to catch listeners' attention. With administration approval, have students deliver PSAs during school announcements.

Thinking Critically Through Visuals

Due to economic slowdowns, many businesses are forced into bankruptcy. Why, do you think, is this store selling its inventory at a deep discount? (Answers may include to raise capital, to pay creditors, and so on.)

▼RETEACH Have students identify which bankruptcy law would be the most appropriate form of relief in each case: **(1) A farmer has $50,000 in debts.** (Ch. 12); **(2) Directors of a corporation do not want to end its existence.** (Ch. 11); and **(3) A homeowner has $65,000 in debts that can't be paid.** (Ch. 7 or 11).

▼ENRICH Have students complete a comparison chart of the four forms of relief for debtors from pp. 396–397. Provide these headings as a guide: **Chapter**, **For Whom Designed**, **Type of Relief**, and **Other Key Points**.

In writing, using a computer, if possible, have pairs of students identify the obligations of the debtor under a Chapter 12 Proceeding, the role and obligations of the trustee, which claims are not dischargeable by bankruptcy, and which of the debtor's assets are exempt from seizure to satisfy creditors' claims. (See pp. 397–398.)

Invite an attorney specializing in bankruptcy to discuss the ethical and financial implications of bankruptcy and to explain how various assets are exempt by state or federal laws. You may also wish to have the guest speaker address the issue of potential bankruptcy abuse, including people who declare bankruptcy in one company and then start another. Before the visit, have the class make up a list of questions to ask.

In writing, using a computer, if possible, have students answer the following question: **For which debts, do you think, should a person who needs protection of the bankruptcy laws still be held liable? Why?** (Answers should reflect independent thinking but will be based, presumably, on the list of claims on p. 398.)

In either voluntary or involuntary bankruptcy proceedings, the debtor must file under oath:

a. a list of all creditors and amounts owed to each;
b. a list of all property owned, including property claimed to be exempt from seizure;
c. a statement explaining the debtor's financial affairs; and
d. a list of current income and expenses.

A trustee is then selected. The trustee's duties are to find and to protect the assets of the debtor, liquidate them, and pay the claims against the debtor's estate with the proceeds. Such claims would include court costs, back wages owed to the debtor's employees, taxes, and claims of the general creditors. Secured creditors would seek payment of the secured debts directly against the collateral. Secured debts would be enforced ahead of any of these other claims. In addition, there are certain types of claims that are not dischargeable by bankruptcy. These include the following:

a. certain taxes;
b. alimony and child support;
c. claims against the debtor for property obtained by fraud, embezzlement, or larceny;
d. judgments against the debtor for willful and malicious injury to the person or property of another (but claims for injuries caused by negligence are discharged);
e. student loans owed to the government or to a nonprofit school of higher learning, unless the loan became due more than five years before the bankruptcy, or an undue hardship would be imposed on the debtor or on his or her dependents;
f. judgments against the debtor resulting from driving while intoxicated; and
g. any claims not listed by the debtor.

In addition, certain assets of the debtor are exempt from seizure to satisfy creditor's claims. Under the federal law these exemptions include the following:

a. up to $7,500 in equity in the debtor's home,
b. up to $1,200 interest in one motor vehicle,
c. up to $750 interest in the debtor's tools of trade, and
d. alimony and support payments, social security payments, and certain welfare and pension benefits.

States may pass legislation disallowing the use of these federal exemptions and some have done so. In such states, only the state exemptions are available.

▼ ASSESS

Learning Objectives 3 & 4 Have students explain, in writing, how a person may file for bankruptcy, yet retain certain assets exempt from seizure by creditors. (Answers may include that federal and state laws prohibit certain assets from being seized, such as a portion of home equity, alimony and support benefits, and so on.)

WHAT SPECIAL LAWS APPLY TO CREDIT CARDS AND THEIR USE?

PROBLEM

Tomlinson applied for and received a gasoline credit card. After using it several times, Tomlinson sold the automobile, bought a bicycle, and laid the card aside. Several weeks later, she received a bill for $79 from the oil company for purchases made by someone else. Tomlinson realized that the card had been lost or stolen and so notified the company. Must she pay the $79?

Instead of carrying large amounts of cash (which could be lost or stolen), or writing checks (which are not accepted by many restaurants and retail stores), millions of consumers buy goods and services by using **credit cards.** A credit card identifies the holder as a person entitled to obtain goods or services on credit. The issuer of the card specifies the limit of available credit, and before a large sale is made, the seller can contact the issuer to determine if this limit has been exceeded.

Usually a credit card is made of plastic, is embossed with the holder's name and identification number, and has a place on the back for the holder's signature (see Figure 19-1). Annually, billions of dollars of credit purchases are made with this "plastic money." Some credit cards are intended for specialized purchases. For example, the AMERICAN EXPRESS®,

Figure 19-1 *These are representative examples of widely used credit cards. An authorized signature validates the card and helps to prevent its misuse by thieves.*

TEACH

Point out to students how easy it is to charge purchases that they cannot afford. Make students aware of how much more they end up paying for goods if they make only the minimum credit card payment each month. Discuss cardholders' liabilities for unauthorized use of their cards and what to do when one loses a credit card.

Summarize points 1–5 on p. 400, which identify a cardholder's liability for unauthorized use of a credit card. Provide various scenarios of credit card abuse, then ask students to determine the cardholder's liability.

Thinking Critically Through Visuals

There are many different kinds of credit cards. Why, do you think, do companies and banks issue credit cards? (Answers may include to entice people to buy things they do not have the cash for, to make it easier to purchase goods, to make money through interest, and so on.)

RETEACH Have students use the information on p. 398 to create a two-column chart. In the first column, entitled *Debts Not Discharged*, have students list those debts not cancelled by bankruptcy. In the second column, called *Assets Exempt from Seizure*, have students identify those assets exempt, by federal law.

ENRICH  Using a computer, if possible, have students explain why the claim of bankruptcy cannot discharge student loans (under most conditions). Ask students to hypothesize the intent of this exception.

APPLY

Secure for each student a credit application form from department stores, credit card companies, or banks. Have students write the word SAMPLE in large print across the application, then complete the sample as fully as possible. Point out what information to look for and have students verbally summarize their obligations and responsibilities to the creditor. **Guided Practice**

Working in groups of two or three, have students role play the opening of a credit/charge account at a department store. Each group should consist of a credit manager and a single person or a couple applying for credit. The applicant(s) should be asked appropriate, legal questions by the credit manager, then complete an application. Be sure payment responsibilities and rates of interest are discussed. **Independent Practice**

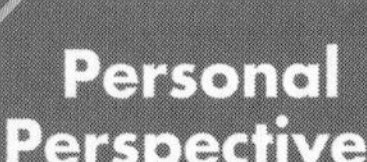

Personal Perspectives

Have students discuss with adult family members the legal and ethical responsibilities that go along with having a credit card. Using this information as a guide, have students make posters in class dealing with wise and unwise uses of credit cards.

Carte Blanche®, and Diners Club International® cards are commonly used for travel and entertainment. Some are limited to use in designated retail outlets, such as identified department stores or gasoline service stations. Some are all-purpose cards, usually issued by banks, and intended for purchases from any cooperating seller. Examples are MasterCard™, VISA®, and DISCOVER® cards.

A credit card is usually issued in response to a consumer's written application. The consumer who signs the card is bound in a contractual relation with the issuer and is liable for all purchases made with the card by the holder or by others with the holder's permission.

Under federal law, the cardholder is also liable for unauthorized use of the credit card by any other person, such as a thief or a dishonest finder. This liability is limited, however, to $50 and is imposed only if:

1. the cardholder had asked for and received the credit card or had signed or used it;
2. the card issuer had given adequate notice of the possible liability for unauthorized use;
3. the card issuer had provided the cardholder with a description of how to notify the card issuer in the event of loss or theft of the card;
4. the card issuer had provided positive means for identification on the card, such as space for the holder's signature or photograph; and
5. the unauthorized use took place before the cardholder had notified the issuer that the card had been lost or stolen.

Thus, the loss or theft of a credit card should be reported immediately to the issuer. In the problem, Tomlinson would probably be liable for only $50 of the charges. The thief would be criminally liable for forgery and larceny.

Most credit card agreements require the cardholder to pay the amount charged on the card within a specified number of days after the closing date shown on the billing statement. If the cardholder fails to do so, he or she is contractually obligated to pay interest or finance carrying charges on the unpaid balance. Some states set limits on the rates that can be charged credit card holders. These limits are relatively high (usually about 18 percent a year) and should be avoided whenever possible by paying the full amount due within the grace period. Fifteen days is common but it may be more or fewer. Customers seldom earn 18 percent on their money when they lend or invest it. Thus credit may be easily obtained but it is *not* cheap.

Credit cards clearly offer convenience and protection from loss for the consumer. But they can cause a significant increase in the cost of goods and services purchased. This is true even when balances due are paid before carrying charges are added. Realistically, the seller must pay the credit card

ASSESS

Learning Objective 5 Have students create a chart listing the pros and cons of using credit cards. (Answers may include: pros—you can carry a limited amount of cash and you can keep better track of expenses; cons—you might overextend yourself financially, you might tend to buy on impulse, and so on.)

company for its service in bookkeeping and in prompt payment for purchases made. Commonly, this cost to the seller is a charge of between 3 percent and 6 percent of the sales prices. Such amounts paid to the credit card company are passed on to customers—both cash and credit—through higher prices for goods sold.

In addition, credit cards have a great potential for abuse through overuse by owners and misuse by thieves or finders of lost cards. Some consumers fail to plan and save for their purchases. Instead, they often use their credit cards impulsively to purchase goods and services not really needed. Sometimes, the payments for these purchases, when added to other living expenses, total more than the debtor's income. As one consequence, debt counseling services now operate in many cities. These services assist debtors in budgeting their income and expenses in a disciplined plan to pay off creditors and to avoid being forced into bankruptcy.

With information from credit card applications, banks, and newspapers, create a chart or poster comparing the current interest rates and finance charges associated with different types of credit cards. Have students decide which credit card offers the best rates. Compare these rates with current interest rates paid on savings accounts.

Preventing Legal Difficulties

Using credit wisely...

1. In applying for credit, always be accurate and honest. Any temporary advantage gained by misleading a creditor can eventually cause serious trouble. Credit information about customers is exchanged freely by stores and other creditors. Thus, lies about one's credit history are often exposed.
2. If you give property as security for a debt, be sure it is returned or properly released when the debt is paid. Otherwise you may later have difficulty selling the property or using it as security again.
3. Protect your rights by learning about them and exercising them when appropriate. The Fair Credit Reporting Act, Fair Credit Billing Act, Equal Credit Opportunity Act, Fair Debt Collection Practices Act, and related statutes are of limited value without consumer demand for their enforcement.
4. Be cautious about entering into a credit agreement as a surety or a guarantor, and be prepared to pay when the bill comes due.
5. A person who repairs your television, watch, car, or other personal property can exercise an artisan's lien on the property, retaining possession until paid, or eventually selling the goods. It helps to get a detailed written estimate of required work and of the anticipated cost before work has begun. Again, be prepared to pay these fees upon completion of the work.

Review the five tips for using credit wisely, listed on p. 401. Have students summarize these points in writing to share at home.

RETEACH Have pairs of students make a poster informing their classmates—current or future credit card holders—what to do if a credit card is stolen or lost. Display posters in visible areas around your school.

As a group, have students create a cartoon strip to illustrate the perils of misusing credit cards. You may wish to bring in sample comics from a daily newspaper for students to use as a guide for format.

▼ CLOSE

To help students who have difficulty summarizing or synthesizing large blocks of information, encourage small groups of students to complete the chapter outline on pp. 177–178 in the Workbook.

Assign the following end-of-chapter materials:
Student text review activities, pp. 402–407
Workbook, pp. 59–60
Chapter Test

Chapter *MicroExam*

▼ REVIEWING IMPORTANT POINTS

1. When one owes money to another, the relationship is that of debtor and creditor.

2. A debt may be secured or unsecured. If secured, the debtor gives the creditor possession of the security, or a nonpossessory lien against specified property until the debt is paid. If unsecured, the creditor does not get a lien against specific property. However, the creditor may successfully sue the debtor, and then have the sheriff seize cash deposits or other available assets of the debtor to satisfy (i.e., pay) the court judgment. To the extent necessary, the assets (real and personal property) are sold by the sheriff at a public sale.

3. A lien gives the creditor the right to sell specified property of the debtor to pay the debt. Any excess money received goes to the debtor. If there is a deficiency or shortage, the creditor normally may sue for the balance due.

4. Goods or documents representing property rights may be delivered to the creditor as security for a loan. This creates a pledge and gives the creditor the right to sell the goods or the documents in case of default. Upon performance of the obligation, the pledgor (debtor) has a right to have pledged property returned.

5. Creditors may proceed against the general assets of the debtor in the following two cases:
   a. when secured debts are in default and are not paid in full by proceeds from sale of the property pledged, and
   b. when unsecured debts are not paid.

6. In answering for the debt of another upon default, the surety assumes a primary liability. The guarantor is liable secondarily after the creditor has exhausted all remedies against the debtor, including judgment of a court and attempted execution.

7. Debtors are protected by usury laws as well as laws (a) requiring disclosure of loan terms, (b) concerning unconscionable contracts, (c) providing equal credit opportunities, (d) requiring fair billing, (e) controlling the collection of debts, (f) regulating fair reporting of credit standing, and (g) allowing debt discharge through bankruptcy.

8. A signed credit card binds the cardholder and the issuer in a contractual relationship. In case of loss or theft of a card, the cardholder generally is liable for unauthorized purchases up to a limit of $50 unless the issuer had been notified previously.

▼ STRENGTHENING YOUR LEGAL VOCABULARY

Match each term with the statement that best defines that term. Some terms may not be used.

artisan's lien
consumer loan
credit card
credit rating
creditor
debt
debtor
discharge
finance charge
garnishment
guarantor
guaranty
involuntary bankruptcy
lien
mechanic's lien
pawn
pawnbroker
pawn ticket
pledge
pledgee (creditor)
pledgor (debtor)
principal debtor
secured debt
security interest
surety
suretyship
unconscionable contract
unsecured debt
voluntary bankruptcy

1. Plastic card that identifies holder as a person entitled to receive goods or services on credit.
2. Debt backed by the debtor's promise to pay, but not by any lien.
3. The creditor's right to enforce the debt against specific property of the debtor.
4. Person to whom a debt is owed.
5. Third party who agrees to be secondarily liable for the debt of another if such other person defaults.
6. Agreement whereby personal property is deposited with a creditor as security for the payment of a debt.
7. Claim that is filed against real property for the unpaid value of labor and materials.
8. Third party who agrees to be primarily liable for the debt of another if such other person fails to pay the debt when due.
9. One who lends money at interest and has possession of personal property as security for the money.
10. Court-granted right of the creditor to intercept wages of the debtor to pay an overdue debt.

▼ **Strengthening Your Legal Vocabulary** ▼

1. credit card
2. unsecured debt
3. security interest
4. creditor
5. guarantor
6. pledge
7. mechanic's lien
8. surety
9. pawnbroker
10. garnishment

APPLYING LAW TO EVERYDAY LIFE

1. When Dodrill started her own copying and duplicating business, she entered into several contractual arrangements. First, she bought $900 worth of paper from Springfield Business Supply, promising to pay the money within thirty days. Then, using her bank credit card, she purchased a computer and word processing software. In addition, she bought several desktop copying units from the manufacturer on a twenty-four-month installment purchase plan. The plan permitted the seller to repossess the machines if Dodrill defaulted on payments. Finally, Dodrill borrowed $2,000 from the Ozark Region National Bank to meet current expenses, giving a U.S. Treasury bond as security for repayment. Which of the transactions entered into by Dodrill involved a debtor-creditor relationship? Which relationships were secured? Which were unsecured?

2. Glenn needs money on short notice. He has an expensive watch and a poor credit rating. Where might he be able to legitimately raise the funds he needs?

3. After graduating from high school, Jack Tern decided to become a driver of heavy-duty trucks. The A-OK Truck Driving Academy offered a two-week, intensive, one-on-one (instructor-student) course with training on two- and three-axle tractors and on forty-five-foot single and double trucks, for $4,000 cash. Since Jack had no money, A-OK agreed to take his written promise to pay the tuition fee in monthly installments of $130 for four years, provided he could get a surety or guarantor to promise to pay if he defaulted. Jack's Uncle Joe signed a guaranty agreement, and Jack enrolled and completed the course. After six months, however, he lost his job as a truck driver and could not continue making the monthly payments. Can A-OK immediately demand payment from Jack's Uncle Joe?

4. Langley had owed $7,340 to St. John's Hospital for more than one year. Finally, the hospital obtained a court order directing Langley's employer to pay a sum of money out of each of Langley's paychecks toward the bill. What creditor protection device has the hospital utilized? What is the maximum amount of Langley's check that is available to the hospital?

5. ETHICS ISSUE During the warranty period, the Arnaudos returned their home computer for repair to the seller, Computerville, Inc. Later, after the express warranty period had expired, the Arnaudos stopped making their regular monthly $100 payments for the computer

Applying Law to Everyday Life

1. All were debtor-creditor relationships. (p. 386) Only the last two transactions (purchase of the desktop copiers and the bank loan) were secured. (p. 387)
2. A pawnbroker would lend money to Glenn on the spot and take the watch as security. (p. 388)
3. No; As guarantor, Joe did agree to pay if Jack defaulted. But, unlike a surety, who is primarily liable and would have to pay immediately upon default, Joe, as a guarantor, is secondarily liable. This means that A-OK must first sue Jack and get a court judgment. Then it must try to enforce the judgment by collecting from Jack. Only if the debt proves to be uncollectible may A-OK demand payment from Uncle Joe, the guarantor. (p. 390)
4. St. John's has used garnishment of the debtor's wages. The maximum amount of wages which can be garnished is limited to 25 percent of Langley's net pay. (p. 391)

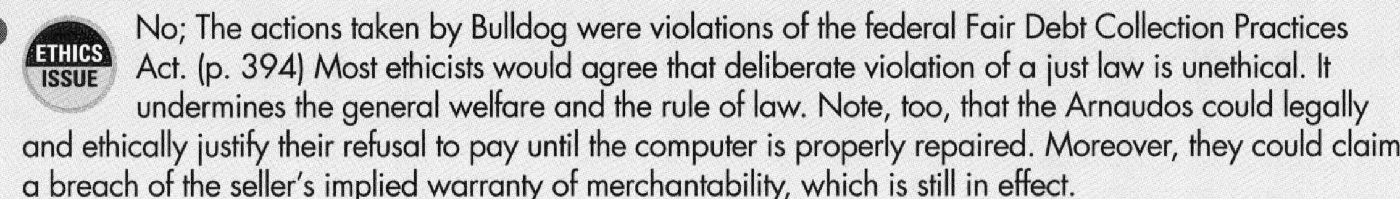
5. ETHICS ISSUE No; The actions taken by Bulldog were violations of the federal Fair Debt Collection Practices Act. (p. 394) Most ethicists would agree that deliberate violation of a just law is unethical. It undermines the general welfare and the rule of law. Note, too, that the Arnaudos could legally and ethically justify their refusal to pay until the computer is properly repaired. Moreover, they could claim a breach of the seller's implied warranty of merchantability, which is still in effect.

because the same problem continued. Computerville then gave its claim for the $1,900 balance to Bulldog Services, a collection agency. Bulldog had a clerk telephone the Arnaudos at least once a day and once a night, usually after 1 a.m. Every Sunday, a uniformed Bulldog agent would park the company truck in front of the Arnaudos's house. The truck had these words in large type on both side panels: "Bulldog Services. We Chase Deadbeats." The agent would then try to talk about the claim with any person entering or leaving the house. Was Bulldog Services acting legally? Was Bulldog Services acting ethically?

6 Shortly after graduation from college, Matilda Smith applied for credit at a local department store. The store denied her application, citing the unfavorable credit report it had received from the Alpha-Omega Credit Bureau. Matilda assumed that the negative report stemmed from a prolonged dispute with a major retail chain over goods she had not ordered. Recently, the retail store acknowledged its error. What can Matilda do to clear her name with Alpha-Omega?

7 McCormack owed the Coopersmith Variety Store $67.50 for purchases. She paid the bill with a personal check after noting the purpose on the face of the check. The check was indorsed and cashed by Coopersmith and returned to McCormack properly canceled. Coopersmith then billed her again for the same obligation. What should McCormack do?

8 ETHICS ISSUE Alex gets paid at the end of the month. A week before payday, Alex ran out of cash. His classmate Roger agreed to lend him "10, for 20 when you get paid." Translated, this means that Roger lends Alex $10 now in exchange for $20 to be paid after seven days. Is this contract legal? Is it ethical?

9 When Lola came home from college for spring break, her mother gave her a credit card. "You can sign my name, but don't spend more than $100," she told Lola. Lola went on a buying spree with her friend Joyce and together they bought $575 worth of clothing using the credit card. Now her mother refuses to pay more than $150, stating, "$100 I authorized, and $50 is the legal maximum for unauthorized purchases." The credit card company sues for $575. Who wins?

10 Mark is greatly upset and wonders if he should report what appears to him to be a flagrant abuse of the bankruptcy law. The individual debtor in question has been living for years in a house that is worth at least $100,000 and maybe much more. Recently, the debtor went through a Chapter 7 liquidation in bankruptcy, yet he and his family still live in the house. Should Mark report this to the Bankruptcy Court?

8 ETHICS ISSUE No; It is an illegal, usurious contract and probably one of adhesion. Alex is required to pay an extra $10 for the use of $10 for seven days. This is 100 percent interest for one week. (p. 393) Such an illegal and outrageously high charge for the loan of money is unconscionable and unethical. Yet it is a common practice, with variations found on school campuses and in the military services.

9 The credit card company; The purchases were valid because the mother authorized Lola to use the card. The misuse was the result of Lola's breach of trust in acting as her mother's representative. (p. 400)

10 No; In all likelihood, the individual debtor has an equity in the house he and his family occupy that is no more than the $7,500 which is exempt from seizure. If his equity was more than $7,500, it is possible that the house was seized, and sold, but now he and his family rent it from the new owner. (p. 398)

6 Matilda may demand to know the general nature of the contents of the Credit Bureau's file, request that they investigate her claims of error, and, if an error is found, report their findings to those who were misinformed of Matilda's credit worthiness as well as correct the Bureau's own record. (p. 395)

7 McCormack should show Coopersmith the canceled check with the notation of purpose which constitutes a receipt. (pp. 395–396) Even without such a notation, the canceled check for $67.50 made payable to Coopersmith would be very persuasive evidence of payment.

Solving Case Problems

1 No; The regulations are not arbitrary and unreasonable. (p. 388) The court noted that "thieves and receivers of stolen property frequently resort to pawnbrokers as an outlet for their ill-gotten means." Where pawnbroking is strictly regulated, larceny is greatly reduced. As to the thumbprints, experience has demonstrated that handwriting may be the subject of forgery, but fingerprints may not.

2 Judgment for plaintiff Sniadach; In this classic case, the U.S. Supreme Court defined what is known in legal circles as the Sniadach doctrine: a debtor is entitled to notice and a fair opportunity to be heard before her or his property is taken. This is true even if a court ultimately renders judgment and the taking proves to be temporary. Here, by freezing the plaintiff's wages, there was an illegal taking of property without the procedural due process required by the Fourteenth Amendment. As stated by Justice William Douglas "… the right to be heard has little … worth unless one is informed that the matter is pending and can choose … whether to appear or default, acquiesce or contest … " the opponent's case. (p. 391)

SOLVING CASE PROBLEMS

1. Medias and other pawnbrokers objected to an Indianapolis city ordinance that regulated their business. The ordinance required an applicant for a pawnbroker's license to establish good character by the certificate of three landowners. The ordinance also provided that the licensee keep specified records and supply information to the chief of police. Finally, the ordinance specified that the licensee hold all pledged articles for ninety-six hours, and it required that the licensee take the thumbprints of all persons from whom he or she bought or received goods. Are these regulations arbitrary and unreasonable? (*Medias v. City of Indianapolis*, 216 Ind. 155, 23 N.E.2d 590)

2. Sniadach owed the Family Finance Corporation (FFC) $420 under a written promise to pay. When this debt became overdue, the creditor obtained a court order that summarily garnished her wages. Her employer had $63 in wages earned by her but not yet paid, and it agreed to hold one-half of them subject to the court order. Sniadach sued the FFC and asked the court to reverse the garnishment order, claiming that it violated her right to due process under the Fourteenth Amendment. She had received the summons and complaint on the same day that her employer was notified and froze her wages. Thus, she had no opportunity to be heard and to present her side of the case before the garnishment took effect. The trial court denied her motion, and the Wisconsin Supreme Court affirmed. She now appeals to the U.S. Supreme Court. How should it rule? (*Sniadach v. Family Finance Corporation*, 395 U.S. 337)

3. Todd was one of seven cosureties. When the principal debtor defaulted, Todd paid the debt and sued the other cosureties. Is Todd entitled to a judgment for one-seventh of the debt against each of the cosureties or to a judgment for six-sevenths of the debt against each? (*Todd v. Windsor*, 118 Ga. App. 805, 165 S.E.2d 438)

4. In his divorce decree, Elliot was ordered to pay $102 of his weekly wages of $467.47 from his job at a General Motors plant for child support. Months later, U.S. Life Credit Corporation (USLC) recovered a judgment against Elliot in municipal court. With court approval, USLC then garnished 25 percent of Elliot's $467.47 per week to pay off the judgment amount. The U.S. Secretary of Labor, whose job it is to see that the provisions of the federal Consumer Credit Protection Act relating to garnishment are properly enforced, then filed a lawsuit against the municipal court and USLC contending that the payments to USLC

3 Todd is entitled only to a judgment for one-seventh of the debt from each of the six cosureties. (p. 390) The right sued on is that of contribution among co-obligors, and each is liable only for an equal, proportionate share of the debt. The creditor, of course, may sue any one or all of the sureties who are jointly and severally liable to such creditor.

and for child support, taken together, violated the 25 percent of disposable income restriction on garnishments imposed by the act. You decide. (*Donovan v. Hamilton County Municipal Court*, 580 F. Supp. 554)

5 When Hardison filed for bankruptcy, one of his main creditors was General Finance Corporation (GFC) to which he owed $2,800. After the GFC debt and others were discharged as a result of the bankruptcy procedure, he received a letter from GFC informing him that his credit was still good with it. By telephone, Hardison then arranged for a $1,200 loan from GFC. However, when he appeared to pick up the money, GFC informed him that it was going to make the loan only if he agreed to pay back not only the $1,200, but also an additional $1,200 from the first loan. Hardison then signed a consumer credit contract agreeing to those terms. Later, Hardison filed a lawsuit claiming that GFC should have included the amount from the previously discharged debt in the "total finance charge" in the truth-in-lending statement shown him at the time of the transaction, rather than as a part of the "total amount financed." Hardison wanted damages available under the Truth in Lending Act. Should he receive them? (*Hardison v. General Finance Corporation*, 738 F.2d 893)

4 Judgment for the Secretary of Labor; The court held that, regardless of its label as child support, the $102 was a garnishment. Therefore, the municipal court violated the Consumer Credit Protection Act by later garnishing the 25 percent for USLC. (p. 391)

5 No; The court held that the purpose of the Act was to ensure that the potential debtor made informed credit management decisions. That purpose was satisfied by the disclosure made by GFC. (p. 392)

CHAPTER 20 ORGANIZER

Chapter Theme

Specific laws govern secured transactions, security interests, and the termination of secured transactions.

DIRECTED STUDY QUESTIONS	SPECIAL FEATURES	PROGRAM RESOURCES: Reteach	Enrich	SN	AM	
What is a secured transaction?	Writing Connections, p. 411	✔	✔			
How are security interests created?	Multicultural Highlights, p. 412 Thinking Critically Through Visuals, p. 412	✔	✔		K	
How does a creditor perfect a security interest?	Thinking Critically Through Visuals, pp. 415, 417 Personal Perspectives, p. 416	✔	✔	✔	V	
How are secured transactions terminated?	Ethics Issue, p. 419 Preventing Legal Difficulties, p. 420	✔	✔		A	

Additional Resources

- Epstein, David G. *Debtor-Creditor Law*, 3rd ed. St. Paul, MN: West Publishing Co., 1986.
- Henson, Ray D. *Henson's Hornbook on Secured Transactions Under the UCC*, 2d ed. St. Paul, MN: West Publishing Co., 1979.
- Hibbs, Bud. *Stop It!: A Consumer's Guide to Effectively Stopping Collection Agency Harassment.* Fort Worth, TX: Equitable Media Services, 1992.
- Walker, Glen. *Credit Where Credit Is Due: A Legal Guide to Your Credit Rights and How to Assert Them.* NY: Holt, Rinehart, and Winston, 1979.

One-semester course	✔	✔	✔					
One-year course	✔	✔	✔	✔				

Chapter Pacing Guide

	ASSESSMENT OPPORTUNITIES			
Cooperative Learning	**Informal Assessment**	**Chapter Review**	**Chapter Test**	**Chapter *MicroExam*** (Media)
	✔	✔	✔	✔
	✔	✔	✔	✔
	✔	✔	✔	✔
✔	✔	✔	✔	✔

Videodiscs

Secured Debt: Right of Repossession

Search Chapter 25, Play To 26

State by State

Alaska, by judicial construction, holds that when goods are delivered on condition that payment is made, the seller may reclaim them if payment is not made.

Teaching Materials

Student text, pp. 408–425

Overhead transparency masters
- *How Can a Lender of Money Be Protected?*
- *Financing Statement for Secured Transaction*

Videos
- *Law for Business* Videodisc

Workbook, pp. 61–66

Outside Resources
- Blank overhead transparencies
- Transparency markers
- Index cards
- Chart paper

- Tape recorder

Assessment
- Chapter Test

- Chapter *MicroExam*

Vocabulary

secured transaction, p. 410
security interest, p. 410
collateral, p. 410
repossession, p. 410
secured parties, p. 410
security agreement, p. 412
perfected security interest, p. 414
financing statement, p. 414
constructive notice, p. 414
consumer goods, p. 415
farm products, p. 415
inventory, p. 415
equipment. p. 415
intangible property, p. 418
termination statement, p. 419

Learning Objectives

When you complete this chapter, you will be able to

1. Describe the difference between secured and unsecured transactions.
2. Discuss how a debtor's property becomes collateral as security for loans and credit sales.
3. Explain how and why creditors may repossess collateral.
4. Recognize four basic types of tangible collateral.
5. Understand the importance of a security interest, and why and how it is perfected.

408

Chapter Self-Test

Assess students' understanding of collateral and repossession before beginning Chapter 20 by asking: **Many of you may have heard the terms *collateral* and *repossession*. In which contexts might you have heard these terms before?** (Answers may include on television, in ads for purchases; or in newspapers, in notices for banks, ads for large purchases, or in legal notices of repossession; and so on.)

CHAPTER 20

COLLATERAL AND REPOSSESSIONS

1 A friend plans to buy a used car advertised in the local paper. How can she be sure that some third party does not have a creditor's claim against the car?

2 You buy a new compact disc read-only memory unit for your personal computer under a contract that permits the seller to repossess it if you miss a payment. The seller has officially recorded these facts. If you sell the memory unit to a friend before you have paid in full for the unit, does your friend get clear title?

3 ETHICS ISSUE Hernández is a recent legal immigrant. He is a gainfully self-employed cabinetmaker. Hernández bought a television in a secured transaction from TV Town and has faithfully made the monthly payments until 55 percent of the sales price has been paid. He suddenly had to return to his native country for five weeks because of the terminal illness of a parent. During the first week, a payment was missed. TV Town immediately repossessed the television and gave written notice of intent to retain the set in full settlement of the debt. Twenty-one days later, TV Town—as permitted by law—resold the set for 80 percent of its original price and kept the full proceeds. Did TV Town act legally? Did TV Town act ethically?

FOCUS

Write the following headings for a two-column chart on the chalkboard: **collateral** and **repossession**. As students take their seats, direct them to copy the chart in their notebooks, then list as many examples of each as they can in the appropriate columns.

As a group, have students review their suggestions for the chart on collateral and repossession. (Answers for both may include tangible property such as cash, cars, property, personal possessions of value, and so on.)

You Decide

1 In some states, a creditor's claim is noted on the title papers for the car. In states where this does not happen, it would be necessary to check with the proper government agency to see if there is a financing statement on file.

2 No; The documents filed by the seller provide constructive notice, and the friend would not have clear title until the unpaid balance was settled.

3 ETHICS ISSUE TV Town acted legally. Hernández should have made arrangements to pay during his absence. Ethically, TV Town could have recognized that Hernández, as a recent immigrant, probably would be limited in his knowledge of the language and laws of the country, and might have acted with more compassion.

Thinking Critically Through Visuals

Businesses may seek to borrow money in order to expand or meet financial obligations. What, do you think, might this business use as collateral for such a loan? (Answers may include inventory, equipment, real property, and so on.)

TEACH

Ensure that students understand the difference between a **secured transaction** and an *unsecured draft* by reviewing the boldfaced vocabulary words in this section. Then, display the overhead transparency, *How Can a Lender of Money Be Protected?* Guide students through the flowchart as you point out which steps a lender can follow (before the loan, during the loan, and after a default on the loan) to protect his or her interests.

APPLY

With the overhead transparency displayed, distribute copies of a blank flowchart similar to the one that follows. Provide students with concrete examples of a sale on credit. For each example, have students complete the flowchart with ways the seller could protect his or her interests in the sale. (Answers should reflect independent thinking.) **Guided Practice**

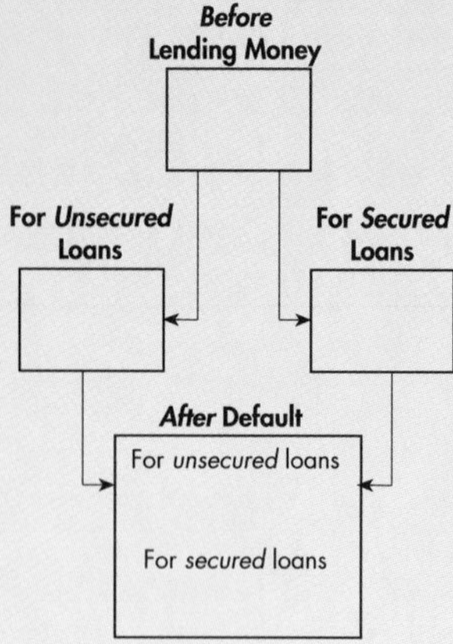

WHAT IS A SECURED TRANSACTION?

PROBLEM

Andrus loaned a friend, O'Shea, $300 cash for a down payment on a new type of videodisc player that would also play compact audiodiscs. O'Shea financed the remaining $900 of the purchase price through the seller, giving the seller a security interest in the goods. Later, O'Shea stopped making payments while she still owed Andrus the $300 and the retailer $500. The retailer repossessed the player and resold it for $480. Would Andrus get a share of the $480 to help pay back the $300 O'Shea borrowed from him?

All purchases are made either with cash or with credit. No debt is involved in a cash transaction. In a credit purchase, however, payment is delayed and a debt, owed by the buyer to the seller or finance company, is created.

In a sale on credit, the seller is understandably concerned about getting paid in full and on time, as promised by the buyer. There is a legal device or method frequently used by sellers on credit that encourages such performance by buyers. It also gives added protection to the sellers and a reassuring sense of security or freedom from anxiety and fear of loss on the sale. That legal device or method is a **secured transaction:** any business deal that creates a security interest in personal property or fixtures. (Fixtures are personal property attached to buildings, as discussed in Chapter 28.) **Security interest** means the interest in or claim against the debtor's property, created for the purpose of assuring payment of the debt. **Collateral** means the property that is subject to the security interest of the creditor.

In a secured transaction, if the debtor-buyer defaults by failing to pay as promised, the creditor-seller, or lender, may exercise the legal right of **repossession**. This means the seller on credit (or the finance company that has provided money for the purchase) takes the goods back, resells them, and uses the net proceeds (after expenses of the repossession and resale) to pay the balance due. If there is any excess, it is returned to the hapless original debtor-buyer. If there is still a deficiency, or remaining balance due, the seller can sue the original debtor-buyer to collect. Clearly, creditors—be they sellers on credit, or lenders of money—are more likely to be paid if they are secured parties. **Secured parties** are the persons who have security interests in collateral owned by the debtor-buyer.

In contrast, a creditor holding a defaulted *unsecured* claim must first sue, get a court judgment, and then execute (i.e., enforce) that judgment against

ASSESS

Media **Learning Objective 1** In writing, using a computer, if possible, have students explain the difference between a *secured* and an *unsecured transaction*. (Secured: If buyer/debtor defaults, seller/creditor may repossess the specific property subject to the security interest; Unsecured: If buyer/debtor defaults, seller/creditor must first sue, get a court judgment, then execute the judgment against debtor's property. The latter is significantly more time consuming, costly, and risky to the seller/creditor.)

the debtor's property. Other creditors of the debtor may have equal rights in that property. If the debtor's financial obligations are discharged in bankruptcy, the unsecured creditor may receive nothing or only a few cents for each dollar of the unpaid debt rightly claimed.

In the problem, the retailer could keep the full $480 because of its security interest in the player. It could also sue O'Shea for the remaining $20 of the $500 owed, for which it would have the right of an unsecured creditor such as Andrus.

HOW ARE SECURITY INTERESTS CREATED?

PROBLEM

Sonia Aponte had to pay a dental bill. She borrowed the needed money from her brother and gave him a paper on which she had written "IOU $575. Sonia Aponte, March 8, 1992." Was this document a pledge, making the loan a secured transaction?

Before the Uniform Commercial Code (UCC) was enacted, many types of legal transactions gave creditors special rights in the property of debtors. Each type had distinct rules for its creation, maintenance, and execution. These rules varied from state to state. Their number and technicality created a situation that enabled unscrupulous individuals to take advantage of the unsuspecting or the uninformed.

The UCC, however, did away with many of the problems by making secured transactions the only legal means of giving a creditor a security interest in another's property. The creditor in such a transaction is the secured party, and the personal property subject to the security interest is the collateral. These UCC provisions apply only to personal property. Contracts involving real property as security, such as mortgages and deeds of trust, are still governed by a variety of other state laws.

A security interest under the UCC can be created only with the consent of the debtor. Such consent is usually given if suitable collateral is available, because otherwise the creditor simply refuses to deal. The agreement may be expressed orally or in writing, depending on which of two basic types of secured transactions is used.

1. When the Creditor Has Possession of the Collateral

In the first type of secured transaction, the creditor obtains possession of the collateral. This transaction, which may be based on an oral or written agreement, is called a pledge (see Chapter 19). The debtor may be buying

Writing Connections

Language Arts
In pairs, have students role-play a buyer/debtor and a seller/creditor who are corresponding about a secured transaction in which the buyer/debtor is about to default. Using a computer, if possible, have the buyer/debtor write to the seller/creditor identifying the transaction, the reason for the default, and asking for assistance. The seller/creditor should respond, also in writing, and inform the buyer/debtor of his or her rights of repossesion.

Independent Practice

TEACH

Point out that the UCC made secured transactions the only legal means of giving a creditor a security interest in another's property. Discuss the two basic types of secured transactions.

Have students label one half of a sheet of paper **Creditor Holds Collateral** and the other half **Debtor Retains Collateral.** Have students note how security interests are created, and what the creditor's legal rights are under default.

Guided Practice

RETEACH Have students construct a spider map with *Transactions* in the center circle and *Secured* and *Unsecured* in two circles radiating from the center. Use this organizer to clarify secured and unsecured transactions.

Media Have students explain in writing, using a computer, if possible, why repossession of tangible collateral must be possible in order to have a secured transaction in tangible property. (Answers may include that there has to be something tangible on which to base the security interest.)

Multicultural Highlights

Following Reconstruction in the South, banks and insurance companies were reluctant to invest in African American businesses. John Merrick (1845–1919), a successful barber, and other African American business owners formed the North Carolina Mutual Life Insurance Company in 1898 and, later, the Mechanics and Farmers Bank. Discuss the kinds of collateral or secured transactions these business owners may have had to provide.

Thinking Critically Through Visuals

Valuables are sometimes used as collateral in a security agreement. What types of problems, do you think, might occur if the secured party had to repossess the antique watch in this photograph in case of default? (Answers may include problems locating and recovering the watch from the personal possessions of the debtor, and so on.)

the property, or the property may already be owned by the debtor but it is now given as security for a loan of money. No pledge was created by Sonia in the problem; her IOU is merely a written acknowledgment of the debt. It is not a formal promissory note (as discussed in Chapter 30), and since she gave no collateral as security for payment, it is not a pledge or other type of secured transaction.

In a pledge, upon default by the debtor, the creditor has a legal right to sell the property and apply the proceeds of the sale to the debt. Any surplus is returned to the debtor. Any deficit remains an obligation of the debtor and is collectible as an unsecured claim through a lawsuit.

2. When the Debtor Retains Possession of the Collateral

In the second type of secured transaction, the debtor retains possession of the collateral under written contract with the secured party. This contract, which creates or provides for the security interest, is a **security agreement.** The security agreement must contain sufficient information to clearly identify the collateral, and it must be signed by the debtor.

It is this second type of secured transaction that enables a consumer to buy an automobile, major kitchen appliances, or other costly items on credit. The debtor gets immediate possession and use of the goods. But the seller, or the bank or finance company that lends money needed for the

ASSESS

Learning Objectives 2 & 3 Have students create a diagram or a flowchart to identify the relationship between the creditor, the debtor, and the collateral in a pledge and in a security agreement. Copy the best examples on the chalkboard or an overhead transparency. Ask volunteers to summarize the visuals aloud to the class.

credit sale, has the right to take the goods back if a payment is missed or if the contract is breached in any way.

In a similar manner, a retail merchant can buy a shipment of goods on credit from a wholesaler or manufacturer. The retailer then routinely sells the goods to customers who get clear title. When the goods are sold to such consumers, the merchant gets paid and in turn pays the supplier. The supplier continues to be protected by the security interest that remains in all of the goods in the shipment that are still unsold.

This second type of secured transaction is also used in borrowing money. More precisely, one might say in *lending* money, because it is the lender who demands the security of collateral. Suppose you want to borrow $1,000 from a bank. By giving the bank a security interest in your car or other valuable personal property, such as your personal computer, your promise to repay the loan is strengthened. This is true because the bank has the legal right to repossess (i.e., seize) the goods in case of default and then to sell them for its own account, applying proceeds of the sale to repay the loan. If the bank approves the loan, which it is very likely to do with this added security, you obtain the desired money and still have the use of your car.

When the debtor retains possession of the collateral, the secured party may have problems repossessing the goods in case of default. Repossession must be accomplished without committing a breach of the peace, that is, without violence, actions likely to produce violence, or other violation of the law. Also the secured party may find that the collateral has been improperly maintained, subjected to the claims of other creditors, or even sold. However, the UCC gives the secured party maximum protection against most such occurrences, provided the security interest has not only been properly created but has also been "perfected."

▼ HOW DOES A CREDITOR PERFECT A SECURITY INTEREST?

PROBLEM

The Old Salt Fishing Supply House sold on credit to Abernathy an expensive sonar device for locating large schools of fish. Abernathy had the sonar installed on his eighty-foot commercial fishing boat. Old Salt retained a security interest in the sonar and filed a financing statement. Before the sonar was paid for, Abernathy sold it to Hoa Tien. Hoa Tien was a purchaser in good faith who knew nothing about Old Salt's security interest and who purchased the sonar for her own fishing boat. Can Old Salt enforce against Hoa Tien its security interest in the sonar?

Divide the class into groups of two or three students. Have each group brainstorm five examples of secured transactions, then list them on a flip chart or an overhead transparency, making one class list. Delete duplicate examples. Then, call on individual volunteers to determine who likely retains possession of the collateral in each example.

Independent Practice

▼ TEACH

Point out that a security interest may be perfected by the creditor having or taking possession of the collateral or, if the debtor has the goods, by filing a financing statement (except for motor vehicles, for which the security interest is usually noted on the title). On the chalkboard, classify the property as *tangible* (either consumer goods, farm products, inventory, or equipment) or **intangible** (the rights to money, goods, or performance). Give examples of each before continuing with the section.

▼RETEACH Copy on the chalkboard the best examples of a *pledge* and a **security agreement** from the ASSESS activity flowcharts or diagrams. Work with the group to create scenarios that show who retains possession of the collateral in each instance.

▼ENRICH Have students brainstorm situations in which they might be expected, realistically, to provide **collateral** for a debt (such as for a personal loan, car loan, major purchase, and so on). Then, have students determine what articles of value they might provide as the collateral.

Display the overhead transparency, *Financing Statement for Secured Transaction*. Use a transparency marker to highlight the following information: names and addresses of both the debtors and the creditor, signature of the debtors and creditor, and a description of the collateral. Have students name the debtors and the creditor, then classify the property as tangible or intangible. (Tangible) **Guided Practice**

In pairs, ask students to role play a creditor and a debtor. After they copy a blank financing statement (see Figure 20-1), have the creditor and debtor complete it to perfect the creditor's interest. "File" statements on a bulletin board entitled *Public Notice*. **Independent Practice**

It is possible for a debtor to agree to give many different creditors, each unaware of the others, a security interest in the same goods. The UCC therefore specifies that the first creditor to perfect a security interest has priority over all other creditors. Upon default, the creditor with priority may repossess and resell the goods even if they are now held by an innocent purchaser, such as Hoa Tien in the problem. Such priority creditor takes as much of the proceeds from the sale of the collateral as is necessary to satisfy his or her claim against the debtor. A **perfected security interest** results when the creditor gives proper notice of the existence of the security interest to all other potential creditors. Such notice may be given in a number of ways. For example, a creditor in possession of the collateral, as in a pledge, needs to take no additional steps for protection. Possession alone is notice to any possible subsequent buyer or creditor of the debtor that a security interest may exist. The creditor who has possession has a perfected security interest. If a creditor is able to repossess collateral upon default, the act of retaking possession also perfects the security interest even though the interest had not been perfected previously.

When the debtor has the goods, it may be necessary for the creditor to file a financing statement to perfect the creditor's interest. A **financing statement** is a brief, written notice of the existence of a security agreement. (See the example in Figure 20-1.) It must include the following:

1. the names and addresses of both the debtor and the creditor,
2. the signature of the debtor (although the creditor may also sign and commonly does), and
3. a statement describing the items of collateral.

If crops or property attached to buildings or land is involved, the land where such property is located must also be described. If the security agreement extends to products to be derived from the original collateral—such as the calves of cows, or proceeds from the resale of such collateral—these facts must be stated. The security agreement itself may be filed instead of the financing statement if it meets the stated requirements.

On the financing statement, any description that identifies the property reasonably well suffices even though it might be necessary to ask questions to determine exactly what property was intended. Of course, a debtor who possesses two automobiles, a motorcycle, a racing bicycle, and a mountain bicycle should not list an unspecified one of these vehicles as "my favorite wheels."

Filing gives constructive notice to the world that a security interest in specific property exists. **Constructive notice** means that the law presumes

▼ ASSESS

Learning Objective 4 & 5 Divide the class into groups of four or five students. Using a blank overhead transparency, have each group outline how a creditor perfects a **security interest,** including the special provisions that depend on whether the property is tangible or intangible. To reinforce and summarize the main points of this important section, have student volunteers orally explain their group's outline for the class, correcting misconceptions, if any.

UNIFORM COMMERCIAL CODE — FINANCING STATEMENT — UCC-1

This FINANCING STATEMENT is presented to a filing officer for filing pursuant to the Uniform Commercial Code. 3 Maturity date (if any):

1 Debtor(s) (Last Name First) and address(es)	2 Secured Party(ies) and address(es)	For Filing Officer (Date, Time, Number, and Filing Office)
Daley, John C. and Ava G. 116 Seashore Drive Biloxi, MS 39534	Adam Cranston 485 Magnolia Street Gulfport, MS 39501	

4 This financing statement covers the following types (or items) of property:

"Smooth Sailin" Houseboat

Check ☒ if covered: ☐ Proceeds of Collateral are also covered ☐ Products of Collateral are also covered No. of additional sheets presented:

Filed with.....

By: John C. Daley Ava G. Daley
Signature(s) of Debtor(s)

By: Adam Cranston
Signature(s) of Secured Party(ies)

Filing Officer Copy — Alphabetical

This form of financing statement is approved by the Secretary of State.

STANDARD FORM—UNIFORM COMMERCIAL CODE—UCC-1

Figure 20-1

A financing statement is a document that must be filed to give public notice of the existence of a security interest in the identified property. Filing perfects the security interest in the property for the creditor who does the filing.

one has knowledge of the facts on file even if one does not. Anyone sufficiently concerned may get actual notice by checking the public records. The place of filing is specified by the state's version of the UCC and also depends on the nature of the collateral. Filing could be done centrally in the office of the secretary of state, or locally in the office of the clerk in the county where the goods are located, or both.

As explained in the following paragraphs, there are special provisions for perfecting the security interest that depend on whether the property in question is tangible or intangible.

1. Tangible Property

When tangible property is used as collateral, the procedure for perfecting the creditor's security interest depends on whether the goods are (a) **consumer goods**—used primarily for personal, family, or household purposes; (b) **farm products**—crops, livestock, unmanufactured products of the farm, and farm supplies; (c) **inventory**—business goods that are intended for sale or lease, or, if they are raw materials, work in process or materials used or consumed in a business; (d) **equipment**—goods used by a business in performing its function, such as specialized telephone switching equipment or computers.

Goods can be in only one of these four classes at a given time. Their classification may change, however, if their use changes. For example, a television is classified as inventory if held by a dealer for resale. If used as a closed

Thinking Critically Through Visuals

This financing statement serves as written notice of the existence of a security agreement. What is the collateral? (Houseboat) **What classification of tangible property might the collateral be?** (Consumer goods, if used for pleasure; inventory, if they are boat dealers; or equipment, if the boat is used for business)

Help visually impaired students by recording key portions of the text on audiotape or providing them in large-print format. You may wish to contact your state department of education, Recording for the Blind (609) 452-0606, or the American Printing House for the Blind (502) 895-2405 to determine whether portions of this

text already exist in alternate formats.

Have students create a four-tier mobile illustrating, through visuals and words, the four classes of goods that are tangible property (consumer goods, farm products, inventory, and equipment). Display the visuals in class.

Have students select their favorite **financing statement** from the ASSESS activity on p. 414 and photocopy it for them. Using a marker, have students circle and identify the three items that must be included. (Names and addresses of debtors and creditors, signature of debtor, description of collateral)

To illustrate how a good's classification can change if its use changes, ask each student to select a good and classify it. Have a second student change the original use of the good, then reclassify it accordingly, such as a computer purchased for office use (equipment) that later gets dedicated for personal use (consumer goods).

Personal Perspectives

Extend the previous activity to include students' families. Have students, with help from family members, make a list of five additional examples of tangible property that they, or family members might reclassify if the use changes, such as purchasing a company car (equipment) for personal use (consumer goods). Have students make a class list, eliminating duplicate suggestions. Review and correct errors before continuing with the lesson.

circuit system in the store for security, it is equipment. If installed in the buyer's home for entertainment, it is a consumer good.

Consumer Goods. Filing is not required to protect the seller's security interest in consumer goods against other creditors of the buyer. This rule relieves retail merchants, who sell many thousands of articles on installment plans, of what would be a heavy burden in paperwork and in payment of filing fees. In case of default in payment, however, the creditor may repossess the goods from the original buyer. Although not legally obliged to do so, most creditors tolerate late payment for perhaps ten or more days. However, they typically impose a penalty charge for use of this privilege.

Filing would be required for consumer goods if the consumer already owned the goods and was simply borrowing against them as security. Filing is also necessary, even in initial purchases, if the seller wants protection against a third person who might innocently buy the good for personal, family, or household use from a dishonest debtor. Such a buyer of consumer goods, who gives value and does not know of the security interest, acquires clear title if there has been no filing. On the other hand, if a filing is in the public records, the third party is bound by the filed security interest even if unaware of its existence. Therefore, the television set that was installed in the buyer's home for entertainment and then sold to a good-faith purchaser for value must nevertheless be returned to the unpaid creditor.

Tokuda bought a household refrigerator for $795 from the Super-Circuit Sales Company in a secured transaction. Super-Circuit did not file a financing statement. When $500 was still owed, Tokuda sold the refrigerator to Goto, a neighbor, who paid $600, honestly assuming that Tokuda had paid for it in full and could therefore transfer it with a clear title. If Tokuda thereafter fails to make any payment as required, Super-Circuit cannot take the refrigerator away from Goto. Instead, it must pursue Tokuda. Goto obtained clear title because Super-Circuit had not filed a financing statement.

In the problem at the beginning of the section, Hoa Tien did not get good title because Old Salt had filed a financing statement. Thus, Old Salt can enforce its security interest by repossessing the sonar. It may do so without compensating Hoa Tien, who must pursue Abernathy for money lost in the deal. In contrast, if Old Salt had not filed the financing statement, Hoa Tien would have acquired clear title. In that case, Old Salt would have to sue Abernathy for damages.

ASSESS

Learning Objective 4 Have students identify the following statements as *True* or *False*. **(1) When tangible property is used as collateral, the procedure for perfecting the creditor's security interest depends on how the goods are classified.** (True); **(2) Goods can be in multiple classes at any given time.** (False); and **(3) Stocks and bonds are intangible property.** (True)

Because there are so many millions of motor vehicles on the roads, most states provide that instead of filing as described above, a special office and procedure are utilized. Thus, the security interest in motor vehicles is perfected by noting its existence on the certificate of title to the vehicle that is registered in the proper state office. An exception to the filing requirement is also made when fixtures are sold on credit. Fixtures are items of personal property that are permanently attached to real property in a manner that makes the law treat them like real property. A filing to protect a security interest in fixtures must include in the financing statement a description of the real property involved.

Farm Products. A security interest in farm products is perfected by filing or by taking possession of the products upon default. This applies both to farm products bought on credit and to those put up as security for loans. Most states require the filing of the financing statement for farm products to be made with the clerk at the courthouse of the county where the products are stored.

Inventory. A security interest in inventory is perfected by filing or by taking possession of the inventory upon default. This is true whether the inventory is bought on credit or is put up as security for a loan. However, since inventory generally is purchased by business firms for the very purpose of reselling, a person buying from such a debtor in the ordinary course of business gets clear title to the goods even if aware of the security interest.

Thinking Critically Through Visuals

Farmers often borrow money on the expectation of a good harvest. How could the security interest in this grain be perfected if the farmer used it as collateral, then was unable to repay the debt? (The creditor may take possession of the crop upon default.)

▼RETEACH Have students identify the four basic types of tangible property, then create four flowcharts to show what happens to the tangible property if the debtor defaults.

▼ENRICH Have students complete the RETEACH activity, then add four examples for each of the four classes of tangible property.

Have students create a graphic organizer like the following to identify sources of intangible property and to determine the procedure used to perfect a security interest in intangible property.

Intangible Property

Intangible Property	How to Perfect Security Interest
Accounts Receivable Rights to Performance	File Financing Statement
Bill of Lading Airbills Warehouse Recepits	File Financing Statement or Take Possession Upon Default
Commercial Paper Bonds Stocks Promissory Notes	Take Possession Upon Default

▼ TEACH

Summarize for students how **secured transactions** are terminated—both when the debtor pays in full (creditor releases security interest in the collateral and files a termination statement, if a financing statement was filed previously) and when the debtor defaults (creditor may take possession then sell, lease, or otherwise dispose of the collateral).

For example, if you buy a stove at an appliance store, you get title to it free of the security interest held by the unpaid manufacturer or wholesaler who originally sold it to the store on credit.

Equipment. A security interest in equipment is perfected by filing or by taking possession of the equipment upon default. This applies whether the equipment is bought on credit or is put up as security for a loan. As stated above, if the equipment is a motor vehicle, a notation on the certificate of title may substitute for filing in perfecting the interest. As with inventory, perfection of a security interest in equipment requires filing with the state government, usually in the office of the secretary of state.

2. Intangible Property

The second major classification of collateral, **intangible property,** represents value in rights to money, goods, or promises to perform specified contracts. Intangible property generally is evidenced by legal documents or other writings. It includes the accounts receivable of a business, the rights to performance under a contract, bills of lading or airbills, warehouse receipts, commercial paper, and bonds or stocks.

As with tangible property, the procedure used in perfecting a security interest in intangible property depends on the classification of that property. A security interest in accounts receivable or contractual rights that cannot be possessed in a physical sense must be perfected by filing unless the transaction does not cover a significant part of the debtor's accounts receivable or other contractual rights. For documents used in bailments, such as bills of lading, airbills, and warehouse receipts (discussed in Chapter 27), the creditor may either file a financing statement or take possession of the goods upon default. To perfect a security interest in commercial paper (e.g., promissory notes, stock certificates, or bonds, discussed in Chapter 30), possession by the creditor, upon default of the debtor, is essential.

▼ HOW ARE SECURED TRANSACTIONS TERMINATED?

PROBLEM

The Nosmans bought a new flat-screen wall television for their recreation room for $2,000 including the credit carrying charge. They paid $400 down and agreed to pay the balance in eight monthly installments of $200 each. The seller, Silitech, Inc., retained a security interest in the television. After making six payments, the Nosmans defaulted. Silitech repossessed the television. What must Silitech do to be able to legally keep the set in settlement of the unpaid $400 balance?

▼ ASSESS

Media **Learning Objective 5** Divide the class into small groups and, in writing, using a computer, if possible, have each group create one scenario depicting the termination of a **secured transaction**—without specifying the outcome of the termination. Ask groups to exchange papers. Then, have the second group summarize how the transaction was terminated.

Most secured transactions are routinely terminated when the debtor pays the debt in full and the creditor releases the security interest in the collateral. If the creditor has filed a financing statement, this release is made when the creditor files an acknowledgment of the full payment, called a **termination statement,** with the governmental office that has the financing statement. Filing the termination statement informs potential buyers and creditors that the property is no longer collateral. For consumer goods, the termination statement must be filed within thirty days of the payoff or within ten days of a written request by the debtor. Otherwise the creditor must pay $100 plus damages to the debtor.

If the debtor defaults by failing to pay as promised, the secured creditor who does not have possession of the collateral may take possession of it. This may be done without legal proceedings, provided it does not involve a breach of the peace. The creditor may then sell, lease, or otherwise dispose of the collateral. (Note that this right of sale also applies after default for the benefit of the secured creditor who has retained possession of the property.) The proceeds of disposition are applied to the reasonable expenses of retaking, holding, preparing for resale, and reselling. They are applied also to payment of reasonable attorney's fees and other legal expenses incurred. What remains of the proceeds then goes to pay off the secured debt. In some cases, other creditors may have subordinate or secondary security interests in the collateral, and these are now paid off if proper claims have been made. Finally, if any surplus remains, it goes to the debtor. If there is any deficiency, the debtor is obligated to pay it unless otherwise agreed.

Even when in default as to payment or other performance of the security agreement, the debtor does not forfeit all rights. For example, the debtor may pay the balance due and the expenses of the creditor and redeem the collateral any time before the creditor has disposed of it or contracted for its disposal.

As an alternative to resale, the secured creditor may retain the collateral in full settlement of the debt. Written notice of the creditor's intention to keep the collateral must be given to the debtor. If the debtor (or any other person entitled to receive notice) objects in writing within twenty-one days, the creditor must dispose of the collateral in a commercially reasonable manner by a public or private sale.

Additional protection is given to consumers who have paid 60 percent or more of the debt. In these situations, the creditor may not keep the collateral in satisfaction of the debt unless the consumer agrees in writing. In the absence of such a written agreement, the creditor must sell the collateral within ninety days after the repossession. This law seeks to protect consumers in situations where the value of the goods exceeds the amount of the debt. In the problem, the Nosmans paid $400 down and $1,200 in monthly installments. The total ($1,600) was far more than the 60 percent

Point out that, even when in default, a debtor does not forfeit all rights. In addition, when consumers paid 60 percent or more of the debt, the collateral must be sold in a commercially reasonable manner to satisfy the debt.

Divide the class into two groups. Ask the first to summarize in writing, using a computer, if possible, what options are available to a creditor if a debtor defaults on a secured transaction and has paid less than 60 percent of the debt. Ask the second group to do the same for transactions in which the debtor has paid at least 60 percent.

Media **Guided Practice**

ETHICS ISSUE

Ethics Issue

Sometimes creditors violate the law during repossession. In small groups, have students create and tape record *20/20*-style (hypothetical) cases where debtors have been illegally victimized. Share the audiotapes with the class, and ask them to comment on the ethics of this conduct.

Independent Practice

Media

▼RETEACH Have students create a graphic organizer with the words **Terminated Transaction** in the center circle. Then, connect two smaller circles, **Paid in Full** and **Defaulted.** Have students provide information about what happens to debtors and creditors when a transaction is terminated in either manner.

Have students write three *True* or *False* statements about how secured transactions are terminated. Have volunteers read their statements as group members answer.

Preventing Legal Difficulties

As a group, have students paraphrase the seven suggestions for buyers or borrowers in a secured transaction. Then, create a class poster of the advice, using simple, clear terms. Display the poster in a hallway, cafeteria, or auditorium.

▼ CLOSE

Assign students to small groups of three or four to role-play one or two debtor(s) and one or two creditor(s) in a secured transaction. Have the members of the group brainstorm the details of the transaction, including the type of collateral, who retains possession, and how the transaction is terminated. Have students prepare paperwork, such as a financing statement, if necessary. Then, have students role-play the entire transaction, from start to finish, for the class.
Cooperative Learning

Assign the following end-of-chapter materials:
Student text review activities, pp. 420–425
Workbook, pp. 61–66
Chapter Test

Chapter *MicroExam*

($1,200). Therefore, Silitech must obtain the Nosmans' written consent before Silitech can keep the television. Without that consent, the television must be resold in a commercially reasonable manner.

When the creditor sells the collateral, reasonable notice must be given to the debtor unless the goods (1) are perishable, (2) threaten to decline speedily in value, or (3) are of a type usually sold on a recognized market where prices are determined openly and fairly. The secured creditor may be the highest bidder and get title. If the proceeds of the sale do not equal the balance due, including all costs of repossession and resale, the debtor is liable for the deficiency unless otherwise agreed. In the unlikely event that a surplus exists, it belongs to the debtor.

Preventing Legal Difficulties

Suggestions for buyer or borrower in a secured transaction...

1. Be sure you understand the entire security agreement before you sign it. If you have any doubts, have the seller, or preferably your lawyer, banker, accountant, or other trustworthy counsel, examine the form and explain it to you.
2. Never sign any security agreement that has blank spaces to be filled in later. Draw lines in any blank spaces not used.
3. Know what any charges are for, especially service charges. Ask for a detailed listing if it is not offered.
4. Find out if there are any penalties for late payment of installments or if there are any discounts for making payments before they are due.
5. Include express warranties or other promises of the seller in the written contract to avoid later difficulty of proof under the parol evidence rule.
6. Always get a copy of the agreement signed by the other party.
7. After payment in full, check to be sure that a termination statement has been properly filed.

▼ REVIEWING IMPORTANT POINTS

1. Secured transactions are of two types: (a) those in which the creditor has possession of the collateral (called pledges) and (b) those in which the debtor has possession.

2 Property used as collateral is classified as either tangible property (called goods) or intangible property. Goods are further classified as (a) consumer goods, (b) farm products, (c) inventory, or (d) equipment. In perfecting a security interest, proper classification of the property must be known. Intangible property includes such things as accounts receivable, bills of lading, airbills, warehouse receipts, notes, bonds, and other contractual rights.

3 A security interest may be perfected by the creditor having or taking possession of the collateral or by the filing of a financing statement. An exception may apply in the case of a motor vehicle; most states provide that such a security interest is perfected by a notation on the certificate of title.

4 The financing statement is used to give notice that a security interest in specific property exists. The statement identifies the parties and the collateral. Usually the financing statement and the security agreement are separate writings. However, the security agreement may be filed in place of the financing statement if it meets the legal requirements.

5 After default in a secured transaction, the debtor has the following rights:

a. To pay all that is owed and to redeem the collateral held or repossessed by the creditor at any time before the creditor arranges to dispose, or actually does dispose, of it.

b. Under certain specified circumstances, to demand that the collateral be sold and the proceeds applied to the payment of the debt.

6 Upon the debtor's default, the secured creditor has the following rights:

a. To sell or otherwise dispose of the property. If the creditor does not have the property, he or she may repossess it.

b. Under certain specified circumstances, to retain the property in settlement of the debt.

7 When the debtor has fully paid the obligation in accordance with the security agreement, the secured party has the responsibility for clearing the official records by filing a termination statement.

STRENGTHENING YOUR LEGAL VOCABULARY

Match each term with the statement that best defines that term. Some terms may not be used.

collateral
constructive notice
consumer goods
equipment
farm products
financing statement

Strengthening Your Legal Vocabulary

1 secured transaction
2 consumer goods
3 constructive notice
4 termination statement
5 collateral
6 secured party
7 financing statement
8 equipment
9 inventory
10 intangible property

Applying Law to Everyday Life

1. No; This was not a secured transaction, because there was no written security agreement, hence, no security interest in the goods. (pp. 410–411)
2. Yes; The pledgee has a perfected security interest by virtue of possession of the pledged goods. In the case of a pledge, the security agreement may be oral, and no filing is required. (p. 414)
3. ETHICS ISSUE No; If the owner of consumer goods borrows, using the goods as security and retaining possession, the creditor's security interest is not perfected until the financing statement is filed. It would be otherwise if the Bartons were buying the consumer goods. In such a case, the perfection is automatic and filing is not required. (pp. 414–418)

intangible property	secured transaction
inventory	security agreement
perfected security interest	security interest
repossession	termination statement
secured party	

1. Business deal in which a creditor is given a security interest in personal property as protection in the event of default by the debtor.
2. Goods to be used primarily for personal, family, or household purposes.
3. Knowledge, presumed by law, of facts on file.
4. Officially filed acknowledgment of the end of a creditor's security interest.
5. Any personal property in which the creditor has a security interest as protection against default by the debtor.
6. Creditor (lender or credit seller) in a security agreement.
7. Brief, written notice of the existence of a security agreement.
8. Goods used by a business in performing its function.
9. Business goods intended for sale or lease, or certain raw materials.
10. Rights to money, goods, or contract promises, usually evidenced by legal documents.

APPLYING LAW TO EVERYDAY LIFE

1. The Lawsons bought a set of color-coordinated bedspreads and draperies at the Mercantile Mart Department Store. They paid for the $987 purchase by using a nationally recognized credit card. When the monthly statement arrived, they defaulted. Could Mercantile Mart repossess the goods?
2. Taft borrowed $50 from a friend, agreeing to repay $5 each week. Although the agreement was informal and oral, Taft gave the friend her high school class ring to hold until the debt was paid in full. Did the friend have a perfected security interest in the ring?
3. ETHICS ISSUE The Bartons were "strapped for cash" but needed to have their child's teeth straightened. The corrective work would cost more and take longer if they waited until a later date. Therefore, they pledged their electric range, refrigerator, microwave oven, television, sofa, two armchairs, and complete dining room set as security for a loan of $1,500 from the Happy Home Finance Company. All of the

listed property was in excellent condition, having been purchased recently with $10,000 the Bartons had won in a lottery. Did Happy Home Finance Company obtain a perfected security interest in these consumer goods as soon as it gave the money to the Bartons? Did Happy Home act ethically in demanding the listed security from the Bartons?

4 Cuisine International sold kitchen equipment on credit to the Shoreline, a large resort. In the security agreement and in the financing statement, the collateral was identified as "food service equipment delivered to the Shoreline resort." When the Shoreline was unable to pay its creditors, including Cuisine, some creditors claimed that the collateral description was too vague to create a valid security interest. Were they correct?

5 Conant was the owner and operator of the Tipperary Tavern. She purchased two color televisions on installment. One set was for home use and the other set was for the tavern. How would each set be classified?

6 Ortega sold Ford a small household robot and retained a security interest. When Ford defaulted after paying 25 percent of the purchase price, Ortega decided that she would keep the robot and give it to some friends for a gift. What must she do to be able to retain the robot in full settlement of the debt?

7 D'Artole, an accountant, bought for her personal use a new portable computer with a hard disk for $7,500. She paid $1,000 down and then paid $150 per month for several months under a security agreement she had signed with the seller, the Computer Clinic. Finally, she paid off the remaining balance with her Christmas bonus. The next May she needed a $5,000 loan to take advantage of a business opportunity. She offered the computer as collateral, but the lender refused, saying there was still a security interest in favor of the Computer Clinic on file. D'Artole did not get the loan as a result. What are her rights in this situation?

8 ETHICS ISSUE Fanno pondered the pros and cons of buying versus leasing a costly integrated computer control system for his business. "There are so many improvements coming along," he said, "that I could be stuck with an obsolete white elephant if I buy. On the other hand, leasing eventually costs more since the lessor earns a profit too." Finally, he bought the needed machine under a five-year secured transaction. He told a friend, "If something better comes along while we're still making payments, I'll simply default and let the seller repossess the obsolete equipment." Could Fanno legally default as planned? Would it be ethical if this shifted the loss on the obsolete gear to the seller? How is it possible that the seller would "have the last laugh" in this mini-drama?

4 Yes; A description must reasonably identify the property. The date, time, and a description of each piece delivered would have been adequate, but this information was not provided. (p. 414)

5 The set for Conant's home would be classified as a consumer good because it is to be used primarily for personal purposes. The set for the tavern would be classified as equipment because it is intended for business use. (p. 415)

6 Ortega must give Ford written notice of her intention to keep the robot in full settlement of the debt. Ford (or any other person entitled to receive notice, such as another creditor) may object in writing within 21 days. Then the creditor must dispose of the goods in a commercially reasonable manner and follow prescribed procedures with reference to the proceeds. If there is an excess over costs and creditors' claims, it goes to the debtor. If there is a deficiency, the debtor is still liable. (p. 419)

7 D'Artole has a right to a termination statement to be filed by the Computer Clinic. Because the Clinic did not file this statement on time, it may be liable for penalties equalling $100 plus damages. (p. 419)

8 ETHICS ISSUE Fanno may default as contemplated, but after the equipment is repossessed and resold, there may still be a balance due. Fanno would be legally liable for this balance. It would not be ethical for Fanno to deliberately shift a loss that he has incurred onto the back of the seller who did not cause it. The seller could have the last laugh if the proceeds of the resale do not cover the total balance due. In that event the seller (creditor) can sue Fanno and get a deficiency judgment against him for the amount still owed. Fanno could end up paying more than the original contract price because he is liable for the unpaid balance plus the costs of repossession and resale. (p. 419)

9 ETHICS ISSUE The repossession was legal, but the sale was illegal and fraudulent. It had not been conducted in a commercially reasonable manner. (pp. 410–411, 419) Bounding Main (Sharko) obviously conspired with Ooze to acquire title to the boat at less than its true value, and to defraud Chabra in the process.

10 ETHICS ISSUE Yes, Gullib had constructive notice of the bank's interest in the animals because the bank had perfected its security interest by filing a copy of the financing statement or security agreement in the county where the cows were kept. Gullib could have, and should have, checked the file of financing statements in the county courthouse before he "bought" the cattle. In the alternative, he should have consulted a lawyer before making such a purchase, and undoubtedly the lawyer would have checked the county files. When Spade sold the cattle, Gullib took title subject to the prior, legally established interest or claim of the bank. (pp. 414–415)

9 ETHICS ISSUE Chabra had purchased a sailboat equipped with an auxiliary outboard engine for $9,500 under a security agreement with the Bounding Main Boat Company. After he had paid $4,000, he was seriously injured at work and had to retire, supported largely by workers' compensation checks. He could no longer afford the sailboat and defaulted on his purchase contract. Sharko, the owner-manager of Bounding Main, repossessed the boat and sold it at a public sale but at a remote lake 200 miles from the city where the sale was advertised. Only two bidders appeared. One was named Ooze. By prior secret agreement with Sharko, Ooze bid $2,250, supplied by Sharko. Sharko then sued Chabra for the balance due of $3,250, waiving, with feigned generosity, any repossession or sales charges. A month after judgment was ordered against Chabra, Sharko gave Ooze $250 for his help and Ooze transferred title to the boat to Sharko. Did Bounding Main (Sharko) act legally in the repossession and sale? Did Bounding Main (Sharko) act ethically?

10 ETHICS ISSUE At the county fair, Gullib used cash to buy two cows and a bull—all pure-bred Holsteins. The seller was Spade, a newcomer in the area. Soon after, Gullib was surprised and chagrined when the local banker told him that Spade had defaulted on a related loan given to Spade in a secured transaction. The bank had a perfected security interest in the animals. When it repossessed them, Gullib protested: "How in the deuce was I to know that? I never had any notice of the bank's interest. Where's the proof?" Did Gullib actually have legal notice of the bank's interest in, and prior claim to, the animals? Did Spade act ethically in their deal? What can Gullib do now?

SOLVING CASE PROBLEMS

1 Shelton purchased an automobile on credit from Erwin. Both Shelton and Erwin clearly intended to create a security interest in the car in favor of Erwin. As a consequence, they signed a bill of sale that set out the terms of payment of the balance due and that also required that Shelton should insure the auto until paid for in full. Shelton later obtained a title certificate from the state that clearly showed Erwin as the holder of a first lien on the car. Did these actions and documents give Erwin a security interest in the car? (*Shelton v. Erwin*, 472 F.2d 1118)

2 Speigle fell behind in his car payments to Chrysler Credit Corporation. He had made fourteen monthly payments on a thirty-six-month contract, and Chrysler had accepted several late payments. Then he was out of work and money, and he was almost a month in default on a current

Solving Case Problems

1 No; In order to do so, the bill of sale would have to comply with the UCC requirements for a security agreement. This requires that the document must contain some language that directly creates or provides for a security interest. In addition, the state involved did not consider the lienholder portion of the automobile title to bring about perfection. (pp. 413, 417)

payment. Speigle visited the Chrysler office to negotiate a solution to his problem. While in the office, one employee of Chrysler parked a car behind Speigle's car, blocking it so it could not be moved. Another employee told him it was repossessed. Speigle sued, claiming that Chrysler's conduct was inequitable and in breach of the peace. Do you agree? (*Speigle v. Chrysler Credit Corporation*, 56 Ala. App. 469, 323 So. 2d 360)

3 The Uniform Commercial Code excludes "money" from its definition of goods. As a consequence, a perfected security interest cannot be obtained in money merely by the creditor's taking possession of it. Midas Coin Company transferred possession of some rare U.S. coins to the St. John's Community Bank as security for a loan. Did the bank have a perfected security interest? (*In re Midas Coin Co.*, 264 F. Supp. 193)

4 The Franklin State Bank repossessed the Parkers' automobile because of the Parkers' delinquency in payments. At the time, Mr. Parker and his son were giving the engine of the car a tune-up in their garage. The vehicle was not mechanically operational because the spark plugs, points, condenser, and air filter had been removed. Franklin did not try to determine why the car was not mechanically operational. Instead, after a three-day notice to the Parkers, the bank sold the car at a private sale to an auto parts dealer for $50. The bank then sued the Parkers to recover the substantial balance of the purchase price remaining and unpaid. You decide. (*Franklin State Bank v. Parker*, 136 N.J. Super. 476, 346 A.2d 632)

2 No; By accepting several late payments, Chrysler did not waive its rights to repossess. There was no breach of the peace in the repossession; therefore, the repossession was legal. (pp. 413, 419–420)

3 Yes; The coins were being treated as commodities rather than as a medium of exchange by both parties to the transaction, so the UCC exclusion of money did not apply. (p. 414)

4 Judgment for the defendant, Parker; The bank did not conduct the private sale following repossession in either good faith or a commercially reasonable manner (pp. 419–420), and did not obtain a fair price from the parts dealer. Three days' notice of the sale was not commercially reasonable. Likewise, the failure to determine why the engine would not start, when only a few dollars in parts and labor would have made the car mechanically operational, also was not commercially reasonable.

Special Section: How and When to Be Your Own Attorney

On chart paper, make a class chart summarizing effective options to the often time-consuming, emotional, and expensive process of litigation.

Nevertheless, some students may someday need to sue in small claims court. Walk them through these four steps:

1. Appear before the clerk of the court in the *defendant's* area and briefly tell your story. Fill out the forms, including the formal complaint and pay the registration fee, if any.
2. The clerk assigns the date for court appearance. The complaint is delivered to the defendant either by the clerk's office or by the plaintiff. Either party may ask for a postponement.
3. The court appearance is informal. Failure to appear will result in a judgment against the absent party.
4. The judge renders a decision, often on the spot, and issues an order to pay the claim or an amount that the court feels is fair, or decides in favor of the defendant.

SPECIAL SECTION

HOW AND WHEN TO BE YOUR OWN ATTORNEY

Sometimes the very nature of a legal cause of action dictates that the parties involved should act as their own attorneys. This may be the only cost-effective alternative when the damages that might be recovered are small. In every state, small claims courts are available to decide such cases. The claim for damages generally may not exceed $1,000. You do not need a lawyer to represent you; indeed, some states ban representation by lawyers in small claims courts.

Small claims courts are ideal to hear disputes involving such matters as:

—the $328.00 security deposit kept by your former landlord when you moved, even though you left the apartment undamaged and in a much cleaner condition than it was when you moved in.

—the $134.70 share of the telephone bill still owed to you by your ex-roommate.

—the $425.00 check that the bank paid regardless of your stop-payment order on it.

But before suing, it is always a good idea to try other means of getting satisfaction. A lawsuit, even in a small claims court, requires the expenditure of much time and energy. Courtroom confrontations can be emotionally and physically exhausting, and there is always the possibility of losing. Therefore, before becoming fully committed to a legal battle, contact the other party and clearly state (preferably in writing) your grievance and specify what you expect in the way of satisfaction. Be reasonable. Give a time deadline and perhaps say that you are considering court action but would much prefer an amicable out-of-court settlement. Be prepared to compromise; that is what will probably happen under court order if you bring the matter before a judge. If you cannot reach a satisfactory solution, pursue the matter in court.

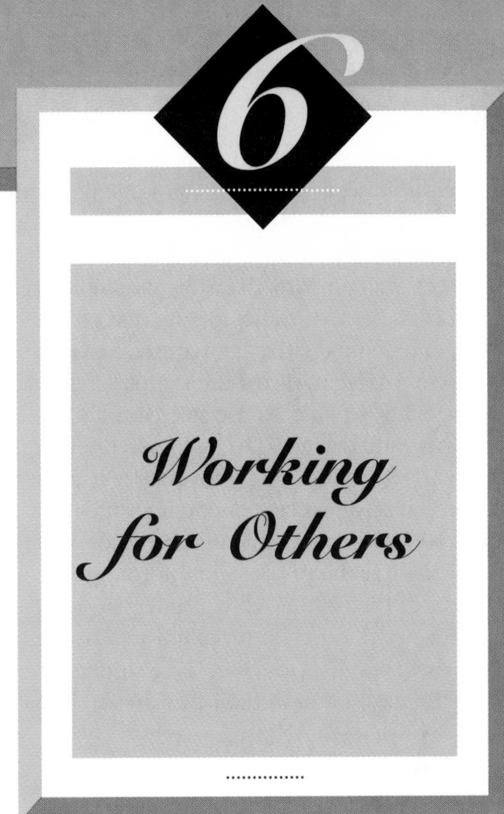

Unit Overview

In Unit 6, *Working for Others,* students will read about employment contracts, unions, employment discrimination, employee injuries, and agents. They also will learn about the Equal Employment Opportunity Commission, workers' compensation laws, and the Occupational Safety and Health Administration.

Specific duties and obligations related to employment and employment contracts are imposed on both employers and employees. In Chapter 21, *Employment Contracts*, students will study what employment is. They will learn where the terms of the employment contract come from, what employee duties are created by law, what duties are imposed by law on the employer, and how an employment contract is terminated.

State and federal governments regulate actions, labor relations, union management, and union workers. In Chapter 22, *Unions,* students will discover how state and federal governments regulate employment and will learn about the history of labor laws. What the National Labor Relations Board is, how unions are established, and how they impact management and workers are additional topics covered in this chapter.

In Chapter 23, *Employment Discrimination*, students will learn about the concept of unjustified discrimination. They will study the types of unjustified discrimination, the scope of protection, how unequal treatment can be proved, when treatment is illegal, and what specific legislation prohibits unjustified discrimination.

In Chapter 24, *Employee Injuries*, students will study how our legal system treats injured employees, how workers' compensation laws work, when an injured employee can recover from his or her employer for negligence, and how OSHA protects employees.

Principals, agents, and agencies are bound by contractually legal relationships, duties, and obligations. In Chapter 25, *Agents*, students will understand what an agency is, how agency authority is created, the fiduciary duties of an agent, what duties a principal owes an agent, when a principal or an agent is liable to third persons, and how an agency is terminated.

At the end of this unit, you'll find a special section, *Dealing With an Attorney*, which can be used at any time during the study of Unit 6. You may wish to assign its accompanying *Teacher Edition* activity to give students an opportunity to investigate finding an appropriate lawyer for a particular legal problem.

Portfolio Assessment

Using a computer, if possible, have students create an employee newsletter based on the information in Unit 6, *Working for Others*. Tell students to write the newsletter for a company that they would like to work for in the future, the company that they work for now, or a company they've worked for in the past. You may wish to distribute sample workplace newsletters for students to use as examples for style, layout, and design. Have students refer to Chapters 21–25 for specific information relating to this aspect of business law. Encourage students to include articles on contracts, unions, discrimination, and injuries—for the purpose of informing employees of their rights. Have students use clip art or draw and paint programs to illustrate the newsletter, if possible. Have students add the newsletter to their portfolios.

Careers

Corporate Human Resources Manager
The complexity of the corporate workplace has significantly expanded the role of the Human Resources Manager. Staff layoffs, sexual discrimination and harassment lawsuits, and affirmative-action programs require that today's Human Resources Manager be knowledgeable in several aspects of business law, including personnel management, pension planning, and insurance.

A four-year college degree in business, economics, or behavioral science is required. Many Human Resources Managers also have an advanced degree, such as a M.B.A. or a Ph.D. Entry-level salaries are about $33,000 and, depending on the company and the responsibilities of the position, can reach $100,000 or higher.

Invite the Human Resources Manager from a community business to speak to your class. Using a copy of his or her job description, if available, ask the speaker to address the challenges of this position.

Annotated Bibliography

- ***Peterson v. Rath Packing Company*, 461 F.2d 312 (1972).**
  No action can be brought under the Labor Management Relations Act authorizing suit for violations of contracts between an employer and a labor organization until the party attempts to exhaust his or her contractual remedies. The purpose of this requirement is to utilize the contract grievance procedure in collective bargaining agreements as an initial method of settling disputes. (Chapter 21)

- ***Heights Thrift-Way, Inc.*, 155 N.L.R.B. 52 52 (1965).**
  A store owner's assaults and threats against union picketers engaging in the peaceful picketing of his store were held to constitute unfair labor practices affecting commerce, even though the store had no union employees. (Chapter 22)

- ***Griggs v. Duke Power Co.*, 401 U.S. 424, 431 (1971).**
  The Court construed Title VII to proscribe "not only overt discrimination but also practices that are fair in form but discriminatory in practice." This basis of liability is known as the "disparate-impact" theory. (Chapter 23)

Working for Others

- Employment Contracts
- Unions
- Employment Discrimination
- Employee Injuries
- Agents

Chapter Theme

Specific duties and obligations related to employment and employment contracts are imposed on both employers and employees.

DIRECTED STUDY QUESTIONS	SPECIAL FEATURES	PROGRAM RESOURCES				
		Reteach	Enrich	SN	AM	
What is employment?		✔	✔			
Where do the terms of the employment contract come from?		✔	✔	✔		
What employee duties are created by the law?	Thinking Critically Through Visuals, p. 433	✔	✔		K	
What duties are imposed by law on the employer?	Thinking Critically Through Visuals, pp. 435, 438 Writing Connections, p. 435 Multicultural Highlights, p. 436 Ethics Issue, p. 438	✔	✔		A	
Is the employer liable for the torts of employees?		✔	✔			
How is the employment contract terminated?	Personal Perspectives, p. 441 Preventing Legal Difficulties, p. 441	✔	✔		V	

Additional Resources

- Joel, Lewin, G. III. *Every Employee's Guide to the Law: Everything You Need to Know About Your Rights in the Workplace—and What to Do If They Are Violated.* NY: Pantheon Books, 1993.
- Tarrant, John J. *Perks and Parachutes: Negotiating Your Executive Employment Contract.* NY: Linden Press/Simon & Schuster, 1985.

One-semester course	✔	✔	✔					
One-year course	✔	✔	✔	✔	✔			

		ASSESSMENT OPPORTUNITIES			
	Cooperative Learning	**Informal Assessment**	**Chapter Review**	**Chapter Test**	**Chapter *MicroExam***
		✔	✔	✔	✔
	✔	✔	✔	✔	✔
		✔	✔	✔	✔
		✔	✔	✔	✔
		✔	✔	✔	✔
		✔	✔	✔	✔

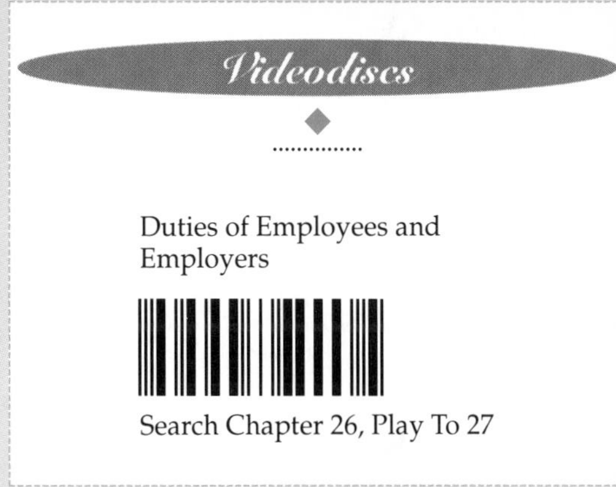

Videodiscs
Duties of Employees and Employers
Search Chapter 26, Play To 27

State by State

In Missouri, children under 16 years of age may not work with power-driven machinery, in a mine, in a foundry, or in a hotel or motel.

Teaching Materials

Student text, pp. 428–447

Overhead transparency masters
- *Work Forbidden for Those Between 14 & 16 Years of Age*
- *Children Younger Than Age 14 May Be Employed in Certain Nonhazardous Occupations*

Videos
- *Law for Business* Videodisc

Workbook, pp. 67–68; 180–182

Outside Resources
- Blank overhead transparency
- Guest speakers: local employer and employment commission representative
- Newspaper or magazine articles on crimes in the workplace
- Federal Minimum Wage poster from U.S. Dept. of Labor
- Help-wanted classified ads
- Empty facial tissue box
- Students' pay stubs
- Work permit applications

- Camcorder

Assessment
- Chapter Test

- Chapter *MicroExam*

Vocabulary

employer, p. 430
employee, p. 430
employment, p. 430
independent contractor, p. 430
employment for a specific period, p. 431
terminable at will, p. 431
duty of obedience, p. 432
duty of reasonable skill, p. 433
duty of loyalty and honesty, p. 433
duty of reasonable performance, p. 434
payroll deductions, p. 436
workers' compensation, p. 436
work permit, p. 437
wrongful discharge, p. 440
unemployment compensation, p. 441

Learning Objectives

When you complete this chapter, you will be able to

1. Define employment and contrast it with other relationships where one person works for another.
2. Describe how the *terms* in employment contracts are created.
3. Discuss the duties imposed by law on employees.
4. Explain the duties imposed by law on employers.
5. Recognize when an employer is liable for an employee's acts.
6. Explain how and when employment contracts can be terminated.

428

Chapter Self-Test

Assess students' understanding of employment contracts before they begin Chapter 21 by posing the following questions orally to the class and having students respond *True* or *False*. Review and discuss students' responses before continuing with the chapter. **(1) An employee may quit a job at any time without being in breach of contract.** (False); **(2) Anyone can collect unemployment compensation.** (False); **(3) Every employee owes a duty of loyalty and honesty to his or her employer.** (True); and **(4) Minimum wage is set by the federal government through the Fair Labor Standards Act.** (True).

CHAPTER 21

EMPLOYMENT CONTRACTS

1 At the beginning of the summer you were hired as a food server by a local restaurant. Unfortunately, neither you nor your employer discussed how long the job would last. You will be starting college soon in a different state. May you quit this job then without legal liability?

2 A friend of yours is hired as a ride operator with a traveling carnival. At a county fair, he carelessly fails to secure the safety bar over the seat on a small roller coaster. Two riders are thrown out and seriously injured. Who is liable for the injuries—the carnival, your friend, or both?

3 ETHICS ISSUE You have been employed as an accounting clerk at a local automobile parts store for the past three years. In formal performance evaluations, your supervisor has consistently ranked you "superior." Now the company is installing a computerized accounting system and plans to fire you and hire someone who has computer experience. Can your employer legally fire you when you have done nothing wrong? Ethically, what should the employer do?

FOCUS

Write the following statement on the chalkboard before class begins and have students jot down their responses on a sheet of paper: **Name any paying jobs you have held and identify the responsibilities that accompanied each job.**

Discuss students' responses. Then discuss the terms of employment for each job, such as how long the job would last, duties and responsibilities, wages, and so on. Keep a class list of responses for later use in this chapter.

You Decide

1 Yes; You may quit because your contract is terminable at will.

2 Both; Your friend is liable because he acted negligently. The carnival is liable because your friend was acting within the scope of his employment when he caused the injury.

3 ETHICS ISSUE Yes, your employer can fire you even though you have done nothing wrong. Most accounting contracts are terminable at will. Ethically, the employer should consider training you to operate the computerized accounting system.

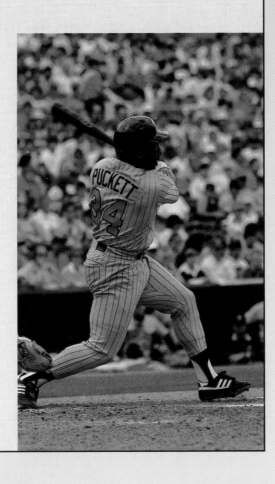

Thinking Critically Through Visuals

All major league baseball players sign employment contracts before they begin playing for a team. What types of terms, do you think, are included in these contracts? (Answers may include salary, number of games to be played, bonuses, trades, how injuries will affect pay, and so on.)

TEACH

Employment is a legal relationship based on a contract. There are requirements for an employment contract to exist. (The employer contracts to pay the employee to do work under the employer's supervision and control.) If a key element is missing, no employment relationship exists.

Help students distinguish between an **employee** (supervised) and an **independent contractor** (unsupervised). (IRS Form SS-8 is used to determine employment status for tax purposes.)

APPLY

Have students give three examples of an employee (such as a server at a restaurant) and three examples of an independent contractor (such as a person hired to build a porch). **Guided Practice**

Have students rewrite the PROBLEM on the top of p. 430 to make it fit the definition of **employment**. **Independent Practice**

TEACH

Point out that employment contracts differ from most other contracts because their terms come from a variety of sources: express agreements, implied agreements, and state and federal laws. Use the outline on pp. 180–182 of the Workbook to summarize.

WHAT IS EMPLOYMENT?

PROBLEM

Phil and his teenaged daughter Elaine trimmed the branches from a large, dead tree in front of their house. They also dug around the base and cut through most of the roots. Then they tried to pull the main trunk out of the ground with a long, heavy rope. Seeing them struggle, their neighbor Steve came out and helped. Is Elaine an employee of Phil? Is Steve an employee of Phil?

Employment is a legal relationship based on a contract. The parties to this contract are the employer and the employee. The party who pays is the **employer**; the party who does the work is the **employee**. In general, **employment** exists when an employer contracts to pay an employee to do work under the employer's supervision and control. If there is no contract to pay for work, or if there is no supervision and control, the relationship between the parties is not one of employment. Thus, in the problem, neither Elaine nor Steve was an employee. There was no contract for pay. Elaine was helping with a family chore; Steve was a friendly volunteer.

Sometimes people use the words "employment" or "hiring" to refer to relationships that are not relationships of employment. This occurs most frequently when someone contracts to have a job done, but does not supervise or control the worker. For example, suppose a homeowner promises to pay $3,500 to a roofing company to install a new roof. There is a contract for pay. However, because the homeowner will not direct and control the workers, this is not a contract of employment. Rather, it is what the law calls hiring an **independent contractor.** In general, an independent contractor agrees to produce a finished job without being supervised, while an employee agrees to do a range of tasks under the direction and control of the employer.

WHERE DO THE TERMS OF THE EMPLOYMENT CONTRACT COME FROM?

PROBLEM

Sid applied for a part-time job as a cook in a Mexican restaurant. Sid and the manager, Leslie, discussed hours and agreed that Sid would work from 3 p.m. to 5:30 p.m. on Mondays, Wednesdays, and Fridays.

ASSESS

Media **Learning Objective 1** Using a computer, if possible, have students define **employment** and identify the terms necessary for an employment contract to exist. (An employer contracts to pay an employee to do work under the employer's supervision and control.) Then have students describe how this differs from an independent contractor. (An independent contractor does a job without being supervised, while an employee performs under the direction and control of the employer.)

Sid was given a company personnel manual that described the pay scale and fringe benefits. It showed that he would be paid $6 per hour. In addition, Leslie told Sid how she wanted the food cooked. What are all the terms of this employment contract?

Employment contracts are unusual because their terms can come from a variety of sources. The terms can be derived from:

a. express agreements between the employer and employee;
b. implied agreements between the employee and employer; and
c. state and federal laws.

1. Express Agreements

Some employment contracts are expressed in detailed written documents. Such contracts are used most often with sports professionals, top-level managers, and union members. These written contracts typically describe all of the elements of the employment relationship. For example, a contract for **employment for a specific period** contains an express term identifying the length of employment. If either party violates that express term, they are liable for breach. Often the contract describes the liability for breach of any of the terms of the contract. However, only a small percentage of employment contracts are *completely* in writing.

Most employment contracts are partly written and partly oral. In the problem, Sid's hours have been orally agreed upon. Thus, this is an express term. The hourly rate and fringe benefits are in writing in the company personnel manual, so these might also be express terms. Compensation is almost always an express term. So are fringe benefits. Often the employer and employee also expressly agree upon the time required for advance notice of termination.

2. Implied Agreements

Notice that Sid and Leslie said nothing about the length of time Sid will be employed. When hiring hourly workers, custom, or trade practice, determines this. Sid, like most other employees, is employed in a job that is **terminable at will.** This means that he can be fired at any time because there has been no agreement about the length of his employment. Employment contracts can always be identified as "at will" or "for a specific period."

Frequently, there are other terms that are implied from the way individual employers supervise their employees. For example, in a particular restaurant there may be an implied term that requires waiters and waitresses to

▼ APPLY

On a transparency or a flip chart, have students create a spider map depicting the three sources of terms of an employment contract. Have students add details in spokes radiating from each of the three sources.

Guided Practice

Using the class list from the FOCUS activity, have students describe terms of employment contracts with which they may be familiar. **Independent Practice**

In pairs, have students role-play an employment interview. Have one student play the applicant, and the other act as the interviewer. Students should ensure that major issues relating to the employment contract are discussed. Videotape the interviews, then play them back so that students can fine-tune their interviewing skills. Ask a local employer to conduct simulated interviews to add more realism to the experience.

Cooperative Learning

As L.E.P. students complete this and other chapters, ask them to make a list in their notebook of the terms they do not know, including any boldfaced vocabulary words. Then, working with a bilingual dictionary, have students write the corresponding native-language words and their definitions in their notebook glossary.

▼RETEACH Have students identify whether the following are likely to be employees (E) or independent contractors (I): a house painter (I), store manager (E), teacher (E), taxi driver (E or I), and freelance photographer (I).

▼ENRICH Using a computer, if possible, have students write and perform two scenarios: one describing an employee/employer relationship and the other describing an independent contractor/client relationship. Have students identify each other's scenarios.

Obtain and display a copy of the Federal Minimum Wage poster (required by federal law to be displayed in every place of employment) from the U.S. Department of Labor, Employment Standards Administration, Wage and Hour Division, Washington, DC 20210. Review the poster with the class, especially the sections, *Child Labor* and *Training Wage*, which may be of immediate interest to your students.

pool their tips and to share them with the people who clear tables. Factory workers may be required to provide their own safety shoes and gloves. Such implied terms come from the rules of a particular employer rather than from customs of the industry or trade group.

3. Laws Provide Many Terms

State and federal laws provide many important terms for each employment contract. The law sometimes becomes a part of each employment contract whether the employer and employee want that or not. In the problem, Sid is entitled to receive, and Leslie is required to pay, at least the minimum wage specified by federal law. Federal law would dictate this part of Sid's employment contract even if Sid and Leslie had expressly agreed upon a lower amount.

Some of the employment laws that are, in effect, part of the employment contract are discussed in other chapters. These include employment discrimination laws, labor union laws, and job safety laws. The balance of this chapter discusses all the other laws that become part of the employment contract.

▼ TEACH

Point out that, in addition to an employee's duties to fulfill agreements made with his or her employer, four other duties are created by state law: **the duties of obedience, reasonable skill, loyalty and honesty, and reasonable performance.** As you summarize these duties, have students complete the corresponding section of the Chapter Outline in the Workbook.

▼ WHAT EMPLOYEE DUTIES ARE CREATED BY THE LAW?

PROBLEM

Vito hired Winston as a welder for a three-year period. Vito required all welders to wear protective helmets and goggles while working. Winston, who had long hair which made it difficult to wear the helmet, refused to do so. Can Vito discharge Winston without liability?

An employee has a duty to fulfill the agreements made with the employer. But in addition, the employee has other duties created by state case law. These duties include the following.

1. Obedience

Each employee is bound by the **duty of obedience.** This means the employee has a duty to obey the reasonable orders and rules of the employer. This duty exists whether or not the employee has expressly agreed to it. Thus, in the problem, the company would be within its rights in discharging Winston because the rule that Winston disobeyed was reasonable. However, an employee cannot be required to act illegally, immorally, or contrary to public policy.

▼ ASSESS

Learning Objective 2 Have students independently make a graphic organizer identifying the three sources of the terms of employment contracts, putting the answers on a separate key. Then, have each student exchange papers with a classmate, complete the organizer, and check his or her responses against the key.

2. Reasonable Skill

The **duty of reasonable skill** requires that those who accept work must possess the skill, experience, or knowledge necessary to do it. The employer need not keep the employee, nor pay damages for discharging the employee, if the employee does not perform with reasonable skill. Thus, a welder whose welds kept breaking could be fired for the lack of reasonable skill.

3. Loyalty and Honesty

PROBLEM

Ash was the assistant to the president of Pinos Point Properties. She had confidential information that her company was going to make an offer on a certain piece of land for $250,000 but would be willing to pay as much as $350,000 for it. Ash told this to the owners of the land, who agreed to give her one-half of any amount over $250,000 that they received. After the purchase was made for $350,000, Pinos Point learned of Ash's action. Pinos dismissed Ash and sued her for damages. Was the company within its rights?

Every employee owes the **duty of loyalty and honesty** to their employer. By committing a fraud upon the employer, or by revealing confidential

APPLY

Thinking Critically Through Visuals

This professional orchestra charges people to hear each performance. Which of the four employee duties described in this section, do you think, is the most important duty of an orchestra member? (Answers may include reasonable skill or reasonable performance, both of which affect the way the orchestra will sound.)

Bring to class the help-wanted classified ads from a recent newspaper and distribute a page, or a part of a page, randomly to each student. After selecting an ad of interest, have each student jot down specific duties created by state case law to which the prospective employee would likely be bound. Share students' selections with the class and correct misconceptions, if necessary. **Guided Practice**

RETEACH

Media: In pairs, have students write, using a computer, if possible, an employment contract that includes clauses derived from the three sources of terms of employment contracts (pp. 430–432). Post them on a bulletin board entitled *Top Jobs for Top Workers.*

ENRICH

Independently, using a computer, if possible, have students write their ideal employment contract in which they specify, at minimum, the length of employment, salary, working hours, and job description.

Video résumés are becoming popular in some fields and parts of the country. Have each student take turns scripting, then filming, his or her video résumé, including how he or she would fulfill his or her legal duties as an employee.

Independent Practice

Have students draw caricatures depicting each of the four employee duties created by law (pp. 432–434). Display the illustrations on a bulletin board created for this chapter.

▼ TEACH

Point out to students that, just as an employee's duties are governed by law, so are an employer's duties. Brainstorm with students what the legal duties for an employer might be. Then, share the six principal duties owed by an employer to an employee. (Reasonable treatment, safe working conditions, fair labor standards, payroll deductions, duties to minors, and military service and voting)

▼ APPLY

Have students read and clip newspaper or magazine articles about incidents or court cases that deal with each of the employer duties. Have students sort their articles by duty and create a collage to be displayed in class.
Guided Practice

information about the business, an employee such as Ash may be justifiably discharged. Such a worker may also be liable for damages.

4. Reasonable Performance

Employees owe the **duty of reasonable performance** to employers. An employer is justified in discharging an employee who fails to perform assigned duties at the prescribed time and in the prescribed manner. Occasional minor failure to perform as expected ordinarily is not sufficient grounds for dismissing an employee. On the other hand, any employee may be discharged if unable to do the work because of illness or injury.

▼ WHAT DUTIES ARE IMPOSED BY LAW ON THE EMPLOYER?

PROBLEM

Dale hired Frey to run her office for one year for $1,800 a month. The agreement provided that Frey was to be paid on the fifteenth and the last business day of each month. One month, Dale had financial problems and temporarily withheld $100 from Frey's paycheck. Dale promised to make it up the next payday, which she did. Three months later, Dale withheld $200, and so Frey quit. Was Frey legally justified in quitting?

Employers owe a variety of duties to employees. Some of these duties arise out of the express terms agreed upon by the parties. Thus, in the problem Dale violated the express term related to pay and Frey was justified in quitting. In other cases, the duty is imposed by the law instead of by agreement. The following are the principal obligations, created by law, which the employer owes to the employee.

1. Reasonable Treatment

PROBLEM

Gerhart had been hired as a vacation replacement for clerical employees of the Dairyland Creamery. He promised to work all summer. When Gerhart made a number of mistakes, his supervisor reprimanded him and called him "stupid." Was Gerhart within his rights in quitting his job?

▼ ASSESS

Learning Objectives 3 & 4 Have students independently create a two column chart with the headings *Employee* and *Employer*. In each column, have students list the duties to which each party is bound by law.

An employer is required to treat workers in a reasonable manner. If the employer commits an assault or battery upon an employee (see Chapter 5), the employee may quit the job without liability. The injured employee may also sue for damages. In the problem, however, there was no assault or battery. There was only an insult and reprimand, which did not constitute unreasonable treatment. Normally under such circumstances, employees like Gerhart who have promised to work for a specific period would have no right to quit and could be held liable for breach of contract if they did.

2. Safe Working Conditions

PROBLEM

Pittman contracted to work for six months as a forklift operator for Corder Moving and Storage Company. The brakes on her forklift were not working properly, and the lift was slipping. On three occasions, Pittman reported these defects to her supervisor. However, no repairs were made. After a near-accident caused by these unsafe conditions, Pittman walked off the job. There were four months left on her employment contract. Did she have a right to quit?

An employee is entitled by law to reasonably safe working conditions (including safe tools, equipment, machinery, and the building itself). The

Thinking Critically Through Visuals

Employers are bound by law to provide safe working conditions for their employees. How, do you think, does the company meet its obligations to the employee in this photograph? (Answers may include through regular safety inspections and by providing protective clothing, safety training, and so on.)

Writing Connections

Health
Have each student write a fictitious newspaper article, using an integrated software package or page layout program, if possible, on an unhealthful or unsafe working condition at school or in a specified place of work. Have students apply their process writing skills to state the problem, the law(s) broken, where the problem is, and what, if anything, should be done to correct the problem.

RETEACH Have students create posters alerting fellow students, as prospective employees, to the four duties to which they are bound by law. Post in a hallway.

ENRICH Decorate an empty facial tissue box to resemble a workplace suggestion box. Then, acting as employees, have students write suggestions to you, their employer, on how any of the six duties owed to employees could be better implemented. After anonymously stuffing the suggestion box, have volunteers read selections aloud to the class.

Have student volunteers bring to class their paycheck stubs showing payroll deductions and display them as an overhead transparency. Guide students to understand what each deduction is for and the formula used to calculate the deductions. (This information is available through your employer or the local office of your state (un)employment commission.)

Multicultural Highlights

In the United States, individuals must meet certain criteria to be legally employed, such as proof of citizenship or employment status (through a Resident Alien card or work permit). Unfortunately, many employers hire illegal workers who, in some cases, are forced to work long hours for less than minimum wage—sometimes under unhealthful and dangerous conditions. Have students debate the pros and cons of hiring illegal aliens in the workplace.

working conditions must not be harmful to the employee's health, safety, morals, or reputation. If the employer does not provide safe working conditions, the employee may quit without breaching the contract. In the problem, Pittman had this right. She also had the right to report the unsafe conditions to the Occupational Safety and Health Administration (OSHA) of the U.S. Department of Labor. (The rights of an employee to proper working conditions and the rights of an employee in case of injury on the job are discussed in Chapter 24.)

3. Fair Labor Standards

The federal government has enacted the Fair Labor Standards Act (also known as the Wage and Hour Act) to establish the minimum wage and maximum hours for all employees under the jurisdiction of the act. Maximum hours that can be worked at regular rates of pay are forty per week (with no daily maximum). If more than forty hours are worked in one week, overtime must be paid at one and one-half times the regular rate.

The minimum wage and overtime requirements of the law do not apply to executives, administrators, and professional workers (including teachers, certain salespeople, and employees of certain small enterprises). In addition, the hourly provisions apply only partially to workers in seasonal industries. Special rules apply to trainees, apprentices, student workers, and handicapped workers. In certain circumstances they may be paid at 85 percent of the minimum wage.

4. Payroll Deductions

Certain governmental programs are financed by payments made by employees. Typically the employer deducts money from the employee's paycheck. These are sometimes called **payroll deductions.** Thus the employer is legally obligated to withhold a percentage of the paycheck to cover the employee's federal and state income tax obligations. Similarly, the employer must withhold certain amounts for the employee's portion of social security payments (sometimes called FICA).

Other payments are often made from the funds of the employer. **Workers' compensation** is an example. This is a payment into an insurance fund that compensates employees for their injuries on the job. On the other hand, workers' compensation insurance coverage deprives the employee of the ability to recover from the employer for on-the-job injuries. Workers' compensation law is discussed in Chapter 24. Similarly, employers must make payments for unemployment insurance. Unemployment insurance pro-

ASSESS

Learning Objective 4 Have students identify in writing the duties imposed by law on employers and explain why these laws are necessary. (Answers may include reasonable treatment, safe working conditions, fair labor standards, payroll deductions, duties to minors, and rules related to military service and voting; They are necessary to ensure that minimum government standards for workers and the workplace are enforced.)

vides short-term income for people who have recently lost their jobs. This is discussed later in this chapter.

5. Duties to Minors

PROBLEM

Cushing, age seventeen, recently graduated from high school and is looking for a summer job. He heard about an opening for a band saw operator on the swing shift (4 p.m. to 12 a.m.) in a lumber mill. Can Cushing qualify for the job?

The federal government and every state government regulate the conditions and types of employment permitted for persons under age eighteen. These are often termed child-labor laws. When state child-labor laws have higher standards than federal laws, the state laws govern. Although these federal and state laws vary, they are all based on the following principles:

a. that a person's early years are best used to obtain an education,
b. that certain work is harmful or dangerous for young people, and
c. that child labor at low wages takes jobs from adults.

The states specify a minimum age for employment during school hours. The most common ages are fourteen or sixteen years. All of the states place a limit on the number of hours a young person may work. In calculating the maximum number of hours, the hours of school are often combined with the hours on the job while school is in session. For example, a common maximum is forty-eight hours (school and outside work combined) in one week. Most states maintain controls over those hours, and most require a **work permit** if the individual is under the age of eighteen years.

In addition, most states have laws that

a. set the maximum number of working hours in one day,
b. prohibit night work,
c. prescribe the grade in school that must be completed before being able to work,
d. set the required age for certain hazardous occupations, and
e. determine whether a child who is working is required to continue school on a part-time basis.

Display the overhead transparency, *Work Forbidden for Those Between 14 & 16 Years of Age.* Have student volunteers suggest why each of these jobs is prohibited to minors between age 14–16. Add these reasons to the transparency.

Assign individual students the responsibility for finding out what the minimum age for employment is in their state and other employment laws pertaining to minors. In an oral presentation, have students report their findings to the class.

Independent Practice

Display the overhead transparency, *Children Younger Than Age 14 May Be Employed in Certain Nonhazardous Occupations.* Discuss why youngsters are allowed to have these jobs. (Answers may include to assist America's farming families; to participate, within legal boundaries, in certain fields or trades; and so on.)

Have students find out how minors in your state obtain a work permit. Students may wish to ask a guidance counselor or local employer whom they know personally for this information, then share their findings with the class.

RETEACH Have students create and complete a graphic organizer of the six duties imposed by law on employers (found on pp. 434–438). Have them include details to explain each duty.

ENRICH Invite a representative from your state (un)employment commission to speak to small groups of students on the rights and obligations of employers and (minor) employees in your state. Have students prepare questions for the speaker in advance of the meeting.

Thinking Critically Through Visuals

Read the list of 12 hazardous occupations. Would a person under age 18 legally be employable as a roofer in his or her family-owned business? (No) Ask: **Why, do you think, are these jobs classified as hazardous?** (Answers may include that they may expose minors to legal and physical risk too great as to be tolerated by society, and so on.)

Ethics Issue

Some employers—illegally—fail to comply with the regulations that were set up to protect minors. Employers who knowingly or unknowingly allow harmful and exploitative working conditions to take place are legally liable. Have students discuss whether or not exceptions should be made to the laws that protect minors and, if so, how these exceptions could be approved and monitored for compliance.

Figure 21-1
Persons under age eighteen are usually prohibited from working in these hazardous occupations.

HAZARDOUS OCCUPATIONS

1. Mining
2. Manufacturing explosives, brick, or tile
3. Operating power-driven hoists
4. Logging and saw milling
5. Driving motor vehicles or acting as an outside helper on such vehicles (except for incidental, occasional, and school bus driving)
6. Working in any job involving exposure to radioactive materials
7. Operating power-driven woodworking, metal-forming, punching, shearing, or baking machines
8. Slaughtering or meat packing
9. Operating circular saws, band saws, or guillotine shears
10. Wrecking or demolishing buildings or ships
11. Roofing
12. Excavating

For example, in some states minors may work only between the hours of 5 a.m. and 10 p.m. Moreover, the job must not be classified as hazardous. Figure 21-1 lists jobs that are often classified as hazardous and thus not available to minors. In the problem, if these laws are in effect where Cushing lives, Cushing cannot qualify for the job.

6. Military Service and Voting

The Military Selective Service Extension Act of 1950 requires that certain military persons must be reemployed by their former employer after honorable discharge from the service. Persons who have (1) been drafted, (2) enlisted, or (3) been called to active duty receive this protection. Veterans must still be able to do their former work to qualify for reemployment.

More than one-half the states provide that workers must be given sufficient time off with pay, at a time convenient to the employer, to vote in regular primary and general elections.

ASSESS

Learning Objective 5 In writing, ask students to identify when an employer is liable for the torts of employees. (If an employee commits a tort while acting within the scope of employment, the employer is liable for damages; whether or not the act was authorized is immaterial.) Then, have students give examples.

IS THE EMPLOYER LIABLE FOR THE TORTS OF EMPLOYEES?

PROBLEM

Walker was an electrician for Centurion Electrical Service. One day Walker was sent to repair mixing machines at Molecular Chemical Company. Walker did the work in a negligent manner, causing several thousand dollars' worth of damage to the machines. Was Centurion liable for the damage? Was Walker liable for the damage?

If an employee, acting *within the scope of employment,* commits a tort (i.e., injures persons or property), the employer is liable for the damages. It is immaterial that the employer did not authorize the act. On the other hand, if an employee commits a tort but is not acting within the scope of the employer's business, the employee alone is liable for any injuries that result. Even if an employee intentionally causes damage, the employer may be held liable if the employee has acted with the intention of furthering the employer's interests. In the problem, Walker was acting within the scope of her employment so both Walker and Centurion are liable for the damage.

Generally, if a person is an independent contractor rather than an employee, the person who hired the contractor is not liable for the contractor's torts. However, if the job is inherently dangerous, such as blasting, the party who hired the independent contractor may be liable to those injured by the inherently dangerous activity.

HOW IS THE EMPLOYMENT CONTRACT TERMINATED?

PROBLEM

After suffering a stroke, Ching hired Vennet as a nurse and companion for one year. Four months later, Ching died. Was Vennet's contract terminated?

Contracts of employment for a specific period are terminated in the same ways as other contracts (see Chapter 14). The usual method is by performance of the contractual obligations. As with other contracts, courts look to the terms of the employment contract to determine the obligations of the parties. The express and implied terms, and those imposed by law, define these obligations. If material obligations are not performed, breach of

TEACH

Employers generally are liable for the intentional and negligent or accidental torts committed by employees (and occasionally independent contractors) as long as the employees were acting within the scope of the employer's business.

APPLY

Copy the following graphic organizer on the chalkboard and have students complete it. **Guided Practice**

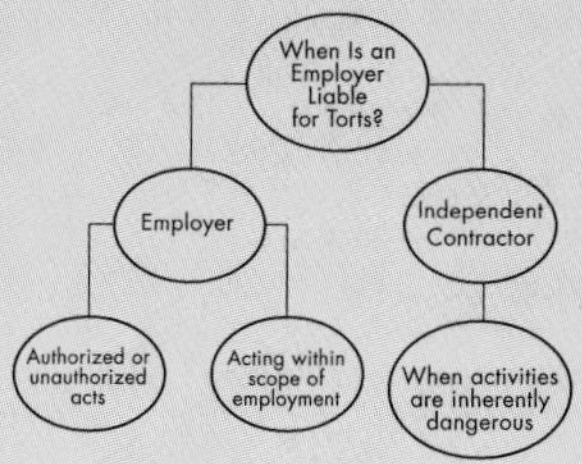

Have students clip articles dealing with crimes in the workplace. Then, have them identify whether the employer would be liable for the employees' act(s) in each case. **Independent Practice**

TEACH

Review these points with the class: **(1)** employment contracts, like others, are usually discharged by performance, **(2)** the terms—express, implied, by law—define the employment obligations, and **(3)** material breach of contract terminates the other party's obligations to the contract without further liability.

RETEACH Have students reread the PROBLEM on the top of p. 439. In writing, have students explain why Centurion is liable. (The employee acted within the scope of her employment. Therefore, both she and her employer are liable.)

ENRICH In pairs, have students write, on a computer, if possible, two scenarios dealing with an employer's liability for the torts of its employees. In the first, the employer should be liable; in the second, the employer should not be liable.

contract occurs. Material breach extinguishes the obligations of the other party to the contract.

Suppose an employer fails to pay the employee the agreed-upon monthly check. This would be a breach of the contract. Because it is material, the employee would be justified in quitting or in abandoning the job without liability for breach of contract. Similarly, if the employee fails to live up to the material obligations of the job, the employer may treat the contract as terminated and discharge the employee without liability. In the problem, the contract was terminated by impossibility of performance. Death made it impossible for Vennet to be a nurse and companion to Ching.

1. Employment Contracts Terminable at Will

As discussed on page 431, many employment contracts, especially with private employers, are terminable at the will of either the employer or the employee. This occurs because the employer and employee generally do not specify a length of time for the employment relationship. The law then assumes that either party may terminate employment at any time without liability. For example, if an automobile repair shop hired a mechanic for $12 per hour and a competitor later offered the mechanic $15 per hour, there would generally be no liability for quitting the $12-per-hour job. On the other hand, the repair shop manager could fire the mechanic without giving any reason for doing so.

There are obvious limitations on this power to terminate without cause. Firing because of race, religion, gender, age, handicap, pregnancy, or national origin is job discrimination and illegal. Further, many states deny the power to terminate at will when it is used to retaliate against those who:

a. refuse to commit perjury at the request of the company,
b. insist on filing a workers' compensation claim,
c. engage in union activity,
d. report violations of law by the company, or
e. urge the company to comply with the law.

When an employer fires an employee for one of the above reasons, it commits the tort of **wrongful discharge.**

2. Employment Contracts for a Specific Length of Time

If the employment contract is for a certain length of time (see page 431), it is breached if one party terminates it early. For example, if a basketball player signed a three-year contract for $600,000 a year to play for a professional club, this would be a contract for a specific length of time. If the player breached the contract by deliberately refusing to come to scheduled games (a breach of the employee's duty of obedience), the employer would

▼ APPLY

As a class, have students scan pp. 439–441, then use this section of the chapter outline in the Workbook to summarize the four numbered points in the section. **Guided Practice**

Using the information from their outline, have students independently complete the following comparison table on notepaper. Then, review and correct answers as a class. **Independent Practice**

	Fact 1	Fact 2
Terminable at will	Answers may include: Either party can terminate if no length of contract is specified	Limitations include firing for discrimination/ illegal practices.
Specific length of time	Contract breached if one party terminates duties before end of contract	Breacher may be liable for damages.
Government contracts	Public (government) employees generally entitled to due process before firing	More difficult to discharge public employees than private.
Unemployment compensation	Terminated workers entitled if discharged without cause; not entitled if for cause	Terms and eligibility determined by each state.

Have students contact the local office of your state's (un)employment commission for information, such as available flyers, bulletins, or pamphlets, on unemployment compensation rights. Have students find out when one is eligible, how to apply, and how payments are made.

▼ ASSESS

Learning Objective 6 As a class, lead a round-robin, collaborative activity to create one scenario in which an employee is terminated. Have the first student begin the verbal brainstorming by offering an employment scenario, such as who the worker is and where he or she works. Have each subsequent student add one piece of information until all students have participated or have covered the four key points of this section in their scenario.

probably be justified in terminating the contract. In addition, since the player caused the termination, the player may be liable for damages. Thus, if the club had to pay $1.4 million to obtain the services of an equally talented replacement, the player might be liable to the club for the difference of $400,000.

3. Employment Contracts With Governments

In general, public employees (i.e., those who work for a government) are entitled to due process before being discharged. This means that they are entitled to notice of the reasons for the discharge along with a hearing, where they are given the opportunity to present their own evidence and to challenge the claims of the governmental employer. For this reason, it is more difficult to discharge public employees than private sector employees.

4. Right to Unemployment Compensation

Workers who have been terminated even though they have complied with all the terms of their employment contract are said to have been discharged *without cause.* This means the cause of the discharge was not the employee's conduct. If an employee is discharged without cause, he or she is entitled to unemployment compensation benefits. **Unemployment compensation** is money paid by the government to workers who have lost their jobs through no fault of their own.

If an employee has been discharged because he or she violated an employment obligation, then the employee is said to be discharged *for cause.* The worker discharged for cause generally is not entitled to unemployment compensation.

Unemployment compensation payments are made by the states in cooperation with the federal government under the Social Security Act of 1935. There is usually a period of one or two weeks after termination before payments begin. Then a percentage of the regular wage is paid to the unemployed person every week for a limited period of time. Unemployment compensation generally is not available to those who quit voluntarily, strike, or refuse to accept similar substitute work. It is often available to part-time workers.

Preventing Legal Difficulties

When you become an employee . . .

1. Realize that you and your employer are parties to a contract in which you both have rights and duties.

Personal Perspectives

Have students interview a family member or friend who has ever terminated, or been terminated from, an employment contract or has experience with wrongful discharge, unemployment compensation, or government contracts (such as public-service employment). Have students report on the interviewee's experience and any advice for handling such situations. Make a class chart of the advice.

Preventing Legal Difficulties

Federal and state regulations often require posting of mandatory notices and posters dealing with employment and employee *rights*. Have students read the four points on pp. 441–442 and make a group poster on employees' *duties* to an employer. Upon completion, ask students who have worked, or currently work, how they might personally apply these suggestions.

▼RETEACH Have a peer-tutor create a scenario covering the four key points of contract termination (pp. 439–441). Pair this student with another who needs reteaching and have him or her identify the criteria.

▼ENRICH Have students select and draw a cartoon that clearly illustrates one aspect of how employment contracts are terminated. Display the cartoons, then use them to summarize this section of the chapter.

▼ CLOSE

As a whole-class activity, wrap up the chapter by having students view role plays of the following five scenarios. First, divide the class into groups of two or three students: employer; employee; and, if necessary, employment negotiator. Then, have each group plan, rehearse, perform, and videotape the scenarios, discussing each after it has been performed.

- An employee and employer discussing terms of an employment contract before hiring
- An employee's duties to an employer, as imposed by law
- An employer's duties to an employee, as imposed by law
- Terminating a contract
- Rights and responsibilities after a contract has been terminated

Assign the following end-of-chapter materials:
Student text review activities, pp. 442–447
Workbook, pp. 67–68
Chapter Test

Chapter *MicroExam*

2. Before you go to work, learn as much as you can about the job. Find out about hours, pay, duties, dress, fringe benefits, and any other related matters.
3. Avoid tardiness and absenteeism.
4. Remember that in addition to reasonable skill and performance, you owe your employer loyalty, honesty, and obedience. However, the duty of obedience does not require employees to engage in illegal, immoral, or unsafe activities.
5. Remember that you are personally responsible for your own negligent acts. This is true even though the injured party may also be able to recover from your employer.

▼ REVIEWING IMPORTANT POINTS

1. Employment is a form of contract.
2. An employee is distinguished from an independent contractor by the fact that an employer has the power to supervise and control the employee's work. An independent contractor is not subject to direction and control, but is only responsible for the finished job.
3. Contracts of employment may be express (oral or written) or implied (shown by conduct).
4. Among the duties imposed by law on the employee are the duties to (a) obey reasonable rules and orders, (b) perform the prescribed duties with reasonable skill, (c) be loyal and honest, and (d) perform the prescribed duties at the proper time and in the proper manner.
5. Among the duties imposed by law on the employer are (a) to ensure reasonable treatment of employees, (b) to provide safe working conditions, (c) to comply with fair labor standards, (d) to withhold payroll deductions, (e) to comply with child-labor laws, (f) to reemploy discharged military personnel, and (g) to give employees time off from work to vote.
6. An employer is liable for injuries to the person or property of third parties if the injuries are caused by employees acting within the scope of their employment. The employee is also liable for such acts.
7. Contracts of employment are terminated in the same ways as are other contracts. Material breach of contract by the employee is cause for discharge. The employee is justified in quitting if the employer does not fulfill an important part of the agreement.

▼ STRENGTHENING YOUR LEGAL VOCABULARY

Match each term with the statement that best defines that term. Some terms may not be used.

due process	employment for a specific period
duty of loyalty and honesty	independent contractor
duty of obedience	payroll deductions
duty of reasonable performance	terminable at will
duty of reasonable skill	unemployment compensation
employee	workers' compensation
employer	work permit
employment	wrongful discharge

1. Governmental payments to those who recently lost their jobs.
2. Payment for injuries that occur on the job.
3. Party who engages another to work for pay.
4. One who contracts to do something for another but is free of the latter's direction and control.
5. Contractual relationship in which one party engages another to work for pay under the supervision of the party paying.
6. Party who works under the supervision of another for pay.
7. The obligation to look out for the best interests of the employer.
8. The obligation to perform the job tasks with competence.
9. A right of employees of the government.
10. Firing an employee in retaliation for reporting violations of law by the company.

▼ APPLYING LAW TO EVERYDAY LIFE

1. ETHICS ISSUE You just interviewed Danny Mitchell for the job of receptionist for your own company. You had intended to pay the person hired $6.25 per hour because that is the competitive rate for receptionists in your community. You decide that Danny is perfect for the job. Before making the offer, you ask, "How much pay do you need to take this job?" Danny responds, "Anything above $5.00 per hour." What pay rate will you use in your offer? What reasons support your decision?

Strengthening Your Legal Vocabulary

1. unemployment compensation
2. workers' compensation
3. employer
4. independent contractor
5. employment
6. employee
7. duty of loyalty and honesty
8. duty of reasonable skill
9. due process
10. wrongful discharge

Applying Law to Everyday Life

1. 

Answers should reflect independent thinking; however, it is unfair to Danny to take advantage of his ignorance about prevailing wages. Also, it may injure you if Danny later discovers that he is being underpaid. (See Chapter 2.)

2 ETHICS ISSUE Suppose you were hired under a contract for three years as a research scientist. After six months on the job, without knowledge of your contract, a competing firm offers you twice the pay. You can breach your current contract, pay damages, and still come out ahead financially. Will you break your contract and your promise? What reasons support your decision?

3 The High Country Lumber Company hired Mason to haul trees from a forest site to a lumber mill twenty-five miles away. Mason used his own truck, began and ended work when he pleased, paid for his own gasoline, and worked by himself. He was paid $8.50 per log. Was Mason an employee of High Country Lumber Company?

4 Chin interviewed Caroline for a position as cashier in her grocery store. She described the job responsibilities, the days and hours Caroline would work, the attitude she wanted Caroline to communicate to customers, and the hourly pay. After the interview, Chin said she would hire Caroline and they shook hands. Describe three terms of this employment contract that are express and three that are imposed by law.

5 Myron owned Crossroads Service Station. He directed Pat, an employee, to put re-refined oil into the unlabeled oil jars displayed for sale. Pat knew that the law required re-refined oil to be labeled "re-refined." Therefore, Pat refused to fill or display the jars. Was Pat's disobedience grounds for discharge? If discharged, could Pat collect unemployment compensation?

6 Amit was the night clerk at the Indian Inn. He had several duties besides working at the main desk. Therefore, he was not allowed to sleep while on the job even if business was slow. On several occasions, the manager of the inn found Amit sleeping and warned him not to do so. If Amit continued to fall asleep on the job, would the manager be justified in discharging him? If discharged, could Amit collect unemployment compensation?

7 Swenson had been employed by a neighborhood meat market as a butcher for twelve years. Her boss had always praised her job performance. After a large grocery store was built nearby, drawing away many of the market's customers and reducing its sales, Swenson was given a thirty-day notice of termination. She protested, claiming she had always been a very good employee. Was Swenson discharged for cause? Can Swenson collect unemployment insurance?

2 ETHICS ISSUE If you breach the existing employment contract, you break the promise you made to your existing employer. Do you keep your promises only when it is in your financial best interest to do so? You decide. (See Chapter 2.)

3 Probably not; however, the IRS may try to prove otherwise. High Country Lumber Company would probably argue that Mason was an independent contractor, not an employee. He was not under the control and supervision of High Country; rather, he was his own boss, entitled to collect $8.50 on the delivery of each log. (p.430)

4 Express terms include: (a) job responsibilities, (b) days worked, (c) hours worked, (d) pay, and (e) desired attitude. All of the duties of the employer imposed by law that are described in the text apply to this relationship except the employee's right to due process. (pp. 431–432, 434–438)

5 Pat's disobedience was not grounds for discharge because Myron asked him to do something which was both illegal and immoral. (p. 440) Pat likely would be entitled to unemployment compensation. (p. 441)

6 The manager would be justified in discharging Amit if he was found sleeping again. Sleeping would be a violation of the duties of obedience and reasonable performance. (pp. 432, 434) If discharged, Amit would probably not be entitled to unemployment compensation because he would have been discharged "for cause;" that is, for violating his employment contract. (p. 441)

7 Swenson was not discharged "for cause." She had not violated her employment contract in any way. Accordingly, she would be able to collect unemployment compensation. (p. 441)

8 Smith and Alonzo agreed that Smith would temporarily be paid less than minimum wage. They did this because Alonzo could not afford to pay more and Smith had no other employment opportunities. They executed an agreement that clearly indicated Smith's consent to the arrangement. Is Smith entitled to the minimum wage or has she waived this right?

9 Inez worked as a cashier in an all-night cafeteria. One night two men followed her home from the swing shift. They assaulted her at her home demanding "the money and the deposits." They thought she took money home from the cafeteria to deposit in the bank the next morning. Inez filed a claim for workers' compensation. Was she "injured on the job"?

10 Jeff was a secretary at Elmhurst Elementary, a public school. Ms. O'Daley, the principal, wanted to fire him because he was often late. Describe how Jeff's employment contract differs from that of a secretary in a private organization. Describe the steps Ms. O'Daley must take to fire Jeff.

▼ SOLVING CASE PROBLEMS

1 Thomas P. Finley worked for Aetna Life Insurance. Aetna had a company personnel manual that stated that employees would "not be terminated so long as their performance is satisfactory." Finley was fired. He sued and asserted that the language in the personnel manual meant that he was not terminable at will but rather entitled to employment as long as he performed satisfactorily. Can a personnel manual supply such terms of the employment contract? (*Finley v. Aetna Life and Casualty Company*, 202 Conn. 190)

2 Gale, an umpire, was a member of the Greater Washington Softball Umpires Association. During a game in which Gale was officiating, a player objected to his decision on a play. The player then struck Gale with a baseball bat, causing injuries to Gale's neck, hip, and leg. Gale claimed that he was an employee of the association and so sought workers' compensation for his injuries. The association asserted that its members were independent contractors. It based this assertion on the fact that the umpires had full charge and control of the games, and that the association did not direct the worker in the performance or manner in which the work was done. The evidence presented showed (a) that the umpires were paid by the association from fees collected from the teams; (b) that the umpires, while assigned to the games by the

8 Smith is entitled to the minimum wage. This right cannot be waived by the employee. (p. 436)

9 Yes, Inez was injured on the job and is entitled to workers' compensation. (p. 436)

10 Because Jeff works for the government, he has the right to due process. Therefore, Jeff must be informed of the reasons for the firing and be given the opportunity to disprove them at a hearing. (p. 441)

Solving Case Problems

1 Yes, company personnel manuals can provide terms of the employment contract. (p. 431)

2 Gale was an independent contractor. The association did not direct the work of the umpire, and it did not have enough control over the umpire's performance or the manner in which the work was done to classify Gale as an employee. (p. 430)

3 No, refusal was not a violation of the duty of obedience. This duty does not require that employees endure unsafe working conditions. (pp. 435–436)

4 Both Gatzke and Walgreen Co. are liable to the Edgewater Motel. Gatzke is liable because he was negligent in not extinguishing his cigarette. Walgreen is liable because Gatzke was acting within the scope of his employment while in Duluth to supervise the opening of the new restaurant. His activities at the bar (discussing the planned restaurant operations) and in sleeping at the motel were designed to advance the employer's (Walgreen's) business. (p. 439)

5 No; Lucky would have been liable had Smith been injured while the letter was being lowered to the ground, because this was inherently dangerous and the risk could not be delegated to an independent contractor. (p. 439) However, the dangerous work on the letter "R" had been completed, and Lucky's responsibility had ended. Both Q.R.I. and its workers were at fault and, therefore, liable.

association, were not obligated to accept the assignments; (c) that the association conducted clinics, administered written examinations, and required members to wear designated uniforms while officiating; and (d) that the umpires had to meet with the approval of committees of the association who observed a member officiating during a probationary period. Under these circumstances, do you believe Gale was an employee of the association or an independent contractor? (*Gale v. Greater Washington Softball Umpires Association,* 311 A.2d 817)

3 Whirlpool operated a manufacturing facility that used overhead conveyors to transport parts around the plant. Because the parts sometimes fell from the overhead conveyor belt, Whirlpool installed a wire screen below the conveyor belts to catch them. Maintenance workers were required to retrieve fallen parts from the screen, which was about twenty feet above the floor of the plant. On two occasions, maintenance workers fell through the screen onto the floor. One of the workers was killed by the fall. Shortly thereafter, Vergil Deemer and Thomas Cornwell asked that the screen be repaired. When repairs were not made, these men complained to OSHA. The next day they were told by their supervisor to climb out onto the screen to retrieve fallen parts. When they refused, they were sent home without pay. Was their refusal a violation of their duty of obedience? (*Whirlpool v. Marshall,* 445 U.S. 1)

4 Walgreen Company planned to open a restaurant in Duluth, Minnesota. A district manager for Walgreen, A. J. Gatzke, was sent to Duluth to supervise preparations for the opening. Gatzke obtained a room—paid for by Walgreen—in a motel owned by Edgewater Motels, Inc. One day, after working many hours, Gatzke left work at 12:30 a.m. and, with another Walgreen employee, went to a bar near the motel. There Gatzke drank four brandy Manhattans (three were doubles) in about one hour. At the bar, Gatzke discussed the planned operations of the new restaurant.

Gatzke went back to his motel room where, apparently, he smoked several cigarettes after completing an expense account report. The butt of one cigarette was apparently thrown into a wastebasket in the room. The room caught on fire and the fire spread to the entire motel. Gatzke escaped uninjured, but the damage to the motel was over $330,000. Edgewater Motels sued both Gatzke and his employer, Walgreen Company. Who is liable? (*Edgewater Motels, Inc. v. Gatzke,* 277 N.W.2d 11)

5 Lucky Stores, Inc., owned a building with a large sign on it spelling out "ARDENS." Lucky hired Q.R.I. Corporation as an independent contractor to remove the sign. The removal work was inherently dangerous

because each letter was about six feet high and two and one-half feet wide and weighed between fifty and sixty pounds. Q.R.I. workers safely removed the letter "A" and loaded it on their truck. They also safely removed the letter "R" and leaned it against the truck. Then, for a moment, one worker negligently released his hold on the letter. A gust of wind blew the letter into contact with seventy-nine-year-old Smith, injuring her seriously. Is Lucky liable to Smith for damages? (*Smith v. Lucky Stores, Inc.*, 61 Cal. App. 3d 826, 132 Cal. Rptr. 628)

CHAPTER 22 ORGANIZER

Chapter Theme

State and federal governments regulate actions, labor relations, union management, and union workers, and determine the legality of strikes, boycotts, and labor practices.

DIRECTED STUDY QUESTIONS	SPECIAL FEATURES	PROGRAM RESOURCES: Reteach	Enrich	S N	A M	
How do state and federal governments regulate employment?		✔	✔			
History of labor laws	Multicultural Highlights, p. 451 Ethics Issue, p. 452	✔	✔			
What is the national labor relations board?		✔	✔			
How are unions established?	Th. Crit. Through Vis., p. 453	✔	✔			
How does union certification affect employees?		✔	✔			
What are unfair labor practices by management?		✔	✔	✔	A	
What are unfair labor practices by unions?	Writing Connections, p. 457 Th. Crit. Through Vis., p. 458	✔	✔		V	
What is collective bargaining?		✔	✔			
When may a union strike?	Per. Pers., p. 460; Th. Crit. Through Vis., p. 461	✔	✔			
When may a union boycott?	Pr. Leg. Dif., p. 462	✔	✔		K	

Additional Resources

- Brennan, Jody. "The $300 Million Litigator." *Forbes,* August 16, 1993, pp. 84–86.
- *Norma Rae*, videotape. Warner Bros.
- *Time Almanac*, CD-ROM. Time-Warner.
- *Union Democracy*, videotape. Chelmsford, MA: Merrimack Films.
- Verespej, Michael A. "Today's Union Leaders." *Industry Week,* July 5, 1993, pp. 28–38.

Chapter Pacing Guide

One-semester course	✔	✔	✔					
One-year course	✔	✔	✔	✔				

	ASSESSMENT OPPORTUNITIES			
Cooperative Learning	**Informal Assessment**	**Chapter Review**	**Chapter Test**	**Chapter *MicroExam*** (Media)
	✔	✔	✔	✔
	✔	✔	✔	✔
	✔	✔	✔	✔
	✔	✔	✔	✔
	✔	✔	✔	✔
	✔	✔	✔	✔
	✔	✔	✔	✔
✔	✔	✔	✔	✔
	✔	✔	✔	✔
	✔	✔	✔	✔

Videodiscs

History of Labor Law

Search Chapter 27, Play To 28

State by State

Tennessee is a right-to-work state.

Teaching Materials

Student text, pp. 448–467

Overhead transparency masters
- *Employees in the Bargaining Unit*
- *The Seesaw of Labor-Management Legislation*

Videos
- *Law for Business* Videodisc

Workbook, pp. 69–70

Outside Resources
- Copies of state employment laws
- Graph paper, index cards, & poster board
- Newspapers and magazines

- *Time Almanac,* CD-ROM from Time-Warner
- *Norma Rae,* videotape from Warner Bros.
- *Union Democracy,* videotape from Merrimack Films
- Camcorder & VCR

Assessment
- Chapter Test

- Chapter *MicroExam*

Vocabulary

yellow-dog contracts, p. 451
ex parte injunction, p. 451
bargaining unit, p. 453
certification, p. 453
decertification election, p. 454
union shop, p. 455
agency shop, p. 455
open shop, p. 455
closed shop, p. 455
right-to-work laws, p. 455
unfair labor practices, p. 455
blacklist, p. 456
featherbedding, p. 457
picket, p. 457
strike, p. 457
lockout, p. 457
collective bargaining, p. 459
deadlocked, p. 460
mediation, p. 460
economic strike, p. 460
unfair labor practice strike, p. 460
cooling-off period, p. 460
national emergency strike, p. 460
boycott, p. 461
primary boycott, p. 461
secondary boycott, p. 461

Learning Objectives

When you complete this chapter, you will be able to

1. Describe the sources of laws that regulate labor relations.
2. Understand the processes for establishing a new union, changing unions, and eliminating union representation.
3. Explain the way union representation affects the relationship between employees and employers.
4. Discuss unfair labor practices.
5. Describe collective bargaining, strikes, and boycotts.

448

Chapter Self-Test

Assess students' understanding of the role of unions before they begin Chapter 22 by asking students to respond briefly in writing to the following statement: **Today there are few federal or state laws regulating employer-employee relations.** (False; Answers may include knowledge of the Americans with Disabilities Act, the Family Leave Act, and so on.) Before continuing with the chapter, review and discuss students' responses.

CHAPTER

22

UNIONS

1 Friends of your family own a large bakery. They claim their workers are not allowed to join a union because all of the workers are paid union-scale wages or better. Are your friends correct?

2 You are employed as a fruit picker at a large orchard. You and your co-workers are dissatisfied with your wages and working conditions. If most of you organize into a union and ask your employer to discuss the disputed issues, must she do so?

3 ETHICS ISSUE Cork did not think his employer was fair in its treatment of women. During a campaign to unionize Cork's workplace, he considered spreading a false rumor about management's "sexist attitudes." He knew if he did this the union would win the campaign. Cork concluded that it would be wrong to spread the false rumor but the result would be good because the union would ensure that women were treated fairly. Is it ethical for Cork to spread the rumor?

FOCUS

As students enter the classroom, have them list on the chalkboard any jobs they have (or have had) outside of school as well as the number of hours they work(ed) each week.

Ask these students what is the maximum number of hours they may work on school days, if they may work at night, and so on. Ask: **Why, do you think, does the government particularly protect young persons from harmful work and unreasonable hours?** (Answers may include that, historically, young people have been exploited in the workplace, prevented from going to school, and so on.)

You Decide

1 No; The National Labor Relations Act gives the employees the right to form a union.

2 Yes; According to law, workers have the right to unionize, and employers must bargain collectively with the union.

3 ETHICS ISSUE Using consequential reasoning, it would seem ethical because the net result would be positive. Deontologically, Cork's spreading a false rumor would be unethical because lying is inherently wrong.

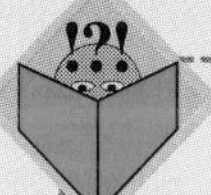

Thinking Critically Through Visuals

The early history of the labor movement could not be told without mentioning the struggles of the coal miners to unionize. Do the concerns of coal miners today differ from the concerns of miners more than 60 years ago? (Students may note that they don't differ very much at all; wages, safety standards, health benefits, and job security are still important.)

TEACH

Tell students that both federal and state laws govern labor-management relations. Make students aware that federal law prevails if there is a conflict between state and federal laws.

APPLY

On the chalkboard or a flip chart, work with students to create a graphic organizer to illustrate the eight labor issues covered by labor relations law. Use the information on p. 450 as a guide. **Guided Practice**

Obtain documents from your state's department of labor regarding employment laws. Make sufficient copies available so that each student has a document. Ask students to classify the laws according to whose rights or needs are the subject of the law—those of the employer or the employee. **Independent Practice**

HOW DO STATE AND FEDERAL GOVERNMENTS REGULATE EMPLOYMENT?

PROBLEM

Jerry is employed as a typist in an electronic component factory which ships its products throughout the United States and to many other countries. Is Jerry's employment subject to state employment law, federal employment law, or both?

The U.S. Constitution gives the federal government certain powers and reserves other powers to the states and to the people themselves. However, in certain areas, such as labor-management relations, both federal and state laws exist. These laws are usually in harmony. In general, however, if there is a conflict between state and federal laws, federal law prevails. State laws are limited to intrastate commerce (i.e., trade within one state). Also, federal guidelines define which employers are not subject to federal jurisdiction even though they are engaged in interstate commerce (i.e., trade between two or more states). Thus, if a retail store sells less than $500,000 worth of goods annually, it is regarded as an intrastate firm for labor relations law and is governed by the state. This is true even if it does business in more than one state.

Labor relations law is just one part of a broad structure of federal and state employment laws covering the following:

1. the right of employees to form, join, and assist labor unions and to bargain collectively with employers over wages, hours, and conditions of employment;
2. the rights of union members in relation to their union;
3. minimum wages and overtime pay (see Chapter 21);
4. protection of young persons from harmful work (see Chapter 21);
5. the right to get a job, be paid, and be promoted without regard to race, color, religion, gender, pregnancy, national origin, handicap, or advanced age (see Chapter 23);
6. training of apprentices in some crafts;
7. safe working conditions and compensation for injury suffered on the job (see Chapter 24); and
8. unemployment compensation (see Chapter 21).

In the problem, Jerry's employment was subject to both state and federal laws governing the items listed above.

ASSESS

Learning Objective 1 Orally and as a group, have students identify and describe the sources of law that regulate labor relations, identified on pp. 451–452. Reinforce key information and have students copy these points in their notebooks.

HISTORY OF LABOR LAWS

PROBLEM

Boston bootmakers formed an association with the intent of negotiating higher wages. The state of Massachusetts prosecuted them, alleging that the bootmakers were engaged in a criminal conspiracy to extort higher wages. Further, the state alleged that the wage increases would be passed on to consumers, thereby injuring them. Is the conduct by the bootmakers criminal?

An understanding of the history of labor law will help you see how the law evolves over time. It will also help you understand the current state of labor law. Labor unions did not engage in strikes in the United States until the 1800s. The law then responded with hostility. One line of reasoning held that an employment contract existed between employers and union members. Strikes then were attempts to pressure, or extort, employers into accepting terms they would otherwise reject. Courts held that strikes, boycotts, and similar tactics were simply actions in breach of the employment contract. Many companies immediately fired any employee suspected of harboring sympathies toward unions. They could do this because employment contracts are terminable at will. Other companies made new employees promise not to join a union. These employment contracts earned the name **yellow-dog contracts.** If an employee working under a yellow-dog contract joined a union, she or he could be fired for breach of the contract.

A second line of legal reasoning held that union activities were criminal conspiracies. Unions were held to be organizing their members to extort higher wages at the expense of the consuming public. This claim was supported by the courts until about 1842. After that time, the courts ceased classifying unions as criminal conspiracies. Thus, in the problem, the bootmakers are not engaged in criminal conduct.

Another response to unions was the **ex parte injunction.** This is an injunction issued by a judge after hearing only one side of an argument. If the employer could show potential injury flowing from a strike, many judges would issue the injunction prohibiting the strike. If employees struck in the face of the injunction, they could be arrested and imprisoned for contempt of court. Also, injunctions were used to prohibit attempts to organize employees into unions when they were working under yellow-dog contracts.

In 1890, Congress passed the Sherman Antitrust Act, which prohibited restraints of trade and made business monopolies illegal. Some judges thought this act also made unions illegal. For example, in the *Danbury Hatters Case,* the U.S. Supreme Court held that the Sherman Antitrust Act *did*

TEACH

The historical relationship between labor laws and unions sometimes has been hostile. Discuss: **strike, breach of contract, yellow-dog contracts, unions, ex parte injunction, Sherman Antitrust Act, monopolies,** and **Clayton Act.**

APPLY

On the chalkboard, draw a cause-and-effect chart of the events that sparked the labor laws on pp. 451–452. Have students add the information to complete it. **Guided Practice**

Multicultural Highlights

José Yglesias, a Cuban American author, was a teenager during the Depression when factory owners cut hours and fired the workers they thought were Communists or union organizers. The remaining workers went on strike. Afterwards, the strike committee was convicted of conspiracy and went to jail for a year. None of the workers got their jobs back. Ask: **Would the actions of these factory owners be legal today?** (No)

RETEACH Have students use the eight terms listed in the TEACH section on p. 451 to create a crossword puzzle and answer key. Exchange papers and complete the puzzle.

ENRICH Media: Time-Warner has produced *Time Almanac,* a CD-ROM that contains more than 5,000 articles from *Time* from its inception in 1923 to 1989. If you have access to this resource, have students use it to create a timeline of the labor movement in the United States.

Ethics Issue

Have students write a paragraph, using a computer, if possible, on the ethical implications of **yellow-dog contracts** and **ex parte injunctions.** (Employees often were not financially able to reject such contracts, decisions based on just one side are more likely to be wrong, and so on)

Independent Practice

TEACH

The National Labor Relations Board (NLRB), resolves many labor problems. The NLRB administers the rights and duties given to workers, employees, and unions.

APPLY

Help students to create a flowchart to show the legal actions Joyce could take to get her job back. (See PROBLEM on top of p. 452.) **Guided Practice**

In small groups, have students list concerns that a terminated, but newly reinstated, employee might have. (Answers may include job security, pay raises, promotions, harassment, and so on.) **Independent Practice**

apply to unions. Congress responded by enacting the Clayton Act, which exempted unions from the Sherman Antitrust Act. The history of U.S. labor law reveals great hostility toward unions.

WHAT IS THE NATIONAL LABOR RELATIONS BOARD?

PROBLEM

Joyce was a union member who frequently complained about working conditions. Even though she did more work than was required of her, she was fired. When she asked why, her boss stated that it was because of her pro-union, anti-management attitude. Must Joyce and/or her union go to court to get this matter settled?

Today, most labor relations problems are resolved through a federal administrative agency instead of through the courts and Congress. That agency, the National Labor Relations Board (NLRB), administers the rights and duties given to workers, employers, and unions. It was created by the National Labor Relations Act. Representatives of the union, employers, and individual workers are entitled to file charges and to take part in hearings before the NLRB. A party that is dissatisfied with the board's order may seek review in the federal courts.

In the problem, Joyce need not go to court. She or her union can file a complaint with the NLRB. The board would probably order the employer to reinstate her.

HOW ARE UNIONS ESTABLISHED?

PROBLEM

Joan felt that her employer did not treat its employees fairly. When she asked the employer to address issues of sexual harassment in the workplace and unsafe working conditions, she was ignored. When she talked with other employees in her machine shop, she discovered that her views were widely shared. Joan decided that the only way to get management to listen was to organize the machine shop workers into a union. Can Joan do this? If so, how could she go about it? Who would be in the union?

Employees may organize into unions and bargain collectively with their employers. Or they may voluntarily decide not to organize into unions and

ASSESS

Learning Objective 2 Have student volunteers read aloud the three sections of the TEACH activity outline students copied in their notebooks. One at a time, have the class identify the information in their text (pp. 452–454) and add supporting details.

bargain individually instead. To establish union representation, workers need to complete a series of steps. One step involves determining which employees should be represented together. Within a unionized company, any group of employees whose employment contract is negotiated together is called a **bargaining unit.** It is common for workers in the same *department* to be in the same bargaining unit. In other instances, persons *doing similar work* in different departments may be in the same bargaining unit. For example, all the janitors working for General Motors might be in the same bargaining unit. Sometimes one union represents several bargaining units in negotiating with a single employer. Each unit is entitled to select its own union to bargain with the employer. Thus, in the problem, all the workers in Joan's machine shop could become a bargaining unit.

To establish a union, the organizers must obtain employee signatures on forms asking the NLRB to conduct a representation election. At least 30 percent of the employees in the bargaining unit must sign the form. If the 30-percent requirement is met, the NLRB will conduct hearings to determine the bargaining unit and to decide who is eligible to vote in the representation election. To select a bargaining representative (i.e., a union), the NLRB conducts a secret vote of the workers in the bargaining unit. Majority vote governs. If a union is selected, it becomes the exclusive negotiator for all the employees in the bargaining unit. The NLRB will then acknowledge that union as the exclusive bargaining agent. This is called **certification.** If the union does not obtain a majority, it may not call for another election for one year.

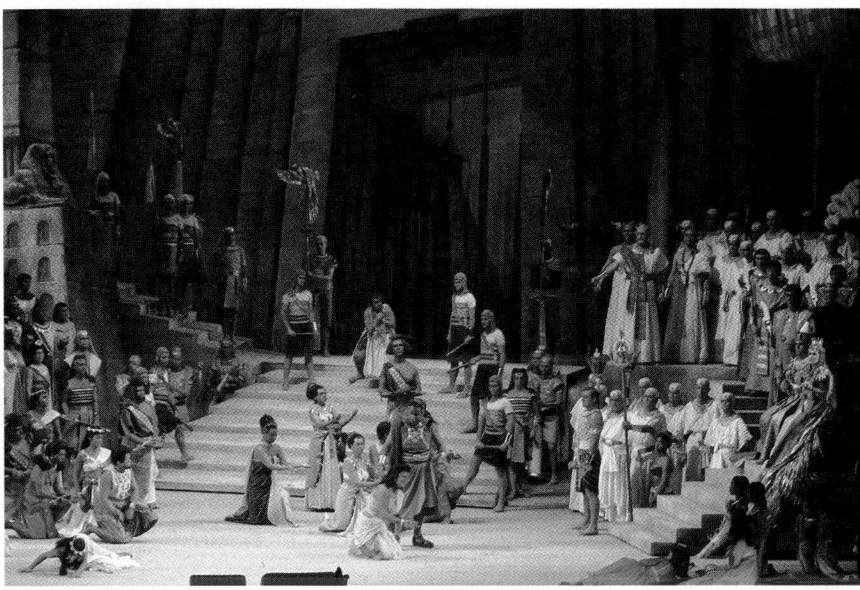

▼ TEACH

On an overhead transparency or on the chalkboard, copy this outline of the steps in establishing a union. Have students copy it in their notebooks.

A. To Establish the Bargaining Unit

1. Determine which employees should be represented

2. Informally determine whether a majority wants union representation

B. To Initiate a Certification Vote

1. Organizers must obtain signatures of at least 30% of employees in the bargaining unit

2. If the 30% requirement is met, NLRB conducts hearings; decides who can vote

C. To Become Exclusive Bargaining Agent

1. NLRB conducts secret vote of workers

2. If union selected, NLRB acknowledges it as bargaining agent

▼ APPLY

Thinking Critically Through Visuals

To what kind of union might these workers belong? (Answers may include the Screen Actors' Guild and so on.)

▼RETEACH

Have students use the information on pp. 452–454 and the outline they copied in their notebooks from the TEACH activity on p. 453 to create their own flowcharts to illustrate how unions are established.

Have students put themselves in Joyce's situation in the PROBLEM (top of p. 452). Using a computer, if possible, ask students to write and file a written complaint with the NLRB. Display students' work on a bulletin board called *Standing Up for One's Rights.*

Before displaying the overhead transparency, *Employees in the Bargaining Unit,* cover *30%* and *50%,* and their brackets. Ask students to determine how many employees in a plant of 50 would have to sign the form for the NLRB to conduct a certification election and how many employees would need to vote in favor of establishing and certifying a union. (15 and 26)

Guided Practice

On a flip chart or on the chalkboard, write the following information:

PERCENTAGE OF TOTAL WORKFORCE AFFILIATED WITH UNIONS

Year	Percentage
1930	11.6
1935	13.2
1940	26.9
1945	35.5
1950	31.5
1955	33.2
1960	31.4
1965	28.4
1970	27.3
1975	25.5
1980	21.9
1985	18.0
1990	16.1

Distribute graph paper or have students use spreadsheet or graphics programs to create a line graph illustrating this information. Discuss the reasons for the growth and decline of labor unions. Ask: **What do you foresee as the future of labor unions in the United States? Why?** (Answers may include that there appears to be a recent small, but steady, decline.)

Media **Independent Practice**

For six weeks, union organizers conducted an intensive campaign to get workers in a particular bargaining unit of the MGM Cabinet Works to join the union. Picketers carried placards that read "MGM IS UNFAIR TO ORGANIZED LABOR." They did this even though the company paid the union-scale wage or higher in all categories of work. An election was finally held under the guidance of the NLRB to determine whether the union should have the exclusive right to represent the workers. By a close margin, the workers in the bargaining unit rejected the union. Under NLRB rules, the union now may not picket or call for another election for at least one year.

If 30 percent of the employees decide they want *different* representation, they can petition the NLRB to conduct a **decertification election.** At this election, employees can reject union representation or select a different union. If a majority rejects representation, workers will negotiate individually with the employers.

Managerial employees are not permitted to vote or to be represented by a union. This is because their duties differ from those of the nonmanagerial employees whom they direct. Moreover, the company owners should be able to rely on the undivided loyalty of their managers in negotiations with unions.

▼ HOW DOES UNION CERTIFICATION AFFECT EMPLOYEES?

PROBLEM

Phil was an employee of Long Distance Trucking, Inc. Union organizers collected signatures from 30 percent of the employees in Phil's department and the NLRB conducted an election. Phil voted against having a union, but by a majority vote of the bargaining unit, the employees chose the union. Phil did not like the contract the union negotiated because the contract required that union dues be deducted from his pay even though Phil was not required to join the union. Phil objected. Further, he tried to make an individual contract with the company. What rights does Phil have in this situation?

Whether or not they are union members, all workers in each bargaining unit are bound by the collective agreement reached between the union and the employer. Thus, in the problem, Phil could not negotiate an individual employment contract with his employer.

▼ ASSESS

Learning Objective 3 Have students reread the PROBLEM on p. 454. Then, ask each student to write a response to Phil, explaining why he could not negotiate an individual employment contract with Long Distance Trucking, Inc. (Answers may include that Phil—despite having voted against the union and the union contract—is bound by the collective agreement reached between the established union and the agency shop.)

Workers are not required to join a union unless the employer has agreed to have a union shop. In a **union shop,** nonunion employees may be hired, but they must join the union within a stated maximum period, usually thirty days. The agency shop is a variation of the union shop. In the **agency shop,** employees are not required to join the union, but if they do not, they must nevertheless pay union dues as a condition of employment. In the problem, Phil is working in an agency shop. The union, in effect, acts as the employees' agent in dealing with the employer. In the **open shop,** employees are not required to belong to a union or to pay dues. The union bargains collectively with the employer and agrees to an employment contract binding union and nonunion workers. In the **closed shop,** the employer agrees that workers must belong to the recognized union before they can be hired. The closed shop was outlawed by the Labor Management Relations Act.

Right-to-work laws have been enacted by a number of states. Such laws prohibit compulsory union membership and ban the union shop, closed shop, and agency shop. In states with right-to-work laws, unions may function, but only with open shops.

▼ WHAT ARE UNFAIR LABOR PRACTICES BY MANAGEMENT?

PROBLEM

Mulroy worked in a factory where leather goods were manufactured. During lunch hour and after work, Mulroy was active as an organizer for a labor union that sought to be recognized as the sole bargaining agent for the employees. Mulroy's employer said she paid better than union-scale wages and did not want to deal with a union. She fired Mulroy because of her organizing efforts. Was Mulroy's employer legally permitted to do so?

The Wagner Act and other federal and state statutes require that employers treat unions fairly by allowing them to organize. These statutes also require that management engage in good-faith negotiations (i.e., collective bargaining) with unions. These laws define certain actions of employers as **unfair labor practices** and prohibit such actions. The following are unfair labor practices.

1. It is an unfair labor practice for management to interfere with employees' efforts to form, join, or assist unions. Such interference can take a variety of forms. For example, it would be an unfair labor

▼ **TEACH**

On the chalkboard, write the following terms: **union shop, agency shop, open shop, closed shop,** and **right-to-work laws.** Explain each term and its effect on employees.

▼ **APPLY**

On an overhead transparency or on the chalkboard, draw a four-column chart and write across the top of it the names of the four kinds of shops: **union, agency, open,** and **closed**. Have students complete the chart with descriptions of each.

Guided Practice

Divide students into four groups and assign one of the four shops to each group: **union, agency, open,** or **closed.** Have each group create a persuasive poster to illustrate the benefits of its shop to employees. Display and have students vote on the best poster. **Independent Practice**

▼ **TEACH**

Tell students that the Wagner Act and other statutes require that employers treat unions fairly by allowing them to organize. On the chalkboard, write the four unfair labor practices by management (pp. 455–456) and discuss each.

▼**RETEACH** Give each student four index cards on which to summarize each of the four kinds of union shops. As a group, have students combine their notes to create a graphic organizer illustrating how union certification affects employees.

▼**ENRICH** Have students explain in writing, using a computer, if possible, how the certification process is an example of the axiom, "*the majority rules.*" Ask: **Why is it important that a union represent all employees, including those who are not members?**

▼ APPLY

Have students respond orally to the following question: **What, in your opinion, was the greatest benefit labor, or workers, received from the Wagner Act and other statutes that define and prohibit unfair labor practices?** (Answers may include the legal right to organize, and so on.) **Guided Practice**

To help visual learners or students with reading comprehension difficulties, you may wish to preview, then show, *Norma Rae*, a videotape from Warner Bros. This video portrays how job conflict affects personal lives.

Divide the class into four groups. Assign each group one of the four unfair labor practices by management (pp. 455–456) and have those students role play it. Have the class identify which practice was depicted.

Independent Practice

practice to refuse to deduct union dues for union members, to disrupt organizing meetings, or to threaten to fire employees to keep them from organizing a union. Similarly, employers may not threaten to stop operations, replace workers with machines, or move the factory just to avoid unionization.

2 It is an unfair labor practice for management to dominate a union or to give it financial or other support. This preserves the ability of unions to represent the interests of employees. In the past, some companies tried to influence certification elections. Sometimes, they wanted the least aggressive union to win. Other times they tried to win favor with union leaders by contributing money to their election campaigns.

3 It is an unfair labor practice for management to encourage or to discourage union membership. Employers may not threaten to blacklist employees. Employers **blacklist** employees by placing their names on a list of pro-union persons and sending it to other employers with the purpose of making it difficult for the employees to find work.

Kent and Rimski were trying to get their co-workers to join a clerical union. The manager of their department threatened to fire them. He also threatened to blacklist them by sending their names as "known trouble-makers" to a trade association for distribution to other employers. Because of these acts of the department manager, the employer was guilty of two unfair labor practices.

Similarly, it is an unfair labor practice to discharge or otherwise discriminate against an employee for filing charges of labor law violations or for testifying about such charges. In the problem, Mulroy's employer was guilty of an unfair labor practice. She could be required to rehire Mulroy and to pay Mulroy the wages lost while Mulroy was barred from the job.

4 It is an unfair labor practice for management to refuse to bargain in good faith with the union. This means management must participate actively in attempting to reach an agreement. It must make honest and reasonable proposals and must listen to the arguments of the union. Management must attempt to find a common ground with the union. However, the law does not require that management *agree* to union proposal; it need only engage in good-faith bargaining.

▼ ASSESS

Learning Objective 4 Have students orally summarize the seven unfair labor practices by unions (pp. 457–458), listing them one by one on the chalkboard, a flip chart, or an overhead transparency as each is offered. Review students' answers for accuracy, then instruct them to copy the information in their notebooks or law journals.

WHAT ARE UNFAIR LABOR PRACTICES BY UNIONS?

PROBLEM

After Paul had voted against forming a union, he tried to negotiate directly with management. He also complained loudly to other employees about how much money was being deducted from his paycheck for union dues. In response, some union officials went to management and asked that Paul be fired. The union officials implied that labor negotiations would go more smoothly if management agreed to this request. As a result, Paul was fired. Does Paul have a claim against the union?

The Taft-Hartley Act and other statutes require that unions treat employees and management fairly. The actions described below are unfair labor practices by unions.

1. It is an unfair labor practice for unions to refuse to bargain collectively in good faith with the employer.

2. It is an unfair labor practice for unions to attempt to force an employer to pay for featherbedding. **Featherbedding** is payment for services not performed. If the work is performed, there is no featherbedding even though the work may be unnecessary.

3. It is an unfair labor practice for uncertified unions to **picket** (i.e., patrol the employer's property with signs) to try to force the employer to bargain with that union. Certifying elections are the appropriate method for compelling an employer to bargain with a particular union. It is also an unfair labor practice for a union to picket in an effort to force employees to select that union as their representative within twelve months after losing a valid representation election.

4. It is an unfair labor practice for unions to engage in certain kinds of strikes and boycotts. A **strike** is a work stoppage by a group to force an employer to give in to union demands. (Its counterpart is a **lockout**, which occurs when an employer temporarily closes down operations to induce the union to agree to the employer's proposals.) Most strikes are legal if they are conducted without violence.

5. It is an unfair labor practice for unions to require payment of an excessive or discriminatory fee for initiation into the union.

TEACH

Tell students that the Taft-Hartley Act as well as other statutes require that unions treat employees and management fairly. On the chalkboard or a flip chart, identify, one at a time, each of the seven unfair labor practices by unions, as noted on pp. 457–458.

APPLY

Writing Connections

Language Arts/ Psychology
Have students read parts of a biography of a labor leader and, using a computer, if possible, write a book report or summary. Possible subjects are John L. Lewis, Walter Reuther, Mother Jones, Jimmy Hoffa, A. Philip Randolph, David Dubinsky, and César Chávez. After following standard book report form, students should concentrate on the psychological character traits of the subject. Have them consider what made him or her the kind of person who could become a leader in the labor movement.

Independent Practice

RETEACH Divide the class in two. Have each group create an illustrative poster. Have one group alert workers to unfair labor practices by management and the other group alert management to unfair labor practices by unions.

ENRICH

Divide students into four groups. Have each group script, present, and videotape an interview in which an action by management, perceived as an unfair labor practice, is disputed by workers.

To help students understand what the Taft-Hartley Act and other similar statutes do, in a positive sense, have students reword each of the seven practices in the affirmative. For example, for the first point, students might respond, "Unions will bargain in good faith with employers." Correct any misconceptions.

Guided Practice

Show the videotape, *Union Democracy* (color, 30 min.), which shows the Wagner and Landrum-Griffin acts in use. Contact Merrimack Films, P.O. Box 127, No. Chelmsford, MA 01863.

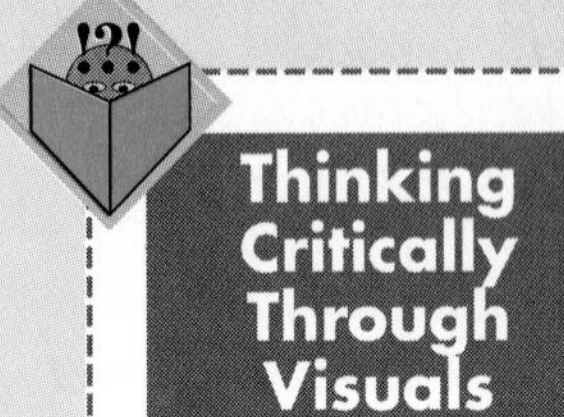

The Union Bill of Rights was written for the protection of union members. **Under what circumstances do union members have the right to use secret ballots?** (Answers may include election of union officials, setting dues, and so on.)

6. It is an unfair labor practice for unions to force or to attempt to force employees to support that union or to restrain employees from supporting competing unions. A union may, however, try to persuade employees to support it.

7. It is an unfair labor practice for unions to cause or to attempt to cause an employer to discriminate against an employee because of union-related activities. Thus, in the problem, Paul could sue the union for engaging in an unfair labor practice.

After congressional testimony about corruption and violence in a few unions, Congress passed legislation designed to limit union corruption. The Landrum-Griffin Act requires that unions operate in a manner that gives members full voice in decision making. The law was intended to ensure that union members themselves could correct abuses of power by entrenched leadership through free and open elections. Figure 22-1 describes rights that union members have in the operation of their unions.

Figure 22-1
Unions are now required to operate in the best interest of their members rather than for the benefit of the union leadership. This "bill of rights" for union members was established by the Landrum-Griffin Act in 1959.

UNION BILL OF RIGHTS	
ELECTIONS:	Union members have the right to equal opportunities for nominating candidates for union offices, and the right to vote by secret ballot in union elections.
MEETINGS:	Union members have the right to meet with other members to express views about candidates or other business.
DUES:	Union members have the right to vote by secret ballot on increases in dues, initiation fees, and assessment levies.
LAWSUITS:	Union members have the right to sue; to testify in court or before any administrative agency or legislative body; and to communicate with any legislator.
DISCIPLINE:	Union members are protected from union disciplinary action, unless the member is served with written charges, given time to prepare a defense, and afforded a fair hearing. (Members may be disciplined for nonpayment of dues without such elaborate due process.)
MANAGEMENT:	Union members have the right to obtain information about union policies and financial matters; to recover misappropriated union funds for the union; to inspect union contracts; and to be informed of provisions of this act.

▼ ASSESS

Learning Objective 5 Have students orally summarize the **collective bargaining** process. Then, have them create a two-column chart on the chalkboard, a flip chart, or an overhead transparency with the headings **Labor** and **Management**. For each, have students add the factors that influence the bargaining power of each side. Verify responses, then have students copy the charts in their notebooks.

WHAT IS COLLECTIVE BARGAINING?

PROBLEM

Ace Automotive Accessories, Inc., manufactures automobile seats for several U.S. car companies. All of its manufacturing employees are represented by the Amalgamated Union of Michigan. Historically, labor and Ace management negotiated five-year contracts. The current round of negotiations was unsuccessful. During one session, union and management representatives began swearing at each other. A chair was thrown across the bargaining table. Because of these incidents and the unlikelihood of reaching an agreement, Ace refused to continue negotiating. It said it was prepared to continue paying workers under the old contract but that it was unwilling to negotiate with the current leaders of the union. What alternatives are available to solve this problem?

Collective bargaining is the process whereby the union and the employer negotiate a contract of employment that binds both sides. Unions are represented by negotiators of their own choosing. The company is typically represented by its management or its lawyers. Pay and fringe benefits are the most commonly negotiated issues. However, grievance procedures, hours, overtime, pensions, health care, working conditions, and safety issues are also frequently negotiated. An employer is not required to bargain over such issues as product prices or designs, plant location, or quality of products. These are strictly management matters even though they do affect the company's ability to pay wages.

A variety of factors influence the bargaining power of labor and management. These include the company's profitability, availability of substitute workers, prevailing labor rates, the competitiveness of the industry, and foreign competition. The union has legal power flowing from the ability to strike, while the employer has legal power flowing from the ability to lock out. But there is great economic pressure on both sides. If there is either a strike or a lockout, employee wages usually cease and production often stops. This economic pressure is reinforced by the legal requirement that both management and labor bargain with each other. Failure to bargain is an unfair labor practice. Thus, in the problem, Ace committed an unfair labor practice by refusing to continue negotiations. The union could file a complaint with the NLRB, which might issue an order compelling management to negotiate in good faith.

TEACH

Tell students that **collective bargaining** is the process whereby the union and the employer negotiate a contract of employment that binds both sides. Describe the factors that influence the bargaining power of both labor and management. Define the terms **deadlocked** and **mediation.**

APPLY

Divide students into two groups: labor (union members) and management. Have students participate in a role-play or discussion of collective bargaining over the issue of safety in the workplace. As the instructor, role-play the mediator, if the negotiations become deadlocked. **Guided Practice**

Divide the class into groups of four or five. Assign the following roles to each group: researcher (one or two) to choose a contemporary, local labor-management issue and to provide information on it; union member to represent the union's views; management representative to express management's views; mediator to speak with both sides to achieve compromise. Have each group engage in collective bargaining techniques to resolve the issue before it. Videotape the negotiations, if possible.

Cooperative Learning

RETEACH

Media: Have students use a desktop publishing program, if possible, to create a brochure explaining to a new employee what collective bargaining is, commonly negotiated issues in the company, and factors that influence the bargaining power of labor and management. Display students' work.

ENRICH

Divide students into two groups and have them debate the topic: *Strikes and Lockouts: Which Is More Powerful?* Have student observers track key issues of the debate and judge the most convincing arguments.

▼ TEACH

On the chalkboard, write the terms **economic strike, unfair labor practice strike, cooling-off period,** and **national emergency strike**. Define and discuss each term. Use the terms to discuss an employer's possible responses to the different kinds of union strikes mentioned on p. 460.

▼ APPLY

Personal Perspectives

Ask members of the class to share any personal recollections of strikes, or experiences of a family member that he or she would be willing to share. **Guided Practice**

Have students hypothesize why some union workers have greater freedom to strike than do others, who also may have sound reasons to strike. Then, ask: **Which of the following could create a national emergency? A steel strike?** (Possibly, since many other industries depend on steel.) **An automobile strike?** (No) **Independent Practice**

Collective bargaining sometimes breaks down or becomes deadlocked. Negotiations are **deadlocked** when the union and employer cannot agree on important issues. When this happens, a governmental representative may try to bring the parties together to settle their differences. In **mediation** (also known as conciliation), a mediator (conciliator) talks with both sides and attempts to achieve a compromise. However, such a person has no power to compel agreement.

▼ WHEN MAY A UNION STRIKE?

PROBLEM

Zeus Computers was deadlocked with the union representing its service technicians. After attempts at mediation, the parties were still far apart on the pay rate for overtime. The union stated that if an agreement was not reached within two weeks, it would strike. Zeus responded that it would hire workers to replace the striking union members. It also stated that those replaced would not be rehired at the end of the strike. Can Zeus legally do this?

An **economic strike** is one where the dispute is over wages, hours, or conditions of employment. An employer may respond to an economic strike by giving any striking employee's job to someone else. Thus, in the problem, Zeus could give replacement workers the jobs of striking union members. However, when there is an economic strike, unions commonly refuse to settle unless striking members are rehired. On the other hand, if the strike is over an unfair labor practice by management, the employer may not permanently give the striking worker's job to someone else. When such an **unfair labor practice strike** is over, the employer must reinstate the striking worker even if this requires transferring or discharging the replacement.

Strikes of public (i.e., governmental) employees are generally prohibited even though such workers may unionize and bargain collectively. Sometimes public workers (including police officers, teachers, and fire fighters) strike, or stay away from work claiming illness. In such cases, the workers and their leaders are subject to court orders directing them to return to work. If they ignore the court order, they may be fired or jailed.

The president of the United States has the power to obtain an injunction in federal court forcing a **cooling-off period** of eighty days when a national emergency strike is threatened. A **national emergency strike** is one that involves national defense or major industries, or would have a substantial effect on the nation's economy.

▼ ASSESS

Learning Objective 5 Have students review the text sections, *When May a Union Strike? and When May a Union Boycott?* (pp. 461–462). Have students use this information to clip pictures from newspapers and magazines to illustrate each section on a two-part bulletin board with the same titles.

Thinking Critically Through Visuals

Firefighters are public employees subject to the no-strike rule. Why, do you think, are firefighters subject to this rule? (Answers may include that a strike by firefighters could result in major property damage or loss of life.)

WHEN MAY A UNION BOYCOTT?

PROBLEM

A union was on strike against a New York manufacturer of women's dresses. Members of the union set up picket lines at retail stores that bought dresses from the manufacturer and tried to persuade their customers not to buy from the stores because they dealt with the New York manufacturer. Is this legal?

A **boycott** is usually a refusal to buy or to use someone's products or services. A **primary boycott** involves the employees' refusals to buy their *employer's* products or services. Primary boycotts are legal. Typically, they are accompanied by a strike and by picketing at the employer's place of business. Usually the striking employees also encourage others, such as customers and suppliers, to boycott the employer.

Sometimes, however, striking employees try to get customers to stop buying the products or services of a third party. Such action against a third party is known as a **secondary boycott.** It is generally illegal. In the problem, the action was an illegal secondary boycott by the union. The picketing would have been legal if the picketers had urged customers of the

TEACH

On a transparency, create a graphic organizer to explain the difference between a **primary boycott** and a **secondary boycott.**

APPLY

Have students research labor-management relations topics, such as collective bargaining, strikes, and boycotts. Evaluate the effectiveness of these methods in achieving desired goals, the advantages and disadvantages for workers, and their effect on the community. **Guided Practice**

Have groups of students prepare written arguments, cartoons, collages, raps, posters, or some other expression to support or oppose a particular boycott.

Independent Practice

RETEACH Pair students and have them use the following terms to create *Jeopardy*-style questions to ask each other: **economic strike, unfair labor practice strike, cooling-off period, national emergency strike, boycott, primary boycott,** and **secondary boycott.**

ENRICH Using a computer, if possible, have students write a short essay explaining when it may be more advantageous for union members to strike rather than boycott an employer's product.

Preventing Legal Difficulties

Tell students that the law is very clear on the rights and duties of employees and employers. It also offers the employee, who is a member of a union, protection from corrupt leadership. Have students create mobiles of important points to remember using pictures from newspapers or magazines, clip-art software, or a paint or draw program, if possible, for their project.

Hang the mobiles in class.

▼ CLOSE

Before displaying the overhead transparency, *The Seesaw of Labor-Management Legislation*, mask out the labels, *Labor* and *Management*. Based on their understanding of labor-relations legislation, have students determine

on which side of the seesaw the labels belong.

Assign the following end-of-chapter materials:
Student text review activities, pp. 463–467
Workbook, pp. 69–70
Chapter Test

Chapter *MicroExam*

stores to stop buying only dresses made by the New York manufacturer, not all products.

Although generally illegal, secondary boycotts are legal when the National Labor Relations Act, or similar state statutes, do not apply. This would be the case with farm labor in most states. Thus, farm workers engaged in labor disputes with farmers have encouraged consumers to not buy anything at grocery stores carrying nonunion grapes and lettuce. This secondary boycott is legal because the farm workers are not covered by the National Labor Relations Act.

Preventing Legal Difficulties

If you are an employee, remember...

1. You and your co-workers generally have the legal right to organize into unions and bargain collectively with your employer.
2. An employer may not legally discharge you for engaging in union activities. An employer that does so is guilty of an unfair labor practice.
3. If you belong to a union, you have a right to vote for your officers in secret elections and to see accurate and timely information on union finances and activities.

If you are an employer, remember...

1. Unions are legal. If they represent your workers, you should cooperate with them in good faith for the common good of all parties involved.
2. You may not discharge or otherwise discriminate against your workers because they join a union or because they refuse to join a union (unless there is a legal union shop).
3. You must bargain collectively in good faith with representatives of any union chosen by a majority of the workers in each bargaining unit. You are not obligated to make any concessions, such as boosting wages, reducing hours, or changing conditions of employment. However, if you refuse to compromise and make some concessions, there may be a strike, and it may continue indefinitely. If it is an economic strike (for higher wages, for example), you are free to hire permanent replacements for the strikers and to resume production, although this is not always a feasible alternative. If it is an unfair labor practice strike, you may not hire permanent replacements for the strikers.

REVIEWING IMPORTANT POINTS

1 The federal government has the power to regulate the employment of persons in enterprises engaged in interstate commerce (i.e., commerce between two or more states).

2 The NLRB is the federal agency charged with administering labor relations laws. It can accept complaints, conduct hearings, and issue orders. Its decisions can be appealed to the federal courts.

3 The NLRB will conduct a certification election if it receives petitioning signatures from 30 percent of the employees in a bargaining unit. If a majority of employees vote for the union, it becomes their exclusive bargaining unit.

4 In a union shop, employees must join the union, usually within thirty days after being employed. In an agency shop, they need not join the union but must pay union dues. In an open shop, employees are not required to join the union or to pay union dues.

5 Common unfair labor practices by management include interfering with employees trying to form a union, favoring one union over another, trying to dominate a union, discriminating against union members, and refusing to bargain in good faith.

6 Common unfair labor practices by unions include refusing to bargain in good faith, featherbedding, picketing an employer when the union is not the exclusive bargaining agent, forcing employees to support the union, and discriminating against employees who do not support the union.

7 If a strike is over economic issues, the employer may hire permanent replacements for the jobs held by strikers. If the strike is over an unfair labor practice, permanent replacements cannot be hired.

8 Primary boycotts are directed against the employer; secondary boycotts are directed against a third party.

9 Primary boycotts are legal; secondary boycotts are often illegal.

STRENGTHENING YOUR LEGAL VOCABULARY

Match each term with the statement that best defines that term. Some terms may not be used.

agency shop
bargaining unit
blacklist
boycott
certification
closed shop

Strengthening Your Legal Vocabulary

1 decertification election
2 right-to-work laws
3 union shop
4 primary boycott
5 strike
6 picket
7 featherbedding
8 mediation
9 lockout
10 open shop

collective bargaining	open shop
cooling-off period	picket
deadlock	primary boycott
decertification election	right-to-work laws
economic strike	secondary boycott
ex parte injunction	strike
featherbedding	unfair labor practices
lockout	unfair labor practice strike
mediation	union shop
national emergency strikes	yellow-dog contracts

1. A process by which a union ceases to be the exclusive bargaining agent for employees.
2. State laws that ban both the union shop and the closed shop.
3. Establishment in which all employees must belong to the union, either when they are hired or within a specified time after they are hired.
4. Boycott by striking employees that is directed mainly against their employer.
5. Concerted stoppage of work to force an employer to yield to union demands.
6. Patrolling by union members with signs alongside the premises of the employer during a labor dispute.
7. Requiring an employer to pay for services not performed.
8. Attempt by a neutral third party to achieve a compromise between disputing parties.
9. Employer's shutdown of operations to bring pressure on employees.
10. Establishment in which nonunion members do not pay union dues.

▼ APPLYING LAW TO EVERYDAY LIFE

1. 
Sharpe was a union leader. In the midst of intense negotiations, she was approached by a stranger who engaged her in a discussion. They agreed to meet for lunch. At lunch, the stranger offered her $20,000 if she would support a management proposal. Although Sharpe knew this was an unfair labor practice, she also recognized that it would be difficult to prove. Would she be morally justified in accepting the money and supporting the proposal? Would she be justified in accepting the money without supporting the proposal?

Applying Law to Everyday Life

1. ETHICS ISSUE Sharpe should not support the proposal in exchange for the bribe. If she did so, she would be acting only for herself and thus unethically.

In evaluating the consequences, she might count herself as positively affected (financially) by the bribe. But those negatively affected are more numerous. They would include all the members of her union who would be injured by the proposal. Another important consequence is that she would be encouraging future attempts to subvert the negotiating process. This may negatively affect many more people. So a consequentialist would reject the bribe as ethically wrong.

Many consequentialists would also argue that Sharpe isn't really benefiting by accepting the bribe. They might argue that by allowing herself to be corrupted she does herself more injury than she benefits herself with the $20,000.

Deontologists would say that accepting the bribe is conduct which would make a lie of her promises to act as a good union leader. It is therefore inherently wrong. (See Chapter 2.)

2 ETHICS ISSUE Alonzo owns his own machine shop and has several close friends among his employees. The NLRB is about to conduct a certification election. Alonzo knows he could persuade his employee friends to spread rumors that if the union is certified, he would move his shop out of the country. He is also certain that such rumors could never be traced back to him. Would it be ethical for Alonzo to spread such rumors if they would cause the union to lose the election and allow him to make an extra $60,000 per year?

3 Jacob was unhappy with his working conditions and wanted to start a union. He knew many other employees were also sympathetic to the idea of union representation. How many co-workers must support an election before the NLRB will conduct a certification election? How many must vote to support a union for it to become the exclusive bargaining agent?

4 When a national union sent organizers to try to persuade Baker's workers to join the union, Baker called three of her most trusted employees to her office. She urged them to organize a new union limited to company employees. She offered to provide the union with office space and time for officers to conduct union business. Baker then gave the three workers money to buy printed notices and refreshments for an organization meeting. Was Baker's action legal?

5 In the first year of its operation, a local union, attempting to increase membership, threatened to slash the tires of nonunion members. Union members followed nonunion members to their homes and picketed there. The union fined a member for accusing the union of an unfair labor practice. Were these actions legal?

6 O'Donnell felt that management at the company where he worked was engaging in unfair labor practices. He complained in public and filed charges with the NLRB. Those charges were dismissed. Later he was called to testify about charges filed by the union. O'Donnell's bosses hinted that they would get even. About two months later, the company decided to abolish O'Donnell's job. Does he have any recourse?

7 Joann and the other members of her union were striking for higher wages. Management made a public announcement that workers who failed to report on the following Monday would be permanently replaced. Can an employer permanently replace striking union members? Can a union continue striking until the employer agrees to rehire the striking employees?

2 

For many of the same reasons discussed in question 1, Alonzo should not spread the false rumor. In both consequentialism and deontology it is wrong. It hurts more people than it helps and it is inherently wrong because it is a form of lying. (See Chapter 2.)

3 Thirty percent of the employees in Jacob's bargaining unit must support a certification election for the NLRB to conduct an election. To win certification, a union needs a majority vote. (p. 453)

4 No; Baker's action violated the National Labor Relations Act, as amended by the Labor Management Relations Act, by favoring one union over another. (p. 456)

5 No; All were unfair labor practices under the National Labor Relations Act. (pp. 457–458)

6 Yes; The company's actions appear to be in retaliation for O'Donnell's exercise of his rights as a union member. Therefore the company has engaged in an unfair labor practice. (pp. 455–456)

7 Joann is engaged in an economic strike, not an unfair labor practice strike. Therefore, she can be replaced by her employer with a permanent employee. On the other hand, her union can continue striking until management agrees to rehire all the strikers. (p. 460)

8 No; A mediator has no power to compel the parties to sign an agreement. As long as Titan has negotiated in good faith, it may reject Pax's recommendations. (p. 460)

9 Yes; In many states, public employees do not have the right to strike. Therefore, if the city of Locale is located in such a state, the strike would be illegal. (p. 460)

10 Yes; Boycotting stores which carry General televisions is secondary boycotting. Secondary boycotts are illegal when the National Labor Relations Act governs the parties. (p. 461)

8 A strike at the Titan Stone Works was in its fifth week when Pax, a federal mediator, was called in. After long discussions with both sides, she persuaded the union representatives to accept certain terms. The terms were a major concession on the part of the union but seemed to her to be fair to all parties involved, including the buying public. Titan rejected the terms even though it was financially able to meet every demand. Can Pax compel Titan to sign the proposed contract?

9 Employees of the city of Locale became dissatisfied with their working conditions. As a result, 35 percent petitioned the NLRB for a representation election. They established a local, unaffiliated union which won the election. When they were unsuccessful in their negotiations with the city council, they went on strike. Is any conduct by these employees illegal?

10 The Electrical Workers Union of Westport represented most of the assembly line workers in the General TV Plant. In a dispute over wages, the union went on strike and began picketing the plant. They also picketed nearby stores that carried the General brand of televisions, asking that shoppers not purchase them. Is any of this conduct illegal?

Solving Case Problems

1 No; The provision is illegal because it restricts the voice of the union members in selecting union leadership. (p. 458)

2 The company is right. Certain persons, such as the secretary of the president of a company, or those considered part of the management team, are not employees within the meaning of the National Labor Relations Act. (p. 454)

▼ SOLVING CASE PROBLEMS

1 The United Steelworkers of America, a national union, had a provision in its constitution that imposed requirements to be satisfied before a member could run for leadership positions in local affiliates. The limitation was that to be eligible to be a local officer, the union member must have attended at least one-half of the regular local meetings for the three years prior to the election. Is this restriction legal? (*Local 3489 United Steelworkers of America v. Usery,* 97 S. Ct. 611)

2 Mary Weatherman was the personal secretary to the president of Hendricks County Rural Electric Membership Corporation. One of her friends, who also worked for the same firm, was involved in an industrial accident that resulted in the loss of one of his arms. Shortly after the accident, he was dismissed. Mary, concerned about the plight of her friend, signed a petition seeking his reinstatement. Because of this conduct Mary was also discharged. Mary filed a charge with the NLRB, alleging an unfair labor practice. The company defended itself by claiming that because Mary was a confidential secretary, she was not covered by the National Labor Relations Act's definition of "employee." Who is right, Mary or the company? (*NLRB v. Hendricks County,* 102 S. Ct. 216)

3 During a union organizing campaign at Portage Plastics Company, some members began wearing union buttons on the job. Because a but-

ton fell into a grinder and caused loss of material and because of the increasing division among the employees, the president of Portage prohibited the wearing of either union or nonunion badges at work. Other jewelry and hair attachments were still permitted even though such ornaments had also fallen into equipment and caused losses on prior occasions. Immediately after the president gave his order, a strike started to protest it. Was the company rule on union badges an unfair labor practice? Would it make any difference if the union agreed, after the order, that its members would not wear badges? (*Portage Plastics Company v. International Union, Allied Industrial Workers of America, AFL-CIO*, 163 NLRB No. 102)

4 Kuebler was a member in good standing of the lithographers union when it struck the Art Gravure Company. Several months after the strike began, Kuebler met in a nonsecret meeting with twelve or thirteen other strikers at the home of one. Their purpose was to discuss "the widening gap" between the labor and management bargaining committees and to "try to straighten this thing out to where we could get back to work." Later, a three-person committee from the group communicated its views to the Union Negotiating Committee. Kuebler returned to the picket line. When the strike finally ended, the trial board of the local union charged and found Kuebler guilty of attending "a meeting . . . held for the purpose of undermining the Union Negotiating Committee." Kuebler was suspended from the union for three months and was fined $2,000. He filed a notice of appeal to the membership and requested several items: copies of charges against him, with supporting facts; names of the persons on the executive board who had accused and tried him; a copy of the decision in writing showing how each member had voted; and a copy of the transcript of the evidence and proceedings at his trial by the union trial board. This information was refused, and so Kuebler sued for relief in the U.S. district court. Had the union violated Kuebler's rights? Had Kuebler been denied a fair hearing? (*Kuebler v. Cleveland Lithographers and Photoengravers Union Local*, 473 F.2d 359)

5 The Greenpark Nursing Home hired First National Maintenance to maintain its facilities. The firm in turn hired employees to work for it on the premises of the nursing home. These employees of First National Maintenance formed a union. Shortly after, First National Maintenance decided, for financial reasons, to cancel its maintenance contract with the nursing home. Anticipating a complete layoff, the union sought to negotiate with management over the decision to terminate this contract. Management refused to negotiate on this issue. Was this refusal to negotiate legal? (*First National Maintenance v. NLRB*, 452 U.S. 666)

3 Yes; The rule banning union badges was an unfair labor practice. It was an attempt on the part of the company to discourage unionizing activities. (p. 456)

4 Yes; Kuebler's rights were violated. He was entitled to meet with other union members and to express his views. He was entitled to a written notice of the charges against him and a fair hearing. (p. 458)

Yes; Kuebler had been denied a fair hearing. He did not even know who was making the decision about him, so he was unable to present his version of the facts to them. (p. 458)

5 Yes; Unions do not have the power to compel management to negotiate over basic business decisions, such as where to locate a plant, which products to manufacture, or whether to do business with someone, such as the Greenpark Nursing Home. (p. 459)

CHAPTER 23 ORGANIZER

Chapter Theme

Our laws govern unjustified discrimination, for which there is both protection for compliant employers and employees and penalties for those convicted.

DIRECTED STUDY ***QUESTIONS***	SPECIAL FEATURES	PROGRAM RESOURCES				
		Reteach	***Enrich***	SN	AM	
What is the concept of unjustified discrimination?		✔	✔			
What are types of unjustified discrimination?	Thinking Critically Through Visuals, p. 471	✔	✔			
What is the scope of protection?	Personal Perspectives, p. 473	✔	✔			
How can unequal treatment be proved?		✔	✔			
When is equal treatment illegal?	Writing Connections, p. 477	✔	✔	✔	A	
How is a pattern and practice of discrimination proved?		✔	✔			
What specific legislation prohibits discrimination?	Ethics Issue, p. 479 Thinking Critically Through Visuals, p. 480 Multicultural Highlights, p. 480 Preventing Legal Difficulties, p. 481	✔	✔		K V	

Additional Resources

- *The Americans with Disabilities Act: Questions and Answers*. Washington, D.C.: U.S. Equal Employment Opportunity Commission and U.S. Dept. of Justice, Civil Rights Division. 1992
- *Episode 12, Affirmative action versus reverse discrimination*, videotape. Chicago, IL: Films Incorporated.
- Petrocelli, William and Repa, Barbara Kate. *Sexual Harassment on the Job*. Berkeley, CA: Nolo Press, 1992.

One-semester course	✔	✔	✔					
One-year course	✔	✔	✔	✔				

		ASSESSMENT OPPORTUNITIES			
	Cooperative *Learning*	**Informal *Assessment***	**Chapter *Review***	**Chapter *Test***	**Chapter *MicroExam*** (Media)
		✔	✔	✔	✔
		✔	✔	✔	✔
		✔	✔	✔	✔
		✔	✔	✔	✔
		✔	✔	✔	✔
		✔	✔	✔	✔
	✔	✔	✔	✔	✔

Videodiscs

Unjustified Discrimination:
Sexual Harassment

Search Chapter 28, Play To 29

State by State

Section 50.0002 of the Texas Code Annotated makes discrimination on the basis of sex, race, religion, national origin, color, or political affiliation illegal in certifying social workers.

Teaching Materials

Student text, pp. 468–485

Overhead transparency masters
- *Protected Classes*
- *Proof of Disparate Impact*

Videos
- *Law for Business* Videodisc

Workbook, pp. 71–72

Outside Resources
- Flip chart
- Blank overhead transparencies
- Transparency markers
- News magazines
- Newspaper classified employment sections
- Local demographic statistics
- Posterboard
- Markers

- *Episode 12, Affirmative Action Versus Reverse Discrimination,* videotape from Films Incorporated
- VCR
- Camcorder
- Tape recorder

Assessment
- Chapter Test

- Chapter *MicroExam*

Vocabulary

discrimination, p. 470
protected classes, p. 470
unequal treatment, p. 473
business necessity, p. 474
bona fide occupational qualification, p. 475
bona fide seniority system, p. 475
neutral on its face, p. 476
disparate impact, p. 476
applicant pool, p. 476
workforce pool, p. 476
causation, p. 476
Equal Employment Opportunity Commission (EEOC), p. 478
sexual harassment, p. 478
affirmative action plan, p. 479

Learning Objectives

When you complete this chapter, you will be able to

1. Define illegal discrimination.
2. Identify the protected classes.
3. Describe how an employer might treat members of a protected class unequally.
4. Explain how an employer might illegally use a policy that appears to be neutral on its face.°
5. Describe how an employer can become liable for employment discrimination based on the composition of its workforce.
6. Explain each of the major defenses available to employers accused of employment discrimination.
7. List the basic statutes that establish employment discrimination law.

468

Chapter Self-Test

Assess students' understanding of the difference between *justified* and *unjustified discrimination.* In large letters, have students write **Justified** on one side of a sheet of paper and **Unjustified** on the other. Have students display their response as you give the following examples: **(1)** a dependable worker receives a favor (Justified); **(2)** Hispanics receive less pay for the same work performed by non-Hispanics at ABC Co. (Unjustified); and **(3)** the smartest, most hard-working people at XYZ Inc. receive the best pay raises. (Justified)

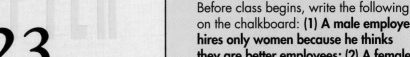

CHAPTER

23 EMPLOYMENT DISCRIMINATION

1 Fidelity reimbursed employees for their job-related educational expenses. Janice applied for reimbursement for a course, but was told, "This isn't job related." She learned that another employee, Gail, had been turned down, too.

Later, Janice met four men with similar jobs who had taken the same course, but they had been reimbursed. Has Fidelity engaged in employment discrimination?

2 As a condition of employment, Duke Moving required a high school education or a satisfactory score on a general intelligence test. Neither requirement was specifically job related. Both requirements were designed to improve the quality of the workforce. Griggs claimed that the test discriminated against him. He said that, as a minority member, he had not had the educational opportunity afforded others. Moreover, he said, the test did not relate to skills and qualifications that were necessary for employment at Duke. Was Griggs legally correct?

3 
Pablo interviewed people to serve as clerks at his dry cleaner. Pablo concluded that he would get more repeat business if he hired attractive clerks. Is Pablo considering all the ethical issues?

FOCUS

Before class begins, write the following on the chalkboard: **(1) A male employer hires only women because he thinks they are better employees; (2) A female employer hires only women because she feels women are usually discriminated against; (3) An employer hires only women who are past the childbearing age;** and **(4) An employer hires only people under 40.** As students enter the classroom, have them write on a sheet of paper which, if any, they think are examples of illegal discrimination. (All are examples.)

Have two students tally the votes. Ask students if they can identify why each is an example of discrimination.

You Decide

1 Yes; Fidelity is not treating women and men equally.

2 Yes; Because these job requirements are not job-related in this situation, they violate the Civil Rights Act of 1964.

3 
The law does allow us to discriminate on the basis of some factors over which we do not have control. But it is not ethical to make factors over which people have no control (such as appearance) an important hiring criterion.

Thinking Critically Through Visuals

This woman holds a job in what was once a male-only profession. Even after women were first hired into police forces, their duties were often restricted to office work. What gives evidence that this is not the case with this woman? (She carries a gun and is working in an outdoor setting.) **What type of employment discrimination, do you think, might she still be subject to because of her gender?** (She might not be promoted as readily as fellow male officers, might be sexually harassed, and so on.)

▼ TEACH

Brainstorm with students the definition of **discrimination**. Write answers on the chalkboard. Then, write the text definition: ***different treatment of individuals***. Explain that this is the legal definition. Point out that it is important to understand the difference between *justified discrimination* and *unjustified discrimination*. Explain each and introduce the term **protected classes**.

▼ APPLY

Provide examples of justified or unjustified discrimination and ask students to label them as such. For example, an employer allows a conscientious hard-worker to take an afternoon off for personal reasons but denies the same privilege to a person with a high absentee record. (Justified) Discuss answers. **Guided Practice**

Have each student make a two-column chart with the headings *Justified* and *Unjustified*. At this time, have students only list examples of justified discrimination in the workplace. (See p. 470 for answers.) Make a class list of students' responses on the chalkboard or on a flip chart. Have students save their charts to use in the next APPLY section. **Independent Practice**

▼ WHAT IS THE CONCEPT OF UNJUSTIFIED DISCRIMINATION?

PROBLEM

Clare had been working at Rich Manufacturing for three years while Lisa had been working there for only two months. They both operated computerized machine-tooling equipment. These machines perform multiple operations, such as drilling, cutting threads, turning, deburring, and surfacing metal objects. Lisa is faster. When a promotion opportunity came along, it was given to Lisa. Clare protested, saying that she was being discriminated against because Lisa would be earning almost 30 percent more money than she would. Is Clare correct? Is she a victim of unjustified discrimination?

Most people's understanding of discrimination is very broad. **Discrimination** is simply *different* treatment of individuals. It is a form of discrimination to pay more money to those who work harder. An important point for understanding this chapter is knowing the difference between justified discrimination and unjustified discrimination. Our law attempts to protect persons against being judged on the basis of their membership in certain *groups*. Being judged simply on the basis of group membership is a form of unjustified discrimination. Instead of judging persons by their group membership, the law compels employers to judge persons as *individuals*. This is a form of justified discrimination.

The law attacks unjustified discrimination in a practical way. It identifies group characteristics that may not be considered when making employment decisions. The courts have attached the label **protected classes** to persons within these groups. Members of protected classes are often, but not always, called minorities. Employment discrimination law is designed to ensure that membership in a protected class is not a significant factor in employment decisions.

Justified discrimination is permitted, even encouraged. Workers fairly judged as dependable, skilled, creative, smart, or hard-working usually receive more favorable treatment. They earn more money and have more job opportunities. Thus, in the problem, Clare is being justifiably discriminated against. She is only pointing out the fact that Lisa is being treated better. If the employer has a good reason for the treatment (e.g., Lisa works faster), the discrimination is justified. Much of employment discrimination law concerns the balancing of justified and unjustified discrimination.

▼ ASSESS

Learning Objective 1 Ask students to orally respond *True* or *False* to the following: **(1) Being judged simply on the basis of group membership is a form of unjustified discrimination.** (True); **(2) The law compels employers to judge persons as individuals. This is a form of justified discrimination.** (True); and **(3) Illegal, or unjustified, discrimination occurs when an employer has a good reason for the treatment.** (False)

WHAT ARE TYPES OF UNJUSTIFIED DISCRIMINATION?

PROBLEM

Stephanos is Greek and has a strong accent. He is living in the United States. He has a Ph.D. in engineering from a Greek university. When Stephanos applies for engineering jobs, he often encounters resistance from those who do not feel that a person with a strong accent can do good engineering work. Stephanos knows that, unlike many countries, the United States has laws that forbid employment discrimination. He assumes that these laws are aimed at helping minority groups in this country like blacks and Hispanics. He does not think these laws could protect him. Is he correct?

A variety of federal statutes define the criteria that an employer cannot consider when making employment decisions. These criteria and the associated protected classes of persons are presented below.

- *Race and Color.* This includes all persons who are not white. So, African-Americans, Asians, Filipinos, Hispanics, native Americans, and others are members of protected classes.
- *Gender.* Employers may not discriminate against females or males. In addition, sexual harassment is illegal.

TEACH

Display the overhead transparency, *Protected Classes.* Cover all the text except the first statement. Discuss that it means that employers may not discriminate against females or males. Sexual harassment is also illegal. One at a time, uncover and discuss the remaining class descriptions.

APPLY

To help students understand that everyone is a member of some protected class, display the overhead transparency used in the preceding TEACH section, and have students categorize themselves into one or more of the classes.

Guided Practice

Thinking Critically Through Visuals

Women who enter traditionally male professions sometimes experience sexual harassment. This photograph shows a male nurse with a patient. Do you think that male nurses might suffer sexual harassment? (Yes, sexual harassment happens to both genders.)

RETEACH

On a transparency, draw two circles. Label one *Individual,* the other *Group Membership.* Draw spokes from each circle. Have students write characteristics (race, color, age, skilled, creative) on the spokes. Relate these to justified and unjustified discrimination.

ENRICH

Pair students. Have each pair write, using a computer, if possible, a short essay supporting why a specific act of unjustified discrimination is wrong.

Have students take out the charts they began in the previous APPLY section completed for justified discrimination. Have students now fill in examples of unjustified discrimination. (See pp. 473–474 for answers.) Complete and review the class chart you began in the previous APPLY section. **Independent Practice**

▼ TEACH

On an overhead transparency or on the chalkboard, list the aspects of employment described on pp. 472–473 and discuss how each might be the basis of employment discrimination. Point out that only employers of 15 or more employees who are engaged in interstate commerce are subject to federal employment discrimination laws.

▼ APPLY

On the chalkboard, draw a three-column chart with the following headings: *Aspect*, *Blatant*, and *Subtle*. Have students write some aspect of employment in column one and then list a blatant and a subtle form of discrimination related to that aspect. For example, hiring; "Under forty only, please" found in a classified ad; and asking ages of a candidate's children in an interview. **Guided Practice**

- *Pregnancy.* Employers may not discriminate because of persons' child-bearing condition or plans.
- *Age.* Persons over the age of forty are protected against discrimination on the basis of their age.
- *Religion.* Persons who hold beliefs about religion, including agnostics and atheists, are members of a protected class. This category could include everyone.
- *Disability.* The physically and mentally disabled are afforded limited protection against discrimination.
- *National Origin.* Persons are protected against discrimination based on their country of origin. So persons who do not speak English or who are not citizens of the United States are protected to a limited extent.

In the problem, Stephanos is being discriminated against because his accent is a signal of his national origin. That is illegal.

▼ WHAT IS THE SCOPE OF PROTECTION?

PROBLEM

Gifford is African-American. He works for a company that has a good reputation for hiring people of both sexes, from all racial groups, and without regard to age, religion, handicap, or national origin. About one-half of Gifford's colleagues and superiors are African-American. Pay rates are equal among the majority and all protected classes. Gifford's only complaint about the company is that white males seem to be assigned overtime much more often than anyone else. Gifford concludes that since the company does such a good job in *hiring* protected classes, he does not have a legal basis for suing. Is he correct?

1. Conditions of Employment

The most blatant forms of employment discrimination arise out of the hiring decision. In the past, this country's employment advertisements often included such language as "men only," "no black people need apply," and "persons between the ages of sixteen and thirty years only, please."

But today the law makes illegal not only unjustified discrimination in hiring, but also unjustified discrimination in any *"term, condition, or privilege of employment."* This means it is illegal to discriminate against protected classes in any aspect of the job. If the unjustified discrimination is displayed

▼ ASSESS

Learning Objective 3 Tell students to jot down answers to the following: **(1) How many employees must a company have to be subject to federal discrimination laws?** (15 or more) and; **(2) In addition to hiring decisions, what other aspects of jobs are protected?** (Pay, promotions, training, overtime, educational opportunities, travel requirements, shift rotations, firings, and layoffs) in pay, promotions, training, overtime, educational opportunities, travel requirements, shift rotations, firings, layoffs, or any other aspect of employment, it is illegal. Thus, in the problem, Gifford could win a suit even if the employer discriminated only in allocating overtime.

2. Organizations Subject to These Laws

Most employers with fifteen or more employees that are engaged in interstate commerce are subject to federal employment discrimination laws. This means that almost all employers except some small businesses are subject to the laws described in this chapter. Agencies of state governments, employment agencies, and labor unions are also generally subject to this body of law. When it passed the major legislation in this area, the U.S. Congress exempted itself from its provision. So our Congress can legally discriminate without justification.

HOW CAN UNEQUAL TREATMENT BE PROVED?

The idea of **unequal treatment** (sometimes called disparate treatment) is that an employer treats members of a protected class less favorably than other employees. Further, this treatment must be *intentional.* Cases based on unequal treatment have taken two forms, based on the nature of the evidence.

1. Direct Evidence

In the past, unequal treatment was often both *intentional and open.* Newspapers carried want ads that listed jobs as "men only." Some firms would publicly refuse to hire African-Americans, Asians, Cajuns, Mexicans, mulattos, Puerto Ricans, or women. Flyers would sometimes state, "no Irish" or "no Jews need apply." Sometimes women would receive letters stating, "I am sorry but we have a policy against hiring women in these positions."

> Pan American World Airways (Pan Am) had a "female only" policy for flight attendants. A male, Diaz, applied for the job and was turned down because of his sex. He sued. At the trial, he offered direct proof of the policy. Pan Am admitted that it had the policy. This was proof of Pan Am's intent to discriminate. Pan Am lost.

To win a case where the discrimination is admitted, the employee need only prove that she or he was denied employment because of membership in a protected class. Today, most direct evidence litigation focuses not on the decision to hire, but on decisions related to other aspects of the employment

Personal Perspectives

Have students discuss with adult family members the reasons for employment discrimination, described on pp. 472–473. Suggest that students ask these individuals if they have personally experienced or witnessed discrimination for any of these reasons and to share the details of the incident. In class, ask student volunteers to share highlights of their discussions, including the ethical and legal nature of each experience. **Independent Practice**

TEACH

Define **unequal treatment**. (When an employer treats members of a protected class less favorably than other employees) Explain that this treatment must be proved intentional using direct or indirect evidence. Explain *direct evidence* and *indirect evidence.* List the four examples of indirect evidence (p. 474) that an employee must show to establish intent. Discuss each, then list and discuss an employer's defenses.

RETEACH Have students create situations of blatant and subtle unjustified discrimination, such as paying different wages for the same job. Ask students to explain why each is an example of unjustified discrimination.

ENRICH Have each student clip an illustration from a magazine of a member of a protected class and tape it to a sheet of paper. Then, ask the student to write a poem telling why an employer who discriminates against that person would be acting unethically and illegally.

APPLY

Make up scenarios like the three boxed cases on pp. 474–475 showing employment discrimination. For example, Bonnie, manages a privately owned ice cream shop. When one of her employees quit at the peak of the busy season, she immediately began interviewing. The first two applicants did not have the necessary skills. Dolores, a Hispanic American who was the third applicant, had all the required skills and displayed a pleasant personality. Still, she was not hired. Bonnie thought that because all the other employees were Anglo American, Dolores wouldn't fit in. Ask: **Was Bonnie's basis for not hiring legal or ethical?** (Neither) **Guided Practice**

Have students, without your direct guidance or support, brainstorm a list of jobs and professions and write them on the chalkboard. Then, have the class discuss and try to agree on at least one example of legitimate **business necessity** and one example of **bona fide occupational qualification** that an employer might rightfully claim as a defense against an accusation of discrimination. **Independent Practice**

relationship. Thus, if an employer offered life insurance as a fringe benefit but the amount was less for women than for men (on the grounds that women outlive men), this would be intentional unequal treatment.

2. Indirect Evidence

Today most cases involve situations where the employer denies any intention to illegally discriminate. To establish a case against such an employer, an employee must show the following:

1. the person was a member of a protected class;
2. the person applied for the job and was qualified;
3. the person was rejected; and
4. the employer held the job open and sought other persons with similar qualifications.

> Geraldo, a Hispanic, had ten years of experience as a finish carpenter. He applied for a job with a local construction company but was turned down. The company continued advertising the position and eventually hired Jake. Jake was white. He did not have as much experience as Geraldo. At the trial, the company was not able to justify its decision to hire Jake instead of Geraldo. Therefore, the court presumed that the discrimination was intentional and Geraldo won the suit.

3. Employer's General Defense: Business Necessity

Once the employee has shown, with either direct or indirect evidence, that unequal treatment occurred, the employer may defend by establishing one of several defenses. All the defenses attempt to show that the unequal treatment was justified by a reason that is legal. Thus, in an indirect proof case, the employer's most common defense is that the employee's skills or work history was the reason for not hiring. This general defense is sometimes called business necessity or job relatedness. **Business necessity** means that the employer's actions were aimed at advancing the business rather than at unjustified discrimination.

> Star Plumbing advertised a position that stated that applicants would be considered only if they had five years of residential plumbing experience. Manuel, a Hispanic, had the experience. He applied for the job but was turned down. Later, Star hired Sue, a white woman, for the job. She also had the experience. Manuel sued and attempted to prove the discrimination with indirect proof: he established in court that he

ASSESS

Learning Objective 6 Ask students to orally respond to the following: **(1) What are the four examples of indirect evidence that an employee must show to establish intent in a discrimination case?** (See enumerated list on p. 474.); **(2) What job requirement compels discrimination against a protected class?** (Bona fide occupational qualification); and **(3) What do you call discrimination resulting from justified attempts to advance business rather than to discriminate unjustifiably?** (Business necessity) was a member of a protected class, that he had the experience, that he applied and was rejected, and that the job was held open for others. At that point in the trial, Star proved that when it checked Manuel's references it discovered that he had been recently fired from other jobs for drinking at work. Star won the suit because it had a valid general defense. It discriminated against Manuel because of business necessity.

4. Defense of Bona Fide Occupational Qualification

Another defense available to an employer is called the bona fide occupational qualification (BFOQ). A **bona fide occupational qualification** is a job requirement that compels discrimination against a protected class. Thus, if an employer hired actors to play parts in a stage show, some of the parts would be for men and the employer could decide to hire only men. Similarly, employers could request only male or female models for a fashion show. But to establish the BFOQ, the discrimination must truly be *essential* to the business. The fact that discrimination is helpful is not enough. When airlines were fighting to preserve female-only flight attendants, they presented surveys showing that a high proportion of their passengers preferred to be served by women. The courts rejected this argument and held that being female is not necessary to perform the job.

5. Defense of Seniority

Seniority can be another justification for unequal treatment. A **bona fide seniority system** is one that rewards employees based on the length of employment rather than merit and is not *intended* to discriminate. In the law, a bona fide seniority system can justify discrimination. If an employer pays union members on the basis of seniority, promotes on the basis of seniority, or lays employees off on the basis of seniority, unequal treatment of protected classes will be tolerated. The Supreme Court will permit seniority to be used even when it perpetuates past discrimination.

▼ WHEN IS EQUAL TREATMENT ILLEGAL?

PROBLEM

Sharron's Machine Shop manufactured fire hydrants. When finished, each hydrant weighed approximately 175 pounds. Part of the job description for hydrant assemblers stated that persons must be able to lift 175 pounds ten times in two minutes. This requirement is quite similar to the actions required in assembling the hydrants. Is this job requirement a form of illegal employment discrimination?

▼ TEACH

Display the transparency, *Proof of Disparate Impact.* Explain each point. Tell students that to win a suit of disparate impact, the employee need not prove an intention to discriminate, but must identify a specific practice

that discriminates against protected classes.

▼ APPLY

Have all students above 5′10″ stand up. Note the number and gender of students standing, then have them sit down. Discuss whether height would eliminate more members of one protected class than another. (In general, men are taller than women.) Have the class brainstorm job requirements, such as height, that would eliminate more members of one or more protected classes than members of the majority. List the requirements on the chalkboard. Then, have students list those jobs where that requirement might be legitimate and jobs where that requirement would not be necessary. For example, an ability to swim would be legitimate for a job as a lifeguard, but questionable for a swimwear salesperson. **Guided Practice**

On a transparency, list the four examples of indirect evidence an employee must show to establish intent in a discrimination case. (See p. 474.) Have students create examples.

In small groups, have students select one of the following scenarios to describe, using a computer, if possible: showing legal employment discrimination because of **business necessity, bona fide occupational qualification,** and **bona fide seniority system.**

On three slips of paper write one of the following: **No intention to discriminate, Disparate impact,** and **Hidden attempt to determine if the applicant is a member of one or more protected classes in order to discriminate.** Have pairs of student volunteers seated back to back simulate telephone job interviews. Have the student who is role-playing the employer draw one of the slips and conduct the interview to achieve the objective. Have the class guess the employer's motive.

Independent Practice

For Basic Education or Compensatory Education students who are having difficulty understanding the statistical proof of disparate impact, make a worksheet such as the following: Qualified applicant pool = 786,000; Special population: women = 392,500; Workforce pool = women 38%. Ask: **Does this situation suggest disparate impact? Why?** (Yes; because women make up about 50% of the qualified applicant pool and only 38% of the workforce.)

Many companies have a policy, like the one at Sharron's, that is regarded as **neutral on its face.** This means that the policy makes no reference to a protected class. But note that in the problem, more men will probably be able to satisfy this job requirement than women. So the policy has a disparate, or different, impact on a protected class. **Disparate impact** indicates that the policy eliminates more members of protected classes than members of the majority. If prison guards are required to be six feet tall, this would eliminate a higher proportion of Asians, Hispanics, and women than white and black males. Agility tests, height tests, weight tests, educational requirements, and tests of clerical abilities will all have a disparate impact on a protected class.

The courts treat cases involving job requirements quite differently from cases involving unequal treatment. To win a suit of disparate impact, the employee need *not* prove an intention to discriminate. But the employee must identify a specific employment practice and show statistically that the practice excludes members of a protected class. Even then the employee will lose if the employer is able to show that there is a legitimate business necessity for the practice.

In the problem, Sharron's weight-lifting test is neutral on its face. But it can be statistically shown that a smaller proportion of women will pass the test. Therefore, it has a disparate impact. However, the test is justified by business necessity because it is clearly job-related.

1. Specific Employment Practices

To win a disparate impact case the employee must identify a specific practice that screens protected classes from jobs. In the past, such practices as requiring high school graduation, written aptitude tests, height and weight tests, and subjective interviews have been attacked by employees.

2. Statistical Proof of Disparate Impact

The employee must establish that there is a difference between the number of protected class members qualified for the job when the challenged employment practice is used and when it is not. This involves examining two groups: (1) the **applicant pool** (i.e., those qualified for the job without regard to the challenged practice) and (2) the **workforce pool** (i.e., persons actually in the workforce). The percentage of protected class individuals in each pool is then compared. If the percentage in the applicant pool is statistically higher than the percentage in the workforce group, this suggests disparate impact. But one other element, causation, must be proven. **Causation** is a linking of the challenged practice and the difference in percentages of protected class persons. After causation is established, the employee has proven disparate impact.

▼ ASSESS

Learning Objective 4 Ask students to jot down answers to the following: **(1) Would a policy regarded as neutral on its face make reference to a protected class?** (No); **(2) Must an employee prove intention to discriminate to win a suit of disparate impact?** (No); and **(3) Do the following statistics suggest disparate impact? Qualified applicant pool = 6,000; Special population: Hispanics = 1,980; Workforce pool = Hispanics 33%** (No; same approximate percentage)

Lenny's Trash Collection Company in Denver, Colorado, advertised an unskilled job—trash collector—paying $11 per hour. It required that applicants be able to lift 130 pounds. This job requirement had been in place for about fifteen years. Of 150 trash collectors, only 3 percent were women. The percentage of women in the unskilled workforce in Denver is approximately 40 percent. Lucy challenged the practice. Her lawyers hired a statistician who proved that the difference between 40 percent (the percentage of women in the unskilled labor pool) and 3 percent (the percentage of women in the workforce) was statistically significant. Lenny's then introduced evidence showing that most women did not want to work in a dirty job like trash collecting. Its survey showed that 90 percent of unskilled women workers in Denver would not apply for a position to collect trash. Lenny's then hired its own statistician, who proved that there was not a statistically significant difference between the percentage of women who would apply (about 4 percent) and the 3 percent in the workforce. Lenny's and Lucy had offered evidence pointing to different *causes* for the small percentage of women in the workforce. Lucy has not established disparate treatment.

3. Employer Defenses

Employers can avoid liability even after the employee has shown disparate treatment. If the challenged practice is justified by business necessity, there is no liability. Thus, if weight lifting is required on the job, it does not legally matter that the requirement excludes a protected class from the job. In addition, an employer can utilize the defenses of bona fide occupational qualification and seniority.

HOW IS A PATTERN AND PRACTICE OF DISCRIMINATION PROVED?

PROBLEM

Beck wanted to be considered for advanced training at her company's headquarters. Employees were nominated for the training by their bosses. In Beck's job classification, there were about eighty men and sixty women. Beck's boss nominated her. Of the twenty people nominated for the home office training, one-half were men and one-half were women. Of the ten persons selected for the training, all were men. Is Beck's employer liable for employment discrimination?

Writing Connections

Language Arts
Have students review the cases of Star Plumbing and Lenny's Trash Collection Company (pp. 474–475 and 477). Have students write, using a computer, if possible, two recruitment ads for each company. The first should simply state the company's needs. The second should actively encourage members of protected classes to apply.

TEACH

Write the terms **isolated case** and **pattern** on the chalkboard. Explain the difference between the two and relate each to employment discrimination. Tell students that a statistically significant difference between the protected class and the workforce is often enough evidence for the government to initiate proceedings for employment discrimination.

APPLY

Have the class brainstorm examples of isolated cases and patterns of behavior. (For example, hitting a home run, always being late, and so on.) **Guided Practice**

RETEACH Pair students who understand how to calculate the statistical proof of disparate impact with students who are having difficulty. Have each student take turns figuring problems that may or may not be examples of statistical proof of disparate impact.

ENRICH Supply students with employment ads and ask them to clip examples that would probably have a disparate impact. Have students read the ads aloud. Then, have students analyze whether the job requirement is justified by business necessity.

Provide students with the following national population statistics: Anglo American 80%, African American 12%, Native American 1%, Asian American 3%, and Hispanic American 9%. (The total is more than 100% because some persons are in more than one group.) Have students determine the workforce percentage cutoff for each of the protected classes that might suggest further investigation to determine whether a pattern of discrimination is suggested. Have students make a chart, using a computer, if possible, showing this data. Display the chart.

Independent Practice

▼ TEACH

Draw a large three-column chart on the chalkboard. In the first column, **Acts**, list the five legislative acts discussed on pp. 478–480. Tell students that these laws have been enacted because of past injustices in the hiring, paying, training, transferring, and discharging of workers. Head the remaining columns: **What Law Does**, and **Who Is Protected**. As you discuss each law, fill in these columns. Discuss the role of the Equal Employment Opportunity Commission (EEOC) and what steps an affirmative action plan might include. Have students copy the completed chart in their notebooks.

In some cases, the government can initiate proceedings against a company for employment discrimination when there is evidence of a pattern and practice of discrimination. In this type of litigation, the government merely shows a statistically significant difference between the protected class composition of the pool of qualified applicants and the workforce. In the problem, Beck's employer would probably be liable under pattern and practice.

▼ WHAT SPECIFIC LEGISLATION PROHIBITS DISCRIMINATION?

PROBLEM

Jannette was employed in a glass factory. Her job was to inspect and pack glass jars in cartons. Men were also employed in the same capacity, but they were occasionally required to lift the packed cartons. The women were paid 10 percent less than the men were. Is the difference in pay illegal?

1. The Civil Rights Act of 1964

With some exceptions, the Civil Rights Act of 1964 forbids employers, employment agencies, and unions from discriminating in hiring, paying, training, promoting, or discharging employees on the basis of race, color, religion, national origin, or sex. An employer may discriminate in selecting one worker over another if the standard set is necessary for proper performance of the job. For example, a prospective pilot of an airplane may be required to understand radar and navigation equipment. That person may also be required to react quickly to emergencies and to be free of potentially fatal heart diseases.

The Civil Rights Act sets up the **Equal Employment Opportunity Commission** (EEOC). The EEOC has the authority to investigate and conciliate complaints of job discrimination and to prosecute suspected offenders.

One form of sex discrimination made illegal by the act is sexual harassment. **Sexual harassment** is unwelcome sexual comments, gestures, or contact in the workplace. The most vivid illustration is when a boss threatens to fire a subordinate unless sex is provided. In instances such as this where a supervisor sexually harasses a subordinate, the employer is strictly liable. Generally, the employer is liable only for the conduct of nonsupervisory employees when the harassment is either known or should have been known to supervisors. Thus, a woman repeatedly subjected to whistles and sexual jokes by male co-workers who complained to her supervisor could recover from her employer if nothing was done to stop it. On the other hand, a

▼ ASSESS

Learning Objective 7 Tell students to orally name the act that the following statements describe: **(1) Forbids employers from discriminating on the basis of race, color, religion, national origin, or sex** (Civil Rights Act of 1964); **(2) Forbids discrimination against workers over the age of 40** (Age Discrimination in Employment Act of 1967); and **(3) Is the principal protection for the handicapped** (Vocational Rehabilitation Act).

woman who encourages sexual comments is unlikely to prevail in a suit for sexual harassment.

When an employer has discriminated in the past, an **affirmative action plan** may be mandated by the courts to remedy the past discrimination. Most employers that contract with the federal government must also submit affirmative action plans. These are positive steps aimed at offsetting past discrimination by bringing the percentages of minorities and women in the workforce up to their corresponding percentages in the pool of qualified applicants. Because the federal government is the biggest buyer of goods and services in the country, most large employers are directly affected by affirmative action.

2. Equal Pay Act of 1963

The Equal Pay Act prohibits wage discrimination on account of sex. Women who do the same work as men must be paid at the same rate. This means that when the same skill, effort, and responsibility are required and when the job is performed under similar working conditions, women must be paid the same as men. Thus, in the problem, the court held that Jannette and the other women were entitled to equal pay for equal work and that "equal work" did not mean identical duties.

3. Age Discrimination in Employment Act of 1967

The Age Discrimination in Employment Act forbids discrimination against workers over the age of forty in any employment practice (e.g., hiring, discharging, retiring, promoting, and compensating). Exceptions are made when age is a necessary consideration for job performance. Such occupations include bus drivers, fire fighters, and police officers.

4. Vocational Rehabilitation Act

The Vocational Rehabilitation Act is the principal protection for the handicapped. It requires that employers that receive federal funding not discriminate against handicapped persons who are *qualified* to perform the job. The act attempts to prevent employers from automatically assuming that handicapped persons cannot perform work. Employers must now make reasonable workplace accommodations for the handicapped worker.

The Vocational Rehabilitation Act defines a handicapped person as one who has a physical or mental impairment that substantially limits a major life activity. Those with significantly impaired sight or hearing, or those without the use of limbs, are clearly handicapped under this act. A person with a communicable disease, such as tuberculosis, is also protected. On the

▼ APPLY

ETHICS ISSUE

Ethics Issue

In 1991, during the Senate confirmation hearings of Supreme Court justice nominee Clarence Thomas, Anita Hill stepped forward to accuse him of past sexual harassment. After a highly controversial, televised hearing, Thomas was the second African American to be seated on the U.S. Supreme Court. However, Hill, a highly respected university law professor, has not recanted her testimony. Many people believe that Anita Hill forever changed the way people view the seriousness of sexual harassment. Ask: **Which relevant protected group did Hill's actions aid?** (Women) **Guided Practice**

Divide the class into pairs. Give each pair a sheet of posterboard and markers. Assign each pair one of the five laws on pp. 478–480 and tell them to create a poster that alerts people to their legal rights protected by that law. Display the posters.

Independent Practice

▼RETEACH

Pair students. Have each pair explain one of the five federal laws prohibiting discrimination, discussed on pp. 478–480, to the other students. Have these peer-tutors field questions, but make sure that the correct information is disseminated.

Show the videotape, *Episode 12, Affirmative Action Versus Reverse Discrimination*, from the series *The Constitution: That Delicate Balance*, distributed by Films Incorporated, Chicago, IL. After showing the video, lead a discussion.

Thinking Critically Through Visuals

The teacher in this photograph has proved that his physical handicap does not interfere with his ability to do his job. Which federal laws protect his employment rights? (Vocational Rehabilitation Act and the Americans With Disabilities Act)

Multicultural Highlights

Dr. Suzanne Ahn, a neurologist in Dallas, TX, came to the U.S. from Korea. She now leads the fight for Asian American rights and equal treatment and equal opportunity for all. An amendment to the Civil Rights Act of 1991, intended to clarify employment discrimination, actually excluded about 2,000 Filipino Americans and Native Americans. Dr. Ahn is working to get the excluded groups included. Discuss the ethical and legal questions that arise from the exclusion of protected classes from federal law.

other hand, alcoholism and drug addiction do not qualify a person as handicapped under the act.

5. Pregnancy Discrimination Act

The Pregnancy Discrimination Act is a statute that makes it illegal to discriminate because of pregnancy, childbirth, or related medical conditions. Accordingly, an employer may not fire, refuse to hire, refuse to promote, or demote a woman because she is pregnant.

The act also makes it illegal for fringe benefits to discriminate on these bases. Thus, an employer cannot carry an insurance policy that insures all physical conditions except pregnancy.

Federal laws—such as the Civil Rights Act, the Equal Pay Act, the Age Discrimination in Employment Act, the Vocational Rehabilitation Act, and the Pregnancy Discrimination Act—have been enacted because of past injustices in the hiring, paying, training, transferring, and discharging of workers. Most states and many cities have enacted similar laws. In addition, the Supreme Court has interpreted the Fourteenth Amendment to apply to employment. The Supreme Court has also extended to employment the civil rights laws passed in 1866 and 1870.

These efforts have modified the old common-law concept that an employer has complete freedom in hiring and, subject to liability for breach of contract, freedom in discharging workers. Essentially, current laws, regulations, and court decisions require that job applicants be judged on their merits as individuals, not as members of any group or class.

▼ ASSESS

Learning Objective 7 Ask students to respond orally to the following: **(1) What is the name of the statute that makes it illegal to discriminate because of pregnancy, childbirth, or related medical conditions?** (The Pregnancy Discrimination Act); and **(2) How does the Pregnancy Discrimination Act affect fringe benefits?** (Employers cannot carry insurance policies that insure all physical conditions except pregnancy.)

Preventing Legal Difficulties

As an employee...

1. Approach every job in a professional manner. Do not seek to be judged on the basis of your race, sex, handicap, national origin, or other group characteristic. Seek to be judged on the basis of your job performance.
2. Do not flirt with co-workers.
3. If you suspect that you are being discriminated against because of your membership in a protected class, contact the EEOC.

As an employer...

1. Do not ask questions on job applications that require the disclosure of race, religion, sex, national origin, handicap, or pregnancy status.
2. Do not ask questions in job interviews about maternity plans, child care abilities, birth control practices, number of children, or other related factors.
3. Carefully train your supervisory employees both to avoid unwanted sexual comments and to respond intelligently to complaints about the unwelcome sexual conduct of co-workers.
4. Train your supervisory employees to focus on the job performance of their subordinates. Help them become sufficiently impartial so that their biases do not play a role in their employment decisions.

REVIEWING IMPORTANT POINTS

1. The law attacks only unjustified discrimination.
2. Discrimination is illegal when it is based on race, color, sex, pregnancy, age, religion, disability, or national origin.
3. Employment discrimination laws generally apply only to firms with fifteen or more employees.
4. There are two ways to prove unequal treatment: directly and indirectly.
5. The employer's principal defenses are business necessity, bona fide occupational qualification, and bona fide seniority system.
6. In a disparate impact case, the employee must show that the challenged practice caused a statistically significant difference in the percentage of protected class members in the pool of qualified applicants and the workforce.

CLOSE

Divide the class into groups of four or five and assign the following roles: facilitator, if necessary; employee; employer; news interviewer, who conducts the interview; and director, who directs and videotapes the broadcast. Ask each group to prepare a script for a news broadcast on specific aspects of employment discrimination, then tape their broadcast. Show the tapes for the class, using each case as an opportunity to summarize one or more key concepts of the chapter.

Cooperative Learning

Assign the following end-of-chapter materials:
Student text review activities, pp. 481–485
Workbook, pp. 71–72
Chapter Test

Chapter *MicroExam*

Preventing Legal Difficulties

Review each of the seven suggestions for preventing legal difficulties. Ask students to discuss the ethical as well as the legal foundations of each point.

RETEACH Have students read the definition of the Pregnancy Discrimination Act (p. 480) and rewrite it in their own words in their notebooks. Have them also include the points about illegal fringe benefits. Discuss students' paraphrased definitions.

ENRICH Have students brainstorm why carrying an insurance policy that insures all physical conditions except pregnancy discriminates against a protected group. (This is true discrimination; pregnant women and, indirectly, their unborn children, are treated differently than other people.)

7 The EEOC is the governmental agency charged with enforcing most employment discrimination laws.

8 Sexual harassment is any unwelcome sexual comment, gesture, or touch in the workplace. When supervisory employees do this, the employer is strictly liable.

9 Employers that have engaged in discrimination in the past and those with federal contracts may be required to implement affirmative action plans.

10 Persons with handicaps should be evaluated only on their ability to do the job.

11 Pregnancy is not a factor that can affect employment or any of its conditions or privileges.

STRENGTHENING YOUR LEGAL VOCABULARY

Match each term with the statement that best defines that term. Some terms may not be used.

affirmative action plan	disparate impact
applicant pool	Equal Employment Opportunity Commission (EEOC)
bona fide occupational qualification	neutral on its face
bona fide seniority system	protected classes
business necessity	sexual harassment
causation	unequal treatment
discrimination	workforce pool

1 All the persons who work for an employer that has been charged with employment discrimination.

2 Unwelcome comments, gestures, or touching of a sexual nature at work.

3 A label for a workplace policy that does not seem on the surface to discriminate against any protected class.

4 When a business practice has the effect of reducing the number of protected class persons in the workforce.

5 A job requirement that, of necessity, requires the hiring of a person of a particular race, sex, or national origin.

6 A linking of a job requirement with underrepresentation of a protected class in the workforce.

Strengthening Your Legal Vocabulary

1 workforce pool
2 sexual harassment
3 neutral on its face
4 disparate impact
5 bona fide occupational qualification
6 causation
7 protected classes
8 bona fide seniority system
9 applicant pool
10 Equal Employment Opportunity Commission (EEOC)

Applying Law to Everyday Life

1 Irene's conduct is illegal. It is unequal treatment of a protected class (persons who are not Jehovah's Witnesses). (pp. 473–474) Even if Irene could prove the members of her religion were more honest, this would not justify the unequal treatment. Everyone has the legal right to be considered as an individual and not as a member of a group. (p. 470)

2 ETHICS ISSUE Yes; Peter is obligated to follow these laws even though they don't apply to him. Employment discrimination laws require treatment which is essential to human dignity. Deontologists therefore conclude that everyone has the ethical right to be judged only as an individual. Consequentialists say the economy will work more efficiently when everyone's talents are used best. So Peter is ethically obligated to follow these laws. (See Chapter 2.)

7 Groups that employment law protects.

8 A system that rewards employees for length of employment rather than merit.

9 Those qualified for the job.

10 Has the authority to investigate and conciliate complaints of job discrimination and to prosecute suspected offenders.

APPLYING LAW TO EVERYDAY LIFE

1 Irene was a Jehovah's Witness. She believed that other members of her religion were more honest than the general population. When she was asked to hire a bank teller for her employer, she advertised the job as one available only for members of her religion. Is Irene's action legal? Would it be legal if Irene could prove in court that members of her religion were in fact more honest?

2 ETHICS ISSUE Peter owned a small restaurant that specialized in Vietnamese food. He had fewer than fifteen employees and therefore knew that most employment discrimination laws did not apply to him. Is Peter ethically obligated to follow these laws anyway?

3 A fast-food restaurant surveyed its customers to determine their preference for food servers. The survey indicated that the customers clearly preferred girls over boys as servers. Therefore the restaurant advertised for and hired female servers only, and this caused its business to increase substantially. Bitt applied for a job but was denied an interview because of his sex. Is Bitt entitled to an interview for this job?

4 ETHICS ISSUE Suppose you were in charge of hiring fifteen workers to assemble very small electrical components to make a toy. If you believed that females of Asian ancestry were most likely to do this type of work well, would you limit your interviews to this group of persons only? Would your decision be different if you were certain there would be no legal risk?

5 Boyce's mother, Martha, went to college after her husband died. She studied accounting and graduated when she was fifty-two years old. When she applied for positions with large accounting firms, she was never seriously considered because of her age. The firms seemed to hire only people in their twenties and thirties. Has Martha been the victim of illegal employment discrimination?

3 interview; customer preference cannot be the basis for a bona fide occupational qualification. The employment practice of this fast-food restaurant constitutes unequal treatment of a protected class (men). (p. 475)

4 ETHICS ISSUE Hiring Asian women based on this highly questionable belief is illegal and unethical. Everyone has the legal right to compete for these jobs. (p. 470) No; If there is no chance of being caught, the employer should still avoid discrimination because ethics demands it.

5 Yes; Martha has been the victim of unequal treatment because of her membership in a protected class (those over forty years old). The conduct of the accounting firms is thus illegal. (p. 479)

6 ETHICS ISSUE No; Jerry faces an ethical dilemma. The insurance company has acted unethically. By increasing Jerry's premiums 1,000 percent, it violated an unspoken understanding that it would bear the medical risks of Jerry's employees. It is using a legal loophole to avoid its ethical obligation. If Jerry had been more experienced in this area he might have obtained a policy that could not be canceled. But now he confronts a very difficult dilemma. He cannot ignore the plight of his AIDS-infected employee; to do so would be to deny the person's basic dignity. Therefore deontologists would not abandon this employee. On the other hand, Jerry's firm will go into bankruptcy if he pays the premiums. If that occurs, Jerry and all the other employees will lose their jobs. So, consequentialists will simply count those affected positively and those affected negatively. This reasoning leads to the conclusion that it is all right to ignore the AIDS-infected employee. The two major styles of ethical

reasoning reach opposite conclusions in this case. That means this is an enormously difficult moral problem to resolve. It is not the kind of problem where our casual thinking will easily guide us to the moral decision. (See Chapter 2.)

7 Yes; The employment requirement of being able to lift 120 pounds is illegal because it produces a disparate impact on a protected class (women) and is not job-related. (p. 476)

8 No; This is not sexual harassment because it only happened once. It will become sexual harassment if Joyce complains to her boss and nothing is done, or if other incidents make it part of a pattern of unwelcome sexual communication. (pp. 478–479)

6 ETHICS ISSUE Jerry owned a small printing shop. He had medical insurance coverage for all his employees. The policy was periodic, renewable once each year. One of Jerry's employees contracted acquired immune deficiency syndrome (AIDS). As the disease progressed, medical expenses for this employee skyrocketed, but they were covered by the insurance. A clause in the policy allowed the insurance company to raise the premium when the policy was renewed by the employer. On the annual renewal date, the insurance company presented Jerry with a 1,000-percent premium increase for continued coverage. If he paid the premiums, it would bankrupt his company. Is Jerry ethically obligated to pay the increase to protect his AIDS-infected employee? Has the insurance company acted ethically?

7 Ajax Trash Removal company had a policy that required employees be able to lift 120 pounds. It also had a policy that trash cans weighing more than 65 pounds would not be picked up. In your opinion, is the employment policy (120 pounds) legal?

8 Joyce was at her first day on the job. When she started up her computer, it automatically drew an explicit picture of a nude woman on the screen. Is this sexual harassment? What should Joyce do to ensure that nothing like this happens again?

Solving Case Problems

1 Yes; Hopkins was evaluated by standards different from those used to evaluate men. This is unequal treatment. (p. 473)

2 No; Antonio was trying to compare the racial composition of two different groups of employees. In order to win a suit based on disparate impact, the difference in racial composition must be established between the pool of otherwise qualified applicants and the workforce. In this case that would mean comparing the racial composition of those in the pool of applicants for the noncannery positions and the composition of the noncannery workforce. Since Antonio did not do this, he lost. (p. 476)

3 Yes, Henderson prevails. The chief conditioned Henderson's career success on sexual favors. When a boss engages in sexual harassment such as this, the employer (the City of Dundee) is strictly liable. Of course the chief himself is also liable. (p. 478)

SOLVING CASE PROBLEMS

1 Ann Hopkins worked for Price Waterhouse, a large accounting firm. It was a practice to make professional employees partners in the firm after several years. Ann had been distinctively successful in the performance of her job. Of about 600 partners in the firm, only eight were women. When Ann was being considered for partnership, a committee of all male partners evaluated her. Several members of the committee made comments such as the following: "She should go to charm school"; "She needs to learn to dress, walk, and talk like a woman"; and "She should wear jewelry and makeup." Ultimately the committee turned her down for partnership. She was also told the comments of the members of the committee. Ann sued, claiming unequal treatment. Will she prevail? (*Price Waterhouse v. Hopkins,* 109 S. Ct. 1775)

2 Wards Cove Packing Company operated canneries in remote areas of Alaska. The workers in the canneries were primarily Filipinos and native Alaskans. These jobs were unskilled and the pay was low. The workers in noncannery jobs were primarily white. These positions were highly skilled and highly paid. Antonio was a canner and he sued for

employment discrimination. He claimed that the difference in the composition of the cannery and noncannery workforces established that Wards Cove was illegally discriminating. Will he prevail? (*Wards Cove Packing Company v. Antonio,* 109 S. Ct. 2115)

3 Henderson worked as a radio dispatcher for the Dundee, Florida, police department. The police chief, she alleged, subjected her to repeated sexual comments and requests that she have sexual relations with him. Because she refused, she said, the chief refused to allow her to attend the police academy. Further, he suspended her for two days for violating a minor office policy that had never been enforced before. She interpreted the suspension as a threat that she would be fired unless she gave in to her boss's advances. Eventually Henderson quit and then sued the city claiming sexual harassment. Will she prevail? (*Henderson v. City of Dundee,* 682 F.2d 897)

4 United Airlines had certain minimum requirements for the position of flight officer. The applicant had to have 500 hours of flight time, be twenty-one to twenty-nine years of age, have a commercial pilot's license and instrument rating, and have a college degree. When Spurlock, a black, applied for the position, no one knew his race. At the time, he had only 204 hours of flight time and only two years of college, mostly in music education. His written application was rejected. Therefore Spurlock sued United, claiming racial discrimination in violation of Title VII of the Civil Rights Act. He pointed out that of approximately 5,900 flight officers in United's employ at the time, only nine were blacks. Was United guilty of illegal discrimination? (*Spurlock v. United Airlines, Inc.,* 475 F.2d 216)

5 Shiela Grove and David Klink were both tellers for Frostburg National Bank. Both were high school graduates. They had worked for the bank for the same length of time performing the same duties. Occasionally, Klink performed miscellaneous tasks that were not assigned to Grove. A male supervisor, David Willetts, set the salaries for both tellers. Klink's salary was significantly higher than Grove's. Has the bank violated the Equal Pay Act? (*Grove v. Frostburg National Bank,* 549 F. Supp. 922)

peak performance ability. Possession of a college degree, particularly in the "hard sciences," indicates that the person has the necessary ability to understand and retain necessary information. However, United would waive the college degree requirements if the applicant's other qualifications were superior, especially if he or she had much flight time in high-speed jet aircraft. The court noted that an employer has a lighter burden of showing employment criteria are job-related when the job clearly requires a high degree of skill and the human and economic risks of hiring an unqualified candidate are great. A United Airlines flight officer has such a job: The plane is worth as much as $40 million, and it transports as many as 300 passengers per flight.

5 Yes; The Equal Pay Act is violated when members of a protected class are paid less than those in the majority. Here Shiela was paid less than David, even though they both performed substantially the same job. This violates the Equal Pay Act. (p. 479)

4 No; Spurlock made a prima facie case of racial discrimination by showing the minuscule number of black flight officers in the employ of United. However, United met the burden of showing that its requirements were job-related and, therefore, valid discrimination against any candidate—black or white—who failed to qualify. (p. 478) United proved through statistics that flight officers who have more than 500 minimum flight hours are more likely to succeed in its rigorous training program. This program begins upon hiring, and successful candidates are required to attend intensive refresher courses every six months to maintain

CHAPTER 24 ORGANIZER

Chapter Theme

Our legal system has legal precedents and policies in place to compensate employees injured at work.

DIRECTED STUDY QUESTIONS	SPECIAL FEATURES	PROGRAM RESOURCES: Reteach	Enrich	SN	AM	
Historically, how has our legal system treated injured employees?	Personal Perspectives, p. 489 Writing Connections, p. 489 Thinking Critically Through Visuals, p. 490	✔	✔		V	
How do workers' compensation laws work?	Personal Perspectives, p. 491 Thinking Critically Through Visuals, p. 492	✔	✔	✔		
When can the injured employee recover from the employer for negligence?	Ethics Issue, p. 494	✔	✔		K	
How does OSHA protect employees?	Ethics Issue, p. 495 Multicultural Highlights, p. 496 Preventing Legal Difficulties, p. 496	✔	✔		A	

Additional Resources

- Lacey, Dan. *Your Rights in the Workplace.* Berkeley, CA: Nolo Press, 1991.
- *Occupational Injuries and Illnesses in the United States by Industry.* Washington, D.C.: Labor Department, Bureau of Labor Statistics, 1993.
- *Silkwood*, videotape. ABC Motion Pictures.
- *United States Government Manual.* Washington, DC: U.S. Government Printing Office.

One-semester course	✔	✔						
One-year course	✔	✔	✔					

	ASSESSMENT OPPORTUNITIES			
Cooperative Learning	**Informal Assessment**	**Chapter Review**	**Chapter Test**	**Chapter *MicroExam*** 
	✔	✔	✔	✔
✔	✔	✔	✔	✔
	✔	✔	✔	✔
	✔	✔	✔	✔

Videodiscs

Workers' Compensation Systems

Search Chapter 29, Play To 30

OSHA: Whistle-Blowing within OSHA Guidelines

Search Chapter 30, Play To 31

State by State

In South Carolina, an independent contractor is generally not covered by workers' compensation. In this state, an independent contractor is defined as one who does work using his or her own methods without the control of the employer.

Teaching Materials

Student text, pp. 486–501

Overhead transparency masters
•History of Worker Protection Laws
•When the Employer Can Be Sued for Negligence

Videos
•*Law for Business* Videodisc

Workbook, pp. 73–74

Outside Resources
•Newspapers
•Butcher paper
•News and business magazines
•Art supplies: scissors, tape, & markers
•Blank overhead transparencies
•Transparency markers

•Camcorder
•VCR
•*Silkwood*, videotape from ABC Motion Pictures
•Tape recorder

Assessment
•Chapter Test

•Chapter *MicroExam*

Vocabulary

common-law defenses, p. 488
negligence suit, p. 488
assumption of the risk, p. 489
contributory negligence, p. 489
co-worker negligence, p. 489
workers' compensation statutes, p. 489
Occupational Safety and Health Administration (OSHA), p. 489
vocational rehabilitation, p. 492
casual workers, p. 492
independent contractor, p. 492

Learning Objectives

When you complete this chapter, you will be able to

1. Describe how the law has changed approaches to protecting employees.
2. Identify the main features of workers' compensation systems.
3. Understand when an employee can sue an employer for negligence.
4. Explain how the Occupational Safety and Health Administration (OSHA) protects employees.

486

Chapter Self-Test

Before they begin Chapter 24, assess students' understanding of employees' options when on-the-job injuries occur by asking them to respond orally to the following questions: **(1) Does every employee who is injured on the job have the right to bring a negligence suit against his or her employer?** (No; in many cases employees covered by workers' compensation are not allowed to sue for negligence.); and **(2) Are the monetary benefits of workers' compensation and the awards won in negligence suits relatively equal?** (No; negligence suits almost always pay much more.) Before continuing with the chapter, review and discuss students' responses.

CHAPTER 24

EMPLOYEE INJURIES

1 Smith started a telephone-answering business in her home. She hired one person, Jones, to work for her for one week. They agreed that Jones would receive a flat fee, no fringe benefits, and no workers' compensation coverage. During her second day on the job, the old chair Jones was sitting in collapsed, and her spinal cord was severely injured. Is Smith liable for Jones's injury?

2 Jameston, a school custodian, is injured when some student lockers fall on him while he is cleaning the hallway. All of the school's employees are covered by the school's workers' compensation insurance policy. What are Jameston's legal rights?

3 

A friend of yours at work complained about fumes that were causing eyeburn, headaches, and nausea. She asked the company to install exhaust fans, but it did not. So she reported the problem to the Occupational Safety and Health Administration (OSHA). Shortly after, she was told that her services were no longer needed, so she left. You are aware that the fumes are causing health problems for many other employees. Are you ethically obligated to complain to OSHA even if that means risking your job? Will the law protect you if you report safety violations to OSHA?

FOCUS

On the chalkboard, write the following statements: **(1) Employers are always partly responsible for on-the-job injuries and should pay; (2) An employee injured on the job deserves to seek as much money as he or she can get; (3) Employers have a right to try to prove other factors contributed to an employee's injury, even when the employee proved that the employer's negligence caused the injury; and (4) I cannot agree with statements 1–3.** As students enter the classroom, have them write their initials after the statement with which they most agree.

Have a student volunteer tally the votes. Ask students to explain their choices. Save the tally to compare with the answers to the same questions in the CLOSE activity—based on law, not emotions—at the end of this chapter.

You Decide

1 Since Jones was not covered by workers' compensation, she may sue the employer for negligence. Whether Smith can use the employers' defenses, such as assumption of risk, depends on the laws of her state.

2 The school's workers' compensation policy would cover the costs of Jameston's medical care and, in most states, a portion of wages if Jameston missed work because of the injury.

3 ETHICS ISSUE Yes, ethically you should report the violation to OSHA, which is legally obligated to try to protect those who inform it of safety violations.

Thinking Critically Through Visuals

This photograph shows a person who has a greater-than-average risk of on-the-job injury. What are two dangers that this job entails? (Answers may include falling, skin burns, eye injuries from welding sparks, and so on.) **What safety precautions are evident?** (A safety hood is being worn to protect the eyes, skin, and hair.)

TEACH

Explain to students that our legal system has developed three ways of dealing with injuries that occur on the job. Display the overhead transparency, *History of Worker Protection Laws.* Discuss **negligence suits,** pointing out that they attempted to make the party at fault bear the financial loss associated with the injury. Then discuss the three common-law defenses listed on the bottom of p. 488. Compare **negligence suits** to **workers' compensation** and to the safety standards enacted and enforced by the **Occupational Safety and Health Administration** (OSHA).

Media

APPLY

Write the terms **negligence suit**, **workers' compensation**, and **OSHA** on the chalkboard. Tell students to imagine that three fictitious countries have each chosen to allow only one of these ways of dealing with injuries to employees. Have them choose the country they think would be the best place in which to be employed. Let groups choosing each country meet to briefly discuss why they made their choice. Then, gather all groups for a panel discussion of the pros and cons of each approach. **Guided Practice**

HISTORICALLY, HOW HAS OUR LEGAL SYSTEM TREATED INJURED EMPLOYEES?

PROBLEM

Crow was a steelworker working on the fifth story of a fifteen-story high-rise apartment project. His employer, Nu-Dimensions, Inc., provided all workers with protective helmets as required by law. One day, because of the intense heat, Crow removed his helmet and worked bareheaded while the supervisor was off-duty. A large bolt fell from the employer's construction crane and hit Crow on the head, fracturing his skull. It was common for objects to fall from the top floor of a construction project. Could Crow recover any money for injuries due to this on-the-job injury?

Our legal system has developed three ways of dealing with injuries to employees.

1. Negligence Suits

The traditional common-law approach involved the employee suing the employer. Employees won the negligence suit if they could prove in court that the employer's negligence caused their injury. This system attempted to make the party at fault bear the financial loss associated with the injury. By making employers liable for the injuries caused by their negligence, the common law encouraged employers to protect employees.

The law imposes on employers the general duty to provide reasonably safe working conditions for employees. This duty may be violated in several ways. For example, an employer might fail to provide a safe workplace, safe tools, or safe machinery. Similarly, the employer would violate the duty if there were an insufficient number of co-workers to do a job safely or if employees were given inadequate safety instructions. When the employer violates the duty to provide safe working conditions and this causes injury to workers, the employer has probably committed the tort of negligence.

However, the common-law system had many problems. The injured worker had several reasons for not suing the employer. For example, the employee had to hire an attorney. And if the employee did sue, he or she risked being fired. Even if an employee proved that the employer's negligence caused the injury, the employee would not collect if the employer proved any one of the following **common-law defenses:**

a. the employee had *assumed the risk* involved,
b. the employee was *contributorily negligent,* or
c. the *negligence of a co-worker* caused the injury.

ASSESS

Learning Objective 1 Have students orally identify whether or not each statement is associated with negligence suits (NS), workers' compensation (WC), or OSHA: **(1) Benefits are paid without regard to fault.** (WC); **(2) Attempts are made to make the party at fault bear the financial loss associated with the injury.** (NS); and **(3) Regulations and inspections are used to make the workplace a safer place.** (OSHA)

Assumption of the risk occurs when a person is aware of a danger that could cause injury, but voluntarily remains in the dangerous situation. In the problem, Crow assumed the risk of being hurt by falling objects when he remained on the job after seeing other objects fall.

Contributory negligence means that the employee carelessly did something that contributed to her or his injury or death. This defense is often effective even when the employee's negligence is very slight in relation to the employer's. In the problem, Crow was contributorily negligent because he removed his safety helmet.

Co-worker negligence means simply that a co-worker is one of the causes of the injury. It also defeats recovery from an employer. Thus, in the problem, if the employer could show that a co-worker caused the bolt to fall, the employer would not be liable. These common-law defenses prevented employees from winning most negligence suits. Until the early 1900s, the negligence suit was the only recourse for workers injured on the job.

2. Workers' Compensation

Because employees had great difficulty in winning negligence suits, around the turn of the century state legislatures enacted laws to help injured employees. These **workers' compensation statutes** require most employers to obtain insurance to pay benefits to injured employees. The benefits are paid without regard to fault. So the insurance pays even when the employer is not a cause of the injury. This statutory system was a substitute for negligence suits; if an injured employee was covered by workers' compensation, no negligence suit was allowed against the employer. Because the amount an employer must pay for workers' compensation insurance is somewhat related to the firm's safety record, employers still had an incentive to maintain a safe workplace.

3. Occupational Safety and Health Administration

The third approach relies on workplace safety standards enacted and enforced by federal and state administrative agencies. The **Occupational Safety and Health Administration (OSHA)** enacts safety regulations and inspects workplaces. It can impose fines and even shut down plants when it finds violations of its laws. OSHA does not allocate loss based on fault or provide money for medical expenses without regard to fault; rather, it seeks to make the workplace safer. It is trying to prevent injury.

In the problem, Crow probably could not recover from his employer in a suit for negligence because Crow's failure to wear his helmet was a cause of his injury. Crow was more at fault than the employer. If the employer had workers' compensation coverage for Crow, then he would not be allowed to sue his employer. Workers' compensation would probably pay some of Crow's lost wages and all of his medical expenses. The injury might lead to an OSHA

Personal Perspectives

Tell students to read and discuss with adult family members the sections about negligence suits and workers' compensation on pp. 488–489. Suggest that students ask adult family members to share direct or indirect experiences they have had with either approach to on-the-job injuries. Have volunteers share their discussions.

Writing Connections

Language Arts
Have students review the PROBLEM on p. 488. Tell them to assume the role of a newspaper reporter who has been called to the scene of the accident just after Crow was injured. Using a computer, if possible, have students write an article including the legal aspects of the incident. Remind students to answer who, what, when, where, why, and how in their articles.

Independent Practice

▼RETEACH Tape paper over the first column on the overhead transparency master, *History of Worker Protection Laws.* Copy and distribute it. Discuss each goal and have students write in the corresponding law. Next, have students summarize the process for each.

▼ENRICH Provide students with newspapers and have them clip articles about injuries to employees. Have them read and orally summarize the articles. Have the class determine which worker-protection approach might play a role in the case.

Thinking Critically Through Visuals

The workers in this photograph are engaged in a potentially dangerous job. What evidence is there that the employer is taking steps to protect workers? (Answers may include that workers are wearing protective clothing, there is a caution label on the equipment, and so on.)

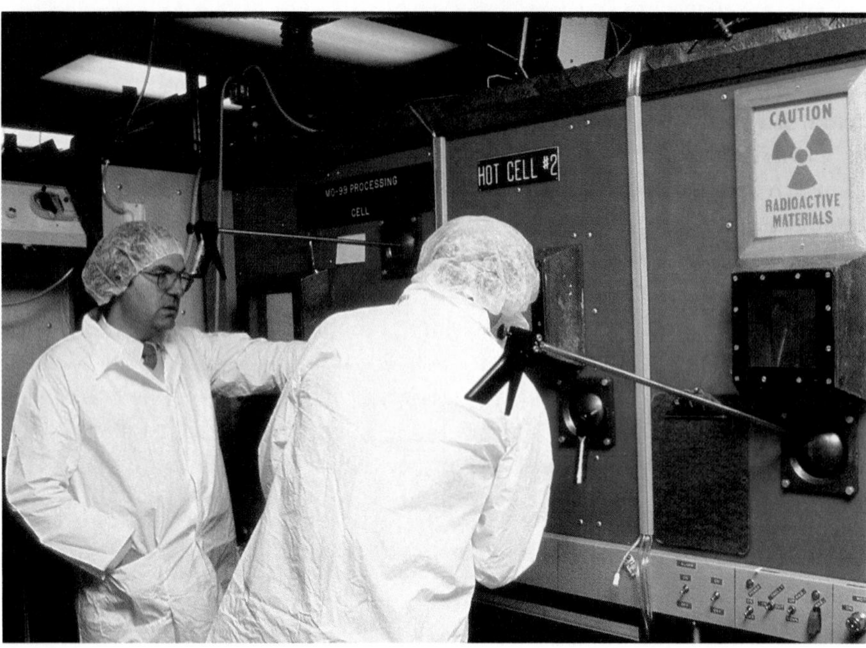

investigation. If OSHA finds that any of its safety regulations have been violated, it would require that the unsafe condition be eliminated and would perhaps fine the employer.

HOW DO WORKERS' COMPENSATION LAWS WORK?

PROBLEM

Turpin was a production-line worker in a steel desk factory. His job was to use a hydraulic shear to cut large pieces of sheet metal into smaller sizes for desk drawers. One morning while Turpin was setting up his shear, Gillis, his friend and co-worker, watched. Gillis believed that the main power supply for the machine was off. As a joke, he pressed the two "ON" buttons while Turpin's arm was under the shear's blade. Turpin's arm was cut off. Can Turpin recover from his employer for the loss of his arm?

Negligence suits under the common law were risky for both employers and employees. Most injured employees collected nothing because of the common-law defenses. However, when employees did win, they sometimes were awarded amounts that would bankrupt the employer. Today's workers'

TEACH

Explain that today's workers' compensation laws reflect a move from allocating costs based on fault to ensuring medical expense and continued income coverage. On the chalkboard, list the three factors (listed on p. 491) that determine whether an employee is protected by workers' compensation. Discuss each. Be sure students are aware that the decision about whether or not a person is entitled to benefits is made at a hearing conducted by a state administrative agency. Define **casual workers** and **independent contractors** and explain why they are not required to be covered by workers' compensation.

ASSESS

Learning Objective 2 Have students jot down answers to the following true or false questions about workers' compensation insurance: **(1) Job-related stress is generally not covered.** (False); **(2) In nearly every case, the payment is less than if the employee had won a negligence suit.** (True); and **(3) Employees are generally protected if they are injured or killed in the course of their employment or from the risks of employment.** (True) compensation laws reflect a public policy objective of moving away from allocating costs based on fault and toward always ensuring that injured employees will recover medical expenses. The cost of this insurance is passed along to consumers in the form of slightly higher prices for goods and services.

Thus, in the problem, Turpin would recover workers' compensation benefits even though the injury was caused by a co-worker and the employer was not at fault. Note that before workers' compensation, no money would have been paid, since Turpin's only right at that time would have been to sue for negligence. He probably would have lost this suit against his employer because of the defense of co-worker negligence. Although the co-worker, Gillis, was legally responsible, he was probably judgment-proof (i.e., had no money to pay a judgment).

1. Recovery Under Workers' Compensation Insurance

PROBLEM

Boal assembled fire hydrants for the Richmond Foundry. The job required him to lift finished fire hydrants weighing up to 140 pounds. One day, while lifting fire hydrants, Boal suffered a hernia. Can he collect workers' compensation benefits?

Employees are generally protected by workers' compensation insurance if they are injured:

1. by accident or disease, including job-related stress;
2. in the course of their employment; and
3. from the risks of that employment.

Generally, these requirements are satisfied if a worker is injured while on the job and the injury is caused by the work. Thus, in the problem, Boal could collect benefits. On the other hand, a clerical worker who suffered a hernia while picking a piece of paper off the floor might not collect benefits. That is because the injury may not have been caused by the job; it was probably caused by weak abdominal muscles.

If a worker covered by workers' compensation is injured because of the job, the worker becomes entitled to benefits. Sometimes there is a lump-sum payment to cover such things as pain and suffering, injuries such as loss of a hand, or loss of life. In nearly every case, the payment is less than if the injured party had won a negligence suit. All medical expenses usually are covered. Most states will also pay a percentage of lost wages; 80 percent is a common amount. If an accident makes it impossible for a worker to

▼ APPLY

Personal Perspectives

Ask students to recall and share incidents that they have experienced or witnessed, involving injuries in school or at work. Ask the class to determine who was at fault and to evaluate if it should be a factor in determining compensation. **Guided Practice**

Divide the class into groups of four or five. Write the following outline on the chalkboard: **Who was injured; The extent of the injury; How he or she was injured; What contributed to the injury; The employer's role; Evidence of the employer's attitude toward employees;** and **What compensation the employee is asking.** Assign the following roles: recorder who writes the scenario; employee's attorney who defends the case; employer's attorney who presents the case; reporter who reads the scenario on camera; and facilitator who keeps everyone on task. Tell students to use the outline to structure a scenario, then prepare and videotape two opposing attorneys' closing arguments. Show videotapes to the class and have students render judgments.

Cooperative Learning

▼RETEACH Pair students who understand how employees are protected by workers' compensation insurance with those who are having difficulty. Have each pair create a graphic organizer showing the important points in the section, *Recovery Under Workers' Compensation Insurance*, on p. 491.

Have students compose, using a computer, if possible, scenarios that would result either in awards under workers' compensation insurance or exceptions to recovery. Have them specify the requirements being met.

Thinking Critically Through Visuals

The man in the photograph is applying for a new job. If his disability occurred from an injury at his past job, what compensation might he have received in addition to medical expenses? (Answers may include lost wages, vocational rehabilitation, and so on.)

Ask students to identify the options employers have for funding workers' compensation benefits. (Private insurance companies, state-administered funds, self-insurance) List each on the chalkboard as it is offered, and have student volunteers explain how each affects workplace safety. **Independent Practice**

Have at-risk students who are having difficulty understanding the relevance of this material, imagine that they are working at their dream jobs. Have them, one by one, orally describe the job and whether or not it would be covered by workers' compensation insurance. Have other students correct any misconceptions.

continue in the former job, most states also pay for vocational rehabilitation. **Vocational rehabilitation** is training for another type of job. Often the amount of the benefit is increased if the employer is grossly negligent or reduced if the employee is grossly negligent. A 10-percent increase or reduction is typical.

Workers' compensation benefits are paid from one of three sources. Employers may purchase a workers' compensation insurance policy from a private insurance company, participate in a state-administered workers' compensation fund, or be self-insured. Insurance companies and state funds charge amounts that reflect the riskiness of the business and each employer's safety history. The amount paid out by those that are self-insured depends on the number and severity of workplace injuries. So employers have an incentive to make the workplace safe to reduce their costs of workers' compensation coverage.

2. The Coverage of Workers' Compensation Laws

Not all workers are required to be covered by a plan of workers' compensation. Frequently, companies with three or fewer employees are not required to provide workers' compensation insurance. Similarly, in most states, casual workers need not be covered. **Casual workers** are those who do not work regularly for one employer. If a company hired a troop of Scouts on a one-time basis to wash all the company cars, the Scouts would be casual workers. In addition, servants, housekeepers, and agricultural workers often are not required to be covered. Also independent contracts need not be covered. An **independent contractor** is someone hired to accomplish a task, but who is not supervised while doing so. If you hired someone to repair your car's broken transmission, he or she would probably be an independent contractor, not an employee.

▼ ASSESS

Have students orally match the boldface terms on p. 492 to the following definitions: **(1) Workers who do not work regularly for one employer.** (Casual workers); **(2) Training after an injury for another type of job.** (Vocational rehabilitation); and **(3) Someone hired to accomplish a task, but who is not supervised while doing so.** (Independent contractor)

Rather than being covered by state workers' compensation laws, employees of railroads, airlines, trucking firms, and other common carriers engaged in interstate commerce are governed by a special federal law. Longshore and harbor workers also operate under a different federal law and are not subject to state workers' compensation laws.

3. Winning a Workers' Compensation Award

The decision about whether a person is entitled to benefits is made at a hearing conducted by a state administrative agency. This agency is often called the Workers' Compensation Board or the Industrial Accident Commission. Hearing procedures are much less complicated than those of a trial. Accordingly, for small claims the injured worker does not need a lawyer. However, when the claim or injury is significant, the person should be represented by a lawyer who is a specialist in the field.

WHEN CAN THE INJURED EMPLOYEE RECOVER FROM THE EMPLOYER FOR NEGLIGENCE?

PROBLEM

Tolbert worked as a secretary for Martin Aerospace in an area secured from the public. While on her way to lunch one day, she was raped by a man who worked for Martin as a janitor. Can Tolbert recover from Martin Aerospace for her injuries?

The general rule is that an employee cannot sue the employer for on-the-job injuries if the employee is covered by workers' compensation. But there are several important exceptions. In these exceptional circumstances, an injured employee (or the family of an employee who is killed on the job) can still sue the employer for negligence. The cases differ in the extent to which they allow use of the common-law defenses. In some situations, no common-law defense is available, in others only assumption of the risk and contributory negligence are available.

1. When the Employer Fails to Provide the Required Workers' Compensation Insurance

If state law requires that an employee be covered but the employer has not purchased workers' compensation insurance, the injured employee can sue the employer for negligence. This may happen when the employer mistakenly classifies someone as an independent contractor or a casual employee. In these cases, the employer generally may not use the employers' common-law defenses of assumption of the risk, contributory negligence, or co-worker negligence. Thus, the employee has the possibility of recovering

TEACH

Explain that, in general, employees cannot sue the employer for on-the-job injuries if the employee is covered by workers' compensation, but there are exceptions. Discuss the four exceptions on pp. 493–494 by showing the overhead transparency, *When the Employer Can Be Sued for Negligence.* Explain each point.

APPLY

You may wish to provide further background on Karen Silkwood (p. 494) by showing parts of the ABC Motion Pictures videotape, *Silkwood,* such as the workers making light of safety, the union meeting, and Karen's discouragement by co-workers. Afterward, discuss students' reactions. You may wish to preview the video before showing it and, using your discretion, censor any scenes that might be objectionable. **Guided Practice**

Secure a large section of butcher paper to a wall. Provide students with a supply of news and business magazines, scissors, tape, and markers. Have them make a collage that depicts the theme: *Labor Rules and Rights.* When completed, have students explain their section to the class.

Independent Practice

RETEACH

Make a two-column chart on butcher paper, or a transparency. Label the columns **Covered Employees** and **Uncovered Employees (Casual Workers/Independent Contractors).** List examples in the corresponding column. (See pp. 492–493 for examples.)

ENRICH

Have students debate the workers' compensation standard practice of reducing the benefit for vocational rehabilitation when either the employee or the employer is found to have been grossly negligent.

Ethics Issue

Read the following: **Plunkett, a casual worker, was working for Winslow Builders on blasting sites. Safety helmets and glasses were available, but not required. Plunkett was not wearing glasses when a charge went off prematurely, and flying dirt seriously injured his eye.** Ask: **What are the legal and ethical issues involved?** (Answers may include that casual workers need not be covered by workers' compensation. Plunkett could sue; however, Winslow could cite assumed risk and contributory negligence. Ethically, Winslow should pay at least part of Plunkett's medical bills.)

▼ TEACH

On the chalkboard, draw a three-column chart. Label the columns **Type, Requirements,** and **Results.** Discuss OSHA's *general duty clause, specific regulations,* and *workplace inspections.* Fill in the chart as you discuss each. Then, discuss the fact that the high cost of OSHA compliance sometimes bankrupts a company.

large sums of money while the employer is almost defenseless. This possibility creates a great incentive for the employer to purchase workers' compensation coverage.

2. When the Employee Is Not Required to Be Covered

If an employee is not required to be covered by workers' compensation and is injured because of the employer's negligence, the employee may sue the employer. In these cases, the employer may usually use the common-law defenses.

3. When the Injury Is Not Covered by Workers' Compensation

In some cases, the employee is injured because of the negligence of the employer but workers' compensation does not cover the injury. In the problem, Tolbert's injury did not arise from a risk of her work. There is nothing about being a secretary that increases the risk of being raped. So the injury was not covered by workers' compensation. But Tolbert could sue Martin for not adequately screening its employees. While the law would allow Martin Aerospace to assert the defenses of contributory negligence or assumption of the risk, neither is likely to be an effective defense. So Tolbert will prevail.

4. When the Employer Commits an Intentional Tort

Even when covered by workers' compensation, an employee may sue the employer for intentional actions that the employer knows will cause injury. This most often occurs when the conduct of the employer is criminal, is an intentional tort, or is an intentional violation of a safety regulation.

> Karen Silkwood worked in a plant that manufactured radioactive materials. She was covered by workers' compensation. The procedures used by the company resulted in employees being systematically exposed to radioactive materials. Karen was one of the employees exposed. After her death, her family sued the employer in tort and recovered a large judgment.

▼ HOW DOES OSHA PROTECT EMPLOYEES?

PROBLEM

Browning Processing Company prepares fruits and vegetables for the market. An OSHA inspector ordered the company to install clutches on the prune-pitting machines and to provide electrical grounding of all electric typewriters and word processors. Must Browning comply?

▼ ASSESS

Learning Objective 3 Ask students to list and explain, in writing and in their own words, the four important exceptions to the general rule that an employee cannot sue employers for on-the-job injuries if the employee is covered by workers' compensation. (See pp. 493–494.)

In 1970, the U.S. Congress enacted a law called the Occupational Safety and Health Administration Act. This law created the Occupational Safety and Health Administration and empowered it to enact rules and regulations designed to achieve safety in the workplace. The law and the federal administrative agency are both commonly referred to as OSHA. The basic policy behind this legislation was to directly prevent injuries by requiring that workplaces be safe.

1. The General Duty Clause

In general, OSHA enforces two types of laws. The first type is the general duty clause. It requires that employers provide a place of employment free from hazards that are likely to cause death or serious physical harm. If this general duty requirement is violated, OSHA can fine the company and/or shut down the plant.

2. Specific Regulations

The second type of OSHA law includes specific workplace safety regulations. Many of these regulations were hastily established shortly after this federal administrative agency was formed. In some cases, OSHA simply adopted private industry and trade association safety standards. As a result, many regulations were poorly worded and inappropriately applied. In recent years, many of these regulations have been revised to make them more clear and practical.

These regulations cover most aspects of work. They spell out safety training requirements; safety clothing and equipment to be worn by workers; and the construction, maintenance, and shielding of equipment. Minimum standards are established for lighting, ventilation, and sanitation. For example, OSHA specifies that spray paint booths must be vented to the exterior of the building and that they must be constructed of metal rather than wood. Another example is the requirement that hair protection (e.g., hair nets) be worn when working near equipment such as drills. Minor violations of OSHA regulations are usually resolved by bringing the workplace into compliance, although employers can be fined. In the problem, Browning Processing would be required to comply with OSHA's demands because the lack of clutches and electrical grounding violates specific OSHA regulations. If the company did not comply, it could be fined.

3. Workplace Inspection

OSHA uses workplace inspections to ensure compliance with its general duty clause and specific regulations. While an employer may deny OSHA inspectors access to the workplace, inspectors can easily obtain a search warrant giving them authority to inspect. Employers are required to file periodic safety reports describing work-related injuries and deaths. These

APPLY

Ethics Issue

Ask the class to debate the possible risks and gains to employees when they decide to report an OSHA violation. Explain that these people are often called *whistle blowers*. Suggest long-range consequences of the violation. Ask: **What are the ethical conflicts inherent in these kinds of situations?** (Answers may include getting fired, being ostracized by fellow employees, and so on.) **Guided Practice**

Pair students. Using a tape recorder, have members of each pair take turns role-playing a telephone conversation between an employee reporting a suspected OSHA violation and an OSHA representative. The employee's objective is to get the message across but to remain anonymous, and the OSHA worker's objective is to gain enough information to determine if a legitimate violation has been committed. Have students record their conversations. **Independent Practice**

Cover the type in the overhead transparency master, *When the Employer Can Be Sued for Negligence*, and duplicate and distribute it to students. Discuss each point. Have students provide examples.

Have students write, using a computer, if possible, two paragraphs listing the pros and cons of awarding sums of money that greatly exceed typical workers' compensation awards in cases where the employer fails to provide required workers' compensation.

Multicultural Highlights

César Estrada Chávez was a labor union organizer and executive director of the United Farm Workers, which organized farm workers. Chávez was personally committed to seeking justice and fair and safe working conditions through nonviolent means. In his lifetime, he became a symbol of social protest for many Hispanic Americans. Ask: **Why, do you think, was Chávez committed to nonviolence?** (Answers may include that seeking justice through unjust methods is ethically illogical, and so on.)

Preventing Legal Difficulties

Review the suggestions to employees and employers for preventing legal difficulties in the workplace. Then, have students brainstorm a list of specific questions to ask in order to carry out the three suggestions for employees. Have students copy them in their notebooks for future reference.

reports often prompt OSHA inspections. Also, employees may anonymously report safety violations simply by calling OSHA, and OSHA will send inspectors to the workplace. Employers may not discriminate against workers who have informed OSHA of safety violations.

4. Dealing With OSHA Violations

In most simple cases involving violations, employers deal with OSHA officials without a lawyer. The problems usually involve technical engineering and safety issues rather than legal issues. Inspectors and company supervisors are best equipped to deal with these problems. However, some OSHA violations become serious because the cost of compliance can be prohibitive, pushing some companies into bankruptcy. In these situations, the employer needs immediate expert legal help. Unless one acts quickly, some rights to appeal the safety citation may be lost.

Preventing Legal Difficulties

As an employee . . .

1. Determine whether you would be covered by workers' compensation insurance before accepting a job involving safety risks.
2. Follow all safety precautions, use all safety devices prescribed for your job, and follow the employer's safety regulations.
3. Think about the elements of your work that might cause injury to you or to a co-worker. If there are serious risks, discuss them in a friendly way with your boss. If your boss is not helpful, consider discussing the situation with the people at OSHA.

As an employer . . .

1. Inspect your workplace to identify and to eliminate risks to the safety and health of your workers.
2. Identify lawyers in your area who specialize in employment law.
3. Verify that all your workers are covered by workers' compensation. If some are not covered, ask your attorney to review their status.
4. If you hire servants, agricultural or casual workers, or independent contractors who are not covered by workers' compensation, ask your lawyer for advice on how to limit your liability for injuries to them.
5. Consider asking OSHA inspectors to conduct an informal inspection of your workplace.

ASSESS

Learning Objective 4 Ask students to respond orally to the following: **(1) What is the basic policy behind OSHA?** (To prevent injuries from occuring by requiring that workplaces be safe); **(2) What action(s) can OSHA take if the general duty requirement is violated?** (Fine the company and/or shut down the plant); and **(3) Are anonymous reports of safety violations accepted by OSHA?** (Yes; If credible, OSHA then will send inspectors to the workplace.)

REVIEWING IMPORTANT POINTS

1. Negligence suits are based on determining who is at fault. These suits generally *cannot* be brought if the injured worker is covered by workers' compensation.
2. Negligence suits *can* be brought by an injured worker if (1) a worker should have been covered by workers' compensation but was not, (2) a worker was not required to be covered by workers' compensation, (3) the injury to the worker is not covered by workers' compensation, or (4) the employer does something that it knows will cause injury.
3. In a suit for negligence, the worker must establish that the employer was negligent and this caused the injury.
4. Even when the employer is negligent, the worker cannot win if the employer can establish any of the common-law defenses.
5. Workers' compensation pays benefits to those injured in the course of their employment from the risks of the job. The benefits usually include all medical payments, some lost wages, and sometimes vocational rehabilitation.
6. The employer pays the workers' compensation premiums. The amount is based in part on the safety record of the employer.
7. OSHA enforces both a general duty clause and specific workplace regulations.
8. OSHA inspectors can obtain search warrants to inspect the workplace. Most violations do not involve a fine if the violation is eliminated. Serious violations can lead to heavy fines and plant closings.

STRENGTHENING YOUR LEGAL VOCABULARY

Match each term with the statement that best defines that term. Some terms may not be used.

assumption of the risk
casual workers
common-law defenses
contributory negligence
co-worker negligence
independent contractor
negligence suit
Occupational Safety and Health Act (OSHA)
Occupational Safety and Health Administration (OSHA)
vocational rehabilitation
workers' compensation statutes

1. When a worker knows there is danger on the job but agrees to do it anyway.

CLOSE

Once again, poll the students to find out if their answers to the questions in the FOCUS activity have changed. Tally their responses and compare them with those from the beginning of this chapter. Discuss differences in the pre- and post-tallies.

As a whole class, create a wallet-size summary of important things for employees to remember about employee injuries. Have a student input this information on a computer, duplicate it on

heavy stock, and distribute a copy to each student.

Assign the following end-of-chapter materials:
Student text review activities, pp. 497–501
Workbook, pp. 73–74
Chapter Test

Chapter *MicroExam*

Strengthening Your Legal Vocabulary

1. assumption of the risk
2. vocational rehabilitation
3. workers' compensation statutes
4. Occupational Safety and Health Administration (OSHA)
5. casual workers
6. contributory negligence
7. independent contractor
8. negligence suit
9. common-law defenses
10. co-worker negligence

RETEACH

On blank overhead transparencies, have small groups make flowcharts that trace examples (fictitious or real) of workplace safety violations, from violation to OSHA action.

ENRICH

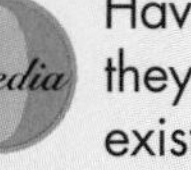

Have students write, using a computer, if possible, an essay in which they imagine what working conditions would be like if OSHA did not exist. Recommend books, such as *History of Standard Oil* by Ida Tarbell, *The Octopus* by Frank Norris, and *The Jungle* by Upton Sinclair.

2 Retraining of an injured worker.

3 Laws that provide compensation for workers (or their dependents) when the workers are injured (or killed) in the course of employment.

4 Federal agency that administers the Occupational Safety and Health Act.

5 Persons who do not work regularly for a certain employer.

6 When a worker does something to partially cause his or her own injury.

7 Someone who is hired to accomplish a task, but who is not supervised while doing it.

8 A suit, brought by an employee against an employer, that claims the employer's carelessness caused the employee's injury.

9 Consists of assumption of risk, contributory negligence, and negligence of a co-worker.

10 A fellow employee is responsible for one part of your injury.

APPLYING LAW TO EVERYDAY LIFE

1 ETHICS ISSUE Smyth, who was just starting a new lumberyard, hired only two employees. He did not purchase workers' compensation insurance for them. When asked why, he said, "There are two reasons: state law doesn't require it and I don't have enough money invested in the business to worry. If someone sues the corporation, I'll just take it into bankruptcy." Is Smyth's conduct ethical?

2 Jerold hired a construction worker to install a shake shingle roof on his home. The work was to be completed within thirty days. All the decisions about materials, methods, and time when the work would be done were left to the contractor. Must Jerold purchase workers' compensation insurance for the contractor? Why or why not?

3 ETHICS ISSUE Owens was hired by Moonglow Drive-in Theater to carry a large banner advertising the theater in a parade. The job was dangerous because it required Owens to walk through many busy intersections carrying the heavy banner. Does the law require that Moonglow purchase workers' compensation insurance for Owens? Ethically, is Moonglow required to carry the insurance? Why or why not?

4 Blake worked for West Oregon Lumber Company as a wood sorter. In violation of Oregon law, the company did not carry workers' compensation insurance. While sorting wood on a table, Blake knocked off a piece, which fell and hit his foot. Blake sued the employer for negligence. The lumber company asserted contributory negligence as an employer's defense. Will Blake win?

Applying Law to Everyday Life

1 ETHICS ISSUE No; Smyth's conduct is not ethical. A consequentialist would count the persons affected by Smyth's conduct. Smyth is positively affected because he saves the money he would otherwise pay for the workers' compensation insurance. But his two employees are injured because they assume risks of injury that will not be compensated. So, two are injured and one is benefited. Thus, consequentialists would say it is wrong. Deontologists would say that Smyth is deceiving the two employees unless he informs them that they are not covered.

2 No; Jerold need not purchase workers' compensation insurance because the roofer is an independent contractor. Jerold neither supervises nor controls the contractor's work.

3 

No; The law does not require Moonglow to provide workers' compensation coverage because Owens is a casual worker. (p. 492) However, unless Moonglow informs Owens of the known dangers of the job, plus the fact that Owens is not covered by workers' compensation, Moonglow may be engaged in deception. Deontologists would say this is unethical.

4 Yes; Blake will win. Since the employer did not have workers' compensation, it may be sued for negligence. Even though Blake was contributorily negligent, West Oregon Lumber Co. will be unable to assert employer's defense since it has not paid for workers' compensation. (p. 493)

5 Lambert hired Mayer to apply anhydrous ammonia, a fertilizer, to the soil on her farm. Lambert was not required to provide workers' compensation insurance, so Mayer was not covered. Lambert said to Mayer, "Be careful when you handle this stuff; it might burn you." However, Mayer had never used this type of equipment before, and Lambert did not explain to him how to handle the tank or the hose or what to do if he was sprayed on his body. Mayer lost control of the hose and was sprayed in the face with the chemical, blinding him in one eye. He sued Lambert for negligence, claiming that he was not properly instructed in how to handle the equipment. Who wins?

6 Atlas Warehouse was equipped with an old-fashioned freight elevator that had a manually operated gate on each floor. Any employee using the elevator could personally operate it. When the elevator reached a floor, the employee had to raise the gate and then lower it after getting off. Lacey, a supervisor delivering a message to Ritter, stepped off the elevator after raising the gate. But she did not lower the gate because she intended to get back on immediately. While she was talking with Ritter, the elevator was moved to another floor. After completing her conversation, Lacey returned to the elevator. Not noticing that it had been moved, she stepped into the shaft and fell to her death. What would be the employer's liability in a suit for negligence? What would be the employer's liability under workers' compensation statutes?

7 Frick and Brack were employed as truck drivers by different companies, and both were covered by workers' compensation. Late one afternoon, Frick was rushing to make a delivery before quitting time. In haste, Frick negligently rammed into Brack's truck. Brack suffered fatal injuries. Brack's widow later received a lump-sum workers' compensation benefit of $55,000. Is this all she can collect?

8 Randle worked at the Hide Tanning Company, which employed only two people. The company did not carry workers' compensation insurance because the state law did not apply to very small firms. A large wooden vat of acid with an open top was mounted on a wooden stand six feet off the ground. Because the stand was old and rickety, the people working near it were afraid that it would collapse and spill the acid on them. An OSHA inspector cited the company for violation of the general duty clause and threatened to close down the production operation. After negotiations, the company was given thirty days to correct the problem. Two days after the citation, the vat broke, spilling acid on Randle. Randle sued the employer and introduced the citation as evidence of the company's negligence. The company objected, claiming that OSHA inspections have nothing to do with suits for employer's negligence. Is the company correct?

5 Mayer wins. The employer has an obligation not merely to warn the worker of danger, but to give instructions that will enable the worker to avoid injury. Thus, Lambert was negligent. Mayer probably was not contributorily negligent because this was his first experience with the equipment and he was probably not fully aware of the risk involved. (pp. 488–489)

6 The employer had no liability in a suit for negligence unless it could be proved that the elevator was not safe. (pp. 488–489) The employee's death was caused by her own negligence. The workers' compensation insurance policy would be liable for the employee's death because the harm arose in the course of the employment from a risk of employment. (pp. 491–492)

7 No; Brack's widow may sue Frick and Frick's employer, and she might collect substantially more. There is no limit to the liability of outside third parties who negligently injure or kill workers on the job. Brack's employer has no further liability, however. (p. 493)

8 No; Violation of OSHA regulations, particularly violation of the general duty clause, is evidence of negligence. (p. 485)

9 Yes; Peery has been discriminated against, and this violates the Occupational Safety and Health Administration Act. He will be entitled to receive his old rate of pay. (p. 496)

9 Circo-Pacific manufactured circuit boards—the base on which electrical components are mounted by soldering. Peery worked as a dip solderer, inserting the bare boards into a small tub of molten solder to coat the copper circuits. The building in which he worked leaked and, when it rained, water dripped into the tub and splashed molten solder onto Peery's arm, causing numerous slight burns—the largest about half the size of a pencil eraser. Peery complained to his boss about the problem several times but his boss dismissed the complaints saying, "Don't be such a sissy." Peery finally complained to OSHA. An inspector arrived at the plant and cited the company. The fine was $500. A month later, Peery was transferred to a job that paid much less than that of dip solderer. He complained to OSHA that he was being discriminated against because of his complaint. Is he correct? What is the result?

Solving Case Problems

1 Yes; Janice is entitled to workers' compensation benefits. Her stress arose from the job and from a risk of the job. (p. 491)

2 No; Abell was a casual worker. The nature, scope, purpose of the hiring, and the duration of employment all indicate that the brothers were not regular employees. Accordingly, the recourse for the death of the worker was limited to wrongful death recovery and not to workers' compensation benefits. (p. 492) (Note: The court awarded the widow $20,000 and the estate $15,000 in damages.)

SOLVING CASE PROBLEMS

1 Janice worked for Drenberg and Associates, an insurance agency in Arizona, for fifteen years. During that time, the agency had grown dramatically and Janice's job responsibilities had been increased dramatically. As the pressures of her job increased, she suffered mental difficulties. One day, after a particularly emotional conversation with a client of the agency, she left the office in tears. Later, she was admitted to a mental hospital and diagnosed as neurotic depressive—as having a mental breakdown. She filed for workers' compensation insurance. Is she entitled to workers' compensation for stress? (*Fireman's Fund Insurance Company v. Industrial Commission*, 579 P.2d 555)

2 Abell and his brother had been hired as laborers to help prepare the grounds for the county fair. They were to be paid by the hour and were to furnish their own tools. No understanding was reached concerning the length of their employment, but it was understood that it would be "for one or two weeks." The work to be done consisted of "odd jobs," such as cleaning up and making minor repairs. Abell died when he was struck by a tractor while working. In light of these facts, were Abell's survivors entitled to workers' compensation benefits? (*Wood v. Abell*, 300 A.2d 665)

3 Thornton was employed as production foreman with the defendant corporation. On several occasions, Thornton had reprimanded an employee, Sozio, for failure to wear safety glasses and had reported this to the employer. On one occasion, Sozio threatened Thornton, saying, "I'll take care of your eyes later." Nine days after Sozio's employment had been terminated, Thornton saw him in a bar. At that time Sozio said, "Remember me, remember me?" and attacked Thornton, causing him to lose

the sight of one eye. Thornton claims that he is entitled to workers' compensation benefits because his injuries arose out of and had their origin in his employment and because the injuries were in the course of the employment. His employer claims that the injuries did not occur on the job even though they did arise out of the employment. Sozio, no longer an employee, had deliberately inflicted the injuries. Therefore, the employer argues, Thornton is not entitled to workers' compensation benefits. Is Thornton entitled to benefits? (*Thornton v. Chamberlain Manufacturing Corporation,* 62 N.J. 235, 300 A.2d 146)

4 Bailey managed a gasoline station. He was required to use his station wagon to make emergency calls for the station. Tools were carried in the car, and the service station paid for the gas and oil it used. Bailey owned another car that was used as a "family car." One morning while driving to work, Bailey was struck and killed by a train. His wife filed a claim for workers' compensation benefits. The Industrial Commission denied the claim, stating that travel to and from work is not covered by workers' compensation insurance. Was Bailey's death caused by his work? Is his widow entitled to the death benefit? (*Bailey v. Utah State Industrial Commission,* 16 P.2d 208, Utah)

5 Eckis, age twenty-two, was a full-time employee of Sea World, an amusement park. Eckis served as secretary for Burgess, the director of animal training. Eckis, who was an excellent swimmer, had worked as a model. When Burgess asked her to ride "Shamu, the Killer Whale" in a bikini for some publicity pictures, she eagerly agreed. Burgess knew Shamu was conditioned to being ridden only by persons wearing wet suits and had attacked riders in bathing suits. Eckis was warned in general terms of the danger, and she fell off during one practice session while wearing a wet suit. When a trainer told Eckis he would not watch her ride Shamu "because it was really dangerous," Burgess reassured Eckis and she rode Shamu three different times. Each time she wore a bikini instead of a wet suit. During the second ride, Shamu's tail was fluttering, indicating that the whale was upset. During the third ride, Eckis fell off and Shamu bit her on her legs and hips and held her in the tank until she was rescued. As an employee, Eckis qualified for modest workers' compensation payments but had no other insurance benefits. Therefore, she sued for more money in a civil action. She claimed that the employer was negligent, had defrauded her, and was liable for the acts of an animal with dangerous tendencies. The jury awarded Eckis damages of $75,000. Sea World appealed. Was workers' compensation Eckis's only remedy? (*Eckis v. Sea World Corporation,* 64 Cal. App. 3d 1, Cal. Rptr. 183)

3 Yes; The fact that the injuries were intentionally inflicted does not take them out of the workers' compensation statute. Also, the injury was sufficiently "work-connected" to bring it within the statute, which the legislature declares is to provide "protection for employees, not because of the fault or failure of the employer, but rather upon the belief that the enterprise should absorb losses which inevitably and predictably are an incident to its operations." (p. 491) Ordinarily, however, harm resulting from grudge fights is not covered by workers' compensation, particularly when occurring after working hours.

4 Yes; The death was caused by a risk of the work, and Bailey's widow is entitled to the death benefit. Generally, driving to and from work is not an activity occurring in the course of the employment. However, when driving to and from work has the purpose of transporting equipment needed to perform the job, it is a part of the job; thus, the death occurred in the course of the employment. (p. 491)

5 Yes, and the judgment was reversed. Eckis was clearly acting as an employee of Sea World at the time; therefore workers' compensation is her only remedy. The fact that the employer may have been negligent makes no difference. (p. 489)

CHAPTER 25 ORGANIZER

Chapter Theme

Principals, agents, and third parties are bound by contractually legal relationships, duties, and obligations.

DIRECTED STUDY QUESTIONS	SPECIAL FEATURES	PROGRAM RESOURCES				
		Reteach	Enrich	SN	AM	
What is agency?	Thinking Critically Through Visuals, p. 505	✔	✔			
Who can be a principal?	Ethics Issue, p. 506	✔	✔			
Who can be an agent?		✔	✔			
How is agency authority created?	Thinking Critically Through Visuals, p. 508 Multicultural Highlights, p. 509	✔	✔		V K	
What are an agent's fiduciary duties?	Writing Connections, p. 512 Thinking Critically Through Visuals, p. 513	✔	✔	✔	A	
What duties does a principal owe an agent?		✔	✔			
When is a principal liable to third persons?		✔	✔			
When is an agent liable liable to third persons?	Personal Perspectives, p. 516	✔	✔			
How is an agency terminated?	Preventing Legal Difficulties, p. 517	✔	✔			

Additional Resources

- Clifford, Denis and Randolph, Mary. *Who Will Handle Your Finances If You Can't?* Berkeley, CA: Nolo Press, 1992.
- Clifford Denis. *The Power of Attorney Book.* Berkeley, CA: Nolo Press, 1986.
- Steffen, Roscoe T. *Agency-Partnership*. St. Paul, MN: West Publishing Co., 1977.

One-semester course	✔	✔	✔					
One-year course	✔	✔	✔	✔	✔			

	ASSESSMENT OPPORTUNITIES			
Cooperative Learning	**Informal Assessment**	**Chapter Review**	**Chapter Test**	**Chapter *MicroExam*** Media
	✔	✔	✔	✔
	✔	✔	✔	✔
	✔	✔	✔	✔
	✔	✔	✔	✔
	✔	✔	✔	✔
	✔	✔	✔	✔
	✔	✔	✔	✔
	✔	✔	✔	✔
✔	✔	✔	✔	✔

Videodiscs

Agent's Authority

Search Chapter 31, Play To 32

State by State

In North Carolina, agents who sell burglar alarms must be licensed by the state.

Teaching Materials

Student text, pp. 502–524

Overhead transparency masters
- *Agency Is a Triangular Relationship*
- *Directions of Agency Relationships*

Videos
- *Law for Business* Videodisc

Workbook, pp. 75–80

Outside Resources
- Newspaper advertisements
- "Junk mail" flyers
- Telephone book "Yellow Pages"
- List of state-licensed agents
- Index cards
- Newspapers and magazines
- Sample business expense account form
- Legal and business notices from newspapers
- Hippocratic Oath
- Blank overhead transparencies

- Blank cassette tapes
- Tape recorders
- Camcorder
- VCR

Assessment
- Chapter Test

- Chapter *MicroExam*

Vocabulary

agency, p. 504
principal, p. 504
agent, p. 504
third party, p. 504
scope of authority, p. 505
fiduciary duties, p. 505
warranty of the principal's capacity, p. 506
gratuitous agency, p. 507
express authority, p. 507
power of attorney, p. 507
implied authority, p. 508
apparent authority, p. 509
ratification, p. 509
duty of loyalty, p. 511
duty of obedience, p. 511
duty of reasonable care and skill, p. 511
duty of confidentiality, p. 512
duty of accounting, p. 512
commingling, p. 512
undisclosed principal, p. 516

Learning Objectives

When you complete this chapter, you will be able to

1. Describe when an agency relationship exists.
2. Tell who is qualified to be a principal and who is qualified to be an agent.
3. Identify the scope of an agent's authority.
4. Name and define the agent's fiduciary duties.
5. Define the principal's duties to the agent.
6. Explain when the principal or agent is liable to a third party.
7. Describe how an agency relationship can be terminated.

502

Chapter Self-Test

Assess students' understanding of agency relationships before they begin Chapter 25 by asking students to respond in writing to the following *True* or *False* statements: **(1) You work at the supermarket after school stocking shelves. You are not an agent of the market.** (True); and **(2) The person who delivers your daily newspaper is an agent.** (True) Before continuing with the chapter, review and discuss students' responses.

CHAPTER 25

AGENTS

1 The Outdoors Equipment Shop has a big sale scheduled for next weekend, but you will be out of town. Can you authorize a friend to buy a pair of binoculars in your name? If your friend buys the binoculars in your name, will you both be liable for the purchase price?

2 You know a friend is looking for a weight-lifting bench and a set of barbells. When you find a good buy, you give the seller a down payment in the name of your friend. Is your friend liable to you for the down payment? Is your friend liable to the seller for the balance? Are you liable for the balance?

3 ETHICS ISSUE Jeff hired Sally as his real estate broker to help sell his home. While she was trying to sell the home, a buyer asked Sally what Jeff's bottom price was. She told the buyer (without Jeff's permission) and the house sold. Has Sally done anything legally wrong? Has Sally done anything ethically wrong?

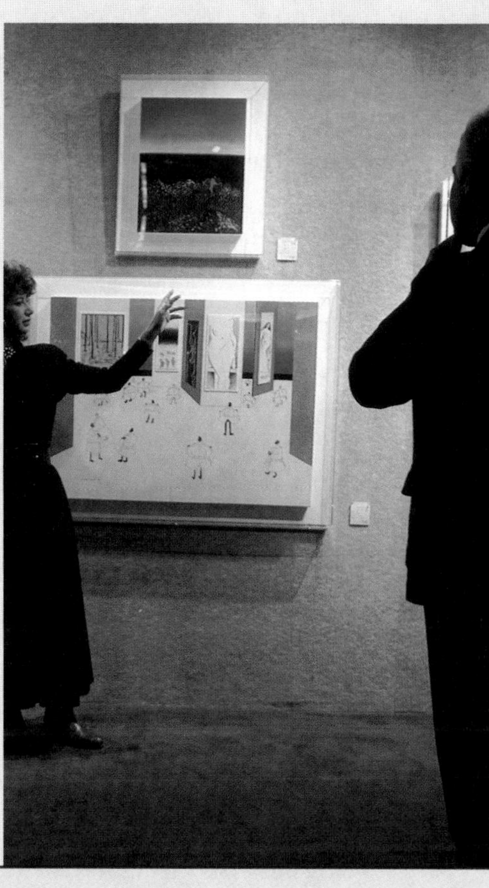

FOCUS

In small groups, have students brainstorm and make a list of as many types of agents as they can. (Answers may include travel agent, actor's agent, business agent, talent agent, lawyer, accountant, and so on.)

Have a student volunteer from each group read aloud the group's list. Ask students to hypothesize what the term **agent** means after discussing the jobs or roles of the agents that they listed.

You Decide

1 Yes, you can authorize another person to buy binoculars in your name. Only you, the principal, would be liable to pay for them.

2 Your friend is not liable to you or to the seller since your friend never asked you to be an agent, You, because you led the seller to accept you as an agent, are liable for the cost of the equipment.

3 ETHICS ISSUE Sally violated her duty of loyalty to the seller and also acted unethically because she did not act in the seller's best interest.

Thinking Critically Through Visuals

When an artist's paintings hang in a gallery, with whom, do you think, is the buyer more likely to deal—the agent or the principal? (The agent; The artist who is the principal has agreed to let the gallery act as an agent in selling the paintings.)

▼ TEACH

Ask if anyone has recently picked up and paid for a pizza ordered by a family member. Identify this as an **agency** relationship. Display the overhead transparency, *Agency Is a Triangular Relationship.* Show how the pizza pickup scenario fits into the triangular relationship. The principal (family member) orders the pizza. The agent (student) picks up the pizza and pays the third party (pizzeria) for it. Emphasize that for this relationship to work successfully, the participants must recognize their **scope of authority** and **fiduciary duties.**

▼ APPLY

Have students use the overhead transparency, *Agency Is a Triangular Relationship,* to identify the people in the following situation: **Mrs. Waters walks into Minervini's Bicycle Shop, says hello to Barbara who runs the repair section, and buys a helmet from Pat, the owner's son. Pat writes out a sales slip, which Mrs. Waters takes to Lisa, the cashier, and pays for the helmet. Who fits into the three categories that make up the agency triangle?** (Agents—Pat and Lisa, principal—owner Minervini, third party—Mrs. Waters) **Guided Practice**

▼ WHAT IS AGENCY?

PROBLEM

Jose worked at the Civic Center Service Station. His duties included selling gasoline, oil, and accessories, for which he either collected cash or made out credit tickets. Jose also changed oil and filters, provided lubrication services, and cleaned the premises. Was Jose an agent or an ordinary employee?

You learned in Chapter 21 that one who does work for pay (e.g., bagging groceries or reading water meters) under the supervision and control of another person is an ordinary employee. But some employees have a special legal status because they make contracts for their employer. When one person is authorized to alter another's legal relationships (e.g., by contracting on their behalf), the relationship of **agency** exists. The person who authorizes another to alter a legal relationship is a **principal**. The party authorized is the **agent**. A **third party** works through an agent to reach an agreement that binds a principal.

In the problem, Jose was just an employee when he changed oil and filters, lubricated cars, and cleaned the premises. But when he sold gas, oil, and accessories, the agency relationship existed. Agency existed because Jose was altering the legal relationships of the service station by making contracts on its behalf. The service station or its owner is the principal. Jose is the owner's agent as well as an employee. Customers are the third parties. Figure 25-1 illustrates these parties and their relationships.

Contracting is the most common way of altering legal relationships. But there are other ways an agent can alter legal relationships. You can use agency to marry someone, divorce someone, sue someone, waive your legal rights, or alter your legal relationships in a variety of other ways.

Sharon was a physician and a member of the Army reserve. She was called to active duty during Operation Desert Storm and sent to Saudi Arabia. She and Dennis wanted to marry but they were separated by over 6,000 miles. So Sharon asked her friend Gail "to stand in for her" during the wedding ceremony. Gail did, and on behalf of Sharon said, "I do." Gail was Sharon's agent because she altered Sharon's legal relationship with Dennis—Gail bound Sharon to the marriage relationship.

▼ ASSESS

Learning Objective 1 Have students brainstorm a series of agency relationships with which they or their families are personally familiar. Share responses and identify the principal, the agent, and the third party.

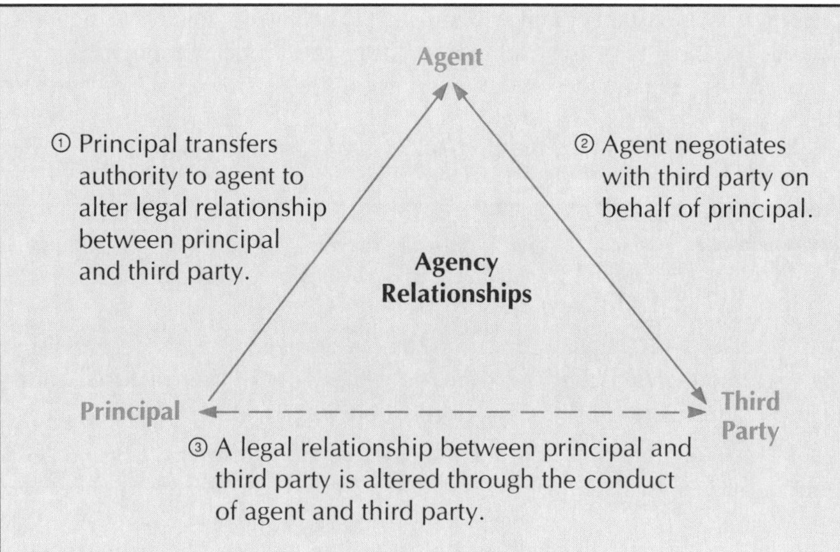
Agent
① Principal transfers authority to agent to alter legal relationship between principal and third party.
② Agent negotiates with third party on behalf of principal.
Agency Relationships
Principal
Third Party
③ A legal relationship between principal and third party is altered through the conduct of agent and third party.

Figure 25-1
In agency relationships, the principal authorizes the agent to alter legal relationships with third parties on the principal's behalf.

Thinking Critically Through Visuals

In an agency relationship, both the principal and the third party deal with the agent. Why is the relationship between the principal and the third party indicated by a broken line in this diagram? (It is not a direct relationship; it is altered by the actions of the agent.)

The agent must act within the scope of authority to bind the principal. The **scope of authority** is the range of acts authorized by the principal.

Smiley bought a motorscooter from The Wheels Shop. The salesperson who sold Smiley the scooter gave her a signed card offering a free engine adjustment anytime within three months of purchase. If the salesperson changed jobs or was out of the shop when such an adjustment was requested, Smiley could look directly to Young, the owner of the shop, for performance. The signature of the salesperson was binding on the owner as principal, just as if the owner had personally signed the card.

If the agent has acted *outside* the scope of authority, the principal is not bound. Thus, in the example, if the salesperson had, without consent, executed a deed to Young's home, the owner would not be bound. The salesperson would have been acting outside the scope of authority. Generally, agents are not personally liable for the contracts that they negotiate on behalf of their principals. However, when the agent acts outside the scope of authority and the third party suffers an injury as a result, the third party can recover from the agent.

All agents have obligations called fiduciary duties. In essence, **fiduciary duties** require that the agent serve the best interests of the principal. The specific fiduciary duties are those of loyalty and obedience, reasonable care

To small groups, distribute newspaper ads, "junk mail" flyers, and the "Yellow Pages" from the telephone directory. Have students examine the material and make lists of agency relationships that they find. (Answers may include car dealers, supermarkets, insurance agents, auction houses, lawn-care franchises, and so on.) As a whole class, review and discuss the lists. **Independent Practice**

RETEACH Have students draw a diagram or flowchart to show a specific agency relationship of their choosing. Refer students to Figure 25-1.

ENRICH Media: Contract law assumes that all parties will look out for their own self-interests, whereas agency law requires the agent to look out for the best interests of the principal. Ask: **Why, do you think, do these bodies of law have such different orientation?** Using the computer, if possible, have students write a short essay.

and skill, confidentiality, and accounting. If an agent violates a fiduciary duty, the principal may sue and recover from the agent any damages.

WHO CAN BE A PRINCIPAL?

PROBLEM

Carey, a minor, wished to sell her surfboard. She agreed to pay Fischer 10 percent of the sales price of $100 if Fischer would sell the board for her. Fischer agreed, but after he had found a buyer, Carey decided not to sell. She claimed that, as a minor, she had the power to avoid the agency agreement and to avoid the contract made by Fischer, her agent. Was Carey correct?

Minors, and others who lack contractual capacity, can be principals and act through agents. However, they may still avoid their contracts. So they may avoid contracts *made with* their agents. Thus, in the problem, Carey may avoid her contract to pay Fischer 10 percent. In addition, minors may avoid contracts *made through* their agent. So Carey can avoid the contract with the buyer of her surfboard. Acting through an agent does not alter the ability of minors, the legally intoxicated, or the insane to avoid contracts.

Because contracts made through agents can still be avoided by those who lack capacity, the law tries to protect third parties with a warranty of capacity. The **warranty of the principal's capacity** is imposed by law on the agent. The law assumes that the agent promised the third party that the principal had capacity. If the principal lacked capacity, avoided the contract, and thus injured the third party, the third party can recover from the agent.

WHO CAN BE AN AGENT?

PROBLEM

Tricia Cousins, a seventeen-year-old minor, was asked to buy a car on behalf of her elderly mother, Mrs. Cousins. Mrs. Cousins signed documents appointing Tricia as her agent for this purpose. Then Tricia found a car and executed a contract to buy it. Later, her mother decided she did not like the color and said she was not bound by the contract because Tricia was underage. Is Tricia's mother correct?

TEACH

Minors, and others who lack contractual capacity, can be principals and act through agents. A third party, however, may be protected by a **warranty of the principal's capacity.** The law assumes that the agent promised the third party that the principal had capacity.

APPLY

Ethics Issue

Ask: **In the PROBLEM on the top of p. 506, were Carey's actions ethical?** (No) Discuss the ethical problems of minors using the law to produce unfair outcome. **Guided Practice**

Have students give their opinion on the fairness of the warranty of the principal's capacity. (Answers may include third parties must have some protection, and so on.)

Independent Practice

TEACH

Minors, and others who lack contractual capacity, may act as agents. These agents, although lacking legal capacity for themselves, can bind adults in contracts.

ASSESS

Learning Objective 2 Have students create a Venn diagram to illustrate who can be a principal and who can be an agent. Suggest the following categories to get students started: *minors, people who lack contractual capacity*, and so on.

Minors, and others who lack contractual capacity, may themselves be agents. Thus, minors who lack legal capacity to act for themselves can generally act for and bind adults in contracts. The adult principals cannot later avoid the resulting contracts simply because of the minority of their agents. Only in the situation where the minor is unable to understand the transaction is the minor unable to act as an agent. In the problem, Tricia's mother is wrong. Mrs. Cousins is bound by the contract even though her agent, Tricia, was a minor.

To protect the public, all states require that agents in certain occupations be licensed. This usually requires passing a professional examination. Licensing is often required of auctioneers, insurance agents, lawyers, and real estate brokers.

HOW IS AGENCY AUTHORITY CREATED?

PROBLEM

In planning a birthday party, Taylor asked her friend Logan to buy the cake. Logan agreed. Taylor told her to charge the cake to Taylor's account at the bakery. Taylor also gave Logan the keys to her car. What type of agency authority does Logan have?

Agency authority is created when a principal authorizes an agent to represent the principal. When the principal agrees to pay the agent, the agency relationship arises from a contract between the agent and the principal. In other instances, there is no contract. One person, such as Logan in the problem, may simply agree to help another in altering relationships with third parties. In cases where the agent receives no consideration, the agency is called a **gratuitous agency.**

Agency authority may be created in a variety of ways. These include (1) an express grant of authority, (2) an implied grant of authority, (3) agency by apparent authority, and (4) ratification.

1. Express Grant of Authority

Express authority is directly communicated by the principal to the agent. It may be oral or written. In the problem, Taylor gave Logan express authority to purchase the cake. If written, the grant may be in an informal letter or a carefully drafted document. Any writing that appoints someone as an agent is called a **power of attorney.**

APPLY

Have students explain why an eight-year-old may act as an agent by going to the market for his or her mother but would not be recognized as a valid agent in the purchase of a lawn mower. (The assumption is that he or she would not have the knowledge to deal competently in the second transaction.)

Guided Practice

Distribute to students a list of agents who must be licensed by your state. In small groups, have students brainstorm the types of questions that might be asked on these agents' licensing exams. **Independent Practice**

TEACH

On a blank overhead transparency or on the chalkboard, draw a four-column chart to explain the ways agency authority may be created: by **express authority**, **implied authority**, **apparent authority**, and **ratification**.

Using the Venn diagram from the ASSESS activity on p. 506, have students brainstorm agency relationships within the same categories students identified.

Using a computer, if possible, have students discuss their legal role, or roles, as a minor in an agency relationship.

▼ APPLY

Thinking Critically Through Visuals

Trade fairs give manufacturers opportunities to display their newest products. Under what kind of agency authority are the manufacturers' representatives probably working? (Most likely under express grants of authority, but situations may arise that could only be covered by implied grants of authority) **Guided Practice**

Keeping the photograph in mind, have students create scenarios that may warrant a representative's use of implied or apparent authority. For example, in the photograph, if the representatives at the thermal plotter booth ran out of paper, they could assume they had implied authority to acquire more paper to continue their demonstrations.

2. Implied Grant of Authority

Implied authority is the power to do anything that is reasonably necessary or customary to carry out the duties expressly authorized. Thus, an agent's implied authority flows out of the express authority. In the problem, there may be implied authority for Logan to buy some gas for the car and charge it to Taylor if it is needed to get to the bakery.

Implied authority may be expanded in an emergency. In the problem, if Taylor's car caught on fire while Logan was driving it on the errand, Logan would have implied authority to promise money to someone to assist in extinguishing the fire. Taylor would be liable to pay for this help.

3. Apparent Authority

PROBLEM

Redman drove into Milton's Motors with the intention of trading her car for another one. The only person present was Davis, who was seated at the sales desk. Davis had been left in charge by Milton. Milton had instructed Davis to answer the telephone and to ask any walk-in customers to wait until he returned from the bank. Davis, upon learning of Redman's purpose, suggested that she inspect the new models on display while he test-drove her car for appraisal purposes. Davis drove Redman's car off the lot and never returned. Would Milton be liable for the value of Redman's car?

Agency authority may sometimes result from the appearance created by the principal. This does not create a conventional authority because there

▼ ASSESS

Learning Objective 3 Have students complete the fourth section, *How Is Agency Authority Created?*, of the Chapter Outline on p. 189 of the Workbook.

has been no agreement between the principal and the agent. **Apparent authority** is created when a principal leads the third party to reasonably believe that a particular person has agency authority. The apparent authority must always come from the principal's words or acts. It can never arise from the words or conduct of the agent alone. Thus, in the problem, Milton's conduct—allowing Davis to take charge of the office—led Redman to reasonably believe that Davis was Milton's agent with authority to make appraisals and sales. A person who intentionally or unintentionally causes another to think that a particular individual has been given agency authority will generally be bound by this apparent authority. Thus, Milton would be liable for the value of Redman's car.

The Wilsons were unhappy with a power lawn mower they had purchased from Lacey's Department Store. It was hard to start. Carla, who was in charge of Lacey's Customer Relations Department, had express authority to handle exchanges and refunds. In this case, she allowed the Wilsons to return the mower, and she gave them a full cash refund. Carla assumed that Lacey's would return the mower to the manufacturer. Later, the store manager told the Wilsons they should have asked the manufacturer for the refund. The Wilsons need not do so because Carla had apparent authority to bind the store. Her apparent authority was created when Lacey's made her the head of its customer relations department.

---

4. Ratification

If a person acts without express, implied, or apparent authority (i.e., acts outside the scope of his or her authority), the principal is not bound. However, a principal who later agrees to the transaction will be bound. This approval of an unauthorized act is called **ratification**. A principal impliedly ratifies an agency transaction by knowingly accepting its benefits.

For a valid ratification, the following conditions must be met:

- **a.** the third person must have believed that by dealing with the principal's agent, he or she was making a contract with the principal;
- **b.** before ratification, the principal must have full knowledge of all material facts;
- **c.** the principal must show an intent to ratify;
- **d.** the principal must ratify the entire act, not just one part of the transaction; and
- **e.** the principal must ratify before the third person withdraws from the unratified transaction.

Divide the class into four or five groups. Have each group create a scenario that depicts one of the four ways, listed on pp. 507–509, in which agency authority may be created. Then, have each group role-play it while the class determines which type of authority is being portrayed.

Independent Practice

Multicultural Highlights

Both an expressed and an implied agency relationship exist between advertising agencies and their clients. After losing her advertising job because she refused to work on a TV commercial she found "tasteless and offensive," Barbara Gardner Proctor, an African American, established her own agency. She vows to handle only those accounts that reflect family values and lend themselves to quality promotional ideas. Proctor's high standards have won her more than 20 advertising awards. Discuss whether Proctor violated her fiduciary responsibilities to the client and to the agency when she refused to work on that particular TV commercial.

▼RETEACH On one set of index cards, write the six vocabulary terms found on pp. 507-509. On another set of cards, write brief situations that describe or define each term. Distribute the cards to students and play a game of *Vocabulary Concentration*, in which students match each word to its meaning.

▼ENRICH Provide students with newspapers and magazines to create a bulletin-board display made up of news ads or articles that describe various types of agency authority.

TEACH

On the chalkboard or an overhead transparency, draw a spider map such as the one that follows to

graphically depict the fiduciary duties of an agent.

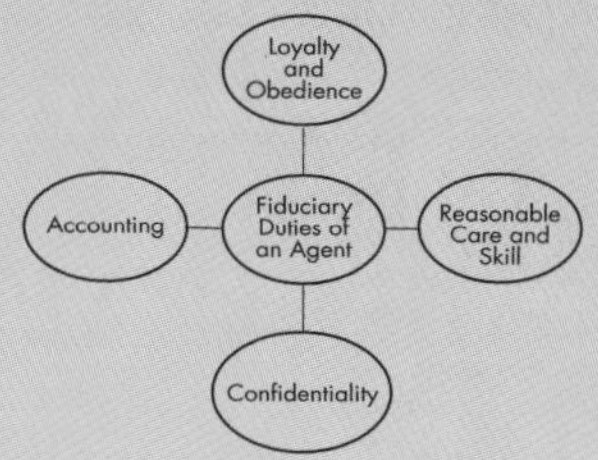

APPLY

In order to help ESL students and students with poor reading skills, audio tape, in random order, each PROBLEM found on pp. 510–512. Make photocopies of the spider map used in the previous TEACH section. Pair stronger and weaker readers. Distribute a pre-recorded cassette, a tape recorder, and a graphic organizer to each pair. Have students listen to the tape. Ask them to identify the fiduciary duty described in each problem and explain the best solution.

Guided Practice

Nora collected music boxes. One day her friend George discovered an attractive Swiss music box that he thought she would want. He bought the music box for $750, making a down payment of $100 in Nora's name but without her knowledge. When George described the transaction, Nora took the music box and paid George the $100. She is liable for the remaining $650 because she has ratified George's unauthorized conduct.

WHAT ARE AN AGENT'S FIDUCIARY DUTIES?

PROBLEM

Marty gave Wallace an antique Chinese bronze mirror to sell for her at the highest possible price. Wallace bought the mirror for his wife. However, he did not reveal that fact when he paid Marty. If Marty discovered what Wallace had done, could she avoid the contract?

In many respects, the agent's duties to the principal are the same as those of an ordinary employee. However, the agent has the power to bind the principal in dealings with others. Therefore, great trustworthiness, loyalty, utmost honesty, and good faith are required of the agent. The law encourages this with the four fiduciary duties mentioned earlier in this chapter. These duties owed by agents to principals are (1) loyalty and obedience, (2) care and skill, (3) confidentiality, and (4) accounting. In general, if an agent violates a fiduciary duty and that injures the principal, the *agent* will be liable for the injury. In the problem, Marty could sue Wallace for any lost profits. However, she could not avoid the contract.

1. Loyalty and Obedience

PROBLEM

Buck was a real estate broker. He obtained a listing on Marlene's home, which made him her agent. Later Buck spent almost two weeks working with a prospective buyer, and they became friends. The buyer, who was interested in Marlene's home, asked Buck, "What is the minimum price Marlene would accept for this property?" Buck knew what that price was. Can he tell it to the buyer?

ASSESS

Learning Objective 4 Display the spider map used in the TEACH activity. Brainstorm with students any number of agents, such as a real estate agent, accountant, and so on. Have students identify examples of the four fiduciary duties specific to each agent.

One of an agent's most basic duties is that of loyalty. The **duty of loyalty** requires that agents must place the interests of their principals above the interests of all others. In the problem, Buck must place Marlene's interests above the interests of his friend the buyer. He may not tell the buyer what Marlene's lowest price is. Further, the duty of loyalty means that the agent may not secretly benefit from the agency transaction. Thus, agents may neither buy from nor sell to themselves (or their relatives or friends) without prior approval by their principals. In addition, any profits the agent earns in performing the agency duties belong to the principal unless otherwise agreed.

The **duty of obedience** means that the agent must obey the instructions of the principal. Of course an agent should not follow instructions to do an illegal or immoral act. For example, a sales agent may not lie about a product even if the principal has ordered such fraudulent conduct. If a principal orders an agent to do something illegal or immoral, the agent should resign from the agency relationship.

Divide students into groups of three or four. Have students choose one of the following roles: principal, agent, third party, or extra actor (optional). Have groups create and role-play scenarios depicting a lack of duty of one of the following: loyalty and obedience, reasonable care and skill, confidentiality, and accounting. Have the class determine which duty was being violated.

Independent Practice

2. Reasonable Care and Skill

PROBLEM

The Merritts owned the Pony Express Inn. Because the inn was located in a high crime area, security was a concern. Therefore, the Merritts told everyone to limit the cash on hand by dropping all excess receipts into a floor safe controlled by an automatic timer. Kate, the weekend manager, thought this was too bothersome, so she simply left the receipts in the cash drawer and dropped the excess in at the end of her shift. One Sunday, Kate was robbed. The robbers escaped with the $3,000 that was in the cash drawer at the time. Is Kate liable to the Merritts for the loss?

In performing a transaction for one's principal, an agent must satisfy the duty of reasonable care and skill. The **duty of reasonable care and skill** requires the agent to exercise the degree of care and skill that a reasonably prudent person would use in a similar situation. At a minimum, this requires the agent to communicate to the principal any information that would affect the principal's decisions. Failing to satisfy the fiduciary duty of reasonable care and skill renders the agent liable to the principal for the resulting loss or injury. Thus, Kate would be held liable for the loss of the $3,000. This is because a prudent manager would not leave so much money in the cash drawer when a safe was available.

▼RETEACH Have students write five quiz questions (with answers on a separate sheet of paper) based on the information on pp. 510–511. Then have students exchange papers and take each other's quizzes.

▼ENRICH Have students brainstorm and write a list of agency relationships in which the duty of reasonable care and skill is particularly important. (Answers may include a delivery-van driver, healthcare providers, and so on.)

Writing Connections

Language Arts Obtain the Hippocratic Oath from the library. Read portions to students and point out that most physicians and healthcare providers feel strongly about their sworn duties. Then, have students choose one of the five PROBLEM scenarios on pp. 510–512. Have students write an agent's oath, expressing an agent's fiduciary duties, detailing how they will be fulfilled, and the consequences if a duty is violated. Encourage students to use a computer, if possible, to prepare their work.

Duplicate a sample business expense account form, found at office supply stores, for each student. On a transparency, write a list of expenses for a fictitious business trip of several days' duration. Be sure to include expenses for travel, hotel, food, entertainment of clients, and so on. Using this information, have students fill out the expense account form. (Point out that personal expenses are usually not allowable.)

3. Confidentiality

PROBLEM

Sue, when acting as the agent of Harry, learned that Harry was about to go into bankruptcy. This information was very valuable. Can Sue tell others about Harry's situation?

Agents owe the fiduciary duty of confidentiality to their principals. The **duty of confidentiality** requires the agent to treat information about the principal with great caution. Information that is obviously confidential must be treated as confidential. In the problem, Harry's impending bankruptcy is obviously confidential. If Sue told people about it and this injured Harry, he could sue her for the injury.

Other information is not obviously confidential. But if a principal asks an agent to treat any information as confidential, the agent must do so. This duty of confidentiality survives the agency relationship. So the duty binds agents even after the agency relationship has ended.

4. Accounting

PROBLEM

Rich, who often donated animals to the city zoo, sent his agent Alice to Africa to buy an elephant. Rich gave Alice $9,500 for travel and other expenses. Upon her return, must Alice report her expenses to Rich?

Agents owe the duty of accounting to their principal. The **duty of accounting** requires that an agent, like Alice in the problem, must account to the principal for all money and property of the principal that comes into the agent's possession. The agent must promptly notify the principal of the receipt of money from third parties and must make an accounting within a reasonable time. An accounting is a formal statement (usually in writing) that tells the principal what happened to all the principal's money or property.

The agent may not commingle. **Commingling** is mixing the funds or property of the agent with those of the principal. If commingling occurs and there is a loss, the agent will bear that loss. Further, if the agent's property is mixed with that of the principal in such a manner that they cannot be separated, all the property may be claimed by the principal. Money of the principal held by the agent must usually be deposited in a bank, in an ac-

ASSESS

Learning Objectives 4 & 5 Have students work in small groups to brainstorm other examples, such as the one in the PROBLEM on p. 513, that illustrate the duties a principal owes to an agent. Have students share their suggestions. Correct misconceptions as necessary.

count separate from that of the agent. These separate accounts for the funds of principals are called trust accounts.

WHAT DUTIES DOES A PRINCIPAL OWE AN AGENT?

PROBLEM

James signed an agreement with Jesse, appointing Jesse to find a buyer who would pay $35,000 for James's antique Ford. If Jesse found a buyer who was ready, willing, and able to buy the car, Jesse was to receive a commission of 10 percent of the price. Jesse found a ready, willing, and able buyer for the car at the agreed price, but James refused to enter into a sales contract. Is Jesse entitled to the commission?

A principal owes many of the same obligations to an agent that an employer owes to an ordinary employee. Failure of the principal to fulfill these obligations gives the agent the right to quit and to sue for any damages. The principal's main obligation is the duty to pay the agent. Thus, if a principal promises to pay for agency services, then the principal, like James in the problem, is legally obligated to pay. In addition, if an agent properly incurs expenses, the principal must reimburse the agent.

Thinking Critically Through Visuals

Works of art are often shipped between dealers and museums. In the situation shown here, what, do you think, was the agent's primary fiduciary responsibility? (Since the agent was the shipper, it probably was to exercise reasonable care and skill.)

TEACH

On the chalkboard, write the following: **principal = employer** and **agent = employee.** A principal owes many of the same obligations to an independent agent that an employer owes to an employee-agent. The principal's main duty is to pay his or her agent.

APPLY

On the chalkboard, draw a chart showing the duties of a principal and the rights of an agent. Have students provide you with the information from this section to complete the chart. **Guided Practice**

Have students create their own cause-and-effect charts to illustrate the relationship between a principal and an agent. **Independent Practice**

RETEACH

In writing, using a computer, if possible, have students explain why the duties of confidentiality and accounting are important fiduciary responsibilities of an agent to the principal.

Have small groups brainstorm a scenario in which a principal defaults on a debt to an agent. Acting (collectively) as the agent, have students write a letter of resignation. Encourage students to use a computer, if possible.

▼ TEACH

Explain to students that a principal is liable to third persons for fraud and torts committed by an agent as long as that agent acts within the scope of his or her authority and any unauthorized acts of the agent were ratified.

▼ APPLY

On an overhead transparency or the chalkboard, draw the base of the following spider map detailing the principal's liabilities to third parties, as long as the agent is acting within the scope of authority. Have students provide the information to complete the diagram. **Guided Practice**

Have students make a two-column chart listing the two subsections on p. 514 in one column and giving an example of each kind of liability in the second column. Label the chart *Principal's Liability to Third Persons.* **Independent Practice**

▼ WHEN IS A PRINCIPAL LIABLE TO THIRD PERSONS?

PROBLEM

Carol authorized Stan, her agent, to sell a quantity of out-of-style ladies' shoes at a very large discount. However, Stan was authorized to sell them for cash only. Stan sold the shoes to the Bargain Mart for 10 percent cash and the balance on three month's credit. When Stan told Carol it was "the best deal I could get for that junk," Carol accepted the cash. Two days later, however, Carol changed her mind. Must she complete the contract and deliver the shoes?

1. Contractual Liability to the Third Party

As long as an agent acts within the scope of the authority, the principal is bound by the agreement with the third party. The principal is also liable when, as in the problem, the unauthorized acts of the agent are ratified. By accepting the cash down payment, Carol ratified the contract made by her agent. Thus, Carol must deliver the shoes or be liable to Bargain Mart.

2. Liability for Fraud, Torts, and Crimes

If torts or fraudulent acts are committed by an agent who is acting within the scope of the authority, the principal is liable to third parties for the actions. For example, if an agent defrauds a customer in order to make a sale, the principal is liable for any damages that result. The agent is also liable for harm caused by any torts or fraudulent acts that he or she personally committed.

Bridges was the credit manager of White Appliances. Bridges wrongfully took possession of Diane's truck while attempting to collect a past-due account from Diane. White Appliances was liable to Diane for damages because Bridges, its agent, had committed the tort of conversion while acting within the scope of his authority. Bridges was also liable for the wrongdoing.

Usually, the principal is not liable for an agent's crime unless the crime itself has been authorized or ratified. As an exception to this rule, the principal is generally liable for the illegal sale, by the agent, of intoxicating liquor or adulterated foods. Thus, the principal, a bar owner, would be liable if the agent, a bartender, illegally served liquor to a minor.

▼ ASSESS

Learning Objective 6 Have students give examples of an agent's liability to third persons, as related to each of the three numbered sections on pp. 515–516.

WHEN IS AN AGENT LIABLE TO THIRD PERSONS?

PROBLEM

Sara was authorized to sell rugs and carpeting for the Magic Carpet Company, Inc., but she was not authorized to make purchases. While on a sales trip to New York, Sara had a rare opportunity to buy a quantity of small oriental rugs at low "distress sale" prices. She did not have enough time to contact her home office. Therefore, she simply signed the contract as a purchasing agent for Magic Carpet. Is Sara liable for the purchase price?

1. Agent Acts Outside the Scope of Authority

If an agent acts without authority from the principal, the agent becomes personally liable to the third party. That is because the agent impliedly warrants the agency authority. This problem usually arises when an agent exceeds the authority given by the principal. For example, in the problem, Sara was personally liable because she exceeded her agency authority. However, if Magic Carpet later ratified the purchase, Sara would no longer be personally liable. In some cases, a person will act as agent for an alleged principal when absolutely no authority has been given for any action. Again, only the "agent" is liable to the third party unless the "principal" ratifies the contract (or unless the principal has given apparent authority).

Alice knew that her friend Jill wanted to sell a matched set of luggage. When Raza revealed that she was about to leave on a trip to South America, Alice sold her Jill's luggage set for $300, promising prompt delivery. Jill refused to ratify the sales contract and so Raza had to buy a comparable set elsewhere for $375. Alice is liable to Raza for $75 in damages.

2. Principal Lacks Capacity

As discussed earlier, the agent warrants the principal's capacity to the third party. If it turns out that the principal does not exist, or that the principal is able to avoid the contract for lack of contractual capacity, the agent will be liable.

Normally, to bind the principal and to avoid personal liability an agent will sign the name of the principal to a contract and add words to indicate that the signature is by an agent.

TEACH

Tell students that an agent is liable to third persons if the agent acts outside the scope of authority or if the principal lacks contractual capacity. Remind students that this agent alone is then liable to the third party unless the principal ratifies the contract or has given apparent authority to the agent.

APPLY

On the chalkboard, draw a cause-and-effect chart (leaving either the cause or effect column blank for each entry). Acting as a scribe, have students dictate either the cause or effect in order to complete the chart relating to an agent's liability to third persons. **Guided Practice**

RETEACH Have students create a graphic organizer to illustrate both a principal's and an agent's liability to third persons.

ENRICH Have students create posters to illustrate third-person protection in agency relationships. Encourage students to think of ways to make the message clear to people with limited English proficiency.

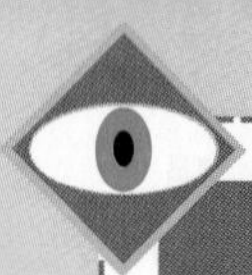

Personal Perspectives

Have students list some experiences they, or family members, have had as third persons in agency relationships when either an agent or a principal defaulted. **Independent Practice**

TEACH

Explain to students that the agent and principal have the power, but not always the right, to terminate the agency at any time. The principal may end the agency relationship but may have to pay damages. The agent may quit but possibly will owe damages to the principal unless the principal has breached the contract. An agency is also terminated upon the death, insanity, or bankruptcy of either the principal or the agent. Point out that principals should notify third persons when an agent has been terminated to avoid any unwanted binding contracts.

APPLY

On the chalkboard, create a chart to illustrate when and how an agency is terminated. Have students provide you with the information from pp. 516–517 to complete it. **Guided Practice**

Maria Costa contracted for a supply of paper bags and cartons for her employer, Tasti-Town Tamales. She properly signed the contract as follows: "Tasti-Town Tamales, by Maria Costa, Purchasing Agent."

Sometimes the agent is not allowed to disclose the principal's identity. The principal in such a case is known as an **undisclosed principal.** With most contracts, when the third party learns the identity of the principal, the third party may generally elect to hold either the principal or the agent to the agreement. But the third party may not enforce the agreement against both.

HOW IS AN AGENCY TERMINATED?

PROBLEM

Daisey entered into a one-year written contract with the Sweet Magnolia Wholesale Nursery as its sales agent in North Carolina, South Carolina, and Georgia. After six months, total company sales dropped far below expectations as a result of a general economic recession. Because Daisey was the last to be hired, she was the first to be fired even though her manager admitted that her performance had been satisfactory. Did the nursery have a legal right to terminate the agency?

Generally, both the agent and the principal have *the power, but not the right,* to terminate the agency at any time. The principal terminates by revoking the agent's authority. Thus, in the problem, the nursery could revoke Daisey's authority. As a result, Daisey could no longer bind the nursery. This illustrates that the nursery had the *power* to terminate the agency. But it did not have the *right.* Therefore, it would be liable in damages for breach of the one-year agency contract. The concept that the principal has the power but not the right means that the principal may end the agency relationship but must pay damages for doing so.

In a similar way, the agent has the power to quit at any time. However, he or she may lack the right to do so unless the principal has breached the contract. If an agent wrongfully terminates the agency before the contract expires, the principal is entitled to damages. An agency is also ordinarily terminated upon the death, insanity, or bankruptcy of either the principal or the agent.

ASSESS

Learning Objective 7 Independently, have each student reread the PROBLEM on p. 516. Then, ask them to summarize in writing, in their own words, how both an agent and a principal each may have the power, but not the right, to terminate an agency relationship.

Recall that a gratuitous agency exists when the agent receives no consideration. There is no difference between the way a gratuitous agency may be terminated and the way an agency created by contract may be terminated. There is, however, a difference in the remedies that are available for wrongful termination. Usually, a gratuitous agent cannot recover any damages if the authority is revoked. Likewise, a principal normally cannot recover any damages from a gratuitous agent who abandons the agency.

When the authority of an agent is terminated by the principal's voluntary act, the principal should promptly notify third persons who have previously dealt with the agent. If the principal does not give such individualized notice, the agent is likely to have apparent authority to make binding contracts between the principal and third persons as long as the third persons do not know of the termination. Others who may have heard of the agency are also entitled to notice, but this can be given by publishing the fact of the termination in a newspaper of general circulation in the area.

Preventing Legal Difficulties

If you are a third person dealing with an agent, remember that...

1. You should learn the extent of the agent's authority from the principal.
2. If you pay an agent money, be sure that the agent has authority to accept it. You should also obtain a receipt with the name of the principal on it. The receipt should state the date, amount, and purpose of the payment and should be signed by the agent.
3. If you are uncertain about the authority or honesty of the agent, make payment by a check payable to the principal.

If you are an agent, remember that...

1. When you sign anything for your principal, make it unmistakably clear that you are signing as an agent. Always write the name of your principal first, then add "by" and your signature followed by the word "agent."
2. You must be loyal to your principal and exercise reasonable care and skill in obeying all proper instructions.
3. If you handle your principal's money or other assets, you should keep them separated from your own.

Distribute copies of a newspaper's legal and business notices to students. Have students skim them for examples of agency termination notices. Using these as models, have students write a termination notice for an agency relationship that they created.
Independent Practice

Preventing Legal Difficulties

Divide the class into groups of five or more. Each group will be responsible for writing, producing, and delivering a segment of a videotaped public service announcement (PSA) about the rights and responsibilities of an agency relationship. The segments should be brief three-minute vignettes that illustrate the suggestions listed on pp. 517–518. Students should select from the following roles: producer, facilitator, director, prop person, camera person, and actors (as needed). The group, as a whole, should write the script. The class, as a whole, should think of a clever title for each PSA.

Cooperative Learning

RETEACH In small groups, have students create a graphic organizer to illustrate ways an agency can be terminated. Have students explain their work to one another. Correct any misconceptions.

In a short essay, using a computer, if possible, have students expand on their interpretation of the phrase having *"the power, but not the right,"* found on p. 516.

▼ CLOSE

Distribute copies of the overhead transparency master, *Directions of Agency Relationships.* Display the transparency and tell students to make notes on their copies as you work through the transparency with them. Have students define terms and explain the impact of each on the relationships

between the three points of the triangle.

Assign the following end-of-chapter materials:
Student text review activities, pp. 518–522
Workbook, pp. 75–80
Chapter Test

Chapter *MicroExam*

▼ Strengthening Your Legal Vocabulary ▼

1. warranty of the principal's capacity
2. duty of loyalty
3. implied authority
4. duty of confidentiality
5. fiduciary duties
6. express authority
7. gratuitous agency
8. ratification
9. power of attorney
10. principal

If you are a principal, remember that...

1. Your agent, in effect, stands in your shoes. Your agent's acts become your acts. Therefore, use care in selecting an agent.
2. If you discharge your agent, protect yourself by notifying those with whom the agent has been dealing in your name. To inform all others who may have heard of the agency, publish a notice in a journal of general circulation in the area.

▼ REVIEWING IMPORTANT POINTS

1. The relationship of principal and agent is created when one person authorizes another to act on his or her behalf in contracting, or assisting in contracting, with third persons.
2. Principals are bound by the contracts negotiated by their agents when the agents have acted within the scope of their agency authority.
3. Agency authority may be created by express grant or by implied grant, or it may result from appearance. Unauthorized action may also be created through ratification.
4. Agents owe fiduciary duties to their principals. These duties include the duties of loyalty and obedience, reasonable care and skill, confidentiality, and accounting.
5. The agent is liable to the third party if the agent acts outside the scope of authority and thereby injures the third party.
6. Both the principal and the agent have the power, but not the right, to terminate most agency relationships.

▼ STRENGTHENING YOUR LEGAL VOCABULARY

Match each term with the statement that best defines that term. Some terms may not be used.

agency
agent
apparent authority
duty of accounting
commingling
duty of confidentiality
duty of loyalty
duty of obedience
duty of reasonable care and skill
express authority
fiduciary duties
gratuitous agency
implied authority
power of attorney
principal
ratification

scope of authority
third party
trust account
undisclosed principal
warranty of the principal's capacity

1. An agent's implied promise that the principal has contractual capacity.
2. Duty that requires an agent to place the interests of the principal above the interests of all others.
3. Authority of an agent to do anything necessary or customary to carry out expressly authorized duties.
4. Duty to treat information about the principal very carefully.
5. A group of duties owed by the agent to the principal.
6. Authority directly granted by a principal to an agent orally or in writing.
7. An agency that is not based on a contract.
8. Principal's assent to unauthorized acts of an agent.
9. A writing that creates agency authority.
10. One who authorizes an agent to make contracts.

APPLYING LAW TO EVERYDAY LIFE

1. Alonzo hired Lawrence to help him sell a valuable Persian rug. He authorized Lawrence to sell it for $400,000 cash. Lawrence did so. Later, Alonzo discovered that the rug was worth over $600,000. Because Alonzo was a minor, he disaffirmed the contract, returned the $400,000 to the buyer, and got the rug back. The buyer sued Lawrence for $200,000—the difference between the $400,000 contract price and the $600,000 value. Will she collect?

2. ETHICS ISSUE Gail, an agent for Summer Farms, sold its fruit every year. Summer Farms trusted Gail completely. Gail knew she could sell its fruit to one of her friends at a price slightly lower than the market price and make about $25,000 for herself. She was absolutely sure there was no way she could be caught. Should she do it? Give reasons why she should or should not.

3. ETHICS ISSUE Bud was a real estate broker. He was acting as the agent in finding a buyer for Mr. Crib's home. A seller made an offer of $250,000 for the property but said, "If Mr. Crib doesn't accept this offer, I will raise it by $15,000." Bud knew that the duty of loyalty compelled him to tell Mr. Crib of the buyer's statement. Is this fair to

Applying Law to Everyday Life

1. Yes, the buyer will recover the $200,000. This is because Lawrence, as an agent, automatically warranted the principal's capacity. When Alonzo disaffirmed, this warranty was violated. So the third party, the buyer, can sue the agent, Lawrence, for any injury. In this case the injury was $200,000 ($600,000–$400,000). (p. 506)

2. ETHICS ISSUE Ethically she should not do it for the following reasons: it injures Summer Farms, it violates her implied promise to treat Summer Farms fairly, it violates her legal obligation, and it corrupts Gail. (See Chapter 2.)

3. 

The duty of loyalty requires Bud to place the interests of the seller above the interests of the buyer. Legally, therefore, the buyer's statement must be disclosed to the seller. (p. 511) If the buyer had a reasonable basis for trusting Bud, then Bud is in a situation where his legal duty (to tell the seller) is in conflict with his ethical duty (to live up to the trust which he created). In the future Bud can avoid these kinds of problems by ensuring that the buyer the buyer? Why or why not? What could Bud do in future transactions to allow him to treat buyers more fairly?

4 Newman authorized Sánchez to sell his car at the highest price possible, but for not less than $2,800. Sánchez received an offer of $3,000 from Hack. Nevertheless, Sánchez sold the car to his buddy Glenn for $2,800. When Newman learned of this, he attempted to collect $200 from Sánchez. Will he succeed? Why or why not?

5 Jane asked Kroger to represent her in selling her real property, which consisted of a farm and certain pastures. She executed a formal power of attorney authorizing Kroger to negotiate a sale and to execute all necessary documents in order to transfer title to her real property. Then Jane left for a three-week vacation. When she returned, she learned that Kroger had sold the farm and pastures at an attractive price. But he had also sold two tractors and a truck. Is Jane bound by Kroger's conduct in selling the farm? In selling the tractors and the truck?

6 Baroni asked her boyfriend, Sid, to help her sell her car. She promised to pay Sid 10 percent of the sales price. Sid agreed. Later, when trying to sell the car, Sid stated that a rebuilt engine had just been installed. This was not true. Kate bought the car. When she discovered the deception, she sued Baroni. Is Baroni legally responsible?

7 Vásquez owned a large clothing store. He hired Sharon, a business broker, to help him sell it. The contract between Vásquez and Sharon authorized Sharon only to "*find* a ready, willing, and able buyer." It did not authorize her to sell the business. Sharon found a buyer, Jerry, who offered an attractive price. Sharon executed the documents of sale on behalf of Vásquez. When Vásquez discovered this, he said the price was too low and that he would not be bound by the contract of sale. Meanwhile, Jerry had moved his family across the country, spending about $5,000 to do so. Is Vásquez bound by the contract of sale? Can Jerry recover his expenses from Vásquez? From Sharon?

8 When Kraus discharged his purchasing agent, Stacey, and terminated their agency relationship, Stacey became angry. To get even, Stacey made three contracts that included terms that were unfavorable to Kraus, yet were reasonable in the competitive market. The first contract was with an old customer, A. The second contract was with a new customer, B, who had heard of the agency but had never been contacted by Stacey. The third contract was with a total stranger, C, who had never heard of the agency. Is Kraus liable on any of these three contracts?

understands that Bud is the agent of the seller and owes the duty of loyalty to that person, not to the buyer. Then buyers won't make disclosures which might injure them. (See Chapter 2.)

4 Yes; Sánchez violated the duty of loyalty and this caused Newman to be injured in the amount of $200. Sánchez will be required to pay that amount to Newman. (p. 511)

5 Yes, Jane is bound by Kroger's conduct in selling the farm; this action was within the scope of Kroger's authority. However, Jane is not bound to the sale of the tractors and truck because these sales were outside Kroger's authority. (p. 505)

6 Baroni is liable to Kate for the fraud committed by Sid. The principal is liable for the agent's fraud committed within the scope of employment. (p. 514)

7 Sharon has acted outside the scope of her authority. The agency contract authorized her only to "find a ready, willing, and able buyer," but Sharon went way beyond this in executing documents of sale. Therefore Vásquez is not bound by the sale. The buyer, Jerry, cannot recover from Vásquez, but he can recover from Sharon, the agent who has acted outside the scope of her authority. (pp. 505, 515)

8 Kraus will be liable to the old customer, A, and to the new customer, B, who had heard of the agency. Kraus is liable because Kraus did not notify A or B of the termination of the agency relationship. Stacey had apparent authority to act on behalf of Kraus and A and B relied on this apparent authority. On the other hand, C, who was unaware of the prior agency relationship, had no basis other than Kraus's conduct for believing that Stacey was Kraus's agent. Therefore Kraus is not liable to C. (p. 517)

SOLVING CASE PROBLEMS

1. Nissan Motor Corporation appointed McKnight as its Denver area agent and dealer for the sale of its automobiles. McKnight purchased automobiles and parts from Nissan. He then sold them as he desired and at prices he set without any control from Nissan. The question arose as to whether an agency existed. What is your judgment? (*United Fire and Casualty Company v. Nissan Motor Corporation,* 164 Colo. 42, 433 P.2d 769)

2. Ronnell Lynch was hired and trained by Nabisco to sell its cookies to grocery stores. Then he was given a territory that included a store managed by Lange. While Lynch was a salesman in the territory, Nabisco received several complaints about his behavior. Some stores complained that he would remove competitors' cookies and put Nabisco cookies in their place without permission from the store. One day Lynch was servicing Lange's store. Lange complained about the quality of service that Lynch provided. Lynch began swearing in front of customers. He became very angry and said to Lange, "I ought to break your neck." Later he dared Lange to fight. When Lange refused, Lynch beat him viciously. Is Lynch an agent of Nabisco? Is Nabisco liable for Lynch's conduct? (*Lange v. Nabisco,* 432 P.2d 405)

3. The manager of a retail butcher shop owned by Serges borrowed $3,500 from David for use in the butcher shop. Serges claimed that the manager had no authority to borrow money. Nevertheless, Serges made payments of $200. Serges also told David on several occasions that the full sum would eventually be paid. Was Serges liable? (*David v. Serges,* 373 Mich. 442, 129 N.W.2d 882)

4. Desfossess was a mobile-home-park developer. He hired Notis, a licensed real estate broker, at a weekly salary. Notis's job was to assist Desfossess with the special assignment of acquiring land for mobile home parks. Desfossess asked Notis to negotiate on his behalf for the purchase of a tract suitable for a mobile home park. Notis suggested a certain parcel and received authority to purchase it in his own name, with Desfossess as the undisclosed principal. Notis reported to Desfossess that the land would cost $32,400, although Notis knew it could be and was purchased for $15,474.62. It also appeared that Notis, before becoming Desfossess's agent, had obtained an option for $1,000 to purchase the land but did not reveal this to Desfossess. Desfossess sued for the difference between what he had paid Notis and the cost of the land. Notis claimed that if Desfossess, as his former principal, had any right

Solving Case Problems

1. There was no agency. Nissan exercised no direction or control over McKnight, who had purchased the automobiles and parts from Nissan and sold them as he desired. (p. 504) McKnight was, in fact, an independent contractor. (p. 430)
2. Yes, Nabisco will be liable to Lange. Lynch was Nabisco's agent. His actions occurred within the scope of his agency authority. Therefore, his principal, Nabisco, is liable. (p. 514)
3. Yes. Even though borrowing money was not within the manager's authority, the principal, Serges, ratified the act by repaying a portion of the loan and promising to pay the rest of it. (p. 509)
4. The plaintiff, Desfossess, is right. The court held that the defendant was guilty of a breach of the fiduciary duty an agent has to the principal. The court pointed out the breach of four such duties: failure to fully disclose material facts, misrepresentation of matters within the scope of the agency, false inducements to obtain money from the principal, and misuse and wrongful intention of the principal's funds. (pp. 510–513) Moreover, the agent is liable for any secret profits. (p. 511)

5 ETHICS ISSUE The sponsors are liable. Agents impliedly warrant the principal's capacity. Since this principal lacked capacity, the agents—the sponsors—are liable. (p. 515) It would not be ethical for the sponsors of the Little League to contract for and to receive $3,900 of merchandise and then avoid making payment for the merchandise. That would be very similar to theft.

6 O'Day is liable for the lettuce. While Kirchberg was not an agent for O'Day, he did have apparent authority to deal with Arakelian Farms. O'Day should have notified Arakelian Farms when the agency relationship with Kirchberg was terminated. (p. 517)

at all, it would be only to rescind the contract and to return the land to Notis. Who was correct? (*Desfossess v. Notis,* 333 A.2d 89)

5 ETHICS ISSUE Smith and Edwards operated a sporting goods shop in Brigham City, Utah. Sponsors of the Golden Spike Little League made arrangements with the store to purchase, at a substantial discount, the players' baseball uniforms and equipment. The sponsors picked up $3,900 worth of merchandise without making any payments. After a demand for full payment, Smith and Edwards sued the sponsors. The sponsors defended by asserting that they were agents of Golden Spike Little League, acting within the scope of their authority, and thus were not personally liable. The trial judge found that Golden Spike Little League was a loosely formed voluntary association and thus not a legal entity upon which liability could be imposed. Are the sponsors liable? If the sponsors avoided liability, do you think this would be ethical? (*Smith and Edwards v. Golden Spike Little League,* 577 P.2d 132, Utah)

6 William Kirchberg was a food broker. He represented O'Day in fifty-five transactions for the purchase of lettuce from Arakelian Farms. For each transaction, Arakelian Farms sent bills to O'Day and he paid them. Then Kirchberg terminated the agency relationship with O'Day. Arakelian Farms was not notified of the termination. Thereafter, Kirchberg placed twenty more orders, purportedly on behalf of O'Day. Arakelian Farms delivered the lettuce and billed O'Day but was not paid. Arakelian Farms sued O'Day. At the trial, O'Day's defense was that Kirchberg was not his agent. What is the result? (*O'Day v. Arakelian Farms,* 540 P.2d 197)

SPECIAL SECTION

DEALING WITH AN ATTORNEY

Although attorneys take some cases at the request of the court or as their conscience dictates without expecting a fee in return, attorneys usually expect to be paid for their services. It is important to determine in advance how your lawyer charges for services. Most attorneys either charge an hourly rate or are paid on a contingency-fee basis.

A typical contingency-fee schedule calls for payment to the attorney of 25 percent of the recovery if the case is resolved without trial. If a trial is required, the attorney might get 33 percent of the recovery, and if the judgment is appealed, the percentage might go up to 40 percent. If the case is lost, the attorney gets nothing. Attorneys often take tort suits, antitrust, and contract actions on a contingency-fee basis, but only if they believe there is a good chance of recovery.

With the hourly rate, the attorney is paid regardless of whether the case is won or lost. To avoid misunderstandings, it is a good idea to have a written agreement about compensation before the attorney begins working on your case.

Some urban areas have legal clinics. These clinics set a flat fee for various types of legal services. For example, a name change might cost $125. Uncontested divorces, simple wills, and other legal services frequently can be obtained through such a clinic. Of course, the more complex the service required, the more expensive it will be and the less likely it can be provided by a clinic.

When dealing with your attorney, you must provide every bit of information that can be used to pursue your interests. When first meeting with your attorney about a problem, bring a detailed, chronological, written summary of relevant events, together with supporting correspondence or other documents. Too often, clients withhold useful information that they consider irrelevant or embarrassing only to find later that without it their attorney was misdirected, and possible success in court was jeopardized.

Always listen to your attorney's advice and weigh it carefully. Never forget, however, that it is your reputation, your resources, or

Special Section: Dealing with an Attorney

Divide the class into five groups. Assign each group a legal problem in which they need to seek counsel. Choose legal problems that fall into one of the five categories: employment contracts, unions, employment discrimination, employee injuries, and agents.

Have students investigate resources in their community to find a suitable attorney to handle their situation. To find appropriate information, suggest students check the reference section of the library for resources such as the *Martindale-Hubbell Law Digests*, obtain references from friends and family, or use a consumer-network service, such as *CompuServe* or *PRODIGY*. Using a computer, if possible, have students create a profile on the attorney or attorneys who they think would best represent their case. (Students may wish to contact attorneys directly for specific information.) Tell students that their profiles should include the attorney's fees, prior case histories, locality, availability, degrees and awards, areas of

specialty, and prior malpractice suits.

your freedom that is at stake — not the attorney's. Therefore ask detailed questions about what is happening. Utilize your attorney's legal experience to the utmost, but also realize that your experience is superior regarding the facts of your case. You must integrate what the attorney says is legally possible into your plan to achieve your ends.

If you feel that your case is being handled carelessly or incompetently, tell your attorney so. Frequently the problem is one of communication, such as the attorney's failure to inform you about the progress of the case. If the problem persists, consult another attorney; you are free to change your counsel. If your dispute is over the fee charged, or other matters, you may contact the local bar association and possibly settle through arbitration. If all else fails, you can sue the attorney for damages, claiming malpractice.

524

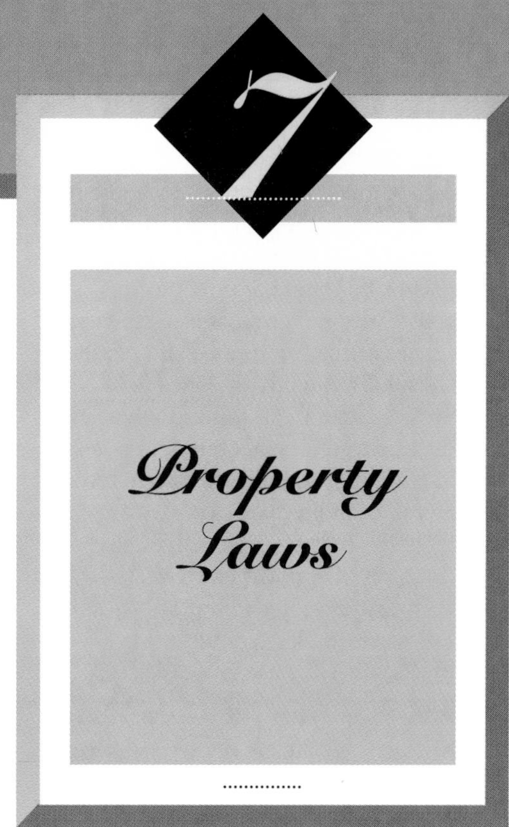

Unit Overview

In Unit 7, *Property Laws*, students will read about personal property, bailments, real property, and the relationships between landlords and tenants. They also will learn about intellectual labor, ownership, deeds, mortgages, escrow, leasing, renting, and eviction—concepts with which they may need to be familiar as adults.

Transactions involving real and personal property—what they are, their forms of ownership, and the limitations on ownership—are regulated by law. In Chapter 26, *Personal Property*, students will study what property is and how property can be acquired. They will learn what the different forms of ownership are, and the limitations on ownership.

Bailors, bailees, and the most common bailments are covered in Chapter 27, *Bailments*. Students will analyze different types of bailments, learn what the bailee's duty of care is, how it can be modified, and the nature of the bailee's duty to return the goods. In addition, students will learn about the bailor's duties, the most common bailments, and how a bailment is ended.

Real property and how it is acquired is the focus of the next chapter, which also covers deeds and financing arrangements for purchasing real property. In Chapter 28, *Real Property*, students will understand what real property is, how it is acquired, and how it is purchased.

Leases and the landlord-tenant relationships form the basis of a chapter of great interest to young adults planning for life "on their own." In Chapter 29, *Landlord and Tenant*, students will learn what a lease is and what types of leasehold estates may be created. Of personal relevance are topics such as the rights and duties of a tenant and a landlord, and how a lease can be terminated.

At the end of this unit you'll find a special section, *Computer Law,* which can be used at any time during the study of Unit 7. You may wish to assign its accompanying *Teacher Edition* activity to give students an opportunity to design a poster warning computer users against illegally copying software.

Portfolio Assessment

Tell students to imagine that they have been invited to be a guest speaker on the topic of property laws at an introductory real estate course at your local college. Using a computer, if possible, have students prepare and write a lecture that is informative, interesting, insightful, humorous, and practical. Tell students to refer frequently to their textbooks for appropriate information on topics such as what real property is, how can it be acquired, how leasing differs from owning, and what the rights and duties of a tenant and a landlord are. Ask students to

include personal experiences, real or fictitious, if applicable. Have students add their lecture notes to their portfolios.

Careers

Real Estate Agent

A real estate agent is needed by employees who relocate for a job and for those who buy property as an investment or for other reasons. Real estate agents negotiate on behalf of the seller with the buyer, help arrange bank loans, organize and perform title searches, and are present when final sale contracts are signed.

To get a job as a real estate agent, a candidate must obtain a state license by passing a written test, which covers real estate transactions and property laws. To get a license, a candidate first needs to take courses in real estate. A real estate agent's average annual salary ranges from $25,000 to $40,000.

Divide the class into groups of three or four and assign the following roles: real estate agent, sellers, and buyer. Have the buyer skim through the real estate section of a newspaper to locate property to purchase. Have the real estate agent negotiate with the buyer, on behalf of the seller, to complete a property transaction.

Annotated Bibliography

- ***Shelley v. Kraemer*, 334 U.S. 1 (1948).**
  State courts may not enforce private agreements or restrictive covenants which have as their purpose the exclusion of persons of designated race or color from the ownership or occupancy of real property. (Chapter 28)

- ***Reitman v. Mulkey*, 64 Cal.2d 529, 413 P.2d 825, 847 (1967).**
  The California legislature added to its Constitution a provision that the enactment of any law that would deny, limit, or abridge a property owner's absolute right to sell, lease, or rent such property to anyone the property owner, in his or her discretion, chooses. The California Supreme Court held this statute to be unconstitutional in violation of the Equal Protection Clause of the Fourteenth Amendment because it will significantly encourage and involve the State in private discriminations. (Chapter 29)

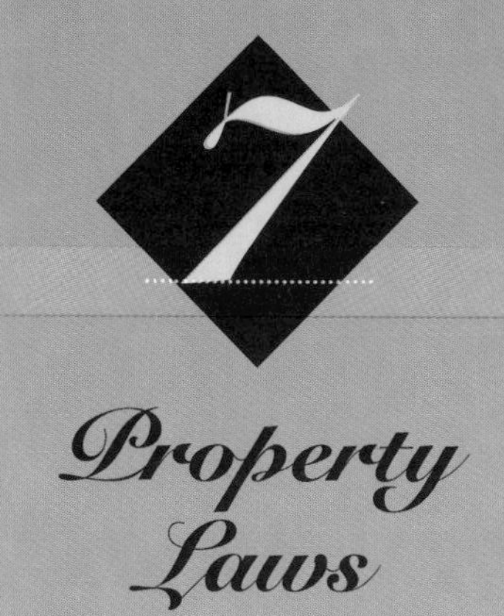

Property Laws

- Personal Property
- Bailments
- Real Property
- Landlord and Tenant

UNIT 7 PROPERTY LAWS

Chapter Theme

Transactions involving real and personal property, what they are, their forms of ownership, and the limitations on ownership are regulated by law.

DIRECTED STUDY QUESTIONS	SPECIAL FEATURES	PROGRAM RESOURCES				
		Reteach	Enrich	SN	AM	
What is property?	Personal Perspectives, p. 528 Thinking Critically Through Visuals, p. 529	✔	✔		V	
How can property be acquired?	Ethics Issue, p. 530 Multicultural Highlights, p. 531	✔	✔	✔	K A	
What are the forms of ownership?	Writing Connections, p. 534 Thinking Critically Through Visuals, p. 536	✔	✔			
What are the limitations on ownership?	Preventing Legal Difficulties, p. 537	✔	✔			

Additional Resources

- Coleman, Bob and Neville, Deborah. *The Great American Idea Book.* NY: W.W. Norton, 1993.
- Rosenthal, Lois. *Partnering: A Guide to Co-owning Anything from Homes to Home Computers.* Cincinnati, OH: Writer's Digest Books, 1983.

One-semester course	✔	✔						
One-year course	✔	✔	✔					

	ASSESSMENT OPPORTUNITIES			
Cooperative Learning	**Informal Assessment**	**Chapter Review**	**Chapter Test**	**Chapter *MicroExam*** 
	✔	✔	✔	✔
	✔	✔	✔	✔
✔	✔	✔	✔	✔
	✔	✔	✔	✔

Videodiscs

Ownership of Property and Copyright

Search Chapter 32, Play To 33

State by State

In Virginia, unclaimed personal property in the possession of a law enforcement agency for 60 days may be sold at a public sale.

Teaching Materials

Student text, pp. 526–541

Overhead transparency masters
- *Ways of Acquiring Ownership of Personal Property*
- *Forms of Co-ownership and Their Legal Characteristics*

Videos
- *Law for Business* Videodisc

Workbook, pp. 81–82

Outside Resources
- Blank overhead transparencies
- Art supplies
- Package labels
- Advertisements in newspapers and magazines
- Butcher paper
- Newspaper articles on property restrictions

- Tape recorder
- Camcorder
- VCR

Assessment
- Chapter Test

- Chapter *MicroExam*

Vocabulary

property, p. 528
real property, p. 528
personal property, p. 528
intellectual property, p. 528
accession, p. 530
copyright, p. 531
patent, p. 531
trade secret, p. 531
trademark, p. 532
servicemark, p. 532
mislaid property, p. 532
lost property, p. 532
occupancy, p. 533
ownership in severalty, p. 534
co-ownership, p. 534
equal rights of possession, p. 534
right of partition, p. 534
joint tenancy, p. 534
right of survivorship, p. 534
tenancy in common, p. 535
tenancy by the entireties, p. 535
community property, p. 535
separate property, p. 536

Learning Objectives

When you complete this chapter, you will be able to

1. Define real and personal property.
2. Describe the various ways ownership of property can be acquired.
3. Explain the legal rights that characterize the different forms of co-ownership.
4. Identify some of the legal limitations on the use of property.

526

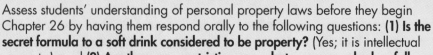

Chapter Self-Test

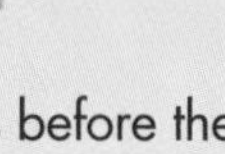

Assess students' understanding of personal property laws before they begin Chapter 26 by having them respond orally to the following questions: **(1) Is the secret formula to a soft drink considered to be property?** (Yes; it is intellectual property.); and **(2) Are there any restrictions on what a person who has fully paid ownership of property can do with that property?** (Yes; property cannot be used or discarded in an unreasonable or unlawful manner.) Review and discuss students' responses before continuing with the chapter.

CHAPTER 26

PERSONAL PROPERTY

❶ ETHICS ISSUE Fran learned that owning property together with someone in joint tenancy allows one co-owner to receive another's interest when that person dies. So Fran asked her seventy-eight-year-old uncle to pay one-half and become a co-owner of resort property with her. When he asked what form of co-ownership they should use, Fran said, "Since we will own it together, we should be joint tenants." Is Fran's conduct ethical?

❷ While on a skiing trip in Vermont, you (a) find a pair of skis in a parking lot, (b) pick up some firewood along the road, and (c) shoot two rabbits for a meal. Do you acquire ownership rights in these things?

❸ You and five friends combine your savings to buy a large sailboat. What form of ownership should your group use?

▼ FOCUS

As students enter the classroom, have them list an example of property on the chalkboard. Have the class verify if each is an example of property and explain why or why not.

You Decide

❶  No, Fran's conduct is unethical. She knows the legal effect of using the words *joint tenants* and her uncle does not. When the uncle asked for Fran's advice, he was asking her to provide all the information she knew that was relevant to the decision to be made. Fran failed to do that, so her action was intended to deceive.

❷ **(a)** No; The skis left in the parking lot have been mislaid, therefore the owner of the parking lot, not you, the finder, is entitled to keep the skis until the owner returns for them.
(b) Yes; If you were on public property you would own the firewood by **occupancy** because there was no prior owner before you took possession.
(c) Yes; assuming you had a valid hunting license and were on public property.

❸ Tenancy in common is best among friends. Because the friends are not married, tenancy by the entireties and community property are not available. Joint tenancy, which has a right of survivorship, is not appropriate because most people want their property to go to their relatives when they die.

Thinking Critically Through Visuals

The girl in this photograph has caught a fish. Can you assume that she now owns the fish? Why or why not? (Yes; If the girl is obeying fishing regulations and is not trespassing, the fish is hers because it is unknown wildlife and was considered unowned before it was caught.)

TEACH

On the chalkboard, write the definition and rights of **property**. Then, on an overhead transparency, draw a graphic organizer to explain the difference between **real** and **personal property.** Tell students that possession of something itself does not always include possession of all rights. Use renting or loaning as examples.

APPLY

On the chalkboard, draw a large two-column chart. Label the chart **Property**, column one **Real**, and column two **Personal**. Divide and label column two into the subcategories—**Tangible** and **Intangible (Intellectual)**. Have the class brainstorm and list examples appropriate for each column. Discuss what rights and interests might be related to the things listed. **Guided Practice**

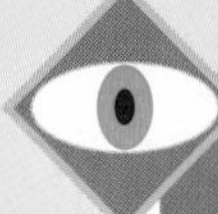

Personal Perspectives

Tell students to list 10 examples of property they own, indicating if they own all or some of the total bundle of rights to that property. Tell them to circle all items that are tangible. **Independent Practice**

WHAT IS PROPERTY?

PROBLEM

Winkler rented her cabin in Ocean City to Hanson for the summer season. Did Hanson acquire property under the lease?

When someone speaks of property, you probably think of many tangible, things (i.e., things you can see or touch). Tangible things include this book, desks, clothing, buildings, land, airplanes, cars, and boats. But thinking about property should also bring to mind intangible things (i.e., things you cannot see or touch). For example, both the goodwill of a brand name and the secret formula by which a product is made are intangible. So are patents for inventions, the copyright of this book, the franchise to open a particular business in your town, and the right to collect money under an automobile insurance policy.

According to the law, **property** is (1) a thing, tangible or intangible, that is subject to ownership and (2) a group of rights and interests related to the thing that are protected by law. For example, suppose you own some land with a house that you correctly call property. Ownership of the land and house gives you a number of legal rights. These include rights to (1) possess, use, and enjoy it; (2) dispose of (by gift or sale), consume, or even destroy it; and (3) give it away by will after death. You also have the right to lease your property to a tenant. Therefore, your tenant does acquire property; that is, a right to use your land and building. In the problem, Hanson acquired a property interest in the cabin. A person may own all or some of the total group or "bundle" of rights to property.

Property can be classified as real or personal. Different rules govern the creation, use, and transfer of real and personal property. **Real property** is land, including not only the surface of the earth, but also the water and minerals on and below the surface. Real property extends down to the center of the earth and, with certain limits, includes the airspace above the land. Real property also includes anything permanently attached to the land, such as buildings. (Real property is discussed more fully in Chapter 28.)

Personal property is property that is movable, such as a car, airplane, musical instrument, sofa, book, or tennis racket. Personal property also includes intangible property. **Intellectual property** is purely intangible; that is, one cannot touch it. Intellectual property discussed in this chapter includes patents, trade secrets, servicemarks, and trademarks. The creation, use, and transfer of interests in intellectual property are generally governed by federal statutes.

ASSESS

Learning Objective 1 Have students respond orally to the following *True* or *False* questions: **(1) According to the law, property includes a bundle of rights and interests that are protected by law.** (True); **(2) Intellectual property is purely tangible.** (False); **(3) Real property includes only the surface land.** (False); and **(4) All property can be classified as real or personal.** (True)

HOW CAN PROPERTY BE ACQUIRED?

PROBLEM

While comparing their wristwatches, five friends explained how each had acquired theirs. Appleton had bought his with earnings from a paper route. Baird had received hers as a graduation gift. Cameron had inherited hers from an aunt who had died. Dawson, a skilled watchmaker, had made his own. Engler had found hers on the street. She had not been able to find the owner. Did each friend have equal ownership rights in their wristwatches?

Real or personal property is most commonly acquired by contract, gift, or inheritance. In addition, personal property may be legitimately acquired by accession, intellectual labor, finding, or occupancy. (Other methods of acquiring real property are discussed in Chapter 28.) In the problem, even though they acquired their watches with different processes, each friend had equal ownership rights in his or her own wristwatch.

1. Acquiring Ownership by Contract

Any kind of property may be acquired and transferred, or bought and sold, by contract. People acquire most of their property by earning money and using it to purchase property.

2. Acquiring Ownership by Gift

To create a valid gift, one must do two things: (1) manifest an intent to transfer ownership and (2) deliver the property. (Delivery is a shift of

Thinking Critically Through Visuals

The couple in the photograph has rented the tandem bike. The car they are passing is owned by its driver. How do the couples' rights to the bike differ from the driver's rights to the car? (The car owner probably holds all legal rights to the car, including the right to enjoy, sell, destroy, or give away, although a lender may also have a security interest in the car. The bike renters have the right

to use for a limited time.)

TEACH

Show the overhead transparency, *Ways of Acquiring Ownership of Personal Property*. As you discuss each section of the pie chart, elicit an example from the class. Point out that most real and personal property is acquired by contract, gift, or inheritance. Explain ownership by accession,

intellectual labor, finding, and occupancy.

RETEACH Write the definitions of **real** and **personal property** (pp. 528–529) on the chalkboard. Then, on an overhead transparency, list examples of real and personal property, including intellectual property. Display the transparency and ask students to orally identify each example as real or personal property and discuss the rights that might be part of each item.

ENRICH Give students art supplies and have them create a collage displaying different forms of real and personal property.

physical possession of the property to the new owner.) Thus you could transfer ownership of a watch by giving it with a birthday card to your niece. This would display both the intent to transfer ownership and the shift in physical possession. Often the law allows a symbol of the thing to be substituted in delivery. Thus, the keys to a car or a deed to real property could be used in place of the thing itself. As you learned in Chapter 11, a mere promise to make a gift creates no legal obligations.

Schuster dangled a certificate for 100 shares of stock in front of his niece, a senior in high school. "Melinda," he said, "you've been doing so well in all your classes that I'm giving you this stock." Melinda had no ownership rights in the stock because, as yet, there was no delivery. If Schuster had given her the indorsed stock certificate, however, there would have been delivery and ownership would have shifted.

Sometimes a gift is *conditional,* as when a man gives his fiancée an engagement ring. If the two mutually agree not to get married after all, or if the woman breaks the engagement, the man may generally reclaim the gift. In most states, if the man breaks the engagement the woman is entitled to keep the ring.

Another type of conditional gift is made when a donor expects to die soon. The gift may be conditional upon the death actually occurring. Donors who survive may change their minds and may take back their gifts.

Three friends were flying across the Rocky Mountains in a small airplane. An unexpected storm caused ice to form on the wings so the plane crashed in an isolated area. Only the pilot, Gary, was hurt and his injuries appeared critical. "I'll never make it, " he said. "Here, Jim, take my diamond ring. Lisa, you take my watch." Gary insisted, and so Jim and Lisa accepted the gifts before Gary lapsed into unconsciousness. Within hours, however, a helicopter rescued them, and Gary survived. He is entitled to the return of his ring and watch.

A gift made in contemplation of death should not be confused with one made by a will. With a will, the transfer of possession and title does not take place until after death occurs.

3. Acquiring Ownership by Accession

Personal property may be acquired by accession. **Accession** is the right of an owner of property to an increase in that property. The increase may be natural or man-made. Thus, farm crops and the offspring of animals belong

APPLY

Ethics Issue

Read aloud the following scenario: **Angela received an impressively expensive engagement ring from Jesse early in their senior year in high school. Jesse worked after school to make the monthly payments for the ring. But by spring, Jesse's feelings had changed. He no longer wanted to marry Angela and he wished he could use the money spent, as well as that still owed on the ring, for college. "So, tell Angela you want out," advised a friend. "No way," replied Jesse, "we are both of legal age. If I break the engagement, she could keep the ring and I would still have to pay for it. But, if I make her want to break the engagement, then I'm legally entitled to get the ring back."** Ask: **Are Jesse's ideas legally correct?** (Yes, in general, in most states) **Is his plan ethical?** (No; Jesse is attempting to manipulate Angela's feelings to his own benefit.) **Guided Practice**

ASSESS

Learning Objective 2 Have students jot down answers to the following: **(1) What two things must you do to make a valid gift?** (Manifest an intent to transfer ownership and deliver the property, or control over it); **(2) If a relative gave you a savings bond in exchange for your promise to not smoke, what kind of gift would this be?** (A conditional gift); and **(3) If your dog had puppies, through what right would you own the puppies?** (Right of accession) to the owner of the land or the animals. When new parts are put into an article, they generally become part of the article. For example, if a modem is connected to your personal computer, it becomes part of the computer.

If, by mistake, someone improves another's property, courts seek to do justice by letting the improver keep the property after paying fair value for the original item. For example, an innocent trespasser increased the value of lumber twenty-eight times by changing the lumber into barrel hoops. That person then acquired title to the new goods after paying a fair price for the original lumber.

4. Acquiring Ownership by Intellectual Labor

One may acquire personal property rights by original production. Authors or inventors have exclusive property rights in their own productions prior to the time their inventions are published or marketed. The author or inventor wishing to keep exclusive rights thereafter may do so for a limited time by properly requesting and obtaining a grant from the federal government.

A **copyright** is a grant to an author, artist, or composer of a creative work of the exclusive ownership of the created material. Copyrights are granted for the life of the author plus fifty years. The author can transfer the copyright to others.

> Martin and two friends were musicians who enjoyed improvising. One day Gardner heard them playing and added lyrics. Together, the four wrote out the music and lyrics. They protected the personal property they had thus created by copyrighting it. Later, they sold the copyright to a publisher, which paid them royalties (i.e., compensation that is usually a percentage of sales).

A **patent** is the grant of the exclusive right to make, use, and sell a *novel, nonobvious, useful* product or process. Like a copyright, it can be transferred to others. A patent is good for seventeen years and is not renewable. However, an inventor will sometimes patent improvements to the original product and thereby extend the length of the patent. Patents are also given for original designs, such as a unique chair, or original processes, such as one for refining oil into rubber. They are also given for certain new and distinct varieties of plants.

Sometimes a business firm will own important trade secrets, which are not patented. A **trade secret** is commercially valuable information that the owner attempts to *keep secret.* If an employee leaves a company and sells a secret formula, process, or customer list, he and the buyer will be liable to the employer.

Multicultural Highlights

In the United States, even very young children are encouraged to choose between alternative purchases. But allowing youths to make personal choices is not a part of all cultures. Guan Keguang, an Asian American journalist born in China, addresses this point in his book, *A Chinese Reporter on Cape Cod.* He writes about a vending machine, "I put in some coins, push a button, and out comes what I want.... But so many decisions!

Such a process epitomizes what I have experienced while struggling hard to adapt my traditional ways of thinking and doing things to an American environment, which demands constantly considering alternatives and making decisions.

This has been no easy job for me. For almost half a century I have lived in a culture where choices and decisions are made by authorities and circumstances rather than by individuals and personal preferences."

▼RETEACH In small groups, have students create and role-play scenarios of acquiring property by contract, gift, conditional gift, and accession. Have students summarize the property related rights they give and receive.

▼ENRICH Explain to students that not all software is copyrighted. Have students investigate the copyright requirements for the following types of software: shareware, commercial software, freeware, and public-domain software.

On the chalkboard, make a three-column chart labeled **Patented**, **Copyrighted**, and **Trademarked or Servicemarked**. Ask students to identify items in view that fall under one of the columns and add them to the chart. For example, General Electric light bulbs are trademarked, textbooks are copyrighted, and an overhead projector may be patented. Some items, such as a computer, may fall into more than one column.

Help students with specific learning disabilities to visually differentiate between the terms **mislaid property** and **lost property** by completing the following chart.

Lost	Mislaid
Unknowingly left	Forgotten
Watch drops unnoticed to ground	Sunglasses forgotten on restaurant table
True owner can reclaim	True owner can reclaim

Business firms may also acquire property rights in trademarks. A **trademark** is a word, mark, symbol, or device that identifies a product of a particular manufacturer or merchant. The mark must be distinctive and identify and distinguish the product. For example, the word "Kodak" is a trademark. It is included in the name of the owner, the Eastman Kodak Company, and it identifies products made by that company. However, descriptive words, such as "35mm camera," may be used by any company. A **servicemark** is a word, mark, or symbol that identifies a service as opposed to a product.

All states and the federal government have trademark registration laws that simplify proof of trademark ownership. However, registration is not essential. Common-law protection lasts forever if the trademark is used continuously. Sometimes leading U.S. manufacturers develop and give unique trademarks to products that are widely used. The originating company loses its exclusive property right to the trademark if it does either of the following:

a. permits competitors to refer to similar products by the unique trademark, or

b. does not object when the trademark is used generally in the press as a descriptive generic term.

Examples of terms that have become generic are "shredded wheat" and "cellophane." In contrast, the terms "Xerox," "Levi's," and "Scotch Tape" remain the property of the original owners.

5. Acquiring Ownership by Finding

Anyone who loses property has the right to recover it from any finder. One must simply prove true ownership. If the true owner is unknown, either the *finder* or the *owner of the place where the property was found* will be able to keep the property until the true owner appears.

Finders keep *lost* property and owners of the place where the property was found keep *mislaid* property. **Mislaid property** is intentionally placed somewhere but then forgotten. If you went into a restaurant and hung your coat on a coatrack while you ate and then you walked out without your coat, it would be mislaid. Anyone finding the coat would be required to turn it over to the restaurant. Since you may come back looking for the coat, this law helps true owners find mislaid property.

Lost property is created when the owner unknowingly leaves it somewhere or accidentally drops it. If, while you are preoccupied with a football game, your coat falls from the bleachers at a football stadium, and someone finds it on the ground, the finder, not the school, is entitled to possession unless you recover the coat. Statutes permit the finder to become the owner if the true owner does not reclaim the property within a stated time.

ASSESS

Learning Objective 2 Have students take turns orally describing examples of property acquisition. Have the rest of the class label the type of acquisition described. Correct any misunderstandings.

6. Acquiring Ownership by Occupancy

Occupancy means acquiring title by taking possession of personal property that belongs to no one else. A common example is personal property that has been discarded by the owner. In such a case, the finder who takes possession gets absolute title.

A national aluminum company offered to buy used aluminum cans for recycling. One Saturday, the members of the Junior Optimist Club picked up three truckloads of cans from along the sides of a heavily traveled country road. The club members acquired property by occupancy and transferred ownership of the property to the company by sale.

Like abandoned property, wildlife is considered unowned. A properly licensed person who takes possession of a wild animal by killing it on public lands becomes the legal owner. Similarly, one may become the owner of shells by picking them up on a public beach, or one may become the owner of firewood by gathering it along public roads. However, property on private lands belongs to the owner of the real property and may not be acquired by occupation.

7. Acquiring Ownership by Inheritance

A person may acquire both real and personal property by inheritance from others after they die. If a person leaves a will, it will specify who gets each item of property. If a person dies without a will, he or she is said to die intestate (see Chapter 8). In that situation, the courts will follow the instructions of a state statute that declares how the deceased's property is to be divided. These statutes generally give the property to surviving relatives.

WHAT ARE THE FORMS OF OWNERSHIP?

PROBLEM

After graduating from high school, Denise became a computer programmer. Her salary was good, and her expenses were low because she lived with her parents. With most of her savings, Denise bought shares in a mutual fund. What form of ownership did she use?

There are various forms of ownership of property. These are examined in detail in the following sections.

Supply students with package labels and advertisements in newspapers and magazines. Have each student collect five trademarks or servicemarks from packages and advertisements. Have them glue their selections on sheets of paper and post them around the classroom.

Independent Practice

Divide the class into groups of three and four. Tell each group to create and record a humorous report of a brief incident that involves acquiring property. Tell students that the incident should be not only humorous but also accurate. Play the tape and have the class identify the way ownership was acquired.

TEACH

Compare **ownership in severalty** (when someone, alone, owns all the ownership rights in property) with **co-ownership** (when two or more persons have the same ownership rights in the same property). Display the transparency, *Forms of Co-ownership and Their Legal Characteristics.* Discuss each of the forms of co-ownership in detail.

RETEACH Have students create a graphic organizer, poster, or chart to illustrate the seven ways property can be acquired (pp. 529–533).

ENRICH Have students create a new trademark or a servicemark for a new or existing product or service or a product. Display students' artwork on a classroom bulletin board entitled *The Marks of Intellectual Labor.*

APPLY

Pair students. Tell each pair that they own something under a specific kind of ownership and ask them to tell what this information tells them about their situation. For example, you might say: **Mark and Linda, you own property by tenancy by the entireties. What does this tell you about your situation?** (Answers may include we are married, one of us cannot sell without the other's consent, and so on.) **Guided Practice**

Writing Connections

Language Arts
Tell students to imagine that they are about to start a window-washing business with a financial banker. Tell them that the partnership will be by tenancy in partnership. Have students write, using a computer, if possible, an agreement for co-ownership of the window-washing equipment, covering what would happen if they sold or dissolved the business or if one of them should die. Tell students to be careful to keep the agreement clear and legal.

Independent Practice

1. Ownership in Severalty

Ownership in severalty exists when someone owns all the ownership rights in property by themselves. This is the most common form of ownership for personal property. If you owned a stamp collection, you would probably own it in severalty. In the problem, Denise held her shares in this way.

2. Co-Ownership

Co-ownership is the opposite of ownership in severalty. **Co-ownership** exists when two or more persons have the same ownership rights in the same property. Thus, one, two, or more persons may all have the same ownership rights to a single piece of land.

Co-ownership differs from situations in which two persons have different legal rights in the same property. For example, landlord and tenant are not co-owners because they have different rights in the realty. The landlord has the right to sell the property and to give it away after death; the tenant has the right to possess the property during the term of the lease. If two persons own the same rights in a house together, they are co-owners. This is the situation with most married owners. Similarly, if you and one of your parents own a car together, you are probably co-owners.

Co-ownership may take one of several forms—joint tenancy, tenancy in common, tenancy by the entireties, or community property. All forms have two attributes in common. The first is that all co-owners have equal rights of possession. **Equal rights of possession** means that no co-owner can exclude any other co-owner from any physical portion of the property. This is the most basic attribute of co-ownership. The second attribute common to all forms of co-ownership is the right of partition. The **right of partition** allows any co-owner to require the division of the property among the co-owners. Sometimes the partition is physical, as when a farm is divided. Usually partition is financial. For example, a co-owned airplane could be sold and the proceeds of sale divided among the co-owners.

Joint Tenancy. **Joint tenancy** is the equal co-ownership of the same property rights with the *right of survivorship*. Each joint tenant's ownership interests must always be equal, for example fifty-fifty with two owners or 25 percent for each of four owners. The **right of survivorship** means that if one of the joint owners dies, the surviving owner or owners automatically divide equally the deceased owner's interest. Each surviving owner gets an equal share.

Since the interest passes automatically on death, joint tenants often use this form of co-ownership to leave property to the other joint tenant(s) without incurring the costs and delays of probate. A joint tenant's interest

ASSESS

Learning Objective 3 Tell students to jot down answers to the following: **(1) If ownership is held with title in severalty, how many persons hold shares?** (One); **(2) What two attributes do all forms of co-ownership have in common?** (Equal rights of possession, right of partition); and **(3) Which two forms of co-ownership are available only to married couples?** (Tenancy by the entireties, community property) may be transferred while the joint tenant still lives. But a transfer would end the joint tenancy with regard to the transferred interest.

Bill, Joe, and Al were brothers. They owned equal interests in joint tenancy in a boat. Al became tired of it and sold his interest to a stranger. Joint tenancy remained between Bill and Joe. On death of either, their interest would pass to the other. But joint tenancy did not exist with the stranger.

Tenancy in Common. In this form of co-ownership the owners are called tenants in common. In **tenancy in common** the shares may be unequal and there is no right of survivorship. Upon the death of any tenant in common, that person's interest passes to the heirs (i.e., relatives entitled to inherit) or to the beneficiaries designated in the will if there is one. The heirs or beneficiaries then become tenants in common with the other owners.

Smith, Locke, and Pitt were friends and co-workers at a local factory. The three friends could not afford to purchase vacation trailers individually. Together, however, they were able to buy one. Smith contributed 50 percent, Locke contributed 10 percent, and Pitt contributed 40 percent. They agreed to allocate the time when they could use the trailer in proportion to their contribution to the purchase price. Tenancy in common would be the appropriate form of ownership for these three friends.

Although all owners have the right of possession, they can agree to give exclusive use to one or the other at certain times. This is true of all forms of multiple ownership.

Tenancy by the Entireties. In some states, tenancy by the entireties is the usual form of co-ownership between husband and wife. **Tenancy by the entireties** is limited to married couples, carries the right of survivorship, and may not be sold or mortgaged without the spouse's consent. Like joint tenancy, the interests must be equal.

Community Property. In Arizona, California, Idaho, Louisiana, Nevada, New Mexico, Texas, and Washington, all property acquired by husband and wife during their marriage is presumed to be community property. With **community property,** each spouse owns a one-half interest in such property. Generally, while the spouses are alive, both must consent to

Group students into groups of three or four. List **joint tenancy**, **tenancy in common**, **tenancy by the entireties**, and **community property** on slips of paper totaling the same number as the groups and place the slips of paper in some type of container. Have each group pick a slip of paper. Explain to each group that they are going to role-play the co-ownership situation listed on the slip of paper. Tell students to include in their skits property descriptions, descriptions of prospective owners, relationships, business and personal objectives, and so on. Students may wish to review the facts about co-ownership on pp. 534–536. Assign the following roles: director, if necessary, who keeps everyone on task; two owners; and a narrator, who summarizes the situation to the class as the two owners act out the skit. When the groups are ready, have each group present its skit. Have each group vote on which type of co-ownership is being displayed. Keep score and reward the group who gets the most correct votes. Videotape the skits and use them as a review at the end of this chapter.

Cooperative Learning

RETEACH Pair a student who understands *co-ownership* (p. 534) with one who is having difficulty. Have pairs of students create a graphic organizer to illustrate the different forms of co-ownership. Then, ask pairs to exchange their organizers and have each pair explain the organizer to the pair who created it.

Have students write, using a computer, if possible, a statement explaining which form of ownership they would choose for a car and a home, if they were married, and why they would choose that form.

Thinking Critically Through Visuals

The couple in the photograph has just purchased a home taking title in tenancy by the entireties. Knowing this, what can you tell about the couple and the property? (They are married; one of them cannot sell or mortgage the property without the consent of the other; if one dies, the survivor gains total ownership; and so on.)

TEACH

Tell students that the government has power to adopt laws to protect the public health, safety, morals, and general welfare, and that this power extends to the use of private property. Give examples, such as dangerous property and animal nuisance laws.

APPLY

Have the whole class brainstorm examples of a property owner's unreasonable or unlawful use of property that might injure another. Ask students to determine whether each example endangers public health, safety, morals, or general welfare. **Guided Practice**

disposal of community property. In some states, there is a right of survivorship. In other community property states, the spouse who dies is permitted to dispose of his or her half through a will.

> All of the property belonging to John and Sally Yaun was community property. Domestic difficulties developed between them. Although there was no divorce, John made a will in which he left all the community property to his nephews and nieces. If John dies, it is clear that he may not legally deprive his widow of at least her half of the community property. In some states, he could will *his half* of the community property to relatives or strangers.

Property owned by either spouse at the time of marriage or received as a gift or inheritance is **separate property.** Such property becomes community property only if the owner formally or informally treats it as community property and mixes it with other community assets.

WHAT ARE THE LIMITATIONS ON OWNERSHIP?

PROBLEM

> Jordan, who lived alone, was very fond of animals. After his retirement, he began to care for stray dogs, which he kept in his home and yard. Within one year, he had twenty-seven animals. Neighbors were reluctant to interfere, but the noise became intolerable. Could the neighbors compel Jordan to dispose of his animals?

ASSESS

Media

Learning Objective 4 Tell students to write a brief paragraph, using a computer, if possible, that gives evidence to support the following statement: **An owner of property does not have unlimited power in the use and disposition of that property.** (Answers may include various statutes and restrictions, such as condition of property, effect of property on others, and restrictions of number of animals in one place, and so on.)

An owner of property is not permitted to use that property in an unreasonable or unlawful manner that injures another. Thus, in the problem, Jordan could be compelled to correct a nuisance. Under its police power, the government may adopt laws to protect the public health, safety, morals, and general welfare. This power extends to the use of property. Thus, a city may require that buildings be maintained at a certain level of livability. It may enact zoning laws that restrict certain neighborhoods to specific uses. Cities or counties may also enact laws that prohibit the keeping of livestock or other animals in certain sections. They may regulate the purity of food and drugs sold to the public. Governments may even destroy private property, such as shipments of canned fish that are infected with deadly botulism. All such laws limit the owner's absolute ownership and freedom of use.

Preventing Legal Difficulties

Manage and use property wisely...

1. Do not misuse your property in any way that injures others.
2. Protect the ecology and conserve resources by avoiding waste; it is one of your social responsibilities.
3. Use public property with care. Vandalism, destruction, and theft deprive innocent persons of the benefits of use and also cause higher taxes, which burden all taxpayers.
4. Do not infringe upon the copyright, trademark, or patent of another.
5. If you become a co-owner, be sure to take title in an appropriate form. Use tenancy in common with strangers, associates, and friends. Use joint tenancy with a spouse or other relative whom you want to have the full ownership by right of survivorship when you die.
6. In community property states, be sure to keep separate property separate, with clear independent records, if you do not want it to become community property.

▼ REVIEWING IMPORTANT POINTS

1. Technically, property means a group of rights or interests that are recognized by society and, therefore, are protected by law. However, the terms may also refer to the things themselves—both real and personal, tangible and intangible—in which one may have legal rights and interests.

Ask students to review Amendment XIV, Section 1, of the U.S. Constitution (found on p. 798). Have students write an essay, using a computer, if possible, discussing the limitations of ownership when it conflicts with the rights of others.

Independent Practice

Preventing Legal Difficulties

Discuss the suggestions for preventing legal difficulties related to property. Ask students to suggest scenarios that reflect the possible consequences of not following each recommendation.

▼ CLOSE

Secure butcher paper to a wall and label it, ***Personal Advice About Personal Property***. Invite students to write, graffiti style, what they consider the most pertinent information discussed in this chapter.

You may wish to replay the videotaped skits from the Cooperative Learning Activity on p. 535 as a chapter review exercise.

Assign the following end-of-chapter materials:

Student text review activities, pp. 537–541
Workbook, pp. 81–82
Chapter Test

Chapter *MicroExam*

▼RETEACH Distribute newspaper articles that discuss recent cases of government restrictions on property. Have students read, discuss, and summarize in writing the articles.

▼ENRICH Have students orally debate the following question: **Since the government has power to restrict use of all property, what does *ownership* really mean?**

Strengthening Your Legal Vocabulary

1 mislaid property
2 tenancy in common
3 ownership in severalty
4 accession
5 patent
6 occupancy
7 copyright
8 real property
9 tenancy by the entireties
10 joint tenancy

Applying Law to Everyday Life

1 ETHICS ISSUE Jerry is ethically obligated to turn the coat and the money over to the owner of the restaurant. Consequentialists might find the theft morally neutral if Jerry and the true owner of the property were the only ones affected. But Jerry may not keep the coat or the money because deontologically that action would be a form of theft, which is inherently wrong. (See Chapter 2.) Both consequential and deontological reasoning compel Jerry to obey the law. The law classifies this property as mislaid and so requires Jerry to leave the coat and money with the restaurant. Consequentialists see obeying the law as generating the greatest good for the greatest number. Deontological reasoning shows that we promise to obey the law, so not complying with the law is a form of promise–breaking. Since promise–breaking is inherently wrong, Jerry can't take the coat and money. (p. 532)

2 No; Steven will not prevail. A trade secret must be kept secret by its owner. Since Steven did not keep the details of his process secret, he lost the protection of trade secrecy. For this reason, most firms treat trade secrets very carefully. Letters and documents related to trade secrets are often stamped in large red letters—CONFIDENTIAL or SECRET. Employees are asked to sign agreements promising to keep trade secrets confidential. (p. 531)

2 Property may be classified as real or personal. Legally, each category includes a group of rights that can be owned.

3 Real property is land, including the surface of the earth, surface and subsurface water and minerals, the airspace above, and anything permanently attached to the land. Personal property is any intangible or tangible property that is movable. Personal property also includes intellectual property—copyrights, patents, servicemarks, trademarks, and trade secrets.

4 Both real and personal property may include intangible rights, as, for example, the right to use land or the right to make and to sell a product.

5 Rights in property may be acquired by (a) contract, (b) gift, (c) accession, (d) intellectual labor, (e) finding, (f) occupancy, or (g) inheritance.

6 Ownership by one person is ownership in severalty. Co-ownership may take the form of joint tenancy or tenancy in common. In some states, husband and wife may hold property by tenancy by the entireties. In some other states, their property acquired during marriage is community property.

7 Individual ownership of property may be limited when necessary to prevent infringement on the rights of others.

STRENGTHENING YOUR LEGAL VOCABULARY

Match each term with the statement that best defines that term. Some terms may not be used.

accession	personal property
community property	property
co-ownership	real property
copyright	right of partition
equal rights of possession	right of survivorship
intellectual property	separate property
joint tenancy	servicemark
lost property	tenancy by the entireties
mislaid property	tenancy in common
occupancy	trademark
ownership in severalty	trade secret
patent	

1 An item that is intentionally placed somewhere but then forgotten.

2. Co-ownership of property without the right of survivorship.
3. Ownership of property by one person alone.
4. Right of an owner of property to an increase in the property.
5. Exclusive, monopolistic right to make, use, and sell an invented product.
6. Means of acquiring title by taking possession of personal property that belongs to no one else.
7. Exclusive, monopolistic right to possess, produce, and publish an intellectual production.
8. Land and things permanently attached to the land.
9. Form of co-ownership, other than community property, where neither co-owner may sell without the consent of the other.
10. Co-ownership of property with the right of survivorship by persons who are not husband and wife.

APPLYING LAW TO EVERYDAY LIFE

1. ETHICS ISSUE Jerry saw another customer in the restroom of a local restaurant place his overcoat on a coat hook but walk out without it. He also saw the customer drive away from the restaurant. Jerry picked up the coat and found $160 in one pocket. What are Jerry's ethical obligations in this situation? What are Jerry's legal duties in this situation?
2. Steven was president of a highly successful chemical company. He had developed a nonpatentable process for making soap a better cleaner. At first he treated his process as secret. But later his pride in developing it caused him to disclose the technique to a variety of people in his community. When one of these people started a competing business using his process, he sued claiming theft of a trade secret. Will Steven prevail?
3. Your mother operates a small lumber business. She owns a tract of land with a stand of trees on it. She cuts down the trees, saws them into construction lumber, and sells the wood to builders. She also is building a house as a business venture. The house is about one-third finished, and one-half of the framing for the walls is completed. Your mother is concerned about her insurance coverage because it covers only personal property. Which parts of her business property are real and which are personal?

3. The land is realty. The trees in the ground are also realty. When cut down, the trees become personal property. The saws are personal property. After the trees are cut into lumber they are personal property until nailed into a house under construction, such as in the house owned by the mother. All the materials permanently attached to the house which the mother is building are realty; the materials stacked at the site are personal. (p. 528)

4. No, Jake does not need to return the stock. When his Aunt Yvette delivered possession of the stock certificates to Jake she intended to shift ownership. Once ownership is shifted, the transferor cannot reverse the transaction. (pp. 529–530)

5. ETHICS ISSUE No; It is illegal and unethical for Jeff to copy the copyrighted computer program for himself or for anyone else without the permission of the owner of the copyright. No; The principal does not own the copyright and therefore does not have the legal power to allow Jeff to copy the program. Copying the program of another without that person's consent is deontologically wrong.

6. Yes, Voila! will prevail. The owner of a trademark has the exclusive right to the use of that trademark. Anyone who sells products bearing the trademark without the owner's consent has misappropriated the trademark and is liable to the owner. (p. 532)

7. No; While co-owners have the right to demand the partitioning of co-owned property, courts will not cut up, or disassemble, an item such as a drag racer. Rather, when the co-owners cannot agree on a way to divide the property, the court will cause the drag racer to be sold and will divide the money among the owners. (p. 534)

8 Trudy will get Bert's share of the apartment house because they co-owned as joint tenants. Joint tenancy carries the right of survivorship. This means that upon the death of one joint tenant, the decedent's interest passes to the surviving co-owners. (pp. 534–535) This will occur even if the will of the decedent co-owner directs otherwise.

9 No; Because the record stores are owned in tenancy by the entireties, Michael cannot sell or mortgage his one-half interest without Julia's consent. This is a distinguishing feature of tenancy by the entireties. (p. 535)

Solving Case Problems

1 Dollar Savings Bank prevails. This is because the money was mislaid, not lost. The court held that the money was mislaid because it was left in a private safety deposit booth which was only available to safety deposit box users. Such a location increases the probability that the true owner will determine that the money was left there and ask the bank for its return. If the money had been left in a public part of the bank, the court reasoned that it would have been lost and the finder then entitled to keep the money instead of the bank. (p. 532)

4 Yvette gave her nephew, Jake, 100 shares of stock in Gold Stake Oil Corporation for his sixteenth birthday. She handed the shares, worth about $2,000 to Jake right after Jake successfully blew out all sixteen candles. Two days later, Gold Stake discovered a very large oil field. The value of the stock increased 100 times to $200,000. As a result, Yvette had second thoughts and demanded the return of the shares. Must Jake return the stock?

5 ETHICS ISSUE Jeff's school has a computer laboratory. Jeff also has a computer at home and decides to copy the school's word processing program for his personal use. The program is copyrighted by its developer. Is it legal for Jeff to make a copy for himself? Would it be ethical for Jeff to make a copy if he obtains permission from the school's principal?

6 Voila!, a French firm, manufactured expensive leather goods. It marked all of its products with a crest or seal that was its registered trademark. Imperial sold six counterfeit handbags bearing the Voila! mark. The purchaser was a private investigator in the employ of Voila!. Voila! sued Imperial for trademark infringement. Imperial did not manufacture the handbags, but only sold them. Will Voila! prevail?

7 Foxx, Flynn, and Hammond were amateur auto mechanics. The three also had equal shares in a drag racer as tenants in common. After a disagreement, Foxx wanted to get out of the arrangement. She demanded the engine as her share of the commonly owned racer. Is she entitled to it?

8 For ten years, Trudy and her brother Bert invested their savings in a twelve-unit apartment house. They held the title as joint tenants. Then Bert got married. Shortly after the wedding, he was killed in an automobile accident. In his will, Bert left all his property to his wife. His sister and his widow are now in a dispute over who should get his share of the apartment house. Who will get Bert's share?

9 Michael and Julia are married. They co-own a chain of record stores as tenants by the entireties. Michael decides he wants to sell the record stores and go into the plumbing business. Can he sell his one-half interest without Julia's consent?

SOLVING CASE PROBLEMS

1 Betty Dolitsky was in a booth of the safety deposit room of the Dollar Savings Bank when she discovered a $100 bill in an advertising folder that the bank had placed in the booth. She turned the money over to

2 Yes, Roberts will prevail. This swimming pool is personal property because it is not permanently attached to the realty. Accordingly, the value of Roberts's real estate should not have been increased. However, the value of his personal property should have been increased. In many counties, this would be subject to a tax similar to the real estate tax. (p. 528)

the bank. A year later after the money had not been claimed by its true owner, Betty asked for it. The bank refused. Betty sued. Who prevails? (*Dolitsky v. Dollar Savings Bank*, 119 N.Y.S.2d 65)

2 Roberts had an above-ground swimming pool installed on his land. The pool was not permanently attached to the realty. It could be easily disassembled and moved to another location. Shortly after the installation, Roberts received a real estate tax assessment bill with an increased assessed value for his realty because of the pool. Roberts sued for a reduction, claiming that the pool was personal property. Will he prevail? (*Roberts v. Assessment Board of Review of the Town of New Windsor*, 84 Misc. 2d 1017, N.Y.)

3 Joseph's aunt sent him $5,000 as a gift. Later, she sent a letter stating that upon her death the money was to be distributed among Joseph and his brothers and sisters. After the aunt died, Joseph kept the money and was sued. Joseph defended by claiming that a valid gift of the money occurred before the letter was sent, so the letter is of no legal significance. Is Joseph correct? (*In re Gordon's Will*, 27 N.W.2d 900, Iowa)

4 Gem Electronic Distributors installed Make-a-Tape systems in their retail stores. Make-a-Tape is a coin-operated magnetic tape duplicating system. In two minutes, it can reproduce on a blank tape the complete musical selections already recorded on another tape that takes thirty-five to forty-five minutes to play. Elektra records sued Gem to restrain it from using Make-a-Tape to produce unauthorized copies of Elektra sound recordings, which are copyrighted. You decide. Would it be ethical for Gem to make the machine available for use by its customers if it knew that 95 percent of its users violated the copyright laws? (*Elektra Records Company v. Gem Electronic Distributors, Inc.*, 360 F. Supp. 821, E.D.N.Y)

5 Hamilton and Johnson were tenants in common of a parcel of land. Hamilton wanted to end the relationship and brought a suit for partition of the property. A forced sale of the property would be inconvenient for Johnson and would cause him some loss. Must the court, nevertheless, order partition? (*Hamilton v. Johnson*, 137 Wash. 92, 241 P. 672)

6 Alejo Lopez was a married man. Without divorcing, he married a second time. He and his second wife, Helen, purchased property and tried to take title as tenants by the entireties. Later, Alejo divorced his first wife and then remarried Helen. When he died, a question arose as to whether the property was owned in tenancy by the entireties. Is it? (*Lopez v. Lopez*, 243 A.2d 588, Md.)

3 Yes, Joseph is correct, the money is his alone. The gift was completed before his aunt tried to attach conditions to it. Her power to attach conditions ended when the gift became final. (pp. 529–530)

4 No, it would be unethical. Gem would be liable if its employees used the Make-a-Tape machine to violate the copyright law by reproducing copyrighted tapes. (p. 531) However, Gem would not be legally liable if its customers did the copying themselves without Gem's direct knowledge. If Gem were aware that 95 percent of the customers using the machine were violating the copyright laws, it would be unethical for Gem to make the machine available to them.

5 Yes; Hamilton, as a tenant in common, has an absolute right to partition, in the absence of a contrary agreement to hold the property in such tenancy for a definite and fixed time. (p. 534) Inconvenience of owners or depreciation in value because of the partition is not a defense.

6 Yes; At the time Alejo and Helen acquired the property, they were not married. Therefore the property was then owned in joint tenancy, not tenancy by the entireties. But when they became validly married, the property became owned in tenancy by the entireties because that was the intent of the married couple. (pp. 534, 535)

CHAPTER 27 ORGANIZER

Bailors, bailees, and common bailments are discussed in this chapter.

DIRECTED STUDY QUESTIONS	SPECIAL FEATURES	PROGRAM RESOURCES				
		Reteach	Enrich	SN	AM	
What is a bailment?		✔	✔	✔		
What are the types of bailments?		✔	✔			
What is the bailee's duty of care?		✔	✔			
How can the bailee's duty of care be modified?	Thinking Critically Through Visuals, p. 549 Personal Perspectives, p. 549	✔	✔			
What is the nature of the bailee's duty to return the goods?		✔	✔			
What are the bailor's duties?		✔	✔		V	
What are the most common bailments?	Ethics Issue, p. 553 Thinking Critically Through Visuals, p. 553 Writing Connections, p. 554 Multicultural Highlights, p. 554	✔	✔		A	
How is a bailment ended?	Preventing Legal Difficulties, p. 556	✔	✔		K	

Additional Resources

- Freese, Marjorie and Duncan, Sylvia. *How to Start a Consignment Shop & Make It Go.* Syracuse, IN: Sylvan Books, 1984.
- Schulman, Margaret B. *The Dow Jones-Irwin Guide to Property Ownership: How to Understand, Control and Protect Your Assets.* Homewood, IL: Dow Jones-Irwin, 1986.

One-semester course	✔	✔	✔					
One-year course	✔	✔	✔	✔				

Chapter Pacing Guide

	ASSESSMENT OPPORTUNITIES			
Cooperative Learning	Informal Assessment	Chapter Review	Chapter Test	Chapter *MicroExam*
	✔	✔	✔	✔
	✔	✔	✔	✔
✔	✔	✔	✔	✔
	✔	✔	✔	✔
	✔	✔	✔	✔
	✔	✔	✔	✔
	✔	✔	✔	✔
	✔	✔	✔	✔

Media

Videodiscs

Bailments: What They Are and What Bailers' Duties Are

Search Chapter 33, Play To34

State by State

In West Virginia, it is a crime (a misdemeanor) for a bailee for hire to willfully damage the bailed property. In Georgia, immoral or illegal contracts are not enforceable.

Teaching Materials

Student text, pp. 542–561

Overhead transparency masters
- *Types of Bailments*
- *Duty of Care in Bailments*

Videos
- *Law for Business* Videodisc

Workbook, pp. 83–84

Outside Resources
- Colored pens, pencils, and markers
- Blank overhead transparencies
- Flip chart, poster paper, index cards
- Articles on damaged bailed goods and bailor's duties

- Camcorder and VCR
- Tape recorder

Assessment
- Chapter Test

- Chapter *MicroExam*

Vocabulary

bailment, p. 544
bailor, p. 544
bailee, p. 544
custody, p. 545
fungible, p. 545
extraordinary bailment, p. 546
common carrier, p. 546
ordinary bailment, p. 546
gratuitous bailment, p. 546
bailment for the sole benefit of the bailee, p. 546
bailment for the sole benefit of the bailor, p. 546
mutual-benefit bailment, p. 547
actual bailment, p. 547
constructive bailment, p. 547
involuntary bailment, p. 547
bailee's duty of care, p. 548
extraordinary care, p. 548
ordinary care, p. 548
minimal care, p. 548
disclaimer, p. 550
bailee's duty to return the property, p. 551
bailee's lien, p. 551
bailor's duty to provide goods fit for the intended purpose, p. 551
demurrage, p. 553
carrier's lien, p. 553
consignment, p. 555
sale on approval, p. 555

Learning Objectives

When you complete this chapter, you will be able to

1. Identify transactions that qualify as bailments.
2. Describe the major types of bailments.
3. Explain how the bailee's duty of care changes with different types of bailments.
4. Discuss how parties can modify the bailee's duty of care.
5. Explain the bailee's duty to return goods.
6. Understand the obligation of the bailor in a bailment.
7. Describe the most common kinds of bailments.
8. Explain how bailments can be ended.

542

Chapter Self-Test

Assess students' understanding of bailments before they begin Chapter 27 by having them brainstorm terms or phrases associated with using someone else's personal property, such as borrowing, lending, leasing, renting, and so on. Review and discuss students' responses. Then, discuss how such property, such as athletic uniforms and equipment, library books and textbooks, and other school property, should be treated. Record students' responses on a flip chart. After students complete the chapter, return to the flip chart and revise any previous misconceptions.

CHAPTER 27

BAILMENTS

1 You need transportation to the senior prom, but your car breaks down. What legal relationship arises if you borrow a friend's car for the evening, without charge? What legal relationship arises if you rent a car from a rental agency?

2 While shopping for lipstick in the cosmetics department of the store, Sara places her purse on the counter. Minutes later she reaches for it, but it is gone—apparently stolen. Is the store liable for her loss?

3 ETHICS ISSUE You know that you have only a minimal duty of care for mail you receive that is addressed to others. Does the law here also define all of your ethical responsibilities?

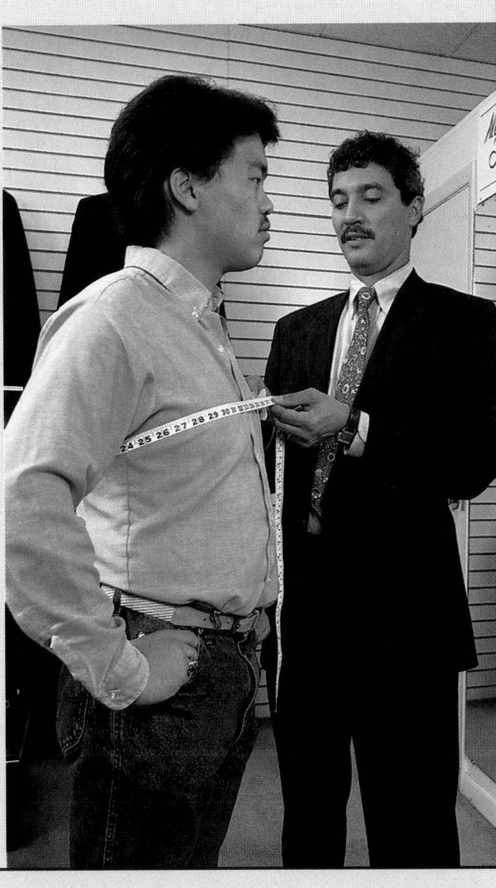

FOCUS

Prior to class, write the following question on the chalkboard for each student to answer on a sheet of paper: **What types of things do you lend to others?** (Answers may include CDs, books, clothes, and so on.)

Discuss how students decide what personal property they will lend, and to whom they will lend that property. Ask: **Are there any things or any people to whom you will not lend? Why?** Discuss responses that focus on the care, or lack of care, given to loaned items.

You Decide

1 If the friend charges you nothing, it is a gratuitous bailment for the sole benefit of you as bailee. If you rent a car from a rental agency, it is a mutual-benefit bailment.

2 No; The store neither received nor accepted the purse for safekeeping and had no duty to guard it.

3 ETHICS ISSUE No, the law does not express all of your ethical obligations in this situation.

Thinking Critically Through Visuals

This young man is being measured for a rental tuxedo. What responsibility, do you think, he has in taking care of the tuxedo? (Answers may include that he is responsible for returning the tuxedo in the same condition in which he received it, and so on.)

TEACH

Have students use the *Glossary of Legal Terms* to define, in their notebooks, the boldfaced terms on pp. 544–545 dealing with bailments. Remind the class that possession and temporary control of personal property are the crux of the bailment relationship.

Summarize the three characteristics of bailments as stated on p. 544–545. Point out how such characteristics differ from those of sales of goods, where both possession and ownership are transferred. Provide examples of bailment and of sales. Be sure students understand the differences between the two exchanges of goods.

APPLY

Verbally provide students with several examples of bailments (such as leaving a car in a park-and-lock lot, taking shoes to be repaired, finding a classmate's ring in the locker room of the gym, storing a coat at the dry cleaner for the summer, borrowing a sweater from a friend, and so on). Guide students in determining whether a bailment exists on the basis of the characteristics of bailments: the type of property (personal), possession and control (shifts from bailor to bailee), and intent to return (same or equal-value goods returned to bailor). **Guided Practice**

WHAT IS A BAILMENT?

PROBLEM

Roberta's parents own a forty-seven-inch television with a built-in videocassette recorder. One evening they rent a video Roberta has been wanting to see. What is the legal relationship between Roberta's parents and the videotape rental store?

If you lend your ballpoint pen to a friend, you create the legal relation of **bailment**. The transaction is neither a sale nor a gift, because your friend is obligated to return the pen to you. Bailments arise only with transfers of *personal property*. Further, the parties must intend that the personal property be *returned* to the person who gave it. *Possession* and temporary control of goods is the central feature of the bailment relationship. The **bailor** is the party who gives up possession of the property. The **bailee** is the party who receives possession and control. In the problem, a bailment was created. The rental store was the bailor, and Roberta's parents were the bailees.

Bailments have three characteristics: (1) the subject is personal property, (2) there is a temporary transfer of possession and control, and (3) the parties intend the identical goods to be returned. These three characteristics are discussed below.

1. The Subject of the Bailment Must Be Personal Property

The subject of the bailment must be personal property. Real property, such as land or buildings, cannot be bailed. Realty is leased under different rules of law (see Chapter 29).

2. A Bailor Gives Temporary Possession and Control of Goods to Another

Usually property is bailed by the owner; that is, the person with title to the goods. However, property may be bailed by any person in possession. This includes an agent or employee, a custodian, a finder, or even a thief.

A robber held up the cashier of a theater located in a shopping center. He stuffed the cash into an attaché case and mingled with the crowd of shoppers in the indoor mall. At an expensive restaurant nearby, he

ASSESS

Learning Objective 1 Independently and in writing, have students prepare a list of five transactions that qualify as bailments. Have students exchange papers, then identify for each transaction, using a different color ink or pencil, the three characteristics of bailments that exist. Discuss students' examples orally, then return papers to the original owner. (Answers may include renting a movie, taking clothes to the dry cleaner, renting a computer, lending tools to a friend, leasing a car, and so on.)

checked the case and his topcoat with an attendant. This was a legal bailment for storage.

For a bailment to arise, both possession and *control* of the goods must shift from the bailor to the bailee. Disputes about control often arise over cars left in parking lots. The car owner who drives into a lot, parks the car, keeps the key, and can later drive the car away without permission from an attendant continues to have control of the car. So there is no bailment. While possession may have been given up, the driver did not give up control. However, if an attendant takes the keys to the car and gives the owner a claim check that must be surrendered to get the car back, there is a bailment. In this situation, both possession and control have been given to the bailee.

Questions also arise as to whether the bailment of a car is a bailment of the articles enclosed in it. If the article is normally included, such as a spare tire in the trunk, the bailment covers it without regard to the bailee's knowledge of its presence.

It is possible for a person to have temporary control of another's personal property, yet not have a bailment. This occurs with **custody**. For example, a person hired to guard the paintings in an art museum has custody, but is not a bailee. Nor is a clerk using an employer's word processing equipment in the company offices a bailee. The owners of the art and the word processor never gave complete control of the goods to another. They merely authorized employees to guard or use goods. The employers retained control.

3. The Parties Must Intend That the Goods Be Returned to the Bailor

The bailor and bailee must intend that the goods be returned to the bailor or someone designated by the bailor. In many instances, the bailor identifies another party to whom the goods must be delivered. These transactions are still bailments. Usually, the bailee must return the identical goods. The goods may be modified somewhat, as by agreed-upon use, repairs, processing, or aging.

Some goods are fungible. **Fungible** means that there is no difference between one unit of the goods and another. For example, one unit of 500 gallons of 90-octane gasoline is the same as, or fungible with, another unit of 500 gallons of 90-octane gasoline. When the subject of the bailment is fungible, the bailee need only return the same *quantity* as received, not the exact same *unit* of the goods.

Provide students with one blank overhead transparency and a number of transparency markers. With the projector on, encourage students to apply their critical thinking skills to prepare a list of businesses in their community that engage in bailments. To verify students' classification of the transaction as a bailment, have them apply the three characteristics of bailment to each business they named.

Independent Practice

Have students who are having difficulty understanding the legal relationship of bailment, through a print modality, work in small groups to create posters that graphically explain the three characteristics of bailment. After checking the posters for accuracy, post them around the room so students can refer to them throughout the chapter. (You may wish to do the same type of exercise for students to more clearly visualize the terms **bailee** and **bailor.**)

Have students independently create a spider map to identify the three characteristics that must be present for a bailment to exist. Then, ask students to brainstorm an example of a bailment and create another map to depict the bailment attributes of the example.

Have students draw an illustration of a bailment transaction. Have them exchange papers with another student who will label the bailor, bailee, the bailment itself, and the three characteristics that make it a bailment.

TEACH

Complete the following graphic organizer as you identify the difference between the three basic types of bailments. Then, explain to students that the type of bailment created determines the degree of care that the bailee must exercise over the goods. Students must understand that the more the bailment benefits the bailee, the greater the bailee's duty of care. Ensure that students understand the boldfaced vocabulary words on pp. 546–547 before continuing with the chapter.

3 Characteristics of Bailments

- Personal property
- Temporary possession and control
- Goods returned to bailor

3 Types of Bailments by Priority

- Extraordinary
  - voluntary bailment
  - with common carrier

  -or-
- Ordinary
  - voluntary bailment
  - with other than commercial or common carriers

  -or-
- Involuntary
  - without consent of bailee

APPLY

Working in pairs, have students write on index cards two examples of each of the three basic types of bailments discussed in this section. In small print, have them identify the type of bailment on the back of the index card. Then, after you verify students' examples, have groups exchange cards to see how many types of bailments they can identify correctly. **Guided Practice**

WHAT ARE THE TYPES OF BAILMENTS?

PROBLEM

In preparing for a professional tennis tournament, Page ordered a new racket from Wilson, a manufacturer. Wilson used an interstate trucking company to ship the racket to Page. Page also took two of her tennis rackets to the Village Racketeer for restringing. Page borrowed four cans of tennis balls from her sister. Another tournament participant planned to jog to the tournament, so Page agreed to keep his equipment and bring it to the tournament. While practicing on a tennis court in her backyard, Page discovered that a friend had left his hat and sunglasses there. What types of bailments have been created?

The three basic types of bailments are discussed in this section. The type of bailment created determines the degree of care that the bailee must exercise over the goods. The more the bailment benefits the bailee, the greater the bailee's duty of care.

1. Extraordinary Bailments

The most basic distinction between types of bailments is between ordinary and extraordinary bailments. A *voluntary* bailment with a common carrier is called an **extraordinary bailment** because the bailee is held to an extraordinarily high standard of care for the bailed property. A **common carrier** is one who agrees, for a fee, to transport goods for anyone who applies, provided the goods are lawful and fit for shipment. When goods are given to common carriers and hotels, an extraordinary bailment arises. In the problem, an extraordinary bailment was created when Wilson gave the new tennis racket to the common carrier.

2. Ordinary Bailments

Ordinary bailments are voluntary bailments with parties *other* than commercial carriers and hotels. The standards of care for ordinary bailments are highly variable. In a **gratuitous bailment,** only one of the parties benefits. There are two types of gratuitous bailments: those for the sole benefit of the bailor and those for the sole benefit of the bailee. It would be a gratuitous **bailment for the sole benefit of the bailee** if you loaned your pocket calculator to a classmate (the bailee) without charge. It would be a gratuitous **bailment for the sole benefit of the bailor** (the neighbor) if your parents accepted a neighbor's house plants and agreed to

ASSESS

Learning Objective 2 Pass out one index card to each student. On it, have students write a one-sentence example of one of the types of bailments and write the answer (the type of bailment) in parentheses. Use the best questions to create a written short-answer quiz on the types of bailments. (You may wish to provide extra credit to those students whose questions you selected.)

care for them without charge while the neighbor was on a vacation. In the problem, gratuitous bailments were created when Page (1) borrowed the tennis balls and (2) transported the equipment for the other participant who wanted to jog. The tennis balls were for the sole benefit of the bailee (Page). However, when Page accepted the jogger's equipment, she created a bailment for the sole benefit of the bailor (the jogger).

When consideration is given and received by both bailor and bailee, the contracts are called **mutual-benefit bailments** because both parties benefit. In the problem, Page received the restringing and paid the price; the Village Racketeer received the money and did the work. Mutual-benefit bailments result from contracts, whereas gratuitous bailments do not because there is no exchange of consideration.

Both extraordinary and ordinary bailments are voluntary. This means that the bailee accepted the goods. There are two ways to voluntarily accept bailed goods. In an **actual bailment,** the bailee receives and accepts the goods themselves. Thus when you rent a truck, get behind the steering wheel, and drive away, you receive and accept the truck in bailment. **Constructive bailment** occurs when the bailee receives and accepts a *symbol* of the actual personal property. For example, if you received only the keys to a truck that was located elsewhere, you would be entering into a constructive bailment.

3. Involuntary Bailments

An **involuntary bailment** arises without the consent of the bailee. For example, this can happen when your neighbor's trash barrels are blown onto your property. In the problem, an involuntary bailment arose with the hat and sunglasses because Page never voluntarily accepted the goods. The duty of care for involuntary bailments is minimal. Notice that involuntary bailments raise the issue of whether the goods are lost or mislaid. This will determine whether the goods may be kept by the finder or the owner of the property (see Chapter 26).

WHAT IS THE BAILEE'S DUTY OF CARE?

PROBLEM

Patricia borrowed her neighbor's small sailboat for the afternoon. While she was sailing, a strong wind ripped the sail. What type of bailment was created and how does that affect Patricia's liability for the damage to the boat?

Have students think of the kinds of bailments into which they, or their family members, have entered. Then, on a class chart, have students individually record their bailments. Tally students' responses to identify the most common types of bailments (either extraordinary, ordinary, or involuntary). Graph students' responses using a computer, if possible.

Independent Practice

Display the overhead transparency, *Types of Bailments*, to underscore that there are different kinds of ordinary bailments (gratuitous and mutual-benefit). Using the headings on the transparency, have students orally give examples of gratuitous bailments (such as taking care of a neighbor's pet for free) and mutual-benefit bailments (such as getting paid to take care of a neighbor's pet).

TEACH

Every bailee has the duty to exercise care, but there are three levels of care, generally, depending on the type of bailment: extraordinary care when the bailment is extraordinary, ordinary care in a mutual-benefit bailment, and minimal care in an involuntary bailment and in a gratuitous bailment for the sole benefit of the bailor.

RETEACH Have students create a four-column chart summarizing the three basic types of bailments. In the first column, have them identify the type of bailment. In the second, have students describe each. In the third, have them provide examples. In the fourth, have students explain what the duty of care is.

Have three groups use a desktop publishing program, if possible, to create one newspaper story (covering extraordinary bailment, ordinary bailment, and involuntary bailment). Publish and circulate the stories.

APPLY

On the chalkboard, present a list of various bailment situations. Working in pairs, have students determine the level of care required in each bailment. Review students' answers. **Guided Practice**

Obtain, or have students obtain, newspaper or magazine articles dealing with bailed goods that were damaged. After reading each article, have students determine the type of bailment involved and the bailee's duty of care. Create a bulletin-board display with the headings *Extraordinary Care, Ordinary Care,* and *Minimal Care.* Then have students post their articles under the appropriate headings. **Independent Practice**

Have students play a *Jeopardy*-style game in which there are only three possible questions: **What is duty of extraordinary care? What is duty of ordinary care?** and **What is duty of minimal care?** Divide the class into teams of four or five students: one or two students to research and write the statements, two to play the game, and one team to announce the statements and judge the game. Videotape students' performance for later viewing.

Cooperative Learning

Most legal problems with bailments arise when something happens to the goods while they are in the possession of the bailee. The **bailee's duty of care** for the goods depends on the type of bailment. In general, there are three levels of care: extraordinary, ordinary, and minimal.

1. Duty of Extraordinary Care

When the bailment is extraordinary, the duty of care is usually extraordinary. In most cases **extraordinary care** means that if there is damage, loss, or injury, the bailee is liable. Thus, a common carrier is strictly liable for injury to the bailed goods. A similar standard applies to bailments for the sole benefit of the bailee. Since the bailment benefits only the bailee, the bailee must exercise extraordinary care. About the only time the bailee is not liable is when the loss is caused by an act of war, unforeseeable acts of God, or acts of the police. In the problem, Patricia is a gratuitous bailee with temporary control over the boat. The bailment is solely for the benefit of the bailee (Patricia). Therefore, she must exercise extraordinary care and will be liable even if she has not acted negligently. The high winds are not acts of God because they are foreseeable. If the damage had been caused by a tornado, that would have been an act of God and Patricia would not be liable.

2. Duty of Ordinary Care

A bailment of mutual benefit creates only the duty of ordinary care. In most instances, **ordinary care** means that the bailee will be liable only if he or she has been negligent in some fashion.

During the fall harvest, most of the Rome Beauty apples picked at Scott's Orchard were immediately placed in the Kool Storage Company's warehouse. Scott's Orchard paid a monthly fee for the storage and the contract specified that the apples would be stored at temperatures between 40 and 55 degrees. When Scott's removed some of the apples three months later, many had begun to rot because Kool Storage had failed to keep the building at the proper temperature. The bailment is one for mutual benefit. Therefore the bailee, Kool Storage, was required to exercise ordinary care. It did not do so and is therefore liable to Scott's Orchard for the loss.

3. Duty of Minimal Care

An involuntary bailment *and* a bailment for the sole benefit of the bailor both create only a minimal duty of care. In general, **minimal care** means

ASSESS

Learning Objective 3 In writing, have students explain the following statement and give examples: **The bailee's duty of care for the goods depends on the type of bailment.** (The type of bailment created determines the degree of care that the bailee must exercise over the goods. Examples may include: extraordinary care [airline baggage], ordinary care [furniture storage], and minimal care [a toddler's swimming pool blows onto your property], and so on.)

that the bailee must not waste or destroy the property. For valuable property, the bailee must make a minimal effort to identify the owner.

During a severe storm on a lake, a rowboat was torn loose from Compton's pier. The next morning, Sprague found the boat on his beach on the other side of the lake. As an involuntary bailee, Sprague is required to act with minimal care for the boat and in seeking the owner. Thus, he should probably tie it up so it would not float farther away. This duty would be violated if he simply pushed the boat back into the water. This type of bailment also arises when mail is delivered to the wrong addressee.

HOW CAN THE BAILEE'S DUTY OF CARE BE MODIFIED?

There are three common ways to modify the nature of the bailee's duty of care: (1) by legislation, (2) by contract, and (3) by disclaimer.

1. Modification by Legislation

Often an industry seeks to avoid the duty of care established by the common law by lobbying for legislation with a state legislature or a regulatory body. For example, under the common law, hotels are held to the standard

TEACH

Many industries want to limit their duty of care to reduce their potential liability. The three common ways to modify the nature of the bailee's duty of care are by legislation, by contract, and by disclaimer.

Thinking Critically Through Visuals

What type of bailment is involved when luggage is checked and what level of care is required? (Extraordinary bailment; extraordinary care limited by legislation)

Personal Perspectives

Have students discuss with their families experiences they have had with modifying duty of care, such as disclaimers in stores or contracts limiting liability. Then, make a class tally sheet to identify the most common experiences people have had with modifying the bailee's duty of care.

RETEACH Distribute individual copies of the overhead transparency master, *Duty of Care in Bailments*, to summarize the duty of care required for various bailments. Have students add one example for each heading. Check students' work.

ENRICH In small groups, have students select and role–play one of the bailee's three levels of care. Present the skits to the class. Have observers identify which level of care is being portrayed.

▼ APPLY

A major U.S. airline supplies the following information to passengers. Read aloud: **Our liability for loss, damage or delays is limited to $1,250 per passenger domestically and $640 per piece of checked baggage for international travel. These limits will apply unless an excess valuation is declared at time of check-in.** Ask: **Why, do you think, does this common carrier limit its liability for lost, damaged, or delayed baggage?** (Answers may include that it is difficult to ascertain the true value of the contents claimed to be in the baggage.)

Help students make a list of 15 or more industries that might want to modify their duty of care. (Answers may include a variety of businesses that provide goods or services to the public.) Discuss why and how they would go about modifying it (by legislation, by negotiated contract, or by disclaimer). **Guided Practice**

Have students each choose an industry from the list made in the previous activity. Then, have students research that kind of business to see if state or federal regulations have been enacted to limit liability for that industry. Have them present their findings. **Independent Practice**

of extraordinary care. But in most states, laws have been enacted that eliminate the hotels' liability. Similarly, airlines are common carriers and would owe the duty of extraordinary care for the luggage of their passengers. But the industry has persuaded the Federal Aviation Administration to adopt a regulation limiting their liability to a small dollar amount per item of luggage. Laundries and dry cleaning establishments often have special legislation limiting their duty of care. On the other hand, the legislature sometimes increases the duty of care or limits the ability of the industry to modify the duty of care.

2. Modification by Negotiated Contract

When the bailor and bailee negotiate a contract, they can usually modify the duty of care. Thus, if General Motors negotiated with an automobile transportation company to deliver its cars to local automobile dealers, the parties could agree in the contract that this bailment for mutual benefit would create a duty of care for the transportation company that was extraordinary. Similarly, they could agree that the duty was minimal. The bailee cannot be relieved of liability for *willful* or *deliberate* injury to the bailed property.

3. Modification by Disclaimer

Often merchants attempt to modify the duty of care with a disclaimer. A **disclaimer** is a sign, label, or warning reducing the bailee's duty of care. Thus, a garage may have a sign on the wall stating that it is not liable for loss of items left in a car. A restaurant may have a sign indicating that it is not responsible for loss of coats left on coatracks. A parking lot might have a ticket with small printing on it stating that it is not liable for any loss or damage to the car.

Disclaimers are often invalid. Usually disclaimers become a part of the contract only when the bailor is aware of the limitation before the purchase. So limitations in small print on claim checks or car parking tickets are insufficient notice unless the bailor has read them or was specifically told about the limitations in advance. Courts often scrutinize disclaimers to find them inapplicable.

Willard Van Dyke Productions was a commercial photographic company. It bought Kodak film for motion pictures it was taking of Alaska. The boxes the film came in contained a disclaimer stating that Kodak was not liable, except for replacing the film, for any "warranty or other liability of any kind." After shooting the pictures, the

▼ ASSESS

Learning Objective 4 Have students identify the modification of the bailee's duty of care in each of the following: **(1) Lobbyists try to increase a day-care's duty of care limits.** (Legislation); **(2) A "Not liable for contents left in car" sign is in a car parking lot.** (Disclaimer); and **(3) Two companies agree to modify the duty of care in an agreement they are preparing to sign.** (Negotiated contract) film was sent to the Eastman Kodak Company for processing. While processing the film, an employee of Kodak made a mistake and much of the film was damaged. Van Dyke Productions sued Kodak. Since this was a bailment for mutual benefit, Kodak owed a duty of ordinary care. The negligence of the employee violated this duty. But the disclaimer attempted to modify Kodak's duty by eliminating the duty of ordinary care. The court interpreted the language of the disclaimer as not applying to negligence because that word was not used in the disclaimer.

WHAT IS THE NATURE OF THE BAILEE'S DUTY TO RETURN THE GOODS?

PROBLEM

During dinner at the Sky Ski Lodge, Blue carelessly left his skis near a blazing fireplace in the main lounge. By the time he returned to the lounge, the heat had caused the laminated wood to separate at several points. Blue took the skis to the Alpine Ski Hut and had them repaired. Now he wants the skis for the coming weekend but does not have the cash to pay for the repair. Must Alpine give him the skis and simply bill him?

The **bailee's duty to return the property** compels the bailee to return the bailed property according to the terms of the bailment agreement. If the bailee is entitled to payment for the bailment, but it has not been paid, he or she may exercise the **bailee's lien** and retain possession until paid. If payment is delayed unreasonably, the bailee may sell the property to recover the fee and related costs. In the problem, Alpine has the right to retain possession until paid and to sell the skis if not paid within a reasonable time.

WHAT ARE THE BAILOR'S DUTIES?

In a mutual-benefit bailment, there is a **bailor's duty to provide goods fit for the intended purpose.** Thus, a rubber raft rental company *must* check carefully for damaged spots and slow leaks. Failure to do so could cause injury—or even death—to a bailee later caught in violent river rapids. The bailor in a mutual-benefit bailment who fails to inform the bailee of reasonably discoverable defects is liable for any resulting injuries.

A bailee who has been told about or discovers a defect is barred from collecting damages if injured because of the defect. The bailee is held to have

TEACH

Explain to students that once the bailee has finished with the bailed property, as per the terms of the bailment agreement, he or she must return the property to the bailor. Define a **bailee's lien** and the reason for such a clause.

APPLY

Help students make a list of situations in which the bailee is supposed to return bailed property. Then, using the list, have students give examples of when the bailee might consider exercising the bailee's lien. **Guided Practice**

Have students survey local businesses (such as a repair shop, animal groomer, dry cleaner, and so on) to see if, or how often, they have exercised the bailee's lien and retained property until paid. **Independent Practice**

TEACH

Point out to students that the bailor, in both a mutual-benefit bailment and a gratuitous bailment, must inform the bailee of reasonably discoverable defects or is liable for resulting injuries.

RETEACH Using poster paper, have students draw their own cartoons of one of the three common ways to modify the nature of the bailee's duty of care: by legislation, by contracts, and by disclaimer. Have students label their work accordingly and display it in class.

ENRICH In pairs, have students role-play one of the three common ways to modify the nature of the bailee's duty of care.

▼ APPLY

Help students create a list of occasions in which the use of defective goods could result in bailor liability. **Guided Practice**

Bring to class, or have students bring, newspaper articles on a bailor's duty to provide goods fit for the intended purpose and the catastrophes that may result from non-compliance. Have students select, clip, and post these articles on a bulletin-board display called *It's Your Duty—It's the Law.*

Independent Practice

▼ TEACH

Explain to students that the four most common bailments are mutual-benefit bailments: bailments for transport, for hire, for services, and for sale. Then, give examples of each to help students understand the classifications, as outlined on pp. 552–554.

▼ APPLY

Have students create a two-column chart. In the first column, have them list: Bailments for transport; Bailments for hire; Bailments for services; and Bailments for sale. In the second column, have students briefly describe each in their own words, using their summaries of pp. 552–554 as a starting point. **Guided Practice**

assumed the risk. This could happen, for example, if a bailee drives a rented truck with defective brakes after being told of the dangerous condition.

On the other hand, suppose your friend went on vacation and left her dog and automobile with you. These are gratuitous bailments for the sole benefit of the bailor. Unless otherwise agreed, you may not use such goods unless the use is necessary for their preservation. Before transferring possession, the bailor should examine the goods for possible defects. Failure to inform the bailee of known or reasonably discoverable defects makes the bailor liable for any possible resulting injury.

In contrast, friends or relatives often borrow equipment and other personal property from one another and are not charged. These are also gratuitous bailments, but they are for the sole benefit of the bailee. For example, one might borrow an extension ladder or jewelry. The bailee-borrower may use the goods, but only as agreed. The bailor-lender is obligated to inform the bailee of known defects. Thus, the bailor who knows of a loose rung in a ladder, yet says nothing, may be liable for any resulting injuries suffered by the bailee.

▼ WHAT ARE THE MOST COMMON BAILMENTS?

The most common bailments are mutual-benefit bailments. The distinctive details of some of these bailments are discussed below.

1. Bailments for Transport

PROBLEM

Shooting Stars Shippers, an interstate trucking company, transported Morgan's large box of valuable machinist tools to New York. Shooting Star, the carrier, refused to release the box until it was paid for its services. Morgan said he needed the tools to work and earn enough to pay the charges, and he demanded credit. Must Shooting Star release the tools?

Although passengers may be transported by common carriers, only their baggage is governed by bailment law. In the problem, the interstate trucking company was a common carrier.

A common carrier has the right to:

1. enforce reasonable rules and regulations for the conduct of its business (e.g., rules stating how goods must be packed);
2. demand compensation for its services, as allowed by law;

▼ ASSESS

Learning Objective 7 Have students create a spider map to identify the four most common mutual-benefit bailments. (Bailments for transport, bailments for hire, bailments for services, and bailments for sale) Then, have them add an example of each to the map.

3. charge **demurrage**; that is, fees for use of the transportation vehicle when the bailor fails to load or unload at the agreed time; and
4. enforce a **carrier's lien;** that is, the right to retain possession of the goods until the charges for transportation and incidental services are paid.

Thus, in the problem, Shooting Star would not be required to release the box of tools to Morgan until he paid for the transportation and any demurrage.

2. Bailments for Hire

PROBLEM

Rosetta rented a Cadillac from Hertz Car Rental for a week's trip with her children. Because they were having so much fun, she wired Hertz and said she would "take the Caddy for another week." This extended use was not authorized. On the way to return the car, a drunken driver crashed into the Cadillac. Rosetta was not at fault for the accident. Is she liable to Hertz?

A bailment for hire arises when the bailor provides personal property (e.g., a car, truck, tool, machine, or other equipment) for use by the bailee.

Ethics Issue

Most car rental companies require drivers to have a valid driver's license, be 25 or older, and possess a valid credit card. Ask: **Is it ethical for rental companies to impose additional requirements on licensed drivers?** (Answers may include yes, because they want to limit their risk, or no, because meeting state driver's requirements should be the limit of the law.)

Have students add a third column to their charts from the GUIDED PRACTICE on p. 552 and list examples of each kind of bailment. **Independent Practice**

Thinking Critically Through Visuals

What kind of bailment arises from a car rental? What duty of care is required? (Bailment for hire; ordinary care, rental agreements usually make the bailee strictly liable for property damage)

RETEACH Working in pairs, have students make an outline of the key details for each of the bailments highlighted on pp. 552–555.

ENRICH As a group, have students make a list of mutual-benefit bailments into which they, their friends, or family members have entered. Then, ask students to identify them as bailments for transport, for hire, for services, or for sale.

Writing Connections

Language Arts Using a computer, if possible, have students respond to this statement: **Demurrage and carrier's liens give bailees an unfair advantage over bailors.**

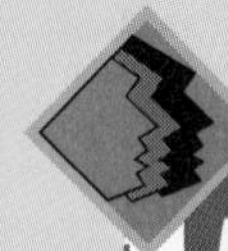

Multicultural Highlights

Nydia M. Velázquez, a Hispanic American, and Eva Clayton, an African American, both serve on the House subcommittee on Small Business. Ask: **How can being directly involved in a small business impact a legislator's ability to make wise policy decisions?** (Answers may include that such individuals bring greater knowledge and understanding of the issues, and so on.)

The bailee is required to act with ordinary care. However, most rental contracts modify the duty of care, making the bailee strictly liable for property damage. So in the problem, Rosetta probably would be liable for the damage to the Cadillac. The bailee must abide by the contract by using the property only for the stated purposes and returning it at the agreed-upon time. In the problem, Rosetta's unauthorized use of the car for the second week made her liable for damages beyond the rental rate.

3. Bailments for Services

PROBLEM

Systematics Unlimited prepared 1,000 copies of its annual catalog and price list on its own word processing machines. Then it sent the materials to the Bocca Bindery for binding into booklets. After the job had been done, a fire broke out in the Bocca plant. All the booklets were ruined by fire, smoke, and water from the automatic sprinkler system. Must Systematics pay for the job? Under what circumstances would Bocca be liable for the loss?

When a person delivers goods to be serviced, repaired, or made into a finished article, a bailment results. For example, the bailor may deliver wool cloth to a tailor to have a suit made. Or a bailor may deliver clothes to a laundry to be washed or a watch to a jeweler to be cleaned and oiled. As in the problem, a bailor may send printed materials to a bindery to be made into books. If the goods are damaged or destroyed, but the bailee has exercised ordinary care in their protection, the loss falls on the bailor who owns them. Moreover, the bailor must pay for any work done by the bailee before the accident. In the problem, Systematics must pay for the job. Only if the fire was caused by Bocca's negligence or intentional wrongful act (e.g., arson) would Bocca be liable.

4. Bailments for Sale

PROBLEM

Werner owned a retail sport shop. Irresistible Lures, Inc., offered Werner a counter card that displayed a new type of fishing lure. Werner agreed to display the card when the sales agent said, "You pay nothing and return any lures not sold. Just deduct 50 percent of each sale for yourself and send the balance to us." Was Werner a bailee?

ASSESS

Learning Objective 8 Have students identify and give examples of the ways a bailment can be ended. (When an agreed upon time has lapsed; when the agreed purpose has been accomplished; by destruction of the subject matter; when the parties mutually agree to end it; and, in certain cases, through death, insanity, or bankruptcy)

Sometimes goods are sent on consignment by a manufacturer to a retailer. A **consignment** is where ownership remains in the manufacturer or wholesaler (the bailor) until the goods are sold. The retailer who displays and sells the consigned goods, like Werner in the problem, is a bailee.

Bailment is also created when a merchant sends goods "on approval" to a prospective buyer. In a **sale on approval,** the prospective buyer is permitted to use the goods to determine whether he or she wants to buy them. During this time, the prospective buyer is a bailee. Ownership shifts if the bailee agrees to buy the goods. At that point the bailment ends. If the bailee rejects the goods, they must be returned. This arrangement is common in national merchandising of books, records, and cassettes.

HOW IS A BAILMENT ENDED?

PROBLEM

Ruden leased a heavy-duty pile driver from Max Power Controls for six months with the right to renew upon thirty days' notice. Three months later, Ruden was killed in an industrial accident. Was the bailment ended?

The bailment ends when the time agreed upon by the parties has elapsed, when the agreed purpose has been accomplished, or when the parties mutually agree to end it. If no time of termination is stated, either party may end the bailment. Thus, the bailor might ask for return of the property. Or the bailee may no longer need the property and return it. If the bailed property is destroyed or damaged so badly that it is not fit for the intended purpose, the bailment ends.

Death, insanity, or bankruptcy of one of the parties terminates the relationship when (1) the bailee's duties cannot be performed by another or (2) the bailment is one that may be ended at will. Normally, however, if there is a contractual bailment for a fixed period, death or incapacity of a party does not end the relationship. The rights and duties of the deceased party are transferred by law to the personal representative of the estate. This rule would apply to Ruden's case in the problem.

Preventing Legal Difficulties

Practical pointers for bailees . . .

1. Before you take possession of or use bailed goods, be sure you are covered by adequate liability and property insurance. You are usually

Have students work in pairs to create, then tape record, a verbal agreement dealing with one of the four most common mutual-benefit bailments. They should decide on the type of bailment and on any stipulations about how the bailment would be rendered. Then have students play their contracts for the class.

TEACH

Point out the ways in which bailments can be ended. Explain that the death or incapacity of either the bailor or bailee does not always end the relationship—the rights and duties of the deceased may transfer to the representative of the estate of the deceased.

APPLY

Have students play a version of *Telephone*, in which each student successively adds information to a bailment scenario, then whispers it to the following student. Have the last participant determine how the bailment in each scenario ended. **Guided Practice**

Have students create visuals to illustrate how a bailment might end.

Independent Practice

RETEACH Have each student create one example of a bailment relationship, with full details. Collaborating with another student, have the pair identify how the bailment logically might end.

ENRICH Working in small groups, have students create and role-play scenarios in which the bailment relationship is ended by any of the following: elapsed time frame, the purpose has been accomplished, the property is so damaged it is unusable, bankruptcy of the parties, or death of one of the parties.

Preventing Legal Difficulties

Review the pointers for bailees and bailors. Then, have students make posters or cartoons highlighting each of the pointers.

CLOSE

Return to the flip chart created in the CHAPTER SELF-TEST at the beginning of the chapter. Revise any misconceptions associated with bailments.

Using a computer, if possible, have each student write a scenario for a bailment. Each scenario must include, at minimum, the three characteristics necessary for a bailment relationship to exist. Make an overhead transparency of the most imaginative, most realistic, and most comical bailments. For each, have the class identify the type of bailment described, the bailee and bailor, the bailee's duty of care, the bailor's duties, and how the bailment ended.

Assign the following end-of-chapter materials:
Student text review activities, pp. 556–561
Workbook, pp. 83–84
Chapter Test

Chapter *MicroExam*

required to pay damages if you damage or destroy the bailed property or injure someone with it.

2. If you have performed services on bailed goods, do not return them until you are paid for your services or are satisfied that the bailor's credit is good.

Practical pointers for bailors . . .

1. Although a bailee may be liable for willful or negligent conduct that damages your goods or injures third parties, it is still wise to carry appropriate property and liability insurance to cover possible losses.
2. Spell out the terms of the bailment contract in writing whenever practicable. Always get a receipt for goods transferred to a bailee.
3. If the bailee is to repair or service the goods, be as precise as practicable about prices and work to be done.
4. If you rent a car or other equipment that could be dangerous if it is in bad condition, inspect it carefully and correct defects before delivering it to the bailee.
5. When you travel by common carrier, you are responsible for clothing and baggage that you retain in your possession. Guard it. Moveover, there are limits on the carrier's liability for baggage you check. For added protection, buy additional coverage from the carrier.

In bailments for your sole benefit . . .

1. If you alone benefit from a bailment, you must exercise an extraordinary degree of care. Failure to exercise an extraordinary degree of care can make you liable for resulting losses even though you received no consideration.
2. If you are the bailee, use the goods only as agreed and protect them carefully from possible loss or harm.
3. If you are the bailor, carefully examine the goods for defects that could cause harm and tell the bailee of any found.

REVIEWING IMPORTANT POINTS

1. In a bailment, the bailee has possession and control of personal property belonging to the bailor.

2. Every bailment has three characteristics: (a) the subject is tangible personal property; (b) the bailor transfers possession and control to the bailee; (c) the identical goods must be returned to the bailor.
3. Bailments created for the benefit of both parties are mutual-benefit bailments. Bailments created for the benefit of only one party are gratuitous bailments.
4. In a mutual-benefit bailment, the bailee must exercise ordinary care. In a gratuitous bailment for the sole benefit of the bailee, the bailee must exercise extraordinary care. In a gratuitous bailment for the sole benefit of the bailor, the bailee need exercise only minimal care.
5. In a bailment for hire, the bailor is liable for damages caused by known or reasonably discoverable defects in the property unless the bailee has specifically been informed of such defects.
6. Common types of mutual-benefit bailments are those for transport, for hire, for services, and for sale.
7. A bailment may be terminated (a) by agreement, (b) by act of either party, (c) by destruction of the subject mattter, or (d) by operation of law.

STRENGTHENING YOUR LEGAL VOCABULARY

Match each term with the statement that best defines that term. Some terms may not be used.

actual bailment
bailee
bailee's duty of care
bailee's duty to return the property
bailee's lien
bailment
bailor's duty to provide goods fit for the intended purpose
bailment for the sole benefit of the bailee
bailment for the sole benefit of the bailor
bailor
carrier's lien
common carrier
consignment
constructive bailment
custody
demurrage
disclaimer
extraordinary bailment
extraordinary care
fungible
gratuitous bailment
involuntary bailment
minimal care
mutual-benefit bailment
ordinary bailment
ordinary care
sale on approval

Strengthening Your Legal Vocabulary

1. sale on approval
2. minimal care
3. fungible
4. bailee's lien
5. common carrier
6. constructive bailment
7. custody
8. gratuitous bailment
9. extraordinary care
10. disclaimer

1. A bailment where the bailee can try out the goods before buying them.
2. The duty of care when the bailment is involuntary.
3. Type of goods that are identical from one unit to another.
4. Right of a bailee to hold goods until paid.
5. One who undertakes, for hire, to transport goods or passengers for anyone who applies.
6. Bailment created by accepting a symbol of the property, such as keys to a car.
7. Control of another's personal property under the owner's direct supervision.
8. Bailment in which one party receives no benefit.
9. The duty of care when the bailment is for the sole benefit of the bailee.
10. A sign, label, or warning that reduces the bailee's duty of care.

APPLYING LAW TO EVERYDAY LIFE

1. Guilt bought and contracted to have delivered to his place of business a large industrial stamping machine that weighed approximately 11,000 pounds. When the common carrier truck arrived with the machine, it took Guilt a week to locate a crane that could lift the machine off the truck. Is Guilt liable for the rental value of the truck while it waited to be unloaded?
2. ETHICS ISSUE Cararro rented a car and treated it harshly. He gunned the engine before engaging it in gear, drag raced, and intentionally burned a cigarette hole in the upholstery. When a friend asked why he did that he said, "Since it isn't mine, who cares? Besides, it's fun. It makes me feel good, kind of powerful." Is Cararro acting ethically? Why or why not?
3. Boyd borrowed a lawn edger from her neighbor Enbanks. The edger's circular blade was defective, but Enbanks did not know this. While Boyd was using the edger, the blade snapped. A piece of metal lodged in Boyd's eye, blinding her in that eye. Was Enbanks liable for the injury?
4. ETHICS ISSUE A neighbor asked Hazel if he could borrow her chain saw. Hazel thought something was wrong with the saw but there was nothing specific she could point to. She thought, "It doesn't

Applying Law to Everyday Life

1. Yes; Guilt is liable for the value of the truck's time. It is demurrage. (pp 552–553)
2. ETHICS ISSUE Cararro is not acting ethically. His answer indicates that he is using his emotions as the guide to his conduct. He also appears hostile toward the owner of the car and this is how he justifies his conduct. Both consequentialists and deontologists would condemn Cararro's conduct. (See Chapter 2)
3. No; Enbanks is not liable because this was a bailment for the sole benefit of the bailee, Boyd. (p. 546) In such case, the bailor is liable to the bailee only for harm caused by a defect which the bailor knew about but did not warn the bailee of the danger. (p. 552)
   Also, note that Boyd may have been guilty of contributory negligence in failing to wear protective goggles or a face mask. Even if Enbanks were liable, in some states Boyd's negligence would bar any recovery. In other states, which use the rule of comparative negligence, it would reduce the collectible damages.
4. 
   Hazel was not legally liable for the injury to Buz. Buz was a gratuitous bailee where the bailment was solely for the benefit of the bailee. That meant that Hazel's duty of care was minimal. She wasn't legally obligated to tell Buz about her nonspecific concerns. (p. 552) Ethically, she should have told Buz about her concerns.
5. Jon Silver is not liable for the loss. He exercised reasonable care in protecting the property, but it was destroyed by an act of God. (p. 548) Since Silver had done the work as agreed, Widdington must pay him the $95,000.

matter because my neighbor Buz will have to look out for himself here." Hazel did not say anything to Buz about her concerns. While Buz was cutting a small log, the saw hit a knot in the wood, bucked back, and hit him in the shoulder, chewing a large gash into his skin and sawing part way into his collar bone. Was Hazel legally liable for the injury? Did she act ethically?

5 Widdington inherited an old ninety-foot former Navy patrol boat. She delivered it to Ol' Jon Silver's Shipyard, which was located near the oceanfront. Widdington contracted with Jon Silver to convert the patrol boat into a houseboat for $95,000. After the work had been completed but before Widdington came to get her boat, a tidal wave destroyed the ship and all the boats in the immediate vicinity. Is Jon Silver liable for the loss of Widdington's boat? Or must Widdington pay the $95,000?

6 Babbitt rented a paint-spraying outfit from Baron. The equipment was in good working condition, and Babbitt knew how to use it properly. However, when Babbitt was shifting position between two buildings, she carelessly sprayed the neighbor's building and the top of the neighbor's car parked below. The neighbor sued Baron. Is Baron liable?

7 Bortez, a sales representative, had a breakfast appointment with a prospective buyer. They were to meet in the restaurant of the Grand Prix Hotel. Bortex left his attaché case, which contained almost $30,000 worth of sample watches, with the clerk in the hotel checkroom. The clerk gave him a receipt that stated in fine print: "Not liable for loss or damage from any cause beyond a maximum of $100." Bortez, in a hurry, stuffed the stub into his pocket without reading it. The clerk left his post briefly to go to the restroom. When he returned, the case was gone. Is the Grand Prix liable? If so, for how much?

8 Burg customized and sold new vans and serviced old ones. Jake and Jayne Slinker were trusted employees who had been carefully hired and trained and had worked for Burg for ten years. Jake did metalworking and woodworking; Jayne did upholstering. One holiday weekend, the Slinkers and an accomplice stole three vans and disappeared. The first van belonged to Adams, who had brought it in to have the engine tuned. The second van belonged to Yates, a friend who had asked Burg if he could leave the van on the lot with a "FOR SALE" sign. Burg had agreed and did not charge Yates. The third van was a very valuable vehicle, built by Burg, and sold to Mox. Mox had loaned the van to Burg, free, for display in the latter's exhibit at a Civic Auditorium show

6 No; Baron is not liable to the neighbor. The bailor normally is not liable for torts committed by the bailee. (pp. 553–54) However, in some states, statutes do make the bailor liable up to a specified limit when a bailee injures another with a rented automobile. Usually the auto insurance of the bailor would cover such loss.

7 Yes; This was a mutual-benefit bailment, even though no prescribed fee was charged. (p. 547) A "tip" was expected, and the hotel was catering to the needs of present and prospective guests. If the clerk directed Bortez's attention to the limitation on the receipt, or if Bortez had read the notice, the limit would apply. (p. 550) Bortez may collect a reasonable sum for the case and its contents. However, it would not be reasonable to assume that an ordinary attaché case would contain $30,000 worth of sample watches. Bortez should have disclosed this fact, and probably would have been told of the $100 limit. Then he might have left the case in the hotel safe, but here again, a limited liability might have been stated. (p. 550)

8 Adams's van was held by Burg in a mutual-benefit bailment. Therefore he was duty-bound to exercise ordinary care in its protection, and this he evidently did. (p. 547) Yates's van was held by Burg in a bailment for the sole benefit of the bailor, Yates. Burg was obligated to use only minimal care and would be liable only for gross negligence. (pp. 548–549) On these facts he is not liable for the loss. Mox's van was held by Burg in a bailment for the sole benefit of the bailee, Burg. Burg was obligated to exercise great care, and would be liable for even the slightest negligence. (p. 548) Here he might have moved the van into a secure garage (with 24-hour attendants), posted a special guard, installed a burglar alarm, or asked the police to check the premises

scheduled for the following week. What is Burg's liability, if any, to Adams? to Yates? to Mox?

▼ SOLVING CASE PROBLEMS

1. Plaintiff Wall drove his car into a self-parking lot at O'Hare Airport, Chicago. He entered through an automatic gate and received a ticket bearing the date and time of arrival. He parked, locked the car, and left with the keys. Normally, when ready to depart, he would walk to his car and, using his keys, would enter the car and drive it to the exit. There, an attendant would take the ticket and compute and collect the parking fee. This time his car had been stolen. He sued the defendant, Airport Parking Company of Chicago, for damages. Is the defendant liable? (*Wall v. Airport Parking Company of Chicago,* 244 N.E.2d 190, 41 Ill. 2d 506)
2. Carter took her fur coat to Reichlin Furriers to be cleaned and stored. She was given a receipt for the coat. On the front of the receipt an employee had written the number "100." On the back of the receipt were written the words, "the . . . amount recoverable for loss or damage to this article shall not exceed . . . the depositor's valuation appearing in this receipt . . . ." Also on the front of the receipt was a place for the customer's signature, but Carter had not signed. The coat was lost. Is Reichlin liable for its market value of $450 or only for the $100? (*Carter v. Reichlin Furriers,* 386 A.2d 648)
3. A student enrolled in flight school. While 900 feet above the ground on a practice flight in the school's aircraft, the student discovered that the rudder was stuck. As a result of the stuck rudder, the plane crashed into the ground and the student was seriously injured. Is the school liable to the student for the injury? (*Aircraft Sales and Service v. Gannt,* 52 A.2d 388)
4. Loden shipped a quantity of perishable cucumbers from Yuma, Arizona, to Los Angeles via the Southern Pacific Company railroad. Heavy rainfall damaged two bridges near Thermal, California, and the repairs delayed the shipment of Loden's cucumbers. When the cucumbers finally arrived in Los Angeles, they were spoiled. Loden sued the railroad for $10,000 in damages. You decide. (*Southern Pacific Company v. Loden,* 19 Ariz. App. 460, 508 P.2d 347)
5. Armored Car Service, Inc., had its employees pick up a locked money bag containing $1,511.25 at the Miami Springs Junior High School.

from time to time. Having failed to do so, he is liable to Mox for the loss. Note that with suitable theft insurance, Burg could pay off Adams, Yates, and Mox.

Solving Case Problems

1. No; Airport Parking Company is not liable. It had merely leased the space to Wall as an invitee for a fee. The lot operator owes a duty of reasonable care in the operation of the lot. But here Wall failed to prove any negligence by the defendant. Moreover, there was no bailment. There was no express agreement, and none can be implied from the circumstances. (p. 545)
2. Carter never agreed to the terms written on the receipt. Therefore, the disclaimer was ineffective. (p. 550)
3. The school is liable because it violated the bailor's duty to provide goods reasonably fit for the purpose intended. (p. 551)
4. Judgment for the plaintiff, Loden; The heavy rainfall was a weather condition "which could foreseeably cause damage" to the facilities of the carrier, and consequently delay transportation. Southern Pacific should have anticipated what happened and taken appropriate corrective measures in time, or refused the shipment temporarily. A rainstorm of unusual duration or intensity is not necessarily an act of God, which would relieve the carrier of liability. (p. 548)

The money was to be deposited in the proper cafeteria fund account at a certain bank. However, the bag was mistakenly deliverd to the First National Bank of Miami. First National provided a receipt for the bag but made no record of the bag's handling or disposition. Presumably, the bag was stolen. Armored Car Service indemnified the high school and now seeks to recover its loss from First National. What kind of bailment was created by the mistake? Is the First National Bank of Miami liable as bailee? (*Armored Car Service, Inc. v. First National Bank of Miami,* 114 So. 2d 431, Fla.)

5 This was an involuntary bailment (p. 547), and the bailee is required to exercise minimal care, the degree to be determined by the facts relating to the bailment. The bank is grossly negligent in failing to exercise minimal care for the bag of money left there by mistake. Therefore, it is liable as bailee. (pp. 548–549)

CHAPTER 28 ORGANIZER

Chapter Theme

Real property and how it is acquired is the focus of this chapter, which also covers deeds and financing arrangements for purchasing real property.

DIRECTED STUDY QUESTIONS	SPECIAL FEATURES	PROGRAM RESOURCES				
		Reteach	Enrich	SN	AM	
What is real property?	Personal Perspectives, p. 565 Ethics, Issue, p. 566 Thinking Critically Through Visuals, p. 566 Writing Connections, p. 567	✔	✔		K	
How is real property acquired?	Ethics Issue, p. 568 Multicultural Highlights, p. 569	✔	✔			
How do we buy real property?	Thinking Critically Through Visuals, p. 571 Preventing Legal Difficulties, p. 573	✔	✔	✔	V A	

Additional Resources

- Jordan, Cora, LL.B. *Neighbor Law: Fences, Trees, Boundaries and Noise.* Berkeley, CA: Nolo Press, 1991.
- Miller, Peter G. and Bregman, Douglas M. *The Common-sense Guide to Successful Real Estate Negotiation: How Buyers, Sellers and Brokers Can Get Their Share—and More—at the Bargaining Table.* NY: Harper & Row, 1987.

One-semester course	✓	✓						
One-year course	✓	✓	✓					

Chapter Pacing Guide

		ASSESSMENT OPPORTUNITIES			
	Cooperative Learning	**Informal Assessment**	**Chapter Review**	**Chapter Test**	**Chapter *MicroExam*** (Media)
		✓	✓	✓	✓
		✓	✓	✓	✓
	✓	✓	✓	✓	✓

Videodiscs

Acquisition of Real Property

Search Chapter 34, Play To 35

Sale of Real Property

Search Chapter 35, Play To 36

State by State

In Florida, the time period for adverse possession without color of title is seven years. However, the possessor must pay property taxes and have cultivated or enclosed the land with a fence.

Teaching Materials

Student text, pp. 562–577

Overhead transparency masters
- *A Sample Warranty Deed*
- *Roles of Parties to Mortgages*

Videos
- *Law for Business* Videodisc

Workbook, pp. 85–86

Outside Resources
- Real property classified advertisement
- Blank overhead transparencies
- Magazines and newspapers
- Tape, scissors, markers, butcher paper
- Business sections of newspapers
- Copies of telephone "Yellow Pages"
- Outside speakers: real estate loan officer and professional surveyor

- Tape recorder

Assessment
- Chapter Test

- Chapter *MicroExam*

Vocabulary

real property, p. 564
land, p. 564
buildings, p. 565
fixtures, p. 565
annexation, p. 566
adaptation, p. 566
test of intent, p. 566
trade fixtures, p. 567
license, p. 567
easement, p. 567
profit, p. 567
deed, p. 568
grantor, p. 568
grantee, p. 568
quitclaim deed, p. 568
warranty deed, p. 568
adverse possession, p. 569
easement by prescription, p. 569
dedication, p. 569
eminent domain, p. 569
condemnation proceeding, p. 569
surveying, p. 570
abstract of title, p. 571
title insurance, p. 571
mortgage, p. 572
mortgagor, p. 572
mortgagee, p. 572
right of foreclosure, p. 572
deed of trust, p. 572
escrow agent, p. 572
escrow, p. 572
recording, p. 572

Learning Objectives

When you complete this chapter, you will be able to

1. Define real property and explain how it differs from personal property.
2. Explain how real property is acquired.
3. List the steps involved in the typical sale of real property.

Chapter Self-Test

Assess students' understanding of real property before they begin Chapter 28 by asking them to respond orally to the following: **(1) How does real property differ from personal property?** (Real property includes land, buildings, things permanently attached to land or buildings, and certain rights to the use of the real property of others. Personal property is any property that is not real property.); and **(2) How, other than by buying, can real property be acquired?** (By gift, by inheritance, by adverse possession, by dedication, or by eminent domain) Before continuing with the chapter, review and discuss students' responses.

CHAPTER

28

REAL PROPERTY

1 ETHICS ISSUE A friend of yours who is selling his home knows about problems in its title. So he is planning to give the type of deed where he has no legal liability for these problems—a quitclaim deed. The buyer does not understand the legal consequence of accepting a quitclaim deed. Is it ethical for your friend to use his legal knowledge this way?

2 Jerry's mother and father entered into a contract for the purchase of a house. The house contained many desirable improvements, such as vertical blinds, a built-in dishwasher, paintings, carpeting glued to the floor, throw rugs, and a built-in workbench in the garage. The contract signed by Jerry's parents stated only that they had purchased the "real property." Which of the improvements stay with the house and become the property of Jerry's family and which can the sellers take with them?

3 Your best friend is about to buy a new house and needs to borrow part of the purchase price from a bank. She has been told that it does not matter whether she gives the bank a mortgage or a trust deed because they are exactly the same. Is this correct?

FOCUS

Before class begins, write on the chalkboard the following heading: **Things I Want to Know Before Buying Real Property.** As students enter the classroom, have them list on the chalkboard an appropriate entry under the heading.

Briefly discuss some of the items that students listed. Ask: **How do these items differ from a list of things to know before buying personal property?**

You Decide

1 ETHICS ISSUE No, it is not ethical for your friend to use his legal knowledge to deceive the buyer. Legally, your friend is only obligated to look out for his own self-interest, but ethically your friend would be engaged in something similar to lying.

2 Jerry's family receives the built-in dishwasher, the glued carpeting, and the built-in workbench. The other items are personal property and the seller will be able to keep them.

3 No; Mortgages generally give borrowers more rights than do deeds of trust.

Thinking Critically Through Visuals

The homes under construction shown in this photograph will soon be purchased. What, in addition to the structure of the house, will the buyers receive with their deed? (Buyers will receive the rights and possession to the land the house is on, including the land beneath it to the center of the Earth and everything permanently attached to the soil, the airspace above it, and all fixtures, such as built-in appliances.)

TEACH

Clip a classified sale advertisement for real property. Make an overhead transparency of the ad and display it. Ask students what they would be buying if they agreed to purchase the property. Explain the legal definitions of **land** and **buildings**. Discuss the meaning of **fixtures** and **trade fixtures**. Tell students to note that there is no single way to determine whether an item is a fixture. Explain, however, the tests of **annexation, adaptation,** and **intent.** Point out the benefits of resolving fixture issues in advance of any transaction. Give examples of **license, easement,** and **profit** as rights in the real property of others.

APPLY

As a whole-class activity have students brainstorm and create a list of items found in the classroom and around the school. Have them take turns classifying items as a fixture, not a fixture, or questionable. Have students cite the test or tests (annexation, adaptation, or intent) they used to justify their classification. **Guided Practice**

WHAT IS REAL PROPERTY?

PROBLEM

The Bryants own a condominium and are required to pay property tax on both the real property and the personal property. The tax rate on the real property is 1 percent of its value. The rate for the personal property is 4 percent. The Bryants also own a stereo system that is wired into each room, with speakers concealed in the walls. The receiver, tuner, amplifier, cassette player, compact disc player, and other items are permanently attached and wired into a closet that has been remodeled to accommodate the equipment. Should the stereo be taxed at 1 percent (as real property) or at 4 percent (as personal property)?

All property can be classified as either real or personal. **Real property** (also sometimes called realty) includes land, buildings, things permanently attached to land or buildings (called fixtures), and certain rights to the use of the real property of others. All of these are in fixed locations. Personal property is any property that is not real property (see Chapter 26). In contrast with real property, personal property is easily movable. In the problem, the Bryants' stereo would be taxed at 1 percent because it was permanently attached to the building and was therefore real property. Although this overview definition of real property may seem simple, its application is not.

1. Land

PROBLEM

The limb of an apple tree growing on Gilbert's land extended over the boundary onto Oster's lot. One day Gilbert discovered that Oster had cut the limb off at the point where it crossed the boundary. Did Oster act illegally?

Land, in a legal sense, includes not only the surface of the earth, but also the airspace above it and whatever is beneath its surface—down to the very center of the planet. Land also embraces everything permanently attached to the soil—such as grass and trees—and things embedded in the soil—such as minerals, gases, and bodies of water on or below the surface.

Annual crops still in the ground are generally held to be personal property because they are not *permanently* attached for more than one year. When any crop is severed from the land, it is personal property because it is then mobile.

ASSESS

Learning Objective 1 Have students jot down answers to the following question: **(1) If you purchase a plot of land on which corn is planted, you would be entitled to the trees on the property but not the corn. Why?** (Corn, an annual crop and not permanently attached for more than one year, is considered personal property.); and **(2) What is the test for deciding if a structure is a building?** (The structure must be permanently attached to the land.)

An owner of land has a right to the peaceful enjoyment and control of it. Airplanes may fly over the property, but they may not fly so low or so often as to interfere unreasonably with the owner's use of the land. Residents in the flight patterns of airports have won damage suits because of noise and vibration caused by jets taking off and landing. Likewise, when limbs or roots of a neighbor's tree overhang or extend into the adjoining property, the owner of the adjacent property has the legal right to cut them off at the property line. This is seldom done because both owners generally benefit from the vegetation. However, in the problem, Oster did act legally.

2. Buildings

PROBLEM

Vader owns a mobile home. She claims that she can change the home into real property by removing its tires, placing it on a concrete foundation, and installing permanent plumbing. Is she correct?

The law defines **buildings** as structures that are permanently attached to the land. A barn built on a foundation is permanently attached and therefore a building. In contrast, a mobile home is generally personal property because it is not permanently attached to the land. If a mobile home is set up as described in the problem, however, it will no longer be movable and therefore will be legally classified as real property—a building.

3. Fixtures

PROBLEM

Sharron rented an apartment for eighteen months. After living there for two months, she spent $3,000 to have a plumber install a jacuzzi in her bathroom. She did not inform her landlord and when the landlord found out she became very irritated. At the end of the eighteen months, Sharron offered to remove the jacuzzi and replace it with the old tub. The landlord refused, saying that she is the owner of the jacuzzi and Sharron must leave it in place. Who is correct, the landlord or Sharron?

Fixtures are things that had been personal property but are treated by the law as real property because they are built into or are closely associated with the realty. The law uses three tests to determine whether an item so associated with real property is personal or real. These are the tests of annexation, adaptation, and intent.

Secure butcher paper to a wall. Provide students with a supply of magazines and newspapers, tape, scissors, and markers. Tell students to clip photographs that depict one or more of the following: land, buildings, and fixtures. Direct students to tape the clippings to the butcher paper to make a collage entitled *Is This Property Real?* Have students label all examples of land, buildings, and fixtures in each photo.

Independent Practice

Personal Perspectives

Have students create a three-column chart with the headings *Personal Property*, *Real Property*, and *Fixtures*. Have students take their charts home and, with adult family members, classify 10–15 family-owned items into either the real or personal property categories. Have them put a check mark in the *Fixtures* column, when appropriate. In class, have students cite examples from their charts and have others determine in which column on the chart they should be listed.

▼RETEACH *Media* On a transparency, draw a simple diagram of a plot of land, including a house, tent, mobile home, garage, trees, garden, the ground below the surface, and airspace above. Have students tell if each would or would not be considered part of the real property.

▼ENRICH Have students brainstorm answers to the following question: **In what places might ownership of water and mineral rights become an important consideration to land buyers?** (Answers may include rural areas, drought areas, oil-rich areas, and so on.)

Ethics Issue

Read the following: **Yamasaki signed an 18-month apartment lease. After a year, he decided that he would like to stay in the apartment. He told his landlord and asked if he could build some cabinets on the living room wall. The landlord agreed. Yamasaki bought materials and built the cabinets. When lease-renewal time came, the landlord told Yamasaki he needed the apartment for a relative. He reminded Yamasaki that the cabinets, as fixtures, were part of the apartment and now belonged to him.** Ask: **Is the landlord acting legally and ethically?** (Yes; His actions are legal. Ethical questions may be debated based on intent.)

Thinking Critically Through Visuals

Which items in the photograph are real property and which are personal property? (*Real*: land, shrubs, and cement wall; *Personal*: dog, hose, dog-house, and hammer)

Annexation (i.e., attachment) is the principal test. An item becomes annexed if it is permanently attached to land or a building and cannot be removed without material damage to the realty. For example, a built-in dishwasher would be real property under this test, while a freestanding refrigerator would be personal property because it is not permanently attached.

Adaptation refers to things that are essential for the purpose for which the real estate is used. Adaptation indicates that the personal property has become part of the realty. For example, cast concrete troughs installed on a dairy farm for feeding and watering the animals would become part of the realty through adaptation.

The third test, the **test of intent,** considers whether persons intended something to become part of the realty. For example, a landlord and a tenant might agree to have the tenant install an under-the-counter dishwasher in an apartment. Normally, under the test of annexation, this would be permanently attached and real property. But if these parties agreed that the tenant would retain the right to remove it at the end of the rental period, it would be personal property under the test of intent.

If a homeowner enters into a contract to sell the real property, then the fixtures go to the buyer. Under the test of intent, the seller and buyer can agree that certain fixtures are to be removed and kept by the seller of the home.

Tenants are obligated, at the end of the lease, to leave all the real property in the leased premises for the landlord. This means that if something such as a built-in bookcase is installed by the tenant, it becomes the property of the landlord and may not be removed at the end of the lease. Thus, in the problem, the landlord is correct and Sharron may not remove the jacuzzi. If, however, the parties had agreed to treat items as personal property, the items would be removable as personal property under the test of intent.

ASSESS

Learning Objective 1 Have students respond orally by indicating if the fixture status of each of the following would be best determined by the test of annexation, adaptation, or intent: **(1) A kitchen light listed in the sales contract as not being part of the real property** (Intent); **(2) A wooden pier on a fishing lake** (Adaptation); and **(3) An air conditioner built into the wall** (Annexation).

When business tenants lease space, they frequently install costly equipment and machinery, such as refrigerated display cases. Since most business landlords and business tenants understand that this will occur, statutes generally treat such items as trade fixtures and prescribe that they are personal property under the test of intent. **Trade fixtures**, then, are a business tenant's fixtures that are treated as personal property even when permanently attached. In summary, fixtures installed by a residential tenant generally become the property of the landlord, while trade fixtures installed by a business tenant generally remain the personal property of the tenant.

4. Rights in the Real Property of Others

PROBLEM

Rudy owned 2,000 acres of land in Texas. After oil was discovered on Rudy's land, an oil company bought the right to pump the oil from the ground. The company also bought the right to drive on the land with tank trucks in order to transport the oil. What are the legal names of the rights the oil company now holds in Rudy's real property?

Rights in the real property of others include licenses, easements, and profits. A **license** is the temporary right to be on another's land because they consent. For example, you are on school property by right of license. A license is revokable at any time. If the principal told you to leave the school and you refused, you could be arrested as a trespasser. An **easement** is the right to a specific use of another's real property even though the other party retains possession. Typically, a person might purchase an easement allowing him or her to drive across another's land. Similarly, a utility company might acquire an easement to hang its power lines over the land of another. On the other hand, a **profit** is the right to extract (remove) something (e.g., trees, oil, or minerals) from someone else's land. In the problem, the oil company held both an easement and a profit in Rudy's land.

HOW IS REAL PROPERTY ACQUIRED?

PROBLEM

Eaton, a land developer, wanted to buy a full square block along Michigan Boulevard in downtown Chicago as the site for a new hotel-office-store complex. The property was owned by twelve different individuals and corporations, some of whom refused to sell. Eaton, therefore, asked the city government to use its power of eminent domain to acquire the entire block and then to transfer the block to her. Eaton

Writing Connections

Language Arts
Tell students to imagine that they are renting an apartment and that they have reached the following agreement with the landlord. They build storage shelves along the hall and install an over-the-stove microwave oven in the wall in the kitchen. The shelves will become fixtures, but the oven will remain personal property. Direct students to write, using a computer, if possible, a document that summarizes this agreement, including all details necessary to avoid misunderstandings. Have students exchange papers and look for "loopholes."

TEACH

Tell students that two principal ways of acquiring real property are by wills (evidencing inheritance) and by deeds (evidence of a purchase or a gift). Write **adverse possession, dedication,** and **eminent domain** on the chalkboard. Point out that these are other ways in which real property may be acquired.

On the chalkboard, write the definitions of the three fixture tests for determining if an item associated with real property is personal or real. Then name an item. Ask students to apply each test, one at a time, to determine if the named item is real or personal.

Have students draw a three-panel cartoon showing the three fixture tests. Each panel should show one of the tests—**annexation, adaptation,** or the **test of intent.** Then, ask students to write a caption for each panel and attach it.

APPLY

Duplicate the overhead transparency master, *A Sample Warranty Deed*, and distribute copies to students. Display the overhead transparency and ask students to answer the following questions: **(1) Who are the sellers of the property?** (Algers); **(2) Who are the buyers?** (McMahons); and **(3) What is warrantable?** (That the Algers own the property: par. 6, lines 6 & 7; there are no undisclosed claims on the property: par. 6, lines 8 & 9; and that the buyer will have quiet enjoyment of the property: par. 6, line 10)

Guided Practice

Ethics Issue

Divide the class into two groups and have them debate the ethics and justification of **adverse possession.** (Answers may include to suppress long-dormant claims, to enable use of land, and to require owners to be diligent.) **Independent Practice**

claimed this was justified because the new complex was desperately needed by the public. Also, she said, construction would provide many jobs, and the neighborhood would be improved. Eaton said she would pay fair market value for the property. Could the city comply with Eaton's request?

Ownership of real property is not transferred in the same manner or with the same ease as ownership of personal property. The two principal ways of acquiring real property are by deed as evidence of a sale or a gift, and by wills or by inheritance. Other common ways are by adverse possession, dedication, or eminent domain.

1. By Deed as Evidence of a Sale or a Gift

If a person buys real property or receives it as a gift, the person should receive a deed as evidence of the transfer. The **deed** is a written document used when an individual transfers ownership and other rights to real property. The individual who conveys the ownership rights is the **grantor**. The individual who receives the rights is the **grantee**.

The two major types of deeds are the quitclaim deed and the warranty deed. The **quitclaim deed** transfers any interest the grantor may have in the real property. If the grantor owned no interest in the property, then the grantee receives nothing. Further, the grantee has no legal claim against the grantor based on the quitclaim deed. The **warranty deed,** however, protects the grantee by providing several enforceable grantor's warranties. Examples of such warranties include the following:

a. that the grantor is either the owner of the real property or a person who has been given the authority by the owner to transfer the property;
b. that there are no undisclosed claims or encumbrances (e.g., liens, mortgages, overdue taxes, etc.) against the property; and
c. that the grantee shall have quiet enjoyment of the property (i.e., no one with superior title will disturb the grantee's possession).

2. By Will or by Inheritance

Title to real property may be willed to or inherited by someone in the distribution of properties from the estate of a deceased person.

3. By Adverse Possession

In some situations, a person who publicly occupies another's land for a number of years may be treated by the law as the new owner of the realty. Suppose you bought a 600-acre farm and the legal description of the boundary included ten adjoining acres that belonged to an absentee neighbor. If

ASSESS

Learning Objective 2 Have students respond orally to the following *True or False* questions: **(1) The individual who conveys ownership is the grantor.** (True); **(2) In a transfer by quitclaim deed, if the grantor owned no interest in the property, the grantee receives nothing.** (True); and **(3) Eminent domain is the power of the government to take private property for public use without payment.** (False)

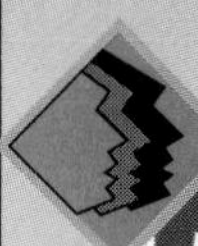

you fenced your farm and included the ten acres, or otherwise occupied the ten acres for the statutory period, you could become the owner of the ten acres. This is because of the doctrine of adverse possession. **Adverse possession** occurs when you "adversely" and exclusively possess in an "open and notorious" way the land of another private person "continuously" for a state's statutory period (five to twenty-one years) under claim of right.

a. *Adverse* means that the occupation is without the consent of the owner. If an owner said you could occupy the land, either for rent or without charge, you could not become an adverse possessor.
b. *Open and notorious* means that the occupation must be visible to the public, including the owner if he or she were to inspect the land. Erecting fences, planting crops, building houses or barns, and grazing cattle all constitute open and notorious occupation.
c. *Continuously* means that the occupation is uninterrupted. This element—and the element of "open and notorious"—is intended to allow the owner who inspects the land at reasonable intervals an opportunity to become aware of the presence of potential adverse possessors and to evict them.

Many states require that adverse possessors pay the property taxes on the occupied land before they can become owners under the doctrine of adverse possession. Some states also require that adverse possessors have a legal basis for concluding that they own the property. To prevent adverse possession, owners of realty, especially raw land, should check it periodically to see if someone is occupying it without their consent.

One can acquire an *easement* through similar uninterrupted adverse use of another's land without the owner's consent for the statutory period. This may happen, for example, when a landowner does nothing over an extended period of time to prevent neighbors from going across the land to reach a main road. An easement thus acquired is said to be an **easement by prescription.**

4. By Dedication or by Eminent Domain

Dedication typically involves giving of real property to the government, such as a city, for use as a park or roadway. As with any other gift, the dedication is effective only if the government accepts the property.

In contrast with dedication (the giving of land to the government), **eminent domain** is the power of the government to take private property for public use in exchange for the fair market price. If the owner is unwilling to sell at a price that the government thinks is fair, the government initiates a condemnation proceeding. A **condemnation proceeding** is a hearing to determine fair compensation for the owner and acquire ownership for the

Multicultural Highlights

The right of eminent domain is a powerful and sometimes controversial tool. Coleman Young, labor organizer, Michigan state senator, Democratic floor leader, and one of the country's first African American mayors of a major city, used this power. General Motors offered to build a plant that would bring thousands of jobs to Detroit if, and only if, the company would be guaranteed a large tract of cleared land inside the city limits within one year. Young, as mayor, applied the power of eminent domain to force relocation of people in a deteriorated neighborhood. He believed that his action was the only way to save his city, which had high unemployment rates. Not everyone agreed. Some challenged that the land use was private, not public, and it did not qualify under eminent domain. Eventually the Supreme Court of Michigan ruled in Young's favor. Ask: **If you were a supreme court judge, how would you have voted?**

Have students create a graphic organizer showing the four ways that real property can be acquired. (See pp. 568–570.)

Have student pairs role–play the acquisition of real property. Have other students determine the type of acquisition portrayed.

▼ TEACH

On a blank overhead transparency, list the steps of a real property transaction. Discuss the type of professionals involved at each step. Next, display the overhead transparency, *Roles of Parties to Mortgages*, to explain each exchange.

▼ APPLY

Invite a real estate loan officer of a local bank or savings and loan association to tell the class how loans are arranged for home buyers and to explain loan officers' roles in real property purchases. Before the speaker arrives, as a whole-class activity, have students brainstorm and generate a list of questions to ask the speaker. **Guided Practice**

Supply students with business sections from newspapers and the "Yellow Pages" from telephone directories. Have students clip ads for businesses that could play a role in the transaction process of purchasing real property. Using these ads, have students create a booklet for their local chamber of commerce, including summaries of what each business does and where in the transaction that business fits. Have students title their projects *How to Buy Real Estate in (name of your town).*

government. If not satisfied with the price offered, the owner may demand a trial by jury to set a just price.

Property taken under eminent domain must be for a public use, such as for highways, airports, parks, or schools. Privately owned railroads and utilities may also exercise this power for such essentials as land for tracks and switching yards and for telephone and electric lines. Eminent domain may not be used for other private purposes even though the public may benefit and a fair price is offered. Thus, in the problem on pages 567–568, the city would not comply with Eaton's request.

▼ HOW DO WE BUY REAL PROPERTY?

PROBLEM

The Webbs want to buy a house. They have saved $34,000. The full purchase price is $100,000, and they have applied for a loan for the difference. What factors will the lending institution consider in determining whether to grant the loan?

Today, real property is most frequently acquired by purchase. The steps that typically make up such a transaction are the following:

1. contracting for the sale of the property;
2. having a survey made of the property;
3. taking steps to ensure the buyer receives good title to the property;
4. obtaining financing if necessary;
5. closing (completing) the transaction; and
6. recording the deed.

1. Negotiating the Contract of Sale

The terms of the contract of sale may result from negotiations between the buyer and the seller. Often real estate agents assist the seller in the negotiations. The resulting contract must be in writing to satisfy the requirements of the statute of frauds (see Chapter 12). Both parties should sign the contract.

2. Surveying the Property

To determine its exact boundaries, the property is often surveyed. **Surveying** is the process of carefully measuring the exact boundaries of real property.

▼ ASSESS

Learning Objective 3 Ask students to respond orally to the following: **(1) Why is a parcel of real property surveyed?** (To determine its exact boundaries); and **(2) What can a buyer do to protect against claims by others to the same land or parts of it?** (Obtain an abstract of title or a policy of title insurance)

3. Protecting the Title

The buyer of real property wants assurance that he or she will receive the title as promised. Therefore, to protect against claims of others to the same land or parts of it, the buyer may obtain an abstract of title or a policy of title insurance.

An **abstract of title** is a condensed history of the ownership of a particular parcel of land. It is abstracted (i.e., taken from) legal records of the "chain of title" over the years. It includes a summary of all conveyances, recorded liens or encumbrances, and other matters that may affect ownership. The buyer may usually rely on the opinion of the attorney who prepares a complete abstract that the title is valid. If the owner has not received the title described in the lawyer's opinion, the lawyer may be liable.

When the title is insured with a policy of **title insurance,** the insurance company guarantees, in exchange for a premium, that the title is good. The pertinent records are first examined by attorneys and other employees of the insurance company. Then the company agrees that it will pay the buyer for damages suffered if title to the property is not clear.

4. Securing Financing

Like the Webbs in the problem, most individuals do not have the full purchase price of the home they wish to buy. So banks, savings and loan associations, and similar institutions will normally lend up to 80 or 90 percent of the value of the property to the buyer. The remaining money must come from the buyer's savings.

Thinking Critically Through Visuals

The professionals in this photograph are surveyors. What, do you think, are they doing? What, do you think, is their role in real property transactions? (Answers may include that they are determining the exact boundaries of the property about to be purchased. This allows the purchaser to know, without misunderstanding or danger of misrepresentation, the exact content of the parcel of land in question.)

Invite a professional surveyor to visit the classroom, bringing the different types of equipment he or she uses on site. Have the surveyor explain the procedures and demonstrate the use of the equipment. Have the surveyor instruct the students, as potential buyers, in details to watch for when contracting with a professional surveyor. Have students prepare questions to ask the speaker. **Independent Practice**

▼RETEACH Arrange studengs in pairs. Have each pair create either a graphic organizer or a two-column chart comparing **abstract of title** and **title insurance.**

▼ENRICH Have students compare, using a computer, if possible, the terms **abstract of title** and **title insurance.** (Abstract of title is a condensed history of the ownership of a particular parcel of land. It includes a summary of all matters that may affect ownership, such as liens. Title insurance is a guarantee by an insurance company that the title is good and clear.)

To extend gifted students' understanding of how mortgages and deeds of trust function, draw on the chalkboard the following graphic organizers. Explain the graphics and have students copy them in their notebook.

Mortgage

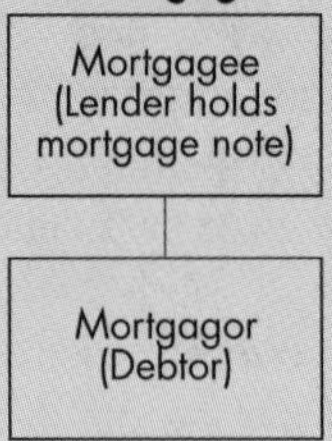

Deed of Trust

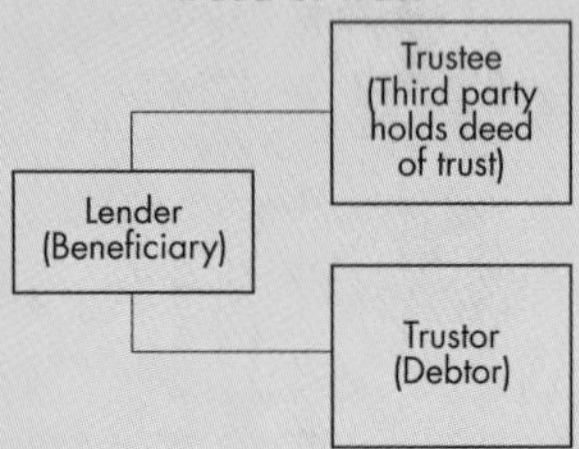

Divide the class into groups of four or five. Assign these roles in each group: facilitator, if necessary, who keeps everyone on task; seller who determines details of property; buyer who negotiates with seller; money lender who asks questions to determine if buyer is a good risk for loan; and title insurance agent who explains services and fees. Have groups create a real-estate scenario and conclude with writing and signing a deed. **Cooperative Learning**

If the loan is made and the real property is purchased, the lender will protect itself with a mortgage or a deed of trust. Whether the lender requires a mortgage or a deed of trust will depend on the laws and the business practices of the state in which the transaction takes place. Both arrangements permit the forced sale of the real property to pay off the loan if the debtor fails to make payments as promised. However, the procedure required to force such a sale under the mortgage arrangement differs greatly from that required under a deed of trust.

The **mortgage** is a written document made out by the **mortgagor** (the debtor) in favor of the **mortgagee** (the lender) that allows the mortgagee the **right of foreclosure.** Thus, if the debtor defaults, the mortgagee has the right to ask the court to sell the property to pay off the loan. The foreclosure procedure also allows the debtor to redeem the property by paying the amount due within a certain time after default. In some states, the debtor can redeem the property for up to one year after it has been sold.

In contrast to a mortgage, a **deed of trust** is handled by a trustee who has the power to cause the sale of the property at a public auction if the debt is not paid as promised. Although the sale must be conducted in a legally prescribed manner, a court generally is not involved. Typically, the sale is carried out swiftly, and the debtor has no right to redeem the property after the sale. For this reason, a lender with a deed of trust can obtain its money more quickly than it could with a mortgage.

5. Closing the Transaction

The closing of the transaction, as required by the sales contract, basically involves the exchange of the purchase price in return for the deed. A variety of other matters must be settled at this time. Property taxes and fire insurance must be prorated. Broker's commissions, attorney's fees, title insurance payments, and recording fees must be paid. Deeds, mortgages, and trust deeds must be recorded.

When there is title insurance, a clerk of the insurance company may act as the closing officer and perform most of these tasks. When there is no title insurance, an **escrow agent,** who is a neutral third party in the business of conducting closings, is often used. Closing officers follow the instructions created for them in the contract of sale. Documents and money delivered by the buyer, seller, or lender to these closing officers are said to be delivered into **escrow.**

6. Recording the Deed

As a part of the closing, the deed should be recorded in the county recorder's office. **Recording** makes a document available to the public at the county recorder's office. This is done to protect the buyer against the possibility of the seller fraudulently reselling the same land to another purchaser.

▼ ASSESS

Learning Objective 3 Hand out butcher paper to students. Have each student create a poster-size flowchart showing the six steps that typically make up a real property transaction. (See enumerated headings on pp. 570–572 for answers.)

Preventing Legal Difficulties

When dealing with real property...

1. If personal property is to be attached to real property (realty) in any transaction, agree in writing who will get it. Put the entire real property agreement in writing, whether the contract involved is a sale, lease, or mortgage.
2. When purchasing real property, protect your interest by:
   a. having the property properly surveyed, particularly if it is an irregularly shaped parcel or has borders that are uncertain;
   b. requiring a deed containing all possible warranties; and
   c. securing title insurance if it is available.
3. Be sure that any deed to land you have purchased is promptly recorded.
4. Realize that the services of an escrow agent, where available, are usually worth the modest cost involved.
5. Inspect your vacant land at reasonable intervals to prevent adverse possession.
6. If you are asked to convey property and want to be free of possible future obligations, use a quitclaim deed.
7. If you have a choice as a borrower, use a mortgage instead of a deed of trust. A deed of trust gives the holder the power to sell your property upon default, with no right of redemption. If you have a choice as a seller or lender, use a deed of trust.
8. If the government seeks to take your land by condemnation under its right of eminent domain, consult a lawyer. You have a constitutional right to a trial by jury to determine the fair price that must be paid.

▼ REVIEWING IMPORTANT POINTS

1. Real property includes land, buildings, fixtures, and certain rights in the land of others, such as easements and profits.
2. The steps in buying or selling real property are commonly (a) contracting for the sale, (b) surveying, (c) protecting the title, (d) obtaining the financing, (e) closing, and (f) recording the deed.
3. Real property usually is acquired by sale or by gift, or by will or by inheritance. Other less common ways include adverse possession, dedication, and eminent domain.
4. Deeds and other instruments affecting the title to land should be recorded promptly.

Preventing Legal Difficulties

Discuss each of the eight suggestions for preventing legal difficulties when dealing with real property. Ask students to orally suggest scenarios that reflect the possible consequences of not following each one.

▼ CLOSE

Have students discuss their plans and ideas for future ownership of real property. Ask students to share ways the information they learned in this chapter had an effect on these plans and ideas.

As a whole-class activity, have students fill in their Chapter Outline for Chapter 28 found in the Workbook. Instruct students to use the completed outline as a study aid for the Chapter Test.

Assign the following end-of-chapter materials:
Student text review activities, pp. 573–577
Workbook, pp. 85–86
Chapter Test

Chapter *MicroExam*

Using the poster-size flowcharts students created in the ASSESS activity, have students add a real-life example to each step in their charts.

Ask students to choose a real-property profession, such as real estate agent, loan officer, title insurance agent, or county recorder of deeds. In small groups, have students brainstorm the pros and cons of their choices of profession. Then have each student write, using a computer, if possible, how each selection matches his or her skills and personality.

5 Two commonly used deeds are the quitclaim deed and the warranty deed.

6 If a financing arrangement is necessary to purchase real property, a mortgage is sometimes more advantageous to the purchaser than a deed of trust.

STRENGTHENING YOUR LEGAL VOCABULARY

Match each term with the statement that best defines that term. Some terms may not be used.

abstract of title
adaptation
adverse possession
annexation
buildings
condemnation proceeding
dedication
deed
deed of trust
easement
easement by prescription
eminent domain
escrow
escrow agent
fixtures
grantee
grantor
land
license
mortgage
mortgagee
mortgagor
profit
quitclaim deed
real property
recording
right of foreclosure
surveying
test of intent
title insurance
trade fixtures
warranty deed

1 A right to a specific limited use of another's land that is acquired through uninterrupted adverse use.

2 Personal property attached to buildings in such a way that it is regarded as real property.

3 Method of acquiring title by occupying land belonging to another, without the other's consent, for a certain uninterrupted period of time under prescribed conditions.

4 The document used to transfer ownership of real property.

5 Making a public record of a document.

6 Condensed history of the ownership of title to real property.

7 Debtor who gives a mortgage as security.

8 Property right allowing one person to extract things, such as minerals and oil, from the land of another.

Strengthening Your Legal Vocabulary

1 easement by prescription
2 fixtures
3 adverse possession
4 deed
5 recording
6 abstract of title
7 mortgagor
8 profit
9 easement
10 eminent domain

Applying Law to Everyday Life

1 

The buyer could protect herself by having the property surveyed. However, this is expensive. (p. 570) Dean is acting only in his self-interest and taking advantage of the buyer's ignorance. Usually market transactions are morally justified because both parties are benefited by the transaction. But, this general assumption disappears when one of the parties is ignorant about an important part of the transaction. That is the case here. The only party to benefit from this transaction would be Dean. The buyer would be injured. So consequential ethics can't justify the sale; there are an equal number of benefited and injured parties. Deontological ethics condemns Dean's action. He acts only for himself and knowingly injures an innocent party. This cannot be universalized; it is inherently wrong. Since consequentialism is neutral, and deontology condemns Dean's acts, the acts are ethically wrong.

9 Property right one has in the land of another, such as a right to cross the other's land.

10 Power of the government to take private property for public use upon payment of the fair market price.

APPLYING LAW TO EVERYDAY LIFE

1 ETHICS ISSUE Dean, who was selling his farm, was engaged in a dispute with his neighbor over the location of the boundary line. A survey would resolve the dispute but it would cost $3,000. So Dean decided to sell the property without telling the buyer about the dispute. How could the buyer protect herself against the risk of buying less than she thought she was getting? Was Dean's conduct ethical?

2 ETHICS ISSUE Marcel was selling her custom-built home, which contained a large Persian rug valued at $6,000. The room with the rug had been designed so it was the same size and shape as the rug, and the wallpaper matched the rug's design. Several buyers asked Marcel if the rug went with the house, and she said no. When others indicated that they assumed the rug was part of the realty, Marcel said she planned to take the rug with her. After the house had been on the market for a year, Marcel gave out this information only when asked directly. Finally, she received an offer for "all the real property." Because she knew the law would not include her rug within this definition, but she did not think the buyer would know it, she decided it was okay not to say anything about this to the buyer. Is Marcel acting ethically?

3 Nikov leased an apartment for one year. During this year, she hung pictures on the walls, replaced the bathroom's chrome faucets with brass ones, installed an under-the-counter trash compactor, and put an oriental rug in the center of the living room floor. At the end of her lease, what must she leave and what can she take?

4 Brand sold property to Alioto and conveyed it with a quitclaim deed. There was a mortgage on the property that neither Brand nor Alioto knew about at the time of the conveyance. Who will lose money because of this mortgage, Brand or Alioto?

5 Atwater sold a farm to Kent. Atwater conveyed with a warranty deed. Later the parties discovered that Atwater was not really the owner of about three acres of the land described in the deed. Is Atwater liable to Kent, and if so for what?

2 ETHICS ISSUE No; Marcel is not acting ethically. Her situation is like that of Dean in the first problem, and all the general statements there hold true here. These questions offer an opportunity to make an important distinction for students: the distinction between legal and ethical. Both the law and ethics seek fairness. But the law is a human institution and always under pressure to use legal resources efficiently. So the law, out of the need for efficiency, tells persons to look out for their own self-interests. That eliminates many problems and keeps many other problems out of court. But when the law does this it also tolerates some unfairness. Personal ethics is not constrained by a need for efficiency. So, if Marcel were to try to justify her action by saying, "It's legal," it would be appropriate to respond, "In this case that doesn't mean it is ethical."

3 At the end of the lease, Nikov must leave those things which are permanently attached—the brass faucets and the trash compactor. She may take the pictures and the oriental rug. (pp. 565–566)

4 Alioto will lose the money because he took title to the property with a quitclaim deed. This deed does not give its grantee (Alioto) any recourse if an encumbrance, such as this mortgage, is later discovered. (p. 568)

5 Atwater is liable to Kent for breach of one of the warranties in the warranty deed. By giving a warranty deed, Atwater promised Kent that he owned all the property described in the deed, and that if he did not, he would pay Kent for any loss suffered. (p. 568)

6 No matter what Swinsen's deed says, Follet owns the property by adverse possession, assuming the statutory period for adverse possession is 20 years or less in her state. She occupied the property openly, notoriously, adversely (without Swinsen's consent), and continuously. In addition, Follet paid the property taxes on the property. (p. 569)

7 Yes, Bentley can be compelled to sell. The government has the power to take private property for public use under the doctrine of eminent domain. However, the government must pay Bentley the reasonable value of her property. (pp. 569–570)

8 Ferrera should select the mortgage because it gives him greater rights in the event he encounters financial difficulties. (p. 572)

9 Yes; The tire changer was a trade fixture and, therefore, personal property. Commercial tenants, like Pete, are allowed to remove personal property at the end of the lease and take it with them. (p. 567)

6 When Follet purchased her home, there was a fence enclosing her property. Nearly twenty years later, a neighbor, Swinsen, had his property surveyed and discovered that his deed's description included a parcel extending ten feet past the fence into Follet's property. Follet had been paying property taxes on the property for the entire twenty years. Who owns this property?

7 Bentley had been in business at a particular location in Cleveland, Ohio, for many years. When the government's Redevelopment Agency sought to buy her land for redevelopment purposes, Bentley refused to sell. Can she be compelled to sell?

8 Ferrera entered into a contract of sale that required him to obtain financing within sixty days after signing the contract. In checking with lenders in the area, he discovered a wide variety of lending policies. The two best opportunities offered the same financial terms. However, one lender wanted a mortgage while the other wanted a deed of trust. Should Ferrera choose a mortgage or a deed of trust?

9 Pete rented a large garage from which to operate his automobile repair business. He installed only one item of equipment—an automatic tire changer (i.e., a machine that removes the rubber tires from the steel wheels on which they are mounted). A large hole had to be drilled in the cement floor and a foundation for the machine built. Also a new specially reinforced cement floor was laid and 220-volt electrical wiring installed. Four months later, business was going so well for Pete that he decided he needed more space. When he left, could he take the tire changer?

▼ SOLVING CASE PROBLEMS

1 The Wakes operated a cattle ranch in Cassia County, Idaho. During the spring and fall, they drove their cattle over land owned by the Johnsons. Eventually the Wakes sold their cattle ranch to the Nelsons. The new owners continued to use the Johnsons' land as a cattle trail twice a year. This had gone on for about sixteen years before the Johnsons objected and locked the gates to the cattle trail. The Nelsons sued, claiming an easement by prescription. Is there an easement by prescription here? (*Nelson v. Johnson*, 679 P.2d 662)

2 The Pentecostal Tabernacle Church had just built a new church building when dissension broke out among the members, and they split into two factions. As a consequence, payments on the building loan were not made, and foreclosure resulted. Williams bought the church build-

Solving Case Problems

1 Yes, there is an easement by prescription. The Nelsons acquired an easement by prescription through the open, notorious, and continuous use (limited for easements) of another's land without the owner's consent. So they have an easement to cross the Johnsons' land with cattle during the spring and fall. (p. 569)

2 Yes, the court held that the pews were a part of the realty. This was evidenced by (a) the testimony of the two ex- trustees on intent; and (b) the harm that was done by removal of some of the pews. (p. 566)

ing at the foreclosure sale. Trustees of the church then brought suit to recover the pews from the building. Williams defended by claiming that the pews were fixtures and were therefore to remain in the building. Evidence disclosed that removal of the pews left holes and broken bolts in the tiled floor. However, the pastor and a trustee of the church testified that when the pews were installed it was intended that they were to be removed later and placed in another wing of the building. Two ex-trustees of the church disputed that intention during their testimony. Are the pews real property? (*Sims v. Williams*, 441 S.W.2d 385)

3. Smith bought two lots along the shore of Lake Pepin and built a cottage, which he mistakenly extended over the boundary line onto a third lot, Parcel X8. Smith cleaned all three lots, seeded X8 with grass, and used it in the sporadic and seasonal manner associated with lakeshore property. Burkhardt had a warranty deed to X8 but did not challenge Smith's possession for more than twenty years. Now Smith claims title to X8 by adverse possession. Burkhardt argues that the entire parcel was not actually occupied nor was it usually cultivated. Burkhardt also argues that Smith's possession was not hostile because it was based on a mistaken boundary line and because Smith paid no taxes on X8. Does Smith get title to Parcel X8 by adverse possession? (*Burkhardt v. Smith*, 17 Wis. 2d 132)

4. Lober sold a parcel of realty to Brown in 1957. A warranty deed was used. Later, Brown tried to sell a portion of the property to Consolidated Coal Company. At that time, Brown learned that he did not own all of the property described in Lober's deed. Can Brown recover from Lober? (*Brown v. Lober*, 75 Ill. 2d 549)

5. In 1942 a deed properly created a perpetual easement of "right to receive light, air, and unobstructed view" over certain property now owned by Friedman. Friedman erected a television antenna, and Petersen—as owner of the property benefited by the easement—sought an injunction to compel removal of the "obstruction." Friedman argues that the parties who created the easement back in 1942 could not have intended to bar such television installations, since they were not even known of at the time. Is the easement valid? (*Petersen v. Friedman*, 162 Cal. 2d 245)

3. Yes; Smith's actions in building the cottage over the boundary line, clearing the land, and putting in a lawn, which extended substantially over Parcel X8, were sufficient "to plant the flag of hostility." "Actual occupancy" means ordinary use of which the land is capable and such use as the owner would make of it. Any actual visual means which give notice of the claimant's dominion over the property and of the exclusion of the true owner or the public is sufficient. Finally, "usually cultivated or improved" means that the land must be put to the exclusive use of the adverse occupant as the true owner might use it if in possession. Smith's actions, taken together over the 20 years, show a continuous use in the usual way an owner would use land surrounding a lake cottage. In this jurisdiction, payment of property taxes was not required to establish ownership using adverse possession. (p. 569)

4. Yes, Brown can recover from Lober for breach of one of the warranties in the warranty deed. By giving a warranty deed, Lober promised that he owned the property described in the deed and, if it turned out that he did not, that he would pay for any injury to the grantee. (p. 568)

5. Yes; Easements of light, air, and unobstructed view may be created by express grant. The language used in creating the easement was clear and left no room for construction or determination of the intent of the parties.

Chapter Theme

Leases and the landlord-tenant relationship form the basis of this chapter, which is of great interest to young adults planning for life "on their own."

DIRECTED STUDY QUESTIONS	SPECIAL FEATURES	PROGRAM RESOURCES				
		Reteach	Enrich	SN	AM	
What is a lease?		✓	✓			
What types of leaseholdestates may be created?	Thinking Critically Through Visuals, p. 581	✓	✓			
What are the rights and duties of a tenant?	Multicultural Highlights, p. 583 Ethics Issue, p. 584	✓	✓	✓	A	
What are the rights and duties of a landlord?	Personal Perspectives, p. 586 Thinking Critically Through Visuals, p. 587 Writing Connections, p. 587	✓	✓		K V	
How can a lease be terminated?	Preventing Legal Difficulties, p. 589	✓	✓			

Additional Resources

- *How to Win Landlord-Tenant Disputes.* Leesburg, VA: Citizens Law Library, 1979.
- Tondorf-Dick, Gary. *How to Be a Landlord: All About Tenant Selection, Rental Agreements, Money Matters, and Sharing Your Space.* Garden City, NJ: Doubleday, 1985.

One-semester course	✔	✔						
One-year course	✔	✔	✔					

	ASSESSMENT OPPORTUNITIES			
Cooperative Learning	Informal Assessment	Chapter Review	Chapter Test	Chapter *MicroExam* (Media)
	✔	✔	✔	✔
✔	✔	✔	✔	✔
	✔	✔	✔	✔
	✔	✔	✔	✔
	✔	✔	✔	✔

Videodiscs

Rights and Duties of Landlords and Tenants

Search Chapter 36, Play To 37

State by State

In Florida, a landlord who has not been paid has a lien on the tenant's personal property for the unpaid rent.

Teaching Materials

Student text, pp. 578–594

Overhead transparency masters
- *Residential Lease*
- *Tenancies in Landlord and Tenant Relationships*

Videos
- *Law for Business* Videodisc

Workbook, pp. 87–92

Outside Resources
- Blank overhead transparencies
- Butcher paper
- Samples of standard lease forms
- Classified ads for apartment and house rentals
- Poster board
- Markers
- Index cards

- Tape recorder

Assessment
- Chapter Test

- Chapter *MicroExam*

Vocabulary

lease, p. 580
rent, p. 580
landlord, p. 580
tenant, p. 580
leasehold estate, p. 580
periodic tenancy, p. 581
tenancy from month to month, p. 581
tenancy for years, p. 581
tenancy at sufferance, p. 582
tenancy at will, p. 582
eviction, p. 583
partial eviction, p. 583
constructive eviction, p. 583
duty of reasonable care, p. 584
assignment of a lease, p. 584
subletting, p. 584
lease covenant, p. 585
lease condition, p. 585

Learning Objectives

When you complete this chapter, you will be able to

1. Describe the legal characteristics of a lease.
2. Describe the various leasehold estates.
3. Define the rights and duties of landlords and tenants.
4. Tell how leases can be terminated.

578

Chapter Self-Test

Assess students' understanding of the laws governing landlord and tenant relationships before they begin Chapter 29 by asking them to respond orally to the following: **(1) Does a tenant have the right to negotiate changes in a printed lease?** (Yes); and **(2) Does a landlord have the right to personally remove a tenant and his or her property if rent is not paid when due?** (No, only the courts have this right.) Review and discuss students' responses before continuing with the chapter.

CHAPTER 29

LANDLORD AND TENANT

1 Several months ago, your brother entered into a nine-month lease for an apartment. All the terms were agreed upon orally. Now, upon discovering that the apartment can be leased for more money, the landlord has told your brother to vacate. The landlord claims that their oral agreement is unenforceable. Is the landlord correct?

2 You moved into an apartment some time ago under a two-year lease. You now plan to move out but do not tell the landlord. Two days before the lease expires, while you are packing, the landlord appears and informs you that since you did not give notice of your intent to leave, you owe rent for an additional month. Is the landlord right?

3 

Three weeks before you are scheduled to move out of an apartment, the landlord tells you that he wants to begin showing the apartment to other prospective tenants. Must you allow him to do this even though your lease says nothing about showing the apartment? Ethically, should you allow the apartment to be shown even if you are not legally obligated to do so?

579

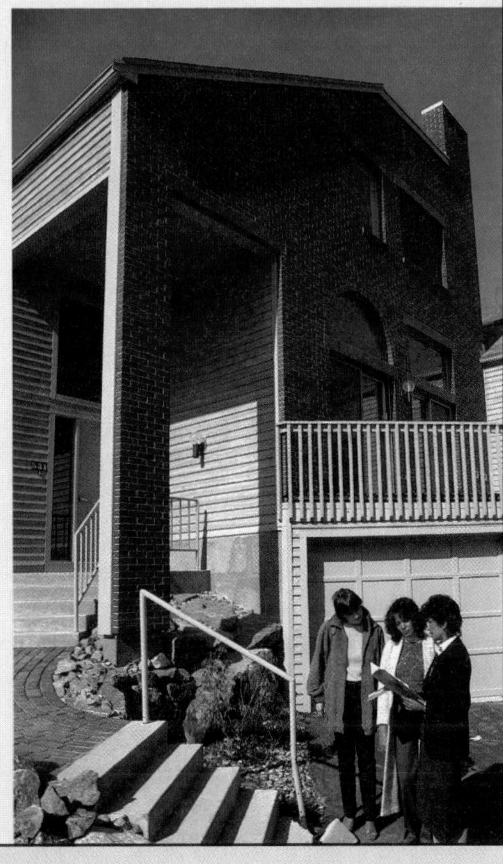

▼ FOCUS

Before class begins, draw two, two-column charts on the chalkboard. Label one chart **Tenant** and the other **Landlord**. On both charts, label one column **Rights** and the other **Duties**. As students enter the classroom, have them make an entry on each chart.

Compare the charts and discuss entries. Copy the finished charts onto butcher paper or an overhead transparency to use throughout this chapter. Ask if any students and their families are tenants or landlords. If so, ask student volunteers to share some experiences or insights with the class.

You Decide

1 No; In most states, an oral lease for less than one year is enforceable.

2 The landlord is wrong. A two-year lease is a tenancy for years, which automatically terminates at the end. Neither the landlord nor the tenant must give notice of termination of a tenancy for years.

3 ETHICS ISSUE No; Tenants have the exclusive right of possession and landlords may not show the property unless that right is created in the lease. Yes; Ethically, you should allow the landlord to show the leased premises. Doing so benefits the lessor and the new tenant greatly and inconveniences you only slightly.

Thinking Critically Through Visuals

The two women on the left in this photograph are making the final agreement with a landlord to lease the house shown. What are some major factors on which they will have to agree? (Answers may include amount of rent and when it is due, security deposit, length of lease, permission to have pets, who pays heating bills, renewal options, and so on.)

TEACH

Compare the temporary and limited rights of a tenant in a leasehold estate to the unlimited, indefinite rights of an owner. Show the overhead transparency, *Residential Lease*. Discuss the terms **rent**, **landlord**, *lessor*, **tenant**, and *lessee*. Discuss verbal leases and their consequences.

APPLY

Distribute to students copies of standard lease forms (long and short versions) from a local realtor, lawyer, or stationery store. Display the overhead transparency, *Residential Lease*. Have students analyze the leases and compare them to each other and to the overhead transparency. Have students point out examples of how leases are generally written primarily to protect the landlord.

Guided Practice

Make copies of the overhead transparency master, *Residential Lease*, and distribute them to pairs of students. Have each pair identify and rewrite the terms of this lease that students, as role-playing tenants, might want to modify. Have each pair make written suggestions that might persuade a lessor to accept their new terms. **Independent Practice**

WHAT IS A LEASE?

PROBLEM

Curtis entered into an oral agreement with Kearne to lease Kearne's cabin for three months during the winter ski season. However, skiing was poor that year because there was little snowfall. Therefore Curtis tried to avoid the contract. Curtis claimed that the lease was not enforceable because it was not in writing and because of the poor skiing conditions. Was Curtis correct?

A **lease** is an agreement in which one party receives temporary possession of another's real property in exchange for rent. **Rent** is the consideration given in return for temporary possession. The lease creates a relationship between the person conveying possession (called the **landlord** or *lessor*) and the person receiving possession (called the **tenant** or *lessee*) of realty. The ownership interest of the tenant is called a **leasehold estate.** In contrast to rental of real property, rental of personal property (covered in Chapter 27) creates the relationship of bailment between bailor and bailee.

A lease may be oral. However, under the statute of frauds, leases that extend for more than one year must be in writing or courts may refuse to enforce them. In the problem, therefore, Curtis was wrong. Because the lease was for only three months, the oral agreement was binding. As the tenant, Curtis was entitled to possession during the three months of the lease. In addition, the landlord had not made a contract to deliver "good snowfall." Even if a writing is not required, it is a good idea to put the important terms of the lease in written form to avoid disputes.

WHAT TYPES OF LEASEHOLD ESTATES MAY BE CREATED?

PROBLEM

The two Adams sisters leased an apartment from Pena. They were to pay rent on the first day of each month. No time limit for the lease was specified. What type of leasehold estate was created?

Depending on the terms, one of the four following basic types of leasehold estates (i.e., tenant's ownership interests) can be created by a lease.

ASSESS

Learning Objective 1 Ask students to respond orally to complete the following statements: **(1) Another term for landlord is ______.** (Lessor); **(2) Another term for tenant is ______.** (Lessee); **(3) The ownership interest of the tenant is called a ______.** (Leasehold estate); and **(4) An agreement in which one party receives temporary possession of another's real property in exchange for rent is a ________.** (Lease)

1. Periodic Tenancy

When a leasehold is for a renewable period of time with rent due at stated intervals, it is a **periodic tenancy.** This is probably the most common type of tenancy. A periodic tenancy may be by the week, the month, the year, or any other period of time agreed upon. If the rent is paid by the month, as in the problem, the tenancy is referred to as a **tenancy from month to month.** Leases that create a periodic tenancy usually identify a rental period, such as from "week to week," "month to month," or "year to year." A periodic tenancy continues for successive time periods until one of the parties ends it by giving proper notice of termination. Usually notice must be given one period in advance. For example, a lessor could terminate a month-to-month tenancy or change the terms of the lease by giving notice one month in advance.

2. Tenancy for Years

When a leasehold is for a definite period of time—such as six months, one year, or ninety-nine years—it creates a **tenancy for years.** It has this name even when the period of the lease is less than one year. The feature that distinguishes a tenancy for years from a periodic tenancy is the identification of a date for the ending of the lease. Thus, if a lease states that the rental period is from May 1 to August 15, this is tenancy for years because

▼ TEACH

Display the overhead transparency, *Tenancies in Landlord and Tenant Relationships.* Discuss and

compare each of the four types of leasehold estates.

▼ APPLY

Pair students. Describe a short scenario involving the creation of a leasehold estate. One student must identify the type of leasehold estate and the other must tell how it can be terminated. For example: **Smith's lease expired last week but Smith is making no effort to vacate.** (Tenancy at sufferance; by eviction or acceptance of additional rent) **Guided Practice**

Thinking Critically Through Visuals

Assume that the man shown in the photograph is moving out of an apartment he held in a periodic tenancy from month to month. How much notice did he probably have to give his landlord of his plans? (Answers may include one month because, in most states, notice must be given one period in advance.)

▼RETEACH

On a blank overhead transparency, have students draw a flowchart that shows the exchange of rights and consideration in a landlord/tenant relationship.

▼ENRICH

Have students brainstorm and list the pros and cons, from a tenant's point of view, of not having a written lease. (Answers may include pros: all topics can be disputed; and cons: no guarantees of continuing availability of the property.)

On slips of paper, write the four types of leasehold estates. Place folded slips in a container. Have pairs of students draw a slip of paper and discuss the type of leasehold estate. Have the rest of the class vote on which type of leasehold estate is being portrayed. Keep track of the number of correct answers.
Independent Practice

Divide the class into groups of four or five. Assign the following roles: facilitator, if necessary, who keeps everyone on task; tenant who creates tenant circumstances; landlord who creates landlord circumstances; recorder who inputs the contract, on the computer, if possible; and legal consultant who checks format and wording for consistency and clarity. Have students use the overhead transparency master, *Residential Lease*, as a model to write a partial contract for the tenancy situation they created.

Cooperative Learning

▼ TEACH

On a blank overhead transparency, create a graphic organizer to illustrate and discuss the six rights and duties of a tenant, listed on pp. 582–585. Compare these to the ones listed by students in the FOCUS activity.

August 15 is specified as the ending date. At the end of the lease period, a tenancy for years terminates automatically without a requirement of notice.

3. Tenancy at Sufferance

If a tenant remains in possession after the lease has expired, a **tenancy at sufferance** arises. The landlord may treat such a tenant as a trespasser. However, if the landlord accepts additional rent, a periodic tenancy is generally created for the same period as the prior lease. If the prior lease was for one year or longer, the landlord can hold the tenant for another full year's rent. If the old lease was for one month, the landlord generally can hold the tenant for another month's rent.

4. Tenancy at Will

If a party possesses land with the owner's permission but without an agreement as to the term of the lease or the amount of the rent, a **tenancy at will** results. Such a leasehold may be terminated at any time by either party.

▼ WHAT ARE THE RIGHTS AND DUTIES OF A TENANT?

PROBLEM

The Bartleys leased a house from Atlas Properties. The lease limited the property to single-family use. To help the family finances, the Bartleys installed bunk beds on the second floor and took in eight college students as boarders. Atlas claims this violates the lease. Is Atlas correct?

Tenants have both rights and duties created by a lease. These are discussed in the following sections.

1. The Right to Possession

The tenant has a right to the possession of the real property starting at the time agreed upon in the lease. In addition, unless otherwise provided in the lease, the tenant's possession is to be exclusive of all other persons and is for the duration of the lease. Landlords generally do not have a right to enter leased premises for inspection unless this right is given in the lease. If a landlord is given the right to enter and inspect the leased premises, most states require that the landlord give reasonable advance notice and that the landlord inspect at a reasonable time of the day.

▼ ASSESS

Learning Objective 2 Have students list in writing the four types of leasehold estates. Have them summarize in their own words how each is created and terminated.

Trip, the landlord of an apartment building, asked to show a tenant's apartment to a prospective renter. Because the lease did not provide for such tours, the tenant could rightfully deny the request. Showing the apartment without the tenant's permission would make Trip a trespasser.

If the landlord removes the tenant from possession of all the real property, an **eviction** has occurred. Depriving the tenant of the possession of only one part (e.g., one room of an apartment) is a **partial eviction.** In either case, the tenant may recover damages from the landlord if the eviction is improper.

In addition, under some circumstances, the tenant may claim **constructive eviction** and refuse to pay rent. This could happen if the landlord failed to perform certain duties as defined in the lease or imposed by statute *and if* the tenant abandoned the premises because of such a breach. Examples include the landlord's failure to make repairs as agreed upon in the lease or failure to heat the premises. If the law requires that the premises be kept in a condition fit for human habitation, an infestation of insects or rodents could amount to constructive eviction if the tenant left the premises because of such condition.

2. The Right to the Use of the Property

The tenant is allowed to use the leased property in the manner specified in the lease. If a particular use is not mentioned in the lease, the tenant may use the property for any purpose for which it is designed or customarily used. A tenant who agrees to lease a house as a single-family residence may not use the building as a boardinghouse. In the problem, the Bartleys were in violation of their lease.

3. The Duty to Pay Rent

A tenant's most important duty is to pay the agreed-upon rent when it is due. Although rent is usually expressed as a fixed sum of money, it may consist of a share of the crops of a farm or a percentage of the profits of a business.

Before leasing property in a tenancy for years or a tenancy from month to month, landlords sometimes require the payment of the first and last months' rent. Thus, if the tenant fails to make prompt payment for the next period's rent, the landlord can use the "last month's rent" for the month during which legal steps are taken to evict the tenant. In residential rentals, a

Multicultural Highlights

The U.S. Constitution guarantees that landlords must offer the same rental opportunities to all potential tenants. In 1967, a Supreme Court landmark decision resulted from efforts of an African American couple in California. That state had adopted a constitutional provision (Section 26) that forbade the state to abridge rights of owners (or their agents) to sell or rent, or refuse to sell or rent, to whomever they chose. The couple was rejected as a tenant and brought suit, claiming that the new rule violated the Fourteenth Amendment. They pursued their case to the California Supreme Court and were successful. The defendants appealed to the U.S. Supreme Court in *Reitman v. Mulkey* (1967). The U.S. Supreme Court upheld the state court's judgment. Justice Potter Stewart said ".... Section 26 was intended to authorize, and does authorize, racial discrimination in the housing market."

RETEACH Have students create a graphic organizer to illustrate the information on the four types of leasehold estates.

ENRICH Media: Create a four-column bulletin board entitled *Types of Leasehold Estates.* Label the columns *Period Tenancies, Tenancy for Years, Tenancies at Sufferance,* and *Tenancies at Will.* Then, using a computer, if possible, have students create scenarios to describe any of the four types of leasehold estates.

"cleaning" or "security" deposit is almost always required. The amount of this deposit should be refunded at the end of the lease period if the property is left as clean and undamaged as it was when first occupied, less ordinary wear and tear.

4. The Duty to Take Care of the Property

A tenant must take reasonable care of the leased property and return it in substantially the same condition it was in when the lease began. The **duty of reasonable care** ordinarily includes responsibility for making all minor repairs. The tenant is not liable for wear and tear caused by ordinary use. However, the tenant is liable for deterioration caused by willful misuse or negligence. In some states by agreement, and sometimes by statute, landlords make all repairs. This includes even such minor repairs as replacing faucet washers and electric fuses.

The tenant normally is under no obligation (in fact, has no right) to make major structural changes or to make improvements without the consent of the landlord. For example, if the roof leaks, the necessary repair and replacement are concerns of the landlord. However, in such circumstances, the tenant is legally expected to act reasonably, taking appropriate steps to prevent avoidable damage until the landlord has been notified and can make needed repairs. The tenant is obligated to notify the landlord when major repairs become necessary. In a few states, the tenant may apply up to a full month's rent toward necessary repairs if the landlord does not make the repairs after reasonable notice.

5. The Right to Assign the Lease or to Sublet

Unless restricted by the terms of the lease, a tenant may assign the lease or may sublet the premises. An **assignment of a lease** takes place when the tenant transfers his or her entire interest in the lease to a third person. Although the assignee becomes liable to the landlord for the rent and performance of other conditions of the lease, the original tenant *also* remains liable.

A **subletting** occurs when the tenant does either of the following:

a. leases *all* of the property to a third person for a period of time that is less than the term remaining on the lease, or

b. leases *part* of the property to a third person for part or all of the term remaining.

When the property is sublet, the original tenant continues to be directly liable to the owner-landlord for performance of the lease.

Leases often require the landlord's prior approval of assignment or subletting. However, courts have held that the landlord must have a valid reason if consent is withheld.

▼ APPLY

Ethics Issue

Read aloud the following scenario: **The landlord has just inspected your apartment and found a few minor damages you caused that allow her to keep most of your security deposit. A friend suggests that, since you are going to lose your deposit anyway, you should completely stop caring for the property.** Ask: **Does this advice propose ethical conduct?** (This is poor advice from both a legal and an ethical viewpoint. You will be legally obligated as a tenant to keep up the property, and you did sign the agreement informing you about the loss of your security deposit.) **Guided Practice**

To help at-risk students relate the rights and duties of tenants to real life, bring to class classified ads for apartment rentals. In small groups, have students list the rights and duties—listed or implied—in each ad. Extend this activity by having students determine the costs for leasing the apartment, including rent, electricity, insurance, and so on.

▼ ASSESS

Learning Objective 3 Have students respond orally to the following: **(1) Do landlords generally have the right to enter leased property without oral or written consent to do so?** (No); **(2) Are tenants legally obligated to pay rent?** (Yes); and **(3) How long are tenants obligated to take reasonable care of the property?** (For the duration of the lease)

6. The Duty to Satisfy Conditions

Leases often contain two types of duties that tenants must fulfill. These are called lease covenants and lease conditions. A **lease covenant** is a promise made by a tenant which, if violated, allows the landlord to sue for damages while the lease remains in effect. In contrast, a **lease condition,** if violated, allows the landlord to terminate the lease and evict the tenant.

Sharon and Bill both rented two-bedroom apartments in the same town, but from different landlords. Both signed written leases containing clauses prohibiting pets in the apartments. Bill's clause was labeled a "condition." Sharon's clause was labeled a "covenant." Later, while attending a dog show together, they fell in love with Springer spaniels. Both bought puppies and took them home. Bill's landlord could evict him while Sharon's could only sue for damages caused by the puppy.

WHAT ARE THE RIGHTS AND DUTIES OF A LANDLORD?

PROBLEM

McElroy leased a store building from Steward for one year. After three months, McElroy moved all her possessions from the building and left town, defaulting on her rent. Steward did not relet the store. Is McElroy liable for the rent for the remaining nine months?

Often, the rights and duties of a tenant find their complements in the rights and duties of a landlord.

1. The Right to the Rent

The landlord's primary right is to the rent agreed upon in the lease. If the tenant fails to pay the rent, the landlord may take legal action to recover the rent and sue to evict the tenant.

Recovery of rent if the tenant vacates early. A tenant who vacates the property before the end of the lease remains liable for the unpaid rent. In some states, the tenant is liable for the rent even if the landlord allows the property to remain empty. Other states require that the landlord make a good-faith effort to rerent the property. If it is not rerented, the original tenant is liable for the rent remaining on the lease. If it is rerented, but at a lower rental amount, the original tenant is liable for the difference.

Bring to class a variety of newspaper classified ads for apartment and house rentals. Pair students. Give one student in each pair a copy of a particular ad. Have the pair role–play and tape record a phone conversation between a potential tenant who has seen the ad and the landlord who placed the ad. The tenant should ask all of the legal and personal questions he or she would want to know before renting. Play the tape and have the class comment on the information exchanged. Ask: **Did both the potential tenant and the landlord get enough information to make an informed decision?**
Independent Practice

TEACH

On a blank overhead transparency or on the chalkboard, label a two-column chart **Landlord** and add the column headings **Rights** and **Duties**. As you discuss the four rights and duties of a landlord, found on pp. 585–587, list them in the appropriate column on the chart. Compare this chart with the one students created in the FOCUS activity.

RETEACH Have students create a graphic organizer showing the six rights and duties of tenants, found on pp. 582–585.

ENRICH Have students role-play renting an apartment. Have students cover the six duties and rights of a tenant in their skits. As each right or duty is covered, write it on the chalkboard.

▼ APPLY

Have students generate a list of minor and major repairs, improvements, and routine maintenance for a rental home or apartment. Then, have the class classify each as the responsibility of the tenant or the landlord. **Guided Practice**

Personal Perspectives

As a class, brainstorm and list on the chalkboard a list of ideal landlord and tenant duties and responsibilities. Have students copy the list and take it home to review with family members. Ask family members to check off duties and rights they have experienced as either a landlord or a tenant, draw an X through the ones they would like to eliminate, and add any they would like to include. In class, revise the ideal list based on input from students' families.

Supply students with poster board and markers. Divide the class into four groups. Ask each group to make a poster illustrating one of the following: rights of tenants, rights of landlords, duties of tenants, or duties of landlords.

Independent Practice

In the problem, McElroy's liability depends on the law of the state where the property is located. In some states, Steward can allow the premises to remain empty and sue McElroy for the unpaid rent. Other states will require that Steward try to re-lease the premises before collecting from McElroy.

Sue to evict the tenant and reenter the property. If the tenant fails to pay rent and remains in possession, the landlord may sue to evict the tenant. The landlord may include the claim for overdue rent in the same suit. However, the landlord may not take the law into his or her own hands, personally evicting the tenant and placing the tenant's belongings on the sidewalk. If the tenant refuses to leave the premises, a court order directing the sheriff or other official to evict the tenant *must* be obtained.

2. The Right to Regain the Realty and Fixtures

At the end of the lease term, the lessor is entitled to regain possession of the real property. If a tenant has added fixtures to the realty, they belong to the landlord. (Remember, however, that this general rule does not apply to trade fixtures [see Chapter 28].) This may provoke a dispute. Therefore it is desirable for parties to agree in advance on which additions are to be considered fixtures and which are to be considered removable personal property.

3. The Duty to Maintain the Premises

The duty to maintain the leased property generally falls on the tenant. However, there are exceptions to this rule. For example, when a number of tenants rent portions of a building, the landlord is responsible for the upkeep of the exterior and the public areas. Public areas are those not under the specific control of any one tenant and include common hallways, stairs, elevators, yards, and swimming pools. One who is injured because of the faulty condition of these areas could bring suit for damages against the landlord. In addition, a landlord may be held liable for injuries that result from defective conditions in the property in the tenant's exclusive possession if the conditions are concealed or are not readily apparent.

Finally, when housing is leased, the landlord is required to provide the quarters in a condition fit for living. In some states and in some cities, the law in the form of a housing code may prescribe in detail the required condition of such properties. A representative city housing code makes provisions such as these:

a. there shall be no exposed electrical wiring;
b. the roof shall not leak;

▼ ASSESS

Learning Objective 3 Have students orally respond to the following *True* or *False* statements: **(1) If a tenant vacates the property before the end of the lease, he or she is liable for rent only for the period of occupancy.** (False); **(2) Fixtures added by tenants belong to the landlord.** (True, except for those covered in previously arranged agreements and for trade fixtures); and **(3) In some places housing codes prescribe, in detail, required maintenance conditions of properties.** (True)

c. every ceiling and wall shall be smooth, free of loose plaster and wallpaper, and easily cleanable;
d. outside doors and windows shall have tight-fitting screens;
e. every unit shall have a private bathroom; and
f. gas stoves shall be properly vented and connected.

4. The Duty to Pay Taxes

In the absence of contrary agreement, the landlord pays all property taxes and assessments on the leased property. However, long-term leases of commercial property commonly provide that the tenant will pay such taxes and assessments, as well as premiums for fire insurance.

Thinking Critically Through Visuals

It is the duty of landlords to provide housing that is in fit condition for living, which is usually specified by city housing code. By looking at this photograph, what city housing codes are probably being violated? (Answers may include that outside doors and windows shall have tight-fitting screens, and so on.)

Writing Connections

Language Arts
Have students imagine that they are disgruntled tenants of a particular housing complex. Have students write, using a computer, if possible, to the local newspaper about their predicament. Their letters should explain tenants' rights and duties as well as those of landlords. Then have students exchange papers and, acting as the landlord, respond in a rebuttal editorial.

▼RETEACH Pair students who understand the four rights and duties of landlords with those who are having difficulty. Have each pair write a series of questions involving a landlord's rights and duties. For example: The light in the stairwell of your apartment has burned out. Whose responsibility is it to change it? (Landlord)

▼ENRICH Pair students. Have each pair role-play a tenant and a landlord who are resolving problems concerning collection of rent and/or upkeep of property. State that the objective is to understand the position of both sides.

TEACH

On the chalkboard or on an overhead transparency, create a graphic organizer to illustrate the ways that a lease can be terminated.

APPLY

Cover up the information under the heading, *How the Tenancy Is Terminated*, on the transparency master, *Tenancies in Landlord and Tenant Relationships*, before displaying it to students. Have students provide you with the information. Uncover the masked information as students suggest it.

Guided Practice

Divide the class into four or five groups. Hand out three blank index cards to each group. On each of the index cards, have each group write three scenarios of tenancy termination. Each should describe a particular tenant/landlord situation and discuss each one's action. When students are finished writing, place the cards in a box or other container. Have student volunteers choose a card and present the scenario to the class. Have the class determine who (tenant, landlord, or both) acted within his or her legal rights. **Independent Practice**

HOW CAN A LEASE BE TERMINATED?

PROBLEM

Harpstein leased in a month-to-month tenancy a store in Marx's Shopping Center. Three days before the end of March, Harpstein told Marx that on the first of April she was moving her business to another shopping center. Was Harpstein legally able to terminate the lease on such short notice?

A lease can be terminated in several ways. If it is made for a definite period of time, it terminates at the end of such time. In a lease for a definite period, neither the lessor nor the lessee is required to give advance notice of termination. A lease can also be terminated by agreement before the expiration of the term, as when the tenant surrenders the lease to the landlord and the landlord accepts. Mere abandonment of the premises without assent to the landlord is not surrender, it is a breach of the lease. Any *material* breach by the tenant generally gives the landlord the right to terminate the lease, and vice versa.

In a periodic tenancy, the party seeking to terminate must notify the other party. There is usually a requirement in the lease that this notice be in writing and be given so many days before the end of the lease period. If the lease is silent about when termination notice must be given, state statutes often control and specify the required time for advance notice. Typical notice time for a tenancy from month to month is thirty days. In the problem, Harpstein could not terminate the lease on such short notice unless Marx was willing.

Preventing Legal Difficulties

If you are a tenant . . .

1. Written residential leases are generally prepared by the landlord or the landlord's attorney. Thus, such leases often contain many clauses that protect the landlord's interest. Read with understanding before you sign. If the terms are unacceptable to you, request a change. If you are refused, go elsewhere.
2. You may not remodel or significantly change the premises without the consent of your landlord.

ASSESS

Learning Objective 4 Beginning with the first student in the first row, have one student orally describe one of the four types of leasehold estates—**periodic tenancy, tenancy for years, tenancy at sufferance,** and **tenancy at will.** Then, have the next student label it, verbally, and describe how it can be terminated. If that student fails to correctly label the leasehold estate and list the correct termination, continue to the next student. Continue describing, labeling, and terminating until all students have participated.

3 You may be held liable if someone is injured because of the faulty condition of the premises if such condition was caused by your negligence. Normally you, the tenant, have the obligation to make necessary *minor* repairs and to notify your landlord of the need for major repairs. Protect yourself with careful maintenance and with adequate liability insurance.

4 When you move, give your landlord proper notice. Such notice is required in periodic tenancies. Failure to give adequate notice may obligate you to pay additional rent even after you vacate the premises.

5 If you are a tenant in a tenancy for years, be sure to vacate, removing all belongings and trade fixtures, before expiration of the lease or arrange to renew the lease. If you stay beyond the lease period without permission, you could be treated as a trespasser or be held liable for as much as another full year's rent.

6 If a "cleaning" or "security" deposit is required, it is a good idea to conduct an inspection of the premises with the landlord and with witnesses both before occupying and immediately after vacating.

Preventing Legal Difficulties

Have students read and discuss each of the six suggestions for tenants. Have students create hypothetical situations in which these issues might arise, then field each other's questions.

REVIEWING IMPORTANT POINTS

1 The relationship between landlord and tenant always involves real property.

2 A landlord-tenant relationship may be a tenancy for years, a periodic tenancy (e.g., a tenancy from month to month or a tenancy from year to year), a tenancy at will, or a tenancy at sufferance.

3 Generally the tenant is responsible for paying the rent, taking reasonable care of the premises, and using the premises only for the purposes agreed upon.

4 To claim constructive eviction, the tenant must vacate the real property.

5 A tenant may assign the lease or sublet the premises unless there is a restriction in the lease.

6 The landlord must make major repairs, see that the tenant is not deprived of the use of the leased property, and pay the taxes.

7 A lease may be terminated by expiration of the lease period, by agreement of the parties, or at the option of either party upon material breach by the other. In a periodic tenancy, either party seeking to terminate must give the other party proper notice.

CLOSE

Have students create and present a poster, rap, or poem that promotes understanding of the laws and the ethics of the tenant landlord relationship. Have students present their project to the class.

Assign the following end-of-chapter materials:
Student text review activities, pp. 589–593
Workbook, pp. 87–92
Chapter Test

Chapter *MicroExam*

Pair students who understand how a lease can be terminated with those who are having difficulty. Have the student who understands write a description of how a (hypothetical) lease was legally terminated and have the other student explain which type of leasehold estate was terminated. Then, alternate roles.

Have students write a letter of termination, using a computer, if possible. In the letter, make sure students identify the type of leasehold estate that is being terminated.

Strengthening Your Legal Vocabulary

1. rent
2. partial eviction
3. tenancy from month to month
4. landlord
5. tenant
6. tenancy for years
7. tenancy at sufferance
8. subletting
9. lease
10. eviction

Applying Law to Everyday Life

1.  Yes; Legally, Perry can give 30 days' notice and end the month-to-month tenancy. (p. 581) No; Ethically, however, his conduct is wrong. When Perry has information needed by another to prevent injury, Perry must provide it. Failure to disclose the information is a form of deception; it is like lying. Deontologically, that is wrong. The fact that Perry's deception creates a financial benefit for him is not an ethical justification. If that were the only factor he weighed, he would be ignoring the effect of his conduct on others. That is an ethical mistake.

STRENGTHENING YOUR LEGAL VOCABULARY

Match each term with the statement that best defines that term. Some terms may not be used.

assignment of a lease	partial eviction
constructive eviction	periodic tenancy
duty of reasonable care	rent
eviction	subletting
landlord	tenancy at sufferance
lease	tenancy at will
lease condition	tenancy for years
lease covenant	tenancy from month to month
leasehold estate	tenant

1. Consideration given by a tenant.
2. Depriving the tenant of possession of *part* of the leased real property.
3. Periodic tenancy in which the rent is paid by the month.
4. One who, through a lease, transfers to another exclusive possession and control of real property.
5. One who, through a lease, is given possession of real property.
6. Lease that exists for a definite period of time.
7. Tenancy created when the tenant remains in possession after the lease has expired.
8. Tenant's transfer of partial interest in the lease to a third person.
9. Agreement that provides that the tenant shall obtain possession of the real property of the landlord in exchange for rent.
10. Legal action taken to remove a tenant from possession of all real property.

APPLYING LAW TO EVERYDAY LIFE

1. ETHICS ISSUE Perry owned apartments in a college town. Apartments were easy to rent when school started in September, but they were often vacant during summer months. Pablo moved to town in the middle of the summer and rented one of Perry's apartments for only $250 per month. The written lease was a periodic tenancy from month to month. Pablo said, "This is such a good deal, you can count on me as a tenant for the next year." Perry said nothing in response. He planned

2.  No; Conner's conduct is not ethical. By allowing the complex to deteriorate so badly that it becomes dangerous, he is shifting risks of injury to his tenants. Unless the tenants consent, that is wrong. In utilitarian reasoning, only Conner benefits while all of his tenants are injured. This makes his actions ethically wrong.

to give Pablo thirty days' notice at the beginning of August so he could rerent the apartment for $400 per month for the academic year. Legally, can Perry do this? Is it ethical?

2 ETHICS ISSUE Conner was the only shareholder of Riverside, Inc., a corporation. The corporation owned a large apartment complex in a poor area of town. Many parts of the apartment complex's public areas did not satisfy the local housing code. Some public areas, such as common stairways, were in such disrepair that they were dangerous for the residents who used them. When Conner was asked why he allowed the property to fall into disrepair, he said it made financial sense. He said improving the complex would not allow him to charge higher rents because his tenants were too poor to pay more. He also indicated that if someone was injured, sued, and won a large judgment, he would just take the corporation into bankruptcy. He said his strategy was the best way to make money on low-income housing. Is Conner's conduct ethical?

3 Strovic *orally* leased a restaurant from Quinn for five years. Within a year, Strovic had built a large following, and business was booming. Quinn then demanded more rent. When Strovic refused, Quinn sought to evict him and to lease the now well-established property to someone else who would pay higher rent. Can Quinn do this?

4 Slovin entered into a month-to-month tenancy of an apartment for $450 per month. When he married, his wife moved in with him. The landlord did not discover this until three months later. The landlord told Slovin that he owed an extra $100 per month for the time during which the wife had also occupied the apartment. In addition, he told Slovin that the rent for the next month would be $600. What are Slovin's legal obligations to the landlord?

5 Hirschey moved away to college and rented a room for nine months, to end on the first of June. After her final examinations were over (on the first of June), she moved out of the room without saying anything to the landlord. The landlord now seeks to collect an additional month's rent because Hirschey did not give notice of termination. Can the landlord collect?

6 In the midst of a very cold winter, the heating unit in Manlie's apartment failed to function for a month. Therefore Manlie refused to pay the rent, claiming constructive eviction. Her landlord, however, claimed that the rent was still due because Manlie had not abandoned the premises. Is the landlord correct?

3 Yes, Quinn can do this. The lease is for five years, but since it was not placed in writing, the oral agreement will not be enforced. Since there is not an enforceable lease, the landlord may terminate with one month's notice. (p. 581)

4 Slovin has no liability for the three months during which his wife occupied the apartment with him. This is because Slovin, as the tenant, may use the property for its intended purpose. (p. 583) However, since this is a month-to-month tenancy, the landlord may terminate the lease with 30 days' notice. In effect, this landlord is terminating the lease and proposing a new one with a higher rent. The landlord under a periodic tenancy has the legal power to do this, provided adequate notice is given. (p. 581)

5 No, the landlord cannot collect. Hirschey was under no obligation to give notice since this was a tenancy for years, which automatically terminated on the first of June. (pp. 581–582)

6 Yes, the landlord is correct. Failure to provide Manlie with heat might be grounds for constructive eviction. However, the tenant must abandon the premises before being able to assert rights arising from constructive eviction. (p. 583)

7 Romero (the tenant) is liable for the damage. The tenant had exclusive possession of the leased premises and was responsible for minor repairs, such as the one required for the window. Further, the tenant was negligent in not closing the window during rainy periods. (p. 584)

8 Yes, Houser is liable. When a lessee assigns a lease, the landlord must attempt to collect the rent from the assignee, in this case Todd, before attempting to collect from the lessee. It appears that this has occurred, so Houser is now liable for the rent. (p. 584)

9 The landlord, Johnson, is liable. Landlords have the legal responsibility to maintain the exterior and the public areas of their property. Failure to remove ice from a sidewalk violated the duty that the landlord owed to those who use it. (p. 586)

7 Romero rented a farm under a three-year lease. At the end of the lease, Romero and the landlord walked through the farmhouse to inspect for damage. In an empty upstairs room the landlord found a window that was jammed open. It was obvious that rain and snow had come through the open window and damaged curtains and carpeting. Who is liable for this damage, Romero or the landlord?

8 Houser opened a hamburger shop in a building that she leased for five years from Livingston. The long hours impaired Houser's health and after one year she sold the business to Todd, assigning the lease as part of the deal. When Todd later defaulted on rent payments, Livingston tried to collect from Houser. Is Houser liable?

9 Moya rented an apartment in a large complex owned by Johnson. Moya's guest, Perkins, was injured when he fell on the icy sidewalk leading up to the building where Moya's apartment was located. Perkins sued both Moya and Johnson. Who is liable, Moya or Johnson?

SOLVING CASE PROBLEMS

1 Platt leased the Arctic Circle Drive Inn to Peterson with a tenancy for years. The term was ten years. At one point Peterson fell two months behind with the rent. In response, Platt let himself into the property after everyone else was gone. He changed the locks and prohibited Peterson and his employees from entering the establishment. Because Peterson was unable to gain access, many of his goods perished. He then sued Platt, claiming that Platt's actions were illegal. He asked that Platt be required to pay for the spoiled goods. Will Peterson prevail? (*Peterson v. Platt,* 678 P.2d 41)

2 Wallenberg leased certain property from Boyar in a tenancy from month to month, beginning October 1. The rent was payable in advance on the first of each month. On November 27, Wallenberg left without notifying the landlord. Is Boyar entitled to rent for the month of December? (*Boyar v. Wallenberg,* 132 Misc. 116, 228 N.Y.S. 358)

3 Lemle rented an expensive home in the Diamond Head area of Honolulu. The home contained six bedrooms and the roof was made in the Tahitian style with corrugated metal covered by woven coconut leaves. After moving in, Lemle and his family discovered the roof was infested with rodents. For two days after moving in, they all slept in the downstairs living room because of their fear of the rodents. After the landlord tried without success to exterminate the rodents, Lemle and his family moved out and demanded return of their deposit and prepaid

Solving Case Problems

1 Yes; Peterson prevails. A lessor must use legal process to evict a tenant. A landlord who personally evicts a tenant may be engaged in criminal conduct. Unless the lease gives the landlord the right to enter, the landlord has committed trespass. In this case, the judge awarded Peterson damages. (p. 586)

2 Yes; To terminate a periodic tenancy, the party who wishes to terminate must give notice. (p. 581) Wallenberg's failure to give notice here made him liable for another month's rent.

rent. Is Lemle entitled to the return of the rent? (*Lemle v. Breeden,* 462 P.2d 470, Hawaii)

4 James Kreidel was engaged to be married and planned to attend school. He entered into a lease of an apartment from May 1, 1972, to April 30, 1974. Before the lease period began, Kreidel's engagement was broken. As a student, Kreidel then had no means of support and therefore had no way to pay the rent. On May 19, 1972, he wrote the landlord explaining his situation and stating that he was abandoning the lease. Although the landlord had the opportunity, he did not rerent the apartment until September 1, 1973. Is James liable for the rent from May 1, 1972, to September 1, 1973? (*Sommer v. Kreidel,* 378 A.2d 767, N.J.)

5 Stockton Realty Company rented to Green an apartment in a three-story building which had on the roof a washroom and clothesline for use by tenants. The clothesline ran near the skylight, but there was no guardrail between the clothesline and the skylight. After Reiman, a fourteen-year-old friend, removed Green's clothes from the line, she tripped on some object and fell against the skylight. The glass was too weak to support her weight, and she dropped to the floor below, sustaining injuries. Is the landlord responsible for the condition of the roof, and thus liable for the injury? (*Reiman v. Moore,* 108 P.2d 452, Cal.)

3 Yes, Lemle is entitled to the return of the deposit and prepaid rent. This is an example of constructive eviction. A rat-infested house is not fit for human habitation and the landlord failed to solve the problem after being notified. Since Lemle moved out, he is entitled to treat the lease as being terminated by the lessor. (p. 583)

4 No, James is not liable for rent for the whole amount of the lease period. In most states, the landlord is under an obligation to rerent the premises after the tenant moves out. Failure to try to rerent eliminates the landlord's right to collect damages from the tenant who breached the lease by early departure. (p. 585)

5 Yes, the landlord is responsible and, thus, liable. The roof with the washroom and clothesline is a common area for which the landlord is responsible. (p. 586)

Special Section: Computer Law

Divide students into groups of four or five. Have each group design a poster warning computer users against illegally copying software. Assign the following roles: illustrator; copywriter; researcher; proofreader; and facilitator, if necessary. Allow approximately 20–25 minutes for each group to produce a poster. Hang the posters next to the computers in class or computer lab. **Cooperative Learning**

As an extension to this section, list on the chalkboard the following terms that deal with computer ethics: **virus**, **antivirus program**, **disinfectant**, **hacker**, **Trojan horse**, **pirate**, **bomb**, **worm**, **freeware**, **shareware**, **copy protect**, and **copyright**. Have students brainstorm what they think each term means, then research its true definition. Have students draw a two-panel cartoon showing the most outrageous misconception they had of one of the terms. Use one panel to show the misconception and the other to show the correct definition of the term. Display the cartoons on a bulletin board called *Copyright or Copywrong?*

SPECIAL SECTION

COMPUTER LAW

The pervasive use of the computer in our society has given rise to new terms and a new area of the law. "Data diddling," "salami slicing," "logic bombs," "hackers," and "viruses" are just some of the ways we refer to the harmful aspects of computer use. How to protect and encourage the positive possibilities of digital technology while winnowing out as illegal, tortious, or both these other activities have proven to be a long-term problem within the law.

According to current law, protection is afforded to computer programs that are part of a patentable process or that are creative works falling under the protection of the Computer Software Copyright Act of 1980. The structuring of the logic sequences that computers use to carry out commands and various operating systems have been afforded protection under recent federal court decisions. Chipmakers are protected under the Semiconductor Chip Protection Act of 1984, if they properly register the circuitry with the U.S. Copyright Office. In addition, the Federal Counterfeit Access Device and Computer Fraud and Abuse Act provides for the punishment of individuals who invade various governmental data bases, the data bases of financial institutions, or consumer reporting agency data bases. State laws on fraud and embezzlement have been amended or new laws added to make the use of a computer to carry out most criminal schemes illegal.

Nonetheless, innovation is the key to our society and the law must continue to change and update in order to keep pace with the computer.

Checks and Other Commercial Paper

Unit Overview

In Unit 8, *Checks and Other Commercial Paper*, students will read about the different kinds of commercial paper, negotiability, and rights and defenses of holders. In this unit, students will learn about drafts, checks, promissory notes, certificates of deposit, indorsements, and electronic fund transfers. Given that your students may not even have their own checking accounts, much less prior academic background in this area, this unit of *Law for Business* delivers the content in relatively small increments. Examples, PROBLEMS, figures, and the text relate closely. You may wish to provide numerous, personally relevant examples of your own to clarify information and "drive home" the key points of these pages.

Checks and other kinds of commercial paper are covered in depth in this chapter. In Chapter 30, *Nature and Kinds of Commercial Paper*, students will study what commercial paper is, the types of commercial paper, and the specialized forms of commercial paper that are available.

Negotiability of commercial paper—and requirements for such transactions—are regulated by law. In Chapter 31, *Negotiability*, students will discover what negotiation is and why it is so important. They will also study a checklist of requirements that a written instrument must fill in order to be negotiable, and how commercial paper is transferred. Blank, special qualified, and restrictive indorsements are all explained in depth, as is the importance of accommodation parties, when they are present.

Holders, holders in due course (HDC), and holders through holders in due course are all subject to universal defenses. In Chapter 32, *Rights and Defenses of Holders*, students will understand who can be a holder in due course and why this status is so important. They will also cover topics such as limited defenses, universal defenses, discharge of commercial paper, and one's rights and duties in an electronic fund transfer.

At the end of this unit, you'll find a special section, *How to Litigate in Small Claims Court*, which can be used at any time during the study of Unit 8. You may wish to assign its accompanying *Teacher Edition* activity to give students an opportunity to role-play a small claims court case.

Portfolio Assessment

Have students create a banking handbook to inform new bank customers, especially minors, of the kinds, use, and negotiability of checks and other commercial paper. Have students refer closely to Chapters 30–32 for information. Then, using a computer, if possible, have students write the handbook in an easy narrative style, following a question-and-answer format. Cover topics that are of interest, importance, or sources of confusion for minors. Have students include the handbook in their portfolios.

Careers

Bank Officer

With the increasing use of commercial paper, the need for bank officers will also increase. Depending on the specific position held, responsibilities include soliciting new accounts, preparing fiscal reports and budgets, servicing customer and business loans, and reviewing credit ratings.

A bachelor's degree in business, economics, finance, accounting, or law is needed for this position. Knowledge of French, Japanese, or another foreign language, as well as geography and history, is helpful since many banks do business internationally. Average annual starting salaries for a bank officer range from $19,000 to $23,000.

Have students write a classified ad on behalf of a bank seeking a bank officer. Tell them to include education and salary requirements and necessary experience. Then, have students exchange ads and write how they could start preparing themselves today to qualify for such a job, if they were to answer that ad five years from now.

Annotated Bibliography

- ***Ashford v. Thomas Cook & Son*, 471 P.2d 530 (1970).**
  A traveler's check is a medium of exchange with negotiable characteristics, and all risk of theft falls on the issuer, who is liable to any bona fide purchaser. (Chapter 30)

- ***Ackerman v. FDIC*, 930 F.2d 3,4 (5th Cir. 1991), certified question accepted sub. nom., *Amberboy v. Société de Banque Privée*, 34 Tex. Sup. Ct. J. 690 (June 22, 1991).**
  A promissory note requiring interest to be charged at a rate that can be determined only by reference to a bank's published prime rate is a negotiable instrument. By a "bank's published prime rate," we intend our answer to include only those rates that are public, either known to or readily ascertainable by an interested person. (Chapter 31)

- ***Williams v. Stansbury*, 649 S.W.2d 293 (Tex. 1983).**
  A holder in due course takes an instrument free from all legal equitable claims by any person to the instrument. (Chapter 32)

Checks and Other Commercial Paper

- Nature and Kinds of Commercial Paper
- Negotiability
- Rights and Defenses of Holders

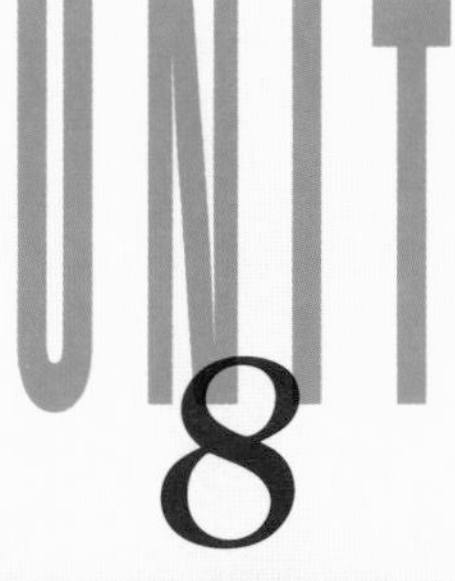

UNIT 8 CHECKS AND OTHER COMMERCIAL PAPER

CHAPTER 30 ORGANIZER

Chapter Theme

Checks and other kinds of commercial paper are covered in depth in this chapter.

DIRECTED STUDY QUESTIONS	SPECIAL FEATURES	PROGRAM RESOURCES: Reteach	Enrich	SN	AM	
What is commercial paper?		✔	✔			
What are the types of commercial paper?	Thinking Critically Through Visuals, pp. 599, 600, 601, 603, 604 Multicultural Highlights, p. 600 Ethics Issue, p. 602 Writing Connections, p. 602 Personal Perspectives, p. 603	✔	✔	✔	V A	
What specialized forms of commercial paper are available?	Thinking Critically Through Visuals, pp. 606, 607 Preventing Legal Difficulties, p. 607	✔	✔		K	

Additional Resources

- Martin, J. Michael. *Life After CDs: The Practical Guide to Safe Investing.* Chicago, IL: Dearborn Financial Publishing, 1993.
- Rosenberg, Jerry M. *Dictionary of Banking.* NY: John Wiley & Sons, Inc., 1993.

One-semester course	✔	✔						
One-year course	✔	✔	✔					

	Cooperative Learning	Informal Assessment	Chapter Review	Chapter Test	Chapter *MicroExam* 
		ASSESSMENT OPPORTUNITIES			
		✔	✔	✔	✔
	✔	✔	✔	✔	✔
		✔	✔	✔	✔

Chapter Pacing Guide

Videodiscs

Basic Types of Commercial Paper

Search Chapter 37, Play To 38

State by State

Currently in approximately 20 states, the term *bank* is defined to include savings and loans and credit unions. In the other states, a bank is an institution governmentally chartered as a bank and nothing more.

Teaching Materials

Student text, pp. 596–613

Overhead transparency masters
•*Anglee Davis's Message to Her Bank in Teaser 2*
•*One Solution to Chapter Opening Teaser 1*

Videos
•*Law for Business* Videodisc

Workbook, pp. 93–94

Outside Resources
•Sample blank checks
•Colored markers or pens
•Flip chart
•Rectangular (6" × 2¾") sheets of paper
•Outside speaker: bank employee
•Bank brochures on CDs and interest rates
•Sample cashier's checks, bank drafts, money orders, and/or traveler's checks
•Poster board
•Blank overhead transparencies

Assessment
•Chapter Test

•Chapter *MicroExam*

Vocabulary

commercial paper, p. 598
draft, p. 600
drawer, p. 600
drawee, p. 600
payee, p. 601
sight draft, p. 601
time draft, p. 601
acceptance, p. 601
check, p. 601
honor, p. 602
dishonor, p. 602
stop payment order, p. 602
promissory note, p. 603
maker, p. 603
comakers, p. 603
collateral note, p. 603
mortgage note, p. 604
certificate of deposit, p. 604
certified check, p. 605
cashier's check, p. 605
bank draft, p. 606
money order, p. 606
traveler's check, p. 606

Learning Objectives

When you complete this chapter, you will be able to

1. Know what commercial paper is.
2. Describe the basic types of commercial paper.
3. Understand the use of certain specialized types of commercial paper.

596

Chapter Self-Test

Assess students' understanding of commercial paper before they begin Chapter 30 by asking them to identify the following types of commercial paper: **(1) certificate of deposit** (A deposit acknowledged by the bank with promise to repay with interest at a specific time); **(2) money order** (A draft issued by a recognized institution); and **(3) certified check** (A personal check that has been accepted by a bank before payment) Before continuing with the chapter, review and discuss students' responses.

CHAPTER 30

NATURE AND KINDS OF COMMERCIAL PAPER

1 Felicia Harms wants to purchase a digital VCR from Dan's Bargain Rack, a discount seller in a distant state. Unfortunately, she does not have any credit cards, Dan's will not take a personal check, and it is too risky to send cash through the mail. What special type of check could she use to send the $385 purchase price to Dan's?

2 When Stew Dent asks Anglee Davis for the $200 she owes him, she writes a message to her bank on a blank sheet of paper. The message directs the bank to pay $200 from her checking account to Dent or to his order whenever he demands it. She signs the paper, dates it, and hands it to Dent. Is the paper a check?

3 ETHICS ISSUE You overdraw your checking account, but the bank honors your check anyway. According to your depositor's contract, a fee of $15 is charged by the bank for such a service. When you get your statement, however, you see that the bank has forgotten to deduct the $15 charge for honoring your check. Should you inform the bank of the error?

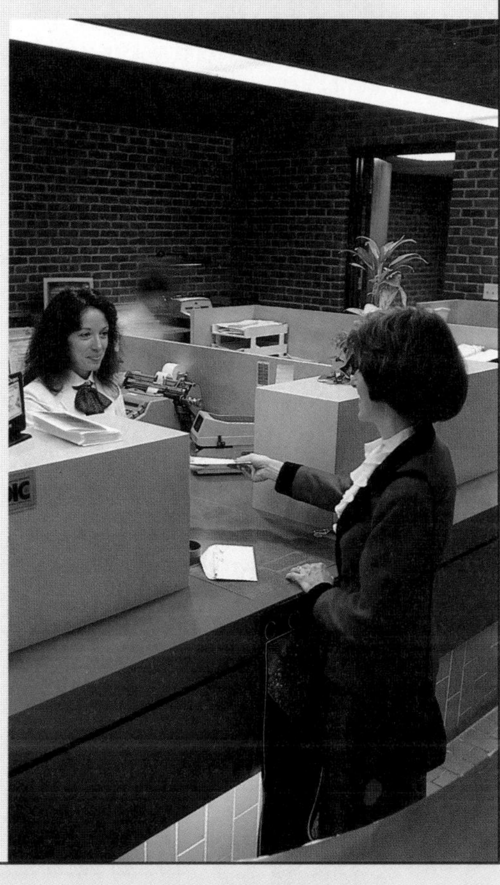

Before class begins, create and duplicate a sample blank check. Then, write the following on the chalkboard: **UpBeat Music Center; (Today's date); (Student's name and address); $45; Forty-five and no/100————.** As students enter the classroom, have them take a blank check and use the information on the chalkboard to write out a check for a purchase of compact discs.

On an overhead transparency, show a sample blank check with the information from the chalkboard filled in correctly. Poll students to determine if

any of them have a checking account. Ask those who do to discuss its use and importance.

You Decide

1 Felicia could send a certified check, a bank check, or a money order to pay for the VCR.

2 Yes, it meets all the standards for a check. Check forms as we know them today are of fairly recent use.

3 ETHICS ISSUE Yes; Not to inform the bank, which violates the contract, would be unethical.

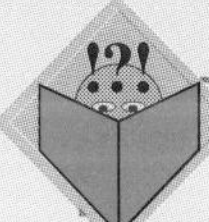

Thinking Critically Through Visuals

The woman in the photograph is handing a check to a bank teller. What, do you think, are the benefits of checking accounts? (Answers may include that checks are much safer than cash, checks provide a receipt for payment, and so on.)

▼ TEACH

Tell students that **commercial paper** is the unconditional written orders or promises to pay money. The check, developed many years ago to serve as a safe substitute for money for traveling merchants, is the most common form of commercial paper. Explain that checks are called demand instruments because they enable depositors to withdraw their money or have it paid out to their creditors. Have students understand that the UCC governs the legitimacy and use of commercial paper.

▼ APPLY

On the chalkboard, draw a two-column chart with the vertical headings **Commercial Paper** and **Money** and the horizontal headings **Advantages** and **Disadvantages.** Ask students to help you complete it by listing advantages and disadvantages of each in their respective columns. **Guided Practice**

In an essay, using a computer, if possible, have students explain why commercial paper was developed and why today's society relies on it so heavily.

Independent Practice

▼ WHAT IS COMMERCIAL PAPER?

PROBLEM

Marsha shocked her friend Benito by claiming that the bank she had her checking account with was really her debtor and that she could collect whenever she wanted. Benito stared at her, then laughed. "Who are you trying to kid?" he asked. "When did a bank ever come to anyone for a loan?" Marsha smiled back and said, "It happens every day." Is she correct?

Unconditional written orders or promises to pay money are collectively defined as **commercial paper.** Most of the laws governing the legitimacy and use of commercial paper are in the Uniform Commercial Code (UCC). However, other laws are important to commercial paper as well. For example, commercial paper is not valid if used in illegal transactions, such as gambling, as defined in criminal codes.

The check is the most common form of commercial paper. Like other forms of commercial paper, it was developed years ago to serve as a relatively safe substitute for money. When traveling and dealing with distant sellers, merchants would leave their valuable gold or silver with their bankers. Then, when the merchants wanted to pay a seller for purchases, they simply wrote an order addressed to their bank. The order directed the bank to deliver a specified amount of the gold or silver to whomever the seller designated. The bank could tell if the order was authentic by comparing the signature (and perhaps the seal) on the order with the signature of the merchant it had on file. The bank then complied with the order because, once the merchant had deposited the gold or silver, the bank was the merchant's debtor. Consequently, if the merchant appeared and demanded the gold or silver, the bank had to give it back.

This is still true today. Banks are the debtors of the depositors, as Marsha correctly stated in the problem. They compete with one another to borrow funds from their depositors and then lend what they have borrowed to others. Checks are called demand instruments because they enable depositors to withdraw their money or have it paid in accordance with their order. Marsha can "collect" what is owed to her by writing a check at any time.

▼ WHAT ARE THE TYPES OF COMMERCIAL PAPER?

PROBLEM

Nightwing purchased a personal computer for her new business. After comparing software, she selected an integrated accounting and inven-

▼ ASSESS

Learning Objective 1 Have students brainstorm a class definition of **commercial paper** and write it on the chalkboard. Then, have students compare their definition with the one found on p. 813 of the *Glossary of Legal Terms*. To clarify the process of writing and cashing a demand instrument, such as a check, have three student volunteers role-play the transaction described on p. 598 (merchant, seller, and banker) as a fourth volunteer reads aloud the passage from the text.

tory program. The program cost more than $700, and she had to borrow the money from her friend Fyffe. In exchange, Nightwing gave Fyffe an IOU for that amount. The IOU was signed and dated. Was it commercial paper?

Today, commercial paper can be grouped into two categories. The first consists of unconditional *orders* to pay money. The second category is composed of unconditional *promises* to pay money.

"Unconditional," as used to define commercial paper, means that the legal effectiveness of the order or promise does not depend on any other event. Accordingly, an instrument that reads in part "Pay to the order of Sam after he delivers the bike to me" would not be commercial paper because its enforceability is conditional upon delivery of the bike. Unlike unconditional orders or promises to pay a sum of money, an IOU, such as the one Nightwing gave to Fyffe in the problem, only acknowledges the debt. The law holds that such an acknowledgment is far short of a promise or order to repay. Therefore, an IOU is not enforceable as commercial paper.

Of the four main types of commercial paper, two—the draft and the check—are unconditional *orders* to pay money. The other two—the promissory note and the certificate of deposit—are unconditional *promises* to pay money. These four main types are discussed below.

▼ TEACH

Explain the four types of commercial paper. (pp. 598–605). On the chalkboard, draw a large four-column chart. Label the first column **Draft** and write these terms and definitions: **draft, drawer, drawee, payee, sight draft, time draft,** and **acceptance**. Label the second column **Check** and write these terms and definitions: **check, honor, dishonor,** and **stop payment order**. Label the third column **Promissory Note** and write these terms and definitions: **promissory note, maker, comakers, collateral note,** and **mortgage note**. Label the fourth column **Certificate of Deposit**, followed by its definition and the following points: offers a relatively high interest rate, has a bank stand behind it, and provides incentive to save money because of the interest penalty for early withdrawal.

▼ APPLY

Thinking Critically Through Visuals

The appliance store employee in the photograph is processing today's receipts. What type of commercial paper is she currently processing? (Check) **Guided Practice**

Based on your class discussions and reading p. 598 of their text, have students orally identify and describe the most important points of commercial paper.

▼ENRICH

In writing, using a computer, if possible, have students discuss the meaning of the phrase, *"Banks are debtors of their depositors."*

1. Drafts

A **draft** is an unconditional written order by one person that directs another person to pay money to a third. The person directed to pay may be a natural person or an artificial "legal" person, such as a corporation.

Sanford bought a used amplifier for her electric guitar from Minton for $600. She paid Minton $100 down and promised to pay the remaining $500 by her next payday. A few days after the sale, Minton bought a state-of-the-art, low-distortion speaker system for $750 at a clearance sale at Downtown Audio. As partial payment to Downtown Audio, Minton drew a draft (see Figure 30-1) on the $500 Sanford owed him. To be sure Sanford had enough time to get the money, Minton made the draft payable to the order of Downtown Audio thirty days after sight. Upon receiving the draft, Downtown immediately presented it to Sanford who indicated her willingness to pay in thirty days by writing the date and her signature on the front of the paper along with the word "accepted."

If it is not necessary to specify that a particular person receive the money, the order may be made payable to "cash" or to "bearer." Then the person in legal possession of the order may collect on it. However, the order must be either effective upon demand or at a definite date, such as the "thirty days after sight" in Figure 30-1.

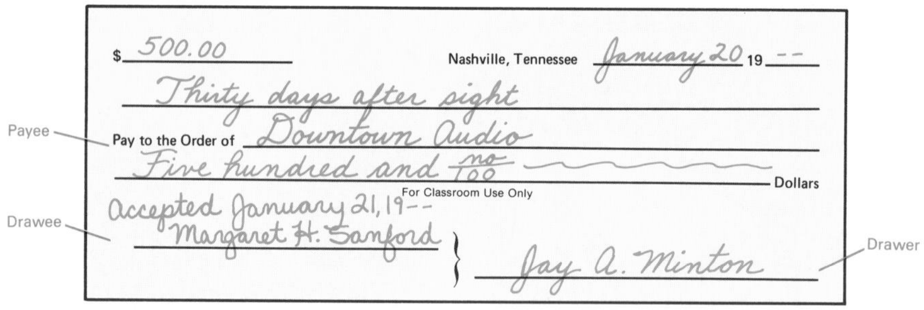

$ 500.00 Nashville, Tennessee January 20 19 --
Thirty days after sight
Pay to the Order of Downtown Audio
Five hundred and no/100 Dollars
For Classroom Use Only
Accepted January 21, 19--
Margaret H. Sanford
Jay A. Minton

Payee
Drawee
Drawer

Figure 30-1
A draft by which Minton directs Sanford to pay $500 to Downtown Audio thirty days after the draft is presented to Sanford for payment.

The person who executes or draws the draft and orders payment to be made is the **drawer**. The **drawee** is the party ordered to pay the draft. The

Multicultural Highlights

Ana María Fernández Haar was nine when her parents moved from Cuba to Miami. She later went on to college at night and worked in a bank during the day. By the mid-1970s, she became the bank vice-president in charge of an advertising campaign to market the Miami Beach Chamber of Commerce to three Latin American countries. In 1978, she opened her own advertising and marketing agency. Today, Fernández Haar employs 25 people in her award-winning agency. Ask: **Why, do you think, would a bank help a local chamber of commerce market itself to other countries?** (To attract depositors, raise customer confidence, and so on)

Thinking Critically Through Visuals

A draft must be payable either at sight or on demand. When is the draft in Figure 30-1 effective? (On February 19—30 days after the draft was presented)

ASSESS

Learning Objective 2 Have students use the necessary elements **(drawer, drawee, payee, sight draft,** and **time draft)** to create their own drafts. Have students exchange papers, explain the scenarios behind each, and have their partner review the draft for accuracy and completeness.

payee is the party to whom commercial paper is made payable. The drawee is usually the debtor of the drawer. In the example above, Minton is the drawer, Sanford is the drawee, and Downtown Audio is the payee.

Drafts are sometimes classified in terms of the time of payment. If the draft is payable at sight or on demand—that is, when presented to the drawee by the one holding the draft—it is a **sight draft.** The drawee is expected to pay when the draft is presented.

If a draft is payable on a set date, at the end of a specified period after sight, or at the end of a specified period after the date of the draft, it is a **time draft.** The commercial paper in Figure 30-1 is a time draft. When a time draft is payable a number of days or months after sight, it must be presented to the drawee for acceptance in order to start the running of the specified time. **Acceptance** is the drawee's promise to pay the draft when due. Such a promise is usually evidenced by the signature of the acceptor on the face of the instrument along with words indicating the acceptance. Also, when a draft states it is payable a number of days or months "after date," the time starts running immediately from the date of the draft.

2. Checks

PROBLEM

Hubble paid Honest John's Auto Repair $385 by check for the repair of his car's transmission. When the job proved defective, Hubble telephoned his bank and ordered it to stop payment on the check. Three weeks later, however, the bank honored the check and paid Honest John's the $385 out of Hubble's account. Did the bank make a mistake?

A **check** is a type of draft by which a bank depositor orders the bank to pay money, usually to a third party (see Figure 30-2). Checks are usually

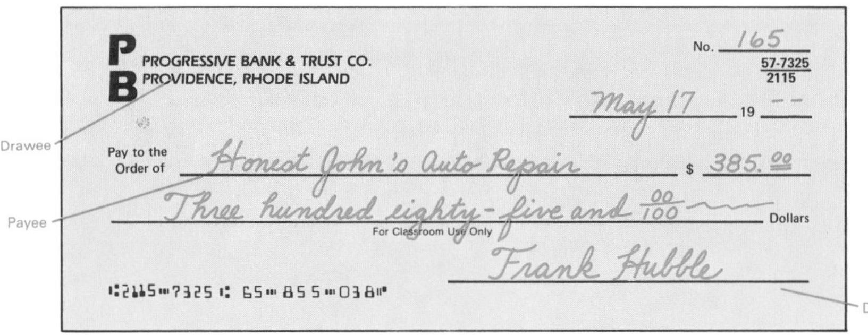

Figure 30-2
Hubble, by issuing this check, is ordering his bank, Progressive Bank & Trust Co., to pay $385 to Honest John's Auto Repair.

Ensure that dyslexic students or students who have difficulty spelling new words focus specifically on the new vocabulary crucial to understanding commercial paper. Create a word search puzzle using the vocabulary terms on pp. 600–601. The definitions of the terms should serve as the clues. Assign the word search to students. After they have completed the puzzle, share the correct  responses and have students spell them aloud.

For a check to be processed, it must be filled out properly. Who is ordered to pay the draft? (Progressive Bank & Trust Co.) **Who is the party to whom the check is made payable?** (Honest John's Auto Repair) **Who is ordering that the payment be made?** (Frank Hubble)

Provide students who need support to understand the concept of process and parties to a draft with one of the drafts prepared in the previous ASSESS activity. Have students use colored markers or pens to identify each of the following: **drawer, drawee,** and **payee.**

Have groups of students demonstrate the process of executing a draft by having them role-play a drawer, drawee, and a payee, using some of the drafts from the ASSESS activity as a guide.

Display the overhead transparency, *Anglee Davis's Message to Her Bank in Teaser 2.* Have students identify the **payee** (Stew Dent), the **drawer** (Davis), and the **drawee** (bank).

Ethics Issue

Ask: **Is it ethical to write a check if you know you have insufficient funds in your account, even though you plan to make a deposit the next day?** (No, it is unethical. In addition, it is illegal and could be costly.

Writing Connections

Language Arts
Using a computer, if possible, ask students to write the letter that Frank Hubble (see PROBLEM, p. 601) should have written to stop payment on his check. Outline proper business letter format on an overhead transparency. Display students' work on a bulletin board entitled *Take a Letter María.*

Independent Practice

written on special forms that are magnetically encoded to simplify check processing for the banking system. However, checks may be written on blank paper, on forms provided by the depositor, on rawhide, or on other materials and still be legally effective. The drawee, though, must always be a bank for the instrument to qualify as a check.

The bank, according to the contract between it and the depositor, agrees to **honor** (i.e., pay when due) each check as long as sufficient funds remain in the depositor's account. The bank owes that duty as a debtor of the depositor in return for being able to use the depositor's funds until the depositor demands their return. This means that the bank must retain a sizable percentage of the deposited funds so that it can pay properly drawn checks when presented. The remainder of the deposited funds is loaned at interest to pay for the bank's operations and to return a profit to the bank's owners.

A person who deliberately issues a check while knowing that there are insufficient funds in his or her account to pay the check when it is presented at the drawee bank is guilty of a crime. The bank will **dishonor** (i.e., refuse to pay when due) the instrument and the payee or current owner of the check will not get money for it from that source. In addition, if a check is issued to pay a debt, the payoff is not effective until the check is presented to the drawee bank and honored.

When a check has been lost or stolen, the drawer should direct the bank not to pay it. Such an instruction is called a **stop payment order.** If the drawee bank still pays the check, the bank must recredit the account, and the bank, not the depositor, must bear any loss. Oral stop payment orders are good for only two weeks unless they are confirmed in writing. Written stop payment orders are good for six months, but lapse at the end of that time unless renewed. In the problem, the bank did not make a mistake; Hubble did. He did not send a written follow-up to his oral stop payment order.

Care must be taken to prevent checks from being altered. When writing a check, do not leave space for someone to insert figures and words that would change the amount of the instrument. Certainly, never sign a blank check. Do not give anything of value in return for a check that appears to have been altered in any manner. In addition, be wary of a check that may have been issued in connection with illegal activities, for example, gambling. Such instruments are usually considered void by courts.

3. Promissory Notes

PROBLEM

Burger was the owner and president of a small surfboard manufacturing company. She also owned the land and buildings the company

ASSESS

Learning Objective 2 On an overhead transparency, provide a blank template of a personal check (top) and a promissory note (bottom). Have students decide which type of commercial paper would best be used for the following examples, then brainstorm and complete each on the transparency: a promise to repay a $7,000 college loan (Promissory note) and an authorization to repay a $7,000 college loan (Personal check).

occupied. When she needed to raise cash to finance a major expansion, her financial advisers told her that the best way to do so was by using the building and land as a source of funds. How could Burger do this?

A **promissory note** is an unconditional written promise by a person or persons to pay money according to the payee's order or to pay money to the bearer of the instrument. The payment may have to be made on demand or at a definite time according to the stated terms on the face of the note (see Figure 30-3). The person who executes a promissory note is the **maker**. If two or more persons execute the note, they are **comakers** and are equally liable for payment.

Eric Gordon was a songwriter. Every February and August, he received checks for the royalties from his published songs. The checks were his only income. Occasionally, he would run low on money just before his next check was to arrive. When he did, Eric borrowed money from his bank. In return, he executed a short-term promissory note payable to the bank. The note was written to mature (i.e., become due) after he received his check, generally in thirty, sixty, or ninety days from the date the note was executed, and payable with interest at that time.

Many financial institutions will not lend money unless some personal or real property is offered as security by the would-be borrower. The security ensures that the loan will be paid when due. If the debtor fails to pay, the creditor can force the sale of the property and then take the money due from the proceeds of that sale. When personal property is offered as security and so indicated on the face of the note, the paper is a **collateral note.** When real property is the security for payment, the paper is a

$ 3,000.00 Las Vegas, Nevada December 20 19 --

Sixty days after date I promise to pay to

Payee — the order of First National Bank

Three thousand and no/100 Dollars

For Classroom Use Only

Payable at First National Bank Building, Las Vegas, Nevada

with interest at 9 % a year.

No. 6 Due February 20, 19-- Eric Gordon — Maker

Figure 30-3
This promissory note shows an unconditional promise by Eric Gordon to pay First National Bank $3,000, sixty days after December 20, 19—.

Personal Perspectives

Ask: **Why might banks be reluctant to take promissory notes from people your age without the signature of a comaker?** (Answers may include that a valid comaker would lessen their financial risk.) Ask: **Are the bank's concerns valid?** (Answers may include yes, minors often are not contractually liable or no, if the minor is earning enough money, the bank should take the risk.)

Thinking Critically Through Visuals

This promissory note is an unconditional written promise to pay money owed, along with interest. How much will Eric Gordon pay on February 20? (About $3,045)

Divide the class into groups of three or four. Assign these roles: facilitator, two comakers to execute a promissory note, and a bank representative. Have each group create a poster-size promissory note and label the key parts. **Cooperative Learning**

▼RETEACH

Media: In small groups, have students use the seven vocabulary terms found on pp. 602–603 to create a group crossword puzzle on the chalkboard or an overhead transparency. Have students exchange and solve each other's puzzles.

▼ENRICH

Distribute rectangular (6″ x 2¾″) sheets of paper. Have students practice creating and writing checks to each other. Have students exchange checks and review them for accuracy, completeness, and security features.

Invite a bank employee to visit your classroom or have your class visit a bank and discuss the four types of commercial paper discussed on pp. 598–605 and the responsibilities and risk of each. Ask the speaker to bring to the presentation examples of each type of commercial paper for students to examine. Have students prepare questions ahead of time to ask the speaker.

Thinking Critically Through Visuals

This certificate of deposit indicates that Kimberly H. Crowson has deposited $10,000 with The Bank of Lewis and Clark. When will Crowson be able to withdraw her money without penalty? (March 15 of the following year) **How much interest will her money have earned?** (Answers will vary, but will be about $700 if compounded monthly.)

mortgage note. In the problem, Burger could borrow funds by signing a mortgage note and giving a mortgage on the land and the buildings as security for repayment.

4. Certificates of Deposit

PROBLEM

Crowson wanted to buy a new car in a year or two. She had just received a large income tax refund, which she planned to use as a down payment. However, she was afraid that she might spend the money before she was ready to purchase the car. Therefore, Crowson was looking for an investment that would pay a good interest rate, allow access to the money in a year, and discourage her from spending it in the interim. Would a certificate of deposit satisfy Crowson's requirements?

A **certificate of deposit** is an instrument bearing a bank's written acknowledgment of the receipt of money, together with an unconditional promise to repay it at a definite future time (see Figure 30-4). A certificate of deposit is often called a CD.

Banks are prohibited by federal law from paying out CDs and other long-term deposits before maturity without a penalty to the depositor. Usually the penalty is a sharp reduction in the amount of interest payable on the funds. This inhibits depositors from withdrawing funds before maturity and permits the banks to lend the funds to others on a long-term basis. Consequently, interest rates on CDs are usually significantly higher than the rates on savings or checking accounts (from which the depositor is far more likely to withdraw funds). Therefore, in the problem, Crowson should strongly consider buying a CD that matures in one year. It would offer (1) a relatively high interest rate, (2) the security of having a bank stand behind

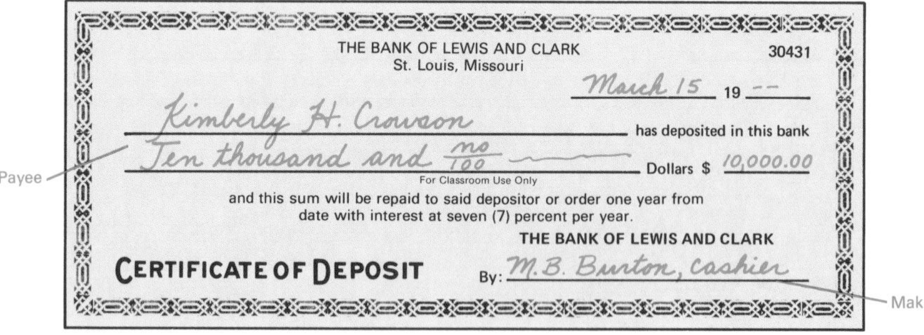
THE BANK OF LEWIS AND CLARK
St. Louis, Missouri
30431
March 15 19 --
Kimberly H. Crowson has deposited in this bank
Ten thousand and no/100 Dollars $ 10,000.00
For Classroom Use Only
and this sum will be repaid to said depositor or order one year from date with interest at seven (7) percent per year.
THE BANK OF LEWIS AND CLARK
CERTIFICATE OF DEPOSIT By: M.B. Burton, cashier

Figure 30-4
This one-year certificate of deposit obligates The Bank of Lewis and Clark to pay Kimberly H. Crowson $10,000 plus 7 percent interest.

ASSESS

Learning Objective 2 Collect and bring to class brochures from commercial banks, S&Ls, and other financial institutions advertising their CDs. Duplicate sufficient copies so that each student has a copy of at least one of the samples. Have students read the brochures carefully, then review the information on CDs on pp. 604–605. Have students highlight the information from the text on each example, such as deposit terms, penalties, rates of interest, maturity dates, and so on.

it, and (3) because of the interest penalty for early withdrawal, an incentive to save money until it is really needed.

WHAT SPECIALIZED FORMS OF COMMERCIAL PAPER ARE AVAILABLE?

PROBLEM

Dr. Sydney Pugh, of Santa Ana, California, needed expensive drugs to treat a patient with a rare nerve disease. Drugtek, the supplier of the drug, was a New York corporation. It would not ship COD, extend credit, or accept personal checks from customers outside the state. What other means of payment could Dr. Pugh use to satisfy Drugtek?

The four types of commercial paper described in the previous sections are the most frequently used. However, certain forms of commercial paper are available to meet specialized needs. Typically, these forms provide for an extremely safe, noncash means of transfer of monetary value. Specialized forms that meet this need include those described in the following sections.

1. Certified Checks

A person offered a personal check as payment may fear the bank will not honor the check because of insufficient funds in the drawer's account. But if the bank has already agreed to pay the check, only if the bank fails will the payee or current owner of the check not receive the money due. A personal check that has been accepted by a bank before payment is a **certified check.** At the time of certification, the bank draws funds from the depositor's account and sets them aside in a special account in order to pay the check when it is presented. In addition, the bank marks the front of the check with either the word "accepted" or "certified," along with the date and an authorized signature of the bank. In the problem, Dr. Pugh could use a certified check if Drugtek will accept it.

2. Cashier's Checks

A check that a bank draws on itself is a **cashier's check** (see Figure 30-5). Banks use such checks to pay their own obligations. They also may be purchased from a bank by persons who wish to pay others but who do not have checking accounts or find it impractical to use their personal checks. Because it is relatively risk-free (since only the bank may stop payment on the

TEACH

Tell students that, in addition to the four types of frequently used commercial paper described on pp. 598–605, five other forms of commercial paper are designed to meet specialized needs. They provide for safe, noncash means of transfer of monetary value. Write on the chalkboard, define, and explain a **certified check, cashier's check, bank draft, money order,** and **traveler's check.**

APPLY

Before displaying the overhead transparency, *One Solution to Chapter Opening Teaser 1*, cover the sentence under the check with masking tape or a strip of paper. Ask: **What type of commercial paper is shown here?** (Certified check) **How does an employee at Dan's Bargain Rack know that the company will receive the $385 that Felicia Harms owes?** (The money has already been withdrawn from Harms' account and held to pay the check when it is cashed.)

Guided Practice

RETEACH

Have students create newspaper ads, using a computer, if possible, for a bank offering CDs, explaining why they are worthwhile investments.

ENRICH

In small groups, have students identify and poll local banks, savings and loans, or other institutions for their current rates of interest on certificates of deposit. Have them prepare charts or graphs, using a spreadsheet or graphing program, if possible, to present their finding of the best choice to the class.

Thinking Critically Through Visuals

A cashier's check is relatively risk-free since only the bank may stop payment on the check. Who is the party ordered to pay the check? (First State Security Bank) **Who is ordering the payment to be made?** (Martha C. Todd) **To whom is the check made payable?** (Drugtek) **Why would Dr. Pugh use a cashier's check to pay Drugtek?** (Drugtek may want to know that such a large sum is available in the account.)

Bring to class multiple photocopies of cashier's checks, bank drafts, money orders, or traveler's checks with SAMPLE written across them. Divide students into pairs and distribute one sample of each of the four specialized forms of commercial paper to each. Have one student role-play a banker and the partner role-play someone who wants to obtain a money order, bank draft, certified check, cashier's check, or traveler's check. After playing out each transaction, have students exchange roles. Correct misconceptions before proceeding with the lesson.

Independent Practice

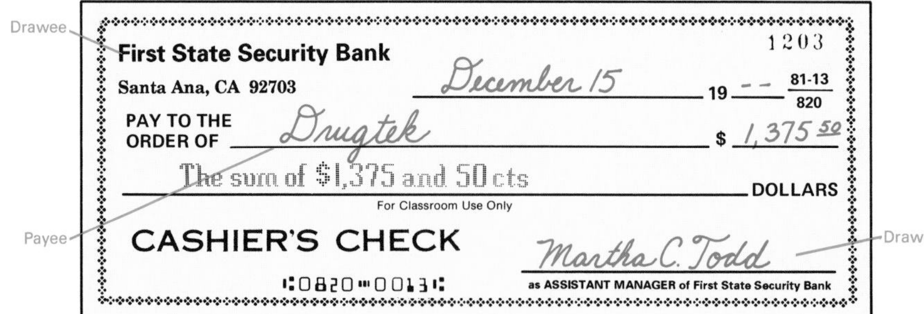

Drawee
First State Security Bank
Santa Ana, CA 92703
1203
December 15
19 - -
81-13
820
PAY TO THE ORDER OF
Drugtek
$ 1,375 50
The sum of $1,375 and 50 cts
DOLLARS
For Classroom Use Only
Payee
CASHIER'S CHECK
Martha C. Todd
Drawer
as ASSISTANT MANAGER of First State Security Bank

Figure 30-5
A cashier's check made out in favor of Drugtek by an official of the First State Security Bank to pay for the medicine Dr. Pugh needs. Dr. Pugh must pay First State Security Bank a service charge and the amount of the check.

check), a payee is usually willing to take such a check. This could be the most appropriate type of check for Dr. Pugh.

3. Bank Drafts

A draft drawn by a bank on funds that it has on deposit at another bank is a **bank draft.** Such a document is a draft drawn by one bank on a second bank. Individuals and business firms may also use these instruments when a substantial sum is involved. The purchase of such a draft is another possibility open to Dr. Pugh.

4. Money Orders

Money orders are often used by persons who do not have checking accounts. A **money order** is a draft issued by a post office, bank, express company, or telegraph company for use in paying or transferring funds for the purchaser. For example, a money order purchased at one post office orders the post office in the hometown of the payee to make payment. A money order could also be used by Dr. Pugh.

5. Traveler's Checks

Travelers are rightfully wary of carrying a lot of cash. Retailers and hotelkeepers worldwide are understandably reluctant to take checks from people from other regions and even other countries. The traveler's check was devised to overcome these problems and meet the needs of both groups. A **traveler's check** is a draft drawn by a well-known financial institution on itself or its agent. When purchased, traveler's checks are signed by the buyer. Later, when they are used to pay for a purchase, the traveler writes in the name of the payee and then signs again, in the presence of the payee. The payee then deposits and collects the traveler's check in the same manner as other checks. The payee's ability to compare the two signatures, coupled with the reputation of the financial institution that issued the instrument,

ASSESS

As a group, have students use the chalkboard, a flip chart, or an overhead transparency to create a fishbone map to visually illustrate the five key specialized forms of commercial paper. After checking the accuracy of the information, have students copy the organizer into their notebooks.

usually reduces the risk to the point where businesses worldwide accept traveler's checks.

Preventing Legal Difficulties

1. Prepare commercial paper accurately and handle it with care knowing it has significant value. Be sure you do not leave enough blank space for someone to insert figures and words that would change the face amount of the instrument.
2. If you lend money, get a promissory note made out in your favor in return. If practical, ask for security for the loan and clearly identify the collateral on the face of the instrument.
3. Use traveler's checks and credit cards on long trips. Do not carry a lot of cash.
4. Never sign a blank piece of commercial paper. Take care not to let your blank checks be stolen. Your negligence may render you liable for any forgeries that consequently occur.
5. Remember that an oral stop payment order is good for only fourteen days unless confirmed in writing. A written stop payment order is good for six months and can be renewed.

Thinking Critically Through Visuals

The tourists in the photograph are paying the entrance fee to a state park. What type of commercial paper does the evidence lead you to believe they are using to pay? (Traveler's check)

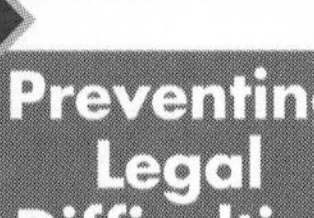

Preventing Legal Difficulties

Divide the class into five groups. Assign each group one of the items in this section. The groups may pick one of the following methods to present the advice—cartoons, poetry, rap, or posters. Display work on a bulletin board titled *Preventing Legal Difficulties When Using Commercial Paper.*

RETEACH Have students take out the fishbone map they completed in the previous ASSESS activity. Ask them to add horizontal lines to each branch of the map, and add examples of each of the five specialized forms of commercial paper.

ENRICH Have students create posters to hang in a local bank or travel agency to advertise the benefits of traveler's checks. Have students include, at minimum, the advantages of traveler's checks, the process for acquiring and using them, and the advantages of this type of commercial paper over cash.

▼ CLOSE

Divide the class into two groups to debate whether society will rely more on commercial paper, cash, or other means, such as electronic mail, to pay bills in the future.

Assign the following end-of-chapter materials:
Student text review activities, pp. 608–613
Workbook, pp. 93–94
Chapter Test

Chapter *MicroExam*

Strengthening Your Legal Vocabulary

1 traveler's check
2 drawee
3 maker
4 promissory note
5 drawer
6 check
7 payee
8 commercial paper
9 acceptance
10 honor

▼ REVIEWING IMPORTANT POINTS

1 Commercial paper was developed hundreds of years ago to serve as a safer, more convenient substitute for precious metals and currency.

2 There are four important types of commercial paper: (a) drafts, (b) checks (a special type of draft), (c) promissory notes, and (d) certificates of deposit (CDs).

3 Drafts, including checks, are unconditional *orders* by one party to another party to pay money on demand or at a specified future time to a third party. Initially, three parties are involved: the drawer, who gives the order to pay; the drawee, who is so ordered; and the payee, to whom payment is to be made.

4 A check is a special type of draft in that
a. the drawee of a check is always a bank,
b. a check is drawn against funds the drawer has on deposit in the bank, and
c. a check is always payable on demand.

5 Promissory notes and certificates of deposit are unconditional *promises* to pay money on demand or at a definite time in the future. Initially, two parties are involved in notes and CDs: the maker, who promises to pay; and the payee, to whom payment is promised.

▼ STRENGTHENING YOUR LEGAL VOCABULARY

Match each term with the statement that best defines that term. Some terms may not be used.

acceptance
bank draft
cashier's check
certificate of deposit
certified check
check
collateral note
comakers
commercial paper
dishonor
draft
drawee
drawer
honor
maker
money order
mortgage note
payee
promissory note
sight draft
stop payment order
time draft
traveler's check

1 Check drawn by a financial institution on itself and then sold to a person who signs it at the time of issue and at the time of use.

2 Party ordered by the drawer to pay a draft.

3 Party who executes a promissory note.

4 Unconditional written promise by a party to pay money to the order of another or to the bearer of the instrument on demand or at a definite future time.

5 One who executes a check.

6 A special form of draft by which a depositor orders his or her bank to pay money according to the terms of the instrument.

7 Party to whom a promissory note, check, or other commercial paper is made payable.

8 An unconditional written order or promise to pay money.

9 Drawee's promise to pay a draft when due.

10 To pay an instrument when due.

APPLYING LAW TO EVERYDAY LIFE

1 Joseph McReynolds gave the following signed instrument to Helen Harrison after borrowing $5,000 from her: "This acknowledges my legal duty to pay Helen Harrison $5,000." It was dated and signed by McReynolds. Is the instrument commercial paper?

2 Briering executed the following commercial paper. Identify the type of paper and the legal title of the parties involved.

Portland, Maine
June 1, 19--

On September 1, 19--, I promise to pay to the order of J. Cameron Curtis one thousand dollars ($1,000).

Anna C. Briering

Anna C. Briering

For Classroom Use Only

3 Thompson executed the commercial paper at the top of page 610. Identify the type of paper and the legal title of the parties to it. Under what circumstances would Calhoun be legally obligated to pay the amount as ordered?

Applying Law to Everyday Life

1 No, it is merely the acknowledgment of a debt without a promise or order to repay. (pp. 599–600)

2 It is a promissory note. Briering is the maker and Curtis is the payee. (p. 603)

3 It is a time draft. Thompson is the drawer, Calhoun is the drawee, and Clifford is the payee. (p. 601) Calhoun will not have any obligation to pay the instrument until she signs the face of it and indicates her acceptance. (p. 601)

4 It is a check. Edwards is the drawer, the Mother Lode Mining & Refining Bank is the drawee, and Cruzan is the payee. (pp. 601–602)
5 Chen could send a cashier's check or a money order. (pp. 605, 606)
6 No; The written stop payment order was good for only six months. (p. 602)
7 **(a)** A collateral note will be used. (p. 603) **(b)** A mortgage note will be used. (pp. 603–604)

Chattanooga, Tennessee
January 15, 19--

Thirty days after date, pay to the order of Corita J. Clifford the sum of fifteen hundred dollars ($1,500) with interest at the rate of seven (7) percent per year.

To: T.C. Calhoun
15 Mountain View Road
Asheville, North Carolina

Walter Thompson
Walter Thompson

For Classroom Use Only

4 Edwards executed the following commercial paper. Identify the type of paper and the legal title of the parties to it.

Mother Lode Mining & Refining Bank
Fairbanks, Alaska

No. 8116
89-73/1252

November 15, 19--

Pay to the Order of Tommy Cruzan $ 300.00

Three hundred and no/100 Dollars

For Classroom Use Only

Anton Edwards

⑆1252⑈0073⑆ 4156⑈2222⑈

5 Chen wanted to order skis that she had seen advertised in a national magazine. The advertisement expressly said, "Do not send cash or personal checks. No COD orders accepted." How could Chen pay?

6 Rivera ordered by mail a programmable electronic doorbell for her townhouse. She paid with a personal check. When the doorbell arrived, it would not work. Rivera immediately called the bank and told it to stop payment on her check. She then shipped the doorbell back to the seller. The next day, she confirmed the stop payment order in writing. Seven months later the seller sent her check through the interbank collection process, and Rivera's bank paid it. Rivera is furious and demands that the bank recredit her account for the amount that was paid in spite of her stop payment order. Must the bank do so?

7 Thruster owns Discovery Electronic Works, a small company that manufactures portable computers. The company is doing well but needs to

expand and update its product line. Thruster plans to use credit to do both. What specific types of commercial paper will be used if:

a. Discovery Electronic Works borrows $15,000 out of the $20,000 needed to pay for a shipment of integrated circuit chips and uses the chips as security for payment?

b. Discovery Electronic Works borrows $65,000 out of the $100,000 needed to buy a building in which a new assembly line is to be housed and uses the real property as security for payment?

8 ETHICS ISSUE You are working as a checkout clerk at Surprise Discount, Inc., a local department store. Sarah Johnson, an elderly lady, comes through your line with what she describes as "the perfect gift for my great-grandson." She says that she never expected to find it for under $200 much less the $110 that it is marked at. She writes out a check for the purchase. After she has left the store, you realize that she has written the check for $15.50 rather than the $115.50 purchase price plus tax. However, there is plenty of room to alter the amount to the correct figure. Should you do so?

9 Marianne Sawyer is getting ready for a European vacation. Because she has a history of financial problems, she has been unable to get a credit card. How would you advise her to carry the cash she must take on the trip?

10 ETHICS ISSUE You loaned Deane Trenton, a single parent of four children, $5,000 last year at this time. To be sure he could repay you, you took an interest in his car as security and had him sign a promissory note to that effect. The note came due today, and he has just told you he cannot pay for at least six months. You know he needs the car to drive to work and to transport his family. Should you exercise your right to have the car sold to pay off the loan?

▼ SOLVING CASE PROBLEMS

1 While in Shreveport, Louisiana, Claypool wanted to play poker for money stakes at the Crystal Bar. He persuaded Parker to stand good (i.e., pay) for any losses he might have. Before the night was over, Claypool's losses amounted to $6,000. Afterwards, Claypool gave Parker a promissory note for $10,473.14 to cover the $6,000 in gambling losses and a legitimate previous loan. When the note came due, Claypool refused to pay. Parker sued, and Claypool defended on the grounds that

8  No; Ethics would preclude such an alteration. As a universal rule, it would be unacceptable. (A replica of the check as originally drawn by Sarah Johnson is at the top of p. 93 of the Workbook.)

9 Traveler's checks, purchased from a local financial institution, would be the best solution. (p. 606)

10 ETHICS ISSUE Answers to this question will vary. Legally, you have the right to have the car sold and thereby recoup the money plus interest. Ethically, some people would have a problem deciding what to do, especially if they need the money Deane owes. Probably the most ethical solution would be to try and renegotiate the loan, if in fact you do not have an urgent and valid need for the money.

Solving Case Problems

1. No; Parker's claim is barred due to the illegal $6,000 portion. Some states might allow the legitimate claim on which to collect the remainder, but this is not likely. (p. 598)
2. No; The instruments were conditional, and, therefore, could not be commercial paper. (p. 598)
3. The bank must pay Lai. A cashier's check is drawn by a bank on itself, so the bank is obligated to pay the holder on demand. Cashier's checks circulate as equivalents of cash because banks stand behind them. To allow a bank to stop payment under such circumstances would greatly limit the usefulness of cashier's checks as substitutes for cash. Gunn's remedy is to sue Tak. (pp. 605–606)
4. For Kleen; The Missouri Supreme Court held that the instrument was not by law a "check" until it contained a certain sum. As a consequence, the alleged illegal act of issuing the check occurred in Tennessee where the check was filled out. (pp. 601–602)

the note was illegal and void, since it originated in a gambling debt. Will Parker recover? (*Parker v. Claypool*, 78 So. 2d 124)

2. Purchasers of land developed by Holiday Interval, Inc., signed writings in which they promised to pay a certain sum of money at a definite time in the future. However, according to the signed instruments, the payments were due only if specified structures were built in the complex within two years of the signings. Some of these instruments were labeled "promissory note." Were any of the writings commercial paper? (*In re Holiday Interval, Inc.*, 94 Bankr. 594)

3. Gunn contracted to sell Tak, a broker from Hong Kong, 60,000 metric tons of UREA, a fertilizer, at $400 a ton. In connection with this $24-million sale, Gunn entered another contract agreeing to pay Tak a commission for all Tak's sales of the fertilizer. After 10,000 tons of UREA had been sold, paid for, and delivered, Gunn bought and delivered to Tak a cashier's check from the Empire Bank of Springfield for $150,000 payable to Tak's order. Shortly after, Gunn learned that the balance of the order for the remaining 50,000 tons of UREA had been canceled by Tak. Consequently, Gunn went to court and obtained an injunction from the court to the bank to stop payment on the cashier's check. Shortly after the court acted, the cashier's check was transferred by Tak to Lai, who now claims the right to collect the face amount. Should the court order the bank to honor the stop payment order, or must the bank pay Lai the face amount of the check? (*Lai v. Powell, Judge*, 536 S.W.2d 14)

4. In a Missouri circuit court, Kleen was convicted of issuing an insufficient funds check. He appealed, pointing out that he had merely signed a blank check form in Missouri and then given the form to his truck driver. The truck driver carried the signed blank check form to Memphis, Tennessee, where someone at the Herring Sales Company filled in the company name as the payee and also filled in the amount. Herring kept the check in return for a truckload of meal that was transported by Kleen's truck and driver back to Kleen's business in Nevada, Missouri. Kleen therefore contended that even though the check was drawn on the Citizen's Bank of Nevada, the alleged criminal act occurred in Tennessee, where the signed blank form was made a check and was issued. Consequently, Missouri had no jurisdiction, and his conviction should be overturned. You decide. (*State v. Kleen*, 491 S.W.2d 244)

5 Henry Thomas purchased a new car on October 22 and gave Frazier Buick Company a check for the full amount. The company then signed over the certificate of title to Thomas. Unfortunately, Thomas died the next day, and Frazier Buick immediately repossessed the car without cashing the check. The administratrix of Thomas's estate then sued the company on behalf of the estate for $500 actual damages, since she "had [the car] sold" for $500 above the price Thomas had paid for it at Frazier Buick. She also asked for $2,500 in punitive damages for the company's abrupt and insensitive action in repossessing the car. Will the estate recover? (*Hickerson v. Con Frazier Buick Company*, 264 S.W.2d 29)

5 No; The court held for Frazier Buick Co. The acceptance of the check was for convenience but, until the check was honored, the debt was still outstanding. Therefore, Thomas had not paid for the car and the company could repossess the vehicle. (p. 602)

CHAPTER 31 ORGANIZER

Chapter Theme

Negotiability of commercial paper—and requirements for such transactions—are regulated by law.

DIRECTED STUDY QUESTIONS	SPECIAL FEATURES	PROGRAM RESOURCES				
		Reteach	Enrich	SN	AM	
What is negotiation and why is it so important?	Personal Perspectives, p. 616 Writing Connections, p. 617	✔	✔			
What is required to make a written instrument negotiable?	Multicultural Highlights, p. 620	✔	✔	✔	K	
How is commercial paper transferred?	Thinking Critically Through Visuals, p. 622	✔	✔		V A	
What are the kinds and respective legal effects of indorsements?	Thinking Critically Through Visuals, pp. 623, 625 Ethics Issue, p. 624	✔	✔			
What is an accomodation party?	Personal Perspectives, p. 626 Preventing Legal Difficulties, p. 627	✔	✔			

Additional Resources

- Smith, Brian W. and Puleo, Frank C. *Banking Law and Regulation.* NY: Practicing Law Institute, 1987.
- Wells, Jean F. *Banks and Thrifts in Transition.* Washington DC.: Congressional Research Service, Library of Congress, 1991.
- White, James J., and Summers, Robert S. *White and Summer's Hornbook on the Uniform Commercial Code,* 3d ed. St. Paul, MN: West Publishing Co., 1988.

One-semester course	✔	✔						
One-year course	✔	✔	✔	✔				

		ASSESSMENT OPPORTUNITIES			
	Cooperative Learning	**Informal Assessment**	**Chapter Review**	**Chapter Test**	**Chapter *MicroExam*** (Media)
		✔	✔	✔	✔
		✔	✔	✔	✔
		✔	✔	✔	✔
	✔	✔	✔	✔	✔
		✔	✔	✔	✔

Videodiscs
Proper Indorsement
Search Chapter 38, Play To 39

State by State

In approximately 20 states, the negotiability of an instrument is still maintained if the word "order" is omitted from the check. In the other states, "pay to the <u>order</u> of" must appear.

Teaching Materials

Student text, pp. 614–631

Overhead transparency masters
- *The Requirements of Negotiability*
- *The Various Types of Indorsements*

Videos
Law for Business Videodisc

Workbook, pp. 95–96

Outside Resources
- Blank overhead transparencies
- Flip chart
- Poster board
- Samples of blank commercial papers
- Art supplies: drawing paper & markers

- Tape recorder
- Camcorder
- VCR

Assessment
- Chapter Test

- Chapter *MicroExam*

Vocabulary

negotiable, p. 616
negotiation, p. 616
antedated, p. 617
postdated, p. 617
money, p. 619
acceleration clause, p. 620
payable on demand, p. 620
payable at a definite time, p. 620
bearer paper, p. 621
bearer, p. 621
order paper, p. 621
indorsement, p. 622
indorser, p. 622
indorsee, p. 622
holder, p. 622
blank indorsement, p. 623
special indorsement, p. 624
qualified indorsement, p. 625
unqualified indorsement, p. 625
restrictive indorsement, p. 626
accommodation party, p. 627

Learning Objectives

When you complete this chapter, you will be able to

1. Understand the importance of negotiation in reducing the risks associated with commercial paper.
2. Determine whether an instrument is negotiable.
3. Know how to transfer a negotiable piece of commercial paper correctly.
4. Competently select the proper indorsement to use in such transfers.

614

Chapter Self-Test

Assess students' understanding of negotiability before they begin Chapter 31 by asking them to respond orally to the following *True* or *False* statements: **(1) Commercial paper is a conditional written order or promise to pay money.** (False; It is unconditional.); **(2) Businesses that accept negotiable commercial paper are not protected.** (False; The UCC provides assurance.); and **(3) Bearer paper and order paper both need to be indorsed to be transferred.** (False; Bearer paper can be negotiated by delivery alone; order paper must be indorsed.)

CHAPTER

31 NEGOTIABILITY

1 Your friend wants to buy a car but his credit rating is poor. He asks you to cosign the note with him so that the transaction will go through. If you do so, could you later be required to pay the full amount of the note?

2 On April Fool's Day, a friend gives you a $25 check that she has deliberately antedated to April 1 of the previous year. If she has adequate funds in her account when you present the check, can you still collect on it?

3 ETHICS ISSUE On August 7, you sell your car to pay for your college tuition. The buyer asks that you not cash the payoff check until his payday on the first of September, since he needs the money in his account for family expenses. You promise not to cash it, but when you go to register for classes you find that the tuition amount must be paid immediately or else you cannot enroll. Your only source of funds is the check, and you did tell the buyer that the money was to go for your tuition. You know that according to the law, a check is a demand instrument. Should you cash it?

Thinking Critically Through Visuals

This photograph shows workers getting paid by check instead of cash. Could these workers, in turn, use the check, instead of cash, to purchase something? (Yes, checks are negotiable.)

FOCUS

Before class begins, list on the chalkboard a variety of consumer products. Include both inexpensive personal items, (pack of gum, magazine) moderately priced items, (compact disc, costume jewelry) and major purchases (condominium, car). List a number of items equal to the number of students in the class. As students enter the classroom, have them write an estimated price beside an item without a price.

Ask**: Based solely on the prices of each item, which would most likely be paid for by cash?** (Lower priced items) **How might consumers pay for the other products?** (Answers may include with commercial paper, such as personal checks, or by credit card.) Point out that if commercial paper is to be accepted, the person or business receiving it must be assured that there is a strong chance the instrument will be paid, and that negotiability provides that assurance.

You Decide

1 Yes; If the friend fails to pay when the note comes due, you could be required to pay it. You could then seek reimbursement from your friend, but there is no guarantee that your friend can, or will, pay you.

2 Yes; Antedating the check does not destroy its negotiability.

3 ETHICS ISSUE Legally, yes; The law of commercial paper would support the cashing of the check. Ethically, however, putting your interests ahead of those of the buyer and his family seems improper, especially after having given your word that you would wait until the first of September to cash it.

WHAT IS NEGOTIATION AND WHY IS IT SO IMPORTANT?

PROBLEM

Montez was preparing to open her new business, a hobby store. However, in talking with her accountant, Montez indicated that she wanted to do business on a cash-only basis because taking checks or promissory notes is too risky. Is this advisable?

If commercial paper is to be accepted instead of cash, the person or business firm receiving it must be assured that there is a strong chance the instrument will be paid. Today, the Uniform Commercial Code (UCC) provides that assurance. To do this, the UCC empowers a qualified owner of commercial paper to overcome many of the legal defenses the person who is obligated to pay the instrument might raise to keep from paying.

Grayson bought a used four-wheel drive vehicle for his canoe rental business. As payment, Grayson signed a $4,000 promissory note. The seller, Dandy Dan's Pre-owned Cars, sold the note to a bank for $3,500. Grayson had driven the vehicle less than 100 miles when the transmission locked and had to be replaced at a cost of $1,700. When Grayson tried to contact Dandy Dan to complain, he found the dealer had gone out of business and disappeared. A few months later, when the bank demanded the $4,000 in payment of the note, Grayson raised the defense of the failed transmission and offered to pay only the $2,300 difference. Using the powers given to it by the UCC, the bank was able to take Grayson to court and collect the full $4,000.

To enable an obligee to overcome most common defenses and collect on commercial paper (as the bank did on Grayson's note), the promise or order to pay money must be negotiable. **Negotiable** means that it must be in writing, contain an unconditional promise or order payable in a sum certain, be payable on demand or at a definite time, and be payable to the bearer or to someone's order. These requirements are prescribed by statute and are discussed in the following section. Realize that an instrument must be negotiable in order to be classified as commercial paper. In addition, the instrument with the promise or order to pay money must be acquired in the correct manner by the party trying to collect on it. This **negotiation** means the proper transfer of negotiable instruments so that the person receiving the instrument has the power to collect on it by overcoming certain de-

TEACH

Define the terms **negotiable** and **negotiation**. Stress that an instrument must be negotiable to classify as commercial paper and it must be acquired in the correct manner by the party trying to collect on it. Have students note that if commercial paper is not negotiated, it is considered to have been only assigned.

APPLY

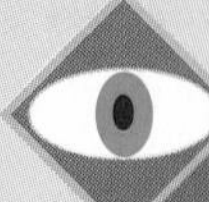

Personal Perspectives

Have the whole class brainstorm and create a list of different situations in which commercial paper might be issued or received instead of cash, such as checks used to pay household bills. If any students have been involved in personal situations involving the transfer of commercial paper, have them share their experiences. **Guided Practice**

ASSESS

Learning Objective 1 Have students respond orally to the following *True* or *False* statements: **(1) *Negotiation* means the proper transfer of a negotiable instrument.** (True); **(2) Negotiable paper is legally transferable to another person.** (True); **(3) Commercial paper must be negotiated and cannot be assigned.** (False); and **(4) The UCC protects people who accept commercial paper.** (True) fenses of the person who must pay it off. Negotiation is discussed in detail later in this chapter.

In the problem, Montez would probably be advised by the accountant that significant protection would be afforded her by the UCC if she were to take properly transferred negotiable instruments. Such protection would drastically reduce the risk of not being able to collect. Refusing to accept commercial paper would probably mean losing customers because they would be denied the safety and convenience of using checks and notes in her store. Also, if commercial paper is not negotiated, it is considered to have been only assigned, as was discussed in Chapter 14. An assignee may still collect in full on commercial paper that is only transferred by assignment unless a valid defense prevents it.

WHAT IS REQUIRED TO MAKE A WRITTEN INSTRUMENT NEGOTIABLE?

PROBLEM

Because he had to sign more than 3,000 company documents each week, Bill Capeci, the company president, had a rubber stamp made that read "Downtown Furniture Factory by Bill Capeci, President." Thereafter, he even used this stamp to sign the company's payroll checks. Is such a practice legal?

According to the UCC, whether an instrument is negotiable is determined by what appears on its face at the time it is issued. In particular, the instrument must:

1. be in writing and be signed by the maker or drawer,
2. contain an unconditional promise or order,
3. be payable in a sum certain in money,
4. be payable on demand or at a definite time, and
5. be payable to the bearer or to someone's order.

Negotiability does not require that the instrument state that something of value has been given for the paper. But identifying such value given is often a good idea and will not defeat negotiability. Likewise, the ability to negotiate (but not the ability to collect on) an instrument is not affected by the fact that it is **antedated** (i.e., dated earlier than the date of issuance), **postdated** (i.e., dated later than the date of issuance), or even undated. If a

Writing Connections

Language Arts
Have students assume the role of a financial advisor who writes a column for the business section of your local newspaper. Have them write, using a computer, if possible, an editorial advising small business owners of the pros and cons of operating on a cash-only basis. Have students exchange papers and write a rebuttal to the editorial.

Independent Practice

TEACH

Explain to students that an instrument is determined to be negotiable by what appears on its face at the time it is issued. To graphically illustrate the five requirements of negotiability, display, or rewrite on the chalkboard, the graphic organizer you created in the previous TEACH section. Then draw spokes branching off the main spokes and add examples and vocabulary words to clarify each requirement. Include the vocabulary terms in boldface on pp. 618–621. Explain what negotiability does not require. Make sure students understand the terms *antedated* and *postdated.*

RETEACH Have students make a poster to show what makes commercial paper negotiable. Display students' work in your classroom.

ENRICH Have students role play or discuss various business transactions involving commercial paper instead of cash. Have the person offering the paper and the person accepting the paper each describe what they are doing and why. For example, "I am agreeing to allow my bank to withdraw money from my account in this amount in exchange for this check."

▼ APPLY

In order to help limited English proficient students understand the terms *antedated* and *postdated,* write the prefixes *ante-* and *post-* on the chalkboard. Have student volunteers look up the two prefixes in the dictionary. (*Ante-* means previous to; *post-* means after in time.) Provide examples of other words that use the same prefix, then have students define each word and use it correctly in a sentence. Correct misconceptions and mispronunciations.

Guided Practice

Distribute to students blank sample copies of various forms of commercial paper on which you have written **SAMPLE** in large letters. Have students complete the forms, incorporating defects that would make each one non-negotiable. Have students exchange papers and circle the sections that make the commercial paper non-negotiable. **Independent Practice**

date is not present, it may be entered by any owner who has possession and who knows the date on which the paper was issued.

Now, let us look at each of the requirements of negotiability in detail.

1. A Writing Signed by the Maker or Drawer

To be negotiable, commercial paper must be in writing and signed by the maker or drawer with the intent that it create a legal obligation. Because of the writing, commercial paper is subject to the parol evidence rule (see Chapter 13) when its terms are challenged at law. However, oral evidence may be utilized to show failure of consideration or breach of contract.

The writing may consist of a printed form with the terms typed or written in. In the alternative, the paper may be totally handwritten. The law is very flexible in this regard. An ink pen, a typewriter, even a pencil may be used, although a pencil is not recommended because it invites alteration. Any medium is satisfactory as a writing surface as long as the result is recognizable as a writing.

If there are conflicting terms within the writing, those written in by hand prevail over both typewritten and printed form terms. Similarly, typewritten terms prevail over printed form terms. In addition, an amount expressed in words prevails over an amount expressed in figures.

C.W. Bean wrote a check payable to Christopher John for the full purchase price of John's used pickup. Bean put "$7,500" in numerals on the payee line for the amount of the check but wrote out "seven thousand eight hundred dollars" below it. If no other evidence were presented as to the sale price, the court would hold the check enforceable for the latter amount as it was written out and therefore more deliberately set down.

As far as the signature is concerned, the form it takes does not alter its legal effectiveness as long as the writer intended for it to be his or her signature. For example, a legally effective signature may be made with a rubber stamp, as in the problem.

A trade or assumed name may be used in signing if it is intended as one's signature. Chris Kringle's Christmas Tree Company would be an example. Also one person may legitimately sign another person's name if authorized to do so as an agent (see Chapter 25). Any individual who is unable to write her or his name because of illiteracy or a physical handicap may sign with a mark, typically an X. It is an advisable practice to have another person then insert the name of the signer next to the mark and sign as a witness.

▼ ASSESS

Learning Objective 2 Ask students to respond orally to the following questions: **(1) Which of the following signatures meet the requirement of negotiability? Handwritten, a rubber stamp, signed by an authorized agent, or an "X" made by someone unable to write** (All); and **(2) Does the following promise to pay meet the requirements of negotiability: I will pay you $75 as soon as I sell my bike? Why or why not?** (No; It is a conditional promise, not an unconditional one.)

The location of the signature is generally immaterial as long as it appears somewhere on the face of the instrument. Thus, the signature may appear anywhere in the body of the instrument as long as the signer's status as maker or drawer is clear.

2. An Unconditional Promise or Order

To be negotiable, a promissory note or a certificate of deposit must contain an unconditional promise to pay money. Similarly, a check or a draft must contain an unconditional order to pay money. Simply acknowledging a debt as in "I owe you $100" is not enough, because there is nothing in such a statement to indicate the money will ever be repaid. The use of the word "unconditional" means that the promise or order to pay money must be absolute, that is, free of any limits or restrictions. "I promise to pay Ann Kiersten $1,000 if my mare foals in the next year" would be conditional upon an event that might not occur; therefore, the instrument that included the statement would not be negotiable.

Likewise, to promise payment out of a certain fund or account "only" or to make payment subject to another agreement would make the obligation conditional on enough money being in the account or on the agreement being properly performed. Such conditions would restrict the free flow of commercial paper by requiring a prospective purchaser of the paper to deal with the uncertainty that the condition might not have been satisfied and, therefore, that collection might not be legally possible. On the other hand, a phrase entitling the holder to reasonable attorney's fees upon default or enhancing the possibility of collection, such as "secured by a mortgage," would improve the potential for negotiation by reducing the uncertainty of collection.

Courteous or considerate language, such as "please pay to the order of" or listing the obligor's bank account number (without the word "only" following) for the convenience of others, does not affect negotiability. However, contrary to rules for privately issued instruments, checks of the government that are restricted to payment from one account (such as "pay out of social security account only") are still negotiable. Finally, instruments that merely acknowledge the source of the obligation, as in "pay to the order of Merrick Miller as per contract," are also negotiable.

3. Payable in a Sum Certain in Money

To be negotiable, commercial paper must call for the payment of a sum certain in money. **Money**, for this purpose, is any official currency or coin acceptable as a medium of exchange either in the United States or in any foreign country at the time the commercial paper is written. Thus, commercial paper that is collectible in the United States but that has the amount

On the chalkboard, draw the outline of the following chart, write the two column headings, and write the information in the first column.

Non-negotiable statement	Reason
"John, I owe you $20."	Nothing to indicate money will be repaid
"I promise to pay you $50 if your softball team makes it to the play-offs."	Conditional; event may never occur
"I will pay you $1,000 out of my savings account."	Conditional; enough money may not be in that account
"If Susan pays me the $500 she owes me, I'll give you the $300 that I owe you."	Conditional; payment subject to another agreement

Have students copy the chart in their notebooks. Ask them to write the reason why the statement is non-negotiable in the second column. Discuss students' answers.

Have students write both a conditional and an unconditional promise to repay a loan of $50 to a friend. Have students exchange papers and identify which promise is conditional and which is unconditional.

In a round-robin format, have the first student in the front row describe an unconditional or conditional promise. Have the next student identify whether it is conditional or unconditional. Correct any misconceptions. Continue until all students have either described or identified a promise.

Multicultural Highlights

To be negotiable, commercial paper must call for the payment of a sum of money. Some of the requirements of commercial paper apply to money, too. All U.S. dollars are signed by the maker, the U.S. Treasury Department. If you look at a dollar, you will see two signatures—those of the treasurer of the United States and the secretary of the treasury. Georgia Neese Clark, a European American, was the first woman to hold the "power of the pen" as treasurer of the United States. Clark was appointed by President Harry S. Truman in 1949. She led the way for many other women who would later serve in that capacity. Ask: **Who signed the currency now in your possession?**

expressed in an acceptable foreign currency is negotiable. Often, the foreign currency is simply changed into U.S. dollars on the day the paper is payable. However, if the paper requires that the foreign currency be used as the medium of payment, the commercial paper is payable in that currency.

Payment must be solely in money and not money plus another good or service. On the other hand, paper that gives the obligee (creditor) a choice of money or something else, for example, "I promise to pay to the order of Vera Spielman $10,000 or thirty-five ounces of gold at the obligee's option" would be negotiable, since the obligee could choose money as payment. If the choice to pay in money or a good or service was the obligor's (debtor's), the instrument is not negotiable because the obligor could choose to make payment in something other than money.

An instrument is still negotiable if it requires that the amount be paid:

a. with a fixed interest or discount, but not if the interest rate may vary in an indeterminate way (e.g., if the instrument reads "interest to be set at 2% plus prime bank rate" it is not negotiable);
b. by installment, perhaps with an **acceleration clause** that makes the entire balance due and payable upon the happening of a certain event (e.g., the obligor's default by missing an installment payment);
c. with bank charges for exchanging one national currency into another; or
d. with costs of collection and reasonable attorney's fees in case the paper is not paid.

In fact, most of these provisions usually tend to make the paper more attractive to prospective owners.

4. Payable on Demand or at a Definite Time

Negotiability also requires that an instrument be payable on demand or at a definite time. **Payable on demand** means that the commercial paper is written so as to be payable immediately upon presentment or at sight. If no time of payment is specified, an instrument is interpreted as being payable on demand.

Payable at a definite time means that the commercial paper is written payable on or before an identified calendar date. It is also acceptable for an instrument to be payable within a set period after an identified calendar date or a fixed period, such as ninety days, after sight. An instrument is not negotiable if it is payable at or after an event that is sure to occur but whose date cannot be determined beforehand. For example, a note payable "30 days after the death of Sam Larue" would not be negotiable. Such a promise might be honored by the person making it or it might be legally enforceable as part

ASSESS

Learning Objective 2 Have students answer *True* or *False* to the following statements. If the statement is false, ask students to change one word or phrase to make it true. **(1) Payable at a definite time means that the commercial paper is written so as to be payable immediately upon presentment or on sight.** (False/payable on demand); **(2) When commercial paper is made payable to the order of a specified payee, it is called bearer paper.** (False/order paper); and **(3) The party in possession of bearer paper is called the bearer.** (True) of a contract, but that has nothing to do with whether the instrument is commercial paper and can therefore be negotiated.

5. Payable to Bearer or to Someone's Order

The final requirement is that the paper contain the words of negotiability by being made payable to bearer or to a specified person's order. When commercial paper is made payable to bearer, that is in such a way as to make the paper legally collectible by the party in possession of it, it is referred to as **bearer paper.** The party in possession of bearer paper is called the **bearer**. To qualify as bearer paper, the face of a piece of commercial paper can read "pay to the order of bearer," "pay to bearer," "pay to (a named party) or bearer," "pay to cash," or any other way that does not identify a specific payee.

In contrast, when commercial paper is made payable to the order of a specified payee, it is called **order paper.** Such phrasing shows the intent of the maker or drawer to have the paper payable to the named payee or to anyone to whom the paper is subsequently negotiated by order of that payee. Order paper may read "pay to the order of Charles Blevins" or whatever specific party the maker or drawer intends. It may also read "pay to Charles Blevins or order." However, if it only reads "pay to Charles Blevins," it is not negotiable.

Order paper may be made payable to the order of more than one party. These parties can be named either jointly, such as "pay to the order of J. J. Adamson *and* Miller School" or, in the alternative, "pay to the order of Ashleigh Adamson *or* Greenwood School." In the former example, both parties have to sign the instrument to negotiate it further. In the latter example, either Ashleigh Adamson or Greenwood School acting alone can sign and cash it.

HOW IS COMMERCIAL PAPER TRANSFERRED?

PROBLEM

Rainqueest awakened one morning with a severe toothache. The pain was worse by noon, so she made an afternoon appointment with her dentist. When Rainqueest arrived at the dentist's office, the receptionist informed her that she still owed $175 for previous treatment. By coincidence, Rainqueest had with her a check made out to her order in that amount. Rainqueest gave it to the receptionist as payment. The receptionist examined it, then returned it to Rainqueest and asked her to sign the back. Is Rainqueest's signature necessary to transfer the check to the dentist?

Pair students. Provide pairs with drawing paper and markers. Ask them to choose an important point about the requirements of negotiability and create a graphic way of communicating that point. Students may create a chart, cartoon, flowchart, or other graphic element. Display students' work on

a bulletin board called *To Pay or Not to Pay?*

TEACH

Discuss the ways commercial paper is transferred. Make sure students understand that commercial paper is usually transferred by negotiation. Explain that to qualify as negotiation, commercial paper must be transferred properly. Discuss the proper transfer of order paper (through indorsement) and define **indorsement, indorser, indorsee,** and **holder.** Explain that bearer paper may be negotiated by delivery alone without indorsement.

RETEACH Before duplicating the overhead transparency master, *The Requirements of Negotiability*, cover the handwritten answers in sections 1–5. Distribute copies to students and ask them, in pairs, to fill in the answers. Uncover the masked-out sections and review students' responses.

ENRICH Have students create replica checks to illustrate: **payable on demand, payable at a definite time, bearer, bearer paper,** and **order paper.** Have students exchange checks and identify each as **negotiable** or **non-negotiable.**

▼ APPLY

Thinking Critically Through Visuals

This photograph of a gold certificate contains visible evidence of all five requirements of negotiability. Locate each. Ask: **Is this certificate payable on demand or at a certain time?** (On demand) **Is it bearer paper or order paper?** (Bearer paper)

On the chalkboard, draw two flowcharts—one showing the transfer of order paper and the other showing the transfer of bearer paper. As a whole-class activity, have volunteers go to the chalkboard and label a step until all steps are labeled. **Guided Practice**

Divide the class into groups of two or three. Have each group create and record public-service announcements (PSAs) for the radio that inform people about the importance of transferring commercial paper correctly and how to make that transfer. Play the tapes and have students comment on the information presented. **Independent Practice**

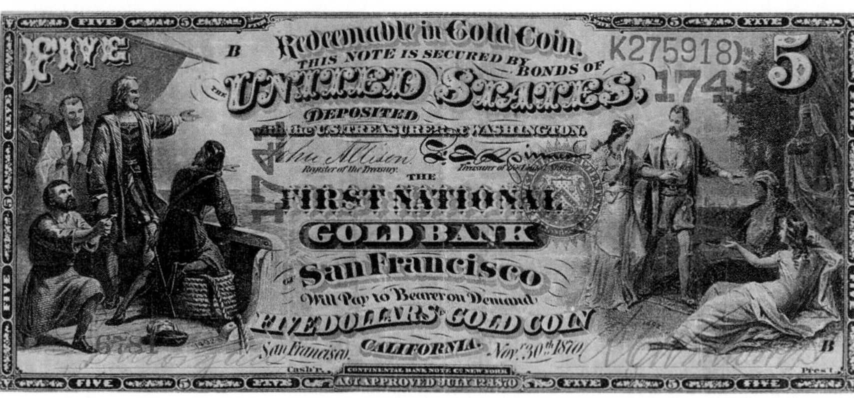

As mentioned previously, commercial paper is usually transferred by negotiation. Negotiation may give the transferee greater rights than if the paper is merely assigned. This is true because, in an assignment, the transferee receives only the rights of the transferor. In negotiation, the transferee, if qualified, may receive additional rights granted under the UCC. In particular, negotiation for value may be to a party who has no knowledge of defects in the original transaction in which the paper was created. This could give that innocent transferee the power to overcome many defenses against payment that the party obligated to pay might have otherwise used. These defenses include breach of contract and failure of consideration, which are explained in Chapter 32.

If the transfer of commercial paper does not qualify as a negotiation, it is legally considered as having been assigned. Therefore, it is critical to know the proper way to transfer commercial paper. Such proper method of transfer depends on whether the instrument is order or bearer paper.

If the instrument is order paper (i.e., payable to the order of a named person), the named person or her or his agent must sign the paper on its reverse side, as properly requested in the problem. Then the paper must be delivered to make the transfer complete and proper. Such a signature is termed an **indorsement**. An owner of commercial paper who signs on its reverse indorses the paper and is an **indorser**. The party to whom the paper is indorsed is the **indorsee**. A party who has physical possession of commercial paper that is payable to his or her order or who is in possession of bearer paper is a **holder**. Therefore, a bearer is a holder, as is a person in possession of paper payable to his or her order.

If the paper is bearer paper, it may be negotiated by delivery alone. The bearer may simply hand the paper to the transferee. Many transferees, however, will require the bearer to indorse the paper. This generally allows the

▼ ASSESS

Learning Objective 3 Have students respond orally to the following *True* or *False* statements: **(1) If the transfer of commercial paper does not qualify as a negotiation, it is legally considered to be assigned.** (True); **(2) Negotiation has no ability to give the transferee rights greater than those available if the paper is merely assigned.** (False); and **(3) Bearer paper may be negotiated by delivery alone.** (True) future holders to pursue the transferor for payment of the paper's value if there are problems collecting it from the maker or drawee.

WHAT ARE THE KINDS AND RESPECTIVE LEGAL EFFECTS OF INDORSEMENTS?

PROBLEM

Gordon Marshall paid his ex-wife, Gloria Marshall, her monthly alimony by indorsing a weekly paycheck with his name only and handing it to her. While shopping, Gloria had her purse stolen. The thief found the check and promptly bought goods with it at the Penny-Ante Quick Shoppe, which accepted it in good faith. Penny-Ante can legally collect on the check. What other kind of indorsement might have protected Gloria from this loss?

All indorsements are either blank or special. However, by the use of appropriate phrases, each of these two basic types may also be qualified and/or restricted in their effect.

1. Blank Indorsements

A **blank indorsement** consists of just the indorser's signature (see Figure 31-1[a]). Because it is quickly written, the blank indorsement is the most common. It does not specify a particular person to whom the paper is being transferred. Therefore, it transforms order paper into bearer paper, which even a finder or a thief may negotiate. A blank indorsement is satisfactory and safe for the indorser if (1) value is immediately received for it or (2) the paper is deposited in a bank at the time of indorsement.

(a)

Gordon Marshall

(b)

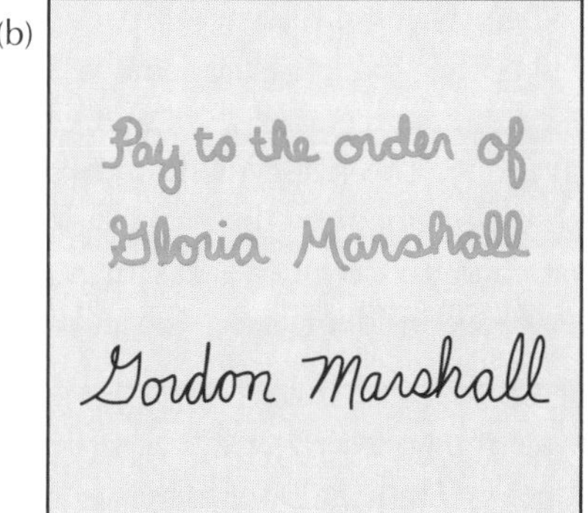

Figure 31-1
A blank indorsement (a) can be converted to a special indorsement (b) by adding the phrase "Pay to the order of . . ." above the indorsement.

TEACH

Display the overhead transparency, *The Various Types of Indorsements.* Discuss each type of indorsement: **blank, special, qualified,** and **restrictive.** Explain that all indorsements are either blank or special. By the use of appropriate phrases, either kind

can become qualified and/or restrictive.

APPLY

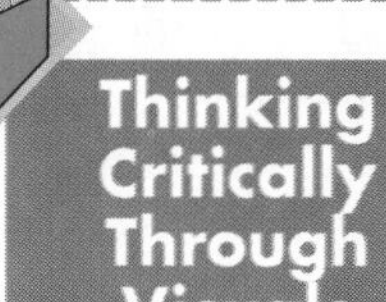

Figure (b) shows additions that convert a blank indorsement into a special indorsement. How could the indorsement shown in (a) be converted to a qualified indorsement? (Add the words "without recourse" over the indorsement.)

Draw a large four-column chart on the chalkboard. Label the columns in order as follows: **Types of Indorsement, Definition, What It Does,** and **Example.** Have students take turns filling out parts of the chart. **Guided Practice**

RETEACH In writing, have students explain the meanings of **indorsement, indorser, indorsee,** and **holder.** Then, have students use each word correctly in a sentence. Verify students' responses.

ENRICH Have students write, using a computer, if possible, two scenarios—one on bearer paper and the other on order paper—describing the steps in transferring each type of commercial paper. Have students exchange papers and label the type of commercial paper being transferred.

Ethics Issue

Read aloud the following scenario: **You and a friend are asked to buy materials for a class project. Instead of cash, your teacher gives you a check made out to her, which she had indorsed by signing her name on the back. Later, you decide to add the words, "pay to the order of" and your name above her indorsement. Your friend said changing indorsements is illegal. Was your friend right?** (No, what you did was legal. Ethically, you are not at fault unless you use your control of the check to gain power over your friend.)

Divide the class into groups of five or six. Assign the following roles: TV talk-show host to lead the presentation; script recorder to write the script; fact checker to check the script for accuracy; one or two TV talk-show guests to tell their experiences; and attorney/expert to give advice on negotiability. Have each group plan and videotape a talk-show segment that features the guests communicating their experiences with indorsements. Play the videotape and discuss.

Cooperative Learning

2. Special Indorsements

A **special indorsement** makes the paper payable to the order of a designated party. Recall that the words "Pay to the order of" must be used on the face of the instrument to achieve the same result. In an indorsement, the more concise wording "Pay to Gloria Marshall" is as effective as "Pay to the order of Gloria Marshall." The paper will be order paper as a result of either wording.

To be properly negotiated, order paper requires the signature of the party named in the indorsement. A forged signature used as an indorsement cannot pass title, so, unlike the situation with paper having a blank indorsement, a thief or a finder of the paper could not legally cash it.

The transferee who receives commercial paper with a blank indorsement may be protected by writing that the paper is payable to him or her above the indorser's signature. This is perfectly legal and restores the order character of the instrument. For example, as shown in Figure 31-1(b), Gloria Marshall could have taken the blank indorsement of Gordon Marshall and written above it "Pay to the order of Gloria Marshall" or "Pay to Gloria Marshall." Then the thief would have had to forge her signature to pass the instrument. The law states that the loss generally falls on the person who takes from the forger. Therefore, if Penny-Ante had accepted the check with a special indorsement, it would have been unable to collect.

It is important to note that there are exceptions to the above rule. Innocent holders may be allowed to collect despite the forgery. These exceptions require negligence on the part of the maker or drawer. For example, suppose that a dishonest employee fraudulently gets an employer to sign a check made payable to a frequent supplier of the business but for a nonexistent shipment. The employee then takes the check, forges the supplier's indorsement, and cashes it. The employer must pay it, because it was the employer's negligence that placed the employee in a position to commit the forgery. The employer can then try to recoup the loss from that dishonest employee.

Another exception occurs when an imposter tricks the maker or drawer of commercial paper into giving the imposter an instrument that is made payable to the person who is being impersonated. The imposter then forges the indorsement of the party being impersonated and cashes the check. The instrument is effective against the maker or drawer, who was negligent in not properly identifying the party to whom the paper was given.

Jean was approached by an imposter representing himself as the campaign chairman for Senator Walton Knudson's reelection. Jean supported Knudson, so she made out a check to the "Walton Knudson Campaign Fund" for $500. The imposter forged the fund's indorsement

ASSESS

Learning Objective 4 Have students answer *True* or *False* to the following statements. If the statement is false, ask students to change one word to make it true. **(1) A special indorsement makes the paper payable to the order of a designated party.** (True); **(2) To be properly negotiated, bearer paper requires the signature of the party named in the indorsement.** (False/order); and **(3) If "without recourse" or equivalent words are added over the indorsement, the result is an unqualified indorsement.** (False/qualified) and cashed the check as partial payment for a new car. The car dealership can enforce the instrument against Jean's checking account because she should have been certain whom she was dealing with.

3. Qualified Indorsements

If the maker or drawee of an instrument fails to pay it, the indorsers may be required to. This potential secondary liability based on signature can be eliminated by adding "without recourse" or equivalent words such as "not liable for payment" over the indorsement. The result is a **qualified indorsement** and the indorser's secondary liability because of his or her signature appearing on the instrument is eliminated. If the maker or the drawee does not add such wording, the result is an **unqualified indorsement,** and the indorser may be liable to subsequent holders.

Even though secondary liability is avoided by qualifying the indorsement, certain warranties still may bind a transferor. These warranties are implied by law against all transferors and may still require the indorser to pay if the instrument cannot be collected. The warranties include the following: (1) that the transferor has good title or is authorized to transfer the paper for another; (2) that all signatures are genuine; (3) that there has been no material alteration of the instrument; (4) that the transferor has no knowledge of a bankruptcy proceeding against the maker, drawer, or drawee; and (5) that there are no defenses of any type good against the transferor. In

Thinking Critically Through Visuals

The people in this photograph are closing a sales transaction. If the buyer signed a note agreeing to pay a certain amount to the dealer every month for two years to pay for the car, can the dealer transfer that note to another institution? (Yes) **What must the dealer do to transfer the note?** (Indorse and deliver the note)

Tape paper strips over the handwritten examples on the overhead transparency master, *The Various Types of Indorsements.* Then duplicate and distribute it to students. Have students fill in examples of each on their copies. Correct students' work using the completed overhead transparency as a guide.

Independent Practice

RETEACH Have students create a graphic organizer to illustrate the four different types of indorsements described on pp. 623–626.

ENRICH In small groups, have students brainstorm things they would do before accepting an indorsed check as payment for goods, services, or cash. (Answers may include see how long the indorser has held the check, get identification, and so on.) Then, have each group write a jingle warning others about how to protect themselves when accepting indorsed checks.

▼ TEACH

Introduce the term **accommodation party** and stress the potential liability associated with being an accommodation party. Elicit from the class circumstances that might necessitate a cosignature by an accommodation party.

▼ APPLY

As a whole-class activity, draw and label a flowchart showing the liability of an accommodation party. Then draw and label another flowchart showing the legal relationship between the accommodation party and the accommodated party when the accommodation party has paid the face amount. **Guided Practice**

Personal Perspectives

In class, have students brainstorm items that they would like to purchase on credit, but would need a cosigner to do so. Have students ask family members whether they would cosign for the purchase. Then, have students explain what they learned in class about the accommodation party's liability.

the case of a qualified indorser, this last warranty is modified to state that the indorser has no knowledge of such defenses. Regardless, the warranties are very broad in coverage.

The transferor of bearer paper who does not indorse it (and therefore does not acquire secondary liability on her or his signature as an indorser) still is accountable for these warranties, but only to the immediate transferee. If the transferor does indorse it, however, the implied warranties are extended to protect the transferees beyond just the immediate transferee.

To be totally without potential liability on a piece of commercial paper, a qualified indorser might add "without warranties" and thus eliminate all warranty liability. However, it will be extremely difficult to find a transferee who will give significant value for the instrument to a potential transferor under such circumstances.

4. Restrictive Indorsements

A **restrictive indorsement** directs the use of the proceeds from the instrument or imposes a condition upon payment of the instrument by the indorser. For example, "Pay to John Webb to be held in trust for his oldest son, Tommy," would be a restrictive indorsement, since it directs what is to be done with the proceeds of the paper. "For deposit only" and "for collection" are also restrictive indorsements.

In addition, a restrictive indorsement might impose conditions on payment such as "Pay to Wallace Turk upon his delivery of his 1965 Mustang to me." Such a condition, if on the face of the instrument, would destroy negotiability, but this is not true if included in an indorsement. However, a future holder is bound by the condition and could not collect the instrument against the restrictive indorser until the condition was satisfied.

▼ WHAT IS AN ACCOMMODATION PARTY?

PROBLEM

After working for several years as an automobile mechanic, Burk decided to return to college to finish the coursework required for his degree. To finance his education, he arranged a loan from his bank. His mother agreed to cosign the promissory note. What is his mother's liability on that instrument?

Sometimes a person who desires to borrow money or to cash a check is not well known in the community or has not established credit. To make her or his commercial paper acceptable, the person might arrange—as in

▼ ASSESS

Learning Objective 4 Read aloud the following scenario: **Pinto was newly hired on his first job. When he tried to buy a used car on monthly payments, the car dealer demanded that he obtain a cosigner. His friend Rivas agreed to be an accommodation party and cosigned.** Ask: **Why is Rivas primarily liable for the car payments?** (Because the dealer does not have to try to collect from Pinto before proceeding against Rivas.)

the problem—for someone who is known and has a good credit rating to join in signing the paper. Such a cosigner is an **accommodation party.** Under such circumstances, a person who signs as a maker (as did Burk's mother), or as drawer, indorser, or acceptor, becomes primarily liable in that role. It is as though they received the value from the transfer of the instrument. The obligee of the instrument does not have to try to collect from the accommodated party (Burk) before proceeding against the accommodation party (his mother). However, if the accommodation party is collected against, he or she has the right to seek compensation from the accommodated party. In the problem, if Burk's mother had to pay the note, she could try to recover from him. However, if the party accommodated is collected against, he or she has no legal right to any contribution from the accommodation party simply because the latter was a cosigner.

Preventing Legal Difficulties

1. Remember that even if an instrument is not negotiable commercial paper, it may still be a valuable contract or creditor's claim and be freely transferable by assignment.
2. If you issue commercial paper that is payable on demand, be ready to pay at any time. Keep funds available to meet such a demand. Civil and even criminal penalties may result from your failure to do so.
3. Only issue bearer paper or create it by indorsement if you immediately transfer it and receive value in exchange or immediately deposit it. Otherwise the bearer paper may be misused by unauthorized persons with the loss falling to you.
4. Where it is a practical option, if you are the payee of commercial paper, include a clause for the payment of reasonable attorney's fees and collection costs by the issuer in case of default.
5. Do not sign as an accommodation party unless you are prepared to pay the full amount of the instrument.

▼ REVIEWING IMPORTANT POINTS

1. To be negotiable, an instrument must
   a. be in writing and signed by the maker or drawer,
   b. contain an unconditional order (if it is a draft or a check) or promise (if it is a note or a CD),
   c. call for payment of a sum certain in money,

Have students use Shakespeare's speech of advice from Polonius to his son Laertes, from *Hamlet*, as a model to create their own personal statement of advice that suits their family values and experiences. *"Neither a borrower nor a lender be: For loan oft loses both itself and friend."* Ask: **Is this always good advice? Why or why not?** In class, have students write their advice statements on a bulletin board. **Independent Practice**

Divide the class into five groups. Assign each group one of the five tips on preventing legal difficulties related to commercial paper. Have each group illustrate their tip as a poster. Post students' posters on a bulletin board called *The Commercial Paper Chase.*

Have students create posters to illustrate to others about the liability associated with being an accommodation party.

Have students brainstorm a list of questions to ask if they were asked to be an accommodation party. Then, working in pairs, have students role-play a situation in which a person is asked to be an accommodation party. Have one student play the accommodation party and ask the list of questions he or she has prepared. Exchange roles.

▼ CLOSE

Have students devise an imaginary sequence of events in a chain of indorsements, showing how different types may be used and how one check, for example, may do the work of many dollars.

Assign the following end-of-chapter materials:
Student text review activities, pp. 627–631
Workbook, pp. 95–96
Chapter Test

Chapter MicroExam

Strengthening Your Legal Vocabulary

1 payable on demand
2 postdated
3 acceleration clause
4 qualified indorsement
5 blank indorsement
6 accommodation party
7 restrictive indorsement
8 special indorsement
9 antedated
10 money

d. be payable on demand or at a definite time, and
e. be payable to the bearer or to the order of a specified person.

2 In conflicts between provisions written by various means, the handwritten version prevails over the typewritten version, and the typewritten version prevails over the printed version. Amounts expressed in words prevail over amounts expressed in figures.

3 Although the order or promise given in commercial paper must be unconditional, certain terms may be added to an instrument without destroying negotiability. An example is a provision for the recovery of collection costs or reasonable attorney's fees in case of default.

4 Commercial paper payable to order may be negotiated only by indorsement and delivery. Commercial paper payable to the bearer may be negotiated by delivery alone.

5 There are two basic forms of indorsement: blank and special. By the use of appropriate phrases, either kind may become qualified and/or restrictive.

6 Qualified indorsers have some potential liability on an instrument unless they add the words "without warranties" above their signatures, along with "without recourse."

7 An accommodation party is liable to all subsequent holders of the paper who give value for it, but an accommodation party is not liable to the party accommodated.

▼ STRENGTHENING YOUR LEGAL VOCABULARY

Match each term with the statement that best defines that term. Some terms may not be used.

acceleration clause	negotiable
accommodation party	negotiation
antedated	order paper
bearer	payable at a definite time
bearer paper	payable on demand
blank indorsement	postdated
holder	qualified indorsement
indorsee	restrictive indorsement
indorsement	special indorsement
indorser	unqualified indorsement
money	

1 A label for paper that is to be paid on presentment or at sight.

2 Dated later than the date of issuance.

3. A statement in the text of a negotiable instrument making the entire balance due upon the occurrence of a specific event, such as a default.
4. An indorsement that eliminates the indorser's secondary liability to pay if the primarily liable party does not.
5. An indorsement consisting only of the signature of the indorser.
6. Person who signs as maker, drawer, acceptor, or indorser to lend name and credit to another person.
7. Indorsement that directs the use of the proceeds from an instrument or imposes a condition on payment.
8. Indorsement that makes a paper payable to a particular party or to his or her order.
9. Dated prior to the date of issuance.
10. The official medium of exchange in the United States or a foreign country at the time a piece of commercial paper is issued.

APPLYING LAW TO EVERYDAY LIFE

1. Campbell wrote the following by hand: "I, Gary Campbell, promise to pay to the order of Allison J. Nagy $2,500." Campbell then delivered it to Nagy. In a dispute that arose later, it was argued that because the instrument lacked Campbell's signature, was not dated, and was without a time of payment, it was not negotiable. Do you agree?
2. Parnell was the maker of a promissory note payable to LaSalle. The note was complete and legally correct in all respects but contained the following additional terms:
   a. "This note is prepared as a result of a service contract between the parties dated 3/13/—."
   b. "This note is secured by a mortgage on the maker's residence at 67 Park Central West, Pierre, South Dakota."
   c. "This note is payable in Canadian dollars, with exchange."

   Do any of the added terms destroy the negotiability of the note?
3. Smith paid Coleman $500 for possession of a bearer note made out in the amount of $750. The note is payable upon the death of Coleman's uncle. Is the note negotiable?
4. Anton drew a check for $750 payable to bearer. Anton gave the check to Brewster. Brewster negotiated it by delivery to Charlois. Charlois negotiated it by delivery to Deltoid. Deltoid tried to collect but found that Anton's bank account lacked the necessary funds for payment. May

Applying Law to Everyday Life

1. No; A signature may appear in the body of the instrument's text. Commercial paper need not be dated to be negotiable. No time of payment need be given. However, a note that does not specify a time of payment is treated as a demand instrument. (pp. 618, 620)
2. No, none of the provisions destroys the negotiability. (p. 620)
3. No; Although the uncle is certain to die eventually, the actual date is uncertain. For negotiability, the instrument must be payable on demand or at a definite time. (p. 620)
4. Yes, but only against Charlois should Deltoid be able to show a breach of one of the implied warranties. (pp. 625–626)

Deltoid collect from either or both of the prior holders, and if so, under what circumstances?

5 Lissa Mona received a promissory note for $1,000 payable to bearer. She indorsed it "to Vince Leonard" and delivered it to him. Later Leonard simply delivered the note to the Renaissance Record Shop for a laser disc player and a collection of greatest hits of the Sixties, Seventies, and Eighties. Was Leonard's action a proper negotiation?

6 Heart indorsed a time draft "without recourse, Jan Heart" and delivered it to Shefner. On the date the draft came due, the drawee refused to pay Shefner because the drawee had proof that the signature of the drawer (a certain L. J. Marks) was a forgery. Shefner sued Heart for payment. Is Heart legally obligated to pay?

7 Krosby was starting a new business and needed cash. He persuaded the Federated Finance Bank to lend him $10,000 against his new equipment. However, the bank insisted that his prominent friend, Hopper, or someone of equal financial means indorse the note as well. What would be the extent of Hopper's potential liability from such an act?

8 Fell sold his collection of baseball memorabilia to his friend Ryun. Ryun gave him a promissory note in partial payment. The note read that it would be paid "as soon as the authenticity of the collection can be established." Is the note negotiable?

9 ETHICS ISSUE Angela Floyd sold Thomas a note with a maturity value of $5,000. Thomas paid $4,750 for it, since the maker, The Teton Company, had a good reputation for sound financial dealings. At the time of the transaction, however, Floyd knew that a bankruptcy proceeding had been initiated against The Teton Company that morning. She said nothing because Thomas would probably not have paid over $500 for the note if he had known. Ethically, should Floyd have told Thomas? Will Thomas have any legal recourse if he can prove Floyd had such knowledge?

10 ETHICS ISSUE Using carefully crafted legal means, the insurance company Raven worked for had avoided paying several claims that she felt were justified. The claimants in each case were elderly and were left destitute. The day before Raven quit her job as special assistant to the president of the company, she prepared payout checks for all of these parties and put them in the stack of instruments that the president always signed without question because of his trust in her. After the signing, she distributed the checks to the payees. Ethically, has Raven acted properly?

5 No; The special indorsement "to Vince Leonard" mandated his signature for a proper subsequent negotiation. (p. 624)

6 Yes; Heart is not liable for nonpayment because of his qualified indorsement. But he is liable on his warranty that all signatures are genuine. A forged signature is not genuine. (p. 625)

7 If Krosby fails to pay the note when due, Hopper is liable to the holder for the full amount. (p. 627) Hopper may then try to recover the full amount from Krosby, but he may have disappeared or gone bankrupt or simply lack sufficient funds to pay.

8 No; Negotiable paper must be unconditional and not payable upon the establishment of the "authenticity of the collection." (p. 619)

9 ETHICS ISSUE Yes; Ethically, Floyd should have mentioned the bankruptcy proceeding. Yes; With proof, Thomas could legally recover against Floyd for a breach of the warranty of no knowledge of bankruptcy proceedings against the maker. (p. 625)

10 ETHICS ISSUE Yes; She has acted properly from the standpoint of the greatest good for the greatest number. She has also helped the poor and destitute. However, she betrayed a trust to do so. This should lead to a lively class discussion.

▼ SOLVING CASE PROBLEMS

1. Associates Discount Corporation sought court enforcement of a note it held. The note stated that Fitzwater owed a large sum of money for a tractor that had been delivered to him. Fitzwater, the signer and obligor on the note, wanted to testify to the effect that the tractor was never delivered. May he do so? (*Associates Discount Corporation of Iowa v. Fitzwater,* 518 S.W.2d 474)

2. On May 8, 1957, Brookshire was convicted of issuing a check with intent to defraud. On January 1, 1957, Brookshire had given a check dated December 31, 1957, to pay his taxes for 1956. On January 7 or 8, 1957, Brookshire's bank dishonored the check due to insufficient funds. Under these circumstances, should an intent to defraud be inferred from Brookshire's issuing a postdated check? If not, the conviction should be overturned. You decide. (*State v. Brookshire,* 329 S.W.2d 252)

3. In May 1963, Ferri executed a note promising to pay $3,000 to Sylvia's order "within ten years after date." Two years later, Sylvia demanded payment. When refused, Sylvia sued Ferri. Is the note due at a definite time? If so, when? If not, why not? (*Ferri v. Sylvia,* 214 A.2d 470)

4. Centerre Bank sued the Campbells for payment on a note the Campbells had issued to the Strand Investment Company. The note, for $11,250 plus interest payable semi-annually "which may vary with bank rates charged to Strand Investment Company," had later been transferred to Centerre for value. Centerre could collect if the note was negotiable. Was it? (*Centerre Bank of Branson v. Campbell,* 744 S.W.2d 490)

5. A $10,000 certificate of deposit (CD) "payable to the Registered Depositor hereof" was issued to John D. Cox by Commercial Bank of Liberty. Cox then used the CD as security for a loan made by the Kaw Valley Bank. When Cox defaulted on the loan, Kaw Valley sought to collect on the CD but Liberty refused to pay. Kaw Valley brought suit but could only collect if the CD was negotiable. Was it? (*Kaw Valley Bank Etc. v. Commercial Bank of Liberty,* 567 S.W.2d 710)

Solving Case Problems

1. Yes; Although the parol evidence rule is applicable to commercial paper, the rule does allow oral evidence to show failure of consideration. (p. 618)
2. No, no intent to defraud should be inferred. Although postdated checks are negotiable (p. 617), they give implied notice there are not sufficient funds currently in the account but that there will be when the check comes due. The conviction was therefore overturned.
3. Yes, the note is due at a definite time. When a commercial paper is payable "within" a certain period of time, it is the same as saying it is due "on or before" the arrival of the fixed due date. (p. 620) In this case, the fixed date is 10 years from the date of the note, and although Ferri may pay before that time, he is not obligated to.
4. No; The interest rate and thus the amount due is uncertain as it is keyed to "bank rates." (p. 620)
5. No; The instrument is not payable to order or to bearer. (p. 621) The words "payable to" are only the equivalent of "pay to."

Chapter Theme

Holders, holders in due course (HDC), and holders through holders in due course are all subject to universal defenses.

DIRECTED STUDY QUESTIONS	SPECIAL FEATURES	PROGRAM RESOURCES: Reteach	Enrich	SN	AM	
Who can be a holder in due course and why is this status so important?		✔	✔	✔		
What are the limited defenses?	Thinking Critically Through Visuals, p. 636 Writing Connections, p. 638	✔	✔		K	
What are the universal defenses?	Ethics Issue, p. 639 Personal Perspectives, p. 640	✔	✔		V A	
How is commercial paper discharged?		✔	✔			
What rights and duties are involved in an electronic fund transfer?	Thinking Critically Through Visuals, p. 644 Multicultural Highlights, p. 644 Preventing Legal Difficulties, p. 645	✔	✔			

Additional Resources

- *Computer Crime: Electronic Fund Transfer Systems and Crime*. Washington, D.C.: U.S. Dept. of Justice, Bureau of Justice Statistics, 1993.
- *Selected Electronic Funds Transfer Issues: Privacy, Security, and Equity.* Washington, D.C.: Congress of the United States, Office of Technology Assessment, 1982.
- Steffen, Roscoe T. *Agency-Partnership*. St. Paul, MN: West Publishing Co., 1977.

Chapter Pacing Guide

One-semester course	✔	✔						
One-year course	✔	✔	✔	✔	✔			

	ASSESSMENT OPPORTUNITIES			
Cooperative Learning	Informal Assessment	Chapter Review	Chapter Test	Chapter *MicroExam* (Media)
	✔	✔	✔	✔
✔	✔	✔	✔	✔
	✔	✔	✔	✔
	✔	✔	✔	✔
	✔	✔	✔	✔

Videodiscs
Electronic Fund Transfers: ATMs
Search Chapter 39, Play To 40

State by State

When is a check overdue? In approximately 20 of our 50 states, the law indicates 90 days after issue. In the remainder, the deadline is set at 30 days.

Teaching Materials

Student text, pp. 632–652

Overhead transparency masters
- *What Are the Limited and Universal Defenses?*
- *How Is Commercial Paper Discharged?*

Videos
- *Law for Business* Videodisc

Workbook, pp. 97–104

Outside Resources
- Blank overhead transparencies
- Flip chart
- Guest speakers: banker, lawyer, or paralegal; judge, attorney, or justice of the peace
- Index cards
- Newspaper or magazine articles on limited defenses
- Poster paper
- 2′ × 2′ sheets of cardboard
- Bell or other signaling device
- Newspaper or magazine photographs of electronic fund transfers
- Business section of newspaper

- Camcorder
- VCR
- Tape recorder

Assessment
- Chapter Test

- Chapter *MicroExam*

Vocabulary

holder in due course (HDC), p. 634
holder through a holder in due course (HHDC), p. 634
limited defenses, p. 634
universal defenses, p. 634
cancellation, p. 642
electronic fund transfer (EFT), p. 643

Learning Objectives

When you complete this chapter, you will be able to

1. Understand the importance of the status of holder in due course.
2. Identify the various limited and universal defenses.
3. Know how to discharge obligations under commercial paper.
4. Recognize the significance of electronic fund transfers in financial operations.

632

Chapter Self-Test

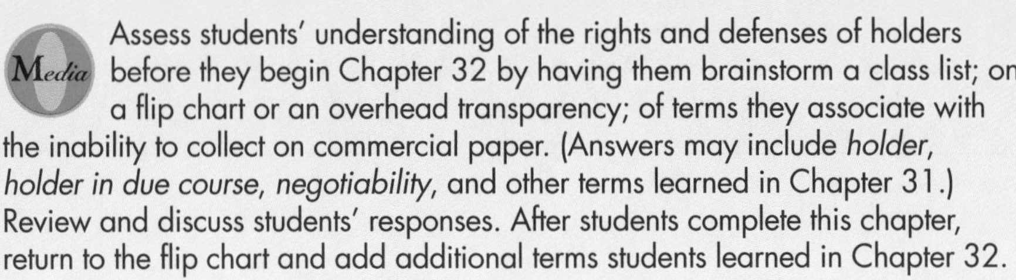

Assess students' understanding of the rights and defenses of holders before they begin Chapter 32 by having them brainstorm a class list; on a flip chart or an overhead transparency; of terms they associate with the inability to collect on commercial paper. (Answers may include *holder, holder in due course, negotiability*, and other terms learned in Chapter 31.) Review and discuss students' responses. After students complete this chapter, return to the flip chart and add additional terms students learned in Chapter 32.

CHAPTER 32

RIGHTS AND DEFENSES OF HOLDERS

1 A seventeen-year-old student contracts to pay $3,000 for a twelve-month modeling course. She pays $500 down and gives a note for the balance, payable in twenty-four monthly installments. Advertisements for the course promised "exciting, high-paying jobs." However, it becomes clear that the only jobs offered are to model clothes at local schools. The student decides to avoid the contract but is told that the note has been transferred to a bank that is a holder in due course. Must she pay as promised?

2 You contract for aluminum siding to be installed on your skateboard manufacturing business. You sign a promissory note for $10,000 payable to the order of the siding company. Later, although the siding company has gone out of business without doing the job, a bank demands payment of the note. The bank purchased the instrument from the siding company for $9,500 and is a holder in due course. Are you legally required to pay the note?

3 ETHICS ISSUE You are the chief executive officer of the bank in number 2 above. You know that if you collect on the note, the skateboard company will go out of business and its eight employees will lose their jobs. Ethically, should you enforce collection of the note?

▼ FOCUS

Before class begins, write the following statement on the chalkboard and have students agree with or refute it in writing: **If someone alters a check you have written, you must still honor it.** (No, you are liable only for the original amount of the check unless your negligence contributed to the possibility of alteration, such as leaving space for the addition of figures.)

Poll students to see how many believe they are obligated to pay the altered check. Discuss students' explanations.

You Decide

1 No; Minority is a universal defense. In addition, under the FTC rule, if the school has fraudulently misrepresented the availability of "exciting, high-paying jobs," the HDC could not collect against a consumer/maker who contracted for the course.

2 Yes; A holder in due course can overcome your limited defense of failure of consideration. Had this been a consumer rather than a business transaction, the FTC rule would be applicable and the note would not have to be paid.

3 ETHICS ISSUE From the perspective of most ethical systems, the answer is a clear *yes.* As CEO of the bank, you have given your word to perform your duties in a manner so as to protect the owners of the bank. However, you might be able to find other options for the skateboard company to pay the note that would benefit your bank, such as financing at a higher interest rate.

Thinking Critically Through Visuals

The owner of these horses does not have the money to repay a debt to you. Do you think he or she can legally offer one of these horses in place of the money? Would you have to accept? (Yes; He or she can offer the horse if it is of approximate equal value, but you do not have to accept the offer.)

TEACH

Discuss with students who can be a **holder in due course** (see qualifications on p. 634) and the importance of this status. Clarify for students the difference between a **holder, a holder in due course (HDC),** and **a holder through a holder in due course (HHDC)** by creating a comparison table on the chalkboard, a flip chart, or an overhead transparency. The table should compare the qualifications of and defenses against a holder, an HDC, and an HHDC. Point out that, legally, it is better to be an HDC or an HHDC than a holder or an assignee because the former have greater legal protection against non-payment.

APPLY

Have students expand the comparison table to include an example of a holder, an HDC, and an HHDC. Have students copy the completed table in their notebooks. **Guided Practice**

Invite a local banker to class for a discussion of the three types of holders and why it is better to be an HDC or an HHDC rather than a holder. In advance of the visit, have each student prepare a list of three or more questions they have about holders. **Independent Practice**

WHO CAN BE A HOLDER IN DUE COURSE AND WHY IS THIS STATUS SO IMPORTANT?

PROBLEM

Donna Tipton paid Alanna Acorn $500 for a promissory note with a face value of $10,000. The note was bearer paper, and Acorn refused to indorse it, saying that she had to leave town and therefore her indorsement would not do any good. Tipton knew Acorn had recently been indicted for participation in a blackmail scheme. When Tipton tried to collect on the note, the maker refused to pay claiming he had signed it only because Acorn had threatened to reveal certain incriminating facts to the Internal Revenue Service. Is Tipton a holder in due course and thereby able to overcome the obligor's defense and collect?

As discussed in Chapter 31, a holder is a person who has physical possession of bearer or order paper. All holders have the right to assign, negotiate, enforce payment, or discharge the paper—with or without payment in return. However, when trying to collect on an instrument, a party who qualifies as either a holder in due course or a holder through a holder in due course is legally placed in a much better position than a mere holder or an assignee. To be a **holder in due course (HDC),** a person has to qualify as a holder and, in addition, take the commercial paper in good faith, give value for it, and not have knowledge of any defense, adverse claim to, or dishonor of the instrument. Also, if the instrument is overdue and the acquirer knew or should have known of its status, that person cannot be an HDC.

A **holder through a holder in due course (HHDC)** is a holder who takes commercial paper anytime after an HDC. An HHDC normally has the same rights as an HDC unless the HHDC is reacquiring the instrument. According to the Uniform Commercial Code (UCC), persons cannot improve their position on commercial paper through reacquisition. So, if Anna Tylon had been a mere holder the first time she had an instrument and she then sold it to a person who qualified as an HDC, reacquiring the instrument from that HDC would still leave Anna with only her original rights as a mere holder, not those of an HHDC. In collecting, either an HDC or an HHDC can overcome more of the defenses that the obligor on an instrument might raise against payment than a mere holder.

Defenses that are good against everyone except an HDC or an HHDC are termed **limited defenses.** (These are labeled *personal defenses* in some jurisdictions.) Defenses that are good against all obligees are called **universal defenses.** (These are also known as *real defenses* in some jurisdictions.) These defenses are discussed in the following sections.

ASSESS

Learning Objective 1 Have students orally explain why it is better to be a holder in due course or a holder through a holder in due course rather than a holder. (An HDC or an HHDC has greater legal protection from defenses that might limit payment of the paper.)

Taking paper in good faith requires that the holder act honestly, not just in the immediate transaction, but in relation to the complete set of circumstances surrounding the paper. In addition, although the courts generally do not consider the adequacy of the value given for commercial paper, the amount given may affect the court's judgment as to the good faith of the parties involved. For example, if the value given is small in relation to the face value of the instrument, fraud or some other unconscionable act that would prevent the holder from being considered an HDC may be implied by the court. In the problem, Tipton's knowledge of Acorn's alleged criminal activities and the small value given will probably disqualify her from being an HDC due to a lack of good faith.

Besides giving value in good faith, an HDC must not know the paper is overdue. For example, a time instrument is overdue the day after the maturity date, or, if payments are to be made in installments, the paper is overdue if even a single installment is late. If an instrument is due on demand, it is overdue a reasonable time after it is issued. However, the UCC specifies that a check is overdue thirty days after issue. Also every holder is charged with knowledge of what is on the instrument, so failing to notice the date is no excuse. Similarly, if the date has been altered, as from May 5 to May 15, and if the alteration is not recognizable by a reasonable person, an innocent holder is accountable only for the date as altered (May 15).

Finally, to qualify as an HDC a holder must not know of any defenses against enforcement of the paper, any claims of ownership from third parties, or any previous dishonors of the paper. Any such knowledge attributable to the holder when he or she acquired the paper would prevent that holder from being considered an HDC. As a consequence, that holder might be legally unable to overcome an obligor's limited defenses against payment of the paper.

WHAT ARE THE LIMITED DEFENSES?

PROBLEM

Santana owned "Hello, Cleveland!," a business that provided touring rock groups with transportation from one concert to another. He bought a large used recreational vehicle (RV) to convert for such a purpose from Trail's Used Car and RV Center. Trail assured Santana that the odometer reading of 25,275 on the RV was correct. Santana paid for the vehicle with $15,000 in cash and by issuing a $45,000 promissory note payable to Trail's order. Santana later learned from state authorities that the true odometer reading was 125,275 miles. Santana wanted to avoid the contract because of the fraud. In the

Much of the content of this chapter revolves around understanding who a holder, an HDC, and an HHDC are. Assist your poor readers and speakers of non-standard English by having students perform the following demonstration. Have three volunteers stand with index cards labeled *holder, HDC,* and *HHDC.* Then have them role-play a scenario in which bearer paper transfers from the person labeled holder to the HDC, and finally to the HHDC. Have each person explain, as the bearer paper is transferred, why he or she is so labeled. Repeat as necessary until students understand the difference between the terms.

TEACH

Although a holder runs the risk of not being able to collect, point out that most commercial paper is promptly paid. Discuss the eight limited (or personal) defenses (pp. 636–639) that may be raised against a holder in case of collection. Explain that these eight limited defenses are ineffective in barring collection against an HDC or an HHDC. As you discuss each defense, write it on the chalkboard or a flip chart. Have students take notes on the information presented, using the chapter outline, *What Are the Limited Defenses?,* on pp. 205–206 of the Workbook as a guide.

RETEACH Have students who have difficulty understanding the different holders reread pp. 634–635. Then review the PROBLEM on p. 634 and explain why Tipton is not a holder in due course. (Her information about Acorn should have prohibited her from taking the paper in good faith, the small value, and so on.)

ENRICH Hand out two index cards to pairs of students. Have the pairs make up two scenarios: one about a holder and one about an HDC or an HHDC. Have students exchange index cards and identify the status of the holder.

▼ APPLY

Make individual copies of the overhead transparency master, *What Are the Limited and Universal Defenses?*, and distribute them to students. Display the overhead transparency. Help students to define each of the eight limited defenses. Then, in pairs, have students provide examples of each defense in use. Have students complete their papers as you fill in the information on the overhead.

Guided Practice

Thinking Critically Through Visuals

The pedal on this woman's brand new bicycle has just snapped off. She paid by check for the bike. Which limited defense might bar the holder from collecting on the check? (Failure of consideration)

meantime, Trail had negotiated the note to the Continental Bank, an HDC, for $41,000. Must Santana pay Continental the $45,000 as promised?

Even though the emphasis in this and the next section is on defenses, it is important to realize that most commercial paper is enforceable according to its terms and is promptly paid. Only in the exceptional case do defenses to collection come into play. In such instances, however, the holder's risk of not being able to collect is greatly reduced if he or she is an HDC and thereby is able to overcome the limited defenses that might be raised against such collection.

Limited defenses, which, as mentioned earlier, are also called personal defenses, are good against all holders except an HDC or an HHDC. Against ordinary holders they are just as effective in barring collection as the universal defenses discussed later in this chapter. The following are limited defenses.

1. Breach of Contract or Failure of Consideration

Often commercial paper is issued as a result of a contractual agreement, as in the problem. Ordinary holders are subject to defenses that arise when the terms of such contract are not fulfilled or the consideration (or partial consideration) is not given to the person who issued the instrument. In the problem, for example, if Trail had failed to deliver the RV on time, it would

▼ ASSESS

Learning Objective 2 In their notebooks, have students create a spider map identifying the eight limited defenses that are good against all holders except an HDC or an HHDC. (See pp. 636–639.) Then, have students add details to the map that explain each defense. Correct students' papers.

have been a breach of contract or, if the RV were defective, a failure of consideration. In either instance only an HDC or an HHDC could have collected on the note regardless. An ordinary holder, like Trail, could not have overcome the defenses.

2. Fraud in the Inducement

If a person uses fraud to induce another to issue commercial paper (as Trail did to Santana in the problem), the party defrauded has a limited defense to use against holders who try to collect. However, in the problem, Continental Bank is an HDC, and therefore Santana must pay the note. Santana can then seek to recover from Trail. Fraud in the inducement occurs when the issuer is aware that an obligation based on commercial paper is being created. This should not be confused with fraud in the execution, where the issuer is unaware that an obligation based on commercial paper is being created or is unaware of the nature or essential terms of the commercial paper. Fraud in the execution is a universal defense covered later in this chapter.

3. Temporary Incapacity to Contract (Excluding Minority)

Contractual obligations made when a person is experiencing a temporary loss of capacity due to insanity or intoxication are voidable. The law establishes a personal or limited defense against commercial paper issued during such periods of temporary loss of capacity. (Please see the discussion of minority as a defense on page 639.)

4. Ordinary Duress

Duress can be either a limited or a universal defense depending on its severity. Ordinary duress does not strip away a person's capacity to contract, but does improperly force him or her to enter into a contract. As a consequence, ordinary duress provides a limited defense against collection of any commercial paper that originates in such a contractual setting.

> Sampson left a bar, got into his car, started it, and drove into the street directly in front of Harrington's pickup. Harrington swerved and crashed into a light pole. Harrington threatened to bring a criminal action for drunken driving against Sampson if Sampson did not buy Harrington's car. Sampson wrote out a check for the amount Harrington wanted and gave it to her. The defense of ordinary duress could be used by Sampson to stop collection on the check by a mere holder.

Obtain, or have students obtain, newspaper or magazine articles dealing with recent cases on limited defenses to collection. After reading each article, have students summarize it aloud for the class and identify the type of defense that applies and highlight the part of the article that led them to their conclusion. Verify students' articles before sharing them with the class. **Independent Practice**

Working in small groups of two or three, have students plan, write, and present a skit in which one of the eight limited defenses against collection is being used against a holder. Allow students to choose their role: the holder who cannot collect, the obligor using the limited defense, or, if necessary, an impartial observer. Videotape students as they present their skits to the class. Then, view the skits so the rest of the class can identify the limited defense being depicted.

RETEACH In eight small groups, have students create a poster, cartoon, or other visual to illustrate one of the eight limited defenses against collection by holders. Encourage students to use drawings, cartoons, photographs, and other materials.

Working in pairs, have students write and record a radio broadcast about a fictitious case in which a limited defense was used to bar collection by a holder. Play the tapes for the class. Have students identify the limited defense used in each.

Writing Connections

Language Arts Using a computer, if possible, have individual students complete the following statement, then provide a justification for their response: **Limited defenses should be changed to apply to _____.** (Answers may include that there should be no difference between a holder and an HDC, and so on.)

Have students brainstorm ideas for a board game about limited defenses against holders of commercial paper. After deciding on the goal of the game, divide the class into three groups. Have one group use a 2′ × 2′ sheet of cardboard to make the game board. Have another group write the game questions and answers on index cards. Have the third group write the rules of the game and make the game pieces. Allow time for students to play the game. **Cooperative Learning**

5. Prior Payment or Cancellation

If the obligee pays the amount due on a piece of commercial paper but does not obtain the instrument or, at least, have it marked paid, the instrument could continue circulating. If it does so and ends up in the hands of an HDC, that party could then enforce it against the obligor a second time because prior payment or cancellation only produces a limited defense.

6. Conditional Delivery or Nondelivery

Assume that a check or a note is delivered under a separate agreement that the instrument is to be negotiated only upon the happening of a certain event. Before the condition is satisfied, the paper is negotiated regardless. The resulting defense of conditional delivery is good only against ordinary holders. For example, concert promoters give a $10,000 earnest money check to the agent of a famous rock group. The agent agrees to cash the check only if the group appears for the promoters' performance. If the group does not appear, yet the agent indorses the check to an HDC in exchange for some new sound equipment, the promoters will have to pay it and try to collect their loss from the agent or the rock group.

Nondelivery is also merely a limited defense. In such a case, an instrument is properly prepared or indorsed but only circulated as a result of theft or negligence. If the instrument is in bearer form, a later HDC could enforce it, but a mere holder could not.

At the beginning of the month, Bradley Post made out a check payable to "cash" for $750.00. He planned to have the Deep-Sweep Rug Cleaning Company clean the rugs in his motel, and $750.00 was its flat fee for such a job. He attached a memo to the check reading "For Deep Sweep Co." and left both memo and check in his desk drawer. Two days later he became ill and was hospitalized. During his illness, Post's brother ran the motel business. The brother found the check and, not knowing the job had not been completed, delivered it to Deep Sweep. In financial distress, the owner of the rug cleaning company used the check to pay for cleaning supplies. The cleaning supply store, an HDC, can collect the instrument against Post's account, although an ordinary holder could not.

7. Unauthorized Completion

A maker or drawer who signs a negotiable instrument but leaves the amount blank runs a great risk. Typically, in such an instance, someone else

ASSESS

Learning Objective 2 Have students each create a spider map identifying the seven universal (real) defenses that are good against all kinds of holders. (Permanent incapacity to contract and minority, illegality, forgery or lack of authority, material alteration, fraud in the execution of the paper or as to the essential terms, duress depriving control, and claims and defenses stemming from a consumer transaction) Then, have students add an example of each defense to the spider map. Review as a class.

is authorized to complete the paper when, for example, a final price is negotiated. If the amount actually entered is not within authorized limits and the instrument is transferred to a holder in due course, the amount would have to be paid to the HDC because unauthorized completion is only a limited defense.

8. Theft

A mere holder cannot collect on the instrument if the holder or a person through whom she or he obtained the instrument acquired it by theft. An HDC can require payment in such circumstances, however.

WHAT ARE THE UNIVERSAL DEFENSES?

PROBLEM

Tomassen threatened Bisque that if Bisque did not issue a promissory note for $5,000 in Tomassen's favor, Bisque's wife would be physically harmed. Bisque signed and delivered the note to Tomassen, who then sold it to an HDC for $4,500. Can the HDC collect on the note against Bisque?

As mentioned previously, defenses that are good against all kinds of holders, including HDCs and HHDCs, are universal defenses. These defenses may also be referred to as real defenses. They include the following.

1. Permanent Incapacity to Contract and Minority

If a person is declared permanently insane or a habitual drunkard by judicial proceeding, the person is not responsible for any obligation incurred thereafter on commercial paper. Either status poses a universal defense to the making, drawing, accepting, indorsing, or accommodating of another party on an instrument.

Just as a minor may avoid contractual responsibilities as discussed in Chapter 12, her or his refusal to pay on a piece of commercial paper is a universal defense. This is true whether the minor signs as maker, drawer, acceptor, indorser, or in any other capacity.

2. Illegality

Commercial paper issued in connection with illegal conduct, such as illegal gambling or prostitution in most states, is unenforceable even by an HDC or an HHDC.

TEACH

Point out to students that while limited defenses are not good against HDCs and HHDCs, universal, or real, defenses are good against all types of holders. Briefly review with the class each of the seven universal defenses (found on pp. 639–641). Discuss students' ideas on why these defenses are necessary.

Ethics Issue

By law, minors cannot legally be held responsible for any contractual responsibilities for commercial paper. Have students discuss the ethics involved and whether or not minors should be able to get out of obligations this easily. Then, have students brainstorm five pieces of advice for holders, HDCs, and HHDCs who knowingly enter into contracts of commercial paper with a minor.

RETEACH

Photocopy the overhead transparency master, *What Are the Limited and Universal Defenses?*, and distribute to students who are having trouble identifying universal defenses. Working with a peer-tutor, have students complete the bottom half of the sheet.

Have students, working in small groups, create posters warning all holders (including HDCs and HHDCs) about the seven universal defenses by giving tips on ways to avoid falling victim to them. Discuss and then display the posters.

▼ APPLY

On the chalkboard or a flip chart, lead the class in a brainstorming activity to provide a series of examples for each universal defense identified on pp. 639–641. **Guided Practice**

Using photographs from newspapers and magazines, as well as their own illustrations, have students create a collage or a mobile that exemplifies the seven universal defenses against holders of commercial paper. Hang students' work in the classroom.

Independent Practice

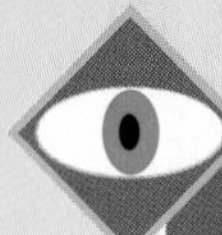

Personal Perspectives

Have students poll family members to see if any of them have experience with universal defenses against holders of commercial paper. Have students determine, for example, if one parent signed the other's signature on a paycheck to deposit it in the bank. For each example they are given, have students identify the respective universal defense. Then, poll the class on which defenses people have experienced. Discuss the results of the poll.

3. Forgery or Lack of Authority

When one person signs the name of another with the intent to defraud, a forgery has been committed. Such an act is a crime and forgery on commercial paper produces a universal defense for the person whose signature has been forged. If the intent to defraud is lacking, but a person signs another's signature without authorization, the signer does not commit forgery. However, the effect on an HDC would be the same unless the person whose name was signed later ratified (i.e., approved) the signing. Both the forger and the unauthorized signer would be liable for the instrument regardless.

While Freed was on vacation and unreachable, the real estate she had been interested in buying came on the market. Although not authorized to do so, Freed's secretary called the seller, negotiated a price for the property, and drew a check on Freed's account by copying Freed's signature from another document. Any HDC to whom the seller might negotiate the check could not collect against Freed unless she ratified the instrument. However, the HDC could collect against the secretary.

4. Material Alteration

When a dishonest holder fraudulently and materially alters commercial paper, parties who held the paper prior to the alteration are generally discharged from liability based on the altered form of its terms. However, they remain liable on the paper's original terms but only to an HDC or HHDC. For example, if the $15 amount payable on a check is altered to read $150, an HDC or HHDC could collect on the instrument, but only $15.

5. Fraud in the Execution of the Paper or as to the Essential Terms

Sometimes trickery is used in such a way that even a careful person who signs does not know and has no reasonable opportunity to learn of the nature or essential terms of the document. Such a person has a defense of fraud against even an HDC or an HHDC. For example, a celebrity signs an autograph on a blank sheet of paper. The "fan" then prints or writes a promissory note around the signature. Or suppose the signer of the paper is not able to read because he or she is illiterate in English or has broken glasses, and the person planning to defraud gives a false explanation of the essential terms or substitutes one paper for another before the signing. Not even an HDC or an HHDC can collect in these cases.

▼ ASSESS

Learning Objective 2 In writing, using a computer, if possible, have students explain the key difference between **limited** and **universal defenses.** (Limited defenses are good against holders but not against HDCs and HHDCs, whereas universal defenses are good against all holders including HDCs and HHDCs.) Then, have students provide concrete examples of the difference between the two types of defenses.

6. Duress Depriving Control

While ordinary duress is a limited defense, duress that deprives control is a universal one. For example, a person who signs a note or draft because another person is threatening to shoot him with a gun has a defense good against even an HDC or an HHDC. In the problem, the threat of physical harm against an immediate family member (or the home) would result in a universal defense being available to Bisque against collection of the paper.

7. Claims and Defenses Stemming From a Consumer Transaction

Although not defined as a universal defense by the UCC, by Federal Trade Commission (FTC) rule any defense a consumer could raise against the seller of a good or service can be raised against commercial paper originating in the same transaction. Defenses—such as breach of contract, failure of consideration, and fraud in the inducement—are thereby made good even against an HDC or HHDC in the proper circumstances. A consumer transaction is one in which a party buys goods or services for personal or household use. A notice stating that a piece of commercial paper originated in a consumer transaction and that the debtor's defenses are good against holders must be given in bold print on the instrument.

HOW IS COMMERCIAL PAPER DISCHARGED?

PROBLEM

Hofstra owed $7,700 on a note held by Duvall. On the due date Hofstra offered Duvall a prize quarterhorse worth more than $7,700 as payment instead of cash. Must Duvall accept the quarterhorse as payment or can he demand cash?

The obligation to pay on commercial paper may be discharged in the following ways.

1. By Payment

The vast majority of commercial paper is paid and discharged according to its terms. A note or a certificate of deposit is usually paid by the maker. A check is usually paid upon demand by the bank on which it is drawn. Other types of drafts are usually paid by the drawees. Regardless of the type of instrument or who is paying, by law the commercial paper terms must dictate that payment be made in money. At maturity or on demand,

You may wish to invite a lawyer or paralegal to class to discuss universal defenses. Have the guest explain what universal defenses are, how they are used, and the legal ramifications of each. Have students prepare individual questions about universal defenses

in advance of the classroom visit.

TEACH

Have students review the definition of *commercial paper* on p. 598 or in the *Glossary of Legal Terms*. Then, discuss students' ideas on what it means to discharge commercial paper (To release the debtor from debt) and review the four ways to discharge commercial paper (by payment, cancellation, alteration, or reacquisition). Write the above four terms on the chalkboard. Display the overhead transparency, *How Is Commercial Paper Discharged?*, and provide students with examples to help explain the four ways a person's obligation to pay on commercial paper can be ended. Have students copy this information in their notebooks.

RETEACH Have students identify a defense that is good against an ordinary holder and one that is good against an HDC or an HHDC. Have them identify each example as being a limited or universal defense. (Ordinary holder: limited defense; HDC or HHDC: universal defense)

ENRICH Have students create a three-column chart comparing limited and universal defenses. Their charts should identify the type of defense, give an example for each, and identify what type of holders each defense is good against.

APPLY

Divide the class into small groups of three or four students and distribute pages from the newspaper's business section to each group. Have each group skim the paper for articles that refer, directly or peripherally, to commercial paper. Then, ask students to brainstorm and write two ways that the commercial paper might be discharged. **Guided Practice**

Based on the examples listed in the GUIDED PRACTICE activity, have students create illustrations showing the various methods of discharging commercial paper. Divide a bulletin board into four columns and label them **payment**, **cancellation**, **alteration**, and **reacquisition**. Have students display their completed illustrations under the appropriate headings. **Independent Practice**

however, the holder (obligee/creditor) may agree to some form of substitution. For instance, the holder may agree to take different kinds of property, such as other commercial paper or even a quarterhorse, as in the problem, in place of a monetary payment. Absent such agreement though, the holder has the right to demand payment in money or to consider the obligor, Hofstra in the problem, in default. If, however, Duvall agreed to the substitution, the note would be discharged.

When an obligor pays a holder the amount due on commercial paper, the obligor should obtain possession of the paper. Otherwise, a dishonest holder who retains the paper might falsely claim that it had not been paid and demand a second payment. Such a dishonest holder could also negotiate it wrongfully to an innocent third party, who then might also be entitled to payment. Even if the amount due on paper is paid only in part, this fact should be shown by appropriate notation on the paper itself. Mistakenly marking a note paid and returning it to the maker does not discharge the obligation by itself. However, it is very difficult evidence for the obligee to overcome in order to still be allowed to collect.

2. By Cancellation

The obligation to pay commercial paper may also be discharged by cancellation. **Cancellation** in this context consists of any act by the current holder that indicates an intent to end the obligation of payment. Knowingly tearing up the paper, burning it, or just drawing a line through the name of a potential obligor, like an indorser, would be excellent evidence of an intent to discharge one or all obligations arising from the instrument.

3. By Alteration

A fraudulent and material alteration of commercial paper by the holder will discharge the obligation of all prior parties. For example, suppose that it is shown to the satisfaction of a court that the holder of a note fraudulently changed the rate of interest due from 7 to 17 percent. In such a case, neither the maker nor any persons who may have previously indorsed the instrument would be obligated to pay it. However, the original parties to the paper would still be bound to make payment in accordance with the original terms if the paper later came into the hands of an HDC or an HHDC.

4. By Reacquisition

When an instrument is returned to or reacquired by a prior party, any intervening party is discharged from liability to the person who has reacquired the instrument or to any subsequent holder who is not an HDC.

ASSESS

Learning Objective 3 Have students independently select and create a graphic organizer to visually identify the four ways commercial paper may be discharged. (Payment, cancellation, alteration, reacquisition) Then, have them add an example of each in additional spokes on the organizer. Have students take turns showing and explaining their choices for the class.

A promissory note payable to James O'Brien was indorsed in blank by him and negotiated to Karen Shaw. She indorsed the note in blank and negotiated it to Tim Leary. Tim Leary indorsed the note, "Pay to James O'Brien, Tim Leary," and negotiated it back to O'Brien, the original payee. If the maker refused to pay on the note, James O'Brien could not collect its value from either Karen Shaw or Tim Leary. They, as intervening parties, were discharged when O'Brien reacquired the instrument.

WHAT RIGHTS AND DUTIES ARE INVOLVED IN AN ELECTRONIC FUND TRANSFER?

PROBLEM

Snyder left her purse in her unlocked car while visiting a friend. When she returned to the car, the purse had been stolen. Her automatic teller card was in the purse. Snyder immediately notified the police of the theft but did not notify her financial institution for three days. During that time the thief took out $2,100 in cash advances using the card. Who is liable for the $2,100 loss?

A transfer of funds that requires a financial institution to debit or credit an account and that is initiated by the use of an electronic terminal, computer, telephone, or magnetic tape is an **electronic fund transfer (EFT).**

EFTs are basically conducted without such instruments as checks or drafts. Automated teller machines, point-of-sale terminals in stores, and automated clearinghouse networks that credit payroll checks directly to accounts are examples of devices that facilitate EFTs.

Commercial paper law, due to its emphasis on the need for a writing, was generally inapplicable to EFTs. Therefore, the Electronic Fund Transfer Act was passed by the federal government. The EFT Act emphasizes that the use of such transfers is to be purely voluntary. When an EFT is used, the consumer must immediately receive a written receipt and later must receive a statement of all transfers during a particular period. If the consumer detects an error of overbilling, it must be reported to the institution responsible for the EFT. The institution then has forty-five days to investigate, during which time the consumer has the funds returned for use. This rule applies unless the institution makes a reasonable determination within ten days of the report.

TEACH

Poll the class to see if anyone has had any experience with **electronic fund transfers (EFTs),** such as bank automatic teller machines, department store computerized registers, and direct-deposit of payroll checks to a specified account. Discuss what the EFT Act covers. Point out that, although they are convenient, there are risks involved in using EFTs. Discuss consumer liability of unauthorized transfers.

APPLY

As a class, list on the chalkboard or a flip chart examples of electronic fund transfers that may be common practice to businesses or adult consumers. Discuss the convenience of using EFTs and steps wise consumers should follow. **Guided Practice**

Using the chalkboard, a blank overhead transparency, a flip chart, or sheets of paper, have students work in small groups to create a flowchart that illustrates how funds (perhaps a payroll check) are transferred electronically from the issuer, to the bearer, to other parties. Have a volunteer from each group explain the process. Correct misconceptions. **Independent Practice**

RETEACH After rereading pp. 641–643 (top), have students work together to write a poem, song, or rap about discharging commercial paper. The lyrics can be general or focus on one particular method of discharge.

ENRICH Independently or in pairs, have students realistically illustrate the four ways commercial paper can be properly discharged. For example, a note torn up by the holder would indicate the intent to end the obligation of payment. Display the visuals at the front of the class. Have students correctly label each method.

Thinking Critically Through Visuals

These people are banking through an automatic teller machine. How could the consumer at left protect herself against a banking error? (Answers may include checking her receipt, verifying her bank statement, and so on.)

Multicultural Highlights

We can thank Frank Annunzio, in part, for legislation protecting users of electronic fund transfers. As Chair of the House Banking Consumer Affairs Subcommittee in the 1970s, he fought to pass the EFT Act so that consumers who were unaware of the risks in using EFT services would be protected. A Democrat of Italian ancestry, Annunzio retired in 1992 after 28 years as a member of Congress. Ask: **How else, do you think, can consumers be made aware of the risks—and liabilities—of using EFTs?** (Answers may include through bank newsletters, PSAs, and so on.)

In the case of unauthorized transfers, Congress rejected the idea present in commercial paper law requiring full liability on the part of a depositor who negligently allows such a transfer (by losing a check, for example). Instead, Congress chose to divide the risk of unauthorized transfers between the consumer and the financial institution, even if the depositor is negligent. As a consequence, as long as notification is given to the financial institution within two days of learning of the loss or theft of the card, the consumer is responsible only for the lesser of $50 or the value obtained in an unauthorized transfer prior to the notification. However, if more than two days have elapsed before notification, the consumer may be responsible for up to a maximum of $500. In the problem, because three days went by before Snyder gave notification of her loss, she will probably have to pay $500 and the financial institution will have to absorb the other $1,600.

Preventing Legal Difficulties

For your protection...

1. When you acquire commercial paper, try to do so in a manner that qualifies you for the rights of a holder in due course. Do this by giving value in good faith for it and by taking only paper that is not overdue or subject to any defense, claim, or dishonor of which you have knowledge.

▼ ASSESS

Learning Objective 4 As a whole-class activity, have students summarize how users of EFTs are protected. (See pp. 643–644.) Then, have students make a two-part poster. The first part should identify the procedures the consumer and institution must follow in an EFT transaction. The second should explain how Congress divides the risk of unauthorized transfers between the consumer and the financial institution.

If that is impossible, become an HHDC by acquiring the paper from an HDC.

2. When you are acquiring commercial paper, require the transferor to give an unqualified indorsement in your presence. Verify the transferor's identity carefully. If the signature is a forgery, the loss would generally fall on the party who took from the forger.

3. When you receive commercial paper, work to minimize defenses that can be used against you if you try to collect.

4. If you pay your obligation on commercial paper in full, have the paper so marked and signed by the holder, then obtain possession of it immediately. Have partial payments noted on the paper as well.

5. When using EFT, retain your receipts and use them to verify your statements. Immediately report any lost or stolen EFT cards or any other breach of security surrounding your use of EFT to the financial institution that issued your card. This will minimize your potential losses.

REVIEWING IMPORTANT POINTS

1. A holder in due course can overcome limited defenses offered against payment of the paper. An ordinary holder's right to collect is subject to such defenses.

2. Ordinary holders, holders in due course, and holders through holders in due course are all subject to universal defenses.

3. Limited defenses include the following:
   a. breach of contract or failure of consideration,
   b. fraud in the inducement,
   c. temporary incapacity to contract (excluding minority),
   d. ordinary duress,
   e. prior payment or cancellation,
   f. conditional delivery or nondelivery,
   g. unauthorized completion, and
   h. theft.

4. Universal defenses include the following:
   a. permanent incapacities to contract and minority,
   b. illegality,
   c. forgery or lack of authority,
   d. material alteration,
   e. fraud in the execution of the paper or as to its essential terms,

Preventing Legal Difficulties

Have students read the five items on pp. 644–645. Then, divide the class into five groups, one for each of the points listed on pp. 644–645. Have students create a newspaper, television, or radio PSA stressing one of the five ways for a consumer to protect himself or herself.

CLOSE

Divide the class into two or three groups. Give each group a bell or some other signaling device. Prepare questions pertaining to the chapter content ahead of time. Then, asking one question at a time, allow the groups one minute, for example, to discuss the question. The first group to signal and correctly answer the question receives one point. The first group to score 10 points wins.

Return to the flip chart created in the CHAPTER SELF-TEST at the beginning of this chapter. Add to the chart the related vocabulary terms learned in this chapter.

Assign the following end-of-chapter materials:
Student text review activities, pp. 645–650
Workbook, pp. 97–98
Chapter Test

Chapter *MicroExam*

Have students, working in pairs, create a collage showing various types of EFTs in use in their community. They may use pictures from magazines or newspapers, illustrations, and/or photographs they have taken.

Have students create cartoon strips highlighting what one should do to limit a consumer's liability against unauthorized EFT transfers. Collect and photocopy the cartoons into an EFT booklet.

Strengthening Your Legal Vocabulary

1. holder through a holder in due course (HHDC)
2. holder in due course (HDC)
3. universal defenses
4. limited defenses
5. cancellation
6. electronic fund transfer (EFT)

Applying Law to Everyday Life

1. Yes, the bank as an HDC can overcome Abbiatti's limited defense of failure of consideration and collect. However, if the purchase had been for her personal/household use instead of for her business, Abbiatti, as a consumer, would have had an effective defense. (pp. 636–637, 641)

f. duress depriving control, and
g. claims and defenses stemming from a consumer transaction.

5. Obligations on commercial paper may be discharged by payment, cancellation, alteration, or reacquisition.

6. If the consumer reports the loss or theft of a card within two business days after learning of it, the consumer's liability on an unauthorized EFT is limited to $50 or the value of the unauthorized use, whichever is the lesser. Otherwise, the consumer's loss is limited to $500.

STRENGTHENING YOUR LEGAL VOCABULARY

Match each term with the statement that best defines that term. Some terms may not be used.

cancellation
electronic fund transfer (EFT)
holder in due course (HDC)
holder through a holder in due course (HHDC)
limited defenses
universal defenses

1. One who takes commercial paper after an HDC and thereby acquires the same rights.
2. Holder who takes commercial paper in good faith without knowledge of any defect or overdue status and who gives value for it.
3. Defenses good against all obligees.
4. Defenses good against all obligees except HDCs and HHDCs.
5. One method by which commercial paper can be discharged.
6. A debit or credit to an account that is initiated by the use of a terminal, computer, telephone, or magnetic tape.

APPLYING LAW TO EVERYDAY LIFE

1. Abbiatti operated her own computer repair business. To work on the newer models, she purchased a set of advanced instruments for $2,300 from CompRepare, Inc. She paid $300 down and signed a 180-day negotiable note payable to CompRepare for the balance. After using the tools, she realized they were not of the precision required or promised and refused to pay. In the meantime, the note had been sold to the People's Commercial Bank, an HDC, for $1,850. Can the bank overcome Abbiatti's defense and collect?

2 When Rebel T. Clef, a rock star, landed at the local airport, a young woman persuaded him to sign his autograph on a blank sheet of paper. The woman was a skilled typesetter. She went home and printed all the essential language of a promissory note around the signature. After filling in the amount of $15,000 and inserting her name as payee, she sold the note to an HDC. Is Clef legally obligated to pay the $15,000?

3 Eaton owed Fobair $1,500 for supplies he purchased the year before for his business. Fobair met Eaton in a restaurant one day and loudly demanded either cash or a signature on an interest-bearing note or he would "haul you into court and sue you for all you've got." Eaton signed, and Fobair promptly sold the note to Livingston, an HDC. Now Eaton refuses to pay the note, claiming it was signed under duress. Will this be a valid defense to payment?

4 Tilly needed another freezer for her ice cream store. She purchased a used one from Worth and paid with a check for $1,275. Worth had assured her that the freezer was in good working order. However, when the unit was installed in Tilly's business, it did not work. Upon removing the back panel, Tilly found that the motor was defective and had not been in working order for several years. What is her defense against collection of the check by Worth? Would Tilly's defense be good against an HDC?

5 The following paper was indorsed in blank by Haddock and delivered to Garner on November 10, 19— in exchange for valuable consideration. Did Garner become an HDC?

Fargo, North Dakota
July 1, 19--

On December 30, 19--, I promise to pay Harvey Haddock three hundred dollars ($300) with interest at nine (9) percent per year.

Mary Ann March
Mary Ann March

For Classroom Use Only

6 Ficklin was an unqualified indorser on a note for $10,000. Dixon, the holder of the note, mistakenly believed that Ficklin was in financial ruin. Thinking that she could not collect on the note, Dixon struck out Ficklin's indorsement. Is Ficklin still potentially liable on the instrument?

2 No, Clef is not obligated to pay. Fraud as to the nature of the paper or its essential terms is a universal defense—good even against an HDC. (p. 640)

3 No; Although duress may be a valid defense, there was no duress here. (pp. 637, 641) A creditor has a right not only to threaten to sue, but to sue in a civil action. Duress requires some threat of personal harm or violence, or of forced confinement. The words *"for all you've got"* were of no consequence because a reasonable person would realize that the creditor could get a judgment only for the amount owed plus interest and court costs. Both an ordinary holder and an HDC could collect on the note from Eaton.

4 Tilly has the defense of fraud in the inducement. (p. 637) No; Fraud in the inducement is a limited defense good against everyone except an HDC. (p. 636)

5 No; To be an HDC one must take a commercial paper under certain prescribed circumstances. Garner could not qualify here because the instrument is not payable to order or to bearer, and therefore it is not negotiable. (pp. 634–635)

6 No; Ficklin's obligation was canceled by Dixon when she struck through Ficklin's name. (p. 642)

7 Yes; According to the EFT Act, Hi-Tech Bank has 45 days to investigate, during which time Crocke has use of the $350 if Hi-Tech has not made a determination of her error claim within 10 days of the report of error. It would be a good idea for Crocke to call Hi-Tech and be sure the funds have been recredited before using them, however. (pp. 643–644)

8 ETHICS ISSUE Yes; Taking unfair advantage of the mistake would be wrong.

9 ETHICS ISSUE No; Cupito's own negligence caused the reaction. She is acting unethically, trying to switch the burden of guilt to her doctor. Legally, an HDC will be able to overcome Cupito's limited defense of ordinary duress and collect. (p. 637)

10 Orr's defense is fraud in the inducement. (p. 637) It will be an effective defense as the purchase was a consumer transaction. (p. 641)

7 Crocke detected a $350 overcharge against her account resulting from an electronic fund transfer. She reported the error to Hi-Tech Bank. The bank had not completed its investigation ten days later. Can Crocke spend the $350?

8 ETHICS ISSUE By mistake, the Downtown Bank returned a $1,000 note to its maker, Hall. Hall knows that the note had not been paid and that it is highly unlikely that the bank discharged his obligation as a gift. Should he contact the bank and inform it of the mistake?

9 ETHICS ISSUE Garringer seeks treatment from Cupito, a local doctor, for some recurrent headaches she has been having. Although Cupito inquires, she negligently forgets to tell him of medicine, prescribed by another doctor, she has been taking for back pain. Cupito prescribes a pain-killer for her headaches. The next day Garringer has a severe reaction to taking both medicines at once. Garringer knows that Cupito is very proud of his professional reputation. She threatens to sue him for malpractice unless he makes out a promissory note in her favor for $35,000. He does so. Has Garringer acted ethically? Will an HDC of the instrument be able to recover against Cupito if the facts are known?

10 Orr bought a riding lawnmower with attachments for his home. The lawnmower was described as brand new by a salesperson but was in fact a used mower that had been rebuilt and repainted. Orr signed a promissory note for the $1,500. The lawnmower broke after two months, and the facts became known. What is Orr's defense against collection? Is this defense good against an HDC?

SOLVING CASE PROBLEMS

1 On May 2, as part of the $96,500 purchase price of some real estate, Collins issued a thirty-day note for $66,500. Just before the due date, Collins ordered his attorney, Sanders, to have money available from Collins's account to pay the note. The attorney had the money and did pay the note, but directed the payees to indorse the instrument in blank rather than mark the note paid. Sanders then, without Collins's knowledge, took the note and, on June 3, pledged it as security to the Oswego Bank for a loan the bank had made to the attorney. When Sanders defaulted on the loan, the bank tried to collect against Collins. Was the Oswego Bank an HDC and therefore able to overcome Collins's defense of prior payment? (*Collins v. First National Bank of Oswego, Kansas*, 746 S.W.2d 424)

Solving Case Problems

1 No; The note was past due when transferred to the bank. Therefore, the bank cannot be an HDC. (p. 634)

2 The Pierces purchased siding for their home from the Globe Remodeling Company, Inc. They gave a promissory note for $3,044.40 in payment. In exchange, they were to receive sufficient siding for the job, properly installed, together with $1,200 in cash. Globe indorsed the note to the Gramatan Company, Inc. Gramatan then sold it without indorsement to its affiliate, the plaintiff, Gramatan National Bank, for $2,250. The bank had previously placed Globe on its "precautionary list" because it knew that in other sales, Globe had not performed as promised. The bank also knew that similar Globe notes were being litigated and that federal law enforcement officials had been investigating Globe's activities. In this case, only about $400 had been paid to the Pierces. In addition, only about one-half the siding had been delivered, and none had been installed. The Pierces refused to pay the note, and the bank sued. Is the bank a holder in due course? (*Gramatan National Bank and Trust Co. v. Pierce,* 159 A.2d 781)

3 The Charltons were approached by a vacuum cleaner sales representative who offered them a business deal called a "club plan." Under its terms, the Charltons were to make appointments in their area for sales representatives to demonstrate the cleaners. For each appointment leading to a sale, the Charltons were to receive $25. After some discussion, the couple read and signed the club plan. Then the sales representative mentioned that since they were to be agents for the company, he wanted to leave a vacuum cleaner with them. He then had them sign a "receipt" for the cleaner. Taking his word for the nature of the document although they could have read the instrument, the Charltons then signed the receipt. Only later, when approached by the Local Finance Company for payment, did the Charltons find out that the receipt was actually a promissory note. Can they successfully defend against payment by claiming fraud in the execution? (*Local Finance Co. v. Charlton,* 289 S.W.2d 157)

4 Cameron State Bank mistakenly believed that credit life insurance had paid an $8,000 note it held. Consequently, it marked it paid and returned it to the heirs of the maker. Having discovered the mistake, the bank now asks the court to void the release and enforce the note against the estate. Has the note been discharged? (*Cameron State Bank v. Sloan,* 559 S.W.2d 564)

5 Ognibene withdrew $20 at an automated teller machine (ATM) through the use of his Citibank card and the entry of his confidential personal identification number. As he did so, he was evidently observed by an individual who was using a telephone between Ognibene's ATM and an

2 No, the bank is not a holder in due course. The bank knew of prior difficulties of the Globe firm and was aware of the investigation of the company by federal officials. These facts should have been sufficient to alarm the bank officers. Therefore they did not buy the note in good faith and do not qualify as an HDC. (p. 634)

3 No; The Charltons did not avail themselves of their reasonable opportunity to learn of the true nature of the instrument by reading it when they had it in their hands. (p. 640)

4 No; Although excellent evidence, the marking of the note "paid" and returning it to the obligor is not conclusive as to the obligation being discharged. If the bank can present evidence as to its mistake and the lack of payment, it can recover against the estate. (p. 642)

⑤ The court held that Ognibene did not authorize the transaction. Ognibene did not initiate or benefit from the transaction. Merely giving his card to the person at the ATM area did not furnish the means of access to the account; Ognibene's personal identification number was necessary as well. Any allegation of negligence on Ognibene's part for letting the other person have the card is irrelevant under the statute. (pp. 643–644)

adjacent ATM. The individual was seemingly reporting to the bank that the adjacent ATM was not working. The person, speaking into the telephone said, "I'll see if his card works in my machine." He then borrowed Ognibene's card and inserted it in the other ATM several times, finally stating, "Yes, it seems to be working." Then he returned Ognibene's card. Later, Ognibene discovered $400 had been withdrawn from his account by the person. Ognibene then sued the bank to have the $400 recredited to his account claiming it was an unauthorized transaction under the EFT Act. The bank refused, stating that by giving the other person the card, Ognibene had "authorized" the transaction and was fully liable even though Ognibene had obviously not benefited from the transaction at all. You decide. (*Ognibene v. Citibank N.A.*, 446 N.Y.S.2d 845)

SPECIAL SECTION

HOW TO LITIGATE IN SMALL CLAIMS COURT

If you cannot achieve a satisfactory out-of-court resolution to a dispute, you may decide to take the case to small claims court. If so, several important steps must be taken.

You Must Decide Whom to Sue

Make sure you are correctly naming as defendant(s) the person(s) responsible for your injury.

Many judgments turn out to be uncollectible due to the defendant's lack of resources. Consequently, it is important to bring suit against someone who can pay if you win. However, even individuals who appear to be judgment-proof (i.e., without any resources from which to pay a judgment) are not likely to remain so forever. Most jurisdictions allow ten to twenty years for a judgment to be collected after it is entered.

You Must Decide the Amount for Which to Sue

The damages you claim must be a reasonable approximation of how much you lost due to the defendant's act. The amount cannot exceed the jurisdictional limit of the small claims court.

You Must Properly Serve the Defendant(s) With Process

To give the court jurisdiction, each defendant must receive a summons and a copy of the complaint in person or by certified mail.

You Must Prepare Your Evidence

Although standards of evidence are somewhat relaxed in small claims courts, the documents, exhibits, and testimony you want to present to the court must be logical, concise, relevant, and persuasive.

Special Section: How to Litigate in Small Claims Court

Review when a person would use small claims courts. You may wish to invite an attorney, judge, or justice of the peace to discuss litigation in small claims court with your class. As a class, brainstorm and write on the chalkboard a list of cases that might be litigated in small claims court. Then divide the class into groups of four or more students to role-play a small claims court case.

Have each group begin by deciding on a case, either from the class list or one they come up with on their own that you approve. Students should decide on the role each person in the group will play: defendant(s), plaintiff(s), witnesses (if appropriate), and judge (who will act as observer to the proceedings and reach a decision *for* or *against* the plaintiff).

As students plan their case, have them refer to the guidelines on how to litigate in small claims court, found on pp. 651–652. Following these guidelines, have students plan, present, and videotape their cases.

After viewing each case, have the class discuss the judge's decision and the strong points of each side. Poll the class to see if they agree with the judgment.

Cooperative Learning

Interview with Court Referee

Search Chapter 40, Play To 41

You Must Appear at the Appropriate Time and Place, Ready to Make Your Case

You may be required to appear more than once, especially if the other party has an attorney who asks for a continuance. This request is not uncommon and is often granted once. When you present your case, do so with firmness and control. Even if an attorney is representing your opponent, do not be intimidated. An attorney does not necessarily have an advantage in presenting a case in small claims court.

If You Win, Collect the Judgment

Most defendants will not voluntarily pay the damages awarded. Therefore a successful plaintiff will often have to seek the help of the sheriff to attach (i.e., seize) property of the defendant. This property can then be sold and the proceeds used to satisfy the judgment. If the defendant is a wage earner, it may be possible to garnish the wages to satisfy the judgment.

If You Lose

Many jurisdictions allow the defendant, but not the plaintiff, to appeal. If the defendant appeals, seek the counsel of an attorney.

Through all of these steps it is important to remember that the personnel of the clerk of court's office can be a good source of help in determining the correct procedure and form for each.

652

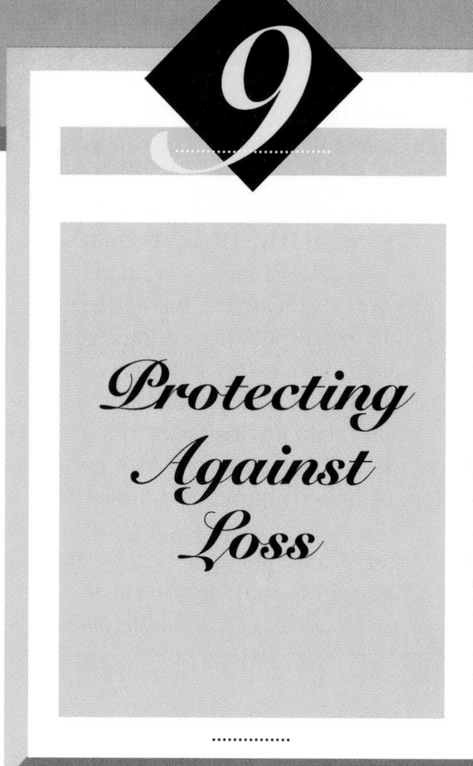

Unit Overview

In Unit 9, *Protecting Against Loss*, students will read about the different kinds of insurance: property and casualty insurance, automobile insurance, life insurance, and social insurance. They will learn about premiums, risks, beneficiaries, endorsements, claims, kinds of coverages, and Retirement, Survivors', Disability, and Health Insurance (RSDHI).

The law of contracts applies, with minor changes, to the most common types of insurance. In Chapter 33, *Nature and Kinds of Insurance*, students will study what insurance is. They will discuss insurable interests, the common types of insurance, how the law of contracts applies to insurance, who may be an insurer, the importance of representations and warranties, and the effect of the concealment of material facts.

Property and casualty insurance contracts contain several clauses, including those related to recovery for a loss, extensions, assignment, termination, and cancellation. In Chapter 34, *Property and Casualty Insurance*, students will discover what property insurance and casualty insurance are and what a comprehensive insurance policy is. They will read what risks are covered by fire, inland marine, liability, and other related policies. The chapter also covers how an insured collects after a loss, and how an insurance policy is terminated.

Automobile insurance policy coverages protect insured, uninsured, and underinsured motorists in a variety of ways. In Chapter 35, *Automobile Insurance*, students will understand what risks of loss can be covered in an automobile insurance policy. They will analyze protection from legal liability available under an automobile policy, learn why we pay for medical payments, and identify the extent of the protection provided. They will learn what protection is provided by collision or comprehensive coverage for an automobile, why we carry uninsured motorists coverage, and how no-fault automobile insurance works.

With thoughtful planning and preparation, a variety of life insurance options and social insurance programs are available to assist people in their greatest times of need. In Chapter 36, *Life Insurance and Social Insurance*, students will learn what life insurance and social insurance are and why they are so important. They will read about provisions commonly found in a life insurance policy, the kinds of life insurance plans that are available, the rights of the beneficiary of a life insurance policy, kinds of social insurance provided under the Social Security Act, how employment benefits are obtained, and how RSDHI benefits are obtained.

At the end of this unit, you'll find a special section, *How to Become an Attorney*, which can be used at any time during the study of Unit 9. You may wish to assign its accompanying *Teacher Edition* activity to give students an opportunity to create a board game that focuses on law students getting through law school.

Portfolio Assessment

Have students use Chapters 33–36 to develop their own hypothesis on some aspect of insurance, such as "Drivers Who Live in States with No-fault Automobile Insurance Have Higher Premiums." Have students go to the library and contact insurance companies to obtain research to prove their hypothesis right or wrong. Then, using a computer, if possible, have students write a thesis on their topic. Tell students that their papers should include these sections in the following order: title page, table of contents, list of illustration or tables (optional), introduction, main body of paper including hypothesis and footnotes, appendices (optional), and bibliography. Ask students to add their thesis to their portfolios.

Careers

Insurance Agent

The market for insurance is steadily growing as more people aim to protect themselves against financial loss. Insurance agents assist clients in selecting the right policy for their needs, explain it and write the policy, set up physical exams, and assist clients in filing claims.

Most insurance agents have a high school degree and many have some college education. Courses in business and economics are useful as is knowledge of computers, since computers are used to provide financial information. All agents must be licensed by the state in which they work. To get a license, candidates usually have to pass a written test. New agents start at an annual salary of $20,000 to $25,000.

Have students skim through the employment classified section of newspapers to find job openings for insurance agents. Have students create fictitious résumés to answer one of the ads they locate.

Annotated Bibliography

- ***Connell v. Indiana Insurance Co.*, 334 F.2d 993 (4th Cir. 1964).**
  An insured's failure to assist and cooperate with an insurance company in defending a claim will defeat recovery on the policy. (Chapter 33)

- ***Delta Lloyds Insurance Co. v. Williamson*, 720 S.W.2d 232 (Tex. App. 1986).**
  The fact that an insured willfully misrepresented the true value of inventory destroyed in a fire did not render the entire fire policy void, as the misrepresentation was not proven material to the insurer's liability under the policy. (Chapter 34)

- ***State Automobile Insurance Co. v. Ellis*, 700 S.W.2d 801 (Kentucky 1985).**
  The court held that an insured's underage daughter, driving without a license and without permission, was insured under a policy providing coverage to any family member. (Chapter 35)

Protecting Against Loss

- Nature and Kinds of Insurance
- Property and Casualty Insurance
- Automobile Insurance
- Life Insurance and Social Insurance

UNIT 9 PROTECTING AGAINST LOSS

CHAPTER 33 ORGANIZER

Chapter Theme

The law of contracts applies, with minor changes, to the most common types of insurance.

DIRECTED STUDY QUESTIONS	SPECIAL FEATURES	PROGRAM RESOURCES				
		Reteach	Enrich	SN	AM	
What is insurance?		✔	✔	✔		
What is an insurable interest?	Personal Perspectives, p. 658	✔	✔			
What are the common types of insurance?	Thinking Critically Through Visuals, pp. 660, 661, 662 Multicultural Highlights, p. 660 Personal Perspectives, p. 661	✔	✔		V	
How does the law of contracts apply to insurance?		✔	✔		A	
Who may be an insurer?		✔	✔		K	
What is the importance of representations and warranties?	Writing Connections, p. 665	✔	✔			
What is the effect of the concealment of material facts?	Ethics Issue, p. 667 Preventing Legal Difficulties, p. 667	✔	✔			

Additional Resources

- Kennedy, David W. *Insurance: What Do You Need? How Much Is Enough?* Tucson, AZ: Knight-Ridder Press, 1987.
- Nader, Ralph and Smith, Wesley J. *Winning the Insurance Game: The Complete Consumer's Guide to Saving Money.* NY: Knightsbridge Publishing Company, 1990.

One-semester course	✔	✔						
One-year course	✔	✔	✔	✔	✔			

		ASSESSMENT OPPORTUNITIES			
	Cooperative Learning	Informal Assessment	Chapter Review	Chapter Test	Chapter *MicroExam*
		✔	✔	✔	✔
		✔	✔	✔	✔
		✔	✔	✔	✔
		✔	✔	✔	✔
		✔	✔	✔	✔
		✔	✔	✔	✔
	✔	✔	✔	✔	✔

Media

Videodiscs

Types of Insurance and Insurers

Search Chapter 41, Play To 42

State by State

A lessee of an apartment in New York was held to have an insurable interest in the whole building.

Teaching Materials

Student text, pp. 654–671

Overhead transparency masters
- *Seven Types of Insurance Policies*
- *Insurance Protection*

Videos
- *Law for Business* Videodisc

Workbook, pp. 105–106

Outside Resources
- Sample insurance policies
- Blank overhead transparencies
- Newspapers and magazines
- Outside speakers: insurance agents
- State insurance statutes
- Poster board
- Blank index cards
- Flip chart

- Camcorder
- VCR

Assessment
- Chapter Test

- Chapter *MicroExam*

Vocabulary

insurance, p. 656
indemnify, p. 656
insurer, p. 656
insured, p. 656
beneficiary, p. 656
policy, p. 656
face value, p. 656
premium, p. 656
risk, p. 656
insurable interest, p. 657
binder, p. 663
stock insurance company, p. 664
mutual insurance company, p. 664
participating policies, p. 664
representations, p. 665
warranties, p. 666
concealment, p. 666
incontestable clause, p. 666

Learning Objectives

When you complete this chapter, you will be able to

1. Understand the practical necessity for insurance.
2. Identify when an insurable interest is present.
3. Know the types of insurance and insurers.
4. Recognize the importance of representations, warranties, and the incontestable clause.

654

Chapter Self-Test

Before they begin Chapter 33, assess students' understanding of insurance by asking the class the following questions. As you read each question aloud, have students write their *True* or *False* responses on a sheet of paper. **(1) No one may be turned down for insurance.** (False); **(2) A person may purchase insurance to protect against loss as a result of negligence.** (True); **(3) Minors generally can void most insurance contracts, unless otherwise specified by state statutes, because of their statutory lack of capacity.** (True); and **(4) Lying on an insurance application could void the policy.** (True) Before continuing with the chapter, review and discuss students' responses.

CHAPTER 33

NATURE AND KINDS OF INSURANCE

1 You buy a car from a person who has just renewed the insurance on it. Will the insurance automatically be transferred to you along with the title to the car?

2 Your parents are concerned about the advancing age of their parents. Consequently, they apply for life insurance on the lives of each of your grandparents, to be used to pay for funeral expenses. Will the applications be accepted?

3 ETHICS ISSUE While in school, you start a successful business. According to the law, you must have fidelity insurance to insure against loss due to the dishonesty of your employees. You apply for it knowing that Joan, one of your managers, has served a prison term for theft. You also know that she stole only to buy food for her family. She has had numerous opportunities to take money from your business since you hired her, but she has not. If you tell the insurance company about Joan's record, your rates will be so high that you will probably have to fire her to stay in business. You are at the meeting with the insurance agent, and she has just asked if you know if any of your employees has a criminal record. What do you tell the agent? What is the legal effect of concealing such information?

▼ FOCUS

Before class begins, write the following question on the chalkboard: **What kinds of insurance do people generally have?** Ask students to answer the question independently on a separate sheet of paper. Ask them not to share responses yet.

When class begins, list students' responses on the chalkboard and discuss the purpose of each type of insurance. Poll students to find out what kinds of insurance they or their families may have. (Answers may include auto, fire, homeowners, life, and so on.) Then, discuss students' ideas on what **insurance** is. (A contractual arrangement in which one party agrees to pay money to help offset a specified type of loss that might occur to another party)

You Decide

1 No; A policy of automobile insurance is not transferable without the consent of the insurer because insurance is a personal contract.

2 Generally not; Most courts rule against adult children having an insurable interest in the lives of their parents.

3 ETHICS ISSUE Legally, such past history of theft would be material in assessing the risk and, therefore, if the employer conceals the fact from a direct question, the insurer would be able to avoid the contract and not pay upon loss. This would injure not only the employer, but also the general public, on whose behalf the indemnification is required.

Thinking Critically Through Visuals

These people live in an area that, obviously, floods. Why, do you think, might they pay high premiums for flood insurance? (Answers may include that insurance companies may charge higher premiums because they will likely have to pay the claims against damages done by flooding. This may not be the only family they insure in a flood area, so the companies' costs are multiplied.)

WHAT IS INSURANCE?

PROBLEM

Bertellino is about to open a bicycle sales, exchange, and repair store. Because she is unsure how large the market is for such an enterprise, she asks an insurance agent to write a policy that would pay back any amount she might lose from business operations. Will the agent be able to sell her a policy that insures her against the risk of doing business?

Insurance is a contractual arrangement in which one party (usually an insurance company) agrees to pay money to help offset a specified type of loss that might occur to another party. The loss may be the death of a person, property damage from fire, damage resulting from exposure, or many other risks. When one party pays to compensate for such harm, that party is said to **indemnify**, or make good, the loss to the suffering party. The party who agrees to indemnify is called the **insurer**. The party covered or protected is the **insured**, and the recipient of the amount to be paid is the **beneficiary**. In some cases, notably under life insurance contracts, the insured will not be the beneficiary.

Insurance makes an important contribution to society. By collecting relatively small premiums from many persons, the insurer builds a fund from which payments can be made to indemnify those who suffer losses.

The written contract of insurance is called a **policy**. The **face value** of a policy is the stated maximum amount that could be paid if the harm insured against occurs. However, a person who suffers a loss covered by insurance recovers no more than the actual value of the loss, even if this amount is less than the face value of the policy.

Carlson carried $10,000 of insurance coverage on his car to pay for repairs to it in the event he alone caused an accident that damaged the vehicle. Driving home from bowling one foggy night, he hit a telephone pole. The repairs cost $4,200. The insurance company would have to pay only this actual loss amount, not the $10,000 face value of the policy.

The consideration for a contract of insurance is the **premium**. The possible loss arising from injury to or death of a person or from damage to property from a specified peril is called the **risk**.

The risk of most financial losses can be covered by insurance. Certain risks, however, cannot. In the problem at the beginning of this section,

TEACH

Explain that **insurance** is a contractual arrangement in which one party agrees to pay money to another party to help offset losses, such as property damage, premature death, medical expenses, catastrophes, and so on. On the chalkboard, write the following basic insurance terms and discuss their meanings: **indemnify, insurer, insured, beneficiary, policy, face value, premium,** and **risk**. Point out that certain risks—such as that of doing business—cannot be covered by insurance.

APPLY

Transfer one sample insurance policy onto a blank overhead transparency. Display it and have students identify the following: **insurer, insured, beneficiary, face value,** and **premium.** Then, divide students into five or six groups and distribute sample copies of different policies on which you have written SAMPLE across the paper. Using their policies, have students repeat the activity.

Guided Practice

ASSESS

Learning Objective 1 In writing, using a computer, if possible, have students explain for what purposes people carry insurance and why this is a practical contractual agreement. (Answers may include that it is practical to guard against possible loss, to avoid having to pay full replacement costs in case of loss, to cover certain expenses, and so on.)

Bertellino cannot be insured against a business loss. This illustrates one of the most important risks for which a policy of insurance cannot be written. The risk of doing business is too unpredictable and too subject to the control of the would-be insured. If she were insured, Bertellino could simply neglect the business and yet collect on the insurance when the store failed. The best protection against the risk of doing business is found in hard work, good products, and excellent service.

WHAT IS AN INSURABLE INTEREST?

PROBLEM

When Sanders bought Dante's only car, she offered to pay him an extra $100 for the two months of protection still remaining on his automobile insurance policy. Dante refused, saying he alone did not have the power to transfer its protection to her. Was he correct?

Insurance is intended to be a personal contract between the insurer and the insured. Consequently, the insured cannot transfer or assign the benefits of the policy to a third person without the permission of the insurer. Certainly, in the problem, Dante was correct. Merely buying goods that have been insured does not automatically transfer the benefits of the insurance policy to the new owner.

A person with contractual capacity is eligible to acquire insurance if he or she has an **insurable interest** or, in general, a direct financial or personal interest in the property or the person insured.

1. Insurable Interest in Property

PROBLEM

Lampson sold Stark a large recreational vehicle for $52,500. However, Lampson forgot to cancel the insurance he held on the vehicle. One month after Stark bought the recreational vehicle, it was totally destroyed by fire. Shocked by the occurrence, Lampson then remembered the policy and immediately filed a claim for the loss of the recreational vehicle with his insurance company. Would he be able to collect?

To insure such things as houses, cars, apartment furnishings, pets, boats, or other property, a person must have an insurable interest in those items.

Divide students into pairs. Have one student in each pair role-play an insurance agent who must explain to the client (second student) what insurance is and why it is a practical necessity. Tell the agents to use the proper terminology; have the client ask questions for clarification. **Independent Practice**

To assist students with limited English proficiency or reading comprehension difficulties to learn the basic insurance terms, have them write the following vocabulary terms in their notebooks: **insurance, indemnify, insurer, insured, beneficiary, policy, face value, premium,** and **risk.** As you explain each term, have students write the definition in their own words in their notebook. Then, have them write a

context sentence using each term correctly.

TEACH

Tell students that **insurable interest** is a direct financial or personal interest in the property or person insured. Explain the difference between *insurable interest in property* and *insurable interest in life*. Point out that with insurable interest in life (unlike property insurance) the insured need only show an insurable interest at the time the policy is taken out, not at the time of the loss.

RETEACH Have students, in pairs, create a crossword puzzle using the following vocabulary terms: **insurance, indemnify, insurer, insured, beneficiary, policy, face value, premium,** and **risk.** Exchange papers and have the student pairs complete each other's puzzle.

Divide the class to debate whether or not insurance companies should offer insurance against the risk of doing business. Videotape the debate for all students to view.

▼ APPLY

On the chalkboard, draw the following chart. Include only the headings *Property* and *Life*.

Property	Life
houses cars jewelry furniture pets boats machinery clothing stamp collection	creditors insuring debtors business partners key employees spouses

As a group, list the types of property and people in which a person may have an insured interest. (See pp. 657–659) **Guided Practice**

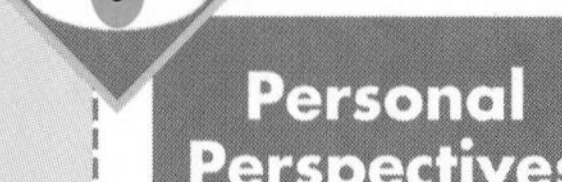

Personal Perspectives

Using a computer, if possible, have students write two scenarios, one in which a person collects on an insurable interest in property, and the other dealing with an insurable interest in life. For example, they may write about the loss of personal belongings in a car accident or a fictitious business partner, whose life they insure. Display student's work on the bulletin board and, as a class, judge whether or not the scenarios are qualified examples.

Independent Practice

Any person who would suffer a direct and measurable monetary loss if certain property were damaged or destroyed has such an interest in that property. However, a person need not hold all the property rights (e.g., a security interest, title, possession, use, or some future interest) in the insured property in order to have an insurable interest. Just one of these rights would be sufficient. Consequently, many individuals may all have an interest in the same property.

> The Saving-by-Paving Company was renting Ruben's asphalt paving machine for use on a large highway job. The First National Bank had a security interest in the paving machine. Saving-by-Paving, Ruben, and First National all had insurable interests in the machine. If the machine were destroyed, they all might collect from their insurers for their respective losses.

In the case of property insurance, for the insurer to be legally obligated to pay, the insurable interest must exist at the time of the loss. In the problem, this was not the case. When Lampson sold the recreational vehicle to Stark, Lampson's insurable interest was terminated. Therefore, he could not collect on the policy.

2. Insurable Interest in Life

PROBLEM

> Buck and Shannon formed a partnership to market a new type of computer memory device that Buck had developed. Shannon, who was in poor health, had all the business contacts that would make the venture a success. Buck worried that she would lose her $250,000 investment if Shannon died. Therefore, Buck insured Shannon's life for $250,000. A year later, Shannon quit the partnership and retired. Buck decided to keep the insurance in force, however, and when Shannon died eight months after she retired; Buck sought to collect the $250,000 from the insurance company. Will she be successful?

Everyone who is qualified and legally competent has an insurable interest in her or his life and may therefore acquire a life insurance policy on herself or himself. Would-be beneficiaries seeking to take out a policy on another person's life, however, must demonstrate that they would suffer direct financial loss if the insured died. Accordingly, creditors may insure their debtors, businesspeople may insure their partners or key employees, and husbands and

▼ ASSESS

Learning Objective 2 In small groups, have students plan and write a brochure on the two types of insurable interest: property and life. Using a computer, if possible, have students identify the factors required for eligibility to acquire the insurance. Print multiple copies of the brochure and circulate them to the other students in school.

wives may insure one another. However, courts frequently rule against adult children having insurable interests in their aging parents or brothers and sisters having insurable interests in each other.

Unlike property insurance, the insured has to demonstrate only an insurable interest at the time the policy is taken out, not at the time of the loss (i.e., not at the time of the death of the person whose life is insured). Therefore, in the problem, Buck should collect the $250,000. Finally, realize that unless the beneficiary contracted for the life insurance, the beneficiary of the policy need not have an insurable interest at any time.

WHAT ARE THE COMMON TYPES OF INSURANCE?

PROBLEM

To raise funds for a trip to the New Year's Day Parade in New Orleans, the Band Boosters planned a Fall Festival complete with contests and games. Some of the planned events involved a risk of injury to participants and spectators alike. What kind of insurance would protect the Band Boosters against liability for negligence or other torts that might result in injury to individuals at the fund-raiser?

There are seven major types of insurance (see Figure 33-1). These are (1) life insurance, (2) fire insurance, (3) casualty insurance, (4) social insurance, (5) marine insurance, (6) inland marine insurance, and (7) fidelity and surety bonding insurance.

1. Life Insurance

Insurance that pays the beneficiary a set amount upon the death of a specified person is life insurance. Life insurance is discussed in Chapter 36.

2. Fire Insurance

Insurance that indemnifies for loss or damage due to fire (and usually smoke as well) is fire insurance. The typical fire insurance policy coverage may be increased to cover losses due to perils such as rain, hail, earthquake, and windstorm. Fire insurance is discussed in Chapter 34.

3. Casualty Insurance

Casualty insurance provides coverage for a variety of specific situations in which the intentional, negligent, or accidental acts of others or mere chance may result in loss. Some of the most important types of casualty insurance include the following.

TEACH

On a blank overhead transparency, draw a fishbone map with seven diagonal branches. List the seven common types of insurance. (Life, fire, casualty, social, marine, inland marine, and fidelity and surety bonding) As you discuss each, fill in the details relating to each type of insurance on lines radiating from the appropriate diagonal branches. Have students copy the completed fishbone map in their notebooks.

APPLY

Before displaying the overhead transparency, *Insurance Protection*, cover the text under the heading "Type of Insurance Offering Protection." Have students determine which insurance would be needed to cover each of the perils listed on the transparency.

Guided Practice

Have students choose one type of insurance coverage to investigate. Have them contact local insurance agents or companies, then create a comparison table of at least three policies. Their tables should compare the type of coverage, the amount of coverage, the premium, and how to collect on the policy. Display, compare, and discuss students' tables. **Independent Practice**

RETEACH Have students independently create a graphic organizer to illustrate insurable interest in property and insurable interest in life.

ENRICH In small groups, have students debate whether or not they think adult children should be able to have an insurable interest in their aging parents. Suggest to students the use of money to cover final illness and burial costs, and to collect death benefits and reduce the burden to the taxpayer for public burial.

Thinking Critically Through Visuals

This diagram shows the common types of insurance that many people carry. Into which category does health insurance fall? (Casualty) **Under which type of insurance might you be covered if**

you lost your job? (Social)

Multicultural Highlights

When homeowners have a mortgage, they are often required by the mortgagee to obtain homeowner's insurance to cover the appraised value of the home in case of destruction. People living in high crime areas are often charged higher rates because of their location. As a result, this often discriminates against people of color and immigrants to the U.S. Insurance companies justify the rates because they often have to pay out more claims in those areas. Have students debate whether or not insurance companies should have the right to charge higher rates in some areas.

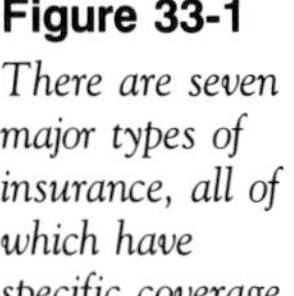

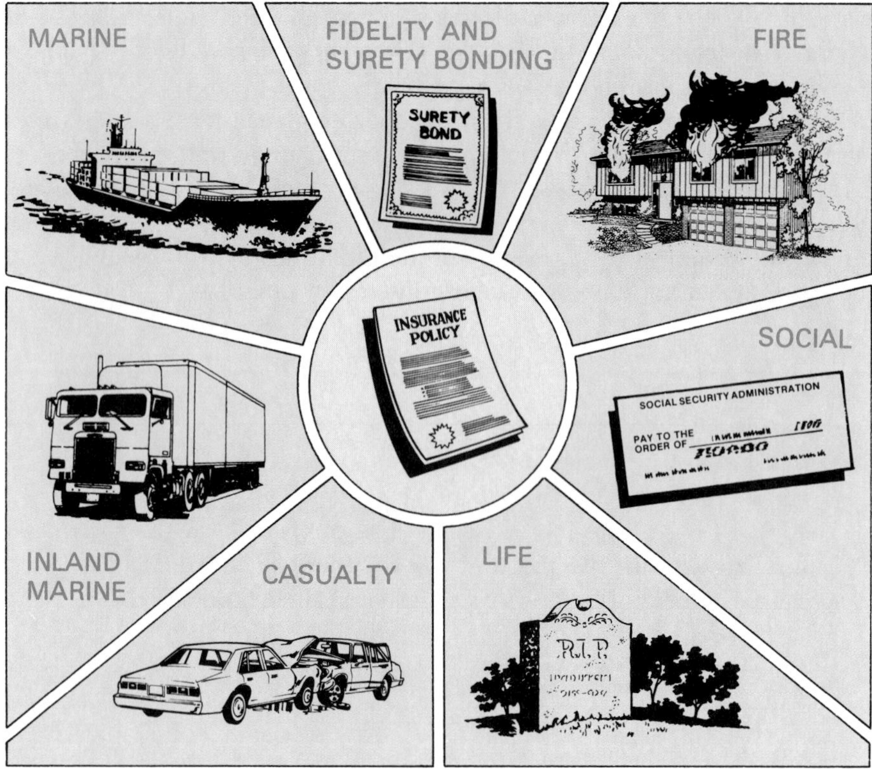

Figure 33-1 *There are seven major types of insurance, all of which have specific coverage.*

Burglary, Robbery, Theft, and Larceny Insurance. Such insurance protects against losses resulting from identifiable criminal behavior. In addition, this form of insurance may also protect against the mysterious disappearance of property (i.e., when the cause of the property's vanishing cannot be ascertained).

Automobile Insurance. This type of insurance indemnifies for losses arising from or connected to the ownership and operation of motor vehicles. Automobile insurance is discussed in Chapter 35.

Liability Insurance. Such insurance provides protection against claims of parties who suffer injury or other loss as a result of negligence or other torts committed by the insured. In the problem, if the Band Boosters were insured under a suitable liability policy, the organization would be protected against claims arising from the fund-raiser.

Disability, Accident, or Health Insurance. These policies protect the insured from the financial consequences of hospital bills and loss of income stemming from accident or illness.

ASSESS

Learning Objective 3 Create a bulletin board entitled *Seven Types of Insurance Policies.* Divide the bulletin board into seven sections, one each for the types of insurance identified on pp. 659–661. Divide the class into seven groups, one for each section. Ask each group to label their section, then scan newspapers and magazines for examples of that type of insurance. Have students paste or staple their examples on the board. Review as a group and adjust, if necessary.

4. Social Insurance

Under the provisions of the Social Security Act and related acts, millions of Americans insure themselves against unemployment, disability, poverty, and medical expense problems typically incurred in their later years. Coverage of the programs set up by our society to handle these problems is provided in Chapter 36.

5. Marine Insurance

Marine insurance indemnifies for loss of or damage to vessels, cargo, and other property exposed to the perils of the sea. It is perhaps the oldest type of insurance, dating back to ancient times.

6. Inland Marine Insurance

Inland marine insurance covers personal property against loss or damage caused by various perils while such property is being transported (other than on the oceans) or wherever such property is located. This insurance is discussed in Chapter 34.

7. Fidelity and Surety Bonding Insurance

This insurance provides coverage against financial loss caused by dishonesty. Such dishonest acts include embezzlement or failure of one person to perform a legal obligation to another, such as constructing a building as promised. Contracts of fidelity insurance are often known as surety bonds.

Thinking Critically Through Visuals

This woman is in the hospital recovering from an automobile accident. What type of insurance would cover her expenses? (Casualty—such as an automobile, accident, or health insurance policy—is the primary coverage although, if she is 65 years of age or older, her social insurance, Medicare, may come into play.)

Personal Perspectives

Have students poll family members, friends, or teachers about the types of insurance they have such as life, health, homeowner's, tenant's automobile, and so on. Have students find out the reasons why people chose each particular kind of insurance. In class, have students create a classroom chart listing the seven common types of insurance. Have students classify their polling results and tally them in the proper column of the class chart. Discuss students' findings.

RETEACH

Media: Before copying the transparency master, *Seven Types of Insurance Policies*, cover the illustrations. Distribute to students and ask them to write a descriptive statement, with examples, under each type of insurance.

ENRICH

Media: Provide newspapers and magazines for students to look for ads promoting various types of insurance. Then, using a computer, if possible, have students prepare their own persuasive ads for one of the seven types of insurance.

Thinking Critically Through Visuals

These emergency workers are trying to rescue the driver of the vehicle. If, in the process, they damage the vehicle, which major type of insurance would cover the damage (assuming coverage is in effect)? (Casualty)

TEACH

Generally, the law of contracts is applicable to the field of insurance, with the four exceptions noted on p. 663. Mutual asssent, consideration, capacity, and proper form are still significant in determining one's rights and responsibilities under insurance contracts. As a point of departure, however, discuss the specific differences when dealing with the insurance industry regarding offer and acceptance, proper form, mutual consideration, and capacity of minors.

HOW DOES THE LAW OF CONTRACTS APPLY TO INSURANCE?

PROBLEM

Addison bought a new sports car at Elegance Cars' downtown sales lot. Before driving off in the $98,000 vehicle, she called her insurance agent and asked for fire, theft, and collision protection. The agent told her to "enjoy driving, you're covered." The car was stolen from Addison a few minutes later when she stopped at a restaurant on the drive home. Will the insurance agent's company cover the loss although it has not received a premium or issued a written policy on the car?

Generally, the law of contracts is applicable to the field of insurance with only minor exceptions. Mutual assent, consideration, capacity, and proper form and legality are all significant in determining rights and responsibilities under insurance contracts. Also, as under contract law, if the insurance contract is ambiguous, its meaning is construed against the drafter of the contract (i.e., the insurer). However, against this backdrop of similarity, the following specific changes, which are due mainly to detailed governmental regulation of the insurance industry, need to be noted.

ASSESS

Divide the class into four groups: offer and acceptance, proper form, mutual consideration, and capacity of minors. Have each group, on an index card, prepare an explanation of their specific change in the law of contracts, as it applies to insurance. Using the "cue" card, have a group spokesperson summarize their category for the class. Listeners should record key points in their notebooks.

1. Offer and Acceptance

In contracting for insurance, the would-be insured becomes the offeror by making out an application for coverage. On the basis of the factual statements in the application and sometimes on the additional basis of further investigation, the potential insurer determines whether it will reject the offer or accept it by issuing the policy.

Most insurance companies operate through well-trained agents who must pass qualifying examinations to acquire the appropriate license to sell. (Read more about the law of agency in Chapter 25.) However, even with their qualifications most agents do not have the authority to alter the written terms that appear in the company's printed form insurance contract. However, in some instances—notably casualty insurance—it is customary for the agent to have the power to make a rudimentary oral agreement to insure an applicant that needs immediate coverage. This was done for Addison in the problem. When this occurs, the insurance is put in force at the moment the oral contract is made, then a written notation called a **binder** is issued as evidence of that oral contract. Unless a loss has occurred in the interim, the company may cancel the policy after it learns more of the facts. In the problem, Addison was covered and she would be able to collect for her loss.

2. Proper Form

State insurance statutes require that a contract of insurance be written, and they mandate much of the wording used in the contract as well. Terms controlling the relationship between the parties are most often dictated by statute. In addition, certain terms, such as exclusions from coverage, must be of a prescribed size, color, or both or they will be voided.

3. Mutual Consideration

Payment of the premium for an insurance contract is usually made in advance of the time for which protection is provided. Installment terms, however, are commonly provided so that large annual or semi-annual premiums can be spread over several months.

4. Capacity of Minors

Minors, because of their statutory lack of capacity, can avoid most contracts, including many types of insurance contracts. However, most states have statutes that prevent minors from avoiding contracts for health, life, or disability insurance.

APPLY

Invite insurance agents from one or more companies to visit your class. Ask the speakers to discuss the important points of insurance contracts, including offer and acceptance, proper form, mutual consideration, and capacity of minors. As a whole group, before the speaker arrives, have students brainstorm questions to ask the speaker.

Guided Practice

Divide the class into groups of three or four students. Provide each group with a copy of your state's insurance statutes. (You can obtain the statutes by contacting your state department of insurance or an insurance company.) Have students read the statutes and highlight what they believe to be the most important points, such as exclusions, information pertaining to minors, who can be covered, and so on. Discuss students' findings. **Independent Practice**

RETEACH In small groups, have students create a graphic organizer to illustrate how the law of contracts applies to insurance.

ENRICH Have students research whether minors in your state can avoid certain insurance contracts because of their statutory lack of capacity. Then, using a computer, if possible, have students write a brief, collective essay that expresses the opinion of the majority.

TEACH

Tell students that there are various state laws that require any organization that contracts to issue insurance to meet high standards of competency and financial reliability. These companies and associations must be chartered by the state and they are grouped according to their type of business. Discuss the difference between (1) **a stock insurance company,** (2) **a mutual insurance company,** and (3) other types of insurers.

APPLY

On the chalkboard, work with students to create a spider map of the three types of qualified insurers. Identify the owners for each. **Guided Practice**

In small groups, using a computer, if possible, have students create a booklet of qualified insurers in their community. Have students begin by collecting ads for the three types of insurers from newspapers, magazines, or the telephone book, or by contacting companies or insurance agents. Have students create a cover, table of contents, and an index for their booklets. Display students' work in your school library or administration office. **Independent Practice**

WHO MAY BE AN INSURER?

PROBLEM

Washam did not carry insurance on his life or on his property because he did not like the fact that the major insurance companies were making huge profits. One day his friend Slyke told him that some insurance companies are owned by the insureds. Is Slyke correct?

The laws of the various states require that any organization that contracts to issue insurance meet high standards of competency and financial reliability. Such organizations must be chartered by the state and consequently come under the close examination of the state insurance commissioner. The companies and associations that are qualified as insurers can be grouped according to their type of business form.

1. Stock Insurance Companies

A **stock insurance company** has capital stock owned by shareholders who contribute the original capital and share the future profits or losses. As a stock company, such an organization is governed by the rules applicable to all corporations as well as by the laws regulating insurance companies.

2. Mutual Insurance Companies

A **mutual insurance company** issues no stock to capitalizing owners. Instead the insureds are the owners, as Slyke correctly noted in the problem. As the members pay their premiums, they contribute to a fund that is used in paying for losses covered by the company's policies as well as for paying the organization's expenses. Because the policyholders are the owners, they are entitled to refunds if losses and expenses are low. These refunds are analogous to the dividends paid to the owners of stock insurance companies but are not taxable income, since the refunds are merely a return of excess premiums paid by the insured. Life insurance policies on which such refunds may be paid are **participating policies.** All mutual company policies are participating policies. Many stock life insurance companies also issue participating policies.

3. Other Types of Insurers

Certain lodges and fraternal societies, such as the Knights of Columbus and the Grange, provide various lines of insurance for their members. State and federal governmental insurance for a variety of perils is also available. For example, workers' compensation insurance, disability insurance, and cer-

ASSESS

Learning Objective 3 Orally, have students identify the three types of companies and associations that are qualified as insurers and explain their type of business. (Stock insurance companies—stock owned by shareholders who contribute the original capital and share the future profits or losses; mutual insurance companies—insureds are the owners; and other types of insurers—fraternal societies, state and federal government issues or sponsors, and Lloyd's of London) tain other forms of casualty insurance are provided by some states. In addition, the federal government issues or sponsors to qualified parties insurance covering risks in areas such as mortgages, deposits in financial institutions, retirement, disability, survivorship, and health.

Finally, as an insurer of last resort, there is Lloyd's of London, England. Lloyd's is famous for assuming a wide diversity of risks, ranging from injury to pianists' fingers to the sinking of massive oil tankers. However, Lloyd's rarely, if ever, handles an ordinary life insurance policy. With that exception, for the customer willing to pay the premium, Lloyd's will issue an insurance policy to cover practically any risk.

WHAT IS THE IMPORTANCE OF REPRESENTATIONS AND WARRANTIES?

PROBLEM

In the application for fire insurance on his building, Phalan stated that the structure had an automatic sprinkler system even though it did not. As a consequence, the insurance policy was issued at a reduced rate. When fire damaged the building shortly thereafter, the insurance company discovered the truth and did not pay for the loss. Was it legally correct in refusing to do so?

An applicant for insurance must provide information about the nature of the risk. For property insurance, this information usually contains statements by the would-be insured about the age, use, and general condition of the property. For life insurance, statements concerning the would-be insured's age, occupation, personal habits, prior illnesses, and the health of his or her parents are pertinent.

If the statements by the applicant are used by the insurer in determining whether to accept the application but are not made part of the final written policy, they are called **representations**. A false representation can render the contract of insurance voidable by the insurer, but only if the statement is material or is so important that it significantly increases the risk. In insurance law, the materiality of a fact usually can be determined by asking: "If this fact had been known, would the insurer have issued the policy on the same terms?" Accordingly, in the problem, because the presence or lack of an automatic sprinkler system would certainly be material, the insurance company was legally justified in avoiding the contract and refusing to pay.

If statements of past or existing fact or promises as to future behavior made by the applicant are included as part of the final written policy, they

Writing Connections

Language Arts
Using a computer, if possible, have students write a (fictitious) letter to Lloyd's of London asking for high-risk coverage. Each letter should give pertinent information about the risk and applicant from which the insurance carrier can determine coverage.

TEACH

Tell students that false **warranties** can render an insurance contract voidable by the insurer. False **representations** will have such an effect only if the facts are material and significantly increase the risk.

APPLY

Orally present several situations in which an insured was deceitful on an insurance application. Have students decide if the lie will render the contract voidable. **Guided Practice**

Divide the class into small groups to write and role-play an insurance fraud news report. Assign the following roles: reporter, insured party, insurer, informant, and facilitator. **Cooperative Learning**

RETEACH

As a group, have students use the chalkboard, a flip chart, or an overhead transparency to create a Venn diagram to compare and contrast **stock insurance companies** and **mutual insurance companies.**

ENRICH

Have students debate which type of organization chartered to sell insurance they think is better—stock, mutual, or other types of insurers. After making this decision, divide the group in half to debate the advantages (pros) and disadvantages (cons) of their selection.

Using a computer, if possible, have pairs of students each write two scenarios in which a person lies on an insurance application. In the first scenario, the lie should render the policy voidable; in the second, the lie should be immaterial.

Independent Practice

▼ TEACH

Failure to disclose material facts is known as **concealment**. An insurance contract may be rescinded if there was concealment with the intent to defraud the insurer. The major exception, with regard to life insurance, is known as an **incontestable clause.** This clause provides that, after two years from the date of issuance, any insurer's claim of misrepresentation of concealment against the insured cannot be used to avoid the contract.

▼ APPLY

Have students brainstorm a list of facts or issues people might conceal from an insurance company. (Answers may include state of health, age, driving or criminal record, and so on.) **Guided Practice**

Have students brainstorm scenarios in which concealment would allow the insurer to rescind the contract and deny the claim and one in which the **incontestable clause** would come into play. **Independent Practice**

are called **warranties**. False warranties make the contract voidable by the insurer whether or not the matter is material. This means that they must be the literal truth or the policy can be avoided even though the insured honestly believed the statements to be true and acted in good faith.

▼ WHAT IS THE EFFECT OF THE CONCEALMENT OF MATERIAL FACTS?

PROBLEM

Salvador applied for and was issued a life insurance policy for $500,000 naming her husband as beneficiary. On the application, she was required to check boxes beside the names of diseases she had previously had. She intentionally did not check the box beside "cancer," although she had been treated for skin cancer. The insurance company discovered this fact three years later, immediately after Salvador had died of cancer. As a consequence, the company refused to pay. Can it legally be forced to pay the $500,000?

The parties to a contract of insurance are required to act with the utmost good faith, especially in regard to material facts. Failure to disclose such facts is known as **concealment**. If a material fact has been concealed with intent to defraud the insurer, the contract may be rescinded and the claim denied.

Where life insurance is concerned, however, there is one major exception to this rule. This exception comes in the form of a statutorily required term called an **incontestable clause.** In most states, this clause provides that after two years from the date of issuance, any insurer's claims of misrepresentation or concealment against the insured cannot be used to avoid the contract. Therefore, in the problem, because the policy was three years old, it is most likely that the insurance company would have to pay the $500,000.

Preventing Legal Difficulties

To have the proper amount of insurance coverage...

1. Make sure your insurance agent is aware of your personal financial situation, property holdings, and insurance needs. Consider your agent's recommendations as to additional types of insurance coverages that may

▼ ASSESS

Learning Objective 4 On index cards, have students write a brief explanation of why is it important to tell the whole truth when filling out an insurance application. (False representations, false warranties, and concealment can void or rescind insurance contracts.) After reviewing the cards for accuracy and completeness of information, have volunteers read aloud their notes to the class. Summarize the key issues and have students record them in their notebooks.

be advisable, but realize that one may prudently assume some risks and should not over-insure.

2. Compare costs and coverages from various companies for the insurance you require and check on the financial stability of these insurance companies.
3. Periodically check the extent and level of your life and property insurance coverage to see if changes need to be made.
4. Be truthful and forthright in answering all questions on insurance applications. Remember that a false representation or warranty or the concealment of a material fact may allow the insurance company to avoid the policy rather than pay for the loss.
5. Carefully read the insurance contract to be familiar with all its terms. Pay special attention to stated exclusions and conditions.
6. Keep an up-to-date itemized list and, if possible, a videotape of insured property away from the reach of fire or thieves. Be sure each item's date of purchase and price are included. In the event of a general loss of your goods, such a list would allow you to recover more fully.

▼ REVIEWING IMPORTANT POINTS

1. Although insurance is an excellent way to protect against possible loss, certain risks—such as that of doing business—cannot be covered.
2. To be indemnified for damage to or destruction of property, the insurable interest of the insured must exist at the time of the loss. To be indemnified for the loss of life, it is necessary that the insurable interest of the applicant exist only at the time the policy is issued; it does not have to exist at the time of loss.
3. Generally, the law of contracts applies to the field of insurance with relatively minor changes.
4. Mutual insurance company insureds can enjoy several advantages, such as nontaxable premium refunds and other privileges of ownership, over the insureds of stock insurance companies.
5. False warranties can render an insurance contract voidable by the insurance company. False representations will have such an effect only if they are of material facts or facts that significantly increase the risk.

Ethics Issue

When applying for insurance coverage, some people opt to conceal information (such as past health problems or family history) because they are afraid that they will not be given the insurance or that their premiums will be too high. Ask: **If your friend were afraid that he or she would not be able to obtain insurance because of a pre-existing medical condition, would you condone lying to get insurance coverage?** Ask students if they think it is ethical for someone to use the identity of an insured person in order to get medical coverage for an operation.

Preventing Legal Difficulties

In small groups, have students create posters explaining the importance of the six points (pp. 666–667) for obtaining the proper amount of insurance coverage. Have students share their knowledge with family and friends.

▼RETEACH Have students make individual, insurance-related cartoons to explain the following terms: *false representations*, **warranties, concealment,** and the **incontestable clause.** You may wish to use a cartoon from the editorial section of your newspaper as a model. Display students' work.

▼ENRICH Have students create a public service announcement (PSA) stressing the importance of telling the truth on insurance applications and the consequences of lying.

CLOSE

Using a computer, if possible, have each student write a position paper on the kinds of policies that insurance companies should sell versus those that they think

the federal government should provide.

Assign the following end-of-chapter materials:
Student text review activities, pp. 667–671
Workbook, pp. 105–106
Chapter Test

Chapter MicroExam

Strengthening Your Legal Vocabulary

1. beneficiary
2. policy
3. premium
4. representations
5. face value
6. warranties
7. indemnify
8. binder
9. insurer
10. mutual insurance company

Applying Law to Everyday Life

1. **(a)** Harvest States Insurance Company, **(b)** Copeland, **(c)** Copeland's home, **(d)** loss by fire, **(e)** $225,000, and **(f)** $1,187. (pp. 656–657)

STRENGTHENING YOUR LEGAL VOCABULARY

Match each term with the statement that best defines that term. Some terms may not be used.

beneficiary	insurer
binder	mutual insurance company
concealment	participating policies
face value	policy
incontestable clause	premium
indemnify	representations
insurable interest	risk
insurance	stock insurance company
insured	warranties

1. Recipient of the amount paid on an insurance claim.
2. Written contract of insurance.
3. Consideration paid for coverage under an insurance contract.
4. Pertinent statements made by the applicant for insurance that are not made a part of the final written policy.
5. Stated maximum amount to be paid in the event the harm insured against occurs.
6. Pertinent statements or promises by the applicant for insurance that are made a part of the final written policy.
7. To make good the actual loss suffered.
8. Written notation given as evidence of a preliminary, oral contract of insurance.
9. Party who agrees to indemnify.
10. Type of insurance company in which the insureds are the owners.

APPLYING LAW TO EVERYDAY LIFE

1. Copeland contracted for fire insurance coverage for the full value of her $225,000 home at an annual cost of $1,187. The policy was issued by Harvest States Insurance Company.
   Identify
   a. the insurer,
   b. the insured,
   c. the subject matter,
   d. the risk,

e. the face value, and

f. the premium.

2 Severson planted a large cucumber crop on her farm. To help her at harvest time, she bought a motorized "pickle picker" from a farm supply store for $7,300. She paid $2,300 in cash and financed the balance. The seller, Equipment Unlimited, retained a security interest in the device. The next summer, Muscando, a neighboring farmer, leased the harvester from Severson. Of these parties, which one(s) had an insurable interest in the "pickle picker?"

3 An abandoned store surrounded by high, dry weeds stood adjacent to a frequently traveled road near Ashleigh's home. She realized that the store would be destroyed if just one cigarette butt were thrown from a passing vehicle. Therefore, even though she did not own it, she decided to insure the building against loss by fire. After she obtained the insurance, there was a fire. Legally, will Ashleigh be allowed to collect?

4 Claudia James took out a $200,000 life insurance policy on her husband and named herself as beneficiary. Three months later they were divorced, and a month after that her ex-husband died in a car accident. Claudia sought to collect on the policy, but the insurance company refused to pay, stating she lacked an insurable interest both at the time the policy was taken out and at the time of death. Is the company legally obligated to pay the $200,000?

5 Stark bought a new car. Before driving away from the dealership in it, he called his insurance agent for coverage. Over the telephone the agent said, "Okay, you're covered. Come in and sign the papers as soon as you possibly can." Stark hung up the telephone, got in the car, drove two blocks, and was involved in a collision that destroyed the vehicle. Must the insurance company indemnify Stark for the loss of the automobile?

6 ETHICS ISSUE Garrett, a minor, took out a personal life insurance policy at age fourteen. One month before reaching majority, Garrett sued to avoid the policy and collect the premiums previously paid. Will Garrett be successful? Ethically, should Garrett be allowed to recover the premiums?

7 Benesh applied for life insurance. The insurance company had him undergo a medical examination. Although he had had diabetes for many years, Benesh, thinking it unimportant because the examiner did not ask about it, did not volunteer the fact. Five years later, Benesh died of complications from the disease. Will the insurance company be able to rescind the contract and deny any claim because of Benesh's failure to volunteer the information?

2 Severson (title), Equipment Unlimited (security interest), and Muscando (possession and use) each had an insurable interest in the "pickle picker." (pp. 657–658)

3 No; Ashleigh did not suffer any direct and measurable monetary loss from the burning of the store. (p. 658)

4 Yes; For life insurance, a person need have an insurable interest only at the time the insurance is taken out. A person generally has such an interest in a spouse. The $200,000 belongs to Claudia. (p. 659)

5 Yes; Agents can issue immediately effective binders for property insurance as a result of oral agreements such as the one entered into by Stark. (p. 663)

6 ETHICS ISSUE The answer to both the legal and ethical questions should be *no*. Although, legally, minors can avoid most contracts and receive their consideration back, an exception is made in the case of a life, health, or disability contract. (p. 663) Ethically, Garrett could not justify such an action from an individual perspective. As a society, however, we would perhaps want such protection afforded to minors due to the complexity of such insurance contracts and the relative inexperience of minors.

7 No; An incontestable clause would not allow such avoidance. (p. 666)

8  Jason had a rare blood disease that he had inherited from his mother. The disease was almost impossible to detect until it entered its terminal phases, and victims usually died in their early forties. When he turned forty, Jason contracted for a $500,000 life insurance policy and named a charity devoted to conquering crippling children's diseases as beneficiary. Before it issued the policy, the insurance company subjected him to an exhaustive physical examination and 173 detailed questions on diseases he might have had. Jason answered each question honestly and none of the answers nor the physical exam produced any indication of the rare disease. Ethically, should Jason have volunteered the information? Legally, was he required to volunteer the information?

9 Angel Flynn was an opera star at the height of her career. Worried that her fame and fortune might evaporate if she lost her singing voice, she sought to insure it. However, every U.S. insurance agent and company she approached declined the opportunity. As a last resort, what company might she apply to for the insurance?

10 McNeely owned a go-cart track on which the public was invited to race the small motorized carts that she provided. Collisions and upsets occurred relatively frequently. What type of insurance would it be advisable for McNeely to have?

SOLVING CASE PROBLEMS

1 Antrell made an offer to purchase a building on the Leech Lake Indian Reservation in Minnesota for $300. He paid $100 in cash at the time he made the offer and received the keys to the structure. Without examining the property, the defendant insurance company issued a policy with a face value of $16,000 covering the building. Several months later, fire totally destroyed the structure. At the time of the loss, Antrell had not paid the balance of the purchase price nor had the title been transferred. The company claims that the plaintiff did not have the required insurable interest and that, therefore, the company was not liable on the policy. You decide. (*Antrell v. Pearl Assurance Company*, 89 N.W.2d 726)

2 Lakin sued the Postal Life and Casualty Insurance Company for its failure to pay him, as beneficiary, under an insurance policy on the life of his business partner, Hankinson. Evidence presented at the trial showed that Hankinson had contributed neither capital nor skills to the alleged partnership, that he could not issue partnership checks, and that

8 ETHICS ISSUE Ethically, a consequentialist might salute Jason's methodology for producing the greatest good for the greatest number. A follower of deontological ethical systems might say that Jason's actions have already become universal law due to the presence of incontestable clauses in most state insurance codes. Legally, if such a material fact has been concealed to defraud the insurer, then the policy can be voided should the truth be discovered within the incontestable clause period. (p. 666)

9 Lloyd's of London is recognized as the insurer of last resort for risks such as that of Angel's voice. (p. 665)

10 It would be highly advisable for McNeely to acquire liability insurance to cover the numerous potential risks. (p. 660)

Solving Case Problems

1 Judgment for Antrell; It is not necessary for one to be an owner of property to have an insurable interest in it. Antrell was the future owner of the property who had paid a substantial part of the purchase price and who therefore had suffered the required monetary loss by the destruction of the property. (pp. 657–658)

2 No; The court held that Lakin was a legal partner of Hankinson but even so suffered no loss from Hankinson's death. Therefore no insurable interest was present when the insurance policy was initiated, and Lakin could not collect the face amount. (pp. 658–659)

he could not hire or fire employees. In addition, it was disclosed that Lakin paid the policy premiums and had made no settlement of "partnership" interests after Hankinson's death. Should the insurance company be ordered by the court to pay the $25,000 face amount to Lakin? (*Lakin v. Postal Life and Casualty Insurance Company*, 316 S.W.2d 542)

3 In the life insurance policy agreed to by James McElroy was a term that read, "if the insured is over the age of fifty-four years at the date hereof, this policy is void...." McElroy was indeed over fifty-four at the time. When he died three years later, his beneficiary sued for the face amount of the policy claiming it should be paid because of a two-year incontestable clause in the same policy. Should the court order the insurance company to pay the policy's face amount? (*Hall v. Missouri Ins. Co.*, 208 S.W.2d 830)

4 Milburn carried automobile damage and theft insurance on his Cadillac sedan as required by the creditor on his car loan. When the payments became burdensome, Milburn turned the car over to an automobile salesperson to sell. The salesperson failed to do so, and ultimately disappeared with the car. The insurer, Manchester Insurance Company, refused to pay, and World Investment Company, Milburn's creditor on the loan, sued Manchester. Manchester claimed that the policy insured against theft which, as larceny, involved a taking against the owner's will. Since Milburn voluntarily delivered the car to the salesperson, no theft had occurred. World Investment Company claimed instead that the word "theft" should be given its common meaning of "steal" and that, as a consequence, the insurance company should pay. You decide. (*World Investment Co. v. Manchester Insurance and Indemnity Co.*, 380 S.W.2d 487)

5 When Wilson and his passenger and fellow employee Davison were injured in an automobile accident, the insurance company stated that the policy on Wilson excluded coverage of more than one person in a single accident. Davison sued, contending that since the exclusion of coverage in the policy was not in a different color or type than the rest of the policy as required by state statute, the term was void, and he could recover. The insurance company pointed out that although the exclusion did not appear in a different color or type of print, it was in a section of the policy clearly labeled "exclusions." Should Davison be allowed to collect? (*Davison v. Wilson*, 239 N.W.2d 38)

3 No; McElroy's age voided the contract, so the incontestable clause is void as well and has no effect. (p. 666)

4 Judgment for the creditor, World Investment Company; When a term in a carefully drafted insurance contract is ambiguous, the court will construe the terms against the maker. "Theft" was therefore given its common meaning of "steal," and the insurance company was ordered to pay. (p. 662)

5 Yes; The statute reflected a public policy that all reasonable steps should be taken to bring the insured's attention to terms that would adversely affect his or her interest. The court noted that the particular exclusion in question was "buried in the obscurity of two paragraphs that dealt exclusively with workers' compensation." Because of the insurance company's failure to comply, the term was void and Davison was allowed to collect. (p. 663)

CHAPTER 34 ORGANIZER

Chapter Theme

Property and casualty insurance contracts contain several clauses, including those related to recovery for a loss, extensions, assignment, termination, and cancellation.

DIRECTED STUDY QUESTIONS	SPECIAL FEATURES	PROGRAM RESOURCES				
		Reteach	Enrich	S N	A M	
What are property insurance and casualty insurance?	Multicultural Highlights, p. 674	✔	✔			
What is a comprehensive insurance policy?	Thinking Critically Through Visuals, p. 675	✔	✔			
What risks are covered by fire insurance and how are losses under such a policy proven?		✔	✔		K	
What is coinsurance?		✔	✔	✔		
What does inland marine insurance cover?		✔	✔		A	
What is the purpose of liability insurance?	Thinking Critically Through Visuals, p. 680	✔	✔		V	
How does an insured collect after a loss?	Personal Perspectives, p. 681 Writing Connections, p. 682 Ethics Issue, p. 682	✔	✔			
How is an insurance policy terminated?	Preventing Legal Difficulties, p. 684	✔	✔			

Additional Resources

- *Insurance Facts: Property, Liability, Marine, Surety.* NY: Insurance Information Institute, 1983.
- *State Solvency Regulation of Property-casualty and Life Insurance Companies: A Commission Report.* Washington, D.C.: United States Advisory Commission on Intergovernmental Relations, 1992.

One-semester course	✔							
One-year course	✔	✔	✔					

		ASSESSMENT OPPORTUNITIES			
	Cooperative Learning	**Informal Assessment**	**Chapter Review**	**Chapter Test**	**Chapter *MicroExam*** (Media)
		✔	✔	✔	✔
		✔	✔	✔	✔
		✔	✔	✔	✔
		✔	✔	✔	✔
		✔	✔	✔	✔
		✔	✔	✔	✔
	✔	✔	✔	✔	✔
		✔	✔	✔	✔

Videodiscs

Property Insurance: Comprehensive, Inland Marine, and Liability

Search Chapter 42, Play To 43

State by State

New York law prohibits an insurer from being liable for damages caused by someone other than the vehicle's lessee driving.

Teaching Materials

Student text, pp. 672–689

Overhead transparency masters
- *Collecting for Losses* Sides 1 & 2

Videos
- *Law for Business* Videodisc

Workbook, pp. 107–108

Outside Resources
- Sample insurance policies (with policy termination information)
- Poster board
- Newspaper articles discussing liability insurance cases
- Past and current catalogs or price lists for the same or similar items
- Art supplies: poster paper, paints or colored markers, and paste or glue
- Blank overhead transparencies

- Tape recorder

Assessment
- Chapter Test

- Chapter *MicroExam*

Vocabulary

property insurance, p. 674
casualty insurance, p. 674
exclusions, p. 674
comprehensive policy, p. 675
standard fire policy, p. 676
forms, p. 676
endorsements, p. 676
extended coverage endorsement, p. 676
hostile fire, p. 677
friendly fire, p. 677
coinsurance, p. 677
inland marine insurance, p. 678
personal property floater, p. 679
floater, p. 679
liability insurance, p. 679
claim, p. 681
notice of loss, p. 681
proof of loss, p. 681
actual cash value, p. 681
replacement cost, p. 682
subrogation, p. 682
prorate, p. 683

Learning Objectives

When you complete this chapter, you will be able to

1. Recognize the importance of property and casualty insurance.
2. Identify the risks covered by a comprehensive, inland marine, or liability insurance policy.
3. Understand the manner in which coinsurance works.
4. Know how to collect from an insurer after a covered loss.
5. Be aware of when and how an insurance policy can be terminated.

672

Chapter Self-Test

Assess students' understanding of property and casualty insurance before they begin Chapter 34 by asking them to respond orally to the following *True* or *False* statements: **(1) The purpose of casualty insurance is to allow victims of loss to recover just a little more than the actual value of the loss.** (False); and **(2) Certain circumstances relieve the insurance company from paying for loss, but these circumstances, known as exclusions, must be expressly stated in the policy.** (True) Before continuing with the chapter, review and discuss students' responses.

CHAPTER

34 PROPERTY AND CASUALTY INSURANCE

1 When lightening strikes your home and starts a fire, you begin moving valuable personal property out of the house. Unfortunately, while moving your new personal computer and monitor, you drop them. They are damaged beyond repair. Will your fire insurance cover the loss of the computer and monitor?

2 Your friend Joe is injured when the small motorized cart he is driving on an amusement park ride loses a wheel and overturns. What kind of insurance would protect the owner of the park if Joe sues?

3 

While you are away on vacation, a fire ravages your house. Upon returning home, you file an insurance claim for all the property you can remember being in the house. Although you are paid fairly by the insurance company, you think you have forgotten to list a claim for many of your belongings. Several weeks later, stuffed behind the spare tire in the trunk of your car, you find an expensive watch you thought had been lost in the fire. You recovered $400 for the watch from your insurance claim. Should you report your error to your insurance company and return the money? How could you have prevented any uncertainty about what property was in the house?

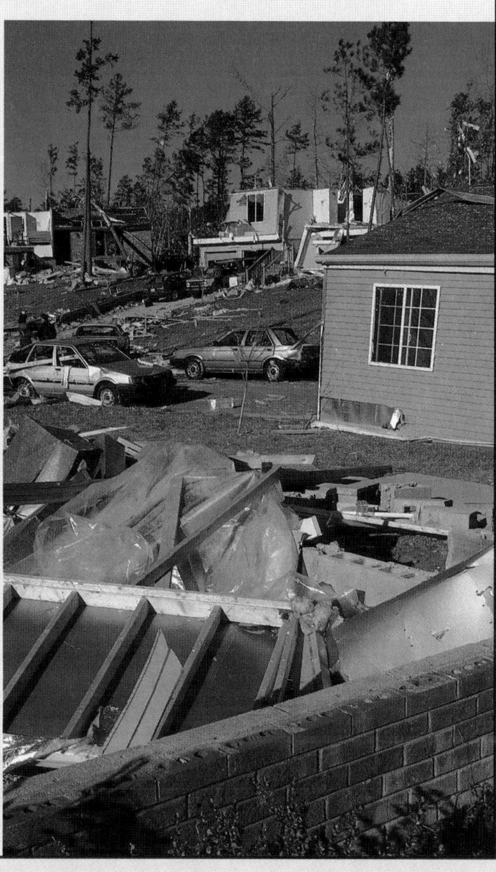

FOCUS

As students enter the classroom, have them gather in groups of two or three, brainstorm, and write on a piece of paper potential dangers to personal or real property, such as fire or theft.

When class begins, make and display a composite list on a blank overhead transparency or on the chalkboard and discuss specific examples of each. Ask students to project the impact that each event would have. Point out that, in addition to other ramifications, substantial expense would result. Tell students that guaranteeing reimbursement for this expense is the idea behind **property** and **casualty insurance.** Media Retain the list for the activity on p. 675.

You Decide

1 Yes; A fire insurance policy will cover not only losses caused by burning and smoke from a hostile fire but also the damage done in fighting the fire and in hastily removing goods to a safe location.

2 Liability insurance would protect the owner of the park from a recovery by your friend in a lawsuit.

3 ETHICS ISSUE A person subscribing to the ethic of honesty, regardless of consequences, would report the finding of the watch. A careful and up-to-date inventory of the property would have greatly reduced the uncertainty surrounding the filing of proof of loss.

Thinking Critically Through Visuals

The photograph shows the aftermath of a storm. Which type of property damage—real or personal—is in evidence? (Both) **What types of damage could be covered by insurance?** (Property and casualty)

▼ TEACH

The purpose of both **property** and **casualty insurance** is to indemnify for a loss; that is, to cover no more than the actual value of the loss. On the chalkboard, make a two-column chart with the headings *Property* and *Casualty*. List examples of each type of insurance under the appropriate columns. Define **exclusions** and discuss common ones.

▼ APPLY

Multicultural Highlights

In the past, some financial institutions and insurance companies sought to control their economic risk by *redlining*. The name grew from the practice of outlining neighborhoods—usually low-income sections inhabited by people of color—on maps in red to indicate areas in which the bank or insurance company would not do business. Redlining was outlawed by Title VIII of the 1968 Civil Rights Act. Discuss how redlining might affect the insurance coverage of residents in redlined areas. **Guided Practice**

WHAT ARE PROPERTY INSURANCE AND CASUALTY INSURANCE?

PROBLEM

Waste Not, Want Not, an environmentally oriented rock group, insured all its $28,000 worth of equipment with each of two companies. When the group's tour bus overturned and the equipment was destroyed, the group tried to collect in full from both companies. Will it be allowed to do so?

The general type of insurance intended to indemnify for harm to the insured's personal or real property brought about by perils such as fire, theft, and windstorm is **property insurance.** The type of insurance that indemnifies for losses resulting from accident, chance, or negligence is **casualty insurance.** There is some overlap between these two. Certain types of casualty insurance (e.g., automotive policies) are written to indemnify for casualty and property losses. Examples of casualty insurance include workers' compensation, disability insurance, and health insurance. Liability insurance, which protects the insured against other parties' claims of negligence or other tortious conduct, is also a type of casualty insurance.

The purpose of all property and casualty insurance is indemnification for loss. This means that a person who experiences a loss recovers no more than the actual value of the loss. In the problem, Waste Not, Want Not's total recovery from both insurance companies could not exceed $28,000.

Although property and casualty insurance can be obtained to indemnify for almost any peril that might cause a loss, certain circumstances relieve the insurance company from paying. These exceptions to coverage, known as **exclusions**, are expressly stated in the policy. Many states make certain that any exclusions are easily noticeable within a policy by requiring them to be set in a different style and larger size of type, in a different color of print, or both. Examples of common exclusions include losses due to war, invasion, insurrection (i.e., rebellion), nuclear disaster, depreciation, and pollution.

WHAT IS A COMPREHENSIVE INSURANCE POLICY?

PROBLEM

The Bernsteins did not want to take the time to evaluate all the different types of insurance coverage they should have. Instead, they bought what their agent called an "all-risk" policy. Later they were dis-

▼ ASSESS

Learning Objective 1 Have students respond orally to the following questions: **(1) Workers' compensation, disability insurance, and health insurance are examples of which kind of insurance?** (Casualty insurance); **(2) Which type of insurance is intended to indemnify for harm brought about by fire, theft, or storms?** (Property insurance); and **(3) What are stated exceptions to insurance coverage called?** (Exclusions) turbed when their neighbor said the policy did not cover all risks. Is the neighbor correct?

A **comprehensive policy** (also called an all-risk package or homeowner's policy) is a policy that may be written to contain all the real property, personal property, and liability coverages needed by the average family. Losses from fire, theft, legal liability, windstorm, hail, vandalism, glass breakage, and other causes may all be insured against under such a policy.

As with all insurance policies, there may be exclusions. Exclusions with this type of policy could include losses caused by termites, earthquakes, floods, and insurrections. Also excluded could be losses that are normally covered by other insurance. Such losses could arise from the ownership and operation of motor vehicles, boats, and aircraft, as well as from business activities. All-risk policies cover losses from all perils except those that are specifically excluded in the policy. In the problem, the neighbor is correct. The Bernsteins should take the time to study their all-risk policy and, where possible, insure against the excluded risks.

In some cases, it may be better to insure against individual risks in separate policies rather than to insure against many risks in a more expensive comprehensive policy. Therefore, it is important to know as much as possible about the individual types of property and casualty insurance.

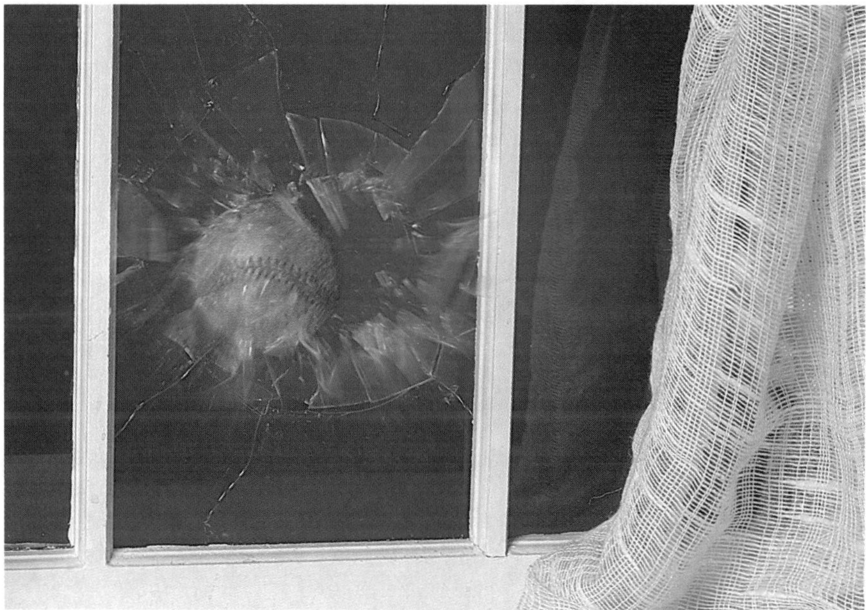

Photocopy and distribute the list of dangers from the FOCUS activity. Have students label each item with the kind of insurance by which it would most likely be covered. **Independent Practice**

▼ TEACH

Explain that a **comprehensive policy** insures against a wide scope of risks under one policy. Display Side 2 of the overhead transparency, *Collecting for Losses*. Discuss the

types of losses covered and the typical exclusions.

▼ APPLY

Thinking Critically Through Visuals

What kind of insurance policy might cover a baseball smashing through a homeowner's window? (Comprehensive or property) **Guided Practice**

Distribute to students copies of insurance policies, including a comprehensive policy, on which SAMPLE is written. In small groups, have students compare coverages and costs. Have each group conclude which policy is more favorable. **Independent Practice**

▼RETEACH

Have students write, in their own words, using a computer, if possible, definitions of **property insurance, casualty insurance,** and **exclusions.** Have students exchange papers and critique each other's work.

▼ENRICH

Ask students to brainstorm reasons for the common exclusions in insurance policies. Then have students write, using a computer, if possible, a scenario in which they need to purchase property or casualty insurance.

TEACH

Explain that fire insurance is a type of property insurance, which covers the risk of direct loss to property resulting from fire. Explain the relationship between a **standard fire policy, forms,** and **endorsements.** Then, list and discuss the three steps on p. 677 that must be taken to prove that a particular loss should be indemnified. Make sure students understand the difference between **hostile** and **friendly fires.**

APPLY

On the chalkboard, draw a graphic organizer to show the relationship between a **standard fire policy, forms,** and **endorsements.** Discuss variations of each. You may wish to have students define each term as you write it on the chalkboard. **Guided Practice**

Divide the class into pairs. Provide pairs with poster board and markers. Tell students to create a poster that graphically illustrates the three steps to prove that a loss should be indemnified. Display students' posters on a bulletin board called *Firing Line: To Pay or Not to Pay?*.

Independent Practice

WHAT RISKS ARE COVERED BY FIRE INSURANCE AND HOW ARE LOSSES UNDER SUCH A POLICY PROVEN?

PROBLEM

Zelmar ran a mail-order computer sales business in a building she owned. Late one night, the building and its contents were destroyed by a fire set by an arsonist. Will Zelmar's fire insurance cover her loss?

The risk that is covered by fire insurance alone is the direct loss to property resulting from fire, lightning strike, or removal from premises endangered by fire. Any fire insurance contract written to cover these risks is composed of a basic or **standard fire policy** and one or more **forms** that modify the standard policy to make it apply to the specific type of property being insured. The standard fire policy itself is composed of basic policy provisions required by the law of the state in which the policy is written. All the states have such provisions. Some forms include a Dwellings and Contents Form for homes and a Mercantile Building and Stock Form for businesses. For those who have no need for policies to cover the building itself, such as renters and tenants, there are special forms covering only the contents and other personal property.

The standard policy and forms may also be modified by **endorsements** (also known as *riders*). These endorsements are attached to the policy and forms to provide for special and individual needs. For example, difficulty often arises in determining whether a loss was the direct result of fire, lightning, windstorm, explosion, or some other peril. Suppose that a truck crashes into a building and explodes, causing a fire. In such a case, it would be hard to tell how much of the loss was caused by the impact of the truck, how much by the explosion, and how much by the resulting fire. To avoid this difficulty, a fire insurance policy may be issued with an **extended coverage endorsement.** This endorsement adds coverage for damage by windstorm, hail, explosion, riot, smoke, aircraft, and vehicles. Therefore, it would not be necessary to determine the exact cause of the damage, since all possible causes would be covered. Because of the frequency of the losses covered by an extended coverage endorsement, such an endorsement usually is added routinely to the Dwellings and Contents Form.

Regardless of the particular forms or endorsements added to the standard fire policy, three steps must be taken to prove that a particular loss should be indemnified.

ASSESS

Learning Objective 1 Have students respond orally to the following *True* or *False* statements: **(1) A store with a standard fire policy could collect for lost profit as well as damage to the building resulting from a hostile fire.** (False); **(2) The term *rider* is another term for *form*.** (False); **(3) An extended coverage endorsement is not usually added to a Dwellings and Contents Form.** (False); and **(4) The first thing the insured must show to indemnify a loss covered by fire insurance is that there was an actual fire.** (True)

First, the insured must show that there was an actual fire. A glow or a flame is required. Damage to an item resulting from scorching, blistering, or smoke due to being too near to another type of heat source is not enough.

Second, the actual fire has to be hostile. A **hostile fire** is either (1) a fire started by accident, negligence, or a deliberate act uncontrolled by the insured or (2) a **friendly fire** (i.e., a fire in its intended place) that becomes uncontrollable.

Third, the hostile fire has to be the natural and foreseeable cause of the loss. In Chapter 6, this is referred to as being the proximate cause of the harm. Generally, a hostile fire is not only considered the proximate cause of damage caused by the burning, but also that caused by scorching, smoke, techniques used in extinguishing the fire, and actions in removing goods endangered by the fire.

In the problem, if she had the appropriate Mercantile Building and Stock Form, Zelmar would be able to recover on her fire policy for the proximate losses to her building, business inventory, and equipment. However, she could not recover for any lost profits caused by the fire nor could she recover if it could be proven that she had hired the arsonist.

▼ WHAT IS COINSURANCE?

PROBLEM

The town of Miller, Missouri, insured its municipal building under a fire insurance policy with an 80-percent coinsurance clause. At the time of a fire that totally destroyed the structure, the building was valued at $100,000 and the face value of the policy was $80,000. How much of the $100,000 loss would the insurance policy cover?

As the capability of fire departments to respond to alarms and quickly suppress fires increased over the years, the number of structures totally lost to fire decreased markedly. Consequently, in recognition of this fact and the needs of their insureds to keep premiums low, insurance companies developed coinsurance.

Coinsurance is a clause in an insurance policy that requires the insured to maintain coverage equal to a certain percentage of the total current value of the insured property. The coverage amount, therefore, must be increased as the property value increases. In the event of loss, the insurance company will fully indemnify up to the face amount of the policy unless the

▼ TEACH

Point out that **coinsurance** is a clause in an insurance policy that requires the insured to maintain coverage equal to a certain percentage (typically 80%) of the total current value of the insured property. Explain that the coverage must be increased as the property value increases or the insurance company will pay for a smaller portion of the loss. Discuss the benefits of coinsurance. Explain how coinsurance works by working out on the chalkboard, step-by-step, the examples that appear on p. 678.

▼ APPLY

For Basic Education and Compensatory Education students who have difficulty with math problems, prepare and distribute a worksheet of problems using the 80% coinsurance clause. For example: **Smyth owned a building with a value of $40,000 and insured it against loss to the extent of $24,000. A $16,000 loss occurred. Would he be indemnified for $16,000?** (No; He would receive only the fractional amount of insurance actually carried, divided by the amount he should have carried [$24,000 ÷ $32,000 = 0.75 of the loss suffered; $16,000 × 0.75 = $12,000]) Allow students time to complete the problems. Then, have them demonstrate their work on the chalkboard. Discuss answers.

Guided Practice

▼RETEACH

Pair students. Using a computer, if possible, have each pair write a one-page article explaining which risks are covered by fire insurance and how losses under such a policy are proven.

▼ENRICH

Have students brainstorm endorsements that the school might carry. If possible, have students check with school administrators to determine actual coverage and report their findings to the class.

Have each student create a problem involving a coinsurance clause and write it, and their name, on a sheet of paper. Have students work out the answers on a separate sheet of paper. Collect the papers with students' problems and redistribute them. Have students work out the problem they receive and then check their answer with the writer. **Independent Practice**

TEACH

Compare the term *inland* with the term *on the high seas.* Discuss the transition from marine insurance to **inland marine insurance** to a **personal property floater.** Explain that inland marine insurance does not cover the carrier, but personal property floater insurance, in which the protection "floats" with the property, does. Give examples of *bailee insurance.*

APPLY

On the chalkboard, with the help of students, create a flowchart to illustrate the transportation of goods. At each stage, have the class discuss what perils may exist that could result in loss. Then have students speculate which type of insurance might provide coverage at each stage. **Guided Practice**

insured has failed to keep that face amount at the proper level. For example, suppose that the insured's property has a current value of $50,000 and that the policy has an 80-percent coinsurance clause. Therefore, the insured will have to have a $40,000 (80 percent of $50,000) face value on the policy. If the insured has this, the insurance company will pay any loss in full up to a limit of $40,000. The insured will have to bear any amount of loss in excess of the $40,000.

If the insured does not increase the face value of the policy as the property value increases, the insurance company will pay for a smaller portion of the loss. For example, assume that the above insured's property value increases from $50,000 to $100,000, yet the insured keeps the face value at $40,000. If a $50,000 loss occurs, the insurance company will not pay the face value of the policy of $40,000. The insurance company will pay an amount equal to the loss ($50,000) times the fraction of insurance actually carried ($40,000) divided by the amount that should have been carried ($100,000 × 80 percent = $80,000). Consequently, the company will pay for one-half of the loss. The insured would have to bear the other $25,000.

Remember that the insurance company will never pay more than the face amount of the policy. In the problem at the beginning of this section, even though the town of Miller was carrying the full amount required by the coinsurance provisions ($80,000), the town would still have to bear $20,000 of the loss ($100,000 − $80,000).

The system of coinsurance is somewhat complex, but it can result in up to a 70-percent savings in premium amounts for policies covering fire-resistant buildings in areas with good fire departments.

WHAT DOES INLAND MARINE INSURANCE COVER?

PROBLEM

While visiting a theme park on their vacation, the Baldnorf family was approached by one of the costumed characters, Slappy the Seal. Slappy offered to videotape the Baldnorfs. Shortly after they gave Slappy their new videocamera, Slappy slipped away with it. Slappy's costume was later found by park officials, and it became clear that the camera had been stolen by an imposter. Will the Baldnorfs' personal property floater cover the loss?

Modeled after insurance covering goods being transported on the high seas, **inland marine insurance** was developed by fire insurance companies

ASSESS

Learning Objective 2 Have students jot down answers to the following: **(1) What is the meaning of the term *floater*?** (The protection floats with, or follows, the property.); **(2) Which came first, *inland marine insurance* or *personal property floater* insurance?** (Inland marine insurance); and **(3) After which type of insurance is inland marine insurance modeled?** (Insurance covering goods being transported on the high seas) to indemnify for loss to most personal property while it is being transported across land. However, the carrier—such as the automobile, airplane, or railroad car—is not covered by this insurance. In response to the changing needs of insureds over time, the basic inland marine policy was altered to produce a second type, called a **personal property floater.** This was issued to cover any and all of an insured's personal property against practically any peril regardless of the location of the property. The term **floater** means that the protection floats with, or follows, the property. Rather than have the policy written to cover all the insured's personal property, it is also possible to contract for coverage of scheduled (i.e., specifically identified) property, such as jewelry, furs, stamp collections, musical instruments, livestock, athletic equipment, wedding presents, and photographic equipment. One can also arrange to insure a single piece of personal property, such as an organ or a neon sign. Mail-order dealers frequently take out a blanket policy to cover all losses, including breakage and mysterious disappearances of shipped goods. Laundries and dry cleaners may take out policies covering possible losses to customers' property in their possession. Such a policy is known as *bailee insurance.*

Although the application of the personal property floater is quite broad, some losses are excluded from coverage; for example, losses caused by wear and tear, repair efforts, dampness, temperature, war, confiscation, and dishonesty of a party to whom the goods have been entrusted. In the problem, because the Baldnorfs entrusted Slappy with the videocamera, their loss would probably be excluded from the coverage of their personal property floater. Personal property insurance may be purchased as a separate policy or as a part of a homeowner's policy.

WHAT IS THE PURPOSE OF LIABILITY INSURANCE?

PROBLEM

Dr. Wilma Lancet is being sued by the family of a man who died of complications after an operation she performed. What type of insurance would protect her from loss?

Liability insurance is a type of casualty insurance that indemnifies against personal injury or property damage claims for which the insured is legally responsible. Generally, liability coverage is limited to harm accidentally caused by the insured. Intentional infliction of harm by the insured is not covered.

Divide the class into three groups. Assign each group one of the following types of insurance: inland marine, personal property floater, and bailee. Have groups create and tape record persuasive radio ads for the type of insurance they were assigned. The ad should make clear to whom the ad is directed, what losses are covered, and what losses are excluded. Play the tapes for the class. **Independent Practice**

TEACH

Define **liability insurance** as a type of casualty insurance that indemnifies against personal injury or property damage claims for which the insured is legally responsible. Explain that the coverage is limited to accidental harm only, not to intentional harm.

APPLY

Before class, obtain a news article discussing a liability insurance case, such as malpractice. Read the news article as an example of the need for this type of insurance. Have students identify what is covered. Give other examples of liability insurance. **Guided Practice**

RETEACH Have students create a graphic organizer to illustrate what inland marine insurance and personal property floaters cover.

ENRICH In small groups, have students make a three-column chart with the headings *Inland marine insurance, Personal property insurance,* and *Bailee insurance.* Have students brainstorm different situations in which each type of insurance would be necessary, then list these situations on their chart.

Thinking Critically Through Visuals

The surgeons in this photograph are performing delicate surgery. What type of insurance might they carry to protect them from the consequences of negligence in pro-fessional performance? (Malpractice insurance, which is a form of liability insurance)

On a sheet of paper, have students create a three-column chart with the following headings: *Businesses/Professions*, *Activities*, and *Liabilities*. Have students brainstorm information to list under each category. (Answers may include physicians, surgery, malpractice, and so on.) **Independent Practice**

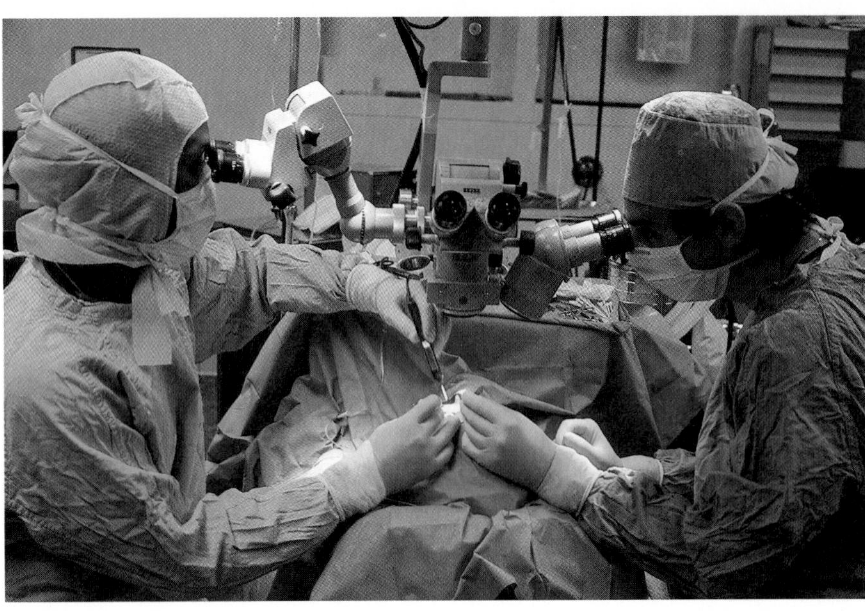

Liability coverage is a major part of most automobile insurance policies and is discussed in Chapter 35. Coverage for liability claims not arising out of the operation of a motor vehicle is often offered as part of a homeowner's or an apartment dweller's insurance policy.

Persons engaged in providing personal services, such as beauty salon operators, usually carry liability insurance. Persons rendering professional services, such as hospital operators and physicians, usually are covered for malpractice by liability insurance. Television and radio broadcasting companies also carry liability insurance to protect against liability for defamation. In the problem, Dr. Lancet would likely have malpractice insurance to protect her from the consequences of negligence in the performance of her duties.

HOW DOES AN INSURED COLLECT AFTER A LOSS?

PROBLEM

Late one summer afternoon, a severe hail and windstorm hit Montez's town. While it was raging, a door to his gift shop was blown open and the expensive etched glass in the door was shattered. What must Montez do to be indemnified under his insurance policy?

TEACH

Display Side 1 of the overhead transparency, *Collecting for Losses*. Discuss each point. Then explain the insurer's option to pay for the loss or to repair, rebuild, or replace the property destroyed or damaged with property of like kind or quality. Compare **actual cash value** with **replacement cost.** Diagram the exchange of rights and money involving **subrogation**.

ASSESS

Learning Objective 4 On a sheet of paper, have students list the five requirements (p. 681) that a sworn statement of proof of loss must include. Beside each, have them write an example of what would satisfy the requirement. Give this example: origin and time of loss: fire starting from electrical system in single-family house at 2 Marvin Gardens Rd., Charlotte, NC, on March 16, 1994, at approximately 2 P.M.

Generally, after an insured suffers a loss covered by an insurance policy, the insured must file a claim with the insurance company. A **claim** is a demand for indemnification. Payment of the claim is then contingent on the insurer receiving both proper notice of loss and proper proof of loss from the insured.

Notice of loss must be made in the way required by the contract or by statute. It is usually given to the agent who wrote the policy. Most insurance contracts require immediate notice of loss, often written, if it is practicable. If not, loss must be reported within a reasonable time. If legal action is commenced against the insured, immediate notice to the insurer is required. Prompt notice enables the insurer to investigate and to take other suitable action while the evidence is fresh and witnesses are available. The insured is required by the insurance contract to cooperate with the insurer not only in such an investigation but also by helping settle claims and by testifying in court, if necessary. However, the insured should not independently settle claims that should legitimately be handled by the insurance company. If the insured does so by making payments or transferring property without proper authorization from the insurer, the insurance company may rightfully refuse to reimburse the insured.

Proof of loss must be in writing and must be submitted within sixty to ninety days of the time of loss. Proof of loss is a sworn statement including information as to:

1. origin and time of loss,
2. value of and damage to any property,
3. injuries suffered,
4. names of any witnesses, and
5. other insurance carried.

In the problem, Montez must give proper notice of loss and furnish the insurer with proof of loss in order to be indemnified. It is extremely helpful to the insured in filling out the insurer's proof-of-loss forms if the insured has kept careful records of the property lost or damaged. Invoices, photographs, and even videotapes of the property are recommended, but not required, by most insurance companies.

Once an effective claim is made, the insurer has the option to pay for the loss or to repair, rebuild, or replace the property destroyed or damaged with property of like kind or quality. Depending on the insurance contract, any payment will be equal either to the actual cash value of the property or to the replacement cost of the property. The **actual cash value** is the purchase

▼ APPLY

On the chalkboard, work with students to create the following flowchart to graphically illustrate how an insured collects after a loss. **Guided Practice**

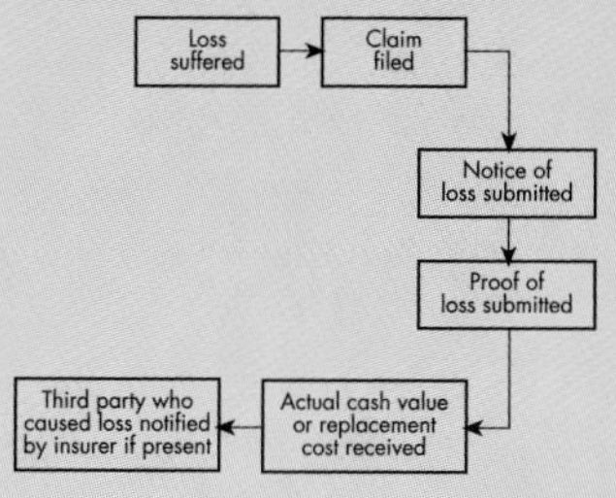

Personal Perspectives

Have students prepare from memory a list of the property that is in their room at home. Then, at home, have students verify their list. In class, ask students how accurate their lists were. Help students draw the conclusion that even without being subject to the anguish that comes after a major loss, they might omit significant items of property. Explain that keeping a proper inventory of property for proof of loss is important. Describe ways of keeping inventories, such as on video; on paper, including bills of sale; and so on.

▼RETEACH Cover the items listed under the headings *Notice of Loss* and *Proof of Loss Including* on Side 1 of the overhead transparency master *Collecting for Losses*. Under *Notice of Loss*, list **When?** and **How?** Under *Proof of Loss Including*, write **What five pieces of information?** Photocopy and distribute to students.

▼ENRICH Have students brainstorm reasons why an insurance company might insist on the prompt reporting of a claim and circumstances that might keep someone from doing so.

Writing Connections

Language Arts
Have students create an insurance loss situation and write, using a computer, if possible, a **proof of loss** statement to report the loss.

Independent Practice

Ethics Issue

Read aloud the following to students: **Your stereo is damaged beyond repair in a fire. Your insurance agent tells you that the purchase of a replacement is covered by your policy. The clerk at the stereo store tells you the model that you are planning to buy is 40% off just for today. After telling her that your insurance company was picking up the tab, she suggests that she charge you the sale price but give you a receipt for the full price. Is her suggestion ethical?** (No; The purpose of insurance is indemnification for actual loss. Also, you will be guilty of insurance fraud if you follow her suggestion.)

price less an allowance for age and use. The **replacement cost** is the amount that it would currently take to replace the damaged or destroyed item. Coverage on terms of replacement cost instead of actual cash value can at times be obtained by the payment of an additional premium. In the problem, the insurer would probably have the door glass replaced or pay for the replacement arranged by Montez rather than pay any money directly to Montez. This method discourages deliberate, fraudulent destruction of property by the insured simply to collect its value.

Once an insurer pays for a loss, it can legally proceed against a third party who caused the loss for the amount the insurer paid out. This **subrogation**, or assignment, by the insured to the insurer of the right to recover damages from a liable third party prevents the insured from potentially recovering twice for a loss.

One day in early spring, Alomar chose a spot for her garden and began digging. Over the next few hours, she uncovered many rocks. Finally, hot and exasperated, she grabbed a large one and angrily hurled it into the air. It crashed through the plate glass front of her neighbor Sampson's specially manufactured solar heat collectors. Sampson's insurance company paid his $3,250 claim for damage to the collectors. By so doing, the insurance company acquired the right to proceed against Alomar for the amount it paid to Sampson. If the insurer had not received this right by subrogation, Sampson could have recovered for the loss from the insurance company and then recovered again by suing Alomar.

After a loss has occurred, an insured may also assign the right to receive payment from the insurance company. The insured does not need the consent of the insurer to do this. However, the insured cannot assign the policy itself to a third party, such as a purchaser of the property covered by the insurance, without the consent of the insurer. Such action is prohibited because property and casualty insurance policies are regarded as personal contracts between the insurers and their insureds.

HOW IS AN INSURANCE POLICY TERMINATED?

PROBLEM

Spitzer's house was destroyed by a tornado. The insurance company paid the $225,000 face value of the policy in settlement. Did this terminate the policy?

ASSESS

Learning Objective 5 Have students respond orally to the following: **(1) How many days' notice to cancel does the standard fire insurance policy prescribe for the insurer?** (Five); **(2) Does payment of loss usually terminate a policy?** (No, it has no effect on coverage); and **(3) If a fire starts during the policy period but causes damage after the time of expiration, is the damage covered?** (Yes)

Generally, property or casualty insurance policies are terminated only by cancellation or expiration of the time period of the coverage. The standard homeowner's policy provides that the full amount of insurance remains in effect despite the payment of any loss. Consequently, Spitzer's policy in the problem was not terminated simply by the payout of the claim. If she rebuilds the house, the coverage may be useful. If not, she may cancel the policy or, if she does nothing, the policy will eventually expire at the end of the coverage period.

1. Termination by Cancellation

A policy may be canceled at any time by mutual consent. Statutes and policies usually provide that either party may cancel a policy upon giving notice in accordance with the terms of the contract. The standard fire insurance policy prescribes five days' notice by the insurer to cancel the coverage. Other types of insurance may require ten or fifteen days' notice by the insurer.

The courts typically require strict compliance with the appropriate contractual or statutory cancellation procedure. This requirement is especially directed at insurance companies that elect to cancel. That is because the notice provided to the insured by the canceling company may be the only one that the insured will receive. Upon receiving such notice, the insured must immediately find other insurance coverage or else run a significant risk. The insured may cancel by giving notice to the insurer at any time.

When a policy is canceled, the insured has a right to the return of the unused portion of the premium if it is not voluntarily tendered by the insurer. The amount varies. When the insurance company cancels a policy, the premium is prorated. **Prorate** means to divide proportionately. For example, if a company cancels a one-year policy at the end of four months, it must return to the insured the premiums paid for the eight remaining months; that is, it must return eight-twelfths of the total premiums paid. If the insured cancels the policy, a part of the premium is returned, but the share is less than if the insurance company had canceled the policy. The amount refundable by the insurer is shown in a short rate table in the policy.

2. Termination by Expiration of the Policy

If not previously terminated, most property or casualty insurance policies will go out of force upon the expiration of the time period for which premiums have been paid. The usual time period is one year. If a fire or other peril commences during the policy period and causes damage either before or after the time of expiration, the policyholder is insured. Likewise, if damage

Divide the class into groups of four or five and assign these roles: facilitator, researcher #1 to research original cost, researcher #2 to research current cost, figure checker, and presenter. Provide students with copies of old and current price lists or catalogs for the same or similar items. Assign items to groups and have them decide if it is better to have actual cash value coverage or replacement cost coverage. Tell students to assume the item is three years old and to figure a 10% per year depreciation deduction when figuring actual cost. **Cooperative Learning**

▼ TEACH

Compare termination by cancellation with termination by expiration of the policy. Define **prorate**. Then discuss the use of the term.

▼ APPLY

Distribute samples of sections of insurance policies, on which you have written SAMPLE, that include policy termination information. Have students locate and read aloud the clauses pertaining to termination. **Guided Practice**

Have students create and role-play scenarios terminating an insurance policy. Have the class determine if the termination was by cancellation or expiration of the policy. **Independent Practice**

▼RETEACH Have students create a graphic organizer to illustrate how an insurance policy is terminated.

▼ENRICH Have students debate whether it is ethical for property insurance companies to refuse to renew high-risk policy holders, such as people who live in "Hurricane Alley" in Florida, after they have been hit by a natural disaster.

Preventing Legal Difficulties

Divide the class into groups of three or four students. Supply each group with poster paper, paints or colored markers, and paste or glue. Have students read and discuss the suggestions for preventing legal difficulties. Have each group create a poster encouraging other students to follow the six steps to prevent legal difficulties when selecting insurance companies and policies. Have students in each group select the following roles: artist to draw the graphics; copywriter to write eye-catching copy; editor/paste-up artist who will edit the copy and paste it onto the poster; and facilitator, if necessary. Encourage students to use a computer to create the graphics and the text.

Cooperative Learning

is sustained during the life of the policy, the policy covers any consequences of the damage realized after the policy expires.

Preventing Legal Difficulties

When purchasing insurance . . .

1. Carefully evaluate the risks of loss that you want to insure against.
2. Select your potential insurers with caution as to their financial reserves and their reputation for good service in case of loss.
3. Obtain comparative price quotations, since the premiums charged by insurers for coverage for the same risk vary from company to company.
4. Read your policies carefully, paying special attention to exclusions.
5. Know and, in the event of loss, comply carefully with the notice-of-loss and proof-of-loss provisions in your policies.
6. Be aware of the expiration dates, cancellation terms, and renewal provisions of your policies. Move quickly to acquire other coverage if a policy lapses or is terminated.

▼ REVIEWING IMPORTANT POINTS

1. Recovery for a loss covered by property and casualty insurance cannot exceed the actual value of the loss.
2. Losses covered by a fire insurance policy will be indemnified only upon a showing that they were proximately caused by a hostile fire.
3. The standard fire insurance policy protection can be extended by appropriate endorsements to cover various other perils, such as windstorm, hail, and smoke damage.
4. The personal property floater of inland marine insurance may be written to cover any and all of an insured's personal property against practically any peril regardless of the location of the property.
5. Liability insurance is a form of casualty insurance that protects an insured against damage claims arising from unintentional torts for which the insured is legally liable.

6 When loss occurs, the insured must normally give notice of loss to the insurer as soon as practicable. Proof of loss must also be submitted by the insured within a specified time from the date of loss.

7 Property and casualty insurance policies are terminated by expiration of the time for which they are written. Both insurer and insured have the right to cancel before the expiration of the policy period.

8 A property or casualty insurance policy can be assigned only with the consent of the insurer. The right to recover from an insurer a loss that has already been sustained may be assigned by the insured without consent of the insurer.

9 Coinsurance requires the insured to keep the face value of the policy equal to a certain percentage (usually 80 percent) of the current value of the insured property. Coinsurance usually requires significantly lower premiums from the insured.

10 When an insurance policy is canceled, the insured has a right to the return of the unused portion of the premium.

▼ STRENGTHENING YOUR LEGAL VOCABULARY

Match each term with the statement that best defines that term. Some terms may not be used.

actual cash value	hostile fire
casualty insurance	inland marine insurance
claim	liability insurance
coinsurance	notice of loss
comprehensive policy	personal property floater
endorsements	proof of loss
exclusions	property insurance
extended coverage endorsement	prorate
floater	replacement cost
forms	standard fire policy
friendly fire	subrogation

1 Policy clause in which the insured shares the risk of loss with the insurer in return for lower premiums.

2 Coverage against claims for damage caused by one's torts.

3 Addition to the standard fire policy giving protection against several other perils.

▼ CLOSE

Have students complete the Chapter Outline on p. 211 of the Workbook. Then, discuss the different ways in which the loss of property to fire or theft can be reduced.

Assign the following end-of-chapter materials:
Student text review activities, pp. 684–689
Workbook, pp. 107–108
Chapter Test

Chapter *MicroExam*

▼ Strengthening Your Legal Vocabulary ▼

1 coinsurance
2 liability insurance
3 extended coverage endorsement
4 hostile fire
5 personal property floater
6 claim
7 subrogation
8 casualty insurance
9 actual cash value
10 endorsements

Applying Law to Everyday Life

1. Yes, insurance covers losses by fire caused by negligence. (p. 677)
2. $80,000; The insurance company will pay all of the loss up to the face amount of the policy, $80,000, because Olivet was keeping the proper amount of insurance on the inventory. Olivet will have to bear $20,000 of the loss, however. (pp. 677–678)
3. Liability insurance protects many professionals from the costs of defending and from judgments awarded in malpractice suits. (p. 680)
4. Perhaps; Most liability policies require the insured to notify the insurer immediately if the insured can do so; if not, as soon as possible. (p. 681) Failure to notify releases the insurer from obligation (breach of contract). Whether six months is a reasonable time under the circumstances probably would have to be determined by a court if the company refused to carry out its obligation under the policy.
5. The standard fire policy is not terminated by payment of a loss. The face value of the policy is reinstated by such payment. Accordingly, Sampers can collect for the windstorm loss. (p. 683)
6. Insurance benefits are payable if the cause of the damage or loss occurs before the policy expires. (pp. 683–684) The insured would be covered for the entire period of hospitalization and until the physician discharges the insured as recovered even though the policy ended the day after the accident.

4. Fire that is accidental or that escapes from its intended place.
5. Policy covering movable personal property wherever located.
6. Demand for indemnification.
7. A right, by operation of law, of the insurer to recover for loss from liable third parties.
8. Protection against losses caused by chance, accident, or negligence.
9. Insured property's purchase price less an allowance for age and use.
10. Modifications of a standard policy that are attached to it to provide for individual insurance needs.

▼ APPLYING LAW TO EVERYDAY LIFE

1. Carnes was insured against fire by Scandinavian Fire Insurance Company. One day while ironing, he left to answer the telephone and negligently forgot to turn off the iron. The iron fell from the ironing board, and the carpet caught fire. The fire then spread to the drapes. As flames engulfed the room, smoke damaged the remainder of the house. Will the loss be covered by the policy?
2. To protect her inventory, Olivet, owner of an appliance store, carried a coinsurance fire policy. The policy required that Olivet carry insurance in the amount of 80 percent of the current inventory value. Late one night, fire totally destroyed the inventory, which was valued at $100,000 when the loss occurred. The face value of Olivet's policy was $80,000. For how much of the $100,000 loss will the insurance company pay?
3. Dr. Bray performed a tympanoplasty (i.e., eardrum replacement) on Azle. The operation appeared to be successful, but one year later the ear canal was found to be completely closed due to the growth of scar tissue from areas where Dr. Bray had drilled improperly. What type of insurance would protect Dr. Bray from a malpractice suit by Azle?
4. Baker was seriously injured when an employee of Jay's Fixit Shop stumbled and pushed her into a glass display case. Jay forgot about the matter and did not notify his insurer until Baker filed suit six months later. Would this delay release the insurer from liability coverage?
5. Following a fire on his property, Sampers was paid the $22,000 face value of his homeowner's policy by the insurer. During the rebuilding of the

property, a windstorm did $4,000 worth of further damage. Could Sampers collect for the second loss, or had his policy been terminated by payment of the fire loss?

6 The day before her medical and hospitalization insurance was to expire, Choate was injured in a skiing accident. Her hospitalization lasted over a month. Did her insurance benefits end after one day, or did they cover her entire stay in the hospital?

7 When he sold his comic book collection, Wallis canceled the insurance contract covering the books. He had paid a year's premium of $120 just three months earlier. Will the insurance company return $90 of the premium?

8 ETHICS ISSUE Canton's glass front door was shattered by a rock thrown by his neighbor's lawnmower. His insurance company paid $350 to replace the door. Would it be ethical for Canton to now sue his neighbor for the loss as well? Legally, does he have the right to do so?

9 ETHICS ISSUE Boyton's young daughter is seriously ill and needs an operation that costs over $50,000. Boyton has $6,500 in savings, but cannot find anyone to give or to lend her the rest. She owns a rental house in a rundown area that is insured for $60,000. A friend tells her that he can set the house afire when her tenants are away and that no one will be able to tell that it was arson. She can then collect the money and pay for her child's operation. What should she do?

10 Klewsuski and Santos were arguing over whether it would be better to have actual cash value or replacement cost coverage for a damaged or destroyed item. Santos believed that the actual cash value coverage was better because it typically paid more. Is she correct?

SOLVING CASE PROBLEMS

1 The Consolidated School District No. 1 of Dallas County, Missouri, contracted for fire insurance to cover its high school buildings. The policy had a 90-percent coinsurance clause. During the term of the policy, a fire caused a partial loss to the buildings, amounting to over $45,000 in damages. At the time of the fire, the structures were valued at approximately $80,000 and the amount of the policy coverage stood at $50,000. How much of the $45,000 loss should the policy cover? (*Templeton v. Insurance Co. of North America,* 201 S.W.2d 784)

9  Ordering the arson might be justified by the far greater good of saving a young girl's life taking precedence over any and all property interests. Such an illegal step might not be acceptable to someone embracing the absolutism of the Judeo-Christian ethic. This case should be the source of a lively discussion of ethics.

10 No; With persistent inflation, the replacement cost is almost always greater than the actual cash value. However, replacement cost coverage typically requires a higher premium. (pp. 681–682)

Solving Case Problems

1 The policy would pay a portion of the $45,000 equal to $50,000 (the actual coverage) divided by $72,000 (the coverage required by the coinsurance clause = 90% of $80,000) or ($50,000/$72,000) × $45,000 = $31,250. (p. 678)

7 Probably not; Most insurance companies will prorate the return when they cancel but will return significantly less than a pro rata share when the insured cancels. (p. 683)

8 ETHICS ISSUE Canton extended his resources to pay for the insurance and the certainty of that indemnification. However, ethically, that contractual set of obligations can be separated from the possibility of recovery at law. Legally, most insurance policies would call for the subrogation of the claim. (p. 682)

2 No; The court pointed out that there was no real claim available against the attorney until after the five years had run out. Therefore the only notice required was given, and the defense was not adequate. (p. 681)

3 As mentioned in Chapter 33, any ambiguity is construed against the writer of the policy. Therefore, it might be decided in court that high winds could constitute a windstorm. The Schaeffers could collect for their loss under their insurance. (p. 676)

4 Yes; The insurance contract clearly states that the insured must cooperate with the company at its request and assist in effecting settlements or in a suit. The insured did not do so and thus breached the contract, relieving the insurer of liability. (p. 681)

2 Sager, who was injured in an automobile accident, hired an attorney to handle his case. The suit was dismissed over three years later for failure to prosecute, due to what the trial court found to be the attorney's negligence. The suit was not reentered, as it could have been, before the five-year statute of limitations had run. Sager sued the attorney and received a judgment for $15,000 plus court costs. Nothing was paid on the judgment, so Sager then sought to recover against the insurance company that insured the attorney with professional liability insurance. It refused to pay, claiming in part that if the attorney had notified it after the suit was dismissed, it would have seen that the suit was reentered before the five-year statute of limitations had run. Instead, the attorney notified the insurer only after the five years had passed. Is this an adequate defense for the insurance company? (*Sager v. St. Paul Fire and Marine Insurance Company*, 461 S.W.2d 740)

3 The Schaeffers' insurance company refused to pay when portions of their roof separated on the third day of a period of high winds, even though coverage against "windstorm" was clearly in the policy. The roof separation allowed rain to fall into the interior of the insured structure and portions of the roof, wood, brick, and plaster followed. The winds were clocked at the nearby Weather Bureau Office at forty, thirty-one, and fourteen miles per hour, respectively, on each of the three days. The insurance company claims that the winds did not constitute a "windstorm" and that since the collapse occurred when the strength of the wind was only fourteen miles per hour, a structural defect caused the damage. You decide. (*Schaeffer v. Northern Assurance Company*, 177 S.W.2d 868)

4 Taff and Hardwick were in an automobile accident that resulted in a $5,000 judgment for Taff against Hardwick. Taff sued to collect the amount of the judgment. The defendant insurance company denied liability, claiming failure of the insured, Hardwick, to cooperate in defending the action, as required in the policy. The policy reads as follows: "Insured shall cooperate with the company and upon the company's request shall attend hearings and trials, and shall assist in effecting settlements, securing and giving evidence, obtaining the attendance of witnesses, and in the conduct of suits." The insurer presented evidence that it had unsuccessfully sought to locate Hardwick by letter and telephone calls, and through the efforts of investigators so that he could cooperate in his defense. Is the insurer released from its obligation to pay the judgment? (*Taff v. Hardwick and Empire Fire and Marine Insurance Company of Omaha*, 419 S.W.2d 482)

5 The Home Insurance Company issued a fire insurance policy that covered Delametter's truck. Several months later, while driving the truck with a trailer attached, Delametter's employee discovered a fire at or near the floor boards. As a result of the fire, the truck crashed into a bridge abutment and sustained a large amount of damage. Should Delametter be able to collect under his fire insurance for the damage done by the collision with the abutment? (*Delametter v. Home Ins. Co.*, 182 S.W.2d 262)

5 Yes; It was reasonably foreseeable that the truck would crash because of an onboard fire. The court held that the fire was the proximate cause of the damage. (p. 677)

Chapter Theme

Automobile insurance policy coverages protect insured, uninsured, and underinsured motorists in a variety of ways.

DIRECTED STUDY QUESTIONS	SPECIAL FEATURES	PROGRAM RESOURCES: Reteach	Enrich	S N	A M	
What risks of loss can be covered in an automobile insurance policy?	Multicultural Highlights, p. 692	✔	✔		K	
What protection from legal liability is available under an automobile policy?		✔	✔			
Why have medical payments coverage and what is the extent of the protection provided?		✔	✔			
What protection is provided by having collision or comprehensive coverage for your automobile?	Ethics Issue, p. 696 Thinking Critically Through Visuals, p. 696	✔	✔	✔	V	
Why carry uninsured motorists coverage?	Writing Connections, p. 698; Thinking Critically Through Visuals, p. 698	✔	✔		A	
How does no-fault automobile insurance work?	Personal Perspectives, p. 700 Preventing Legal Difficulties, p. 701	✔	✔			

Additional Resources

- "Auto Insurance." *Consumer Reports,* August 1992, pp. 489–500.
- *Reducing the Toll: Strategies to Reduce the Frequency and Severity of Auto Crashes and to Improve Auto Safety.* NY: Insurance Information Institution, 1989.

One-semester course	✔							
One-year course	✔	✔	✔					

	ASSESSMENT OPPORTUNITIES			
Cooperative Learning	**Informal Assessment**	**Chapter Review**	**Chapter Test**	**Chapter *MicroExam*** Media
	✔	✔	✔	✔
	✔	✔	✔	✔
	✔	✔	✔	✔
	✔	✔	✔	✔
✔	✔	✔	✔	✔
	✔	✔	✔	✔

Videodiscs

Automobile Insurance: Liability, Medical Payments, Comprehensive, and Collision Coverage

Search Chapter 43, Play To 44

No-Fault Insurance: Uninsured Motorist

Search Chapter 44, Play To 45

State by State

Maine requires the production of *proof* of good and sufficient automobile liability insurance before license issuance.

Teaching Materials

Student text, pp. 690–705

Overhead transparency masters
- *What Does Comprehensive Automobile Insurance Indemnify For?*
- *What Are the Basic Types of Automobile Insurance?*

Videos
- *Law for Business* Videodisc

Workbook, pp. 109–111

Outside Resources
- Butcher paper
- Blank overhead transparencies
- Poster board
- Markers
- Samples of sections of automobile insurance policies that discuss coverage and cost
- Newspapers
- Blank automobile insurance claim forms
- Index cards

- Camcorder
- VCR
- Tape recorder

Assessment
- Chapter Test

- Chapter *MicroExam*

Vocabulary

omnibus clause, p. 693
bodily injury coverage, p. 694
guest laws, p. 694
property damage coverage, p. 694
medical payments coverage, p. 695
collision coverage, p. 696
comprehensive coverage, p. 696
uninsured motorists coverage, p. 698
underinsured motorists coverage, p. 699
unsatisfied judgment funds, p. 699
financial responsibility laws, p. 699
assigned risk plan, p. 699
no-fault insurance, p. 700

Learning Objectives

When you complete this chapter, you will be able to

1. Know the differences between the various coverages available in an automobile insurance policy.
2. Understand how liability, medical payments, comprehensive, and collision coverage protect the insured.
3. Realize the advantage of having uninsured and underinsured automobile insurance.
4. Recognize the importance of no-fault insurance to the insured, the insurance industry, and the legal system.

Chapter Self-Test

Assess students' understanding of automobile insurance before they begin Chapter 35 by asking them to respond orally to the following *True* or *False* statements: **(1) Automobile insurance has multiple purposes including paying accident-related medical expenses for the occupants of the insured's vehicle.** (True); **(2) Presently, there is no defense against uninsured motorists.** (False); and **(3) Can your driving record affect your ability to buy insurance and its cost?** (Yes) Before continuing with the chapter, review and discuss students' responses.

CHAPTER 35

AUTOMOBILE INSURANCE

1. You receive a new pickup truck from your parents as a graduation gift. You immediately purchase insurance on the vehicle. Two days later, you allow your best friend to take it for a test drive. He carelessly loses control on a curve and demolishes your truck. Unfortunately, your friend has no financial resources or insurance to cover the loss. What part of your insurance policy should indemnify you?

2. Your insurance company pays you for the loss in Number 1 above. You search the car lots and find another truck identical to the first. You buy it and drive down to the department of motor vehicles to register your truck. When you walk back to your truck, you notice that it has been sideswiped by a hit-and-run driver. The driver is never apprehended. Repairs to your truck will cost over $3,000. What part of your insurance policy should indemnify you for your loss?

3. 

While driving your repaired pickup truck home from the garage, you see a woman and her two young children on the shoulder of the freeway walking away from a disabled car. It is a mile to the nearest aid station. Should you give them a ride? Will your insurance cover them if they are injured in an accident while riding in your truck?

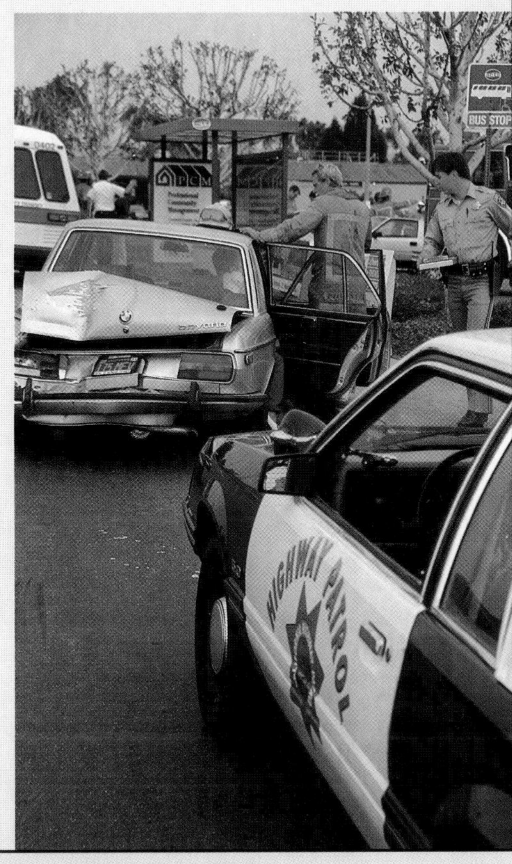

691

▼ FOCUS

Before class begins, secure a piece of butcher paper to a wall. On the butcher paper, draw a large two-column chart. Label the first column **Questions About Automobile Insurance,** and the second column **Answers.** As students enter the classroom, have them list at least one question in the first column.

When class begins, ask students if they can answer any of the questions listed. Have these students write their answers in the appropriate column on the chart. Keep the chart on the wall and have students answer the questions during the course of this chapter.

You Decide

1. Your insurance policy's collision coverage will cover the amount of the loss that is in excess of your deductible.
2. Again, the collision coverage of your policy would cover the loss. Your deductible would again have to be satisfied but, beyond that, the policy should cover the damage in full. If you do not have collision coverage, you will have to pay for the entire loss.
3. ETHICS ISSUE Most people would consider it ethical, but possibly dangerous, to stop and give the woman and her children a ride. If your state has a guest law, it might preclude recovery by the mother and children for injuries they received due to the negligent operation of your vehicle. They would, however, be eligible for medical payments coverage, regardless.

Thinking Critically Through Visuals

The photograph shows the aftermath of an automobile accident. Judging only from visible evidence, would you think that the driver of the gray car in front of the patrol car was at fault? Why or why not? (No; The gray car has been smashed from the rear, indicating that it was probably hit from behind)

TEACH

On a blank overhead transparency or on the chalkboard, list the four risks of loss or liability for which automobile insurance offers protection. Display and discuss each.

Multicultural Highlights

In 1953, Ernesta G. Procope started her own insurance company, E. G. Bowman, in storefront offices in the Bedford-Stuyvesant section of Brooklyn, NY. She started by handling home and auto insurance for African Americans who lived nearby. Her personal drive and skill are credited as the major factors in the company's climb to Wall Street headquarters in the heart of the financial district and to its status as the largest African American-owned insurance brokerage agency.

APPLY

On the chalkboard, create a spider map to illustrate the four risks of loss or liability that can be covered by an auto insurance policy. Have students help you complete it. **Guided Practice**

WHAT RISKS OF LOSS CAN BE COVERED IN AN AUTOMOBILE INSURANCE POLICY?

PROBLEM

Reed drove into the city to see a night baseball game. She parked her new convertible on the street three blocks from the stadium. After a sixteen-inning marathon, she returned to the car to find the top ripped and her new under-dash compact disc player stolen. Will Reed's full-coverage automobile insurance policy cover the loss?

Automobile insurance offers protection to the insured from loss or liability in the following four major instances:

1. When the insured is liable for injury to or death of other people, or for damage to the property of others, resulting from the ownership, maintenance, or use of the specified motor vehicle.
2. When the insured must pay for the medical treatment of occupants of the insured's car who are injured in an accident.
3. When the insured's vehicle is destroyed, damaged, or stolen. Therefore, in the problem, Reed's insurer would pay for the loss of the convertible top and, if Reed has paid a required additional premium, for the loss of the compact disc player.
4. When the insured is involved in an accident with a driver who is liable, but uninsured and potentially insolvent, or who is a hit-and-run criminal.

WHAT PROTECTION FROM LEGAL LIABILITY IS AVAILABLE UNDER AN AUTOMOBILE POLICY?

PROBLEM

Elster was the head of the prom committee. She asked one of the committee members, Arnold, to drive her car to a local department store to buy additional materials for decorations. In his haste, Arnold followed another car, driven by Greene, too closely. When Greene's car stopped, Arnold negligently crashed into it with Elster's car. Elster's automobile policy covered anyone driving her car with permission. Arnold's parents had an automobile policy that covered him while he was driving someone else's car. Which insurer will have to pay for the property and personal damage liability claims made by Greene?

ASSESS

Learning Objectives 1 & 2 Have students respond orally to the following: **(1) What clause extends automobile coverage to all members of the named insured's household and to any person not in the household given permission to drive the insured's auto?** (Omnibus clause); and **(2) Does liability insurance commonly provide coverage for the insured and members of the insured's family when they are operating nonowned automobiles?** (Yes)

An automobile insurance policy's liability coverage obligates the insurer to represent and provide for the insured's defense if the insured is accused of or sued for negligent ownership, maintenance, or use of the motor vehicle. In addition, if necessary, the coverage indemnifies for the payment of damages resulting from such negligence.

Liability coverage is generally found in a personal or family automobile policy. Such a policy may be augmented by an **omnibus clause,** which extends coverage to all members of the named insured's household and to any person not in the household who is given proper permission to drive the insured's car.

Liability insurance also commonly provides coverage for the insured and members of the insured's family when such persons are operating nonowned vehicles with the owner's permission. This coverage applies to all borrowed or substitute automobiles. Examples include automobiles used when the car described in the policy has broken down or is being repaired or serviced. Also, if one purchases another automobile to replace the insured car, generally all the coverages under the policy apply to the replacement car for a limited time as specified in the policy.

When one becomes liable for damage or injury while driving a vehicle he or she does not own, the car owner's policy provides the primary coverage. The driver's policy then provides coverage up to its face amount for any excess liability. In the problem, Elster's insurer would pay any liability claims up to the policy limit and the remainder would have to be paid by the family policy of Arnold's parents.

Because insurers are contractually liable for legitimate claims against their insured, the insurers have the right either to settle such claims out of court or to defend their insured in court. Since the insurer has potential liability under the policy, only the insurer can make a settlement with claimants against the insured. If the insurer requires the presence of the insured as a witness at any legal hearings, most automobile insurance policies provide for payment of lost wages to the insured.

Liability claims against the insured that the insurer may have to pay include bodily injury or death of third parties (i.e., persons other than the insured or insurer) and damage to the property of third parties.

1. Bodily Injury and Death Coverage

PROBLEM

Angela asked Charles to her senior prom. While driving to the dance with Charles as a passenger, Angela negligently forgot to signal her turn and was smashed into by another car. Charles sustained head injuries and his tuxedo was ruined. The other driver was not negligent. Can Charles recover against Angela?

Supply student pairs with poster board and markers. Tell them to create a poster that graphically summarizes the four major instances of automobile insurance protection.

Independent Practice

▼ TEACH

Explain to students that an automobile insurance policy's liability coverage obligates the insurer to represent in court and provide for the insured's defense if the insured is accused of or sued for negligent ownership, maintenance, or use of the motor vehicle. Explain that the two types of coverage provided by automobile liability insurance are for (1) bodily injury and death to third parties and (2) property damage to third parties. Explain how **guest laws** limit the legal right of a nonpaying rider, or *guest*, to sue the driver. Show students how to decipher insurance coverage "shorthand." For example, 25/50/25 means bodily injury coverage of $25,000 for each person, $50,000 for each occurrence, plus property damage coverage of $25,000.

▼RETEACH Make up scenarios like the following example that cover various circumstances involving liability insurance. As you explain each scenario, ask students who would have to pay. For example, **You are driving your friend's car and you injure someone. Who pays?** (The car owner's insurance company because your friend's policy provides the primary coverage) Correct any misconceptions.

▼ENRICH Have students conduct a panel discussion on the following question: **How much responsibility to help defeat or settle a claim does the insured owe the insurer?**

APPLY

Before class, obtain sample automobile insurance policies. Make and display overhead transparencies of sections of the policies that provide information on coverage and cost. Have the class, as a whole, compare the value received for money paid.

Guided Practice

On a sheet of paper, draw and photocopy the base and headings of the following comparison chart:

	Bodily Injury Coverage	Property Damage Coverage
Provided by	Liability insurance	Liability insurance
Covers	Bodily injury or death of other person	Damage to a third person's property
Limits	For each injured person and for each occurrence	Coverage based on premiums

Distribute the chart to students and have them complete it to compare bodily injury coverage with property damage coverage. **Independent Practice**

The first of two major types of coverages provided by automobile liability insurance is for bodily injury. **Bodily injury coverage** protects the insured against liability for bodily injury to or death of other persons. This type of coverage is usually issued with top limits for each injured person and for each *occurrence* (i.e., accident). For example, coverage of $25,000 for each person and $50,000 for each occurrence may be obtained. In the insurance industry's "shorthand," this is called 25/50. By paying additional premiums, an insured may purchase higher limits, such as 50/100 or 100/300. Damages in excess of the policy limits would have to be paid for by the insured.

A few states have statutes known as guest laws. **Guest laws** deny a guest (i.e., nonpaying rider) in a car the legal right to sue the driver unless the driver was *grossly* negligent or *willfully* caused the accident. Ordinary negligence would not be enough to allow suit against the driver in such a state. However, if, for example, the driver was intoxicated or willfully disregarded the fact that the vehicle had no brakes, these states would allow recovery. If the accident described in the problem occurred in a state with a guest law, Charles could not recover from Angela for his losses, since she was only ordinarily negligent. In states without guest laws, he could recover.

2. Property Damage Coverage

PROBLEM

Balboa left his truck parked on a steep hill. In a hurry, he forgot to set the parking brake properly. Unoccupied, the truck rolled down the hill, glanced off the side of the Burks' car, and rammed into their house. The Burks claimed damages of $7,300 to their car, $14,750 to their house, and over $2,000 to their furniture. In addition, they also claimed the cost of renting a substitute car at $43 per day while their own was being repaired. Was Balboa's insurer required to pay for all these claims?

The second of the two major types of coverage provided by automobile liability insurance is for property damage. **Property damage coverage** indemnifies the insured against claims from damage the insured does to a third person's property as a consequence of operating a motor vehicle. This coverage includes compensating for the damaged property and for any related losses caused by the insured's operation of a motor vehicle. Therefore, in the problem, the Burks were correct in claiming not only the cost of damages to their house, car, and furniture, but also the cost of renting the substitute car.

Property damage liability coverage may be written for $10,000. However, this amount may not cover the loss. Higher coverage is available for a small additional premium. A policy with bodily injury coverage of $25,000 and

ASSESS

Learning Objectives 1 & 2 Have students respond orally to the following *True* or *False* statements: **(1) Property damage coverage indemnifies the insured against claims for damage the insured does to a third person's property as a consequence of operating a motor vehicle.** (True); and **(2) Guest laws give passengers the legal right to sue the driver for negligence.** (False)

$50,000 and property damage coverage of $25,000 would be indicated as 25/50/25.

WHY HAVE MEDICAL PAYMENTS COVERAGE AND WHAT IS THE EXTENT OF THE PROTECTION PROVIDED?

PROBLEM

While sledding on a snow-covered street, Bean was hit by an automobile. The driver was not at fault. When Bean's medical bills began to mount up, she wondered if she could use the medical payments coverage in her own automobile insurance policy to help pay them. Can she?

Medical payments coverage pays for the reasonable medical claims of occupants of the insured's vehicle who are injured in an automobile accident. An *occupant* is one who is in, upon, entering, or leaving a vehicle. The coverage also applies to the insured and the insured's family members while such persons are driving or riding in another's automobile. This kind of coverage is mainly for car occupants. However, it also covers the named insured and the family members if such persons are struck by an automobile while walking, riding bikes, roller skating, or sledding. Therefore, in the problem, Bean's automobile insurance policy would help pay for her medical expenses.

The important thing to remember about medical payments coverage is that payment for necessary medical, surgical, dental, X-ray, and even funeral expenses will be made even if the insured is not at fault. Payment will also be made if the state has a guest law. Usually there is a per-person limit in the policy, for example $5,000 per person, but no limit per accident. Typically, however, the expenses must be incurred within one year from the date of the accident.

WHAT PROTECTION IS PROVIDED BY HAVING COLLISION OR COMPREHENSIVE COVERAGE FOR YOUR AUTOMOBILE?

PROBLEM

While driving, Williams was momentarily blinded by the sun reflecting off a passing car's rear window. Consequently, he went into an upcoming curve too fast, and his car overturned. Although his vehicle was totally destroyed, Williams was uninjured because he was wearing his seatbelts. What type of insurance coverage would compensate Williams for the loss of his vehicle in this one-car accident?

TEACH

Explain that **medical payments coverage** is mainly for anyone who is an *occupant,* or a person who is in, upon entering, or leaving a vehicle. It pays for the reasonable medical claims of occupants of the insured's vehicle who are injured in an automobile accident. Coverage also applies to the insured and the insured's family members while such persons are driving or riding in the automobile of another. Necessary medical payments will be made even if the insured is not at fault. Point out that it also covers the named insured and the family members if they are struck by an automobile while walking, riding bikes, roller skating, or sledding.

APPLY

As a whole-class activity, create a bulleted wall chart of the major points in the section on medical payments. **Guided Practice**

Supply students with newspapers. In small groups, have them locate articles about injuries involving automobiles. Have students read the articles aloud and speculate on the role and impact that medical payments coverage could play. **Independent Practice**

RETEACH Have students create two graphic organizers. Show the characteristics of bodily injury coverage in one and property damage coverage in the other. Have students exchange graphic organizers and explain them.

ENRICH In small groups, have students role-play the legal resolution of a motor vehicle accident that involves bodily injury to a passenger. Have students include or exclude in their role-plays the use of guest laws.

▼ TEACH

There are two types of insurance coverage: **collision** and **comprehensive.** Display the overhead transparency, *What Does Comprehensive Automobile Insurance Indemnify For?* Explain the use of deductibles.

▼ APPLY

ETHICS ISSUE

Ethics Issue

Read aloud the following: **A car backs into your car. The only damage to your car is a dent you made earlier. What would you do?** (It would be unethical to do anything other than tell the person that your car was already damaged. Letting that driver's insurance pay for the damage would also be illegal.) **Guided Practice**

Thinking Critically Through Visuals

The boy in the photograph has damaged the woman's car. What kind of insurance would cover the damage? (Comprehensive)

Two types of automobile insurance coverages indemnify insureds for damage to their own vehicles. The first, **collision coverage,** protects against direct and accidental damage due to (1) colliding with another object, such as a tree or bridge abutment, and (2) upset, such as the overturn suffered by Williams in the problem. Only the actual cash value (i.e., the cost new minus an allowance for age and use) of the vehicle or its damaged parts less any deductible is paid. Thus, for each loss the insured pays up to the amount of the deductible, and the insurer pays the rest up to the policy limit.

Deductibles are utilized to lower the premiums the insured must pay for the coverage. Deductibles are especially effective in bringing lower premiums for collision insurance because most "fender bender" collision claims are relatively small compared with the relatively high costs of investigating, inspecting, and settling such claims.

In the event of loss from collision or upset, the insured must notify the insurer "as soon as practicable." Failure to do so releases the insurer from its obligation. The insured also has an obligation to protect the automobile from further loss. Once proper notice of loss and proof of loss have been received, the insurance company has the option of either paying for the loss or repairing or replacing the lost or damaged property.

The second type of automobile insurance coverage indemnifying insureds for damage to their own vehicles is comprehensive coverage. (Sometimes it is also listed as *other than collision* insurance.) **Comprehensive coverage** indemnifies against all damage to the insured's car *except* that caused by collision or upset. The causes covered by comprehensive insurance, which could

▼ ASSESS

Learning Objectives 1 & 2 Have students respond orally to the following: **(1) What types of insurance coverage indemnify insureds for damage to their own vehicles?** (Collision and comprehensive); **(2) What is actually paid by the insurance company in a loss?** (Only the actual cash value of the vehicle or its damaged parts less any deductible); and **(3) Against what does comprehensive coverage indemnify?** (All damage except that caused by collision or upset) occur for any reason, include fire, theft, water, vandalism, hail, and glass breakage. Theft includes loss of the car and any part of the car, such as hubcaps. However, loss of clothing and other personal property left in the car generally is not covered unless the loss is by fire. Similarly, most policies require extra premiums to cover citizens' band radios and stereos. Any damage done to a car, such as broken locks, is covered.

Like collision insurance, comprehensive insurance will pay only the actual cash value of the loss. Also, a deductible is usually written into the policy so that the insured will have lower premiums.

Julianne loved bingo. A large charitable organization in a nearby state advertised a night-long bingo session for large stakes. To attend, Julianne bought a ticket on a chartered bus. The night of the big bingo binge, she parked her car in a mall parking lot and boarded the bus. When she returned the next day her car had been broken into. The passenger-side window had been smashed. Her spare tire and jack, 35-mm camera, and expensive set of golf clubs had been stolen. Under her comprehensive coverage, Julianne could recover for the loss of her window, tire, and jack. However, the loss of the golf clubs and camera would not be indemnified under the comprehensive coverage. She might, however, be able to recover for them under a personal property floater if she had such coverage.

Prompt notice of loss must be provided to the insurer under the comprehensive coverage. Also, if the covered vehicle is stolen, the insured must notify the police as well. In the case of such a theft, most policies provide for the reimbursement of up to a specified amount per day for the insured's expenses in renting a substitute vehicle.

WHY CARRY UNINSURED MOTORISTS COVERAGE?

PROBLEM

Sarnof took a summer job to earn money for his college education. On Sarnof's way home from work late one evening, a drunken driver ran a red light and smashed into his car. Sarnof's medical bills totaled over $45,000 and his injuries prevented him from working for the rest of the summer. Unfortunately, the drunken driver had only the minimum state-required liability coverage ($10,000) and little or no assets or income to pay for Sarnof's losses. Must Sarnof absorb the majority of his medical bills and losses himself?

Before class, obtain samples of blank automobile claim forms furnished by insurers for insureds to report claims. Distribute to students the blank forms and index cards. Have students independently make a list of the information that is required on the form that needs to be obtained at the accident site. Have students, especially at-risk students who are having a difficult time relating the information in this chapter to real life, make a wallet-size card listing the necessary information to carry with them in case they are involved in an auto accident.

Independent Practice

TEACH

Compare **uninsured motorists coverage** with **underinsured motorists coverage.** Explain that **unsatisfied judgment funds** and **financial responsibility laws** are attempts to solve the problems caused by hit-and-run, uninsured, and underinsured motorists. Give examples of people who might have difficulty obtaining liability insurance, (very young, very old, bad driving record) and explain the role of an **assigned risk plan** to provide them with insurance. Point out that the premiums are usually much higher than those charged to other drivers for similar coverage.

RETEACH Have students create a graphic organizer to illustrate the differences between collision and comprehensive coverages.

ENRICH On a sheet of paper, have students answer the following question: **Is it ethical for younger people, without blemishes on their driving records, to be charged more for their automobile insurance just because of their age? Why or why not?** (Answers may include yes or no, but should reflect an understanding of the accident and speeding statistics on which premiums are based.)

On a blank overhead transparency, assist students in creating flowcharts that demonstrate the chain of events in the resolution of an automobile accident where the party who caused harm is uninsured. In the first chart, illustrate what happens if the adequately insured driver has uninsured motorists coverage. In the second chart, illustrate what happens if that same driver does not carry that coverage.

Guided Practice

Writing Connections

Language Arts
Using a computer, if possible, have students write an essay on the ethical issues of driving while uninsured or underinsured.

Independent Practice

Thinking Critically Through Visuals

If the woman in the photograph has had several accidents and has trouble getting liability insurance, where might she apply? (To an assigned risk plan)

When an accident is caused by the negligence of a driver who is uninsured and potentially insolvent or who leaves the scene and cannot be found, innocent parties involved in the accident may have to bear their own losses. Certainly their collision and medical payments coverages may help, but significant amounts of loss, for example, lost wages and the medical payments that exceed the limit of their policy, may not be indemnified.

Consequently, many car owners carry a supplemental coverage to their regular policy. This additional coverage, called **uninsured motorists coverage,** allows the insured to collect damages from his or her own insurance company when they are not collectible from the person who caused the harm. In most states, the coverage is limited to compensation for bodily injury, death, lost wages or support, and pain and suffering. Indemnification for property damage is generally excluded from this coverage.

The liability of the insurer in uninsured motorist cases depends on establishing that the uninsured motorist, or the hit-and-run driver, was negligent and would be liable if sued. In addition, in an accident with a hit-and-run driver, the collision must have been immediately reported to the police. Also, a reasonable attempt to find the hit-and-run driver must have been made. Such requirements help to prevent fraud, such as a driver involved in a one-car accident reporting it as a hit-and-run accident. Finally, for uninsured motorists coverage to apply, actual contact with another car is required. Thus, injuries to the insured caused by the insured swerving off the road to avoid a collision with another car would not be covered.

ASSESS

Learning Objectives 1 & 3 Have students jot down the best answer to the following: **(1) Which kind of coverage protects against people who drive without insurance: uninsured motorists coverage or underinsured motorists coverage?** (Uninsured); and **(2) What helps people who need liability insurance but are having difficulty getting it: unsatisfied judgment funds or an assigned risk plan?** (Assigned risk plan)

In an accident where the negligent motorist does have some insurance, but it is a minimal amount, the uninsured motorist coverage does not apply. This is the situation for Sarnof in the problem. In these accidents, the innocent driver would be more fully indemnified if the party at fault did not have *any* insurance. To combat this eventuality, many insurance companies are now offering underinsured motorists coverage. **Underinsured motorists coverage** compensates the insured when the negligent driver does not have *sufficient* insurance to cover damages. In the problem, if Sarnof had such coverage, he could recover the balance of the medical payments and the lost wages from his own insurance company. Like uninsured motorists coverge, underinsured motorists coverage excludes payment for property damage.

In an attempt to solve the problems caused by hit-and-run drivers and uninsured motorists, a few states have **unsatisfied judgment funds.** Such a fund is financed by taxes on insurance companies and by automobile license fees. Under this plan, a party suffering damage must first obtain a court judgment. If the judgment is not collectible, a claim may be made to the fund to satisfy the judgment.

In addition, most states have **financial responsibility laws.** These laws require that in an accident resulting in injury, death, or property damage greater than a specified amount, the driver or owner must show proof of the ability to pay a liability judgment. In some states, the showing may be accomplished by producing an insurance policy in a specified amount. In other states, either a security deposit large enough to pay any judgment that might be rendered or a signed release from the other driver is required. Failure to comply typically results in the suspension of the driver's license, suspension of the vehicle registration, or suspension of both. Unfortunately these statutes do little to protect the victim of the first accident of a financially irresponsible person. In addition, there are only a very few states that require that liability insurance be obtained before a driver's license is issued.

Some car owners find it difficult to obtain liability insurance to satisfy the requirements of the financial responsibility law of their state. Such difficulty may be due to the person's age, driving record, traffic violations, or other reasons. To enable such persons to comply with this law, an **assigned risk plan** has been devised. (It is also known as an *automobile insurance plan*). Under such a plan, a person who has been refused insurance can apply to be assigned to an insurance company that will issue to that person the minimum liability insurance required by the state. The premium, however, is usually much higher than that charged other drivers for similar coverage. Often this type of insurer voluntarily will insure such a person at regular rates if there has been a clear record for a year or two.

Divide the class into groups of five or six and assign the following roles in each group: driver one (D1) who tells his or her version and seeks to protect self, insurance agent one who represents D1, driver two (D2) who is the counterpart of D1, insurance agent two who represents D2, police officer who investigates accident scene (optional), and legal advisor who guides process to adhere to law by checking facts against text information. Direct each group to create, role–play, and videotape a motor vehicle accident where one of the drivers is uninsured or underinsured. Tell them to provide enough information in the dialogue to clearly show the circumstances and process. Play the videotapes to the class and have students comment on their accuracy.

Cooperative Learning

Divide the class into groups of two or three. Have groups create and record a rap, poem, or song about financial responsibility as it relates to insurance. Play back the tapes for the class.

On the chalkboard, write the terms **uninsured motorists coverage, underinsured motorists coverage, unsatisfied judgment funds, financial responsibility laws,** and **assigned risk plan.** Have students write their own definitions for each.

ENRICH

Ask students to debate the following question: **Should drivers in all states be required to obtain liability insurance before a driver's license is issued?** (Answers should reflect an understanding of how this requirement helps to reduce the number of uninsured drivers.)

TEACH

Explain that **no-fault insurance** requires that people involved in an automobile accident be indemnified by their own insurance company regardless of who is at fault. Discuss the cost savings of such a system.

APPLY

Have students discuss or prepare a panel discussion on fault and no-fault versions of the same accident. **Guided Practice**

Personal Perspectives

Have students share with the class any experiences they have had as a person involved in an auto accident. Ask these students whether it was easy to determine who was at fault. Emphasize how difficult it is to show fault if parties involved in an accident have conflicting stories. Then, at home, have students ask family members about their family's automobile insurance and find out whether they have fault or no-fault insurance. In class, have students tally the results. **Independent Practice**

HOW DOES NO-FAULT AUTOMOBILE INSURANCE WORK?

PROBLEM

Horton made an illegal turn in front of Verona's car. In the ensuing wreck, both Horton and Verôna suffered serious injuries, were hospitalized, and unable to work for several months. Horton's medical bills totaled $26,000 and his lost wages were $7,245. Verona's medical bills were $38,570 and her lost wages were $4,490. How will these losses be indemnified in a state with a no-fault insurance system?

To curtail the growing case load of our court system, over one-half of the states have instituted no-fault insurance systems. **No-fault insurance** requires that parties to an automobile accident be indemnified by their own insurance company regardless of who is at fault. Therefore, a court trial to determine who is at fault in an accident may be avoided. The indemnification of the losses by the insurance company takes the place of the damages that might have been awarded. However, if the medical claims of an injured person are larger than a set amount or the injuries are permanent, a suit can be brought for all alleged damages, including pain and suffering.

Generally, property damage is not covered at all by a no-fault system. This is because it is not likely that people will sue for the amounts involved, since insurance companies tend to resolve such claims fairly and efficiently without court involvement.

In the problem, under the standard no-fault system, the medical bills and lost wages for each of the parties would have to be indemnified by their own insurers unless they exceeded the statutorily set figure beyond which a suit for all the damages would be allowed.

Preventing Legal Difficulties

For automobile insurance, remember that . . .

1. One of the most frequently incurred and potentially disastrous liabilities results from a lawsuit based on bodily injury and property damage in an automobile accident. To protect yourself, carry adequate automobile liability coverage.
2. Many drivers fail to carry insurance. Often such drivers are potentially insolvent and without assets. Consequently, it is advisable to carry un-

ASSESS

Learning Objectives 1 & 4 On a sheet of paper, have students write a brief example of a typical procedure that could be expected after an automobile accident involving minor injuries in a state that has no-fault insurance.

insured motorists coverage or, if your state requires it, no-fault coverage. Finally, consider carrying underinsured motorists coverage, since many drivers maintain only the minimum liability coverage required by law.

3 If you are sued as a result of an accident and you have complied with the policy requirements, your insurer is required to defend you. Therefore, if you are involved in an accident, report it to your insurer immediately no matter how trivial it may appear. Failure to notify the insurer may release the insurer from liability on your policy. Such failure may also excuse the insurer from defending the suit against you.

4 You should deal with a reputable insurance agent. In selecting the proper coverage, and especially in case of an accident, your agent can be of great help.

5 You should read your policy carefully; it is your contract. If you wait until an accident occurs, it may be too late. If there is something about your policy that you do not understand, ask your agent to explain it.

6 If you buy a car in a secured transaction, you will probably be required to protect the seller's interest with collision and comprehensive coverages.

REVIEWING IMPORTANT POINTS

1 The basic purposes of automobile insurance are the following:
  a. to pay claims for personal injury or property damage resulting from an automobile accident that was caused by the insured's negligence,
  b. to pay accident-related medical expenses for occupants of the insured's vehicle,
  c. to indemnify the insured for damage to the insured's vehicle, and
  d. to indemnify the insured when he or she is involved in an accident with a driver who is liable but is underinsured, uninsured, without adequate financial resources, or is a hit-and-run driver.

2 Under an omnibus clause, insurance coverage may be extended to others who drive the insured's car as well as to members of the insured's family who drive the cars of others with permission.

3 With uninsured motorists coverage, the insured can collect from his or her insurer damages for bodily injury or death caused by negligent drivers who are uninsured and financially limited or who are hit-and-run drivers.

4 Most states require motorists to furnish evidence of their ability to pay damages when they are involved in an accident. For those persons unable to obtain insurance, assigned risk plans are available.

Preventing Legal Difficulties

Have students create a consumer's handbook on automobile insurance incorporating the six points in this section. Encourage students to use a computer, if

possible, to produce the handbook.

CLOSE

Cover the first two columns on the overhead transparency, *What Are the Basic Types of Automobile Insurance?* Display the overhead transparency and have students determine the type and purpose of insurance indicated by the illustration. Uncover the

correct answer after each is discussed.

Review the chart that students created in the FOCUS activity. Have students finish answering the questions and review for accuracy the answers that students provided in the beginning of the chapter.

Assign the following end-of-chapter materials:
Student text review activities, pp. 701–705
Workbook, pp. 109–111
Chapter Test

Chapter *MicroExam*

RETEACH

Using the PROBLEM on p. 700 as a model, have students create, using a computer, if possible, a scenario involving an accident. Be sure that one of the people involved is clearly at fault. Ask students to compare the result of the accident in a state with no-fault insurance to that of a state that does not have no-fault.

ENRICH

Have students conduct a panel discussion on the following question: **What ethical issues are there to consider regarding no-fault insurance?**

Strengthening Your Legal Vocabulary

1. property damage coverage
2. omnibus clause
3. assigned risk plan
4. medical payments
5. uninsured motorists coverage
6. comprehensive coverage
7. no-fault insurance
8. guest laws
9. collision coverage
10. bodily injury coverage

Applying Law to Everyday Life

1. No; The insurance company alone has the right to either settle claims out of court or defend its insured against civil suits in court. (p. 693)
2. The plaintiff, Stafford, would probably collect $10,000 from Dalton's insurance because Dalton's policy provides the primary coverage. If a judgment or settlement exceeds the amount of insurance carried by Dalton, as in this problem, the excess amount of the judgment (which in this case is also $10,000) would be paid by Polk's insurance. (p. 693)

5. No-fault insurance, which indemnifies the insured for various losses sustained in an automobile accident regardless of who had legal responsibility for the accident, is now required by some states.
6. The amount that the insurer pays on a claim under collision or comprehensive insurance is reduced if one chooses to carry deductibles to hold down premium costs.

STRENGTHENING YOUR LEGAL VOCABULARY

Match each term with the statement that best defines that term. Some terms may not be used.

assigned risk plan
bodily injury coverage
collision coverage
comprehensive coverage
financial responsibility laws
guest laws
medical payments coverage
no-fault insurance
omnibus clause
property damage coverage
underinsured motorists coverage
uninsured motorists coverage
unsatisfied judgment funds

1. Insurance that protects the insured against liability for damage to the property of third persons resulting from his or her operation of a motor vehicle.
2. Extends insurance coverage to all drivers who are members of the insured's household and any person who is not a member but who has permission to drive the insured's car.
3. Arrangement that enables a person whose application for automobile insurance has been rejected to obtain the minimum amount of coverage.
4. Coverage that pays the medical claims of occupants of the insured's vehicle who are injured in an automobile accident.
5. Insurance coverage that allows insured motorists to collect damages for bodily injury and death from their own insurers if the accidents are caused by the negligence of uninsured motorists with limited resources or hit-and-run drivers.
6. Coverage for loss or damage to the insured's car from all causes other than collision or upset.
7. Type of automobile insurance program in which recovery of most losses is sought from an insured's own insurance company regardless of who was legally responsible for the accident.

8 Laws in certain states that deny a nonpaying rider in a car the right to sue the driver unless the driver was grossly negligent or willfully caused the accident.

9 Coverage for direct and accidental loss to the insured's car caused either by hitting another object or by upset.

10 Coverage that protects the insured against liability for injury to or death of third parties resulting from his or her operation of a motor vehicle.

▼ APPLYING LAW TO EVERYDAY LIFE

1 Olsen negligently backed into Sabatino's car. Olsen was very apologetic and, after a few minutes of negotiating, paid Sabatino for the damage. Olsen then asked his automobile insurance company to reimburse him under its liability coverage for the amount he had paid Sabatino. Must the insurance company do so?

2 Polk carried 25/50/10 liability insurance. Polk borrowed the pickup of his brother-in-law, Dalton, to get a load of firewood. Dalton had the minimum liability coverage required in his state, 10/25/5. Polk struck a pedestrian, Stafford, who sued and received judgment for $20,000. How would Stafford collect on this judgment?

3 Michelson was injured when she lost control of her panel truck on a curve and ran off the road. Michelson was insured for bodily injury and property damage. She sought to collect from her insurance company for hospital and medical expenses, loss of wages, and damage to her truck. Will she be able to collect?

4 Temerant's son, Carl, sustained a broken arm in an accident while riding in Smith's car. There was a guest law in the state, and Smith was not grossly negligent. Smith had the minimum liability insurance coverage required by law. What other insurance coverage might be available to cover the expenses of treating the broken arm?

5 Bouton took a shortcut over a graveled road while driving home one evening. A piece of gravel hit and broke his windshield. The windshield cost $400 to replace. Bouton's collision deductible was $500 and his other than collision deductible was $400. How much of the damage amount would his insurer pay?

6 Forestal's car was hit broadside by Scott's sports car. Forestal had the car repaired for $480. However, she was indemnified by her insurer for only $380, since she had a $100 deductible. When Scott's insurer declined to pay, Forestal filed suit in small claims court and received judgment for $480. Could Forestal keep the entire $480?

3 No; The insurance Michelson carried was liability coverage. To be indemnified for her loss she would need collision (p. 696) and medical payments coverage (p. 695) and even then she would not be indemnified for her total losses.

4 The medical payments coverage of Temerant's policy would pay for the reasonable medical claims of Carl for an injury sustained while riding in another's auto. (p. 695)

5 None; Although glass breakage may be included under collision insurance, many policies exclude it from collision coverage and compensate for it instead under other than collision insurance. In either case, however, Bouton's deductibles were either equal to or greater than the loss. (p. 696)

6 No; Forestal was obligated to reimburse the insurer for the $380 which it had paid to settle the claim. Forestal's only loss was the amount of the deductible. (p. 696)

7 Blount can apply for insurance under the state's assigned risk plan. (p. 699) However, it should be expressly noted in any answer that Blount's premium will be much greater than normal.

8 ETHICS ISSUE Ethically, you should give respect to the law and not bring outside considerations to bear. A utilitarian would focus on the enforcement of the speeding laws and the distribution of the fine as being the greatest good for the greatest number.

9 ETHICS ISSUE Ethically, you should call the ambulance regardless of the consequences. Legally, there is no requirement to do so.

10 Comprehensive coverage would indemnify Thomas. Usually there is a deductible that must be satisfied first, however. (p. 696)

7 While in high school, Blount had received several traffic tickets and had been at fault in several automobile accidents. Therefore his driver's license was revoked. A few months after graduation, he again became eligible for a license. To obtain a license, he needed liability insurance. However, no company would voluntarily insure him even though he needed to be able to drive to work. What can Blount do to obtain the needed insurance?

8 ETHICS ISSUE A highway patrol officer sitting in an unmarked car on a side road clocks you traveling seventy-three miles per hour in a sixty-five-mile-per-hour zone. She pulls you over. As she gets out of the patrol car, you realize that she is the mother of a good friend of yours. However, she does not recognize you. You know that if you get another ticket, your automobile insurance rates will go up several hundred dollars. Should you mention your relationship with her son in hopes of getting leniency?

9 ETHICS ISSUE You have been late for work for two consecutive days. Today you will be on time with just seconds to spare if nothing goes wrong over the next ten miles of driving. One-quarter mile ahead of you on the freeway, a car spins out of control and hits another, and the two cars come to rest in the median. The vehicle between you and the wreck, a large semitrailer truck, pulls off to help. The truck driver runs up to the wreckage, then yells to you as you move slowly past, "They're badly hurt. Phone for an ambulance. There's a call-in box about a half-mile ahead on your right. Hurry." You realize you'll probably be fired if you are late for work again. What should you do? Could you incur any legal liability for not acting?

10 Some of the underdash wiring in Thomas' car shorted out and started a fire. Before the blaze could be extinguished the car was destroyed. What type of automobile insurance coverage would indemnify Thomas?

▼ SOLVING CASE PROBLEMS

1 Gary Stallings was on active duty with the National Guard when the three-quarter-ton truck he was driving overturned and caused a fellow Guard member and passenger, Robert Ward, bodily injury. Stallings was the named insured in Michigan Mutual Liability Company's "Auto-Guard" Family Insurance Policy. When Ward sued Stallings for the injuries, Michigan Mutual refused to defend Stallings and denied responsibility to pay any judgment that might result. In addition to other coverages, the policy obligated the company to defend and pay judgments up to the policy limit if the insured was driving a "nonowned

Solving Case Problems

1 The court held for Stallings. Construing the ambiguity against the party who drew up the contract, the court decided that the common meaning of the word automobile was "a self-propelled vehicle suitable for use on a street or roadway." Therefore the truck was an automobile within the meaning of the policy. (p. 693)

automobile." The company maintained that the three-quarter-ton army truck with canvas top and doors was not an automobile. You decide. (*Michigan Mutual Liability Company v. Stallings,* 523 S.W.2d 539)

2 Jackson purchased a 1968 Chevrolet Caprice automobile and insured it with Teachers Insurance Company. Four months after her purchase, the car was reclaimed from her by members of the Los Angeles Police Department. The car previously had been stolen from the National Research Chemical Company and was returned to its rightful owner. Jackson then filed a claim under the Teachers policy for loss due to theft. Although the Teachers policy included theft coverage, the company refused to pay. Therefore Jackson brought suit. Should she recover? (*Jackson v. Teachers Insurance Company,* 106 Cal. Rptr. 208)

3 A service station attendant did not properly replace the radiator cap on the Sacketts' automobile. This allowed the coolant to escape, causing extensive damage when the engine overheated. The Sacketts' insurer, Farmers Insurance Exchange, refused to cover the $336 loss under the comprehensive clause in the automobile policy. The comprehensive portion of the policy covered "loss . . . by any accidental means except collision" but excluded "loss . . . due to mechanical failure." The Sacketts brought suit against the insurer. The insurer justified its refusal to pay by claiming that the damage was due to mechanical failure. You decide. (*Sackett v. Farmers Insurance Exchange,* 47 Cal. Rptr. 350)

4 Nancy Brake's husband was killed in an automobile accident negligently caused by Donald Miller. Miller maintained the minimum amount of liability coverage as required by state law. This meant that Nancy Brake was able to recover from Miller and his insurance company only $4,000 of her alleged $50,000 damages. The Brakes had $40,000 of uninsured motorists coverage available under their own policies. Consequently, Nancy Brake sued her own insurer claiming that uninsured should be construed to mean underinsured as well. Did she collect the $40,000? (*Brake v. MFA Mutual Insurance Company,* 525 S.W.2d 109)

5 Donald Chitwood had a one-car accident that injured his passenger, Denna Lundry. Donald was driving his father's car but was thirty miles outside of the area his father had given him permission to drive in and over an hour late in returning the vehicle to his father. Therefore, his father's insurer, MFA Mutual Insurance Company, claimed that Donald was uninsured and that Denna's injuries should be compensated by the uninsured motorist's protection under a policy written by Cameron Mutual Insurance Company for Denna's mother. You decide which company should compensate Denna. (*Cameron Mutual Insurance Company v. Chitwood,* 609 S.W.2d 492)

2 No; The court held that theft should be given its usual meaning as used by persons in the ordinary walks of life. Therefore, under the policy, theft meant a felonious taking with the intent to deprive the insured permanently of the car. This did not occur since Jackson was not the insured at the time of the taking. "Plaintiff's actual loss ... were the funds paid by her for the stolen automobile." No theft, no recovery. (pp. 696–697)

3 Judgment for the Sacketts; The court held that although the harm was mechanical in nature, the cause of the loss was the accidental failure to properly replace the cap. (pp. 696–697)

4 As uninsured motorists protection is required by state law to be offered by insurers, the courts used the rules of statutory construction to strictly construe the word "uninsured" to mean without any insurance coverage whatsoever. (p. 699) As a consequence, Nancy Brake could not recover from her insurance company under her policy's uninsured motorists coverage.

5 Cameron Mutual Insurance Company must compensate Denna Lundry. Donald Chitwood had so far exceeded the range of his father's permission as to be deemed uninsured. (pp. 693, 698)

Chapter Theme

With thoughtful planning and preparation, a variety of life insurance options and social insurance programs are available to assist people in their greatest times of need.

DIRECTED STUDY QUESTIONS	SPECIAL FEATURES	PROGRAM RESOURCES				
		Reteach	Enrich	SN	AM	
What are life insurance and social insurance and why are they so important?		✔	✔		V	
What provisions are commonly found in a life insurance policy?		✔	✔			
What kinds of life insurance plans are available?	Personal Perspectives, p. 711	✔	✔		A	
What are the rights of the beneficiary of a life insurance policy?		✔	✔			
What kinds of social insurance are provided under the Social Security Act?	Thinking Critically Through Visuals, p. 714	✔	✔			
How are unemployment benefits obtained?	Ethics Issue, p. 715	✔	✔			
How are RSDHI obtained?	Thinking Critically Through Visuals, pp. 717, 719 Writing Connections, p. 719 Multicultural Highlights, p. 720 Preventing Legal Difficulties, p. 720	✔	✔	✔	K	

Additional Resources

- "Life Insurance." *Consumer Reports,* July, 1993, pp. 431–450.
- Matthews, Joseph L. *Social Security, Medicare and Pensions,* 5th ed. Berkeley, CA: Nolo Press, 1991.

One-semester course	✔	✔						
One-year course	✔	✔	✔	✔	✔			

		ASSESSMENT OPPORTUNITIES			
	Cooperative Learning	Informal Assessment	Chapter Review	Chapter Test	Chapter *MicroExam* Media
		✔	✔	✔	✔
		✔	✔	✔	✔
		✔	✔	✔	✔
		✔	✔	✔	✔
		✔	✔	✔	✔
		✔	✔	✔	✔
	✔	✔	✔	✔	✔

Videodiscs

Life Insurance Coverages

Search Chapter 45, Play To 46

Importance of Social Insurance

Search Chapter 46, Play To 47

State by State

Maryland allows a lack of insurable interest defense to be raised after its incontestable clause period has run.

Teaching Materials

Student text, pp. 706–728

Overhead transparency masters
- *What Makes Life Insurance Unique?*
- *Social Insurance Coverages*
- *Law for Business* Videodisc

Workbook, pp. 113–123

Outside Resources
- Sample life insurance policies, ads, and application forms
- Pay stubs with payroll deductions
- Poster paper and flip charts
- Articles about RSDHI and Medicare

- Camcorder
- VCR
- Tape recorder

Assessment
- Chapter Test
- Chapter *MicroExam*

Vocabulary

Learning Objectives

When you complete this chapter, you will be able to

1. Explain the various life insurance coverages available.
2. Describe the social insurance programs in this country.
3. Understand how the various life insurance plans are structured and be able to select the one most appropriate for the circumstances.
4. Realize the importance of social insurance in its various forms.
5. Explain the eligibility requirements for the various social insurance programs.

706

Chapter Self-Test

Assess students' understanding of life and social insurance before they begin Chapter 36 by listing the following Social Security Act programs on the chalkboard. Have students brainstorm the purpose of each program to the best of their knowledge. **(1) unemployment compensation** (Temporary income for persons laid off from paying jobs); **(2) retirement insurance** (Supplementary income for workers, age 62 and over, and their dependents); **(3) survivors' insurance** (Income for widows, widowers, and their dependents); **(4) disability insurance** (Income for disabled workers and their dependents); and **(5) health insurance.** (Hospitalization and medical care for persons over 65 and certain others under 65 who are disabled)

CHAPTER 36

LIFE INSURANCE AND SOCIAL INSURANCE

1 When she entered graduate school three years ago, one of your acquaintances took out a $250,000 personal life insurance policy and named her mother as beneficiary. Last week, severely depressed over personal problems, she committed suicide. Must the insurance company pay $250,000 to her mother?

2 Your uncle is just turning sixty-five years old and is looking forward to receiving social security benefits. However, he has not applied for them. Will he lose them if he fails to make a timely application?

3 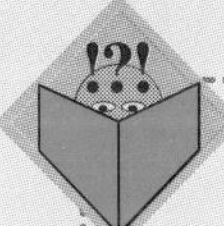

Patricia Jensen took out a $500,000 life insurance policy on her husband Tom. Two years later, a contested divorce proceeding left them very hostile to one another. They had no children and neither was charged with paying support to the other by the divorce decree. However, Patricia continues to pay the premiums. Should the insurance company allow her to keep the policy in effect?

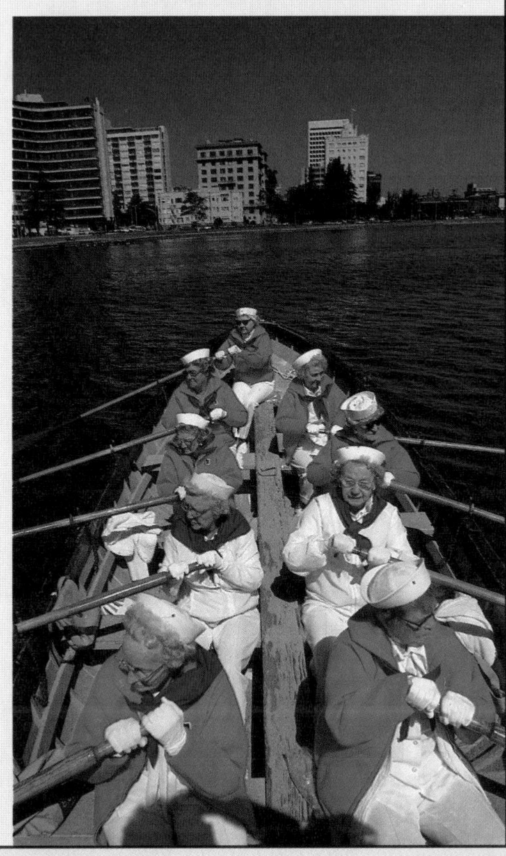

FOCUS

Write the following question on the chalkboard before class begins and have students add their answers: **At your age why, do you think, should you worry about life, social, and retirement insurance?** (Answers may include to prepare for the future, to assist aging parents, and so on.)

Begin class by discussing students' responses. Discuss what students know about life, social, and retirement insurance: its purpose, who would use it, and so on.

You Decide

1 Yes; Generally, however, if the suicide occurs within one to two years after the policy is issued, only the premiums paid to the date of the suicide are payable to the beneficiary.

2 No; However, failure to sign up for Medicare within three months before or after the 65th birthday may result in a delay in protection.

3 ETHICS ISSUE Yes; But, as Patricia no longer has a dependency on Tom for any type of support, maintaining the insurance on him amounts to a wager. However, the law requires an insurable interest to be present only when a life insurance policy is taken out, not when the loss occurs. Therefore, she can legally maintain the coverage as long as she pays the premiums.

Thinking Critically Through Visuals

These active senior citizens probably depend on more than one type of insurance. What types of insurance, do you think, would they need? (Answers may include life, health, retirement, disability, or survivors' insurances.)

TEACH

Define **life insurance** and **social insurance**. Point out the purposes of each.

APPLY

Have students make a two-column chart in their notebooks. Have them label the first column *Life Insurance* and the second column *Social Insurance* and have them write the definition of each term. As students progress in the chapter, have them add to their charts the various types of life and social insurance under the appropriate headings.

Guided Practice

Have students research and write a brief essay on the Social Security Act, including why it began and how it protects the American people. Have students share their findings with the class. **Independent Practice**

TEACH

Review the provisions commonly found in a life insurance policy (pp. 708–709) and discuss why these provisions may be necessary. Provide examples of each provision.

WHAT ARE LIFE INSURANCE AND SOCIAL INSURANCE AND WHY ARE THEY SO IMPORTANT?

PROBLEM

Borrego worries what would happen to her and her family if she lost her job. What kind of insurance would help her if that happened?

Life insurance is a contractual arrangement under which an insurer promises to pay an agreed-upon amount of money to a named party upon the death of a particular person. Given the uncertainties of today's world and its fast-paced mode of living, such insurance is crucial to families, businesses, and responsible individuals throughout our society.

Social insurance indemnifies persons at least partially from the harsh financial consequences of unemployment, disability, death, or forced retirement. Since the late 1930s, programs under the federal government's Social Security Act have been instrumental in providing such protection. In the problem, Borrego would likely be assisted during a time of unemployment by compensation provided under the Social Security Act.

Certainly without the protection of life and social insurance, the potentially adverse impact of death, disability, unemployment, or advancing age would have to be borne solely by the individuals directly affected. Because of the importance of doing as much as possible to protect against the adverse consequences of such occurrences, this chapter covers both life insurance and social insurance.

WHAT PROVISIONS ARE COMMONLY FOUND IN A LIFE INSURANCE POLICY?

PROBLEM

Edmonton was the beneficiary of her uncle's term life insurance policy. When her uncle, a Navy pilot on active duty, was killed in a terrorist bomb explosion overseas, the insurance company refused to pay the policy's face value of $100,000. Can it legally be forced to do so?

ASSESS

Learning Objective 1 Have students identify, in writing, the purpose for and the most common provisions of life insurance. (It is a contractual arrangement under which an insurer promises to pay an agreed-upon amount of money to a named party upon the death of a particular person. The policy may contain: provisions that exempt the insurer from liability when death is due to certain causes, an incontestable clause, a grace period, double indemnity coverage, or disability coverage.)

The insurer of life agrees to pay to a named beneficiary or to the insured's estate the amount stated in the policy, in accordance with the policy provisions. However, life insurance policies sometimes contain provisions that exempt the insurer from liability when death is due to certain causes, such as the crash of a private airplane. Policies may also provide for exemption from liability in case of the policyholder's death during military service abroad or at home. Therefore, in the problem, if such an exemption were in Edmonton's uncle's policy, the insurance company could not legally be forced to pay the $100,000. In cases where death occurs under an exemption, the insurer is liable for return of the premiums paid or cash value (less an indebtedness), instead of the proceeds.

In addition to exemptions, a life insurance policy usually contains an **incontestable clause** that prohibits the insurer from refusing to perform due to fraud or misrepresentation after the policy has been in effect for one or two years. However, if the fraud or misrepresentation involves the age of the insured, the policy is not voided regardless of the length of time it has been in effect. Instead the insurer provides the face amount of insurance that the premium would have bought if the insured's correct age had been known.

A similar clause requires the insurer to pay even if the insured commits suicide after one or, in some states, two years from the date the policy was issued. If the suicide occurs before the one- or two-year limit, the insurer is required to return only the premiums paid.

By statute, most life insurance contracts must also provide for a period of time, called the **days of grace,** during which an overdue premium can be paid to keep the policy in force. Typically, this period is one month. If an insured fails to pay the premium before the days of grace expire, the policy terminates, or **lapses**. A policyholder who is in good health and who pays the back premiums can revive or **reinstate** the policy even after it lapses.

In addition to these common provisions, it is possible to write two additional coverages into a life insurance policy. The first is **double indemnity coverage,** which requires the insurer to pay twice (triple or quadruple coverage may also be purchased, if desired) the face amount of the policy if the death of the insured is accidental. Such coverage usually excludes certain causes of death, such as suicide, illness or disease, wartime military service, and certain airplane accidents. It also is inapplicable after age sixty-five or seventy.

The second additional coverage, **disability coverage,** provides for protection against the effects of total permanent disability. At a minimum, it cancels the requirement for payment of premiums on the life insurance policy while the insured is totally disabled.

▼ APPLY

Pair more able students with those who may experience difficulty with this activity. Together, have students look through samples of various types of life insurance policies (available through local insurance agents). Discuss the following terms, then have students identify and highlight them on the policies: **exemptions, incontestable clauses, days of grace, double indemnity coverage,** and **disability coverage. Guided Practice**

Have students work in pairs to research and report on the insurance laws and regulations in your state. Have students contact the state insurance board, a local insurance company, or your school or public librarian to gather information. Have students tabulate their findings and present them to the class as a chart. **Independent Practice**

Have students write a scenario, using a computer, if possible, in which an insurance policy would not be paid because of a provision in the policy. Refer students to the PROBLEM on the bottom of p. 708.

Have students write life insurance scenarios in which a named party is trying to collect benefits. Encourage students to focus on issues such as why the policy might not be paid, such as due to a lapse in the policy, an exemption such as dying while in a private plane crash, and so on.

▼ WHAT KINDS OF LIFE INSURANCE PLANS ARE AVAILABLE?

PROBLEM

Oxferd wants a life insurance policy that provides adequate coverage on her life and also builds up a cash value that earns interest comparable to other investment opportunities. What type of insurance plan would be best for her?

Various life insurance plans have been developed by the insurance industry to meet the demands of competition from other investment opportunities offering a savings function. Underlying all of the life insurance plans, however, are the two basic types that have been offered for decades.

1. Term Life Insurance Policies

The first type involves the payment of the minimum premium necessary to buy only life insurance on the insured for stated periods of time, generally one, five, or ten years. At the end of that period or upon payment of the face value at the death of the insured, the contract ends with no further obligation on either party. This type is generally called **term life insurance.**

There are two basic types of term insurance. The first, **level term life insurance,** requires the payment of the same premium amount throughout the term in return for a face value that will not change during that term. The second and less expensive type is **decreasing term life insurance.** It requires the payment of the same premium amount throughout the term in return for a face value that will steadily decrease during that term. Decreasing term can be used to insure that a credit instrument, such as a mortgage (which steadily declines in amount), would be paid off if the primary wage earner dies.

Group life insurance, which is sold to cover many similarly situated people (e.g., all employees of a particular business), is typically term insurance. **Credit life insurance,** which pays a lender the amount of an outstanding debt upon the death of the debtor, and **travel insurance,** which covers the life of the traveler during the journey, are also kinds of term insurance.

2. Combination Policies

The second basic type of life insurance plan, **combination policies,** requires the policyholder to pay a premium significantly larger than the minimal premium necessary for term insurance coverage. The surplus amount of

▼ TEACH

Help students to understand the difference between **term life insurance policies** and **combination policies.** (Term: pay minimum premiums to buy only insurance for stated periods of time; Combination: pay higher than minimum premium required to purchase only life insurance; excess is contribution to savings, or similar, plan) Then display and discuss the overhead

transparency, *What Makes Life Insurance Unique?*

▼ APPLY

Have students add to the chart they began in the APPLY activity on p. 708. Under the head, *Life Insurance*, have them add the various types of term and combination policies. **Guided Practice**

Have students each brainstorm one example of a client's need for insurance, such as a young mother's desire to provide for her young son should she die. Then pair students to role-play an insurance agent and the client and determine which type of insurance best meets the client's current needs, without over-insuring him or her. **Independent Practice**

▼ ASSESS

Learning Objective 3 Have students create two graphic organizers, one for term life insurance and another for combination policies, that summarize the different types of basic insurance plans.

the premium is then placed in one of the various savings, investment, or endowment plans run by the insurance company.

For many years, two basic combination policies, endowment and whole life, dominated the market. **Endowment life insurance** requires the insurer to pay the beneficiary upon the death of the insured the policy's face amount during the period of coverage (usually for twenty years or until the insured reaches retirement age). However, if the insured lives to the end of the coverage period, the owner of the policy (usually the insured) is paid the face value. The premiums are quite high, but the necessity of having a large lump sum of money available at a set point in time, for example, to buy a retirement home upon reaching age sixty-five, has attracted many to this type of insurance.

Whole life insurance, another standard type of policy, is somewhat like an endowment policy. It provides for the payment of premiums for as long as the insured lives, or until age 100, rather than for a specified period, such as the twenty years mentioned previously. Obviously, few people live to be 100 and therefore eligible to collect the face value. However, the amount of the premium of a whole life policy is set significantly higher than what would be required for term insurance of the same face value. The surplus goes into a savings program that pays a low but nontaxable return. Gradually over the years, the whole life policy acquires a cash value from this savings function. This cash value provides a savings reserve for the insured that can be borrowed against at a relatively low interest rate. If the insured dies, the face value of the policy, plus the accumulated cash value (less any outstanding loans against it), is paid to the beneficiary.

These combination policies were favored because the necessity of maintaining the life insurance protection by paying the premium forced participation in the savings or investment plan. Without such a discipline, many families would not have put money aside as a reserve. During times of inflation, however, the rates paid on other forms of savings, for example certificates of deposit or money-market funds, increased much more rapidly than did the rates paid on the funds held by the insurance companies. Consequently, the established types of combination policies declined in popularity. Instead many people bought term insurance as cheaply as possible and invested the difference.

The insurance industry responded with a variety of new types of insurance, the most successful of which has been universal life. A **universal life policy** offers death coverage from term insurance plus a minimum guaranteed return on the cash value roughly the same as in a whole life policy (4 to 4.5 percent). However, over short periods, such as one year, the policy may pay higher rates. A similar type of plan, **variable life insurance,** allows

Personal Perspectives

Have students find out from family members, friends, or neighbors if, when, and why they purchased life insurance, and what type of policy was purchased. In class, have students tabulate the results by identifying the types of insurance and adding the number of subscribers to each. Then, identify the most common reasons for purchasing life insurance.

Invite a local insurance agent to discuss the various types of life insurance and how to choose a plan that best fits a person's needs and budget. Then, have the agent discuss life insurance as an investment, compared to other possible investment vehicles.

RETEACH Have students identify the most appropriate type of life insurance policy: **Mary wants a policy that would help her meet expenses when she retires.** (Endowment, universal, or variable life); **Joe is looking for something that would keep his family from losing their home if he dies.** (Level or decreasing term life)

ENRICH

Have students identify, using a computer, if possible questions they might be asked by an agent they consult for life insurance and the kinds of questions they should ask about the insurance plan(s).

Have students collect ads, pictures, or information for various types of life insurance. As a whole-class activity, discuss and sort the ads by type and have students use them to create a bulletin board display entitled *You Bet Your Life.*

▼ TEACH

Review the types, roles, and rights of beneficiaries. Discuss why it is important to identify a **contingent beneficiary** as well as a **primary beneficiary** of a life insurance policy.

▼ APPLY

Have students identify who may be a beneficiary of a life insurance policy. (The insured's estate; partnerships, corporations, or individuals who would suffer the loss of the insured's services if he or she died; named third parties) **Guided Practice**

Independently and in writing, have students explain why it is important to name a beneficiary on a life insurance policy. Have students determine how a beneficiary should be chosen. **Independent Practice**

the insured to invest in several types of funds, such as common stocks, bonds, and money-market instruments. The premium amount is fixed, but the death benefit varies depending on the success of the investments.

The possibility of a relatively high return, combined with the forced savings, tax-free cash buildup, and flexibility of the policy, has caused a renewal of interest in combination term and savings policies. In the problem, Oxferd could consider these new types of combination policies.

▼ WHAT ARE THE RIGHTS OF THE BENEFICIARY OF A LIFE INSURANCE POLICY?

PROBLEM

Sanchez was worried that his insurer would have no one to pay if he and his wife, whom he had named as his life insurance beneficiary, died simultaneously in an accident. What should he do to avoid this possibility?

A **life insurance beneficiary** is the recipient of the proceeds of the policy that are paid upon the death of the insured. Possible beneficiaries include the following:

1. the estate of the insured;
2. partnerships, corporations, or individuals who have taken out life insurance on the insured because they would suffer the loss of the insured's services if the insured died; and
3. third persons who are named in the policy but are not otherwise parties to the insurance contract (e.g., a spouse or the children of the insured).

It is also possible to have two or more beneficiaries. They may share equally, or they may be primary and contingent beneficiaries. A **primary beneficiary** is the one designated by the policy to receive the proceeds if that person is still alive when the insured dies. A **contingent beneficiary** is one designated to receive the proceeds if the primary beneficiary dies before the insured. In the problem, Sanchez could solve his problem by naming a contingent beneficiary, such as a relative, a friend, or a charity. If there was no contingent beneficiary, the insurance proceeds would go to his estate to be distributed under his will or as provided by law if he left no will.

Policies generally give the insured the right to change the beneficiary by giving the insurance company written notice. As a precaution, state law typically provides that any beneficiary who has feloniously killed the insured is not entitled to the policy proceeds.

▼ ASSESS

Learning Objectives 2 & 4 As a group, have students orally identify the five types of Social Security programs and explain why we need such programs. (Unemployment compensation, retirement insurance, survivors' insurance, disability insurance, and health insurance; to help provide for predictable needs, and lessen financial hardships from major disasters)

The **proceeds** of a life insurance policy equal the face of the policy less any amount borrowed against it. When payable to a living beneficiary, the proceeds of insurance are not subject to any claims of creditors of the insured.

WHAT KINDS OF SOCIAL INSURANCE ARE PROVIDED UNDER THE SOCIAL SECURITY ACT?

PROBLEM

Farley had just started college when his mother died unexpectedly. Her paycheck had been the Farley family's sole source of support for over a decade. Is there a Social Security Act program that might help Farley and the rest of his family?

The primary source for social insurance coverages in this country is the federal government's Social Security Act. Coverages provided under the act are frequently labeled **RSDHI** (for Retirement, Survivors', Disability, and Health Insurance). **Unemployment compensation,** which is designed to lessen the financial hardship of losing one's job, is also provided indirectly through programs under the act that are controlled by the individual states (see Figure 36-1). In the problem, it is likely that assistance could be provided to Farley and his family by survivors' insurance benefits.

The Social Security Act is important. Before beginning their first job, everyone should report to or write to the nearest office of the Social Security Administration. This office will assign a permanent number and will provide a card—called a Social Security Account Number Card—which bears one's name, a line for signature, and a nine-digit number. When a person's name is changed by marriage, adoption, or court order, he or she must apply for a new card, which is issued showing the new name, but the number always remains the same. Because of the possibility of errors, it is important for individuals to check periodically with the Social Security Administration to make sure they are receiving the proper credit for wages earned.

The financing for these social insurance programs, except for unemployment and medical insurance, comes primarily from payroll taxes on both workers and employers. The workers' taxes are withheld from their pay by the employers. These **payroll deductions** are then matched in amount by employer contributions, and the total is paid into the appropriate governmental trust fund. The amounts of the taxes and the benefits usually are set as recommended by the Standing Committee on Social Security in Congress. However, the taxes and benefits from unemployment insurance are determined by the various states that administer them in coordination with

RETEACH Have students independently create a graphic organizer that identifies and explains the purpose of each program under the Social Security Act. Have students refer to Figure 36-1 on p. 714 if they need assistance.

ENRICH Invite a guest speaker from, or have students contact (orally or in writing), their local Social Security Administration office to find out how they can review their account (now or for future reference) to ensure that proper credits have been recorded. Encourage students to share the SSA's responses.

Obtain life insurance application forms from a local insurance agent and write SAMPLE on each. Make copies for students and review how to fill out the forms.

TEACH

Review the specific coverages under the federal Social Security Act (pp. 713–714) and discuss the new terms presented in this section.

Display the overhead transparency, *Social Insurance Coverages*, as you discuss the coverages under **RSDHI** and the need for such programs. Provide students with examples of people who need each type of social insurance, such as **unemployment compensation:** Mike Smith is laid off from his job after eight years due to lack of work.

APPLY

Bring to class, have students bring, or create a fictitious payroll stub that shows the various employee payroll deductions that help pay for RSDHI programs. Discuss each one. **Guided Practice**

Divide the class into four groups to spell out the acronym R-S-D-HI. Have each group create an illustration that explains what their letter stands for. Link the illustrations and the letters of the acronym together and display in class. **Independent Practice**

Thinking Critically Through Visuals

Review the coverage of each program then ask: **Which programs do you think would be most important to: a newly retired person who needs income to live on** (Retirement); **a woman whose husband died suddenly** (Survivors'); and **a 17-year old who was permanently injured in a skiing accident** (Disability).

Figure 36-1
This figure shows the specific coverages under the Social Security Act's various programs.

Program	Coverage
1. Unemployment Compensation	Temporary income for persons laid off from paying jobs
2. Retirement Insurance	Supplementary retirement income for workers, age 62 and over, and their dependents
3. Survivors' Insurance	Income for widows, widowers, and their dependents
4. Disability Insurance	Income for disabled workers and their dependents
5. Health Insurance	Hospitalization and medical care (popularly known as Medicare) for persons over 65 and certain others under 65 who are disabled

the federal government. The taxes that support the unemployment insurance programs are paid by the employers only.

TEACH

After you discuss the qualifications and procedures for collecting unemployment benefits (pp. 714–715), have students add this form of insurance under the heading *Social Insurance* on the chart they began in the APPLY activity on p. 708. Review the lists of four qualifications and eight reasons why someone might be denied benefits or have them reduced.

HOW ARE UNEMPLOYMENT BENEFITS OBTAINED?

PROBLEM

After repeated warnings, Speilman and Brown were fired for racing their forklifts around the company loading dock in violation of safety regulations. Were they entitled to unemployment compensation?

The procedures for obtaining benefits under RSDHI, which are described in the following section, vary greatly from the procedures required to receive unemployment compensation through most state governments. However, the self-employed and certain domestic help are generally not covered.

ASSESS

Learning Objective 5 Have students work together to summarize orally in their own, collective, words the generally applicable qualifications for obtaining unemployment benefits as well as circumstances that would warrant a reduction or denial of an unemployment compensation claim. Have students record the information in their notebooks or law journals as it is presented.

Also, benefits are generally available only for twenty-six weeks with a possible further extension during periods of high unemployment.

To obtain unemployment benefits, generally a worker must:

1. be totally unemployed for a specified period of time;
2. register for a job at a public employment office;
3. be ready, willing, and able to work if a suitable job is offered, and in most states, actually be looking for work. To be considered suitable, a job offered must be one in which the worker is trained or experienced even if it pays less than the former work. It must be within a reasonable distance from home; and
4. file a claim for the benefits.

Under certain circumstances, an otherwise qualified unemployed person may have benefits reduced or denied. Typical state rules provide that benefits are partly or completely denied if a worker:

1. quits work voluntarily without good cause;
2. refuses to apply for, or to accept, suitable work;
3. loses the job through an economic strike or a labor dispute in which the worker is involved;
4. intentionally misrepresents the facts about his or her job qualifications;
5. is discharged for misconduct connected with the work, (e.g., refusal to obey proper orders or company regulations);
6. is discharged for criminal conduct;
7. is attending school full-time; or
8. receives other payments (e.g., a company pension or social security retirement benefits).

In the problem, Speilman and Brown were fired for work-related misconduct. As a consequence, they would be barred from receiving any of the unemployment compensation to which they might otherwise have been entitled.

The remaining four major programs under the Social Security Act currently provide various benefits to more than 40 million Americans. Unlike unemployment compensation, the benefits from these programs are uniform throughout the United States, and all are administered by the federal government.

▼ APPLY

Orally present various scenarios in which a person might apply for unemployment insurance benefits, such as being laid off or terminated, quitting in hope of getting a better job, or resigning because of a bad work environment. Have students debate if the worker in each case is, or is not, entitled to collect unemployment insurance. Have students explain their decisions. **Guided Practice**

Have students contact the local office of their state (un)employment commission to find out their state's policies and regulations for eligibility to collect unemployment benefits. Discuss circumstances in your state that differ from those described on p. 715. **Independent Practice**

Ethics Issue

Many people who collect unemployment insurance benefits need the money and are honestly trying to find another job. In some instances, however, people collect benefits while accruing unreported income or turn down jobs because they have money from unemployment. Have students discuss whether these people are acting legally and ethically.

▼RETEACH Have students work independently or in small groups to create a poster identifying the requirements a person must meet in order to obtain unemployment benefits.

▼ENRICH 

Have students write (using a computer, if possible) two scenarios dealing with unemployment insurance claims. In one, the person filing the claim should be qualified; in the other, the claimant should not be eligible. Have students exchange scenarios and decide which claims are likely to be honored.

HOW ARE RSDHI BENEFITS OBTAINED?

PROBLEM

Lansing, who was thirty-three years old, had been working steadily for a construction company for ten years and was fully insured. Then she lost a leg and an arm as a result of an accident while on the job. Does she qualify for disability benefits?

A person becomes eligible to receive the RSDHI benefits by obtaining credit for a specified number of quarters of coverage. A quarter of coverage is awarded, up to a maximum of four per year, each time an employee earns more than a set minimum amount ($540 in 1991). Today, forty quarters are needed to receive retirement benefits at age sixty-two. For disability and survivors' benefits, there is a sliding scale running from a requirement of six quarters if the employee is twenty-eight or younger to forty for an employee age sixty-two or older. Medicare requires only that a person be sixty-five or older or be eligible for the disability program if under sixty-five. Once a person establishes eligibility by receiving the appropriate number of quarters of coverage, he or she is then subject only to the dictates of each of the separate RSDHI programs.

1. Retirement Insurance Requirements

An eligible person may elect to begin receiving retirement insurance checks as early as age sixty-two or may wait until age sixty-five. However, the amount of the monthly income differs considerably between the two options, in favor of the person who retires at age sixty-five. Also, it is important to remember that whatever option is chosen, the checks from the social security retirement insurance program are meant to provide supplemental income only. Too often, individuals rely solely on the checks for their retirement income. This is not the purpose of the program. During the working years, each individual is responsible for accumulating savings to provide enough income that, when added to the social security retirement amount, will allow an adequate standard of living during the retirement years.

All too often, persons retire only to find that they have to return to some form of employment to make ends meet. This working income, earned after retirement, may or may not reduce the worker's retirement insurance payments, depending on the worker's age and the amount of the income from the job. Generally, a retired worker older than age seventy will not have his or her benefits reduced regardless of the amount of income earned.

TEACH

Point out the purposes of the Social Security Act's RSDHI programs and who is eligible to receive benefits under each (pp. 716–720). Discuss specific requirements for receiving retirement, survivors', disability, and health (including Medicare and Medicaid) insurance benefits.

If possible, have someone from the nearest Social Security Administration office explain to students how the quarter system of coverage actually works.

APPLY

Help students use the information on pp. 716–720 to create on the chalkboard, a flip chart, or an overhead transparency a spider map identifying benefits and requirements for the four RSDHI programs mentioned. Have students add supporting details relating to each type of benefit. **Guided Practice**

Divide the class into four groups, one for each of the RSDHI programs. Have students in each group collectively write scenarios describing three fictitious people who would qualify for that RSDHI program. Read scenarios aloud and discuss whether or not the individuals would indeed qualify. **Independent Practice**

ASSESS

Learning Objectives 2 & 5 Independently and in writing, have students identify the four types of RSDHI benefits and to whom each is payable. (Retirement, Survivors', Disability, Health; Refer to pp. 716–720 for requirements and eligibility for benefits' payouts.)

Thinking Critically Through Visuals

This couple has just retired. How, do you think, could they supplement their retirement insurance benefits? (Have students speculate what people could do to supplement retirement income, such as rely on savings, IRAs and private pension plans, relatives, other sources of income, and so on.)

However, individuals between retirement age and age seventy may have their social security retirement checks reduced if they work and receive earnings that exceed a certain amount.

2. Survivors' Insurance Requirements

Survivors' benefits are payable to:

1. a widow or widower age sixty or older (or, if disabled, age fifty or older);
2. a dependent parent age sixty-two or older;
3. a widow or widower of any age if caring for a child under age eighteen, a child that is disabled, or dependent children;
4. a dependent child.

For payments to parties in the latter two categories, it is required only that the deceased worker have six quarters of coverage in the last three years.

Divide the class into groups of five or more students. Have each group brainstorm ideas for a board game on social insurance benefits. For example, they could base the game on working and paying for benefits through payroll deductions, then collect these benefits. Assign one student to make cards that list catastrophes, such as being laid off or getting hurt on the job. Have a second student plan bonus cards that qualify players for full coverage or provide a free pass on a catastrophe, and so on.

After deciding on the basic idea, have two or more students make the game board, and one or two write down the rules. Have groups exchange and play the games. **Cooperative Learning**

In small groups, have students create and tape record a public service announcement (PSA) alerting listeners to eligibility requirements of one of the four RSDHI programs discussed in this section.

Have students discuss the possibility of failure of the Social Security System in our country. As a group, ask students to list reasons for the problem, and possible solutions to it.

Working in pairs, have students write and role-play a scenario in which a person files a claim for benefits under one of the RSDHI programs. One person will act as the applicant and one person will act as the investigator who determines if the claimant qualifies for the program. The investigator should make a list of questions to determine if the person qualifies. Videotape students' skits and discuss each one as you play it back. Discuss how the applicant felt during the interview.

Have students research the appeals process for a decision in which a person's benefits are denied, limited, or terminated. Have students compile their findings as a flowchart.

3. Disability Insurance Requirements

To be eligible for disability benefits, a worker must:

1. be under age sixty-five;
2. be fully insured;
3. have worked at least five years (twenty quarters) in a covered occupation during the ten-year period ending when he or she becomes disabled;
4. have a severe and long-lasting disability, and;
5. have filed an application for benefits.

If disabled before reaching the age of twenty-four, the worker needs credit for only one and one-half years of work in the three years before becoming disabled. From ages twenty-four to thirty-one, the worker needs credit for one-half the time between age twenty-one and the time when unable to work. A worker disabled by blindness needs enough credit to be fully insured but does not need to meet the requirement for recent work.

Benefits for the disabled worker's family are also available and are the same as though the worker were age sixty-five and retired. Disabled widows and widowers age fifty or older receive benefits if their disability begins not later than seven years after the death of the insured husband or wife or the end of a widow's or widower's right to benefits as a mother or father caring for her or his children.

A severe, long-lasting disability is one that prevents the worker from being able to "engage in any substantial gainful activity." Before any payments can be made, it must be established that the condition is physical or mental, is expected to continue indefinitely or result in death, and has lasted—or is expected to last—for at least twelve months. The worker must not refuse reasonable medical treatment. The following ordinarily are considered severe enough to meet the test of disability: loss of both arms, both legs, or a leg and an arm; heart and lung diseases that cause pain or fatigue on slight exertion; progressive cancer; brain damage that results in loss of judgment or memory; loss of vision; inability to speak; and deafness. In the problem, Lansing qualified for disability benefits because of being severely disabled, being under age sixty-five, having worked in a covered occupation for more than five of the past ten years, and being fully insured.

4. Health Insurance (Medicare) Requirements

In the last two decades, the costs of medical care have risen so dramatically that a major illness involving extended hospitalization and treatment threatens not only the physical well-being but the financial livelihood of the

ASSESS

Learning Objectives 2 & 4 Divide the class into two groups. Have students debate Americans' needs for each of the RSDHI programs vs. the cost to all of us of these plans or the cost of not having them. Students may wish to focus on benefits to special populations, such as the elderly or the unemployed, or discuss the high costs for maintaining each program, especially health insurance, in which costs are rising rapidly.

patient and the patient's family. As a consequence, **health insurance,** which indemnifies against the cost of medical care necessary to regain physical well-being after an illness, has become very important. **Medicare** provides such coverage primarily for those over age sixty-five, and private insurance companies provide similar coverage for those not protected by the Social Security Act.

Medicare consists of two basic programs. The first, **hospital insurance,** helps pay for hospital expenses and the costs of follow-up treatment. To receive payments under this program, an eligible person (nearly all persons over age sixty-five, those with severe kidney problems, or those covered for extensive periods by the disability program if under age sixty-five are eligible) must enter a hospital for necessary treatment. After a hospital stay, this program will also help pay for care in a skilled nursing facility or in the home by a home health agency for a period of time. Current benefit figures are available from any Social Security office.

Not all costs of hospital and extended care are covered by Medicare. Many individuals take out supplemental insurance from a private company to pay what Medicare's hospital insurance does not.

Medical insurance, the second basic Medicare program, helps pay for items not covered by the hospital insurance. These include services of physicians and surgeons. Also included are such services as ambulance charges, X-rays, radium treatments, laboratory tests, surgical dressings, casts, and home visits by nurses or therapists as ordered by a doctor. The patient pays

Writing Connections

Social Studies
Have students draft a letter to their state senator or representative, using a computer, if possible, to support or rebut any of the RSDHI programs. Students should state why it is needed or why it should be discontinued, and outline the reasons for their opinion. Have volunteers read their letters aloud.

Thinking Critically Through Visuals

These senior citizens all qualify for Medicare. If someone falls getting out of the pool and breaks a leg, what benefits will Medicare pay? (Medicare will help pay for a portion of all approved hospital and medical costs, minus applicable co-payments and deductibles. The balance must be paid out-of-pocket by the claimant or by the claimant's supplemental insurance carrier, if he or she has this additional coverage.)

RETEACH In small groups, have students identify in writing how they would change the current benefits or qualifications for any of the RSDHI programs and summarize how that program works.

ENRICH Have students independently create a proposal for a new social insurance program, such as youth job training, child care support, employee burnout, and so on. They should provide details on eligibility requirements, how to file, and the purpose of the program. Discuss.

relatively small yearly deductibles, and then medical insurance generally pays either a large percentage or all of the costs of the covered services. All of these items can be extremely expensive.

Unlike hospital insurance coverage, which is financed primarily from the social security tax, the contracting for medical insurance coverage and the payment of the premiums are voluntary. Each person currently enrolled in the medical insurance plan pays a monthly premium. An equal amount is paid by the federal government out of general revenues.

A person must apply for Medicare, just as one must apply for all other social security benefits. However, Medicare differs from other Social Security Act benefits in that application must be submitted within three months before or after the month in which one's sixty-fifth birthday falls. Failure to sign up within the prescribed period results in a six- to nine-month delay in protection, and the premium for medical coverage will then cost more.

Not all medical costs are covered by Medicare. For example, ordinary dental care; routine physical examinations; eye or ear examinations for prescribing, fitting, or changing eyeglasses or hearing aids; strictly cosmetic surgery; and drugs that are not furnished as part of hospitalization are excluded. Therefore most persons should consider buying supplemental private health insurance coverage.

In addition to the Medicare program, the **Medicaid** program assists those in financial need in covering medical costs. Medicaid is federally sponsored but is administered by the states, generally through their divisions of family services.

Preventing Legal Difficulties

1. When considering life insurance, first study your needs and then get competitive bids on the type of policy that will fit them best.
2. Review your policy periodically or whenever there is any significant change in your familial, occupational, or financial situation to see if there is a need to update it.
3. Consider buying decreasing term life insurance to age sixty-five and investing the premium savings if you can discipline yourself to do so. If not, evaluate the term plus savings options in universal and similar life policies.
4. If you have not already secured a Social Security Account Number Card, do so now. You must have one before beginning your first covered job.

Multicultural Highlights

The Department of Health and Human Services (HHS) has been headed by Donna E. Shalala since 1993. Shalala, of Lebanese descent, held several high-level education positions, including becoming the first woman to head a "Big Ten" university: the University of Wisconsin-Madison. As secretary of HHS, Shalala's priorities include making health care more affordable and extending coverage to more than 37 million Americans who are currently uninsured. Ask: **What health care priorities would you add to Shalala's concerns?** (Answers may include AIDS awareness, prevention programs, and so on.)

Preventing Legal Difficulties

After reading and discussing the eight hints for preventing legal difficulties with health or social insurance, have students brainstorm four more items to add to the list.

ASSESS

Learning Objectives 1, 2, 3, & 4 Individually and in writing, using a computer, if possible, have students complete this sentence and then give reasons for their answer: **Of all the types of insurance studied in this chapter I think ________ and ______ are the two most important because ________.**

5 Be informed and aware of the benefits to which you or members of your family might be entitled as a result of dependency, unemployment, disability, or old age.

6 Unemployment benefits may be reduced or denied under certain circumstances. Be sure that you do not jeopardize your rights to unemployment benefits by actions on your part.

7 Try to maintain, at a minimum, a status of having received credit for one quarter of coverage out of the last two possible until you become fully insured under the social security program.

8 Check your social security earnings record for accuracy about every three years. Your social security office will provide you with a free postcard form for this purpose.

REVIEWING IMPORTANT POINTS

1 Life insurance policies may be either pure term insurance or involve a combination of term and a savings or endowment function.

2 It is possible and prudent to specify a primary and one or more contingent beneficiaries to a life insurance policy.

3 Most policies contain an incontestable clause and provide for days of grace and reinstatement in case of lapse.

4 Every employee and self-employed person in covered work needs a Social Security Account Number Card. This number is used all the worker's life to assure that contributions are properly credited to the individual's account.

5 Unemployment compensation provides weekly benefits for a limited period for workers on covered jobs who have been employed a minimum time and have then been discharged.

6 Retirement insurance provides monthly benefits for a worker and dependents when the worker retires at age sixty-two or later.

7 Survivors' insurance provides benefits for dependents when the worker dies.

8 Federal disability insurance provides monthly benefits for a worker and dependents if a severe, long-lasting disability is suffered.

9 Most individuals over age sixty-five and those disabled under age sixty-five are eligible to receive social security payments under Medicare's

CLOSE

Help remedial readers develop a better understanding of the content and vocabulary terms of this chapter by pairing them with a print-dominant partner. Have them write, using a computer, if possible, a collaborative short story. The story is to be about a fictitious person and his or her needs and uses of various types of insurance, both life and social, such as purchasing life insurance, collecting as a beneficiary on a policy, being unemployed, or collecting disability or retirement insurance. Students should try to use as many of the important points of the chapter without making the story too cumbersome. Have students take turns reading their short stories aloud to the class.

Assign the following end-of-chapter materials:
Student text review activities, pp. 721–726
Workbook, pp. 113–123
Chapter Test

Chapter *MicroExam*

RETEACH

In small groups, have students cut and paste pictures, words, or photographs from newspapers and magazine to create a bulletin-board collage depicting Medicare programs, what they cover, eligibility requirements and benefits to insureds. Display the collages in class.

ENRICH

Have students gather magazine and newspaper articles about various RSDHI programs such as changes in laws, problems, fraud charges, and so on. Discuss the articles and have students create a bulletin board display.

Strengthening Your Legal Vocabulary

1. days of grace
2. term life insurance
3. universal life insurance
4. life insurance beneficiary
5. proceeds
6. payroll deduction
7. RSDHI
8. unemployment compensation
9. Medicare
10. contingent beneficiary

hospital insurance. Such payments greatly aid in meeting the cost of necessary hospitalization and nursing care.

10 An important supplement to the hospital insurance under Medicare is the medical insurance available to eligible parties upon the payment of a monthly premium. The medical insurance helps meet costs for which assistance is not available under the hospital insurance (e.g., doctor bills and X-rays).

STRENGTHENING YOUR LEGAL VOCABULARY

Match each term with the statement that best defines that term. Some terms may not be used.

combination policies
contingent beneficiary
credit life insurance
days of grace
decreasing term life insurance
disability coverage
double indemnity coverage
endowment life insurance
group life insurance
health insurance
hospital insurance
incontestable clause
lapse
level term life insurance
life insurance
life insurance beneficiary
Medicaid
medical insurance
Medicare
payroll deduction
primary beneficiary
proceeds
reinstate
RSDHI
social insurance
term life insurance
travel insurance
unemployment compensation
universal life insurance
variable life insurance
whole life insurance

1. Period during which a policy remains in effect even though a premium is overdue.
2. Insurance that pays only if death occurs within the specified period for which the policy was purchased.
3. A type of combination life insurance policy that includes term insurance and a savings program that guarantees a minimum return close to that of a whole life policy but may, on a period by period basis, pay a much higher return on savings.
4. Party to whom the proceeds of a life insurance policy are payable.

5 The amount due to be paid under a life insurance contract equaling the face value plus any cash value and dividends, less any loans against the policy.

6 Money withheld from worker's pay by employer for taxes or for other purposes.

7 Retirement, Survivors', Disability, and Health Insurance.

8 Payments designed to lessen the financial hardship of temporary involuntary job loss.

9 Federal health insurance program that includes both hospital and medical benefits.

10 Person designated to receive the amount due under a life insurance contract if the primary beneficiary dies before the insured.

APPLYING LAW TO EVERYDAY LIFE

1 The Beans disagreed on the relative merits of term versus combination life insurance policies. Mr. Bean maintained that it was better to buy the same amount of term insurance (at a lower rate) and invest the difference between that rate and the higher whole life rate. Mrs. Bean pointed out that they probably would spend the premium savings rather than invest them and that the insurance company would have better investment opportunities. What is your opinion?

2 Driving while intoxicated, Baxter ran over and killed his wife. He was convicted of vehicular manslaughter, a felony. Can he still collect the proceeds as beneficiary of his wife's $100,000 double indemnity policy?

3 When Henecker took out his life insurance policy, he misrepresented his age as twenty-seven. In reality, he was thirty-four. Will the insurance company be required to pay on the policy when Henecker dies?

4 Shuster had a $100,000 triple indemnity policy. Three years after contracting for it, she committed suicide. Will the insurance company have to pay $300,000?

5 Podesta was laid off when the fruit and vegetable canning plant where she worked cut back on production. After a week she began receiving unemployment benefit checks. Shortly after, a new semester began at the local state college. Podesta enrolled as a full-time student, but continued to accept the benefit checks because she said she was ready, willing, and able to go back to work full-time. If called, she would either

Applying Law to Everyday Life

1 The answer may vary depending on individual situations. This question can be the basis for a good discussion. (pp. 710–711)

2 No; State laws typically provide that a beneficiary who has feloniously killed the insured is not entitled to the policy proceeds. (p. 712)

3 Yes; However, the face amount due will be reduced to the amount of insurance the premiums should have purchased had the correct age been known. (p. 709)

4 No; A suicide occurring after one or two years from the initiation of the policy compels the insurer to pay only the face amount (here $100,000). (p. 709)

5 No; A person who is attending school full-time is not available for employment and hence is not eligible for unemployment benefits. (p. 715)

rearrange her classes or quit school. Was she entitled to unemployment benefits?

6 Chadwick began working full time when he graduated from high school at age eighteen. He joined a union and got a job driving a heavy caterpillar-type tractor in road construction. By putting in many hours of overtime, he earned about $15,000 a year for four years. He married and within one year his wife gave birth to a child. Then tragedy struck. Chadwick's tractor overturned on a mountainside, throwing him from the tractor. His lower body was permanently paralyzed. Will social security help Chadwick and his family?

7 When the cost of living rose, Bollinger's employer refused to boost the wages of his workers, saying costs were up and sales down. After weeks of fruitless negotiations, Bollinger and other members of his union went on strike, demanding a pay boost. This cut Bollinger's income to nothing and he applied for unemployment compensation. Does he qualify?

8 McMurty, who was age seventy and covered by Medicare, slipped and fell down a flight of steps. She broke her hip and her jaw, and required dental surgery as well as plastic surgery to restore her face. Would the necessary medical attention be covered under Medicare?

9 ETHICS ISSUE To be able to pay social security retirement benefits to the disproportionately large number of Americans born between 1945 and 1965, the government is building up a huge surplus of funds in the Social Security Trust Accounts. Critics say that such an accumulation of funds hurts the economy. The critics desire instead to reduce or eliminate retirement benefits for the "baby boomer bulge." What should our society do?

10 ETHICS ISSUE Currently, a retiree between the ages of sixty-five and seventy loses $1 of social security retirement benefits for every $3 the retiree earns. Is it ethical to penalize a person for working if he or she desires to do so?

SOLVING CASE PROBLEMS

1 While married to his first wife, Lavender took out a $5,000 life insurance policy on his own life. He named his wife beneficiary and his three minor children as contingent beneficiaries. Marital difficulties later resulted in divorce. The court decreed that Lavender was to keep the policy "in full force and effect" with his former wife as beneficiary and the three children as contingent beneficiaries in the event the

6 Yes; Chadwick is entitled to disability benefits and, if he should die, his wife and child could qualify for benefits as dependents. (p. 718)

7 No; A worker who loses his or her job through an economic strike or labor dispute in which he or she is involved may not collect unemployment insurance benefits. (p. 715)

8 Yes; After McMurty pays the applicable deductibles, Medicare would cover the cost of any hospital stay and a large percentage of any treatment by physicians and surgeons, including plastic surgeons, when necessary because of an accidental injury. (pp. 718–720)

9 The generation in question has supported social security retirees and other programs longer than any other. It has done so with the idea that it will be compensated in like manner when its members reach retirement. Regardless, any changes to decrease or eventually eliminate such benefits should be made shortly to allow the individual members of the generation to prepare accordingly.

10 

Both the policy of penalizing additional income and the amount of the penalty imposed are in question today. The individuals upon whom this policy has its greatest proportional impact can little afford it, and it provides a counterincentive to deciding to retire and vacating a position to be filled by a younger worker.

plaintiff (wife) remarried or died. Both parties remarried, and Lavender changed the beneficiary of the policy to his new wife. Lavender and his second wife were later divorced, but the divorce decree made no mention of the life insurance policy. When Lavender died, the proceeds were claimed by the children, now adults, and the second wife. The first wife made no claim to the proceeds of the policy. The insurer, being aware of both the first divorce decree and the change of beneficiary, paid the proceeds into the court with a request that the court determine the rights of the parties. You decide. (*Travelers Insurance Company v. Lewis,* 531 P.2d 484)

2 After their purchase of all the capital stock of the Laclede Packing Company, the new stockholders, Mickelberry's Food Products Company and others, sought to collect the cash surrender value of $36,945.51 on two life insurance policies. The two policies were on the lives of the former president and the former secretary-treasurer of the Packing Company, Haeussermann and Ackermann. Haeussermann and Ackermann were the principal stockholders and officers in the Packing Company from its inception until the new stockholders took over. When the policies were taken out, several years before the takeover by the new stockholders, the stockholders were obligated to pay the premiums and were also named as the beneficiaries. The defendants, Haeussermann and Ackermann, claim that the new stockholders have no insurable interest in the lives of the former officers and that as a consequence, the new stockholders are not entitled to the proceeds. You decide. (*Mickelberry's Food Products Co. v. Haeussermann,* 247 S.W.2d 731)

3 One month after his release from the Missouri State Penitentiary, Frank Bird insured his own life in a double indemnity policy issued by John Hancock Mutual Life Insurance Company. A little over two months later, the insured was killed while attempting to hold up a cocktail lounge. The insurance company refused to pay the proceeds to the beneficiaries, Harry and Edna Bird, even though the policy contained no provision excluding liability if the insured died as a result of a violation of the law. John Hancock stated that to pay even innocent beneficiaries under such circumstances would be against public policy and might foster criminal behavior. You decide. (*Bird v. John Hancock Mutual Life Insurance Company,* 320 S.W.2d 955)

4 Dawkins had been employed as a sheet metal worker by the Sun Shipbuilding and Dry Dock Company. When World War II ended and shipyard work declined, he expected to be laid off. Therefore, he quit to go into business for himself as a roofing contractor. Within four months he

Solving Case Problems

1 The court held for the children, pointing out that the first wife had remarried and under the divorce decree was prevented from taking the proceeds. The description "minor children" was held to describe the status of the children at the time of the settlement. The children, as opposed to the second wife, took the insurance money because of the court decree to keep the policy in effect with the first wife as beneficiary and the children as contingent beneficiaries. (p. 712)

2 Judgment for the new stockholders; The insurable interest need only exist at the time the policies were taken out. Shareholders do have such interests in the lives of corporate officers. In addition, the assignee of the interest in such a policy need not have an insurable interest as long as the policy is not assigned for wagering purposes. (p. 712)

3 Judgment for the beneficiaries (the Birds); The court held that, absent a policy provision to the contrary, payment could not be withheld from innocent beneficiaries. The contract is to be construed against its maker unless the defendant insurance company can show

that the insured procured the policy in contemplation of taking his life in a felony. (Note: The beneficiaries did not ask for the double indemnity portion to be placed into effect, in part because such a felony death would be from intentional exposure to danger and therefore not accidental.) (p. 712)

4 No; It is not good cause when an employee leaves to become an independent businessperson or a professional. (p. 715)

5 No; Joe has the right to refuse to take the myelogram test or to submit to an operation. However, if his ailment could be remedied by treatment and he refuses such treatment, he forfeits his rights to disability benefits. Here, without a test, a diagnosis cannot be made nor treatment given. (p. 718)

had to shut down because he could not get materials. Now he asks for unemployment compensation, claiming he left his job at the shipyard for good cause. Is he entitled to unemployment benefits? (*Sun Shipbuilding and Dry Dock Co. v. Unemployment Compensation Board of Review*, 56 A.2d 254)

5 Joe Fitzgerald, a laborer, injured his back. Physical therapy did not help, and his doctor recommended injecting oil into his spinal canal for X-rays (myelogram), a painful but safe procedure. If the results were positive, the doctor would recommend surgery, which would require six months for recovery. Joe refused this treatment and claimed disability benefits. Is he entitled to such benefits? (*Fitzgerald v. Finch*, No. 1862, E.D. of Ky.)

SPECIAL SECTION

HOW TO BECOME AN ATTORNEY

If this course and other contacts with the law and legal professionals spark a desire in you to pursue a career as an attorney, now is a good time to start planning. While in high school, take courses in English, political science, and history. If available, take specialized courses dealing with legal issues and perspectives. Latin will improve your command of English and provide some useful understanding of legal terminology.

Be aware that although a college degree is a prerequisite for admission to many law schools, some schools allow you to combine your senior year in college with your first year in law school. This reduces from seven to six the years of formal higher educational preparation necessary for entry into the profession. Being an undergraduate at a given university sometimes helps in obtaining admission to that institution's law school.

During your college years, a concentration in liberal arts and fundamental business courses will assist your future performance in law school and beyond. In addition, many undergraduate institutions offer courses that complement courses offered in most law schools. Advice on identifying such courses and other valuable assistance can be obtained through participation in any pre-law club or similar organization on campus.

Most law schools reduce the number of applicants who are acceptable candidates for admission by setting minimum standards for grade point averages and scores on the Law School Admission Test (LSAT). The LSAT is a standardized examination which tests a person's aptitude for the study of law.

In law school, you will be required to take basic courses in contracts, torts, and crimes, as well as courses in property, wills, trusts

Special Section: How to Become an Attorney

Divide the class into groups of four to create a board game about how to become a lawyer. Each group should think of a title for its game, such as *Three Years 'Till the Boards*. The game will focus on getting through the years of law school, starting with pre-admission preparation and ending with taking the bar exam in your state.

You may want to contact a law school near you for a summary of the required courses before students begin making their game. Review prerequisites to and information on law school, such as how to apply, the type of courses, or grades needed to graduate, and so on.

Have students begin by deciding the basic premise of the game and how one determines the winner, such as being the first to travel from one end of the board to the other as he or she picks up completed course cards. Then have students in each group decide who will make the game board, write the rules, create the game cards, and so on. Have each group play, then explain, their game to the rest of the class. If time allows, have students try out some of the other games and vote for their favorite one.

and estates, legal procedure, evidence, and constitutional law. You may also choose courses that may lead to specialization in a particular field, such as labor law, family law, or tax law.

Law school graduates cannot practice law until they pass the bar exam in the state where they intend to practice. Because most law schools do not emphasize the law of any particular state but instead concentrate on imparting general principles, most law school graduates must take a bar exam preparation course before taking the exam.

Upon passing the bar exam, each potential practitioner's record is examined by a committee of the state bar to ensure that the person is of sound character. Typically, any felony convictions will prevent the applicant from being admitted to practice.

Unit Overview

In Unit 10, *Business Organizations*, students will read about sole proprietorships, partnerships, and corporations. In this unit, students will learn about the different types of partners and partnerships, types of stock, board of directors, bylaws, bonds, proxies, consolidations, and mergers. As they study the legal forms of business organization, students will also learn about the kinds of activities in which all businesses engage. They will also experience to what extent business entities are subject to administrative agency regulations at the local, state, and federal government levels.

The actions of sole proprietors and partners are governed by the state and federal laws that structure these two forms of business ownership. In Chapter 37, *Sole Proprietorships and Partnerships*, students will study what sole proprietorships and partnerships are. They will learn about different kinds of partnerships and partners, the duties of a partner, the rights of partners as owners, authority of a partner and his or her liabilities, and how a partnership is ended.

Corporations have certain advantages and disadvantages over other forms of business ownership. In Chapter 38, *Corporations,* students will discover what a corporation is. They will learn about specifics relating to the corporate form of business ownership, such as the disadvantages of corporations, the different types of corporations, how one is formed, and what shares of stock are. They will study who directs the business of the corporation, the powers and duties of the corporate officers and the corporation, the rights of shareholders and their liability as owners, how corporate existence ends, and the impact of law on business.

At the end of this unit, you'll find a special section, *Rules of Professional Conduct and Discipline for Attorneys*, which can be used at any time during the study of Unit 10. You may wish to assign its accompanying *Teacher Edition* activity to give students an opportunity to present oral reports to the class after reading a novel, listening to an audiotape, or viewing a film that deals with the professional conduct and discipline of attorneys.

Portfolio Assessment

Have students brainstorm a creative idea on which to base their own business. After reviewing Chapters 37 and 38, have them determine the legal structure of their business—a proprietorship, partnership, or corporation. Then, using a computer, if possible, have students outline a simple business plan to determine if their idea could be the basis for a reasonable business venture. Tell students to research and include the following sections in their plan: Table of Contents, Summary of Business Idea, Legal Structure, Management Team, Product or Service, Market for Product or Service, Marketing Plan, Operational Plan, Financial Analysis, Objectives and Milestones, Ownership and Equity, and Appendices. Be sure to have students add their business plans to their portfolios.

Careers

Small Business Owner

With small businesses growing steadily in the United States, the need to be familiar with business law is greater than ever. It is expected that, by the year 2000, 15 percent of the workforce will consist of small business owners. Their responsibilities depend on the nature of the company, but their main functions are planning; managing finances; marketing; and hiring, training, and supervising employees.

To be a successful small business owner, you must be a good manager, have a combination of formal education and practical experience in the business you want to own, and know federal and state tax laws—or hire the services of someone who does. The earnings of small business owners depend on the success of the business itself. Generally, small businesses must be in operation for several years before they show a healthy profit.

Using a computer, if possible, have students write an essay explaining why they do or do not think they would be a successful business owner.

Annotated Bibliography

- ***National Biscuit Co. v. Stroud*, 106 S.E.2d 692 (1959).**
  All partners are jointly and severally liable for the acts and obligations of the partnership, and the acts of a partner on behalf of the partnership are binding on the partnership and the other partners. (Chapter 37)

- ***Dirks v. SEC*, 463 U.S. 646 (1983).**
  If a corporate officer discloses nonpublic corporate information for his or her own personal gain, it is a violation of his or her fiduciary duty to the shareholders, and thus a violation of the Securities & Exchange Commission Rule 10(b)(5). (Chapter 38)

- ***Walkovsky v. Carlton*, 223 N.E.2d 6 (1966).**
  Broadly speaking, courts will disregard the corporate form, "pierce the corporate veil," and find a stockholder personally liable for corporation acts, when, in reality, the shareholder is carrying on the business for purely personal rather than corporate ends. (Chapter 38)

Business Organizations

- Sole Proprietorships and Partnerships
- Corporations

CHAPTER 37 ORGANIZER

Chapter Theme

The actions of sole proprietors and partners are governed by the state and federal laws that structure these two forms of business ownership.

DIRECTED STUDY QUESTIONS	SPECIAL FEATURES	PROGRAM RESOURCES				
		Reteach	Enrich	SN	AM	
What is a sole proprietorship?	Thinking Critically Through Visuals, p. 732	✔	✔			
What is a partnership?	Thinking Critically Through Visuals, p. 734 Personal Perspectives, p. 735	✔	✔		V K	
What are the kinds of partnerships and partners?	Multicultural Highlights, p. 736 Ethics Issue, p. 737	✔	✔	✔		
What are the duties of a partner?		✔	✔			
What rights do the partners have as owners?	Writing Connections, p. 742	✔	✔		A	
What authority does a partner have?		✔	✔			
What are a partner's liabilities?		✔	✔			
How is a partnership ended?	Preventing Legal Difficulties, p. 747	✔	✔			

Additional Resources

- Alarid, William and Berle, Gustav, Ph.D. *Free Help from Uncle Sam to Start Your Own Business (Or Expand the One You Have).* Santa Maria, CA: Puma Publishing Co., 1992.
- Bryan, Cynthia, and Wasserman, Paul. *Small Business Information Source Book.* Phoenix, AZ: Onyx Press, 1987.
- Howell, John, C. *Forming Corporations and Partnerships: An Easy, Do-It-Yourself Guide,* Blue Ridge Summit, PA: Liberty House, 1986.

One-semester course	✔	✔						
One-year course	✔	✔	✔	✔	✔			

Chapter Pacing Guide

	ASSESSMENT OPPORTUNITIES			
Cooperative Learning	Informal Assessment	Chapter Review	Chapter Test	Chapter *MicroExam* (Media)
	✔	✔	✔	✔
	✔	✔	✔	✔
	✔	✔	✔	✔
	✔	✔	✔	✔
	✔	✔	✔	✔
	✔	✔	✔	✔
✔	✔	✔	✔	✔
	✔	✔	✔	✔

Videodiscs

Sole Proprietorship

Search Chapter 47, Play To 48

General Partnership vs.
Limited Partnership

Search Chapter 48, Play To 49

State by State

Partners' fiduciary duties connote the "punctilio of honor most sensitive," a moral standard stricter than the marketplace, in Vermont, New York, Oregon, and Pennsylvania.

Teaching Materials

Student text, pp. 730–753

Overhead transparency masters
- *Kinds of Partnerships*
- *Kinds of Partners*

Videos
Law for Business Videodisc

Workbook, pp. 125–128

Outside Resources
- Butcher paper
- Blank overhead transparencies
- Markers
- Flip chart
- Index cards

Assessment
- Chapter Test

- Chapter *MicroExam*

Vocabulary

sole proprietorship, p. 732
partnership, p. 733
general partners, p. 733
partnership agreement, p. 734
nontrading partnership, p. 736
trading partnership, p. 736
special partnership, p. 736
joint venture, p. 737
general partnership, p. 737
limited partnership, p. 737
limited partners, p. 737
silent partner, p. 738
secret partner, p. 738
dormant partner, p. 738
nominal partner, p. 738
confess judgment, p. 740
tenancy in partnership, p. 742
dissolution, p. 745
winding-up period, p. 746
termination, p. 746
partnership at will, p. 746

Learning Objectives

When you complete this chapter, you will be able to

1. Define sole proprietorship and understand why sole proprietorships are the most numerous form of business organization.
2. Discuss what a general partnership is and explain how it differs from a limited partnership.
3. Recognize that both sole proprietors and general partners are exposed to unlimited personal liability for the debts of their business firms.
4. Understand how a limited partnership can protect investors from the problem of unlimited liability.
5. Understand why the choice of general partners is important.
6. Distinguish between a joint venture and a true partnership.

730

Chapter Self-Test

Assess students' understanding of business organizations before they begin Chapter 37 by having them respond orally to the following questions: **(1) What are the three principal forms of business organization?** (Sole proprietorship, partnership, and corporation); **(2) Do all general partners carry the same basic liability to outside creditors for business debts regardless of agreements among themselves?** (Yes); and **(3) What legal requirements are there for organizing and conducting a sole proprietorship?** (None in particular, other than acquiring a tax identification number and securing any required business licenses) Before continuing with the chapter, review and discuss students' responses.

CHAPTER 37 SOLE PROPRIETORSHIPS AND PARTNERSHIPS

1 At the end of the school year, you buy more than 100 books from other students. During the summer, you clean all the books and rebind some. In September, you sell them at a profit to incoming students. What legal form of business organization are you probably using?

2 ETHICS ISSUE Three friends take auto shop in school. The following summer, they combine their savings and buy three old cars of the same make from an automobile dismantling company. They plan to use the best parts to produce two cars, repainted, and equipped with new tires. Their expenses, excluding payment for their own labor, total $1,200. Are they associated in a legally recognized business relationship? If they sell the two cars for a total of $3,600, how should this money be divided? Would it be ethical to advertise the cars as "newly manufactured"?

3 Four partners own a profitable chain of one-hour film-processing shops. One partner is seriously injured in a motorcycle accident and is permanently disabled. Is the partnership automatically dissolved because one partner can no longer work?

FOCUS

On the chalkboard, write the following headings in a horizontal list: **Sole Proprietorship** and **Partnership.** As students enter the classroom, have them write their name under the business organization heading that they think offers the most advantages. Tell them to be ready to defend their choice.

Give each student an opportunity to briefly state the rationale or motivation for his or her choice. Copy the information from the chalkboard onto a sheet of paper and retain it for use in the CLOSE activity at the end of the chapter.

You Decide

1 Sole proprietorship; You alone own and control the business.

2 ETHICS ISSUE Yes, they are associated in a joint venture, which is similar to a general partnership. Of the $3,600, the $1,200 investment of capital is returned first, each joint venturer receiving $400. The balance of $2,400 is divided equally, with each getting $800. No; It would not be ethical to advertise the cars as newly manufactured because it is likely that many would interpret the phrase to mean that the cars are actually new.

3 No; However, the partners may voluntarily agree to dissolve the partnership. Or, one or more of the uninjured partners could petition a court to order dissolution, if it is proved that the disabled person could not perform partnership duties as agreed. The remaining partners may agree to continue the business in a new partnership.

Thinking Critically Through Visuals

The man in the photograph operates a one-person business. What, do you think, are the major advantages and disadvantages of such an enterprise? (Advantages: he has unlimited control and keeps all the profit; disadvantages: he has unlimited personal responsibility for all debts and for other liabilities the business may incur.)

TEACH

Tell students that there are three types of business organizations: *sole proprietorship, partnership,* and *corporation*. Explain that the **sole proprietorship** is owned by one person who not only has relatively unlimited control over the business and keeps all profits but also has unlimited personal responsibility for all business debts. Sole proprietorships are by far the most numerous legal forms of business organization.

APPLY

Discuss the pros and cons of sole proprietorship and list them on the chalkboard in a two-column chart. **Guided Practice**

Thinking Critically Through Visuals

The chimney sweep shown in this photograph is a sole proprietor. If she damages the roof while working, to what extent is she responsible? (If she does not have enough business assets and liability coverage to cover the damage, then she is required to use personal assets.)

WHAT IS A SOLE PROPRIETORSHIP?

PROBLEM

Sico plans to open a sporting goods store. She hesitates because she thinks the expenses would be prohibitive. She lists the costs of renting or buying required space, hiring help, buying a computer to keep records, buying a large inventory, obtaining a charter from the state, paying for licenses, and legal and accounting fees. Should these problems cause her to drop her plans?

There are three principal forms of business organization: (1) the sole proprietorship, (2) the partnership, and (3) the corporation. Of the three, the simplest, most flexible, and easiest to start is the **sole proprietorship,** which is owned by one person. The owner has relatively unlimited control over the business and keeps all the profits. However, the sole proprietor (owner) also has unlimited personal responsibility for all debts and for other liabilities that the business may incur. In case of breach of contract by the proprietor, or a tort, his or her nonexempt personal property as well as all of the business property may be seized to pay damages awarded by courts. But careful management, coupled with adequate public liability insurance, limits those risks and makes them tolerable.

ASSESS

Learning Objectives 1 & 3 Have students respond orally to the following questions: **(1) What are the three principal forms of business organization?** (Sole proprietorship, partnership, and corporation); **(2) Which is the most numerous legal form of business organization?** (Sole proprietorship); and **(3) In general, are there any limits to the personal liability for which a sole proprietor can be held accountable?** (No)

Sole proprietorships are by far the most numerous legal form of business organization. Most independent contractors listed in the Yellow Pages of telephone directories are sole proprietors. Many expand their businesses with the help of ordinary employees and agents. Nevertheless, although corporations are fewer in number, they have a much larger sales dollar volume and employ many more workers.

There are no particular legal requirements for organizing or conducting a sole proprietorship. When started, many sole proprietorships are conducted out of the owner's home, garage, or van. No help need be hired, no computer is required for the simple records, and inventory may be limited and may often be purchased on credit. No charter is needed from the state, although a local business license—and perhaps a permit to collect sales taxes for transmittal to the state—may be required. Some types of businesses, such as those selling food or securities, are subject to special governmental regulations regardless of the legal form of organization. In the problem, Sico should not necessarily drop her plans. She should survey her potential market to confirm the need for such a business in that location at the present time. She should also be reasonably sure that she has the necessary knowledge and ability, as well as sufficient capital, for the venture. Usually, it is highly desirable to have prior experience as an employee in a similar business.

WHAT IS A PARTNERSHIP?

PROBLEM

Bard and Chung organized and operated the DDD-Dusk t' Dawn Discotheque. They agreed to share profits and losses equally. They also agreed to pay rent of either $500 a month or 6 percent of their gross revenues, whichever amount was greater, for use of Allyn's warehouse. In addition, Kardine was hired as manager for $1,000 a month plus 3 percent of the net profits. Are Bard, Chung, Allyn, and Kardine all partners in the DDD business?

According to the Uniform Partnership Act (UPA)[1] a **partnership** is an association of two or more persons (who are called **general partners**) to carry on, as co-owners, a business for profit. The general partners share all profits equally, as well as all losses if any are suffered. The partners may agree among themselves to a different distribution, but each remains fully liable without limit to outside creditors for debts owed by the firm. This

[1]The UPA has been adopted in all states except Louisiana. In Alabama's and Nebraska's versions, there are minor deviations from the original text.

Using a computer, if possible, have students write about opening their own business. In the essay, have them describe the type of business and explain what tasks would need to be done to run the business, such as accounting, sales, buying equipment; what employees they would hire, if any; and what tasks they would enjoy doing in the business.

Independent Practice

TEACH

Tell students that two or more persons who associate as co-owners of a business for profit legally are partners even if there is no written agreement and they do not call or consider themselves such. Also, point out that, regardless of agreements partners make among themselves, they all remain fully liable without limit to creditors for debts owed by the firm. Explain that if two persons agree in writing at the time they form their partnership that it is to last longer than one year, then they have made a formal **partnership agreement**. Discuss the advantages of having the partnership agreement in writing.

Have students create a graphic organizer illustrating the characteristics of a sole proprietorship.

ENRICH Have students brainstorm a list of common chores they do at home or at work. Then, have them indicate by voting, whether they prefer to do that chore alone or with a partner. Have students look for patterns and decide whether they are more suited to a partnership or a sole proprietorship.

▼ APPLY

Thinking Critically Through Visuals

These children are learning to work together as partners. If, after reaching adulthood they decide to form a legal partnership, would they be required to have a written partnership agreement? (No) **If the partnership lasted longer than one year, would an oral agreement be enforceable?** (No, it must be in writing to be enforceable under the statute of frauds.)

Guided Practice

Secure a large section of butcher paper to a classroom wall. Provide students with markers. Have the class work together to create a graphic organizer that graphically presents the circumstances under which a partnership is legally treated as an *entity* and the circumstances under which it is legally treated as an *aggregation*, or a group of individual partners. Refer students to the enumerated lists on pp. 735–736.

unlimited liability restricts the popularity and utility of the general partnership form of business organization.

In the problem, Bard and Chung were partners, but the others were not. Neither Allyn nor Kardine owned part of the business. Their sharing of the gross revenue or net profits was merely a method of paying them rent and salary.

The agreement of the partners need not be in writing unless required by the statute of frauds. As discussed in Chapter 13, the statute of frauds requires a writing signed by the party being sued to make the contract enforceable if it cannot be performed within one year from the date it is made. Therefore, if two persons agree at the time they form their partnership that it is to last longer than one year, their agreement must be in writing and signed by both persons to be enforceable by both. If the persons do not agree on a specific length of time for their partnership to continue, their agreement need not be in writing. After all, the contract could be performed within one year, even though it could last for many years. The time, resources, and detail involved make it highly desirable to reduce every partnership agreement to a signed writing, preferably with the assistance of a lawyer. This encourages thoughtful review of the many potential problems of the new business. It also helps to avoid future costly controversies by spelling out rights and duties of the partners in advance. The resulting document is called the **partnership agreement.**

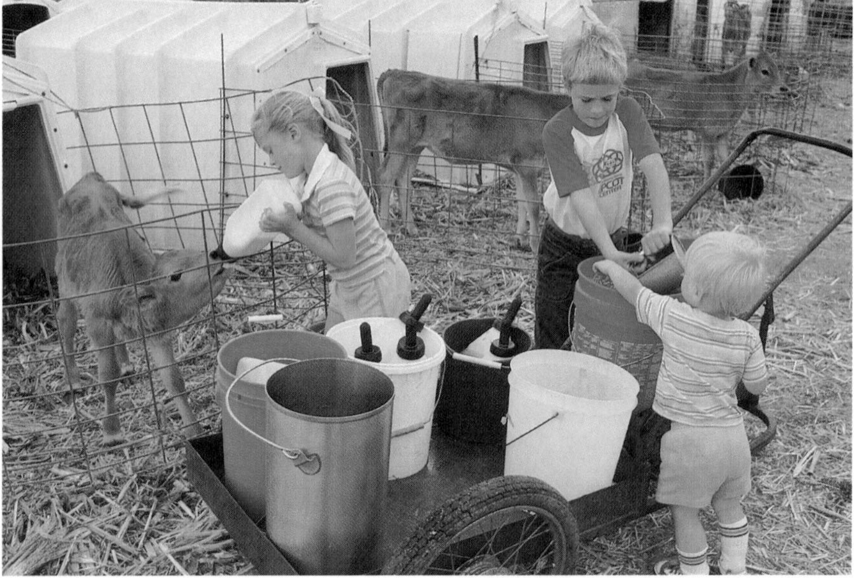

▼ ASSESS

Learning Objectives 2, 3, & 5 Have students respond orally to the following *True* or *False* statements: **(1) If partner *A* agrees that partner *B* will not be held liable for debts owed by the firm resulting from a high-risk business move, outside creditors cannot hold partner *B* liable.** (False); and **(2) In some respects, a partnership is legally treated as an entity.** (True)

A partnership combines the capital, labor, skill, and knowledge of two or more persons. Often the resulting combination serves to multiply the strength of the parties: one plus one equals three or more in talent and productivity. Unique abilities can be better developed and utilized through specialization; bigger projects become manageable.

Because of their close relationship and ability to bind each other legally in contracts and torts involving third parties, partners should be selected with painstaking care. If possible, one should choose as partners only persons who are socially compatible, financially responsible, ethical and morally trustworthy, professionally competent, physically fit, and willing to work hard. As with sole proprietors, competence and integrity, coupled with adequate public liability insurance, make the risks of unlimited liability tolerable.

Kirk and Kevin had been buddies since kindergarten. After graduation from college, each spent a year as a sales representative in Europe. Kirk cultivated a knowledge of French language and business practices, while Kevin became fluent in Spanish and became familiar with Spanish business practices. When Kirk and Kevin returned to the United States, they formed the K & K Company, an export-import trading partnership. It ended within a year because Kirk was constantly in trouble with personal creditors and kept proposing ways to evade export and import laws to boost profits. Kevin, on the other hand, was almost always "last-in and first-out" from their office and resisted any change or expansion.

Under the UPA, a partnership is legally treated, in some respects, as an entity. This means that it is a distinct, real being in the eyes of the law. A partnership:

1. may take title to, and transfer property in its own name;
2. is regarded as a principal, for which each partner may act as agent, making contracts in the firm's name; and
3. must use its own assets to pay its creditors before any individual partner's assets may be seized.

For most purposes, a partnership is legally treated as an aggregation or group of individual partners, with the following results:

1. Each partner must pay income taxes on her or his share of the net profits even if they are not distributed but are retained in the business. The firm pays no income tax but files an information return. This enables

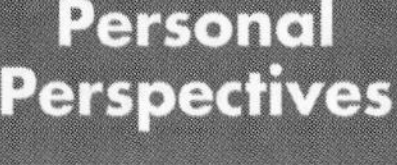

Personal Perspectives

Draw a three-column chart on the chalkboard or a flip chart. Label the three columns as follows: **Types of Partnerships**, **Desirable Partner Characteristics**, and **Partnership Problems**. As a whole-class activity, brainstorm business and nonbusiness partnerships in which students have been involved. List these in the first column of the chart. Save this chart. Then have students discuss business and nonbusiness partnerships with adult family members in which they may be or have been involved. Ask family members to list the most important qualities to look for in a partner and the most likely problems to arise in a partnership. Then, in class, have students list on the class chart the desired characteristics and problems cited most by their family members.
Independent Practice

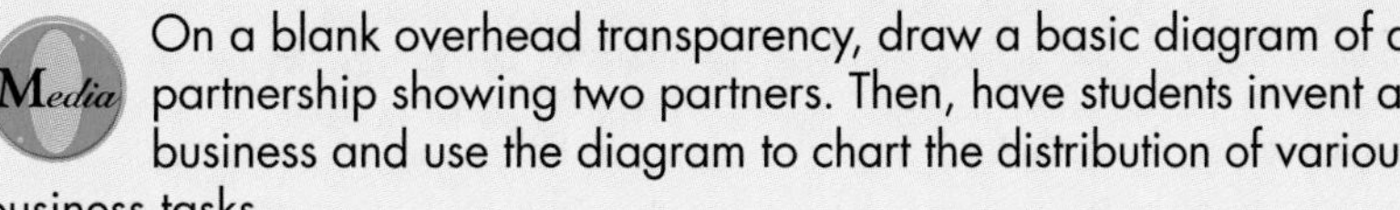

On a blank overhead transparency, draw a basic diagram of a partnership showing two partners. Then, have students invent a business and use the diagram to chart the distribution of various business tasks.

In small groups, have students brainstorm ways that a family is treated as an *entity* (merchant's offers—one per family) and as an *aggregation* in business and law. (If one member breaks the law, the other members are not guilty by association.)

the Internal Revenue Service (IRS) to cross-check the accuracy of the partners' individual tax returns.

2. The firm, in the absence of a permissive statute, must sue and be sued in the name of all the partners.
3. All debts of the firm not paid out of firm assets are chargeable to every partner. (This reflects the unlimited liability of general partners, which many persons understandably fear.)
4. When any partner drops out of the firm for any reason, the partnership is dissolved. (However, prior arrangements can be made to continue operations without interruption.)

Persons often join together for social, political, charitable, educational, or general welfare purposes. They do not conduct business for profit, although they may raise money for their activities. Examples are churches, private schools, civic clubs, fraternities and sororities, labor unions, and volunteer fire departments. Such groups may be unincorporated, nonprofit associations. Participating members generally are not liable for debts of the organization. Officers and individual members may voluntarily guarantee its debts. Sometimes such groups organize as nonprofit corporations.

WHAT ARE THE KINDS OF PARTNERSHIPS AND PARTNERS?

PROBLEM

Avery invested $100,000 as a limited partner in a partnership organized to operate an amusement park. On opening day, an accident on a roller coaster severely injured seventeen people. The damages awarded to the accident victims totaled nearly $7 million. That amount far exceeded the value of the partnership's assets and insurance coverage. Will Avery be held liable for unpaid liability claims against the partnership?

Partnerships may be classified according to their purpose and according to the extent of the liability of the partners. Classified by purpose, partnerships are either trading or nontrading and are either general or special. A **trading partnership** buys and sells goods and services commercially. A **nontrading partnership** provides professional and noncommercial assistance, such as legal, medical, or accounting advice. A general partnership conducts a general business, such as a retail store; a **special partnership** may be formed for a single transaction, such as the purchase and resale of a farm.

TEACH

On the chalkboard, draw a large graphic organizer to illustrate the different kinds of partnerships and partners that exist in business. Title it *Kinds of Partnerships and Partners.* Include the following types of partnerships: **trading, nontrading, special, general,** and **limited;** and the following types of partners: **limited, silent, secret, dormant,** and **nominal.** Explain the difference between a **joint venture** that normally ends when the project is completed and a **partnership** that continues from project-to-project.

Multicultural Highlights

Minority-owned businesses have become an important part of the U.S. business scene. According to the 1987 Survey of Minority-Owned Businesses, Hispanic firms grew in number from 233,975 firms in 1982 to 422,373 in 1987—an increase of 81 percent. Sole proprietorships accounted for 94 percent of Hispanic-owned business in 1987. Partnerships and small corporations each made up three percent of the remaining firms.

ASSESS

Learning Objectives 2, 4, & 6 On the chalkboard, list the following terms, one at a time: **Nontrading partnership, trading partnership, special partnership, joint venture, general partnership,** and **limited partnership.** As each is written, have students orally provide a definition and an example of that term. Have students copy key information in their notebooks.

Sometimes a proposed project (e.g., construction of the Hoover Dam at the Arizona-Nevada border) is too big for a single person or business firm to handle alone. Two or more persons or firms then associate together, combining their resources and skills in a **joint venture** to do the one complex project. Because the joint venture is so similar to a general partnership (which may also be formed to do a single project), many courts as well as the IRS treat it as such. However, unlike the rule for general partnerships, death of a participant does not cause dissolution of the joint venture. The joint venture normally continues until the project is completed.

Classified by extent of liability of partners, partnerships are either general or limited. In a **general partnership,** all the partners assume full personal liability for debts of the firm, as does a sole proprietor. In a **limited partnership,** at least one partner must be a general partner, with unlimited liability. However, one or more partners may be **limited partners,** who are liable only to the extent of their investment in the business.

The Uniform Limited Partnership Act (ULPA) has been adopted (as written, or substantially as written) in all states except Georgia and Louisiana. Unlike a general partnership, a limited partnership can be created only by proper execution, recording, and publication of a certificate that identifies the partners and states basic facts about their agreement. Limited partners contribute capital and share profits and losses with general partners. Because limited partners do not share in the managerial control of the business, their liability for firm debts and losses is limited to the amount of capital they invest. Limited partners who participate in management lose their status and become liable without limit as general partners.

This rule has been relaxed and defined by the Revised Uniform Limited Partnership Act (RULPA), which has been adopted by thirty-six states as of the writing of this edition. Under the resulting act, a limited partner does *not* participate in the managerial control of the business, solely by doing such things as:

1. being an independent contractor for, or an agent or employee of the limited partnership;
2. consulting with or advising a general partner;
3. attending a meeting of the general partners;
4. proposing, approving, or disapproving (by vote or otherwise) the dissolution, change in the nature of the business, admission or removal of a general or limited partner, or amendment to the partnership agreement.

In the problem, then, presuming that the limited partnership had been properly formed and that Avery had not participated in the management of the business, she would be liable only to the extent of her $100,000 investment.

▼ APPLY

Before displaying the overhead transparency, *Kinds of Partnerships,* mask out the text under the three headings: *Classified by Extent of Liability, Classified by Scope of Operations,* and *Classified by Purpose.* Ask students to provide you with the information. Reveal the answers as they are given.

Guided Practice

ETHICS ISSUE

Ethics Issue

Read aloud the following scenario: **Although still under legal age, you talk a friend who is a legal adult into accepting you as a general partner in her booming pet-and house-sitting business. Everything goes well until your partner inadvertently forgets to activate a home alarm system after a visit and a client's home is burglarized. The client decides to sue you. You have the option of pleading age of minority as a defense. Is this an ethical solution?** (No; Although it is legal, it is unethical to leave your friend "holding the bag" since you shared equally in profits.)

▼RETEACH Hand out index cards to students. Have students write a *Jeopardy*-style question on one side of the card and the answer on the other side that covers the information found in this section of the text. In small groups, have one student role play the master of ceremonies and ask the other students the questions.

▼ENRICH

In writing, using a computer, if possible, have students create a partnership and decide which type of partner they would want to be—general, silent, secret, dormant, nominal, or limited.

To assist specific learning disabled students who are having difficulties understanding the different types of partners, help them devise symbols for each type. For example, a circle around a pair of lips with a diagonal line through it could symbolize a silent partner. Have students share their symbols with the class and correct any misconceptions. Then have students use their symbols to write a summary paragraph or a scenario.

Before photocopying the overhead transparency master, *Kinds of Partners*, cover the text under the second, third, and fourth columns. Distribute the chart to students to complete. Then, display the overhead transparency for students so they can compare their answers to those on the chart.

Independent Practice

General partners may be further classified as silent, secret, or dormant. A **silent partner** may be known to the public as a partner but takes no active part in management. A **secret partner** is not known to the public as a partner yet participates in management. A **dormant partner** is neither known to the public as a partner nor active in management. All such partners, when identified, can be held liable without limit for partnership debts. A **nominal partner** is not a partner. However, such persons hold themselves out as partners, or let others do so. Parents sometimes become nominal partners to assist children who have taken over the family business. Consequently, if a partnership liability arises, they are liable as partners. A third party, acting in good faith, may rely on the reputation of the nominal partner and therefore extend credit to the firm. If so, all partners who consented to the misrepresentation are fully liable. If all members consent, the firm is liable.

A minor who enters into a partnership agreement generally has special status. In most states, such a partner retains all of the rights and privileges of a minor. Thus, the minor normally can plead minority as a defense and not pay if sued by a creditor of the partnership. The minor may also withdraw and thus dissolve the partnership without being liable for breach of contract. Some states, however, do hold a minor liable on contracts made in connection with business as an individual proprietor or as a partner.

WHAT ARE THE DUTIES OF A PARTNER?

PROBLEM

Fineman was one of five partners in a firm of certified public accountants. Her duties included management of the office. As such, she bought all office equipment. Recently, she purchased an advanced word processing system for $25,000, a competitive price. Several days later, she met the seller, Fisher, at a dinner party. Fineman convinced Fisher to give her a 5-percent discount on the price because clients of her accounting firm might be inclined to buy similar equipment when they learned of its use from her. Fineman now claims the $1,250 discount belongs to her alone because she obtained it on her own time after the original contract was signed. Is she right?

By law or by agreement each partner has a duty to do the following.

1. Adhere to the Partnership Agreement and Decisions

Each partner must comply with the partnership agreement, including later provisions properly added and related decisions properly made.

TEACH

On the chalkboard, list the following five duties of a business partner: adhere to the partnership agreement and decisions, use reasonable care, act with integrity and good faith, refrain from participating in a competing business, and keep accurate records. Discuss each duty.

ASSESS

Learning Objective 5 Have students respond orally to the following *True* or *False* statements: **(1) A partner may keep important information that concerns the firm's business from other partners if he or she thinks that information may be of personal benefit in the future.** (False); **(2) A partner is free to perform partnership duties as casually as he or she sees fit.** (False); and **(3) No partner may personally keep any profit or benefit unless the other partners consent and are informed.** (True)

2. Use Reasonable Care

In performing partnership duties, each partner must use reasonable care. However, he or she is not personally liable for the full loss caused by errors in judgment, mistakes, and incompetence. Any resulting financial burden rests on the firm and is shared by all of its members. This harsh reality affirms the importance of selecting competent persons as partners.

3. Act With Integrity and Good Faith

A partnership is a fiduciary relationship of utmost trust and confidence. Each partner is legally bound to act with the highest integrity and good faith in dealing with the other partner(s). No partner may personally retain any profit or benefit unless the other partners are informed and consent. In the problem, Fineman was wrong in claiming the discount. All profits or benefits flowing from business of the firm belong to the firm, to be shared by all partners equally or as otherwise agreed.

4. Refrain From Participating in a Competing Business

Unless there is a contrary agreement, a partner may not do any business that competes with the partnership or prevents performance of duties to the firm. A partner may, however, attend to personal affairs for profit, as long as the firm's business is not sacrificed. A partner who withdraws from the firm may compete with it unless validly prohibited by the partnership agreement.

5. Keep Accurate Records

A partner should keep accurate records of all business done for the firm and give the firm all money belonging to it. Moreover, every partner should disclose to the other partner(s) all important information that concerns the firm's business.

▼ WHAT RIGHTS DO THE PARTNERS HAVE AS OWNERS?

PROBLEM

Palm, a partner in the Bobbin' Cork Bait Shops, normally purchased the inventory for the business. Unknown to her, the other three partners voted to no longer deal with Trout Attractions, Inc., one of their main suppliers. Before finding out about their decision, Palm contracted for $1,000 worth of lures from Trout. Is the partnership bound by the contract?

▼ APPLY

Create, or have students create, scenarios and questions concerning the duties of a partner. For example, **Osborn came up with most of the ideas for a partnership agreement between him and his partner Yu. Are both equally bound by the agreement?** (Yes) Read aloud the scenarios and questions to the class and have students provide you with the correct answers. Correct any misconceptions. **Guided Practice**

Divide the class into groups of two or three students. Using a computer, if possible, have groups write a rap, poem, or narrative summarizing the duties of a partner.

Independent Practice

▼ TEACH

On the chalkboard, draw a large, four-column chart called **Rights of Partners** and add the following headings: **Participate in Management**; **Profits**; **Property**; and **Extra Compensation**. Discuss with students the important points for each of the rights and list them in the appropriate column.

▼RETEACH On butcher paper, draw the base of a graphic organizer to illustrate the five duties of a partner. Then divide the class into five groups. Assign each group one of the five duties of a partner. Have each group add information.

▼ENRICH Pair students. Assign each pair one of the five duties of a partner. Have one student role-play a partner who has violated that duty and the other student role-play the partner who has been violated. As a group, discuss the possible ramifications of *not* carrying out the duties of a partner.

▼ APPLY

Discuss with students the important points of this section. On the chalkboard, work with students to outline the rights of partners. Have students take turns coming up to the chalkboard and filling in the outline. **Guided Practice**

In the absence of contrary agreement, legal rights of partners are shared equally. Partners may, however, agree as to who shall have particular rights and duties. The principal rights are the following.

1. Right to Participate in Management

Every partner, as a co-owner of the business, has an equal right to participate in its management. Acting alone, a partner may buy, sell, hire, fire, and make other routine decisions in carrying on the ordinary day-to-day activities of the firm. In effect, each partner acts as an agent for the firm and for the other partners (see Chapter 25). All are bound, unless the partner lacked the necessary authority, and the person with whom the contract was made knew this. In the problem, the $1,000 contract resulted from a routine decision by Palm, a partner with apparent authority. Consequently, the partnership is bound.

In addition to routine decisions, each partner may do the things normally done by managers in similar firms. This includes the right to inspect the partnership books at all times, unless otherwise agreed.

When a difference of opinion arises as to ordinary matters connected with the business, a majority vote of the partners decides the issue. Unless otherwise agreed, each partner has one vote regardless of the amount of capital contributed. If there is an even number of partners and they split equally on a question, no action can be taken. A pattern of such deadlocks can eventually lead to dissolution. To forestall such an outcome, it is often helpful to provide in the partnership agreement that deadlocks over specified matters shall be settled by arbitration.

For several years, Gohegan and Briddle had been partners in Dealing In Wheeling, a bicycle retail and repair business. Gohegan wanted to hire two well-qualified mechanics in order to divide the shop work and to give the partners more time for sales promotion. Briddle objected, saying "If you hire, I'll fire.... We can't afford it now." With the partners deadlocked, no one was hired.

Unanimous agreement of all the partners is required to make any change in the written partnership agreement, however minor it may be. All partners must also agree to any fundamental change that affects the very nature of the business (e.g., changing its principal activity or location). In addition, under the UPA, unanimous agreement is required for decisions to:

a. assign partnership property to creditors,
b. **confess judgment** (i.e., allow a plaintiff to obtain a judgment against the firm without a trial),

▼ ASSESS

Have students respond orally to the following questions: **(1) Can one partner make minor changes in the written partnership agreement without checking with other partners?** (No); and **(2) If there is no other agreement, do partners share equally in losses, no matter which partner may be primarily at fault in causing the losses?** (Yes)

c. submit a partnership claim or liability to arbitration, and
d. do any act that would make it impossible to carry on the business.

The preceding rules governing the use of managerial authority may be changed by agreement. Often, by agreement, certain partners have exclusive control over specific activities, such as selling, purchasing, or accounting and finance. By specializing according to talents and interests, work is divided and efficiency and productivity are increased.

2. Right to Profits

PROBLEM

Laird and Ball were partners in an indoor tennis center. Laird, a wealthy surgeon, contributed all the capital. Ball, a former tennis champion with an international reputation, contributed her name and agreed to work full time at the center. They agreed to split the profits equally. The losses, however, were all to be charged to Laird. Can the partners legally receive different proportions of the losses than the profits?

Partners are entitled to all profits earned. In the absence of contrary agreement, both profits and losses are shared equally regardless of different amounts of capital contributed or time spent. However, the partners may agree to divide the profits and/or the losses in any percentages desired. Often, as in the problem, profits will be shared equally, but a partner with a large amount of outside income may agree, for tax purposes, to take all the losses. Outsiders, however, are not bound by such internal agreements and may hold any or all general partners liable without limit for all partnership debts.

3. Right in Partnership Property

PROBLEM

Adams, Starnes, and Williams were partners in a burglar and fire alarm service. Adams would mount his own camper cabin on the back of one of the company's pickup trucks every weekend and drive it into the country on overnight fishing trips. Starnes would take the company's word processing machine home every weekend to work on her version of the "great American novel." On weekends, Williams used the company's duplicating machine to run off copies of the weekly bulletins for his church. No partner was aware of any other partner's action. Did each have a legal right to borrow the firm's equipment?

Have students imagine that they are starting a partnership. Have them jot down individual preferences for each of the four rights that partners have as owners. For example, a student may prefer an agreement that allows him or her a larger share of the profit because of an exceptional talent. Then, have student volunteers conduct mock partnership interviews. Have the partner interview at least two potential partners. Have the class listen carefully to each interview and discuss the logic of the preferences and questions. Then have students vote on which potential partner would be the best match.

Independent Practice

Have students individually create a graphic organizer to illustrate the rights of partners. Have students display and explain their work. Correct misconceptions, as necessary.

ENRICH

Have students rank the four rights of partners, from most important to the least important. Then, using a computer, if possible, explain why they ranked these rights in that order.

Writing Connections

Language Arts
Divide the class into pairs of students. Have each pair assume the role of a potential business partner. Using a computer, if possible, have the pair draft a partnership agreement, paying particular attention to wording and details. Direct students to address the following points: type of business, type of partnership, duties of each partner, and rights of each partner.

Partnership property consists of all cash and other property originally contributed by the partners as well as all property later acquired by the firm. The property is held in a special form of co-ownership called tenancy in partnership. In **tenancy in partnership,** each partner is a co-owner of the entire partnership property and is not the sole owner of any part of it. For example, if a firm of two partners owns two identical trucks, neither partner may claim exclusive ownership of either vehicle. Therefore, a partner has no salable or assignable interest in any particular item of property belonging to the partnership. However, the interest of a partner *in the firm* may be sold or assigned to another party. The buyer or assignee is not a partner but is entitled to that partner's share of the profits, and of the assets upon dissolution.

Each partner has an equal right to use firm property for partnership purposes, but no partner may use firm property for personal purposes unless all other partners consent. Accordingly, in the problem, all three partners were violating their duties to the firm. The breach of one did not excuse the breach of any other.

4. Right to Extra Compensation

PROBLEM

Hudson, De Soto, and Auburn were partners in an advertising agency. Hudson, who spent days playing golf, tennis, or raquetball with prospective clients and friends, brought in most of the firm's accounts. De Soto, a brilliant artist and copywriter, did most of the production and often worked ten-hour days as well as weekends. Auburn, who had no creative talent and little energy, spent no more than four hours a day delivering and picking up copy and layouts. Are Hudson and De Soto entitled to a larger share of the profits than Auburn?

A partner who invests more capital, brings in more business, or works longer and harder than his or her associates is not entitled to extra pay or a larger share of the profits—unless all the partners so agree. Thus, in the problem, Hudson and De Soto get no more than Auburn, unless all so agree. Common sense and fairness often dictate that a partner who gives more should receive more, but this must be agreed to by all.

WHAT AUTHORITY DOES A PARTNER HAVE?

PROBLEM

Aki, Degas, and Kline were partners in an air-conditioning business. They obtained a $275,000 contract to install units in a candy factory.

TEACH

Explain to students that, unless otherwise agreed, each partner has an equal right to participate in management and to act as an agent for the firm. Each partner has the necessary authority to conduct business. Draw three columns on the chalkboard with the following headings: **Partner, Authority,** and **Example**. Discuss the authority that each partner has by reviewing, one at a time, the ones listed on pp. 743–744. List each authority in column one. Save this chart to complete in the following APPLY activity.

ASSESS

Learning Objectives 2 & 5 Have students respond to the following statements concerning one partner acting alone by indicating thumbs up for acting within authority and thumbs down for exceeding authority: **(1) Borrows money for partnership purposes** (Up); **(2) Makes binding contracts for the firm** (Up); and **(3) Cancels a client's debt to the firm in exchange for the client cancelling a personal debt owed by the partner** (Down).

Long before the job was finished, Kline accepted the final payment of $100,000 and absconded with the money. Must Aki and Degas absorb the loss and complete the job for the $175,000 already paid to them, without being paid an additional $100,000 by the candy factory?

Unless otherwise agreed, each partner has an equal right to participate in management and to act as an agent for the firm. Generally, the law implies to each member the authority necessary to carry on the business. This includes the right to do the following.

1. Make Binding Contracts for the Firm

Acting within the scope of the particular business, each partner can make binding contracts deemed necessary or desirable, regardless of the possible folly of the deals. Any internal agreement limiting powers of a partner is binding on the partners, but not on third parties who do not know about the limitation. However, a partner who violates such internal agreement is liable to the other partners for any resulting loss. No partner can bind the firm in contracts that are beyond the scope of the firm's business as publicly disclosed. Partners engaged in an aerial photography business, for example, would not be bound by a contract by one of the partners to use the plane for air ambulance service. Even if a partner has acted beyond authority in making a contract, the other partners may choose to ratify the act. If they do, the partnership is bound as a principal would be in an ordinary agency.

2. Receive Money Owed to the Firm and Settle Claims Against the Firm

In the eyes of the law, all partners are assumed to have received any payments to the firm even if the partner who actually received the money absconds. Thus, in the problem, the partnership claim against the factory owners ended when Kline accepted the final payment. Aki and Degas must complete the job. Their claim is against Kline if he can be found.

Also, each partner may adjust debts of the firm by agreement with creditors. Each may compromise firm claims against debtors, settling for less than is due. Understandably, however, a partner may not discharge a personal debt by agreeing to offset it against a debt owed to the partnership.

3. Borrow Money in the Firm's Name

In a trading partnership, any partner can borrow for partnership purposes. In such borrowing, the partner can execute promissory notes binding the firm and can pledge or mortgage partnership property as security. Partners in a nontrading partnership generally do not have such power.

▼ APPLY

Using the chart created in the preceding TEACH activity, have students, working as a whole class, brainstorm an example of each of the eight authorities (pp. 743–744). Write the examples in the second column on the chart on the chalkboard. Have students copy the completed chart in their notebook. **Guided Practice**

Have students list the eight types of authority partners possess and, beside each one, have them indicate what special agreements, if any, they would require of a partner regarding that authority. Have them explain their answers. For example, concerning the authority to hire and fire, a student might want his or her partner to agree that both partners must consent in writing on new hires, but either could fire without prior discussion. **Independent Practice**

Have students work in pairs to outline the eight types of partner authority (pp. 743–744). Have students use a computer, if possible, to make their outlines.

In small groups, have students create a chart to compare partner rights with partner duties. Have each group present its findings to the class as a whole.

4. Sell

A partner can sell in the regular course of business any of the firm's goods and give customary warranties. Acting alone, however, a partner may not sell the entire inventory in a bulk transfer because this could end the business.

5. Buy

Any partner can buy for cash or credit any property within the scope of the business.

6. Draw and Cash Checks and Drafts

A partner can draw checks and drafts for partnership purposes and indorse and cash checks payable to the firm.

7. Hire and Fire Employees and Agents

Each partner has the authority to hire and fire employees, agents, and independent contractors to help carry on the business.

8. Receive Notice of Matters Affecting the Partnership

When one partner is served with a summons and complaint against the firm, all are deemed to have received the notice, even if they are not informed. Likewise, one partner's declarations and admissions in carrying on the business bind all partners even when contrary to the best interests of the firm.

WHAT ARE A PARTNER'S LIABILITIES?

PROBLEM

Pinell and Cotter were in the business of buying and selling used farm equipment. They had privately agreed that Cotter would do all the buying because he was a better judge of value. Nevertheless, one day Pinell had a golden opportunity to buy all the equipment of an elderly farmer who was retiring. Pinell and the farmer agreed on a price and completed the sale. Is the firm bound?

Between or among themselves, partners may make any agreements they choose regarding authority to run the business. Outsiders, however, may not be aware of such secret internal agreements. When this is the case, the partnership firm and all of its members are liable without limit for all obligations of the firm that arise out of contracts made by any partner within the scope of the firm's business. Thus, in the problem, the firm and both part-

TEACH

Discuss with students the following points regarding a partner's liabilities: all members are liable for obligations that arise out of contracts made by any partner; laws governing civil and criminal liability are applied to the partnership and all partners if the tort or crime was committed during the course of ordinary business; a partner cannot escape liability by withdrawing from the partnership; and a new partner who joins the firm is liable for both pre-existing and new debts, but liability for old debts is limited to action against only the new partner's share of the partnership property.

APPLY

On the chalkboard, work with students to make a flowchart showing a sequence of events and associated liability. For example, action is brought against a firm in May, a new partner joins the firm in June; outcome: new partner's liability is limited to his or her share of partnership property. **Guided Practice**

Have students role-play various partnership liability situations based on the points listed in the preceding TEACH activity. At the close of each presentation, have the class explain who is liable. **Independent Practice**

ASSESS

Learning Objective 3 Have students respond orally to the following question: **(1) When Bill's firm started to fail, he withdrew from the partnership. Is he free from responsibility for firm debts to that point?** (No); **(2) Hanna, unbeknownst to her partner, broke a criminal law while carrying out firm business. Is her partner criminally liable?** (No); and **(3) Is Hanna's partner civilly liable for damages?** (Yes) ners are bound. If a loss results, Cotter could seek full recovery from Pinell because Pinell had violated their agreement in buying the equipment.

The partnership and all partners are liable when any partner commits a tort (e.g., negligence or fraud) while acting within the ordinary course of the business. The wrongdoer would be obligated to indemnify the partnership for any damages it had to pay to the injured party. If the other partners had authorized or participated in the tort, all would share the blame and no indemnity would be payable.

Liability for certain crimes committed in the course of business, such as selling alcoholic beverages to minors, is also imposed on the partnership and all the partners. Generally, however, if the business of the firm does not require the criminal activity, neither the partnership nor the partners who do not authorize or take part in the crime are held criminally liable. Thus, a partner who kills a pedestrian while negligently driving a company car on firm business will alone be *criminally* liable. However, the wrongdoer as well as the firm and the other partners are *civilly* liable for damages.

When a judgment is obtained against a partnership, and the partnership assets are exhausted, the individually owned property of the general partners may be legally seized and sold to pay the debt. Creditors of the respective individual partners, however, have first claim to such property. Any partner who pays an obligation of the firm with personal assets is legally entitled to recover a proportionate share from each of the other partners.

A partner cannot escape responsibility for firm debts by withdrawing from the partnership. One who withdraws remains liable for all debts incurred while a member. A new partner who joins the firm is liable for both existing and new debts of the business. However, creditors with claims that arose before the new partner joined the firm are limited, with respect to the new partner, to action against only the new partner's share of partnership property.

Divide the class into groups of four or five students and assign these roles in each group: facilitator (optional) to keep everyone on task; writer to write an advice column using the computer, if possible; editor to check for form and clarity of writing; fact checker to check for accuracy of advice; and presenter to present article to class. Have groups assume the task of composing an advice column for the business section of a newspaper. Direct them to compose a column that addresses at least one question involving partner's liabilities and at least one additional question that involves duties, rights, or authority of partners. Have groups present their work. Ask the class to comment on the quality of advice offered.

Cooperative Learning

HOW IS A PARTNERSHIP ENDED?

PROBLEM

Paradiso is a partner in a highly successful firm of certified public accountants. She becomes personally liable for very heavy damages as the result of her negligence in an automobile accident while vacationing. She therefore files for bankruptcy and has these and other debts discharged. What effect will this have on the partnership?

When any partner ceases to be associated in the ordinary carrying on of the business, **dissolution** of the partnership occurs. Dissolution is normally

TEACH

On the chalkboard, write the following in a horizontal line: **dissolution → winding-up period → termination.** Explain the terminology and tell that this is the usual sequence of events in the ending of a partnership. Then, discuss dissolution of a partnership, which can be caused by any of the following: action of one or more of the partners, operation of law, and court decree.

RETEACH Have students create a graphic organizer, illustration, or cartoon to illustrate a partner's liabilities.

ENRICH In small groups, have students create a four-panel cartoon illustrating partner's liabilities. Post cartoons on a bulletin board called *To Be or Not to Be (Liable)*.

▼ APPLY

On a blank overhead transparency or a flip chart, create a cause-and-effect chart. Divide the class into two groups. Have one group brainstorm a cause for a partnership ending. Write it on the chart while the other group decides on the effect. Have the groups switch roles back and forth to list on the chart as many examples as possible. Media **Guided Practice**

Divide the class into groups of three or four students. Have each group create an example for one of the three causes of dissolution of a partnership. Have groups present their scenarios to the class and have students identify the dissolution, winding-up period, and termination stages. **Independent Practice**

followed by a **winding-up period,** which concludes with the actual **termination** or ending of the partnership. During the winding-up period, all partnership business in process at the time of dissolution is concluded, creditors of the business are satisfied if possible, and each partner's share is accounted for and distributed. When the winding-up process is completed, termination of the legal existence of the partnership actually occurs.

Zeno, Smith, and Cospit were partners in Fly by Night, an overnight, small-parcel delivery service. When they formed their partnership, they provided for continuation of the business if any partner should die. (This is permitted by statute in a number of states.) Their written agreement specified that the business would continue uninterrupted, under the same name, with management and control by a new partnership composed of the surviving partners. They also provided that the value of each partner's share in the firm would be updated annually. This figure would be used for payments over a five-year period to the decedent's estate or beneficiaries designated in his or her final will.

Dissolution of a partnership may be caused by any of the following.

1. Action of One or More of the Partners

A partnership may be dissolved by agreement of the parties. For example, if the original agreement is for one year, the partnership concludes at the end of that year. Sometimes a firm is organized for a specific purpose, such as the development of a large tract of farm land into a subdivision for houses. Sale of the last lot and house would end the partnership. Also, as in any contract, the parties may unanimously agree at any time to terminate their relationship.

Withdrawal of a partner for any reason dissolves the partnership. The partnership agreement may permit such withdrawal without penalty, preferably after a reasonable advance notice. In such case, the withdrawing partner would not be liable to the remaining partner(s) for any drop in profits that might result. However, if the withdrawal violates their agreement, the withdrawing partner would be liable in damages for any injury resulting from the breach of contract. If the organization is a **partnership at will,** a partner normally may withdraw at any time without liability to associates. Under unusual circumstances, the withdrawing partner could be liable for resulting losses if the sudden withdrawal was unreasonable.

2. Operation of Law

Death of any partner dissolves the partnership. This is a serious disadvantage of the partnership form of organization. Prudent partners simply

▼ ASSESS

Have students respond orally to the following *True* or *False* statements: **(1) Withdrawal of a partner from a partnership for any reason dissolves the partnership.** (True); **(2) One partner may petition a court to order dissolution under certain circumstances.** (True); and **(3) If one partner dies, the partnership continues through the surviving partners.** (False) anticipate this inevitable event and specify what action shall be taken when it happens. For example, they may agree that the surviving partner(s) will continue with a new firm and pay for the decedent's share over a period of years. Bankruptcy, a kind of financial death, also automatically dissolves the partnership. This is true whether the bankruptcy is suffered by any of the partners (such as Paradiso in the problem) or by the firm itself. Although uncommon, subsequent illegality also dissolves the partnership. For example, a professional partnership of doctors would be dissolved if any member lost the license to practice.

3. Court Decree

Partners, if living, usually arrange for dissolution privately. If necessary, however, one partner may petition a court to order dissolution if another partner has become insane, is otherwise incapacitated, or is guilty of serious misconduct affecting the business. Also a court may act if continuation is impracticable, or if the firm is continuously losing money and there is little or no prospect of success. This could happen, for example, when there are irreconcilable differences between the partners. For example, irreconcilable differences could be the result of decisions to add or drop a major line of merchandise or to move a factory to another location to reduce labor costs.

Preventing Legal Difficulties

Before going into business as a sole proprietor or partner...

1. Be reasonably sure that your formal education and experience (preferably in a similar established business) have prepared you to do a competent job.
2. Be sure to comply with applicable licensing, registration, and other legal requirements.
3. If a partner, put the partnership agreement in writing, with the aid of a qualified lawyer. Include appropriate language covering each partner's:
   a. duties and authority,
   b. share of profits and losses, if not intended to be equal,
   c. salary or right to withdraw earnings (drawing account),
   d. vacation and sick-leave rights, and
   e. rights to withdraw from the partnership.
4. In the partnership agreement, include provisions covering:
   a. periodic valuation of each partner's interest,
   b. methods for raising additional capital if needed,
   c. possible addition or withdrawal of a partner,

Preventing Legal Difficulties

Discuss each of the four suggestions for preventing legal difficulties when involved as a sole proprietor or partnership in a business. Have students suggest the possible consequences of not following each point on pp. 747–748.

CLOSE

Review the list made in the FOCUS activity at the beginning of this chapter. Poll students to determine if their choice remains the same. Analyze the results.

Have students conduct a panel discussion to answer the following question: **What are the most important points to consider when starting a business and, if necessary, when choosing a business partner?** List these points on the chalkboard. Then, have students create a poster to illustrate them.

Assign the following end-of-chapter materials:
Student text review activities, pp. 748–753
Workbook, pp. 125–128
Chapter Test

Chapter *MicroExam*

Have students create a graphic organizer to illustrate how a **partnership** ends or is dissolved.

Have students describe, using a computer, if possible, the advantages and disadvantages of a **partnership at will.**

d. amicable resolution of disputes, as by arbitration, and
e. possible continuation of the business after dissolution.

▼ REVIEWING IMPORTANT POINTS

❶ Sole proprietorships are the most simple and most numerous form of business organization. The owner makes all decisions, keeps all the profits, and is liable without limit for all losses.

❷ A partnership is an association of two or more persons to carry on, as co-owners, a business for profit. Profits and losses are shared equally unless otherwise agreed. Every general partner is liable without limit to creditors for debts of the business.

❸ Unless otherwise agreed, all partners have a right to participate in management with equal authority.

❹ Any partner, acting alone, may normally make routine business decisions for the firm. A majority must resolve disputes about ordinary matters. All must unanimously agree on:
a. changes in the partnership agreement,
b. fundamental changes in the business of the firm, and
c. certain matters prescribed by the UPA.

❺ In dealings with one another, partners are bound to act with the highest integrity and good faith. They must keep one another informed about the business, maintain accurate records, and take no secret profits.

❻ Partners own firm property as tenants in partnership. Each may use the property for company business but not for personal purposes without consent of the other partners.

❼ Limited partnership is a special form in which one or more limited partners contribute capital but not managerial services. The financial liability of a limited partner for debts of the firm cannot exceed the amount of capital such a partner has invested.

❽ There must be at least one general partner (with unlimited liability) in a limited partnership.

❾ Partnerships may be terminated by:
a. action of the partners,
b. operation of law, or
c. decree of court.

❿ In sole proprietorships and in partnerships, appropriate public liability insurance significantly reduces the risk of unlimited liability.

Strengthening Your Legal Vocabulary

❶ winding-up period
❷ general partners
❸ limited partner
❹ silent partner
❺ tenancy in partnership
❻ termination
❼ dissolution
❽ sole proprietorship
❾ partnership at will
❿ partnership

Applying Law to Everyday Life

❶ Each partner gets one-third of the profits, or $40,000. In the absence of a contrary agreement, profits and losses are shared equally regardless of time devoted or capital contributed to the business. (p. 741)

The loss is divided equally, since there was no agreement to the contrary, and neither Brinkley nor Chapman had promised to pay Dodge's share of any loss. (p. 741) Thus, each partner must take a loss of $30,000 ($90,000/3 = $30,000). Since Dodge made no initial investment, he must pay $30,000 to the partnership. Brinkley receives only $70,000 of his original investment of $100,000. Chapman receives only $170,000 of his original investment of $200,000.

▼ STRENGTHENING YOUR LEGAL VOCABULARY

Match each term with the statement that best defines that term. Some terms may not be used.

confess judgment
dissolution
dormant partner
general partners
general partnership
joint venture
limited partner
limited partnership
nominal partner
nontrading partnership
partnership
partnership agreement
partnership at will
secret partner
silent partner
sole proprietorship
special partnership
tenancy in partnership
termination
trading partnership
winding-up period

1. Time during which all business affairs of a partnership are concluded.
2. Persons who associate as co-owners to carry on a business for profit, and who are liable for all firm debts.
3. Partner who is not active in the management and whose liability is limited to the amount of capital invested.
4. Partner who takes no active part in the management of the business but is known to the public as a partner.
5. Legal form of co-ownership of firm property by partners.
6. Actual legal ending of a partnership.
7. When any partner ceases association in carrying on the business.
8. Business that is owned and controlled by one person.
9. Type of partnership in which a partner may withdraw at any time.
10. Association of two or more persons to carry on, as co-owners, a business for profit.

▼ APPLYING LAW TO EVERYDAY LIFE

1. Brinkley, Chapman, and Dodge orally agreed to become partners in a road-paving company. Nothing was said about profits or losses. Brinkley contributed $100,000 in working capital. Chapman contributed used construction equipment with a resale value of $200,000. Dodge, a brilliant civil engineer, contributed no capital. By agreement, Brinkley did

2 ETHICS ISSUE Each of the limited partners is liable only to the extent of his or her investment ($10,000) in the business. (p. 737) The general partner, Brick, is liable to the extent of her investment ($5,000) plus all of her personal fortune not exempt from the execution of judgment. (pp. 735, 737)

It is false and misleading advertising, and as such it is illegal. It also goes beyond innocuous puffing and boldly misrepresents results from an exercise program that evidently can cause serious permanent injury.

3 No; Their partnership agreement called for arbitration of disputes between the partners only. This was a dispute between the partnership and a creditor. Every partner is entitled to "a day in court" for the resolution of such disputes by judge and possibly by jury. Therefore, unanimous consent of the partners is needed to submit a firm claim or liability to arbitration. (pp. 740–741) Here, Bingham must get Freeman to agree to arbitration before the process may be used.

4 No; Because Brooke was a minor, he could avoid his contract without liability. (p. 738)

5 Yes; Internal agreements on sharing losses do not bind outside creditors. All the partners are liable, without limit, to the creditors for payment of firm debts. (pp. 733, 737)

6 No, she could not sell out to Topper without consent of her partner, Jonnas. To withdraw without obtaining such permission would be a breach of the partnership agreement, causing dissolution, and Schmidt would be liable in damages to her partner. (p. 746) Yes; After assignment of her interest, Topper would receive her share of the profits. Schmidt would have to continue to perform her duties and would continue to be personally liable for debts of the firm, so an assignment would not accomplish the result Schmidt desires. Perhaps Schmidt could convince Jonnas to agree to a dissolution. Then, Jonnas could form a new partnership with Topper or another person of Jonnas's choice. (pp. 746–747)

no work for the firm, but Chapman and Dodge devoted full time to the business. A profit of $120,000 was earned during the first year. How should the profit be divided? After ten years, business declines and the firm is dissolved. During the winding-up period, all assets are liquidated. Before the return of invested capital ($300,000), there is only $210,000 in cash. How is the $90,000 loss divided?

2 

Gilmore and nine others each invested $10,000 as limited partners in a physical fitness and jazz exercise studio for men and women. Brick, who promoted the business, invested $5,000 as general partner and agreed to manage the studio. An employee explained to a customer how to do bench presses on the exercise machine. As a result, the customer's back was severely injured and he sues for damages. What is the possible liability of each of the partners? In newspaper advertisements, the partners used pictures of muscular, paid models who never actually patronized the studio. The advertisement said, "You too will look like this satisfied client after six short months in our exercise program!" Is such advertising legal? Is such advertising ethical?

3 Freeman and Bingham were partners in a wholesale drug company. Their agreement required arbitration of all disputes between the partners. While Freeman was away on a cruise, Stuart, a creditor of the firm, threatened to sue over a disputed supply contract. To save time and money for all concerned, Stuart proposed to avoid litigation by submitting the claim to arbitration. Can Bingham agree to arbitrate without Freeman's approval?

4 Brooke was seventeen years old when he entered into a partnership with Beale, age twenty-two. Their agreement to operate a dog training (obedience) school was for three years. After six months, Brooke decided to withdraw. Was he liable for breach of contract?

5 Gary, Mayer, and Solli were general partners in a business that organized fund drives for nonprofit organizations. They received a small percentage of all contributions solicited. When Gary heard of an opportunity to present an outdoor concert by a famous rock group, he proposed that the partners, "Do this on our own—we'll make a mint." This went beyond the purposes of the firm as stated in their written agreement. Mayer agreed, but Solli said he would go along only if the others promised to take total responsibility for any liability in case the project failed. They agreed, and the project did fail. As a result, the partnership went bankrupt. Debts exceeded firm assets as well as personal assets of Gary and Mayer. Can creditors seize Solli's personal assets?

7 No, a majority cannot make such decisions. These terms were included in the partnership agreement, and cannot be changed without unanimous consent. (p. 740) The dissenting partner could seek a court order to enjoin the proposed action. As an alternative, the dissenting partner might elect to claim a material breach if the proposals are implemented, and call for dissolution of the partnership. (p. 746)

6 Jonnas and Schmidt entered into a partnership for five years to conduct a catering business. It proved to be very successful. However, after two years, Schmidt's husband was offered a promotion and transfer by his employer to corporate headquarters in Los Angeles, 2,000 miles away. Schmidt and her husband decided that he should accept the promotion and they would move. Could she sell out to Topper, a trustworthy, well-qualified assistant, transferring all duties and assigning all her rights, title, and interest in the firm? Could she simply assign her interest to Topper?

7 The written agreement of a professional partnership stated that, during the first year of operations, no partner could draw more than $100 earnings per week, and that no partner could take a vacation. All members would have to rely on personal savings and credit if they needed more funds. The business prospered beyond expectations. After six months, four of the five partners agreed to increase the permitted draw to $200 a week, and three of the five voted to permit up to one week of vacation without pay. Are these modifications legal and binding?

8 ETHICS ISSUE Starto and Tokun agree to work together as partners for a year. Both are experienced in treating wooden shingle and shake roofs to make them fire resistant and waterproof, which prevents rotting and extends the life of the roof. Starto puts up the $20,000 capital needed for equipment and supplies. Both agree to work full time, and each draws a salary of $2,500 a month. Starto does all of the difficult sales work, as well as helping on site. Tokun is slow on the job and repeatedly fails to show up, falsely claiming to be sick. In fact, he goes fishing and hunting on long weekends. At the end of the year, the firm shows a net profit of $25,000 after all expenses and the return of Starto's capital contribution. How should the net profit be divided? Has Tokun acted ethically in their business relationship? What can Starto do without becoming liable to Tokun?

9 In the previous question, assume that the same facts exist except that the firm's certified public accountant reports a loss of money for the year's operations. All of Starto's capital contribution had been spent and outside creditors have outstanding claims for $4,000. Thus, the total loss is $24,000. How should it be divided?

10 ETHICS ISSUE A, B, and C majored in computer science when they attended college in a distant city. A was especially talented in programming and trouble-shooting, and worked part-time for several clients in the area while still in school. Immediately after graduation A,

8  The profit of $25,000 must be divided equally, since the parties made no agreement to the contrary. (p. 741) No; Tokun has acted unethically in their business. He could be a slow worker by nature, and so Starto has to tolerate this conduct. However, his repeated "long weekends" with the false excuse of being sick constitute a breach of contract and clearly dishonest, unethical conduct. Starto can dissolve this partnership, wind up the business, and terminate his relationship with Tokun. Since the duration of their partnership was just one year and a year has elapsed, Starto can withdraw without liability to Tokun. If so disposed, he could sue Tokun for breach of contract, but it would be difficult to prove damages, and the cost probably would not justify the effort. (p. 746)

9 In the absence of a contrary agreement, as in this case, losses are divided equally among the partners. Thus the loss of $24,000 requires that each suffer a $12,000 share of the loss. This means that Tokun is legally obligated to pay Starto $10,000, and the outside creditors $2,000, for a total of $12,000. Starto has lost $20,000 minus the $10,000 he receives from Tokun, or $10,000, plus the $2,000 he is legally obligated to pay the outside creditors, for a total of $12,000. (p. 741)

B, and C became associated as general partners in their own computer consulting firm in their home town. Neither B nor C were aware of A's continuing work with her old clients, located near the campus of her alma mater. She serviced these accounts by means of telephone and facsimile transmissions, usually before coming to work and on weekends, but sometimes during regular working hours. Is she obliged to share with B and C the income received from her old clients?

10 ETHICS ISSUE Yes; *A's* work with her former clients is essentially the same as her current partnership work, and therefore competes with the partnership and prevents full performance of duties to the firm. *A* should disclose the facts to her partners, and either get them to agree to permit continuation of the practice, or share with them all fees received. It is unethical to continue the practice which could eventually result in a dispute and a law suit, followed by dissolution of the partnership and payment of damages. (pp. 739, 746–747)

SOLVING CASE PROBLEMS

1. Lewis owned a vacant building. He persuaded Dinkelspeel to open and to conduct a business called The Buffet in the property. Together, they purchased furniture, fixtures, and merchandise. They agreed that Dinkelspeel was to run the business and that profits were to be divided equally. The interest of Lewis was not to be disclosed to the public, although he was to raise necessary funds and provide the building space. When the International Association of Credit Men sued both parties for goods sold to The Buffet, Lewis denied liability as a partner. Is he a partner? If so, what kind? If he is a partner, what is his liability? (*International Association of Credit Men v. Lewis,* 50 Wyo. 380, 62 P.2d 294)

2. On January 1, 1969, Vernon and Engel became partners in a food brokerage business. Later, they disagreed about the way profits were being divided and expenses were being paid. On August 1, 1970, they dissolved the partnership by mutual agreement. Vernon ran the business during the winding-up period. He claimed that Engel had violated their agreement and therefore was not entitled to his share of the profits. Vernon also argued that since he had carried on the business during the winding-up period, Engel was not entitled to any commissions collected during that time. Is Vernon right? (*Engel v. Vernon,* 215 N.W.2d 506)

3. Gast brought suit for back wages against a partnership headed by general partner Petsinger. To improve his chances of recovering a court award, Gast maintained that the limited partners in the business were really general partners and were fully liable along with Petsinger. Gast based his claim on the partnership agreement that gave the limited partners the rights and powers to receive distributions of profits and dissolution funds; prevent the transfer of assets of the firm; examine the books and records; attend meetings; hear reports of the general partner; and transfer, sell, or assign their interests to third parties. Should the limited partners in the agreement be considered general partners? (*Gast v. Petsinger,* 228 Pa. Super. 394, 323 A.2d 371)

Solving Case Problems

1. Yes, Lewis is a dormant partner—neither known to the public as a partner nor active in management. (p. 738) He is fully liable as a general partner to third parties, even though he had concealed his connection with the firm and took no active part in management. This is true even if his existence were not known by creditors when their claims were created, and in spite of any agreement between the partners purporting to limit his liability. (p. 738)

2. No, Vernon is wrong. Breaches of partnership articles, whether or not committed in bad faith, ordinarily do not cause a partner to lose his or her share of the profit. Of course, as in any contract, the victim of the breach is entitled to damages if they can be proved. Moreover, unless otherwise clearly agreed, a partner who withdraws is entitled to his or her share of commissions received during the winding-up period. (p. 745)

4 Cooper and Isaacs were partners in a business that sold and distributed janitorial supplies. Their written agreement provided that the partnership "shall continue until terminated by sale of interests, mutual consent, retirement, death or incompetency of a partner." After eight years, Cooper filed an action seeking dissolution because of irreconcilable differences between the partners regarding matters of policy. He also asked for appointment of a receiver to manage the partnership property until the business was wound up. Isaacs claimed such dissolution was in violation of the partnership agreement. Was Cooper's action a wrongful dissolution? (*Cooper v. Isaacs*, 448 F.2d 1202, D.C.)

3 No; The court held that these rights and powers did not approximate managerial control. (pp. 736–738)

4 No; Irreconcilable differences between partners are proper grounds for dissolution under the Uniform Partnership Act (UPA). (p. 747) Even if the parties had expressly agreed that this would not be valid grounds for dissolution (which they did not), perhaps it would not be binding as a matter of public policy. The dissolution provisions of the UPA "were clearly designed to allow partners to extricate themselves from business relationships which they felt had become intolerable without exposing themselves to liability in the process." Note, moreover, that mere filing of the complaint by Cooper was not a dissolution. The court must order the dissolution. Pending that decision, it was appropriate to appoint a receiver to preserve the firm assets (as was done here). Their agreement "may have been intended only to prevent a partner from dissolving the partnership … without good cause."

CHAPTER 38 ORGANIZER

Chapter Theme

Corporations have certain advantages and disadvantages over other forms of business ownership.

DIRECTED STUDY QUESTIONS	SPECIAL FEATURES	PROGRAM RESOURCES				
		Reteach	Enrich	SN	AM	
What is a corporation?		✔	✔			
What are disadvantages of corporations?		✔	✔			
What are the different types of corporations?	Thinking Critically Through Visuals, pp. 759, 760	✔	✔			
How is a corporation formed?		✔	✔			
What are shares of stock?	Th. Cr. Through Vis., p. 763; Per. Perspectives, p. 764	✔	✔	✔	V K	
Who directs the business of the corporation?	Multicultural Highlights, p. 764 Ethics Issue, p. 765	✔	✔			
What are the powers and duties of the corporate officers?		✔	✔		A	
What are the powers of the corporation?	Writing Connections, p. 767	✔	✔			
What are the rights of the shareholders?	Th. Cr. Through Vis., p. 770 Ethics Issue, p. 771	✔	✔			
How does corporate existence end?		✔	✔			
What is the impact of law on business?	Th. Cr. Through Vis., pp. 775, 776; Preventing Legal Difficulties, p. 777	✔	✔			

Additional Resources

- Nader, Ralph and Taylor, William. *The Big Boys: Power & Position in American Business.* NY: Pantheon Books, 1986.
- *NYSE: A Portrait*, videotape. Syosset, NY: New York Stock Exchange, Educational Products.

One-semester course	✔	✔						
One-year course	✔	✔	✔	✔	✔			

		ASSESSMENT OPPORTUNITIES			
	Cooperative Learning	**Informal Assessment**	**Chapter Review**	**Chapter Test**	**Chapter *MicroExam*** (Media)
		✔	✔	✔	✔
		✔	✔	✔	✔
		✔	✔	✔	✔
	✔	✔	✔	✔	✔
		✔	✔	✔	✔
		✔	✔	✔	✔
		✔	✔	✔	✔
		✔	✔	✔	✔
		✔	✔	✔	✔
		✔	✔	✔	✔
		✔	✔	✔	✔

Videodiscs

Basics and Differences of Sole Proprietorships, Partnerships, and Corporations

Search Chapter 49, Play To 50

Takeovers: AT&T and NCR

Search Chapter 50, Play To 51

State by State

In Delaware, a stockholder could sue the board over a stock purchase plan in which a majority of the directors stood to gain.

Teaching Materials

Student text, pp. 754–784

Overhead transparency masters
- *What Is the Legal Involvement of Government in Business?*
- *Legal Form of Business You Will Work for—or Own—Some Day*

Law for Business Videodisc
Workbook, pp. 129–136

Outside Resources
- Stock certificates, index cards, flip chart, butcher paper, graph paper
- *NYSE: A Portrait*, videotape

Assessment
- Chapter Test
- Chapter *MicroExam*

Vocabulary

corporation, p. 756
S corporations, p. 758
domestic corporation, p. 759
foreign corporation, p. 759
public corporation, p. 760
private corporation, p. 760
close or closely held corporation, p. 760
profit-making corporation, p. 760
nonprofit corporation, p. 760
public service corporation, p. 760
promoters, p. 761
articles of incorporation, p. 761
incorporators, p. 761
shares of stock, p. 762
shareholder, p. 762
stock certificate, p. 762
no-par stock, p. 762
market price, p. 762
par value, p. 762
common stock, p. 763
dividends, p. 763
preferred stock, p. 763
liquidation, p. 763
cumulative stock, p. 763
participating stock, p. 764
directors, p. 764
board of directors, p. 764
inside board, p. 765
outside board, p. 765
mixed board, p. 765
perpetual succession, p. 766
bylaws, p. 767
bonds, p. 767
debentures, p. 767
cumulative voting, p. 769
proxy, p. 769
preemptive right, p. 770
consolidation, p. 772
merger, p. 772

Learning Objectives

When you complete this chapter, you will be able to

1. Describe what a corporation is and why it is the preferred form of organization for big business firms.
2. Explain how the corporation, a legal entity, can be liable without limit for its debts while its stockholders have limited liability.
3. Compare the pros and cons of sole proprietorships, partnerships, and corporations.
4. Explain how and when the S corporation can be used to combine unique advantages of the partnership and the corporation.
5. Define different types of capital stock and distinguish stocks from bonds.
6. Understand the distinct contributions of promoters, shareholders, directors, officers, and other employees of a corporation.

754

Chapter Self-Test

Assess students' understanding of corporations before they begin Chapter 38 by asking them to answer the following *True* or *False* statements: **(1) All corporations are privately-owned businesses.** (False); **(2) Owners of stock in a corporation must be involved in the day-to-day running of the company.** (False); and **(3) In the eyes of the law, a corporation is an artificial person.** (True) Before continuing with the chapter, review and discuss students' responses.

CHAPTER 38

CORPORATIONS

1 Several juniors at Metropolitan High School plan to organize a corporation named Teenage Noteworthy Talent, Inc., or TNT for short. Drawing on the talents of high school students, they hope to arrange for part-time jobs and for full-time summer employment as tutors, models, playground instructors, keyboard operators, tour guides, clerks, and management trainees. Can they incorporate their business?

2 ETHICS ISSUE Several high school teachers are the incorporators, directors, officers, employees, and shareholders of a small corporation that runs boats through the white-water rapids of a nearby river every summer. If a customer is injured because of the negligence of an employee, who is liable for the damages? Would it be ethical to operate such a business without having adequate public liability insurance?

3 As trustees for you, your parents hold 100 shares of stock in the General Electric company. Can your parents vote for directors of the corporation in the annual election without going to the meeting that is held in a city far from your home? Could you vote?

FOCUS

Before class begins, prepare and photocopy a generic stock certificate for each student. On each certificate, print the name of a different major corporation whose stock is traded on the New York Stock Exchange or the American Stock Exchange. Make a list on a flip chart of the most recent closing prices of the stocks. As students enter the classroom, have them take a stock certificate. Tell them to find their company on the flip chart list and note the price for which their stock was selling.

Have available several copies of a local newspaper that carries stock market information. Using the chalkboard or a flip chart, show students how to read the stock market page. Tell them to keep a record for a week of the opening and closing amounts for which their stock is selling. Students will use these records in the PERSONAL PERSPECTIVES activity on p. 764.

You Decide

1 No, the incorporators cannot all be minors. Also, incorporation is not a matter of private agreement; there are formal legal procedures that must be followed.

2 ETHICS ISSUE Both the employee and the corporation are liable without limit. Considering the very high risk of injury, it would not be ethical to operate such a business without proper public liability insurance.

3 Yes, the parents can vote by proxy; the minor can vote when he or she becomes an adult and the stock is transferred.

Thinking Critically Through Visuals

Most of the nation's large corporations have their headquarters in one of the major U.S. cities. These main office buildings are often architectural statements of the corporation's power. What do the buildings in the photograph tell you about the corporation it houses? (Answers may include that the corporations are likely to be large and profitable to occupy such prestigious buildings.)

TEACH

Explain to students that a **corporation** is a legal entity or artificial person in the eyes of the law. It has an existence distinctly separate from the real persons who organize, own, and run it. Tell students that although sole proprietorships and partnerships far outnumber corporations, corporations do most of the business in this country. Explain to students that corporations have recognizable attributes that are essential for large-scale businesses: *perpetual life, limited liability, transferability of ownership interests, ability to attract capital,* and *professional management.* On the chalkboard or a flip chart, list these attributes and explain each one.

WHAT IS A CORPORATION?

PROBLEM

Krug, a prosperous banker, and Erikson, an engineer, agreed to invest in a promising fiberglass boat manufacturing business. Krug was too busy to devote a lot of time to the new business, but Erikson wanted the benefit of her business judgment on major decisions. At the same time, Krug and Erikson could not afford the risk of unlimited liability to third parties. What form of business organization would be appropriate?

A **corporation** is a legal entity or artificial person in the eyes of the law. It has an existence distinctly separate from the real persons who organize, own, and run it. But a corporation is created by and for people, and it cannot do anything without the aid of human incorporators and operators who conduct the corporation's business.

Most corporations obtain authority to exist as corporations by complying with the incorporation statutes of one of the fifty state governments. Congress, by special legislative acts, also creates some corporations (e.g., the Federal Deposit Insurance Corporation, or FDIC) to serve specific national interests.

Although they are far outnumbered by sole proprietorships and partnerships, corporations do most of the business in this country. This is because the corporation has the following attributes that are essential for large-scale enterprises (some of the attributes are attractive to small business ventures, too).

1. Perpetual Life

Unlike the sole proprietorship and the partnership, a corporation is a legal entity separate and distinct from its owners and managers. Therefore it can continue to function after they die. Under the law, it may continue indefinitely with new owners, managers, and employees.

2. Limited Liability

Creditors normally cannot collect claims against the corporation from persons who own shares in the corporation. The corporation itself is liable without limit for its debts; all of its assets may be seized under court order to pay delinquent claims. But the individual stockholders stand to lose only

ASSESS

Learning Objective 1 Have students create a graphic organizer to illustrate what a corporation is and what the five recognizable attributes are. Have students exchange papers and correct each other's work.

the amount they have invested. It is this limited liability that makes the corporation an appropriate form of business organization for investors such as Krug and Erikson in the problem. They are willing to assume risks entrepreneurs face. But they want a ceiling or limit on the amount they might lose if someone successfully sues the business for heavy damages or if the business fails and cannot pay its debts.

3. Transferability of Ownership Interests

A major advantage of the corporate form over the partnership form is the ease of transferring ownership interests in the firm. Normally, individual owners can sell their interests in the corporation without disturbing the company's operations or getting the consent of other owners. The stock of most large corporations is traded (i.e., bought and sold) on the New York Stock Exchange or the American Stock Exchange. By contacting a stockbroker, any person may buy or sell a reasonable number of shares of any listed stock within minutes when the exchanges are open.

4. Ability to Attract Large Sums of Capital

Many investors feel comfortable and reasonably secure when buying stock in corporations. This is because their liability as owners of the corporation is limited to the amount they have invested. Moreover, as owners they may readily sell their individual shares, or buy more. Finally, the corporation may have perpetual life, outlasting present owners, directors, and employees, all of whom may be replaced without terminating the business. As a result, large sums of money may be raised. Small and large investments by thousands of persons and institutions are combined to fund giant corporations.

5. Professional Management

Because they can and do raise substantial amounts of capital, efficient corporations generally have greater financial strength than do other forms of business organization. This enables such corporations to attract superior workers by offering generous salaries and fringe benefits. Moreover, because the corporation is not automatically dissolved by the death of any owner or manager, it usually provides better assurance of continued employment.

In the problem, this advantage would appeal to Erikson, who would probably become a salaried manager. Nevertheless, Krug could participate in major policy decisions as a voting shareholder, and possibly as a director, elected by the shareholders to oversee the general operation of the corporation.

▼ APPLY

Have students participate in a version of *$20,000 Pyramid*. Divide the class into five groups, one for each of the attributes described on pp. 756–757. Ask each group to write short answer clues to identify their attribute, without directly mentioning the key words in the title. Have groups rotate volunteers to sit face-to-face. One student provides the clues and the other student guesses the attribute. Impose a time limit for each round, such as 30 seconds. **Guided Practice**

In their notebooks, have students independently write two benefit statements for each of the five attributes. After they have completed their lists, have students share their benefits aloud. Encourage students to add additional benefits to their lists as they are offered. **Independent Practice**

▼ RETEACH

Media: Using a computer, if possible, have students briefly describe in writing the basic attributes of a corporation. (Answers should mention perpetual life, limited liability, transferability of ownership interests, ability to attract capital, and professional management.)

▼ ENRICH

Have students create and manage a daily bulletin board of articles dealing with corporations. Supply newspapers, such as the *Wall Street Journal*, and magazines, such as *Fortune, Business Week, Forbes,* and *Money*.

▼ TEACH

Tell students that one of the major disadvantages of the corporate form is multiple federal and state taxation. Explain how this can be avoided by small corporations that elect to be treated as **S corporations.**

▼ APPLY

On the chalkboard, draw a three-column chart. Have the class compare the disadvantages of a regular *Corporation*, *S corporation*, and a *Partnership*. Use this information to complete the chart. **Guided Practice**

In writing, have students respond positively or negatively to the following statement: **Subchapter S of the Internal Revenue Code has had a positive effect on U.S. business.** (Answers may be affirmative, because it allows many small businesses to be taxed at personal, not corporate, federal income tax rates, or negative, because the Code allows for different tax burdens for similar businesses.) **Independent Practice**

WHAT ARE DISADVANTAGES OF CORPORATIONS?

PROBLEM

Dorn and several other persons plan to start a business. They reject the partnership form of organization because none of them is willing to become liable without limit for the firm's debts. They consider the corporate form of organization, but reject it also because they know it could require payment of higher income taxes. Is there an alternative legal form of organization that they could use?

There are some important disadvantages to the corporate form. Net income is taxed by the federal government when earned, and then is taxed again after distribution to the shareholders. Some states also tax the corporation's income, and then the shareholders, on income received. The multiple federal taxation can be avoided by small corporations that elect to be treated as S corporations. **S corporations** are organized under Subchapter S of the Internal Revenue Code. To qualify, the corporation can have only one class of stock and no more than thirty-five shareholders (husband and wife are considered one), all of whom must be U.S. citizens or resident aliens. For tax purposes only, the business is then treated as a partnership. The S corporation form would provide a good solution to the problem of Dorn and her associates.

It is costlier and more troublesome to organize a corporation than it is to organize a sole proprietorship or partnership (see Figure 38-1). Large corporations are subject to extensive regulation of the sale of their securities to the public. Juries sometimes tend to favor individuals in legal disputes with corporations. But, overall, advantages outweigh disadvantages, especially for big enterprises.

WHAT ARE THE DIFFERENT TYPES OF CORPORATIONS?

PROBLEM

Appleberry, Jackson, and Smythe urge members of their service club to create a separate organization for a special project. They plan to open a permanent, year-round country farm and camp for underprivileged city children. The planners hope that the farm will be self-supporting. Practically, however, they anticipate that expenses will exceed revenues because so many people are expected to visit and use the place simply for rest and recreation. All edible fruits and vegetables produced

▼ ASSESS

Learning Objectives 3 & 4 In small groups, using the chalkboard or a flip chart, have students create graphic organizers to compare and contrast sole proprietorships, partnerships, S corporations, and (regular) corporations. Have students explain their organizers to the other groups.

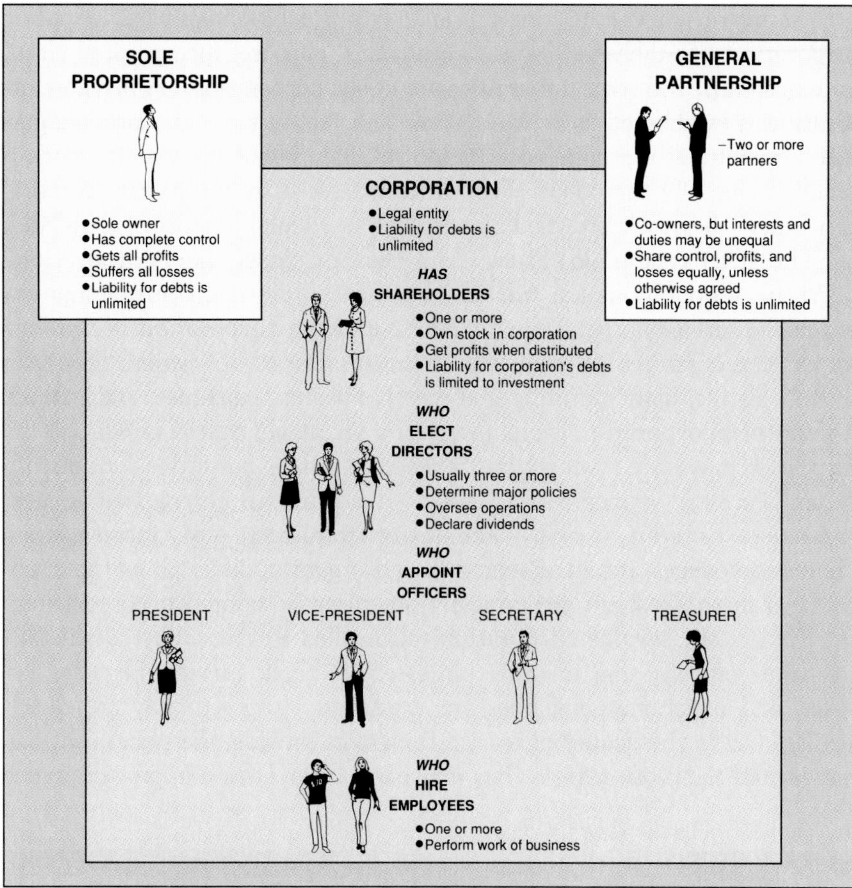

Figure 38-1
The sole proprietorship, partnership, and corporation are the principal legal forms of business organization.

are to be used to feed the campers or to be given to the poor. Field crops, such as corn and hay, are to feed the cattle and hogs. All excess costs are to be covered by anticipated donations obtained in an annual fund-raising auction. Would a corporation be suitable for the group?

Corporations are classified according to their place of incorporation and purpose. If a corporation is chartered in a particular state, it is a **domestic corporation** in that state. Any other corporation doing business in that state is a **foreign corporation** there because it was chartered elsewhere.

Koba, Ltd., a South Korean corporation, and Tarpon Chasers, Inc., a U.S. corporation incorporated in New Jersey, do business in Florida. Both are foreign corporations in Florida.

▼ TEACH

On the chalkboard, create a graphic organizer to illustrate and explain the eight different types of corporations discussed in the section on pp. 758–761: **domestic, foreign, public, private, closely held, profit-making, nonprofit,** and **public service.**

▼ APPLY

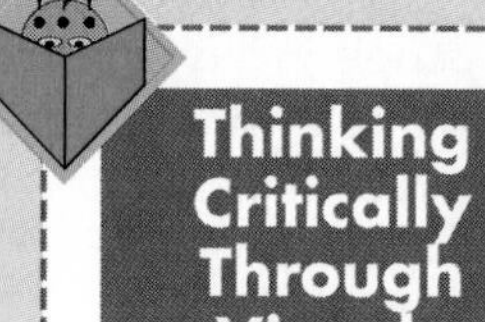

Thinking Critically Through Visuals

This chart compares and contrasts forms of business organizations. Is there a minimum or maximum limit to the number of shareholders in a corporation? (No; a corporation may have one shareholder or as many as there are shares of stock.) **Who elects the directors?** (Shareholders) **Who hires employees for the corporation?** (Usually an officer, according to the chart) **Guided Practice**

▼RETEACH Draw a diagram on the chalkboard that consists of three tiers, one above the other: *Corporate profits, Dividends,* and *Shareholders,* with arrows pointing down from the first tier to the third. Have students summarize the important disadvantages of incorporation. (Corporations experience multiple federal taxation, more costly to organize, subject to more legislation, and so on.)

▼ENRICH  Using a computer, if possible, have students speculate why more partnerships don't take advantage of S corporation status.

On a sheet of paper, have students create a three-column chart. Label the first column, *Type of Corporation*, the second column *Description*, and the third column *Example*. Have them work in pairs to complete it with information from pp. 759–761. **Independent Practice**

Thinking Critically Through Visuals

The people in this photograph work in the Franchise Development department of a major corporation. A *franchise* is the right given to a private person or corporation to market another's product within a certain area. What franchises can you name? (McDonald's, Jazzercise, and so on)

In terms of purpose, a corporation is either public or private. A **public corporation** is established for a governmental purpose. Incorporated cities, state hospitals, and state universities are public corporations. A **private corporation** is established by private citizens for business or for charitable purposes. Sometimes a private corporation is called public because its stock is broadly owned by the public. This differentiates it from a private corporation, where the stock is owned by only one or a small number of shareholders. The latter type is also known as a **close** or **closely held corporation.**

Private corporations are further classified as profit-making, nonprofit, and public service corporations. A **profit-making corporation** is a private corporation organized to produce a financial profit for its owners. Examples abound: banks, manufacturing and merchandising companies, and airlines. A **nonprofit corporation** is organized for a social, charitable, or educational purpose. It may have revenues that exceed expenses, but it does not distribute any earnings to members as profits. If a nonprofit corporation engages in business for profit, it must—like any other business—pay income taxes. Churches, colleges, fraternal societies, and organizations such as the country farm in the problem are typically organized as nonprofit corporations. Finally, a **public service corporation** (also called a *public utility*) is generally a private company that furnishes an essential public service. Electric, gas, water, and telephone companies are examples. However, they are closely regulated as to the quality of service they must provide, the prices they can charge, and the profit margin they may earn. Competition in providing such

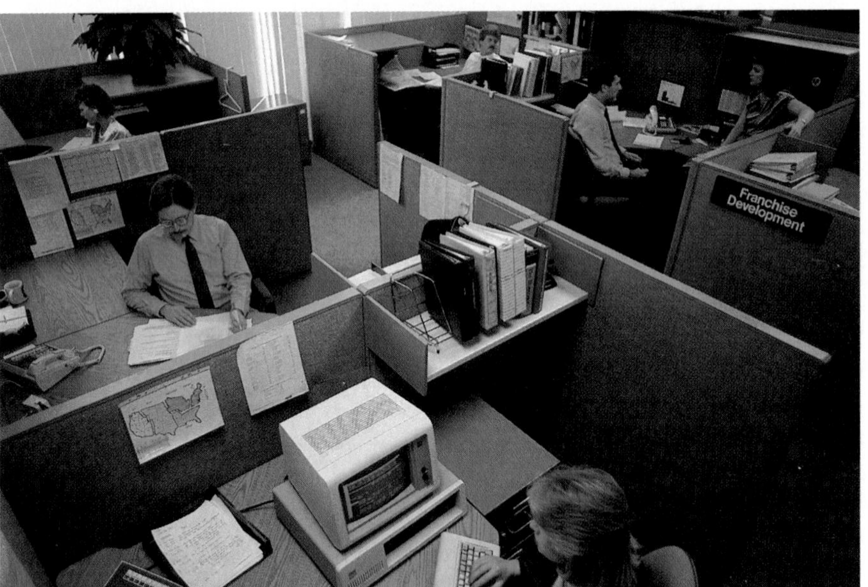

ASSESS

Learning Objective 1 Distribute one index card to each student. On it, have the student jot down a profile of a corporation using one or more of the types of corporations, then read it aloud. Have classmates name the type(s) of corporation described. Suggest this example: a Texas-based corporation established by two women develops custom clothing designs for sale to a select Texas clientele. (Domestic, private, profit-making and possibly, an S Corporation) services needed by most persons would be needlessly wasteful. Therefore such public utilities usually receive monopolistic franchises and special powers of eminent domain to acquire needed real estate.

HOW IS A CORPORATION FORMED?

PROBLEM

Delatronics, Inc., a Delaware corporation, wants to incorporate a subsidiary corporation in another state. The subsidiary will make electronic component parts for Delatronics's products. Could Delatronics serve as an incorporator of another corporation?

Typically, a corporation is formed as a result of the efforts of one or more persons called **promoters**. These individuals bring together interested persons and take preliminary steps to form a corporation. Regardless of the promoters' efforts, however, the resulting corporation is not liable on any contract made on its behalf. The promoters cannot bind an organization that is still to be created. Usually, though, once it comes into being, the corporation adopts the contracts and is bound by them.

Articles of incorporation are drafted, and when submitted to the proper state official (usually the Secretary of State), they are a plan that serves as an application for incorporation. In most states, when the articles are properly filed, the corporate existence begins. The articles are signed and submitted by one or more persons called **incorporators**. At least one of the incorporators must have legal capacity to enter into a binding contract. Thus, the incorporators cannot all be minors. A foreign corporation, such as Delatronics in the problem, or a domestic corporation may be an incorporator. Articles of incorporation filed by the incorporators serve as the basic plan of operation. They generally contain

1. the name of the corporation;
2. the period of duration, which may be indefinite or perpetual;
3. the purpose, or purposes, for which the corporation is organized, which may be broadly stated (e.g., "any purposes legal for a corporation in this state");
4. the number and kinds of shares of capital stock to be authorized for issuance;
5. the location of the corporation's principal office and the name of its agent to whom legal notices may be given;

TEACH

On the chalkboard, create a flowchart to illustrate how a corporation is formed. Make sure students understand the new vocabulary terms: **promoters, articles of incorporation**, and **incorporators**. Then, as you discuss the eight points that are generally found in the articles of incorporation, have students copy them in their notebooks or law journals.

APPLY

Secure butcher paper to a classroom wall. Draw the base of a spider map or other graphic organizer and label it *How a Corporation Is Formed.* One at a time or in small groups, have students add information to the organizer until it is complete. **Guided Practice**

Divide the class into groups of five or six. Assign the following roles: facilitator, promoter, two or three incorporators, and Secretary of State. Have each group role-play the formation of a corporation, including creating articles of incorporation. Have each group perform their work for the class. **Cooperative Learning**

RETEACH Have students create their own crossword puzzle (with answers) using the vocabulary terms on pp. 759–760. Have students exchange papers and complete each other's puzzle.

ENRICH Provide sufficient background, without bias, to allow students to debate the following statement: **The results of the breakup of the communications monopoly held by AT&T proves that monopolistic public service corporations benefit the consumer.**

In writing, have students express their opinion on why all the incorporators in a corporation cannot be minors, recalling information learned in previous chapters. **Independent Practice**

▼ TEACH

On the chalkboard, write the following terms: **shares of stock**, **shareholder**, **stock certificate**, **par value**, **no-par stock**, **market price**, **common stock**, **dividends**, **preferred stock**, **liquidation**, **cumulative**, and **participating stock**. Use each term to explain how corporations issue, and shareholders acquire, different kinds of stock.

In order to help limited English proficient or dyslexic students, create a word search puzzle using the vocabulary terms on pp. 762–763. Distribute copies to the class. Review correct responses by spelling the terms aloud and writing them on the chalkboard as reinforcement.

Guided Practice

6. the number of directors or the names and addresses of the persons who are to serve as directors until the first annual meeting of shareholders or until their successors are elected (in some states, the incorporators serve as directors until the shareholders elect their replacements);
7. the name and address of each incorporator; and
8. any other provision consistent with the law.

In some states, the incorporators file a *certificate of incorporation* instead of articles of incorporation, but with the same result. Many years ago, when a corporation was created by a special act of the legislature, a *charter* was issued. Today the word charter refers broadly to the articles (or certificate) of incorporation taken in connection with the governing statutory law. It also may refer to the contract that exists between the state and the corporation.

▼ WHAT ARE SHARES OF STOCK?

PROBLEM

A is an incorporator of the newly formed Galaxy Space Research Corporation. *B* is a director. C is the president. *D*, *E*, and *F* are shareholders who own most of the stock. If the corporation buys an electronic microscope, who owns it?

Corporations issue units of ownership known as **shares of stock.** A person who owns one or more shares of stock is a **shareholder** (also called a *stockholder*).

The corporation uses the money received from the initial sale of stock to buy equipment, supplies, and inventory; to hire labor; and to pay other expenses. As goods and services are produced and sold, more income flows into the business. Often earnings are reinvested. Also more shares of stock may be sold and money may be borrowed to provide for further expansion.

A shareholder receives a **stock certificate,** which is written evidence of ownership and rights in the business. Stock ownership does not transfer title to specific corporate property to the holder. The corporation, as a legal person, remains the owner of all corporate property. Thus, in the problem, Galaxy Corporation owns the electronic microscope.

Stock may have a **par value,** which is the face value printed on the certificate. If it does not have a par value, it is **no-par stock** and is originally sold at a price set by the board of directors of the corporation. When either par or no-par stock changes hands in later transfers, the price may be higher or lower. This **market price** is determined by many factors, including past

▼ ASSESS

Learning Objective 5 On a sheet of paper, have students determine if the following statements are *True* or *False*. If a statement is false, have students change one word to make it true. **(1) Liquidation of a corporation occurs when all of its business assets are bought, debts are paid, and the corporate existence is ended.** (False; sold); **(2) Par value is the face value printed on a stock certificate.** (True); and **(3) Dividends are distributions of losses by the corporation.** (False; profits)

and anticipated future profits. Profits, in turn, are affected by general economic conditions of the country and of the particular field of endeavor.

Corporations may have one or more kinds of stock. **Common stock** is the basic type, with the right to vote in corporate elections. Shareholders of common stock typically have one vote per share owned, and they generally receive dividends. **Dividends** are distributions of profits earned by the corporation.

To attract additional funds from investors who want greater assurance of payment of dividends, some corporations also issue **preferred stock.** Owners of preferred stock usually have no voting power, but they are legally entitled to a stated dividend—if it is earned—before the common shareholders get anything. For example, by contract with the corporation, the preferred shareholder may be entitled to receive $7 per share each year before any distribution of profits is made to the common shareholders. If profits are high, the common shareholders may get more money than the preferred shareholders. Preferred shareholders also generally have a priority right to be repaid the face value of their stock from the corporation's funds obtained in a liquidation. **Liquidation** occurs when all of the business assets are sold, all debts are paid, and the corporate existence is ended.

Preferred stock may be **cumulative**. This means that if the promised dividend is not paid in a given year, it remains due and payable in the future. Each year the unpaid dividends *cumulate* (i.e., add up) and must be paid in full before the common shareholders receive any dividends. (The

Thinking Critically Through Visuals

Many stocks in the United States are traded on the New York Stock Exchange or the American Stock Exchange. By looking at the photograph, what do you think the work environment is like at the NYSE? (Answers may include that the many computers, many people, and paper on the floor may indicate a busy, fast-paced environment.)

The New York Stock Exchange offers a 12-minute videotape that explains how the exchange functions. Leonard Nimoy is the narrator of *NYSE: A Portrait.* Write to the New York Stock Exchange, Educational Products, P.O. Box 4191, Syosset, NY 11791–4191 for information on this and other educational materials.

RETEACH Write each of the vocabulary words in this section on individual flashcards or sheets of paper. Distribute one or more in random order to each student in the group. Have students stand, facing the class and displaying their flashcards. Have remaining students define the terms, then orally summarize what stocks are.

ENRICH Supply students with copies of stock market information from newspapers and have them list the prices of common and preferred stock in corporations, such as AT&T and General Motors.

Personal Perspectives

Distribute graph paper to students and have them plot this week's progress of the stock they selected for the FOCUS activity.

 **Independent Practice**

▼ TEACH

Tell students that shareholders elect **directors**, the top officials of the corporation, who together form the corporation's **board of directors.** Explain that some of the directors' functions are to determine basic policies, set major goals, appoint officers, and make policy decisions.

Multicultural Highlights

One of the United States' most prosperous African American corporations is Johnson Publishing Company, Inc., of Chicago. Owned by John H. Johnson and managed by his daughter, Linda Johnson Rice, the company publishes books and periodicals, such as *Ebony* and *Jet*.

corporation must earn profits before it can pay dividends.) In some cases, the preferred stock is also participating. For example, in a given year, if dividends are distributed, the **participating stock's** preferred shareholder receives the basic dividend as contractually agreed, and the common shareholder receives an equal amount per share. Then any remaining profit to be distributed that year is divided equally between the preferred and common shareholders or in any ratio as previously agreed.

▼ WHO DIRECTS THE BUSINESS OF THE CORPORATION?

PROBLEM

Max Mogul organized the Integral Cable TV Corporation and owned most of its stock. However, he was no longer actively employed in its management or operations. Nevertheless, during a trip to London he claimed he was "acting for his company" when he contracted for services of an English theater group to present five Shakespearean dramas for Integral. Is Integral bound by Mogul's contract?

As noted earlier, a corporation is a legal person in the eyes of the law. It must act through human agents elected by the shareholders, appointed by the directors, or hired by the officers. No shareholder, not even one who owns most or all the stock, can act for the corporation or bind it by contract merely because of such ownership. In the problem, Mogul had no authority to represent the corporation and therefore Integral is not bound.

Shareholders indirectly control the affairs of a corporation by electing the directors. They also have the power to vote on major issues, such as changing the corporate articles, merging with another company, or selling out in a corporate take-over. Antitrust laws do not forbid acquisitions or mergers of dissimilar companies. Large size in itself is not illegal.

As their name indicates, **directors** are responsible for overall direction of the corporation. Elected by shareholders, they serve as the corporation's **board of directors.** They are fiduciaries and as such are duty bound to act in good faith and with due care, oversee the corporation, and formulate general policies. They must not act fraudulently or illegally. (See Chapter 25 for a discussion of fiduciaries.) Most states apply the standard of the Model Business Corporation Act. This requires that the director act "in a manner he reasonably believes to be in the best interests of the corporation, and with such care as an ordinary prudent person in a like position would use

▼ ASSESS

Learning Objective 6 Have students draw their own organization flowcharts of a fictitious corporation listing the typical hierarchy of directors and officers. The chart should include sidebars explaining **inside, outside,** and **mixed boards.** Post them on a bulletin board entitled *Life at the Top*.

under similar circumstances,"[1] Failure to do so can make the director liable in damages to the shareholders.

The directors are the top officials of the corporation. They set major goals and determine basic policies (e.g., whether to sell for cash, credit, or both, and whether to expand or reduce operations in a given area). They appoint and set the salaries of the top officers of the company: typically the president, vice president, secretary, and treasurer. Acting together, the directors have the power to make contracts for the corporation, but they delegate the day-to-day duties of running the business to the officers they have selected. However, the directors are expected to exercise their own best judgment in appointing the officers and in overseeing their work. The directors alone may declare dividends and authorize major policy decisions. Therefore they may not have other persons serve as substitutes at board meetings, and deliberate and vote for them.

The number of directors varies among corporations. Most states allow the shareholders to determine the number. Some states require at least three. Other states require only one director, who can also be the sole officer and sole shareholder. This gives the corporation the attributes of a sole proprietorship plus the advantage of limited liability for its owner. Statutes sometimes require that directors be shareholders. A few states require that directors be adults. Some states require that the president of the company serve as a director, while in many corporations all the directors are officers. This is called an **inside board** and is not considered ideal because the directors naturally tend to approve their conduct as officers. Better results are sometimes obtained from an **outside board,** which has no officers in its membership and which presumably scrutinizes corporate performance more objectively and critically. Probably the best form is a **mixed board,** with some officers to provide information and detailed understanding and some outsiders "to ask the embarrassing questions."

WHAT ARE THE POWERS AND DUTIES OF THE CORPORATE OFFICERS?

PROBLEM

After Karporev was selected as vice-president of a large U.S. electrical products company, it was disclosed that he was a citizen of the Soviet Union. Several shareholders sought a court order to compel his dismissal. Was Karporev legally qualified to serve in the position?

[1] Model Business Corporation Act, Section 35.

APPLY

On the chalkboard, draw the base of the following graphic organizer and have students complete it with information on the responsibilities of a board of directors (pp. 764–765): **Guided Practice**

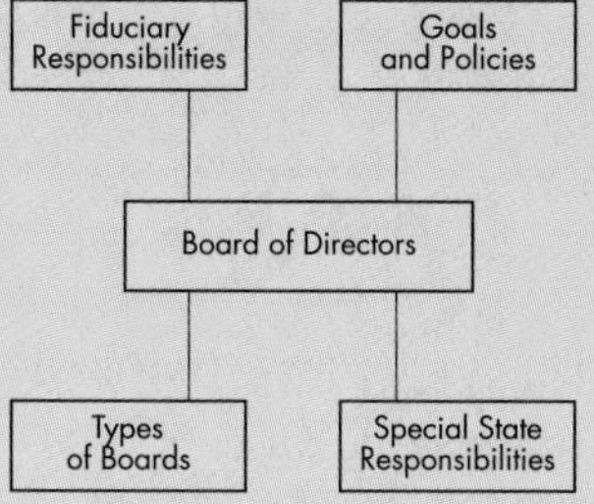

Using a computer, if possible, have students summarize the duties and responsibilities of a corporate director by writing a job description for the position.

Independent Practice

Ethics Issue

It is not unusual for well-known individuals to serve on the board of directors of more than one corporation. Ask: **Is it ethical for a person to serve as a director for several corporations in the same line of business?** (Answers may include that, ethically, it might be difficult to act impartially; legally, it might be difficult to avoid monopolistic policies.)

RETEACH In small groups, have students use library resources, interviews, or corporate statements to support the most important points in this section.

ENRICH Media Tell students that many top corporate officers worked their way up through the ranks of the corporation they now run. Today, many managers do not have the first-hand experience at the lowest employee levels required to effectively manage the work of others. Ask students to comment about this trend, using a computer, if possible.

▼ TEACH

Corporate officers are usually appointed by the board of directors. There are no restrictions in the selection of officers, who act as agents for the corporation and have fiduciary responsibilities.

▼ APPLY

Using Figure 38-1 (p. 759) as a model, draw a graphic organizer and have students describe how the people at each level are chosen and what their responsibilities are. **Guided Practice**

Have students assume the role of a member of the board of directors of a major corporation. Tell them to prepare a list of questions for a prospective officer of the corporation. Pair students and have them role-play the director and the prospective officer.

Independent Practice

▼ TEACH

On the chalkboard, create a chart to facilitate your explanation of the powers of a corporation, as listed in the headings on pp. 766–768.

Directors generally employ managing officers and delegate to them necessary authority to conduct the firm's day-to-day business. Corporate managing officers commonly include a president, a vice president, a secretary, and a treasurer. However, the duties of two or more of these positions may be combined. Other positions may be created as required. Many states and the Model Business Corporation Act permit one person to hold two or more offices, except that the president may not also serve as secretary. This helps to prevent falsification of records. Officers are usually appointed by the board of directors, although in some corporations they are elected by the shareholders. Generally there are no restrictions on the selection of officers. Thus, they do not necessarily have to be shareholders or directors, have certain qualifications, or be a certain age. Accordingly, in the problem, Karporev was legally qualified to serve as vice president.

Because the officers of a corporation are its agents, they are fiduciaries governed by applicable principles of agency law. (See Chapter 25 for a discussion of agency law.) Limitations may be imposed by the articles of incorporation, by the governing rules of the corporation, and by the board of directors. Neither directors nor officers are liable for honest errors of judgment, however costly, but they are legally accountable for willful or negligent acts that cause loss to the corporation.

▼ WHAT ARE THE POWERS OF THE CORPORATION?

PROBLEM

Ruiz organized a corporation in which he owned all the stock. His wife and two daughters were directors with him, and they served as vice-president, treasurer, and secretary, respectively, under his direction as president. If Ruiz died, could the business continue indefinitely because it is a corporation?

In general, a corporation can be formed for any lawful purpose. The corporation is then allowed to exercise all powers that are necessary, convenient, and lawful in achieving that purpose.

Powers vary among corporations, but some are inherent in almost every corporation. These powers include the following.

1. Perpetual Succession

In most jurisdictions, the corporation is the only form of business organization that may be granted the power of perpetual succession. **Perpetual succession** means that regardless of changes in the shareholders (i.e., own-

▼ ASSESS

Learning Objective 1 Have students respond to the following *True* or *False* statements: **(1) A corporation may both borrow and lend money.** (True); **(2) A corporation may not under any circumstances buy back its own stock.** (False); and **(3) The power of perpetual succession is unique to corporations.** (True) ers), the corporation may continue indefinitely or for whatever period originally requested by the incorporators. During this time, the death or withdrawal of a director, manager, or shareholder has no legal effect on the corporation's continuity. Thus, in the problem, Ruiz's business could continue. But even a corporate business may end when a majority of its owners decide to end it or upon the death or retirement of an officer whose services were essential.

2. Corporate Name

A corporation can select any name to identify itself unless that name is identical or deceptively similar to the name of another business already operating in that geographical area. Most states require that the name selected indicate that the business is a corporation, to alert the public of the limited liability of its owners. This can be done by including a descriptive word in the name, such as Corporation, Incorporated, or Limited, or their abbreviations (Corp., Inc., or Ltd.).

Any business organization has the legal power to use a fictitious name. However most states require that fictitious names be registered in a designated government office, along with information about the natural owners.

3. Bylaws

A corporation can make its own reasonable rules and regulations for the internal management of its affairs. Called **bylaws**, these rules specify times for meetings of shareholders and directors, for example, and define duties of officers.

4. Power to Conduct Its Business

In achieving its purpose(s), a corporation may use any legal means to conduct authorized business. Thus, the corporation has the power, in its own name, to:

a. make contracts;
b. borrow money and incur other liabilities;
c. lend money and acquire assets, including all forms of real and personal property;
d. make, indorse, and accept commercial paper;
e. issue various types of stock and bonds. **Bonds** are long-term notes issued in return for money borrowed and usually secured by a mortgage or deposit of collateral. Unsecured bonds are **debentures**;
f. mortgage, pledge, lease, sell, or assign its property;
g. buy back from owners its own stock unless this would make it impossible for the corporation to pay its debts or to pay off any superior

▼ APPLY

Mask out the left and right columns (Sole Proprietorship and Partnership) of the overhead transparency master, *Legal Form of Business You Will Work for—or Own—Some Day* and photocopy it for students. Have students add a subhead, *LEGAL FORM*, and a new column labeled *POWERS*. Have students add the powers of a corporation to the chart. Review responses. **Guided Practice**

Writing Connections

Economics/ Language Arts
Assign students to their cooperative learning activity groups (p. 761). Have students extend the activity by writing bylaws for the corporation, and assigning it a name and undertaking some aspect(s) of authorized corporate business, as identified on pp. 766–768. **Independent Practice**

Have students create posters to show the powers a corporation has to conduct its business. Encourage students to add illustrations or computer graphics to illustrate their points.

▼RETEACH Have students work in small groups to create a fishbone map of the powers of a corporation. After a group discussion, add details on the diagonal branches of the map. Rotate among the groups as you have students explain their work.

▼ENRICH Invite officer(s) of a local corporation to speak to students about the powers and duties of the corporate officers, the type of business they conduct, and the powers the officers exercise to achieve its business purposes.

▼ TEACH

Create a graphic organizer to illustrate and explain the following shareholders' rights: to a stock certificate; to transfer shares; to attend shareholder meetings and, in some cases, to vote; to increase the capital stock; to get a portion of the distributed profits; to participate in distributions of capital; and to inspect corporate books of account. Be sure students understand the terms **cumulative voting, proxy,** and **preemptive right.**

class of stock. Such purchases are sometimes made to boost the market price of the stock, to eliminate dissident shareholders, to acquire shares for employee purchase and bonus plans, or simply to reduce the size of the corporation.

h. acquire and hold stock in other corporations provided this does not violate antitrust laws;

i. make reasonable donations or gifts for civic or charitable purposes to promote goodwill in accord with corporate social responsibility;

j. hire and fire agents, independent contractors, and ordinary employees;

k. establish pension, profit sharing, and other incentive plans for employees; and

l. sue and be sued.

5. Other Implied Powers

A corporation may do any legal act that is necessary or convenient for the execution of its express powers. This would extend to such matters as doing pure and applied research and development (R & D) work, leasing space and equipment, advertising, and buying life and health and liability insurance for officers and other employees.

▼ WHAT ARE THE RIGHTS OF SHAREHOLDERS?

PROBLEM

Berling owns 400 shares of stock in a corporation that has 1,000 voting shares. Niles and Piper, who together own the remaining 600 shares, decide to keep Berling from electing any one of the three directors. Can they do so?

Status as a shareholder does not give one the right to possess any corporate property or to participate directly in management. However, shareholder status does confer the following important rights.

1. The Right to a Stock Certificate

A shareholder has the right to receive a stock certificate as evidence of ownership of shares in the corporation. One certificate may represent one or more shares. For the safety and convenience of shareholders, many large corporations have an independent trust company serve as registrar and transfer agent for the corporation's securities. Often shareholders give such trust companies, or the corporation, the right to retain possession of the shares for safekeeping.

▼ ASSESS

Learning Objective 6 Ask students to discuss as a group why it is important for shareholders to exercise their right to take part in regular corporate meetings, either in person or by proxy. (Answers may include shareholders' have both the right and the responsibility to participate in the major decisions of the corporation.)

2. The Right to Transfer Shares

A shareholder generally has the right to sell or to give away any shares owned. This right is sometimes restricted in closely held corporations, where the owners may want to limit ownership to employees or to members of a given family. Accordingly, the corporation's charter may provide that an owner who wants to sell shares must first offer them to the corporation or to other stockholders.

3. The Right to Attend Shareholder Meetings and, in Some Cases, to Vote

A shareholder may attend shareholder meetings and vote shares owned in any class of stock that has the right to vote. Regular meetings are usually held annually at the place and time designated in the articles or bylaws. Notice of the regular meetings usually is not required. Reasonable notice is required for special meetings.

In a corporate election, a shareholder usually is entitled to the number of votes that equals the number of shares of voting stock held. Having a *minority position* means owning less than 50 percent of the voting shares. To safeguard the interests of such shareholders, many states provide for **cumulative voting** in the election of directors. Under this plan, each shareholder has the right to cast as many votes as the number of shares of stock held, multiplied by the number of directors to be elected. The shareholder may cast all available votes for one candidate or distribute them among two or more candidates. Thus, in the problem, if three directors are to be elected by cumulative voting, Berling could concentrate his 1,200 votes on one candidate (400 shares × three positions). Niles and Piper have a combined voting power of 1,800 votes (600 × three positions). They can elect two directors by dividing their votes and casting 900 for each. If cumulative voting were not in effect, Niles and Piper could keep Berling from electing anyone to the board because, with only 400 votes for each position, he would be outvoted each time.

A shareholder who does not wish to attend meetings and to vote in person ordinarily has the right to vote by **proxy** (see Figure 38-2). Most of the millions of persons who individually own comparatively few shares of stock in various corporations cast their votes in this manner. The management, or anyone seeking control of the corporation, mails the necessary proxy forms to all shareholders and solicits their votes. The shareholders may then sign and return the forms. Shareholders who are satisfied with the corporation's performance, typically give their proxies to incumbent managers who are also directors, giving them authority to cast the votes. Federal law requires that the proxy form give the shareholder an opportunity to specify by ballot

▼ APPLY

As a whole-class activity, hold a shareholder's meeting of Kit 'N KaPoodle Inc., a large retail pet store chain in which all students (except for three) are shareholders. These three students will role-play the potential directors of the corporation. On slips of paper, write arbitrary numbers between 50 and 1,000. Fold the slips of paper in half and place them in a bag or box. Have each shareholder choose a slip. Tell students that the number on the slip of paper represents how many shares of stock they now own in Kit 'N KaPoodle, Inc. Hold a corporate election to elect the director-candidates, using a cumulative voting plan, as identified on p. 769. **Guided Practice**

Using a computer, if possible, ask students to write an essay to answer the following question: **If you disagree with some of the practices of the corporation, what are your options as a shareholder?** (Answers may include selling the stock, attending and participating in stockholder meetings, and so on.)

Independent Practice

As a group, have students summarize the seven rights of shareholders, as presented on pp. 768–771. Then, have members of the group supply details to support each of the rights.

Supply students with magazines and ask them to find articles about an annual shareholder meeting of a major corporation in which there has been some unrest. Have students assume the roles of shareholders and prepare brief statements of their position.

Thinking Critically Through Visuals

Voting by proxy allows participation by shareholders who cannot personally attend a shareholder meeting. What specific authority does Hogan's proxy give Kinnard and Connerly? (The right to vote as they choose in Hogan's name)

Have students imagine that they are a shareholder who cannot attend the shareholders' meeting for the election of directors for Kit 'N KaPoodle, Inc. (See the GUIDED PRACTICE activity on p. 769.) Using Figure 38-2 as a model, have them draw up a proxy, then vote by proxy.

Figure 38-2
Example of a proxy that authorizes a designated person to vote in place of the signer at a meeting of the corporation's shareholders.

THE BACK-PACK CORPORATION

Proxy

The undersigned hereby appoints GEORGE KINNARD and MARY ANN CONNERLY and each of them, proxies, and with power of substitution (i.e., power to name replacements), to attend the Annual Meeting of shareholders of The Back-Pack Corporation, at the company's main office in Green Bay, Wisconsin, on April 15,19--, commencing at 10 a.m. and any adjournment thereof, and there to vote all the shares of the undersigned for election of Directors, and on any other business that may properly come before the meeting.

Dated: March 20, 19-- Roberta J. Hogan (L.S.)
Signature

Proxy # 125413 Roberta J. Hogan
37 Winona Lane
Account # 0590363 Des Moines, Iowa

approval or rejection of particular proposals. Proxy voting, especially when there is no right of cumulative voting, usually enables present directors and officers of large corporations to remain in control indefinitely and then to name their successors. The power of proxy should be exercised with a sense of social responsibility, recognizing the rights not only of owners, but also of employees, customers, and others.

4. The Right to Increase the Capital Stock

Shareholders alone have the right to increase the *capital stock* (i.e., total shares of stock) of the corporation. This is usually done by majority vote, on the recommendation of the board of directors. In some corporations, when the capital stock is increased, each shareholder may have a right to purchase additional shares to maintain the percentage of interest in the corporation owned before the increase. This is called the **preemptive right,** and it enables shareholders to protect their:

a. proportionate interest possessed in past and future profits, and
b. proportionate voting power.

Practically, if there is no preemptive power, little usually is lost. Most individual shareholders in large corporations own too few shares to be concerned about their voting power. The sale of new shares to outsiders brings in new capital which should increase the total profits, thus benefiting all shareholders. Sometimes large blocks of unissued shares are needed by the directors to purchase whole companies; the preemptive right could prevent such action.

ASSESS

Learning Objective 6 Tell students to write five matching questions (with answers on the back) about the rights of shareholders. Have pairs of students exchange papers and answer the questions. Review errors and guide students to an understanding of the correct responses.

5. The Right to a Share of the Profits

Each shareholder is entitled to a proportionate share of the profits which are distributed on the class of stock owned. These dividends are usually paid in money, but they may be shares of stock. Occasionally products of the corporation are distributed as dividends. Even when profits are earned, the board of directors may decide to retain them in the business for future needs of the firm. In effect, the stockholders are thus forced to make an additional investment in the business. Ideally, this should cause the price of stock to go up, and the stockholders can sell out if they so choose. Under unusual circumstances, courts will intervene to compel distribution of dividends at the request of shareholders who claim that there is an unreasonably large surplus of retained and unused or underutilized earnings.

6. The Right to Share in Distributions of the Capital

If a corporation is dissolved, its creditors have first claim upon the assets of the business. After their claims have been satisfied, any remaining assets or proceeds from the sale of assets (i.e., liquidation funds) are distributed to the shareholders. Preferred stockholders generally have priority over common stockholders in such distribution.

7. The Right to Inspect Corporate Books of Account

A shareholder has the right to inspect and to make appropriate records of the accounting books of the corporation. However, this inspection right may be denied if it is not made at a reasonable time and place, in good faith, and with proper motive. This is in contrast to the open inspection permitted to partners. Yet this restriction is understandable when one realizes that many thousands of persons own shares in large corporations. If the books were open to all without restriction, competitors could buy a few shares simply to gain an unfair advantage by such inspection.

HOW DOES CORPORATE EXISTENCE END?

PROBLEM

According to its articles of incorporation, Fun Foods, Inc., was created to operate restaurants and food stands at the state fair for the duration of the event. When the fair ended, how was the corporate existence terminated?

Ethics Issue

In a corporation, stockholders are liable for corporate debts only up to the amount of their financial investment. The corporation, however, has unlimited liability. Creditors, if their claims prove to be uncollectable, stand to lose a portion, or even all, of what is owed to them. Ask: **Is it fair for creditors to have greater exposure to loss than the shareholders?** (Answers may include yes, because the creditors are aware of this business risk, or no, because shareholders should be held more accountable than unknowing creditors for a corporation's liabilities.)

RETEACH

Media: Have students use word processing or page layout software to create a brochure for prospective stockholders on their rights, as identified on pp. 768–771. Encourage students to use concrete examples to explain each of the seven points as they apply to the stockholder.

ENRICH

Have students create a shareholders' proxy, using Figure 38-2 as a model, to reflect the position they articulated earlier when they assumed the identity of stockholders. (See pp. 769–770.)

TEACH

List the five ways a corporation can be terminated or dissolved: specifications by the incorporators or by agreement of the shareholders, forfeiture of the charter, **consolidation** or **merger**, bankruptcy, or court order. Explain each cause in detail, supplying examples as necessary.

APPLY

Create a cause-and-effect chart using the five causes of dissolution or termination of a corporation (pp. 772–773). Write a cause or an effect in its appropriate column. Ask students to provide you with its counterpart. Continue the activity until at least one cause and effect for each of the five items has been listed on the chart.
Guided Practice

A variety of causes may bring about the dissolution or termination of a corporation. These include the following.

1. Specification by the Incorporators or by Agreement of the Shareholders

A corporation terminates upon expiration of the agreed-upon period of its existence. In the problem Fun Foods, Inc., was automatically terminated when the fair ended, as specified in the articles of incorporation. A corporation may also end before the agreed-upon time if the shareholders (usually those with a majority of the voting power) voluntarily vote to do so.

2. Forfeiture of the Charter

The state may bring judicial proceedings for the forfeiture of the charter of a corporation that has been guilty of certain acts. Examples of such acts are (1) fraudulent submission of articles of incorporation, (2) flagrant misuse of corporate powers, and (3) repeated violation of the law. Forfeiture is rare because the state does not monitor corporate affairs, and aggrieved persons can seek private relief in court.

3. Consolidation or Merger

A **consolidation** of corporations can occur with the approval of the boards of directors and a majority of the shareholders in each of the corporations involved. The two corporations cease to exist and a new corporation is formed.

In a **merger** one corporation absorbs the other. The surviving corporation retains its charter and identity; the other disappears. Again, approval must be given by the directors and by the shareholders of the merging corporations.

A combination through either consolidation or merger must not violate antitrust laws by interfering unreasonably with free competition. An illegal monopoly occurs when one company controls the supply of goods, excludes competitors, and sets prices. It is also illegal for two or more companies to conspire to set prices or to allocate exclusive marketing areas, because this reduces free competition. However the antitrust laws have been amended to permit competing companies to form partnerships for joint research in order to meet global competition. Thus General Motors, Ford, and Chrysler do joint research on materials, oil and reformulated fuel, batteries, and electronic systems for control of vehicles.

ASSESS

Learning Objective 3 Have students determine if the following statements are *True* or *False*. If a statement is false, then have students change one word to make it true. **(1) A consolidation occurs when one corporation absorbs another.** (False/merger); **(2) A court order is a usual way to dissolve a corporation.** (False/unusual); and **(3) Forfeiture of the charter is a legal way to end a corporation's existence.** (True)

4. Bankruptcy

Bankruptcy of a corporation does not in itself cause dissolution. However, a bankruptcy proceeding typically leaves the corporation without assets with which to do business. In addition, some state statutes provide that when a corporation is insolvent, its creditors may force dissolution. Recall that a Chapter 11 bankruptcy proceeding is designed to prevent termination of a corporation that is in financial distress (see Chapter 19).

5. Court Order

Occasionally a corporation's assets are seriously threatened with irreparable harm because an internal dispute cannot be resolved by the board of directors or the shareholders. In some states a court can order dissolution if interested parties petition for dissolution. This rarely happens.

WHAT IS THE IMPACT OF LAW ON BUSINESS?

PROBLEM

In a high school "bull session," Jason maintained that, happily, he was not affected by the continuing public debate on the proper role of government and the laws it should make. "Include me out," he said. "I don't pay taxes, I don't bother no one [sic], and no one bothers me." Is Jason correct?

In completing this textbook you have become better informed than most of your fellow Americans about the far-reaching impact of law on business. These final paragraphs (1) briefly review the content of the preceding chapters and (2) list principal objectives of our government and the administrative agencies created to achieve those legal objectives.

1. Review of the Textbook Coverage

Beginning with Chapter 1, Shield of the Constitution, you learned how economic and business problems helped to bring about the American Revolution. However, after victory, the founders of our country retained the English common law. To this day, the constantly updated common law meets our business and noncommercial needs. In those early times as well as now, crimes and torts, and especially contracts, affect business. The law governs sales, whether for cash or on credit. All who work for hire are employed under

In small groups, have students create examples of a **merger** or a **consolidation**. Encourage students to use various methods of presentation, such as advertisements, videotaped or tape recorded public service announcements, cartoons, and so on. Have each group present its work to the class.

Independent Practice

TEACH

Explain to students how business and law interact hand-in-hand. Remind students that English common law, which developed hundreds of years ago, is—updated, of course—the foundation of business law today. Tell students that the law and regulations govern business transactions, the production of money, negotiable instruments, employment, and so on. Remind students that the government allows three basic forms of legal business organization: sole proprietorships, partnerships, and corporations. Give examples of how the government has passed laws and set up agencies, rules, and regulations to protect the rights of all who do business.

RETEACH Have students independently draw cartoons to illustrate one of the five ways a corporation's existence may end. (See pp. 771–773.)

ENRICH Have students debate the following statement: **Corporations have become too powerful because of mergers and consolidations.** (Students should be aware of the leveraged buyouts and other corporate combinations of the 1980s and use this to guide their responses.)

APPLY

Have students review the Table of Contents of *Law for Business* (pp. iii–v). Poll students on which unit or chapter they found most interesting. Begin a class discussion by asking students to explain how this information is, or will be, relevant and pertinent to their lives. **Guided Practice**

Photocopy the overhead transparency master, *What Is the Legal Involvement of Government in Business?*, and distribute it to students. Have them prioritize the 15 items in ascending order (from least to most) according to their importance. Using a computer, if possible, have students write an essay discussing why they selected their first three choices as the most important and their last three as the least important choices to them.

Independent Practice

legal contract. Because sales and employment affect so many people, numerous regulations control both. This encourages such transactions while protecting against abuse and exploitation.

We are a prosperous and productive nation and much of our wealth is found in property, both real and personal. Again the law governs the countless related business transactions for both buyers and sellers, lessors and lessees, landlords and tenants. Ordinary money (cash and coin) is still very much in use, with its production controlled by law. But it has proved to be inadequate for the volume and complexity of our business dealings. Therefore negotiable instruments and other credit extension devices are used to facilitate the production and distribution of goods—all under rules of law. Persons who own valuable economic rights and interests are protected from possible calamitous losses by insurance. In the final two chapters you learned how government encourages business enterprise by permitting several alternative forms of legal organization: sole proprietorships, partnerships, and corporations.

2. Governmental Objectives Achieved Through Administrative Agencies

Since the Great Depression of 1929–39, Americans have increasingly looked to the government for solutions to social and economic problems. Much of our expanded body of law has been created by independent administrative agencies that combine legislative, executive, and judicial functions. Their rules and regulations are usually directed toward business enterprises—be they sole proprietorships, partnerships, or corporations.

Following is a selected list of primary objectives of such governmental action, with the related law or concerned government agency identified.

To maintain free and fair competition:

- The Sherman Antitrust Act
- The Clayton Act

To guarantee the rights of labor and management in collective bargaining over wages, hours, and conditions of employment:

- The National Labor Relations Act
- The National Labor-Management Relations Act

To aid farmers and encourage production of wholesome food:

- Laws that control output, quality, and price of basic crops and dairy products

ASSESS

Have students determine if the following statements about governmental objectives achieved through administrative agencies are *True* or *False*: **(1) The Clayton Act was created to help maintain free and fair competition.** (True); **(2) To aid farmers, the government created the National Labor Relations Act.** (False); and **(3) The Federal Reserve Board was created to promote social and economic well-being by controlling credit and the money supply.** (True)

To promote the social and economic well-being of all:

- The Federal Reserve Board and its control over credit and money supply
- Government-built facilities for air, highway, and sea transportation
- Governmental commitment to public-supported education from kindergarten through college and beyond

To provide a wholesome and stable social environment:

- The vast social security program
- The legal commitment to equal employment opportunity
- The provision of government "safety nets" for the unemployed and others in need
- The availability of police and firefighters on the domestic front and of efficient armed services on the international front

You can think of many additions to the above list (see Figure 38-3). Many of these governmental activities are controversial. Over the years a

Federal Administrative Agency	*Area of Action*
Equal Employment Opportunity Commission (EEOC)	Employment rights
Federal Aviation Admin. (FAA)	Airplane and airport safety
Federal Communications Commission (FCC)	Radio, television, interstate telephone, and telegraph communication
Federal Trade Commission (FTC)	Unfair trade practices and monopolies
Internal Revenue Service (IRS)	Income tax collection
Interstate Commerce Commission (ICC)	Railroad, truck, bus, and inland waterway transportation
National Labor Relations Board (NLRB)	Labor-management relations
Occupational Safety and Health Admin. (OSHA)	Employees' protection from on-the-job hazards
Securities and Exchange Commission (SEC)	Stocks and bonds sales
Small Business Admin. (SBA)	Advice and aid to small businesses
Social Security Admin. (SSA)	Retirement, survivors', disability, and health insurance

Figure 38-3
Activities of sole proprietorships, partnerships, and corporations are regulated by governmental administrative agencies at the federal, state, and local levels.

Thinking Critically Through Visuals

This chart shows some of the federal administrative agencies that regulate the business of partnerships, sole proprietorships, and corporations. Which agency might you contact if you needed a loan to open up a local store? (Small Business Administration) **Which agency would you notify if you experienced discrimination by your employer?** (Equal Employment Opportunity Commission)

Have students orally summarize in their own words what they have learned in this course about the far-reaching impact of law on business.

Have students create a poster-size chart to summarize the primary objectives of government action with the related laws or agencies identified on pp. 774–775.

Thinking Critically Through Visuals

States, counties, and cities have administrative agencies that govern certain areas of business. Which agencies handle transportation concerns? (Airport Board and Transit Authority) **What types of transportation would fall under the Transit Authorities' jurisdiction?** (Subways, trains, buses)

Have students recategorize the agencies, using the information from Figure 38-3 (Continued), and place them in the following chart:

	Agency	Action	Federal(F) State(S) County/ City(C)
Business			
Education			
Transportation			
Housing			
Environment			
Communication			
Consumer Products			

Figure 38-3
(Continued)

State Administrative Agency	***Area of Action***
Agricultural Price Stabilization Board	Food production quotas and prices
Alcoholic Beverage Control Board	Liquor licenses and sales
Public Utilities Commission	Electricity, gas, and telephone rates and service
Workers' Compensation Board	Services for work-related diseases, injuries, and deaths

County and City Administrative Agencies	***Area of Action***
Air Pollution Control Board	Air purity
Airport Board	Operation of airports
Library Board	Operation of libraries
Parks and Recreation Board	Operation of parks
Planning Commission	Land use and development
Public Housing Authority	Construction and operation of public housing projects
Redevelopment Agency	Clearance and redevelopment of slum areas
School Board	Construction and operation of local public schools
Transit Authority	Construction and operation of local mass transit systems

debate has gone on between persons who want more government taxing-spending-regulating, and those who want less of all three. In the problem at the beginning of this section, Jason is quite wrong. Directly or indirectly everyone pays taxes, and to a greater or lesser degree everyone is affected by the great variety of laws that govern us.

With your knowledge of "Law for Business," you are better prepared to participate intelligently in this continuing debate.

Preventing Legal Difficulties

With the corporate form of business organization . . .

1. Directors, even if outsiders, should take their work seriously. They should obey all laws, carefully study the corporate records, and use indepen-

dent judgment on policy decisions. To "rubber stamp" management proposals is to invite lawsuits by disgruntled shareholders if losses occur.

2 Officers of the corporation should be selected with great care because they make most of the day-to-day management decisions. Moreover, directors tend to rely on the advice of the officers.

3 Shareholders should not casually sign proxies that give directors continued control. When feasible, shareholders should exercise their voting rights intelligently after studying the annual reports of the corporation and comparing the corporation's progress with that of similar corporations.

4 Shareholders with a minority position have a better chance to be represented on the board if the company uses cumulative voting.

5 It is usually risky to buy stock in new or small, closely held corporations because:
a. they are more likely to fail,
b. the majority of shareholders may favor themselves with high salaries as officers and pay low or no dividends, and
c. it may be difficult to sell the shares to others.

6 The buyer of preferred stock who desires greater assurance of receiving dividends should seek cumulative and participating shares.

REVIEWING IMPORTANT POINTS

1 A corporation can be created only by government grant—available routinely under incorporation statutes in all states—or under unique circumstances, by special legislative acts of the U.S. Congress.

2 In most states, corporate existence begins when properly prepared articles of incorporation are filed in the office of the Secretary of State. (In some states, charters or certificates of incorporation are issued.)

3 Corporations are favored as a form of business organization because of advantages of (a) potential perpetual life, (b) limited liability of shareholders, (c) easy transferability of shares, (d) better access to capital, and (e) professional management. A major disadvantage is double taxation. Small corporations may eliminate double federal taxation by electing to be taxed like partnerships, as S corporations under a subchapter of the Internal Revenue Code.

Preventing Legal Difficulties

Using a computer, if possible, have students work in small groups to create brochures for prospective entrepreneurs considering forming new corporations. Encourage students to include the advice in parts 1–6 on pp. 776–777.

CLOSE

Before displaying the overhead transparency, *Legal Forms of Business You Will Work for—or Own—Some Day*, mask key context words, such as the number *35* under the number of owners permitted in an S corporation, under the headings *SOLE PROPRIETORSHIP*, *CORPORATION*, and *PARTNERSHIP*. Photocopy and distribute the page to students and have them fill in the blanks as an end-of-chapter review activity.

Assign the following end-of-chapter materials:
Student text review activities, pp. 777–782
Workbook, pp. 129–136
Chapter Test
Chapter *MicroExam*

Strengthening Your Legal Vocabulary

1 preferred stock
2 articles of incorporation
3 board of directors
4 shareholder
5 stock certificate
6 corporation
7 dividends
8 closely held corporation
9 proxy
10 merger

4 Shareholders generally have a right to:
- **a.** receive a properly executed stock certificate;
- **b.** freely transfer their shares of stock;
- **c.** attend shareholder meetings, and vote if they hold voting stock;
- **d.** maintain their ownership percentage by buying an appropriate portion of new stock issues, if there is a preemptive right;
- **e.** receive a proportionate share of the profits when dividends are declared;
- **f.** share proportionally in distributions of capital, and
- **g.** inspect the corporate books, subject to reasonable restrictions.

5 Certain classes of shares may be nonvoting. If preferred, they have priority in the distribution of dividends and capital upon termination.

6 The directors can enter into any contract necessary to promote the business for which the corporation was formed. They are liable only for willful or negligent acts that injure the corporation or its owners. They are not liable for honest mistakes of judgment regardless of how costly the mistakes may be. As fiduciaries, however, they must act with scrupulous good faith and in the best interests of the corporation and its shareholders.

7 Officers of a corporation, governed by the law of agency and employment, are also fiduciaries who must act with good faith for the best interests of the corporation and its shareholders. However, like directors, they are not liable for honest mistakes of judgment, however costly, but only for willful or negligent acts that injure the corporation or its owners.

8 The powers of a corporation include those granted by law, those incidental to corporate existence, and those listed in the articles of incorporation.

9 A corporation's existence may be ended by (a) specification by incorporators, or agreement (i.e., vote) of the shareholders, (b) forfeiture of the charter, (c) consolidation or merger, (d) bankruptcy, or (e) court order.

STRENGTHENING YOUR LEGAL VOCABULARY

Match each term with the statement that best defines that term. Some terms may not be used.

articles of incorporation
board of directors
bonds
bylaws
closely held corporation
common stock
consolidation
corporation
cumulative stock
cumulative voting

debentures
directors
dividends
domestic corporation
foreign corporation
incorporators
inside board
liquidation
market price
merger
mixed board
nonprofit corporation
no-par stock
outside board
participating stock
par value
perpetual succession
preemptive right
preferred stock
private corporation
profit-making corporation
promoters
proxy
public corporation
public service corporation
shareholder
shares of stock
stock certificate
S corporation

1. Stock (usually nonvoting) that has priority with respect to dividends and distribution of assets upon liquidation of the company.
2. Plan submitted to the state as an application for incorporation. When properly filed, corporate existence begins.
3. Governing body of a corporation that determines major policies, declares dividends, and appoints officers.
4. Person who owns one or more shares of stock.
5. Written evidence of ownership in a corporation.
6. Legal entity, created by governmental grant, existing separate from its owners, directors, officers, or other employees.
7. Distributions of corporate profits to shareholders.
8. Private corporation whose stock is held by one person or by a small group.
9. Written authorization designating some person to vote in place of the signer in a corporate election.
10. When one corporation absorbs and eliminates another corporation.

APPLYING LAW TO EVERYDAY LIFE

1. The Lacklands bought 5,000 shares of stock in Space Age Motion Pictures, Inc., a speculative company created to imitate the fabulous success of producers of such space dramas as *Star Wars*. Were the

Applying Law to Everyday Life

1. No; If the corporation earns profits and the directors decide not to distribute them, and then the corporation later fails, the Lacklands would lose their share of those undistributed profits. Also, if the stock pays no dividends and does not increase in market value, they lose imputed interest which they could have earned on their money if placed in some other investment. Beyond such exceptions, however, shareholders stand to lose only what they have invested in the corporation. (pp. 756–757)
2. Yes; This is a proper purpose for inspecting the corporate books. As shareholders, they have a good-faith interest in who runs the company and a right to promote the election of their own slate of directors. Without the corporate register, ledger, or list of shareholders, they may not be able to contact most of the other shareholders. (p. 771)

3 No, the corporation is a legal entity, separate from its shareholders, and they are not liable for its debts. (pp. 756–757) This is true even if, as here, one shareholder owns a majority, or all, of the shares.
4 No; Directors may name themselves officers. (p. 766) Moreover, as officers they may solicit proxies (pp. 769–770) from shareholders and then vote to keep themselves in power as directors.
5 No; Distribution of the product of the corporation as a dividend is permitted by law. (p. 771) Lane could presumably sell or give away his dolls if he so chose. There was added justification for the action of the directors in the fact that the dolls were in short supply and very popular.
6 Yes; Cox and Cook bought the land in their own names. They might have protected themselves against liability by making payment contingent on organization of the corporation, and also on subsequent adoption of the contract by the corporation. (p. 761) No; The corporation is not liable unless it adopts the contract, or enters into a novation. (p. 761)
7 No; Neither as directors nor as officers are they liable for losses caused by such honest errors of judgment. (p. 766) There was no fraud or illegality.

Lacklands correct when they said, "At $25 a share, we can't lose more than $125,000; one big hit and we're millionaires!"?

2 Lomax and Widener were among some 5,000 common shareholders of the Commonwealth Commodities Corporation. They owned 15 percent of the stock and were dissatisfied with the performance of the directors and managers because the company had shown a loss on operations for three successive years. Therefore they decided to solicit proxies from the other shareholders in order to elect a new "management team." The incumbent managers refused to let the two inspect the books to get the current list of shareholders. The managers called Lomax and Widener "meddlesome troublemakers" and said that "losses were caused by world overproduction of grains and the strong U.S. dollar which priced us out of the export market." This was true, according to most experts. Can Lomax and Widener get a court order to compel disclosure of the names?

3 Hull organized a corporation to manufacture antibiotics for cattle. She owned most of the capital stock. All went well until a faulty batch of drugs caused the serious illness or death of more than 3,000 cows. After a series of lawsuits, the corporation was forced into bankruptcy with some $200,000 in debts unpaid. Could Hull be held personally liable for these debts?

4 In a discussion with friends, Fascill insisted that a director of a corporation could not also serve as an officer because this would be "a conflict of interest." "Directors select officers," she argued, "and could keep themselves on the payroll as officers this way." Was Fascill right?

5 Plush Play Products, Ltd., produced toy animals and dolls. A new doll called "Tootsie Twins" proved to be so popular that the factory could not meet the demand. The dolls were commanding premium prices in toy stores. Shortly before Christmas, the board of directors of Plush Play Products voted a dividend that was to include one pair of the "Twins"—valued at the low $10 cost of production—for each stockholder. All shareholders with more than one share would receive the balance of their dividends in cash. Lane, a stockholder, sued the directors to prohibit the doll distribution. He claimed that the corporation could earn more by selling the dolls. Should the injunction be issued?

6 Cox and Cook had an idea for a natural waterslide. They planned to build a small dam and then to release water for the slide as needed. Keeping their plans secret to be certain that the needed stream would be available, they bought a 2,000-acre tract of land for their Wet n' Wild Ride, Inc., a corporation soon to be formed. At this time, are Cox and Cook liable on the contract? Two months later they organized the corporation. Is the corporation now liable on the contract?

7 All directors of the ABC Avionics Corporation were also officers of the corporation. As directors, all were involved in the unanimous decision to follow the advice of De Moreal, the dynamic president of ABC. He had presented engineering and marketing studies in support of a proposal to build a small helicopter that could also be used as a large automobile on public highways. After further study, the directors, as officers, proceeded with the plan to design, produce, and market the novel vehicle. Unfortunately, many unforeseen problems caused abandonment of the project after the corporation had spent, and thus lost, more than $25 million in development costs. Acting on behalf of the corporation, several stockholders sued the directors/officers for the full amount. Are they liable?

8 ETHICS ISSUE Fleecer was employed as a director and vice president of Mt. Everest Productions, a manufacturer of outdoor sports equipment. Without informing the other directors of the corporation, she bought control of a small company that manufactured specialty nylon and composite fabrics. It sold large quantities of its products to Mt. Everest at a profit. Its prices were fair and competitive, and the quality superior. Was Fleecer's conduct legal? Was it ethical?

9 ETHICS ISSUE In 1990, X, Y, and Z were directors and management officers of Gilded Lily Savings and Loan Association. Savings of depositors were insured against loss (for up to $100,000 per qualified account) by the Federal Savings and Loan Insurance Corporation (FSLIC), a federal agency. X, Y, and Z had negligently approved numerous mortgage loans to friends on real estate properties that were grossly overvalued by incompetent appraisers. When the loans came due, the borrowers simply defaulted, and Gilded Lily repossessed the properties. This in turn prevented the S&L from repaying its depositors. The FSLIC then closed the Gilded Lily but paid the depositors' insured account claims. This and similar S&L failures shifted the financial loss to all federal taxpayers. The final cost over thirty years will be an estimated total of more than $500 billion dollars including interest on money the U.S. Treasury Department must borrow. Was the negligent conduct of X, Y, and Z legal? Was it ethical?

10 The O'Brien adult children—two daughters and three sons—shared unusual talents in poetry and prose, as well as in humor, graphic arts, and salesmanship. The business of writing, manufacturing, and marketing a broad line of greeting cards appealed to all. Accordingly they formed a corporation: BLARNEY, INK., B'GOSH. How could they assure themselves that ownership and control of the business would remain within their family quintet?

8 ETHICS ISSUE No, her conduct was illegal. Even though the prices charged were fair and the quality was superior, Fleecer violated her fiduciary duty to the corporation in making a secret profit by means of the sales. (p. 764) She also probably violated her duty of loyalty because she acted simultaneously for the buyer, Mt. Everest, and for the seller, the fabric business. Her conduct was clearly unethical.

9 ETHICS ISSUE No, their conduct was illegal. (pp. 764, 766) X, Y, and Z might argue that continued inflation (and a resulting increase in real estate values) would eventually boost the true market value of the mortgaged properties to the level of their appraised values. This is not a valid argument. The loans should have been based on the genuine present values of the properties when the loans were made. There is no guarantee that inflation will continue, or that real estate values will continue to rise. Nor is there any way of predicting when such changes will take place. Their conduct was unethical.

10 The articles of incorporation could provide that when any owner died, retired, or withdrew, his or her shares of the common stock would have to be offered first to the corporation, or to the other stockholders in equal numbers. (p. 761) They could also facilitate payment to heirs or retirees without hurting the business by sudden withdrawal of a substantial amount of capital. This could be done by giving a suitable amount of nonvoting preferred stock to the heirs or retirees. (p. 763) Or, money, equal to a fair value, could be paid in installments over a period of perhaps five years.

Solving Case Problems

1 No; Pillsbury did not have a proper economic purpose in seeking the records which were germane to his interest as a shareholder. Rather, he was motivated by social and political beliefs that the corporation should not be manufacturing munitions for use in Vietnam, irrespective of economic benefits to himself or the corporation and other shareholders. (p. 771) To qualify for the right to inspect the corporate books, the shareholder must have an economic concern for the well-being of the corporation or the shareholder.

2 Yes; The evidence in this case indicated that the managing directors were imprudent, wasteful, careless, negligent, and unwise in their conduct of the business. (pp. 764–765) Loss in assets alone does not prove liability, however. Corporate directors are not insurers that their acts will result in profits; indeed, they are expected to take calculated business risks. Officers and directors should manage the business to promote the interests of all the shareholders.

SOLVING CASE PROBLEMS

1 Pillsbury believed that the U.S. involvement in the Vietnam War was wrong. When he learned that Honeywell, Inc., had a large governmental contract to produce antipersonnel fragmentation bombs, he became determined to stop such production. Pillsbury learned that a trust set up by his grandmother for his benefit owned 242 shares of the stock, but these shares were voted by the trustee. Therefore Pillsbury bought just one share in his own name. As a shareholder, he petitioned the court to order Honeywell to produce its shareholder ledgers and all records dealing with weapons manufacture. He wanted to communicate with other shareholders to change the board of directors and then to have the corporation stop making munitions. Should the court grant his request? (*Pillsbury v. Honeywell, Inc.*, 291 Minn. 322, 191 N.W.2d 406)

2 A group of shareholders of the Manganese Corporation of America sued the corporation and four officers who were also directors. The group of shareholders sought to recover damages for the corporation and all its shareholders. Evidence indicated that the officers and directors had negligently caused the corporation's assets to drop from $400,000 to $30,000 in less than two years by being wasteful, careless, and unwise. Are the officers and directors liable for the losses? (*Selheimer v. Manganese Corporation of America*, 423 Pa. 563, 224 A.2d 634)

3 General Telephone Company of Florida owned more than 1 percent of the stock of Florida Telephone Corporation. General sought to examine the latter's stock records in order to make a list of the names, addresses, and holdings of all shareholders. Florida refused, claiming that General intended to gain this information in order to buy more shares and thus get control of the corporation. Can General get a court order to compel the disclosure? (*Florida Telephone Corporation v. State ex rel. Peninsular Telephone Company*, 111 So. 2d 677, Fla.)

4 This is a derivative suit, brought on behalf of all the shareholders of the corporation. Schlensky, a minority stockholder in the Chicago National League Ball Club (Inc.) — owner of the Chicago Cubs — sued the corporation and its board of directors, including Philip K. Wrigley. Wrigley also was president and owned about 80 percent of the voting stock. Schlensky alleged negligence and mismanagement for failure to install floodlights to permit night games. He claimed that funds for the installation could be obtained and would be far more than recaptured by increased ticket sales. Allegedly Wrigley thought that baseball was a daytime sport and that night games would have a deteriorating effect on the neighborhood surrounding the ball park, and the other directors acquiesced. The trial court dismissed the complaint, and Schlensky appealed. How should the appellate court rule? (*Schlensky v. Wrigley*, 237 N.E.2d 776, Ill.)

3 Yes; Although a shareholder might be barred from confidential records which could be useful to competitors (for example, cost figures), he or she may not be barred from seeing a list of shareholders for purposes of contacting them. (p. 771)

4 Judgment affirmed for defendant Wrigley, et al. The decision about the lights is a proper one for the directors to make. Courts will not step in and interfere with the honest business judgment of directors,

SPECIAL SECTION

RULES OF PROFESSIONAL CONDUCT AND DISCIPLINE FOR ATTORNEYS

The Model Rules of Professional Conduct adopted by the House of Delegates of the American Bar Association define a lawyer's responsibilities to the profession, to clients, and to the public. These responsibilities fall into different categories. For example, many rules cover the lawyer-client relationship. Others cover the lawyer's role as counselor and advocate, transactions with persons other than clients, the lawyer's role in law firms and associations, public service by lawyers, the communication of information about the legal services that lawyers provide, and the maintenance of the integrity of the profession.

The rules governing the lawyer-client relationship call for the lawyer to provide competent representation and to act with reasonable diligence and promptness in representing clients. The lawyer must keep the client reasonably informed about the status of the matter at hand and provide understandable explanations to permit the client to make informed decisions regarding the representation. Fees charged must be reasonable, and, when the lawyer has not regularly represented the client, the basis or rate of the fee must be communicated to the client before or within a reasonable time after commencing the relationship. A lawyer cannot reveal information relating to the representation unless the client consents or the lawyer has to do so to prevent the client from committing a criminal act likely to result in imminent death or substantial bodily harm. Potential conflict of interest situations are also closely regulated by the rules.

Under the rules governing the lawyer as an advocate, the lawyer is called on to make reasonable efforts to expedite litigation — as long as the client's interests are not jeopardized — and to refrain from bringing frivolous matters before the court. The lawyer must act with candor in relations with the court and must not unlawfully obstruct access to or falsify evidence. Publicity initiated by the

Special Section: Rules of Professional Conduct and Discipline for Attorneys

Have students read excerpts from a novel, listen to portions of an audiotape, or view scenes from a film that deals with the professional conduct and discipline of attorneys. Recommend the following novels: *The Firm, The Pelican Brief,* or *The Client,* all by John Grisham; *Presumed Innocent* by Scott Turow; *The Road to Omaha* by Robert Ludlum; *Final Agreement* by Clifford Irving, and others you may find appropriate and timely.

Then, have students give oral reports relating the following responsibilities of lawyers to their clients, to the public at large, and to their profession to the book, tape, or movie they have selected:

- Provide competent representation and act with reasonable diligence and promptness in representing the client;
- Maintain confidentiality;
- Make reasonable efforts to expedite litigation;
- Inform appropriate professional authorities concerning a lawyer's or judge's misconduct.

unless there is a showing of fraud, illegality, or conflict of interest. (pp. 764–765) Here, none is shown in the alleged motives, or otherwise. Schlensky did not allege or prove that a net benefit would result for the corporation, considering all the costs involved or that profits of other teams in the league were directly related to the number of night games they played. His allegations that the corporation and the minority stockholders have been damaged by wrongful conduct of the directors is merely his personal conclusion and is not based on well-pleaded facts.

lawyer that might materially prejudice a trial is prohibited in many instances.

The rules call on the lawyer to render public-interest legal aid by providing professional services at no charge or for reduced fees to persons of limited means, to public service groups, and to charitable organizations.

Every lawyer who knows that another lawyer has committed a serious violation of the Rules of Professional Conduct is required to inform the appropriate professional authority. Also, any lawyer with knowledge of similar misconduct by a judge must inform the appropriate authority.

The Rules of Professional Conduct are the foundation of an internal control system designed to maintain the integrity of the legal profession.

784

APPENDIX A

CONSTITUTION OF THE UNITED STATES

We the People of the United States, in Order to form a more perfect Union, establish Justice, insure domestic Tranquility, provide for the common defence, promote the general Welfare, and secure the Blessings of Liberty to ourselves and our Posterity, do ordain and establish this Constitution for the United States of America.

ARTICLE I.

Section 1. All legislative Powers herein granted shall be vested in a Congress of the United States, which shall consist of a Senate and House of Representatives.

Section 2. The House of Representatives shall be composed of Members chosen every second Year by the People of the several States, and the Electors in each State shall have the Qualifications requisite for Electors of the most numerous Branch of the State Legislature.

No Person shall be a Representative who shall not have attained to the Age of twenty five Years, and been seven Years a Citizen of the United States, and who shall not, when elected, be an inhabitant of that State in which he shall be chosen.

[Representatives and direct Taxes shall be apportioned among the several States which may be included within this Union, according to their respective Numbers, which shall be determined by adding to the whole Number of free Persons, including those bound to Service for a Term of Years, and excluding Indians not taxed, three fifths of all other Persons.][1] The actual Enumeration shall be made within three Years after the first Meeting of the Congress of the United States, and within every subsequent Term of ten Years, in such Manner as they shall by Law direct. The number of Representatives shall not exceed one for every thirty Thousand, but each

[1]Changed by section 2 of the Fourteenth Amendment.

785

State shall have at Least one Representative; and until such enumeration shall be made, the State of New Hampshire shall be entitled to chuse three, Massachusetts eight, Rhode-Island and Providence Plantations one, Connecticut five, New-York six, New Jersey four, Pennsylvania eight, Delaware one, Maryland six, Virginia ten, North Carolina five, South Carolina five, and Georgia three.

When vacancies happen in the Representation from any State, the Executive Authority thereof shall issue Writs of Election to fill such Vacancies.

The House of Representatives shall chuse their Speaker and other Officers; and shall have the sole Power of Impeachment.

Section 3. The Senate of the United States shall be composed of two Senators from each State, [chosen by the Legislature thereof,][2] for six Years; and each Senator shall have one Vote.

Immediately after they shall be assembled in Consequence of the first Election, they shall be divided as equally as may be into three Classes. The Seats of the Senators of the first Class shall be vacated at the Expiration of the second Year, of the second Class at the Expiration of the fourth Year, and of the third Class at the Expiration of the sixth Year, so that one third may be chosen every second Year; [and if Vacancies happen by Resignation, or otherwise, during the Recess of the Legislature of any State, the Executive thereof may make temporary Appointments until the next Meeting of the Legislature, which shall then fill such Vacancies.][3]

No Person shall be a Senator who shall not have attained to the Age of thirty Years, and been nine Years a Citizen of the United States, and who shall not, when elected, be an Inhabitant of that State for which he shall be chosen.

The Vice-President of the United States shall be President of the Senate, but shall have no Vote, unless they be equally divided.

The Senate shall chuse their other Officers, and also a President pro tempore, in the Absence of the Vice-President, or when he shall exercise the Office of President of the United States.

The Senate shall have the sole Power to try all Impeachments. When sitting for that Purpose, they shall be on Oath or Affirmation. When the President of the United States is tried, the Chief Justice shall preside: And no Person shall be convicted without the Concurrence of two thirds of the Members present.

Judgment in Cases of Impeachment shall not extend further than to removal from Office, and disqualification to hold and enjoy any Office of

[2]Changed by the Seventeenth Amendment.

[3]Changed by the Seventeenth Amendment.

honor, Trust or Profit under the United States: but the Party convicted shall nevertheless be liable and subject to Indictment, Trial, Judgment and Punishment, according to Law.

Section 4. The Times, Places and Manner of holding Elections for Senators and Representatives, shall be prescribed in each State by the Legislature thereof; but the Congress may at any time by Law make or alter such Regulations, except as to the Places of chusing Senators.

The Congress shall assemble at least once in every Year, and such Meeting shall be [on the first Monday in December,][4] unless they shall by Law appoint a different Day.

Section 5. Each House shall be the Judge of the Elections, Returns and Qualifications of its own Members, and a Majority of each shall constitute a Quorum to do Business; but a smaller Number may adjourn from day to day, and may be authorized to compel the Attendance of absent Members, in such Manner, and under such Penalties as each House may provide.

Each House may determine the Rules of its Proceedings, punish its Members for disorderly Behaviour, and, with the Concurrence of two thirds, expel a Member.

Each House shall keep a Journal of its Proceedings, and from time to time publish the same, excepting such Parts as may in their Judgment require Secrecy; and the Yeas and Nays of the Members of either House on any question shall, at the Desire of one fifth of those Present, be entered on the Journal.

Neither House, during the Session of Congress, shall, without the Consent of the other, adjourn for more than three days, nor to any other Place than that in which the two Houses shall be sitting.

Section 6. The Senators and Representatives shall receive a Compensation for their Services, to be ascertained by Law, and paid out of the Treasury of the United States. They shall in all Cases, except Treason, Felony and Breach of the Peace, be privileged from Arrest during their Attendance at the Session of their respective Houses, and in going to and returning from the same; and for any Speech or Debate in either House, they shall not be questioned in any other Place.

No Senator or Representative shall, during the Time for which he was elected, be appointed to any civil Office under the Authority of the United States, which shall have been created, or the Emoluments whereof shall have been encreased during such time; and no Person holding any Office

[4]Changed by the Twentieth Amendment.

under the United States, shall be a Member of either House during his Continuance in Office.

Section 7. All Bills for raising Revenue shall originate in the House of Representatives; but the Senate may propose or concur with Amendments as on other Bills.

Every Bill which shall have passed the House of Representatives and the Senate, shall, before it becomes a Law, be presented to the President of the United States; If he approve he shall sign it, but if not he shall return it, with his Objections to that House in which it shall have originated, who shall enter the Objections at large on their Journal, and proceed to reconsider it. If after such Reconsideration two thirds of that House shall agree to pass the Bill, it shall be sent, together with the Objections, to the other House, by which it shall likewise be reconsidered, and if approved by two thirds of that House, it shall become a Law. But in all such Cases the Votes of both Houses shall be determined by yeas and Nays, and the Names of the Persons voting for and against the Bill shall be entered on the Journal of each House respectively. If any Bill shall not be returned by the President within ten Days (Sundays excepted) after it shall have been presented to him, the Same shall be a Law, in like Manner as if he had signed it, unless the Congress by their Adjournment prevent its Return, in which Case it shall not be a Law.

Every Order, Resolution, or Vote to which the Concurrence of the Senate and House of Representatives may be necessary (except on a question of Adjournment) shall be presented to the President of the United States; and before the Same shall take Effect, shall be approved by him, or being disapproved by him, shall be repassed by two thirds of the Senate and House of Representatives, according to the Rules and Limitations prescribed in the Case of a Bill.

Section 8. The Congress shall have Power To lay and collect Taxes, Duties, Imposts and Excises, to pay the Debts and provide for the common Defence and general Welfare of the United States; but all Duties, Imposts and Excises shall be uniform throughout the United States;

To borrow Money on the credit of the United States;

To regulate Commerce with foreign Nations, and among the several States, and with the Indian Tribes;

To establish an uniform Rule of Naturalization, and uniform Laws on the subject of Bankruptcies throughout the United States;

To coin Money, regulate the Value thereof, and of foreign Coin, and fix the Standard of Weights and Measures;

To provide for the Punishment of counterfeiting the Securities and current Coin of the United States;

To establish Post Offices and post Roads;

To promote the Progress of Science and useful Arts, by securing for limited Times to Authors and Inventors the exclusive Right to their respective Writings and Discoveries;

To constitute Tribunals inferior to the supreme Court;

To define and punish Piracies and Felonies committed on the high Seas, and Offenses against the Law of Nations;

To declare War, grant Letters of Marque and Reprisal, and make Rules concerning Captures on Land and Water;

To raise and support Armies, but no Appropriation of Money to that Use shall be for a longer Term than two Years;

To provide and maintain a Navy;

To make Rules for the Government and Regulation of the land and naval Forces;

To provide for calling forth the Militia to execute the Laws of the Union, suppress Insurrections and repel Invasions;

To provide for organizing, arming, and disciplining, the Militia, and for governing such Part of them as may be employed in the Service of the United States, reserving to the States respectively, the Appointment of the Officers, and the Authority of training the Militia according to the discipline prescribed by Congress;

To exercise exclusive Legislation in all Cases whatsoever, over such District (not exceeding ten Miles square) as may, by Cession of particular States, and the Acceptance of Congress, become the Seat of the Government of the United States, and to exercise like Authority over all Places purchased by the Consent of the Legislature of the State in which the Same shall be, for the Erection of Forts, Magazines, Arsenals, dock-Yards and other needful Buildings; — And

To make all Laws which shall be necessary and proper for carrying into Execution the foregoing Powers, and all other Powers vested by this Constitution in the Government of the United States, or in any Department or Officer thereof.

Section 9. The Migration or Importation of such Persons as any of the States now existing shall think proper to admit, shall not be prohibited by the Congress prior to the Year one thousand eight hundred and eight, but a Tax or duty may be imposed on such Importation, not exceeding ten dollars for each Person.

The Privilege of the Writ of Habeas Corpus shall not be suspended, unless when in Cases of Rebellion or Invasion the public Safety may require it.

No Bill of Attainder or ex post facto Law shall be passed.

No Capitation, or other direct, Tax shall be laid, unless in Proportion to the Census or Enumeration herein before directed to be taken.

No Tax or Duty shall be laid on Articles exported from any State.

No Preference shall be given by any Regulation of Commerce or Revenue to the Ports of one State over those of another: nor shall Vessels bound to, or from, one State, be obliged to enter, clear, or pay Duties in another.

No Money shall be drawn from the Treasury, but in Consequence of Appropriations made by Law; and a regular Statement and Account of the Receipts and Expenditures of all public Money shall be published from time to time.

No Title of Nobility shall be granted by the United States: And no Person holding any Office of Profit or Trust under them, shall, without the Consent of the Congress, accept of any present, Emolument, Office, or Title, of any kind whatever, from any King, Prince, or foreign State.

Section 10. No State shall enter into any Treaty, Alliance, or Confederation; grant Letters of Marque and Reprisal; coin Money; emit Bills of Credit; make any Thing but gold and silver Coin a Tender in Payment of Debts; pass any Bill of Attainder, ex post facto Law, or Law impairing the Obligation of Contracts, or grant any Title of Nobility.

No State shall, without the Consent of the Congress, lay any Imposts or Duties on Imports or Exports, except what may be absolutely necessary for executing its inspection Laws: and the net Produce of all Duties and Imposts, laid by any State on Imports or Exports, shall be for the Use of the Treasury of the United States; and all such Laws shall be subject to the Revision and Controul of the Congress.

No State shall, without the Consent of Congress, lay any Duty of Tonnage, keep Troops, or Ships of War in time of Peace, enter into any Agreement or Compact with another State, or with a foreign Power, or engage in War, unless actually invaded, or in such imminent Danger as will not admit of delay.

ARTICLE II.

Section 1. The executive Power shall be vested in a President of the United States of America. He shall hold his Office during the Term of four Years, and, together with the Vice-President, chosen for the same Term, be elected, as follows

Each State shall appoint, in such Manner as the Legislature thereof may direct, a Number of Electors, equal to the whole Number of Senators and Representatives to which the State may be entitled in the Congress: but no Senator or Representative, or Person holding an Office of Trust or Profit under the United States, shall be appointed an Elector.

[The Electors shall meet in their respective States, and vote by Ballot for two Persons, of whom one at least shall not be an Inhabitant of the same

State with themselves. And they shall make a List of all the Persons voted for, and of the Number of Votes for each; which List they shall sign and certify, and transmit sealed to the Seat of the Government of the United States, directed to the President of the Senate. The President of the Senate shall, in the Presence of the Senate and House of Representatives, open all the Certificates, and the Votes shall then be counted. The Person having the greatest Number of Votes shall be the President, if such Number be a Majority, of the whole Number of Electors appointed; and if there be more than one who have such Majority and have an equal Number of Votes, then the House of Representatives shall immediately chuse by Ballot one of them for President, and if no Person have a Majority, then from the five highest on the List the said House shall in like Manner chuse the President. But in chusing the President, the Votes shall be taken by States, the Representation from each State having one Vote; A quorum for this Purpose shall consist of a Member or Members from two thirds of the States, and a Majority of all the States shall be necessary to a Choice. In every Case, after the Choice of the President, the Person having the greatest Number of Votes of the Electors shall be the Vice-President. But if there should remain two or more who have equal Votes, the Senate shall chuse from them by Ballot the Vice-President.][5]

The Congress may determine the Time of chusing the Electors, and the Day on which they shall give their Votes; which Day shall be the same throughout the United States.

No Person except a natural born Citizen, or a Citizen of the United States, at the time of the Adoption of this Constitution, shall be eligible to the Office of the President; neither shall any person be eligible to that Office who shall not have attained to the Age of thirty five Years, and been fourteen Years a Resident within the United States.

[In Case of the Removal of the President from Office, or of his Death, Resignation, or Inability to discharge the Powers and Duties of the said Office, the Same shall devolve on the Vice-President, and the Congress may by Law provide for the Case of Removal, Death, Resignation or Inability, both of the President and Vice-President, declaring what Officer shall then act as President, and such Officer shall act accordingly, until the Disability be removed, or a President shall be elected.][6]

The President shall, at stated Times, receive for his Services, a Compensation, which shall neither be increased nor diminished during the Period for which he shall have been elected, and he shall not receive within that Period any other Emolument from the United States, or any of them.

[5]Superseded by the Twelfth Amendment.

[6]Modified by the Twenty-Fifth Amendment.

Before he enter on the Execution of his Office, he shall take the following Oath or Affirmation: — "I do solemnly swear (or affirm) that I will faithfully execute the Office of President of the United States, and will to the best of my Ability, preserve, protect and defend the Constitution of the United States."

Section 2. The President shall be Commander in Chief of the Army and Navy of the United States, and of the Militia of the several States, when called into the actual Service of the United States; he may require the Opinion, in writing, of the principal Officer in each of the executive Departments, upon any Subject relating to the Duties of their respective Offices, and he shall have Power to grant Reprieves and Pardons for Offenses against the United States, except in Cases of Impeachment.

He shall have Power, by and with the Advice and Consent of the Senate, to make Treaties, provided two thirds of the Senators present concur; and he shall nominate, and by and with the Advice and Consent of the Senate, shall appoint Ambassadors, other public Ministers and Consuls, Judges of the supreme Court, and all other Officers of the United States, whose Appointments are not herein otherwise provided for, and which shall be established by Law: but the Congress may by Law vest the Appointment of such inferior Officers, as they think proper, in the President alone, in the Courts of Law, or in the Heads of Departments.

The President shall have Power to fill up all Vacancies that may happen during the Recess of the Senate, by granting Commissions which shall expire at the End of their next Session.

Section 3. He shall from time to time give to the Congress Information of the State of the Union, and recommend to their Consideration such measures as he shall judge necessary and expedient; he may, on extraordinary Occasions, convene both Houses, or either of them, and in Case of Disagreement between them, with Respect to the Time of Adjournment, he may adjourn them to such Time as he shall think proper; he shall receive Ambassadors and other public Ministers; he shall take Care that the Laws be faithfully executed, and shall Commission all the Officers of the United States.

Section 4. The President, Vice-President and all civil Officers of the United States, shall be removed from Office on Impeachment for, and Conviction of, Treason, Bribery, or other high Crimes and Misdemeanors.

ARTICLE III.

Section 1. The judicial Power of the United States, shall be vested in one supreme Court, and in such inferior Courts as the Congress may from time to time ordain and establish. The Judges, both of the supreme and inferior Courts, shall hold their Offices during good Behaviour, and shall, at stated Times, receive for their Services, a Compensation, which shall not be diminished during their Continuance in Office.

Section 2. The judicial Power shall extend to all Cases, in Law and Equity, arising under this Constitution, the Laws of the United States, and Treaties made, or which shall be made, under their Authority;—to all Cases affecting Ambassadors, other public Ministers and Consuls;—to all Cases of admiralty and maritime Jurisdiction;—to Controversies to which the United States shall be a Party;—to Controversies between two or more States; between a State and Citizens of another State;—between Citizens of different States—between Citizens of the same State claiming Lands under Grants of different States, and between a State, or the Citizens thereof, and foreign States, Citizens or Subjects.

In all Cases affecting Ambassadors, other public Ministers and Consuls, and those in which a State shall be Party, the supreme Court shall have original Jurisdiction. In all the other Cases before mentioned, the supreme Court shall have appellate Jurisdiction, both as to Law and Fact, with such Exceptions, and under such Regulations as the Congress shall make.

The Trial of all Crimes, except in Cases of Impeachment, shall be by Jury; and such Trial shall be held in the State where the said Crimes shall have been committed; but when not committed within any State, the Trial shall be at such Place or Places as the Congress may by Law have directed.

Section 3. Treason against the United States, shall consist only in levying War against them, or in adhering to their Enemies, giving them Aid and Comfort. No Person shall be convicted of Treason unless on the Testimony of two Witnesses to the same overt Act, or on Confession in open Court.

The Congress shall have Power to declare the Punishment of Treason, but no Attainder of Treason shall work Corruption of Blood, or Forfeiture except during the Life of the Person attained.

ARTICLE IV.

Section 1. Full Faith and Credit shall be given in each State to the public Acts, Records, and judicial Proceedings of every other State; And the

Congress may by general Laws prescribe the Manner in which such Acts, Records and Proceedings shall be proved, and the Effect thereof.

Section 2. The Citizens of each State shall be entitled to all Privileges and Immunities of Citizens in the several States.

A Person charged in any State with Treason, Felony, or other Crime, who shall flee from Justice, and be found in another State, shall on Demand of the executive Authority of the State from which he fled, be delivered up, to be removed to the State having Jurisdiction of the Crime.

[No Person held to Service or Labour in one State, under the Laws thereof, escaping into another, shall, in Consequence of any Law or Regulation therein, be discharged from such Service or Labour, but shall be delivered up on Claim of the Party to whom such Service or Labour may be due.][7]

Section 3. New States may be admitted by the Congress into this Union; but no new State shall be formed or erected within the Jurisdiction of any other State; nor any State be formed by the Junction of two or more States, or Parts of States, without the Consent of the Legislatures of the States concerned as well as of the Congress.

The Congress shall have Power to dispose of and make all needful Rules and Regulations respecting the Territory or other Property belonging to the United States; and nothing in this Constitution shall be so construed as to Prejudice any Claims of the United States, or of any particular State.

Section 4. The United States shall guarantee to every state in this Union a Republican Form of Government, and shall protect each of them against Invasion; and on Application of the Legislature, or of the Executive (when the Legislature cannot be convened) against domestic Violence.

ARTICLE V.

The Congress, whenever two thirds of both Houses shall deem it necessary, shall propose Amendments to this Constitution, or, on the Application of the Legislatures of two thirds of the several States, shall call a Convention for proposing Amendments, which, in either Case, shall be valid to all Intents and Purposes, as Part of this Constitution, when ratified by the Legislatures of three fourths of the several States, or by Conventions in three fourths thereof, as the one or the other Mode of Ratification may be proposed by the Congress; Provided that no Amendment which may be made prior to the Year One thousand eight hundred and eight shall in any

[7]Superseded by the Thirteenth Amendment.

Manner affect the first and fourth Clauses in the Ninth Section of the first Article; and that no State, without its Consent, shall be deprived of its equal Suffrage in the Senate.

ARTICLE VI.

All Debts contracted and Engagements entered into, before the Adoption of this Constitution, shall be as valid against the United States under this Constitution, as under the Confederation.

This Constitution, and the Laws of the United States which shall be made in Pursuance thereof; and all Treaties made, or which shall be made, under the Authority of the United States, shall be the supreme Law of the Land; and the Judges in every State shall be bound thereby, any Thing in the Constitution or Laws of any State to the Contrary notwithstanding.

The Senators and Representatives before mentioned, and the Members of the several State Legislatures, and all executive and judicial Officers, both of the United States and of the several States, shall be bound by Oath or Affirmation, to support this Constitution; but no religious Test shall ever be required as a Qualification to any Office or public Trust under the United States.

ARTICLE VII.

The Ratification of the Conventions of nine States, shall be sufficient for the Establishment of this Constitution between the States so ratifying the Same.

Done in Convention by the Unanimous Consent of the States present the Seventeenth Day of September in the Year of our Lord one thousand seven hundred and Eighty seven and of the Independence of the United States of America the Twelfth In Witness whereof We have hereunto subscribed our Names,

G.° Washington—Presid.
and deputy from Virginia

AMENDMENT I.[8]

Congress shall make no law respecting an establishment of religion, or prohibiting the free exercise thereof; or abridging the freedom of speech, or of the press, or the right of the people peaceably to assemble, and to petition the Government for a redress of grievances.

[8]The first ten Amendments (Bill of Rights) were ratified effective December 15, 1791.

AMENDMENT II.

A well regulated Militia, being necessary to the security of a free State, the right of the people to keep and bear Arms, shall not be infringed.

AMENDMENT III.

No Soldier shall, in time of peace be quartered in any house, without the consent of the Owner, nor in time of war, but in a manner to be prescribed by law.

AMENDMENT IV.

The right of the people to be secure in their persons, houses, papers, and effects, against unreasonable searches and seizures, shall not be violated, and no Warrants shall issue, but upon probable cause, supported by Oath or affirmation, and particularly describing the place to be searched, and the persons or things to be seized.

AMENDMENT V.

No person shall be held to answer for a capital, or otherwise infamous crime, unless on a presentment or indictment of a Grand Jury, except in cases arising in the land or naval forces, or in the Militia, when in actual service in time of War or public danger; nor shall any person be subject for the same offence to be twice put in jeopardy of life or limb, nor shall be compelled in any criminal case to be a witness against himself, nor be deprived of life, liberty, or property, without due process of law; nor shall private property be taken for public use without just compensation.

AMENDMENT VI.

In all criminal prosecutions, the accused shall enjoy the right to a speedy and public trial, by an impartial jury of the State and district wherein the crime shall have been committed; which district shall have been previously ascertained by law, and to be informed of the nature and cause of the accusation; to be confronted with the witnesses against him; to have compulsory process for obtaining witnesses in his favor, and to have the assistance of counsel for his defence.

AMENDMENT VII.

In Suits at common law, where the value in controversy shall exceed twenty dollars, the right of trial by jury shall be preserved, and no fact tried by a jury shall be otherwise re-examined in any Court of the United States, than according to the rules of the common law.

AMENDMENT VIII.

Excessive bail shall not be required, nor excessive fines imposed, nor cruel and unusual punishments inflicted.

AMENDMENT IX.

The enumeration in the Constitution of certain rights shall not be construed to deny or disparage others retained by the people.

AMENDMENT X.

The powers not delegated to the United States by the Constitution, nor prohibited by it to the States, are reserved to the States respectively, or to the people.

AMENDMENT XI.[9]

The Judicial power of the United States shall not be construed to extend to any suit in law or equity, commenced or prosecuted against one of the United States by Citizens of another State, or by Citizens or Subjects of any Foreign State.

AMENDMENT XII.[10]

The Electors shall meet in their respective states, and vote by ballot for President and Vice-President, one of whom, at least, shall not be an inhabitant of the same state with themselves; they shall name in their ballots the person voted for as President, and in distinct ballots the person voted for as Vice-President, and they shall make distinct lists of all persons voted for as President, and of all persons voted for as Vice-President, and of the number of votes for each, which lists they shall sign and certify, and transmit sealed to the seat of the government of the United States, directed to the President of the Senate;—The President of the Senate shall, in the presence of the Senate and House of Representatives, open all the certificates and the votes shall then be counted;—The person having the greatest number of votes for President shall be the President, if such number be a majority of

[9]The Eleventh Amendment was ratified February 7, 1795.

[10]The Twelfth Amendment was ratified June 15, 1804.

the whole number of Electors appointed; and if no person have such majority, then from the persons having the highest numbers not exceeding three on the list of those voted for as President, the House of Representatives shall choose immediately, by ballot, the President. But in choosing the President, the votes shall be taken by states, the representation from each state having one vote; a quorum for this purpose shall consist of a member or members from two-thirds of the states, and a majority of all the states shall be necessary to a choice. [And if the House of Representatives shall not choose a President whenever the right of choice shall devolve upon them, before the fourth day of March next following, then the Vice-President shall act as President, as in the case of the death or other constitutional disability of the President—][11] The person having the greatest number of votes as Vice-President, shall be the Vice-President, if such number be a majority of the whole number of Electors appointed, and if no person have a majority, then from the two highest numbers on the list, the Senate shall choose the Vice-President; a quorum for the purpose shall consist of two-thirds of the whole number of Senators, and a majority of the whole number shall be necessary to a choice. But no person constitutionally ineligible to the office of President shall be eligible to that of Vice-President of the United States.

AMENDMENT XIII.[12]

Section 1. Neither slavery nor involuntary servitude, except as a punishment for a crime whereof the party shall have been duly convicted, shall exist within the United States, or any place subject to their jurisdiction.

Section 2. Congress shall have power to enforce this article by appropriate legislation.

AMENDMENT XIV.[13]

Section 1. All persons born or naturalized in the United States and subject to the jurisdiction thereof, are citizens of the United States and of the State wherein they reside. No State shall make or enforce any law which shall abridge the privileges or immunities of citizens of the United States; nor shall any State deprive any person of life, liberty, or property, without due process of law; nor deny to any person within its jurisdiction the equal protection of the laws.

[11]Superseded by section 3 of the Twentieth Amendment.

[12]The Thirteenth Amendment was ratified December 6, 1865.

[13]The Fourteenth Amendment was ratified July 9, 1868.

Section 2. Representatives shall be apportioned among the several States according to their respective numbers, counting the whole number of persons in each State, excluding Indians not taxed. But when the right to vote at any election for the choice of electors for President and Vice-President of the United States, Representatives in Congress, the Executive and Judicial officers of a State, or the members of the Legislature thereof, is denied to any of the male inhabitants of such State, being twenty-one years of age, and citizens of the United States, or in any way abridged, except for participation in rebellion, or other crime, the basis of representation therein shall be reduced in the proportion which the number of such male citizens shall bear to the whole number of male citizens twenty-one years of age in such State.

Section 3. No person shall be a Senator or Representative in Congress, or elector of President and Vice-President, or hold any office, civil or military, under the United States, or under any State, who, having previously taken an oath, as a member of Congress, or as an officer of the United States, or as a member of any State legislature, or as an executive or judicial officer of any State, to support the Constitution of the United States, shall have engaged in insurrection or rebellion against the same, or given aid or comfort to the enemies thereof. But Congress may by a vote of two-thirds of each House, remove such disability.

Section 4. The validity of the public debt of the United States, authorized by law, including debts incurred for payment of pensions and bounties for services in suppressing insurrection or rebellion, shall not be questioned. But neither the United States nor any State shall assume or pay any debt or obligation incurred in aid of insurrection or rebellion against the United States, or any claim for the loss or emancipation of any slave; but all such debts, obligations and claims shall be held illegal and void.

Section 5. The Congress shall have power to enforce, by appropriate legislation, the provisions of this article.

AMENDMENT XV.[14]

Section 1. The right of citizens of the United States to vote shall not be denied or abridged by the United States or by any State on account of race, color, or previous condition of servitude.

[14]The Fifteenth Amendment was ratified February 3, 1870.

Section 2. The Congress shall have power to enforce this article by appropriate legislation.

AMENDMENT XVI.[15]

The Congress shall have power to lay and collect taxes on incomes, from whatever source derived, without apportionment among the several States, and without regard to any census or enumeration.

AMENDMENT XVII.[16]

The Senate of the United States shall be composed of two Senators from each State, elected by the people thereof, for six years; and each Senator shall have one vote. The electors in each State shall have the qualifications requisite for electors of the most numerous branch of the State legislatures.

When vacancies happen in the representation of any State in the Senate, the executive authority of such State shall issue writs of election to fill such vacancies; *Provided,* That the legislature of any State may empower the executive thereof to make temporary appointments until the people fill the vacancies by election as the legislature may direct.

This amendment shall not be so construed as to affect the election or term of any Senator chosen before it becomes valid as part of the Constitution.

AMENDMENT XVIII.[17]

Section 1. After one year from the ratification of this article the manufacture, sale, or transportation of intoxicating liquors within, the importation thereof into, or the exportation thereof from the United States and all territory subject to the jurisdiction thereof for beverage purposes is hereby prohibited.

Section 2. The Congress and the several States shall have concurrent power to enforce this article by appropriate legislation.

Section 3. This article shall be inoperative unless it shall have been ratified as an amendment to the Constitution by the legislatures of the several States, as provided in the Constitution, within seven years from the date of the submission hereof to the States by the Congress.]

[15]The Sixteenth Amendment was ratified February 3, 1913.

[16]The Seventeenth Amendment was ratified April 8, 1913.

[17]The Eighteenth Amendment was ratified January 16, 1919. It was repealed by the Twenty-First Amendment, December 5, 1933.

AMENDMENT XIX.[18]

The right of citizens of the United States to vote shall not be denied or abridged by the United States or by any State on account of sex.

Congress shall have power to enforce this article by appropriate legislation.

AMENDMENT XX.[19]

Section 1. The terms of the President and Vice-President shall end at noon on the 20th day of January, and the terms of Senators and Representatives at noon on the 3rd day of January, of the years in which such terms would have ended if this article had not been ratified; and the terms of their successors shall then begin.

Section 2. The Congress shall assemble at least once a year, and such meeting shall begin at noon on the 3rd day of January, unless they shall by law appoint a different day.

Section 3. If, at the time fixed for the beginning of the term of the President, the President elect shall have died, the Vice-President elect shall become President. If a President shall not have been chosen before the time fixed for the beginning of his term, or if the President elect shall have failed to qualify, then the Vice-President elect shall act as President until a President shall have qualified; and the Congress may by law provide for the case wherein neither a President elect nor a Vice-President elect shall have qualified, declaring who shall then act as President, or the manner in which one who is to act shall be selected, and such person shall act accordingly until a President or Vice-President shall have qualified.

Section 4. The Congress may by law provide for the case of the death of any of the persons from whom the House of Representatives may choose a President whenever the right of choice shall have devolved upon them, and for the case of the death of any of the persons from whom the Senate may choose a Vice-President whenever the right of choice shall have devolved upon them.

Section 5. Sections 1 and 2 shall take effect on the 15th day of October following the ratification of this article.

[18]The Nineteenth Amendment was ratified August 18, 1920.

[19]The Twentieth Amendment was ratified January 23, 1933.

Section 6. This article shall be inoperative unless it shall have been ratified as an amendment to the Constitution by the legislatures of three-fourths of the several States within seven years from the date of its submission.

AMENDMENT XXI.[20]

Section 1. The eighteenth article of amendment to the Constitution of the United States is hereby repealed.

Section 2. The transportation or importation into any State, Territory, or possession of the United States for delivery or use therein of intoxicating liquors, in violation of the laws thereof, is hereby prohibited.

Section 3. This article shall be inoperative unless it shall have been ratified as an amendment to the Constitution by conventions in the several States, as Provided in the Constitution, within seven years from the date of the submission hereof to the States by the Congress.

AMENDMENT XXII.[21]

Section 1. No person shall be elected to the office of the President more than twice, and no person who has held the office of President, or acted as President, for more than two years of a term to which some other person was elected President shall be elected to the office of the President more than once. But this Article shall not apply to any person holding the office of President when this Article was proposed by the Congress, and shall not prevent any person who may be holding the office of President, or acting as President, during the term within which this Article becomes operative from holding the office of President or acting as President during the remainder of such term.

Section 2. This article shall be inoperative unless it shall have been ratified as an amendment to the Constitution by the legislatures of three-fourths of the several States within seven years from the date of its submission to the States by the Congress.

AMENDMENT XXIII.[22]

Section 1. The District constituting the seat of Government of the United States shall appoint in such manner as the Congress may direct:

[20]The Twenty-First Amendment was ratified December 5, 1933.

[21]The Twenty-Second Amendment was ratified February 27, 1951.

[22]The Twenty-Third Amendment was ratified March 29, 1961.

A number of electors of President and Vice-President equal to the whole number of Senators and Representatives in Congress to which the District would be entitled if it were a State, but in no event more than the least populous State; they shall be in addition to those appointed by the States, but they shall be considered, for the purposes of the election of President and Vice-President, to be electors appointed by a State; and they shall meet in the District and perform such duties as provided by the twelfth article of amendment.

Section 2. The Congress shall have power to enforce this article by appropriate legislation.

AMENDMENT XXIV.[23]

Section 1. The right of citizens of the United States to vote in any primary or other election for President or Vice-President, for electors for President or Vice-President, or for Senator or Representative in Congress, shall not be denied or abridged by the United States or any State by reason of failure to pay any poll tax or other tax.

Section 2. The Congress shall have power to enforce this article by appropriate legislation.

AMENDMENT XXV.[24]

Section 1. In case of the removal of the President from office or of his death or resignation, the Vice-President shall become President.

Section 2. Whenever there is a vacancy in the office of the Vice-President, the President shall nominate a Vice-President who shall take office upon confirmation by a majority vote of both Houses of Congress.

Section 3. Whenever the President transmits to the President pro tempore of the Senate and the Speaker of the House of Representatives his written declaration that he is unable to discharge the powers and duties of his office, and until he transmits to them a written declaration to the contrary, such powers and duties shall be discharged by the Vice-President as Acting President.

Section 4. Whenever the Vice-President and a majority of either the principal officers of the executive departments or of such other body as

[23]The Twenty-Fourth Amendment was ratified January 23, 1964.

[24]The Twenty-Fifth Amendment was ratified February 10, 1967.

Congress may by law provide, transmit to the President pro tempore of the Senate and the Speaker of the House of Representatives their written declaration that the President is unable to discharge the powers and duties of his office, the Vice-President shall immediately assume the powers and duties of the office as Acting President.

Thereafter, when the President transmits to the President pro tempore of the Senate and the Speaker of the House of Representatives his written declaration that no inability exists, he shall resume the powers and duties of his office unless the Vice-President and a majority of either the principal officers of the executive department or of such other body as Congress may by law provide, transmit within four days to the President pro tempore of the Senate and the Speaker of the House of Representatives their written declaration that the President is unable to discharge the powers and duties of his office. Thereupon Congress shall decide the issue, assembling within forty-eight hours for that purpose if not in session. If the Congress, within twenty-one days after receipt of the latter written declaration, or, if Congress is not in session, within twenty-one days after Congress is required to assemble, determines by two-thirds vote of both Houses that the President is unable to discharge the powers and duties of his office, the Vice-President shall continue to discharge the same as Acting President; otherwise, the President shall resume the powers and duties of his office.

AMENDMENT XXVI.[25]

Section 1. The right of citizens of the United States, who are eighteen years of age or older, to vote shall not be denied or abridged by the United States or by any State on account of age.

Section 2. The Congress shall have power to enforce this article by appropriate legislation.

[25]The Twenty-Sixth Amendment was ratified July 1, 1971.

APPENDIX B

DECLARATION OF INDEPENDENCE

IN CONGRESS, JULY 4, 1776. **A DECLARATION** BY THE REPRESENTATIVES OF THE UNITED STATES OF AMERICA, IN GENERAL CONGRESS ASSEMBLED.

WHEN in the Course of human Events, it becomes necessary for one People to dissolve the Political Bands which have connected them with another, and to assume among the Powers of the Earth, the separate and equal Station to which the Laws of Nature and of Nature's God entitle them, a decent Respect to the Opinions of Mankind requires that they should declare the causes which impel them to the Separation.

WE hold these Truths to be self-evident, that all Men are created equal, that they are endowed by their Creator with certain unalienable Rights, that among these are Life, Liberty, and the Pursuit of Happiness—That to secure these Rights, Governments are instituted among Men, deriving their just Powers from the Consent of the Governed, that whenever any Form of Government becomes destructive of these Ends, it is the Right of the People to alter or to abolish it, and to institute new Government, laying its Foundation on such Principles, and organizing its Powers in such Form, as to them shall seem most likely to effect their Safety and Happiness. Prudence, indeed, will dictate that Governments long established should not be changed for light and transient Causes; and accordingly all Experience hath shewn, that Mankind are more disposed to suffer, while Evils are sufferable, than to right themselves by abolishing the Forms to which they are accustomed. But when a long Train of Abuses and Usurpations, pursuing invariably the same Object, evinces a Design to reduce them under absolute Despotism, it is their Right, it is their Duty, to throw off such Government, and to provide new Guards for their future Security. Such has been the patient Sufferance of these Colonies; and such is now the Necessity which constrains them to alter their former Systems of Government. The History of the present King of Great-Britain is a History of repeated Injuries and Usurpations, all having in direct Object the Establishment of an absolute

805

Tyranny over these States. To prove this, let Facts be submitted to a candid World.

HE has refused his Assent to Laws, the most wholesome and necessary for the public Good.

HE has forbidden his Governors to pass Laws of immediate and pressing Importance, unless suspended in their Operation till his Assent should be obtained; and when so suspended, he has utterly neglected to attend to them.

HE has refused to pass other Laws for the Accommodation of large Districts of People, unless those People would relinquish the Right of Representation in the Legislature, a Right inestimable to them, and formidable to Tyrants only.

HE has called together Legislative Bodies at Places unusual, uncomfortable, and distant from the Depository of their public Records, for the sole Purpose of fatiguing them into Compliance with his Measures.

HE has dissolved Representative Houses repeatedly, for opposing with manly Firmness his Invasions on the Rights of the People.

HE has refused for a long Time, after such Dissolutions, to cause others to be elected; whereby the Legislative Powers, incapable of Annihilation, have returned to the People at large for their exercise; the State remaining in the mean time exposed to all the Dangers of Invasion from without, and Convulsions within.

HE has endeavoured to prevent the Population of these States; for that Purpose obstructing the Laws for Naturalization of Foreigners; refusing to pass others to encourage their Migrations hither, and raising the Conditions of new Appropriations of Lands.

HE has obstructed the Administration of Justice, by refusing his Assent to Laws for establishing Judiciary Powers.

HE has made Judges dependent on his Will alone, for the Tenure of their Offices, and the Amount and Payment of their Salaries.

HE has erected a Multitude of new Offices, and sent hither Swarms of Officers to harrass our People, and eat out their Substance.

HE has kept among us, in Times of Peace, Standing Armies, without the consent of our Legislatures.

HE has affected to render the Military independent of and superior to the Civil Power.

HE has combined with others to subject us to a Jurisdiction foreign to our Constitution, and unacknowledged by our Laws; giving his Assent to their Acts of pretended Legislation:

FOR quartering large Bodies of Armed Troops among us:

FOR protecting them, by a mock Trial, from Punishment for any Murders which they should commit on the Inhabitants of these States:

FOR cutting off our Trade with all Parts of the World:

FOR imposing Taxes on us without our Consent:

FOR depriving us, in many Cases, of the Benefits of Trial by Jury:

FOR transporting us beyond Seas to be tried for pretended Offences:

FOR abolishing the free System of English Laws in a neighbouring Province, establishing therein an arbitrary Government, and enlarging its Boundaries, so as to render it at once an Example and fit Instrument for introducing the same absolute Rule into these Colonies:

FOR taking away our Charters, abolishing our most valuable Laws, and altering fundamentally the Forms of our Governments:

FOR suspending our own Legislatures, and declaring themselves invested with Power to legislate for us in all Cases whatsoever.

HE has abdicated Government here, by declaring us out of his Protection and waging War against us.

HE has plundered our Seas, ravaged our Coasts, burnt our Towns, and destroyed the Lives of our People.

HE is, at this Time, transporting large Armies of foreign Mercenaries to compleat the Works of Death, Desolation, and Tyranny, already begun with circumstances of Cruelty and Perfidy, scarcely paralleled in the most barbarous Ages, and totally unworthy the Head of a civilized Nation.

HE has constrained our fellow Citizens taken Captive on the high Seas to bear Arms against their Country, to become the Executioners of their Friends and Brethren, or to fall themselves by their Hands.

HE has excited domestic Insurrections amongst us, and has endeavoured to bring on the Inhabitants of our Frontiers, the merciless Indian Savages, whose known Rule of Warfare, is an undistinguished Destruction, of all Ages, Sexes and Conditions.

IN every stage of these Oppressions we have Petitioned for Redress in the most humble Terms: Our repeated Petitions have been answered only by repeated Injury. A Prince, whose Character is thus marked by every act which may define a Tyrant, is unfit to be the Ruler of a free People.

NOR have we been wanting in Attentions to our British Brethren. We have warned them from Time to Time of Attempts by their Legislature to extend an unwarrantable Jurisdiction over us. We have reminded them of the Circumstances of our Emigration and Settlement here. We have appealed to their native Justice and Magnanimity, and we have conjured them by the Ties of our common Kindred to disavow these Usurpations, which, would inevitably interrupt our Connections and Correspondence. They too have been deaf to the Voice of Justice and of Consanguinity. We must, therefore, acquiesce in the Necessity, which denounces our Separation, and hold them, as we hold the rest of Mankind, Enemies in War, in Peace, Friends.

WE, therefore, the Representatives of the UNITED STATES OF AMERICA, in GENERAL CONGRESS, Assembled, appealing to the Supreme Judge of the World for the Rectitude of our Intentions, do, in the Name, and by Authority of the good People of these Colonies, solemnly Publish and Declare, That these United Colonies are, and of Right ought to be, FREE AND INDEPENDENT STATES; that they are absolved from all Allegiance to the British Crown, and that all political Connection between them and the State of Great-Britain, is and ought to be totally dissolved; and that as FREE AND INDEPENDENT STATES, they have full Power to levy War, conclude Peace, contract Alliances, establish Commerce, and to do all other Acts and Things which INDEPENDENT STATES may of right do. And for the support of this Declaration, with a firm Reliance on the Protection of divine Providence, we mutually pledge to each other our Lives, our Fortunes, and our sacred Honor.

Signed by ORDER *and in* BEHALF *of the* CONGRESS,

JOHN HANCOCK, President.

ATTEST.

CHARLES THOMSON, SECRETARY.

PHILADELPHIA: PRINTED BY JOHN DUNLAP.

Glossary of Legal Terms

abstract of title: history of transfers of title to a parcel of land

acceleration clause: a clause stating that the entire balance is due and payable upon the happening of a certain event

acceptance: drawee's promise to pay the draft when due; also, affirmative response to an offer; also, buyer's approval of goods

acceptance of goods: the buyer's agreement, by words or by conduct, that the goods received are satisfactory

accession: the right of an owner of property to an increase in that property

accommodation party: a person who cosigns a commercial paper for someone who is not well known in the community or has not yet established credit

accord: an agreement to change the obligation required by the original contract

accord and satisfaction: agreement to change a contractual obligation, followed by the agreed-upon substituted performance

actual bailment: the bailee's receipt and acceptance of the goods themselves

actual cash value: property's purchase price less allowance for age and use

adaptation: process by which things that are essential for the purpose for which the real estate is used become part of the realty

administrative agencies: governmental bodies which administer certain statutes

administrative laws: rules and regulations created by administrative agencies to which legislative powers have been given by legislatures

administrator or administratrix: court-appointed representative of an intestate

adoption: legally taking another's child as one's own

adulterated: designating a product that does not meet the minimum standards for purity and quality set by the FDA

adverse possession: means of getting title to another's land by occupation without the owner's permission

affirmative action plan: a plan mandated by the courts to remedy the past discrimination of an employer

agency: relationship in which one person represents another in making contracts

agency shop: establishment in which nonunion members must pay union dues

agent: the person authorized to alter a legal relationship

alimony: support paid by the wage earner of the family to the other spouse according to the terms of the separation agreement

alteration: a material change in the terms of a written contract without consent of the other party

amendment: a change or alteration

809

annexation: an item's becoming annexed (attached) by permanent attachment to land or a building; it cannot be removed without material damage to the realty

annulled: declared legally void

annulment: judicial declaration that a marriage never existed

answer: defendant's statement in reply to the plaintiff's complaint

antedated: dated earlier than the date of issuance

anticipatory breach: notification, before the time of performance, of refusal to perform the contractual terms as agreed

antitrust laws: laws prohibiting business practices that interfere with free competition

apparent authority: power the agent appears to have

appellate court: court that reviews trial court decisions

appellate review: review of the results of a trial by a higher court

applicant pool: those qualified for a particular job

arbitrator: one who makes a decision that is binding on parties in a dispute

arson: the willful and illegal burning of a building

Articles of Confederation: the charter by which the original thirteen sovereign states united loosely in 1781

articles of incorporation: plan submitted to the state as an application for incorporation

artisan's lien: the right of persons who have not been paid for services to retain possession of any goods involved and sell them if payment is not made

assault: placing another in fear of harmful or offensive touching

assigned risk plan: an automobile insurance plan under which a person who has been refused insurance can apply to be assigned to an insurance company that will issue to that person the minimum liability insurance required by the state

assignee: the party to whom the assignment is made

assignment: transfer of contractual rights

assignment of a lease: the transaction which takes place when a tenant transfers his or her entire interest in a lease to a third person

assignor: the party who makes the assignment

assumption of the risk: choosing to remain in a situation despite awareness of a danger that could cause injury

auction: a public sale in which goods go to the highest bidder

bailee: a person having temporary possession of another person's goods, holding them in trust for a specified purpose

bailee's duty of care: care of goods while they are in the possession of the bailee. The three levels of care include: extraordinary, ordinary, and minimal

bailee's duty to return the property: the bailee's obligation to return the bailed property according to the terms of the bailment agreement

bailee's lien: right of a bailee to retain possession of the bailed property until payment is made

bailment: transfer of possession of personal property without transfer of ownership

bailment for the sole benefit of the bailee: a type of gratuitous bailment in which a bailor transfers an item to the bailee without charge and the bailee gains the service

bailment for the sole benefit of the bailor: a type of gratuitous bailment in which the bailor transfers the item to the bailee and the bailor gains a service without charge

bailor: the party who gives up possession of the property

bailor's duty to provide goods fit for the intended purpose: the bailor's obligation in a mutual-benefit bailment to check for damage and inform the bailee of discoverable defects, or be liable for any resulting injuries

bait and switch: a business's use of an understocked, low-priced "come-on" to lure prospective buyers into the store. Once there, the buyers find that the advertised item has been sold out and are then deftly redirected to a better but more expensive (and more profitable) product

bank draft: draft drawn by one bank as a depositor in a second bank

bankruptcy: a legal proceeding whereby a debtor's assets are distributed among his or her creditors to discharge the debts

bargaining unit: group of workers joined together to select a bargaining representative and to negotiate with an employer

barter: exchange of goods for goods

battery: harmful or offensive touching of another

bearer: the party in possession of bearer paper

bearer paper: paper issued or indorsed so as to be collectible by the party in possession of it

beneficiary: person who receives real or personal property under a will; also, recipient of insurance policy proceeds

bigamist: a person who knowingly marries a second spouse while still married to the first

bilateral contract: agreement in which both parties make promises

Bill of Rights: the name popularly given to the first ten amendments to the U.S. Constitution

bill of sale: receipt serving as written evidence of the transfer of ownership of goods

binder: agent's written notation of an oral agreement to insure

blacklist: a list of names of employees identified by management as pro-union and sent to other employers to make it difficult for the employees to find work; an unfair labor practice prohibited by law

blank indorsement: indorsement that consists of the indorser's signature only

board of directors: top governing body of a corporation

bodily injury coverage: insurance which protects against liability for bodily injury to or death of others

bona fide occupational qualification (BFOQ): a job requirement that compels discrimination against a protected class

bona fide seniority system: a system that rewards employees based on length of employment rather than on merit

bonds: long-term secured notes

boycott: refusal to deal with the goods or services of an employer

breach of contract: failure to perform the terms as agreed

bribery: offering, giving, or receiving money to influence official action

buildings: structures that are permanently attached to the land

bulk transfer: transfer of all or a major part of the goods of a business

burglary: illegally entering a building with the intent to commit a crime

business law: rules that apply to business situations and transactions

business necessity: a defense against charges of unequal treatment in which an employer's actions are justified as necessary to advance the business

bylaws: rules for the internal management of a corporation

cancellation: ending a contract for sale of goods because of breach, while retaining other remedies; also, any act that shows an intent to end the obligation of payment of commercial paper

capacity: ability to understand the nature and effects of one's actions

carrier's lien: the carrier's right to retain possession of the goods until the charges for transportation and incidental services are paid

case law: law created by appellate courts

cashier's check: check drawn by a bank on itself

casual seller: one who sells only occasionally or otherwise does not meet the definition of merchant

casualty insurance: insurance that indemnifies the insured for loss due to accident, chance, or negligence

casual workers: those workers who do not work regularly for one employer

causation: a linking of the challenged practice and the difference in percentages of protected class persons; establishing causation is a proof of disparate impact

caveat emptor: let the buyer beware

caveat venditor: let the seller beware

cease-and-desist order: an order requiring the company to stop the specified conduct

certificate of deposit: unconditional written promise of a bank to repay with interest a deposit of money at a certain future date

certification: the selection of a bargaining representative by a majority secret vote of the workers in the bargaining unit, which then becomes the exclusive negotiator for all the employees in the bargaining unit and is acknowledged as such by the NLRB

certified check: personal check accepted by the bank in advance of payment

check: a type of draft in which a depositor orders his or her bank to pay deposited funds to a third party or to bearer

checks and balances: specific authority given to each of the three basic branches of government: the legislative, the executive, and the judicial

civil disobedience: peaceful violation of a law thought to be unjust

civil law: law concerned with private wrongs against individuals

civil rights: personal, natural rights guaranteed by our Constitution

claim: a demand for indemnification

class actions: legal suits brought on behalf of large groups

closed shop: the employer's agreement that workers must belong to the recognized union before they can be hired

closely held corporation: private corporation whose stock is held by one or a few persons

closing statements: in a trial, each attorney's summary of the case, which attempts to persuade the judge (and the jury if there is one) to favor his or her side

COD: collect on delivery

codicil: a modification of a will, executed with the same formality as the will

coinsurance: policy clause resulting in the insurer and the insured sharing the risk of fire loss

collateral: personal property subject to a security interest

collateral note: a note which indicates on its face that personal property is offered as security

collective bargaining: negotiations between representatives of employees and employers

collision coverage: coverage that protects against direct and accidental damage due to colliding with another object or upset

comakers: two or more persons who execute a promissory note and are equally liable for payment

combination policies: life insurance plans that require the policyholder to pay a premium significantly higher than the minimum premium necessary for term insurance coverage

commercial paper: unconditional written orders or promises to pay money

commingling: mixing the funds or property of the agent with those of the principal

common carrier: one who agrees, for a fee, to transport goods for anyone who applies, provided the goods are lawful and fit for shipment

common law: case law, reflecting customs of the people

common-law defenses: in a negligence suit, an injured employee's not being able to collect from the employer if (a) the employee had "assumed the risk" involved, (b) the employee was "contributorily negligent," or (c) the "negligence of a co-worker" caused the injury

common-law marriage: a marriage recognized by law when a single woman and a single man live together, share common property, and hold themselves out as husband and wife over a prolonged period of time

common stock: a basic type of stock that comes with the right to vote in corporate elections

community property: property owned equally by spouses

comparative negligence: system in which damages are awarded in proportion to the plaintiff's negligence

compensatory damages: amount awarded to make good the plaintiff's loss

complaint: first paper in a civil action, filed by the plaintiff, stating the claim for judgment

composition of creditors: agreement of all creditors

to accept a proportion of their claims as full payment

compounding a crime: accepting something of value for a promise not to prosecute a suspected criminal

comprehensive coverage: indemnification against all damage to the insured's car except that caused by collision or upset

comprehensive policy: a policy that may be written to contain all the real property, personal property, and liability coverages needed by the average family; also called an all-risk package or homeowner's policy

compromise of a disputed claim: mutual promises to refrain from bringing suit

concealment: failure to reveal material facts

condemnation proceeding: a hearing to determine fair compensation for the owner of real property that the government wishes to acquire and convert to public use

confess judgment: to allow a plaintiff to obtain a judgment without a trial

confidence game: a fraudulent device whereby the victim is persuaded to trust the swindler with the victim's money or other valuables in hopes of a quick gain

consent order: voluntary agreement to stop an illegal practice

consequential reasoning: a style of ethical reasoning in which particular acts have no moral character; rightness or wrongness is based only on "consequences," or the results of the action

consideration: what one gives and receives in a contract

consignment: bailment for sale purposes

consolidation: the action occurring when a new corporation is formed from two separate corporations; $A + B = C$

conspiracy: agreement to commit a crime

constitutional: fitting within the scope of powers delegated by the state

constitutional law: law created when constitutions are adopted or amended, or when courts interpret constitutions

constructive bailment: bailment created by law when there is no agreement

constructive eviction: when property becomes so unfit for habitation through fault of landlord that the tenant is forced to abandon it

constructive notice: knowledge, presumed by law, of facts on file

consumer: a buyer of goods primarily intended for personal, family, or household use

consumer goods: goods used primarily for personal, family, or household purposes

consumer loan: a loan that arises when a person borrows money primarily for personal, family, household, or agricultural purposes

contempt of court: willfull disrespect to a court or disobedience of its orders

contingent beneficiary: beneficiary designated to receive the policy proceeds if the primary beneficiary dies before the insured

contract: legally binding agreement

contract of adhesion: contract in which the more powerful party dictates all the important terms

contract to sell: a contract in which the ownership of goods is to transfer in a sale in the future

contributory negligence: system in which recovery is barred if the injury is partly the result of carelessness by the plaintiff

conversion: wrongfully depriving another of possession of personal property

cooling-off period: cessation of a labor dispute by federal court order for a period of eighty days when a national emergency strike is threatened

co-ownership: the ownership existing when two or more persons have the same ownership rights in the same property

copyright: government grant of exclusive right to possess, produce, and publish an intellectual production

corporation: artificial legal person, separate and distinct from its owners, created under the laws of a state or the nation

corrective advertising: advertising ordered by the FTC to correct a false or misleading impression created by previous advertising for that product or service

counteroffer: reply to an offer, with new terms; ends the original offer

court: tribunal established to administer justice

co-worker negligence: a co-worker's being one of the causes of the injury for which the employer is being sued; a common-law defense used by employers to defeat a negligence suit

credit card: a card identifying the holder as a person entitled to obtain goods or services on credit

credit life insurance: coverage that pays a lender the amount of an outstanding debt upon the death of the debtor

creditor: one to whom a debt is owed

credit rating: evaluation of one's ability to pay debts

credit sale: sale in which, by agreement, payment for goods is made at a later date

crime: a punishable offense against society

criminal act: breach of duty; the specific conduct that violates the statute

criminal action: a lawsuit brought by the state (also known as "the people") against a person accused of a crime

criminal battery: the intentional causing of bodily harm to another person

criminal insanity: the mental state in which the accused does not know the difference between right and wrong

criminal intent: the defendant's intention to commit the act and intention to do evil

criminal law: law concerned with public wrongs against society

cumulative stock: stock in which the promised dividend is not paid in a given year but remains due and payable in the future

cumulative voting: plan which gives minority shareholders representation on the board of directors

custody: care and present control of another's personal property, under the owner's direction

damages: monetary compensation for loss or injury

days of grace: period during which an insurance policy remains in force after the premium is due

deadlocked negotiations: negotiations that do not move forward because the union and employer cannot agree on important issues

debentures: unsecured bonds

debt: that which is owed

debtor: a person or business that owes money, goods, or services to another

decertification election: an election, sanctioned by the NLRB, in which employees deciding if they want different representation can reject union representation or select a different union

Declaration of Independence: a document formally adopted on July 4, 1776, by delegates from the thirteen original American colonies, meeting in Philadelphia, that proclaimed independence from Great Britain

decreasing term life insurance: a basic type of term insurance that requires the payment of the same premium amount throughout the term in return for a face value that will steadily decrease during that term

dedication: the giving of real property to the government

deed: writing which conveys title and other rights of ownership to real property

deed of trust: document that is equivalent to a mortgage but that involves a more expedient remedy for default

defamation: injury of a person's reputation by false statements, oral or written

defendant: person against whom a criminal (or civil) action is brought

defense: the attempt to escape criminal liability by proving the innocence of the defendant

delegation of duties: turning over to another party one's routine contractual duties

demurrage: fees for delay by consignor in loading or by consignee in unloading

Democratic political party: one of the two major political parties in the United States

deontology: a style of moral reasoning that asserts that acts are inherently right or wrong; good consequences cannot justify wrong or bad acts

deposition: pretrial questioning of the opposing party and witnesses under oath

diminished value rule: the difference in the value of the product as it stands substantially completed, and its value if built in strict compliance with the contract plans and specifications

directors: persons elected by shareholders who are responsible for overall direction of the corporation

disability coverage: protection against the effects of total permanent disability

disaffirmance: refusal to carry out a voidable contract

discharge: the release of the debtor from debt

discharge of contract: a termination of obligations that occurs when the parties perform as promised

disclaimer: notice of exclusion

discovery procedures: court-ordered means of getting facts about the dispute from the opposing party and witnesses before the trial

discrimination: "different" treatment of individuals

dishonor: to refuse to pay an instrument when due

disparate impact: a different impact on members of protected classes than on members of the majority

dissolution: when any partner ceases association in carrying on the business

dividends: distributions of corporate profits to shareholders

divorce: a court action that terminates a marriage and divides the property and remaining responsibility between the parties

domestic corporation: chartered in the state in which it is doing business

dormant partner: partner who is neither known to the public nor active in management

double indemnity coverage: coverage which requires the insurer to pay twice the face amount of the policy if the death of the insured is accidental

draft: unconditional written order by one party to a second party to pay a third party a certain sum on demand or at a definite time

drawee: one directed to pay a draft

drawer: one who executes a draft

due process of law: the constitutional requirement that investigations and trials be conducted in fair and orderly ways

duress: overpowering of another's free will through coercion or by illegal imprisonment

duty of accounting: an agent's requirement to account to the principal for all money and property of the principal that comes into the agent's possession

duty of confidentiality: the requirement that the agent treat information about the principal with great caution

duty of loyalty: the requirement that the agent place the interests of his principal above the interests of all others

duty of loyalty and honesty: the duty that the employee should not commit a fraud upon the employer or reveal confidential information about the business

duty of obedience: the duty that the employee should obey all reasonable orders and rules of the employer

duty of reasonable care: the duty of a tenant to take reasonable care of the leased property and return it in substantially the same condition it was in when the lease began

duty of reasonable care and skill: the duty an agent must exercise, in performing a transaction for one's principal, involving the degree of care and skill that a reasonably prudent person would use in a similar situation

duty of reasonable performance: the duty of an employee to perform assigned duties at the prescribed time and in the prescribed manner

duty of reasonable skill: the duty that those who accept work must possess the skill, experience, or knowledge necessary to do it

easement: right to use land owned and possessed by another party

easement by prescription: the acquisition of an easement, or interest in land, through uninterrupted adverse use of another's land without the owner's consent for a statutory period

economic strike: a work stoppage in which the dispute is over wages, hours, or conditions of employment

electronic fund transfer (EFT): a transfer of funds initiated by the use of an electronic terminal, computer, telephone, or magnetic tape

emancipation: release by parents of their parental rights

embezzlement: fraudulent taking of money or other property entrusted to one's care

eminent domain: governmental power to take private property for public use in exchange for the fair market price

employee: the party in an employment contract who does the work

employer: the party in an employment contract who pays

employment: a contract to pay for supervised work

employment for a specific period: employment contract which contains an express term identifying the length of employment

encumbrances: claims of third parties

endorsements: riders attached to a standard insurance policy to provide for special and individual needs

endowment life insurance: coverage that requires the insurer to pay the beneficiary upon the death of the insured the policy's face amount during the period of coverage

Equal Employment Opportunity Commission (EEOC): agency set up by the Civil Rights Act that has the authority to investigate and conciliate complaints of job discrimination and to prosecute suspected offenders

equal rights of possession: an attribute of co-ownership which means that no co-owner can exclude any other co-owner from any physical portion of the property

equipment: goods used by a business in performing its function

equity: form of justice administered when there is no suitable remedy available in common law courts

escrow: money or papers delivered to a third party to hold until certain conditions are fulfilled

escrow agent: a neutral third party in the business of conducting closings

estate: all the property owned by a decedent at death

ethics: the determination of what is a right or wrong action in a reasoned, impartial manner

eviction: removal of the tenant from possession of all real property by action of the landlord

evidence: anything that provides information used to prove or disprove alleged facts

exclusions: exceptions to coverage in property and casualty insurance that relieve the insurance company from paying

executed contract: contract that has been fully performed

executor or executrix: personal representative named by the testator to carry out the directions in the will

executory contract: a contract that has not been fully performed; something agreed upon remains to be done

existing goods: goods that are physically in existence and are owned by the seller

ex parte injunction: an injunction issued by a judge after hearing only one side of an argument

expert witness: a witness who possesses superior knowledge about important facts

express authority: the oral or written power to do anything directly communicated by the principal to the agent

express contract: an agreement that is stated in words, written or spoken

express warranty: an assurance of quality or promise of performance explicitly made by the seller

extended coverage endorsement: added coverage for damage by windstorm, hail, explosion, riot, smoke, aircraft, and vehicles

extortion: obtaining property wrongfully by force, fear, or the power of office

extraordinary bailment: bailment requiring an unusually high standard of care

extraordinary care: the duty arising from an extraordinary bailment in which the bailee is liable for all damage, loss, or injury

face value: stated maximum amount to be paid in the event of the insured loss

false and misleading advertising: untrue claims of quality or effectiveness about goods or services offered for sale

false imprisonment: depriving a person of freedom of movement without consent and without privilege

false pretenses: obtaining property by lying

false rights: claims based on the desires of a particular individual instead of the basic needs of humanity

farm products: crops, livestock, unmanufactured products of the farm, and farm supplies

featherbedding: forcing an employer to pay for work not done or not to be done

felony: serious crime punishable by death or imprisonment for more than one year

fidelity bond: an insurance policy that pays the employer in case of theft by an employee

fiduciary duties: duties which require one to serve the best interests of another

finance charge: added cost for the payment in installments for goods or services

financial responsibility: proof of the ability to pay at least a specified minimum amount of damages if at fault in an auto accident

financial responsibility laws: laws requiring that in an accident resulting in injury, death, or property damage greater than a specified amount, the driver or owner must show proof of the ability to pay a liability judgment

financing statement: brief, written notice of the existence of a security agreement

firm offer: a binding offer stating in writing how long it is to be held open

fixtures: personal property so closely associated with realty that it becomes part of the real estate

floater: insurance protection that follows the property

FOB: free on board

forbearance: refraining from doing what one has a right to do

foreign corporation: a corporation chartered in a state other than the one in which it is doing business

forgery: making or materially altering any writing, with intent to defraud

formal contract: written contract that must be in a special form to be enforceable

forms: modifications to the standard insurance policy to make it apply to the specific type of property being insured

fraud: intentional misrepresentation of fact, relied upon by another to her or his injury

friendly fire: fire in its intended place

full warranty: warranty that obligates a seller to repair or to replace a product without cost and within a reasonable time

fungible goods: goods of a homogeneous nature

future goods: goods that are either not existing or not identified

garnishment: court-granted right to intercept a debtor's wages for the purpose of paying a debt

general partners: two or more persons who carry on, as co-owners, a business for profit

general partnership: partnership in which all partners are fully liable; also, a partnership formed to conduct a general business

genuine assent: consent that is not negated by fraud, duress, undue influence, or mistake

gift: voluntary transfer of ownership without consideration

the Good: the primary goal toward which human life ought to be directed

good faith: honesty in business conduct and transactions

good-faith purchaser: an innocent third party who has given value and acquired rights in goods fraudulently exchanged

goods: items of tangible, movable personal property

grantee: the person who receives the rights and transfer of ownership to real property

grantor: the person who conveys the rights and transfer of ownership to real property

gratuitous agency: agency relationship in which the agent receives no consideration

gratuitous bailment: bailment which benefits only one party

group life insurance: insurance that covers all members of a group

guarantor: the third party who agrees to pay if the principal debtor fails to do so

guaranty: relationship in which a third party becomes secondarily liable for a debt upon default of the principal debtor

guardian: person who acts in place of parents

guardian ad litem: adult named to sue or defend on behalf of a minor

guest laws: claims which disallow suits based on ordinary negligence, brought by guests against drivers

health insurance: indemnification against the cost of medical care necessary to regain physical well-being after an illness

holder: a party in possession of bearer paper or paper payable to the possessor's order

holder in due course (HDC): a holder who takes in good faith, for value, and without notice of defect or dishonor

holder through a holder in due course (HHDC): a holder who takes commercial paper anytime after an HDC (holder in due course)

holographic will: will written entirely in the testator's or testatrix's own handwriting

honor: to pay an instrument when due

hospital insurance: a program that helps pay for hospital expenses and the costs of follow-up treatment

hostile fire: fire started by accident, negligence, or arson; or friendly fire that becomes uncontrollable

House of Representatives: one of the two bodies of the national legislature in the United States; the Senate is the other

identified goods: goods that have been specifically designated as the subject matter of a particular sales contract

immunity: freedom from prosecution

impartiality: applying the same ethical standards to everyone

implied authority: the power to do anything that is reasonably necessary or customary to carry out the duties expressly authorized

implied contract: an agreement that is not stated in words; the parties instead express their intent by conduct that is appropriate under the circumstances

implied warranty: an implicit, unstated warranty obligation imposed on all sellers in order to ensure minimal standards of contractual performance

incidental beneficiary: one who benefits from a contract but is not a party to it and cannot enforce it

incontestable clause: clause that disallows insurer's avoidance of a contract due to misrepresentations or concealment by the applicant

incorporators: persons who sign and submit the articles of incorporation

indemnify: to make good a loss

independent contractor: one retained to accomplish a specific result without supervision

indorsee: the party to whom a paper is indorsed

indorsement: the signature on the reverse side of an order paper of the named person or his or her agent

indorser: an owner of commercial paper who signs on its reverse

infraction: minor misdemeanor punishable by a fine

inheritance tax: tax imposed on the right to receive property from a decedent at death

injunction: order of a court to do or not to do a specified thing

inland marine insurance: indemnification for loss to most personal property while it is being transported across land

inside board: board of directors in which all the directors are officers

instructions to the jury: instructions given by the judge that tell the jury what rules of law apply to the case

insurable interest: direct financial interest in the life of the insured or in the insured property

insurance: contract to pay for a specified loss if the loss occurs

insured: the party covered or protected

insurer: the party who agrees to indemnify

intangible property: real value in rights to money, goods, or contractual performance

integrity: the capacity to do what is right even in the face of temptation or pressure to do otherwise

intellectual property: a purely intangible personal property that one cannot touch or move

intentional torts: offenses in which the defendant intended either the injury or the act

interference with contractual relations: a third party's enticing or encouraging a breach of contract, in which the third party may be liable in tort to the nonbreaching party

interstate commerce: commerce between two or more states which can be regulated by the federal government

intestate: one who dies without a valid will

intrastate commerce: commerce occurring within one state which cannot be regulated by the federal government

invasion of privacy: unlawful intrusion into another's private life causing mental or emotional injury

inventory: business goods that are intended for sale or lease

involuntary bailment: a bailment which arises without the consent of the bailee, and raises the issue of whether the goods are lost or mislaid

involuntary bankruptcy: liquidation of personal or business assets forced by inability to pay debts of $5,000 or more

joint tenancy: co-ownership with the right of survivorship

joint venture: association of two or more firms or persons to do a single project

judgment: final result of a trial

jurisdiction: the authority to decide types of cases

jury: a body of impartial citizens (usually twelve) who listen to the witnesses, review physical evidence, and decide the issues of fact in a trial

juvenile delinquent: a child under a specified age who commits a criminal act or is incorrigible

juveniles: persons under the age of majority

land: surface of, matter beneath, and airspace above the earth, along with things permanently attached or embedded

landlord: person conveying possession of real property through a lease

lapse: to no longer be in effect

larceny: wrongful taking of money or other personal property

lease: agreement in which possession of real property is exchanged for rent

lease condition: a promise made by a tenant which, if violated, allows the landlord to terminate the lease and evict the tenant

lease covenant: a promise made by a tenant which, if violated, allows the landlord to sue for damages while the lease remains in effect

leasehold estate: the ownership interest of the tenant in real property

legal duties: obligations or conduct toward other persons that is enforceable by law

legally competent: having the capacity to contract

legal rate of interest: rate of interest set by statute

legal rights: the benefits to which a person is justly entitled by law

legal tender: United States currency or coins

level term life insurance: a basic type of term insurance that requires the payment of the same premium amount throughout the term in return for a face value that will not change during the term

liable: describing a defendant who loses a civil case and must pay money to the plaintiff

liability insurance: a type of casualty insurance protecting against claims arising from the insured's negligence

libel: written defamation

license: the temporary right to be on another's land because consent has been given

lien: a security interest giving the creditor the right to force the sale of the property to recover the debt amount

life insurance: insurance in which an insurer promises to pay a specified amount upon the death of a person

life insurance beneficiary: the recipient of the proceeds of the policy that are paid upon the death of the insured

limited defenses: defenses good against all but an HDC or a holder through an HDC

limited partners: one or more partners in a business relationship who are liable only to the extent of their investment in the business

limited partnership: partnership in which certain partners have limited liability

limited warranty: any warranty that provides less protection than a full warranty

liquidated damages: amount agreed upon in advance of possible breach

liquidation: sale of corporate assets upon termination

litigate: to take a dispute to court

lockout: shutdown of operations by an employer to bring pressure on employees

loss leaders: selected items sold at a loss to attract customers to buy costlier goods

lost property: property that the owner unknowingly leaves somewhere or accidentally drops

lottery: gamble involving a payment to play, a winner determined by luck, and a prize to some participants

Magna Carta: Latin for "Great Charter." In 1215, it provided protection against unreasonable acts by kings

majority: age at which one is legally bound to contracts

majority rule: the requirement that elected representatives must vote for laws acceptable to over half of the people they represent

maker: one who executes a promissory note or a certificate of deposit

marital consortium: the mutual obligations, both practical and legal, of the husband and wife in a marriage contract

market price: the price of stock involved in later transfers that is determined by many factors, including past and anticipated future profits

material fact: fact that influences a decision

maximum rate of interest: the highest rate of interest that state law permits lenders of money to charge

mechanic's lien: a legal claim or charge against a home, building, or other real property improvement filed by a person who has not been paid for labor or materials furnished to build it

mediation: attempt by a neutral third party to achieve a compromise between two parties in a dispute

mediator: an independent third party who tries to develop a solution acceptable to both sides of the dispute

Medicaid: state-administered program for those without the income or resources to meet medical expenses

medical insurance: a basic Medicare program that helps pay for items not covered by hospital insurance

medical payments coverage: coverage that pays for the reasonable medical claims of occupants of an insured's vehicle who are injured in an automobile accident

Medicare: governmental program to help pay hospital and other bills for eligible persons

merchant: one who regularly sells a particular kind of goods

merger: absorption of one corporation by another; $A + B = A$ (or B)

minimal care: the duty arising from a bailment in which the bailee must not waste or destroy the property

minor: person who is under the age to have full adult rights and duties

misdemeanor: crime of a less serious nature punishable by fine and/or jail up to one year

mislaid property: property that is intentionally placed somewhere but then forgotten

mitigate: to reduce damages if reasonably possible

mixed board: board of directors composed of both officers and outsiders

money: any official currency or coin acceptable as a medium of exchange either in the United States or in any foreign country at the time the commercial paper is written

money damages: a court-ordered payment by the defendant to the plaintiff

money order: a draft issued by a post office, bank, express company, or telegraph company for use in paying or transferring funds for the purchaser

moral rights: legitimate claims on other persons, which flow from each person's status as a human being

mortgage: written document allowing the right of foreclosure

mortgagee: the lender who receives the right of foreclosure in the mortgage

mortgage note: a note using real property as security for payment

mortgagor: the debtor who makes out the mortgage and allows the mortgagee (lender) the right of foreclosure

mutual-benefit bailment: bailment which benefits both bailor and bailee

mutual insurance company: insurance company owned by the insureds

mutual mistakes: the situation in which both parties are wrong about some important facts; either party may disaffirm

national emergency strike: a strike that involves national defense or major industries, or would have a substantial effect on the nation's economy

natural laws: laws which reflect ethical principles

natural rights: rights to which all persons are entitled because they are human beings

necessaries: goods and services essential to maintain one's lifestyle

negligence: causing injury by failing to act as a reasonable person

negligence suit: a suit, brought by an employee against an employer, that claims the employer's carelessness caused the employee's injury

negotiable: legally transferable to another person; to be negotiable, a promise or order to pay money must be in writing, contain an unconditional promise or order payable in a sum certain, be payable on demand or at a definite time, and be payable to the bearer or to someone's order

negotiation: the proper transfer of a negotiable instrument

neutral on its face: characterizing a company employment policy that makes no reference to a protected class

no-fault divorce: divorce granted without any listing of grievances or attempt to establish blame

no-fault insurance: coverage requiring that parties to an automobile accident be indemnified by their own insurance company regardless of who is at fault

nominal consideration: a token amount ("consideration") identified in a written contract when parties either cannot or do not wish to state the amount precisely

nominal damages: damages granted in recognition of the fact that rights have been violated; may consist of a few cents or a dollar

nominal partner: person who is held out as a partner but is not one

nonprofit corporation: private corporation organized for a social, charitable, or educational purpose; does not return a financial profit to its members

nontrading partnership: a business relationship that provides professional and noncommercial assistance, such as legal, medical, or accounting advice

no-par stock: share with no face value specified

notary public: a public officer who formally certifies that the signatures on deeds and other documents are authentic

notice of loss: a report, usually written, identifying a loss covered by an insurance policy

novation: substitution of a party, creating a new contract

nuncupative (oral) will: an oral will proclaimed during the maker's last illness or by service personnel on active duty, which must be witnessed and is often limited to controlling the distribution of personal property

obligor: debtor

occupancy: the acquisition of title by taking possession of personal property that belongs to no one else

Occupational Safety and Health Administration (OSHA): the federal agency that enacts safety regulations, inspects workplaces, imposes fines, and even shuts down plants when it finds violations of its laws

offer: proposal to enter into a legal agreement

offerees: persons to whom an offer is made

offeror: the person who makes an offer

omnibus clause: insurance clause which covers all drivers who are members of the insured's household and any person who is not a member but is permitted to drive the insured's car

opening statement: the remarks by the attorneys which briefly outline what the plaintiff or the defendant will try to prove in the trial

open shop: establishment in which nonunion members do not pay union dues

option: underlying contract to keep an offer open

order paper: paper that is issued or indorsed to the order of a specified person

ordinance: statutory law created by a town, city, or county

ordinary bailments: voluntary bailments with parties other than commercial carriers and hotels and having highly variable standards of care

ordinary care: the duty created by a mutual-benefit bailment in which the bailee is liable only if he or she has been negligent in some fashion

outlawed debt: debt for which a creditor cannot sue as the injured party because of failure to sue within the time permitted by law

outside board: board of directors with no corporate officers

ownership in severalty: ownership of all the ownership rights in property by oneself; the most common form of personal property ownership

parol evidence rule: rule that bars use of prior written or spoken words to alter a written contract which appears to be complete

partial eviction: depriving the tenant of the possession of only one part (e.g., one room of an apartment) of the real property

participating policies: life insurance policies on which dividends are paid

participating stock: shares in which after regular dividends are received, preferred stockholders share in further distribution of profits with common stockholders

partnership: association of two or more persons to carry on, as co-owners, a business for profit

partnership agreement: a written document that spells out rights and duties of the partners of a business organization

partnership at will: a type of partnership permitting withdrawal by a partner at any time without liability to associates

par value: face value printed on a stock certificate

past consideration: value given before a contract is made

patent: government grant of exclusive right to make, use, and sell a product or process which is novel, non-obvious, and useful

pawn: pledge of tangible personal property

pawnbroker: a person who lends money at interest and takes possession of tangible personal property from the borrower as security for repayment

pawn ticket: a receipt for pawned goods obtained by the borrower

payable at a definite time: payable on or before an identified calendar date

payable on demand: payable immediately upon presentment or at sight

payee: one to whom commercial paper is payable

payment: buyer's delivery and seller's acceptance of the price

payroll deduction: a legal obligation of the employer to withhold a percentage of the paycheck to cover the employee's federal and state income tax obligations

perfected security interest: protected interest resulting from the creditor's possession of collateral or the creditor's filing of a financing statement

performance: fulfillment of an agreement as promised

periodic tenancy: a lease for a renewable period with rent due at stated intervals

perjury: lying under oath

perpetual succession: power by which a corporation continues despite changes in its shareholder membership

personal opinions: in the buyer-seller relationship, a seller's claims about a product that are not statements of fact and should not be taken as a serious endorsement

personal property: tangible, movable property and intangible property

personal property floater: coverage of any and all of an insured's personal property against practically any peril regardless of the location of the property

picket: to walk with signs at employer's business to publicize dispute or influence opinion

plaintiff: one who brings a civil action

plea bargaining: pleading guilty to a less serious crime

pledge: situation in which personal property is given to a creditor as security

pledgee: the creditor who gets possession of the property

pledgor: the debtor who voluntarily gives up possession of the property

policy: written contract of insurance

political party: a group of citizens who are loosely affiliated in a private organization to select and promote for election to public office candidates who agree with them on important governmental policies and legislation

postdated: dated later than the date of issuance

power of attorney: writing that appoints an agent

preemptive right: shareholder's right to buy a proportionate number of shares in a new issue of capital stock

preferred stock: shares with priority claims to dividends and liquidation funds; usually nonvoting

premium: consideration for an insurance contract

prenuptial contract: a contract by which the marital partners-to-be typically give up any future claim they might have to part or all of the other's property

preponderance of the evidence: a majority (fifty-one percent) of the evidence

price: consideration for a sale or a contract to sell

primary beneficiary: beneficiary designated to receive the policy proceeds if still alive at the time of death of the insured

primary boycott: boycott directed mainly against the struck employer

principal: one who authorizes an agent to make contracts

principal debtor: one who originally owes a debt in a three-party arrangement

private corporation: corporation established by private citizens for a business or charitable purpose

privity of contract: relationship of persons who are parties to the same contract

procedural defenses: defenses based on problems with the way evidence is obtained or the way the accused person is arrested, questioned, tried, or punished

procedural law: rules for enforcement of legal rights and duties

proceeds: money paid to the beneficiary of the policy

product liability: responsibility for injury caused by a defective product, based on warranty, fraud, negligence, or strict liability

profit: right to extract something from another's land

profit-making corporation: private corporation organized to produce a financial profit for its owners

promisee: the person to whom the promise or action is given in exchange for the other person's promise or action

promisor: the person who gives the promise or action in exchange for the promise or action of another

promissory estoppel: when a promise is enforced even though no consideration is given for it

promissory note: unconditional written promise by one party to pay a certain sum of money to the order of another party on demand or at a definite time

promoters: persons who bring together interested persons and take preliminary steps to form a corporation

proof beyond a reasonable doubt: a standard of proof in which the vast majority of the evidence (perhaps ninety percent) supports the guilty verdict

proof of loss: a written, sworn statement including information as to (1) origin and time of loss, (2) value of and damage to any property, (3) injuries suffered, (4) names of any witnesses, and (5) other insurance carried

property: things and the corresponding group of legal rights and interests

property damage coverage: coverage that indemnifies the insured against claims from damage the insured does to a third person's property as a consequence of operating a motor vehicle

property insurance: insurance intended to indemnify for harm to the insured's personal or real property brought about by perils such as fire, theft, and windstorm

prorate: to divide proportionately

protected classes: persons whose group characteristics may not be considered when making employment decisions

proximate cause: reasonably foreseeable cause of injury

proxy: written authorization designating some person to vote in place of the signer in a corporate election

public corporation: established for a governmental purpose

public service corporation: a private company that furnishes an essential public service

puffing: exaggerated sales talk

punishment: penalty imposed for committing a crime

punitive or exemplary damages: added damages intended to punish and make an example of the defendant

pure democracy: a government in which every adult citizen may vote on all issues

qualified indorsement: an indorsement that eliminates an indorser's signature-based liability to later transferees

quasi contract: circumstances under which the parties are bound as in a valid contract to prevent unjust enrichment

quitclaim deed: deed which conveys the grantor's interest without warranties

ratification: approval of a voidable contract; also, approval of a previously unauthorized act

real property: land and things permanently attached to the land

reasonable-man standard: a general duty imposed by negligence law that requires that we act with the care, prudence, and good judgment of a reasonable person so as not to cause injury to others

receipt of goods: buyer's taking of physical possession or control of goods

receiving stolen property: receiving or buying property known to be stolen, with intent to deprive the rightful owner of the property

reckless driving: driving by anyone who fails to exercise reasonable care, unreasonably interferes with the use of a public road by others, or deliberately disregards his or her own safety or that of others

recording: the process which makes a document available to the public at the county recorder's office; deeds to real property are such documents

reinstate: to place an insurance policy back in force

remedy: means used to enforce a right or compensate for an injury

rent: the consideration given in return for temporary possession of another's real property

replacement cost: the amount that it would currently take to replace a damaged or destroyed item

repossession: the act in which the seller on credit (or the finance company that has provided money for the purchase) takes the goods back, resells them, and uses the net proceeds (after expenses of the repossession and resale) to pay the balance due

representations: statements of an applicant which are not part of the final insurance contract

republic: a representative democracy in which the voters democratically select persons to represent them in the legislative, executive, and judicial branches of government

Republican political party: one of the two major political parties in the United States

rescission: return of parties to position before contract was made with no damages

restitution: restoring or making good a loss; repayment of money illegally obtained

restrictive indorsement: indorsement that indicates the use of the proceeds or imposes a condition on payment

revocation: withdrawal of an offer before acceptance

right of foreclosure: right to have property that is subject to a mortgage sold to satisfy the debt

right of partition: an attribute of co-ownership which allows any co-owner to require the division, usually financial, of the property among the co-owners

right of survivorship: right of one joint tenant to ownership of property when the other joint tenant dies

right-to-work laws: state laws which ban both the union shop and the closed shop

risk: possible loss covered by an insurance contract

robbery: taking of property by force from the person or presence of another

Roman civil law: body of regulations imposed by emperors of ancient Rome

RSDHI (Retirement, Survivors', Disability, and Health Insurance): coverages provided under the Social Security Act

rules and regulations: administrative laws created by administrative agencies given legislative powers by legislatures

sale: contract in which ownership of goods passes immediately from the seller to the buyer for a price

sale of an undivided interest: a transaction involving the sale of a fractional interest in a single good or in a number of goods that are to remain together

sale on approval: delivery of goods to the buyer "on trial" or "on satisfaction"

sale or return: a transaction in which goods are delivered to a merchant buyer who assumes ownership and risk of loss upon delivery but who has a right to return the goods to the seller within a fixed or a reasonable amount of time, passing ownership and risk of loss back to the seller

satisfaction: performance of a new contractual obligation

scofflaw: a person who does not respect or comply with certain laws

scope of authority: within the range of authorized acts

S corporations: organizations under Subchapter S of the Internal Revenue Code that can have only one class of stock and no more than thirty-five shareholders, all of whom must be U.S. citizens or resident aliens

seal: an impression on a document, a paper, or wax affixed to the document, or the word "Seal" or the letters "L.S." on the document indicating that the parties intend to be legally bound

secondary boycott: boycott directed mainly against third parties who deal with the struck employer

secret partner: partner who is not known to the public but is active in management

secured debt: the debt related to the legal interest in a specific property of the debtor

secured parties: the persons who have security interests in the collateral owned by the debtor-buyer

secured transaction: business deal in which a creditor gets a security interest in personal property

security agreement: a transaction in which the debtor retains possession of the collateral under written contract with the secured party

security interest: the creditor's right to enforce the debt against specific property of the debtor

self-defense: reasonable and lawful resistance to attack

Senate: one of the two bodies of the national legislature in the United States; the House of Representatives is the other

separate property: property owned by either spouse at the time of marriage or received as a gift or inheritance

separation: the first step toward divorce, in which the spouses maintain separate living quarters, but their marital rights and obligations remain intact

servicemark: a work, mark, or symbol that identifies a service as opposed to a product

sexual harassment: unwelcome sexual comments, gestures, or contact in the workplace

shareholder (stockholder): a person who owns one or more shares of stock in a business

shares of stock: units of ownership in a corporation

sight draft: draft payable on sight

silent partner: partner who may be known to the public but is not active in management

simple contract: contract that is not formal

slander: oral defamation

small claims court: a court in which a civil action for a small amount, typically up to $3,000, can be filed

small loan rate of interest: a high rate of interest (typically 36 percent a year) that the state permits licensed loan companies and pawnbrokers to charge on small loans; established as a means to protect people against the unconscionably high rates (often 100 percent or more annually) charged by criminal loan sharks

social insurance: indemnification from financial consequences of unemployment, retirement, and other social concerns

sole proprietorship: unincorporated business owned by one person

sovereignty: freedom from external control

special indorsement: an indorsement that makes the paper payable to the order of a designated party

special or consequential damages: money damages for loss caused by improper or partial performance or by total failure to perform as promised

special partnership: formed to carry out a single transaction

specific performance: completion of an agreement as promised

standard fire policy: any fire insurance contract written to cover direct loss to property resulting from fire, lightning strike, or removal from premises endangered by fire

stare decisis, doctrine of: the principle that new cases must be decided in ways consistent with prior case law

state constitution: document setting forth powers retained by the states that have not been delegated to the federal government

statute: law enacted by a state or federal legislature

statute of frauds: law requiring certain contracts to be in writing and signed by the defendant in order to be enforceable

stock certificate: written evidence of ownership and rights in a corporation

stock insurance company: profit-making insurance company owned by shareholders

stop payment order: an order directing a bank not to pay on a check

strict liability: responsibility for injury regardless of negligence or intent

strike: concerted work stoppage by employees to bring pressure on the employer

subletting: tenant's transferring part of interest to another

subpoena: written order commanding a person to appear in court as a witness

subrogation: assigned right, by operation of law, to recover damages

substantial performance: incomplete but acceptable performance of contractual terms

substantive defenses: defenses that disprove, justify, or excuse the alleged crime

substantive law: rules that define legal rights and duties

substitution: replacement of a contract with a new one because the original is not what the parties want

summons: court order directing the defendant to answer the plaintiff's complaint

supremacy: supreme power or authority; a point to be determined when laws of the differing levels of government conflict

surety: the third party who promises to be liable in case of default by the principal debtor

suretyship: relationship in which a third party becomes primarily liable for a debt upon default of the principal debtor

surveying: the process of carefully measuring the exact boundaries of real property

tenancy at sufferance: remaining in possession after the lease has expired

tenancy at will: possession of land with the owner's permission but without an agreement as to the term of the lease or the amount of the rent

tenancy by the entireties: the usual form of co-ownership between husband and wife, carrying the right of survivorship; the interests must be equal

tenancy for years: a period of tenancy for a definite period of time, such as six months, one year, or ninety-nine years, with identification of a date for the ending of the lease

tenancy from month to month: a period of tenancy in which the rent is paid by the month

tenancy in common: a form of co-ownership in which the shares may be unequal and there is no right of survivorship

tenancy in partnership: a business relationship in which each partner is a co-owner of the entire partnership property and is not the sole owner of any part of it

tenant: the person receiving possession of real property

tender: offer to perform an obligation

tender of delivery: situation in which the seller (1) places (or authorizes a carrier to place) the proper goods at the buyer's disposal and (2) notifies the buyer so that delivery can be received

terminable at will: describes a job in which there is no agreement concerning length of employment

termination: the ending of a partnership

termination statement: publicly filed acknowledgment that a secured debt has been paid off

term life insurance: coverage that involves the payment of the minimum premium necessary to buy only life insurance on the insured for stated periods of time

testamentary capacity: knowledge by the maker of a will of the kind and extent of the property involved and the persons who stand to benefit, and awareness that he or she is making arrangements to dispose of his or her property after death

testamentary intent: clear intention to make one's will, free of pressure or undue influence from others

testate: leaving a valid will upon death

testator or testatrix: a person who makes a will

testimony: statements made by witnesses under oath

test of intent: a test used by the law to determine whether an item associated with real property is personal or real; this test considers whether persons intended something to become part of the realty

third party: a person who works through an agent to reach an agreement that binds a principal

third-party beneficiary: one who is not a party to a contract but benefits from it and can enforce it

time draft: draft payable at a specified time or after a specified period

title insurance: a policy in which the insurance company guarantees, in exchange for a premium, that the title is good

tort: an offense against an individual

trade fixtures: business appliances attached to rented real property used in a business

trademark: distinctive word, device, or symbol

that identifies a product or service

trade secret: unpatented formula or process not known to others and which is valuable in business

trading partnership: formed to buy and to sell commercially

transcript: copy of the written record of a trial

traveler's check: a draft drawn by a well-known financial institution on itself or its agent

travel insurance: a kind of term insurance that covers the life of the traveler during the journey

trespass: wrongful interference with the use of another's property

trial court: court where a dispute is first heard

truants: minors who do not attend school when lawfully required to do so

unconscionable contract: a contract or a clause of a contract that is grossly unfair and oppressive

unconstitutional: invalid because in conflict with a constitution

underinsured motorists coverage: coverage that compensates the injured when the negligent driver does not have sufficient insurance to cover damages

undisclosed principal: a principal whose identity is kept secret from the third party by the agent

undue influence: overpowering another's free will to take unfair advantage in a contract

unemployment compensation: governmental payment to lessen consequences of job loss

unenforceable contract: a valid contract that can be voided when a time limit for filing suit to enforce it has passed

unequal treatment: treating members of a protected class less favorably than other employees; sometimes called disparate treatment

unfair labor practices: union or employer acts which violate the rights of employees with respect to union activity

unfair labor practice strike: a strike in which the dispute is over unfair labor practices

unfair trade practice: dishonest or illegal method of business competition

Uniform Commercial Code (UCC): a large set of business statutes which simplified, clarified, and modernized many laws relating to commercial transactions

unilateral contract: agreement in which only one of the parties makes a promise

unilateral mistake: important contractual mistake made by only one of the parties

uninsured motorists coverage: additional coverage that allows the insured to collect damages from his or her own insurance company when they are not collectible from the person who caused the harm

union shop: establishment in which all workers must join the union within a prescribed period

U.S. Constitution: a document adopted in 1789 that is the supreme law of the United States

universal defenses: defenses good against all obligees

universalizing: a mental test that magnifies the illogical character of acts to make this lack of logic easier to see

universal life insurance: insurance that offers death coverage from term insurance plus a minimum guaranteed return on the cash value roughly the same as in a whole life policy

unqualified indorsement: an indorsement made without the addition of "without recourse" or equivalent words that eliminate potential secondary liability

unsatisfied judgment funds: pools of money used to pay uncollectible judgments

unsecured debt: debt based only on a promise to pay

usury: charging a higher interest rate than that permitted by law

valid contract: a contract that is legally effective and enforceable in court

variable life insurance: coverage that allows the insured to invest in several types of funds

vendee: buyer

vendor: seller

verdict: decision of a jury

vicarious criminal liability: responsibility of a corporate officer for a crime committed by one of the corporation's employees

vicarious liability: responsibility of one person for the torts of another

vocational rehabilitation: the training of employees for another type of job

voidable contract: a contract in which only one of the parties has the power to compel legal enforcement; withdrawal by that party cancels the contract

voidable marriage: a marriage contract having fraudulent grounds which may end the marriage; the contract remains valid until termination

void agreement: an invalid agreement that cannot be enforced in court by either party; it has no force or effect

void marriage: a marriage which occurs whenever laws are violated by the matrimonial union; considered invalid from the beginning

voluntary bankruptcy: voluntary liquidation of the assets of a person or business to discharge debts

wager: a bet on the uncertain outcome of an event

waiver: voluntarily giving up a legal right

War of Independence: the war of 1775–1783 by which the American colonies won their independence from England

warranty: a statement of product qualities which the seller assures is true; also, statement of an applicant that is part of the final insurance contract

warranty deed: a written document which protects the grantee by providing several enforceable grantor's warranties

warranty of merchantability: the requirement that goods are fit for the ordinary purposes for which such goods are used

warranty of the principal's capacity: a warranty imposed by law on the agent so that if the principal injured the third party, the third party could recover from the agent

white-collar crimes: nonviolent crimes committed by respected persons or corporations

whole life insurance: a standard type of policy that provides for the payment of premiums for as long as the insured lives, or until age 100, rather than for a specified period

will: legal expression of how a person's property is to be distributed after the person dies

winding-up period: time during which all business affairs of a partnership are concluded

witness: person who has personal knowledge of the facts

workers' compensation: laws requiring most employers to obtain insurance to pay benefits to injured employees

workforce pool: persons actually in the workforce

work permit: a document given by the state allowing a person under eighteen years old to work

writ of execution: the process by which a judgment for money is enforced

wrongful discharge: firing an employee for one of the following reasons: (1) refusing to commit perjury at the request of the company, (2) insisting on filing a worker's compensation form, (3) engaging in union activity, (4) reporting violations of law by the company, or (5) urging the company to comply with the law

yellow-dog contracts: employment contracts in which the employee could be terminated for joining a union

Index

Italic page numbers are used to indicate the page(s) on which terms are defined.

837

O

P

Photo Credits

p. 1, John Feingersh/Stock Boston; p. 3, Wally McNamee/Woodfin Camp & Associates; p. 8, © Bob Daemmrich/Stock Boston; p. 14, Robert Hutchings/Photo Researchers; p. 25, Wally McNamee/Woodfin Camp; p. 33, Angelina Lax/Photo Researchers; p. 39, AP/Wide World Photo; p. 47, Richard Hutchings/Photo Researchers; p. 50, Bob Daemmrich/Stock Boston; p. 52, Bob Daemmrich/Stock Boston; p. 65, Owen Franken/Stock Boston; p. 66, Richard Pasley/Stock Boston; p. 72, Mary Wolf/TSW; p. 85, Comstock; p. 87, Alan Oddie/PhotoEdit; p. 109, Copyright 1991, Los Angeles Times. Reprinted by permission. By Paul Conrad; p. 113, Tony Freeman/PhotoEdit; p. 127, Bob Daemmrich/Stock Boston; p. 129, Jose Carrillo; p. 134, Richard Pasley/Stock Boston; p. 143, John Lei/Stock Boston; p. 146, Chris Minerva/Telephoto; p. 149, Ellis Herwig/Stock Boston; p. 164, Reprinted with special permission of King Features Syndicate, Inc.; p. 173, N. R. Rowan/Stock Boston; p. 183, Jim Pickerell/West Light; p. 185, Rafael Macia/Photo Researchers; p. 188, Bob Daemmrich/Stock Boston; p. 193, Renee Lynn/Photo Researchers; p. 209, Jose Carrillo; p. 210, Rhonda Sidney/Stock Boston; p. 217, Laima Druskis/Photo Researchers; p. 227, Spencer Grant/Stock Boston; p. 236, Chuck Fishman/Woodfin Camp; p. 241, Charles Teil/Stock Boston; p. 253, Charles Gupton/TSW; p. 256, David Young-Wolff/Don Murie/Meyers Photo-Art; p. 258, David Young-Wolff/PhotoEdit; p. 277, Chris Brown/Stock Boston; p. 282, Matthew Neal McVay/Stock Boston; p. 287, Stephen Dunn/AllSport; p. 297, John Livzey; p. 298, Mike Mazzaschi/Stock Boston; p. 301, John Livzey; p. 317, Dwight Cindrowski/Telephoto; p. 319, John Livzey; p. 321, Mike Jaeggi/Meyers Photo-Art; p. 331, Mike Mazzaschi/Stock Boston; p. 339, Marc Pokempter/TSW; p. 340, Jose Carrillo; p. 347, Odyssey/Woodfin Camp; p. 361, Richard Hutchings/Photo Researchers; p. 368, John Livzey; p. 373, Laurie Rubin/TSW; p. 383, David Young-Wolff/PhotoEdit; p. 385, Grant Heilman Photography; p. 389, John Running/Stock Boston; p. 397, Freda Leinwand/Woodfin Camp; p. 409, Deni McIntyre/Photo Researchers; p. 412, Cotton Coulson/Woodfin Camp; p. 417, Don Murie/Meyers Photo-Art; p. 427, Robert Frerck/Woodfin Camp; p. 429, J. Zerschling/Telephoto; p. 433, Oliver Benn/TSW; p. 435, Cary Wolinsky/Stock Boston; p. 449, Tony Stone Worldwide; p. 453, Moldvay/TSW; p. 461, Tony Stone Worldwide; p. 469, Stacy Pick/Stock Boston; p. 471, James Holmes/Photo Researchers; p. 480, Bob Daemmrich/Stock Boston; p. 487, Terry Vine/TSW; p. 490, John Coletti/Stock Boston; p. 492, Bob Daemmrich/Stock Boston; p. 503, Phil Cantor/Telephoto; p. 508, Michael Grecco/Stock Boston; p. 513, Joseph Nettis/Stock Boston; p. 525, Barbara Filet/TSW; p. 527, © Adamsmith Productions/Westlight; p. 529, Stacy Pick/Stock Boston; p. 536, © Chip Henderson/Telephoto; p. 549, David Weintraub/Photo Researchers; p. 553, Jose Carrillo; p. 563, George Hall/Woodfin Camp; p. 566, Stephen Frisch/Stock Boston; p. 571, Robert Rathe/Stock Boston; p. 579, Michael Grecco/Stock Boston; p. 581, Cathlyn Melloan/TSW; p. 587, Victor Englebert/Photo Researchers; p. 595, Will McIntyre/Photo Researchers; p. 599, Jose Carrillo; p. 607, Jose Carrillo; p. 615, Jose Carrillo; p. 622, courtesy of Wells Fargo Bank; p. 625, Jose Carrillo; p. 636, Jose Carrillo; p. 644, Mike Mazzaschi/Stock Boston; p. 653, Craig Aurness/Woodfin Camp; p. 655, Frank Cezus/TSW;p. 661, Bill Gallery/Stock Boston; p. 662, Bob Daemmrich/Stock Boston; p. 672, Billy E. Barnes/Stock Boston; p. 675, Runk/Schoenberger/Grant Heilman; p. 680, Paul Solomon/Woodfin Camp; p. 691, Ellis Herwig/Stock Boston; p. 698, Jose Carrillo; p. 707, Peter Menzel/Stock Boston; p. 717, courtesy EASTMAN KODAK COMPANY; p. 719, Alon Reininger/Woodfin Camp; p. 729, Susan Lapides/Woodfin Camp; p. 731, Robert Frerck/TSW; p. 732, Michael Heron/Woodfin Camp; p. 734, Michael Heron/Woodfin Camp; p. 755, J. L. Winstead/Telephoto; p. 760, Lawrence Migdale/Stock Boston; p. 763, Alex Bartel/Science Photo Library/Photo Researchers

849